THE OXFORD

Essential
Thesaurus

AMERICAN EDITION

THE OXFORD

Essential
Thesaurus

AMERICAN EDITION

BERKLEY BOOKS, NEW YORK

THE OXFORD ESSENTIAL THESAURUS

A Berkley Book / published in mass-market paperback
by arrangement with Oxford University Press, Inc.

PRINTING HISTORY
Berkley edition / August 1998

Copyright © 1998 by Oxford University Press, Inc.
Oxford is a registered trademark of Oxford University Press, Inc.
The *Oxford Essential Thesaurus* is an adaptation and
abridgment of *The Oxford Paperback Thesaurus*.
All rights reserved. No part of this publication may be reproduced,
stored in a retrieval system, or transmitted, in any form or by any
means, electronic, mechanical, photocopying, recording, or otherwise,
without the prior written permission of Oxford University Press, Inc.
For information contact: Oxford University Press,
198 Madison Avenue, New York, New York 10016.

The Penguin Putnam Inc. World Wide Web site address is
http://www.penguinputnam.com

ISBN: 0-425-16421-7

BERKLEY®
Berkley Books are published by
The Berkley Publishing Group, a division of Penguin Putnam Inc.,
375 Hudson Street, New York, New York 10014.
BERKLEY and the "B" design are trademarks
belonging to Penguin Putnam Inc.

PRINTED IN THE UNITED STATES OF AMERICA

OPM 20 19 18 17 16 15 14 13 12

Contents

Project Staff

Editor: Christine A. Lindberg

Project Editors: Nancy LaRoche, Laurie H. Ongley

Editorial Assistant: Deborah Argosy

Proofreaders: Linda Costa, Adrienne Makowski, Ruth Handlin Manley, Julie Marsh

Data Entry: Kimberly Roberts

Editor-in-chief: Frank R. Abate

Managing Editor: Elizabeth J. Jewell

Guide to
The Oxford Essential Thesaurus: American Edition

HEADWORDS

The text of *The Oxford Essential Thesaurus: American Edition* is organized under headwords, which are printed in bold type. The headwords are listed in strict alphabetical order.

Many English words have two or more acceptable spellings; in this book, the one used is the one regarded as being the most common. Occasionally, two spellings share nearly equal usage; in such cases, the headwords include both forms. For example:

> **cagey, cagy** adjective guarded, secretive, noncommittal, cautious, chary, wary, careful, shrewd, wily.

PARTS OF SPEECH

A headword is always followed by its part of speech. When a word has two or more different parts of speech, it is listed more than once with separate entries for each. For example:

> **obscure** adjective **1** *obscure references* unclear, indeterminate, opaque . . . .
>
> **obscure** verb **1** *obscure the main issue* confuse, blur, muddle . . . .

Not all parts of speech of a word are necessarily included as headwords. For example, many words that function as adjectives can also function as adverbs. In such cases, the adverbial senses are included only when they have useful sets of synonyms.

HOMOGRAPHS

Certain words have the same spelling but different meanings and different etymologies (origins). Such words, known as homographs, are treated as separate headwords, even when they have the same part of speech. For the purposes of cross-referencing, homograph numbers are included in order to distinguish identical headwords with the same part of speech. For example,

> **bank**[1] noun **1** *a grassy bank* slope, rise, incline, ...
>
> **bank**[2] noun **1** *empty the child's bank* piggy bank, cashbox, safe, ...

If two or more headwords are identical in spelling but have different parts of speech, homograph numbers are not used. This does not necessarily imply that these entries share the same etymology.

ENTRIES

Each entry contains a list of words that are synonyms of the headword: i.e., the words can be used in place of the headword in most (although not all) contexts. When a word has more than one meaning, the different senses of the word are numbered. In many instances, example phrases (in italic type) indicate the particular sense and illustrate the use of the word. In some cases, two or more examples are given; these are separated by a vertical bar (|). For example:

> **contribute** verb **1** *contribute money/time to*
> *the charity* | *happy to contribute* give, donate,
> hand out, ...

Note that a slash (/) is used to separate alternative words in order to save space. The slash applies only to the two words it separates; thus "contribute time/money" can be read as "contribute time" and "contribute money."

SUBENTRIES

Verb phrases are included as subentries (in bold type) under a main entry. For example:

> **chance** verb **1** *it chanced that they arrived*
> *last* happen, occur, take place, come about.
> **2** *have to chance it* risk, hazard, gamble . . . .
> **chance on/upon** come across, stumble
> on, come upon, encounter; *inf.* bump into,
> run into.

GROUPS WITHIN SENSES

In general, the synonyms in an entry are separated by commas. However, there are cases in which the words fall naturally into two or more distinct groups, which are separated by semicolons. There are various reasons for subdividing a sense in this way:

Grammatical Differences

Within a given sense, some synonyms may function differently from others. For example:

> **acclaim** noun . . . praise, commendation,
> approval, approbation, homage, tribute;
> cheers, congratulations, plaudits, bouquets.

In the **acclaim** entry, the semicolon separates the singular nouns from the plural nouns. There are other grammatical reasons for subdividing synonym groups; for instance, a headword may function as both a transitive verb (taking a direct object) and an intransitive verb (without an object), whereas some of the synonyms may be only intransitive or only transitive.

Relationship of Meanings

Within a given sense, there sometimes are synonyms whose meanings share a relationship that sets them apart from the other synonyms in that sense. For example:

> **age** verb mature, ripen, grow up, come of
> age; grow old, decline, wither, fade.

> **bag** noun receptacle; handbag, pocketbook,
> purse, shoulder bag; suitcase, grip, flight
> bag; . . . .

In the entry for *age*, a semicolon is used to separate the "maturing" senses of *age* from the "growing old" senses. In the **bag** entry, semicolons separate the general synonym "receptacle" from the specific synonyms, which themselves are separated into categories of bags.

Restricted Usage

Some synonyms are separated into labeled groups of restricted usage. Such groups are always set off by semicolons. For example:

> **acquit** verb . . . vindicate, liberate, free,
> deliver; *fml.* exculpate.

> **work** noun . . . effort, exertion, labor, toil,
> sweat, drudgery, trouble, industry; *lit.*
> travail; *inf.* grind, elbow grease.

The usage labels used in this thesaurus are abbreviated as follows:

derog.	derogatory
fml.	formal
inf.	informal
lit.	literal
Med.	Medicine
TM	trademark

CROSS-REFERENCES

A cross-reference to a main entry is indicated by small capitals and is preceded by "See." Where necessary, the part of speech and sense number are also given. For example:

> **abridge** verb shorten, cut down, con-
> dense, contract, compress. *See* ABBRE-
> VIATE.

> **alternate** adjective every other, every se-
> cond; . . . .*See* ALTERNATIVE adjective 1.

A cross-reference to a subentry follows the same format but also includes the main entry (given in parentheses). For example:

> **transcend** verb. . . . **2** *her performance*
> *transcended that of her opponents* surpass,
> excel. *See* TOWER ABOVE (TOWER) verb.

Aa

abandon verb **1** *abandon one's family* desert, leave, forsake, depart from, leave behind, cast aside, jilt; *inf.* run out on. **2** *abandon hope* give up, renounce, relinquish, dispense with, forgo. **3** *abandon a country to the enemy* yield, surrender, give up, cede, deliver up. **4** *abandon smoking* stop, give up, cease, drop, forgo, desist from, dispense with.

abandon noun recklessness, lack of restraint/inhibition, unrestraint, carelessness, wildness, impulse, impetuosity, immoderation, wantonness.

abandoned adjective **1** *an abandoned child* deserted, forsaken, cast aside. **2** *an abandoned ship* vacated, evacuated, deserted, unoccupied, empty, unused.

abase verb humiliate, humble, belittle, lower, degrade, disparage, debase, demean, discredit.

abashed adjective embarrassed, ashamed, shamefaced, mortified, humiliated; taken aback, disconcerted, nonplussed, discomfited.

abate verb **1** *the storm/pain abated* die down, lessen, ease, subside, let up, decrease, diminish, moderate, decline, fade, slacken, wane. **2** *abate the pain/noise* ease, lessen, decrease, diminish, moderate, soothe, relieve, dull, blunt, alleviate, mitigate, allay, assuage, palliate, appease, reduce, lower.

abbreviate verb shorten, reduce, cut, contract, condense, compress, abridge, truncate, clip, crop, shrink, summarize, abstract, synopsize.

abbreviation noun shortening, reduction, cutting, contraction, condensation, compression, abridgment.

abdicate verb **1** *the king abdicated due to illness* resign, stand down, retire, quit. **2** *abdicate the throne* give up, renounce, resign from, relinquish. **3** *abdicate responsibility* reject, disown, waive, yield, forgo, refuse, abandon, turn one's back on, wash one's hands of.

abduct verb kidnap, carry off, run away/off with, make off with, seize, hold as hostage.

aberrant adjective deviant, divergent, anomalous, abnormal, irregular, atypical, freakish.

aberration noun **1** *a statistical aberration* deviation, divergence, anomaly, abnormality, variation, freak. **2** *in a moment of aberration* abnormality, irregularity, eccentricity, deviation, straying, aberrancy. **3** *a mental aberration* disorder, disease, irregularity, instability.

abet verb assist, aid, help, support, back, second, encourage, promote, cooperate with, connive at, endorse, sanction, succor.

abhor verb detest, loathe, hate, abominate, feel aversion to, shrink/recoil from.

abhorrent adjective detestable, loathsome, hated, abominable, repellent, repugnant, repulsive, revolting, disgusting, distasteful, horrible, horrid, heinous.

abide verb **1** *abide by the rules* keep to, comply with, observe, follow, obey, agree to, hold to, stick to. **2** *I cannot abide his smoking* stand, tolerate, bear, put up with, endure, stomach.

abiding adjective lasting, everlasting, eternal, unending, constant, enduring, persisting, unchanging, steadfast, immutable.

ability noun **1** *a person of outstanding ability* talent, competence, competency, proficiency, skill, expertise, expertness, adeptness, aptitude, cleverness, flair, gift, knack, *savoir faire; inf.* know-how. **2** *the ability to cope* capacity, capability, potential, potentiality, power, aptness, facility, faculty, propensity.

abject adjective **1** *abject poverty* wretched, miserable, hopeless, pathetic, pitiable. **2** *an abject coward* base, low, vile, worthless, contemptible, despicable. **3** *an abject apology* obsequious, groveling, servile, cringing, ingratiating, sycophantic, submissive.

ablaze adjective **1** *the house was ablaze* on fire, burning, blazing, flaming; *lit.* afire, aflame. **2** *the house was ablaze with lights* lit up, alight, gleaming, glowing, aglow, illuminated, radiant, shimmering, sparkling.

able adjective competent, capable, talented, skillful, skilled, clever, intelligent, accomplished, gifted, proficient, apt, fit, expert, adept, efficient.

able-bodied adjective healthy, fit, robust, strong, sound, sturdy, vigorous, hardy, hale and hearty, muscular, strapping, rugged, burly, stalwart.

abnormal adjective unusual, strange, odd, peculiar, uncommon, curious, queer, weird, eccentric, extraordinary, unexpected, exceptional, irregular, unnatural, erratic, singular, atypical, nontypical, anomalous, deviant, deviating, divergent, aberrant; *inf.* oddball, off the wall, wacko.

abode noun home, house, dwelling place, domicile, dwelling, accommodations, quarters; *inf.* pad.

abolish verb do away with, put an end to, end, stop, terminate, eliminate, eradicate, exterminate, destroy, annihilate, stamp out, obliterate, wipe out, extinguish, quash, expunge, extirpate, annul, cancel, invalidate, nullify, void, rescind, repeal, revoke.

abolition noun ending, termination, elimination, extermination, destruction, annihilation, obliteration, extirpation, annulment, cancellation, nullification, invalidation, repeal.

abominable adjective hateful, loathsome, detestable, odious, obnoxious, base, despicable, contemptible, damnable, cursed, disgusting, revolting, repellent, repulsive, repugnant, abhorrent, reprehensible, foul, vile.

aboriginal adjective indigenous, native, original, earliest, first, ancient, primitive.

abort verb 1 *abort a pregnancy/plan* terminate, halt, stop, end, arrest. 2 *the space mission aborted* come to a halt, end, terminate, fail, miscarry.

abound verb be plentiful, proliferate, thrive, flourish. **abound with/in** be full of, overflow with, teem with, be alive with, swarm with; *inf.* be crawling/lousy with.

aboveboard adverb/adjective honest, fair, open, frank, straight, overt, candid, forthright, unconcealed.

abrasion noun 1 *skin abrasion* graze, scrape, scratch, sore, ulcer. 2 *the abrasion of the rock* erosion, wearing down/away, corrosion, rubbing, scraping.

abrasive adjective 1 *an abrasive substance* erosive, eroding, corrosive, chafing, rubbing, coarse, harsh. 2 *an abrasive manner* caustic, cutting, grating, biting, rough, harsh, irritating.

abridge verb shorten, cut down, condense, contract, compress. *See* ABBREVIATE.

abridgment noun summary, synopsis, précis, abstract, digest, shortening, cutting, condensation, summarization.

abroad adverb 1 *go abroad for the summer* overseas, out of the country, across the ocean. 2 *spread a rumor abroad* far and wide, everywhere, publicly, extensively.

abrupt adjective 1 *an abrupt ending* sudden, quick, hurried, hasty, swift, rapid, headlong, instantaneous, surprising, unexpected, unanticipated. 2 *an abrupt manner* curt, blunt, brusque, gruff, snappish, unceremonious, rough, rude. 3 *an abrupt slope* steep, sheer, precipitous, sudden, sharp. 4 *an abrupt writing style* jerky, disconnected, rough.

abscess noun ulcer, ulceration, boil, pustule, carbuncle, pimple.

abscond verb *abscond with the funds* run away, bolt, clear out, flee, make off, escape, take flight, fly, decamp, disappear, take to one's heels, make a quick getaway.

absence noun 1 *the teacher noted their absence* nonattendance, nonappearance, truancy, absenteeism. 2 *an absence of proof* lack, want, nonexistence, unavailability.

absent adjective 1 *the workers are absent* away, off, out, gone, missing, truant, unavailable. 2 *an absent expression* absentminded, distracted, preoccupied, faraway, blank, empty, vacant, inattentive, vague, absorbed.

absentminded adjective forgetful, oblivious. *See* ABSENT 2.

absolute adjective 1 *absolute trust* complete, total, utter, out and out, perfect, entire, undivided, unqualified. 2 *the absolute truth* certain, positive, definite, unquestionable, undoubted, unequivocal, decisive, unconditional, infallible. 3 *an absolute standard* fixed, rigid, established, set, definite. 4 *absolute power* unlimited, unrestricted, unrestrained, ultimate, total, supreme, unconditional, sovereign, omnipotent, despotic, dictatorial, autocratic, tyrannical, authoritarian.

absolutely adverb 1 *absolutely correct* completely, totally, utterly, perfectly, entirely, wholly, fully, thoroughly. 2 *absolutely the worst driver* certainly, positively, definitely, unquestionably, without a doubt, unequivocally, unconditionally, conclusively, unreservedly, actually, in actual fact, really, in truth. 3 *ruling absolutely* despotically, dictatorially, autocratically, tyrannically.

absolve verb 1 *absolve from blame* acquit, exonerate, discharge, release, free, deliver, liberate, let off, clear, exculpate. 2 *absolve sinners* forgive, pardon, excuse, reprieve, clear, set free, vindicate.

absorb verb 1 *absorb liquid* soak up, suck up, draw up/in, take up/in, blot up, mop, sponge up, sop up. 2 *absorb their attention* occupy, engage, preoccupy, captivate, engross, monopolize, rivet.

absorbent adjective porous, spongy, permeable, pervious, penetrable, receptive, blotting.

absorbing adjective fascinating, gripping, interesting, captivating, engrossing, riveting, spellbinding.

abstain verb *abstain from voting/pleasure/drinking* refrain, decline, hold back, keep from, refuse, renounce, avoid, shun, eschew; teetotal, be/stay sober, take the pledge; *inf.* be on the wagon.

abstinence noun teetotalism, temperance, sobriety, refraining, forbearing, renunciation.

abstract adjective **1** *abstract beliefs* theoretical, conceptual, notional, intellectual, metaphysical, philosophical. **2** *abstract theories* complex, abstruse, recondite, obscure, deep.

abstract noun summary, synopsis, précis, abridgment, condensation, digest.

absurd adjective ridiculous, foolish, silly, idiotic, stupid, nonsensical, senseless, inane, crazy, ludicrous, funny, laughable, comical, preposterous, farcical, harebrained, asinine; *inf.* daft.

absurdity noun ridiculousness, foolishness, silliness, idiocy, stupidity, inanity, folly, incongruity, irrationality, ludicrousness, funniness, comedy, humor, joke, farce; nonsense, rubbish, gibberish, drivel.

abundance noun plenty, profusion, copiousness, amplitude, affluence, lavishness; *inf.* heaps, lots, tons, oodles.

abundant adjective plentiful, large, great, huge, ample, well-supplied, well-provided, profuse, copious, lavish, bountiful, teeming, overflowing; *inf.* galore.

abuse verb **1** *abuse power/alcohol* misuse, misapply, misemploy, mishandle, exploit. **2** *abuse children* mistreat, maltreat, ill-use, ill-treat, injure, hurt, harm, beat, wrong, oppress, torture. **3** *abuse trespassers* insult, swear at, curse, scold, rebuke, upbraid, reprove, castigate, revile, vilify, slander.

abuse noun **1** *the abuse of power/alcohol* misuse, misapplication, misemployment, mishandling, exploitation. **2** *child abuse* mistreatment, maltreatment, ill-use, ill-treatment, manhandling, injury, hurt, harm, beating, oppression. **3** *torrents of abuse* swearing, cursing, scolding, upbraiding, vilification, vituperation, defamation, slander, insults, curses, expletives, swearwords.

abusive adjective insulting, rude, blasphemous, offensive, vulgar, vituperative, reproachful, reproving, derisive.

abut verb adjoin, border, verge on, join, touch, meet, impinge on.

abysmal adjective extreme, utter, complete, thorough, profound, deep, endless, unfathomable, bottomless.

abyss noun chasm, gorge, cavity, void, pit, bottomless pit, hole, hellhole, gulf, depth, depths, ravine, canyon, crevasse.

academic adjective **1** *academic considerations* educational, scholastic, instructional,

pedagogical. **2** *an academic turn of mind* scholarly, studious, intellectual, erudite, learned, pedantic, professorial, cerebral; *inf.* brainy. **3** *an academic solution* theoretical, hypothetical, notional, impractical, unrealistic, speculative, ivory-towerish.

academic noun scholar, lecturer, teacher, tutor, professor, fellow, pedant, pedagogue; *inf.* bookworm, egghead.

accede verb **accede to 1** *accede to the request* agree to, consent to, accept, assent to, acquiesce to, comply with, go along with, concur with, grant. **2** *accede to the throne* succeed to, assume, attain, inherit.

accentuate verb **1** *the black dress accentuated her paleness* emphasize, stress, highlight, underline, draw attention to, give prominence to, heighten, point up, underscore, accent. **2** *accentuate the pulse of the music* stress, put the stress/emphasis on, emphasize, accent.

accept verb **1** *accept the award* receive, take, get, gain, obtain, acquire. **2** *accept the decision* accede to, agree to, consent to, acquiesce in, concur with, comply with, go along with, defer to. **3** *accept the responsibility* take on, undertake, assume, bear, tackle. **4** *accept their story* believe, trust, credit, have faith in. **5** *accepted as one of the family* welcome, receive, embrace, integrate.

acceptable adjective **1** *an acceptable present* welcome, agreeable, delightful, pleasing, desirable. **2** *an acceptable standard of work* satisfactory, good enough, adequate, passable, tolerable. **3** *an acceptable risk* allowable, tolerable, admissible, bearable.

access noun **1** *access to the building* entry, entrance, way in; admittance, admission. **2** *access to the prisoner | access to information* admission, admittance, entrée, right of entry, permission/opportunity to enter; accessibility, attainability.

accessory noun **1** *his accessory in the raid* accomplice, associate, confederate, abettor, helper, assistant, partner. **2** *bicycle accessories* attachment, extra, addition, adjunct, appendage, supplement. **3** *clothing accessories* adornment, ornament, ornamentation, embellishment, trappings.

accident noun **1** *an industrial/automobile accident* mishap, casualty, misfortune, misadventure, injury, disaster, tragedy; crash, collision; *inf.* pileup. **2** *met by accident* chance, fate, twist of fate, fortune, luck; *inf.* fluke.

accidental adjective **1** *accidental death | an accidental meeting* chance, unintentional, unintended, inadvertent, unexpected, unforeseen, unlooked-for, fortuitous, unanticipated, unplanned. **2** *an accidental* *consideration* nonessential, inessential, incidental, extraneous, extrinsic, supplementary, subsidiary, subordinate, secondary, irrelevant.

acclaim verb **1** *acclaim his victory* applaud, cheer, celebrate, salute, welcome, approve, honor, praise, commend, hail, extol. **2** *acclaim her queen* declare, announce, proclaim.

acclaim noun *the acclaim of the crowd* applause, ovation, praise, commendation, approval, approbation, homage, tribute; cheers, congratulations, plaudits, bouquets.

acclimate verb adjust, adapt, accustom, get used, accommodate, accustom/habituate oneself, become seasoned, familiarize oneself.

accommodate verb **1** *we can accommodate four people* put up, house, cater for, board, lodge, provide shelter for, shelter, harbor, billet. **2** *accommodate our plans to suit yours* adapt, adjust, modify, reconcile, fit, harmonize, conform. **3** *accommodate you with a loan* provide, supply, furnish, grant. **4** *accommodate her whenever possible* help, assist, aid, lend a hand to, oblige.

accommodating adjective obliging, cooperative, helpful, adaptable, pliable, compliant, complaisant, considerate, willing, kindly, hospitable, kind.

accommodations plural noun housing, lodging, board, shelter; residence, house, billet; rooms, quarters; *inf.* digs.

accompany verb **1** *accompany her to the dance* escort, go with, squire, usher. **2** *vegetables accompany the meat* go with, go together with, coexist/occur/coincide with, supplement.

accomplice noun confederate, accessory, collaborator, abettor, associate, partner, ally, assistant, helper, henchman, right hand, right-hand man, fellow conspirator, partner in crime; *inf.* sidekick.

accomplish verb **1** *accomplish an aim* achieve, carry out, fulfill, perform, attain, realize, succeed in, bring off, bring about. **2** *accomplish a task* finish, complete, carry through, do, conclude, effect, execute, consummate.

accomplished adjective **1** *an accomplished player* skilled, skillful, expert, gifted, talented, proficient, adept, masterly, polished, practiced, capable, able, competent, experienced, professional, deft, consummate. **2** *an accomplished aim* achieved, fulfilled, realized. **3** *an accomplished task* finished, completed, executed.

accomplishment noun **1** *a woman of accomplishment* talent, ability, attainment, achievement, proficiency. **2** *the army's proud accomplishments* achievement, act, deed, exploit, performance, attainment, feat. **3** *the accomplishment of aims* achievement, fulfillment, attainment, realization. **4** *the accomplishment of tasks* completion, conclusion, execution, consummation.

accord verb **1** *his statement does not accord with hers* agree, concur, fit, correspond, match, conform, harmonize, be in tune. **2** *accord them permission/welcome* give, grant, confer, bestow, tender, offer, present.

accord noun agreement, harmony, rapport, unison, concord, amity, sympathy, unanimity, accordance. **of one's own accord** of one's own free will, volition, voluntarily, willingly, freely, unforced. **with one accord** unanimously, with one mind, of one voice.

according adverb **according to 1** *according to the manager* as stated/maintained by, as claimed by, on the authority of, on the report of. **2** *acting according to their principles* in accordance with, in agreement with, in line with, in keeping with, in compliance with, in harmony with, in conformity with, in obedience to. **3** *salary according to experience* in proportion to, commensurate with, in relation to.

accordingly adverb **1** *know the truth and act accordingly* appropriately, correspondingly, suitably, properly, fitly, consistently. **2** *they could not pay the rent and accordingly left* as a result, consequently, therefore, so, thus.

accost verb address, speak to, confront, approach, solicit, importune.

account noun **1** *a full account of the accident* statement, report, description, record, narration, narrative, story, recital, explanation, tale, chronicle, history. **2** *pay your account on time* bill, invoice; charges, debts. **3** *the firm's accounts are in good order* ledger, balance sheet, financial statement, books. **4** *of no account* importance, consequence, significance. **on account of** because of, owing to, on (the) grounds of. **on no account** not under any circumstances, under no circumstances, certainly not, absolutely not.

account verb *account her guilty* consider, regard, reckon, believe, think, look upon, view as, judge, count, deem. **account for 1** *he must account for the delay* explain, explain away, give reasons for, show grounds for, justify. **2** *oil accounts for most of their exports* be responsible for, make up, supply, provide.

accountable adjective **1** *accountable for one's actions* responsible, answerable, liable. **2** *accountable to the manager* responsible, answerable. **3** *his actions are not accountable* explicable, explainable, understandable, comprehensible.

accredit verb **1** *accredited with the invention* credit with, have ascribed/attributed to, receive the credit for. **2** *accredited to Shakespeare* ascribe, attribute.

accredited adjective **1** *our accredited representative* official, authorized, legal, appointed, approved, recognized, certified. **2** *accredited theories* accepted, recognized, believed, endorsed, orthodox. **3** *an accredited day-care center* certified, licensed.

accrue verb **1** *bank interest accrued* accumulate, build/mount up, amass, collect, gather, grow, increase. **2** *medical advances accrued from the new technology* arise, follow, ensue, result/emanate from.

accumulate verb **1** *dust accumulated over the weeks* gather, pile/build up, collect, increase, accrue. **2** *accumulate antiques* amass, gather, collect, stockpile, pile/heap up, store, hoard.

accumulation noun stockpile, pile, heap, mass, collection, buildup, gathering, stock, store, hoard, stack; amassing, building up, stockpiling.

accuracy noun correctness, precision, exactness, rightness, validity, closeness, faithfulness, truth, truthfulness, authenticity, factuality, veracity, carefulness, meticulousness.

accurate adjective correct, precise, exact, right, errorless, without error, valid, close, faithful, true, truthful, authentic, factual, literal, careful, meticulous, painstaking.

accusation noun charge, allegation, attribution, incrimination, imputation, denouncement, indictment, arraignment, impeachment, citation.

accuse verb **accuse of** charge with, indict for, arraign for, impeach for, summon with/for, cite for, inculpate for, blame for, lay the blame on, hold responsible/accountable/answerable for.

accustom verb **accustom to** adapt to, adjust to, acclimatize to, get used to, make familiar/acquainted with, habituate to.

ace noun expert, champion, master, star, winner, genius, virtuoso; *inf.* whiz, pro.

ace adjective expert, champion, brilliant, great, superb, outstanding, excellent, first-rate, fine, skillful, adept; *inf.* crack, A-1, tip-top, hotshot.

acerbic adjective **1** *an acerbic wit* harsh, sarcastic, sharp, biting, stinging, caustic, trenchant, bitter, vitriolic, mordant. **2** *an acerbic taste* sour, tart, bitter, acid, sharp, acrid, pungent.

ache noun **1** *an ache in my back* pain, dull pain, soreness; pang, throb, twinge, smarting, gnawing, stabbing, spasm. **2** *an ache in my heart* suffering, sorrow, misery, distress, grief, anguish, affliction, woe, mourning. **3** *an ache for old times* longing, yearning, craving, desire, hunger, hungering, pining, hankering.

ache verb **1** *my head aches* hurt, be sore, be painful, be in pain, pain; throb, pound, twinge, smart. **2** *my heart aches* grieve, be sorrowful, be distressed, be in distress, be miserable, mourn, agonize, suffer. **ache for** *she aches for sunshine* long for, yearn for, crave, desire, hunger for, pine for.

achieve verb **1** *achieve success* attain, reach, arrive at, gain, earn, realize, win, acquire, obtain, procure, get, wrest. **2** *achieve all the tasks begun* complete, fulfill, perform. *See* ACCOMPLISH 2.

achievement noun **1** *the achievement of success* attainment, gaining, realization. **2** *the achievement of tasks begun* completion, finishing. *See* ACCOMPLISHMENT 4. **3** *proud of their child's achievement* accomplishment, feat, performance, deed, effort.

acid adjective **1** *an acid taste* sour, tart, bitter, sharp, biting, acrid, pungent, acerbic, vinegary, vinegarish, acetic, acetous, acidulous. **2** *an acid wit* biting, sarcastic. *See* ACERBIC 1.

acknowledge verb **1** *acknowledge the need for reform* admit, grant, allow, recognize, accept, concede. **2** *acknowledge him with a wave* greet, recognize, notice. **3** *acknowledge a letter* answer, reply to, respond to, react to. **4** *acknowledge help* show appreciation for/of, express gratitude for, give thanks for, thank.

acknowledgment noun **1** *acknowledgment of the need for reform* admission, granting, recognition, acceptance, agreement. **2** *acknowledgment of his presence* recognition, notice. **3** *acknowledgment of a letter* answer, reply, response. **4** *acknowledgment of help* expression of appreciation/gratitude, thanks.

acme noun peak, pinnacle, zenith, climax, culmination, height, high point, crown, summit, optimum, apex.

acquaint verb familiarize, make familiar/conversant, make known to, make aware of, advise of, inform, apprise of, enlighten, let know.

acquaintance noun **1** *an acquaintance, not a close friend* associate, colleague, contact. **2** *our acquaintance with them* association, relationship, contact, fellowship, companionship. **3** *have some acquaintance with his poetry* familiarity, knowledge, awareness, understanding, cognizance.

acquiesce verb consent, agree, accept, concur, approve, assent, allow, comply, conform, concede, go along with, bow to, yield.

acquiescent adjective **1** *an acquiescent response* consenting, concurrent, compliant, concessionary. **2** *an acquiescent personality* submissive, servile, subservient, obsequious, ingratiating, self-effacing; *inf.* bootlicking.

acquire verb obtain, come by, get, receive, gain, procure, earn, win, secure, take possession of, gather, collect, pick up, achieve, attain, appropriate, amass.

acquisition noun **1** *the museum's recent acquisition* purchase, buy, possession, accession, addition, accretion, property. **2** *the acquisition of money* obtaining, procurement, collecting, collection.

acquit verb *acquit the suspect* clear (of charges), absolve, exonerate, discharge, release, vindicate, liberate, free, deliver; *fml.* exculpate. **acquit oneself** *they acquitted themselves well* perform, act, behave, conduct oneself, comport oneself.

acrid adjective **1** *an acrid taste* pungent, sharp, sour, bitter, tart, harsh, acid, stinging, burning, irritating, vinegary, acerbic, acetic. **2** *an acrid wit* acerbic, sarcastic, sharp, stinging, caustic, astringent, trenchant, vitriolic, virulent.

acrimonious adjective bitter, caustic, cutting, sarcastic, harsh, sharp, acid, acerbic, virulent, trenchant, stringent, spiteful, crabbed, vitriolic, venomous.

acrimony noun bitterness, sarcasm, harshness, sharpness, acidity, acerbicity, virulence, spitefulness.

act noun **1** *acts of bravery/cowardice* deed, action, feat, performance, undertaking, operation, execution, exploit, enterprise, achievement, accomplishment. **2** *acts of Congress* bill, law, decree, statute, edict, dictum, enactment, resolution, ruling, judgment, ordinance, measure. **3** *a music hall act* performance, turn, routine, show, sketch, skit. **4** *putting on an act* pretense, sham, fake, make-believe, show, feigning, affectation, counterfeit, front, posture, pose.

act verb **1** *you must act now* take action, do, move, be active, perform, function, react, behave, be employed, be busy. **2** *the painkiller will act soon* work, take effect, operate, function, be efficacious. **3** *she's acting in a play* perform, play, play a part; portray, enact, represent, characterize, personify, stage. **4** *he's not ill but just acting* pretend, fake, feign, pose. **act on/upon 1** *alcohol acts on the brain* affect, have an effect on, influence, alter. **2** *act on instructions* act in accordance with, follow, obey, comply with. **act up** misbehave, give/cause trouble, malfunction.

acting noun **1** *a career in acting* the theater, drama, the performing arts, dramatics, stagecraft, theatricals, performing, portraying. **2** *acting now will save trouble* taking action, moving, functioning, reacting. **3** *the quick acting of the pills* action, working, taking effect. **4** *the acting of the cast* performance, playing, portrayal, enacting. **5** *his acting fools no one* pretending, pretense, faking, feigning, play-acting, posturing.

acting adjective *an acting head of the department* deputy, substitute, temporary, interim, provisional, pro tem, *pro tempore*.

action noun **1** *their prompt action saved lives* act, deed, move, effort, operation, performance, undertaking, maneuver, exploit. **2** *put ideas into action* activity, doing, motion, operation, work, functioning, performance, effort, exertion. **3** *men of action* activity, energy, vitality, vigor, forcefulness. **4** *the action of acid on metal* effect, influence, power, result, consequence. **5** *the action of the play is set in Spain* events, happenings, incidents, episodes. **6** *a piece of the action* activity, excitement, bustle, happenings, incidents; *inf.* goings-on. **7** *soldiers seeing action* conflict, combat, warfare, fighting, battle. **8** *the military action at Gettysburg* battle, engagement, clash, encounter, skirmish, affray.

actions plural noun behavior, conduct, activity, comportment, deportment, ways.

activate verb switch on, turn on, start, set going, trigger, set in motion, energize.

active adjective **1** *an active member of the team* | *an active volcano* working, functioning, operating, operative, in action, in operation, in force, effective. **2** *people leading active lives* mobile, energetic, vigorous, vital, sprightly, lively, spry, busy, bustling, occupied, involved; *inf.* on the go/move. **3** *active ingredients* effective, effectual, operational, nonpassive, noninert.

activity noun **1** *markets are places of great activity* business, bustle, hustle and bustle, liveliness, movement, life, stir, animation, commotion, flurry, tumult; *inf.* comings and goings. **2** *schoolwork and outside activities* interest, hobby, pastime, pursuit, occupation, venture, undertaking, enterprise, project.

actor, actress noun performer, player, dramatic artist, thespian, film star, starlet, leading man/woman, trouper, tragedian.

actual adjective real, true, factual, genuine, authentic, verified, confirmed, veritable, existing.

actually adverb really, in fact, in point of fact, as a matter of fact, in reality, indeed, truly, in truth.

acumen noun astuteness, shrewdness, sharpness, cleverness, smartness, judgment, discernment, wisdom, perspicacity, ingenuity, insight, sagacity.

acute adjective **1** *an acute sense of hearing | an acute mind* sharp, keen, penetrating, discerning, sensitive, incisive, astute, shrewd, clever, smart, perceptive, perspicacious, discriminating, sagacious, judicious. **2** *an acute shortage* severe, critical, crucial, grave, serious, urgent, pressing. **3** *an acute pain* sharp, shooting, piercing, keen, penetrating, stabbing, intense, excruciating, fierce, racking.

adage noun saying, maxim, axiom, proverb, aphorism, saw, dictum, precept, truism, platitude; *fml.* apothegm.

adamant adjective resolute, determined, firm, immovable, unshakable, uncompromising, unrelenting, unyielding, unbending, inflexible, obdurate, inexorable, intransigent.

adapt verb **1** *adapt a dress/novel* adjust, tailor, convert, change, alter, modify, transform, remodel, reshape. **2** *adapt to a new environment* adjust, conform, acclimatize, accommodate, familiarize oneself with, habituate oneself.

adaptable adjective **1** *an adaptable design* adjustable, convertible, alterable, modifiable, variable, versatile. **2** *try to be adaptable* flexible, pliant, compliant, malleable, versatile, resilient, easygoing, conformable.

adaptation noun **1** *the adaptation of a dress/novel* adjustment, tailoring, converting, alteration, changing, modification, remodeling, reshaping. **2** *adaptation to a new environment* adjustment, conformity, acclimatization, accommodation, familiarization, habituation.

add verb **1** *he added an extra sentence* include, put on/in, attach, append. **2** *add all the numbers* add up, add together, total, count, count up, compute; *inf.* tot up. **3** *"That's fine," he added* go on to say, state further; *inf.* tack on. **add to** increase, magnify, amplify, augment, intensify, aggravate, exacerbate. **add up** *it doesn't add up* make sense, be/seem reasonable, be/seem plausible; *inf.* ring true, hold water, stand to reason. **add up to 1** *it adds up to $100* amount to, come to, total. **2** *it all adds up to a disaster* amount to, constitute, comprise, signify; *inf.* spell, spell out.

addendum noun addition, appendix, codicil, postscript, appendage.

addict noun **1** *a drug/heroin addict* abuser, user; *inf.* junkie, head, fiend. **2** *a movie addict* fan, enthusiast, devotee, follower, adherent; *inf.* buff, freak, nut.

addiction noun dependency, craving, devotion, obsession, dedication, enslavement, habit.

addition noun **1** *the addition of an extra sentence* inclusion, attachment, appendage. **2** *the addition of a row of figures | check

my addition adding up, counting, totaling, computation, calculation. **3** *an addition to the family* increase, increment, extension, augmentation, gain, supplement, appendage. **in addition** additionally, besides, as well, as well as.

additional adjective extra, supplementary, further, more, other, over and above.

address noun **1** *the address on the envelope* inscription, label, superscription. **2** *a new address* house, home, location, place, residence, abode, domicile, dwelling. **3** *an address to the crowd* speech, lecture, talk, discourse, oration, sermon, harangue, diatribe.

address verb **1** *address an envelope* direct, label, inscribe, superscribe. **2** *address the audience* talk to, speak to, give a talk to, make a speech to, lecture, preach to, declaim to, harangue; *inf.* spout to. **3** *address someone across the street* greet, speak to, hail, salute. **4** *how to address the mayor* name, call, speak to, write. **5** *address any remarks to the manager* direct, send, communicate, convey, forward, remit. **6** *address the golf ball* take aim at, aim at, face. **address oneself to** apply oneself to, attend to, turn to, get down to, devote oneself to, concentrate on.

adept adjective proficient, skillful; *inf.* top-notch, A-1. *See* ACCOMPLISHED 1.

adequate adjective **1** *an adequate salary* sufficient, enough, ample, reasonable, satisfactory, requisite. **2** *your work is adequate* passable, tolerable, acceptable, fair, middle-of-the-road, mediocre, unexceptional, indifferent, average, so-so. **adequate to** *he did not feel adequate to the task* up to, equal to, capable of (doing/performing), competent for, suited to.

adhere verb **adhere to** stick to, stick fast to, cling to, hold fast to, cohere to, be fixed to, be pasted/glued to; hold to, abide by, comply with, stand by, be faithful to, follow, obey, fulfill.

adherent noun supporter, follower, upholder, advocate, disciple, votary, partisan, sectary, member; fan, admirer, follower, enthusiast, devotee, lover, addict, aficionado; *inf.* buff, freak, fiend.

adherent adjective sticky, adhering. *See* ADHESIVE adjective.

adhesive adjective sticky, sticking, adhering, adherent, clinging, tacky, gluey, gummy, cohesive, viscous, viscid, glutinous, mucilaginous.

adhesive noun glue, fixative, gum, paste, cement, mucilage.

adjacent adjective adjoining, neighboring, next door, abutting, bordering, alongside, contiguous, attached, touching, conjoining.

adjoining adjective connected, connecting. *See* ADJACENT.

adjourn verb break off, discontinue, interrupt, suspend, dissolve, postpone, put off, defer, delay, shelve; break, pause, take a recess; withdraw, retire, retreat, repair.

adjournment noun discontinuation, interruption, suspension, postponement, deferral, delay; breaking-off, break, pause, recess; withdrawing, retirement, retreat; *fml.* repairing.

adjudicate verb judge, arbitrate, referee, umpire; decide on, settle, determine, pronounce on, give a ruling on.

adjunct noun extra, addition, attachment, accessory, appendage, add-on.

adjust verb adapt, become accustomed, get used (to), accommodate, acclimatize, reconcile oneself, habituate oneself, assimilate; rearrange, alter, modify, change, remodel, regulate, fix, repair, rectify.

adjustable adjective alterable, adaptable, modifiable, movable, accommodating, amenable, obliging, flexible.

adjustment noun adaptation, accommodation, acclimatization, alteration, modification, regulating, fixing, repair, change, rearrangement.

ad lib verb extemporize, improvise, speak off the cuff, speak impromptu.

administer verb 1 *administer the firm's financial affairs* manage, direct, control, conduct, run, govern, operate, superintend, supervise, oversee, preside over. 2 *administer justice* dispense, hand out, allot, deal, distribute, mete out, disburse, provide. 3 *administer a remedy* apply, give, dispense.

administration noun 1 *he's in hospital administration* management, direction, operation, supervision. 2 *the Nixon administration* government, regime, term of office. 3 *the administration of justice* dispensation, discharge, allotment, dealing, distribution. 4 *the administration of a remedy* application, dispensation, provision.

administrative adjective managerial, management, directorial, executive, organizational, supervisory, regulatory.

administrator noun manager, director, executive, head, chief, superintendent, supervisor.

admirable adjective worthy, commendable, praiseworthy, laudable, good, excellent.

admiration noun approval, regard, high regard, respect, approbation, appreciation, praise, esteem, veneration.

admire verb approve of, respect, think highly of, appreciate, applaud, praise, hold in high regard/esteem, venerate, like, sing the praises of, be taken with, adore, love, idolize.

admirer noun enthusiast, fan, devotee, aficionado, supporter, follower; suitor, wooer, beau, sweetheart, lover, boyfriend, girlfriend.

admissible adjective allowable, allowed, permissible, permitted, acceptable.

admission noun 1 *admission to the university* admittance, entry, right of entry, entrance, access, entrée. 2 *admission is $3* entrance fee, ticket, cover charge. 3 *an admission of guilt* acknowledgment, confession, revelation, disclosure, divulgence.

admit verb 1 *one ticket admits two people* let in, allow/permit entry to, give access to. 2 *they admitted their guilt* acknowledge, confess, reveal, make known, disclose, divulge, declare, avow. 3 *admit that you may be right* concede, accept, grant, agree, allow, concur.

admittance noun entry, access. *See* ADMISSION 1.

admonish verb 1 *admonish the boys for smoking* reprimand, rebuke, scold, reprove, upbraid, chide, censure, berate. 2 *she admonished us to seek help* advise, urge, counsel, exhort.

admonition noun 1 *deliver an admonition to the culprits* reprimand, rebuke, scolding. 2 *gave them an admonition to seek help* piece of advice, warning, exhortation; advice.

ado noun fuss, trouble, bother, commotion, upset, agitation, hubbub, confusion, disturbance, flurry, to-do.

adolescent adjective teenage, youthful, pubescent, immature, juvenile, childish, puerile.

adolescent noun teenager, youngster, young person, youth.

adopt verb 1 *adopt Eastern customs* assume, take on, affect, embrace, espouse, appropriate. 2 *adopt a candidate* select, choose, vote for. 3 *adopt the new measures* approve, endorse, accept, ratify.

adoption noun 1 *the adoption of Asian customs* assumption, taking on, affecting, espousal, appropriation. 2 *the adoption of the candidate* selection, choosing, voting for. 3 *the adoption of the new measures* approval, endorsement, acceptance, ratification.

adorable adjective lovable, appealing, charming, sweet, enchanting, captivating, dear, darling, delightful, attractive, winsome, winning, fetching.

adoration noun 1 *the adoration of their children* love, doting, devotion, idolization. 2 *the adoration of God* worship, glorification, praise, homage, exaltation, veneration. 3 *their adoration of travel* love, liking, enjoyment.

adore verb **1** *adore their children* love, be devoted to, dote on, cherish, hold dear, idolize. **2** *let us adore God* worship, glorify, praise, revere, reverence, exalt, magnify, laud, extol, venerate. **3** *they adore ice cream* like, love, be fond of, enjoy, delight in, relish.

adorn verb decorate, embellish, ornament, trim, enhance, beautify, bedeck, deck, array, grace, emblazon.

adornment noun decoration, embellishment, ornamentation, trimming, enhancement, beautification, enrichment, ornament, frills, accessories, trimmings.

adrift adjective drifting, unmoored, unanchored, aimless, purposeless, directionless, awry, amiss, astray, off course.

adroit adjective skillful, skilled, expert, adept, dexterous, deft, clever, able, capable, competent, masterly, proficient, quick-thinking, quick-witted, cunning, astute, shrewd.

adulation noun worship, hero-worship, idolization, adoration, glorification; praise, flattery, blandishments.

adult adjective **1** *an adult tree* mature, grown-up, full-grown, fully developed; *fml.* of age. **2** *adult magazines* sexually explicit, obscene, pornographic.

adulterate verb debase, degrade, spoil, contaminate, taint, doctor, water down.

advance verb **1** *the army advanced* move forward, proceed, go ahead, move along, press on, push forward, make headway, forge ahead, gain ground. **2** *advance the building schedule* speed up, accelerate, step up, hasten, expedite, hurry, quicken, forward. **3** *advance his chances of promotion* further, forward, help, assist, facilitate, boost, improve. **4** *her career advanced rapidly* progress, develop, improve. **5** *advance a theory* put forward, suggest, propose, submit. **6** *the company advanced him $500* lend, supply on credit.

advance noun **1** *the advance of the army* movement forward, progress, headway. **2** *the advance of civilization* progress, development, advancement, improvement, betterment, furtherance. **3** *recent medical advances* development, discovery, breakthrough, finding, invention.

advance adjective **1** *the advance party* sent ahead, leading, first. **2** *advance warning* early, previous, prior, beforehand.

advanced adjective progressive, forward, highly developed, modern, ultramodern, avant-garde, ahead of the times.

advances plural noun approaches, overtures, moves, proposals, propositions.

advantage noun **1** *its main advantage is size* benefit, asset, good point, boon, blessing. **2** *the advantage of age* benefit, superiority, dominance, supremacy, power, mastery, upper hand, trump card. **3** *not to one's advantage* benefit, profit, gain, good.

advantageous adjective **1** *an advantageous position* favorable, superior, dominant, powerful. **2** *advantageous to your career* beneficial, helpful, useful, valuable, profitable.

advent noun arrival, coming, appearance, approach, occurrence.

adventure noun **1** *a spirit of adventure* risk, hazard, danger, peril, gamble, gambling. **2** *the sailor's adventures* exploit, deed, feat, experience.

adventurous adjective daring, daredevil, bold, intrepid, audacious, adventuresome, venturesome, risky, dangerous, perilous, hazardous.

adversary noun opponent, antagonist, rival, enemy, foe, competitor.

adverse adjective **1** *adverse circumstances* unfavorable, unlucky, disadvantageous, inauspicious, unpropitious. **2** *adverse criticism* hostile, unfriendly, unfavorable, antagonistic, negative. **3** *adverse to health* harmful, dangerous, injurious, detrimental, hurtful.

adversity noun misfortune, ill luck, bad luck, trouble, hardship, distress, disaster, suffering, affliction, sorrow, misery, tribulation, woe, hard times, mishap, accident, shock, reverse, setback, catastrophe, calamity.

advertise verb **1** *advertise the results* make known, publicize, announce, broadcast, proclaim, call attention to, promulgate. **2** *advertise a product* promote, publicize, give publicity to, display, tout; *inf.* push, plug.

advertisement noun **1** *a newspaper advertisement* notice, announcement; *inf.* ad; display ad, want ad, classified ad. **2** *a television advertisement* promotion, commercial, blurb; *inf.* ad, plug. **3** *product advertisement* advertising, promotion, publicizing, touting; *inf.* plugging, pushing.

advice noun guidance, counseling, counsel, help, recommendations, suggestions, hints, tips.

advisable adjective desirable, sensible, sound, prudent, proper, appropriate, suitable, fitting, apt, judicious, expedient, politic.

advise verb **1** *cannot advise you on your affairs | advise caution* guide, counsel, instruct; suggest, recommend, urge. **2** *advise you of the facts* inform, notify, apprise, acquaint with, warn.

adviser, advisor noun counselor, mentor, guide, consultant, coach, teacher, therapist.

advocate verb recommend, advise, favor, support, uphold, back, subscribe to, champion, speak for, campaign on behalf of, argue/plead/press for, urge, promote.

advocate noun 1 *an advocate of political freedom* supporter, upholder, backer, champion, spokesman, spokeswoman, speaker, campaigner, pleader, promoter, proponent, exponent, apostle, apologist. 2 *the defendant's advocate* counsel, lawyer, attorney.

aegis noun protection, guardianship, support, patronage, sponsorship, auspices.

affable adjective friendly, amiable, genial, congenial, cordial, pleasant, agreeable, easygoing, good-humored, good-natured, sociable.

affair noun 1 *that's my own affair* concern, business, matter, responsibility. 2 *forget the sad affair* event, happening, occurrence, incident, episode, circumstance, adventure, case. 3 *an informal affair* party, function, reception, gathering; *inf.* get-together, do. 4 *an affair with a married man* love affair, relationship, romance, liaison, affair of the heart, intrigue, amour.

affect verb 1 *it affected his health* have an effect on, influence, act on, work on, have an impact on, change, alter, transform. 2 *the disease affected his lungs* attack, strike at, infect. 3 *the experience deeply affected us* move, touch, upset, disturb.

affectation noun pretense, pretension, pretentiousness, affectedness, artificiality, insincerity, posturing.

affected adjective 1 *an affected style of writing* pretentious, artificial, unnatural, assumed, high-flown, ostentatious, contrived, pompous, mannered. 2 *an affected politeness* pretended, feigned, fake, counterfeit, sham, simulated.

affection noun love, liking, fondness, warmth, devotion, caring, attachment, friendship, amity, warm feelings.

affectionate adjective loving, fond, devoted, caring, tender, doting.

affiliate verb associate, unite, combine, join, ally.

affiliation noun connection, link, bond, tie, relationship.

affirm verb state, assert, declare, aver, proclaim, pronounce, swear, attest.

afflict verb trouble, burden, distress, beset, harass, oppress, torment, plague, rack, smite.

affliction noun trouble, distress, pain, misery, suffering, wretchedness, hardship, misfortune, sorrow, torment, tribulation, woe, disorder, disease, trial, ordeal, scourge, plague.

affluence noun wealth, prosperity, opulence, fortune, richness, riches, resources.

affluent adjective rich, wealthy, prosperous, opulent, well off, moneyed, well-to-do, comfortable; *inf.* well-heeled, in the money, loaded.

afford verb 1 *afford a house* pay for, meet the expense of, spare the price of. 2 *afford the loss* bear, sustain, stand. 3 *the tree affords shade/fruit* provide, supply, offer, give, impart, bestow, furnish, yield, produce, bear.

affront noun insult, offense, indignity, slight, snub, outrage; *inf.* slap in the face.

afraid adjective 1 *noises made them afraid* frightened, scared, terrified, apprehensive, fearful, nervous, alarmed (at), intimidated (by), terror-stricken. 2 *I'm afraid I can't help* sorry, regretful, apologetic, unhappy.

aftermath noun aftereffects, effects, consequences, results; end result, outcome, upshot, issue, end.

against preposition 1 *people against the movement* opposed to, in opposition to, hostile to, at odds with, in disagreement with, versus. 2 *rowing against the tide* in opposition to, counter to, resisting. 3 *leaning against the fence* touching, in contact with, close up to, up against, abutting. 4 *his age is against him* disadvantageous to, unfavorable to, damaging to, detrimental to, prejudicial to.

age noun 1 *what is his age?* number of years, lifetime, duration, stage of life, generation. 2 *wisdom comes with age* maturity, seniority, elderliness, old age, advancing years, declining years, senescence. 3 *the Elizabethan age* era, epoch, period, time.

age verb mature, ripen, grow up, come of age; grow old, decline, wither, fade.

aged adjective old, elderly, superannuated; *fml.* senescent; *inf.* as old as the hills.

agency noun 1 *advertising agency* business, organization, company, firm, office, bureau, concern. 2 *brought together through the agency of friends* mediation, intervention, intercession.

agenda noun program, schedule, timetable, plan, list, scheme.

agent noun 1 *an insurance agent* representative, negotiator, emissary; *inf.* rep. 2 *an enemy agent* spy, secret agent; *inf.* mole. 3 *a cleansing agent* factor, cause, instrument, vehicle, means, power, force.

ages plural noun a long time, an eternity, an eon; hours, days, months, years, eons, hours/days/months on end.

aggravate verb 1 *aggravate the situation* worsen, exacerbate, inflame, intensify, increase, heighten, magnify. 2 *aggravate the* *teacher* irritate, irk, get on one's nerves, rub the wrong way; *inf.* needle. *See* ANGER verb.

aggravation noun **1** *the aggravation of the situation* worsening, exacerbation, intensification. **2** *the aggravation of the teacher* annoyance, irritation, angering, exasperation, provocation. **3** *just one more aggravation* irritant, nuisance, pest, thorn in the flesh; *inf.* headache.

aggression noun attack, assault, injury, encroachment, offense, onslaught, foray, raid, sortie, offensive, invasion.

aggressive adjective **1** *an aggressive person/act* quarrelsome, argumentative, belligerent, pugnacious, militant, warring, hostile, combative, bellicose, invasive, intrusive. **2** *aggressive sales promotion* assertive, forceful, insistent, vigorous, energetic, dynamic, bold, enterprising, zealous; *inf.* pushy.

aggressor noun attacker, assaulter, invader, assailant, provoker, instigator, initiator.

agile adjective active, nimble, spry, lithe, fit, supple, sprightly, in good condition, lively, quick-moving, limber.

agility noun activeness, nimbleness, litheness, fitness, suppleness.

agitate verb **1** *she was agitated by the delay* upset, work up, perturb, fluster, ruffle, disconcert. **2** *agitate the mixture* stir, whisk, beat, churn, shake, toss. **3** *agitate the crowd* stir up, rouse, arouse, excite, inflame, incite, foment.

agitator noun troublemaker, instigator, agent provocateur, inciter, rabble-rouser, provoker, fomenter, firebrand, revolutionary, demagogue.

agonizing adjective excruciating, harrowing, racking, painful, acute, insufferable, torturous.

agony noun suffering, pain, hurt, distress, torture, torment, anguish, misery, woe; pangs, throes.

agree verb **agree on** settle on, arrange, arrive at, decide on. **agree to** consent to, accept, approve, acquiesce in, assent to, concede to, allow, admit, grant. **agree with 1** *agree with you* concur with, be of the same mind/opinion with, see eye to eye with. **2** *the statements do not agree with each other* match, correspond to, conform to, harmonize with. **3** *the warm climate agrees with me* suit, be good for.

agreeable adjective **1** *agreeable occasion/manner* pleasant, pleasing, delightful, enjoyable, pleasurable, likable, charming, amiable, nice, friendly, good-natured. **2** *if you want us to go, we are agreeable* willing, amenable, compliant.

agreement noun **1** *in total agreement* accord, assent, concurrence, harmony, unity, concord. **2** *a business agreement* contract, compact, treaty, covenant, concordat, pact; *inf.* deal. **3** *the agreement of the statements* correspondence, conformity, harmony.

aid verb **1** *aid us in our effort* help, assist, support, lend a hand, succor, sustain. **2** *aid recovery* hasten, facilitate, promote.

aid noun **1** *give aid to a motorist* help, assistance, support, a helping hand, succor, encouragement. **2** *foreign aid* contribution, subsidy, gift, donation.

aide noun assistant, helper, help; *inf.* right arm, girl/man Friday.

ailing adjective ill, unwell, sick, sickly, poorly, weak, indisposed, under the weather.

ailment noun illness, disease, disorder, sickness, complaint, infection.

aim verb **1** *aim a gun* point, direct, take aim, train, sight, focus, position. **2** *aim to increase profits* plan, intend, resolve, propose. **aim at/for** set one's sights on, try for, strive for, work toward, aspire to.

aim noun **1** *the archer's aim* pointing, directing, training; line of sight. **2** *our aim is to win* goal, ambition, objective, object, end, target, intention, plan, purpose.

aimless adjective purposeless, pointless, goalless, undirected, unambitious, drifting, wandering.

air noun **1** *propelled through the air* atmosphere, sky, heavens, aerospace. **2** *let's get some air* breeze, breath of air, gust/movement of wind, zephyr, draft. **3** *an air of peace* impression, appearance, look, atmosphere, mood, ambience, aura, manner, feeling. **4** *playing an old air* tune, melody, song, theme, strain.

air verb **1** *air the room* ventilate, aerate, freshen. **2** *air one's views* express, voice, publish, vent, communicate, reveal, proclaim.

airs plural noun affectedness, posing, posturing; affectations, pretensions.

airy adjective **1** *an airy day* breezy, windy, gusty. **2** *an airy office* well-ventilated, spacious, open. **3** *an airy being* delicate, insubstantial, ethereal, flimsy, wispy, incorporeal. **4** *an airy reply* lighthearted, breezy, flippant, blithe, nonchalant.

akin adjective akin to related to, similar to, corresponding to.

alarm noun **1** *a burglar alarm* warning, signal, bell, siren, alert. **2** *rumors causing alarm* fear, fright, terror, apprehension, panic, trepidation, nervousness, anxiety.

alarm verb **1** *crowds alarm her* frighten, scare, terrify, panic, unnerve, distress, intimidate. **2** *saw the fire and alarmed the neighborhood* warn, alert, arouse, signal.

alarming adjective frightening, disturbing, terrifying, startling, shocking, distressing.

alcohol noun liquor, spirits; *inf.* booze, firewater, hooch, rotgut, hard stuff.

alcoholic adjective intoxicating, inebriating, strong, hard.

alcoholic noun hard/heavy drinker, dipsomaniac, drunk, drunkard, tippler, sot, toper, inebriate, imbiber; *inf.* boozer, lush, alky, tosspot, wino.

alert adjective wide awake, sharp, bright, quick, keen, perceptive; *inf.* on the ball, on one's toes. **alert to** wide awake to, on the lookout for, aware of, heedful of, watchful of, attentive to, wary of, on one's guard for; *fml.* on the qui vive for.

alias noun assumed/false name, pseudonym, stage name, nom de plume, sobriquet, nom de guerre.

alibi noun defense, plea, justification, explanation, reason, vindication, excuse, pretext.

alien adjective **1** *an alien culture* foreign, overseas, nonnative, strange, unfamiliar, unknown, remote, exotic. **2** *alien to his principles* opposed, conflicting, contrary, adverse, incompatible, inimical.

alien noun **1** *aliens deported in wartime* foreigner, outsider, stranger. **2** *aliens from Mars* extraterrestrial, *inf.* E.T., little green man.

alienate verb estrange, set against, turn away, make hostile, sever, divorce, separate, cut off, divide.

align verb **1** *align the books on the shelves* line up, arrange, put in order. **2** *align with a political party* affiliate, ally, associate, join, side, sympathize, agree.

alike adjective like, similar, the same, indistinguishable.

alike adverb *think alike* similarly, the same, identically, in like manner.

alive adjective **1** *the captives are still alive* living, live, breathing; *inf.* in the land of the living, alive and kicking; *fml.* animate. **2** *interest is still very much alive* active, continuing, going on, existing, in the air/wind, in operation. **3** *seeming very much alive today* lively, active, energetic, alert, animated, vivacious, vigorous, vital, spirited. **4** *alive to the possibilities* alert to, awake to, aware/cognizant of. **5** *alive with vermin* overflowing, teeming, crowded, packed, swarming; *inf.* crawling, hopping.

all noun everyone, everybody, every/each person/thing, everything, the whole/total amount, the entirety; *inf.* the whole lot; lock, stock, and barrel.

allay verb *allay suffering* lessen, diminish. *See* ASSUAGE 1.

allegation noun claim, charge, accusation, declaration, statement, assertion.

allege verb claim, profess, declare, state, assert, aver, avow, affirm.

alleged adjective supposed, so-called, claimed, designated.

allegiance noun loyalty, obedience, fidelity, faithfulness, duty, devotion, constancy, adherence, homage; *fml.* fealty.

alleviate verb *alleviate poverty* reduce, ease, abate. *See* ASSUAGE 1.

alley noun alleyway, lane, passage, passageway, path, pathway, corridor, backstreet.

alliance noun **1** *form an alliance* union, association, coalition, league, confederation, federation, partnership. **2** *the alliance between physics and math* affinity, association, relationship.

allocate verb allot, assign, distribute, give out, share/mete/parcel out, dispense, apportion.

allot verb **1** *we allotted money for expenses* set aside, designate, earmark, assign, appropriate. **2** *allot portions to everyone* distribute, dispense. *See* ALLOCATE.

allow verb **1** *allow them to enter* permit, let, authorize, sanction; *inf.* give the go-ahead to, give the green light to. **2** *allow $50 for expenses* allocate, allot, assign. **3** *I allow that you won* admit, acknowledge, concede, grant. **allow for** *allow for wastage* plan for, take into consideration/account, make provision for, provide for.

allowable adjective permissible, admissible, authorized, sanctioned, justifiable, legitimate; *inf.* legit.

allowance noun **1** *father gives her an allowance* remittance, payment, subsidy, grant, contribution. **2** *our book allowance* allocation, quota, share, ration, portion. **3** *tax/business allowances* rebate, discount, deduction, reduction, concession. **make allowances for** take into consideration/account, bear in mind, have regard to; make excuses for, excuse, forgive, pardon.

alloy noun compound, mixture, amalgam, blend, combination, admixture, composite.

all right adjective **1** *the children are all right* safe, safe and sound, secure, unharmed, well, fine; *inf.* OK. **2** *the coffee's all right?* satisfactory, acceptable, adequate, passable; *inf.* OK.

all right adverb **1** *reached home all right* safely; *inf.* OK. **2** *worked out all right* satisfactorily, acceptably, fine; *inf.* OK.

allude verb *allude to* refer to, mention, touch upon, mention in passing, cite.

allure verb attract, fascinate, entice, seduce, charm, enchant, bewitch, beguile, captivate, tempt, lure.

allusion noun reference, citation, mention, hint, intimation, suggestion.

ally noun confederate, partner, associate, accomplice, colleague, helper, accessory, abettor.

almost adverb nearly, close to, just about, not quite, all but, not far from, approximately, practically, as good as, virtually, approaching, verging on, bordering on.

alone adjective/adverb **1** *be alone in the house* by oneself, solitary, unaccompanied, unattended, unescorted, companionless. **2** *succeed alone* single-handed, single-handedly, unassisted, unaided. **3** *left (all) alone* solitary, lonely, deserted, abandoned, forsaken, forlorn, desolate, isolated. **4** *house standing alone* separate, detached, apart, unconnected. **5** *in his field the professor stands alone* unique, unparalleled, unequaled, unsurpassed, matchless, peerless. **6** *you alone can help* only, solely, just, exclusively, no one else but, nothing but.

aloof adjective distant, detached, unresponsive, remote, unapproachable, standoffish, indifferent, unsympathetic, unsociable, unfriendly, cold, chilly.

alter verb change, make different, adjust, adapt, modify, convert, remodel, vary, transform, metamorphose.

alteration noun change, adjustment, adaptation, modification, revision, transformation, metamorphosis.

alternate adjective every other, every second; in rotation, rotating, occurring in turns, following in sequence, sequential; different. *See* ALTERNATIVE adjective 1.

alternate verb take turns, rotate, interchange, oscillate.

alternative adjective **1** *an alternative route* another, other, second, different. **2** *alternative medicine* nonstandard, unconventional, nonconventional.

alternative noun choice, option, preference, election, substitute.

altitude noun height, elevation; tallness, loftiness.

altogether adverb **1** *altogether content* completely, thoroughly, totally, entirely, absolutely, fully, utterly. **2** *altogether the day was fine* on the whole, all things considered, all in all, by and large. **3** *nine of us altogether* in all, all told, *in toto*, taken together.

altruistic adjective unselfish, selfless, public-spirited, philanthropic, humanitarian, benevolent, charitable.

always adverb **1** *he always comes early* every time, on every occasion, consistently, invariably, without exception, unfailingly. **2** *she's always complaining* continually, constantly, forever, repeatedly, perpetually, incessantly. **3** *he will love her always* forever, forever and ever, evermore, eternally, ever.

amass verb accumulate, pile/heap up, hoard, store up, assemble, garner; *inf.* stash away.

amateur noun nonprofessional, dilettante, layman, tyro, dabbler.

amateurish adjective unprofessional, inexperienced, incompetent, clumsy, bungling.

amaze verb astonish, astound, surprise, dumbfound, flabbergast, shock, stun, startle, stupefy; *inf.* bowl over.

amazement noun astonishment, surprise, shock, bewilderment, stupefaction, wonder.

ambassador noun diplomat, consul, envoy, emissary, legate, attaché, plenipotentiary.

ambiguity noun doubtfulness, obscurity, vagueness, uncertainty, abstruseness, equivocation, double-talk, puzzle, enigma, paradox.

ambiguous adjective equivocal, two-edged; cryptic, obscure, doubtful, unclear, vague, abstruse, puzzling, enigmatic.

ambition noun **1** *ambition to succeed* desire, aspiration, drive, eagerness, zeal, longing; *inf.* get-up-and-go. **2** *an ambition to be boss* goal, aim, objective, wish, dream.

ambitious adjective **1** *an ambitious man* aspiring, forceful, enterprising, zealous, purposeful, assertive. **2** *an ambitious task* challenging, demanding, exacting, formidable, arduous, difficult, bold.

ambivalent adjective *an ambivalent attitude* uncertain, doubtful, fluctuating, vacillating, opposing, conflicting, clashing.

amenable adjective **1** *amenable to suggestion* agreeable, responsive, pliant, flexible, adaptable, manageable. **2** *amenable to the law* accountable, answerable, subject, liable, responsible.

amend verb **1** *amend a text* revise, alter, correct, modify. **2** *amend the situation* improve, remedy, ameliorate, better, fix, set right.

amendment noun **1** *amendment of the text* revision, alteration, correction, modification. **2** *amendment of the situation* improvement, amelioration, betterment, fixing. **3** *amendment to the bylaws* alteration, addendum, attachment, appendage.

amends plural noun *make amends for the mistake* compensation, recompense, reparation.

amiable adjective friendly, pleasant, agreeable, pleasing, charming, delightful, good-natured.

amicable adjective *an amicable settlement* friendly, civil, harmonious, nonhostile.

amiss adjective *something was amiss* wrong, awry, faulty, out of order, unsatisfactory, inappropriate.

ammunition noun **1** *ammunition for the guns* bullets, cartridges, shells, shot, slugs, grenades, gunpowder, bombs, missiles. **2** *his speech ran out of ammunition* information, data, points, arguments.

amnesty noun pardon, reprieve, absolution, forgiveness, dispensation.

amorous adjective loving, passionate, sexual, lustful, erotic, amatory.

amorphous adjective formless, shapeless, unstructured, indeterminate, ill-organized, vague, nebulous; *fml.* inchoate.

amount noun **1** *a large amount of experience* quantity, measure, mass, volume, bulk, expanse. **2** *calculate the (full) amount* total, grand/sum total; *inf.* whole kit and caboodle, whole shebang.

amount verb **amount to 1** *the bill amounted to $50* add up to, total, come to, run to. **2** *their silence amounts to a confession* equal, add up to, be equivalent to. **3** *he never amounted to anything* become, grow/develop/mature into, progress/advance to.

ample adjective **1** *ample food to live on* enough, sufficient, adequate, more than enough. **2** *an ample supply of wine* plentiful, abundant, copious, generous, liberal, bountiful, plenteous. **3** *an ample bed* substantial, extensive, wide, spacious, roomy, capacious, commodious.

amplify verb increase, boost, magnify, intensify, heighten, augment, expand, enlarge on, elaborate on, add to, develop, flesh out, expound on.

amuse verb **1** *the clowns amused them* entertain, gladden, cheer, please, charm, delight, divert, beguile. **2** *amuse yourselves when I'm out* occupy, interest, entertain, divert, absorb, engross.

amusement noun **1** *smile with amusement* mirth, laughter, fun, merriment, gaiety, hilarity, enjoyment, pleasure, delight. **2** *a range of amusements* entertainment, diversion, interest, recreation, sport, pastime, hobby.

amusing adjective humorous, funny, comical, witty, entertaining, facetious, droll, jocular.

analogy noun similarity, parallel, correspondence, likeness, resemblance, correlation.

analysis noun breakdown, dissection, examination, study, investigation, review, evaluation, interpretation.

analytical, analytic adjective investigative, inquiring, dissecting, inquisitive, critical.

analyze verb break down, dissect, separate out, examine, study, investigate, inquire into, review, evaluate, interpret.

anarchist noun revolutionary, nihilist, rebel, insurgent, terrorist.

anarchy noun lawlessness, misgovernment, misrule, revolution, riot, disorder, chaos, rebellion, mutiny, tumult, mayhem.

anatomy noun **1** *the anatomy of dogs* structure, makeup, composition, framework. **2** *the anatomy of crime* analysis, examination, study, investigation, scrutiny, research, inquiry.

ancestor noun forebear, progenitor, forerunner, precursor, prototype.

ancestry noun lineage, descent, extraction, parentage, origin, derivation, genealogy, pedigree, blood, stock, ancestors, antecedents, forefathers, forebears, progenitors, family tree.

anchor noun mooring, stability, security, mainstay, support, protection.

anchor verb secure, fasten, moor, attach, connect, bind.

ancient adjective **1** *ancient times* earliest, early, primeval, prehistoric, primordial. **2** *an ancient custom* age-old, time-worn, antique, long-lived. **3** *ancient ideas* antiquated, old-fashioned, outmoded, archaic, obsolete, passé, superannuated, atavistic.

anecdote noun story, tale, narrative, yarn, sketch, reminiscence.

anemic adjective weak, pale, wan, colorless, pallid, ashen, feeble, powerless, impotent, ineffective, ineffectual, enervated.

anesthetic noun narcotic, opiate, soporific, stupefacient, painkiller, sedative, analgesic.

anesthetic adjective numbing, deadening, dulling, narcotic, soporific, stupefacient, painkilling, sedative, analgesic.

anew adverb again, afresh, once more, once again.

angel noun **1** *heavenly angels* messenger of god, heavenly messenger, archangel, seraph, cherub. **2** *thanks! you're an angel* darling, dear, gem, saint. **3** *the play depends on angels* backer, supporter, benefactor, promoter.

angelic adjective celestial, heavenly, ethereal, virtuous, innocent, pure, good, saintly.

anger noun annoyance, rage, fury, indignation, temper, wrath, exasperation, irritation, vexation, ire, outrage, pique, spleen, choler.

anger verb annoy, infuriate, enrage, exasperate, irritate, incense, madden, vex, outrage, provoke, nettle, rile, pique, gall.

angle noun **1** *the angle of the walls* intersection, projection, corner, bend, fork, recess, elbow. **2** *a news angle* slant, spin, approach, viewpoint.

angry adjective annoyed, furious, infuriated, indignant, enraged, irate, wrathful, exasperated, irritated, heated, incensed, maddened, ill-humored, hot-tempered, choleric, outraged, vexed, provoked; *inf.* mad, hot under the collar.

angst noun anxiety, fear, apprehension, foreboding, disquiet.

anguish noun suffering, sorrow, grief. *See* AGONY.

animate verb give life to, enliven, liven up, cheer up, gladden, vitalize; encourage, hearten, inspire, fire, rouse, stir, energize; *inf.* pep up.

animate adjective living, alive, live, moving, breathing.

animated adjective lively, energetic, active, vigorous, excited, enthusiastic, spirited, fiery, forceful, vital, vivacious.

annex verb **1** *annex a garage to the house* add, attach, join, connect. **2** *annex a country* take over, occupy, seize, conquer.

annex noun *a school annex* extension, wing, ell.

annihilate verb destroy, wipe out, exterminate, decimate, eliminate, liquidate, abolish, obliterate, eradicate, extinguish, erase.

announce verb **1** *announce the results* make known/public, give out, declare, proclaim, report, disclose, reveal, divulge, publicize, broadcast, publish, advertise, promulgate. **2** *announce a guest* name, herald, usher in. **3** *cigar smoke announced his approach* signal, indicate, signify, give notice of, warn, foretell, herald.

announcement noun declaration, proclamation, disclosure, report, statement, bulletin, communiqué, message.

announcer noun commentator, presenter, newscaster, broadcaster, reporter, anchor, master of ceremonies, emcee.

annoy verb irritate, exasperate, vex, ruffle, rile, irk, provoke, displease, anger, madden, rub one the wrong way, get on one's nerves, bother, disturb, pester, worry, harry, get to; *inf.* bug.

annul verb nullify, declare null and void, quash, cancel, invalidate, rescind, revoke, repeal, abrogate, void, negate.

anonymous adjective unnamed, nameless, unidentified, unknown, unspecified, undesignated.

answer noun **1** *receive an answer* reply, response, acknowledgment, rejoinder, retort, riposte; *inf.* comeback. **2** *the answer to the clue* solution, explanation, resolution. **3** *his answer to the charge* defense, plea, refutation, rebuttal, vindication.

answer verb **1** *answer a letter* reply to, respond to, acknowledge, react to. **2** *answer our requirements* meet, satisfy, fulfill, fill, measure up to. **3** *answer for her crimes* pay, suffer, atone. **4** *cannot answer for my sister* vouch for, be responsible for, be liable for, take the blame for; *inf.* take the rap for. **answer back** talk back, be impertinent, contradict, argue with, disagree with. **answer to** fit, match, correspond to, be similar to, conform to, correlate to.

answerable adjective responsible, accountable, liable.

antagonism noun hostility, opposition, animosity, antipathy, enmity, rivalry, competition, dissension, friction, conflict.

antagonist noun adversary, enemy, foe, opponent, rival, competitor, contender.

antagonistic adjective hostile, ill-disposed, opposed, dissenting, adverse, antipathetic, inimical, at odds with.

antagonize verb alienate, put against, estrange.

anthem noun hymn, psalm, song of praise, paean, chorale, chant, canticle.

anthology noun collection, compendium, treasury, compilation, miscellany; *lit.* garland.

anticipate verb **1** *anticipate trouble* expect, foresee, predict, forecast; count on, look for, prepare for, await; look forward to, look toward. **2** *anticipate his chess move* forestall, intercept, prevent. **3** *anticipate the invention of radio* antedate, predate.

anticipation noun expectation, prediction, preparation, awaiting, expectancy, hope, hopefulness.

antics plural noun pranks, capers, larks, tricks, romps, frolics, horseplay.

antidote noun cure, remedy, corrective, countermeasure, counteragent, antitoxin.

antiquated adjective out-of-date, old-fashioned, outmoded, passé, archaic, obsolete, antediluvian.

antique adjective **1** *antique furniture* antiquarian, old, vintage. **2** *antique customs* age-old, timeworn, early, earliest, prehistoric, primeval, primordial. **3** *antique attitudes* old-fashioned, passé.

antique noun heirloom, relic, curio, collectible, collector's item.

antiseptic adjective **1** *antiseptic surface* sterile, germ-free, uncontaminated, aseptic, sanitary, hygienic. **2** *antiseptic surroundings* clinical, characterless, undistinguished, unexciting.

antithesis noun opposite, converse, reverse, inverse, reversal.

anxiety noun **1** *anxiety about the future* worry, concern, uneasiness, apprehension, disquiet, nervousness, tenseness, misgiving, angst. **2** *full of anxiety to win* eagerness, desire, longing.

anxious adjective **1** *anxious about the future* worried, concerned, uneasy, apprehensive, fearful, nervous, disturbed, tense. **2** *anxious to please* eager, keen, avid.

apart adverb **1** *a person/house standing apart* to one side, aside, to the side, distant, isolated. **2** *blow/break apart* to pieces, in pieces, to bits, asunder. **apart from** *no one apart from him* except, but, other than, aside from, excluding.

apartment noun quarters, rooms, suite, flat; *inf.* pad, digs.

apathetic adjective uninterested, unconcerned, unfeeling, unemotional, unresponsive, indifferent, impassive, passive, listless.

apathy noun unconcern, unresponsiveness, indifference, impassivity, passivity, dispassion, dispassionateness, listlessness.

ape verb imitate, mimic, copy, echo, mock, parody, parrot.

aperture noun opening, gap, hole, orifice, window, crack, slit, space, chink, fissure, eye, interstice.

apex noun top, summit, peak, pinnacle, tip, crest, vertex, acme, zenith, apogee.

aplomb noun poise, assurance, self-confidence, self-assurance, composure, equanimity, levelheadedness, sang-froid.

apocryphal adjective unverified, unsubstantiated, spurious, debatable, questionable, dubious, doubtful, mythical, fictitious, false.

apologetic adjective sorry, regretful, contrite, remorseful, penitent, repentant, rueful.

apologize verb express regret, ask forgiveness, beg pardon; *inf.* eat humble pie.

apology noun **1** *deliver an apology* expression of regret; regrets. **2** *the apology for their beliefs* defense, justification, argument, apologia. **apology for** *an apology for a man* travesty of, poor excuse for, substitute for.

appall verb shock, dismay, horrify, outrage, astound, alarm.

appalling adjective shocking, horrifying, frightful, outrageous, dreadful.

apparatus noun **1** *gymnastic apparatus* equipment, gear, tackle, mechanism, appliance, machine, device, contraption, instruments, tools. **2** *government apparatus* structure, system, organization, network, setup.

apparel noun clothing, dress, attire, outfit, wear, costume, garb, habit; clothes, garments, robes, vestments; *inf.* gear, togs.

apparent adjective **1** *apparent from the start* clear, plain, obvious, evident, perceptible, manifest, patent. **2** *apparent calmness* seeming, ostensible, outward, superficial.

apparition noun **1** *frightened of the apparition* ghost, specter, phantom, spirit; *inf.* spook. **2** *the sudden apparition of the figure* manifestation, visitation. *See* APPEARANCE 1.

appeal noun **1** *an appeal for help* request, call, plea, entreaty, petition, supplication. **2** *an appeal of the decision* reconsideration, reexamination, review. **3** *hold little appeal* attraction, attractiveness, allure, charm, interest.

appeal verb **appeal for** *appeal for money* ask for, request, put in a plea for, entreat, beg/beseech/plead for, implore. **appeal to** **1** *appeal to a higher authority* seek reconsideration/reexamination/review/another opinion from. **2** *appeals to her* attract, charm, interest, engage, fascinate.

appear verb **1** *a messenger/solution appeared* come into view/sight, emerge, come forth, arrive, turn/show/crop up, materialize, surface, loom. **2** *she appeared sad* seem, look, have the appearance/air of being. **3** *the new line of spring fashions has appeared* come into being/existence, come out, become available, come on the market.

appearance noun **1** *the appearance of the messenger/solution* emergence, arrival, advent, materialization, attendance, presence. **2** *an appearance of sadness* look, air, expression, manner, demeanor, bearing, mien. **3** *the appearance of being rich* semblance, guise, show, pretense, image, impression.

appease verb **1** *appease the enemy* placate, pacify, conciliate, tranquilize, soothe, quiet down, mollify, propitiate. **2** *appease one's appetite* satisfy, assuage, blunt, relieve, quench, diminish.

append verb add, attach, affix, adjoin.

appendix noun *appendix to a book* supplement, addendum, postscript, extension, codicil.

appetite noun hunger, taste, palate, desire, relish, thirst, need, liking, inclination, passion, longing, craving.

appetizer noun starter, hors d'oeuvre, antipasto, canapé.

appetizing adjective mouthwatering, tasty, succulent, delicious, palatable, tempting, inviting, enticing, appealing, alluring.

applaud verb **1** *the audience applauded* clap, cheer, whistle; *inf.* give someone a big hand. **2** *applaud their courage* praise, admire, compliment on, commend, acclaim, extol, laud.

applause noun 1 *the applause of the audience* clapping, handclapping, cheering, whistling, standing ovation; cheers, whistles, encores, bravos, curtain calls. 2 *won the applause of the neighborhood* praise, admiration, approval, approbation, acclaim; compliments, accolades, plaudits.

applicable adjective appropriate, pertinent, apposite, fitting, suitable, useful.

applicant noun candidate, interviewee, competitor, petitioner, suitor.

application noun 1 *the application of force* use, exercise, administration, employment, practice. 2 *a remark having no application to the case* relevance, bearing, significance, pertinence, aptness. 3 *an application for a job* request, claim, appeal, petition, entreaty.

apply verb 1 *apply the brakes* use, put to use, employ, utilize, administer, exercise. 2 *the remark did not apply to the situation* be relevant/significant/pertinent, be apt/apposite/germane. 3 *apply ointment* put on, rub in, cover with, spread, smear. **apply for** *apply for tax relief* put in for, try for, inquire after, request, seek, solicit. **apply oneself** be industrious/diligent/assiduous, study, work hard, make an effort.

appoint verb 1 *appoint him manager* name, designate, nominate, select, choose, elect. 2 *appoint a time* set, fix, arrange, establish, assign, designate, allot.

appointment noun 1 *cancel an appointment* meeting, engagement, date, interview, rendezvous, assignation, tryst. 2 *his appointment as manager* job, post, position, situation, place, office, station.

appraise verb *appraise his ability* assess, evaluate, sum up, estimate, gauge, judge, review; *inf.* size up.

appreciable adjective considerable, substantial, significant, sizable, visible, goodly.

appreciate verb 1 *appreciate your help* be thankful/grateful for, be indebted/beholden for. 2 *appreciate good work* value, prize, cherish, treasure, rate highly, respect, think highly of. 3 *appreciate its importance* recognize, acknowledge, realize, know, be aware of, be conscious/cognizant of, comprehend. 4 *appreciate in value* increase, gain, grow, rise, mount, inflate, escalate.

appreciation noun 1 *appreciation for their help* gratitude, thankfulness, indebtedness, obligation, thanks. 2 *appreciation of its importance* recognition, acknowledgment, realization, knowledge, awareness, cognizance. 3 *the appreciation of housing values* increase, rise, growth, inflation, escalation.

appreciative adjective grateful, thankful, indebted; responsive, supportive, sympathetic.

apprehend verb 1 *apprehend the criminal* arrest, catch, seize, capture, take prisoner, take into custody, haul in, detain; *inf.* collar, nab, nail, run in, bust. 2 *apprehend the significance* understand, grasp, realize, recognize, appreciate, comprehend.

apprehension noun 1 *full of apprehension* anxiety, dread, alarm, worry, unease, nervousness, fear, misgiving, disquiet, concern, trepidation, foreboding, presentiment, angst; *inf.* butterflies in the stomach, the willies, the heebie-jeebies. 2 *the apprehension of criminals* arrest, seizure, capture, detention.

apprehensive adjective anxious, alarmed, worried, uneasy, nervous, frightened, fearful.

apprentice noun trainee, learner, beginner, probationer, cub, greenhorn, tyro, novice, neophyte; *inf.* rookie.

apprise verb inform, notify, tell, let know; *inf.* clue in, fill in.

approach verb 1 *approach the house* draw near/nearer, come/go close/closer, draw nigh, catch up, gain on, near, advance. 2 *don't approach strangers* talk/speak to, greet, address, salute, hail. 3 *approach them for a contribution* broach the matter to, make advances/overtures to, make a proposal to, sound out. 4 *approach the task with care* set about, tackle, begin, start, commence, embark on, undertake. 5 *a price approaching $600* approximate, be comparable/similar to.

approach noun 1 *the approach of footsteps* advance, advent, arrival. 2 *the approach to the estate* driveway, drive, access, road, avenue, street, passageway. 3 *make an approach to | make approaches* appeal, proposal, proposition; advances, overtures. 4 *a new approach to teaching* method, procedure, technique, manner, modus operandi.

appropriate adjective suitable, fitting, befitting, proper, seemly, right, apt, relevant, pertinent, apposite, applicable, germane.

appropriate verb 1 *appropriate a country* take possession of, take over, seize, commandeer, expropriate, annex, arrogate. 2 *appropriate money for education* set apart/aside, assign, allot, allocate, earmark. 3 *appropriate company money* embezzle, misappropriate, steal, pilfer, pocket; *inf.* pinch, swipe; *fml.* peculate.

approval noun 1 *look on with approval* favor, liking, approbation, admiration. 2 *give approval to the plan* acceptance, agreement, consent, assent, sanction, endorsement, blessing, permission, confirmation, ratification; *inf.* the go-ahead, the green light, the OK.

approve verb accept, pass, agree to, sanction, consent/assent to, ratify, authorize, validate, accede to, acquiesce in, concur in; *inf.* give the go-ahead to, give the OK to, give the green light to, buy. **approve of** think well of, look on with favor, give one's blessing to, be pleased with.

approximate adjective rough, estimated, near, close, inexact.

approximate verb come close/near to, approach, border on, verge on, resemble, be similar to.

approximately adverb roughly, about, just about, around, circa, or so, more or less, in the neighborhood of, nearly, almost.

approximation noun **1** *200 is an approximation* guess, estimate, conjecture, rough idea, guesswork; *inf.* guesstimate. **2** *an approximation to the truth* semblance, similarity, likeness, correspondence.

apropos adjective appropriate, pertinent, relevant, apposite, apt, applicable, germane. **apropos of** concerning, with reference to, regarding, on the subject of, re.

apt adjective **1** *an apt remark* suitable, fitting, appropriate, felicitous, apropos. **2** *apt to get angry* inclined, given, likely, liable, disposed, prone. **3** *an apt student* quick, bright, sharp, clever. *See* ABLE.

aptitude noun talent, bent. *See* ABILITY 1, 2.

aquatic adjective water, sea, river, marine, maritime, fluvial.

arable adjective plowable, tillable, cultivable, farmable; fertile, productive, fruitful, fecund.

arbitrary adjective **1** *an arbitrary decision* discretionary, subjective, random, chance, whimsical, capricious, unreasonable, unsupported, irrational. **2** *an arbitrary ruler* despotic, tyrannical, tyrannous, absolute, autocratic, dictatorial, imperious, domineering, high-handed.

arbitrate verb adjudicate, judge, referee, umpire, settle, decide, determine.

arc noun curve, bow, arch, bend, crescent, half-moon, semicircle, curvature.

arcane adjective secret, mysterious, hidden, concealed, recondite, covert, enigmatic, inscrutable, abstruse, esoteric, cryptic, occult.

arch- prefix *archbishop | archenemy* chief, foremost, principal, leading, main, prime, primary, first, top, highest, greatest, preeminent.

archaic adjective old, obsolete, out-of-date, old-fashioned, outmoded, bygone, passé, antiquated, antique; *inf.* old hat.

architect noun designer, planner, author, engineer, creator, originator, deviser, instigator, founder, prime mover.

archives plural noun records, annals, chronicles, papers, documents, registers, rolls; history, documentation.

arctic adjective polar, freezing, frigid, frozen, icy, gelid, glacial, frosty, chilly, cold.

ardent adjective passionate, avid, impassioned, fervent, zealous, enthusiastic, intense, fierce, fiery, profound, consuming.

ardor noun passion, fervor, zeal, eagerness, enthusiasm, intensity, fierceness, fire.

arduous adjective taxing, difficult, hard, onerous, heavy, laborious, burdensome, exhausting, wearying, fatiguing, tiring, strenuous, grueling, punishing, Herculean.

area noun **1** *the area around the city* region, district, zone, sector, territory, tract, stretch, domain, realm, sphere. **2** *the area of the room* extent, size, expanse, scope, compass, range, measurements. **3** *in the area of finance* field, sphere, discipline, realm, domain.

arena noun **1** *circus/boxing arena* grounds, field, stadium, ballpark, ring, stage, amphitheater, coliseum; *inf.* park, bowl. **2** *the political arena* battleground, battlefield, area, scene, sphere, realm, domain.

argue verb **1** *please don't argue* disagree, quarrel, squabble, bicker, fight, dispute, feud. **2** *argue that they are right* assert, declare, maintain, insist, hold, claim, contend. **3** *argue the point* debate, dispute, discuss.

argument noun **1** *the couple had an argument* disagreement, quarrel, squabble, fight, difference of opinion, dispute, clash, altercation, controversy, feud; *inf.* tiff, falling out. **2** *stick to the argument that they are right* assertion, declaration, claim, plea, contention. **3** *the argument against capital punishment* reasoning, logic, case, defense, evidence, argumentation, polemic; reasons, grounds.

argumentative adjective quarrelsome, disputatious, contentious, combative, litigious.

arid adjective **1** *arid areas* dry, dried up, desert, parched, baked, scorched, barren. **2** *arid discussion* uninspiring, unstimulating, dull, dreary, drab, dry, colorless, flat, boring, uninteresting, lifeless, tedious.

arise verb **1** *a difficulty arose* appear, come to light, crop/turn up, spring up, emerge, occur. **2** *accidents arising from carelessness* result, proceed, follow, stem, originate. **3** *arise and go* rise, stand up, get up. **4** *birds arising* ascend, mount, climb, fly, soar.

aristocrat noun nobleman, noble, noblewoman, lord, lady, peer, peeress, patrician, Brahmin; *inf.* blue blood.

aristocratic adjective **1** *an aristocratic family* noble, titled, blue-blooded, highborn, upper-class, patrician, elite. **2** *aristocratic bearing* well-bred, dignified, courtly, refined, elegant, stylish, gracious, fine.

arm noun **1** *arms and legs* limb, forelimb, member, appendage. **2** *arm of the sea* inlet, estuary, channel, strait. **3** *an arm of the civil service* branch, offshoot, section, department, division.

arm verb **1** *arm with information* provide, supply, equip, furnish, issue. **2** *arm oneself against criticism* prepare, forearm, make ready, brace, steel, fortify, gird one's loins.

armistice noun truce, ceasefire, peace, suspension of hostilities.

arms plural noun **1** *carrying arms* weapons, firearms, guns, armaments, weaponry. **2** *the family arms* coat of arms, emblem, crest, insignia, escutcheon, shield, blazonry.

army noun **1** *the invading army* armed/military force, soldiery, infantry, troops, soldiers, land forces, military. **2** *an army of tourists* horde, pack, host, multitude, mob, crowd, swarm, throng, array.

aroma noun smell, scent, odor, bouquet, fragrance, perfume, redolence.

aromatic adjective fragrant, sweet-smelling, perfumed, balmy, spicy, savory, pungent, odoriferous.

around preposition **1** *around the tree* on all sides of, on every side of, circling, encircling, surrounding, encompassing. **2** *thrown around the room* about, here and there, all over, everywhere, in all parts of. **3** *around 9 o'clock* about, roughly. *See* APPROXIMATELY. **4** *turn around* in the opposite direction, in reverse, backward, to the rear.

arouse verb **1** *arouse them at dawn* rouse, awaken, waken, wake, wake up. **2** *arouse panic* cause, induce, stir up, inspire, kindle, provoke, foster, sow the seeds of. **3** *arouse the crowd* rouse, incite, excite, provoke, goad, prompt, spur on, egg on, animate, inflame.

arrange verb **1** *arrange the books* put in order, order, set out, group, sort, organize, tidy, dispose, align, line up, rank, file, classify, categorize, array, systematize. **2** *arrange to meet* settle on, decide, determine, agree, schedule, devise, contrive, make preparations, prepare, plan. **3** *music arranged for the piano* score, adapt, orchestrate.

arrangement noun **1** *the arrangement of flowers* order, ordering, grouping, organization, positioning, system, marshalling, alignment, classification, categorization, array. **2** *make an arrangement* preparation, plan, provision; agreement, contract, compact. **3** *a musical arrangement* score, adaptation, orchestration, instrumentation, harmonization.

array noun **1** *an array of bottles* collection, arrangement, assemblage, formation, disposition, muster, amassing, display, aggregation. **2** *in silken array* attire, apparel, clothing, dress, garments, garb, finery.

array verb **1** *array the troops* assemble, arrange, draw up, group, order, line up, place, position, dispose, muster, amass, agglomerate, aggregate. **2** *she arrayed herself in silk* attire, clothe, dress, fit out, garb, deck, robe, apparel, accoutre.

arrest verb **1** *arrest the thief* apprehend, take into custody, take prisoner, detain, seize, capture, catch, lay hold of, haul in; *inf.* run in, nab, pinch, collar, bust, nail, pick up. **2** *arrest the spread of disease* stop, halt, end, check, block, hinder, prevent, obstruct, inhibit, stay. **3** *arrest their attention* attract, capture, catch, catch hold of, grip, engage, absorb.

arrest noun **1** *the arrest of the thieves* apprehension, detention, seizure, capture. **2** *the arrest of the disease* stoppage, halt, ending, end, check, prevention, obstruction.

arrival noun **1** *the arrival of winter* coming, advent, appearance, entrance, entry, occurrence, approach. **2** *several recent arrivals* newcomer, visitor, visitant, guest.

arrive verb **1** *arrive on time* come, appear, enter, happen, occur, turn/show up; *inf.* blow in. **2** *the actor has really arrived* succeed, make good, reach the top, prosper, flourish, become famous, achieve recognition; *inf.* make it.

arrogance noun haughtiness, pride, self-importance, conceit, egotism, snobbishness, snobbery, pomposity, superciliousness, high-handedness, condescension, disdain, imperiousness, lordliness, presumption, pretentiousness; *inf.* uppitiness.

arrogant adjective haughty, proud, self-important, conceited, egotistic, snobbish, pompous, supercilious, overbearing, overweening, high-handed, condescending, disdainful, imperious, lordly, presumptuous, pretentious, insolent; *inf.* stuck-up, uppity, high and mighty.

arrow noun **1** *bow and arrow* shaft, bolt, dart. **2** *follow the arrows* pointer, indicator, marker.

arsenal noun arms depot, magazine, armory, ammunition dump, ordnance depot, repository; store, supply, stock, stockpile, storehouse.

art noun **1** *study art* painting, drawing, design, visual arts. **2** *the art of conversation* skill, craft, artistry, mastery.

artful adjective cunning, deceitful, wily, sly, crafty, duplicitous, designing, shrewd, politic.

article noun **1** *three black articles* object, thing, item; *inf.* thingamajig, thingamabob, watchamacallit. **2** *a newspaper article* item, piece, story, feature, report, account, write-up. **3** *an article in the document* clause, section, paragraph, division.

articulate adjective **1** *an articulate speaker* eloquent, fluent, coherent, lucid, expressive, silver-tongued. **2** *an articulate speech* eloquent, clear, intelligible, comprehensible, lucid.

articulate verb enunciate, pronounce, voice, say, utter, express, vocalize.

artifice noun **1** *an artifice to mislead* trick, stratagem, ruse, dodge, subterfuge, machination, tactic, contrivance. **2** *win by using artifice* trickery, cunning, deceit, craftiness, artfulness, wiliness, duplicity, guile, chicanery.

artificial adjective **1** *artificial flowers* manmade, manufactured, synthetic, imitation, simulated, pseudo, ersatz, plastic, mock, sham, fake, bogus, counterfeit; *inf.* phony. **2** *an artificial smile* feigned, false, affected, unnatural, assumed, insincere, forced, strained.

artist noun painter, drawer, sculptor, craftsman, craftswoman, expert, adept, genius, past master, maestro.

artistic adjective **1** *an artistic person* creative, talented, gifted, imaginative, sensitive, cultivated. **2** *an artistic flower arrangement* decorative, beautiful, attractive, lovely, tasteful, graceful, stylish, elegant, aesthetic.

artistry noun art, skill, ability, talent, genius, brilliance, expertness, flair, gift, creativity, proficiency, virtuosity, craftsmanship, workmanship.

artless adjective natural, simple, childlike, naïve, ingenuous, guileless, sincere.

ascend verb climb, go/move up, mount, scale, rise, levitate, fly up, soar, slope upward.

ascertain verb find out, establish, discover, learn, determine, settle, verify, confirm; *inf.* pin down.

ascetic noun recluse, hermit, solitary, anchorite, abstainer, celibate, nun, monk, dervish, yogi.

ascetic adjective self-denying, abstinent, abstemious, self-disciplined, austere, frugal, rigorous, strict, celibate, spartan, puritanical.

ascribe verb attribute, assign, credit, put/set down to, chalk up to, impute, charge with, lay on, blame.

ashamed adjective **1** *ashamed of his conduct* humiliated, conscience-stricken, sorry, mortified, abashed, crestfallen, shamefaced, remorseful, discomfited, embarrassed, distressed, sheepish, redfaced. **2** *ashamed to say* reluctant, unwilling, hesitant.

ashen adjective pale, pale-faced, pallid, wan, white, colorless, anemic, washed out, bleached, ghostly, deathlike.

asinine adjective stupid, silly, idiotic, foolish, brainless, nonsensical, senseless, halfwitted, fatuous, inane, imbecilic, moronic; *inf.* daft, dopey, balmy.

ask verb **1** *ask about it* inquire, question, query, interrogate, quiz, cross-examine; *inf.* grill, pump. **2** *ask the boss for a raise* request, demand, appeal to, entreat, beg, implore, beseech, plead, supplicate. **3** *ask them to dine* invite, bid, summon.

askew adverb/adjective sideways, awry, out of line.

asleep adjective/adverb sleeping, fast/sound asleep, slumbering, napping, catnapping, dozing, resting, dormant, comatose; *inf.* snoozing, dead to the world; *lit.* in the arms of Morpheus.

aspect noun **1** *every aspect of the problem* feature, facet, side, angle, slant, viewpoint, standpoint, light. **2** *a fierce aspect* appearance, look, expression, countenance, demeanor, bearing, features, mien. **3** *the southern aspect of the house* direction, situation, position, location, exposure. **4** *affording a pleasant aspect* outlook, view, scene, prospect.

aspersions plural noun *cast aspersions* disparagement, deprecation, denigration, defamation, slander.

asphyxiate verb choke, suffocate, smother, stifle, throttle, strangle, strangulate.

aspiration noun desire, longing, yearning, hankering, wish, ambition, hope, dream.

aspire verb desire, long to/for, yearn to/for, dream of, hunger for, seek, pursue.

assail verb **1** *assail the enemy with blows* attack, assault, set about, lay into, set upon, accost; *inf.* jump. **2** *assail with insults* bombard, berate, lash, abuse, criticize, harangue, revile, lambaste.

assailant noun attacker, mugger, aggressor, assaulter, accoster.

assassin noun murderer, killer, slayer, executioner, liquidator; *inf.* hit man, contract man.

assassinate verb murder, kill, slay, execute, liquidate, eliminate; *inf.* hit.

assault noun attack, onslaught, onset, charge, offensive.

assault verb attack, charge, strike, hit, mug, molest, rape.

assemble verb **1** *assemble the children* bring together, gather, collect, round up, marshal, muster, summon, accumulate, amass. **2** *the crowd assembled* come together, meet, congregate, convene. **3** *assemble the parts* put together, piece/fit together, build, fabricate, construct, connect, join.

assembly noun *talking to a crowded assembly* gathering, meeting, group, crowd, throng, congregation.

assent noun agreement, concurrence, acceptance, approval, consent, acquiescence, compliance, approbation, permission, sanction.

assert verb **1** *assert her innocence* declare, state, maintain, proclaim, contend, aver, swear, affirm, allege, claim. **2** *assert one's rights* uphold, press/push for, insist upon, stand up for, defend.

assertive adjective confident, self-assured, aggressive, forceful, dominant; *inf.* pushy.

assess verb **1** *assess the quality* evaluate, judge, gauge, rate, estimate, appraise. **2** *assess taxes* fix, evaluate, levy, impose.

assessment noun **1** *the assessment of quality* evaluation, judgment, gauging, estimation, appraisal. **2** *tax assessment* levy, charge, rate, toll, tariff, fee.

asset noun advantage, benefit, blessing, strong point, strength, boon, aid, help.

assets plural noun property, estate, capital, wealth, resources, holdings, possessions, effects, goods, belongings, chattels.

assign verb **1** *assign duties to all* allocate, allot, distribute, give out, dispense, apportion. **2** *assign him to the post* appoint, select, install, designate, nominate, name, delegate. **3** *assign Thursdays for trips* fix, appoint, decide on, determine, set aside/apart, stipulate, appropriate. **4** *assign her behavior to jealousy* ascribe, put down, attribute.

assignment noun **1** *carry out an assignment* task, job, duty, commission, charge, mission, responsibility, obligation. **2** *the assignment of duties* allocation, allotment, apportionment. **3** *his assignment to the post* appointment, selection, installation, nomination.

assimilate verb *assimilate food/facts* absorb, take in, incorporate, digest, ingest.

assist verb *assist the police* help, aid, lend a hand, succor, support, cooperate/collaborate with, abet, work with, play a part, help out, support, back, second.

assistance noun help, aid, succor, support, reinforcement, cooperation; a helping hand.

assistant noun **1** *her assistant is in charge* subordinate, deputy, auxiliary, second in command; *inf.* right-hand man/woman. **2** *an assistant in the project* helper, colleague, associate, partner, confederate, accomplice, accessory.

associate verb **1** *associate wine with France* link, connect, relate, think of together, couple. **2** *associate with criminals* mix, keep company, mingle, socialize, hobnob, fraternize; *inf.* run around, hang out.

assorted adjective mixed, varied, miscellaneous, diverse, motley, sundry, heterogeneous.

assortment noun mixture, variety, miscellany, selection, medley, mélange, jumble, mishmash, hodgepodge, potpourri.

assuage verb **1** *assuage the pain* relieve, ease, alleviate, soothe, mitigate, lessen, allay, moderate, diminish, calm, palliate, abate. **2** *assuage their thirst* appease, satisfy, relieve, slake, quench, dull, blunt, take the edge off.

assume verb **1** *assume he's coming* suppose, take for granted, presuppose, presume, imagine, expect, suspect, understand, gather, guess. **2** *assume a thorough knowledge* feign, pretend, simulate, put on. **3** *assume an air of authority* adopt, take on, acquire, come to have. **4** *assume a position of responsibility* undertake, set about, take on/up, embark on, take upon oneself, accept, shoulder. **5** *the invaders assumed power* seize, appropriate, usurp, commandeer.

assumed adjective *an assumed name* false, fictitious, fake, made-up, bogus; *inf.* phony.

assumption noun **1** *on the assumption that you're right* supposition, presupposition, presumption, premise, theory, hypothesis. **2** *the invaders' assumption of power* seizure, appropriation, usurpation. **3** *amazed at his assumption* arrogance, presumption, conceit, impertinence.

assurance noun **1** *you have my assurance that I'll be there* word of honor, word, guarantee, promise, pledge, affirmation. **2** *no assurance of her success* certainty, guarantee.

assure verb **1** *I assure you that he's wrong* declare to, affirm to, give one's word to, guarantee, promise, swear to, certify to, pledge to, vow to, attest to. **2** *they assured him of their ability* convince, persuade, reassure, prove to. **3** *assure their success* ensure, secure, guarantee, seal, clinch, confirm.

astonish verb amaze, astound, dumbfound, stagger, surprise, stun, take aback, confound, take one's breath away, flabbergast; *inf.* floor.

astonishing adjective amazing, astounding, staggering, surprising, breathtaking, striking, impressive, bewildering, stunning.

astound verb amaze, surprise. *See* ASTONISH.

astounding adjective amazing, surprising. *See* ASTONISHING.

astute adjective shrewd, sharp, perceptive, discerning, crafty, wily, perspicacious, sagacious.

asylum noun *seek political asylum* refuge, sanctuary, shelter, safety, safekeeping, protection; haven, retreat, harbor, port in a storm.

atheist noun nonbeliever, unbeliever, heretic, heathen, freethinker, nihilist, infidel.

athletic adjective muscular, powerful, robust, able-bodied, sturdy, strong, strapping, brawny.

atmosphere noun *a friendly atmosphere* environment, surroundings, milieu, medium, background, setting, air, ambience, aura, climate, feeling, character, tone.

atom noun iota, jot, bit, whit, particle, scrap, shred, trace, speck, spot, grain, morsel, mite.

atone verb make amends/reparation, compensate, recompense, expiate, do penance.

atonement noun reparation, compensation, recompense, redress, indemnity, restitution, expiation, penance, redemption.

atrocious adjective 1 *atrocious crimes* brutal, barbaric, barbarous, savage, vicious, wicked, cruel, ruthless, merciless, villainous, murderous, heinous, monstrous, fiendish, diabolical, flagrant, outrageous. 2 *atrocious weather* unpleasant, appalling, dreadful.

atrocity noun *the atrocity of war* abomination, enormity, outrage, horror, evil, monstrosity, brutality, cruelty, barbarity.

attach verb 1 *attach a label to the briefcase* fasten, fix, affix, join, connect, couple, link, secure, tie, stick, adhere, pin, hitch, bond. 2 *attach no significance to it* ascribe, assign, attribute, accredit. 3 *attaching their property* seize, confiscate, appropriate.

attack verb 1 *attack the enemy* assault, set/fall upon, strike at, rush, storm, charge, pounce upon, beset, besiege, beleaguer; strike, begin hostilities; *inf.* lay into, let one have it. 2 *attack the writer* criticize, censure, berate, reprove, rebuke, impugn, revile, fulminate against, vilify; *inf.* knock, slam. 3 *attack the work* set about, get/go to work on, get started on, undertake, embark on.

attack noun 1 *an attack on the enemy* assault, onslaught, offensive, onset, strike, charge, foray, rush, incursion, inroad. 2 *an attack on his writing* criticism, censure, rebuke, reproval, blame, revilement, vilification. 3 *an asthmatic attack* fit, bout, seizure, spasm, convulsion, paroxysm, stroke.

attacker noun assailant, aggressor, assaulter, mugger.

attain verb achieve, accomplish, obtain, gain, procure, secure, get, grasp, win, earn, acquire, reach, realize, fulfill, bring off.

attempt verb try, strive, aim, venture, endeavor, seek, undertake, essay, tackle, have a go/shot at; *inf.* have a crack at, give it a whirl.

attempt noun effort, try, endeavor, venture, trial, experiment, essay.

attend verb 1 *attend a meeting* appear, put in an appearance, turn up, visit, frequent, haunt; *inf.* show up, show. 2 *attend the sick* look after, care for, tend, nurse, mind, minister to. 3 *the president attended by top aides* accompany, escort, guard; chaperon, squire, convoy. **attend to** *attend to this matter* deal/cope with, see to, handle, take care of.

attendance noun 1 *attendance is not compulsory* presence, appearance. 2 *attendances vary* turnout, crowd, audience, house, gate.

attendant noun 1 *parking attendant* assistant, helper, auxiliary, steward, waiter, servant, menial. 2 *the queen and her attendants* companion, escort, aide, guard, custodian, guide.

attention noun 1 *give more attention to the problem* concentration, attentiveness, observation, heed, regard, contemplation, deliberation, scrutiny, thought. 2 *attract their attention* notice, awareness, observation, consciousness, recognition. 3 *for the personal attention of the manager* consideration, action, notice, investigation.

attentive adjective 1 *keen and attentive* alert, aware, awake, watchful, observant, heedful, mindful, vigilant, on guard, on the qui vive. 2 *an attentive host* considerate, thoughtful, courteous, gracious, conscientious, obliging, accommodating.

attest verb affirm, aver, asseverate, confirm, testify to, vouch for, bear witness to, bear out, endorse, back up, support, corroborate, verify, authenticate. **attest to** prove, demonstrate, evince, display, exhibit, show, manifest.

attire noun clothing, ensemble, costume, array, habiliments, accoutrements; *inf.* threads, glad rags. *See* APPAREL.

attire verb dress, clothe, dress up, garb, robe, array, deck out, costume; *inf.* doll up.

attitude noun *his attitude toward marriage* point of view, viewpoint, opinion, frame of mind, outlook, perspective, stance, position, thoughts, ideas.

attract verb 1 *magnets attract iron filings* draw, pull, magnetize. 2 *attracted by beauty* allure, entice, tempt, fascinate, charm, engage, enchant, captivate, bewitch.

attractive adjective **1** *an attractive proposal* appealing, agreeable, pleasing, inviting, tempting. **2** *an attractive woman/man* good-looking, striking, beautiful, handsome, pretty, stunning, gorgeous, prepossessing, fetching, comely, captivating, charming, fascinating, interesting, appealing, enchanting, alluring.

attribute noun quality, feature, characteristic, property, mark, trait.

attribute verb ascribe, assign, accredit, put down, chalk up.

audacious adjective **1** *an audacious scheme* bold, daring, fearless, intrepid, brave, courageous, adventurous, plucky, daredevil, reckless; *inf.* gutsy, spunky. **2** *an audacious youth* impudent, impertinent, insolent, presumptuous, forward, rude, brazen.

audacity noun **1** *the audacity of the scheme* boldness, daring, fearlessness, bravery, courage, pluck, recklessness; *inf.* guts, spunk. **2** *the child had the audacity to swear* impudence, impertinence, insolence, rudeness, brazenness.

audience noun **1** *a concert audience* listeners, spectators, viewers, onlookers; assembly, gathering, house, turnout, congregation, gallery. **2** *publications aimed at a wide audience* public, market, following. **3** *an audience with the pope* interview, meeting, hearing, reception.

audit verb inspect, examine, go over/through, scrutinize, investigate, review, check.

augment verb increase, boost, build up, enlarge, grow, add to, expand, extend, amplify, raise, enhance, heighten, multiply, magnify, elevate, swell, inflate, escalate, intensify.

augur verb foretell, forecast, predict, prophesy, bode, foreshadow, promise, presage, portend, herald, betoken.

august adjective dignified, solemn, majestic, stately, magnificent, imposing, impressive, exalted, awe-inspiring.

aura noun ambience, atmosphere, air, character, tone, suggestion, emanation, vibrations; *inf.* vibes.

auspices plural noun patronage, guidance, influence, responsibility, control, protection.

auspicious adjective propitious, favorable, promising, bright, optimistic, encouraging, opportune, timely, fortunate, providential.

austere adjective **1** *an austere manner* harsh, stern, severe, strict, unfeeling, hard, rigorous, stringent, grim, formal, stiff, aloof, forbidding. **2** *monks lead an austere life* strict, self-denying, self-abnegating, ascetic, Spartan, abstemious, abstinent, celibate, chaste, puritanical. **3** *an austere style* plain, simple, severe, unadorned, unornamented, stark, somber.

authentic adjective **1** *an authentic painting* genuine, bona fide, rightful, legitimate, valid; *inf.* the real McCoy, kosher. **2** *an authentic statement* reliable, dependable, trustworthy, truthful, honest, credible.

authenticate verb **1** *authenticate an agreement* validate, ratify, confirm, certify, seal, endorse, guarantee, warrant, underwrite. **2** *authenticate the work as being Shakespeare's* verify, substantiate, support, prove, evidence.

author noun writer, composer, novelist, dramatist, playwright, screenwriter, poet, essayist, biographer, librettist, lyricist, songwriter, journalist, columnist, reporter.

authoritative adjective **1** *an authoritative biography* official, approved, authorized, sanctioned, validated. **2** *authoritative information* sound, dependable, reliable, trustworthy, valid, certified, attested, definitive, accurate. **3** *an authoritative manner* self-assured, confident, assertive, imposing, masterful, arrogant, commanding, domineering.

authorities plural noun administration, the establishment, government, officialdom, management, legislation, the police, the powers that be.

authority noun **1** *have the authority to decide* authorization, right, power, might, sanction, influence, force, control, prerogative, jurisdiction, rule, command, sovereignty; *inf.* say-so. **2** *an authority on ecology* expert, specialist, professional, master, scholar, pundit; *inf.* walking encyclopedia. **3** *have his authority to act* permission, authorization, sanction. **4** *have the news on their authority* testimony, evidence, witness, attestation, word, avowal, deposition.

authorize verb **1** *authorize them to represent us* commission, empower, entitle, enable, accredit, license, certify, validate. **2** *authorize the sale* permit, allow, approve, assent to, agree to, sanction, ratify, warrant; *inf.* give the green light to, give the go-ahead for.

autocratic adjective despotic, dictatorial, tyrannical, authoritarian, domineering, imperious, omnipotent, all-powerful, absolute, draconian, oppressive, high-handed; *inf.* bossy.

automatic adjective **1** *an automatic washing machine* automated, mechanized, mechanical, push-button, robotic, self-activating, self-regulating. **2** *an automatic reaction* instinctive, spontaneous, involuntary, unconscious, reflex, natural.

available adjective accessible, obtainable, at hand, convenient.

avarice noun greed, acquisitiveness, covetousness, miserliness.

average noun mean, median, midpoint, center; norm, standard, yardstick, rule.

average adjective **1** *the team played an average game* ordinary, normal, typical, everyday. **2** *his ability was only average* mediocre, moderate, unexceptional; second-rate, banal, pedestrian.

aversion noun dislike, distaste, hatred, repugnance.

avid adjective keen, eager, enthusiastic, fervent, zealous, passionate.

avoid verb shun, eschew, steer clear of, evade, elude, shirk, dodge, abstain from, refrain from.

aware adjective awake, watchful, vigilant, alert, cautious. **aware of** *aware of the problem* conscious of, informed of, familiar with, sensitive to; *inf.* clued in on, in the know about.

awe noun amazement, wonder, astonishment, stupefaction; reverence, honor, veneration; dread, fear.

awful adjective **1** *an awful cough* nasty, unpleasant, distressing, horrible, ugly, unattractive, foul, disgusting. **2** *the awful power of the gods* awesome, venerable, impressive, daunting.

awkward adjective **1** *they arrived at an awkward time* inconvenient, difficult, problematic, annoying, vexatious. **2** *an awkward child* clumsy, ungainly, inelegant, inept, gauche.

awry adjective lopsided, uneven, unequal, asymmetrical, askew, crooked.

Bb

babble verb **1** *babble away unintelligibly* jabber, chatter, mutter, mumble, prate, drivel, cackle; *inf.* run on. **2** *the stream babbled quietly* murmur, whisper, gurgle.

baby noun infant, newborn, child, babe, tiny tot.

baby verb pamper, spoil, indulge, pet, humor, coddle, mollycoddle, overindulge, spoonfeed.

back noun **1** *hurt one's back* spine, backbone, spinal column; *Med.* dorsum. **2** *the back of the building* rear, rear end, far end, end, reverse side, other side; hind part, posterior, tail end, backside, hindquarters. **behind one's back** secretly, deceitfully, slyly, sneakily, surreptitiously, covertly.

back adjective **1** *back garden/teeth* rear, hind, end, hindmost, posterior. **2** *back copies* past, previous, earlier, former, bygone.

back verb **1** *back the proposal* support, endorse, approve, favor, advocate, help, aid, promote, champion, encourage, second. **2** *back the theatrical venture* sponsor, finance, subsidize, underwrite. **3** *back her statement* support, confirm, corroborate, substantiate, endorse, second, vouch for, attest to, sanction. **back away** withdraw, retire, retreat, fall back, turn tail. **back down** yield, submit, surrender, give in, concede, backtrack, back-pedal, retract. **back out** go backwards, reverse; go back

on, withdraw from, cancel, renege on, get cold feet, recant; *inf.* chicken out.

backbiting noun slander, libel, defamation, abuse, scandalmongering, disparagement, denigration, detraction, malice, spite, spitefulness, cattiness, vilification, vituperation, calumny.

backbone noun **1** *an injured backbone* spinal/vertebral column. *See* BACK noun 1. **2** *the backbone of the organization* framework, mainstay, support, foundation, structure. **3** *lacking backbone* strength of character, firmness, determination, resolve, courage, grit, nerve, mettle, pluck, fortitude.

backer noun **1** *the theater's backers* sponsor, patron, benefactor, subsidizer, underwriter; *inf.* angel. **2** *backers of the candidate* supporter, advocate, promoter, champion.

backfire verb *the plan backfired* miscarry, rebound, recoil, boomerang, fail, disappoint; *inf.* flop.

background noun **1** *in the background of the painting* distance, rear, horizon. **2** *posing against a white background* setting, backcloth, backdrop, scene, stage. **3** *check the employee's background* upbringing, rearing, education, history, class, culture, experience, family, circumstances, qualifications, credentials. **4** *the political background* conditions, circumstances, environment, factors, influences.

backing noun support, approval, help, assistance, aid, encouragement, cooperation, endorsement, sponsorship, financing, grant, subsidy; funds.

backlash noun reaction, counteraction, repercussion, recoil, kickback, boomerang, retaliation.

backlog noun accumulation, stockpile, heap, stock, supply; arrears, reserves; *inf.* mountain.

backpedal verb retract, take back, withdraw, retreat, backtrack, back down, renege, do an about-face.

backslide verb relapse, lapse, regress, retrogress, revert, fall back, stray, degenerate, deteriorate.

backward adjective **1** *a backward area* slow, behind, behindhand, underdeveloped, undeveloped, retarded, unprogressive, unsophisticated. **2** *rather backward in a crowd* bashful, shy, retiring, hesitant, shrinking, timid.

bad adjective **1** *bad workmanship* poor, unsatisfactory, inadequate, deficient, imperfect, defective, inferior, substandard, faulty, unacceptable, worthless; *inf.* lousy, crummy. **2** *smoking is a bad habit* harmful, hurtful, damaging, injurious, detrimental, destructive, ruinous, deleterious, unhealthy, unwholesome. **3** *a bad man* immoral, wicked, wrong, evil, sinful, corrupt, base, reprobate, depraved, dishonest, dishonorable, crooked. **4** *a bad child* naughty, mischievous, disobedient, unruly, refractory. **5** *bad weather* disagreeable, unpleasant, unwelcome, uncomfortable, nasty, terrible, dreadful, grim, gloomy, unfortunate, unfavorable, distressing. **6** *a bad time for house-buying* adverse, difficult, unfavorable, unsuitable, inappropriate. **7** *a bad mistake/accident* serious, severe, grave, disastrous, terrible, critical, acute. **8** *bad eggs* rotten, decayed, moldy, putrid, tainted, spoiled, contaminated. **9** *an invalid feeling bad* ill, unwell, sick, poorly, indisposed, ailing, weak, feeble, diseased; *inf.* under the weather, below par. **10** *feeling bad about their actions* sorry, apologetic, regretful, conscience-stricken, contrite, remorseful, guilty, penitent, rueful, sad, upset. **11** *a bad check* worthless, invalid, counterfeit, false, spurious, fraudulent, fake; *inf.* bogus, phony. **not bad** all right, quite good, passable, tolerable, fair, average; *inf.* OK, so-so.

badge noun **1** *badge on a uniform* crest, emblem, insignia, device, shield, escutcheon. **2** *badge of honor* mark, sign, symbol, indication, indicator, signal, characteristic, trademark.

badger verb pester, harass, plague, torment, bother, provoke, hound, nag, goad, bully; *inf.* bug, hassle.

badly adverb **1** *do the job badly* poorly, wrongly, incorrectly, unsatisfactorily, inadequately, imperfectly, defectively, faultily, ineptly, inefficiently, shoddily, carelessly. **2** *work out badly* unsuccessfully, unfortunately, unhappily, unfavorably. **3** *badly hurt/defeated* greatly, deeply, severely, seriously, extremely, intensely, exceedingly, acutely. **4** *behave badly* naughtily, wrongly, immorally, wickedly, improperly, criminally. **5** *want something badly* greatly, exceedingly, extremely, enormously, tremendously, considerably.

baffle verb **1** *baffled by the problem* puzzle, perplex, mystify, nonplus, stump, flummox, confound, bewilder, confuse. **2** *baffle their plans* thwart, frustrate, foil, check, block, hinder, obstruct.

bag noun receptacle; handbag, pocketbook, purse, shoulder bag; suitcase, grip, flight bag, backpack, rucksack, haversack, satchel, duffel bag.

bag verb **1** *bag three pheasants* catch, capture, shoot, kill, trap, snare, land. **2** *the pants bagged* sag, hang loosely.

baggage noun luggage, gear, equipment, pack; belongings, things, suitcases, bags, effects, paraphernalia, trappings, accoutrements.

baggy adjective loose, slack, roomy, oversize, oversized, shapeless, ill-fitting, sagging.

bail noun surety, security, bond, guarantee, warranty, pledge, collateral.

bail verb **bail out 1** *bail him out* help, assist, aid, rescue, relieve. **2** *bailed out before the crash* escape, get out, withdraw, retreat.

bait noun *low prices as bait for the consumer* attraction, lure, incentive, snare, temptation; allurement, enticement, incitement, inducement.

bait verb torment, persecute, badger, plague, harry, harass, tease, annoy, irritate; *inf.* hassle, needle.

bake verb *earth baked by the sun* scorch, burn, sear, parch, dry, desiccate, fire.

balance noun **1** *the balance of power* equilibrium, evenness, symmetry, parity, equity, equipoise, correspondence, uniformity, equivalence. **2** *I tripped and lost my balance* steadiness, stability. **3** *people of ability and balance* composure, poise, equanimity, aplomb, stability, coolness, levelheadedness, sang-froid. **4** *her practicality acts as a balance to his genius* counterbalance, countercheck, counterweight, stabilizer, compensation, recompense, ballast. **5** *pay the balance of the account* remainder, rest, residue, difference. **in the balance** uncertain, at a turning point, critical, at a crisis.

balance verb **1** *balance the book on her head* steady, stabilize, poise. **2** *advantages balance the disadvantages* counterbalance, counteract, offset, neutralize, compensate for, make up for, counterpoise. **3** *the profit and loss columns must balance* correspond, match, be level/parallel. **4** *balance the advantages and disadvantages* weigh, compare, evaluate, consider, assess, appraise.

bald adjective **1** *a bald man* hairless, bald-headed, depilated. **2** *a bald landscape* barren, treeless, bare, stark, exposed, bleak. **3** *a bald statement* blunt, direct, forthright, straightforward, downright, outright, plain, simple, unadorned, stark, severe.

balderdash noun nonsense, rubbish, twaddle, drivel, foolishness, gibberish, bunkum, claptrap; *inf.* bunk, hot air, bilge, poppycock, rot.

balk verb refuse, hesitate over, draw back from, flinch/recoil/shrink/shy from, evade, dodge, resist, eschew.

ball noun sphere, globe, orb, globule, spheroid.

balloon verb swell out, puff out, fill out, billow, blow up, inflate.

ballyhoo noun fuss, commotion, to-do, hullabaloo, racket; publicity, propaganda, promotion, buildup; *inf.* hype.

balm noun **1** *apply balm to the burns* ointment, lotion, cream, salve, emollient, embrocation, liniment, unguent. **2** *balm for a troubled mind* remedy, curative, cure, restorative, palliative, solace, consolation, comfort.

balmy adjective **1** *balmy breezes* mild, gentle, temperate, calm, soothing, soft, fragrant, perfumed. **2** *you're balmy* silly, eccentric, peculiar, weird; *inf.* daft, batty, nutty, loony, loopy.

bamboozle verb trick, cheat, deceive, delude, hoodwink, mislead, hoax, fool, dupe, defraud, swindle; *inf.* gull, con.

ban verb prohibit, forbid, veto, disallow, bar, debar, outlaw, proscribe, suppress, reject, restrict, banish.

ban noun prohibition, veto, bar, embargo, boycott, proscription, interdict, interdiction, suppression, stoppage, restriction, taboo.

banal adjective hackneyed, trite, clichéd, commonplace, platitudinous, stock, stereotyped, pedestrian, unoriginal, unimaginative, stale, uninspired, tired, inane, jejune.

band[1] noun **1** *iron/rubber band* bond, binding, cord, strap, tie, link, chain, fetter, manacle, ligature, ring, hoop. **2** *a band round the waist/hair* belt, cord, braid, sash, girdle, ribbon, fillet, cincture. **3** *a band of white on the black* strip, stripe, streak, line, bar, striation.

band[2] noun **1** *a band of robbers* group, troop, company, gang, mob, pack, bunch, assembly, assemblage, association, club, set, coterie. **2** *a brass/jazz band* combo, ensemble, orchestra.

band[3] verb join, group, unite, merge, combine, team up, gather, ally, affiliate, associate.

bandage verb bind, bind up, dress, cover, plaster.

bandit noun robber, brigand, outlaw, desperado, hijacker, plunderer, marauder, gangster, criminal, gunman, highwayman, pirate, racketeer.

bane noun ruin, death, ruination, scourge, torment, plague, affliction, calamity, misery, woe, nuisance, trial, burden, blight, curse, bête noir.

bang noun **1** *a loud bang* report, burst, boom, clash, peal, clap, pop, thud, thump. **2** *a bang on the head* blow, bump, hit, slap, punch, smack, whack, rap, cuff; *inf.* wallop, sock.

bang verb hit, strike, beat, thump, hammer, knock, rap, pound, thud, pummel, whack, slam, crash; *inf.* bash.

banish verb exile, deport, expel, eject, drive away, expatriate, cast out, outlaw, transport, oust, evict, throw out, exclude, dismiss, send away, dispel, get rid of, ban, bar, eliminate, dislodge.

banishment noun exile, deportation, expulsion, expatriation, transportation, proscription.

bank[1] noun **1** *a grassy bank* slope, rise, incline, gradient, mound, hillock, knoll. **2** *the bank of a river* edge, side, shore, brink, margin, embankment.

bank[2] noun **1** *empty the child's bank* piggy bank, cashbox, safe, strongbox, coffer. **2** *a bank of information* store, reserve, accumulation, stock, stockpile, reservoir, supply, fund, hoard, storehouse, repository, depository.

bankrupt adjective insolvent, failed, ruined, financially embarrassed, distressed, in the red; *inf.* on the rocks, broke, hard up. **bankrupt of** *bankrupt of ideas* wanting, without, deprived of, bereft of.

bankruptcy noun insolvency, liquidation, indebtedness, failure, ruin, ruination, penury.

banner noun flag, standard, colors, pennant, pennon.

banner adjective *a banner year* excellent, red-letter, outstanding, notable, exceptional.

banquet noun dinner, dinner party, feast, meal, party, repast, treat, revel.

banter noun repartee, badinage, teasing, joking, jesting, raillery; *inf.* kidding, ribbing, joshing.

banter verb tease, joke, jest, mock; *inf.* kid, rib, rag, josh.

baptize verb christen, name, immerse, sprinkle; initiate, introduce, inaugurate, launch.

bar noun **1** *an iron bar* rod, pole, stake, stick, shaft, rail, spar, crosspiece. **2** *a bar of soap* block, brick, cake, wedge, lump. **3** *no bar to promotion* obstacle, hindrance. *See* BARRIER 2. **4** *bar of light* band, strip, line, belt, streak, stripe. **5** *a ship stuck on a bar* sandbar, shoal, shallow, reef, sandbank, ridge, ledge, shelf. **6** *drinking in a bar* tavern, saloon, pub, lounge.

bar verb **1** *bar the door* bolt, lock, fasten, padlock, secure, latch. **2** *bar from entering* prohibit, preclude, forbid, ban, exclude, keep out, block, impede; obstruct, hinder, restrain, check, stop, defer.

barb noun insult, sneer, gibe, affront; scoffing, scorn, sarcasm; *inf.* dig.

barbarian noun savage, brute, wild man/woman, troglodyte, ruffian, lout, vandal, hooligan, boor, ignoramus, philistine, yahoo.

barbarian adjective savage, uncivilized, primitive, brutish, wild, loutish, hooligan, boorish, uncivilized, wild, rough, coarse, uncouth, vulgar, philistine.

barbaric adjective **1** *barbaric tribes* savage, uncivilized. **2** *barbaric customs* brutal, savage, cruel, vicious, fierce, ferocious, bestial, barbarous, murderous, inhuman, ruthless.

barbarity noun brutality, savagery, cruelty, viciousness, bestiality, inhumanity, ruthlessness; atrocity, outrage, enormity.

bare adjective **1** *sunbathing bare* naked, stark naked, nude, exposed, unclothed, undressed, unclad, stripped, denuded. **2** *a bare room* empty, vacant, unfurnished, unadorned, stark, austere, unembellished. **3** *a bare landscape* bleak, unsheltered, unprotected, unshielded, desolate, barren. **4** *the bare facts* simple, plain, bald, basic, essential, straightforward, stark, unembellished, cold, literal. **5** *the bare minimum* mere, basic, meager, scanty, inadequate.

bare verb reveal, uncover, expose, lay bare, unveil, disclose, show, divulge, unmask, bring to light.

barefaced adjective blatant, flagrant, glaring, arrant, shameless, brazen, bold, impudent, insolent, audacious, brash, open, undisguised, unconcealed, transparent, patent, manifest, palpable.

barely adverb hardly, scarcely, only just, just, by the skin of one's teeth.

bargain noun **1** *make a bargain* agreement, pact, transaction, deal, treaty, negotiation, arrangement, compact, promise, engagement. **2** *get a bargain* discount, reduction, good buy; *inf.* steal, giveaway.

bargain verb haggle, barter, deal, trade, traffic. **bargain for** expect, anticipate, be prepared for, allow for. **bargain on** rely on, depend on, count on.

barge verb **barge in** *barge in during prayers* burst in, break in, intrude, interrupt; *inf.* butt in, horn in. **barge into** *people barging into each other* bump into, crash into, collide with, plow into, smash into.

bark verb **1** *the dog barked* howl, woof, yelp, yap, bay, growl, snarl. **2** *the teacher barked at the students* shout, yell, bawl, thunder, scream, screech, shriek, snap, snarl, bluster.

baron noun noble, nobleman, aristocrat, peer, lord; tycoon, magnate, executive, industrialist, financier, captain of industry.

baroque adjective ornate, elaborate, embellished, ostentatious, showy, florid, convoluted, rococo.

barrage noun bombardment, shelling, volley, salvo; deluge, stream, torrent, onslaught, avalanche, burst, abundance, superabundance, plethora, profusion.

barrel noun cask, keg, butt, vat, tun, tub, tank, hogshead.

barren adjective **1** *a barren woman* | *barren land* infertile, sterile, childless, unproductive, unfruitful, arid, desert, waste. **2** *barren discussion* uninteresting, boring, dull, uninspiring, prosaic, futile, worthless, useless, vapid, lackluster.

barricade noun obstacle, obstruction. *See* BARRIER 1.

barricade verb block, blockade, obstruct, bar, shut off/in, fence in, defend, fortify.

barrier noun **1** *the barrier in the parking lot* barricade, bar, fence, railing, obstacle, blockade, roadblock. **2** *a barrier to success* obstacle, hindrance, impediment, drawback, check, hurdle, restriction, stumbling block, difficulty.

barter verb **1** *barter his horse for food* trade, exchange, swap. **2** *barter for a better price* bargain, haggle.

base noun **1** *the base of a column* foundation, support, prop, stand, pedestal, rest, bottom, bed, foot, substructure, plinth. **2** *paints with an oil base* basis, core, essence, component, essential, fundamental, root, heart. **3** *mountaineers setting up a base* headquarters, center, camp, site, station, settlement, post.

base verb **1** *based on historical facts* found, build, construct, form, establish, ground, rest, root, derive. **2** *based in Chicago* locate, station, situate, post, place, install.

base adjective **1** *base motives* low, mean, sordid, immoral, dishonorable, evil, wicked, nefarious, debased, sinful, disreputable, corrupt, depraved, vile, ignoble, vulgar, foul, despicable, contemptible. **2** *base servitude* menial, subservient, servile, lowly, slavish, groveling, sniveling, cowering.

baseless adjective groundless, unfounded, unsubstantiated, uncorroborated, unjustifiable.

bashful adjective shy, reserved, diffident, retiring, modest, coy, demure, reticent, hesitant, shrinking, timid, blushing.

basic adjective fundamental, elementary, rudimentary, primary, radical, key, central, essential, indispensable, intrinsic, underlying.

basically adverb fundamentally, at heart, intrinsically, inherently, mostly.

basics plural noun fundamentals, (bare) essentials, rudiments, principles, practicalities, realities, ABCs; *inf.* brass tacks, nuts and bolts.

basis noun **1** *no basis for the statement* support, foundation, base, footing, reasoning, grounds. **2** *the basis of the discussion* starting point, premise, fundamental point/principle, main ingredient, core, essence. **3** *on a part-time basis* footing, procedure, condition, status, position.

bask verb **1** *bask in the sunshine* lie, laze, lounge, relax, loll, sunbathe. **2** *bask in their admiration* luxuriate, revel, wallow, enjoy, relish, savor.

bastard noun **1** *born a bastard* illegitimate child, love child. **2** *a rotten bastard* scoundrel, cad, blackguard, villain, rascal.

bastard adjective *a bastard language* adulterated, impure, hybrid, alloyed, inferior, imperfect, spurious, counterfeit.

bastardize verb debase, degrade, devalue, depreciate, corrupt, adulterate, defile, contaminate.

bastion noun bulwark, rampart, fortress, citadel, keep, stronghold, protection, protector, defense.

batch noun group, quantity, lot, bunch, cluster, set, collection, assemblage, pack, crowd, aggregate, conglomeration.

bathe verb **1** *bathe every day* have/take a bath, wash, soak, shower. **2** *bathe the wound* clean, cleanse, wash, steep, immerse, wet, moisten, rinse, suffuse.

bathroom noun toilet, men's/ladies' room, facilities, lavatory, washroom; *inf.* john.

baton noun stick, bar, wand, rod, staff, club, truncheon, mace.

batter verb **1** *battering their prisoners* hit, strike, beat, bash, assault, wallop, thump, thrash, lash, pound, pummel. **2** *countries battered by war* damage, injure, hurt, harm, bruise, wound, crush, shatter, destroy, demolish, ruin.

battery noun **1** *a battery of tests* series, sequence, set, cycle, chain, string. **2** *convicted of assault and battery* attack, mugging, beating, striking, thumping, thrashing, bashing.

battle noun **1** *battle between enemy forces* war, armed conflict, conflict, fight, skirmish, engagement, encounter, confrontation, collision, campaign, crusade, tussle, scuffle, scrap, melee. **2** *a battle of wills* clash, contest, competition, tournament, struggle, disagreement, argument, dispute, controversy, debate, dissension, altercation, strife.

battle verb **1** *battle for fair wages* fight, struggle, strive, combat, contend, labor, push. **2** *neighbors constantly battling* fight, war, feud, argue, quarrel, bicker, wrangle.

battle cry noun war cry, rallying call, slogan, motto, watchword, catchword, shibboleth.

battlefield noun battleground, front, battlefront, field of operations, combat zone, theater/arena of war, war zone.

batty adjective foolish, silly, eccentric; *inf.* daft, bonkers, loony.

bauble noun trinket, knickknack, trifle, ornament, toy, gewgaw, gimcrack, bagatelle.

bawdy adjective obscene, vulgar, blue, racy, titillating, crude, coarse, ribald, lewd, dirty, smutty, off-color, suggestive, salacious, erotic, prurient, lascivious, licentious, risqué, pornographic; *inf.* raunchy.

bawl verb **1** *a child bawling* cry, sob, weep, wail, blubber, snivel, squall. **2** *he bawled a reply* shout, call/cry out, yell, roar, bellow, screech, scream, howl. **bawl out** *bawled me out for being late* rebuke, chastise, yell at, scold.

bay¹ noun *ships moored in the bay* cove, inlet, indentation, gulf, basin, sound, arm.

bay² noun *a table in the bay* alcove, recess, niche, opening, nook.

bay³ verb *hounds baying* howl, bark, yelp, cry, growl.

bazaar noun market, marketplace, mart, exchange, fair, sale.

beach noun seaside, coast, seashore, shore, water's edge, coastline, sands, sand, strand.

beacon noun signal fire/light, flare, beam, lighthouse.

bead noun **1** *glass beads* ball, pellet, pill, globule, spheroid, oval. **2** *beads of sweat* drop, droplet, bubble, blob, dot, glob, dewdrop, teardrop.

beam noun 1 *the roof beams* board, timber, plank, joist, rafter, girder, spar, support, lath. 2 *a beam of light* ray, shaft, stream, streak, flash, gleam, glow, glimmer, glint.

beam verb 1 *light beamed from the window* emit, radiate, shine. 2 *beam radio/television programs* broadcast, transmit, direct, aim. 3 *beam from ear to ear* smile, grin.

bear verb 1 *bear gifts* carry, bring, transport, move, convey, take, fetch, haul; *inf.* tote. 2 *bear tales* spread, transmit, carry. 3 *bear a signature/inscription* carry, display, exhibit, show, be marked with. 4 *bear a crop* yield, produce, give forth, give, provide, supply, generate. 5 *bear a son* give birth to, breed, bring forth, beget, engender. 6 *bear the cost* carry, sustain, support, shoulder, uphold. 7 *cannot bear his attitude* stand, endorse, tolerate, abide, stomach, brook. 8 *much pain to bear* suffer, endure, undergo, experience, go through, support, weather. 9 *bear a grudge* have, hold, harbor, possess, entertain, cherish. 10 *bear left* veer, curve, go, move, turn, fork, diverge, deviate, bend. **bear out** *bear out the facts* confirm, corroborate, substantiate, endorse, vindicate, give credence to, support, ratify, warrant, uphold, justify, prove, authenticate, verify. **bear up** cope, persevere, manage, endure. **bear with** tolerate, put up with, endure, make allowances for, be patient with.

beard noun whiskers, bristle, stubble, five o'clock shadow; goatee, Vandyke, sideburns, muttonchops.

bearing noun 1 *a distinguished bearing* deportment, posture, carriage, gait. 2 *her bearing throughout the trial* attitude, behavior, manner, demeanor. 3 *have a bearing on the case* relevance, pertinence, connection. 4 *lose one's bearings* orientation, location, position, situation, track, way.

beast noun 1 *a beast of the jungle* animal, creature, mammal, quadruped. 2 *a cruel beast to his family* brute, monster, savage, swine, pig, ogre.

beastly adjective 1 *a beastly apparition* beastlike, bestial, animal-like, brutal. 2 *a beastly cold* awful, terrible, horrible, rotten, nasty, foul, vile.

beat verb 1 *he would never beat the dog* hit, strike, batter, thump, wallop, hammer, punch, knock, thrash, pound, pummel, slap, smack, flay, whip, lash, chastise, thwack, cuff, bruise, buffet, box, cudgel; *inf.* belt, bash, whack, clout, slug, lay into, knock about, rough up. 2 *their hearts beating* throb, pound, thump, pulsate, pulse, palpitate, vibrate. 3 *the bird's wings beat* flap, flutter, quiver, tremble, vibrate. 4 *beat the eggs* mix, blend, whip, whisk, stir. 5 *waves beating against the shore* strike, dash, break against, lap, wash. 6 *beat metal into rods* hammer, forge, form, shape, work, stamp, fashion, model. 7 *beat a path* tread, tramp, trample, wear, track, groove. 8 *beat the opposition* defeat, conquer, vanquish, trounce, rout, quash; *inf.* lick. 9 *beat the record* outdo, surpass, exceed, eclipse. **beat up** assault, attack, mug, batter, thrash; *inf.* work over, clobber, rough up.

beat noun 1 *the beat of the drum* bang, banging, stroke, striking, blow, hit. 2 *the beat of his heart* throb, throbbing, pounding, pulsating, thumping, palpitating, vibrating, vibration. 3 *musical beat* rhythm, stress, meter, time, measure, accent, cadence. 4 *policeman's beat* round, circuit, course, route, way, path, orbit.

beat adjective exhausted, tired, worn out, fatigued, wearied, spent.

beatific adjective blessed, blissful, heavenly, celestial, paradisiacal; rapturous, joyful, ecstatic, blissful.

beautiful adjective ravishing, gorgeous, stunning, alluring, lovely, attractive, pretty, handsome, good-looking, pleasing, comely, charming, delightful, glamorous, appealing, fair, fine, becoming, seemly, winsome, graceful, elegant, exquisite.

beautify verb adorn, embellish, enhance, decorate, ornament, garnish, gild, smarten, prettify, glamorize, primp, preen; *inf.* do/doll oneself up.

beauty noun 1 *the beauty of the surroundings* loveliness, attractiveness, prettiness, handsomeness, allure, allurement, charm, glamour, grace, artistry, symmetry; *fml.* pulchritude. 2 *the sisters were all great beauties* belle, charmer, enchantress, seductress, femme fatale, Venus, goddess; *inf.* good-looker, lovely, stunner, knockout, dish. 3 *the beauty of the scheme* attraction, good thing, advantage, benefit, asset, strong point, boon, blessing.

beckon verb 1 *beckon to the waiter* signal, gesture, gesticulate, motion, wave, nod, call, summon, bid. 2 *the sea beckons him* draw, pull, call, attract, tempt, entice, allure.

become verb 1 *she became rich* come to be, turn out to be, grow, grow into, mature into, evolve into, pass into, change into, turn into. 2 *the dress becomes her* suit, flatter, look good on, set off, enhance. 3 *it ill becomes you to behave like that* befit, behoove, suit, be suitable/fitting to.

becoming adjective 1 *a becoming hat* flattering, comely, attractive, lovely, pretty, handsome, stylish, elegant, chic, tasteful. 2 *hardly becoming behavior* suitable, fitting, appropriate, apt, proper, right, decent, seemly, decorous, graceful.

bed noun **1** *she liked to sleep in her own bed* bunk, cot, couch; *inf.* sack. **2** *a flower bed* plot, area, lot, patch, space, border, strip, row. **3** *a bed of concrete* base, basis, foundation, bottom, support, substructure.

bed verb **1** *stones bedded in concrete* embed, set, fix into, insert, inlay, implant, bury. **2** *desiring to bed her* go to bed with, have sex with, sleep with, spend the night with. **bed down** go to bed/sleep, retire, settle down, have a nap; *inf.* turn in, hit the sack/hay.

bedeck verb deck, decorate, adorn, ornament, trim, festoon, array, embellish.

bedevil verb afflict, torment, beset, plague, harass, distress, annoy, vex, irritate, irk, pester.

bedlam noun uproar, pandemonium, commotion, confusion, furor, hubbub, clamor, disorder, chaos, tumult.

bedraggled adjective muddy, muddied, wet, dirty, messy, sodden, soaking, soaking wet, soaked, drenched, saturated, dripping, soiled, stained, disheveled, untidy.

beefy adjective **1** *beefy wrestler* brawny, muscular, hefty, burly, thickset, solid, strong, powerful, heavy, robust, sturdy, stocky. **2** *a beefy youngster* heavy, solid, fat, chubby, plump, overweight, stout, obese, fleshy, portly, corpulent, paunchy, dumpy.

beer noun ale, stout, lager, malt liquor, porter; *inf.* brew, suds.

befall verb happen, occur, take place, chance, arise, come about, come to pass, transpire.

befitting adjective fitting, suitable. *See* APPROPRIATE.

before adverb **1** *we've met before* previously, earlier, formerly, hitherto, in the past. **2** *they went on before* ahead, in front, in advance, in the lead.

beforehand adverb in advance, in readiness, ahead of time.

befriend verb make friends with, help, assist, aid, stand by, succor, advise.

befuddled adjective **1** *befuddled from the anesthetic* confused, dazed, groggy, muddled, numbed; *inf.* woozy. **2** *befuddled partygoers* drunk, drunken, intoxicated, inebriated, stupefied; *inf.* blotto, bombed, out of it, smashed, wasted, wrecked, zonked.

beg verb **1** *beg in order to live* solicit money, seek charity/alms, cadge, scrounge; *inf.* sponge, bum, mooch. **2** *beg for money/mercy* ask for, request, seek, look for, plead for, beseech, entreat, importune.

beggar noun tramp, vagrant, mendicant, cadger, vagabond, pauper, down-and-out, derelict; *inf.* scrounger, sponger, bum, moocher, bag lady, hobo.

begin verb **1** *begin work* start, commence, set about, embark on, initiate, set in motion, institute, inaugurate. **2** *trouble began immediately* arise, come into existence/being, happen, occur, spring up, crop up, emerge, dawn, appear, originate.

beginner noun novice, trainee, learner, apprentice, student, recruit, tyro, fledgling, neophyte, initiate, tenderfoot; *inf.* greenhorn, rookie.

beginning noun **1** *from the beginning of time* start, starting point, commencement, onset, outset, dawn, birth, inception, conception, emergence, rise; *inf.* kickoff. **2** *the beginning of the book* first part, opening, prelude, preface, introduction. **3** *philosophy has its beginnings in religion* origin, source, fountainhead, spring, mainspring, embryo, germ, roots, seeds.

begrudge verb *begrudge him his success* grudge, envy, resent, hold against, be jealous of.

beguile verb **1** *the comedian beguiling the audience* delight, please, enchant, bewitch, seduce, occupy, engage, distract. **2** *beguile the hours* pass, while away, spend.

beguiling adjective charming, enchanting, bewitching, seductive.

behalf noun **on behalf of 1** *acting on behalf of his client* for, representing, in the interests of, in the name of, in place of. **2** *collecting on behalf of the blind* for, for the benefit/good/sake of, to the advantage of, on account of, in support of.

behave verb **1** *they behaved well/badly* act, perform, conduct oneself, acquit oneself, comport oneself. **2** *she behaves like a dictator* act, perform, function, operate. **behave oneself** *the children must behave themselves* act correctly/properly, conduct oneself well, act in a polite way, show good manners, mind one's manners.

behavior noun conduct, comportment, deportment, bearing, actions, manners, ways; performance, functioning, operation, reaction, response.

behead verb decapitate, guillotine, decollate.

behest noun order, command, decree, edict, directive, instruction, request, charge, bidding, wish.

behind preposition **1** *behind the woodshed* at the rear of, beyond, on the other side of, in back of. **2** *running behind us* after, to the rear of, following, in the wake of, close upon, hard on the heels of. **3** *behind the others in English* less advanced than, slower than, weaker than, inferior to. **4** *he's behind the trouble* at the bottom of, responsible for, causing, giving rise to, instigating. **5** *we're behind you all the way* backing, supporting, in agreement with, financing.

behold verb look at, see, observe, view, gaze at, stare at, regard, contemplate, take note of, mark, consider.

beholden adjective indebted, under obligation, obligated, bound, owing, thankful, grateful.

behoove verb 1 *it behooves him to reconsider* be necessary for, be expected of, be advisable for, be wise for, be fitting, be suitable, be seemly, be proper.

beige adjective fawn, mushroom, neutral, buff, sand, oatmeal, ecru, coffee.

being noun 1 *the purpose of our being* existence, living, life, vital force, entity. 2 *shocked to the depths of her being* spirit, soul, nature, essence. 3 *a sentient being* creature, person, human being, human, individual, mortal, living thing.

belabor verb 1 *belabor the actor* criticize, attack, berate, censure, castigate, lay into, flay. 2 *belabor the point* overelaborate, discuss at length, harp on.

belated adjective late, overdue, behind time, delayed, tardy, unpunctual.

beleaguered adjective 1 *a beleaguered city* besieged, under siege, surrounded, blockaded, encircled, hemmed in, under attack. 2 *a movie star beleaguered by fans* harassed, bothered, beset, pestered, plagued, tormented.

belie verb 1 *her smile belied her anger* contradict, deny, disprove, refute, gainsay, confute. 2 *the official report belies the situation* misrepresent, falsify, distort, conceal, disguise.

belief noun 1 *it is my belief that she is dead* opinion, feeling, impression, view, conviction, judgment, thinking, theory, notion. 2 *no belief in his powers* faith, credence, trust, reliance, confidence. 3 *political beliefs* doctrine, teaching, creed, dogma, ideology, principles, tenet, canon, credence, credo.

believable adjective credible, plausible, likely, creditable, probable, conceivable, imaginable.

believe verb 1 *don't believe his story* accept, credit, be convinced by, trust; *inf.* swallow, fall for, buy. 2 *I believe he's retired* think, be of the opinion that, understand, suppose, assume, presume, surmise, reckon, guess. **believe in** *believe in alternative medicine* have faith in, trust, set store by, value, swear by.

belittle verb disparage, decry, deprecate, undervalue, underrate, underestimate, minimize, make light of, slight, detract from, downgrade, play down, scoff at, sneer at.

belligerent adjective 1 *in a belligerent mood* aggressive, antagonistic, pugnacious, quarrelsome, argumentative, disputatious, combative, quick-tempered, hot-tempered, irascible. 2 *belligerent nations* warring, battling, militant, martial, warlike, warmongering.

bellow verb roar, shout, yell, shriek, howl, screech, cry out, whoop, ululate; *inf.* holler.

belly noun 1 *a stabbing pain in the belly* stomach, abdomen, paunch; intestines, innards; *inf.* tummy, insides, guts, pot, bread basket, potbelly, beer belly. 2 *the belly of the plane* underside, underpart, underbelly.

belong verb fit in, be suited to, have a rightful place, be part of; *inf.* go, click. **belong to** 1 *the house belongs to them* be owned by, be the property of, be held by, be at the disposal of. 2 *she belongs to the sailing club* be a member of, be affiliated to/with, be allied to, be associated with, be included in, be an adherent of. 3 *this lid belongs to that box* be part of, be an adjunct of, go with, relate to.

belongings plural noun possessions, effects, goods, accoutrements, appurtenances; property, paraphernalia; *inf.* gear, things, stuff, junk.

beloved adjective adored, much loved, precious, cherished, treasured, prized, worshiped, idolized; admired, respected, valued, esteemed, revered.

beloved noun sweetheart, fiancé, fiancée, boyfriend, girlfriend, love, lover, betrothed; paramour, inamorato, inamorata.

belt noun 1 *a leather belt* girdle, sash, cummerbund, waistband, band. 2 *America's corn belt* zone, region, area, district, tract, stretch, extent.

belt verb 1 *with her waist belted* encircle, gird, encompass, bind, tie, fasten. 2 *belt prisoners on their backs* strap, flog, whip, lash, cane, thrash, scourge, flail.

bemused adjective confused, bewildered, puzzled, perplexed, dazed, stupefied, preoccupied, absentminded, engrossed.

benchmark noun standard, point of reference, gauge, criterion, test, norm, guideline, specification, model, pattern, touchstone, yardstick.

bend verb 1 *bend the little finger* curve, crook, flex, twist, bow, arch, warp, contort. 2 *the road bends to the right* curve, turn, twist, swerve, veer, incline, diverge. 3 *bend down over the sink* stoop, crouch, lean down/over, bow, hunch. 4 *bend them to our will* mold, shape, direct, force, influence, persuade, sway, subjugate. 5 *bend our minds to the task* direct, point, aim, turn, train.

bend noun curve, turn, corner, twist, angle, arc, swerve, incline, divergence, crook, deviation, deflection, coiling, spiral, loop, hook; dogleg, hairpin turn, zigzag.

beneath preposition **1** *sank beneath the waves* below, under, underneath, lower than. **2** *people beneath her socially* inferior to, secondary to, subservient to. **3** *beneath him to behave like that* unworthy of, undignified for, unbefitting, unbecoming.

benefactor noun helper, patron, backer, sponsor, supporter, promoter, contributor, subsidizer, donor, philanthropist, sympathizer, well-wisher.

beneficial adjective advantageous, favorable, propitious, promising, helpful, accommodating, obliging, useful, serviceable, valuable, profitable, rewarding, gainful.

beneficiary noun heir, inheritor, recipient, receiver, legatee, payee, assignee.

benefit noun advantage, good, gain, profit, help, aid, assistance, interest, welfare, well-being, betterment, asset, avail, use, service.

benefit verb **1** *discoveries benefiting society* do good to, be of service to, serve, be of advantage to, help, aid, assist, better, improve, advance, further. **2** *criminals benefiting from their deeds* profit, gain, reap benefits, make money; *inf.* cash in, make a killing.

benevolence noun kindness, kindheartedness, goodness, generosity, altruism, goodwill, compassion, humanitarianism.

benevolent adjective kindhearted, friendly, generous, magnanimous, considerate, thoughtful, altruistic, humane, compassionate, caring, sympathetic, humanitarian, philanthropic.

benign adjective **1** *a benign attitude* kindly, gracious, benevolent, gentle. **2** *a benign climate* health-giving, wholesome, salubrious, temperate, pleasant, mild, agreeable, refreshing. **3** *benign circumstances* favorable, advantageous, propitious, auspicious, opportune.

bent adjective **bent on** *bent on winning* determined to, set on, insistent on, resolved to, fixed on, inclined to, disposed to.

bent noun inclination, predisposition, disposition, leaning, tendency, penchant, bias, predilection, proclivity, propensity, aptitude, facility.

bequeath verb leave, will, cede, endow on, bestow on, consign, commit, entrust, grant, transfer, hand down, pass down/on, impart, transmit.

bequest noun legacy, inheritance, endowment, estate, heritage, bestowal, bequeathal, gift, settlement.

berate verb scold, rebuke, reprimand, chide, reprove, upbraid, castigate, censure, criticize, rail at, harangue, lambaste, fulminate against, vituperate; *inf.* tell off, bawl out.

bereavement noun loss, deprivation, dispossession, death, passing, demise.

bereft adjective **bereft of** deprived of, robbed of, cut off from, parted from, devoid of, wanting, lacking, minus.

berserk adjective frenzied, mad, insane, crazed, hysterical, maniacal, manic, raving, wild, enraged, raging, uncontrollable, amok, unrestrainable, out of one's mind.

berth noun **1** *book a berth in the ship* bed, bunk, billet, hammock, cot. **2** *ships at their berths* anchorage, mooring, docking site. **3** *a well-paid berth* job, post, position, employment, appointment. **give a wide berth to** avoid, keep a careful distance from, stay away from.

beseech verb beg, implore, entreat, plead with, pray, petition, appeal to, supplicate.

beset verb **1** *beset with fears* attack, worry, plague, trouble, torment, pester, bedevil, harry. **2** *beset by enemy forces* surround, besiege, encircle, enclose, encompass, hem in.

beside preposition **1** *walking beside him* alongside, abreast of, next to, with, by, adjacent to, close to, near, neighboring. **2** *beside her work, his is poor* compared with, next to, against, in contrast to/with. **beside oneself** frantic, crazed, distraught, hysterical, uncontrolled, unrestrained. **beside the point** irrelevant, not applicable, immaterial.

besiege verb **1** *the castle was besieged by the enemy* lay siege to, beleaguer, blockade, surround, encircle, encompass. **2** *movie stars besieged by reporters* surround, enclose, beleaguer, beset. **3** *besieged with doubts* harass, assail. *See* BESET 1.

best adjective **1** *the best player* foremost, finest, leading, top, chief, principal, highest, worthiest, supreme, superlative, unsurpassed, unexcelled, excellent, first-class, first-rate, outstanding, preeminent; *inf.* ace. **2** *the best way to get there* most fitting, most suitable, most desirable.

best noun **1** *only the best may enter* finest, first class, top, cream, pick, flower, choice, elite. **2** *do your best* utmost, hardest; *inf.* damnedest. **3** *at his best in the morning* peak, prime, top form, height, apex. **4** *dressed in her best* best clothes, finery, finest clothes; *inf.* Sunday best, best bib and tucker. **5** *give him my best* best wishes, regards, kindest regards, greetings, love.

best verb *best the opposition* defeat, beat, conquer, get the better of, triumph over, get the upper hand of, prevail over, outdo, surpass, outwit.

bestial adjective **1** *bestial treatment of prisoners* brutish, savage, brutal, inhuman, barbarous, abominable, cruel, primitive.

2 *bestial sexual practices* depraved, vile, sordid, degenerate, carnal, lustful, lecherous, prurient.

bestow verb give, present, confer on, grant, donate, endow with, hand over, allot, assign, consign, apportion, distribute, bequeath, impart, accord, award, honor with.

bet verb **1** *I bet $100 that he wins* wager, gamble, stake, pledge, risk, venture, hazard, chance. **2** *he never bets* gamble, wager, speculate. **3** *you can bet they've gone* be certain/sure, state confidently, predict.

bet noun **1** *enter into a bet* wager, gamble, speculation, venture, game of chance, lottery, sweepstake. **2** *place a bet of $100* wager, stake, ante, pledge. **3** *my bet is that they'll go* prediction, forecast, opinion, belief, feeling, view, theory. **4** *that's our best bet* choice, option, alternative, selection, course of action.

betray verb **1** *betray one's friends/wife* be disloyal/unfaithful to, treat treacherously, break faith with, break one's promise to, abandon, desert, forsake; *inf.* tell on, double-cross, stab in the back, sell down the river, walk out on, jilt. **2** *betray a secret* reveal, disclose, divulge, give away, let slip, blurt out, blab, lay bare, bring to light, uncover, expose.

betrayal noun **1** *betrayal of friends* informing on/against, being disloyal to, breaking faith with, breach of faith, bad faith, disloyalty, perfidy, treachery, duplicity, double-dealing; *inf.* double-crossing. **2** *betrayal of a secret* revelation, disclosure, divulgence, giving away.

betrothal noun engagement, marriage contract, espousal, pledge, promise, compact, covenant.

better adjective **1** *better players* finer, greater, superior, worthier, fitter. **2** *better course of action* more fitting, more suitable, more appropriate, more desirable, more advantageous, more useful. **3** *feeling better* healthier, fitter, less ill, stronger, well, cured, recovered; *inf.* mending, on the mend.

better verb **1** *better the conditions of the poor* raise, improve, ameliorate, advance, amend, rectify, relieve, reform, enhance. **2** *better the previous record* improve on, beat, surpass, exceed, top, outstrip, outdo.

bevel noun slope, slant, oblique, tilt, angle, cant, bezel.

beverage noun drink, potation, potable; refreshment, liquid, liquor; *inf.* libation.

beware verb be careful/wary, be cautious, be on one's guard, take heed, watch out, look out, be on the lookout/alert for.

bewilder verb confuse, mix up, muddle, puzzle, perplex, baffle, mystify, nonplus, disconcert, confound, bemuse, daze, stupefy.

bewitched adjective charmed, enchanted, beguiled, captivated, entranced, fascinated, spellbound, mesmerized.

bias noun **1** *cut on the bias* slant, cross, diagonal. **2** *a bias in favor of socialism | a musical bias* tendency, inclination, leaning, bent, partiality, penchant, predisposition, propensity, proclivity, predilection, prejudice, bigotry, intolerance.

bias verb prejudice, influence, sway, predispose, distort, bend, twist, warp, weight.

bicker verb wrangle, quarrel, argue, squabble, fight, disagree, dispute, spar; *inf.* scrap.

bid verb **1** *bid $100* offer, tender, proffer, propose. **2** *they bade him go* command, order, ask, direct, demand, require, invite.

bid noun **1** *put in a bid* offer, proposition, proffer, proposal, submission, price, sum, amount. **2** *a bid for power* attempt, effort.

bidding noun **1** *at his father's bidding* command, order, direction, demand, request, call, behest, invitation. **2** *present at the bidding* auction; offers, tenders, proposals.

big adjective **1** *a big garden/car* large, sizable, great, huge, enormous, immense, vast, massive, extensive, substantial, spacious, colossal, gigantic, mammoth, prodigious. **2** *a big man* large, tall, bulky, burly, hulking, huge, enormous, muscular, beefy, brawny, strapping, thickset, heavy, solid, corpulent, fat, obese, stout, gargantuan. **3** *a big boy now | a big sister* grown-up, adult, grown, mature, elder. **4** *a big decision* important, significant, serious, momentous. **5** *a big figure in the movement* influential, powerful, prominent, outstanding, leading, well-known, principal, foremost, noteworthy, notable, eminent, distinguished. **6** *big ideas/talk* arrogant, pretentious, ambitious, inflated, pompous, proud, haughty, conceited, boastful, bragging, bombastic. **7** *a big heart* generous, kindly, kindhearted, benevolent, magnanimous, unselfish.

bigot noun fanatic, zealot, sectarian, dogmatist, chauvinist, jingoist, racist, sexist.

bigoted adjective prejudiced, intolerant, fanatical, narrow-minded, biased, partial, one-sided, dogmatic, chauvinistic, jingoistic, racist, sexist.

bigotry noun prejudice, intolerance, fanaticism, narrow-mindedness, bias, partiality, dogmatism, discrimination, unfairness, injustice, chauvinism, jingoism, racism, sexism, provincialism.

bigwig noun VIP, dignitary, notable, personage, celebrity; *inf.* somebody, heavyweight, big shot, big gun.

bilge noun *don't talk bilge* rubbish, nonsense, drivel, gibberish, balderdash, hogwash; *inf.* rot.

bilious adjective **1** *feeling bilious* out of sorts, queasy, nauseated, sick. **2** *a bilious temperament* bad-tempered, ill-tempered, ill-humored, cross, irritable, crotchety, grumpy, peevish, crabby, testy, nasty; *inf.* grouchy.

bilk verb swindle, cheat, defraud, fleece, deceive, trick, bamboozle, gull; *inf.* con, do.

bill noun **1** *pay the bill* account, invoice, statement, reckoning, check; *inf.* tab. **2** *post no bills* poster, advertisement, flyer, notice, announcement, leaflet, circular, handout, handbill, brochure, placard, bulletin; *inf.* ad. **3** *top of the bill* program, playbill, list, listing, agenda, card, schedule, timetable. **4** *a congressional bill* proposal, measure, piece of legislation.

bill verb **1** *bill them for the goods* invoice, charge, debit, send a statement to. **2** *billed as the year's best musical* advertise, announce, post, give notice of, put up in lights.

billet verb accommodate, put up, house, quarter, station, shelter.

billow verb puff up, swell, fill out, balloon, belly, surge, roll.

bin noun container, receptacle, box, can, crate.

bind verb **1** *bind the twigs together* tie, tie up, fasten, secure, attach, rope, strap, truss, lash, tether, fetter, chain, hitch, wrap. **2** *bind the wound* bandage, dress, tape, wrap, cover, swathe. **3** *bind the surfaces together* stick, glue, cement, paste. **4** *bind the seams with gold* edge, trim, hem, border, finish. **5** *bind to secrecy* compel, obligate, oblige, constrain, force, impel, engage, require, prescribe. **6** *bound by family ties* constrain, restrain, restrict, hinder.

bind noun quandary, dilemma, predicament, difficulty, spot, tight spot.

binding adjective irrevocable, unalterable, compulsory, obligatory, imperative, mandatory.

binge noun spree, orgy, drinking bout, fling; *inf.* bender, jag.

biography noun life history, life, life story, memoir, profile, account; *inf.* bio.

birth noun **1** *present at the child's birth* childbirth, delivery, parturition, nativity. **2** *the birth of jazz* origin, beginnings, start, source, emergence, commencement, fountainhead, genesis. **3** *of noble birth* origin, descent, ancestry, lineage, line, extraction, derivation, family, parentage, house, blood, breeding, heritage, stock, strain, background.

birthright noun right, due, privilege, heritage, patrimony, legacy.

bisect verb halve, cleave, bifurcate, dichotomize.

bisexual adjective hermaphrodite, androgynous, epicene; *inf.* AC/DC, swinging both ways, switch-hitting, bi.

bit noun **1** *bits of bread* small piece, piece, section, part, segment, portion, particle, fragment, atom, flake, sliver, chip, crumb, grain, speck, scrap, shred, trace, morsel, iota, jot, whit, modicum, shard, hint, tinge, suggestion. **2** *see you in a bit* little, little while, short time, moment, minute, second, instant, short spell, flash, blink of an eye; *inf.* jiffy.

bitch noun **1** *the boss is a bitch* shrew, vixen, virago, harpy. **2** *this job's a real bitch* problem, difficulty, predicament, dilemma.

bitch verb complain, grumble, moan, carp, grouse, whine; *inf.* gripe, beef, bellyache.

bitchy adjective nasty, mean, spiteful, malicious, catty, vindictive, rancorous, venomous, snide, shrewish.

bite verb **1** *bite one's nails* chew, nibble at, gnaw at. **2** *dogs biting people* sink one's teeth in, nip, snap at, tear at. **3** *insects are biting* sting, prick, wound. **4** *biting on his grip* clamp, grip, hold on to. **5** *measures beginning to bite* take effect, work, have results. **6** *fish/new clients not biting* take the bait, be lured, be enticed, be tempted. **7** *what's biting you?* annoy, irritate, bother, peeve, provoke, vex; *inf.* bug. **bite into** **1** *bite into the food* bite, masticate, chew, munch, crunch, nibble. **2** *acids biting into the metal* eat into, corrode, burn, eat away at, erode, wear away.

bite noun **1** *the dog's playful bite* nip, snap. **2** *insect bites* sting, prick, puncture, wound, itch, smarting. **3** *a bite of the food* mouthful, piece, morsel, bit. **4** *a bite to eat* snack, refreshment. **5** *the sauce had bite* sharpness, spiciness, piquancy, pungency, edge; *inf.* kick, punch.

biting adjective **1** *biting winds* sharp, freezing, bitterly cold, harsh, nipping, stinging, piercing, penetrating. **2** *biting words* sharp, bitter, cutting, caustic, sarcastic, scathing, trenchant, mordant, stinging.

bitter adjective **1** *bitter substance* acid, pungent, acrid, tart, sour, biting, harsh. **2** *bitter old woman* resentful, embittered, rancorous, acrimonious, sullen, crabbed, sour, morose, begrudging. **3** *bitter experience* painful, distressing, distressful, harrowing, heartbreaking, heart-rending, agonizing, poignant, grievous, tragic, galling, vexatious. **4** *bitter winds* biting, sharp, harsh, stinging, piercing, penetrating, fierce. **5** *bitter quarrels* virulent, acrimonious, hostile, antagonistic, spiteful, vicious, rancorous, vindictive, malicious.

bitterness noun **1** *the bitterness of the medicine* acidity, pungency, acridity, tartness, sourness. **2** *the bitterness of the old woman* resentment, rancor, animosity, acrimony, sullenness, sourness. **3** *the bitterness of the memories* pain, painfulness, distress, agony, sadness, poignancy. **4** *the bitterness of the wind* sharpness, harshness, coldness, intensity. **5** *the bitterness of the quarrel* acrimony, hostility, spitefulness, rancor, malice, venom.

bizarre adjective strange, weird, peculiar, odd, unusual, uncommon, curious, abnormal, extraordinary, queer, freakish, offbeat, outlandish, unconventional, fantastic, *outré*, eccentric, grotesque, ludicrous, comical, ridiculous, droll, deviant, aberrant; *inf.* oddball, wacky, way-out, off-the-wall.

blab verb **1** *blab a secret* blurt out, let slip, reveal, disclose, divulge, tell, inform, report, let the cat out of the bag, tattle; *inf.* squeal, sing. **2** *blabbing on the phone* gossip, chat, chatter, blabber.

black adjective **1** *black horses* dark, pitch-black, pitch-dark, pitch, jet-black, jet, ebony, raven, sable, inky, coal-black. **2** *the black race* African-American, Negro, Negroid, colored, dark-skinned. **3** *black skies* dark, starless, moonless, unlit, unlighted, unilluminated, gloomy. **4** *children with black hands* dirty, grubby, filthy, grimy, unclean, muddy, sooty, soiled, stained, dingy. **5** *a black day* sad, melancholy, depressing, dismal, distressing, gloomy, somber, doleful, mournful, lugubrious, funereal. **6** *a black mood* angry, threatening, menacing, hostile, belligerent, resentful, sullen. **7** *black hearts* evil, wicked, sinful, bad. **8** *black humor* cynical, sick, macabre.

black noun **in the black** solvent, without debt. **in black and white** in print, written down, clearly/plainly/explicitly defined; in absolute terms, unequivocally, categorically, uncompromisingly.

blackball verb blacklist, bar, ban, exclude, shut out, expel, drum out, oust, cashier, ostracize, reject, repudiate, boycott, snub, shun.

blacken verb **1** *smoke blackening the walls* make black, darken, make dirty/sooty/smoky, besmudge. **2** *the sky blackened* darken, grow dim. **3** *they blackened his character* defame, speak ill/evil of, slander, libel, denigrate, disparage, slur, sully, vilify, defile, smear, besmirch, tarnish, stain.

blacklist verb debar, ban. *See* BLACKBALL.

blackmail noun extortion, exaction, extraction, intimidation, bribery, wresting, wringing, milking, bleeding, bloodsucking.

blackmail verb extort, exact, extract, bribe, wrest, force, hold to ransom, threaten, coerce, compel.

blame verb **1** *blame him for the accident* hold responsible/accountable, condemn, assign fault/liability/guilt. **2** *they're always blaming the child* find fault with, criticize, censure, reprimand, reproach, reprove, upbraid, scold, chide, berate, take to task. **blame on** ascribe to, attribute to, lay at the door of; *inf.* pin on, stick on.

blame noun **1** *put the blame on him* responsibility, guilt, accountability, liability, onus, culpability, fault; *inf.* rap. **2** *incur much blame for his behavior* censure, criticism, incrimination, accusation, condemnation.

blameless adjective innocent, guiltless, above reproach/suspicion, in the clear, without fault, virtuous, irreproachable, unimpeachable, unoffending, sinless.

bland adjective **1** *bland food* tasteless, flavorless, mild, insipid. **2** *a bland speech* dull, middle-of-the-road, mediocre, nondescript, humdrum, boring, uninteresting, monotonous, unexciting. **3** *a bland manner* smooth, affable, amiable, agreeable, gentle. **4** *bland breezes* mild, soft, calm, temperate, balmy, soothing.

blank adjective **1** *a blank paper/expression* void, empty, vacant, deadpan, impassive, poker-faced, vacuous. **2** *my mind went blank* uncomprehending, without ideas, at a loss, confused, puzzled. **3** *a blank refusal* outright, absolute, unqualified, utter, complete.

blank noun space, gap, emptiness, void, vacuum.

blanket noun **1** *cover with a blanket* coverlet, bedcover, spread, afghan; *inf.* throw. **2** *a blanket of snow* covering, mass, layer, coat, coating, film, sheet, carpet, cloak, mantle.

blanket adjective across the board, overall, inclusive, all-inclusive, comprehensive, general, wide-ranging, sweeping.

blanket verb *snow/mist blanketing the hills* cover, overlay, coat, carpet, conceal, hide, mask, cloud, cloak, veil, shroud, envelop, surround. **blanket out** *the storm blanketed out the broadcast* obscure, suppress, extinguish, stifle, smother.

blare verb trumpet, blast, clamor, boom, roar, bellow, resound, honk, toot, peal, clang, screech.

blasé adjective indifferent, apathetic, uninterested, unexcited, nonchalant, uncaring, unmoved, emotionless, phlegmatic, lukewarm, unconcerned, offhand, bored, weary, world-weary, jaded.

blaspheme verb profane, desecrate, swear, curse, revile, abuse, utter profanities.

blasphemous adjective profane, sacrilegious, irreligious, irreverent, impious, ungodly, godless, unholy.

blasphemy noun profanity, sacrilege, irreverence, impiety, impiousness, profaneness, ungodliness, unholiness, desecration, execration, cursing, swearing; curses, oaths, profanities.

blast noun 1 *a blast of cold air* gust, rush, draft, blow, gale, squall, storm. 2 *heard a blast of noise* blare, blaring, trumpeting, clamor, bellowing, boom, roar, clang, screech, wail, toot, honk, peal. 3 *killed by the blast* explosion, detonation, discharge, blow-up, blowing-up, eruption. 4 *receive a blast from the teacher* reprimand, rebuke, reproof.

blast verb 1 *car horns blasting away* boom, roar. See BLARE 1. 2 *blast the building to bits* blow, demolish, shatter, explode, break up. 3 *poverty blasted their hopes* blight, kill, destroy, wither, shrivel, crush, dash, blight, wreck, ruin, spoil, annihilate. 4 *blast the pupils for being late* reprimand, rebuke, criticize, upbraid, berate, castigate.

blatant adjective flagrant, glaring, obtrusive, obvious, overt, manifest, conspicuous, prominent, pronounced, bare-faced, naked, sheer, outright, out-and-out, unmitigated, brazen, shameless.

blaze noun 1 *destroyed in the blaze* fire, conflagration, holocaust, flames. 2 *a blaze of light* beam, flash, flare, glare, streak, glitter; brightness, radiance, brilliance. 3 *a blaze of anger* outburst, burst, eruption, flare-up, explosion.

blaze verb 1 *the logs blazed* burn, be ablaze, flame. 2 *lights blazed in the street* shine, beam, flash, flare, glare, glitter. 3 *blaze with fury* flare up, blow up, explode, seethe, boil, smolder; *inf.* see red.

bleach verb make white/whiter, make pale/paler, lighten, blanch, fade, wash out.

bleak adjective 1 *a bleak landscape* bare, barren, desolate, exposed, unsheltered, open, windswept, windy, chilly, cold, waste, arid, desert. 2 *bleak surroundings/prospects* dreary, dismal, dark, gloomy, depressing, grim, miserable, cheerless, joyless, disheartening, unpromising, hopeless.

bleary adjective 1 *bleary eyes* blurred, blurry, tired, weary. 2 *bleary view* indistinct, dim, hazy, foggy, fuzzy.

bleed verb 1 *the wounded were bleeding* shed/lose blood, emit blood. 2 *sap bleeding from a cut in the trunk* flow, run, ooze, seep, exude, trickle, weep, gush, spurt. 3 *bleeding money from the old man* extort, extract, squeeze, fleece. 4 *bleeding their resources* drain, exhaust, sap, deplete. 5 *hearts are bleeding for them* ache, grieve, mourn, sorrow, suffer, agonize, feel.

blemish noun defect, flaw, blot, taint, stain, smirch, dishonor, disgrace; mark, blotch, spot, patch, bruise, scar, speck, imperfection, discoloration, disfigurement, birthmark, nevus, pimple; *inf.* zit.

blemish verb damage, mar, spoil, flaw, mark, spot, speckle, blotch, disfigure, discolor, deface, sully, tarnish, blot, taint, stain, besmirch, injure, damage, impair, flaw.

blend verb 1 *blend the ingredients* mix, combine, intermix, admix, mingle, commingle, unite, merge, compound, alloy, homogenize. 2 *colors blending with each other* harmonize, go with, complement, fit, suit.

blend noun mixture, mix, combination, amalgamation, amalgam, union, merging, compound, alloy, composite.

bless verb 1 *bless the altar* consecrate, sanctify, hallow, dedicate. 2 *bless God's name* glorify, praise, laud, extol. 3 *bless you for helping* give thanks for/to, thank. 4 *blessed with good looks* endow, bestow, favor, provide, grace. 5 *bless the enterprise* sanction, approve, endorse, support.

blessed adjective 1 *a blessed place* consecrated, sanctified, hallowed, sacred, holy, revered. 2 *blessed with talent* favored, endowed. 3 *blessed time* happy, joyful, joyous, blissful.

blessing noun 1 *utter a blessing* benediction, dedication, thanksgiving, consecration, invocation, grace. 2 *give the plan his blessing* approval, approbation, sanction, endorsement, support; good wishes. 3 *the blessing of good health* advantage, benefit, help, boon, godsend, favor, gift, luck, good fortune.

blight noun 1 *plants killed by blight* disease, canker, infestation, pestilence, fungus, mildew. 2 *the blight that destroyed the city* affliction, plague, scourge, bane, woe, curse, misfortune, calamity, trouble, tribulation.

blight verb kill, destroy, crush, ruin. See BLAST verb 3.

blind adjective 1 *blind people* unsighted, sightless, visually impaired, visionless, unseeing, stone-blind. 2 *he must be blind not to know* imperceptive, slow, slow-witted, dim-witted, obtuse, dense, thick. 3 *blind loyalty* unreasoned, uncritical, unthinking, mindless, injudicious, undiscerning, indiscriminate. 4 *a blind rage* rash, impetuous, hasty, reckless, uncontrolled, unrestrained, violent, furious, irrational. 5 *a blind entrance* concealed, hidden, obscured, out of sight. **blind to** unmindful of, heedless of, oblivious to, indifferent to, unaware of, ignorant of, insensitive to.

blind verb **1** *blinded in the accident | blinding the driver* deprive of sight/vision, render unsighted/sightless, obscure/block (one's) vision, get in (one's) line of vision, dazzle. **2** *blinded by love* deprive of judgment/reason, deceive, delude, beguile, hoodwink.

blind noun **1** *a window blind* screen, shade, curtain, shutter; venetian blind. **2** *the duck hunters' blind* camouflage, screen, façade, cover.

blindly adverb **1** *feeling his way blindly* without sight, sightlessly. **2** *rushing on blindly* unmindfully, carelessly, heedlessly, rashly, impetuously, recklessly, irrationally. **3** *loving him blindly* uncritically, injudiciously, undiscerningly, indiscriminately.

blink verb **1** *eyes blinking in the light* flutter, flicker, wink, bat, peer, squint. **2** *city lights blinking* flicker, twinkle, waver, wink, glimmer, glitter, sparkle, shimmer, gleam, shine. **3** *blink at corruption* turn a blind eye to, take no notice of, disregard, overlook, ignore, condone.

bliss noun ecstasy, joy, elation, rapture, euphoria, happiness, delight, heaven, paradise, seventh heaven, blessedness, beatitude.

blister noun **1** *blisters on the skin* pustule, pimple, boil, cyst, abscess, carbuncle, ulcer. **2** *blisters on the painted surface* bubble, swelling, bulge, protuberance.

blithe adjective **1** *a blithe mood* happy, cheerful, cheery, lighthearted, jolly, merry, carefree, buoyant, jaunty, sprightly. **2** *blithe disregard for others* casual, indifferent, careless, nonchalant, uncaring, unconcerned.

blitz noun bombardment, attack, assault, raid, offensive, onslaught, strike, all-out effort, endeavor.

bloat verb swell, puff up/out, blow up, distend, inflate, balloon, enlarge, expand, dilate.

blob noun **1** *a blob of whipped cream* globule, glob, bubble, pellet, dollop, lump. **2** *a blob of paint* spot, dab, splash, daub, blotch, blot, smudge.

bloc noun alliance, coalition, union, federation, league, ring, group, syndicate, combine, entente, party, wing, faction, cabal, clique, coterie.

block noun **1** *block of chocolate/soap* bar, cake, brick, chunk, hunk, lump, cube, ingot, wedge. **2** *building a new science block* building, complex. **3** *block of seats/shares* group, batch, band, cluster, set, section, quantity. **4** *a block in the pipe* blockage, obstruction, stoppage. **5** *a block to progress* deterrent, stumbling block. *See* BARRIER 2.

block verb **1** *block the pipe* clog, stop up, choke, plug, close, obstruct. **2** *block progress* hinder, impede, halt, stop, bar, check, arrest, deter, thwart, frustrate.

blockade noun *a blockade at the border* barrier, obstacle, obstruction, hindrance.

blockhead noun dunce, numskull, dolt, fool, simpleton, oaf, ass, dullard, idiot, ignoramus, bonehead, nincompoop; *inf.* chump, dingbat.

blond, blonde adjective fair, fair-haired, golden-haired, flaxen, tow-headed; fair-skinned, fair-complexioned, light.

blood noun **1** *blood was flowing* lifeblood, vital fluid. **2** *of noble blood* ancestry, kinship. *See* BIRTH 3. **3** *own flesh and blood* relations, kin, kindred.

bloodshed noun killing, slaughter, slaying, carnage, butchery, massacre, murder, blood-letting, blood bath, gore.

bloodthirsty adjective murderous, homicidal, savage, vicious, ruthless, barbarous, barbaric, brutal, bloody, sadistic, slaughterous, warlike, bellicose, sanguinary.

bloody adjective **1** *a bloody cloth* blood-stained, blood-soaked, blood-marked, blood-spattered. **2** *bloody actions/thoughts* savage, vicious. *See* BLOODTHIRSTY.

bloom noun **1** *perfect blooms* flower, blossom, floweret; flowering, blossoming, efflorescence. **2** *beauty losing its bloom* freshness, glow, luster, sheen, radiance.

bloom verb **1** *plants blooming* flower, blossom, open, open out, bud, burgeon. **2** *they've bloomed since moving to the country* flourish, thrive, prosper, succeed.

blossom noun flowers, flowerets. *See* BLOOM noun 1.

blossom verb **1** *trees blossoming* flower, burgeon. *See* BLOOM verb 1. **2** *she blossomed in her new environment* flourish, thrive. *See* BLOOM verb 2.

blot noun **1** *blots of ink/grease* spot, blotch, smudge, patch, dot, mark, speck, smear. **2** *a blot on his character* fault, imperfection. *See* BLEMISH noun.

blot verb **1** *paper blotted with ink-spots* spot, blotch, smudge, dot, smear, bespatter. **2** *the event blotted his reputation* besmirch, blacken. *See* BLEMISH verb. **blot out 1** *blot out the typist's mistake* erase, obliterate, delete, rub out. **2** *blot out the view* hide, conceal, obscure, obliterate. **3** *blot out memories* wipe out, erase, efface, obliterate, expunge. **blot up** *blot up the grease* soak up, absorb, dry up, take up.

blotch noun **1** *blotch of ink* smudge, dot, spot, speck, blot, stain, smear. **2** *blotch on the skin* patch, blemish, eruption, birthmark, nevus.

blow verb **1** *the wind was blowing* puff, flurry, bluster, blast, gust. **2** *hair blowing in the breeze* wave, flap, flutter, waft, stream, drift, whirl. **3** *wind blowing the leaves/boats* toss, sweep, whisk, drive, buffet, whirl, transport, convey. **4** *blow cigarette smoke* exhale, emit, expel. **5** *he was blowing a bit* puff, pant, wheeze, gasp, huff and puff. **6** *blow the trumpet* sound, play, toot, blare, blast. **7** *blow $100 on a meal* squander, fritter away, spend freely. **8** *blow one's chances* spoil, ruin, bungle, muff; *inf.* botch. **blow out 1** *blow out the candle* put out, extinguish, snuff, douse. **2** *the walls suddenly blew out* break open, burst, shatter, rupture, crack. **blow over** *their anger had blown over by morning* pass, die down, be forgotten, disappear, cease, subside. **blow up 1** *the bombed building blew up* explode, burst open, shatter, rupture. **2** *the bomb blew up* explode, go off, detonate, erupt. **3** *blow up the building* bomb, detonate, explode, blast. **4** *blow up the tire* inflate, pump up, swell, enlarge, distend. **5** *blow up the story* exaggerate, overstate, embroider, expand on. **6** *he blew up at the news* lose one's temper, go wild, rage; *inf.* hit the roof, fly off the handle.

blow noun **1** *a blow on the head* hit, knock, bang, punch, thump, smack, whack, thwack; *inf.* sock, wallop. **2** *her death was a blow* shock, upset, calamity, setback, jolt, reversal.

blowzy adjective **1** *a blowzy young woman* disheveled, slovenly, unkempt, untidy, sloppy, bedraggled. **2** *a blowzy drunk* coarse-looking, florid, ruddy-complexioned, red-faced.

bludgeon verb **1** *bludgeoned to death* club, cudgel, strike, hit, beat, beat up; *inf.* clobber. **2** *bludgeoned into agreeing* coerce, force, compel, browbeat, bully, railroad, steamroll, pressure; *inf.* strong-arm.

blue adjective **1** *a blue dress* azure, sky-blue, powder-blue, deep blue, royal blue, sapphire, ultramarine, navy, indigo, cyan, cobalt, cerulean. **2** *feeling blue* depressed, gloomy, dejected, downcast, unhappy, sad, melancholy; *inf.* down in the dumps. **3** *blue jokes* obscene, indecent, coarse, vulgar, bawdy, lewd, risqué, smutty, offensive.

blueprint noun plan, design, prototype, draft, outline, sketch, pattern, layout.

blues plural noun *a case of the blues* depression, dejection, despondency, unhappiness, sadness, melancholy, glumness, moroseness.

bluff[1] verb **1** *he's only bluffing* pretend, fake, feign, put on, lie. **2** *he's bluffing you* deceive, delude, mislead, trick, hoodwink, bamboozle; *inf.* put one over on.

bluff[2] noun deception, deceit, pretense, sham, subterfuge, feint, delusion, hoax, fraud.

bluff[3] noun cliff, headland, ridge, promontory, peak, crag, bank, slope, escarpment.

blunder noun mistake, error, fault, slip, oversight, *faux pas*, gaffe; *inf.* slipup, booboo.

blunder verb **1** *management blundered badly* make a mistake, err; *inf.* slip up, screw up, blow it. **2** *blunder about in the dark* stumble, flounder, lurch, stagger, falter.

blunt adjective **1** *a blunt knife* unsharpened, dull, dulled. **2** *a blunt remark/person* frank, candid, outspoken, plainspoken, direct, bluff, to the point, brusque, curt.

blunt verb dull, take the edge off, deaden, dampen, numb, weaken.

blur verb **1** *blur the view* make indistinct/vague/hazy, obscure, dim, bedim, befog, fog, cloud, mask, veil. **2** *blur the windshield* smear, smudge, spot, blotch. **3** *blur one's judgment/memory* dull, numb, dim.

blur noun **1** *just a blur on the landscape* haze, haziness, indistinctness, dimness. **2** *a blur on the windshield* smear, smudge, spot, blotch.

blurt verb **blurt out** call out, cry out, exclaim, ejaculate, blab, disclose, divulge, let slip, let the cat out of the bag; *inf.* spill the beans.

blush verb redden, turn red/crimson/scarlet, flush, be red-faced.

bluster verb **1** *wind blustering* blast, gust, storm, roar. **2** *bullies blustering* rant, bully, domineer, harangue, threaten, boast, brag, swagger.

bluster noun **1** *the bluster of the wind* noise, roar, tumult. **2** *the bullies' bluster* ranting, bravado, bombast, boasting, bragging, swaggering, braggadocio; empty threats.

board noun **1** *a wooden board* plank, beam, panel, slat. **2** *pay for one's board* food, sustenance, meals, provisions, victuals; *inf.* grub, nosh. **3** *the board met to discuss policy* committee, council, panel, directorate, advisory group.

board verb **1** *they board with her* lodge, live, room. **2** *she boards three people* take in, put up, accommodate, house, feed. **3** *board the plane/train* get on, enter, embark. **board up** cover up/over, close up, shut up, seal.

boast verb **1** *boasting about his achievements* brag, crow, exaggerate, swagger, blow one's own trumpet, sing one's own praises, congratulate oneself, pat oneself on the back. **2** *the town boasts two museums* possess, own, enjoy, pride oneself/itself on.

boat noun vessel, craft; yacht, dinghy, sloop, sailboat, motorboat, speedboat, rowboat, punt, canoe, kayak.

bob verb move up and down, float, bounce, nod, jerk.

bode verb augur, presage, portend, betoken, foretell, prophesy, predict, forebode, foreshadow, indicate, signify, purport.

bodily adjective physical, corporeal, corporal, carnal, fleshly.

body noun 1 *well-formed bodies* frame, form, figure, shape, build, physique, framework, skeleton, trunk, torso. 2 *a body in the morgue* corpse, cadaver, carcass, remains; *inf.* stiff. 3 *more bodies than the room could hold* person, individual, being, human, creature. 4 *the body of the plane* main part, hub, core. 5 *a body of water* mass, expanse, extent, aggregate. 6 *the body of opinion* majority, preponderance, bulk, mass. 7 *the ruling body* group, party, band, association, company, confederation, bloc. 8 *material with little body* substance, firmness, solidity, density, shape, structure.

bog noun marsh, marshland, swamp, mire, quagmire, morass, slough, fen.

bogged verb **bogged down** stuck, impeded, halted, stopped, delayed, slowed down; trapped, entangled.

bogeyman noun monster, evil spirit, ghost, apparition, specter, phantom, goblin, hobgoblin; *inf.* spook.

bogus adjective fraudulent, counterfeit, fake, spurious, false, forged, sham, artificial, mock, make-believe, quasi, pseudo; *inf.* phony.

bohemian adjective unconventional, unorthodox, nonconformist, offbeat, avantgarde, eccentric, alternative, artistic; *inf.* arty, way-out.

bohemian noun nonconformist, hippie, beatnik, dropout.

boil verb 1 *the soup is boiling* | *boil the soup* bubble, simmer, cook, seethe, heat. 2 *the sea was boiling* seethe, bubble, churn, froth, foam. 3 *the teacher boiled with impatience* rage, fume, seethe, rant, rave, flare up.

boil noun carbuncle, furuncle, abscess, pustule, pimple.

boiling adjective 1 *boiling hot* | *boiling weather* scorching, roasting, baking, blistering, sweltering, searing, torrid. 2 *she was boiling at his insults* furious, angry, incensed, fuming, in a rage, enraged, infuriated, seething, irate.

boisterous adjective 1 *boisterous children/parties* noisy, loud, rowdy, unruly, wild, unrestrained, romping, disorderly, rambunctious. 2 *boisterous winds* blustery, gusty, stormy, rough, turbulent.

bold adjective 1 *a bold explorer* | *bold deeds* daring, intrepid, audacious, courageous, brave, valiant, fearless, adventurous, undaunted, valorous. 2 *a bold youth* brazen, shameless, forward, brash, impudent, saucy, immodest. 3 *bold colors* striking, vivid, showy, flashy, eye-catching, conspicuous, prominent.

bolster verb strengthen, reinforce, support, boost, prop up, buoy up, shore up, buttress, aid, invigorate.

bolt noun 1 *window bolts* bar, catch, latch, lock, fastener, hasp. 2 *bolt of lightning* flash, shaft, streak, burst, discharge, flare. 3 *make a bolt for it* dash, dart, run, bound, spring, jump.

bolt verb 1 *bolt the door* bar, lock, fasten, latch. 2 *bolt the pieces together* rivet, pin, clamp, fasten, batten. 3 *bolt from the room* dash, dart, run, sprint, hurtle, rush, flee, fly, spring, leap. 4 *bolting his food* gulp, gobble, devour, wolf, guzzle.

bolt adverb **bolt upright** straight up, very straight, rigid, stiff, completely upright.

bomb noun 1 *dropped a bomb on the target* explosive, incendiary, blockbuster, grenade, shell, missile, torpedo, letter bomb, nuclear bomb. 2 *the movie was a bomb* flop, failure, fiasco; *inf.* washout, turkey.

bomb verb 1 *bomb the target* bombard, blow up; shell, torpedo, blitz, strafe, cannonade. 2 *the movie bombed at the box office* flop, fail, fall flat, founder; *inf.* go up in smoke, go belly up.

bombard verb 1 *bombard military establishments* bomb, shell, torpedo, pound, blitz, strafe, pepper, fire at, attack, assault, raid. 2 *bombard with questions* assail, attack, besiege, beset, bother, hound.

bombardment noun bombing, shelling, strafing, blitz, blitzkrieg, air raid, strafe, cannonade, fusillade, attack, assault.

bombast noun pomposity, rant, bluster, turgidity, pretentiousness, ostentation, rodomontade.

bona fide adjective genuine, authentic, real, true, actual, sterling, sound, legal, legitimate.

bonanza noun windfall, godsend, stroke/run of luck, boon, bonus.

bond noun 1 *the bond/bonds of friendship* tie, link, binding, connection, attachment, union. 2 *sign a bond* agreement, contract, pact, covenant, compact, pledge, promise. **bonds** *freed from his bonds* chains, fetters, shackles, manacles.

bond verb join, connect, fasten, stick, unite, attach, bind; glue, gum, fuse, weld.

bondage noun slavery, enslavement, captivity, servitude, serfdom, oppression.

bonus noun **1** *the pleasant company was a bonus* extra, plus, gain, benefit, boon, perquisite, dividend, premium. **2** *a Christmas bonus* gratuity, tip, gift, perk, honorarium, reward.

bony adjective angular, rawboned, gaunt, scraggy, scrawny, skinny, skeletal.

book noun volume, tome, work, publication, title, opus, treatise, manual; booklet, pad, notebook, ledger, log.

book verb **1** *book a room/speaker* reserve, engage, charter. **2** *book the meeting* arrange, program, schedule, line up.

bookish adjective studious, scholarly, academic, literary, intellectual, brainy, highbrow, erudite, learned.

boom verb **1** *guns booming | the teacher boomed* resound, bang, blast, blare, roar, rumble, thunder, shout. **2** *the housing market boomed* burgeon, flourish, thrive, prosper, succeed, grow, expand, increase.

boom noun **1** *the boom of the guns/orator's voice* explosion, blast, blare, roar, bellow, rumble, reverberation, thundering. **2** *the boom in low-income housing* increase, upturn, upsurge, upswing, advance, growth, spurt, expansion, improvement, boost.

boomerang verb rebound, come back, spring back, return, recoil, reverse, ricochet, backfire.

boon noun benefit, advantage, gain, blessing, godsend, windfall.

boor noun lout, oaf, philistine, vulgarian, yahoo, barbarian; *inf.* clodhopper, clod, peasant.

boorish adjective rough, rude, coarse, ill-bred, ill-mannered, uncouth, churlish, gruff, uncivilized, unsophisticated, unrefined, crude, vulgar.

boost verb **1** *boost him up the tree* lift, raise, hoist, push, thrust, shove, heave, elevate. **2** *boost morale* raise, increase, improve, encourage, heighten, help, promote, foster. **3** *boost sales* increase, expand, improve, amplify, enlarge, inflate, develop, further, foster. **4** *boost their products* promote, advertise, publicize; *inf.* plug.

boost noun **1** *give him a boost into the tree* lift (up), push, thrust, shove, heave. **2** *a boost to morale* uplift, shot in the arm, help, inspiration, stimulus. **3** *a boost in sales* increase, expansion, rise, improvement, advance.

boot verb *boot the ball* kick, punt. **boot out** *boot him out* throw out, kick out, dismiss, sack, expel, eject, oust.

booth noun stall, stand, kiosk; cubicle, compartment, enclosure.

booty noun spoil, loot, plunder, pillage, prize, haul; spoils, profits, pickings, takings, winnings; *inf.* swag, boodle, the goods.

border noun **1** *the border of the lawn* edge, verge, perimeter, boundary, margin, skirt; fringes, bounds, limits, confines. **2** *passport checks at the border* frontier, boundary, divide.

border verb **1** *woods border the fields* edge, skirt, bound. **2** *Portugal borders Spain* adjoin, abut (on), be adjacent to, be next to, neighbor, touch. **border on** *his reply borders on rudeness* verge on, approach, come close to, near/similar to, resemble.

bore[1] verb pierce, perforate, puncture, penetrate, drill, tap, tunnel, burrow, mine, dig out, gouge out, sink.

bore[2] verb weary, tire, fatigue, send to sleep, exhaust, wear out; bore to tears, bore to death, bore out of one's mind.

bore[3] noun tiresome person/thing, tedious person/thing, nuisance, bother, pest; *inf.* drag.

boredom noun tedium, tediousness, dullness, monotony, flatness, sameness, dreariness, weariness, ennui, world-weariness, malaise.

boring adjective tedious, dull, monotonous, humdrum, repetitious, unvaried, uninteresting, unexciting, flat, dry as dust, weary, wearisome, tiring, tiresome.

borrow verb **1** *borrow money* ask for the loan of; *inf.* cadge, mooch, scrounge, sponge, beg, bum. **2** *borrow another's ideas* appropriate, commandeer, copy, plagiarize, pirate, take, adopt, steal, filch; abstract, imitate, simulate.

bosom noun **1** *woman with a large bosom* breasts, bust, chest. **2** *bosom of the family* heart, center, core, midst, circle, protection, shelter. **3** *nurturing warm feelings in their bosoms* heart, soul, being; emotions, affections.

bosom adjective close, intimate, boon, confidential, dear, inseparable, faithful.

boss noun head, chief, manager, director, chief executive, administrator, leader, superintendent, supervisor, foreman, overseer, employer, master, owner; *inf.* honcho, top dog.

boss verb. **boss around** order about/around, bully, push around, domineer, dominate, ride roughshod over, control.

bossy adjective domineering, dominating, overbearing, dictatorial, authoritarian, despotic, imperious, high-handed, autocratic.

botch verb *botch (up) the situation/repair* bungle, make a mess of, spoil, mar, muff, mismanage, mangle, fumble; *inf.* mess up, foul up, screw up, blow, louse up.

bother verb **1** *don't bother your father* disturb, trouble, worry, pester, harass, annoy, upset, irritate, vex, inconvenience, provoke, plague, torment, nag. **2** *don't bother yourself with that* concern oneself, trouble oneself, inconvenience oneself, worry oneself. **3** *it bothers me that I lost it* upset, trouble, worry, concern, distress.

bother noun **1** *don't go to any bother* trouble, effort, inconvenience, exertion, strain; pains. **2** *what a bother we've missed it* nuisance, pest, annoyance, irritation, inconvenience, difficulty.

bottle noun flask, carafe, decanter, pitcher, flagon, demijohn, magnum.

bottle verb **bottle up** keep back, suppress, restrain, curb, contain, shut in, conceal.

bottleneck noun constriction, narrowing, obstruction, congestion, blockage, jam, gridlock.

bottom noun **1** *the bottom of the hill/pile* foot, lowest part/point, base. **2** *the bottom of the pillar* base, foundation, support, pedestal, substructure, underpinning. **3** *the bottom of the car* underside, underneath, undersurface, belly. **4** *the bottom of the sea* floor, bed, depths. **5** *the bottom of the class* lowest level, least important part, least honorable/valuable part. **6** *sitting on his bottom* hindquarters, buttocks, rear end, rear, rump; *inf.* backside, behind. **7** *his jealousy was at the bottom of it* origin, cause, root, source, starting point. **8** *get to the bottom of it* core, center, heart, base, basis, foundation, reality, essence, nitty-gritty, essentials.

bottomless adjective **1** *bottomless pit* deep, immeasurable, fathomless, unfathomable. **2** *bottomless reserves of energy* boundless, inexhaustible, infinite, unlimited, immeasurable, endless, limitless.

bough noun branch, limb, twig.

boulevard noun avenue, drive, road, thoroughfare, promenade.

bounce verb **1** *the ball bounced* rebound, spring back, bob, recoil, ricochet. **2** *children bouncing about* leap, skip, caper. *See* BOUND verb. **3** *bounce the troublemakers* throw out, eject, remove, expel, oust, evict; *inf.* kick out, boot out.

bounce noun **1** *ball without much bounce* spring, springiness, rebound, recoil, resilience, elasticity, give. **2** *losing bounce over the years* vitality, vigor, energy, vivacity, liveliness, spirit, dynamism; *inf.* go, get-up-and-go, pep, oomph. **3** *with a run and a bounce* leap, spring. *See* BOUND².

bound¹ verb leap, jump, spring, bounce, hop, vault, hurdle, prance, romp, caper, frolic, gambol.

bound² noun leap, jump, spring, bounce, hop, vault, hurdle; skip, bob, dance, prance, romp, caper, frolic, gambol.

bound³ verb **1** *views bounded by prejudice* limit, confine, restrict, cramp, straiten,

restrain, demarcate, define. **2** *estates bounded by walls* enclose, surround, wall in, encircle, hem in. **3** *Germany is bounded on the west by France* border, adjoin, abut.

boundary noun **1** *the boundary between the countries* border, frontier, partition, dividing/bounding line. **2** *the boundary of the forest* fringes, periphery. *See* BOUNDS. **3** *the boundary between sentiment and sentimentality* dividing line, borderline, demarcation line. **4** *push back the boundaries of knowledge* bounds, limits, outer limits, confines, extremities, barriers.

boundless adjective limitless, without limit, unlimited, unbounded, endless, unending, inexhaustible, infinite, interminable, unceasing, untold, immeasurable, immense, vast.

bounds plural noun limits, boundaries, confines, restrictions, borders, margins, edges, fringes; periphery, perimeter, precinct, pale.

bountiful adjective **1** *a bountiful hostess* generous, magnanimous, liberal, giving, openhanded, unstinting, unsparing, munificent. **2** *a bountiful supply of food* ample, abundant, bumper, plentiful, copious, lavish, prolific, profuse, bounteous.

bounty noun *a bounty for finding the treasure* reward, recompense, remuneration, gratuity, tip, premium, bonus.

bouquet noun **1** *the bride's bouquet* bunch/spray of flowers, spray, posy, wreath, garland, fringes, nosegay, boutonnière, chaplet, corsage. **2** *the wine's bouquet* aroma, smell, fragrance, perfume, scent, redolence, savor, odor. **3** *bouquets from the management* compliment, commendation, tribute, praise, congratulations.

bourgeois adjective **1** *bourgeois values* materialistic, capitalistic, money-oriented. **2** *bourgeois way of life* conventional, ordinary, uncultured, philistine, uncreative, unimaginative.

bout noun **1** *bouts of inactivity* spell, period, time, stretch, stint, turn, fit, run, session. **2** *a bout of flu* attack, fit, paroxysm. **3** *defeated in the last bout* match, contest, round, competition, encounter, fight.

bovine adjective cowlike, sluggish, stolid, phlegmatic, dull, dense, doltish.

bow verb **1** *bow to the queen* make obeisance, nod, curtsy, genuflect, bend the knee, salaam, kowtow, prostrate oneself. **2** *age had bowed his back* bend, stoop, curve, arch, crook. **3** *bow to the inevitable* give in, yield, submit, surrender, capitulate, acquiesce. **bow out** leave, resign, withdraw, step down, give up, get out, quit, pull out.

bowels plural noun **1** *an infection affecting the bowels* intestines, entrails, viscera, guts; *inf.* insides, innards. **2** *the bowels of the earth/machine* interior, inside, core, belly, cavity, depths.

bowl noun **1** *a bowl of fruit* dish, basin, vessel. **2** *dust bowl* hollow, crater, hole, depression, valley.

bowl verb **bowl over** overwhelm, astound, amaze, dumbfound, stun, surprise; *inf.* floor.

box¹ noun **1** *a box of cigars | a box shipped from Hawaii* crate, case, carton, pack, package, chest, trunk, bin, casket. **2** *a theater/jury box* compartment, cubicle, enclosure.

box² verb **box in/up** enclose, shut in, hem in, confine, restrain, constrain, cage in, coop up.

box³ verb **1** *he boxes professionally* fight, spar, grapple. **2** *box him on the ears* strike, hit, thump, cuff, slap, punch, knock, wallop, batter, pummel, thwack, buffet; *inf.* belt, sock, clout, whack, slug, slam, whop.

boxer noun fighter, pugilist, prizefighter, sparring partner.

boy noun youth, lad, youngster, kid, junior, stripling.

boy interjection *boy, what a great book* wow, gosh, gee, god, Lord, holy cow, jeepers, goodness.

boycott verb spurn, avoid, eschew, shun, reject, blackball, blacklist, ban, bar, embargo, prohibit, outlaw.

boyfriend noun sweetheart, young man, lover, man, suitor, beau, admirer; *inf.* steady, date.

boyish adjective youthful, young, childlike, immature, adolescent, juvenile, childish, callow, green, puerile.

brace noun **1** *hold in a brace* clamp, vice, fastener, coupling. **2** *the wall's brace* support, prop, beam, strut, stay, truss, buttress.

brace verb **1** *beams firmly braced* support, strengthen, reinforce, fortify, shore up, prop up, hold up, buttress. **2** *brace oneself for the results* prepare, steady, strengthen, fortify, tense.

bracing adjective invigorating, refreshing, stimulating, energizing, exhilarating, reviving, fortifying, strengthening, restorative.

bracket noun **1** *a wall bracket* support, prop, buttress. **2** *in a different financial bracket* group, grouping, category, grade, classification, class, set, section, division.

brag verb boast, crow, show off, bluster, blow one's own trumpet, sing one's own praises, pat oneself on the back.

braggart noun boaster, brag, show-off, trumpeter, braggadocio.

braid verb weave, interweave, plait, entwine, twine, intertwine, interlace, twist.

braid noun **1** *trim it with braid* cord, thread, tape, twine, yarn, edging, rickrack. **2** *hair in braids* plait, pigtail.

brain noun **1** *studying the brain* cerebral matter, encephalon. **2** *a good brain* mind, intellect, brainpower, intelligence, wit, head; *inf.* gray matter. **3** *one of the brains of our group* genius, intellectual, intellect, thinker, mind, scholar, mastermind; *inf.* highbrow, egghead.

brains plural noun intellect, intelligence, wit, head, sense, cleverness, brightness, understanding, shrewdness, sagacity, acumen, capacity, capability; *inf.* savvy.

brainwashing noun indoctrination, inculcation, persuasion, conditioning.

brainy adjective clever, intelligent, bright, brilliant, smart, gifted.

brake noun curb, check, damper, restraint, constraint, rein, control.

brake verb reduce speed, slow, slow down, decelerate.

branch noun **1** *the branch of a tree* bough, limb, stem, twig, shoot, sprig, arm. **2** *the branch of the deer's antlers* offshoot, prong. **3** *the local branch of the bank* division, subdivision, section, subsection, department, part, wing, office.

branch verb *the road branches before the village* fork, divide, furcate, bifurcate, divaricate; separate, diverge. **branch off** diverge, deviate, depart, turn aside. **branch out** extend, spread out, widen, broaden, diversify, expand, enlarge.

brand noun **1** *a brand of soup/comedy* make, line, label, trade name, trademark; kind, type, sort, variety, style, stamp, cast. **2** *recognize the cow by its brand* tag, marker, earmark. **3** *a brand on him for life* stigma, stain, blot, taint, slur.

brand verb **1** *identifying marks branded on cattle* burn, burn in, scorch, sear. **2** *experiences branded on his mind* stamp, imprint, print, engrave, impress, fix. **3** *branded as a thief* stigmatize, mark, disgrace, discredit, denounce.

brandish verb wave, flourish, wield, raise, swing, display, flaunt.

brash adjective **1** *a loud, brash young man* bold, self-assertive, audacious, aggressive, brazen, forward, cocky, impudent, insolent. **2** *brash actions* hasty, rash, impetuous, impulsive, reckless, heedless. **3** *brash colors* loud, showy, garish, gaudy, vulgar, tasteless.

brassy adjective **1** *a brassy teenager* loud, self-assertive, flashy, vulgar, showy, garish. *See* BRAZEN. **2** *brassy music* blaring, noisy, thundering, deafening, harsh.

brat noun imp, rascal, little devil, urchin, minx, whippersnapper.

bravado noun swagger, swaggering, blustering, boasting, boastfulness, bragging, bombast, braggadocio.

brave adjective **1** *brave soldiers* courageous, valiant, intrepid, fearless, plucky, gallant, bold, daring, undaunted, dauntless, lion-hearted, valorous, *inf.* gutsy, spunky. **2** *a brave show* splendid, fine, grand.

brave verb face, stand up to, endure, put up with, bear, suffer, withstand, defy, challenge, confront.

bravery noun courage, courageousness, valor, fearlessness, pluck, pluckiness, gallantry, boldness, daring, grit, mettle, spirit, dauntlessness; *inf.* guts, spunk.

brawl noun fight, fracas, wrangle, melee, rumpus, scuffle, altercation, squabble, free-for-all, tussle, brouhaha, commotion, uproar, donnybrook.

brawl verb fight, wrangle, wrestle, scuffle, tussle, clash, battle, quarrel, argue; *inf.* scrap.

brawn noun muscle, muscularity, burliness, heftiness, huskiness, strength, might; *inf.* beefiness, beef.

brawny adjective muscular, burly, hefty, strong, powerful, strapping, husky, sinewy.

brazen adjective bold, audacious, defiant, forward, brash, presumptuous, impudent, insolent, impertinent, brassy, pert, saucy, shameless, immodest, unashamed, unabashed; *inf.* pushy.

breach noun **1** *a breach in the seawall* break, rupture, split, crack, fissure, fracture, rent, rift, cleft. **2** *a breach of confidence* breaking, violation, infringement, transgression. **3** *a breach between the two families* breaking-off, estrangement, separation, severance, rift, schism, disunion, alienation, dissension, falling-out, quarrel, discord.

breach verb **1** *breach the enemy defenses* break/burst through, rupture, split. **2** *breach the contract* break, violate, infringe, defy, disobey.

breadth noun **1** *the breadth of the room* width, broadness, wideness, thickness, span. **2** *the breadth of her knowledge* extent, extensiveness, scope, range, scale, degree, spread, vastness, expanse, magnitude, measure. **3** *breadth of spirit* liberality, broad-mindedness, freedom, latitude, magnanimity.

break verb **1** *break the cup/rope* smash, shatter, crack, fracture, split, burst, fragment, splinter, shiver, crash, snap, rend,

tear, divide, sever, separate, part, demolish, disintegrate. **2** *break the law* contravene, violate, infringe, breach, defy, disobey. **3** *break for lunch* stop, pause, discontinue, rest; *inf.* knock off, take five. **4** *break one's concentration/journey* interrupt, suspend, discontinue, disturb, interfere with. **5** *break his resolve* overcome, crush, subdue, defeat, weaken, impair, undermine, cripple, enfeeble. **6** *he broke under questioning* crack, collapse, give in, yield, cave in. **7** *the recession broke him* ruin, crush, humble, degrade, bankrupt. **8** *break the news gently* tell, announce, impart, reveal, disclose. **9** *break the record* beat, surpass, outdo, better, exceed, top; *inf.* cap. **10** *break the code* decipher, decode, unravel, solve, figure out. **11** *the day/scandal broke* begin, emerge, erupt, appear. **12** *the weather broke* change, alter, vary, shift. **13** *break one's fall* cushion, soften, lessen, diminish. **break away** make a break for it, flee, make off, escape, decamp; detach oneself, secede, part company, leave. **break down 1** *the talks broke down* fail, collapse, founder, fall through. **2** *he broke down and cried* lose control, collapse, cave in, crumble, be overcome, go to pieces, come apart at the seams; *inf.* crack up. **3** *break down the figures in the budget* separate out, analyze, dissect, itemize. **break in 1** *break in hurriedly* burst in, barge in. **2** *he broke in with his own comments* interrupt, butt in, intervene, cut in, intrude. **3** *he broke in last night* break and enter, burgle, rob. **4** *break in the horse* train, tame, condition, prepare, initiate, show the ropes to. **break into** *break into song* commence, launch into, burst into, give way to. **break off 1** *break off a branch* pull off, snap off, detach, separate, sever. **2** *break off diplomatic relations* end, terminate, stop, cease, finish, discontinue, call a halt to. **break out** *war/fighting broke out* start/commence/occur suddenly, erupt, burst out, set in, arise. **break out of** *break out of prison* escape from, make one's escape from, break loose of/from, burst out of, get free of/from, free oneself of/from. **break up 1** *the meeting broke up at midnight* adjourn, end, come to an end, stop, discontinue, terminate. **2** *the crowd broke up* disperse, go their separate ways, part company. **3** *the police broke up the crowd* scatter, disband, separate, put to rout, send off. **4** *the couple have broken up* separate, part, divorce, split up, come to a parting of the ways. **5** *jealousy broke up their marriage* bring to an end, end, terminate, bring to a halt, kill, destroy. **6** *break up at his jokes* laugh, guffaw, double up, split one's sides, hold one's sides; *inf.* in stitches.

break noun **1** *a break in the seawall* crack, hole, gap, opening, gash, chink, fracture, split, fissure, tear, rent, rupture, rift, chasm, cleft. **2** *a break for lunch* interval, stop, pause, halt, rest, respite, lull, interlude, intermission, recess; coffee break; *inf.* breather, breathing spell, letup, time out, down time, vacation, time off, recess. **3** *a break in their education* interruption, discontinuation, suspension, hiatus. **4** *a break in the weather* change, alteration, variation. **5** *a break in diplomatic relations* rift, breach, split, rupture, schism, chasm. **7** *although losing, we got a break* lucky break, stroke of luck, advantage, chance, opening.

breakable adjective fragile, frangible, frail, delicate, flimsy, insubstantial, brittle, crumbly, friable, destructible.

breakdown noun **1** *the car's breakdown* failure, malfunctioning; *inf.* conking out. **2** *the breakdown of the talks* failure, collapse, foundering, falling through; *inf.* fizzling out. **3** *suffer a breakdown* collapse, nervous breakdown, loss of control, going to pieces, disintegration; *inf.* crack-up. **4** *a breakdown of the figures* itemization, analysis, dissection, categorization, classification.

breakneck adjective fast, rapid, speedy, swift, reckless, dangerous.

breakup noun end, termination, cessation, dissolution, disintegration, splitting up, breakdown, failure, collapse, foundering.

breath noun **1** *take a deep breath* inhalation, inspiration, exhalation, expiration, pant, gasp, wheeze; breathing, respiration. **2** *no breath left in him* breath of life, life, life force, vital force. **3** *hardly a breath of air* breeze, puff, gust, waft, zephyr. **4** *a breath of spring* hint, suggestion, whiff, trace, touch, whisper. **5** *stop for breath* pause, lull, rest, respite; *inf.* breather.

breathe verb **1** *she breathed deeply* respire, inhale, inspire, exhale, expire, puff, pant, gasp, wheeze, gulp. **2** *the wind breathing through the trees* blow, whisper, murmur, sigh.

breather noun stop, pause. *See* BREAK noun 2.

breathless adjective **1** *find myself breathless when climbing stairs* out of breath, wheezing, panting, puffing, gasping, choking, gulping, winded. **2** *breathless with excitement* agog, avid, eager, excited, on edge.

breathtaking adjective spectacular, impressive, magnificent, awesome, awe-inspiring.

breed verb **1** *lions breeding in captivity* reproduce, procreate, multiply, give birth, beget, propagate. **2** *breed horses* raise, rear, nurture. **3** *born and bred in the town* bring up, rear, raise, develop, educate, train, nurture. **4** *breed discontent* cause, bring about, give rise to, create, produce, generate, arouse, stir up, induce, occasion, make for.

breed noun **1** *a breed of cows* family, variety, strain, stock, line, race, lineage, extraction, pedigree. **2** *a new breed of doctor* kind, type, variety, class, brand, strain.

breeding noun **1** *the season for breeding* reproduction, generation, propagation. **2** *a lady by breeding* upbringing, rearing, education, training, nurture. **3** *people of breeding* refinement, cultivation, culture, polish, civility, gentility, courtesy, manners.

breeze noun zephyr, flurry, waft, draft.

breezy adjective **1** *a breezy day* windy, blustery, gusty. **2** *a breezy manner/individual* jaunty, cheerful, lighthearted, carefree, blithe, free and easy, easygoing, casual, airy, sprightly, lively, spirited, animated.

brevity noun **1** *the brevity of the report* shortness, briefness, conciseness, succinctness, compactness, terseness, pithiness. **2** *the brevity of summer* shortness, transitoriness, transience, impermanence, ephemerality.

brew verb **1** *brew beer* make, ferment. **2** *brew tea* infuse, steep, prepare. **3** *trouble is brewing* gather, gather force, form, loom, threaten, impend. **4** *brewing something evil* plot, scheme, hatch, plan, devise, invent, concoct, stir up, foment; *inf.* cook up.

bribe noun inducement, enticement, lure, subornation, carrot; *inf.* graft, hush money, protection money, boodle, kickback, payola.

bribe verb buy off, corrupt, suborn; *inf.* grease/oil the palm of, get at, pay off.

bridal adjective nuptial, marital, matrimonial, connubial, conjugal.

bride noun wife; newlywed, honeymooner, blushing bride; war bride.

bridge noun **1** *a bridge over the river* arch, span, overpass, viaduct. **2** *a bridge between the two families* bond, link, tie, connection, cord, binding.

bridge verb span, cross, cross over, go over, pass over, traverse, extend across, reach across, arch over.

bridle verb **1** *bridle your tongue/anger* curb, restrain, hold back, keep control of, keep in check, put a check on, govern, master, subdue. **2** *she bridled at his insults* bristle, become indignant, rear up, draw oneself up, feel one's hackles rise.

brief adjective **1** *a brief report* short, concise, succinct, to the point, terse, pithy, crisp, condensed, compressed, thumbnail, epigrammatic, sparing, compendious. **2** *a brief life* short, short-lived, fleeting, momentary, passing, transitory, transient, temporary, impermanent, ephemeral, evanescent. **3** *the boss was rather brief with him* short, abrupt, curt, brusque.

brief verb instruct, inform, direct, guide, advise, prepare, prime; *inf.* give someone the rundown/low-down, fill in.

briefly adverb concisely, succinctly, to the point, tersely, economically, sparingly.

brigand noun robber, ruffian, freebooter. *See* BANDIT.

bright adjective **1** *a bright light* shining, brilliant, vivid, intense, blazing, dazzling, beaming, sparkling, flashing, glittering, scintillating, gleaming, glowing, twinkling, glistening, shimmering; illuminated, luminous, lustrous, radiant, effulgent, incandescent, phosphorescent. **2** *bright colors* vivid, brilliant, intense, glowing, bold, rich. **3** *bright children/minds* clever, intelligent, sharp, quick-witted, quick, smart. **4** *a bright smile/personality* happy, genial, cheerful, jolly, joyful, vivacious, lively, buoyant. **5** *a bright future* promising, optimistic, favorable, auspicious, providential, fortunate, golden.

brighten verb **1** *lights brighten the room* light up, lighten, illuminate, illumine, irradiate. **2** *brighten her day/mood* cheer up, gladden, enliven, buoy up, animate; *inf.* buck up, pep up.

brilliant adjective **1** *a brilliant light* blinding, resplendent, coruscating. *See* BRIGHT 1. **2** *brilliant children* brainy, intellectual, gifted, talented, accomplished, learned, erudite, cerebral. **3** *a brilliant course of action* clever, intelligent, smart, astute, masterly. **4** *a brilliant display* magnificent, splendid, superb, impressive, remarkable, exceptional, glorious, illustrious.

brim noun **1** *the brim of the cup* rim, lip, brink, edge. **2** *the brim of the hat* visor, shield, shade.

bring verb **1** *bring books/water* carry, bear, take, fetch, convey, transport, deliver, lead, guide, conduct, usher, escort. **2** *war brought hardship* cause, create, produce, result in, wreak, effect, contribute to, engender, occasion. **3** *his job brings good wages* make, fetch, yield, net, gross, return. **bring about** cause, create, produce, give rise to, achieve, result in, effect, occasion. **bring down** **1** *bring down prices/the government* cause to fall, lower, reduce, overthrow, pull down, lay low. **2** *the bad news brought her down* depress, sadden, cast down, make desolate, weigh down. **bring forward** raise, put forward, propose, suggest, bring to/put on the table. **bring in** **1** *his son brings in $3000* earn, yield, gross, net, return, realize. **2** *bring in a new bill* introduce, launch, inaugurate, initiate, institute. **bring off** pull off, carry off, achieve, succeed in,

accomplish. **bring up** **1** *bring up the children* rear, raise, train, educate, nurture, foster, develop. **2** *bring up the subject* raise, broach, introduce, mention, touch upon.

brink noun **1** *the brink of the cliff* edge, verge, margin, rim, extremity, limit, border, boundary, fringe, skirt. **2** *the brink of disaster* verge, threshold, point.

brisk adjective **1** *at a brisk pace* quick, rapid, fast, swift, speedy, energetic, lively, vigorous, agile, sprightly, spirited. **2** *brisk weather* bracing, crisp, keen, biting, invigorating, refreshing. **3** *a brisk manner* nononsense, brusque, abrupt, sharp, curt, snappy. **4** *business was brisk* rapid, busy, bustling, active, hectic.

bristle noun stubble, whiskers; prickle, spine, quill, thorn, barb.

bristle verb **1** *the dog's hair bristled* stiffen, rise, stand up, stand on end. **2** *she bristled at the insults* bridle, become indignant, rear up, draw oneself up.

brittle adjective **1** *a brittle substance/relationship* breakable, splintery, shatterable, crisp, fragile, frail, delicate, frangible, weak, unstable. **2** *a brittle laugh* harsh, hard, sharp, strident, grating, rasping.

broach verb introduce, bring up, raise, mention, open, put forward, propound, propose, suggest, submit.

broad adjective **1** *a broad street* wide, large. **2** *broad plains* extensive, vast, spacious, expansive, sweeping, boundless. **3** *a broad range of subjects* wide-ranging, broad-ranging, general, comprehensive, inclusive, encyclopedic. **4** *the broad outline of the plan* general, nonspecific, vague, loose. **5** *a broad hint* clear, obvious, direct, plain, explicit, unmistakable. **6** *broad daylight* full, complete, total, clear, open. **7** *a woman of broad views* liberal, tolerant. *See* BROAD-MINDED. **8** *broad humor* coarse, vulgar, gross, unrefined, indelicate.

broadcast verb **1** *broadcast a program* transmit, relay, beam, send out, put on the air, radio, televise, telecast. **2** *broadcast the news of his downfall* make public, announce, report, publicize, publish, advertise, proclaim, air, spread, circulate, pass around, disseminate. **3** *broadcast seed* scatter, sow, disperse, strew.

broadcast noun program, show, transmission, telecast.

broaden verb widen, expand, enlarge, extend, increase, augment, amplify, fill out, develop.

broad-minded adjective open-minded, liberal, tolerant, forbearing, indulgent, impartial, unprejudiced, unbiased, unbigoted, undogmatic, catholic, flexible, dispassionate, just, fair, progressive, free-thinking.

brochure noun booklet, leaflet, pamphlet, folder, handbill, handout, circular, notice, advertisement, flyer.

broke adjective penniless, bankrupt, insolvent, poverty-stricken, impoverished, impecunious, penurious, indigent, destitute, stone-broke, flat broke; *inf.* cleaned out, strapped for cash.

broken adjective **1** *a broken cup* smashed, shattered, cracked, fractured, split, burst, fragmented, splintered, shivered, crushed, snapped, rent, torn, severed, destroyed. **2** *the machine is broken* damaged, faulty. *See* BROKEN-DOWN 1. **3** *broken laws* contravened, violated, infringed, disobeyed, ignored, transgressed. **4** *a broken sleep/chain of thought* interrupted, disconnected, disrupted, discontinuous, intermittent, spasmodic. **5** *a broken man* beaten, defeated, subdued, crushed, humbled, ruined, demoralized, dispirited. **6** *broken businesses* ruined, crushed, bankrupt. **7** *broken English* halting, hesitating, disjointed, faltering, imperfect.

broken-down adjective **1** *a broken-down machine* broken, damaged, faulty, defective, out of order/commission, nonfunctioning, inoperative; *inf.* on the blink, kaput, bust, busted. **2** *a broken-down old shack* dilapidated, in disrepair, ramshackle.

brokenhearted adjective heartbroken, grief-stricken, desolate, devastated, inconsolable, miserable, overwhelmed, wretched, sorrowing, mourning, forlorn, woeful, crestfallen.

broker noun agent, negotiator, middleman, intermediary, factor, dealer.

brood noun young, offspring, progeny, family, hatch, clutch, nest, litter, children.

brood verb *brood about the problem* worry, fret, agonize, think, ponder, meditate, muse, mull, dwell (on/upon), ruminate.

brook noun stream, streamlet, creek, rivulet, rill, brooklet, runnel.

brook verb tolerate, stand, bear, allow.

brothel noun bordello, house of ill repute, bawdy house, whorehouse.

brother noun **1** *she has two brothers* sibling, blood-brother; kinsman; *inf.* sib, bro. **2** *brothers in crime* associate, colleague, companion, partner, comrade; *inf.* pal, chum.

brotherhood noun **1** *feelings of brotherhood* comradeship, fellowship, companionship, camaraderie, friendship, esprit de corps. **2** *a brotherhood of merchants* association, alliance, society, union, league, fraternity, lodge.

brotherly adjective fraternal; friendly, affectionate, amicable, cordial, benevolent, neighborly, philanthropic.

browbeat verb intimidate, terrorize. *See* BULLY verb.

brown adjective **1** *brown hair* chocolate, cocoa, umber, reddish-brown, auburn, copper, copper-colored, bronze, henna, mahogany, walnut, rust, brick, terra-cotta, tan, tawny, ginger, cinnamon, hazel, fawn, beige. **2** *brown bodies on the beach* tanned, sunburned, bronze, bronzed.

browse verb **1** *not reading/buying, just browsing* scan, skim, glance/look through, thumb/leaf/flip through, look around, have a look, window-shop. **2** *cows browsing* graze, feed, eat, nibble, pasture.

bruise verb **1** *bruise the skin/fruit* discolor, mark, blemish, contuse, injure, damage. **2** *her feelings are easily bruised* hurt, upset, offend, insult, wound, displease, distress.

bruise noun black-and-blue mark, mark, blemish, contusion, injury, swelling.

brunt noun full force, force, impact, shock, burden, thrust, violence, pressure, strain, stress; repercussions, consequences.

brush noun **1** *sweep/paint with a brush* broom, besom, whisk. **2** *with a brush of his arm* touch, stroke; *inf.* swipe. **3** *a brush with the law/enemy* encounter, clash, conflict, confrontation, fight, battle.

brush verb **1** *brush one's clothes/teeth* sweep, groom, clean, buff. **2** *breeze brushing her cheek* touch, caress, glance, contact, stroke. **brush aside** dismiss, shrug off, disregard, ignore, forget about, have no time for. **brush off** cold-shoulder, give the cold shoulder to, rebuff, snub, spurn, disregard, reject, scorn, disdain. **brush up/brush up on** refresh one's memory of, relearn; *inf.* bone up.

brusque adjective abrupt, curt, blunt, sharp, caustic, gruff, bluff, hasty, discourteous, rude.

brutal adjective **1** *a brutal attack* savage, cruel, bloodthirsty, vicious, ruthless, merciless, pitiless, uncivilized, inhuman, barbarous. **2** *brutal instincts* bestial, brutish, beastly, animal, coarse, carnal, sensual.

brute noun **1** *the howling brutes of the jungle* beast, wild beast, wild animal, animal, creature. **2** *a murderous brute* monster, savage, sadist, barbarian, devil, fiend, ogre, lout, oaf, boor, churl, dolt.

bubble noun **1** *blowing soap bubbles* globule, glob, bead, blister, drop, droplet. **2** *misled by the real-estate bubble* illusion, delusion, fantasy, dream, chimera.

bubble verb **1** *champagne bubbling* fizz, effervesce, sparkle, foam, froth, spume. **2** *stew bubbling on the stove* boil, simmer, seethe, percolate. **3** *bubble with happiness* overflow, brim over, be filled.

bubbly adjective **1** *bubbly soda* fizzy, effervescent, carbonated, sparkling, foamy, frothy, sudsy. **2** *a bubbly personality* vivacious, effervescent, animated, ebullient, bouncy, buoyant, lively.

buccaneer noun pirate, corsair, sea rover, freebooter, Viking.

buck verb **buck up** cheer up, perk up, take heart; *inf.* shake it off.

bucket noun pail, scuttle, can.

buckle noun **1** *the belt buckle* clasp, clip, catch, fastener, fastening, hasp. **2** *a buckle in the floorboards* kink, warp, curve, distortion, wrinkle, bulge.

buckle verb **1** *buckling his belt* fasten, hook, secure, clasp, catch, clip. **2** *the floorboards buckled* warp, bulge, crumple, cave in.

bucolic adjective rural, rustic, pastoral, country, agricultural.

bud noun shoot, sprout, flowerlet, floret.

budding adjective promising, developing, beginning, fledgling, incipient, embryonic.

budge verb **1** *the car won't budge* move, shift, stir, go, proceed. **2** *he's obstinate so he won't budge* change one's mind, give way, give in, yield, acquiesce. **3** *you won't budge him as he's determined* influence, sway, convince, persuade, bend.

budget verb **1** *budget money/time* plan, schedule, allocate, ration, apportion. **2** *budget for a new car* allow, save, set aside.

buff verb polish, burnish, rub, smooth, polish, shine.

buff noun *a theater buff* fan, enthusiast, devotee, aficionado, addict, admirer, expert; *inf.* freak. **in the buff** naked, nude, bare, in the raw, buck naked, au naturel, undressed; *inf.* in one's birthday suit.

buffer noun cushion, bulwark, guard, safeguard, shield, screen, intermediary.

buffet verb **1** *winds buffeting the trees* batter, beat/knock against, strike, hit, bang, push against. **2** *the fighter buffeted his opponent* slap, smack, thump, wallop, clout, whack, thwack.

buffoon noun **1** *the buffoons in Shakespeare's plays* clown, jester, comic, comedian, wit, wag, merry andrew. **2** *he's just a buffoon* fool, dolt, idiot, nincompoop.

bug noun **1** *bitten by bugs* insect, beetle, fly, flea, mite; *inf.* creepy-crawly. **2** *an illness caused by a bug* bacterium, germ, virus, microorganism; infection. **3** *he's caught the dancing bug* craze, fad, mania, obsession, passion, fixation. **4** *get rid of all the bugs in the machine* fault, flaw, defect, imperfection; *inf.* glitch, gremlin.

bug verb **1** *bug a phone/conversation* tap, wiretap, listen in on, eavesdrop on. **2** *he really bugs me* annoy, irritate, exasperate, anger, irk, vex, try one's patience; *inf.* get on one's nerves.

bugbear noun bane, abomination, pet hate, nightmare, dread, bête noire; goblin, bogeyman, hobgoblin.

build verb **1** *build a house/road* construct, erect, put up, assemble, set up, raise, make, manufacture, fabricate, form. **2** *hopes built on false premises* found, base, establish. **3** *build a new career* start, begin, inaugurate, initiate, develop. **build up 1** *build up a business* establish, develop, expand. **2** *build up her morale/strength* boost, strengthen, increase, improve, develop. **3** *build up the product* advertise, promote, publicize; *inf.* plug, hype.

build noun body, frame, physique, figure, form, structure, shape.

building noun structure, construction, edifice, erection.

buildup noun **1** *the buildup of resources* expansion, increase, growth, enlargement, escalation, development. **2** *the buildup of paperwork* accumulation, stockpile, accretion, mass, heap, stack, pile. **3** *the product's buildup* promotion, publicity, advertising; *inf.* hype, ballyhoo.

bulge noun **1** *a bulge in her pocket* swelling, bump, lump, protuberance, protrusion, prominence, projection. **2** *a population bulge* boost, increase, rise, surge, intensification.

bulge verb swell, swell out, puff up/out, stick out, bag, balloon, balloon up/out, protrude, distend, expand, dilate, bloat.

bulk noun **1** *the sheer bulk of the packages/work* size, volume, bulkiness, quantity, weight, extent, mass, substance, massiveness, hugeness, amplitude; dimensions. **2** *the bulk of the applicants are women* majority, preponderance, lion's share.

bulky adjective large, substantial, huge, enormous, massive, immense, voluminous, hulking, heavy, weighty, stout, thickset, awkward-shaped, awkward, unwieldy, cumbersome.

bulldoze verb **1** *bulldoze the area/buildings* demolish, flatten, level, raze. **2** *bulldoze his way through* force, push, drive, shove, propel. **3** *they bulldozed him into going* coerce, steamroll, railroad; *inf.* strong-arm. *See* BULLY *verb.*

bullet noun pellet, ball, slug, shot, missile, projectile. **bullets** ammunition *inf.* ammo, lead.

bulletin noun **1** *a television bulletin* report, statement, announcement, flash, account, message, communiqué, dispatch. **2** *an in-house bulletin* newspaper, newsletter, pamphlet, leaflet.

bully noun browbeater, intimidator, oppressor, tyrant, tormentor, tough, ruffian, thug, hooligan, rowdy; *inf.* hood.

bully verb browbeat, intimidate, coerce, oppress, domineer, persecute, cow, tyrannize, pressurize, pressure, bulldoze; *inf.* push around, strong-arm.

bulwark noun **1** *a bulwark against flooding* rampart, fortification, buttress, bastion, embankment. **2** *a bulwark of classical education* support, mainstay, defense, safeguard; defender, protector.

bum noun **1** *a bum begging for money* tramp, vagrant, beggar, derelict, mendicant; bag lady, hobo. **2** *just a lazy bum* loafer, idler, good-for-nothing, ne'er-do-well.

bum verb *bum money* borrow, scrounge, sponge; *inf.* mooch. **bum around** loaf, lounge, idle, laze, wander; *inf.* hang out.

bum adjective **1** *a bum stereo | gave me a bum deal* useless, worthless, inferior, unsatisfactory, low-grade, poor, bad. **2** *a bum leg* lame, game, bad.

bumbling adjective clumsy, blundering, awkward, bungling, incompetent, inept, lumbering, foolish.

bump verb **1** *bump his head on the bar* hit, bang, strike, knock, slam, injure, damage. **2** *the wagon bumping along the road* bounce, jolt, jerk, rattle, shake. **3** *bumped from their seats* displace, supplant, remove, eject. **bump into 1** *the cars bumped into each other* collide with, crash/smash into, run into. **2** *we bumped into old friends* run into, come across, meet, meet up with, encounter. **bump off** kill, murder, do away with, assassinate, eliminate, liquidate.

bump noun **1** *hear a bump* thud, thump, bang, crash. **2** *land with a bump* jolt, crash, smash, bang, thud, thump, impact. **3** *a bump on his head* lump, swelling, injury, contusion, protuberance. **4** *a bump in the road* bulge, hump, lump, knob, knot, protuberance.

bumper adjective *a bumper crop* large, big, abundant, bountiful, exceptional.

bumptious adjective self-assertive, overbearing, puffed up, cocky, presumptuous, pompous, forward; *inf.* pushy.

bumpy adjective **1** *a bumpy road* uneven, rough, potholed, rutted, pitted, lumpy, knobby. **2** *a bumpy flight* choppy, jolting, jerky, jarring, bouncy, rough.

bunch noun cluster, assemblage, collection, batch, pile, bundle, mass, quantity, accumulation, agglomeration, group, collection, gathering, band, crowd, multitude.

bundle noun **1** *a bundle of papers* collection, quantity. *See* BUNCH. **2** *send bundles of clothes* package, pack, bale, parcel, packet.

bundle verb **1** *bundle them up* tie, tie up, tie together, package, wrap, bind, fasten together, bale, truss. **2** *bundle people*

inside/outside hurry, hustle, rush, push, shove, thrust, throw. **3** *bundle children up in warm clothes* clothe, wrap, cover.

bungle verb botch, muff, spoil, make a mess of, mess up, mishandle, mismanage, fudge, mar, ruin; *inf.* louse up, screw up, foul up.

bungling adjective clumsy, incompetent, inept, unskillful, inexpert, maladroit; *inf.* ham-handed.

bunk noun nonsense, rubbish. *See* BUNKUM.

bunkum noun nonsense, rubbish, balderdash, twaddle, claptrap, humbug, tomfoolery; *inf.* rot, poppycock, baloney, piffle, bilge, bosh, hogwash, hooey.

buoy verb **buoy up** cheer, cheer up, hearten, encourage, support, sustain, raise, boost, uplift, lift.

buoyant adjective **1** *a buoyant mood/personality* cheerful, cheery, lighthearted, bouncy, carefree, vivacious, animated, lively, sprightly, jaunty, breezy.

burden noun **1** *the donkey's burden* load, cargo, weight, freight. **2** *the burden of parenthood* responsibility, onus, charge, duty, obligation, tax, trouble, care, worry, anxiety, tribulation, difficulty, strain, stress, weight, encumbrance, millstone.

burden verb **1** *donkeys were burdened with heavy loads* load, lade, weight, charge, weigh down, encumber, hamper. **2** *burdened with sorrow* oppress, trouble, worry, distress, bother, afflict, torment, strain, stress, tax, overwhelm.

bureau noun **1** *a travel bureau* agency, office, service. **2** *a government bureau* department, division, branch. **3** *polish the bureau* dresser, chest of drawers, highboy.

bureaucracy noun **1** *rule by bureaucracy* civil service, central administration, directorate; government officials. **2** *cut through the bureaucracy to get a passport* red tape, officialdom, formalities, rules and regulations.

burgeon verb **1** *flowers burgeoning* bud, sprout, put forth shoots, shoot, germinate. **2** *the population burgeoned* grow, develop, flourish, thrive, mushroom, proliferate, snowball.

burglar noun housebreaker, cat burglar, thief, robber, picklock; *inf.* second-story man.

burial noun interment, entombment, inhumation, sepulture; funeral, obsequies, exequies, **burial ground** cemetery, graveyard, churchyard; *inf.* potter's field.

burlesque noun parody, caricature, travesty, farce, mockery, imitation, satire, lampoon; *inf.* send-up, takeoff, spoof.

burly adjective thickset, brawny, muscular, strapping, hulking, hefty, beefy, bulky, sturdy, stocky, stout.

burn verb 1 *watching the house burn* be on fire, be afire, be ablaze, blaze, go up, smoke, flame, flare, flash, flicker, glow. 2 *he burned the papers* set on fire, ignite, put a match to, light, kindle, incinerate, reduce to ashes. 3 *burn the shirt with the iron* scorch, singe, sear, char. 4 *burn with fever* be hot, be warm, feel hot, be feverish; *inf.* be on fire. 5 *burn with pain* smart, sting, tingle. 6 *liquid burning his throat* sting, bite, prickle, irritate. 7 *burn with excitement* be aroused, simmer, smolder, seethe. 8 *burn to get the prize* long, yearn, desire, hunger after, lust, itch. 9 *burn energy* use, use up, consume, expend, eat up.

burning adjective 1 *a burning house* blazing, flaming, flaring, raging, ignited, glowing, flickering, smoldering, scorching. 2 *a burning sensation* smarting, stinging, biting, prickling, caustic, searing, corrosive. 3 *a burning desire* intense, fervent, ardent, eager. 4 *the burning issues of the day* crucial, significant, urgent, pressing.

burnish verb polish, shine, brighten, rub, buff, buff up, smooth.

burrow noun *rabbit burrows* tunnel, hole, hollow, excavation, lair, den, retreat.

burrow verb 1 *burrow holes* dig, tunnel, excavate, hollow out, gouge out, scoop out. 2 *burrow under the blankets* go under, hide, shelter, conceal oneself.

burst verb 1 *the pipe has burst* split, split open, break open, rupture, crack, fracture, fragment, shatter, fly open. 2 *the grenade burst* blow up, explode, detonate, fulminate. 3 *the water burst through the dam* break out, pour forth, gush out, surge out, rush out. 4 *burst into tears/laughter* break out, erupt. **burst out** 1 *"coward!" she burst out* exclaim, cry out, call out, shout, yell. 2 *burst out crying* begin/start suddenly.

bury verb 1 *bury the corpse* inter, lay to rest, consign to the grave, entomb. 2 *bury her head in her hands* conceal, hide, put out of sight, sink, secrete, enshroud. 3 *bury the nail in the wood* drive in, embed, implant, sink, submerge. 4 *bury yourself in your work* absorb oneself, immerse oneself, engross oneself, engage oneself.

bushy adjective thick, shaggy, fuzzy, fluffy, luxuriant, unruly, rough.

business noun 1 *what business is he in?* occupation, line, profession, career, trade, work, employment, job. 2 *do business with the French* trade, commerce, trafficking, buying and selling, merchandizing, bargaining; dealings, transactions. 3 *running her own business* firm, company, concern, enterprise, organization, store, shop, venture. 4 *that's none of your business* concern, affair, responsibility, duty, function,

task, problem. 5 *the main business of the meeting* matter, subject, topic, point of discussion, theme, issue, question. 6 *it was a peculiar business* affair, matter, thing, case.

businesslike adjective 1 *businesslike behavior* professional, efficient, orderly, organized, practical, pragmatic, thorough, painstaking, meticulous, correct. 2 *the businesslike performance of the play* workaday, routine, prosaic, conventional, unimaginative.

bust verb 1 *the crash will bust him* bankrupt, ruin, impoverish, pauperize, break. 2 *the police busted him* arrest, capture, catch, seize; *inf.* collar, nab.

bustle verb hurry, rush, dash, scuttle, scurry, hasten, scamper, scramble, flutter, fuss; *inf.* tear.

bustle noun activity, flurry, stir, commotion, tumult, excitement, agitation, fuss; *inf.* to-do.

bustling adjective active, full of activity, energetic, lively, busy, brisk, animated.

busy adjective 1 *the doctor's busy* occupied, engaged, working, at work, on duty, in a meeting, otherwise engaged. 2 *a busy day/person* active, energetic, strenuous, full, hectic, exacting, bustling, industrious, lively; *inf.* on the go. 3 *busy patterns* ornate, overelaborate, overdetailed, overdecorated, cluttered, fussy.

busy verb *busy himself in the garden* occupy, engage, employ, absorb, immerse, engross, involve, interest.

busybody noun meddler, interferer, snooper, snoop, gossip, scandalmonger.

butcher verb 1 *butcher cattle* slaughter, cut up, carve up, slice up, prepare, dress. 2 *butcher the enemy* slay, massacre, murder, kill, exterminate, liquidate. 3 *butcher the piano concerto* botch, make a mess of, wreck, ruin, spoil, bungle; *inf.* louse up, screw up, foul up.

butchery noun slaughter, massacre, slaying, murder, mass murder, homicide, bloodshed.

butt¹ noun 1 *the butt of a gun* handle, shaft, hilt, haft. 2 *the butt of a cigarette* stub, end, remnant; *inf.* roach. 3 *sitting on his butt* bottom, rump. *See* BUTTOCKS.

butt² noun *the butt of his jokes* scapegoat, dupe, target, victim, laughingstock, object, subject.

butt³ verb push, thrust, shove, ram, bump, prod, poke, jab. **butt into** *butt into a conversation* interrupt, intrude/interfere in, put one's oar into; *inf.* stick one's nose into.

buttocks noun bottom, posterior, rump; hindquarters; *inf.* behind, backside, butt, can, ass.

buttonhole verb accost, waylay, take aside, importune, detain, grab, catch, talk at.

buttress noun **1** *a stone buttress* prop, support, abutment, strut, reinforcement. **2** *a buttress to the family* mainstay, upholder, sustainer, cornerstone, pillar.

buttress verb strengthen, reinforce, prop up, support, shore up, underpin, brace, uphold, defend, back up.

buxom adjective plump, large-bosomed, big-bosomed, full-bosomed, shapely; *inf.* busty.

buy verb **1** *buy a house* purchase, pay for, invest in, procure. **2** *he bought his way in* bribe, suborn, corrupt; *inf.* fix, rig.

buy noun purchase, acquisition, deal, bargain.

buzz noun **1** *the buzz of the bees* hum, murmur, drone, whirr, hiss, sibilation, whisper. **2** *the buzz is he's gone* rumor, gossip, talk, scuttlebutt, report, whisper, scandal, hearsay.

buzz verb **1** *bees buzzing* hum, murmur, drone, whirr, hiss, whisper, sibilate. **2** *tongues buzzing* gossip, chatter, tattle. **3** *people buzzing about* rush, dash. *See* BUSTLE verb.

buzzing adjective active, alive. *See* BUSTLING.

bygone adjective past, departed, former, one-time, previous, forgotten, olden, ancient, obsolete, out-of-date, outmoded.

bypass verb *bypass the city/difficulty/boss* go around, pass around, get around, circumvent, avoid, evade, ignore, pass over, go over the head of.

bystander noun onlooker, looker-on, observer, eyewitness, witness, spectator, gaper, passerby; *inf.* rubberneck.

byword noun proverb, maxim, adage, aphorism, apothegm. **byword for** *a byword for reliability* slogan for, catchword for, example of, personification of, embodiment of.

Cc

cab noun **1** *order a cab* taxi, taxicab, hackney carriage, hackney, *inf.* hack. **2** *the driver's cab* cabin, compartment, quarters, cubicle.

cabin noun **1** *a cabin by the lake* log cabin, hut, chalet, cottage, shack, shanty, shed. **2** *a first-class cabin in the ship* stateroom, room, sleeping quarters, berth, compartment.

cabinet noun **1** *a china cabinet | a filing cabinet* cupboard, chest, locker, dresser, closet, chiffonier, case, container. **2** *the president's cabinet* advisers, council, committee, board, administration.

cable noun **1** *tied with cable* rope, cord, wire, line, cordage. **2** *send a cable* cablegram, telegram, telegraph, wire.

cache noun **1** *hide the treasure in a cache* hiding place, hide-out, secret place, hole. **2** *find the cache of jewels* hoard, store, collection, fund, supply, hidden treasure, treasure, loot; *inf.* stash.

cackle verb **1** *hens cackling* cluck, clack, squawk. **2** *the audience cackling at his jokes* chuckle, chortle, laugh, giggle, titter, snigger, tee-hee. **3** *people cackling at the bus stop* chatter, jabber, prattle, babble, gibber, blather, blab; *inf.* spout away.

cad noun scoundrel, rat, rogue, rascal, double-crosser; *inf.* bounder, heel.

cadence noun **1** *musical/metrical cadence* rhythm, beat, pulse, rhythmical flow/pattern, measure, meter, tempo, swing, lilt. **2** *the cadence of her speech* intonation, inflection, accent, modulation.

café noun coffee shop, snack bar, tearoom, restaurant, cafeteria, bar, bistro; *inf.* greasy spoon.

cage noun enclosure, pen, corral, pound, lockup, coop; birdcage, aviary.

cage verb confine, shut in, impound, pen, corral, lock up, incarcerate, imprison, coop, coop up, hem in, restrict, restrain.

cagey, cagy adjective guarded, secretive, noncommittal, cautious, chary, wary, careful, shrewd, wily.

cajole verb wheedle, coax, beguile, seduce, entice, tempt, inveigle, maneuver, humor; *inf.* sweet-talk, soft-soap, butter up.

calamitous adjective disastrous, catastrophic, cataclysmic, devastating, ruinous, dire, tragic.

calamity noun disaster, catastrophe, tragedy, misfortune, cataclysm, devastation, scourge, mishap, ruin, tribulation, woe.

calculate verb **1** *calculate the sum* work out, compute, estimate, count up, figure out, evaluate, enumerate, determine.

2 *calculate the chances* estimate, gauge, judge, measure, weigh, reckon, rate. **3** *a proposal calculated to appeal to investors* design, plan, aim, intend.

calculated adjective *a calculated risk* considered, planned, premeditated, deliberate, intentional, intended, purposeful.

calculating adjective scheming, designing, devious, shrewd, manipulative, sharp, sly, crafty, Machiavellian.

calculation noun **1** *by their calculations it will cost $3000* computation, estimation, estimate, reckoning, figuring, forecast, gauging, judgment. **2** *the calculation is wrong* result, answer. **3** *got the job by sheer calculation* scheming, designing, deviousness, shrewdness.

caliber noun *statesmen of his caliber* quality, worth, distinction, stature, excellence, merit, ability, competence, endowments, scope.

call verb **1** *call out in pain* cry, cry out, shout, exclaim, yell, scream, shriek, roar. **2** *call him in the morning* awaken, waken, arouse, rouse. **3** *call her tomorrow* call up, phone, telephone, give one a ring; *inf.* give one a buzz. **4** *call at the house* pay a call, pay a visit, pay a brief visit, stop by; *inf.* drop in, pop in. **5** *call a meeting* call together, convene, summon, order, convoke, assemble, announce, declare, proclaim, decree. **6** *call a doctor/taxi* send for, ask for, summon, contact, order, bid, fetch. **7** *they called the baby Jane* name, christen, designate, dub, entitle, denominate, label, term. **8** *I call it disgraceful* consider, think, regard, judge, estimate. **9** *called to the bar | he was called to the church* appoint, elect, ordain. **call for 1** *this calls for a celebration* need, require, be grounds for, justify, necessitate, demand, entail. **2** *call for the packages* collect, pick up, fetch, go for. **call off 1** *call off the dogs* order off, order away, stop, hold back, check, rein in. **2** *call off the date* cancel, postpone, countermand, rescind, revoke. **call on/upon 1** *call on his aunt* visit, pay a visit to, go and see; *inf.* look up, look in on, drop in on. **2** *call on them to help* appeal to, ask, request, entreat, urge, supplicate, invoke. **call up 1** *call me up* phone, telephone. *See* CALL verb 3. **2** *call up painful memories* recall, bring/call to mind, summon up, evoke. **3** *call up all the young men* enlist, recruit, sign up; draft.

call noun **1** *a call of pain* cry, shout, exclamation, yell, scream, shriek, roar. **2** *the call of the bird* cry, song, chirp, chirping, tweet. **3** *have a prearranged call* signal, hail, whoop. **4** *give me a call* ring; *inf.* buzz. **5** *paid her a call* visit, brief visit. **6** *a call for unity* summons, invitation, request, plea, bidding, order, command, appeal, notice. **7** *there's no call to be rude* need, occasion, reason, cause, justification, grounds, excuse. **8** *there's no call for expensive wine here* demand, request, want, requisition. **9** *the call of the wild* attraction, lure, allurement, fascination, appeal.

calling noun vocation, occupation, career, profession, business, work, employment, job, trade, craft, line, line of work, pursuit, métier, walk of life, province, field.

callous adjective **1** *a callous jail warden* hardened, tough, cold, insensitive, unfeeling, hard-hearted, heartless, hard-bitten, cruel, obdurate, inured, uncaring, unsympathetic. **2** *callous skin* hard, hardened, thickened, leathery.

callow adjective immature, inexperienced, uninitiated, naive, unsophisticated, innocent, undeveloped, adolescent.

calm adjective **1** *a calm day* still, windless, mild, tranquil, balmy, halcyon, peaceful, restful. **2** *a calm sea* still, smooth, motionless, placid, waveless, unagitated, stormfree. **3** *be/remain calm during the trouble* composed, collected, cool, coolheaded, controlled, self-controlled, self-possessed, unruffled, relaxed, serene, unflappable, undisturbed, imperturbable, unemotional, unmoved, equable, stoical; *inf.* together.

calm noun **1** *the calm before the storm* stillness, tranquillity, serenity, quietude, peace, restfulness, repose. **2** *nothing disturbs her calm* composure, coolness, self-control, tranquillity, serenity, equanimity, imperturbability, poise, sang-froid; *inf.* cool.

calm verb *calm the child* soothe, quieten, pacify, hush, lull, mollify, appease, still, settle, settle down, relax.

camp[1] noun **1** *soldier's/Scout camp* encampment, camping ground, campsite, tents, bivouac, cantonment. **2** *the right-wing camp* faction, party, group, clique, coterie, set, sect, cabal.

camp[2] verb *we camped in a field* pitch tents, pitch camp, set up camp, encamp, tent. **camp out 1** *we camped out in that field* sleep out, camp. **2** *we're camping out here till the house is rebuilt* live simply; *inf.* rough it, slum it.

camp[3] verb *camp it up* overdo it, overact, behave theatrically/affectedly, posture, ham it up, lay it on.

campaign noun **1** *Grant's Vicksburg Campaign* war, battle, expedition, offensive, attack, crusade. **2** *a campaign against litter* operation, promotion, strategy, set of tactics, drive, push, crusade, movement.

campaign verb fight, battle, work, push, crusade, strive, struggle, agitate.

cancel verb **1** *cancel a vacation/date/contract* call off, stop, discontinue, give up, withdraw from, revoke, rescind, annul, declare void, nullify, quash, invalidate, set aside, retract, negate, repudiate, repeal, abolish. **2** *cancel that last paragraph* delete, cross out, erase, strike out, rub out, blot out, expunge, eliminate. **3** *his friendliness cancels out her hostility* counterbalance, balance, offset, compensate, make up for, neutralize, redeem.

candid adjective **1** *candid remarks* frank, open, honest, truthful, sincere, forthright, direct, outspoken, blunt, unequivocal, bluff; *inf.* straight from the shoulder. **2** *candid snapshots* unposed, spontaneous, impromptu, uncontrived, informal, unstudied.

candidate noun applicant, job applicant, office seeker, contender, nominee, contestant, aspirant, possibility; *inf.* runner.

candor noun frankness, openness, honesty, truthfulness, sincerity, forthrightness, directness, outspokenness, bluntness, bluffness, brusqueness.

candy noun sweet, sweets, confectionery, confection, bonbon.

cane noun **1** *a walking cane* stick, staff, rod, stave; walking stick, shepherd's crook. **2** *pruning the raspberry canes* stem, stalk, shoot, reed.

canon noun **1** *the canons of good taste* principle, standard, criterion, test, measure, yardstick, benchmark, precept, norm, convention. **2** *a Church canon* law, rule, regulation, statute, decree, edict, dictate. **3** *the canon of Shakespeare's plays* official list, list, catalog, enumeration, litany, roll.

canopy noun awning, shade, sunshade, cover, covering, tarpaulin.

cant[1] noun **1** *thieves' cant* slang, jargon, patter, lingo, terminology, argot. **2** *religious cant* hypocrisy, insincerity, sanctimony, sanctimoniousness, humbug, pretense.

cant[2] noun *the table is on a cant* slant, slope, tilt, angle, inclination.

cantankerous adjective bad-tempered, crabby, surly, irascible, grumpy, difficult, disagreeable, quarrelsome, touchy, testy, peevish, crusty; *inf.* grouchy, crotchety, cranky.

canter noun amble, saunter, trot, jog, lope, gallop.

canvass verb **1** *canvassing during the general election* solicit votes, campaign, electioneer, drum up support, persuade, convince. **2** *canvass buying habits* survey, scan, poll.

canyon noun ravine, gully, valley, gorge, chasm, gulf, abyss.

cap noun **1** *doffing his cap* hat, bonnet, headgear. **2** *the cap on the bottle* top, lid, stopper, cork, plug. **3** *mountain caps* top, crest, peak, summit, apex, pinnacle.

cap verb **1** *mountains capped with snow* cover, top, crown, overlie, overspread, coat, blanket. **2** *cap the high-jump record* beat, better, surpass, excel, outshine, transcend, eclipse, outdo, outstrip, exceed. **3** *cap the price* limit, set a limit to, restrict, curb.

capability noun **1** *the capability to do well* ability, capacity, potential, aptitude, faculty, facility, power, competence, efficiency, effectiveness, proficiency, accomplishment, talent, adeptness, skill, skillfulness, experience, cleverness, intelligence, smartness. **2** *offer capabilities* talent, gifts, skill, aptitude, flair, knack.

capable adjective able, competent, adequate, efficient, effective, proficient, accomplished, talented, gifted, adept, skillful, masterly, experienced, practiced, qualified, clever, intelligent, smart. **capable of 1** *capable of murder/lying* tending to, inclined to, predisposed to, prone to, liable to, likely to do. **2** *capable of improvement* requiring, wanting, susceptible to, admitting of, receptive of.

capacity noun **1** *the capacity to seat twenty* space, room, size, largeness, ampleness, amplitude, facility, scope, magnitude, dimensions, proportions, extent. **2** *the capacity to do the job* ability, intelligence. *See* CAPABILITY. **3** *in his capacity as a teacher* position, post, job, office, function, role, appointment.

cape[1] noun cloak, mantle, shawl, wrap, poncho, pelisse.

cape[2] noun headland, head, point, promontory, neck, peninsula.

caper verb frolic, frisk, romp, skip, gambol, cavort, prance, dance, leap, hop, jump, bound, spring, bounce.

caper noun **1** *the energetic capers of the children* frolics, romping, skipping, gambols, cavorting, prancing, leap. **2** *tired of their mischievous capers* prank, trick, practical joke, antic, high jinks, mischief, escapade, stunt; *inf.* shenanigans.

capital adjective **1** *our capital concern* principal, chief, main, major, prime, paramount, foremost, predominant, overruling, leading, cardinal, central, key. **2** *a capital error* grave, vital, important, serious, crucial, fatal. **3** *a capital piece of work* splendid, excellent, first-rate, outstanding.

capital noun *enough capital to buy the firm* money, finance, finances, funds, cash, hard cash, wherewithal, means, assets, liquid assets, wealth, resources, reserves, principal.

capitalize verb *capitalize the firm* finance, back, provide backing for, fund, sponsor. **capitalize on** *capitalize on her rival's mistakes* take advantage of, put to advantage, profit from, cash in on, make the most of, exploit.

capitulate verb surrender, yield, submit, give in, give up, come to terms, succumb, accede, back down, cave in, relent, acquiesce; *inf.* throw in the towel.

caprice noun whim, whimsy, vagary, fancy, notion, fad, freak, humor, impulse, quirk; changeableness, fickleness, volatility, inconstancy.

capricious adjective changeable, unpredictable, fickle, variable, inconstant, unstable, mercurial, volatile, impulsive, erratic, fanciful, whimsical, wayward, quirky.

capsize verb overturn, turn over, upset, upend, knock over, tip over, invert, keel over.

capsule noun *pain-relieving capsules* pill, tablet, lozenge.

captain noun *the captain of the ship/team* commander, master, leader, head, skipper; *inf.* honcho.

caption noun heading, title, wording, head, legend, inscription.

captivate verb charm, delight, enchant, bewitch, fascinate, beguile, enthrall, entrance, enrapture, attract, allure, lure, infatuate, seduce, ensnare, dazzle, hypnotize, mesmerize.

captive noun prisoner, prisoner of war, hostage, slave, bondsman, convict, jailbird, detainee; *inf.* con.

captivity noun imprisonment, custody, detention, confinement, internment, incarceration, restraint, constraint, committal, bondage, slavery, servitude, enslavement, subjection.

capture verb catch, arrest, apprehend, take prisoner, take captive, take into custody, seize, take, lay hold of, trap; *inf.* nab, collar, pinch, nail, bag.

car noun vehicle, motor vehicle, automobile, motorcar; sedan, station wagon, hatchback, coupe; *inf.* wheels, heap, crate, jalopy, limo, auto.

caravan noun *caravan of pilgrims* convoy, troop, band, company, group, cavalcade, procession.

carcass noun **1** *vultures searching for carcasses* corpse, dead body, body; remains, cadaver; *inf.* stiff. **2** *move your carcass* body, person, self.

card noun **in the cards** likely, possible, probable; most likely, certain.

cardinal adjective *cardinal sins/errors* main, chief, principal, greatest, vital, key, central, foremost, leading, prime, paramount, fundamental, basic.

care noun **1** *free from care* worry, anxiety, disquiet, unease, distress, sorrow, anguish, grief, sadness, hardship, tribulation, responsibility, stress, pressure, strain; burdens. **2** *no care for others* concern, regard, interest, solicitude. **3** *arrange the flowers with care* carefulness, attention, thought, regard, mindfulness, conscientiousness, painstakingness, pains, precision, meticulousness, fastidiousness. **4** *cross the road with care* caution, heedfulness, alertness, vigilance, wariness, circumspection, prudence. **5** *in the care of her uncle* charge, protection, custody, keeping, safekeeping, control, management, supervision.

care verb *she cared about her work* be concerned, be interested, have regard, worry, trouble, bother, mind; *inf.* give a damn, give a hoot. **care for 1** *he cares for his colleagues* be fond of, like, find congenial. **2** *would you care for tea?* wish, want, desire, fancy, hanker after, long for; *inf.* have a yen for. **3** *care for the children* take care of, look after, mind, watch, tend, attend to, minister to, nurse, provide for.

career noun **1** *choose a career* occupation, profession, vocation, calling, employment, job, métier. **2** *watch the career of the political party* course, progress, progression, procedure, passage, path. **3** *stop the horse in mid-career* rush, onrush, run, race, bolt, dash, gallop, impetus.

carefree adjective lighthearted, happy-go-lucky, cheerful, cheery, happy, merry, jolly, buoyant, breezy, easygoing, blithe, airy, nonchalant, unworried, untroubled, insouciant.

careful adjective **1** *be careful crossing the road* cautious, heedful, alert, aware, attentive, watchful, vigilant, wary, on guard, chary, circumspect, prudent, mindful. **2** *be careful of your reputation | be careful about what you say* mindful, heedful, protective; solicitous, thoughtful, attentive, concerned. **3** *a careful worker* attentive, conscientious, painstaking, meticulous, accurate, precise, scrupulous, punctilious, fastidious.

careless adjective **1** *a careless driver* inattentive, negligent, remiss, irresponsible, lax, slack. **2** *a careless piece of work* hasty, cursory, perfunctory, inaccurate, disorganized, slapdash, slipshod; *inf.* sloppy. **3** *a careless remark* unthinking, thoughtless, insensitive, indiscreet, unguarded. **4** *careless elegance* unstudied, artless, casual.

caress noun touch, stroke, fondling, pat, embrace, cuddle, hug, nuzzle, kiss.

caress verb cuddle, fondle, pet, pat, embrace, hug, nuzzle, kiss.

cargo noun freight, freightage, load, lading, haul, consignment, contents, goods, merchandise, baggage; shipment, shipload, boatload, truckload.

caricature noun cartoon, parody, burlesque, mimicry, travesty, distortion, satire, farce, lampoon; *inf.* send-up, takeoff, spoof.

carnage noun slaughter, butchery, massacre, bloodshed, blood bath.

carnal adjective sexual, sensual, fleshly, erotic, lustful, lascivious, lecherous, lewd, prurient, salacious, lubricious.

carouse verb binge, party, paint the town red, overindulge, live it up, go on a bender.

carp verb complain, faultfind, find fault, criticize, cavil, pick on, quibble, censure, reproach, nag; *inf.* nitpick.

carriage noun 1 *an elegant carriage* posture, bearing, stance, comportment, manner, presence, air, demeanor. 2 *free carriage* transport, freight, conveyance, delivery.

carry verb 1 *carry a package* transport, convey, move, take, bring, bear, lug, haul, fetch; conduct, pass on, transmit, relay. 2 *carry responsibilities* support, sustain, bear, shoulder. 3 *carry the day* win, capture, gain, secure, accomplish. 4 *a store carrying a brand* sell, stock, offer, retail. 5 *carry the latest news* communicate, give, release, publish, broadcast. 6 *carry the audience* influence, affect, motivate, stimulate. 7 *carry themselves well* bear oneself, hold oneself, comport oneself. **carry on** 1 *carry on talking* go on, continue, keep on, persist in, persevere in. 2 *carry on a business* run, operate, conduct, manage, administer. 3 *he's carrying on with his secretary* have an affair, commit adultery; *inf.* fool around. 4 *children carrying on* cause a fuss/commotion; cry, create a scene. **carry out** 1 *carry out a promise/threat* fulfill, carry through, implement, realize, execute. 2 *carry out an experiment* conduct, perform.

cart noun handcart, wheelbarrow, pushcart.

cart verb 1 *cart away the trash* transport, convey, haul, transfer, move, shift. 2 *cart the luggage* lug, tote, carry.

carton noun box, package, cardboard box, container, case.

cartridge noun case, container, cylinder, capsule, cassette, magazine.

carve verb 1 *carve a figure out of stone* sculpt, sculpture, cut, chisel, hew, whittle, chip, form, shape, fashion. 2 *carve initials on a tree* engrave, etch, notch, incise. 3 *carve meat* slice, cut up. **carve up** divide, partition, parcel out, apportion.

cascade noun waterfall, falls, fountain, shower, cataract, torrent, flood, deluge, outpouring.

cascade verb tumble, descend, pour, gush, surge, spill, overflow.

case¹ noun 1 *a cigarette case* container, box, receptacle, holder, canister. 2 *a case of wine* crate, box, carton; coffer, casket. 3 *bullet case* | *tape case* casing, covering, sheath, sheathing, wrapper, cover, envelope, housing.

case² noun 1 *as has been the case* position, situation, circumstances, occurrence, happening, occasion, conditions, plight, predicament. 2 *a case of cheating* instance, occurrence, example, illustration, specimen. 3 *the case comes up next week* lawsuit, suit, action, trial, proceedings. 4 *his case was that he was elsewhere* statement, plea, claim, alibi, explanation, exposition, thesis.

cash noun 1 *no cash with me* money, ready money, coinage, notes, bank notes, currency; specie, legal tender. 2 *he has no cash of any kind* money, finance, wherewithal, resources, funds, capital; *inf.* dough, bread, cabbage.

cash verb exchange, change, turn into cash/money.

cask noun barrel, keg, tun, vat, vessel, hogshead.

casket noun 1 *funeral casket* coffin, pall, sarcophagus; *inf.* box. 2 *a jewel casket* chest, coffer. *See* CASE 1.

cast verb 1 *cast a stone in the lake* throw, toss, fling, pitch, hurl, sling, let fly. 2 *cast their skins/coats* shed, discard, slough off, peel off, throw off. 3 *cast a glance* shoot, direct, turn, send out. 4 *cast a soft light* emit, give off, send out, shed, radiate. 5 *cast doubt* throw, bestow, impart, confer, give, grant. 6 *cast figures in bronze* shape, fashion, form, mold, sculpt.

cast noun 1 *the cast of the dice* throw, toss, fling, pitch, hurl, lob. 2 *cast of features/mind* sort, kind, style, type, stamp, nature. 3 *plaster cast* figure, shape, mold, form.

caste noun class, social class, order, social order, grade, station, place, standing, position, status.

castigate verb punish, discipline, chastise, rebuke, scold, reprimand, upbraid, berate, chide, admonish, criticize, chasten, take to task, dress down, rake over the coals.

castle noun stronghold, fortress, keep, hold, citadel, palace, chateau.

casual adjective 1 *a casual meeting* chance, accidental, unintentional, unexpected, unforeseen, fortuitous, serendipitous. 2 *a casual remark* offhand, random, impromptu, spontaneous. 3 *a casual read* cursory, perfunctory, superficial, desultory, hasty. 4 *a casual attitude* indifferent, apathetic, uncaring, uninterested, unconcerned, lackadaisical, blasé. 5 *casual clothes* informal, relaxed, leisure; *inf.* sporty. 6 *a casual acquaintance* slight, superficial, shallow.

casualties plural noun *the casualties of the war* dead, fatalities, losses, dead and wounded, wounded, injured, missing in action, missing.

casualty noun **1** *a war casualty* fatality, dead/wounded/injured person, victim. **2** *the firm was a casualty of the recession* victim, sufferer, loser, loss.

cat noun feline; *inf.* pussy, pussy cat, puss; tabby, tomcat, tom, tortoiseshell, kitten, mouser, alley cat.

catalog noun list, record, register, inventory, directory, index, roll, table, calendar, classification, guide, brochure.

catalog verb list, classify, categorize, index, inventory, record, register, file, alphabetize.

catapult verb launch/propel rapidly, hurtle, shoot, fling.

catastrophe noun disaster, calamity, tragedy, blow, adversity, trouble, trials, mishap, misfortune, mischance, misadventure, failure, reverses, affliction, distress.

catch verb **1** *catch the ball* grasp, snatch, grab, seize, grip, clutch, clench, pluck, receive, acquire, come into the possession of, intercept. **2** *catch the prisoner* take captive, arrest, snare. *See* CAPTURE. **3** *catch what he said* understand, follow, comprehend, take in; *inf.* get the drift of. **4** *catch him unawares* surprise, discover, come across, startle, detect. **5** *catch pneumonia* contract, get, become infected with, develop, succumb to, come down with. **6** *catch his attention* capture, attract, draw, captivate, bewitch. **7** *catch a likeness* reproduce, represent, photograph, draw, paint. **catch on 1** *sports catching on* become popular/fashionable, come into fashion/vogue; *inf.* become trendy. **2** *did not understand at first, but eventually caught on* grasp, understand, comprehend, see the light; *inf.* get the picture.

catch noun **1** *the catch of the door/suitcase* bolt, lock, fastener, fastening, clasp, hasp, hook, clip, latch. **2** *what's the catch?* snag, disadvantage, drawback, hitch, fly in the ointment, trap, trick.

catching adjective **1** *is the disease catching?* contagious, infectious, communicable, transmittable, transmissible. **2** *a catching manner* attractive, winning, captivating, charming, fetching, enchanting.

catchword noun slogan, motto, password, watchword, byword, shibboleth, formula, refrain.

catchy adjective memorable, popular, appealing, captivating.

categorical adjective unqualified, unconditional, unequivocal, explicit, unambiguous, absolute, direct, downright, emphatic.

categorize verb classify, class, group, grade, order, arrange, sort, rank, break down, catalog, list, tabulate.

category noun class, classification, group, grouping, head, heading, list, listing, designation, type, sort, kind, variety, grade, grading, order, rank, status, division.

cater verb provide food, feed, provision. **cater to** provide, furnish, supply, purvey.

cathartic adjective purgative, purifying, cleansing, release-bringing.

catholic adjective **1** *of catholic interest* universal, widespread, global, comprehensive, all-encompassing. **2** *catholic tastes/views* wide, broad, eclectic, liberal, tolerant.

cattle plural noun bovines, steer, oxen; stock, livestock.

cause noun **1** *the cause of the fire* origin, root, source, beginning, genesis, occasion, mainspring, originator, author, creator, producer, agent, prime mover, maker. **2** *no cause for alarm* reason, grounds, justification, call, basis, motive, motivation. **3** *the cause of human rights* principle, ideal, belief, conviction, tenet. **4** *plead his cause* case, point of view, contention.

cause verb make happen, bring about, give rise to, begin, create, produce, originate, occasion, generate, effect, engender, lead to, result in, precipitate, provoke.

caustic adjective **1** *caustic chemical substances* corrosive, corroding, burning, destructive. **2** *caustic wit* sarcastic, cutting, biting, mordant, stinging, trenchant.

caution noun carefulness, attention, attentiveness, watchfulness, guardedness, discretion, forethought. *See* CARE noun 4.

caution verb warn, advise, counsel, urge, admonish.

cautious adjective wary, shrewd, discreet, guarded; *inf.* cagey. *See* CAREFUL 1.

cavalier adjective condescending, haughty, arrogant, disdainful, patronizing, contemptuous.

cavalry noun mounted troops, horse soldiers, horsemen, horse, troopers, dragoons, lancers; reinforcements.

cave noun cavern, grotto, hollow, tunnel, cellar, dugout, den.

caveat noun warning, caution, admonition, monition; *inf.* red flag.

cavern noun grotto, hollow. *See* CAVE.

cavernous adjective large, huge, deep, hollow, sunken, yawning, unfathomable, dark.

cavity noun hole, hollow, crater, pit, orifice, aperture, gap, dent.

cease verb **1** *cease working* stop, discontinue, desist, desist from, end, finish, leave off, quit, conclude, terminate, suspend, break off. **2** *the rain ceased* come to a stop, come to an end, let up, die away, abate, terminate.

cede verb yield, surrender, concede; relinquish, renounce, forsake, abandon, turn over, transfer, deliver up, grant, bequeath.

celebrate verb **1** *celebrate their anniversary | celebrate after the exams* commemorate, observe, honor, mark, keep, drink to, toast, rejoice, party, paint the town; *inf.* go on a spree, go out on the town, whoop it up. **2** *celebrate his achievement* proclaim, make known, herald, announce, publicize, broadcast, advertise. **3** *a poem celebrating the joys of love* praise, laud, extol, glorify, exalt, eulogize. **4** *celebrate a religious ceremony* perform, solemnize, ceremonialize.

celebrated adjective famous, famed, noted, renowned, well-known, prominent, distinguished, great, eminent, preeminent, illustrious, acclaimed, legendary, lionized.

celebration noun commemoration, observance, honoring, keeping, remembrance; party, carousal, festival, fête, carnival, gala; festivity, merrymaking, revelry; *inf.* spree, binge, bash.

celebrity noun **1** *celebrities at a charity ball* VIP, dignitary, big name, name, personality, star, superstar, lion, notable, luminary, personage; *inf.* bigwig, big shot, big wheel. **2** *his celebrity spread far* fame, renown, notability, popularity, reputation, honor, prominence, prestige, distinction, eminence, preeminence.

celestial adjective **1** *celestial beings* heavenly, divine, godly, godlike, ethereal, sublime, paradisiacal, elysian, spiritual, angelic. **2** *celestial bodies/navigation* heavenly, astronomical, extraterrestrial, stellar.

celibacy noun chastity, singleness, abstinence, self-denial, self-restraint, continence, asceticism, virginity, bachelorhood.

cell noun **1** *a prison/monastic cell* cubicle, room, apartment, compartment, chamber, stall, enclosure, dungeon, lockup. **2** *a political cell* faction, nucleus, clique, coterie, group, unit.

cement noun adhesive, bonding, binder, glue, superglue, gum, paste.

cement verb bind, bond, stick, join, unite, attach, cohere, combine, affix, glue, gum, paste, solder, weld.

cemetery noun graveyard, burial ground, burial place, churchyard.

censor verb expurgate, bowdlerize, cut, delete, make cuts/changes to, blue-pencil.

censure verb criticize, condemn, blame, castigate, denounce, disapprove of, berate, upbraid, reproach, rebuke, scold, chide.

censure noun criticism, condemnation, blame, castigation, denunciation, disapproval, berating, upbraiding, reproach, rebuke, reprimand.

center noun middle, middle point, midpoint, nucleus, heart, core, hub, focus, focal point.

center verb *her interests center on basketball* concentrate, focus, pivot, converge, close in.

central adjective **1** *a central position* middle, mid, median, mean; inner, interior. **2** *a central issue* fundamental, basic, key, essential, pivotal, focal, core.

ceramics plural noun pottery, earthenware, clay pots, crocks.

ceremonious adjective **1** *a ceremonious occasion* ceremonial, formal, ritual. **2** *behave in a ceremonious manner* punctilious, precise, scrupulous, stately, courtly, courteous, civil, deferential, stiff, rigid; *inf.* just-so.

ceremony noun **1** *a wedding ceremony* rite, service, formality, observance, function, custom, sacrament, show. **2** *conducted with ceremony* formalities, niceties, pomp, protocol, decorum, etiquette, propriety.

certain adjective **1** *I'm certain he's guilty* sure, positive, confident, convinced, assured, satisfied, persuaded. **2** *her success/failure is certain* destined, fated, inevitable, reliable, inescapable, bound to happen, inexorable; *inf.* in the bag. **3** *it is certain that he will go* definite, unquestionable, beyond question, indubitable, undeniable, irrefutable, obvious, evident, clear. **4** *no certain cure | a certain sign* unfailing, unquestionable, undisputed, dependable, reliable, trustworthy, sound, foolproof; *inf.* sure-fire. **5** *there is no certain date yet* definite, decided, settled, fixed, established, determined. **6** *a certain lady/place that will remain anonymous* particular, specific, individual, special, precise. **7** *to a certain extent* indeterminate, moderate, minimum.

certainly adverb surely, definitely, assuredly, undoubtedly, undeniably, obviously, plainly, clearly.

certainty noun **1** *I cannot say with certainty* sureness, assuredness, positiveness, confidence, conviction, reliability, validity, conclusiveness, authoritativeness, truth, fact, factualness. **2** *it's a certainty that they will lose* inevitability, indubitability, inescapability, fact; *inf.* sure thing, cinch.

certificate noun document, authorization, credentials, testimonial, warrant, license, voucher, diploma.

certify verb **1** *a document certifying their marriage* testify to, attest, corroborate, substantiate, verify, confirm, endorse, validate, vouch for, guarantee, authenticate, document, bear witness to, ratify. **2** *she has been certified to teach* accredit, license, authorize, qualify.

cessation noun end, termination, finish, conclusion, pause, break, respite, letup.

chafe verb **1** *his shirt chafed his neck* rub, abrade, graze, excoriate, scrape, scratch, rasp. **2** *fabric chafed by the rock* wear, abrade, wear away/down, wear out, wear to shreds, fray, tatter, erode. **3** *the passengers were chafed by the delay* annoy, anger, irritate, exasperate, vex, worry, peeve, irk, ruffle.

chaff noun **1** *chaff from the grain* husks, hulls, pods, shells, cases, casing. **2** *chaff for the cattle* straw, hay, fodder, silage. **3** *throw away the chaff* rubbish, refuse, waste, garbage, trash, dregs, remains, debris, junk, dross, detritus.

chagrin noun annoyance, irritation, vexation, displeasure, dissatisfaction, resentment, rankling, smarting, disquiet, embarrassment, mortification, humiliation, shame.

chain noun *a chain of events* series, succession, string, sequence, train, progression, course, set, cycle, line, row, concatenation.

chain verb fasten, secure, tie, bind, tether, shackle, fetter, manacle; handcuff, confine, restrain, trammel, gird, imprison.

chains plural noun bonds, fetters, shackles, manacles, trammels.

chair noun seat; stool, bench, pew, stall, throne.

chair verb *chair the meeting* preside over, lead, direct, manage, control, oversee, supervise.

chalk verb *chalk up chalk it up to experience* put down, ascribe, attribute, accredit, impute, charge.

challenge noun **1** *accept a sporting challenge* summons, call, invitation, bidding. **2** *a new challenge in his life* difficult task/venture, hazard, risk, obstacle. **challenge to** *a challenge to tradition* questioning of, opposition to, defiance of, confrontation with.

challenge verb **1** *challenge someone to a competition* dare, summon, invite, bid, throw down the gauntlet to. **2** *challenge their authority* question, call into question, dispute, protest against. **3** *the job really challenges him* test, tax, stimulate, arouse, inspire, excite, spur on.

chamber noun **1** *the judge's chambers* room, apartment, compartment, cubicle. **2** *the princess retiring to her chamber* bedroom, bedchamber, boudoir. **3** *the chambers in the caves* compartment, cavity, hollow, cell.

champion noun **1** *the champion of the competition* winner, title-holder, victor, conqueror, hero. **2** *the champion of the cause* defender, protector, upholder, supporter, advocate, backer.

champion verb defend, protect, uphold, support, fight for, advocate, promote.

chance noun **1** *meet by chance* accident, coincidence, serendipity, fate, luck. **2** *a good chance that he'll win* prospect, possibility, probability, likelihood. **3** *a second chance* opportunity, opening, occasion; *inf.* shot. **4** *take a chance and run* risk, gamble, hazard, venture, speculation.

chance verb **1** *it chanced that they arrived last* happen, occur, take place, come about. **2** *have to chance it* risk, hazard, gamble, venture, speculate, try one's luck, take a leap in the dark. **chance on/upon** come across, stumble on, come upon, encounter; *inf.* bump into, run into.

chance adjective accidental, unexpected, unanticipated, unforeseen, unintended, unpremeditated, fortuitous, serendipitous.

chancy adjective risky, uncertain, hazardous, speculative, dangerous; *inf.* dicey, iffy.

change verb **1** *change one's attitude* alter, modify, transform, convert, vary, remodel, recast, reconstruct, reorganize, metamorphose, transmute, permutate. **2** *she's changed* move on, evolve, fluctuate; *inf.* do an about-face. **3** *change a pair of pants* exchange, interchange, substitute, switch, replace, trade, barter; *inf.* swap.

change noun **1** *a change in plan* difference, alteration, modification, transformation, conversion, variation, reconstruction, reorganization, innovation, metamorphosis, vicissitude, mutation, permutation. **2** *a change of jobs* exchange, interchange, substitution, switch. **3** *he needs a change* diversion, variation; *inf.* break. **4** *have no change* coins, coinage, cash, silver, petty cash.

changeable adjective **1** *changeable weather* variable, chameleonlike, protean, shifting, vacillating, volatile, mercurial, capricious, fluctuating, fluid, kaleidoscopic, fitful, wavering, unstable, unsettled, irregular, erratic, unreliable, inconstant, fickle, mutable, unpredictable. **2** *changeable laws* alterable, modifiable, convertible, mutable.

channel noun **1** *the channel connecting the seas* passage, sea passage, strait, neck, narrows, waterway, watercourse, fiord. **2** *rainwater running through the channels* gutter, groove, furrow, conduit, duct, culvert, ditch. **3** *new channels for their energy* course, way, direction, path, route, approach. **4** *channels of communication* means, medium, agency, vehicle, route.

chant verb sing, recite, intone, cantillate.

chaos noun disorder, confusion, pandemonium, bedlam, tumult, uproar, disarray, anarchy, lawlessness.

chaotic adjective disordered, confused, tumultuous, disorganized, jumbled, topsy-turvy, in disarray, anarchic, lawless.

chaperon, chaperone verb accompany, escort, watch over, keep an eye on, protect, guard, safeguard.

chapter noun **1** *the next chapter in the book* division, section, part. **2** *a tragic chapter in our history* period, time, phase, stage, episode. **3** *a chapter of the society* branch, division, wing, offshoot.

char verb scorch, singe, sear, toast, carbonize, cauterize.

character noun **1** *her character has changed* personality, nature, disposition, temperament; ethos, individuality, constitution, makeup, attributes, bent, genius. **2** *a person of character* moral strength/fiber, strength, honor, integrity, rectitude, uprightness. **3** *damage his character* reputation, name, standing, position, status. **4** *a local character* eccentric, oddity, original, individual; *inf.* oddball. **5** *they're all friendly characters* person, individual, human being, fellow; *inf.* guy, sort, type, customer.

characteristic noun quality, attribute, feature, trait, property, mannerism, mark, trademark, idiosyncrasy, peculiarity, quirk.

characteristic adjective typical, distinguishing, distinctive, particular, special, individual, specific, peculiar, idiosyncratic, singular.

characterize verb **1** *the landscape is characterized by hills and rivers* typify, distinguish, identify, denote, designate, mark, stamp, brand. **2** *the witness characterized the scene as shocking* portray, depict, present, represent, describe.

charade noun pretense, travesty, fake, farce, pantomime.

charge verb **1** *what do you charge for a room?* ask, expect, impose, levy. **2** *charge it to my account* debit, put down to, bill. **3** *charge the murder suspect* accuse, indict, arraign, impeach. **4** *charge the enemy* attack, storm, assault, rush, open fire on, fall on. **5** *charged with the guardianship of the child* entrust, tax, weigh, weigh down, load, burden, encumber, hamper, saddle. **6** *charged with emotion* fill, load, imbue, suffuse, infuse, instill.

charge noun **1** *what is the charge for a room?* cost, price, fee, amount, rate, expense, levy, toll. **2** *murder charge* accusation, allegation, indictment, arraignment, citation, imputation. **3** *a cavalry charge* attack, storming, assault, onrush, onslaught. **4** *have charge of the children* responsibility, care, custody, guardianship, trust. **5** *your charge is to drive the car* duty, task, job, responsibility, office, obligation, assignment. **6** *pay for his charge's education* ward, protégé, dependent, minor.

charitable adjective **1** *be charitable toward the poor* philanthropic, giving, benevolent, generous, liberal, openhanded, kind, magnanimous, beneficent, munificent. **2** *a charitable interpretation* tolerant, broad-minded, understanding, sympathetic, compassionate, lenient, indulgent.

charity noun **1** *rely on charity for survival* financial assistance, donations, contributions, handouts, endowments, financial relief. **2** *behave with charity toward others* goodwill, compassion, humanity, humanitarianism, kindliness, love, sympathy, tolerance, indulgence, liberality, benevolence.

charlatan noun quack, sham, fraud, fake, impostor, pretender, cheat, deceiver, swindler; *inf.* con man.

charm noun **1** *the charm of the resort/hostess* attractiveness, attraction, appeal, allure, fascination, captivation, desirability, delightfulness; beauty, wiles, blandishments. **2** *the sorcerer's charm* spell, magic formula, magic word, abracadabra; sorcery, magic. **3** *the charms on her bracelet* trinket, ornament, bauble, souvenir. **4** *a lucky charm* amulet, talisman, fetish.

charm verb delight, please, attract, win, win over, captivate, allure, lure, draw, fascinate, bewitch, beguile, enchant, enrapture, seduce, cajole.

charming adjective delightful, pleasing, pleasant, appealing, attractive, winning, fetching, taking, captivating, winsome, engaging, lovely, agreeable, alluring, fascinating, bewitching, beguiling, enchanting, irresistible, seductive.

chart noun graph, table, map, diagram, plan, blueprint, guide, scheme.

chart verb tabulate, map, map out, plot, graph, delineate, diagram, sketch.

charter noun **1** *privileges granted by royal charter* authority, authorization, sanction, warrant, document, covenant, deed, bond, permit, prerogative, privilege, right. **2** *the charter of the United Nations* constitution, code, canon, body of laws; principles, rules, laws.

chase verb pursue, run after, follow, hunt, hound, track, trail, tail. **chase away** *chase away the blues* put to flight, drive away, send away, send packing.

chasm noun **1** *a landscape full of chasms* gorge, abyss, canyon, ravine, pit, crater, crevasse, gap, fissure, crevice, cleft, rift. **2** *a chasm between their points of view* schism, breach, gulf.

chaste adjective **1** *nuns leading a chaste life* virgin, virginal, vestal, celibate, abstinent, unmarried. **2** *chaste conduct/speech* virtuous, pure, decent, moral, decorous, modest, wholesome, righteous, upright. **3** *a chaste style* simple, plain, unadorned.

chasten verb **1** *chastened by the experience* subdue, restrain, tame, curb, check, humble, cow, tone down. **2** *chasten the students* discipline, punish. *See* CHASTISE 2.

chastise verb **1** *mutineers chastised the harsh captain* punish, discipline, castigate, beat, thrash, smack, flog, whip, strap, cane, lash, scourge; *inf.* wallop, thump, tan one's hide. **2** *the staff were chastised for tardiness* scold, upbraid, reprimand, reprove, chide, take to task, haul over the coals, chasten, castigate.

chastity noun **1** *nuns take vows of chastity* virginity, celibacy, abstinence, singleness. **2** *chastity of conduct/speech* virtue, goodness, innocence, purity, decency, morality, decorum, modesty, wholesomeness, righteousness.

chat verb talk, gossip, chatter, converse, prattle, jabber, prate; *inf.* have a confab, jaw, chew the fat, rap.

chat noun talk, conversation, chatter, heart-to-heart, tête-à-tête; *inf.* confab.

chatty adjective **1** *a chatty person* talkative, gossipy, garrulous, loquacious, voluble, glib, effusive. **2** *a chatty style* informal, conversational, colloquial, familiar, friendly, lively.

cheap adjective **1** *cheap prices/housing* inexpensive, low-priced, low-cost, economical, reasonable, moderately priced, bargain, economy, sale, reduced, marked-down, slashed, discounted; *inf.* bargain-basement. **2** *cheap and gaudy jewelry* poor-quality, inferior, shoddy, common, trashy, tawdry, paltry, worthless, second-rate, gimcrack; *inf.* tacky. **3** *he felt cheap after what he had done* ashamed, shameful, embarrassed, humiliated, mortified, debased, degraded, abashed, discomfited, disconcerted. **4** *he's too cheap to buy a raffle ticket* stingy, parsimonious, tight-fisted, niggardly, penny-pinching, frugal.

cheapen verb **1** *cheapen the cost of travel* lower, reduce, cut, mark down, slash, discount, depreciate. **2** *cheapening herself by working in that club* degrade, debase, demean, devalue, lower, belittle, denigrate, discredit.

cheat verb **1** *cheat his partner* deceive, trick, swindle, defraud, dupe, hoodwink, double-cross, gull; exploit, take advantage of, victimize; *inf.* con, bamboozle, finagle, bilk; rip off, fleece, take for a ride. **2** *cheat death* avoid, elude, evade, dodge, escape.

cheat noun cheater, swindler, fraud, confidence man/woman, trickster, deceiver, double-crosser, crook, rogue, shark, charlatan; *inf.* con man.

check verb **1** *check the roof for holes* examine, inspect, look at, look over, scrutinize, test, monitor, investigate, probe, study; *inf.* give the once-over to. **2** *check that the door's locked* confirm, make sure, verify, corroborate, validate, substantiate. **3** *check the disease* stop, arrest, halt, bring to a standstill, slow down, brake, bar, obstruct, impede, block, retard, curb, delay. **4** *check one's laughter/tears* restrain, suppress, repress, contain, control, bridle, inhibit. **5** *their stories don't check* correspond, agree, tally, dovetail, harmonize. **check up on** investigate, examine, inspect, research, scrutinize, probe.

check noun **1** *a security check* examination, inspection, scrutiny, scrutinization, test, monitoring, investigation, probe, inquiry, study; *inf.* once-over. **2** *a check in the production rate* stop, stopping, stoppage, arrest, halt, slowing-down, retardation, delay. **3** *act as a check to the celebration* restraint, constraint, control, deterrent, impediment, obstruction, limitation, curb. **4** *the customer asked for his check* bill, account, invoice, reckoning, tally; *inf.* tab.

checkered adjective *a checkered career* mixed, varied, diverse, diversified, eventful; full of ups and downs.

checkup noun examination, inspection, appraisal, assessment, analysis, scrutinization, scrutiny, exploration, probe.

cheek noun **1** jowl, chop, gill. **2** *have the cheek to appear* impudence, audacity, temerity, brazenness, effrontery, nerve; *inf.* gall.

cheeky adjective impudent, audacious, impertinent, insolent, forward, pert, disrespectful, fresh, insulting; *inf.* saucy, sassy.

cheer verb **1** *crowds cheered the president* hail, acclaim, hurrah, hurray, applaud, shout at, clap for. **2** *his arrival cheered her* raise the spirits of, brighten, buoy up, perk up, enliven, animate, elate, exhilarate, hearten, uplift, give a lift to, gladden, encourage, incite, stimulate, arouse, comfort, solace, console, inspirit; *inf.* buck up.

cheer noun **1** *the cheers of the crowd* acclaim, acclamation, hurrah, hurray, applause, ovation, plaudit, hailing, shouting, clapping. **2** *a time of cheer* cheerfulness, gladness, happiness, merriment, mirth, gaiety, joy, pleasure, high spirits, lightheartedness, glee, merrymaking, rejoicing, revelry, festivity. **3** *tables laden with seasonal cheer* fare, food, provisions, foodstuffs, drink; *inf.* eats.

cheerful adjective **1** *a cheerful disposition* happy, bright, merry, glad, gladsome, gay, sunny, joyful, jolly, blithe, buoyant, lighthearted, sparkling, carefree, happy-go-lucky, breezy, cheery, sprightly, jaunty, smiling, laughing, bright-eyed and bushy-tailed, optimistic, hopeful, positive. **2** *a cheerful room* pleasant, agreeable, friendly, happy. **3** *his cheerful acceptance of the situation* willing, obliging, cooperative, compliant.

cheerless adjective gloomy, dreary, miserable, dull, depressing, dismal, bleak, drab, grim, austere, desolate, dark, dingy, somber, uninviting.

cheers interjection here's to you, good luck, to your health, skol, prosit; *inf.* here's mud in your eye, bottoms up, down the hatch.

cheery adjective happy, merry. *See* CHEERFUL 1.

cherish verb **1** *cherish a friendship* treasure, prize, hold dear, adore, revere, indulge; care for, look after, tend, protect, preserve, shelter, support, nurture, foster. **2** *cherish hopes* entertain, harbor, cling to.

chest noun **1** *injured her chest* thorax, breast, sternum. **2** *pack belongings in chests* box, crate, case, trunk, container, coffer, casket.

chew verb masticate, munch, champ, crunch, bite, gnaw, grind. **chew over** meditate on, ruminate on, mull over, consider, deliberate upon, reflect upon.

chic adjective stylish, fashionable, smart, elegant, modish, voguish; *inf.* trendy.

chicanery noun deception, deceitfulness, duplicity, guile, cheating, duping, hoodwinking, dishonesty, subterfuge, craftiness, wiles, sophistry.

chide verb scold, reproach, lecture, call to account. *See* CASTIGATE.

chief noun head, headman, leader, chieftain, ruler, overlord, lord and master, commander, sachem; principal, director, chairman, chairperson, chief executive, manager, superintendent, master, foreman; *inf.* boss, boss man, kingpin, top dog.

chief adjective **1** *chief priest* supreme, head, foremost, highest, leading, superior, premier, directing, governing. **2** *the chief point* main, principal, most important, uppermost, primary, central, key, vital, essential, predominant, preeminent.

chiefly adverb mainly, in the main, principally, primarily, predominantly, especially, particularly, essentially, mostly, for the most part, on the whole, above all.

child noun **1** *two adults and a child* youngster, young person, young one, little one, boy, girl, baby, babe, infant, toddler, tot, tiny tot, adolescent, youth, juvenile, minor; *derog.* brat; *inf.* kid, shaver. **2** *parents and their children* offspring, progeny, issue; descendant, scion; son, daughter.

childhood noun youth, infancy, babyhood, preteens, minority, immaturity; boyhood, girlhood.

childish adjective **1** *the childish behavior of the adults* immature, infantile, juvenile, puerile, silly, foolish, irresponsible, jejune. **2** *childish laughter* children's, childlike, youthful.

childlike adjective **1** *childlike activities* children's, youthful. **2** *childlike reactions* ingenuous, innocent, artless, guileless, simple, naive, trusting, trustful.

chill noun **1** *a chill in the air* chilliness, coldness, iciness, crispness, rawness, sharpness, nip, bite. **2** *a chill in her manner* aloofness, distance, coolness, unresponsiveness, lack of sympathy, frigidity, hostility, unfriendliness. **3** *cast a chill over the proceedings* cloud, depression, damper.

chill verb *chill the enthusiasm* lessen, reduce, dampen, depress, dispirit, discourage, dishearten.

chilly adjective **1** *a chilly breeze* cold, cool, icy, crisp, brisk, fresh, raw, sharp, biting, penetrating, freezing, frigid; *inf.* nippy. **2** *a chilly manner* cold, cool, aloof, distant, unresponsive, unsympathetic, frigid, unwelcoming, hostile, unfriendly.

chime verb ring, peal, toll, sound, ding, ding-dong, clang, boom, tinkle, resound, reverberate. **chime in** *he's always chiming in when we're talking* interrupt, cut in, interpose; *inf.* butt in; jump in.

chimes plural noun bells, carillon, wind chimes.

china noun porcelain, faience, ceramics, pottery; dishes, tableware, dinner/tea service.

chip noun **1** *chips on the sawmill's floor* shaving, paring, shard, flake, shred, sliver, splinter, fragment, snippet, scrap. **2** *the cup with a chip in it* nick, crack, notch, flaw. **3** *gambling chips* counter, token, disk.

chip verb **1** *chip a glass* nick, crack, damage. **2** *the paint chips easily* break off, crack, fragment, crumble. **3** *chipping away at a chunk of wood* whittle, chisel, hew. **chip in 1** *he's always chipping in with suggestions* interrupt, cut in, interpose; *inf.* chime in, butt in. **2** *chip in to buy a present* contribute, make a contribution, donate.

chirp verb chirrup, cheep, twitter, tweet, warble, trill, chatter.

chitchat noun small talk, idle gossip, gossip, chatter.

chivalrous adjective **1** *behaving in a chivalrous way toward women* gallant, gentlemanly, courteous, gracious, mannerly, well-mannered, polite, thoughtful, protective, courtly. **2** *chivalrous followers of King Arthur* knightly, courtly, bold, courageous, brave, valiant, heroic, daring, intrepid, honorable, high-minded, just, fair, loyal, constant, true, gallant, magnanimous.

chivalry noun **1** *chivalry toward women* gallantry, gentlemanliness, courtesy, courteousness, graciousness, mannerliness, politeness, thoughtfulness, protectiveness, courtliness. **2** *the chivalry of King Arthur's followers* courtliness, boldness, valor, honor, high-mindedness, integrity, justness, fairness, loyalty, constancy.

choice noun **1** *the choice of candidates* selection, picking, preference, election, adoption. **2** *no choice but to resign* alternative, option, possibility, solution, answer, way out. **3** *a wide choice of candy* range, variety, supply, store. **4** *he was considered the right choice* selection, appointment, appointee, nominee, candidate.

choice adjective **1** *choice fruit* best, select, superior, first-class, first-rate, excellent, prime, prize. **2** *a few choice phrases* well-chosen, select, handpicked, appropriate, apt.

choke verb **1** *choked to death* strangle, strangulate, throttle. **2** *smoke choking him* asphyxiate, suffocate, smother, stifle. **3** *he choked on a bone* gag, gasp, retch, asphyxiate, suffocate. **4** *the storm drains are choked with leaves* clog, block, obstruct, occlude, plug, dam up. **choke back** *choke back tears* contain, suppress, control, repress, curb, bridle.

choose verb **1** *choose a book/career* select, pick, pick out, handpick, take, opt for, settle on, decide on, fix on, single out, adopt, designate, elect, espouse. **2** *do as you choose* prefer, like, wish, want, desire, fancy, favor.

choosy adjective fussy, finicky, persnickety, fastidious, particular, exacting, discriminating.

chop verb cut up, cube, dice, fragment, crumble. **chop down** cut down, fell, hew, bring down, saw down. **chop off** *chop off branches* cut off, lop, sever, hack off.

choppy adjective rough, bumpy, turbulent, blustery, stormy, tempestuous.

chore noun task, job, duty, errand, burden.

chortle verb chuckle, cackle, guffaw, laugh uproariously, roar/shake with laughter.

chorus noun **1** *sing in a chorus* choir, ensemble, choral group; choristers, singers, vocalists. **2** *the chorus of the song* refrain, strain, response. **in chorus** *give a reply in chorus* in unison, in concert, in harmony.

christen verb baptize, sprinkle, immerse; give a name to, name, call, dub, style, term, designate, denominate.

chronic adjective *a chronic illness/habit* persistent, long-lasting, long-standing, constant, continual, continuous, incessant, lingering, deep-rooted, deep-seated, ingrained, inveterate, confirmed, habitual, hardened.

chronicle noun register, record, annals, calendar, diary, journal, log, account, archive, history, story.

chronicle verb record, put on record, set down, document, register, report, enter, note, relate, tell about.

chronological adjective sequential, consecutive, progressive, serial, historical.

chubby adjective plump, tubby, rotund, stout, portly, round, dumpy, fat, fleshy, flabby, paunchy.

chuck verb **1** *chuck it in the bucket* toss, fling, throw, cast, pitch, hurl, shy, heave, sling, let fly. **2** *chuck his job/girlfriend* abandon, give up, relinquish, quit, forsake; *inf.* drop.

chuckle verb laugh quietly, laugh to oneself, chortle, giggle, titter, cackle.

chum noun friend, bosom friend, companion, comrade, crony, alter ego; *inf.* pal, buddy.

chunk noun lump, hunk, block, slab, mass, square, wedge, dollop, piece, portion, part.

church noun place of worship, the house of God, the Lord's house; cathedral, minster, chapel, temple, tabernacle, mosque, synagogue.

churn verb beat, whip up, agitate, disturb, stir up, shake up.

cinema noun films, pictures, movies, motion pictures; *inf.* big screen, silver screen.

circle noun **1** *draw a circle* ring, disk, loop, circumference, ball, globe, sphere, orb. **2** *move in different circles* sphere, domain, province, realm, region, circuit, orbit, compass. **3** *her circle of friends* group, set, company, crowd, ring, coterie, clique.

circle verb **1** *vultures circling above* rotate, revolve, circulate, wheel, whirl, gyrate, pivot, swivel. **2** *circle the estate/world* surround, encircle, ring, enclose, envelop, hem in, gird, belt, circumscribe; orbit, circumnavigate.

circuit noun **1** *run a circuit of the track* lap, turn, beat, cycle, loop. **2** *the circuit of the estate/field* border, boundary, bounds, compass, limits, circumference.

circuitous adjective roundabout, winding, meandering, tortuous, twisting, rambling, indirect, maze-like, labyrinthine.

circular adjective round, ring-shaped, annular, spherical, spheroid, globular.

circulate verb **1** *circulate the news* spread, disseminate, propagate, distribute, transmit, give out, make known, make public, broadcast, publicize, advertise. **2** *blood/air* *circulating* flow, move round, go round, rotate, revolve, whirl, gyrate.

circumference noun perimeter, periphery, border, boundary, bounds, limits, confines, outline, circuit, compass, extremity, edge, rim.

circumlocution noun periphrasis, tautology, redundancy, discursiveness, verbosity, wordiness, prolixity, long-windedness.

circumscribe verb **1** *circumscribe the area* enclose, encircle, bound, encompass, gird; define, delineate, outline, demarcate, delimit, mark off. **2** *activities circumscribed by poverty* restrict, limit, curb, confine, restrain.

circumspect adjective wary, cautious, careful; prudent, judicious, politic.

circumstances plural noun **1** *I know nothing of the circumstances* situation, state of affairs, conditions, position, event, occurrence, background. **2** *living in poor circumstances* financial plight, predicament, means, resources, lifestyle, station.

circumstantial adjective **1** *circumstantial evidence* indirect, incidental, evidential, deduced, presumed, inferential, conjectural. **2** *a circumstantial account* detailed, precise, particular, exact, accurate, minute.

citation noun **1** *citations from the classics* quotation, quote, extract, excerpt, reference, illustration, allusion, passage, source. **2** *a citation for heroism* commendation, award, honor, mention. **3** *a citation from the courts* summons, subpoena, arraignment.

cite verb **1** *cite the statistics as evidence* quote, mention, name, enumerate, refer to, allude to, exemplify, excerpt, extract. **2** *cited for heroism* commend, recommend, pay tribute to, mention.

citizen noun resident, inhabitant, dweller, denizen, townsman, townswoman, taxpayer, voter, constituent, subject.

city noun metropolitan area, conurbation, metropolis, municipality, town.

civic adjective municipal, public, community, local, civil, communal, urban, metropolitan.

civil adjective **1** *civil responsibilities* municipal, public. *See* CIVIC. **2** *civil government/rulers* civilian, lay, nonmilitary, nonreligious, secular. **3** *in a civil manner* polite, courteous, well-mannered, mannerly, well-bred, gentlemanly, ladylike, refined, urbane, polished, civilized.

civility noun **1** *treat even his opponents with civility* courtesy, courteousness, politeness, good manners, mannerliness, graciousness, cordiality, geniality, pleasantness, gallantry. **2** *exchange civilities* courtesy, etiquette, protocol, propriety, decorum.

civilization noun **1** *a threat to modern civilization* development, advancement, progress, enlightenment, culture, cultivation, edification, refinement, sophistication. **2** *ancient civilizations* society, community, nation, country, people, way of life.

civilized adjective developed, modern, socialized, educated, cultured, cultivated, sophisticated, enlightened, urbane.

claim verb **1** *claim the prize* lay claim to, ask as one's right, demand, request, requisition. **2** *claim that he's innocent* profess, maintain, assert, declare, protest, avow, aver, allege.

claim noun **1** *a claim for damages* demand, request, application, petition, call. **2** *his claim to the crown* right, rights, title, prerogative, privilege, heritage, inheritance, legacy. **3** *dispute his claims of innocence* profession, assertion, declaration, protestation, avowal, allegation.

claimant noun applicant, candidate, petitioner, supplicant, suppliant, suitor, postulant, pretender, plaintiff.

clairvoyance noun second sight, psychic powers, extrasensory perception, ESP, telepathy, sixth sense.

clamor noun **1** *the clamor of children's voices* uproar, noise, din, racket, shout, shouting, yelling, blaring, commotion, hubbub, hullabaloo, outcry, vociferation. **2** *answer their clamors for more money* demand, call, petition, request, urging, protest, complaint, insistence.

clamp noun vice, press, brace, clasp, fastener, hasp.

clamp verb **1** *a pipe clamped between his teeth* grip, hold, fix, clench, press, squeeze, secure, make fast, brace. **2** *clamp a curfew on the city* impose, inflict, lay on, set, charge, burden. **clamp down on** hold in check, crack down on, be severe with, suppress, prevent.

clan noun **1** *tired of the clan of socialites* set, circle, crowd, in-crowd, gang, band, group, faction, clique, coterie. **2** *our clan gathers for every holiday* family, kin, kinfolk, relatives, kith and kin.

clandestine adjective secret, undercover, surreptitious, cloak-and-dagger, back-alley, furtive, concealed, hidden, underhand.

clang noun ring, clank, clash, clangor, bong, chime, toll, clink, clunk, jangle.

clang verb ring, resound, reverberate, clank, clash, bong, clink, chime, toll, peal.

clarify verb clear up, resolve, make plain, explain, elucidate, illuminate, throw light on, make simple, simplify.

clarity noun **1** *the clarity of his prose* clearness, lucidity, lucidness, plainness, simplicity, intelligibility, comprehensibility, unambiguity, precision. **2** *the clarity of the water* clearness, transparency, limpidity, translucence, pellucidity, glassiness.

clash verb **1** *clash the cymbals* strike, bang, clang, crash, clatter, clank, clink, rattle, jangle. **2** *the two sides clashed* be in conflict, war, fight, contend, do battle, come to blows, feud, grapple, wrangle, quarrel, cross swords, lock horns. **3** *the appointments clash* coincide, conflict. **4** *the colors clash* be discordant, jar, be incompatible.

clash noun **1** *the clash of cymbals* striking, bang, clang, crash, clatter, clank. **2** *the clash of the opposing sides* conflict, collision, confrontation, brush, warring, fighting, contending, feud, grappling, wrangling, quarreling. **3** *the clash of the colors* discordance, discord, lack of harmony, incompatibility, jarring.

clasp noun **1** *the clasp of the necklace* catch, fastener, fastening, clip; hook, hook and eye, snap, buckle, hasp. **2** *engage in a loving clasp* embrace, hug, cuddle, hold, grip, grasp.

class noun **1** *professional class* social order/division, stratum, rank, level, status, sphere, grade, group, grouping, set, caste. **2** *degrees divided into three classes* category, classification, division, section, group. **3** *a class of objects* kind, sort, type, collection, denomination, order, species, genre, genus. **4** *a woman of class* quality, excellence, distinction, stylishness, elegance.

classic adjective **1** *a classic performance* first-rate, first-class, excellent, brilliant, finest, outstanding, exemplary, masterly, consummate. **2** *a classic case/example* typical, standard, model, guiding, archetypal, stock, true-to-form, paradigmatic, prototypical. **3** *classic styles* simple, traditional, timeless, ageless, long-lasting, enduring, abiding, long-standing.

classic noun great work, established work, masterpiece.

classical adjective **1** *a classical scholar|classical architecture* Greek, Grecian, Hellenic, Attic, Greco-Roman, Roman, Latin. **2** *classical music* orchestral, symphonic. **3** *a classical style of design* simple, plain, restrained, pure, understated, harmonious, well-proportioned, balanced, symmetrical, elegant.

classification noun categorizing, categorization, grouping, grading, arrangement, codification, taxonomy.

classify verb categorize, class, group, grade, arrange, order, sort, type, rank, rate, designate, codify, catalog.

clause noun section, paragraph, article, note, item, point, passage, part, heading.

claw noun nail, talon, pincer, nipper, chela.

claw verb scratch, tear, lacerate, scrape, graze, rip, dig into, maul.

clean adjective **1** *clean hands/clothes* unsoiled, unstained, unspotted, unsullied, unblemished, spotless, immaculate, speckless, hygienic, sanitary, washed, cleansed, laundered, scrubbed. **2** *clean air* pure, clear, natural, unpolluted, unadulterated, uncontaminated, untainted. **3** *clean lives* good, upright, honorable, respectable, virtuous, righteous, moral, reputable, upstanding. **4** *a clean piece of paper* unused, unmarked, blank, vacant, void. **5** *the clean lines of the airplane* streamlined, smooth, well-defined, definite, clean-cut, regular, simple, elegant, graceful, uncluttered. **6** *a clean break* complete, thorough, total, conclusive, decisive, final.

clean verb **1** *clean one's hands/walls* wash, cleanse, wipe, sponge, scrub, scour, swab. **2** *clean one's clothes* dry-clean, launder. **3** *clean the room* tidy, pick up; vacuum, dust, mop, sweep.

cleanse verb **1** *cleanse the wound* clean, wash, bathe, rinse, disinfect. **2** *cleanse of sin* purify, purge, absolve.

clear adjective **1** *a clear day* bright, cloudless, unclouded, fair, fine, light, undimmed, sunny, sunshiny. **2** *clear glass* transparent, limpid, translucent, crystalline. **3** *it was clear that he was guilty* obvious, evident, plain, apparent, sure, definite, unmistakable, indisputable, patent. **4** *a clear account of the incident* understandable, comprehensible, intelligible, plain, explicit, lucid, coherent. **5** *a clear thinker* astute, keen, sharp, quick, perceptive, discerning, perspicacious. **6** *a clear view* open, empty, free, unobstructed, unimpeded, unhindered, unlimited. **7** *a clear conscience* untroubled, undisturbed, innocent, guiltless, guilt-free.

clear verb **1** *the weather cleared* clear up, brighten, lighten, break. **2** *clear the plates* remove, take away, tidy up/away. **3** *clear the drains* unblock, unclog, unstop. **4** *clear the room of objects* empty, vacate, evacuate, void, free, rid. **5** *clear the accused of charges* absolve, acquit, discharge, let go, exonerate, vindicate. **6** *clear the fence* jump, vault, leap, hop, pass over. **7** *clear $500* net, make a profit of, realize a profit of, gain, earn, make, bring, reap. **8** *the ship was cleared* authorize, sanction, pass, approve, permit/allow to pass. **clear out 1** *clear out the cupboard* empty, evacuate, tidy, tidy up. **2** *clear out the trash* get rid of, throw out, throw away, eject, eliminate. **3** *boys told to clear out* go away, get out, leave, depart, make oneself scarce, decamp. **clear up 1** *clear up the mystery* solve, resolve, straighten out, find an answer to, unravel, untangle, explain, elucidate; *inf.* crack. **2** *the weather cleared up* improve, brighten. *See* CLEAR verb 1.

clearance noun **1** *slum clearance* clearing, removal, evacuation, eviction, emptying. **2** *the clearance under the bridge* clearing, space, gap, allowance, margin, headroom, leeway. **3** *clearance for the plans* authorization, consent, permission, sanction, go-ahead, leave; *inf.* green light.

clear-cut adjective definite, specific, precise, explicit, unambiguous, unequivocal.

clearly adverb obviously, undoubtedly, without doubt, indubitably, plainly, undeniably, decidedly, surely, certainly, irrefutably, incontestably, patently.

cleave verb cleave to cling to, stick to, hold to, stand by, abide by, adhere to, be loyal/faithful to.

cleft noun split, crack, gap, fissure, crevice, rift, break, fracture.

clemency noun mercy, leniency, compassion, humanity, pity, sympathy, kindness, magnanimity, fairness.

clench verb **1** *clench the teeth* close, shut, seal, fasten. **2** *clench the table edge* grip, grasp, clutch, hold, seize.

clergy noun priests, clerics, ecclesiastics; ministry, priesthood, the cloth, first estate.

clergyman, clergywoman noun churchman, churchwoman, man/woman of the cloth, man/woman of God, cleric, ecclesiastic, divine; vicar, parson, pastor, priest, father, padre, reverend, rector, rabbi, chaplain.

clerical adjective **1** *clerical duties* secretarial, office, writing, typing, filing, bookkeeping. **2** *clerical clothes* ecclesiastical, churchly, priestly, pastoral, sacerdotal, apostolic, canonical.

clever adjective **1** *clever people* intelligent, bright, sharp-witted, quick-witted, talented, gifted, smart, capable, able, competent, knowledgeable, educated; *inf.* brainy. **2** *a clever move* shrewd, astute, adroit, canny, cunning, ingenious, artful, wily, inventive. **3** *clever with their hands* dexterous, skillful, adroit, nimble, deft, handy.

cliché noun hackneyed phrase, platitude, banality, truism, saw, bromide; *inf.* chestnut.

click verb **1** *the key clicked in the lock* clink, clack, chink, snap, tick. **2** *it suddenly clicked* become clear, fall into place, come home to one, make sense. **3** *the two girls clicked immediately* get on, take to each other, hit it off, be compatible, be on the same wavelength, feel a rapport. **4** *the new toys clicked with the children* make a

hit, prove popular, be successful, succeed, go down well.

client noun customer, patron, regular, habitué, buyer, purchaser, shopper; patient.

cliff noun precipice, rock face, face, crag, bluff, escarpment, scarp, overhang, tor.

climate noun **1** *temperate climate* weather, temperature. **2** *visit various climates* clime, country, place, region, area, zone. **3** *the political climate* atmosphere, mood, temper, spirit, feeling, feel, ambience, aura, ethos.

climax noun culmination, height, peak, pinnacle, high point, summit, top, highlight, acme, zenith, apex, apogee, crowning point; orgasm.

climb verb **1** *climb up the ladder* | *climb to the top* go, ascend, mount, scale, clamber. **2** *prices are climbing* go up, rise, increase, shoot up, soar. **3** *the road climbs steeply* slope upward, incline, bank.

clinch verb **1** *clinch the deal* settle, secure, seal, set the seal on, complete, assure, cap, close, wind up; *inf.* sew up. **2** *clinch a nail* fasten, make fast, secure, fix, clamp, bolt, rivet. **3** *boxers/lovers clinching* hug, embrace, squeeze, clutch, grasp, grapple.

cling verb the surfaces clung together stick, adhere, hold, grip, clasp, clutch. cling to **1** *cling to the rope* hold on to, hang on to, clutch, grip, grasp, clasp, cleave to. **2** *cling to one's beliefs* stick to, hold to, stand by, abide by, adhere to, be loyal/faithful to, remain true to, remain attached to; *inf.* stick with.

clinical adjective **1** *a clinical attitude* objective, dispassionate, detached, uninvolved, cold, unsympathetic, unfeeling. **2** *clinical designs* plain, simple, unadorned, stark, austere, severe.

clip verb **1** *clip hair/hedges* cut, crop, snip, trim, shear, prune. **2** *clip him across the jaw* hit, strike, box, cuff, smack, wallop, thump, punch, knock; *inf.* clout, whack. **3** *the train was clipping along* speed, race, gallop, rush, dash, zoom.

clique noun coterie, circle, crowd, incrowd, set, gang, group, clan, faction, pack, band, ring, fraternity.

cloak noun **1** *wearing a black cloak* cape, mantle, wrap, shawl, pelisse, coat. **2** *a cloak of secrecy* cover, screen, blind, mask, mantle, veil, shroud, shield, front, camouflage, pretext.

cloak verb hide, conceal, cover, cover up, screen, mask, veil, shroud, shield, cloud, camouflage, obscure, disguise.

clock noun timekeeper, timepiece, timer; chronometer, chronograph.

clog verb **1** *leaves clogging the drains* block, obstruct, dam, congest, jam, occlude; stop up, dam up. **2** *clog the system with red tape* hinder, impede, hamper.

cloister noun *walking in the cloisters* covered walk, walkway, corridor, aisle, arcade, gallery, piazza.

cloistered adjective secluded, sheltered, sequestered, confined, restricted, reclusive, hermitic.

close verb **1** *close the door* shut, slam, fasten, secure, lock, bolt, bar, latch, padlock. **2** *close the bottle* stop up, plug, seal, clog, choke, obstruct, occlude. **3** *close the meeting* bring to an end, end, conclude, finish, terminate, wind up. **4** *close the bargain* complete, settle, clinch, seal. **5** *the gap closed* narrow, lessen, grow smaller, dwindle, reduce. **6** *his arms closed around her* come together, join, connect, come into contact, unite.

close noun end, finish, conclusion, termination, cessation, completion, culmination, finale, wind-up.

close adjective **1** *our two houses are close* near, adjacent, in close proximity, adjoining, neighboring, abutting. **2** *a close resemblance* near, similar, like, alike, comparable, parallel, corresponding, akin. **3** *a close friend* intimate, dear, bosom, close-knit, inseparable. **4** *close formation* dense, condensed, compact, crowded, packed, solid, tight, cramped, congested. **5** *a close game* evenly matched, well-matched, hard-fought, sharply contested, neck-and-neck, nose-to-nose; *inf.* fifty-fifty. **6** *a close description* accurate, true, faithful, literal, exact, precise. **7** *close attention* intense, keen, thorough, rigorous, searching. **8** *under close arrest* strict, stringent, rigorous, thorough, tight. **9** *close weather* humid, muggy, stuffy, heavy, oppressive, stifling, suffocating. **10** *he's very close about his affairs* uncommunicative, reserved, private, unforthcoming, secretive. **11** *close with money* miserly, stingy, niggardly, parsimonious, tight-fisted, tight.

closure noun termination, finish, conclusion.

clot verb coagulate, set, congeal, jell, thicken, cake, curdle.

cloth noun *silk cloth* fabric, material, stuff; textiles, dry goods, soft goods.

clothe verb **1** *clothed in pure wool* dress, attire, rig, rig out, apparel, fit out, outfit, robe, garb, array, deck out, drape; *inf.* doll up. **2** *hills clothed in clouds* cover, wrap, cloak, envelop, swathe.

clothing noun clothes, garments; dress, attire, apparel, outfit, costume, garb, ensemble, vestments, raiment; *inf.* gear, togs, get-up.

cloud noun **1** *clouds in the sky* rain cloud, storm cloud, thundercloud, billow; haze, cloudbank. **2** *a cloud of smoke* pall, shroud, mantle, cloak, screen, cover. **3** *a cloud on their happiness* shadow, threat; gloom, darkness. **4** *a cloud of insects* swarm, flock, mass, multitude, host, horde, throng.

cloudy adjective **1** *a cloudy sky* overcast, hazy, dark, gray, somber, leaden, heavy, gloomy, dim, lowering, sunless, starless. **2** *cloudy recollections* blurred, vague, indistinct, hazy, indefinite, nebulous, obscure, confused, muddled. **3** *cloudy liquids* opaque, murky, muddy, milky, emulsified, opalescent, turbid.

clout noun **1** *give him a clout* smack, slap, thump. **2** *because of your clout in the firm* influence, power, pull, weight, authority, prestige, standing.

clown noun **1** *circus clowns* jester, fool, buffoon, zany, harlequin. **2** *he's a real clown* joker, comedian, comic, humorist, funnyman, wag, wit, prankster.

club noun **1** *hit him with a club* cudgel, bludgeon, stick, staff, truncheon, bat, baton, blackjack. **2** *a swimming/bridge club* society, group, association, organization, affiliation, league, union, federation.

clue noun hint, indication, sign, intimation, pointer, guide, lead, tip, tip-off, inkling.

clump noun group, cluster, bunch, collection, assembly, assemblage; mass, lump, clod, glob, agglutination.

clump verb **1** *houses clumped together* group, cluster, bunch, collect, assemble, congregate, mass, lump, bundle, pack. **2** *clump around in heavy boots* clomp, stamp, stomp, thump, thud, tramp, lumber, plod, trudge.

clumsy adjective **1** *clumsy and always breaking things* awkward, uncoordinated, ungainly, bumbling, inept, maladroit, unhandy, unskillful, like a bull in a china shop; *inf.* ham-handed, butter-fingered. **2** *a clumsy piece of furniture* unwieldy, hulking, heavy, solid, unmaneuverable. **3** *a clumsy apology* awkward, gauche, graceless, tactless, unpolished, crude.

cluster noun bunch, clump, collection, knot, group; gathering, band, company, body, assemblage, congregation.

cluster verb gather, collect, assemble, congregate, group, flock together.

clutch verb **1** *clutching her purse* grip, grasp, clasp, cling to, hang on to, clench. **2** *clutch at the branch* reach for, snatch at, grab, make a grab for, seize.

clutches plural noun hands, power, control, hold, grip, grasp, claws.

clutter noun mess, muddle, disorder, chaos, disarray, state of confusion/untidiness; heap, litter; *inf.* junk, stuff.

clutter verb litter, make a mess of, mess up, be strewn about, be scattered about.

coach noun instructor, trainer, teacher, tutor, mentor.

coach verb instruct, train, teach, tutor, drill, put one through one's paces.

coagulate verb congeal, gel. *See* CLOT.

coalesce verb unite, combine, merge, amalgamate, integrate, affiliate, blend, fuse.

coalition noun union, alliance, affiliation, league, association, federation, confederacy, bloc.

coarse adjective **1** *coarse material* rough, bristly, scratchy, prickly, hairy, shaggy. **2** *coarse features* heavy, rugged, craggy, unrefined. **3** *coarse flour* crude, unrefined, unprocessed, unpurified. **4** *coarse manners* rude, ill-mannered, uncivil, rough, boorish, loutish, churlish, crass. **5** *coarse humor* bawdy, earthy, blue, ribald, vulgar, smutty, obscene, lewd, pornographic, prurient; *inf.* raunchy.

coast noun coastline, shore, seashore, shoreline, seacoast, beach, strand, seaboard, water's edge.

coast verb freewheel, cruise, taxi, drift, glide, sail.

coat noun **1** *a winter coat* overcoat, topcoat, jacket. **2** *animals' coats* fur, hair, wool; fleece, hide, pelt, skin. **3** *a coat of paint/dust* layer, covering, overlay. *See* COATING.

coating noun covering, layer, film, coat, dusting, blanket, sheet, glaze, skin, veneer, finish, lamination, patina, membrane.

coax verb wheedle, cajole, talk into, beguile, flatter, inveigle, entice, induce, persuade, prevail upon, win over; *inf.* sweet-talk, soft-soap.

cocky adjective arrogant, conceited, egotistical, swellheaded, cocksure, swaggering, brash.

coddle verb pamper, mollycoddle, indulge, spoil, baby, humor.

code noun **1** *a message in code* cipher, secret writing, cryptograph. **2** *code of honor|legal code* laws, rules, regulations, system, canon.

coerce verb compel, force, pressure, drive, impel, constrain, oblige; *inf.* twist one's arm, lean on, put the screws on, strongarm.

coffin noun casket, box, sarcophagus.

cogent adjective convincing, forceful, effective, persuasive, compelling, powerful, strong, potent, authoritative.

cogitate verb think, ponder, contemplate, consider, deliberate, meditate, reflect, mull over, muse, ruminate.

cognate adjective **1** *cognate words* related, kindred, akin, allied, consanguine. **2** *cognate sciences* allied, affiliated, associated,

similar, alike, connected, corresponding, correlated, analogous.

cognizant adjective aware, conscious, knowing, alive to, sensible of, familiar with, acquainted with, conversant with; *inf.* wise to.

coherent adjective logical, rational, reasoned, lucid, articulate, systematic, orderly, organized, comprehensible, intelligible.

cohort noun troop, brigade, legion, squad, squadron, column, group, company, body, band.

coil verb wind, spiral, loop, curl, twist, twine, entwine, snake, wreathe, convolute.

coin noun coins, coinage, change, specie, silver, copper, gold.

coin verb *coin a word* invent, create, make up, devise, conceive, originate, formulate, fabricate.

coincide verb **1** *dates coinciding* be concurrent, occur simultaneously, happen together, coexist, concur, synchronize. **2** *stories coinciding* accord, agree, correspond, concur, match, square, tally, harmonize.

coincidence noun accident, chance, a fluke, luck, fortuity, serendipity.

coincidental adjective **1** *a coincidental meeting* accidental, chance, unplanned, unintentional, casual, lucky, fortuitous, serendipitous; *inf.* fluky. **2** *coincidental concerts* simultaneous, concurrent, synchronous.

cold adjective **1** *a cold day* chilly, freezing, bitter, raw, icy, frigid, wintry, frosty, arctic, windy, glacial, polar; *inf.* nippy. **2** *feeling cold* chilly, chilled, cool, freezing, frozen, frozen stiff, frozen/chilled to the bone/marrow. **3** *a cold person/attitude* unresponsive, unfeeling, unemotional, unmoved, indifferent, apathetic, aloof, distant, reserved, standoffish, unsympathetic, heartless, callous, cold-hearted. **4** *the story is cold* dead, gone, extinguished, finished, defunct.

cold-blooded adjective savage, inhuman, barbaric, heartless, pitiless, merciless.

collaborate verb cooperate, work together/jointly, join forces, join, unite, combine; conspire, fraternize, collude.

collaborator noun coworker, associate, colleague, partner, confederate; conspirator, traitor, quisling, turncoat.

collapse verb **1** *the roof collapsed* fall in, cave in, give way, come apart, fall to pieces, crumple. **2** *the onlooker collapsed* faint, pass out, lose consciousness, keel over, swoon. **3** *the business/talks collapsed* break down, fall through, fail, disintegrate, fold, founder, miscarry; *inf.* flop.

collapse noun **1** *the collapse of the roof* cave-in, giving way. **2** *the collapse of the onlooker* fainting, passing out, swooning, swoon. **3** *the collapse of the talks/firm* breakdown, failure, disintegration, foundering. **4** *suffer a collapse* breakdown, nervous breakdown, attack, seizure, prostration; *inf.* crack-up.

collate verb *collate pages/information* arrange, put in order, order, sort, categorize.

collateral noun security, surety, guarantee, pledge.

colleague noun associate, partner, teammate, workmate, fellow worker, coworker, collaborator, confederate, comrade.

collect verb **1** *collect all sorts of stuff* gather, accumulate, assemble, amass, pile up, stockpile, save, store, hoard, heap up, aggregate. **2** *a crowd collected* congregate, converge, cluster, convene. **3** *collect money* gather, solicit, raise, secure, obtain, acquire. **4** *collect one's wits* get together, muster, summon.

collection noun **1** *a collection of junk* accumulation, pile, stockpile, store, supply, stock, hoard, heap, mass, aggregation. **2** *a collection of people* gathering, assembly, assemblage, crowd, body, group, cluster, company, number, throng, congregation, flock, convocation. **3** *a collection of stamps* set, series, array, assortment. **4** *a collection of essays* anthology, corpus, compilation, miscellanea. **5** *the amount of the collection* subscription, donation, contribution, gift, alms; offering, offertory, tithe.

collective adjective joint, united, combined, shared, common, concerted, cooperative, corporate, collaborative.

college noun **1** *she went to college* school, technical college, community college, university. **2** *the college of thespians* association, fellowship, society, academy.

collide verb **1** *cars colliding* crash, crash head on, smash, bump, bang. **2** *views collide* conflict, be in conflict, clash, differ, disagree, be at variance.

collision noun **1** *a highway collision* crash, accident, smash, pileup, impact. **2** *a collision of views* conflict, clash, difference, disagreement, variance, opposition.

colloquial adjective conversational, informal, everyday, casual, familiar, chatty, idiomatic, vernacular.

collusion noun connivance, complicity, collaboration, intrigue, plotting; *inf.* cahoots.

colony noun **1** *the king visited the colony* settlement, territory, province, dominion, protectorate, dependency, possession, satellite state. **2** *the Chinese colony in San Francisco* community, section, ghetto, district, quarter. **3** *a colony of artists* community, group, association, commune, settlement.

color noun **1** *a red color* hue, shade, tint, tone, tinge. **2** *add color to her cheeks* pinkness, rosiness, redness, ruddiness, blush, flush, glow, bloom. **3** *nations of different colors* skin color, complexion, coloring, pigmentation. **4** *add color to the description* vividness, life, animation, richness. **5** *under the color of friendship* guise, show, semblance, pretense, pretext.

color verb **1** *color the fabric yellow* tint, paint, dye, stain, tinge. **2** *she colored with embarrassment* blush, flush, redden, go red, burn. **3** *attitude colored by childhood experiences* influence, affect, prejudice, distort, slant, taint, pervert, warp. **4** *color the facts* exaggerate, overstate, embroider, varnish, misrepresent, falsify.

colorful adjective **1** bright-colored, deep-colored, bright, brilliant, intense, vivid, rich, vibrant, multicolored, many-colored, variegated, psychedelic; *inf.* jazzy. **2** *a colorful description* vivid, graphic, interesting, lively.

colorless adjective **1** *colorless fabric* uncolored, achromatic, white, bleached, faded. **2** *colorless city people* pale, wan, anemic, washed-out, ashen, sickly. **3** *colorless accounts* uninteresting, dull, lifeless, dreary, lackluster, insipid, vapid.

colors plural noun **1** *raised the colors* flag, standard, banner, ensign. **2** *a club's colors* badge, uniform, insignia, ribbon, rosette. **3** *saw his true colors* nature, character, identity, aspect.

colossal adjective huge, gigantic, immense, enormous, massive, vast, gargantuan, mammoth, prodigious, mountainous, elephantine, monumental.

column noun **1** *marble columns* pillar, support, upright, post, shaft; pilaster, obelisk. **2** *a column of people* line, file, row, rank, string, procession, train.

coma noun unconsciousness, insensibility, stupor, oblivion, blackout.

comatose adjective **1** *comatose after the accident* in a coma, unconscious, insensible, out cold, blacked-out. **2** *feeling comatose after the night shift* sluggish, lethargic, somnolent, torpid.

comb verb **1** *comb one's hair* groom, untangle, curry, arrange. **2** *comb the area for clues* search, scour, ransack, go over with a fine-tooth comb.

combat noun battle, fight, conflict, clash, skirmish, single combat, hand-to-hand combat; fighting, hostilities.

combat verb fight, do battle, wage war, clash, take up arms (against), grapple, oppose, strive against, make a stand against, resist, withstand, defy.

combatant noun fighter, soldier, serviceman, servicewoman, warrior, battler; adversary, antagonist, contender, opponent, enemy, foe, rival.

combative adjective pugnacious, belligerent, aggressive, militant, bellicose, warlike, quarrelsome, argumentative, contentious.

combination noun **1** *in combination with others* cooperation, association, union, alliance, partnership, coalition, league, consortium, syndication, federation. **2** *a combination of guilt and grief* mixture, mix, blend, amalgam, amalgamation, compound, alloy, composite.

combine verb **1** *combine to finish their work* join forces, unite, team up, cooperate, associate, ally, pool resources. **2** *combine their efforts* join, put together, unite, pool, merge, integrate, fuse, marry, unify. **3** *combine ingredients* mix, blend, admix, amalgamate, bind, bond, compound, alloy, homogenize.

combustible adjective inflammable, flammable, incendiary, explosive, conflagratory.

combustion noun burning, firing, fire, kindling, igniting, ignition.

come verb **1** *they came last night* arrive, appear, put in an appearance, turn up, enter, materialize; *inf.* show up, blow in. **2** *Easter came in March* occur, fall, take place, happen, transpire, come about, come to pass. **3** *the dress comes to her ankles* reach, extend, stretch. **4** *the car comes in red* be available, be made, be produced, be offered. **come about** arise, come to pass, transpire, result, befall. **come across 1** *come across an old friend* meet, encounter, run into, run across, chance upon, happen upon, find, discover, unearth; *inf.* bump into. **2** *his message came across* be communicated, be understood, be clear, be perceived. **come across with** *come across with the money* hand over, deliver, produce, pay up; *inf.* come up with, fork over, cough up. **come along 1** *patients coming along well* progress, make progress, develop, improve, show improvement, make headway, get better, pick up. **2** *come along!* hurry, hurry up, make haste, speed up; *inf.* get a move on, move it, step on it, make it snappy. **come apart** break up, fall to pieces, disintegrate, come unstuck, crumble, separate, split, tear. **come around 1** *coming around annually* occur, take place, happen. **2** *come around after fainting* come to, regain consciousness, revive, wake up, recover. **3** *come around in the evening* come round, visit, call; *inf.*

drop in, drop by, stop by, pop in. **come around to** *come around to one's way of thinking* be converted to, be persuaded by, give way to, yield to. **come by** get, obtain, acquire, procure, get possession of, get/lay hold of, get one's hands on, secure, win. **come clean** own up, confess. **come down** *the report came down against punishment* decide, reach a decision, recommend, choose, opt. **come down on** rebuke, reprimand, criticize, berate. **come down to** amount to, boil down to, end up as, result in. **come down with** fall ill with, become sick with, catch, contract, fall victim to, be stricken with. **come forward** volunteer, offer one's services. **come into** *come into money* inherit, be left, be willed, acquire, obtain. **come off** *the attempt did not come off* succeed, be successful, be accomplished, work out, transpire, take place. **come out 1** *the newspaper comes out daily* be published, appear. **2** *the full story came out* become known, become common knowledge, be revealed, be disclosed, be released. **3** *come out all right* end, finish, conclude, terminate. **come out with 1** *coming out with a new movie* release, bring out, circulate, publish. **2** *come out with a surprise confession* reveal, let out, blurt out. **come through** *come through the war* get through, survive, outlast, outlive. **come to 1** *the bill comes to $5* total, add up to, amount to. **2** *come to after fainting* regain consciousness, awaken. *See* COME AROUND 2. **come up** *something came up* arise, crop up, turn up, spring up. **come up to 1** *she came up to his shoulder* come to, reach, extend to. **2** *come up to standards* reach, measure up to, match up to, compare with, bear comparison with, hold a candle to. **come up with** *come up with a plan* suggest, propose, submit, put forward, present, offer.

comeback noun **1** *the actor making a comeback* return, rally, resurgence, recovery, revival, rebound. **2** *making witty comebacks* retort, reply, rejoinder, response, retaliation, riposte.

comedian noun **1** *television comedian* comic, funny man, funny woman, comedienne, humorist. **2** *he's a real comedian* joker, wit, wag, jester, clown; *inf.* card, laugh.

comedown noun loss of status, loss of face, demotion, downgrading, degradation, humiliation, deflation, decline, reversal, anticlimax.

comedy noun **1** *theaters staging both comedy and tragedy* farce, burlesque, pantomime, slapstick, satire, vaudeville, comic opera; *inf.* sitcom. **2** *the comedy of the situation* humor, funniness, hilarity, levity, facetiousness.

comely adjective **1** *a comely young woman* attractive, good-looking, pretty, beautiful, handsome, lovely, fair, winsome, pleasing. **2** *not comely behavior* fit, fitting, suitable, proper, seemly, decent, decorous.

come-on noun inducement, lure, enticement, allurement, temptation.

comeuppance noun just deserts, deserts, retribution, punishment, recompense, requital.

comfort noun **1** *live in comfort* contentment, well-being, coziness, plenty, sufficiency, luxury, opulence. **2** *bring comfort to the bereaved* consolation, solace, condolence, sympathy, commiseration, help, support, succor, relief.

comfort verb **1** *comfort the bereaved* console, solace, give sympathy to, succor, reassure, soothe, assuage, cheer. **2** *comforted by the fire* ease, soothe, refresh, revive, hearten, cheer.

comfortable adjective **1** *a comfortable room* homey, cozy, snug. **2** *comfortable clothes/shoes* well-fitting, loose-fitting, roomy. **3** *a comfortable lifestyle* pleasant, adequate, free from hardship, well-off, well-to-do, affluent, opulent. **4** *feeling comfortable* at ease, relaxed, serene, tranquil, contented, cozy.

comforting adjective consoling, soothing, reassuring, encouraging.

comic adjective funny, humorous, amusing, entertaining, diverting, droll, jocular, joking, facetious, comical, witty, farcical, hilarious, zany, sidesplitting, priceless, waggish, whimsical.

comic noun **1** *worked as a comic* stand-up comic, humorist. *See* COMEDIAN 1. **2** *he's a real comic* joker, wag. *See* COMEDIAN 2. **comics** comic strips, comic books; *inf.* funnies.

comical adjective **1** *a comical performance* funny, amusing. *See* COMIC adjective. **2** *a comical hat* absurd, ridiculous, silly, laughable, ludicrous.

command verb **1** *command you to go* order, give orders to, direct, charge, instruct, bid, enjoin, adjure, summon, prescribe, require. **2** *he commands the unit* have charge of, control, rule, govern, direct, preside over, head, lead, manage, supervise.

command noun **1** *follow the commands* order, decree, dictate, edict, instruction, directive, direction, bidding, injunction, behest, mandate, fiat, precept, commandment. **2** *under the command of the French* charge, control, authority, power, government, direction, management, administration, supervision, dominion, sway, domination.

commandeer verb seize, take possession of, requisition, expropriate, appropriate, hijack.

commander noun leader, head, director, chief, boss; officer, captain; commander in chief, commanding officer; *inf.* top dog, kingpin, big cheese.

commanding adjective controlling, directing, dominating, dominant, superior, advantageous; authoritative, autocratic, masterful, assertive, peremptory, imposing, impressive, august.

commemorate verb celebrate, pay tribute to, remember, honor, salute, memorialize.

commemorative adjective memorial, remembering, in memory of, in remembrance of.

commence verb **1** *ready to commence* begin, start, go ahead, be off, embark, set sail, set the ball rolling, get something off the ground; *inf.* get the show on the road. **2** *commence the proceedings* open, enter/embark upon, inaugurate, initiate, originate.

commend verb **1** *commend his work* praise, applaud, speak highly of, approve, acclaim, extol, laud, eulogize. **2** *commend action* recommend, approve, endorse, advocate. **3** *commend her to your care* entrust, trust, deliver, commit, hand over, give, consign, assign.

commendable adjective praiseworthy, admirable, laudable, estimable, worthy, deserving.

commendation noun praise, applause, acclaim, acclamation, approval, approbation, credit, eulogies, laudation, encomium, panegyric.

commensurate adjective **1** *a commensurate amount of water to wine* equivalent, equal, corresponding, comparable, proportionate. **2** *a salary commensurate with experience* in accordance with, proportionate to, appropriate to, consistent with.

comment verb **1** *he commented unfavorably on her actions* remark, speak, express an opinion on. **2** *"Good," he commented* say, remark, state, observe, interpose. **3** *comment on the text* annotate, explain, interpret, elucidate, clarify, shed light on.

comment noun remark, opinion, observation, view, statement, criticism; annotation, note, footnote, gloss, marginalia, interpretation, elucidation.

commentary noun account, review, analysis, interpretation, exegesis, critique.

commentator noun reporter, broadcaster, correspondent; interpreter, critic.

commerce noun **1** *work in commerce* business, trade, buying and selling, merchandising, dealing, finance, marketing,

commercial · compact

traffic. **2** *everyday (social) commerce* social relations, socializing, communication, dealings.

commercial adjective **1** *commercial training* business, trade, marketing, merchandising, sales, mercantile. **2** *a commercial proposition* profitable, profit-making, profit-oriented, money-oriented, mercantile, materialistic, mercenary.

commission noun **1** *a commission on the sale* percentage, brokerage, share, fee, compensation; *inf.* cut. **2** *the commission of designing the building* task, employment, duty, charge, mission, responsibility. **3** *a commission of inquiry* committee, board, council, advisory body, delegation. **4** *the commission of a crime* execution, perpetration, performance.

commission verb **1** *commission an artist* employ, engage, contract, appoint, book, authorize. **2** *commission a portrait* order, put in an order for, place an order for, contract for, pay for, authorize.

commit verb **1** *commit a crime* perform, carry out, execute, enact, perpetrate, effect, do. **2** *commit to one's care* entrust, trust, deliver, hand over, give, consign, assign. **3** *commit oneself to take part* pledge, promise, engage, bind, covenant, obligate, dedicate. **4** *commit the thief/patient* imprison, jail, confine, lock up, put into custody, put away; hospitalize, institutionalize, confine.

commitment noun **1** *too many commitments* undertaking, obligation, responsibility, duty, liability, tie, task, engagement. **2** *have no commitment to the job* dedication, devotion, loyalty, allegiance, adherence. **3** *make a commitment* pledge, promise, vow, assurance, covenant.

commodity noun thing, item, article, product, article of merchandise.

common adjective **1** *the common people* ordinary, average, normal, typical, unexceptional, run-of-the-mill, plain, simple. **2** *a common style* unexceptional, undistinguished, workaday, mediocre, pedestrian, humdrum. **3** *a common occurrence* usual, ordinary, everyday, frequent, customary, habitual, routine, standard, repeated, commonplace. **4** *a common response* familiar, routine, stock, standard, conventional, traditional. **5** *a common belief* widespread, general, universal, popular, accepted, prevalent, prevailing. **6** *for the common good* communal, collective, community, public, popular. **7** *a common young woman* low, vulgar, coarse, uncouth, inferior.

commonplace adjective **1** *a commonplace novel/youngster* ordinary, unexceptional. *See* COMMON 2. **2** *air travel is now commonplace | commonplace events* ordinary, routine. *See* COMMON 3.

common sense noun good sense, sense, practicality, judgment, levelheadedness, prudence, discernment, astuteness, shrewdness, judiciousness, wisdom; *inf.* horse sense.

commotion noun disturbance, racket, uproar, rumpus, tumult, clamor, riot, hubbub, hullabaloo, brouhaha, furor, disorder, confusion, upheaval, agitation, excitement, fuss, disquiet, to-do.

communal adjective common, collective, shared, joint, general, public, community.

commune verb communicate, speak, have a tête-à-tête, confer, confide; feel in close touch, feel at one, empathize, identify.

communicable adjective infectious, contagious, catching, transmittable, transferable.

communicate verb **1** *communicate information* transmit, pass on, transfer, impart, convey, relay, spread, disseminate, make known, publish, broadcast, announce, report, divulge, disclose. **2** *not to communicate with him* be in touch, be in contact, have dealings, interface. **3** *you must be able to communicate* get one's ideas/message across, be articulate, be fluent, be eloquent.

communication noun **1** *communication is difficult* information transmission/transfer, dissemination, contact, getting in touch, radio/telephone link, connection, interface. **2** *received the communication* message, letter, report, statement, dispatch.

communicative adjective expansive, forthcoming, talkative, loquacious, voluble, chatty.

communion noun rapport, empathy, sympathy, accord, affinity, fellowship, togetherness, harmony, closeness, agreement, sharing, concord.

communism noun collectivism, Sovietism, Bolshevism, Marxism, Leninism.

community noun **1** *move to a new community* locality, district, neighborhood. **2** *the community condemned her* residents, inhabitants; population, populace. **3** *work for the community* society, public, general public, body politic, nation, state. **4** *the Jewish community in New York* group, section, body, company, set, ghetto. **5** *community of interests* similarity, likeness, agreement, affinity.

commute verb **1** *commute from the suburbs* travel to and from, travel back and forth, shuttle. **2** *commute a sentence/penalty* lessen, reduce, shorten, curtail, mitigate, modify. **3** *commute an annuity to a lump sum* exchange, change, interchange, substitute, trade, barter, switch.

compact adjective **1** *a compact parcel* dense, packed close, pressed together, close, firm, solid, compressed, condensed. **2** *a compact style* concise, succinct, terse, brief, condensed, pithy, to the point, epigrammatic, compendious.

compact verb pack down, press down, compress, press together, condense, tamp.

compact noun contract, agreement, covenant, pact, indenture, bond, treaty, alliance, bargain, deal.

companion noun **1** *the girl and her companions* partner, escort, consort, friend, crony, comrade, colleague, associate, ally, confederate; *inf.* buddy, pal. **2** *the princess and her companion* attendant, aide, chaperon, duenna, squire. **3** *the companion of this bookend* fellow, mate, twin, match, counterpart, complement. **4** *the Reader's Companion* guide, handbook, manual.

companionship noun friendship, fellowship, company, society, togetherness, social intercourse, comradeship, camaraderie, intimacy, rapport.

company noun **1** *enjoy their company* friendship, fellowship. *See* COMPANIONSHIP. **2** *address the company* assembly, assemblage, gathering, meeting, audience, group, crowd, throng, congregation, convention. **3** *a company of actors* group, band, party, body, association, society, fellowship, troupe, collection, circle, league, crew, guild. **4** *a retail company* business, firm, concern, corporation, house, establishment, conglomerate; *inf.* outfit. **5** *expecting company* guest(s), visitor(s), caller(s).

comparable adjective equivalent, commensurable, corresponding, proportional, proportionate, similar, like, parallel, analogous, related. **comparable to** as good as, equal to, on a par with, in the same class/league as/with.

compare verb **1** *compare the two styles* contrast, juxtapose, weigh/balance/measure the differences between, collate, differentiate. **2** *the island has been compared to heaven* liken, equate, analogize. **compare with** *his work does not compare with hers* bear comparison to, be comparable to, be on a par with, be in the same class with, compete with, approach, come up to, hold a candle to.

comparison noun **1** *make a comparison* contrast, juxtaposition, collation, differentiation. **2** *no comparison between their works* resemblance, likeness, similarity, correlation.

compartment noun **1** *luggage compartment* section, part, partition, bay, chamber, niche. **2** *compartments of one's life* part, section, division, department, area.

compassion noun tender-heartedness, pity, softheartedness, tenderness,

gentleness, mercy, leniency, understanding, sympathy, concern, humanity, kindness.

compassionate adjective softhearted, tender, gentle, merciful, lenient, understanding, sympathetic, pitying, humanitarian, humane, kindly, kindhearted.

compatible adjective **1** *compatible couples* well-suited, suited, like-minded, of the same mind, in agreement, in tune, in harmony. **2** *views not compatible with actions* consistent, in keeping, reconcilable, consonant, congruous, congruent.

compel verb **1** *compel them to leave* force, make, coerce, drive, pressure, dragoon, constrain, impel, oblige, necessitate, urge; *inf.* bulldoze, railroad, twist one's arm, strong-arm, put the screws on. **2** *compel obedience* force, enforce, exact, insist upon, necessitate, extort.

compelling adjective **1** *a compelling story* fascinating, gripping, enthralling, irresistible, hypnotic, mesmeric. **2** *compelling reasons* cogent, convincing, forceful, powerful, weighty, telling, conclusive, irrefutable.

compensate verb **1** *compensate for his evil deed* make amends, make restitution, make reparation, make up for, atone, expiate. **2** *compensate her for her loss* recompense, repay, reimburse, requite, indemnify. **compensate for** counterbalance, counterpoise, counteract, balance, cancel out, neutralize, nullify.

compensation noun **1** *receive compensation for her loss* recompense, repayment, reimbursement, requital, indemnification, indemnity, damages. **2** *make compensation for his deed* amends, restitution, redress, atonement, expiation.

compete verb contend, vie, strive, struggle, fight, pit oneself (against); *inf.* throw one's hat in the ring, be in the running.

competence noun capability, ability, capacity, proficiency, adeptness, expertise, skill.

competent adjective capable, able, proficient, qualified, efficient, adept, accomplished, skillful; adequate, appropriate, suitable.

competition noun **1** *a chess competition* contest, match, game, tournament, event, meet, quiz. **2** *the competition between opponents* rivalry, vying, contest, opposition, struggle, contention, strife. **3** *the competition is poor* field, opposition; challengers, opponents, rivals.

competitive adjective ambitious, combative, aggressive, dog-eat-dog, cutthroat.

competitor noun rival, opponent, adversary, antagonist; contestant, contender, challenger, participant.

compilation noun collection, anthology, album, corpus, ana.

compile verb gather, collect, accumulate, amass, assemble, put together, collate, marshal.

complacent adjective smug, self-satisfied, pleased with oneself, satisfied, contented, self-contented, pleased, placid.

complain verb 1 *complain about the service* lodge a complaint, criticize, find fault, carp, make a fuss. 2 *always complaining* grumble, grouse, gripe, moan, grouch, whine; *inf.* bellyache, beef, bitch.

complaint noun 1 *manager attending to complaints* criticism, grievance, charge, accusation, protest, remonstrance. 2 *a painful complaint* illness, disease, ailment, disorder, sickness, affliction, malady.

complement noun 1 *the perfect complement to the food* companion, addition, supplement, accessory, final/finishing touch. 2 *the school's full complement* amount, allowance, total, capacity, quota.

complementary adjective complemental, completing, finishing, perfecting, culminative, consummative.

complete adjective 1 *the complete collection* entire, whole, full, total, intact, unbroken, undivided, uncut, unabridged, plenary. 2 *the task is complete* finished, ended, concluded, accomplished, finalized. 3 *a complete fool* absolute, out-and-out, thoroughgoing, thorough, utter, total, perfect, consummate, unqualified, dyed-in-the-wool.

complete verb 1 *complete the task* finish, end, conclude, finalize, realize, accomplish, achieve, fulfill, execute, effect, discharge, settle, clinch, do; *inf.* wrap up, polish off. 2 *complete the outfit* finish off, round off, perfect, crown, cap, add the finishing touch to.

completely adverb totally, utterly, absolutely, thoroughly, quite, wholly, altogether.

completion noun finish, ending, conclusion, close, finalization, realization, accomplishment, achievement, fulfillment, execution, consummation.

complex adjective 1 *a complex subject* complicated, difficult, involved, intricate, convoluted, knotty, perplexing. 2 *a complex structure* composite, compound, compounded, multiple, manifold, multiplex, heterogeneous.

complex noun 1 *building complex | complex of regulations* structure, scheme, composite, conglomerate, aggregation, network, system. 2 *a complex about her nose* obsession, phobia, fixation, preoccupation, idée fixe.

complexion noun 1 *ruddy complexion* skin color, skin tone, coloring, pigmentation. 2 *put a new complexion on it* aspect, appearance, guise, look, angle. 3 *his brother is of a different complexion* character, nature, disposition, cast, stamp.

complexity noun complication, difficulty, intricacy, convolution.

compliance noun yielding, submissiveness, deference, passivity, subservience, servility. **compliance with** obedience to, observance of, abiding by, conforming to.

complicate verb make difficult, make involved/intricate, confuse, muddle, jumble, snarl up, entangle.

complicated adjective difficult, entangled, Byzantine. *See* COMPLEX adjective 1.

complication noun 1 *meet complications* difficulty, problem, drawback, snag, obstacle. 2 *a great deal of complication* difficulty, intricacy, complexity, confusion.

complicity noun collusion, conspiracy, collaboration, connivance, abetment.

compliment noun **compliments** praise, tribute, homage, admiration, flattery, commendation, laudation, eulogy.

compliment verb congratulate, felicitate, speak highly of, praise, sing the praises of, pay tribute/homage to, salute, admire, flatter, commend, honor, acclaim, laud, eulogize.

complimentary adjective 1 *complimentary remarks* congratulatory, admiring, appreciative, approving, flattering, commendatory, laudatory. 2 *complimentary tickets* free, gratis; *inf.* on the house.

comply verb **comply with** obey, observe, abide by, adhere to, conform to, acquiesce to, assent to, consent to, follow, respect, yield, submit.

component noun part, piece, section, constituent, element, unit, module.

compose verb 1 *compose a poem* write, make up, create, think up, devise, concoct, invent, compile, contrive, formulate, fashion, produce. 2 *compose one's dress/plans* put together, arrange, put in order, align, organize, assemble, collate, systematize. 3 *peoples composing a nation* make up, form, constitute, comprise. 4 *compose oneself* calm, calm down, quiet, collect, control, soothe.

composed adjective calm, cool, collected, serene, tranquil, relaxed, poised, at ease, unruffled, untroubled, confident, self-possessed; *inf.* together.

composite adjective compound, complex, combined, blended, mixed.

composite noun compound, amalgam, blend, mixture, complex, combination, fusion, conglomerate, synthesis.

composition noun **1** *the composition of the soil* structure, constitution, makeup, conformation, configuration, organization, arrangement, layout, character. **2** *the composition of a poem* writing, creation, concoction, invention, compilation. **3** *a brilliant composition* work of art, creation, literary/musical/artistic work. **4** *students writing a composition* essay, theme. **5** *admire the painting's composition* arrangement, proportions, harmony, balance, symmetry.

composure noun aplomb, poise, self-possession, presence of mind, sang-froid, equanimity, equilibrium, self-control, calm, calmness, coolness, serenity, tranquility.

compound noun alloy, conglomerate, synthesis, medley, hybrid. *See* COMPOSITE noun.

compound verb **1** *compound the two substances* mix, blend, combine, put together, amalgamate, unite, coalesce, alloy, fuse, mingle, intermingle, synthesize. **2** *compound the problem* worsen, add to, augment, exacerbate, magnify, aggravate, intensify, heighten.

comprehend verb understand, grasp, take in, assimilate, fathom, perceive, discern, apprehend, conceive, imagine.

comprehensible adjective intelligible, understandable, graspable, fathomable, discernible.

comprehension noun understanding, grasp, perception, ken, discernment, conception.

comprehensive adjective inclusive, all-inclusive, all-embracing, complete, full, encyclopedic, exhaustive, thorough, extensive, broad, widespread, far-reaching, blanket.

compress verb **1** *compress the pile of sand* squeeze together, squash, crush, cram, constrict. *See* COMPACT verb. **2** *compress the text* abbreviate, shorten, abridge, contract, reduce.

comprise verb consist of, contain, include, be composed of, take in, embrace, encompass.

compromise verb **1** *compromise on the wording* come to terms, come to an understanding, make a deal, make concessions, find a happy medium, find the middle ground, strike a balance, meet halfway. **2** *compromise his reputation/chances* endanger, jeopardize, imperil, prejudice, damage, injure, weaken.

compromise noun understanding, deal, happy medium, middle course, balance, trade-off.

compulsion noun **1** *under no compulsion to go* obligation, force, duress, constraint, coercion, pressure. **2** *feel a compulsion to travel* urge, need, desire, preoccupation, obsession.

compulsive adjective **1** *compulsive viewing* fascinating, gripping. *See* COMPELLING 1. **2** *a compulsive desire to wash/eat/drink* obsessive, uncontrollable, irresistible, driving, overwhelming, addictive, obsessional, out of control, ungovernable.

compulsory adjective obligatory, mandatory, required, forced, necessary, de rigueur.

compunction noun remorse, regret, guilt, contrition, penitence, repentance; scruples.

compute verb calculate, reckon, count, add up, total, figure out, enumerate, sum, tally.

comrade noun companion, friend, colleague, partner, associate, coworker, fellow worker, mate, teammate, ally, confederate, compatriot; *inf.* pal, buddy.

con verb swindle, deceive, cheat, hoodwink, mislead, delude, bamboozle.

con noun con man, confidence man, swindler, deceiver, cheater.

concave adjective curved in, hollowed out, depressed, sunken, indented.

conceal verb hide, cover, keep out of sight, keep hidden, screen, obscure, disguise, camouflage, mask; keep secret, keep dark, hush up, cover up, dissemble; *inf.* keep the lid on.

concede verb **1** *concede defeat* acknowledge, admit, accept, own, allow, grant. **2** *concede territory* give up, yield, surrender, relinquish, cede, hand over.

conceit noun **1** *the winner full of conceit* pride, arrogance, vanity, self-admiration, self-love, self-importance, self-adulation, narcissism, egotism, vainglory. **2** *exchanging clever conceits* witticism, quip, bon mot. **3** *a mind occupied with conceits* fancy, notion, whim; fantasy, imagination, whimsy, vagary.

conceited adjective proud, arrogant, vain, self-important, cocky, haughty, supercilious, narcissistic, egotistical, puffed up, self-satisfied, complacent, boastful, vainglorious; *inf.* bigheaded, swellheaded, stuck-up.

conceivable adjective credible, believable, imaginable, thinkable, possible, comprehensible.

conceive verb **1** *conceive a plan* think up, draw up, form, formulate, produce, develop, devise, contrive, conjure up. **2** *cannot conceive that/how he lost* imagine, think, believe, realize, understand, comprehend, perceive, grasp.

concentrate verb **1** *concentrate one's efforts on* focus, center, converge, centralize,

concentrated · concurrent

consolidate, bring to bear, congregate, cluster, amass. **2** *concentrate the liquid* condense, boil down, reduce, compress, distill. **concentrate on** be absorbed in, focus attention on, be engrossed in.

concentrated adjective intensive, intense, consolidated, rigorous, vigorous; *inf.* all-out.

concentration noun close attention, absorption, application, engrossment, single-mindedness, heed.

concept noun idea, notion, abstraction, conceptualization, conception, hypothesis, theory.

conception noun **1** *when conception took place* fertilization, impregnation, fecundation. **2** *at the conception of the project* inception, beginning, origin, birth, initiation, formation, launching, outset. **3** *a brilliant conception* plan, design, invention, creation, project, scheme, proposal. **4** *no conception of how to behave* idea, notion, appreciation, understanding, clue, inkling.

concern verb **1** *affairs that concern you* be the business of, affect, be relevant to, involve, apply to, pertain to, have a bearing on, touch. **2** *a report concerning cancer* be about, deal with, relate to. **3** *you should not concern yourself (in/with)* interest/involve oneself (in), take/have a hand (in), busy oneself (with), devote one's time (to), be busy (with). **4** *their behavior concerned us* worry, disturb, trouble, bother, perturb, distress.

concern noun **1** *none of your concern* business, affair, interest, involvement, responsibility, charge, duty, job, task, department, field. **2** *news of concern to all* interest, importance, relevance, bearing, applicability. **3** *parents full of concern* worry, anxiety, disquiet, distress, apprehension. **4** *parents demonstrating their concern* care, solicitude, attentiveness, attention, consideration, regard. **5** *start a publishing concern* business, firm. *See* COMPANY 4.

concerned adjective **1** *concerned parties* interested, involved, implicated. **2** *concerned citizens* caring, responsible, solicitous; worried, disturbed, anxious, troubled, apprehensive.

concerning preposition about, on the subject of, relating to, regarding, with reference to, with respect to, in the matter of, re.

concert noun **in concert** *act in concert* together, jointly, in combination, cooperatively, in unison.

concerted adjective combined, cooperative, joint, coordinated, united, collaborative, synchronized.

concession noun **1** *the concession of defeat* acknowledgment, admission, acceptance, recognition. **2** *the concession of territory* yielding, surrender, relinquishment, ceding, giving up. **3** *as a concession to their youth* allowance, adjustment, modification, indulgence, exception. **4** *price concessions* reduction, cut, discount, decrease. **5** *grant the concession* franchise, license, permit, authorization.

conciliate verb placate, appease, pacify, propitiate, mollify, assuage, calm down, soothe, humor, reconcile.

conciliatory adjective appeasing, pacifying, propitiative, mollifying, assuaging, reconciliatory, peacemaking.

concise adjective succinct, short, crisp, summary, synoptic. *See* COMPACT adjective 2.

conclude verb **1** *we concluded the meeting* end, finish, close, halt, cease, terminate, discontinue; *inf.* wind up. **2** *conclude an agreement* negotiate, come to terms on, bring about, pull off, work out, accomplish, effect, establish, engineer. **3** *conclude that he had won* deduce, infer, decide, gather, reckon, judge, assume, surmise.

conclusion noun **1** *the conclusion of the meeting* end, discontinuance. *See* CLOSE noun. **2** *a predictable conclusion* outcome, result, upshot, issue, culmination, consequence. **3** *reach the conclusion that he was guilty* deduction, inference, decision, opinion, judgment, verdict, conviction. **in conclusion** in closing, to sum up, finally, lastly.

conclusive adjective decisive, clinching, definitive, final, categorical, incontestable, convincing.

concoct verb **1** *concoct a meal/stew* prepare, put together, cook, mix, blend, brew; *inf.* rustle up. **2** *concoct an excuse* devise, invent, make up, think up, dream up, fabricate, hatch; *inf.* cook up.

concoction noun **1** *a tasty concoction* preparation, mixture, blend, combination, brew, creation. **2** *don't believe that concoction* invention, fabrication, plot, scheme.

concrete adjective **1** *concrete evidence* actual, real, factual, definite, genuine, substantial, material, tangible, specific. **2** *a concrete substance* solid, solidified, firm, compact, dense, compressed, coalesced, calcified.

concur verb **1** *they concur on/over the verdict* agree, be in accord/harmony, be of the same mind, be in concord. **2** *the two events concurred* coincide, be simultaneous, coexist, synchronize. **3** *they concurred in the attempt* cooperate, combine, unite, collaborate, join forces.

concurrent adjective **1** *concurrent sentences* simultaneous, parallel, coincident, contemporaneous, synchronous, side-by-side. **2** *concurrent lines* converging, convergent, meeting, intersecting. **3** *concurrent attitudes* agreeing, in accord, in harmony, harmonious, assenting, of the same mind, like-minded, compatible. **4** *concurrent action* cooperative, combined, united, joint, collaborative.

condemn verb **1** *condemn all violence* censure, denounce, deprecate, disapprove of, criticize, berate, upbraid, reprove, reproach, blame. **2** *condemn him to death/poverty* sentence, pass sentence on, convict; doom, damn, force, compel, coerce, impel.

condensation noun **1** *the condensation of the sauce* concentration, reduction. **2** *the condensation of steam* liquefaction, liquidization, deliquescence, precipitation, distillation. **3** *the condensation of the report* abridgment, summarization, summary, précis, digest, abstract, synopsis.

condense verb **1** *condense the sauce by boiling* concentrate, thicken, boil down, reduce, solidify, coagulate. **2** *steam condensing on the mirror* liquefy, liquidize, deliquesce, precipitate. **3** *condense the report* shorten, abridge, abbreviate, cut, compress, contract, compact, encapsulate.

condescend verb **1** *condescend to speak to him* lower oneself, deign, stoop, descend, vouchsafe; *inf.* come down from one's high horse. **2** *condescend to younger people* patronize, talk down to, look down one's nose at.

condescending adjective patronizing, disdainful, supercilious, superior, snobbish, lofty, lordly; *inf.* snooty, snotty, uppity.

condition noun **1** *the human condition* state, circumstance, situation. **2** *in a miserable condition* position, plight, predicament, quandary. **3** *athletes in good/poor condition* shape, form, order, fitness, health, fettle, kilter, trim, working order. **4** *a condition of the job* qualification, requirement, necessity, essential, demand, prerequisite, stipulation. **5** *the conditions of the agreement* restriction, rule, provision, proviso, contingency, stipulation. **6** *a heart condition* disease, disorder, illness, complaint, problem, ailment.

condition verb **1** *lotions conditioning the skin/leather* improve, tone up, prepare, make ready. **2** *cats conditioned to live in apartments* accustom, adapt, habituate, inure. **3** *childhood experiences conditioning later responses* influence, affect, govern, determine.

conditional adjective *a conditional offer* qualified, with reservations, restrictive, provisional, provisory, stipulatory.

conditions plural noun circumstances, surroundings, environment, situation.

condolence noun commiseration, sympathy, compassion, pity, solace, comfort.

condone verb overlook, disregard, let pass, turn a blind eye to, wink at, excuse, pardon, forgive.

conducive adjective contributing, helpful, instrumental, favorable.

conduct noun **1** *guilty of evil conduct* behavior, comportment, bearing, deportment; actions, ways, habits, practices, manners. **2** *the conduct of the war* direction, running, management, administration, control, guidance, supervision.

conduct verb **1** *conduct oneself well/badly* behave, act, comport, deport, acquit. **2** *conduct the proceedings* direct, run, be in charge of, manage, administer, handle, control, supervise, lead, preside over. **3** *conduct us to our seats* show, guide, lead, escort, accompany.

conduit noun duct, pipe, tube, channel, canal, trough, passageway.

confederacy noun alliance, federation, partnership, union, collaboration, association, league, coalition.

confederate noun accomplice, abettor, accessory, ally, associate, collaborator, colleague, partner.

confer verb **1** *confer a title/favor* bestow, present, grant, award, give, give out, hand out, accord. **2** *confer with her colleagues* discuss, talk, consult, converse.

conference noun meeting, congress, convention, seminar, symposium, colloquium, forum, convocation.

confess verb **1** *confess her guilt* admit, acknowledge, make a clean breast of, own up to, declare, make known, disclose, reveal, divulge, blurt out, expose. **2** *I must confess I don't know* admit, concede, grant, allow, own.

confidant, confidante noun friend, crony, intimate, familiar, alter ego; *inf.* chum, pal, mate, bosom buddy.

confide verb **1** *confide a secret to | confide in a friend* disclose, reveal, divulge, impart, tell, open one's heart to, unburden oneself to, tell one's all to. **2** *confide a task* entrust, consign, hand over, commit, commend, assign.

confidence noun **1** *candidates full of confidence* self-confidence, self-assurance, assurance, self-reliance, self-possession, aplomb, poise. **2** *have no confidence in them* trust, reliance, faith, dependence, belief, credence. **3** *exchange confidences* secret, confidentiality, intimacy.

confidential adjective **1** *confidential information* secret, private, classified, off-the-record, restricted, personal, intimate, privy; *inf.* hush-hush. **2** *a confidential friend* close, bosom, intimate, trusted, trustworthy, reliable, dependable.

confidentially adverb in confidence, in secret, in private, privately, behind closed doors, sub rosa.

confine verb 1 *birds confined in a cage* enclose, shut up, shut, cage, keep, coop up, pen, box up, lock up, imprison, incarcerate, impound. 2 *remarks confined to the discussion* restrict, limit.

confinement noun custody, imprisonment, detention, captivity, internment, incarceration.

confirm verb 1 *evidence confirms her statement* bear out, verify, corroborate, prove, endorse, validate, authenticate, substantiate, give credence to. 2 *confirm that he would appear* reassert, give assurance, affirm, pledge, promise, guarantee. 3 *confirm his appointment* ratify, endorse, approve, sanction, underwrite. 4 *confirm my doubts* strengthen, reinforce, fortify.

confirmation noun 1 *confirmation of her statement/booking* verification, corroboration, proof, evidence, endorsement, validation, authentication. 2 *confirmation of the appointment* ratification, endorsement, approval, sanction, authorization.

confiscate verb seize, impound, take possession of, appropriate, commandeer, expropriate, sequester, arrogate.

conflict noun 1 *the military conflict* battle, fight, war, warfare, clash, engagement, encounter, hostilities, contest, combat, collision, struggle, strife, tussle, scuffle; *inf.* set-to. 2 *bitter conflict between the families* dissension, hostility, feud, discord, antagonism, antipathy, ill will, bad blood, contention. 3 *the conflict between love and duty* clash, variance, opposition, friction.

conflict verb clash, differ, disagree, be at variance, be in opposition, be at odds, be incompatible, collide.

conflicting adjective clashing, differing, disagreeing, contradictory, contrary, opposing, incompatible, inconsistent, discordant, at odds.

conform verb follow convention, comply, adapt, adjust, follow the crowd, run with the pack. **conform to** *conform to accepted standards* comply with, fall in with, follow, obey, adapt, accommodate to, adjust to, observe.

conformist noun conventionalist, traditionalist, conservative; *inf.* yes-man, stick-in-the-mud, square.

conformity noun 1 *noted for their conformity* conventionality, traditionalism, orthodoxy. 2 *their conformity to accepted standards* compliance, obedience, observance, adaptation, adjustment, accommodation. 3 *having a certain conformity*

likeness, similarity, resemblance, correspondence, agreement, compatibility, congruity, consonance.

confound verb 1 *confounded at the news* dumbfound, astound, amaze, astonish, stun, flabbergast, disconcert, perplex, puzzle, mystify, baffle, nonplus, confuse, bewilder, dismay. 2 *confound the argument* refute, contradict, demolish, annihilate, explode.

confront verb 1 *confronting the enemy* defy, oppose, challenge, attack, assault, accost, waylay. 2 *confront one's problems* face, tackle, come to grips with, meet head on. 3 *confront them with the proof* bring face to face, show, present. 4 *problems confront us* threat, trouble, harass, annoy, molest.

confrontation noun conflict, clash, contest, collision, encounter; *inf.* set-to, showdown.

confuse verb 1 *confused by all the questions* bewilder, bemuse, perplex, baffle, puzzle, confound, mystify. 2 *confuse the issue* muddle, mix up, throw into disorder, disorder, disarrange, tangle up; *inf.* snarl up. 3 *confuse the twins with each other* mistake, mix up.

confused adjective 1 *a confused recollection* unclear, blurred, indistinct, hazy, foggy. 2 *a confused mess* muddled, jumbled, untidy, disorderly, chaotic, disorganized, upset, topsy-turvy. 3 *a confused old woman* muddled, addled, dazed, disoriented, at sea, unbalanced, unhinged, demented; *inf.* discombobulated.

confusing adjective unclear, puzzling, baffling, ambiguous, misleading, inconsistent.

confusion noun 1 *people in a state of confusion* bewilderment, perplexity, bafflement, puzzlement, mystification, disorientation, befuddlement. 2 *the room in a state of confusion* untidiness, disorder, chaos, shambles, disarrangement, disorganization. 3 *frightened by the confusion at the airport* bustle, commotion, upheaval, turmoil.

congeal verb solidify, harden, coagulate, thicken, set, concentrate, cake.

congenial adjective 1 *a congenial companion* sympathetic, compatible, like-minded, kindred. 2 *congenial work/places* agreeable, pleasant, pleasing, nice, suitable, well-suited, fit, favorable.

congenital adjective inborn, inbred, innate, inherent, constitutional, inherited, hereditary.

conglomerate noun corporation, multinational, joint concern, cartel.

congregate verb gather, assemble, group, flock together, convene, meet, amass, crowd, cluster, throng, rendezvous.

congregation noun gathering, assembly, group, convention, congress, mass, throng, conclave, convocation; flock, parishioners, parish.

congress noun *an international congress* assembly, meeting, gathering, conference, convention, convocation, council, synod.

conjecture noun guess, inference, fancy, notion, suspicion, presumption, theory, hypothesis; guessing, surmise, surmising, speculation, theorizing; *inf.* guesstimate.

conjugal adjective connubial, matrimonial, nuptial, marital, married, wedded, spousal.

conjunction noun *the conjunction of events* coincidence, co-occurrence, simultaneousness, coexistence, contemporaneousness, concomitance.

conjure verb summon, call up, invoke, rouse, raise up. **conjure up** recall, bring/call to mind, evoke, re-create.

connect verb **1** *connect the hose to the faucet* join, attach, fasten, affix, couple, clamp, secure, rivet, fuse, solder, weld. **2** *a road connecting the towns* join, link, unite, bridge. **connect with** *she connects him with sadness* associate with, link with/to, relate to, identify with, equate with.

connection noun **1** *the connection has come loose* attachment, fastening, coupling, clamp, clasp, joint. **2** *the connection between the events* link, relationship, relation, relatedness, association, bond, tie-in, correspondence, parallel, analogy. **3** *in that connection* context, reference, frame of reference, relation. **4** *get a job through a connection* contact, friend, acquaintance, ally, associate, sponsor.

connive verb conspire, collaborate, collude, be in collusion, intrigue, plot, scheme, be a party to, be an accessory to.

connoisseur noun expert, authority, specialist, pundit, cognoscenti (pl.), savant.

connotation noun undertone, nuance, hint, intimation, suggestion, implication, allusion, insinuation.

conquer verb **1** *conquer the enemy* defeat, beat, overpower, overthrow, vanquish, subdue, rout, trounce, subjugate, crush, quell. **2** *conquer the territory* seize, occupy, invade, annex, appropriate. **3** *conquer one's fears* overcome, get the better of, master, surmount, rise above, prevail over.

conqueror noun victor, winner, champion, hero, lord, master, conquistador.

conquest noun **1** *the conquest of/over the enemy* victory, defeat, overpowering, overthrow, vanquishment, rout, triumph. **2** *the conquest of the territory* seizing, possession, occupation, invasion, annexation, appropriation. **3** *the conquest of the audience* captivation, enchantment, bewitching, seduction, enticement, enthrallment.

4 *yet another of her conquests* admirer, fan, adherent, follower, supporter, worshiper.

conscience noun morals, scruples, principles, ethics.

conscience-stricken adjective contrite, penitent, repentant, remorseful, sorry, regretful, guilty, guilt-ridden, troubled, ashamed.

conscientious adjective diligent, careful, attentive, thorough, meticulous, punctilious, painstaking, hard-working, dedicated; precise, accurate, detailed.

conscious adjective **1** *a conscious attempt at humor* deliberate, calculated, premeditated, on purpose, reasoned, willed, volitional. **2** *in a conscious state* awake, aware, sentient, responsive, alert. **conscious of** *conscious of the problem* aware of, alert to, cognizant of.

consciousness noun **1** *regain consciousness* awareness, sentience, responsiveness, alertness. **2** *lack consciousness of the situation* realization, cognizance, perception, apprehension, recognition.

consecrate verb **1** *consecrate the building* sanctify, bless, make holy, hallow, dedicate to God. **2** *a life consecrated to science* dedicate, devote, pledge, commit.

consecutive adjective successive, succeeding, following, in sequence, sequential, serial, continuous, uninterrupted, unbroken.

consensus noun agreement, consent, common consent, unanimity, unity, concurrence.

consent verb **consent to** agree to, accept, approve, go along with, acquiesce in/to, accede to, concede to, yield to, give in to, submit to, comply with.

consent noun acceptance, approval, permission, sanction, acquiescence, compliance, concurrence.

consequence noun **1** *the consequence of the decision* result, effect, upshot, outcome, issue, aftermath, repercussion. **2** *a matter of consequence* importance, note, significance, import, moment, weight. **3** *a person of consequence* distinction, standing, status, prominence, prestige, eminence, rank.

consequent adjective resulting, resultant, ensuing, following, subsequent, successive, sequential.

consequently adverb as a result, therefore, thus, hence, subsequently, accordingly, ergo.

conservation noun preservation, protection, safeguarding, safekeeping, care, custody, upkeep, maintenance.

conservative adjective **1** *politically conservative* right-wing, reactionary, traditionalist. **2** *a conservative hairstyle* conventional, traditional, cautious, prudent, moderate, middle-of-the-road, temperate, stable, unchanging, old-fashioned, unprogressive.

conserve verb preserve, save, keep, protect, take care of, hoard, store up, husband, reserve.

consider verb 1 *consider your application* think about, give thought to, examine, ponder, contemplate, deliberate over, cogitate about, chew over. 2 *consider the feelings of others* take into consideration, take into account, make allowances for, respect, bear in mind, have regard to. 3 *consider you suitable* think, believe, regard as, deem, hold to be, judge. 4 *consider the horizon* contemplate, observe, regard, survey, scrutinize, scan.

considerable adjective 1 *a considerable amount* sizable, substantial, appreciable, goodly, tolerable, fair, ample, plentiful, noticeable, decent, great, large. 2 *a considerable artist* noteworthy, important, significant, influential, illustrious.

considerate adjective thoughtful, attentive, concerned, solicitous, mindful, heedful, kind, kindly, unselfish, compassionate, sympathetic.

consideration noun 1 *give consideration to the proposal* thought, attention, heed, notice, regard, deliberation, reflection, contemplation, examination, inspection, scrutiny, analysis, review. 2 *show consideration to their parents* thoughtfulness, attentiveness, concern, solicitousness, kindness, compassion, sympathy, patience, charity. 3 *money a major consideration* issue, factor, point, concern. 4 *for a small consideration* payment, fee, remuneration, compensation, recompense. 5 *take age into consideration* account, reckoning, allowance.

consign verb 1 *consign her to his care* hand over, give over, entrust, commend, remit, bequeath. 2 *consign to the junk pile* assign, deliver, commit.

consist verb **consist of** *consist of flour and water* comprise, contain, include, incorporate, embody, involve.

consistency noun 1 *mix to the right consistency* thickness, density, firmness, solidity, viscosity, cohesion. 2 *attitudes lacking consistency* dependability, constancy, uniformity.

consistent adjective 1 *consistent attitudes* steady, dependable, constant, uniform, unchanging, undeviating. 2 *testimony consistent with the facts* compatible, congruous, agreeing, accordant, consonant.

consolation noun 1 *words of consolation* compassion, pity, encouragement, soothing. *See* COMFORT noun 2. 2 *the baby is a consolation to her* comfort, solace, support.

console verb commiserate with, cheer, encourage. *See* COMFORT verb 1.

consolidate verb 1 *consolidate his position* strengthen, make secure, stabilize, reinforce, fortify, cement. 2 *consolidate the territories* combine, unite, merge, amalgamate, join.

conspicuous adjective 1 *conspicuous changes* obvious, evident, apparent, noticeable, observable, recognizable, discernible, manifest, vivid. 2 *conspicuous colors* obtrusive, blatant, flagrant, showy, garish, bold, ostentatious.

conspiracy noun 1 *a conspiracy to overthrow the government* plot, scheme, stratagem, plan, machination; collusion, connivance, collaboration.

conspirator noun conspirer, plotter, schemer, intriguer, colluder, collaborator, confederate.

conspire verb 1 *conspire against the leader* plot, scheme, intrigue, collude, collaborate, cabal, machinate; *inf.* be in cahoots with. 2 *events conspire against us* act together, work together, combine, unite, join forces, gang up (on).

constancy noun 1 *her lover's constancy* faithfulness, fidelity, devotion, loyalty, staunchness, dependability, adherence. 2 *constancy of purpose* firmness, steadfastness, resoluteness, fixedness, determination, perseverance, tenacity, doggedness. 3 *constancy of temperature* uniformity, evenness, regularity, stability, immutability.

constant adjective 1 *at a constant speed/temperature* uniform, even, regular, stable, steady, fixed, unvarying, unchanging, immutable. 2 *a constant stream of people/chatter* continuous, unbroken, uninterrupted; continual, never-ending, endless, unending, nonstop, incessant, unceasing, persistent, interminable, unremitting, relentless, unrelenting. 3 *a constant lover* faithful, devoted, loyal, staunch, dependable, true, trustworthy, trusty. 4 *constant in his purpose* firm, steadfast, steady, resolute, determined, persevering, tenacious, dogged, unwavering.

constantly adverb always, all the time, continually, continuously, endlessly, nonstop, incessantly, persistently, interminably, relentlessly.

consternation noun astonishment, dismay, bewilderment, confusion, anxiety, distress, alarm, panic, dread.

constitute verb 1 *the countries that constitute the alliance* form, make up, compose, comprise. 2 *his suggestion constitutes a warning* be tantamount to, be the equivalent of, be, be regarded as, act as. 3 *constitute a committee* appoint, establish, authorize, commission, charter.

constitution noun **1** *the society's constitution* system of laws/rules, code, charter, canon; laws, rules, fundamental principles. **2** *the constitution of the committees varies* composition, makeup, structure, organization. **3** *people having a strong constitution* state of health, physique, physical condition. **4** *people of a nervous constitution* disposition, temperament, temper, nature, character, mood.

constrain verb **1** *feel constrained to cooperate* force, compel, coerce, drive, impel, oblige, press, pressure. **2** *research constrained by lack of resources* hold back, restrict, hinder, impede, hamper, limit, curb, check, restrain. **3** *constrain political opponents* confine, chain, shut in, lock up, imprison, incarcerate.

constraint noun **1** *act under constraint* force, compulsion, coercion, obligation, pressure, impulsion. **2** *no constraints on their activities* restriction, hindrance, impediment, limitation, curb, check, restraint, damper. **3** *subject political opponents to constraint* confinement, imprisonment, incarceration. **4** *constraint of manner* forcedness, unnaturalness, inhibition, reservedness.

constrict verb **1** *a medication that constricts the blood vessels* narrow, compress, contract, squeeze, strangle, strangulate. **2** *constrict the flow of traffic* impede, obstruct, hinder, hamper, limit, restrict, check, curb, inhibit.

construct verb **1** *construct a bridge* build, erect, put up, set up, assemble, manufacture, fabricate, make. **2** *construct a plan/theory* form, formulate, devise, design, invent, compose, fashion, shape, frame, forge, engineer.

construction noun **1** *a bridge under construction* building, erection, establishment, assembly, manufacture, fabrication. **2** *an impressive construction* structure, building, edifice, assembly, framework. **3** *put a different construction on her words* interpretation, reading, meaning, explanation, inference.

constructive adjective useful, helpful, productive, practical, positive, valuable.

consult verb **1** *consult an expert | consult a reference book* ask, seek advice/information from, call in, turn to, take counsel from, look up in, check (in), refer to, turn to. **2** *consult with his colleagues* confer, discuss, talk over, exchange views, deliberate, parley.

consultant noun adviser, expert, authority, specialist.

consultation noun **1** *have a consultation with one's adviser* meeting, talk, discussion, interview, session, audience, tête-à-tête, parley. **2** *international consultations* conference, convention, symposium, forum, session, seminar.

consume verb **1** *consume dinner/lemonade* eat, drink, devour, ingest, swallow, gobble, guzzle, snack on; *inf.* tuck into, scoff, down, put away, polish off. **2** *consumed by a desire* absorb, engross, obsess, grip. **3** *buildings consumed by fire* destroy, demolish, lay waste, wipe out, annihilate, devastate, raze, gut, ravage. **4** *cars consuming too much gasoline* use up, expend, deplete, exhaust; waste, squander, dissipate, fritter away.

consumer noun user, buyer, purchaser, customer, shopper, client, patron.

consuming adjective absorbing, compelling, preoccupying, engrossing, devouring, obsessive, gripping, overwhelming.

consummate adjective complete, total, utter, absolute, perfect; accomplished, expert, proficient, masterly, talented, gifted.

consumption noun **1** *unfit for human consumption* eating, drinking, ingestion. **2** *consumption by fire* destruction, demolition, annihilation, devastation, razing, gutting, ravaging. **3** *the consumption of fuel* utilization, expenditure, depletion, exhaustion, waste, draining, dissipation.

contact noun **1** *following contact with chemicals* touch, touching, proximity, exposure, contiguity, junction, union, tangency. **2** *be in contact with* touch, communication, connection, correspondence, association. **3** *get a job through contacts* connection, acquaintance.

contact verb get/be in touch with, get hold/ahold of, communicate with; write to, write, notify, phone, call, speak to, reach.

contagious adjective catching, communicable, transmittable, spreadable, infectious, epidemic, pandemic.

contain verb **1** *the cabin contained four people* hold, have capacity for, carry, accommodate. **2** *the committee contains six members* include, comprise, embrace, take in, incorporate, involve. **3** *contain your laughter* hold in, restrain, control, keep in check, suppress, repress, curb, stifle.

contaminate verb pollute, adulterate, defile, debase, corrupt, taint, infect, foul, spoil, soil, sully, tarnish, stain, befoul, vitiate.

contemplate verb **1** *contemplate the portrait* look at, view, regard, examine, survey, scrutinize, scan, stare at, gaze at. **2** *contemplate the future* think about, meditate over, ponder, reflect over, mull over, muse on, deliberate over, cogitate over, ruminate over, turn over in one's mind. **3** *he is contemplating going* consider, intend, plan, propose.

contemplation noun **1** *his contemplation of the painting* viewing, examination, inspection, observation, scrutiny, regard. **2**

contemplation of the future pondering, reflection, rumination, deliberation, cogitation. **3** *lost in contemplation* thought, meditation, reflection; *inf.* brown study.

contemplative adjective thoughtful, pensive, reflective, meditative, musing, ruminative, introspective.

contemporary adjective **1** *contemporary writers* contemporaneous, coexisting, co-existent, concurrent, synchronous. **2** *contemporary fashion* modern, present-day, current, up-to-date, up-to-the-minute, latest, recent, ultramodern, newfangled; *inf.* with it.

contemporary noun *Shakespeare and his contemporaries* peer, compeer, fellow.

contempt noun scorn, disdain, disrespect, condescension, derision, mockery, disgust, loathing, abhorrence.

contemptible adjective despicable, detestable, ignominious, lamentable, pitiful, low, mean, shameful, base, vile, sordid, degenerate.

contemptuous adjective scornful, disdainful, disrespectful, insulting, insolent, derisory, derisive, mocking.

contend verb **1** *armies contending with each other* compete, oppose, vie, contest, clash, strive, struggle, grapple, scuffle, skirmish, battle, combat, fight, war. **2** *contend that he's mad* assert, maintain, hold, claim, profess, allege. **contend with** cope with, face, grapple with, take on, pit oneself against.

content noun **1** *the content of the mixture* component parts/elements. *See* CONTENTS 1. **2** *the content of the essay* subject matter, subject, material, substance, theme, ideas, gist. **3** *foods with a low sodium content* amount, proportion, quantity.

content adjective *content with life* contented, satisfied, pleased, happy, cheerful, glad, gratified, fulfilled, at ease, at peace, comfortable, serene, tranquil, unworried, untroubled, complacent.

contented adjective satisfied, pleased. *See* CONTENT adjective.

contention noun **1** *two groups in contention for the title* competition, contest, rivalry, opposition, striving, struggle, combat, battle. **2** *much contention between the families* discord, feuding, hostility, enmity, strife, dissension. **3** *it was her contention that she won* assertion, claim, stand, position, opinion, view, belief.

contentious adjective **1** *contentious people* argumentative, quarrelsome, bickering, wrangling, disputatious, factious, litigious, combative, pugnacious. **2** *a contentious subject* controversial, disputable, debatable, controvertible.

contentment noun content, contentedness, satisfaction, pleasure, happiness, cheerfulness, gladness, gratification, fulfillment, ease, comfort, peace, equanimity, serenity, tranquillity.

contents plural noun **1** *the contents of the mixture/box* constituents, components, ingredients, elements, items; content, load. **2** *the contents of the book* text, subject matter, theme.

contest noun **1** *a sport/dancing contest* competition, match, game, event, tournament, meet, trial. **2** *a leadership contest* struggle, conflict, battle, fight, combat, tussle.

contest verb *contest the decision/point* challenge, question, call into question, oppose, doubt, dispute, argue, debate, quarrel over.

contestant noun competitor, entrant, candidate, participant, player, contender, rival, opponent, adversary, antagonist, aspirant.

context noun **1** *in the present financial context* circumstances, conditions, situation, state of affairs, background, environment. **2** *take a statement out of context* text, frame of reference, subject.

contiguous adjective touching, in contact, meeting, joining, connecting, abutting, bordering, neighboring, adjacent.

contingent adjective chance, accidental, fortuitous, random, haphazard; uncertain, possible. **contingent on/upon** dependent on, subject to, hinging on.

continual adjective **1** *continual complaints* frequent, repeated, constant, regular, persistent, habitual, recurrent, repetitive, oft-repeated. **2** *continual noise* perpetual, endless. *See* CONTINUOUS.

continue verb **1** *the desert continues for miles* go on, extend, keep on, carry on, maintain course, drag on. **2** *the firm may continue* last, remain, stay, endure, survive, live on, persist, abide. **3** *continue the session as long as possible* maintain, sustain, retain, prolong, protract, perpetuate, preserve. **4** *continue trying* keep on, keep at, persist in, persevere in; *inf.* stick with/at. **5** *continue the search after a break* resume, renew, recommence, start again, carry on with, return to, take up, proceed, pick up where one has left off.

continuity noun **1** *continuity of supplies* continuousness, uninterruptedness, flow, regular flow, progression. **2** *continuity in the prose* cohesion, coherence, connection, interrelatedness, linkage, sequence.

continuous adjective uninterrupted, unbroken, consecutive, constant, nonstop, perpetual, ceaseless, incessant, unceasing, unremitting, endless, everlasting, interminable.

contort verb twist, wrench/bend out of shape, warp, deform, misshape.

contour noun outline, silhouette, profile, figure, shape, form; lines, curves.

contraband noun smuggling, trafficking, black marketing, black marketeering, bootlegging.

contract noun agreement, compact, covenant, pact, settlement, arrangement, transaction, bargain, deal.

contract verb 1 *metals contracting | contracting metals* get/make smaller, become/make shorter, shrink, reduce, shrivel. 2 *blood vessels contracting | muscles contracting* constrict, become narrower, narrow, tighten, become tighter, tense, draw in. 3 *contract a word/text* shorten, abbreviate, abridge, compress, condense. 4 *contract (with) them to do the work* arrange, agree, come to terms, negotiate, bargain, strike a bargain, close/clinch a deal, close, engage. 5 *contract a disease* catch, get, come down with, develop. 6 *contract a debt* incur, acquire, fall into.

contraction noun shrinking, narrowing, tightening, constricting, tensing.

contradict verb 1 *contradict his father* say the opposite of, oppose, challenge, counter, be at variance with; deny, dispute, refute, rebut, controvert, impugn, confute. 2 *the statements contradict each other* disagree with, be in conflict with, clash with, contravene, run counter to, be inconsistent with, negate.

contradiction noun 1 *the contradiction of his statement* disputing, countering, refuting, rebuttal, controverting, impugning, confutation. 2 *the contradiction between the two statements* disagreement, conflict, clash, inconsistency, dissension, contravention, negation.

contradictory adjective 1 *hold a contradictory view* opposing, opposite, dissenting, contrary, dissident; at variance, at odds. 2 *contradictory statements* conflicting, contrasting, incompatible, irreconcilable, inconsistent, antithetical.

contraption noun device, machine, mechanism, gadget, contrivance, apparatus, invention, appliance; *inf.* thingamajig, thingamabob, whatsit, doodad, gizmo.

contrary adjective 1 *holding contrary views* opposite, opposing, incongruous. *See* CONTRADICTORY 2. 2 *a contrary young woman* willful, obstinate, stubborn, headstrong, pigheaded, intractable, recalcitrant, intransigent, refractory.

contrast noun 1 *a marked contrast between them* difference, dissimilarity, distinction, disparity, dissimilitude, differentiation, distinguishment. 2 *he is a complete*

contrast to his brother opposite, antithesis.

contrast verb 1 *contrast the two writers* compare, juxtapose, set side by side, distinguish, differentiate, discriminate. 2 *theories and actions contrast sharply* contradict, be at variance, be contrary, diverge, differ.

contravene verb 1 *contravene a law* disobey, break, infringe, violate, transgress. 2 *evidence contravenes that theory* contradict, be in conflict with, be in opposition to, clash with, be at variance with, run counter to, refute, rebut.

contribute verb 1 *contribute money/time to the charity | happy to contribute* give, donate, hand out, present, grant, endow, bestow, accord, confer, provide, supply, furnish; *inf.* chip in, pitch in. 2 *sensible eating contributes to good health* be conducive to, lead to, be instrumental in, promote, advance.

contribution noun 1 *contributions to the fund* donation, gift, offering, present, grant, bestowal, allowance, subsidy, endowment. 2 *appreciated your contribution during the discussion* input, participation; *inf.* two cents' worth.

contributor noun giver, donor, patron, supporter, backer, benefactor, subsidizer.

contrite adjective penitent, repentant, remorseful, regretful, sorry, chastened, conscience-stricken, guilt-ridden, in sackcloth and ashes.

contrivance noun 1 *a contrivance for plowing* device, invention, gadget, contraption, appliance, apparatus, implement, tool, machine, mechanism, equipment, gear, tackle. 2 *fooled by a clever contrivance* stratagem, scheme, ruse, trick, plot, machination, fabrication, artifice. 3 *the contrivance of the schemer* inventiveness, ingenuity, creativity, originality.

contrive verb 1 *contrive a brilliant scheme* devise, concoct, engineer, invent, originate, create, construct, design, plan, work out, think/dream up, plot, fabricate. 2 *contrive to win* manage, find a way, engineer, maneuver, scheme.

contrived adjective unnatural, artificial, forced, strained, labored, nonspontaneous.

control verb 1 *control the organization* be in charge of, head, manage, direct, preside over, conduct, command, rule, govern, lead, supervise, superintend, oversee, dominate, master, reign over, be in the driver's seat of, be in the saddle of. 2 *control prices* keep in check, restrain, curb, contain, hold back, restrict, limit, regulate, constrain, subdue, bridle.

control noun 1 *have control over the organization* charge, management, authority, power, command, direction, rule, government, jurisdiction, supervision, dominance, mastery, reign, supremacy. **2** *get control of oneself* self-control, self-restraint, restraint, hold. **3** *arms control | import controls* limitation, restriction, regulation, check, curb.

controversial adjective disputed, disputable, debatable, under discussion, at issue, contentious, contended, controvertible.

controversy noun dispute, argument, polemic, debate, disagreement, dissension, altercation, wrangling, quarreling, squabbling, bickering.

contusion noun bruise, discoloration, blemish, injury, bump, lump.

conundrum noun riddle, puzzle, word game; problem, enigma, mystery; *inf.* brainteaser.

convalescence noun recovery, recuperation, improvement, rehabilitation, mending, restoration.

convene verb **1** *convene a meeting* call, call together, summon, convoke, round up, rally. **2** *the meeting convened* assemble, gather, collect, congregate, meet, muster.

convenience noun **1** *the convenience of the time/arrangement* accessibility, availability, suitability, appropriateness, fitness, fittingness, favorableness, favorability, advantageousness, opportuneness, propitiousness, expedience, usefulness, utility, serviceability. **2** *do it at your convenience* suitable opportunity, leisure, spare moment, free time. **3** *for the convenience of all* service, use, benefit, advantage, accommodation, enjoyment, comfort, ease. **4** *few conveniences in the kitchen* gadget, labor-saving device, appliance, appurtenance, amenity.

convenient adjective **1** *stores convenient to the highway* accessible, handy, at hand, close at hand, within reach, nearby, just around the corner, at one's fingertips, available. **2** *choose a convenient time/setting* suitable, suited, appropriate, fit, fitting, favorable, advantageous, opportune, expedient, useful, serviceable.

convention noun **1** *a medical/political convention* conference, congress, gathering, meeting, assembly, convocation, synod, conclave. **2** *follow convention* protocol, propriety, code, custom, tradition, usage, practice. **3** *a convention between countries* agreement, contract, pact, treaty.

conventional adjective **1** *conventional behavior/attitudes* accepted, customary, usual, standard, normal, ordinary, decorous, proper, orthodox, traditional, prevailing, prevalent, conformist, conservative; *inf.* square, straight, straitlaced. **2** *conventional works of art* run-of-the-mill, commonplace,

ordinary, everyday, garden-variety, prosaic, routine, pedestrian, hackneyed, unoriginal.

converge verb meet, intersect, join, merge, unite, come together, become one.

conversant adjective acquainted with, familiar with, knowledgeable about, well-versed in, informed about; *inf.* (well) up on.

conversation noun discussion, dialogue, discourse, communication, conference, colloquy; talk, chat, exchange, gossip, tête-à-tête; *inf.* confab, rap session.

converse verb talk, speak, discuss, chat, communicate.

converse noun opposite, contrary, reverse, antithesis, obverse.

conversion noun **1** *the conversion of liquid to gas* transformation, metamorphosis, transfiguration, transmutation; *inf.* transmogrification. **2** *the conversion of the building* alteration, adaptation, modification, reshaping, refashioning, remodeling. **3** *religious conversion* reformation, regeneration, proselytization. **4** *conversion of pounds to dollars* change, exchange, substitution, switch.

convert verb **1** *convert liquid to gas* change, transform, metamorphose, transfigure, transmute; *inf.* transmogrify. **2** *the sofa converts to a bed* change (into), make (into), adapt, transform (into). **3** *convert the building* alter, adapt, modify, reshape, refashion, remodel, restyle. **4** *convert the heathens* reform, regenerate, bring to God, baptize, proselytize. **5** *convert yards to meters* change, turn into; exchange for, substitute by.

convey verb **1** *convey the goods* transport, carry, bring, fetch, bear, move, shift, transfer, cart, lug. **2** *convey information* transmit, pass on, send, dispatch, communicate, make known, impart. **3** *convey property* transfer, transmit, devolve, lease, bequeath, will.

conveyance noun **1** *by public conveyance* transport, transportation, carriage, transfer, transference, transmission, haulage, portage, cartage, shipment, freightage. **2** *the conveyance of information* transmission, passing on, communication, imparting. **3** *conveyance of property* transfer, granting, ceding, cession.

convict noun prisoner, criminal, offender, lawbreaker, felon; *inf.* crook, con, jailbird.

conviction noun **1** *she spoke with conviction* confidence, assurance, certainty, certitude, firmness, earnestness. **2** *my conviction is that he is dead* belief, opinion, view, persuasion. **3** *a person of conviction* principle, belief, faith, creed.

convince verb **1** *she convinced me that I was wrong* prove to, satisfy, assure, reassure.

2 *convince him to vote for them* persuade, prevail upon, sway, bring around.

convincing adjective cogent, powerful, persuasive, plausible, incontrovertible, conclusive; plausible, credible.

convivial adjective genial, cordial, sociable, friendly, affable, amiable, congenial, agreeable.

convoy noun **1** *the convoy set off* assemblage, line, fleet, cortege, caravan. **2** *a fleet/company under convoy* escort, protection, guard, bodyguard, defense.

convulse verb **1** *convulsed with laughter* shake, churn up, discompose, unsettle. **2** *a city convulsed with rioting* agitate, disturb, upset, disorder, unsettle, wrack.

convulsion noun **1** *the child went into convulsions* fit, seizure, paroxysm, spasm, contractions. **2** *political convulsions in the city* turmoil, tumult, commotion, upheaval, agitation, unrest, upset, disorder, chaos.

cook verb **1** *cook a dish/meal* prepare, put together, concoct. **2** *cook the books* falsify, forge, alter. **3** *what's cooking?* happen, occur, take place. **cook up** concoct, contrive, fabricate, improvise.

cool adjective **1** *cool weather* coldish, chilly, chilled, nippy, unheated, sunless, windy, breezy, drafty. **2** *keep cool in an emergency* calm, composed, collected, self-possessed, self-controlled, levelheaded, unexcited, unperturbed, unmoved, unruffled, unemotional; *inf.* together. **3** *a cool welcome* chilly, impassive, undemonstrative, unresponsive, unenthusiastic, indifferent. **4** *the cool method of the killer* calculated, premeditated, planned, deliberate, dispassionate, cold, cold-blooded. **5** *thinks he's really cool* sophisticated, suave, stylish, urbane, cosmopolitan. **6** *what a cool idea* great, superb, excellent, splendid; *inf.* awesome, far-out.

cool verb **1** *cool the milk* cool down, chill, refrigerate, freeze. **2** *the milk cooled* become cold/colder, lose heat. **3** *cool his passion* lessen, abate, moderate, temper, diminish, reduce, dampen.

cool noun **1** *lose one's cool* self-control, control, calmness, composure, poise. **2** *the cool of the evening* coolness, freshness, crispness, coldness, chill.

coop noun cage, pen, enclosure, hutch, pound, lockup.

coop verb **coop up** cage, cage/pen in, confine, enclose, hem in, shut/lock up, imprison.

cooperate verb **1** *cooperate in the venture* work together, act/pull together, join forces, unite, combine, collaborate, pool resources. **2** *he'll be released if he cooperates* assist, help, contribute, participate, go along; *inf.* pitch in, play ball.

cooperation noun **1** *cooperation between the departments* collaboration, coordination, teamwork, give and take, synergy. **2** *thank you for your cooperation* assistance, help, aid, contribution, helping hand, participation.

cooperative adjective **1** *a cooperative venture* joint, united, shared, unified, combined, concerted, coordinated, collaborative. **2** *the public's being cooperative* helpful, obliging, accommodating, participating, responsive.

coordinate verb **1** *coordinate the effort* organize, order, integrate, synchronize, correlate. **2** *coordinating for the common good* unite, combine, collaborate, interrelate.

cope verb manage, succeed, survive, carry on, get through, get on, get along, get by, subsist. **cope with** handle, deal with, weather, contend with, grapple with, wrestle with.

copious adjective abundant, superabundant, plentiful, ample, profuse, full, extensive, generous, lavish, rich, liberal, bounteous, bountiful.

copy noun **1** *a copy of the document* transcript, facsimile, duplicate, duplication, carbon, carbon copy, photocopy; *TM* Xerox, Photostat. **2** *a clever copy of the vase* imitation, reproduction, replica, likeness, counterfeit, forgery, fake. **3** *three copies of the book* specimen, example, sample, issue.

copy verb **1** *copy the document* duplicate, photocopy, Xerox (*trademark*), Photostat (*trademark*), transcribe. **2** *copy the vase/painting* reproduce, replicate, forge, counterfeit; imitate, mimic, emulate, follow, echo, mirror, simulate, ape, parrot.

cordial adjective **1** *a cordial welcome* warm, friendly, genial, affable, amiable, pleasant, gracious, warmhearted, sincere, hearty, wholehearted, heartfelt. **2** *cordial dislike* intense, acute, strong, fierce, keen.

cordon verb **cordon off** close off, fence off, shut off, enclose, encircle, surround.

core noun center, heart, nucleus, nub, kernel, crux, heart of the matter, essence, quintessence, substance, gist, pith; *inf.* nitty-gritty.

corner noun **1** *the corner of the road* angle, bend, curve, crook, turn; intersection, junction, fork, convergence, juncture. **2** *hidden in secret corners* nook, cranny, niche, recess, hideaway, hide-out. **3** *in a remote corner of Maine* part, region, area, district, section, quarter. **4** *in a difficult corner* predicament, plight, tight spot; *inf.* pickle. **5** *a corner of the property market* dominance, monopoly.

corner verb **1** *corner the enemy* block off, trap, bring to bay. **2** *corner the market* gain control, dominate, monopolize.

corny adjective banal, trite, hackneyed, stale, commonplace, platitudinous, inane, fatuous, jejune, sentimental, mawkish; *inf.* old hat.

coronation noun crowning, enthronement, enthroning, accession to the throne, investiture, anointing, inauguration.

coronet noun crown, circlet, garland, wreath, chaplet.

corporal adjective bodily, fleshly, physical, corporeal, material, carnal.

corporate adjective 1 *review corporate finances* company, organization, business. 2 *for the corporate good* communal, collective, shared, collaborative.

corporation noun company, firm, trust, partnership, combine, conglomerate.

corps noun 1 *an army corps* unit, division, detachment, company, troop, contingent, squad, squadron. 2 *diplomatic/press corps* group, body, band, contingent, pack, crew.

corpse noun cadaver, carcass, skeleton; remains; *inf.* stiff.

corpulent adjective fat, obese, plump, portly, stout, overweight, beefy, thickset, heavy, heavyset, well-padded, fleshy, rotund, roly-poly.

correct adjective 1 *the correct answer* right, accurate, true, actual, exact, precise, unerring, close, faithful, strict, faultless, flawless; *inf.* OK, on the mark, on the beam. 2 *correct behavior* proper, suitable, fit, fitting, befitting, appropriate, apt, seemly, conventional, approved, accepted, standard, usual, customary.

correct verb 1 *correct the errors* rectify, right, amend, remedy, redress, cure, improve, better, ameliorate, repair. 2 *correct a defect* counteract, offset, counterbalance, compensate for, make up for, neutralize. 3 *correct an instrument* adjust, regulate, fix, set, standardize. 4 *correct the children* scold, rebuke, chide, reprimand, reprove, admonish, discipline, punish, chastise.

correction noun 1 *the correction of the text* amendment, emendation, rectification, improvement, modification, alteration, amelioration, repair. 2 *a house of correction* punishment, discipline, castigation, reformation.

corrective adjective 1 *corrective surgery* remedial, therapeutic, restorative, curative, reparative, rehabilitative. 2 *corrective training* punitive, penal, reformatory.

correctly adverb 1 *answer correctly* accurately, unerringly, precisely, faultlessly. 2 *dressed correctly* properly, suitably, fittingly, appropriately, aptly.

correlate verb 1 *subjects correlating with each other* correspond, tie in, equate, interact, relate, agree, coordinate. 2 *correlate the facts* bring together, compare, show a connection/relationship, connect.

correlation noun correspondence, equivalence, reciprocity, interrelationship, interdependence, connection, relationship.

correspond verb 1 *the accounts do not correspond* agree, be in agreement, accord, concur, coincide, conform, match, fit together, square, tally, dovetail, correlate. 2 *Congress corresponds to Parliament* be analogous, be similar, be comparable.

correspondence noun 1 *lack of correspondence between the accounts* agreement, accordance, accord, concurrence, conformity, harmony. 2 *a backlog of correspondence* mail, communication; letters, notes, messages, E-mail.

correspondent noun 1 *her brothers are regular correspondents* letter writer, pen pal. 2 *newspaper correspondent* reporter, journalist; *inf.* stringer.

corridor noun passage, passageway, aisle, hallway.

corroborate verb back up, support. *See* CONFIRM 1.

corrode verb eat away, wear away, erode, gnaw, abrade, destroy, consume, rust, oxidize, oxidate; waste away, disintegrate, crumble, fragment, be destroyed.

corrosive adjective corroding, eroding, erosive, abrasive, biting, caustic, acrid, destructive.

corrugated adjective furrowed, grooved, ridged, fluted, crinkled, wrinkled, crumpled, striate.

corrupt adjective 1 *corrupt officials* dishonest, bribable, crooked, fraudulent, dishonorable, unscrupulous, untrustworthy, venal; *inf.* bent, shady. 2 *a corrupt young man* immoral, depraved, wicked, evil, sinful, degenerate. 3 *a corrupt substance* adulterated, impure, alloyed, contaminated, tainted.

corrupt verb 1 *corrupt the official* bribe, suborn, buy, buy off; *inf.* pay off, grease the palm of. 2 *corrupt the young boy* deprave, pervert, warp, debauch. 3 *corrupt the atmosphere* pollute, putrefy, taint, infect, contaminate. 4 *corrupt the substance* adulterate, alloy, contaminate, taint, defile, debase. 5 *corrupt the text* alter, tamper with, falsify, doctor.

corruption noun 1 *officials involved in corruption* bribery, subornation, extortion, dishonesty, crookedness, fraud, fraudulence, unscrupulousness, shadiness, profiteering, criminality, venality; *inf.* graft. 2 *guilty of moral corruption* immorality, depravity, vice, wickedness, evil, sin, iniquity, turpitude, degeneracy. 3 *corruption of the atmosphere* pollution, contamination.

cortege noun **1** *a funeral cortege* procession, column, file, line, parade, cavalcade. **2** *the bride and her cortege* retinue, entourage, train; attendants.

cosmetic adjective **1** *a cosmetic improvement* superficial, surface. **2** *cosmetic surgery* beautifying, nonessential, nonmedical.

cosmic adjective **1** *cosmic laws* universal, worldwide. **2** *disasters of cosmic proportion* vast, huge, immense, enormous, immeasurable, measureless, infinite, limitless.

cosmopolitan adjective **1** *a cosmopolitan city* international, multiethnic, universal, global, worldwide. **2** *a cosmopolitan attitude* sophisticated, urbane, worldly, worldly-wise, well-traveled, jet-setting, globe-trotting, unprovincial, cultivated.

cost verb **1** *the book costs $30* be priced at, sell for, fetch, come to, amount to; *inf.* set one back. **2** *tragedy costing lives | work costing effort* involve, result in, lead to, involve the loss/expense/sacrifice of, necessitate.

cost noun **1** *the cost of the house* price, asking price, selling price, charge, amount, value, valuation, quotation, rate, worth, payment, expenditure, expense, outlay; *inf.* damage. **2** *work done at great cost* sacrifice, expense, loss, penalty, suffering, harm, damage, deprivation.

costly adjective **1** *a costly house* expensive, high-cost, high-priced, valuable, exorbitant, extortionate, extravagant; *inf.* steep. **2** *a costly victory* ruinous, catastrophic, disastrous, damaging, harmful.

costume noun **1** *dressed in national costume* style of dress, fashion, clothing, attire, apparel, garb, uniform, livery, habit; *inf.* get-up, gear, togs. **2** *a woman in a green costume* suit, outfit, ensemble.

coterie noun clique, set, crowd, circle, gang, club, league, faction.

cottage noun cabin, chalet, hut, bungalow, shack.

couch noun sofa, settee; ottoman, *chaise longue*, chesterfield, davenport, divan, day bed, love seat.

council noun **1** *the governor's council* advisory body, board, board of directors, committee, assembly, panel, trustees. **2** *the council of committee members* conference, conclave, assembly, convocation; meeting, gathering.

counsel noun **1** *seek expert counsel* advice, guidance, direction, recommendation, information; opinion, suggestion. **2** *hold counsel with a friend* consultation, discussion, conference, deliberation, dialogue. **3** *counsel handling his case* lawyer, attorney, advocate.

counsel verb advise, give guidance/direction, guide, direct, recommend, give one's opinion/suggestions.

counselor noun adviser, guidance counselor, director, mentor, confidant, guide.

count verb **1** *count the numbers* add up, total, sum up, calculate, compute, enumerate, tally. **2** *counting everyone* include, take into account, embrace. **3** *count himself lucky* consider, regard, hold, judge, rate, deem. **4** *his presence does not count* matter, enter into consideration, be of account, be of consequence, have effect, signify, carry weight, mean anything, amount to anything, make a difference, rate; *inf.* carry (any) weight/clout. **count on** rely on, depend on, lean on, bank on, trust. **count out** exclude, disregard, ignore, pass over.

count noun **1** *after the ballot count* counting, enumeration, calculation, computation, tally. **2** *know the calorie count* total, sum total, amount, aggregate, whole.

countenance noun **1** *angry countenance* face, features, facial expression, expression, look, appearance, aspect, air, complexion, visage, physiognomy, mien. **2** *not give countenance to the plan* support, backing, encouragement, endorsement, assistance, aid, approval. **3** *lose countenance* composure, calmness, coolness, poise, self-possession, self-control, equanimity.

counter verb oppose, resist, rebut, combat, dispute, contradict, retaliate, ward off.

counteract verb thwart, frustrate, foil, impede, check, counterbalance, offset, neutralize, annul, negate.

counterfeit adjective fake, faked, copied, forged, imitation, feigned, simulated, fraudulent, sham, spurious, bogus, ersatz; *inf.* phony, pseudo.

counterfeit noun fake, copy, forgery, reproduction, imitation, fraud, sham; *inf.* phony.

counterfeit verb fake, copy, reproduce, imitate, simulate, feign, falsify, sham.

countermand verb cancel, annul, revoke, rescind, reverse, repeal, retract.

counterpart noun equivalent, equal, opposite number, match, twin, mate, fellow, analog, correlative.

countless adjective innumerable, incalculable, immeasurable, endless, limitless, boundless, infinite, inexhaustible, untold, legion, myriad.

country noun **1** *countries at war* nation, state, sovereign state, kingdom, realm, people, community, commonwealth. **2** *love for one's country* native land, homeland, fatherland, motherland, mother country. **3** *driving through rough country* terrain, land, territory; region, area, district, part, neighborhood; parts; *inf.* neck of the woods. **4** *the will of the country* people, nation, public, population, populace, citizenry; inhabitants, residents, citizens, electors, voters. **5** *live in the country, not the city* countryside, rural area, farmland, great outdoors; *derog.* backwoods, sticks, wilds, wilderness, middle of nowhere; *inf.* boondocks, boonies.

coup noun **1** *pull off quite a coup* feat, masterstroke, deed, accomplishment, stroke, stroke of genius, maneuver, stratagem, stunt. **2** *a military coup* overthrow, seizure of power, coup d'état, revolt, revolution, rebellion, mutiny, insurgence.

couple noun pair, duo, twosome, dyad; partners, lovers, husband and wife, cohabitees.

couple verb connect, unite, hitch together, join, link, associate, ally.

courage noun bravery, valor, gallantry, heroism, fearlessness, intrepidity, lionheartedness, stoutheartedness, pluck, nerve, boldness, daring, mettle; *inf.* spunk, guts, grit, moxie.

courageous adjective brave, valiant, valorous, gallant, heroic, fearless, intrepid, lionhearted, plucky, bold, daring, audacious, dauntless.

courier noun messenger, carrier, bearer, runner, conveyor, envoy, emissary, harbinger, herald.

course noun **1** *the course of history* progression, advance, march, furtherance, unfolding, flow, movement, continuity. **2** *go a bit off course* route, way, track, direction, tack, path, line. **3** *pursue a different course (of action)* method, way, process, procedure, manner, mode of behavior/conduct. **4** *in the course of an hour* duration, passage, lapse, period, term, span. **5** *an English course* course of study, curriculum, program, schedule; classes, lectures, studies. **6** *a course of treatment* sequence, series, system, regimen. **7** *a waterlogged course* racecourse, track, circuit, ground. **in due course** in time, sooner or later, eventually. **of course** naturally, obviously, certainly, definitely, undoubtedly.

course verb flow, move, run, rush, surge, gush, race, hurry, speed, charge, dash.

court noun **1** *appear before the court* court of law, bench, bar, court of justice, justiciary, tribunal. **2** *the queen's court* royal household, retinue, entourage, train, suite, cortege; attendants. **3** *situated near the queen's court* royal residence, palace, castle, manor, hall, chateau. **4** *paying court to the young lady* attention, homage, deference, suit, wooing, courtship. **5** *walking in the campus court* atrium, esplanade, patio, piazza.

court verb **1** *he's courting her sister* woo, pursue, chase, run after, set one's cap for, pay suit to. **2** *the couple are courting* go

out, go steady, date, keep company. **3** *court the manager* curry favor with, pander to, fawn over; *inf.* soft-soap, butter up. **4** *court fame* seek, solicit, ask for, crave. **5** *court disaster* invite, risk, provoke, bring on, elicit.

courteous adjective polite, well-mannered, mannerly, civil, chivalrous, gallant, gracious, diplomatic, politic, well-bred, polished, refined, urbane.

courtesy noun **1** *have the courtesy to wait* politeness, civility, chivalry, gallantry, good breeding, gentility, graciousness, kindness, consideration, respect, deference, decorum, refinement, elegance; good manners, manners. **2** *your tickets are by courtesy of the management* generosity, benevolence, indulgence, favor.

courtyard noun quadrangle, square, cloister, esplanade, court.

covenant noun contract, agreement, pledge, promise, commitment, compact, pact, arrangement, treaty, concordat.

cover verb **1** *cover the potatoes* place under cover, protect, shield, shelter, conceal, hide, house, secrete, bury. **2** *snow covering the fields* overlay, overspread, blanket, carpet, coat. **3** *girls covered in silk* clothe, attire, outfit, garb, robe, wrap. **4** *cover all the entrances* protect, defend, guard, shield, safeguard. **5** *cover several issues* include, deal with, involve, provide for, embrace, incorporate, refer to, consider, examine. **6** *money to cover expenses* offset, balance, counterbalance. **7** *cover against fire* insure, indemnify, protect. **8** *cover 30 miles* travel, travel/pass over, traverse, cross. **cover for** **1** *doctors covering for each other* relieve, substitute for, take over for/from, fill in for. **2** *the thief's sister covering for him* give an alibi, provide an alibi, shield, protect. **cover up** conceal, hide, keep secret, hush up, keep dark, suppress, stonewall; *inf.* whitewash.

cover noun **1** *take cover from the storm* protection, shield, shelter, concealment, housing, refuge, sanctuary, haven, hiding place. **2** *the cover for the pot/box* lid, top, cap, covering. **3** *a cover of dust/snow* layer, coating, film, blanket, overlay, carpet. **4** *the business is a cover for spying* front, pretense, façade, pretext, false front, screen, smokescreen, mask, cloak. **5** *under plain cover* envelope, wrapper, package. **6** *protecting the cover for wildlife* undergrowth, woods, shrubbery, thicket, copse.

coverage noun **1** *news coverage* reporting, reportage; reports, accounts, articles, pieces, stories. **2** *coverage against fire* insurance, protection, compensation, indemnification, indemnity.

covering noun **1** *provide covering for the children* protection, shelter. *See* COVER noun 1. **2** *a covering of dust/snow* layer, coating. *See* COVER noun 3. **3** *the boiler covering* casing, case, sheath, sheathing, jacket, housing.

covers noun bedclothes, sheets, blankets; bedcovers, quilts, comforters, duvets, bedspreads.

covert adjective secret, concealed, hidden, surreptitious, furtive, stealthy, underground.

covet verb desire, want, yearn for, crave, hanker/lust after, thirst for, hunger after, set one's heart on.

coward noun poltroon, craven, dastard, recreant, renegade; *inf.* chicken, scaredy-cat, yellowbelly, sissy, big baby.

cowardly adjective lily-livered, fainthearted, chickenhearted, craven, spineless, timorous, timid, shrinking, pusillanimous, dastardly, afraid of one's (own) shadow; *inf.* chicken, yellow, gutless, yellow-bellied.

cowboy noun cowhand, cattleman, cowherd, herdsman, drover, stockman, rancher, ranchero; *inf.* cowpuncher, cowpoke, broncobuster; gaucho.

cower verb cringe, shrink, flinch, draw back, recoil, crouch, wince, blench, quail, quake, tremble, quiver, grovel.

coy adjective coquettish, flirtatious, kittenish, shy, modest, bashful, reticent, shrinking, timid, demure.

cozen verb cheat, deceive, beguile, trick, double-cross, swindle, take advantage of, dupe, defraud, fleece, hoodwink.

cozy adjective snug, comfortable, warm, homelike, homey, sheltered, secure, safe, at ease; *inf.* comfy, snug as a bug.

crabby adjective crabbed, bad-tempered, ill-tempered, ill-natured, ill-humored, cross, cantankerous, crotchety, irritable, touchy, testy, grouchy, snappy, peevish, churlish, surly, sour, morose.

crack verb **1** *crack the cup* chip, fracture, fragment, break, split, splinter, snap, cleave. **2** *the rifle cracked* ring out, go bang, pop, snap, crackle, boom, explode, detonate. **3** *crack his head on a beam* hit, bang, bump, strike, knock, smack, whack, thump; *inf.* wallop, clout, clip. **4** *crack under questioning* give way, break down, collapse, go to pieces, lose control, yield, succumb, founder; *inf.* fall/come apart at the seams. **5** *crack the problem* solve, work out, get the answer to, find the solution to, fathom, decipher. **crack up** break down, have a breakdown, go out of one's mind, go mad; *inf.* freak out.

crack noun **1** *a crack in the cup/wall* chip, fracture, break. *See* CREVICE. **2** *the crack of the gun* bang, report, pop, snap, crackle, boom, explosion, detonation. **3** *a crack on the head* blow, hit, bang, bump, strike, knock, smack, whack, thump; *inf.* wallop, clout, clip. **4** *another crack at the competition* attempt, try, shot, opportunity; *inf.* go, stab. **5** *laugh at his cracks* wisecrack, joke, quip.

cradle verb hold, rock, nestle, shelter, support.

craft noun **1** *admire the artist's craft* skill, skillfulness, expertise, expertness, ability, mastery, artistry, art, technique, workmanship, aptitude, dexterity, talent, flair, knack. **2** *use craft to get his way* craftiness, cunning, artifice, guile, subterfuge, stratagem, slyness, wiliness, shrewdness, trickery, duplicity, deceit; wiles, ruses. **3** *take up a new craft* occupation, trade, vocation, pursuit, line. **4** *pilot a craft* vessel, ship, boat, aircraft, plane, spacecraft.

crafty adjective cunning, artful, scheming, designing, calculating, wily, sly, devious, guileful, tricky, duplicitous, deceitful, crooked, fraudulent, underhanded.

crag noun cliff, bluff, escarpment, scarp, ridge, peak, pinnacle, tor.

cram verb **1** *cram clothes into the suitcase* stuff, push, shove, force, pack in, ram down, press, squeeze, jam, crush, compress, compact, condense. **2** *a bus crammed with people* stuff, fill, fill to overflowing, stuff to the gills, fill to the brim, overcrowd.

cramped adjective **1** *cramped accommodations* narrow, small, restricted, limited, confined, closed in, hemmed in, tight, crowded, packed, squeezed, jammed in. **2** *cramped handwriting* small, squeezed, crabbed, illegible, unreadable, indecipherable.

cranky adjective **1** *a cranky old man | a cranky diet* eccentric, unconventional, odd, peculiar, queer, strange, bizarre, idiosyncratic, quirky; *inf.* funny, wacky. **2** *a cranky teacher* bad-tempered, cross. *See* CRABBY.

crash verb **1** *the glass crashed on the floor* smash, batter, dash, shatter, break, disintegrate, shiver, splinter, fracture, fragment. **2** *the cymbals crashed* clash, clang, clank, clatter, bang, boom, thunder, explode. **3** *the business crashed* collapse, fail, fold, fold up, go under, founder, be ruined, cave in; *inf.* go broke/bust. **4** *crash the party* gatecrash, intrude, sneak/slip into,

crash noun **1** *the crash of cymbals* clash, clank, clang, clatter, bang, smash, clangor, racket, din, boom, thunder, explosion. **2** *involved in a crash* accident, smash, smash-up, collision, pileup. **3** *the market crash* collapse, failure, bankruptcy, fold, smash, fall, ruin, ruination, downfall, depression, debacle.

crass adjective boorish, coarse, gross, vulgar, crude, rude, uncouth, unsophisticated, unrefined; insensitive, stupid, dense.

crave verb **1** *crave a chocolate bar* long/yearn for, desire, hanker after, need, hunger/thirst for, be dying for, cry out for, lust after, pant for. **2** *crave pardon* plead/beg for, entreat, beseech, implore, petition.

craven adjective chickenhearted, lily-livered. *See* COWARDLY.

craving noun longing, yearning, desire, hankering, need, urge, hunger, thirst, lust, appetite, addiction; *inf.* yen.

crawl verb creep, go on all fours, move on hands and knees, inch, drag/pull oneself along, drag, slither, squirm, wriggle, writhe, worm one's way, advance slowly/stealthily, sneak.

craze noun fad, vogue, trend, fashion, obsession, mania, fixation, fancy, novelty, whim, rage; *inf.* thing, the latest.

crazy adjective **1** *a crazy person* crazed, of unsound mind, insane, mad, mad as a hatter, mad as a March hare, lunatic, wild, unbalanced, demented, deranged, berserk, unhinged, touched, maniacal, delirious, out of one's mind/head; *inf.* cracked, daft, bats, batty, loony, loopy, screwy, flaky, nuts, nutty, nutty as a fruit cake, cuckoo, bonkers, mental, not all there, out to lunch, off one's nut/rocker, around/round the bend. **2** *a crazy idea* absurd, idiotic, stupid, silly, ridiculous, foolish, peculiar, odd, strange, queer, weird, eccentric, bizarre, fantastic, outrageous, wild, fatuous, inane, puerile, impracticable, senseless, unworkable, foolhardy, unrealistic, unwise, imprudent, ill-conceived, preposterous; *inf.* screwy, screwball, harebrained, cockeyed, half-baked. **crazy about** *crazy about opera* enthusiastic about, mad about, wild about, avid about, keen about, infatuated with, passionate about, smitten with/by, fanatical about, devoted to, fond/enamored of, zealous about/for, fervent, fervid about, excited about; *inf.* nuts about/on.

creak verb squeak, screech, squeal, groan, grate, grind, jar, rasp, scrape, scratch.

cream noun **1** *beauty/antiseptic cream* lotion, emulsion, emollient, paste; cosmetic, ointment, salve, unguent, liniment. **2** *the cream of the college* best/choice part, flower, elite, pick, prime, crème de la crème.

create verb **1** *create a new environment* generate, originate, invent, initiate, engender, produce, design, devise, make, frame, fabricate, build, construct, erect, develop, shape, form, mold, forge, concoct, hatch. **2** *create a good impression* produce, make, result in, cause.

creation noun **1** *the creation of a new environment* generation, origination, invention, initiation, inception, design, devising, formation, production, fabrication, building, shaping, hatching. **2** *everything in creation* the world, the living/natural world, the universe, the cosmos, nature, life; all living things. **3** *the poet's creation* work, work of art, achievement, production, opus, invention, handiwork.

creative adjective inventive, imaginative, original, artistic, inspired, visionary, talented, gifted, resourceful, ingenious, clever, productive, fertile.

creator noun *the creator of the series* author, inventor, originator, initiator, maker, designer, producer, architect, prime mover, begetter, generator.

creature noun living thing/entity, being; animal, beast; person, human being, human, individual, character, fellow, soul, mortal; *inf.* critter, body.

credentials plural noun testimonial, proof of identity/qualifications, evidence, documentation, references.

credibility noun **1** *the credibility of the story* plausibility, tenability. **2** *the government lacks credibility* trustworthiness, reliability, dependability, integrity.

credible adjective **1** *a scarcely credible story* believable, conceivable, imaginable, plausible, tenable. **2** *the more credible party* acceptable, trustworthy, reliable, dependable.

credit noun **1** *receive credit for his performance* acknowledgment, tribute, kudos, glory, recognition, regard, respect, merit; thanks. **2** *he gained credit in the city* reputation, prestige, influence, standing, status, regard, esteem; *inf.* clout. **3** *a credit to the town* source of honor/pride, feather in the cap, asset, boast, glory. **4** *the story gaining credit* belief, believability, credence, faith, trust, reliability, reliance, confidence. **on credit** in installments, by deferred payment, on account.

credulous adjective gullible, naïve, green, dupable, deceivable, unsuspicious, unskeptical, uncritical; *inf.* wet behind the ears.

creed noun beliefs, principles, rules, articles of faith, maxims.

creek noun stream, brook, rivulet, small river, channel; *inf.* crick.

creep verb **1** *creeping along the ground* go on all fours, move on hands and knees. *See* CRAWL. **2** *creep up on them* move stealthily, steal, sneak, tiptoe, approach unnoticed, slink, skulk.

creepy adjective horrifying, horrific, frightening, terrifying, hair-raising, disturbing, eerie, sinister, weird, nightmarish, macabre, menacing, ominous, threatening, disgusting, repellent, repulsive, revolting; *inf.* scary.

crest noun 1 *a cock's crest | the helmet crest* cockscomb, comb, tuft, plume, topknot, tassel, mane, panache. 2 *the crest of the hill* summit, top, pinnacle, peak, crown, apex, ridge. 3 *the club crest* regalia, insignia, badge, emblem, device, coat of arms.

crestfallen adjective downcast, dejected, depressed, glum, downhearted, disheartened, discouraged, dispirited, disappointed, disconsolate, in the doldrums, down in the dumps.

crevice noun fissure, cleft, chink, crack, cranny, split, rift, slit, gash, rent, fracture, opening, gap, hole, interstice.

crew noun 1 *the camera crew* team, company, party, working party, gang, squad, force, corps. 2 *that crew over there* crowd, lot, gang, troop, band, group, bunch, set.

crime noun 1 *convicted of the crime* offense, misdemeanor, misdeed, wrong, felony, violation, transgression, trespass. 2 *a crime against humanity* sin, evil, evil action, wrong, wrongdoing, vice, iniquity. 3 *crime is on the increase* lawbreaking, delinquency, wrongdoing, villainy, malefaction, illegality, misconduct, corruption.

criminal adjective 1 *a criminal act* unlawful, illegal, lawbreaking, illicit, lawless, felonious, indictable, delinquent, culpable, wrong, villainous, corrupt, evil, wicked, iniquitous, nefarious; *inf.* crooked. 2 *a criminal waste of resources* deplorable, scandalous, shameful, reprehensible, senseless, foolish, ridiculous, sinful, immoral.

criminal noun lawbreaker, offender, wrongdoer, felon, delinquent, miscreant, malefactor, culprit, villain, gangster, bandit, transgressor, sinner, trespasser; *inf.* crook, con.

cringe verb cower, shrink, draw back, quail, flinch, recoil, start, shy, blench, dodge, duck, crouch, wince, tremble, quiver, shake.

cripple verb 1 *the accident crippled him* make lame, disable, incapacitate, debilitate, impair, maim, enfeeble, paralyze. 2 *businesses crippled by the recession* injure, ruin, destroy, weaken, impair, hamstring, hamper, impede, cramp, spoil.

crippled adjective lame, disabled, incapacitated, physically impaired/handicapped, deformed.

crisis noun 1 *the crisis of the fever | reach a crisis* turning point, critical/decisive point, crux, climax, culmination, height, moment of truth, zero hour; *inf.* crunch. 2 *a financial crisis* extremity, predicament, plight, mess, trouble, difficulty, dilemma, quandary, exigency; dire straits; *inf.* fix, pickle, scrape.

crisp adjective 1 *crisp toast* brittle, crispy, crumbly, crunchy, breakable. 2 *crisp lettuce* firm, fresh, unwilted, unwithered. 3 *crisp weather* brisk, bracing, fresh, refreshing, invigorating, dry, cool, chilly. 4 *a crisp account* brief, terse, succinct, concise, short, incisive, clear, pithy. 5 *a crisp manner* brisk, vigorous, decisive. 6 *a crisp appearance* clean-cut, neat, smart, spruce, trim, well-groomed; *inf.* snappy.

criterion noun measure, gauge, scale, yardstick, standard, norm, benchmark, touchstone, barometer, model, exemplar.

critic noun 1 *theater critics* reviewer, commentator, pundit, arbiter, evaluator, analyst, judge. 2 *answer his critics* faultfinder, attacker, detractor, backbiter; *inf.* nitpicker.

critical adjective 1 *a critical point in history* crucial, deciding, decisive, climacteric, pivotal, important, momentous, high-priority, urgent, pressing, compelling. 2 *in a critical condition* dangerous, grave, serious, risky, perilous, hazardous, touch-and-go, uncertain, precarious; *inf.* chancy. 3 *a critical attitude* faultfinding, captious, censorious, carping, quibbling, judgmental, hypercritical; *inf.* nitpicking. 4 *a critical essay* evaluative, analytic, interpretative, expository, commentative, explanatory.

criticism noun 1 *actions receiving criticism* faultfinding, censure, reproof, condemnation, disapproval, disparagement, captiousness, carping; *inf.* nitpicking, flak, bad press, bad notices, knocking, panning, slamming. 2 *studying literary criticism* evaluation, comment, assessment, appreciation, appraisal, interpretation, explanation, explication, elucidation, annotation. 3 *read the criticism* review, notice, commentary, critique, analysis, appraisal.

criticize verb find fault with, censure, denounce, blame, condemn, pick holes in, disapprove of, disparage, carp at, cavil at, excoriate; *inf.* nitpick, hand out brickbats, give flak to, knock, pan, slam.

critique noun evaluation, commentary. *See* CRITICISM 2, 3.

crony noun friend, companion, chum, comrade, associate, confederate; *inf.* pal, buddy.

crook noun 1 *crooks imprisoned* thief, robber, swindler, cheat, racketeer; *inf.* shark, con man. 2 *the crook of one's arm* bend, curve, curvature, angle, bow.

crooked adjective 1 *a crooked branch/road* bent, curved, twisted, contorted, warped, irregular, angled, bowed, hooked, flexed, winding, twisting. 2 *a crooked back* deformed, misshapen, disfigured, crippled. 3 *the picture is crooked* tilted, angled, slanted, aslant, slanting, sloping, askew, awry, to one side, off-center, lopsided, uneven, asymmetrical. 4 *a crooked politician/deal* criminal, dishonest, corrupt, dishonorable, unscrupulous, unprincipled, fraudulent, illegal, unlawful, underhanded; *inf.* shady.

crop noun **1** *the apple crop* harvest, yield, produce, vintage, gathering, reaping, gleaning, garnering. **2** *the year's crop of students* batch, lot, collection, assortment, selection, supply.

crop verb cut short, lop. See CUT verb 4.

crop up happen, occur, arise, turn up, spring up, emerge, appear, come to pass.

cross noun **1** *the sign of the cross* crucifix, rood. **2** *a cross to bear* trouble, worry, burden, trial, disaster, tribulation, affliction, misfortune, adversity, misery, woe, pain, suffering. **3** *a cross between two breeds/types* crossbreed, hybrid, mixture, amalgam, blend, combination, mongrel, cur.

cross verb **1** *the bridge crossing the river* span, extend/stretch across, pass over, bridge, ford. **2** *cross the road* go/travel across, cut across, traverse. **3** *the roads/lines crossed there* intersect, meet, join, converge, crisscross, interweave, intertwine. **4** *hates being crossed* oppose, resist, thwart, frustrate, deny, contradict. **5** *cross two species* crossbreed, interbreed, cross-fertilize, crosspollinate, hybridize, mix, blend. **cross out** delete, strike out, blue-pencil, cancel, eliminate, obliterate.

cross adjective **1** *she was cross at/with the children* angry, annoyed, irritated, in a bad mood, peeved, vexed, upset, piqued, out of humor. **2** *a cross old woman* irritable, short-tempered, bad-tempered, ill-humored, surly, churlish, disagreeable, irascible, touchy, snappish, peevish, petulant, fractious, crotchety, grouchy, grumpy, querulous, cantankerous, testy, captious, splenetic, waspish. **3** *cross purposes* contrary, opposing, opposite, adverse, unfavorable.

crouch verb squat, bend, bend down, hunker, stoop, hunch over, cower, cringe.

crow verb boast, brag, trumpet, gloat, show off, swagger, bluster, strut; *inf.* blow one's own horn.

crowd noun **1** *a crowd of people* throng, horde, mob, rabble, mass, multitude, host, army, herd, flock, drove, swarm, pack, flood, collection, company, gathering, assembly, assemblage. **2** *nonconformists don't follow the crowd* majority, multitude, common people, populace, general public, mob, rank and file, hoi polloi, proletariat; riff-raff; masses. **3** *the late-night crowd* group, set, lot, gang, bunch, clique. **4** *the show played to a capacity crowd* gate, house, turnout, audience, attendance; spectators, listeners, viewers.

crowd verb **1** *crowd around the teacher* gather, cluster, congregate, flock, swarm, throng, huddle. **2** *people crowding into the*

hall push, shove, thrust forward, elbow, squeeze. **3** *tourists crowding the streets* throng, pack, fill, overfill, congest. **4** *crowd people into the trains* pack, squeeze, cram, jam, stuff, pile.

crowded adjective full, overfull, busy, overflowing, packed, jam-packed, crushed, cramped, congested, teeming, swarming, thronged, populous, mobbed.

crown noun **1** *the king's crown* diadem, coronet, coronal, tiara. **2** *the champion wins the crown* prize, trophy; honor, distinction, glory, kudos; laurels. **3** *the power of the Crown* monarchy, monarch, sovereignty, sovereign, king, queen, emperor, empress. **4** *the crown of the hill* top, crest, summit, apex, head, tip, pinnacle. **5** *the crown of his achievements* height, culmination, pinnacle, zenith, acme.

crown verb **1** *crown the queen* invest, inaugurate, induct, install. **2** *crown his career* cap, round off, be the culmination/climax of, consummate, top off, complete, perfect. **3** *the steeple crowning the church* top, surmount, overtop.

crucial adjective determining, central, essential, vital. See CRITICAL 1.

crude adjective **1** *crude oil/flour* raw, unrefined, natural, coarse, unprocessed. **2** *a crude sculpture/dwelling* rudimentary, primitive, rough, rough-hewn, makeshift, unfinished, unpolished, unformed, undeveloped, rude. **3** *a crude manner* coarse, vulgar, rude, uncouth, indelicate, boorish, crass, tasteless.

cruel adjective **1** *a cruel dictator* savage, brutal, inhuman, barbarous, vicious, ferocious, fierce, evil, fiendish, callous, cold-blooded, sadistic, ruthless, merciless, pitiless, unfeeling, heartless, inhumane, severe, harsh, stern. **2** *a cruel stroke of fate* unkind, painful, distressing, harrowing, harsh, grim, heartless.

cruelty noun **1** *the cruelty of the dictator* savageness, savagery, brutality, inhumanity, viciousness, ferocity, fierceness, evil, callousness, sadism, ruthlessness, pitilessness, severity, harshness. **2** *the cruelty of the blow* unkindness, painfulness, grimness, heartlessness.

crumb noun bit, fragment, morsel, particle, grain, atom, speck, scrap, shred, sliver, mite.

crumble verb **1** *crumble the crackers* break up, crush, pulverize, pound, grind, powder. **2** *the empire was crumbling* disintegrate, fall to pieces, fall apart, collapse, decay, deteriorate, degenerate, go to rack and ruin, rot, rot away, molder, perish, vanish, fade away.

crunch verb **1** *crunching carrots* munch, champ, chomp, gnaw, masticate. **2** *crunch* *the snow* crush, grind, pulverize, pound, smash.

crusade noun campaign, war, drive, push, struggle, cause, movement.

crusade verb campaign, fight, work, do battle, take up arms.

crusader noun campaigner, fighter, battler, champion, advocate, reformer.

crush verb **1** *crush the grapes* squash, squeeze, mash, press, press down, compress, bruise. **2** *crush the material* crease, crumple, rumple, wrinkle, crinkle. **3** *crush the stones* smash, shatter, pound, pulverize, grind, crumble, crunch. **4** *crush the rebellion* put down, quell, quash, suppress, subdue, overcome, overwhelm, defeat, conquer. **5** *crushed by his criticism* mortify, humiliate, abash, quash, shame, chagrin; *inf.* put down. **6** *crush her in his arms* embrace, enfold, hug.

cry verb **1** *babies crying* weep, sob, wail, snivel, blubber, whimper, whine, bawl, howl. **2** *he cried out her name* call out, exclaim, yell, scream, screech, bawl, shout, bellow, howl.

cry noun call, exclamation, scream, screech, yell, shout, bellow, howl. **cries** weeping, sobbing, sniveling, blubbering, wailing, lamenting, lamentation; sobs, wails, howls.

cuddle verb **1** *cuddling his wife* hug, embrace, enfold, clasp. **2** *cuddling by the fire* embrace, pet, fondle; *inf.* neck, smooch. **3** *cuddle (up) in bed* snuggle, nestle, curl up.

cuddly adjective cuddlesome, huggable, warm, soft.

cue noun **1** *"away" is your cue* catchword, keyword, prompt, reminder. **2** *your cue to begin* signal, sign, indication, hint, suggestion, intimation.

cuff noun **off the cuff** impromptu, ad lib, extempore, extemporaneous, extemporaneously, off the top of one's head, unrehearsed, improvised, offhand.

culmination noun high point, consummation, completion, close. *See* CLIMAX.

culpable adjective at fault, in the wrong, guilty, answerable, blameworthy, blamable, to blame, censurable, reproachable, reprovable.

culprit noun guilty party, wrongdoer, evildoer, lawbreaker, criminal, miscreant, delinquent, reprobate, transgressor, felon, sinner, malefactor; *inf.* bad guy.

cult noun **1** *belong to a secretive cult* sect, religion, faith, belief, persuasion, faction, clique. **2** *the rap music cult* craze, fashion, fad; admiration, devotion, obsession, homage, worship, idolization.

cultivate verb **1** *cultivate the fields* till, farm, work, plow, dig, prepare, fertilize. **2** *cultivate a crop* plant, raise, tend, bring

on, produce. **3** *cultivate the mind* culture, educate, train, civilize, enlighten, enrich, improve, better, develop, refine, polish. **4** *cultivate a friendship* pursue, foster, promote, encourage, support.

cultivated adjective cultured, educated, civilized, enlightened, refined, polished, sophisticated, discerning, discriminating, urbane.

cultural adjective **1** *cultural interests* artistic, enlightening, enriching, broadening, edifying, civilizing, elevating. **2** *cultural differences* lifestyle, ethnic, folk, racial.

culture noun **1** *a woman of culture* cultivation, education, enlightenment, accomplishment, edification, erudition, refinement, polish, sophistication, urbanity, discernment, discrimination, good taste, taste, breeding, politeness, gentility, *savoir faire*. **2** *belong to a different culture* civilization, way of life, lifestyle; customs, habits, ways, mores.

cultured adjective cultivated, artistic, educated, enlightened, learned, knowledgeable, intellectual, highbrow, scholarly, well-informed, well-read, erudite, accomplished, well-versed, refined, genteel, polished, sophisticated, urbane.

cumbersome adjective **1** *cumbersome packages* awkward, unwieldy, bulky, hefty, clumsy, unmanageable, burdensome, inconvenient. **2** *cumbersome procedures* slow, slow-moving, inefficient, unwieldy.

cumulative adjective accumulative, increasing, growing, enlarging, accruing, snowballing.

cunning adjective **1** *a cunning thief* crafty, devious, deceitful, wily, sly, shifty, artful, foxy, tricky, guileful, shrewd, astute, sharp, knowing, subtle, Machiavellian. **2** *a cunning device/artist* clever, ingenious, resourceful, inventive, imaginative.

cunning noun **1** *the cunning of the thief* craftiness, deviousness, deceitfulness, deceit, wiliness, slyness, artfulness, foxiness, trickery, guile, shrewdness, astuteness. **2** *admire the cunning of the process/artist* cleverness, ingenuity, resourcefulness, inventiveness, imaginativeness, skill, dexterity, ability, capability.

curb verb restrain, check, control, constrain, contain, hold back, bite back, repress, suppress, moderate, dampen, impede, retard, subdue, bridle.

curb noun *curbs on expenditure* restraint, check, control, constraint, limitation, limit, damper, brake, rein.

cure noun remedy, curative, medicine, cure-all, panacea, restorative, corrective, antidote, nostrum; treatment, therapy.

cure verb **1** *cure the patient* heal, restore to health, rehabilitate, treat. **2** *cure*

the disease remedy, doctor, fix, repair.
3 *cure meat* preserve, smoke, salt, dry,
pickle.

curiosity noun **1** *curiosity about the past*
inquisitiveness, interest, questioning, prying, snooping; *inf.* nosiness. **2** *the curiosities
on display* novelty, oddity, phenomenon,
rarity, wonder, marvel, sight, spectacle.

curious adjective **1** *curious to know the facts*
inquisitive, inquiring, interested, investigating, searching, questioning. **2** *curious about others' affairs* prying, snooping,
meddling, meddlesome, interfering, intrusive; *inf.* nosy, snoopy. **3** *a curious
site* strange, unusual, rare, odd, peculiar, extraordinary, remarkable, singular,
novel, queer, bizarre, unconventional,
unorthodox, weird, freakish, marvelous,
prodigious, exotic, mysterious.

curl verb **1** *the smoke curled upward* spiral,
coil, twist, twist and turn, wind, curve,
bend, loop, twirl, wreathe, meander, snake,
corkscrew. **2** *curl the hair* crimp, crinkle,
kink, frizz, wave.

curl noun **1** *put curls in one's hair* kink,
ringlet, coil, wave, curlicue, corkscrew.
2 *curls of smoke* spiral, coil, twist, whorl,
helix.

currency noun **1** *foreign currency* money,
legal tender, cash, coinage, coin, specie, paper money; coins, bank notes,
notes, bills. **2** *story gaining currency* prevalence, acceptance, popularity, vogue, circulation.

current adjective **1** *current fashions* present, present-day, contemporary, ongoing,
extant, existing, popular, modern, up-to-
date, up-to-the-minute. **2** *ideas no longer
current* prevalent, accepted, in circulation, going around, common, popular,
widespread.

current noun **1** *current of air* steady flow,
draft, updraft, downdraft, wind, thermal.
2 *swimmers swept away by the current* stream,
tide, channel. **3** *disturb the even current
of their life* course, flow, progression. **4**
currents of opinion trend, drift, tendency,
tenor.

curse noun **1** *a voodoo curse* malediction, evil eye, execration, imprecation,
anathema, damnation, excommunication;
inf. jinx. **2** *angrily uttering curses* oath,
swearword, expletive, profanity, obscenity; swearing, blasphemy; *inf.* cussword.
3 *the curse of poverty* evil, affliction, burden, cross, bane, scourge, plague, torment.

curse verb **1** *the sorcerer cursed them* accurse,
put the evil eye on, execrate, imprecate,
anathematize, damn, excommunicate; *inf.*
put a jinx on, jinx. **2** *curse at the policeman*
swear, blaspheme; *inf.* cuss. **3** *poverty*

cursed his childhood blight, afflict, trouble,
beset, plague, torment.

curt adjective abrupt, brusque, blunt, short-
spoken, short, snappy, snappish, sharp,
crisp, tart, rude, impolite, unceremonious,
brief, concise.

curtail verb reduce, cut short, truncate,
shorten, abbreviate. *See* CUT *verb* 6.

curtain noun **1** *hang curtains* drape, dra-
pery, window hanging; screen, blind. **2**
a curtain of secrecy screen, cover, shield,
cloak, veil.

curve noun arc, bend, arch, turn, bow,
loop, hook, half moon, crescent.

curve verb bend, arc, arch, bow, turn,
inflect, swerve, twist, wind, hook, loop,
spiral, coil.

cushion noun pillow, throw pillow, bolster,
pad; hassock, mat, beanbag.

cushion verb **1** *cushion her head* pillow,
bolster, cradle, support, prop up. **2**
cushion the blow soften, lessen, diminish,
mitigate, allay, deaden, muffle, stifle. **3**
cushion the child from reality protect, shield,
buttress.

custody noun **1** *in the custody of his mother*
guardianship, wardship, trusteeship,
charge, care, keeping, keep, safekeeping,
protection, guidance, supervision. **2** *sus-
pects in custody* imprisonment, detention,
confinement, incarceration.

custom noun **1** *it was their custom to leave
early* habit, practice, routine, way, wont,
policy, rule. **2** *local customs* practice,
convention, ritual, procedure, ceremony,
form, usage, observance, way, fashion,
mode, style.

customary adjective accustomed, usual,
regular, common, habitual, traditional,
routine, fixed, set, established, everyday.

customer noun patron, client, buyer, purchaser, shopper, consumer; clientele; *inf.*
regular.

cut verb **1** *cut his finger/throat* gash, slash,
lacerate, slit, nick, notch, pierce, penetrate, wound, lance, incise, score. **2** *cut
the logs/meat* chop, sever, divide, cleave,
carve, slice. **3** *cut a key/gem* shape, fashion,
form, mold, chisel, carve, sculpt, sculpture, chip away, whittle, engrave, incise,
score. **4** *cut their hair | cut the hedge/grass*
trim, clip, snip, crop, prune, dock, shear,
shave, pare, mow. **5** *cut some flowers* detach, gather, harvest, reap. **6** *cut expendi-
tures* reduce, curtail, curb, retrench, cut
back/down on, decrease, lessen, lower,
diminish, contract, ease up on, prune,
slash, slim down, slenderize, economize
on. **7** *cut the text* shorten, abridge, condense, abbreviate, summarize, epitomize.
8 *cut the unsuitable parts* delete, edit out,

blue-pencil, excise. **9** *his behavior cut me* hurt, offend, wound, distress, grieve, pain, sting. **10** *his old friend cut him* shun, ignore, snub, spurn, give the cold shoulder to. **11** *cut the engine* stop, halt, turn off, switch off. **12** *cut a record/tape* record, put on disk/tape, make a tape of, tape-record. **cut across** *cut across national prejudices* transcend, go beyond, rise above. **cut down 1** *cut down a tree* fell, saw down, hew, chop/hack down. **2** *cut down in his prime* kill, slay, slaughter, massacre, mow down, dispatch. **cut in** *cut in on a conversation* interrupt, interpose, break in, intervene, intrude; *inf.* butt in. **cut off 1** *cut off supplies/communication* break off, disconnect, interrupt, suspend, discontinue, halt, stop. **2** *cut off from the town by snow* isolate, separate, sever. **3** *cut off without a penny* disinherit, disown, renounce. **cut out 1** *cut out eating chocolate* give up, refrain from, stop, cease. **2** *cut out the middleman* leave out, omit, eliminate, exclude, do away with. **3** *the engine cut out* stop, malfunction. **4** *not cut out for teaching* suit, equip/design for. **cut short** *cut short a vacation* interrupt, break off, leave unfinished, truncate, abort. **cut up** verb **1** *cut up in a street fight* slash, knife, stab, lacerate, wound, injure. **2** *the teacher really cut up his essay/friend* criticize, ridicule, find fault with, tear to pieces/shreds, take apart.

cut noun **1** *a cut on his finger* gash, slash, laceration, incision, slit. **2** *a cut in expenditure/salary* cutback, decrease, reduction, lessening, curtailment, retrenchment, contraction. **3** *I want my cut* share, portion, proportion.

cutthroat adjective **1** *a cutthroat attack* murderous, death-dealing, homicidal, savage, violent, bloody, bloodthirsty, fierce, ferocious, barbarous, cruel. **2** *a cutthroat business* ruthless, merciless, pitiless, unfeeling, relentless, dog-eat-dog, fiercely competitive.

cutting adjective **1** *a cutting wind* biting, bitter, piercing, raw, keen, penetrating, stinging, sharp, chill, chilling, icy. **2** *a cutting remark* hurtful, wounding, caustic, acid, barbed, acrimonious, trenchant, mordant, scathing.

cycle noun **1** *occur in cycles* rotation, round, revolution. **2** *compare the completed cycles* series, sequence, succession, run.

cynic noun pessimist, skeptic, scoffer, doubter, doubting Thomas, misanthrope.

cynical adjective pessimistic, skeptical, scoffing, doubting, unbelieving, disbelieving, distrustful, suspicious, misanthropic, critical, sardonic.

cynicism noun pessimism, skepticism, scoffing, doubt, unbelief, disbelief, distrust, suspicion, misanthropy.

Dd

dab verb pat, press, touch, blot, smudge.

dab noun *add a dab of paint/butter* touch, bit, spot, drop, dash, tinge, suggestion, hint, modicum.

dabble verb **dabble in** *dabble in politics* toy with, dip into, flirt with, trifle with, play with, fiddle with.

daft adjective silly, absurd, stupid, foolish, idiotic, fatuous, ridiculous, ludicrous, asinine, simple, simpleminded, feebleminded, slow-witted; crazy, insane, mad.

dagger noun stiletto, dirk, bayonet, knife, blade.

dainty adjective **1** *dainty china figures* petite, neat, delicate, exquisite, refined, tasteful, fine, elegant, graceful, pretty. **2** *a dainty morsel* tasty, delicious, appetizing, choice, delectable, luscious. **3** *a dainty eater* particular, discriminating, fastidious, fussy, choosy, finicky, refined.

dam noun barricade, barrier, embankment, obstruction, hindrance.

damage verb harm, injure, hurt, impair, abuse, spoil, mar, deface, defile, vandalize.

damage noun harm, injury, hurt, impairment, abuse, defacement, detriment, vandalism, destruction, ruin, loss.

damages plural noun *receive damages from the court* compensation, indemnity, reparation, restitution.

damn verb **1** *damned for his blasphemy* curse, doom, execrate, imprecate, excommunicate, anathematize. **2** *damned by the neighbors/critics* condemn, censure, criticize, castigate, denounce, attack, flay; *inf.* pan, slam.

damn interjection *inf.* darn, rats, shoot.

damned adjective **1** *damned souls* cursed, accursed, doomed, lost, condemned, exe-

crated, excommunicated, anathematized.
2 *this damned machine/weather* annoying,
confounded, nasty, hateful, detestable,
odious.

damp adjective wettish, moist, dank, soggy,
rainy, drizzly, humid, clammy, muggy,
misty, foggy.

dampen verb **1** *dampen the clothes/atmosphere* wet, moisten, humidify. **2** *dampen
their enthusiasm* discourage, dull, dash,
check, curb, restrain, stifle, inhibit, deter.

dampness noun damp, wetness, moisture,
dankness.

dance verb move/sway to music, twirl,
pirouette; caper, skip, prance, hop, frolic,
gambol, jump, jig, romp, bounce, whirl,
spin.

danger noun risk, peril, hazard, jeopardy,
precariousness, menace, threat.

dangerous adjective risky, perilous, hazardous, chancy, precarious, insecure, unsound, unsafe; menacing, threatening,
alarming, ominous, treacherous.

dangle verb **1** *keys dangling from her waist*
hang, hang down, swing. **2** *dangle the keys*
swing, wave, brandish, flourish, flaunt.

dare verb **1** *dare to go* have the courage, be
brave enough, have the nerve, risk, hazard, venture. **2** *dare him to go* challenge,
provoke, goad, taunt.

daredevil adjective daring, adventurous,
bold, audacious, courageous, intrepid, fearless, rash, heedless, foolhardy, impetuous,
incautious.

daredevil noun adventurer, stunt man,
exhibitionist; *inf.* show-off.

daring adjective bold, adventurous, brave,
courageous, audacious, intrepid, fearless,
rash, reckless.

daring noun *the daring of the explorers* bravery, courage, valor, audacity, nerve, pluck,
temerity; *inf.* guts.

dark adjective **1** *a dark night* black, pitch-black, inky, unlit, unlighted, dim, indistinct, shadowy, shady, murky, overcast,
sunless. **2** *dark thoughts* dismal, gloomy,
somber, bleak, drab, dreary, depressed, dejected, melancholy, grave, morose, mournful, doleful. **3** *a dark mood* angry, moody,
brooding, sullen, dour, glum, morose,
sulky, frowning, scowling, glowering, forbidding, threatening, ominous. **4** *dark
deeds* evil, wicked, sinful, villainous, vile,
base, foul, horrible, atrocious, abominable, nefarious, sinister. **5** *a dark secret*
concealed, hidden, veiled, mysterious.

dark noun **1** *sitting in the dark* darkness,
blackness, gloom, murkiness, shade. **2**
when dark comes night, nighttime, dead of
night, evening, twilight.

darken verb **1** *the sky darkened* grow
dark/darker, blacken, cloud over, dim,
grow dim. **2** *darken the room* make dim,
shade. **3** *darken one's skin* tan, blacken.
4 *his mood/face darkened* blacken, grow
angry, become gloomy, sadden.

darkness noun blackness, gloom; night.
See DARK noun.

darling noun dear, dearest, dear one, love,
sweetheart, beloved, honey, charmer,
favorite, pet; *inf.* sweetie.

darling adjective **1** *his darling wife* dear, beloved, adored, cherished, treasured, precious. **2** *a darling little girl* adorable, sweet,
lovely, charming, enchanting; *inf.* cute.

dart noun **1** *throwing a poisoned dart* arrow,
barb. **2** *make a sudden dart* dash, rush,
run, bolt, bound, spring, leap, start.

dart verb **1** *dart into the bushes* dash, rush,
bolt, sprint, tear, run, bound, spring,
leap, start; *inf.* scoot. **2** *dart an angry
look* throw, cast, shoot, send, fling, toss,
flash, hurl.

dash noun **1** *make a dash for freedom* rush,
bolt, run, race, flight, dart, sprint, spurt.
2 *a dash of salt* bit, drop, pinch, sprinkling,
splash, grain, trace, suggestion.

dash verb **1** *dash into the road* rush, hurry,
hasten, bolt, run, race, fly, dart, sprint,
tear. **2** *waves dashing against the shore*
strike, beat, break, crash, smash, batter.
3 *dash the plate to the floor* smash, crash,
throw, hurl, fling, slam, cast. **4** *dash her
hopes* shatter, destroy, ruin, spoil, frustrate,
thwart.

dashing adjective debonair, stylish, smart,
jaunty, sporty, elegant, fashionable, showy,
flamboyant; gallant, bold, daring.

data plural noun facts, figures, statistics,
details; information, material, input.

date noun **1** *a lunch date* appointment, engagement, meeting, rendezvous, tryst. **2**
who is his date? partner, escort, girlfriend,
boyfriend, beau; *inf.* steady. **to date** so
far, as of now, up to now.

date verb *dating the girl next door* go out
with, go with, take out; *inf.* go steady with.

dated adjective out-of-date, outdated, old-fashioned, outmoded, passé.

daub verb smear, plaster, smudge, spatter, slap.

daunt verb intimidate, frighten, scare,
alarm, dismay, disconcert, unnerve, discourage, dishearten, dispirit, deter, put off.

dawdle verb go slowly, loiter, dally, linger,
delay, idle; *inf.* dilly-dally.

dawn noun **1** *get up at dawn* daybreak,
break of day, sunrise, first light, sunup.

2 *the dawn of civilization* dawning, beginning, birth, start, rise, emergence, origin, inception, genesis, outset, onset, advent, unfolding.

dawn verb *day dawned* begin, break, lighten, brighten. **dawn on** *the truth suddenly dawned on them* occur to, strike, hit.

day noun **1** *when day dawns* daytime, daylight hours, broad daylight. **2** *in this modern day* period, time, age, era, epoch, generation. **3** *the steam train has had its day* prime, heyday, peak, zenith, ascendancy. **day after day** *raining day after day* continuously, relentlessly, persistently, ceaselessly, regularly. **day by day** *grow bigger day by day* daily, gradually, steadily, progressively.

daybreak noun break of day, sunrise. *See* DAWN noun 1.

daydream noun reverie, fantasy, fancy, hallucination; dream, wishful thinking; castles in the air.

daydream verb dream, muse, fantasize, hallucinate; *inf.* space.

daylight noun light of day, natural light, sunlight, daytime, broad daylight; dawn, daybreak, sunrise. **see daylight** understand, comprehend, see the light; *inf.* catch on, get the picture.

daze verb stun, stupefy, shock, confuse, bewilder, numb, paralyze; amaze, astonish, astound, dumbfound.

daze noun stupor, state of shock; confusion, bewilderment, distraction, numbness.

dazzle verb daze, overpower, overwhelm, awe, hypnotize, amaze, astonish; *inf.* bowl over, take one's breath away.

dead adjective **1** *the dead man/flower* deceased, late, departed, lifeless, expired, extinct. **2** *dead matter* inanimate, lifeless. **3** *a dead language* obsolete, outmoded, outdated, extinct, passé, discontinued. **4** *dead fingers* numb, unfeeling, paralyzed. **5** *a dead time of day* dull, boring, tedious, tiresome, uneventful, humdrum. **6** *feeling dead* tired, exhausted, worn out, fatigued, spent; *inf.* pooped.

dead adverb *dead right/serious/tired* completely, absolutely, totally, entirely, utterly, thoroughly, categorically.

deaden verb blunt, dull, muffle, weaken, diminish, reduce, suppress, moderate, abate, mitigate, alleviate, smother, stifle, numb, mute, desensitize, anesthetize.

deadlock noun stalemate, impasse, standstill, stand-off, tie, draw.

deadly adjective fatal, lethal, mortal, dangerous, destructive, harmful, pernicious, noxious, malignant, venomous, toxic, poisonous, virulent.

deaf adjective unhearing, hard of hearing, stone deaf. **deaf to** *deaf to their pleas* unmoved by, indifferent to, oblivious to, heedless of, unmindful of.

deafening adjective earsplitting, earpiercing, overpowering, booming, thunderous, resounding, reverberating, ringing.

deal verb **1** *deal with a problem* attend to, see to, take care of, cope with, handle, manage, sort out. **2** *the book deals with Mozart* be about, have to do with, concern, discuss, consider. **3** *deal in stocks and bonds* trade, traffic, buy and sell, negotiate. **4** *deal cards* distribute, hand out, dole out, mete out, allocate, dispense.

deal noun arrangement, transaction, agreement, negotiation, bargain, contract, pact.

dealer noun trader, salesman, saleswoman, salesperson, retailer, wholesaler, vendor, trafficker.

dealings plural noun *have dealings with the firm* business, trade, commerce; transactions, relations, negotiations.

dear adjective **1** *his dear wife* beloved, loved, darling, adored, cherished, intimate. **2** *her dearest possessions* precious, treasured, valued, prized, cherished, favorite. **3** *what a dear child* sweet, darling, endearing, lovable, enchanting. **4** *the car was too dear for me* expensive, costly, high-priced, overpriced; *inf.* pricey, steep.

dear noun love, beloved, darling, sweetheart, honey, precious, angel.

dearth noun lack, scarcity, want, deficiency, shortage, insufficiency, paucity, sparseness, meagerness.

death noun **1** *death by drowning* dying, demise, end, passing, eternal rest. **2** *the death of his hopes* end, termination, cessation, extinction, destruction, eradication, obliteration. **3** *the death on the battlefield* killing, slaying, murder, slaughter, fatality; bloodshed, massacre, carnage.

debacle noun fiasco, failure, downfall, collapse, disintegration, disaster, catastrophe, ruin, devastation, defeat, rout.

debatable adjective arguable, disputable, questionable, controversial, contentious, doubtful, dubious, undecided.

debate noun **1** *a formal debate* discussion, argument, dispute, altercation, controversy, contention. **2** *after some debate* consideration, deliberation, reflection, contemplation.

debate verb **1** *debate the issue* discuss, argue, dispute, contend, contest. **2** *debated in his mind* consider, think over, deliberate, reflect, contemplate.

debauchery noun dissipation, dissoluteness, corruption, immorality, profligacy, licentiousness, promiscuity, wantonness.

debonair adjective suave, urbane, elegant, refined, well-bred, genteel, dashing, dapper, gallant, chivalrous; carefree, jaunty, lighthearted, cheerful, vivacious, buoyant.

debris noun rubble, wreckage, detritus, rubbish, litter; remains, ruins, fragments.

debt noun indebtedness, obligation, liability; arrears.

debut noun premiere, beginning, introduction, coming-out, entrance.

decadence noun 1 *the decadence of the empire* decay, degeneration, deterioration, decline, retrogression. 2 *the decadence of the wealthy set* dissipation, debauchery, immorality, self-indulgence, licentiousness, hedonism, epicureanism, corruption, depravity.

decadent adjective 1 *a decadent empire* decaying, degenerating, deteriorating, declining. 2 *decadent behavior* dissolute, debauched, degenerate, immoral, self-indulgent, licentious, hedonistic, epicurean, corrupt, depraved.

decay verb 1 *food decaying* rot, go bad, decompose, putrefy, spoil, perish, corrode. 2 *an empire decaying* degenerate, deteriorate, decline, dwindle, crumble, disintegrate, collapse, wither, die, atrophy.

decay noun 1 *the decay of the food* rotting, decomposition, putrefaction, putrescence, spoilage, corrosion. 2 *spot the decay in the teeth* rot, decomposition; caries, gangrene. 3 *the decay of the empire* degeneration, deterioration, decline, failure, disintegration, collapse.

deceased adjective late, departed. *See* DEAD adjective 1.

deceit noun deception, duplicity, fraud, fraudulence, cheating, trickery, chicanery, underhandedness, pretense, artifice, treachery; trick, stratagem, ruse, subterfuge, swindle, sham, hoax, misrepresentation; *inf.* hanky-panky.

deceitful adjective lying, untruthful, dishonest, mendacious, insincere, false, untrustworthy; deceptive, duplicitous, misleading, fraudulent, crooked.

deceive verb take in, mislead, delude, fool, misguide, trick, hoodwink, dupe, swindle, bamboozle, seduce; betray; *inf.* con.

decency noun propriety, decorum, seemliness, modesty, good taste, respectability, etiquette, delicacy, dignity, appropriateness, fitness, suitability.

decent adjective 1 *a scarcely decent exhibition* decorous, seemly, modest, proper, nice, tasteful, polite, respectable, dignified, appropriate, fitting, fit, suitable, becoming. 2 *a decent person* obliging, helpful, accommodating, generous, kind, thoughtful, courteous, civil, honorable, worthy, respectable. 3 *a decent salary* acceptable, adequate, sufficient, ample, competent.

deception noun duplicity, fraud. *See* DECEIT.

deceptive adjective 1 *appearances can be deceptive* deceiving, misleading, false, illusory, fallacious, ambiguous, specious, spurious. 2 *deceptive practices* deceitful, duplicitous, fraudulent, crooked; *inf.* sneaky, tricky.

decide verb 1 *decide to go* reach/make a decision, resolve, choose. 2 *decided the matter* settle, resolve, determine, clinch. 3 *the judge decided the case* judge, adjudicate, arbitrate, referee, pass/pronounce judgment.

decided adjective 1 *a decided difference* distinct, clear, clear-cut, definite, marked, pronounced, obvious, unmistakable, undeniable, unequivocal, indisputable, unquestionable. 2 *a decided effort* determined, resolute, firm, dogged, purposeful, unswerving, emphatic.

decision noun 1 *come to a decision* resolution, conclusion, determination, settlement. 2 *the judge announced his decision* judgment, ruling, pronouncement, verdict, adjudication, arbitration; findings. 3 *a man of decision* decisiveness, determination, resoluteness, resolve, purpose, purposefulness.

decisive adjective 1 *a decisive person* determined, resolute. *See* DECIDED adjective 2. 2 *a decisive factor* deciding, determining, definitive, conclusive, final, settling, critical, crucial, significant, influential, important.

declaration noun 1 *declaration of war* announcement, statement, proclamation, notification, pronouncement, edict, manifesto. 2 *his declaration that he was innocent* statement, assertion, insistence, protestation, affirmation, contention, claim, avowal.

declare verb 1 *declare war* announce, proclaim, pronounce, publish, broadcast, promulgate, trumpet, blazon. 2 *he declared that he was innocent* state, assert, maintain, aver, affirm, profess, claim, allege, swear.

decline verb 1 *decline an invitation* turn down, rebuff, refuse. 2 *his influence declined* lessen, decrease, diminish, wane, dwindle, fade, ebb. 3 *the empire is declining* deteriorate, degenerate, decay, fail, fall, wither, weaken, ebb. 4 *the terrain declines here* descend, slope/slant down.

decline noun 1 *the decline of his influence* decrease, downturn, downswing, ebb, slump, plunge. 2 *the decline of the empire* deterioration, degeneration, decay, failure, fall, wane. **3** *hikers sighting a decline* slope, declivity, dip.

decompose verb decay, rot, putrefy, fester; break up, fall apart, disintegrate, crumble.

decorate verb trim, embellish, garnish, festoon, beautify, enhance; renovate, refurbish; *inf.* spruce up.

decoration noun **1** *holiday decorations* adornment, ornamentation, beautification, enhancement; furnishing; ornament, trinket, bauble; trimming. **2** *a decoration for bravery* award, medal, badge, star, ribbon; colors, insignia.

decorum noun propriety, decency, good taste, correctness, politeness, courtesy, refinement, dignity, respectability; etiquette, protocol.

decoy noun lure, bait, enticement, entrapment, snare, trap.

decrease verb lessen, grow less, diminish, reduce, drop, fall off, decline, dwindle, abate, subside, taper off, peter out.

decrease noun **1** *the decrease in numbers/amount* lessening, lowering, reduction, drop, decline, falling off, downturn, cutback, curtailment, shrinkage. **2** *the decrease in the wind* dying down, abatement, subsidence, letting up, letup, slackening.

decree noun edict, order, law, statute, act, ordinance, regulation, rule, injunction, mandate, proclamation, dictum.

decree verb ordain, rule, order, command, dictate, lay down, prescribe, pronounce, proclaim.

decrepit adjective **1** *decrepit old men* doddering, tottering, aged, old, elderly, feeble, enfeebled, infirm, weak, weakened, weakly, frail, wasted, debilitated. **2** *decrepit houses* dilapidated, rickety, brokendown, tumbledown, ramshackle, rundown, worn-out, battered, decayed, deteriorated.

decry verb disparage, criticize, carp at, cavil at, censure, blame, condemn, denounce, run down, rail against.

dedicate verb **1** *dedicate her life to the poor* devote, commit, pledge. **2** *dedicate a church* bless, consecrate, sanctify, hallow.

dedicated adjective devoted, committed, wholehearted, single-minded, enthusiastic, zealous.

dedication noun devotion, devotedness, commitment, wholeheartedness, single-mindedness, enthusiasm, zeal.

deduce verb conclude, infer, reason, gather, glean.

deduct verb subtract, take away, take off, withdraw, discount; *inf.* knock off.

deduction noun **1** *the detectives' sound de-*

duction conclusion, inference, reasoning, assumption, presumption. **2** *the deduction of tax* subtraction, withdrawal, removal.

deed noun *brave deeds* act, action, feat, exploit, performance, achievement, accomplishment, undertaking, enterprise.

deem verb think, believe, consider, judge, feel, imagine, conceive, regard, see, hold.

deep adjective **1** *a deep hole/wound* cavernous, yawning, profound, bottomless, immeasurable, fathomless, unfathomable. **2** *a deep voice* low, low-pitched, full-toned, bass, resonant, sonorous. **3** *a deep red* dark, intense, vivid, rich, strong. **4** *deep distrust* profound, extreme, intense, great, grave, deep-seated, deep-rooted. **5** *a deep thinker/person* learned, wise, sagacious, sage, discerning, penetrating, perspicacious. **6** *deep affection* intense, heartfelt, fervent, ardent, impassioned. **7** *a deep mystery/secret* obscure, abstruse, unfathomable, recondite, esoteric, enigmatic, arcane.

deepen verb grow, increase, intensify, magnify, strengthen, heighten, reinforce.

deeply adverb greatly, extremely, profoundly, intensely, keenly, acutely, sharply.

deface verb spoil, disfigure, mar, blemish, deform, ruin, sully, tarnish, damage, vandalize, injure.

defamation noun slander, libel, character assassination, aspersion, calumny, vilification, defilement, obloquy, contumely, denigration, detraction, derogation; smear, slur, insult; *inf.* mudslinging.

defame verb slander, libel, cast aspersions on, asperse, blacken the name/character of, malign, smear, vilify, traduce, besmirch, disparage, denigrate; *inf.* do a hatchet job on, drag through the mud; bad-mouth.

defeat verb **1** *defeat their team/army* beat, conquer, vanquish, rout, trounce, thrash, overcome, overpower, overthrow, over whelm, crush, quash, quell, subjugate, subdue, repulse; *inf.* clobber, zap. **2** *defeat your own purpose* hinder, prevent, ruin, thwart, frustrate, foil.

defeat noun **1** *suffer defeat by the enemy* conquest, vanquishment, rout, beating. **2** *the defeat of their plans* failure, ruin, abortion, miscarriage; undoing, reverse, disappointment, setback.

defect noun **1** *a defect in the machine/writing* fault, flaw, imperfection, weak spot/point, snag, kink, blemish, mistake, error; *inf.* bug. **2** *defects in the educational system* deficiency, inadequacy, insufficiency, shortcoming, lack, want, omission, weakness, failing.

defect verb **1** *soldiers defected* desert, turn traitor, change sides/allegiances, shift ground, break faith, apostatize. **2** *defect from one's party* abandon, forsake, renounce, repudiate, secede from.

defective adjective **1** *a defective machine* faulty, flawed, imperfect, weak, deficient. **2** *defective in character* lacking, wanting, deficient, inadequate, insufficient. **3** *mentally defective* impaired, retarded, abnormal, subnormal.

defector noun deserter, turncoat, traitor, renegade, apostate, recreant; *inf.* rat, Benedict Arnold.

defend verb **1** *defend the city* protect, guard, safeguard, watch over, keep from harm, preserve, secure, shield, fortify, garrison, fight for. **2** *defend one's ideas* vindicate, justify, argue/speak for, make a case for, plead for, explain, give reasons for. **3** *the newspaper defended its journalist* support, back, stand by, stand/stick up for.

defendant noun accused, appellant, litigant, respondent.

defender noun protector, guard, bodyguard, guardian, preserver; supporter, backer, champion.

defense noun **1** *a defense against the enemy* protection, shield, safeguard, guard, security, cover, shelter, screen, fortification; barricade, rampart, bulwark, buttress, fortress. **2** *published a defense of his ideas* vindication, justification, apologia, apology, argument, explanation, explication. **3** *the accused gave his defense* denial, rebuttal, plea, declaration, case, excuse, alibi.

defenseless adjective undefended, unprotected, unguarded, unfortified, unarmed, helpless, vulnerable, weak, powerless, impotent, wide open, exposed, endangered.

defer[1] verb *defer the meeting* postpone, put off, adjourn, delay, hold over, shelve, put on ice, put on the back burner, pigeonhole, suspend, table, stay, hold in abeyance, prorogue.

defer[2] verb *defer to the expert* yield, submit, bow, give way, give in, surrender, accede, capitulate, acquiesce.

deference noun **1** *deference for the old* respect, regard, consideration, thoughtfulness, courteousness, courtesy, dutifulness, reverence, veneration. **2** *deference to the expert* submission, capitulation, accession, acquiescence, complaisance, obeisance.

defiance noun **1** *treat the enemy with defiance* resistance, opposition, confrontation, noncompliance, disobedience, recalcitrance, rebelliousness, insubordination, contempt, scorn, insolence. **2** *a spirit of defiance* challenge, provocation, daring, boldness, audacity, bravado, aggression, truculence.

defiant adjective **1** *defiant opposition* resistant, rebellious, insubordinate, mutinous, refractory, contemptuous, scornful, insolent. **2** *a defiant air* challenging, provocative, bold, audacious, aggressive, truculent.

deficiency noun **1** *vitamin deficiency* lack, want, shortage, dearth, insufficiency, inadequacy, scarcity, deficit, scantiness, paucity, absence. **2** *a deficiency in the system* weakness, failing, shortcoming. *See* DEFECT noun 1.

deficient adjective **1** *deficient in vitamins* lacking, wanting, short of, low on. **2** *deficient quantities* insufficient, inadequate, scanty, meager, skimpy, sketchy. **3** *a deficient system* defective, faulty, flawed, imperfect.

deficit noun shortfall, deficiency, shortage.

defile verb **1** *streets defiled by filth* pollute, foul, befoul, dirty, soil. **2** *defile young minds* corrupt, contaminate, taint, infect, tarnish, sully, pervert, vitiate. **3** *defile reputations* defame, blacken, denigrate, besmirch, stigmatize. **4** *defile young girls* ravish, rape, deflower, violate, dishonor.

define verb **1** *define one's terms/position* spell out, describe, explain, expound, elucidate, clarify, set out, outline, detail, specify, designate. **2** *define the boundary* mark out, fix, establish, settle, demarcate, bound, delimit, delineate, circumscribe.

definite adjective **1** *definite plans* specific, particular, precise, exact, defined, well-defined, clear, clear-cut, explicit, express, determined, fixed, established, confirmed. **2** *it's definite that he's going* certain, sure, positive, guaranteed, settled, decided, assured, conclusive, final. **3** *definite boundaries* fixed, marked, demarcated, delimited, circumscribed.

definitely adverb certainly, surely, for sure, without doubt/question, undoubtedly, indubitably, positively, absolutely, undeniably, unmistakably, plainly, clearly, obviously.

definition noun **1** *the definition of terms* meaning, description, explanation, exposition, expounding, interpretation, elucidation, clarification. **2** *the definition of boundaries* fixing, settling, establishment, determination, demarcation, delineation, circumscribing. **3** *the definition of the image* precision, sharpness, distinctness, clearness, clarity, contrast, visibility, focus.

definitive adjective **1** *the definitive answer* conclusive, final, ultimate, decisive, unconditional, unqualified, absolute, categorical. **2** *the definitive edition* authoritative, most reliable, most complete, exhaustive.

deflate verb **1** *deflate the air mattress* let down, collapse, flatten, void, puncture. **2** *deflate the pompous man* humble, humiliate, mortify, chasten, subdue, dispirit; *inf.* put down, debunk. **3** *deflate a currency* devalue, depreciate, depress, diminish, reduce.

deflect verb turn aside/away, turn, alter course, change course/direction, diverge, deviate, veer, swerve, slew, drift, bend.

deformed adjective **1** *deformed bodies* misshapen, malformed, distorted, contorted, twisted, crooked, curved, gnarled, crippled, maimed, disfigured, damaged, marred, mutilated, mangled. **2** *deformed minds* twisted, warped, perverted, corrupted, depraved, vile, gross.

defraud verb cheat, swindle, rob, fleece, sting, dupe, rook, bilk; *inf.* gyp, con, rip off.

deft adjective dexterous, adroit, handy, nimble, nimble-fingered, agile, skillful, skilled, proficient, adept, able, clever, expert.

defunct adjective **1** *defunct ancestors* dead, deceased, departed, extinct, gone. **2** *defunct organizations* obsolete, expired, nonexistent, inoperative.

defy verb **1** *defied their parents* disobey, disregard, ignore, slight, flout, fly in the face of, thumb one's nose at, spurn, scoff at, deride, scorn. **2** *defy the enemy forces* resist, withstand, brave, stand up to, confront, face, meet head-on, square up to, repulse, repel, thwart. **3** *I defy you to stay* challenge, dare, throw down the gauntlet to.

degeneracy noun corruption, decadence, immorality, depravity, dissoluteness, debauchery, profligacy, wickedness, vileness, sinfulness, baseness, turpitude.

degenerate verb deteriorate, decline, worsen, decay, rot, fail, fall off, sink, slip, slide, go downhill, regress, retrogress, lapse; *inf.* go to pot, go to the dogs, hit the skids.

degradation noun **1** *the degradation of his family* debasement, discrediting, demeaning, deprecation, shaming, disgracing, dishonoring, humiliation, mortification. **2** *a scene of degradation* degeneracy, corruption, decadence, depravity, squalor.

degrade verb **1** *his family was degraded by his behavior* discredit, belittle, demean, deprecate, deflate, devalue, lower, reduce, shame, disgrace, humble, humiliate, abase. **2** *officers were degraded* downgrade, demote, cashier, depose, unseat, dethrone; *inf.* drum out. **3** *degraded by her immoral associates* debase, corrupt, pervert, defile, sully, debauch.

degrading adjective debasing, discrediting, cheapening, belittling, demeaning, lowering, shaming, shameful, humiliating, mortifying, disgraceful.

degree noun **1** *a high degree of competence* stage, level, grade, step, gradation, rung, point, mark, measure, notch, limit. **2** *to a marked degree* extent, measure, magnitude, level, amount, quality, intensity, strength, proportion, ratio. **3** *people of higher degree* rank, class, standing, status, station, position, grade, level, order, condition, estate. **by degrees** gradually, slowly, step by step, little by little, bit by bit.

dehydrate verb dry, dry up/out, sun-dry, desiccate, parch, sear.

deify verb idolize, exalt, worship, adore, venerate, revere, pay homage to.

deign verb condescend, stoop, lower oneself, think/see fit, deem worthy, consent.

deity noun god, goddess, divine being, celestial being, supreme being, divinity; godhead.

dejected adjective depressed, dispirited, disheartened, downhearted, crestfallen, cast down, downcast, down, disappointed, unhappy, sad, miserable, blue.

delay verb **1** *delay our meeting* postpone, put off. See DEFER[1]. **2** *visitors delayed by the traffic* hold up/back, detain, slow up, set back, hinder, obstruct, hamper, impede, bog down, check, hold in check, restrain. **3** *don't delay!* linger, loiter, dawdle, dally, dilly-dally, lag/fall behind, tarry.

delay noun **1** *the delay to the meeting* postponement, adjournment, deferment, suspension, tabling, stay. **2** *holiday traffic delays* holdup, wait, setback, detainment, detention, hindrance, obstruction, impediment, check, stoppage, halt, interruption. **3** *the delay between trains* wait, interval, lull, interlude, intermission.

delectable adjective **1** *delectable food* appetizing, tasty. See DELICIOUS 1. **2** *delectable manner/appearance* delightful, charming, enchanting, captivating, winning, engaging, winsome, pleasing, agreeable.

delegate noun representative, deputy, agent, spokesman, spokeswoman, spokesperson, ambassador, envoy, legate, messenger, go-between, proxy, emissary, commissary.

delegate verb **1** *delegate tasks* pass on, hand over, transfer, give, commit, entrust, assign, relegate, consign. **2** *delegate him leader* authorize, deputize, commission, empower.

delete verb cross/strike out, cut out, erase, blue-pencil, edit out, remove, take out, expunge, eradicate; *inf.* scratch, kill.

deleterious adjective harmful, injurious, hurtful, damaging, destructive, ruinous, bad, disadvantageous, noxious.

deliberate adjective **1** *a deliberate act* intentional, planned, considered, calculated, designed, studied, studious, painstaking, conscious, purposeful, willful, premeditated, preplanned, prearranged, preconceived, predetermined, aforethought. **2** *deliberate speech/steps* careful, unhurried, cautious, thoughtful, steady, regular, measured, determined, resolute, ponderous, laborious.

deliberate verb **1** *looking out of the window deliberating* ponder, think, muse, meditate, reflect, cogitate, ruminate, brood, excogitate. **2** *deliberate the advantages* think over, consider, reflect on, mull over, evaluate. **3** *deliberate with colleagues* discuss, debate, confer, consult.

delicate adjective **1** *delicate china/material* fine, exquisite, fragile, slender, slight, elegant, graceful, dainty, flimsy, silky, gauzy, gossamer, wispy. **2** *his wife is delicate* frail, sickly, weak, debilitated, infirm. **3** *delicate colors* pastel, pale, muted, subtle, soft, subdued, understated, faint. **4** *a delicate matter/situation* difficult, tricky, sensitive, ticklish, critical, precarious, touchy; *inf.* sticky, dicey. **5** *require delicate handling* careful, considerate, tactful, discreet, diplomatic, politic, kid-glove. **6** *a delicate palate* discriminating, discerning, refined, perceptive, critical, fastidious, finicky, persnickety, squeamish. **7** *a delicate mechanism* sensitive, precise, accurate, exact. **8** *a delicate touch* deft, skilled, skillful, expert.

delicious adjective **1** *delicious food* tasty, appetizing, mouthwatering, delectable, choice, savory, flavorsome, flavorful, luscious, palatable, toothsome, ambrosial, ambrosian; *inf.* scrumptious, yummy. **2** *a delicious evening* delightful, exquisite, enjoyable, pleasurable.

delight noun pleasure, joy, happiness, gladness, gratification, bliss, rapture, ecstasy, elation, jubilation, excitement, entertainment, amusement, transports.

delight verb **1** *delighted by the news* please, gladden, cheer, gratify, thrill, excite, transport, enchant, captivate, entrance, charm, entertain, amuse, divert. **2** *delight in reading* take/find pleasure, indulge, glory.

delighted adjective pleased, joyful, happy, glad, gratified, overjoyed, blissful, enraptured, ecstatic, jubilant, thrilled, transported, excited, enchanted, captivated, entertained, amused, diverted.

delightful adjective pleasant, pleasing, agreeable, enjoyable, amusing, entertaining, diverting, pleasurable, gratifying, delectable, joyful, exciting, thrilling, rapturous, enchanting.

delinquent noun *damage done by delinquents* offender, wrongdoer, culprit, lawbreaker, criminal, hooligan, vandal, ruffian, hoodlum, miscreant, malefactor, transgressor.

delirious adjective **1** *delirious patients* raving, incoherent, babbling, light-headed,

irrational, unhinged. **2** *delirious at the good news* ecstatic, euphoric, beside oneself, carried away, transported, hysterical, frenzied.

deliver verb **1** *deliver the mail/groceries* distribute, carry, bring, take, transport, convey. **2** *deliver the prisoners to the enemy* hand over, turn over, transfer, commit, grant, make over, give up, yield, surrender, relinquish. **3** *deliver them from enemies* free, liberate, release, save, rescue, set loose, loose, extricate, discharge, ransom, emancipate, redeem. **4** *deliver a speech* utter, speak, express, pronounce, enunciate, proclaim, announce, declare. **5** *deliver a blow* direct, aim, administer, launch, inflict, throw, strike, hurl, pitch, discharge. **6** *deliver better sales figures* come up with, achieve, attain, provide, supply.

deliverance noun **1** *deliverance from prison/evil* liberation, release, rescue, escape, discharge, ransom, emancipation, salvation, redemption, manumission. **2** *deliverances from the pulpit* pronouncement, declaration, announcement, proclamation, report, lecture, sermon, speech.

delivery noun **1** *delivery is extra* distribution, carriage, transporting, transport, conveyance, dispatch. **2** *receive a delivery* consignment, load, batch. **3** *admire his clear delivery* enunciation, articulation, intonation, elocution, utterance, presentation. **4** *the pitcher's delivery* directing, aiming, launching, throwing, pitching.

delude verb mislead, deceive, fool, take in, trick, dupe, cheat, hoodwink, beguile, outwit, misguide, lead on, bamboozle, defraud, swindle, double-cross, cozen; *inf.* con, pull a fast one on, take for a ride, put one over on, two-time.

deluge noun **1** *houses swept away by the deluge* flood, spate, inundation, overflowing, flash flood, cataclysm; downpour, torrent, torrential rain, cloudburst. **2** *a deluge of correspondence* flood, rush, spate, torrent, avalanche, barrage, outpouring.

deluge verb **1** *towns deluged with polluted water* flood, inundate, swamp, engulf, submerge, drown, soak, drench, douse. **2** *deluged by correspondence* inundate, flood, overrun, overwhelm, engulf, swamp, overload.

delusion noun **1** *delusions of grandeur* false impression, false belief, misconception, misapprehension, misbelief, self-deception, illusion, fancy, phantasm, fool's paradise. **2** *victims of their own delusion* deluding, misleading, deception, fooling, tricking, duping.

deluxe adjective luxurious, sumptuous, palatial, opulent, lavish, superior, exclusive, choice, select, elegant, splendid, costly, expensive; *inf.* plush, upscale, upmarket.

demand verb 1 *workers demanding a raise* press for, insist on, urge, clamor for. 2 *"What's that?" he demanded* ask, inquire, question, interrogate, challenge. 3 *work demanding care* require, need, necessitate, call for, take, involve, want, cry out for. 4 *demand payment* expect, insist on, exact, order, requisition.

demand noun 1 *give in to demands* request, entreaty, claim, requisition; insistence, pressure, clamor. 2 *answer his demand* inquiry, question, interrogation, challenge. 3 *the demands of the job* requirement, need, necessity, want, claim, imposition, exigency. **in demand** sought-after, popular, in vogue, fashionable; *inf.* trendy.

demanding adjective 1 *demanding children* nagging, harassing, clamorous, importunate, insistent, imperious. 2 *demanding jobs* challenging, taxing, exacting, exigent, tough, hard, difficult, tiring, wearing, exhausting.

demean verb debase, demote. *See* DEGRADE 1.

demeanor noun behavior, conduct, bearing, air, appearance, mien, deportment, carriage, comportment.

demented adjective insane, mad, crazy, crazed, deranged, of unsound mind, out of one's mind, unhinged, unbalanced, touched, *non compos mentis*, maniacal, manic, frenzied, distraught, foolish, idiotic, crackbrained, lunatic; *inf.* daft, balmy, loopy, batty, dippy, wacky.

demolish verb 1 *demolish the building* knock down, pull/tear down, bring down, flatten, raze, level, bulldoze, dismantle, break up, pulverize. 2 *demolish his self-confidence* destroy, put an end to, ruin, wreck, undo. 3 *demolish the opposition* defeat, conquer, vanquish, overthrow, overturn, quell, quash, annihilate.

demolition noun 1 *the demolition of the buildings* razing, leveling, bulldozing. 2 *the demolition of the argument/opposition* destruction, ruin, ruination, undoing, defeat, conquest, overthrow, destruction, annihilation.

demon noun 1 *demons from hell* devil, fiend. 2 *a demon for work* hard worker, powerhouse, dynamo, workaholic; *inf.* whiz kid, eager beaver, busy bee. 3 *a demon at sailing* master, wizard; *inf.* ace, wiz.

demonic, demoniac, demoniacal adjective 1 *demonic spirits* diabolic, diabolical, devilish, fiendish, satanic, hellish, infernal, evil, wicked, Mephistophelian. 2 *demonic eyes/laughter* maniacal, manic, mad, crazed, frenzied, frantic, feverish, hysterical.

demonstrate verb 1 *demonstrate the proof of the proposition* determine, prove, validate, confirm, verify, establish. 2 *blushes demonstrating embarrassment* show, indicate, display, exhibit, express, manifest, evince, evidence. 3 *demonstrate putting on a bandage* illustrate, teach (about), describe, explain (about), expound on. 4 *demonstrate against war* protest, march, parade, rally, sit in, picket.

demonstration noun 1 *demonstration of the proof of the proposition* substantiation, confirmation, affirmation, verification, validation. 2 *a gymnastics demonstration* illustration, description, explanation, presentation, exhibition; *inf.* expo. 3 *an anti-war demonstration* protest, march, parade, rally, sit-in, picket.

demonstrative adjective *a demonstrative person* emotional, unreserved, unrestrained, expressive, open, effusive, expansive, gushing, nonreticent, affectionate, loving, warm.

demur verb object, take exception, express reluctance/reservations/doubts, be unwilling, protest, dispute, dissent, balk at, hesitate, cavil.

demure adjective 1 *demure young girls* modest, unassuming, decorous, meek, reserved, quiet, shy, bashful, retiring, diffident, reticent, timid, shrinking. 2 *demure young ladies* overmodest, coy, prim, priggish, prissy, prudish, goody-goody, straitlaced.

den noun 1 *the fox's den* lair, hole, hollow, shelter, hide-out. 2 *den of thieves* site, haunt; *inf.* dive, joint. 3 *writing in his den* study, retreat, sanctum, *sanctum sanctorum*, sanctuary, hideaway.

denial noun 1 *a denial of the statement* contradiction, repudiation, disclaimer, retraction, abjuration, disaffirmation; negation, dissent. 2 *the denial of the request* refusal, rejection, dismissal, rebuff, repulse, veto, turndown; *inf.* thumbs down. 3 *denial of beliefs* renunciation, renouncement, disowning, repudiation, disavowal.

denote verb 1 *a smile denoting delight | the color yellow denoting happiness* indicate, signify, betoken, symbolize, represent, stand for, typify. 2 *the word bankruptcy denotes financial ruin* mean, convey, designate.

denounce verb 1 *denounce the council's policies* condemn, criticize, attack, censure, castigate, decry, rail/inveigh/fulminate against, declaim against. 2 *denounce his partner* accuse, inform against, incriminate, implicate, inculpate, charge.

dense adjective 1 *a dense forest/crowd* close-packed, tightly packed, crowded, thickset, closely set, jammed together, crammed, compressed, compacted. 2 *dense fog/smoke*

thick, concentrated, opaque, impenetrable. **3** *too dense to understand* thick, slow, dull-witted, blockish, obtuse; *inf.* dim.

deny verb **1** *deny the charge/statement* contradict, negate, nullify, dissent from, disagree with, repudiate, refute, controvert, disclaim. **2** *deny the request* refuse, reject, turn down, dismiss, repulse, decline, veto; *inf.* give the thumbs down to, give the red light to. **3** *to deny one's citizenship* renounce, disown, turn one's back on, repudiate, discard, disavow.

depart verb **1** *they departed at noon* leave, go, go away/off, take one's leave, withdraw, set off/out, start out, get going, get under way, quit, make an exit, exit, break camp, decamp, retreat, retire; *inf.* make tracks, shove off, split, cut out, vamoose, hightail it. **2** *depart from the norm* deviate, diverge, differ, vary, digress, veer, branch off, fork, swerve, turn aside.

departure noun **1** *the hour of their departure* leaving, leave-taking, going, going away/off, withdrawal, setting off/out, starting out, exit, exodus, decamping, retreat. **2** *a departure from the norm* deviation, divergence, variation, digression, veering, branching off, swerving. **3** *a new departure for the firm* change of direction, change, difference of emphasis, shift, innovation, branching out, novelty.

depend verb **1** *success depends on hard work* turn/hinge on, hang on, rest on, be contingent upon, be subject to, be controlled/determined by, be based on, revolve around, be influenced by. **2** *depend on him for help* rely on, count/bank on, lean on, cling to, trust in, put one's faith in, have confidence in, swear by, be sure of.

dependable adjective reliable, trustworthy, faithful, responsible, steady, stable, sure, unfailing, true, steadfast.

dependence noun **1** *pity the children's dependence* helplessness, weakness, defenselessness, vulnerability, exposure. **2** *alcohol dependence* addiction, overuse, abuse.

dependent adjective **1** *dependent on circumstances* depending on, conditional on, contingent on, determined by, subject to. **2** *dependent children* helpless, weak, defenseless, vulnerable, immature. **3** *dependent countries* subsidiary, subject, subservient.

dependent on/upon *dependent on their mother* relying on, reliant on, counting on, leaning on, supported by, sustained by.

depict verb **1** *the painting depicts him sitting* portray, represent, draw, paint, sketch, illustrate, delineate, outline, reproduce, render, limn, chart, map out. **2** *the account depicts his faults* describe, set forth/out, detail, relate, narrate, recount, record, chronicle.

deplete verb exhaust, use up, consume, ex-

pend, spend, drain, empty, milk, evacuate, bankrupt, impoverish, reduce, decrease, diminish.

depletion noun exhaustion, consumption, expenditure, draining, emptying, reduction, decrease, dwindling, diminution, lessening.

deplorable adjective **1** *deplorable behavior* disgraceful, shameful, dishonorable, blameworthy, disreputable, scandalous, reprehensible, despicable, abominable. **2** *in deplorable circumstances* lamentable, regrettable, unfortunate, wretched, dire, miserable, pitiable, pathetic, distressing, grievous.

deplore verb **1** *deplore his behavior* be scandalized/shocked by, disapprove of, condemn, censure, deprecate, denounce, decry. **2** *deplore the passing of steam trains* regret, lament, mourn, rue, bemoan, bewail, pine for.

deploy verb arrange, position, dispose, spread out, extend, redistribute, station, utilize, set out/up, bring into play.

deport verb **1** *deport the refugees* banish, expel, exile, evict, transport, oust, expatriate, extradite. **2** *deport oneself badly* behave, conduct oneself, act, acquit oneself, comport oneself.

depose verb *depose the ruler* remove, unseat, dethrone, oust, displace, dismiss, discharge, cashier, demote.

deposit verb **1** *deposit the package on the floor* put, lay, set, set/put/lay down, drop, let fall. **2** *deposit money/jewels in the safe* bank, entrust, consign, save, store, hoard, stow, put away, lay in, squirrel away.

deposit noun **1** *a chemical deposit* precipitation, sediment, sublimate, accumulation, deposition; dregs, lees; silt, alluvium. **2** *coal/iron deposits* bed, vein, lode, layer. **3** *put a deposit on the goods* down/part payment, installment, security, retainer.

depot noun **1** *buses/trains returning to the depot* terminal, terminus; bus/railroad station, garage. **2** *stored in the depot* storehouse, warehouse, repository, depository, magazine, cache, arsenal.

depraved adjective corrupt, corrupted, immoral, unprincipled, dissolute, perverted, degenerate, profligate, debased, degraded, wicked, sinful, vile, base, iniquitous, lewd, licentious, lascivious, lecherous, prurient.

depravity noun corruption, immorality, debauchery, dissoluteness, perversion, degradation, degeneracy, profligacy, contamination, wickedness, sinfulness, vileness, baseness, iniquity, criminality, viciousness, brutality, brutishness, lewdness, licentiousness, lasciviousness, lechery, prurience.

deprecate verb **1** *deprecate the commit-*

tee's actions disapprove of, deplore, frown upon, censure, condemn, protest against, inveigh/rail against, denounce; *inf.* knock. **2** *deprecate his achievement* belittle, disparage, denigrate, decry, discredit, deflate, diminish, depreciate.

depreciate verb **1** *depreciate the value | depreciate the furniture* devalue, reduce, lower in value/price, mark down, cheapen, cut, slash. **2** *depreciate efforts to help* belittle, make light of, discredit, underrate, undervalue, underestimate, deflate, detract from, diminish, minimize, run down.

depress verb **1** *news that depressed her* sadden, deject, cast down, dispirit, dishearten, discourage, dampen the spirits of, weigh down, oppress. **2** *depress economic activity* slow down/up, weaken, lower, reduce, sap, impair, enfeeble, exhaust, drain. **3** *depress prices* reduce, lower, cut, cheapen, slash, depreciate, devalue, diminish, downgrade.

depressed adjective **1** *depressed spirits* sad, gloomy, blue, glum, dejected, downhearted, cast down, downcast, down, crestfallen, despondent, dispirited, low, melancholy, disheartened, discouraged, desolate, moody, morose, pessimistic, weighed down, oppressed; *inf.* down in the dumps. **2** *a depressed section of land* sunken, hollow, concave, indented, dented, pushed in, recessed, set back. **3** *a depressed economy* weak, weakened, slow, enervated, debilitated, devitalized, impaired. **4** *depressed prices* reduced, lowered, cut, cheapened, slashed, devalued, marked-down, discounted. **5** *a depressed area* poverty-stricken, poor, destitute, disadvantaged, deprived, needy, distressed, rundown.

depressing adjective *depressing news* saddening, sad, unhappy, gloomy, dismal, bleak, somber, grave, melancholy, dispiriting, disheartening, discouraging, distressing, painful.

depression noun **1** *bad news caused her depression* sadness, unhappiness, despair, gloom, glumness, dejection, downheartedness, despondency, dispiritedness, melancholy, discouragement, desolation, dolefulness, moodiness, moroseness, pessimism, hopelessness; melancholia; low spirits, blues; *inf.* the dumps. **2** *a depression in the landscape* hollow, indentation, dent, cavity, concavity, dip, valley, pit, hole, bowl, sink, sinkhole, excavation. **3** *an economic depression* slump, recession, decline, slowdown, standstill; paralysis, inactivity, stagnation.

deprivation noun **1** *the deprivation of their rights* withholding, denial, withdrawal, removal, dispossession, stripping, expropriation, seizure, confiscation, robbing,

appropriation, divestment, divestiture, wresting. **2** *areas of social deprivation* poverty, hardship, privation, destitution, disadvantage, need, neediness, want.

deprive verb dispossess, strip, expropriate, divest, wrest, rob.

depth noun **1** *measure the depth of the hole* deepness, drop, vertical extent, profundity. **2** *a person of depth* profundity, wisdom, understanding, sagacity, discernment, insight, awareness, intuition, penetration, astuteness, acumen, shrewdness, acuity. **3** *an issue of great depth* gravity, seriousness, weight, importance, complexity, intricacy, obtuseness, abstruseness, obscurity, reconditeness. **4** *the depth of the color* intensity, richness, darkness, vividness, strength, brilliance. **5** *the depths of the sea* remotest area, bottom, floor, bed, abyss, back, pit; bowels. **in depth** thoroughly, extensively, comprehensively, intensively.

deputy noun substitute, stand-in, representative, second in command, assistant, surrogate, proxy.

deputy adjective assistant, substitute, stand-in, representative, surrogate, proxy, subordinate.

deranged adjective unbalanced, unhinged, insane, mad, crazy, crazed, demented, disturbed, irrational, of unsound mind, *non compos mentis*, berserk, frenzied.

derelict adjective **1** *derelict factories/ships* abandoned, forsaken, deserted, discarded, rejected, cast off, relinquished, ownerless. **2** *derelict properties* dilapidated, ramshackle, tumbledown, rundown, broken-down, in disrepair, crumbling, falling to pieces, rickety, neglected. **3** *derelict officers* negligent, neglectful, remiss, lax, careless, sloppy, slipshod, slack, irresponsible, delinquent.

derelict noun vagrant, tramp, beggar, bum, hobo, outcast, pariah, ne'er-do-well, good-for-nothing, wastrel.

deride verb mock, ridicule, jeer at, scoff at, sneer at, make fun of, poke fun at, laugh at, scorn, pooh-pooh, lampoon, satirize.

derision noun mockery, ridicule, jeering, scoffing, sneering, scorn, contempt, taunting, ragging, teasing, raillery, disdain; jeers, sneers, taunts, insults; satire, lampoon.

derivative adjective *derivative research* imitative, unoriginal, uninventive, noninnovative, copied, plagiaristic, plagiarized, secondhand, secondary, rehashed.

derive verb **1** *happiness deriving from marriage* originate, stem, proceed, flow, emanate, issue. **2** *derive satisfaction* acquire, obtain, get, gain, procure, extract. **3** *derive sufficient facts* draw out, elicit, educe, deduce, infer.

derogatory adjective disparaging, denigratory, belittling, slighting, deprecatory, depreciatory, detracting, deflating, discrediting, dishonoring, unfavorable, disapproving, uncomplimentary, unflattering, insulting, offensive.

descend verb 1 *descend the hill/stairs* go down, come down, move down, climb down, pass down; drop, fall, sink, subside, plummet, plunge, tumble, slump. 2 *the hill descended to the valley* go down, slope, incline, dip, slant. 3 *will not descend to talk to servants* condescend, stoop, lower/abase oneself. 4 *descend in quality/values* degenerate, deteriorate, decline, sink, go downhill; *inf.* go to pot, go to the dogs. 5 *enemies/visitors descending on us* pounce, raid, swoop, charge, come in force, arrive in hordes. 6 *houses descending from father to son* be handed/passed down, pass by heredity.

descendants plural noun offspring, progeny, issue, family; scions.

descent noun 1 *the descent of the balloon* going down, drop, fall, sinking, subsiding, plummeting, plunge. 2 *walk down the descent* slope, incline, dip, drop, gradient, declivity, declination, slant. 3 *descent in quality/values* deterioration, decline, debasement, degradation, sinking, decadence. 4 *of German descent* ancestry, parentage, lineage, extraction, genealogy, heredity, succession, stock, line, blood, strain; origins.

describe verb 1 *describe the incident* narrate, put into words, detail, tell, express, recount, relate, report, set out, chronicle, define, explain, elucidate, illustrate. 2 *he was described as brilliant* characterize, portray, depict, style, label. 3 *describe a circle* draw, delineate, mark out, outline, trace, sketch.

description noun 1 *a description of the incident* account, detailed statement, report, setting out, chronicle, narration, recounting, relation, commentary, explanation, elucidation, illustration; details. 2 *the description of him as dishonest* characterization, portrayal, depiction. 3 *the description of a circle* drawing, delineation, outline, tracing. 4 *vegetables of every description* kind, sort, variety, type, brand, breed, category, class, designation, genre, ilk, mold.

descriptive adjective graphic, vivid, striking, expressive, detailed, explanatory, elucidatory, illustrative, pictorial, depictive, picturesque.

desecrate verb violate, defile, profane, treat sacrilegiously, blaspheme, debase, degrade, dishonor.

desert verb 1 *desert one's wife/post* abandon, forsake, give up, cast off, leave,

turn one's back on, leave high and dry, leave in the lurch, throw over, betray, jilt, strand, leave stranded, maroon, neglect, shun, relinquish, renounce; *inf.* walk/run out on. 2 *the soldier has deserted* abscond, defect, run away, make off, decamp, flee, fly, bolt, turn tail, go AWOL, depart, quit, escape.

desert noun wasteland, waste, wilderness, barrenness, solitude; wilds.

desert adjective arid, dry, moistureless, parched, scorched, dried up, burnt, hot, burning, torrid; desolate, barren, bare, wild, empty, uninhabited, solitary, lonely, uncultivable, infertile, unproductive, sterile, uncultivated, untilled.

deserter noun 1 *army deserters* defector, runaway, fugitive, truant, escapee, derelict. 2 *deserters from the cause* defector, renegade, turncoat, traitor, betrayer, apostate, derelict; *inf.* rat.

deserve verb merit, be worthy of, warrant, rate, justify, earn, be entitled to, have a right to, have a claim on, be qualified for.

deserved adjective well-earned, merited, warranted, justified, justifiable, earned, rightful, due.

deserving adjective worthy, meritorious, commendable, praiseworthy, laudable, admirable, estimable.

design verb 1 *architects designing the structure* plan, draw, sketch, outline, map out, plot, block out, delineate, draft. 2 *design clothes/schemes* create, invent, originate, think up, conceive, fashion, fabricate, hatch, innovate; *inf.* dream up. 3 *a course designed for beginners* intend, aim, devise, contrive, tailor.

design noun 1 *the design was inadequate* plan, blueprint, drawing, sketch, outline, map, plot, diagram, delineation, draft, depiction, scheme, model. 2 *admire the fabric designs* pattern, motif, style, arrangement, composition, makeup, constitution, configuration, organization, construction, shape, figure. 3 *a clever design to defeat the enemy* scheme, plot, intrigue, expedient, stratagem, device, artifice. 4 *with the design of entering* intention, aim, purpose, objective, goal, end, target.

designate verb 1 *a new atomic particle designated "quark"* call, name, entitle, term, christen, dub, style, label, denominate, nickname. 2 *designated ambassador* appoint, nominate, depute, delegate, select, choose, elect, ordain, induct. 3 *at designated times* state, appoint, specify, define, stipulate, particularize, earmark, set aside, pinpoint. 4 *arrows designating direction* show, indicate, point out, mark, denote.

designing adjective scheming, plotting,

intriguing, conspiring, conniving, calculating, Machiavellian, cunning, crafty, artful, wily, devious, shrewd, sly, underhand, deceitful, tricky; *inf.* crooked.

desirable adjective **1** *a desirable job* attractive, sought-after, in demand, popular, covetable, enviable, agreeable, appealing, pleasant, admirable, worthwhile, profitable, good, excellent. **2** *it is desirable that no one knows* preferable, advisable, advantageous, beneficial, expedient. **3** *a desirable young woman* seductive, alluring, erotic, fetching, fascinating, beguiling; *inf.* sexy.

desire verb **1** *desire happiness* wish for, want, long/yearn for, crave, set one's heart on, hanker after, have a fancy for, fancy, be bent on, covet, lust after, burn for; *inf.* have a yen for; lech after, have the hots for. **2** *desire a cup of tea* request, ask for, want.

desire noun **1** *her desire for success* wish, want, fancy, inclination, preference; wanting, longing, yearning, craving, eagerness, enthusiasm, hankering, predilection, aspiration, proclivity, predisposition. **2** *overcome by desire* lust, lustfulness, sexual appetite, passion, carnal passion, concupiscence, libido, sensuality, sexuality, lasciviousness, lechery, libidinousness; *inf.* the hots.

desired adjective **1** *fitted to the desired length* required, necessary, proper, right, correct, appropriate, fitting, suitable, preferred, expected. **2** *the desired prize* wished for, longed for, craved, coveted.

desirous adjective **desirous of** *desirous of success* desiring, wishing (for), wishful of, hopeful of, avid/eager/anxious for, craving, ambitious for.

desist verb stop, cease, discontinue, abstain, give up, forbear/refrain from, break/leave off.

desolate adjective **1** *desolate plains* bare, barren, bleak, dismal, desert, waste, wild. **2** *desolate farms* deserted, uninhabited, unoccupied, depopulated, forsaken, abandoned, unpeopled, untenanted, unfrequented, unvisited, solitary, lonely, isolated. **3** *desolate at the news* sad, unhappy, wretched, downcast, disconsolate, forlorn, cheerless, distressed, grieving, bereft.

despair noun **1** *unemployed and full of despair* hopelessness, dejection, depression, desperation, disheartenment, discouragement, despondency, disconsolateness, defeatism, pessimism, melancholy, gloom, melancholia, misery. **2** *the boy is the despair of the teacher* hopeless case, bane, burden, bother, scourge.

despair verb lose hope, give up hope, give up, lose heart, be discouraged, be despondent, be pessimistic, resign oneself, throw in the towel.

desperado noun outlaw, bandit, gunman, criminal, lawbreaker, gangster, terrorist, thug, ruffian, hooligan, villain, hoodlum, mugger.

desperate adjective **1** *a desperate criminal/act* reckless, rash, hasty, impetuous, foolhardy, bold, madcap, wild, violent, frantic, mad, frenzied; risky, hazardous, precipitate, harebrained, imprudent, incautious, injudicious, indiscreet, ill-conceived. **2** *in desperate need* urgent, pressing, compelling, acute, critical, crucial, drastic, serious, grave, dire, extreme, great. **3** *the desperate state of the country* grave, appalling, outrageous, intolerable, deplorable, lamentable. **4** *trying to help desperate people* despairing, hopeless, wretched. **5** *desperate measures* last-ditch, last-resort, do-or-die.

despicable adjective contemptible, beyond contempt, reprehensible, vile, base, low, mean, scurvy, abominable, loathsome, hateful, detestable, odious, disreputable, ignoble, shameful, ignominious.

despise verb scorn, look down on, spurn, shun, disdain, slight, undervalue, deride, scoff/jeer at, sneer at, mock, revile, hate, detest, loathe, abhor, abominate, execrate, contemn.

despite preposition in spite of, notwithstanding, regardless of, in defiance of, in the face of.

despondent adjective hopeless, in despair, despairing, downcast, down, low, disheartened, discouraged, disconsolate, low-spirited, dispirited, downhearted, melancholy, gloomy, glum, morose, doleful, woebegone, miserable, wretched, distressed.

despot noun absolute ruler, autocrat, dictator, tyrant, oppressor.

despotic adjective absolute, autocratic, dictatorial, tyrannical, oppressive, totalitarian, domineering, imperious, arrogant, high-handed, authoritarian, arbitrary.

destined adjective **1** *a plane destined for Chicago* bound for, en route for, heading for/toward, directed/routed to, scheduled for. **2** *destined for the state* designed, intended, meant, set, set apart, designated, appointed, allotted. **3** *destined to die young* fated, ordained, preordained, foreordained, predestined, predetermined, doomed, foredoomed, certain, sure, bound, written in the cards.

destiny noun **1** *couldn't escape his destiny* fate, fortune, lot, portion, cup, due, future, doom. **2** *destiny drew them together* fate, divine decree, predestination, luck, fortune, chance, karma, kismet; the stars.

destitute adjective **1** *destitute refugees* poverty-stricken, indigent, impoverished, penurious, impecunious, penniless, insolvent, beggarly, down-and-out, poor, needy, hard up, badly off, on the breadline, pauperized; *inf.* up against it. **2** *destitute of ideas* devoid of, without, bereft of, deficient in, lacking, wanting, deprived of, empty, drained.

destroy verb **1** *destroy the bridge* demolish, knock down, pull down, tear down, level, raze, fell, dismantle, wreck, smash, shatter, crash, blow up, blow to bits, explode, annihilate, wipe out, bomb, torpedo. **2** *destroy the countryside* ruin, spoil, devastate, lay waste, ravage, wreak havoc on, ransack. **3** *destroy their confidence* terminate, quash, quell, crush, stifle, subdue, squash, extinguish, extirpate. **4** *destroy the herd/tribe* kill, kill off, slaughter, put to sleep, exterminate; slay, murder, assassinate, wipe out, massacre, liquidate, decimate. **5** *destroy the enemy/opponents* defeat, beat, conquer, vanquish, trounce, rout, drub; *inf.* lick, thrash.

destruction noun **1** *the destruction of the building* demolition, knocking down, pulling down, tearing down, leveling, razing, dismantling, wrecking, smashing, blowing up, wiping out, annihilation. **2** *the destruction of the countryside* ruination, ruin, spoiling, devastation, laying waste, desolation, ransacking, ravaging. **3** *the destruction of their confidence* termination, quashing, quelling, crushing, stifling, squashing, extinguishing, extirpation, extinction. **4** *the destruction of the herd/tribe* killing, slaughter, slaying, murder, assassination, massacre. **5** *the destruction of the enemy/opponents* defeat, beating, conquest, vanquishing, trouncing, rout.

destructive adjective **1** *destructive winds/wars* ruinous, devastating, disastrous, catastrophic, calamitous, cataclysmic, ravaging, fatal, deadly, dangerous, lethal, damaging, pernicious, noxious, injurious, harmful, detrimental, deleterious, hurtful. **2** *destructive comments* discrediting, invalidating, derogatory, denigrating, disparaging, disapproving, discouraging, undermining, negative, adverse.

desultory adjective haphazard, random, aimless, rambling, erratic, irregular, unmethodical, unsystematic, chaotic, inconsistent, inconstant, fitful, capricious.

detach verb **1** *detach the collar* unfasten, disconnect, unhitch, remove, separate, uncouple, loosen, free, sever, tear off, disengage, disjoin, disunite. **2** *detach oneself from the group* separate, move off, dissociate, segregate, isolate, cut off, disconnect, divide.

detached adjective **1** *a detached collar* unfastened, disconnected, unhitched, separate, loosened, free, severed. **2** *observing in a detached way* dispassionate, aloof, indifferent, unconcerned, reserved, unemotional, impersonal, cool, remote. **3** *detached commentators* objective, disinterested, unbiased, unprejudiced, impartial, nonpartisan, neutral, fair.

detail noun item, particular, fact, point, factor, element, circumstance, aspect, feature, respect, attribute, part, unit, component, member, accessory; unimportant point, insignificant item, trivial fact. **details** *fill in the details* particulars, fine points, niceties, minutiae, trivia. **in detail** comprehensively, fully, thoroughly, exhaustively.

detail verb specify, set forth, set out, list, enumerate, tabulate, catalog, spell out, delineate, relate, recount, narrate, recite, rehearse, describe, cite, point out, indicate, portray, depict, itemize, particularize, individualize.

detailed adjective **1** *a detailed bill/description* itemized, particularized, full, comprehensive, thorough, exhaustive, all-inclusive, circumstantial, precise, exact, specific, particular, meticulous. **2** *a detailed picture/story* complex, involved, elaborate, complicated, intricate, convoluted, entangled.

detain verb **1** *detained by business* hold/keep back, hold up, delay, keep, slow up/down, hinder, impede, check, retard, inhibit, stay. **2** *detain the accused* put/keep in custody, confine, imprison, lock up, incarcerate, impound, intern, restrain, hold.

detect verb **1** *detect hostility/smoke* notice, note, discern, perceive, make out, observe, spot, become aware of, recognize, distinguish, identify, catch, decry, sense, see, smell. **2** *accountants detected the error* discover, find out, turn up, uncover, bring to light, expose, unearth, reveal, unmask, unveil.

detective noun investigator; private investigator, FBI agent, police officer; *inf.* sleuth, tec, dick, private eye, tail, shadow, cop, gumshoe, G-man.

deter verb put off, prevent, stop, discourage, dissuade, talk out of, check, restrain, caution, frighten, intimidate, daunt, scare off, warn against, hold back, prohibit, hinder, impede, obstruct, block, inhibit.

deteriorate verb **1** *moral values deteriorating* get worse, worsen, decline, degenerate, sink, slip, go downhill, slide, lapse, fail, fall, drop, ebb, wane, retrograde, retrogress, slump, depreciate; *inf.* go to pot, go to hell, go to the dogs. **2** *buildings/food deteriorating* decay, decompose, disintegrate, become dilapidated, decline, degenerate, crumble, fall apart, fall to pieces, fall down, break up.

determination noun **1** *behave with determination* firmness, firmness of purpose, resoluteness, steadfastness, tenacity, single-mindedness, resolve, drive, push, thrust, fortitude, dedication, backbone, stamina, mettle, strong will, persistence, perseverance, conviction, doggedness, stubbornness, obduracy, intransigence. **2** *the committee's determination | the legal determination* decision, conclusion, judgment, verdict, opinion, diagnosis, prognosis.

determine verb **1** *determine the place of meeting* settle, fix, decide, agree on, establish, judge, arbitrate, decree, ordain. **2** *determine the argument* resolve, conclude, end, terminate, finish. **3** *determine the room dimensions* find out, discover, learn, establish, ascertain, check, verify, certify. **4** *determine to go alone* decide, resolve, choose, elect. **5** *conditions determining the nature of the soil* affect, influence, act/work on, decide, control, direct, rule, dictate, govern.

determined adjective **1** *a determined person/attitude* firm, resolute, steadfast, tenacious, purposeful, single-minded, dedicated, strong-willed, mettlesome, plucky, persistent, persevering, dogged, unflinching, unwavering, stubborn, obdurate, intransigent, indomitable, inflexible. **2** *determined on going* bent, intent, set.

deterrent noun disincentive, discouragement, curb, check, restraint, obstacle, hindrance, impediment, obstruction, block, barrier, inhibition.

detest verb loathe, abhor, hate, despise, abominate, execrate, feel aversion/hostility/animosity toward, feel disgust/distaste for, recoil/shrink from, feel repugnance toward.

detract verb **detract from** *their conduct detracts from their achievement* diminish, lower, devalue, devaluate, depreciate.

detriment noun injury, harm, damage, impairment, hurt, loss, disadvantage, disservice, ill, wrong, mischief.

detrimental adjective injurious, harmful, damaging, hurtful, deleterious, destructive, pernicious, disadvantageous, adverse, unfavorable, inimical, prejudicial.

devastate verb **1** *fire devastated the warehouse* lay waste, leave desolate, destroy, ruin, demolish, wreck, raze, level, annihilate, ravage, ransack, sack, despoil, spoil. **2** *devastated by the news* overcome, overwhelm, shock, traumatize, disconcert, discompose, discomfit, perturb.

devastation noun **1** *a scene of devastation* desolation, destruction, waste, ruin, wreckage, demolition, razing, annihilation. **2** *her complete devastation* shock, traumatization,

bewilderment, discomposure, discomfiture, perturbation.

develop verb **1** *cities developing rapidly* grow, evolve, mature, expand, enlarge, spread, advance, progress, prosper, flourish, make headway. **2** *develop a plan* begin, commence, start, set in motion, originate, invent, form, establish, institute, fashion, generate. **3** *develop a cough* begin to have, acquire, contract, pick up. **4** *develop a theme* elaborate (on), unfold, work out, enlarge on, expand (on), broaden, amplify, add to, augment, magnify, supplement, reinforce. **5** *an argument developed* come about, follow, happen, result, ensue, break out.

development noun **1** *the development of cities* growth, evolution, maturing, expansion, spread, progress, headway. **2** *the development of a plan* originating, invention, forming, establishment, institution; generation, propagation, rearing, cultivation. **3** *the development of themes* elaboration, unfolding, enlarging, expansion, augmentation. **4** *new developments in the affair* event, turn of events, occurrence, happening, circumstance, incident, situation, issue, outcome, upshot. **5** *a housing development* complex, estate, structure, conglomeration.

deviant adjective deviating, aberrant, divergent, abnormal, irregular, nonstandard, anomalous, peculiar, curious, queer, bizarre, eccentric, idiosyncratic, unorthodox, offbeat, wayward, perverse, warped, twisted, perverted; *inf.* bent, kinky, quirky.

deviate verb diverge, turn aside, step aside, depart from, digress, deflect, differ, vary, change, veer, swerve, bend, drift, stray, tack.

deviation noun divergence, departure, digression, deflection, variation, veering, straying, fluctuation, aberration, abnormality, irregularity, anomaly, inconsistency, discrepancy; change, shift, veer, swerve, bend, drift.

device noun **1** *a handy device* appliance, gadget, implement, utensil, tool, piece of equipment/apparatus, apparatus, instrument, machine, contrivance, contraption, invention; *inf.* gizmo. **2** *win by a cunning device* design, plot, scheme, ploy, project, stratagem, trick, artifice, ruse, dodge, gambit, maneuver, machination, strategy, intrigue, wile. **3** *the club device* emblem, symbol, insignia, crest, coat of arms, seal, badge, token, motif, design, mark, figure, motto, slogan, legend, logo, colophon, trademark.

devil noun **1** *the Devil defeated by God* Satan, Lucifer, Prince of Darkness, the Evil One, the Archfiend, Beelzebub, Lord of the Flies, *inf.* Old Nick. **2** *tempted by devils* demon, fiend, evil spirit. **3** *the master was* *a devil* brute, savage, beast, monster, ogre, demon, fiend, barbarian, rogue, scoundrel, villain, bully, knave. **4** *the child's a little devil* imp, scamp, rascal, rogue, mischief-maker, troublemaker. **5** *feel pity for the poor devils* wretch, unfortunate, beggar, creature, thing, sad case.

devilish adjective **1** *devilish practices* diabolic, diabolical, demonic, demoniacal, fiendish, satanic, infernal, hellish. **2** *a devilish creature* wicked, evil, abominable, atrocious, detestable, villainous, sinister, accursed, damnable.

devious adjective **1** *a devious merchant* underhand, underhanded, cunning, crafty, sly, wily, artful, guileful, scheming, designing, calculating, dishonest, deceitful, double-dealing; *inf.* crooked. **2** *go by a devious route* indirect, roundabout, deviating, circuitous, tortuous, rambling, wandering, erratic, digressive, excursive.

devise verb concoct, contrive, work out, plan, form, formulate, plot, scheme, project, invent, originate, create, compose, construct, frame, think/dream up, conceive, imagine, fabricate, hatch, put together, arrange.

devote verb assign, allot, allocate, set aside, set apart, reserve, commit, apply, consign, pledge, give, offer, dedicate, surrender.

devoted adjective **1** *a devoted follower* loyal, faithful, true, true blue, staunch, steadfast, constant, committed, dedicated, devout, fond, loving, admiring, affectionate, caring, attentive, warm, ardent. **2** *time devoted to reading* assigned, allotted, set aside, dedicated. **3** *buildings devoted to God* dedicated, consecrated, blessed, sanctified, hallowed.

devotee noun enthusiast, fan, admirer, addict, follower, adherent, disciple, supporter, champion, advocate, votary, fanatic, zealot; *inf.* buff, freak.

devotion noun **1** *the devotion of his followers* loyalty, faithfulness, fidelity, steadfastness, constancy, commitment, adherence, allegiance, dedication; fondness, love, admiration, affection, attentiveness, care, caring, warmness, closeness. **2** *churchgoers full of devotion* devoutness, piety, religiousness, spirituality, godliness, holiness, sanctity, saintliness.

devour verb **1** *devour the feast* eat greedily/hungrily, eat up, consume, swallow up, gulp down, gobble up, bolt, wolf down, guzzle, stuff down, cram in, gorge oneself on, feast on; *inf.* tuck into, pack away, polish off, stuff one's face with, pig out on. **2** *flames devoured the house* consume, engulf, envelop, destroy, devastate, lay waste, demolish, wipe out, ruin, wreck, annihilate. **3** *children devouring books* feast on, revel in, delight in, enjoy, relish, ap-

preciate. **4** *devoured by anxiety/jealousy* consume, swallow up, engulf, swamp, overcome, overwhelm.

devout adjective **1** *a devout Christian* pious, religious, reverent, churchgoing, godly, saintly, holy, prayerful, orthodox, pure, righteous. **2** *devout hope* sincere, genuine, deep, profound, heartfelt, earnest, fervent, fervid, intense, ardent, vehement, passionate, zealous.

dexterity noun **1** *craftsmen showing dexterity* deftness, adroitness, nimbleness, agility, skillfulness, skill, knack, adeptness, handiness, facility, proficiency. **2** *crisis management requires dexterity* cleverness, shrewdness, smartness, astuteness, cunning, craft, sagacity, sharp-wittedness, acuteness, ingenuity, resourcefulness, inventiveness.

dexterous adjective **1** *dexterous craftsmen* deft, adroit, nimble, agile, skillful, skilled, adept, handy, proficient, expert, talented, accomplished, artistic. **2** *a dexterous businessman* clever, shrewd, smart, astute, cunning, crafty, wily, artful, sagacious, sharp-witted, acute, ingenious, resourceful, inventive.

diabolic, diabolical adjective **1** *diabolic forces* devilish, fiendish, demonic, demoniacal, satanic, infernal, hellish. **2** *a diabolic slave master* fiendish, wicked, evil, sinful, savage, brutish, cruel, malevolent, malicious, black-hearted, nasty, abominable, hateful, damnable. **3** *a diabolic task* difficult, complicated, complex, tricky, nasty, unpleasant, dreadful, vile.

diagnose verb identify, determine, distinguish, recognize, detect, pinpoint, pronounce.

diagram noun drawing, sketch, draft, illustration, picture, representation, outline, delineation.

dialogue noun conversation, talk, tête-à-tête, chat, chitchat, gossip, communication, debate, argument, exchange of views, discourse, discussion, conference, converse, colloquy, interlocution, duologue, confabulation, parley, palaver; *inf.* powwow, confab, rap session.

diaphanous adjective sheer, fine, delicate, light, thin, silken, chiffony, gossamer, gauzy, cobwebby, translucent, transparent, see-through.

diary noun day-by-day account, daily record, journal, chronicle, log, logbook.

diatribe noun tirade, harangue, denunciation, philippic, reproof, reprimand, rebuke, upbraiding; invective, vituperation, abuse, castigation, criticism, stricture; *inf.* tongue-lashing, knocking.

dicey adjective uncertain, risky, chancy,

difficult, tricky, dangerous, ticklish; *inf.* hairy.

dictate verb **1** *dictate the letter* read aloud, speak, say, utter, recite. **2** *dictate terms* prescribe, lay down, impose, set down, order, command, decree, ordain, direct, pronounce, enjoin, promulgate. **3** *always dictating to others* give orders, order about, lay down the law, impose one's will, boss about, domineer; *inf.* call the shots, throw one's weight around.

dictator noun absolute ruler, despot, autocrat, tyrant, oppressor.

dictatorial adjective **1** *dictatorial government* absolute, unlimited, unrestricted, arbitrary, omnipotent, all-powerful, autocratic, totalitarian, authoritarian, despotic, tyrannical, autarchic. **2** *dictatorial bosses* tyrannical, despotic, oppressive, ironhanded, imperious, overbearing, domineering, peremptory, high-handed, authoritarian, dogmatic, high and mighty; *inf.* bossy.

dictatorship noun autarchy, totalitarian state, absolute monarchy, absolute rule; despotism, autocracy, tyranny, authoritarianism, totalitarianism, absolutism.

diction noun **1** *learn diction through elocution lessons* enunciation, articulation, elocution, pronunciation, speech, intonation, inflection, delivery. **2** *impressed by the writer's diction* style, language, phraseology, phrasing, wording, expression, idiom.

didactic adjective *didactic prose* instructive, instructional, preceptive, pedagogic, pedantic, moralistic.

die verb **1** *she died last night* pass away, pass on, lose one's life, depart this life, expire, decease, breathe one's last, meet one's end, lay down one's life, be no more, perish, go to one's last resting place; *inf.* give up the ghost, kick the bucket, push up the daisies, bite the dust, snuff it, croak, turn up one's toes, cash in one's chips. **2** *hope died* come to an end, end, vanish, disappear, pass, fade, fall away, dwindle, melt away, dissolve, subside, decline, sink, lapse, ebb, wane, wilt, wither, evanesce. **3** *the engine died* stop, halt, fail, break down, peter out, fizzle out, run down, fade away, lose power. **4** *I nearly died laughing* collapse with, be overcome with, be overwhelmed/overpowered by, succumb to. **5** *dying to see you* be eager, be desperate, long.

differ verb **1** *tastes differ* be different, be unlike, be dissimilar, be distinguishable, vary, diverge. **2** *parties agreeing to differ* disagree, fail to agree, dissent, be at variance, be in dispute/opposition, oppose, take issue, conflict, clash, quarrel, argue, wrangle, quibble, squabble, altercate. **differ from** *results differing from the norm*

vary from, diverge from, deviate from, depart from, run counter to, contravene, contradict, contrast with.

difference noun **1** *the difference between/in their lifestyles* dissimilarity, unlikeness, dissimilitude, contrast, distinction, distinctness, differentiation, variance, variation, divergence, deviation, disparity, incongruity. **2** *spot the difference* distinction, peculiarity, oddity, idiosyncrasy, singularity, eccentricity, individuality. **3** *the two had a difference* disagreement, dispute, disputation, argument, debate, misunderstanding, quarrel, row. **4** *pay the difference* balance, remainder, rest, residue, residuum, excess.

different adjective **1** *tastes different from ours* unlike, dissimilar, contrasting, diverse, divergent, deviating, disparate, incompatible, inconsistent, opposed, at variance, at odds, clashing, conflicting, discrepant. **2** *a different dress every day* separate, other, nonidentical, distinct, individual, discrete. **3** *available in different colors* various, several, many, numerous, assorted, varied, miscellaneous, diverse. **4** *looking for something different* unusual, out of the ordinary, uncommon, distinctive, rare, unique, novel, special, singular, unconventional, atypical, odd, strange, bizarre.

differentiate verb distinguish, discriminate, make a distinction, contrast, see/discern a difference; tell apart, set apart, separate, mark off.

difficult adjective **1** *digging in this soil is difficult* hard, strenuous, arduous, laborious, demanding, formidable, tough, onerous, burdensome, exhausting, tiring, wearisome, backbreaking, painful, oppressive; *inf.* no picnic. **2** *a difficult problem* complicated, complex, involved, intricate, puzzling, problematic, baffling, perplexing, knotty, thorny, ticklish, delicate, obscure, abstract, abstruse, recondite, enigmatic, profound, deep. **3** *a difficult child* troublesome, tiresome, demanding, unmanageable, intractable, perverse, recalcitrant, obstreperous, refractory, fractious, unaccommodating, uncooperative, uncompliant, unamenable. **4** *difficult people to choose presents for* hard to please, fussy, particular, fastidious, perfectionist, critical, hypercritical, finicky. **5** *arrive at a difficult time* inconvenient, ill-timed, disadvantageous, unfavorable. **6** *go through difficult times* hard, straitened, hard-pressed, bad, tough, grim, dark.

difficulty noun **1** *dig with difficulty* difficultness, strenuousness, arduousness, laboriousness, toughness, struggling, awkwardness; labor, strain, struggle. **2** *the difficulty of the problem* complexity, intricacy, perplexity, knottiness, delicacy, obscurity, abstruseness. **3** *encounter a difficulty* complication, problem, snag, hitch, hindrance, obstacle, pitfall, hurdle, impediment, obstruction, barrier. **4** *raise difficulties* protest, objection, complaint, gripe, demur, cavil. **5** *in difficulty | in financial difficulties* predicament, quandary, dilemma, plight, distress, embarrassment, trouble, hot/deep water; straits; *inf.* fix, jam, spot, scrape. **6** *the difficulty of the times* hardship, trial, tribulation, ordeal, exigency.

diffident adjective shy, bashful, modest, sheepish, unconfident, unassertive, timid, timorous, apprehensive, fearful, shrinking, reserved, withdrawn, hesitant, reluctant, doubtful, unsure, insecure.

diffuse adjective **1** *diffuse light* diffused, spread out, scattered, dispersed, not concentrated. **2** *a diffuse style* verbose, wordy, prolix, long-winded, copious, profuse, discursive, rambling, wandering, meandering, digressive, circuitous.

diffuse verb spread around, scatter, disperse, disseminate, dissipate, dispel.

dig verb **1** *enjoy digging | dig the earth* break up soil/ground; work, break up, loosen up, turn over, spade, delve, till, cultivate, harrow, plow. **2** *dig a tunnel/hole* dig out, excavate, quarry, hollow out, scoop out, gouge, tunnel, burrow, mine, channel. **3** *dig someone in the ribs* poke, prod, jab, thrust, drive, push, punch. **4** *dig into the history* delve, search, probe, investigate, research. **5** *dig potatoes* unearth, dig up. **6** *dig the music* like, love, enjoy, appreciate. **7** *I dig what you're saying* understand, comprehend, follow, grasp, make out; *inf.* get. **dig up** *dig up new information* uncover, root out, extricate, bring to light, come up with, discover, find, come across.

dig noun **1** *a dig in the ribs* poke, prod, jab, thrust, push, punch. **2** *tired of digs at/about his baldness* gibe, jeer, taunt, sneer, insult, slur, quip; *inf.* wisecrack, crack.

digest verb **1** *digest food* assimilate, absorb, break down, dissolve, macerate. **2** *digest the facts* take in, understand, comprehend, grasp, master, consider, think about, contemplate, mull over, weigh up, reflect on, ponder, meditate on, study. **3** *digest the information* shorten, reduce, condense, abridge, compress, compact, summarize, précis.

digest noun summary, synopsis, abstract, précis, résumé, outline, abridgment, epitome, review, compendium.

dignified adjective stately, noble, solemn, grave, formal, decorous, reserved, ceremonious, courtly, majestic, august, lofty, exalted, regal, lordly, imposing, impressive, grand.

dignify verb add dignity/distinction to, distinguish, honor, grace, adorn, exalt, enhance, ennoble, glorify, elevate, make lofty, aggrandize, upgrade.

dignitary noun public figure, notable, notability, worthy, personage, luminary, VIP, pillar of society, leading light, celebrity, big name, somebody, star, lion; *inf.* bigwig, top brass, big gun, big shot, big wheel, celeb.

dignity noun **1** *the dignity of the occasion* stateliness, nobleness, nobility, solemnity, gravity, formality, decorum, propriety, reserve, ceremoniousness, courtliness, majesty, augustness, loftiness, exaltedness, regalness, regality, lordliness, impressiveness, grandeur. **2** *the dignity of work* worthiness, honorability, nobility, excellence, respectability; worth, merit, virtue. **3** *achieve dignity in social affairs* high rank, high standing, high station, status, elevation, eminence, honor, glory, greatness, importance.

digress verb get off the subject, stray from the point, deviate/deflect from the topic, go off at a tangent, diverge, turn aside, depart, drift, ramble, wander, meander.

dilapidated adjective rundown, broken-down, tumbledown, ramshackle, in ruins, ruined, falling to pieces, falling apart, in disrepair, shabby, battered, rickety, shaky, crumbling, decayed, decaying, decrepit, worn-out, neglected, uncared-for.

dilatory adjective delaying, dallying, dilly-dallying, procrastinating, postponing, deferring, putting off, stalling, time-wasting.

dilemma noun devil and the deep blue sea, Catch-22, vicious circle, quandary, predicament, plight, difficulty, tight corner/spot, problem, puzzle.

diligent adjective assiduous, industrious, conscientious, hardworking, painstaking, meticulous, thorough, careful, attentive, heedful, intent, earnest, studious, constant, persevering, sedulous, persistent, dogged, plodding, slogging, laborious.

dim adjective **1** *a dim light* faint, weak, feeble, pale, dull, dingy, lusterless, muted. **2** *dim skies* dark, darkish, gray, overcast, leaden, gloomy, somber, dusky, lowering, cloudy, hazy, misty, foggy, crepuscular, tenebrous. **3** *dim corridors* dark, darkened, gloomy, badly lit, poorly lit, dingy, dismal. **4** *a dim shape/recollection* vague, ill-defined, indistinct, unclear, shadowy, blurred, blurry, fuzzy, imperceptible, nebulous, obscured, bleared, bleary, hazy, confused, imperfect. **5** *prospects are rather dim* unpromising, unfavorable, discouraging, disheartening, depressing.

dim verb **1** *dim the stage lights* turn down, lower. **2** *the light dimmed* grow dim, fade, grow faint/feeble, dull, pale, blur. **3** *the skies dimmed* grow dark, darken, cloud over, grow leaden. **4** *memories/recollections dimming* grow dim, fade, blur, become blurred/confused.

dimension noun **1** *of huge dimension | the dimensions of the tank* extent; length, width, breadth, depth, area, size, volume, capacity, bulk; proportions. **2** *add another dimension to entertainment* aspect, side, feature, facet, element. **dimensions** *the dimensions of the problem* size, extent, scope, measure, scale, range, magnitude, greatness, importance.

diminish verb **1** *their power diminished | time diminished their power* lessen, grow less, decrease, reduce, shrink, contract, abate, grow weak/weaker, lower, curtail, cut, contract, narrow. **2** *diminish his reputation* belittle, disparage, denigrate, depreciate, deprecate, derogate, devalue, demean, detract from.

diminutive adjective small, little, tiny, petite, slight, elfin, minute, miniature, mini, small-scale, compact, microscopic, midget, undersized, dwarfish, pygmy, Lilliputian; *inf.* wee, baby.

din noun uproar, row, racket, commotion, hullabaloo, hubbub, tumult, clangor, outcry, brouhaha, crash, clatter, clash, shouting, yelling; clamor, noise, pandemonium, bedlam, babel.

dine verb eat, sup, feed, feast, banquet. **dine on** eat, consume, feed on.

dingy adjective dark, dull, dim, gloomy, drab, dismal, dreary, cheerless, dusky, somber, murky, hazy, smoggy, smoky, sooty, dirty, discolored, grimy, soiled, faded, shabby, worn, seedy, rundown.

dip verb **1** *dip the garment in dye* immerse, submerge, plunge, duck, dunk, lower, sink, souse, douse, soak, drench, steep, bathe, rinse. **2** *the sun dipping behind the horizon* sink, set, descend, fade, disappear, subside. **3** *profits dipping* fall, go down, drop, drop/fall off, decrease, decline, slump. **4** *the road dips* slope, descend, fall, slant down, droop, sag. **5** *dip water* scoop up, scoop, spoon, ladle. **dip into 1** *dip into a book* skim, browse, glance at. **2** *dip into art* dabble in, scratch the surface of, play at, sample. **3** *dip into one's savings* draw on, take out of, use/spend part of.

dip noun **1** *give the garment a dip | take a dip* immersion, plunge, ducking, dunking, sousing, dousing, soaking, drenching; swim, dive, plunge. **2** *a dip in profits* fall, falling-off, drop, dropping-off, decrease, decline, lowering, slump. **3** *a dip in the terrain* slope, incline, decline, slant, descent, hollow, concavity, depression, basin.

diplomacy noun **1** *ministers skilled in di-*

plomacy statesmanship, statecraft, international relations/politics; negotiations. **2** *treating her objections with diplomacy* tactfulness, tact, subtlety, discretion, judiciousness, prudence, delicacy, sensitivity, finesse, *savoir faire*, politeness, cleverness, artfulness, cunning, skill.

diplomat noun **1** *an international meeting of diplomats* ambassador, foreign minister, envoy, emissary, legate, consul, attaché. **2** *the diplomat of the firm* conciliator, reconciler, peacemaker, mediator, negotiator, tactician, arbitrator.

diplomatic adjective **1** *a diplomatic post* ambassadorial, consular. **2** *diplomatic handling* tactful, discreet, judicious, prudent, careful, delicate, sensitive, politic, clever, skillful, artful.

dire adjective **1** *in dire straits | dire poverty* terrible, dreadful, appalling, frightful, awful, horrible, atrocious, grim, cruel, grievous, disastrous, ruinous, miserable, wretched, woeful, calamitous, catastrophic, cataclysmic, distressing, harrowing, shocking. **2** *dire warnings* ominous, sinister, portentous, gloomy, gloom-and-doom, grim, dreadful, dismal, unpropitious, inauspicious, unfavorable, pessimistic. **3** *in dire need of money* urgent, desperate, drastic, pressing, crying, vital, grave, critical, crucial, extreme, compelling, exigent.

direct verb **1** *direct the operation* administer, manage, be in charge/control/command of, lead, run, command, control, govern, conduct, handle, preside over, rule, supervise, superintend, oversee, guide, mastermind, regulate, orchestrate, engineer; *inf.* be the boss of, run the show, call the shots. **2** *directed to work late* command, order, instruct, charge, bid, dictate, adjure, enjoin. **3** *direct them to the station* give directions to, guide, steer, lead, conduct, accompany, usher, escort, navigate, pilot. **direct at** aim at, address to, intend/mean for, destine for, focus on, train at, turn on, fix on.

direct adjective **1** *a direct road* straight, undeviating, unswerving, uncircuitous, shortest. **2** *a direct approach* immediate, firsthand, personal, face-to-face, head-on, noninterventional. **3** *a direct statement/manner* frank, blunt, straightforward, straight, straight to the point, explicit, clear, plain, unequivocal, unambiguous, honest, candid, open, sincere, plainspoken, outspoken, forthright, downright, point blank, matter-of-fact, categorical. **4** *the direct opposite* exact, absolute, complete, downright, thorough, diametrical. **5** *a direct quotation* exact, precise, word for word, verbatim, accurate, correct.

direction noun **1** *his direction of the project* administration, management, government, supervision, superintendence, regulation, orchestration; control, command, conduct, handling, running, overseeing, masterminding, disposal; leadership, guidance. **2** *ignore the teacher's direction* command, order, instruction, bidding, charge, dictate, enjoinment, prescription. **3** *which direction did they take?* way, route, course, path, track, road, line, run, bearing, orientation. **4** *the direction of their policy/statement* drift, aim, tack, scope, bent, bias, tendency.

directive noun ruling, regulation, decree, edict, notice, ordinance, mandate, fiat. *See* DIRECTION 2.

directly adverb **1** *travel directly* straight, in a straight line, as the crow flies, by the shortest route, without deviation. **2** *leave directly* immediately, at once, instantly, right/straight away, without delay/hesitation, quickly, speedily, promptly; *inf.* pronto. **3** *speak directly* frankly, bluntly, straightforwardly, explicitly, clearly, plainly, unequivocally, unambiguously, sincerely, truthfully, outspokenly, forthrightly, pointblank, matter-of-factly. **4** *talk directly to the manager* at first hand, firsthand, personally, face to face, head on. **5** *it's directly opposite* exactly, immediately, diametrically.

director noun administrator, controller, manager, executive, chairman, chairwoman, chairperson, chair, head, chief, principal, leader, governor, president, superintendent, supervisor, overseer, organizer, producer; *inf.* boss, kingpin, top dog, honcho.

dirge noun elegy, lament, funeral song/chant, burial hymn, dead march, requiem, keen, threnody.

dirt noun **1** *clean the dirt from the room* grime, dust, soot, smut, muck, mud, filth, mire, sludge, slime, ooze, waste, dross, pollution; smudge, stain, tarnish; *inf.* crud, yuck, grunge. **2** *piles of dirt by the roadside* earth, soil, loam, clay, silt. **3** *disapprove of the dirt in modern novels* obscenity, indecency, smut, sordidness, coarseness, bawdiness, ribaldry, salaciousness, lewdness, pornography; *inf.* sleaze, sleaziness. **4** *spreading dirt about the neighbors* scandal, gossip, talk, rumor.

dirty adjective **1** *dirty rooms/clothes* unclean, soiled, grimy, begrimed, grubby, messy, dusty, sooty, mucky, muddy, filthy, bedraggled, slimy, polluted, sullied, foul, stained, spotted, smudged, tarnished, defiled, nasty; *inf.* cruddy, yucky, grungy. **2** *dirty jokes* blue, obscene, indecent, vulgar, smutty, coarse, bawdy, suggestive, ribald, salacious, risqué, prurient, lewd, lascivious, licentious, pornographic, off color; *inf.* sleazy. **3** *a dirty cheat* nasty, mean, base, low, vile, contemptible, des-

picable, cowardly, ignominious, sordid, beggarly, squalid. **4** *a dirty trick* | *dirty play* unsporting, unfair, dishonorable, unscrupulous, dishonest, crooked, illegal, deceitful, double-dealing, corrupt. **5** *a dirty look* malevolent, smoldering, resentful, bitter, angry, indignant, annoyed, peeved, offended. **6** *a dirty rumor* nasty, unkind, scandalous, defamatory, slanderous, libelous.

dirty verb soil, stain, muddy, begrime, blacken, mess up, spatter, smudge, smear, spot, splash, spoil, sully, pollute, foul, defile, besmirch.

disability noun impairment, disablement, infirmity, defect, handicap, disorder, affliction, ailment, complaint, illness, malady; incapacity, unfitness, weakness, incapability, inability, incompetence, ineptitude, disqualification.

disable verb incapacitate, impair, damage, put out of action, debilitate, indispose, weaken, enfeeble, cripple, lame, handicap, immobilize, hamstring, paralyze, prostrate.

disabled adjective incapacitated, impaired, handicapped, debilitated, unfit, out of action, infirm, weak, weakened, enfeebled, crippled, lame, immobilized, bedridden, paralyzed.

disadvantage noun **1** *the disadvantages of the situation* drawback, snag, downside, weak spot/point, weakness, flaw, defect, fault, handicap, trouble, liability; *inf.* minus, fly in the ointment. **2** *people suffering from financial disadvantage* deprivation, privation, hardship, lack, burden. **3** *to their disadvantage* disservice, detriment, prejudice, harm, damage; loss, injury, hurt, mischief.

disagree verb **1** *the two sides disagreed* differ, fail to agree, dissent, stand opposed, be at variance/odds, diverge, disaccord. **2** *the stories disagreed* differ, vary, conflict, clash, contrast, diverge, be discordant. **3** *children constantly disagreeing* quarrel, argue, bicker, wrangle, squabble, spar, dispute; *inf.* fall out, have words.

disagreeable adjective **1** *a disagreeable experience* unpleasant, displeasing, nasty, horrible, dreadful, hateful, detestable, abominable, odious, objectionable, offensive, obnoxious, repugnant, repulsive, repellent, revolting, disgusting, distasteful, nauseating, unsavory, unpalatable. **2** *a disagreeable old man* bad-tempered, illnatured, nasty, cross, irritable, rude, surly, discourteous, impolite, churlish, peevish, contrary.

disagreement noun **1** *the disagreement of the two sides* difference of opinion, dissent, dispute, contention, disaccord, discord. **2** *the disagreement of/between the* *accounts* difference, dissimilarity, variation, variance, discrepancy, disparity, dissimilitude, incompatibility, incongruity, contradiction, conflict, clash, contrast, divergence, deviation. **3** *the disagreement between the children* quarrel, argument, wrangle, squabble, altercation, dispute, debate, disputation, discord, strife, conflict, war of words; bickering, sparring, contention, dissension, disharmony; *inf.* falling out.

disappear verb **1** *the sun disappearing below the horizon* pass from sight, vanish, be lost to view/sight, recede from view, fade, fade/melt away, withdraw, depart, retreat, ebb, wane, dematerialize, evanesce, evaporate; *inf.* vamoose. **2** *customs that have disappeared* die out, die, cease to be/exist, end, pass away, expire, perish, become extinct.

disappoint verb **1** *sorry to disappoint you* let down, fail, dishearten, depress, dispirit, upset, sadden, dash the hopes of, chagrin, dismay, disgruntle, disenchant, disillusion, dissatisfy, vex. **2** *disappoint their plans* thwart, frustrate, foil, defeat, baffle, hinder, obstruct, hamper, impede, interfere with.

disappointed adjective upset, saddened, let down, disheartened, downhearted, cast down, downcast, depressed, dispirited, chagrined, disenchanted, disillusioned, discontented, dissatisfied; thwarted, frustrated, foiled, defeated, failed, baffled.

disappointment noun **1** *hide one's disappointment* sadness, regret, distress, chagrin, disgruntlement, displeasure, disenchantment, disillusionment, discontent, dissatisfaction, vexation. **2** *the disappointment of their plans* thwarting, frustration, foiling; defeat, failure, unfulfillment. **3** *the event was a disappointment* letdown, failure, fiasco, setback, blow, misfortune, disaster; *inf.* washout.

disapprove verb **1** *disapprove of their behavior* find unacceptable, be against, deplore, criticize, frown on, take a dim view of, look askance at, censure, blame, condemn, denounce, object to, take exception to, reproach, rebuke, reprove. **2** *disapprove the plans* turn down, reject, veto, disallow, set aside; *inf.* give the thumbs down to.

disarray noun disorder, untidiness, confusion, chaos, dishevelment; mess, muddle, clutter, jumble, mix-up, tangle; shambles.

disaster noun **1** *natural disasters* catastrophe, calamity, cataclysm, tragedy, act of God, accident, mishap, misadventure, mischance, stroke of ill-luck, setback, reverse/reversal of fortune, reversal, heavy blow, shock, buffet; adversity, trouble, misfortune, ruin, ruination. **2** *the play was*

a disaster failure, fiasco; *inf.* flop, bomb, dud, washout.

disastrous adjective catastrophic, calamitous, cataclysmic, tragic, devastating, ravaging, dire, terrible, shocking, appalling, dreadful, black, harmful, injurious, detrimental, ruinous, unfortunate.

disbelief noun unbelief, lack of belief, skepticism, incredulity, doubt, discredit, distrust, mistrust, questioning, agnosticism, atheism, nihilism.

discard verb throw away/out, get rid of, dispose of, toss out, jettison, scrap, dispense with, cast aside, reject, repudiate, abandon, relinquish, forsake, drop, have done with, shed; *inf.* dump, ditch.

discern verb see, notice, observe, perceive, make out, distinguish, detect, descry, recognize, determine, differentiate.

discernible adjective visible, noticeable, observable, perceptible, perceivable, distinguishable, detectable, recognizable, apparent, obvious, clear.

discerning adjective discriminating, astute, shrewd, ingenious, clever, intelligent, perceptive, sharp, quick, perspicacious, penetrating, critical, percipient, judicious, subtle, prudent, sound, wise, knowing, sagacious, sapient.

discharge verb **1** *discharge the patient/soldier* set free, free, let go, release, liberate. **2** *discharge from employment* dismiss, remove, get rid of, oust, expel, cashier; *inf.* sack, fire, ax, send packing, give the ax/sack/boot to, boot out. **3** *discharge a weapon* fire, shoot, let/set off, explode, detonate. **4** *discharge pus/fumes* exude, ooze, excrete, give off, leak, dispense, emit, send out, send/pour forth, eject, release, gush, void. **5** *discharge a duty* carry out, perform, do, accomplish, achieve, fulfill, execute, observe, abide by. **6** *discharge a load* unload, disburden, remove, unburden, off-load, relieve. **7** *discharge a debt/obligation* pay, settle, clear, honor, meet, liquidate, satisfy; *inf.* square.

discharge noun **1** *soldiers receiving a discharge* release, liberation, clearance. **2** *his discharge from the firm* dismissal, removal, ejection, ousting, expulsion, cashiering, *inf.* firing, axing, sacking. **3** *the discharge from a weapon* firing, shooting, explosion, detonation, blast, burst, pop, report, volley, salvo, fusillade. **4** *the discharge of pus/fumes* excretion, emission, ejection, release, voidance. **5** *a watery discharge* excretion, exudate, emission, flow, secretion, ooze, suppuration, pus, seepage. **6** *discharge of duty* carrying out, performing, accomplishment, achievement, fulfillment, execution, observance, performance. **7** *discharge of a debt* payment, settlement, clearance, honoring, meeting.

disciple noun apostle, follower, pupil, student, believer, adherent, devotee, votary, upholder, supporter, advocate, proponent, satellite, partisan.

discipline noun 1 *yoga is a useful discipline* training, drilling, exercise, regimen, routine, method; instruction, coaching, teaching, indoctrination, inculcation. 2 *discipline required for the exercise* control, self-control, self-restraint, strictness, orderliness, regulation, direction, government, restriction, limitation; restraint, check, curb. 3 *students in need of discipline* punishment, chastisement, castigation, correction; penalty, reprimand, rebuke, reproof. 4 *literature and other disciplines* field of study, field, branch of knowledge, course of study, course, area, subject, specialty.

discipline verb 1 *discipline the troops* train, drill, break in, exercise, instruct, coach, teach, educate, tutor, prepare, ground, indoctrinate, inculcate, inure, toughen. 2 *discipline oneself* control, restrain, regulate, govern, restrict, limit, check, curb. 3 *discipline the children* punish, chastise, castigate, correct, penalize, reprimand, rebuke, reprove.

disclose verb 1 *disclose confidential details* reveal, divulge, tell, impart, communicate, make public, broadcast, publish, release, unveil, leak, let slip, blurt out, blab, admit, confess, avow; *inf.* spill the beans about, let the cat out of the bag about, blow the lid off, squeal about. 2 *disclose the contents of the box* uncover, show, exhibit, expose, lay bare, unveil, bring to light.

discomfit verb 1 *discomfited by personal questions* embarrass, disconcert, make uncomfortable, take aback, nonplus, abash, confuse, ruffle, fluster, upset, disturb, perturb, discompose, discomfort; *inf.* faze, rattle, discombobulate. 2 *discomfit the enemy's plans* thwart, frustrate, foil, obstruct, hinder, hamper, check, upset.

disconcert verb 1 *disconcerted by the silence in the room* unsettle, shake, disturb, perturb, daunt, bewilder, upset, agitate, worry, perplex, confound, distract, throw off balance; *inf.* throw, faze, rattle. See DISCOMFIT 1. 2 *disconcerting their plans* thwart, upset, undo. See DISCOMFIT 2.

disconnect verb sever, uncouple, disengage, detach, unhook, unhitch, unlink, disjoin, disunite, separate, part, split up, interrupt.

disconsolate adjective despondent, wretched, miserable, heartbroken, forlorn, grief-stricken, inconsolable, woebegone, dejected, low, low-spirited, dispirited, down, depressed, downcast, gloomy, melancholy, blue; *inf.* down in the mouth/dumps.

discontent noun discontentment, dissatisfaction, restlessness, impatience, fretfulness, displeasure, unhappiness, envy, regret, umbrage, disaffection, disquiet.

discontented adjective dissatisfied, fed up, restless, impatient, fretful, complaining, displeased, disgruntled, querulous, unhappy, envious, regretful, disaffected, exasperated.

discontinue verb stop, end, put an end/stop to, finish, bring to a halt, terminate, cease, abandon, give up, break off, cancel, drop, refrain from, quit, suspend, interrupt; *inf.* cut out.

discord noun 1 *bitter discord between the leaders* dissension, conflict, friction, contention, strife, opposition, hostility, wrangling, clashing, incompatibility, variance, disunity, rupture. 2 *the discord of the instruments* disharmony, dissonance, cacophony, harshness, jarring, jangling, din, racket.

discount verb 1 *discount what he says* disregard, ignore, pass over, overlook, pay no attention to, take no notice of, brush off, gloss over. 2 *discount $5 from the price* deduct, take off, rebate; *inf.* knock off. 3 *discount the regular price* reduce, lower, lessen, mark down; *inf.* knock down.

discount noun markdown, deduction, price cut, cut, rebate, price concession, reduction.

discourage verb 1 *the outcome discouraged him* dishearten, dispirit, deject, cast down, depress, demoralize, disappoint, daunt, intimidate, cow, unnerve. 2 *discourage them from applying* put off, dissuade, deter, talk out of, advise against, urge against, caution against, restrain, inhibit. 3 *discourage the idea* oppose, disapprove of, repress, deprecate, put a damper on, throw cold water on. 4 *a preparation discouraging mildew* prevent, check, curb, hinder, obstruct, suppress, inhibit.

discourse noun 1 *engage in discourse* conversation, talk, dialogue, communication, discussion, conference, colloquy, converse, chat, chitchat, confabulation; *inf.* confab. 2 *a discourse on art* address, speech, lecture, oration, sermon, homily, essay, treatise, dissertation, paper, study.

discourteous adjective rude, impolite, ill-mannered, bad-mannered, unmannerly, uncivil, curt, abrupt, brusque, short, gruff, boorish, churlish, ungracious, ungentlemanly, unladylike, ill-bred, uncouth, disrespectful, ungallant, insolent, impertinent, impudent.

discover verb 1 *discover new talent* find, come across/upon, stumble upon, chance upon, light upon, locate, bring to light, uncover, unearth, turn up; *inf.* dig up. 2

discover that he was lying find out, come to know, learn, realize, detect, determine, ascertain, recognize, see, spot, notice, perceive, reveal, disclose; *inf.* get wise to the fact. **3** *discover a new drug* invent, originate, devise, pioneer, design, contrive, conceive of.

discovery noun **1** *the discovery of a quiet village* finding, locating, location, uncovering. **2** *the discovery that they lied* realization, detection, determination, recognition, revelation, disclosure. **3** *discovery of new drugs* invention, origination, devising, pioneering, introduction. **4** *recent discoveries* find, invention, breakthrough, innovation, findings.

discredit verb **1** *discredit their rivals* detract from, bring into disrepute, defame, slur, slander, cast aspersions on, vilify, disparage, deprecate, denigrate, devalue, devaluate, degrade, belittle, decry, dishonor, disgrace, censure. **2** *evidence to discredit the research* disprove, invalidate, refute, dispute, challenge, destroy the credibility of, shake one's faith in, reject, deny. **3** *the jury discredited the witness* disbelieve, give no credence to, discount, doubt, distrust, mistrust.

discredit noun **1** *bring discredit on the neighborhood* disrepute, ill repute, infamy, disgrace, dishonor, shame, humiliation, ignominy, stigma, harm, damage, censure, blame, reproach, scandal, odium. **2** *regard the story with discredit* disbelief, lack of credence, incredulity, question, doubt, distrust, mistrust, skepticism, suspicion.

discreet adjective prudent, judicious, careful, cautious, circumspect, wary, guarded, chary, tactful, reserved, diplomatic, considerate, politic, strategic, wise, sensible.

discrepancy noun inconsistency, variance, variation, disparity, deviation, divergence, incongruity, difference, disagreement, dissimilarity, contrariety, conflict, discordance, gap.

discrete adjective separate, distinct, individual, detached, unattached, disconnected.

discretion noun **1** *act with discretion* prudence, judiciousness, care, carefulness, caution, circumspection, wariness, guardedness, chariness, tactfulness, tact, reserve, diplomacy, consideration, discrimination, wisdom, sense, good sense, discernment, sagacity, acumen, forethought. **2** *at the discretion of the manager* choice, option, volition, will, preference, inclination, pleasure, liking, wish, desire.

discrimination noun **1** *wine lovers of discrimination* discernment, perception, perspicacity, acumen, astuteness, shrewdness, selectivity, fastidiousness, judgment, taste, refinement, sensitivity, cultivation, cul-

ture. **2** *guilty of discrimination* prejudice, bias, unfairness, inequity, intolerance, bigotry, narrow-mindedness, favoritism.

discuss verb talk over, talk/chat about, converse about, confer about, debate, exchange views on/about, deliberate, consider, go into, thrash out, examine, review, study, scrutinize, analyze; *inf.* kick around.

discussion noun talk, conversation, dialogue, chat, conference, debate, discourse, exchange of views, symposium, seminar, consultation, deliberation, parley; *inf.* confab.

disdain noun scorn, scornfulness, contempt, contemptuousness, derision, sneering, deprecation, disparagement, denigration, arrogance, superciliousness, haughtiness, hauteur, snobbishness, aloofness, indifference.

disdain verb scorn, show contempt for, spurn, reject, refuse, rebuff, disregard, sneer at, deride, belittle, undervalue, slight, despise, look down on; *inf.* pooh-pooh, look down one's nose at.

disdainful adjective scornful, contemptuous, sneering, derisive, slighting, disparaging, arrogant, proud, supercilious, haughty, superior, snobbish, aloof, indifferent; *inf.* high and mighty, hoity-toity.

disease noun illness, sickness; disorder, complaint, malady, ailment, affliction, condition, indisposition, infirmity, disability, abnormality; infection, contagion, pestilence, plague, canker, blight.

disenchanted adjective disillusioned, disabused, undeceived, set straight, disappointed, let down, blasé, cynical, soured.

disentangle verb **1** *disentangle the knotted yarn* unravel, unwind, untwist, undo, unknot, untie, unsnarl, unkink, smooth out, straighten, comb, card. **2** *disentangle oneself* extricate, disentwine, release, loosen, detach, unfasten, unclasp, free, set free, liberate, disconnect.

disfavor noun **1** *look upon with disfavor* disapproval, disapprobation, dislike, displeasure, dissatisfaction, disregard, low opinion, low esteem. **2** *fall into disfavor* disapproval, unpopularity, discredit, disrepute, ill repute, ignominy, disgrace, shame.

disfigure verb deface, deform, mutilate, blemish, flaw, scar, uglify, spoil, mar, damage, injure, maim, vandalize, ruin.

disgorge verb **1** *volcanoes disgorging lava | disgorging phlegm* spit out, spew out, belch, discharge, spout, vomit, regurgitate, throw up, eject, emit, expel, empty. **2** *disgorging their booty* give up, surrender, yield, cede, relinquish, hand over.

disgrace noun **1** *the disgrace of being in*

prison shame, humiliation, dishonor, scandal, degradation, ignominy, infamy, discredit, debasement. **2** *brought him disgrace* disfavor, discredit, disrepute, loss of face, disrespect, disapproval, disapprobation, disesteem.

disgrace verb **1** *disgrace the family* shame, humiliate, dishonor, discredit, degrade, debase, sully, besmirch, taint, stigmatize, brand, drag through the mud. **2** *the soldier was publicly disgraced* discredit, disfavor, humiliate, mortify, disparage, demean, denigrate, belittle.

disgraceful adjective shameful, shameless, dishonorable, disreputable, degrading, ignominious, blameworthy, culpable, contemptible, despicable, reprehensible, appalling, dreadful, terrible, shocking, improper, unseemly, unworthy.

disgruntled adjective discontented, dissatisfied, displeased, annoyed, exasperated, vexed, irritated, peeved, put out, resentful, sulky, sullen, petulant, grumpy, churlish, testy; *inf.* ticked off, fed up.

disguise verb **1** *disguised as a policeman* camouflage, conceal, hide, mask, screen, shroud, veil, cloak, dress up, be under cover, be incognito. **2** *disguise the truth* cover up, misrepresent, falsify, fake, fudge, feign, dissemble, gloss over, varnish.

disgust verb **1** *the slimy food disgusted me* sicken, nauseate, turn one's stomach, revolt, repel; *inf.* turn off. **2** *her behavior disgusted me* offend, outrage, shock, appall, scandalize, displease, dissatisfy, annoy, anger.

disgust noun **1** *look with disgust at the food* revulsion, repugnance, repulsion, aversion, nausea, distaste, abhorrence, loathing, detestation. **2** *disgust at her behavior* outrage, shock, disapproval, displeasure, dissatisfaction, annoyance, anger.

disgusting adjective **1** *disgusting odor* sickening, nauseating, nauseous, revolting, repellent, unpalatable, foul, nasty, unappetizing, distasteful, abhorrent, loathsome, detestable, obnoxious, odious. **2** *disgusting behavior* offensive, objectionable, outrageous, shocking, shameless, shameful, appalling, scandalous, vulgar, gross, vile, displeasing, annoying.

dishearten verb discourage, cast down, dispirit, depress, crush, make crestfallen/downhearted, dash, dampen, put a damper on, daunt, disappoint, deter, sadden, weigh down.

disheveled adjective untidy, tousled, rumpled, bedraggled, disordered, disarranged, messy, in a mess, unkempt, uncombed, slovenly, slatternly, blowzy, frowzy; *inf.* mussed.

dishonest adjective fraudulent, cheating, untrustworthy, false, untruthful, dishonorable, unscrupulous, unprincipled, corrupt, swindling, deceitful, deceiving, deceptive, lying, crafty, cunning, designing, mendacious, double-dealing, underhand, underhanded, treacherous, perfidious; *inf.* crooked, shady.

dishonesty noun fraud, fraudulence, cheating, chicanery, untrustworthiness, falseness, falsity, falsehood, untruthfulness, dishonor, unscrupulousness, corruption, criminality, deceit, deception, duplicity, lying, craft, cunning, trickery, wiliness, guile, double-dealing, underhandedness, treachery, perfidy, graft, improbity, rascality, knavishness; *inf.* crookedness, shadiness.

dishonor noun **1** *bring dishonor to the regiment* disgrace, shame, humiliation, scandal, discredit, degradation, ignominy, infamy, disrepute, ill repute, loss of face, disfavor, debasement, abasement, odium. **2** *do him a dishonor* indignity, insult, affront, offense, abuse, outrage, slight, discourtesy. **3** *a dishonor to his profession* disgrace, blot, blemish, stigma.

dishonor verb **1** *dishonor the flag* disgrace, bring dishonor/shame to, shame, humiliate, discredit, degrade, debase, sully, stain, stigmatize. **2** *dishonor their hosts* insult, affront, abuse, slight, offend.

dishonorable adjective **1** *a dishonorable act* disgraceful, shameful, shameless, shaming, disreputable, degrading, debasing, ignominious, ignoble, blameworthy, contemptible, despicable, reprehensible, base. **2** *a dishonorable man* unprincipled, blackguardly, unscrupulous, corrupt, untrustworthy, treacherous, perfidious, traitorous, disreputable, discreditable; *inf.* shady.

disillusion verb disabuse, disenchant, open the eyes of, shatter the illusions of, undeceive, set straight, enlighten, disappoint, make sadder and wiser.

disinclined adjective reluctant, unenthusiastic, not in the mood, hesitant, unwilling, loath, averse, antipathetic, resistant, opposed, recalcitrant.

disinfect verb sterilize, sanitize, clean, cleanse, purify, fumigate, decontaminate.

disingenuous adjective insincere, duplicitous, false, lying, untruthful, artful, cunning, crafty, wily, sly, shifty, scheming, calculating, designing, insidious.

disintegrate verb fall apart, fall to pieces, break up, break apart, shatter, splinter, crumble, decompose, decay, rot, molder, erode, dissolve, go to wrack and ruin.

disinterested adjective **1** *disinterested judges* unbiased, unprejudiced, impartial, detached, objective, uninvolved, dispassionate, impersonal, open-minded, neutral, outside, fair, just, equitable, evenhanded, unselfish. **2** *disinterested in the lecture* uninterested, unconcerned, uninvolved, unresponsive, indifferent, bored, apathetic, blasé.

disjointed noun **1** *a disjointed talk* incoherent, unconnected, disconnected, ununified, discontinuous, disorganized, disordered, fitful, spasmodic, aimless, directionless. **2** *disjointed limbs* dislocated, displaced, severed, separated, disarticulated.

disloyal adjective unfaithful, faithless, false, false-hearted, untrue, inconstant, untrustworthy, treacherous, perfidious, traitorous, disaffected, subversive, seditious, unpatriotic, renegade, apostate, dissident, two-faced, double-dealing, deceitful.

dismal adjective **1** *dismal weather/surroundings* gloomy, miserable, wretched, forlorn, lugubrious, dreary, bleak, drab, dingy, cheerless, desolate, depressing, grim, funereal, comfortless, inhospitable, uninviting. **2** *a dismal piece of work* bad, poor, inept, bungling, disgraceful.

dismay verb disconcert, upset, jolt, unsettle, unnerve, alarm, frighten, scare, dishearten, dispirit, daunt.

dismiss verb **1** *dismissed from the firm for theft* discharge, expel, cashier, remove, oust, eject, lay off; *inf.* sack, fire, give one one's marching orders, send packing, give the boot/heave-ho to, boot out. **2** *dismiss an assembly/army* disband, disperse, dissolve, discharge, send away, let go, release, free. **3** *dismiss foolish thoughts* put away, banish, think no more of, put out of one's mind, set/lay aside, abandon, have done with, reject, drop, disregard.

dismissal noun **1** *his dismissal from the firm* notice, discharge, expulsion, removal, ejection; *inf.* sacking, firing. **2** *the dismissal of the assembly* dispersal, dissolution, discharge, permission to go/depart/leave, release.

disobedient adjective insubordinate, unruly, wayward, undisciplined, rebellious, defiant, mutinous, recalcitrant, intractable, willful, refractory, disorderly, delinquent, noncompliant, perverse, naughty, mischievous, contrary.

disobey verb defy, disregard, flout, contravene, infringe, overstep, resist, rebel against, fly in the face of, transgress, violate.

disorder noun **1** *tidy up the disorder* untidiness, mess, chaos, muddle, clutter, jumble, confusion, disorderliness, disarray, disorganization; *inf.* shambles. **2** *police quelling the disorder* disturbance, disruption, tumult, riot, breach of the peace, fracas, rumpus, brouhaha, melee, unrest.

3 *a disorder of the kidneys* disease, ailment, complaint, affliction, malady, sickness, illness.

disorderly adjective **1** *disorderly rooms* untidy, messy, chaotic, cluttered, jumbled, muddled, out of order, out of place, in disarray, confused, deranged, upsidedown, at sixes and sevens. **2** *disorderly crowds* unruly, boisterous, rough, rowdy, disobedient, undisciplined, lawless, wild, unmanageable, uncontrollable, ungovernable, refractory, rebellious, mutinous, turbulent, tumultuous, rioting.

disorganized adjective random, unorganized, unmethodical, unsystematic, haphazard, disorderly, chaotic, out of order, in disarray, confused; *inf.* hit-or-miss.

disown verb repudiate, renounce, reject, cast off, abandon, forsake, turn one's back on, disclaim, deny, disallow, abnegate, disavow, disinherit.

disparage verb **1** *disparage their efforts* belittle, slight, depreciate, devalue, devaluate, downgrade, demean, detract from, discredit, deprecate, denigrate, derogate, deflate, minimize, undervalue, underestimate, make light of, play down. **2** *disparage their competitors* defame, run down, slander, libel, malign, cast aspersions on, impugn, calumniate, vilify, traduce; *inf.* do a hatchet job on, bad-mouth, trash.

disparity noun discrepancy, inequality, unevenness, inconsistency, imbalance, incongruity, difference, dissimilarity, contrast, gap.

dispassionate adjective **1** *a dispassionate demeanor* unemotional, emotionless, unmoved, unexcited, unexcitable, unflappable, unperturbed, nonchalant, unruffled, cool, collected, cool and collected, calm, composed, self-possessed, level-headed, self-controlled, temperate, sober, placid, equable, tranquil, serene; *inf.* laid-back, together. **2** *dispassionate judges* indifferent, uninvolved, impersonal. *See* DISINTERESTED 1.

dispatch verb **1** *dispatch a letter* send, send off, post, mail, forward, transmit, consign, remit, convey. **2** *dispatch the task in an hour* finish, dispose of, discharge, execute, perform, expedite, push through, accelerate, hasten, speed up, hurry on; *inf.* make short work of. **3** *a flurry of bullets dispatched the terrorists* kill, put to death, slay, finish off, slaughter, murder, assassinate, execute; *inf.* bump off, do in, knock off, eliminate, erase.

dispatch noun **1** *carried out with dispatch* promptness, promptitude, speed, alacrity, quickness, haste, hurry, swiftness, rapidity, expedition, expeditiousness. **2** *military dispatches | a journalist's dispatch* communication, communiqué, bulletin, report, account, document, missive, letter, epistle, message, item, piece, article, news, instruction.

dispel verb drive away, drive off, chase away, banish, rout, expel, disperse, scatter, dissipate, disseminate, dismiss.

dispensable adjective expendable, disposable, unnecessary, unessential, nonessential, needless, superfluous, uncalled-for.

dispense verb **1** *dispense supplies* distribute, hand out, deal out, dole out, share out, divide out, parcel out, allocate, allot, apportion, assign, bestow, confer, supply, disburse. **2** *dispense justice* administer, discharge, carry out, execute, implement, apply, enforce, effectuate, operate, direct. **3** *dispense medicines* make up, prepare, mix, supply. **4** *dispense him from that obligation* exempt, excuse, except, release, relieve, reprieve, absolve; *inf.* let off. **dispense with 1** *dispense with the formalities* waive, do without, omit, forgo, give up, relinquish, renounce, ignore, disregard, pass over, brush aside. **2** *dispense with their services* do away with, get rid of, dispose of, abolish, revoke, rescind, cancel, shake off, manage without.

disperse verb **1** *the crowd dispersed* break up, disband, separate, scatter, dissolve, leave, vanish; dissipate, dispel, drive away, banish. **2** *disperse seeds* scatter, disseminate, distribute, sow, sprinkle, spread, diffuse, strew, bestrew. **3** *disperse information* circulate, broadcast, publish, publicize, spread, diffuse.

dispirit verb dishearten, discourage, cast down, make dejected, depress, crush, dash, dampen the spirits of, daunt, disappoint, deter, sadden; *inf.* throw cold water on.

displace verb **1** *displace the tribe* move, shift, relocate, transfer, resettle. **2** *displace from office* remove, depose. *See* DISMISS 1. **3** *displaced the aging chairman* replace, take the place of, take over from, supplant, oust, supersede, succeed; *inf.* crowd out.

displaced adjective **displaced person** refugee, DP, exile, émigré, fugitive.

display verb **1** *display the goods* show, exhibit, put on view, present, unveil, set forth, arrange, dispose, array, demonstrate, advertise, publicize. **2** *display their military power* show off, flaunt, parade, flourish, boast, vaunt; *inf.* flash. **3** *display emotion* evince, manifest, reveal, disclose.

display noun **1** *a display of sculpture* show, exhibition, exhibit, presentation, demonstration, spectacle, array. **2** *military display* show, spectacle, parade, pageant; pomp, flourish, ostentation.

displease verb put out, annoy, irritate, anger, irk, vex, provoke, offend, pique, peeve, gall, nettle, exasperate, perturb, aggravate.

displeasure noun dissatisfaction, discontentment, disgruntlement, disapproval, distaste, annoyance, irritation, anger, pique, chagrin, indignation, exasperation, perturbation.

disposable adjective **1** *disposable plates* throwaway, nonreturnable, paper, plastic, biodegradable. **2** *disposable assets* available, usable, accessible, obtainable.

dispose verb **1** *troops disposed in rows* arrange, order, place, put, position, array. **2** *behavior not disposing me to believe him* incline, predispose, prompt, lead, induce, motivate, bias, influence, condition. **dispose of 1** *dispose of the trash* get rid of, throw away/out, clear out, discard, eject, unload, scrap, destroy, dump. **2** *dispose of the business* deal with, settle, determine, decide, finish, conclude, end. **3** *dispose of his estate* distribute, allot, allocate, assign, part with, transfer, give away, bestow. **4** *dispose of his enemy* kill, do away with, put to death, slay, murder, slaughter; *inf.* bump off, knock off.

disposition noun **1** *people of a calm disposition* nature, character, temperament, humor, makeup, constitution, spirit, temper, mood. **2** *a disposition to/for moodiness* inclination, tendency, proneness, propensity, leaning, proclivity, bias, bent, predilection, weakness, habit, readiness. **3** *the disposition of the troops* disposal, arrangement, positioning, placement, lining-up, marshaling, grouping. **4** *disposition of property* disposal, distribution, allocation, transfer, transference, bestowal.

dispossess verb **1** *dispossess them of their property* deprive, divest, strip, bereave. **2** *dispossess the tenants* dislodge, oust, eject, drive out, evict, turn out, dismiss.

disprove verb prove false, invalidate, refute, negate, rebut, confute, contradict, discredit.

dispute verb **1** *dispute with colleagues* debate, discuss, argue, disagree, clash, quarrel, wrangle, bicker, squabble. **2** *dispute his right to go* question, call into question, challenge, contest, deny, doubt, contradict, oppose, controvert, impugn, gainsay.

dispute noun **1** *open to dispute* debate, discussion, argument, controversy, contention, disagreement, dissension, conflict, friction, discord, litigation. **2** *a dispute over boundaries* argument, row, altercation, clash, quarrel, wrangle, squabble, feud, disturbance, fracas, brawl.

disqualify verb declare ineligible, rule out, preclude, debar, reject, prohibit, disentitle.

disregard verb **1** *disregard the consequences* ignore, take no notice/account of, pay no attention/heed to, discount, set aside, neglect, forget, never mind, overlook, turn a blind eye to, pass over, gloss over, brush aside, laugh off, make light of; *inf.* play down. **2** *disregard their achievement* slight, disparage, denigrate, disdain.

disregard noun **1** *treat danger with disregard* inattention, heedlessness, carelessness, neglect, negligence, indifference. **2** *treat staff/achievements with disregard* scorn, contempt, disparagement, denigration, disdain, disrespect, disesteem.

disrepair noun dilapidation, deterioration, decay, collapse, shabbiness, ruin, ruination, decrepitude.

disreputable adjective dishonorable, dishonest, unprincipled, villainous, notorious, ignominious, corrupt, unworthy, base, low, mean, questionable, unsavory, unscrupulous, rascally, contemptible, reprehensible, despicable, discreditable, disgraceful, shameful, shocking, outrageous, scandalous; *inf.* crooked, shady.

disrepute noun notoriety, discredit, ill repute, disfavor, ill favor, disesteem, disgrace, shame, dishonor, infamy, ignominy, degradation, odium.

disrespect noun discourtesy, incivility, impoliteness, unmannerliness, rudeness, ungraciousness, irreverence, lack of consideration, disregard, insolence, impudence, scorn, contempt; ill manners.

disrespectful adjective discourteous, uncivil, impolite, unmannerly, ill-mannered, rude, irreverent, inconsiderate, insolent, impudent, impertinent, scornful, contemptuous, insulting.

disrupt verb throw into disorder/disarray, disorder, disorganize, cause confusion/turmoil in, disarrange, disturb, upset; interrupt, suspend, discontinue, interfere with, obstruct, impede, hamper; *inf.* throw a monkey wrench in/into (the works of).

disruptive adjective *disruptive children* troublemaking, troublesome, divisive, unruly, disorderly, undisciplined, upsetting, disturbing, distracting, noisy.

dissatisfaction noun discontent, discontentment, disapproval, disappointment, frustration, unhappiness, dismay, vexation, annoyance, irritation.

dissatisfied adjective discontented, displeased, disgruntled, disapproving, unsatisfied, disappointed, unfulfilled, frustrated, unhappy, regretful, vexed, angry, resentful, restless.

dissect verb *dissect the information* analyze, break down, examine, study, inspect, scrutinize, probe, explore, investigate.

disseminate verb spread, circulate, broadcast, publish, publicize, proclaim, promulgate, propagate, dissipate, scatter, distribute, disperse, diffuse.

dissension noun disagreement, dispute, argument, dissent, nonconformity, variance, conflict, friction, strife, discord, contention, quarreling, wrangling, bickering.

dissent verb **dissent from 1** *dissent from official policy* disagree with, differ from, be at variance with, decline/refuse to support, protest against, object to, dispute. **2** *dissent from established practice* reject, repudiate, renounce, abjure, secede from, apostatize.

dissenter noun dissident, objector, protester, protestant, disputant, rebel, revolutionary, nonconformist, apostate, sectarian, heretic.

dissertation noun treatise, thesis, discourse, essay, critique, exposition, disquisition.

disservice noun bad/ill turn, dirty trick, disfavor, unkindness, injury, harm, hurt, damage, wrong, injustice; *inf.* kick in the teeth.

dissident noun protester, nonconformist. *See* DISSENTER.

dissimilar adjective unlike, unalike, different, varying, variant, disparate, unrelated, divergent, deviating, diverse, various, contrasting, mismatched, distinct.

dissipate verb **1** *dissipate one's fears | the crowd dissipated* dispel, dissolve. *See* DISPERSE 1. **2** *dissipate their resources* squander, fritter, misspend, lavish, waste, exhaust, drain, deplete, spend, expend, burn up, use up, consume, run through.

dissipated adjective **1** *a dissipated young man* dissolute, debauched, intemperate, profligate, abandoned, rakish, licentious, promiscuous, drunken, self-indulgent, wild, unrestrained, wanton, depraved, degenerate, corrupt. **2** *dissipated resources* squandered, frittered away, wasted, exhausted, depleted, consumed.

dissolute adjective debauched, intemperate. *See* DISSIPATED.

dissolve verb **1** *salt dissolves in water* liquefy, melt, deliquesce. **2** *his hopes dissolved* disappear, vanish, melt away, evaporate, dissipate, disintegrate, crumble, decompose, perish, die, evanesce. **3** *dissolve a partnership* end, terminate, break up, discontinue, wind up, disband, dismiss, suspend, ruin. **4** *the crowds dissolved* separate, sever, disunite, disjoin, disperse, scatter, go their separate ways. **5** *dissolve in tears/mirth* break into, collapse into, be overcome with.

distance noun **1** *the distance between the fields* space, interval, span, gap, separation, stretch, extent; length, width, depth.

2 *the distance of the farm from the highway* remoteness, farness. **3** *upset by her colleague's distance* aloofness, reserve, remoteness, reticence, coolness, coldness, frigidity, stiffness, formality, restraint, unresponsiveness. **in the distance** far away, far off, on the horizon, afar, yonder.

distant adjective **1** *a distant place* far, far-away, far off, remote, out of the way, outlying, abroad, far-flung. **2** *a distant time* far-off, long ago. **3** *three miles distant from each other* away, off, apart, separated. **4** *a distant relative/likeness* not close, remote, indirect, slight. **5** *a distant memory* vague, faint, indistinct, obscure, uncertain. **6** *a distant smile* aloof, reserved, remote, uncommunicative, unapproachable, standoffish, restrained, cool, unresponsive, unfriendly.

distasteful adjective unpleasant, disagreeable, displeasing, undesirable, uninviting, objectionable, offensive, obnoxious, revolting, repugnant, abhorrent, loathsome, detestable; unpalatable, unsavory, unappetizing, disgusting, sickening, nauseating, nauseous.

distinct adjective **1** *a distinct resemblance* clear, clear-cut, well-defined, sharp, marked, decided, definite, unmistakable, recognizable, obvious, plain, plain as day, evident, apparent, manifest, patent, palpable, unambiguous, unequivocal. **2** *two distinct jobs* separate, individual, different, unconnected, unassociated, detached, discrete, dissimilar, unalike, disparate.

distinction noun **1** *make the distinction between right and wrong* differentiation, contradistinction, discrimination, division, separation, dividing line, contrast. **2** *fail to notice the identifying distinctions* difference, dissimilarity, dissimilitude, contrast, differential, subtlety, nicety, nuance. **3** *the distinctions of wealth and rank* feature, characteristic, mark, individuality, peculiarity. **4** *pass the exam with distinction* honor, credit, excellence, merit. **5** *people of distinction* note, consequence, importance, account, significance, prestige, prominence, eminence, repute, reputation, renown, fame, honor, excellence, glory.

distinctive adjective distinguishing, characteristic, typical, individual, particular, peculiar, special, different, uncommon, unusual, remarkable, singular, extraordinary, noteworthy, original, idiosyncratic.

distinctly adverb **1** *distinctly annoyed* obviously, plainly, evidently, manifestly. **2** *speak distinctly* clearly, plainly, intelligibly, precisely.

distinguish verb **1** *distinguish one color from another* tell apart, differentiate, discriminate, determine; tell the difference

between, decide between. **2** *his hair distinguishes him from the others* make distinctive, set apart, separate, single out, mark off, characterize, individualize, designate, categorize, classify. **3** *distinguish a black shape* make out, see, discern, perceive, observe, notice, detect, recognize, identify, pick out. **4** *distinguish himself in battle* bring fame/honor to, ennoble, dignify, glorify, win acclaim for, lionize, immortalize.

distinguished adjective *a distinguished scientist* famous, famed, eminent, renowned, prominent, well-known, noted, notable, esteemed, acclaimed, illustrious, celebrated, legendary.

distinguishing adjective *a distinguishing mark* distinctive, determining, individualistic, peculiar, singular, characteristic, typical.

distort verb **1** *distort their features* twist, warp, contort, bend, buckle, deform, misshape, disfigure, mangle, wrench, wring, wrest. **2** *distort the facts* misrepresent, pervert, twist, falsify, garble, slant, bias, color, tamper with, alter, change.

distortion noun **1** *a distortion in the metal* twist, warp, contortion, bend, buckle, curvature, deformation, deformity, malformation, gnarl, knot. **2** *a distortion of the truth* misrepresentation, perversion, twisting, falsification, garbling, coloring, alteration.

distract verb **1** *distract them from work* deflect, divert, sidetrack, turn aside, draw away. **2** *distract the children* amuse, entertain, divert, beguile, absorb, engage, occupy. **3** *bright lights distracting her* confuse, bewilder, fluster, agitate, disconcert, discompose, confound. **4** *grief distracting her* make frantic, drive/make mad, madden, derange, throw into a frenzy.

distracted adjective **1** *rushing around in a distracted way* confused, bewildered, agitated, flustered, harassed, worried; *inf.* hassled. **2** *distracted women mourning their sons* grief-stricken, distraught, frantic, frenzied, raving, wild, hysterical, overwrought, mad, maddened, crazed, deranged.

distraction noun **1** *distraction from their work* diversion, interruption, disturbance, interference, obstruction. **2** *distractions for the children* amusement, entertainment, diversion, pastime, recreation, hobby, game, occupation. **3** *a look of distraction amid the crowds* confusion, bewilderment, befuddlement, perplexity, disturbance, agitation, perturbation, harassment. **4** *pity the distraction of the widow* frenzy, hysteria, distress, madness, insanity, derangement, delirium.

distress noun **1** *the lost child's distress* anguish, suffering, pain, agony, ache, affliction, discomfort, heartache, heartbreak, sorrow, grief, woe, sadness, desolation, trouble, worry, anxiety, perturbation, uneasiness, angst; tribulations, cries, wails. **2** *old people in distress* hardship, adversity, misfortune, need, want, poverty, lack, privation, destitution, indigence, impoverishment, penury; difficulties, dire straits.

distress verb **1** *the news distressed her* pain, upset, make miserable/wretched, grieve, sadden, trouble, worry, bother, perturb, disturb, vex, harrow, torment. **2** *distress the furniture* dent, scratch, antique, simulate age/wear in.

distribute verb **1** *distribute rations to the crowd* give out, hand out, allocate, allot, issue, dispense, administer, apportion, assign, deal out, dole out, measure out, mete out, parcel out, dispose. **2** *distribute advertising leaflets* circulate, pass out/around, hand out, deliver, convey, transmit. **3** *distribute seeds evenly* disseminate, disperse, diffuse, scatter, spread, strew, sow. **4** *luggage distributed by size* arrange, organize, group, class, classify, categorize, file, assort.

distribution noun **1** *distribution of rations* allocation, allotment, dispensation, administering, assignment, dealing out, division. **2** *distribution of seeds* dissemination, dispersal, diffusion, scattering. **3** *the distribution of luggage by size* organization, grouping, classification. **4** *in charge of sales and distribution* handling, delivery, transport, transportation, conveyance, mailing.

district noun area, region, place, locality, neighborhood, quarter, sector, vicinity, community, territory, domain; county, ward, parish, constituency, department, canton.

distrust verb mistrust, be suspicious of, be wary/chary of, be skeptical of, have doubts about, doubt, have misgivings about, be leery of, wonder about, question, suspect, disbelieve, discredit.

distrust noun mistrust, lack of faith, suspicion, wariness, chariness, skepticism, doubt, doubtfulness, dubiety, misgiving, questioning, qualms, leeriness.

disturb verb **1** *disturb them while they are working* interrupt, butt in on, distract, bother, trouble, pester, intrude on, interfere with, hinder, plague, harass, molest; *inf.* hassle. **2** *disturb papers on a desk* disarrange, muddle, disorganize, disorder, confuse. **3** *the news disturbed them* trouble, worry, upset, agitate, fluster, discomfit, disconcert, alarm, frighten, startle, dismay, distress, ruffle, shake.

disturbance noun **1** *please excuse the disturbance* interruption, distraction, intrusion, interference, hindrance, harassment. **2** *police called to a disturbance* uproar, commotion, row, rumpus, hullabaloo, tumult, turmoil, fracas, affray, brawl, riot; *inf.* ruckus.

disturbed adjective *emotionally disturbed* unbalanced, disordered, maladjusted, neurotic, psychotic; *inf.* screwed up.

disturbing adjective troubling, worrying, upsetting, disconcerting, alarming, disquieting, startling, dismaying, frightening, distressing, unsettling, bewildering.

ditch noun trench, channel, watercourse, dike, canal, drain, gutter, gully, moat, furrow, rut.

ditch verb **1** *ditch the plan* abandon, throw out, discard, drop, scrap, jettison, get rid of, dispose of, dump. **2** *ditch the police* evade, escape, elude, shake off.

dive verb **1** *dive from the springboard* plunge/descend into water, plummet, nosedive, fall, descend, submerge, drop, swoop, dip, bellyflop. **2** *dive out of sight* jump, lunge, rush, dart, dash, duck, dodge.

diverge verb **1** *the roads diverged* separate, divide, subdivide, split, part, disunite, fork, branch off, radiate, spread out, bifurcate, divaricate. **2** *opinions diverge* differ, disagree, be at variance/odds, conflict, clash. **3** *diverge from the norm* deviate, digress, depart, veer, stray, drift, turn aside, wander.

diverse adjective various, miscellaneous, assorted, mixed, diversified, variegated, varied, varying, heterogeneous, different, differing, distinct, unlike, dissimilar, distinctive, contrasting.

diversify verb vary, variegate, modify, assort, mix, alter, change, transform.

diversion noun **1** *the diversion of the stream* redirection, deflection, digression, deviation, divergence. **2** *diversions for the children* amusement, entertainment, pastime, distraction, recreation, fun, relaxation.

diversity noun diverseness, variety, miscellany, assortment, mixture, range, medley, multiplicity, variegation, heterogeneity, difference, unlikeness, dissimilarity, contrast.

divert verb **1** *divert the stream* turn aside, deflect, draw away, avert, redirect. **2** *divert him from his work* distract, detract, sidetrack, lead away, turn aside. **3** *clowns diverted the children* amuse, entertain, distract, delight, beguile, enchant, interest, occupy, absorb.

diverting adjective amusing, entertaining, humorous, fun, enjoyable, pleasurable, recreational, beguiling, interesting, absorbing.

divest verb **1** *trees divested of their leaves* unclothe, undress, disrobe, strip, denude.

2 *divest them of property* deprive, strip, dispossess, relieve, bereave.

divide verb **1** *divide the apple in two* cut up, sever, split, shear, bisect, halve, quarter, cleave, rend, sunder, rive; separate, part, segregate, partition, detach, disconnect, disjoin. **2** *the road divides here* diverge, branch, fork, split in two, divaricate. **3** *divide the food* share, allocate, allot, apportion, portion out, distribute, dispense, deal out, hand out, dole out, measure out, parcel out, *inf.* divvy (up/out). **4** *politics divided them* estrange, alienate, separate, split up, disunite, disaffect, set/pit against one another, cause disagreement between, sow dissension between. **5** *divide into types* classify, sort, arrange, order, group, grade, rank, categorize.

divine adjective **1** *a divine being* godly, godlike, heavenly, celestial, holy, angelic, seraphic, spiritual, saintly. **2** *divine worship* religious, holy, sacred, sanctified, consecrated, spiritual. **3** *divine music* supernatural, superhuman, mystical, exalted, beatific, blissful, ethereal, transcendental, transcendent. **4** *looking divine | a divine evening* lovely, beautiful, charming, perfect, excellent, superlative, wonderful, glorious, marvelous, admirable; *inf.* super, stunning.

divine verb **1** *divine their plans* guess, surmise, conjecture, speculate, suspect, deduce, infer, theorize, hypothesize. **2** *divine their need* intuit, discern, perceive, understand, grasp, apprehend, comprehend. **3** *divine the future* foretell, predict, foresee, forecast, presage, augur, portend, prognosticate, forebode.

division noun **1** *the division of the groups* parting, separation, segregation, partitioning, disconnection, detachment. **2** *the division of rations* allocation, allotment, apportionment, distribution. **3** *cross the division* dividing line, divide, boundary, border, partition. **4** *divisions of equal size* section, part, portion, piece, bit, segment; compartment, category, class, group, grade, family. **5** *divisions of the firm* branch, department, section, sector, arm. **6** *a bitter division between the families* disagreement, feud, breach, rupture, split; dissension, conflict, discord, variance, disunion, estrangement, alienation.

divorce verb split up, break up, separate, part, disconnect, divide, dissociate, detach, disunite, sever, disjoin, split.

divulge verb disclose, reveal, make known, expose, uncover, bring into the open, let slip, leak, let the cat out of the bag about, confess, betray; *inf.* spill the beans about.

dizzy adjective **1** *get dizzy on top of the ladder* light-headed, faint, vertiginous, weak at/in the knees, shaky, wobbly, off-balance, reeling, staggering; *inf.* woozy. **2** *feeling dizzy at the amount of information* dazed, bewildered, confused, muddled, bemused, befuddled, puzzled, perplexed. **3** *dizzy young girls* giddy, scatterbrained, featherbrained, flighty, foolish, silly, capricious, inconstant.

do verb **1** *do as you know you should* act, behave, conduct oneself, comport oneself. **2** *do the job* perform, carry out, undertake, discharge, execute, accomplish, implement, achieve, complete, finish, conclude, bring about, effect, effectuate, realize, produce, engineer. **3** *this amount will do* be enough, be sufficient, be adequate, suffice, be satisfactory, be of use, fill/fit the bill, answer/serve the purpose, meet the needs, pass muster, measure up. **4** *do the meals* make, prepare, get ready, fix, produce, see to, arrange, organize, be responsible for, be in charge of, look after, take on. **5** *do a large picture* create, make, produce, originate, form, fashion, design, fabricate, manufacture. **6** *they're doing three plays* put on, perform, act, present, produce, give. **7** *do me a favor* render, afford, give, bestow, grant, pay. **8** *can't do this math problem* solve, resolve, work out, figure out, decipher. **9** *what does he do?* work at, be employed at, earn a living at. **10** *how are you doing?* get on/along, progress, fare, make out, manage, continue. **11** *the play was done in Russian* translate, put, render, adapt, transform. **12** *the car was doing 90 mph* travel at, go/proceed at, be driven at. **13** *we did 50 miles* travel, journey, cover, traverse. **14** *they're doing the museums today* sightsee, look at, visit, tour. **do away with 1** *do away with the penalty* abolish, get rid of, discard, remove, discontinue, eliminate, repeal, revoke, rescind, cancel, annul, nullify. **2** *do away with his enemy* kill, put to death, slay, murder, slaughter, liquidate, assassinate, execute, dispatch; *inf.* do in, bump off, knock off, eliminate. **do in 1** *do in his business* ruin, reduce to nothing, wreck, destroy, smash, crush, wreak havoc on. **2** *the walk did me in* tire out, exhaust, wear out, fatigue, weary. **do out of** prevent from having, deprive of, swindle/cheat/trick out of; *inf.* con out of. **do without** forgo, dispense with, abstain from, give up, refrain from, eschew.

docile adjective manageable, controllable, tractable, malleable, amenable, accommodating, compliant, pliant, obedient, biddable, dutiful, submissive, yielding, ductile.

dock noun pier, quay, wharf, jetty, marina, waterfront.

docket noun agenda, roster, schedule, slate, program.

doctor verb **1** *doctor the patients* treat,

prescribe for, attend to, minister to, care for, cure, heal. **2** *doctor the machinery* patch up, repair, fix, mend, botch. **3** *doctor the drinks* adulterate, contaminate, dilute, water down, weaken, mix, cut, lace; *inf.* spike. **4** *doctor the evidence* tamper with, interfere with, alter, change, falsify, disguise, fudge, pervert, misrepresent.

doctrine noun creed, credo, dogma, belief, conviction, teaching; tenet, principle, precept, maxim; articles of faith, canons.

document noun paper, form, certificate, record, report, deed, voucher, instrument, charter; paperwork, documentation.

document verb **1** *document their statement* prove, back up, support, corroborate, substantiate, authenticate, verify, validate, certify. **2** *the war was well documented in the press* report, record, detail, tabulate, chart, register, cite, instance.

doddering adjective tottering, staggering, shuffling, faltering, shaky, unsteady, trembling, trembly, quivering, infirm, decrepit, aged, in one's dotage, senile.

dodge verb **1** *dodge behind the door* dart, duck, dive, swerve, sidestep, veer, jump away, move aside. **2** *dodge the police* evade, elude, escape, fend off, avoid, stay/steer clear of, deceive, trick; *inf.* give the slip to. **3** *dodge the question/work* evade, get out of, parry, fend off, fudge, shirk, shun, stay/steer clear of.

dodge noun **1** *a dodge to the right* dart, duck, dive, swerve, jump. **2** *a tax dodge* ruse, ploy, scheme, stratagem, subterfuge, trick, wile, deception, maneuver, device, machination, contrivance, artifice, expedient.

dog verb pursue, follow, track, trail, shadow, hound, plague, trouble, haunt; *inf* tail.

dogged adjective determined, resolute, obstinate, stubborn, tenacious, relentless, intent, single-minded, unshakable, unflagging, indefatigable, tireless, unfaltering, unwavering, persistent, persevering, pertinacious, unyielding, obdurate, firm, steadfast, steady, staunch.

dogma noun creed, credo, conviction, teaching; belief, tenet, principle, precept, maxim; articles of faith, canons.

dogmatic adjective **1** *dogmatic religious tenets* doctrinal, canonical, authoritative, *ex cathedra.* **2** *dogmatic statement/manner* assertive, insistent, doctrinaire, emphatic, categorical, authoritarian, opinionated, peremptory, domineering, imperious, arrogant, overbearing, dictatorial, intolerant.

doldrums plural noun **1** *a fit of the doldrums* downheartedness, dejection, depression, melancholy, gloom, inertia, apathy, listlessness, malaise, boredom, tedium, ennui; blues, low spirits. **2** *a business in*

the doldrums inactivity, inertia, flatness, stagnation, dullness, sluggishness, torpor.

dole verb **dole out** deal out, allocate, allot, apportion, share (out), mete out, distribute, divide up, dispense, hand out, give out, issue, assign, administer.

doleful adjective mournful, sorrowful, sad, dejected, disconsolate, depressed, gloomy, melancholy, blue, miserable, wretched; *inf.* down in the mouth/dumps.

dolt noun blockhead, dunderhead, thickhead, numskull, nitwit, dunce, fool, idiot, ass, simpleton, nincompoop, ignoramus, dullard; *inf.* dope, chump, clod, boob, jerk, dimwit, nerd, airhead.

domain noun **1** *the king's domain* realm, kingdom. *See* DOMINION 2. **2** *the scientific domain* area, field, region, province, sphere, section, discipline.

dome noun cupola, rotunda; hemisphere.

domestic adjective **1** *an unhappy domestic life* home, family, household, domiciliary, residential, private. **2** *preferring domestic people* housewifely, stay-at-home, home-loving. **3** *a domestic animal* domesticated, tame, pet, house-trained, housebroken, trained. **4** *domestic markets/plants* home, internal; native, indigenous, homegrown, home-bred.

domesticate verb **1** *domesticate an animal* tame, house-train, housebreak, train, break in, gentle. **2** *domesticate a foreign tree* naturalize, acclimatize, habituate, accustom, familiarize, assimilate.

domicile noun home, house, residence, residency, dwelling, dwelling place, abode, habitation, lodging, accommodation.

domicile verb settle, make one's home, take up one's abode, ensconce oneself.

dominant adjective **1** *the dominant member of the committee* ruling, governing, controlling, commanding, ascendant, presiding, supreme, authoritative, most influential, superior, most assertive, domineering. **2** *the dominant issue* predominant, most important, chief, main, principal, leading, primary, paramount, preeminent, outstanding, prominent, prevailing.

dominate verb **1** *dominate the council* rule, govern, control, command, direct, preside over, have ascendancy/mastery over, master, domineer, tyrannize, intimidate, have the upper hand over, ride roughshod over; have under one's thumb, be in the driver's seat, be in the saddle, wear the pants; *inf.* boss, call the shots. **2** *the hill dominates the town* overlook, tower above, stand over, project/jut over, hang/loom over, bestride.

domineering adjective overbearing, imperious, authoritarian, high-handed, autocratic, peremptory, arrogant, haughty, dictatorial, coercive, tyrannical, despotic, oppressive, subjugating, iron-fisted, iron-handed; *inf.* bossy, pushy.

dominion noun **1** *have dominion over smaller states* supremacy, ascendancy, sway, mastery, sovereignty, jurisdiction, control, command, direction, authority, power, domination, suzerainty. **2** *the king's dominions* realm, kingdom, empire, domain, country, province, territory, region, estate.

donate verb give, contribute, make a contribution of, subscribe, make a gift of, gift, present, pledge, put oneself down for, bestow; *inf.* chip in, kick in.

donation noun contribution, subscription, gift, present, grant, offering, gratuity; alms; charity, benefaction, largesse.

done adjective **1** *the job is done* accomplished, complete, completed, executed, perfected, finished, ended, concluded, terminated, realized, consummated. **2** *such behavior is not done* acceptable, proper, seemly, decorous, conventional, de rigueur.
done for finished, ruined, destroyed, broken, wrecked, undone, doomed, lost, defeated, beaten, foiled; *inf.* washed-up.
done in worn out, exhausted, tired out, weary, fatigued, played out, on one's last legs; *inf.* dog-tired, all in, dead beat, bushed, pooped.

donor noun contributor, donator, grantor, benefactor, benefactress, supporter, backer, philanthropist; *inf.* angel.

doom noun **1** *companies facing doom* ruin, ruination, rack and ruin, downfall, destruction, catastrophe, disaster, extinction, annihilation, death, termination. **2** *the prisoner hearing his doom* condemnation, sentence, judgment, pronouncement, decree, damnation. **3** *predicting doom* the Last Judgment, Judgment Day, doomsday, Armageddon, end of the world.

doom verb **1** *children doomed to be poor* fate, destine, predestine, ordain, preordain, foreordain, consign, condemn. **2** *prisoners doomed to die* condemn, sentence, judge, pronounce, decree, damn.

doomed adjective *doomed plans/lovers* ill-fated, star-crossed, foredoomed, unlucky, damned, bedeviled, ruined, crushed.

door noun **1** *wooden doors* doorway, portal, entrance, entry, exit, barrier. **2** *doors to academic success* access, opening, entrée, gateway, way, path, road, ingress. **out of doors** outside, outdoors, out, in/into the open air, alfresco.

dormant adjective sleeping, asleep, inactive, inert, latent, fallow, quiescent, inoperative, hibernating, comatose, stagnant.

dot noun spot, speck, fleck, point, mark, dab, particle, atom, iota, jot, mote, mite;

period, decimal point. **on the dot** *arrive on the dot* to the minute, on time, punctually, promptly; *inf.* on the button.

dot verb spot, fleck, bespeckle, mark, dab, stud, bestud, stipple, pock, freckle, sprinkle, scatter, pepper.

dote verb *dote on/upon* idolize, adore, hold dear, love dearly, treasure, prize, make much of, lavish affection on, indulge, spoil, pamper.

doting adjective adoring, devoted, loving, fond, indulgent, pampering.

double noun *the double of his cousin* look-alike, twin, clone, doppelgänger, duplicate, replica, copy, facsimile, counterpart, match, mate, fellow; *inf.* spitting image, dead ringer, ringer. **on the double** at full speed, as fast as possible, with haste, in double time, post-haste, right away, immediately, without delay, straight away; *inf.* p.d.q.

double-cross verb betray, cheat, defraud, trick, hoodwink, mislead, deceive, swindle; *inf.* two-time, take for a ride.

double-dealing noun duplicity, treachery, betrayal, double-crossing, bad faith, perfidy, breach of trust, fraud, fraudulence, underhandedness, cheating, dishonesty, untrustworthiness, mendacity, deception, trickery, deceit, two-facedness, hypocrisy; *inf.* crookedness.

doubt verb **1** *doubt his motives* suspect, distrust, mistrust, lack confidence in, have misgivings about, feel uneasy/apprehensive about, call in question, query, question. **2** *doubt that it is genuine* be dubious, hesitate to believe, feel uncertain, be undecided, lack conviction.

doubt noun **1** *have doubts about his motives* distrust, mistrust, skepticism, uneasiness, apprehension; reservations, misgivings, suspicions, qualms. **2** *express doubt that it is genuine* dubiousness, lack of certainty/conviction, incredulity; queries, questions. **3** *full of doubts* uncertainty, indecision, hesitation; hesitancy, wavering, vacillation, irresolution, lack of conviction. **in doubt** *the issue is still in doubt* undecided, unsettled, unresolved, confused, open to question. **no doubt** *no doubt he will win* doubtless, certainly, of course, surely.

doubter noun skeptic, questioner, disbeliever, doubting Thomas, unbeliever, agnostic, scoffer, dissenter, pessimist.

doubtful adjective **1** *it is doubtful that he will come* in doubt, uncertain, unsure, unconfirmed, unsettled, improbable, unlikely. **2** *doubtful of/about his motives* suspicious, distrustful, mistrustful, skeptical, apprehensive, uneasy, unsure. **3** *its genuineness is doubtful* dubious, open to question, questionable, debatable, disputable, not definite, inconclusive. **4** *doubtful about his religious convictions* uncertain, indecisive, hesitating, irresolute, wavering, vacillating.

dour adjective unsmiling, sullen, morose, sour, gruff, churlish, forbidding, grim, stern, severe, austere, harsh, dismal, dreary, gloomy.

douse, dowse verb **1** *douse the walls with soapy water* drench, saturate, soak, souse, flood, deluge, wet, splash, hose down. **2** *douse the clothes in the tub* plunge, immerse, submerge, dip, dunk. **3** *douse the light/candle* extinguish, put out, blow out, quench, snuff.

dowdy adjective frumpish, frumpy, unfashionable, inelegant, shabby, untidy, dingy, frowzy.

down adjective **1** *feeling down* downhearted, dejected. *See* DOWNCAST. **2** *prices are down* lower, reduced, of lower/less value. **down on** *wish I hadn't been so down on school* against, prejudiced against, set against, antagonistic to/toward, hostile to/toward, negative toward/about.

down verb **1** *down three of the enemy* knock/throw/bring down, floor, fell, tackle, trip up, overthrow, defeat, conquer, subdue. **2** *down three glassfuls* drink, gulp down, swallow; *inf.* put away, chug (down), chug-a-lug, swill.

downbeat adjective *too many downbeat stories in the news* depressing, sad, gloomy, disheartening, dreary, dispiriting, bleak.

downcast adjective *downcast at the news* disheartened, dispirited, downhearted, dejected, depressed, discouraged, daunted, dismayed, disappointed, disconsolate, crestfallen, despondent, sad, unhappy, miserable, wretched, down, low, blue, gloomy, glum, melancholy, sorrowful, doleful, mournful.

downfall noun fall, collapse, undoing, ruin, ruination, crash, destruction, debasement, degradation, disgrace, overthrow, defeat.

downgrade verb **1** *downgrade the officers* demote, degrade, humble, debase; *inf.* take down a peg or two. **2** *downgrade their achievement* disparage, denigrate, detract from, run down, decry, belittle, make light of, minimize.

downhearted adjective disheartened, dispirited. *See* DOWNCAST.

downpour noun rainstorm, snowstorm, deluge, torrential/pouring rain, cloudburst, downfall; torrents of rain.

downright adjective **1** *a downright lie* complete, total, absolute, out and out, outright, utter, sheer, thorough, thoroughgoing, categorical, unmitigated, unqualified, unconditional, positive, simple, wholesale, all out, arrant, rank. **2** *a downright person* frank,

forthright, straightforward, open, candid, plainspoken, matter-of-fact, outspoken, blunt, brusque.

downright adverb *downright rude* completely, totally, absolutely, utterly, thoroughly, profoundly, categorically, positively.

down-to-earth adjective practical, sensible, realistic, matter-of-fact, no-nonsense, hardheaded, sane, mundane, unromantic, unidealistic.

downtrodden adjective oppressed, burdened, weighed down, overwhelmed, tyrannized, ground down, helpless, powerless, prostrate, poor, miserable, wretched, distressed.

doze verb nap, take a nap, catnap, slumber, take a siesta; *inf.* nod off, drift off, snooze, have a snooze, catch forty winks, get some shut-eye, catch/grab some Z's.

drab adjective **1** *drab clothes/surroundings* dull, dull-colored, colorless, mousy, gray, grayish, dingy, dreary, dismal, cheerless, gloomy, somber, depressing. **2** *a drab talk* uninteresting, boring, tedious, dry, dreary, lifeless, lackluster, uninspired.

draft verb **1** *draft a proposal* outline, plan, draw (up), frame, sketch (out), design, delineate. **2** *drafted by/into the army* recruit, conscript, call up, induct.

drag verb **1** *drag the body from the sea* haul, pull, draw, tug, yank, trail, tow, lug. **2** *time dragged* go/move slowly, creep/limp along, crawl, go at a snail's pace. **3** *the movie dragged* go on too long, go on and on, become tedious. **drag out** *drag out the lecture* protract, prolong, draw out, spin out, stretch out, lengthen, extend.

drain verb **1** *drain the water from the tank* draw off, extract, withdraw, remove, pump off, milk, bleed, tap, filter. **2** *drain the tank* empty, void, evacuate. **3** *the liquid drained (away)* flow out, ooze, trickle, seep out, leak, discharge, exude, effuse. **4** *legal costs draining resources* use up, exhaust, deplete, consume, expend, empty, sap, strain, tax, bleed.

drain noun **1** *a sewage drain* channel, conduit, culvert, duct, gutter, sewer, trench, ditch, dike, pipe, outlet. **2** *a drain on resources* exhaustion, depletion, consumption, expenditure, outflow, sapping, strain, tax.

drama noun **1** *studying drama* dramatic art, stagecraft, theater, acting, dramatics. **2** *a Chekhov drama* play, show; stage play, screenplay, radio play, television play, stage show, theatrical work, theatrical piece. **3** *the drama at the police station* exciting/emotional scene, thrilling/tense spectacle, excitement, crisis; dramatics, theatrics, histrionics.

dramatic adjective **1** *dramatic art* theatrical, stage, thespian. **2** *dramatic scenes in court* exciting, sensational, spectacular, startling, unexpected, thrilling, tense, suspenseful, electrifying, stirring, affecting. **3** *a dramatic view/description* striking, impressive, vivid, spectacular, breathtaking, moving, affecting, emotive, graphic, effective, powerful. **4** *a dramatic gesture* theatrical, artificial, exaggerated, overdone, stagy, histrionic.

dramatist noun playwright, scriptwriter, screenwriter, tragedy writer, comedy writer, dramaturgist, dramaturge.

drape verb **1** *drape the walls in tapestry* cover, envelope, blanket, overlay, cloak, veil, shroud, decorate, adorn, array, deck, festoon. **2** *drape a shawl around her* hang, arrange, let fall in folds. **3** *drape an arm on the chair* hang, let fall, place loosely, lean, dangle, droop.

drastic adjective extreme, severe, desperate, dire, radical, harsh, sharp, forceful, rigorous, draconian.

draw verb **1** *draw a chair up | draw the table away* pull, haul, tow, trail, tug, yank. **2** *draw alongside | drew to a close* move, go, come, proceed, approach. **3** *draw a sword/gun* pull out, take out, bring out, extract, withdraw, produce, unsheathe. **4** *draw the curtains* shut, close, pull together. **5** *draw attention* attract, allure, lure, entice, invite, engage, interest, win, catch the eye of, capture, captivate, fascinate, tempt, seduce. **6** *draw a breath* breathe in, inhale, suck in, inspire, respire. **7** *draw a salary* take, take in, receive, be in receipt of, get, procure, obtain, earn. **8** *draw a conclusion* deduce, infer, conclude, derive, gather, glean. **9** *draw liquid* drain, siphon off, pump off, tap, milk, bleed, filtrate. **10** *draw lots/straws* choose, pick, select, opt for, make a choice of, decide on, single out. **11** *draw a house* sketch, portray, depict, delineate, represent, trace, map out, mark out, chart, paint, design. **draw on** *draw on experience* make use of, use, have recourse to, exploit, employ, rely on. **draw out 1** *draw out the talk* prolong, protract. *See* DRAG. **2** *draw the child out* induce to talk, persuade to speak, put at ease. **draw up** *draw up a document* compose, formulate, frame, write out, put in writing, put down on paper, draft, prepare.

draw noun **1** *the draw of the circus* attraction, lure, allure, pull, enticement, magnetism. **2** *the match ended in a draw* tie, dead heat, stalemate.

drawback noun disadvantage, snag, catch, problem, difficulty, trouble, flaw, stumbling block, hitch, handicap, hindrance, obstacle, impediment, hurdle, obstruction, barrier, curb, check, deterrent, damper,

inconvenience, nuisance, detriment, fault, weak spot, weakness, imperfection, defect; *inf.* fly in the ointment.

drawing noun sketch, picture, illustration, representation, portrayal, delineation, depiction, composition, study, diagram, outline.

drawn adjective *pale and drawn* pinched, haggard, hollow-cheeked, strained, stressed, fatigued, tired, worn, drained, wan, sapped.

dread verb fear, be afraid of, be terrified by, tremble/shudder about, cringe/shrink from, quail/cower/flinch from; worry about, be anxious about, have forebodings about.

dread noun fear, fright, alarm, terror, apprehension, trepidation, horror, anxiety, concern, foreboding, dismay, perturbation, trembling, shuddering, flinching; *inf.* blue funk, heebie-jeebies.

dreadful adjective **1** *a dreadful sight/accident* terrible, frightful, horrible, grim, awful, dire, frightening, terrifying, alarming, distressing, shocking, appalling, harrowing, ghastly, fearful, hideous, horrendous, gruesome, tragic, calamitous, grievous. **2** *dreadful weather* nasty, unpleasant, disagreeable, frightful, shocking, very bad, distasteful, repugnant, odious. **3** *a dreadful waste of time* shocking, outrageous, inordinate, great, tremendous.

dream noun **1** *saw his mother in a dream* nightmare; vision, fantasy, hallucination. **2** *his dream to become rich* ambition, aspiration, goal, design, plan, aim, hope, yearning, desire, wish, notion, daydream, fantasy. **3** *the car was a dream* beauty, vision, delight, pleasure to behold, joy, marvel. **4** *go around in a dream* daydream, reverie, trance, daze, fog, stupor.

dream verb **1** *he thought he saw a ghost but he was dreaming* hallucinate, have a vision, imagine things, fantasize. **2** *she was dreaming instead of working* daydream, be in a trance/reverie, be lost in thought, muse, be preoccupied. **3** *never dream that they would go* think, consider, visualize, conceive, suppose. **dream up** *dream up new schemes* conjure up, think up, invent, concoct, devise, create, hatch, fabricate; *inf.* cook up.

dreamer noun daydreamer, visionary, fantasist, fantasizer, romantic, romancer, idealist, theorizer, Utopian, Don Quixote.

dreamland noun land of make-believe, never-never land, fairyland, fantasy world.

dreary adjective **1** *a dreary day* gloomy, dismal, bleak, somber, dull, dark, overcast, depressing. **2** *lead a dreary life* dull, drab, uninteresting, flat, dry, colorless, lifeless, tedious, wearisome, boring, humdrum, routine, monotonous, uneventful, run-of-the-mill, prosaic, commonplace, unvaried, repetitive. **3** *in a dreary frame of mind* gloomy, glum, sad, miserable, wretched, downcast, dejected, depressed, despondent, doleful, mournful, melancholic.

dregs plural noun **1** *the dregs of the wine* sediment, deposit, residue, precipitate, sublimate, scum, debris, dross, detritus, refuse, draff; lees, grounds. **2** *the dregs of society* scum, riff-raff, rabble, refuse; down-and-outs, good-for-nothings, outcasts, deadbeats, tramps, vagrants.

drench verb soak, saturate, permeate, drown, inundate, flood, steep, douse, souse, wet, slosh.

dress noun **1** *wearing a black dress* gown, garment, robe. **2** *with her dress in disarray* clothes, garments; clothing, attire, apparel, costume, outfit, ensemble, garb; *inf.* gear, get-up, togs, duds. **3** *birds/trees in their winter dress* covering, outer covering, plumage, feathers, pelt.

dress verb **1** *she was dressed in black* clothe, attire, garb, fit out, turn out, array, apparel, robe. **2** *dress poultry* prepare, get ready, clean; stuff. **3** *dress a wound* cover, bandage, bind up, put a plaster on. **dress down** reprimand, scold, upbraid, rebuke, reprove, berate, castigate, rake over the coals; *inf.* tell off. **dress up 1** *dress up for the occasion* dress formally/smartly, wear evening dress; *inf.* doll oneself up, dress to the nines, put on one's glad rags. **2** *dress the room up* decorate, adorn, ornament, trim, embellish, beautify, prettify.

dressing noun **1** *a dressing for the salad* relish, sauce, condiment. **2** *a dressing on the wound* covering, bandage, gauze.

drift verb **1** *boats/leaves drifting along* be carried away/along, be borne, be wafted, float, go with the current, coast. **2** *people drifting about* wander, roam, rove, meander, stray. **3** *snow drifting* pile up, bank up, accumulate, gather, amass.

drift noun **1** *a drift to the right* movement, deviation, digression, variation. **2** *the drift of his argument* gist, essence, meaning, substance, core, significance, import, purport, tenor, vein, direction, course, tendency, trend.

drill noun **1** *military drill* training, instruction, coaching, teaching, grounding, indoctrination. **2** *early morning drill* exercises, workout. **3** *not know the drill* procedure, routine, practice.

drink verb **1** *drink the water* swallow, gulp down, drain, quaff, imbibe, partake of, swill, guzzle, sip; *inf.* swig. **2** *her husband drinks* tipple, indulge; *inf.* hit the bottle, bend one's elbow, booze. **drink in** be absorbed/rapt/lost in, be fascinated by. **drink to** toast, propose a toast to, salute.

drink noun **1** *food and drink* beverage, drinkable/potable liquid, liquid refreshment; thirst-quencher. **2** *no drink at the dance* alcohol, liquor, spirits; *inf.* booze, hard stuff, hooch. **3** *take a drink from the cup* swallow, gulp, sip, swill; *inf.* swig, slug.

drinker noun social drinker, heavy/hard drinker, serious drinker, alcoholic, problem drinker, alcohol abuser, drunk, drunkard, dipsomaniac, tippler, toper, sot, inebriate, imbiber; *inf.* boozer, soak, lush, wino, alky, elbow-bender.

drip verb drop, dribble, trickle, splash, sprinkle, plop, leak, ooze, exude, filter, percolate.

drive verb **1** *drive a car* operate, steer, handle, guide, direct, manage. **2** *he drove us here* chauffeur, run, give one a lift. **3** *drive cattle to the barn* urge, press, push, impel, propel, herd, round up. **4** *driven to steal/despair* force, compel, constrain, impel, oblige, coerce, make, pressure, goad, spur, prod. **5** *drove himself too hard* work, overwork, tax, overtax, overburden. **6** *drive the stake into the ground* hammer, ram, bang, sink, plunge, thrust, stab. **drive at** *what are you driving at?* mean, suggest, imply, hint at, refer to, allude to, intimate; *inf.* get at.

drive noun **1** *go for a drive* run, trip, jaunt, outing, journey, excursion, tour, turn; *inf.* spin, joyride. **2** *the tree-lined drive* driveway, road, roadway, avenue. **3** *a sales drive* effort, push, campaign, publicity campaign, crusade, surge. **4** *a young man with drive* energy, vigor, verve, ambition, push, enterprise, motivation, initiative, action, aggressiveness; *inf.* get-up-and-go, zip.

drivel noun **1** *speak drivel* nonsense, twaddle, gibberish, balderdash, rubbish, mumbo jumbo; *inf.* rot, poppycock, garbage, tripe, bunk, hogwash, crap. **2** *wipe away the drivel* saliva, drool, drooling, dribble, slaver, slobber.

droll adjective amusing, comical, waggish, witty, whimsical.

drone[1] noun *the drone of aircraft* hum, buzz, whirr, whirring, purr.

drone[2] noun *the workers and the drones in the firm* idler, loafer, layabout, lounger, do-nothing, sluggard, parasite, leech; *inf.* lazybones, scrounger, sponger.

droop verb **1** *flowers drooping* hang, hang down, bend, bow, stoop, sag, sink, slump, fall down, drop. **2** *drooping after the news|spirits drooping* flag, fade, languish, falter, weaken, wilt, shrivel, wither.

drop noun **1** *a drop of water* droplet, globule, bead, bubble, blob, spheroid, oval. **2** *add just a drop* little, bit, dash, spot, dribble, splash, sprinkle, trickle, taste, trace, pinch, dab, speck, particle, modicum; *inf.* smidgen, smidge, tad. **3** *a drop in prices* decline, decrease, reduction, cut, cutback, lowering, falling-off, downturn, depreciation, devaluation, slump. **4** *the path ended in a sudden drop* descent, incline, declivity, slope, plunge; abyss, chasm, precipice, cliff.

drop verb **1** *water dropping from the trees* fall, drip, dribble, trickle, plop, leak. **2** *the plane dropped out of the sky* drop down, descend, plunge, plummet, dive, tumble. **3** *she dropped from exhaustion* fall/sink down, collapse, faint, swoon, drop/fall dead. **4** *prices dropped* fall, decrease, lessen, diminish, depreciate, go into decline, dwindle, sink, slacken off, plunge, plummet. **5** *drop singing lessons* give up, discontinue, end, stop, cease, terminate, finish with, withdraw/retire from, quit, abandon, forgo, relinquish, dispense with. **6** *drop his girlfriend* desert, abandon, forsake, leave, throw over, jilt, discard, reject, repudiate, renounce, disown; *inf.* ditch, chuck, run out on, leave flat. **7** *drop half the workforce* dismiss, discharge, let go; *inf.* sack, fire, boot out. **8** *drops the second syllable in "mathematics"* omit, leave out, eliminate, elide, contract, slur. **drop off 1** *drop the goods/passengers off* deliver, deposit, set down, unload, leave. **2** *people dropping off* fall asleep, doze, doze off, have a nap, catnap, drowse; *inf.* nod off, snooze, take forty winks, get some shut-eye.

drove noun **1** *a drove of cattle/sheep* herd, flock, pack. **2** *droves of people going shopping* crowd, horde, swarm, multitude, mob, throng, host, collection, gathering, assembly, company, herd.

drown verb **1** *the cornfields were drowned when the dam burst* flood, submerge, immerse, inundate, deluge, swamp, engulf, drench. **2** *outside noise drowning her speech* drown out, muffle, deaden, stifle, overpower, overwhelm, overcome, engulf, swallow up. **3** *drowning his grief in work* suppress, quash, quench, extinguish, obliterate, wipe out, get rid of.

drowsy adjective **1** *feeling drowsy* sleepy, half asleep, tired, weary, heavy-eyed, yawning, lethargic, sluggish, somnolent, dazed, drugged; *inf.* dopey. **2** *drowsy weather* sleepy, sleep-inducing, soporific, somniferous, lulling, soothing, dreamy.

drubbing noun beating, thrashing, walloping, thumping, battering, trouncing, whipping, flogging, pounding, pummeling, bludgeoning; *inf.* hammering, licking, clobbering, working-over.

drudgery noun menial/hard work, toiling, toil, labor, hard labor, chores; *inf.* grind.

drug noun **1** *a new cancer drug* medicine, medication, medicament, remedy, cure,

cure-all, panacea, physic. **2** *addicted to drugs* narcotic, opiate; *inf.* dope.

drug verb anesthetize, knock out, make/render unconscious, make/render insensible, stupefy, befuddle; *inf.* dope (up).

drugged adjective anesthetized, knocked out, comatose, stupefied, insensible, befuddled; *inf.* doped, stoned, dopey, on a trip, spaced out, zonked, high, high as a kite, turned on, flying, charged up.

drum verb **1** *drum one's fingers* tap, beat, rap, knock, strike. **2** *drum information into the students* drive home, instill, hammer, inculcate. **drum out** expel from, dismiss/discharge from, throw out, oust from. **drum up** obtain, get, attract, canvass, solicit, petition, bid for.

drunk adjective drunken, blind drunk, dead drunk, intoxicated, inebriated, inebriate, under the influence, tipsy, soused; *inf.* tight, tiddly, woozy, pie-eyed, three sheets to the wind, under the table, out of it, legless, plastered, smashed, sloshed, stoned, well-oiled, blotto, blitzed, lit up, stewed, pickled, tanked up, bombed.

drunk noun drunkard, inebriate, heavy/hard drinker, sot, toper, tippler, alcoholic, dipsomaniac, serious/problem drinker; *inf.* boozer, lush, alky, wino, elbow-bender.

dry adjective **1** *dry ground/regions* arid, parched, scorched, waterless, unwatered, moistureless, rainless, torrid, thirsty, droughty, barren, unproductive, sterile. **2** *dry leaves* withered, shriveled, wilted, dehydrated, desiccated, wizened, sapless, juiceless. **3** *a dry talk* dull, uninteresting, boring, tedious, tiresome, wearisome, dreary, monotonous, flat, unimaginative, commonplace, prosaic, run-of-the-mill, humdrum, vapid. **4** *a dry wit* subtle, lowkey, deadpan, laconic, sly, sharp, ironic, droll, waggish. **5** *a dry response/greeting* unemotional, indifferent, cool, cold, aloof, remote, impersonal.

dry verb **1** *the sun drying the earth/leaves* dry out/up, parch, scorch, dehydrate, desiccate, dehumidify, sear, wither, shrivel, wilt, wizen, mummify. **2** *dry the wet patch* dry off, mop up, blot up, towel, drain. **dry up** *inspiration dried up* fail, become unproductive, grow barren/sterile, cease to yield.

dual adjective double, twofold, duplicate, duplex, binary, twin, matched, paired, coupled.

dub verb call, name, christen, designate, term, entitle, style, label, denominate, nominate, tag, nickname.

dubious adjective **1** *dubious about going* doubtful, uncertain, hesitant, undecided, wavering, vacillating; *inf.* iffy. **2** *the outcome is dubious* unsure, unsettled, undetermined, indefinite, unresolved, up in the air, open.

3 *a dubious reply* equivocal, ambiguous, indeterminate, indefinite, unclear, vague, imprecise, enigmatic, cryptic. **4** *a dubious character* questionable, suspicious, suspect; *inf.* shady, fishy.

duck verb **1** *duck behind the wall* bend, bow down, bob down, stoop, crouch, squat, hunch down, hunker down. **2** *duck one's head* bow, lower, drop. **3** *duck him in the pond* immerse, submerge, plunge, dip, souse, douse, dunk. **4** *duck the police/work* dodge, evade, sidestep, avoid, steer clear of, elude, escape, shirk, shun.

duct noun pipe, tube, conduit, channel, passage, canal, culvert.

dud noun failure, flop; *inf.* washout, lemon, loser.

dudgeon noun **in high dudgeon** angry, annoyed, furious, in a temper, indignant, enraged, fuming, vexed, offended.

due adjective **1** *money/thanks due (to) them* owing, owed, payable, outstanding. **2** *recognition due (to) a hero* deserved by, merited by, earned by, justified by, appropriate to, fit for, fitting to, suitable for, right for. **3** *treat with due respect* proper, right and proper, correct, rightful, fitting, appropriate, apt, adequate, sufficient, enough, ample, satisfactory, requisite, apposite. **4** *the essay is due tomorrow* scheduled, expected, required, awaited, anticipated.
due to *due to uncertainty* attributable to, ascribed to, ascribable to, caused by, assignable to, because of, owing to.

due noun *receive only his due* rights, just deserts, deserts; *inf.* comeuppance.

dull adjective **1** *dull of wit* dull-witted, slow, slow-witted, unintelligent, stupid, dense, doltish, stolid, vacuous; *inf.* dim, dim-witted, thick, dumb, birdbrained. **2** *a dull reaction* insensitive, unfeeling, unemotional, indifferent, unresponsive, apathetic. **3** *feeling dull in the winter* inactive, inert, slow, slow-moving, sleepy, drowsy, idle, sluggish, stagnant, lethargic, listless, languid, heavy, apathetic, torpid, phlegmatic, vegetative. **4** *a dull speech* uninteresting, boring, tedious, tiresome, wearisome, dry, monotonous, flat, bland, unimaginative, humdrum, uneventful, vapid. **5** *dull weather* overcast, cloudy, gloomy, dark, dim, dismal, dreary, bleak, somber, leaden, murky, sunless. **6** *dull colors* drab, dreary, somber, dark, subdued, muted, toned-down, lackluster, lusterless, colorless, faded, washed-out. **7** *a dull sound* muffled, muted, indistinct, feeble. **8** *a dull edge* blunt, blunted, unsharpened, dulled, edgeless.

dull verb **1** *dull the appetite* take the edge off, blunt, lessen, decrease, diminish, reduce, deaden, mute, tone down, allay, ease, soothe, assuage, alleviate, palliate.

2 *drugs dull the senses* numb, benumb, stupefy, drug, sedate, tranquilize. **3** *time dulling the colors* fade, bleach, wash out. **4** *the sky dulled by clouds* darken, dim, bedim, obscure. **5** *spirits dulled by the bad news* dispirit, dishearten, depress, deject, sadden, discourage, cast down, dampen, put a damper on, cast a pall over.

dumb adjective **1** *struck dumb at the sight* speechless, wordless, silent, mute, at a loss for words, voiceless, soundless, inarticulate, taciturn, uncommunicative, tongue-tied; *inf.* mum. **2** *dumb people and clever people* stupid, dull, dull-witted, slow, slow-witted, unintelligent, dense, foolish, doltish; *inf.* dim, dim-witted, thick.

dumbfound verb astound, astonish, amaze, startle, surprise, stun, take aback, stagger, overwhelm, confound, shock, confuse, bewilder, baffle, nonplus, perplex, disconcert; *inf.* flabbergast, throw, shake, throw for a loop.

dump verb **1** *dump the goods on the floor* drop, let fall, throw down, fling down. **2** *dump the unwanted goods* dispose of, get rid of, throw away/out, scrap, jettison. **3** *the tanker dumped its load* discharge, empty out, pour out, tip out, unload, jettison. **4** *dump his wife* abandon, desert, leave, leave in the lurch, forsake, walk out on.

dump noun **1** *take the debris to the dump* refuse/rubbish dump, rubbish heap, junkyard, scrapyard; transfer station. **2** *what a dump!* hovel, shack, slum, shanty, pigsty; *inf.* hole, joint.

dunce noun dolt, blockhead, dunderhead, thickhead, numskull, nincompoop, ninny, simpleton, halfwit, idiot, moron, ass, ignoramus, dullard; *inf.* dimwit, dummy.

dungeon noun cell, lockup, black hole, oubliette; keep.

duplicate noun **1** *a duplicate of the chair* copy, replica, facsimile, reproduction, twin, double, clone, match, mate, fellow, counterpart, look-alike, spitting image; *inf.* ringer, dead ringer. **2** *make a duplicate of the document* copy, carbon copy, carbon, photocopy, facsimile, fax; Photostat *(trademark)*, Xerox *(trademark)*.

duplicate verb **1** *duplicate the documents* copy, make a carbon/facsimile of, photocopy, fax, reproduce, make a replica of, replicate, clone; Photostat *(trademark)*, Xerox *(trademark)*. **2** *duplicate the task* repeat, do over again, perform again, replicate.

duplicity noun deceitfulness, doubledealing, trickery, guile, chicanery, artifice, dishonesty, knavery.

durable adjective **1** *durable affection* lasting, enduring, abiding, continuing, constant, stable, fast, firm, fixed, permanent, unfading, changeless, unchanging, invariable, dependable, reliable. **2** *durable clothing/goods* long-lasting, hard-wearing, strong, sturdy, sound, tough, resistant, substantial, imperishable.

duress noun force, compulsion, coercion, pressure, pressurization, constraint, arm-twisting, enforcement, exaction.

dutiful adjective respectful, filial, deferential, obedient, compliant, pliant, docile, submissive.

duty noun **1** *a sense of duty to one's country/parents* responsibility, obligation, allegiance, loyalty, faithfulness, fidelity, respect, deference, reverence, homage. **2** *share the duties* task, job, chore, assignment, commission, mission, function, office, charge, part, role, requirement, work, burden. **3** *pay duty* tax, levy, tariff, excise, toll, fee, impost; customs, dues.

dwarf verb **1** *dwarfed by the effects of a drug* stunt, arrest/check growth, atrophy. **2** *a novelist who dwarfs his contemporaries* tower above/over, overshadow, stand head and shoulders over, dominate, diminish, minimize.

dwell verb reside, live, be domiciled, lodge, stay, abide. **dwell on/upon** spend time on, linger over, harp on, discuss at length, expatiate on, elaborate on, expound on, be preoccupied with/by, be obsessed with/by.

dwelling noun residence, home, house, abode, domicile, establishment.

dwindle verb **1** *savings/hope dwindling* decrease, lessen, diminish, shrink, contract, fade, wane. **2** *the Roman empire dwindling* decline, fail, sink, ebb, degenerate, deteriorate, decay, wither, rot, disappear, vanish, die out; *inf.* peter out.

dyed-in-the-wool adjective entrenched, inveterate, established, deep-rooted, confirmed, complete, absolute, through and through, utter, thoroughgoing.

dying adjective **1** *a dying woman* terminally ill, breathing one's last, on one's deathbed, passing away, sinking fast, expiring, moribund, *in extremis*; *inf.* in the jaws of death, having one foot in the grave, on one's/its last legs, at death's door. **2** *dying customs* passing, fading, vanishing, failing, ebbing, waning. **3** *dying words* final, last.

dynamic adjective energetic, active, lively, alive, spirited, vital, vigorous, strong, forceful, powerful, potent, effective, effectual, high-powered, magnetic, aggressive, go-ahead, driving, electric; *inf.* zippy, peppy.

dynasty noun line, succession, house, regime, rule, reign, dominion, empire; sovereignty, ascendancy, government, authority, administration, jurisdiction.

Ee

eager adjective **1** *eager students* keen, enthusiastic, impatient, avid, fervent, earnest, diligent, zealous, passionate, wholehearted, ambitious, enterprising; *inf.* bright-eyed and bushy-tailed. **2** *eager for news* agog, anxious, intent, longing, yearning, itching, wishing, desirous, hopeful, thirsty, hungry, greedy; *inf.* hot.

ear noun *have the ear of the president* attention, attentiveness, notice, heed, regard, consideration.

early adjective **1** *an early crop/birth* advanced, premature, untimely. **2** *an early reply* prompt, quick, speedy, rapid, fast, expeditious, timely. **3** *early man* primitive, primeval, primordial, prehistoric.

earmark verb *earmark the money for a vacation* set/lay aside, keep back, allocate, reserve, designate, label, tag.

earn verb **1** *earn a good salary* make, get, receive, obtain, draw, clear, collect. **2**

earn their admiration gain, win, rate, merit, achieve, secure, deserve.

earnest adjective **1** *an earnest young man* serious, solemn, grave, intense, staid, studious, thoughtful, dedicated, assiduous. **2** *her earnest request* sincere, fervent, ardent, passionate, heartfelt, wholehearted, zealous.

earnest noun **in earnest 1** *in earnest about the punishment* serious, not joking, sincere. **2** *working in earnest* zealously, ardently, fervently, fervidly, passionately, wholeheartedly, resolutely.

earnings plural noun income, salary, wage, pay, take-home pay, remuneration, revenue, yield, profit, gain, return; wages.

earth noun **1** *earth, moon, and stars* globe, world, planet, sphere, orb. **2** *dig up the earth* soil, loam, clay, dirt, sod, turf, ground. **3** *between the earth and the sky* ground, dry ground, land.

earthly adjective *earthly joys* worldly, temporal, secular, mortal, human, material, materialistic, corporeal.

earthy adjective **1** *earthy people* down-to-earth, unsophisticated, simple, plain, unpretentious, rough, robust. **2** *an earthy sense of humor* bawdy, crude, coarse, ribald.

ease noun **1** *succeed with ease* facility, simplicity, effortlessness, deftness, adroitness, proficiency, mastery. **2** *his ease of manner* naturalness, informality, amiability, affability, composure, aplomb, nonchalance, insouciance, urbanity, suaveness. **3** *a life of ease* comfort, affluence, wealth, prosperity, luxury, opulence; bed of roses.

ease verb **1** *ease the pain* mitigate, lessen, reduce, lighten, moderate, abate, ameliorate, relieve, assuage, allay. **2** *ease her mind* comfort, console, soothe, calm, pacify. **3** *ease his promotion* facilitate, expedite, assist, help, aid, advance, further. **4** *ease it into position* guide, maneuver, steer, slide, slip.

easy adjective **1** *an easy task* simple, effortless, uncomplicated, straightforward, undemanding, painless, facile. **2** *easy prey* compliant, susceptible, docile, gullible, tractable, trusting, acquiescent. **3** *an easy manner* natural, casual, informal, easygoing, amiable, affable, composed, carefree, nonchalant; *inf.* laid-back. **4** *an easy pace* even, steady, regular, comfortable, moderate, unhurried.

easygoing adjective happy-go-lucky, relaxed, carefree, nonchalant, amiable; *inf.* laid-back.

eat verb **1** *eat chocolate* consume, devour, munch, gulp down, bolt, wolf; dine; *inf.* snack, graze. **2** *eating the rock away* erode, corrode, wear, dissolve, rot, decay, destroy.

ebb verb **1** *the tide ebbed* go out, retreat, fall back, recede, abate, subside. **2** *its popularity ebbed* decline, fade away, die out, lessen, wane, decrease, diminish, flag, dwindle, deteriorate, decay.

ebullient adjective exuberant, buoyant, exhilarated, elated, euphoric, animated, vivacious.

eccentric adjective odd, queer, strange, peculiar, weird, anomalous, unconventional, singular, idiosyncratic, capricious, quirky.

echo verb **1** *echo around the room* reverberate, resound, reflect, ring. **2** *echo a statement* copy, imitate, reproduce, repeat, reiterate, parrot.

economical adjective **1** *economical with resources* thrifty, sparing, careful, prudent, frugal, scrimping, stingy, parsimonious. **2** *an economical vacation* cheap, inexpensive, reasonable, low-cost, low-budget, budget.

economize verb cut back, retrench, budget, scrimp, save; *inf.* cut corners, tighten one's belt, pinch pennies.

ecstasy noun bliss, rapture, elation, euphoria, joy.

ecstatic adjective blissful, joyful, joyous, jubilant, elated, on cloud nine, in seventh heaven.

edge noun **1** *the edge of the lake* border, side, boundary, rim, margin, fringe, verge, brink, lip, perimeter, periphery. **2** *a voice with an edge* sting, bite; sharpness, severity, pointedness, acidity, acrimony. **3** *have the edge on her* advantage, upper hand, dominance, superiority. **on edge** nervous, tense.

edge verb **1** *edge with lace* trim, hem, border, fringe. **2** *edge one's way through the crowd* inch, elbow, worm, work, sidle; creep, steal.

edgy adjective nervous, tense, ill at ease, anxious, on tenterhooks, restive, uneasy, irritable, touchy; *inf.* uptight, wired.

edict noun decree, order, command, ruling, statute, injunction, mandate, manifesto, proclamation, dictate, dictum, fiat.

edifice noun building, structure, construction.

educate verb instruct, teach, school, tutor, train, inform, enlighten.

educated adjective literate, schooled, well-read, informed, knowledgeable, enlightened, lettered, erudite, cultivated, cultured, refined; *inf.* highbrow.

education noun schooling, teaching, instruction, tuition, tutelage, enlightenment; edification, cultivation, development.

eerie adjective uncanny, mysterious, strange, unnatural, frightening, spine-chilling, blood-curdling; *inf.* spooky, scary, creepy.

effect noun **1** *the effect of the changes* result, outcome, consequence, conclusion; results, fruits. **2** *the law goes into effect tomorrow* force, implementation, execution, action. **3** *speak to great effect* effectiveness, success, influence, efficacy, weight, power, cogency. **4** *or words to that effect* sense, meaning, drift, significance, essence. **in effect** effectively, actually, really, in reality, in essence.

effect verb *effect a plan* carry out, cause, make, produce, create, achieve, accomplish, complete, fulfill, implement, execute.

effective adjective **1** *effective administration* successful, productive, competent, capable, able, efficient, adequate. **2** *effective lighting* striking, impressive, exciting, attractive. **3** *effective arguments* powerful, forceful, cogent, compelling, persuasive, convincing, moving. **4** *rules become effective tomorrow* valid, operative, active.

effects plural noun belongings, (personal) possessions, goods, accoutrements, paraphernalia; property, gear, equipment; *inf.* things, stuff.

efficient adjective **1** *an efficient person* capable, able, competent, effective, productive, adept, organized, businesslike. **2** *an efficient office* organized, well-run, streamlined.

effort noun **1** *put effort into it* exertion, force, energy, work, muscle, labor, toil, struggle, strain; *lit.* travail; *inf.* elbow grease. **2** *admire his artistic efforts* achievement, accomplishment, attainment, creation, production, opus, feat.

effortless adjective easy, simple, uncomplicated, undemanding, painless, facile.

egg verb **egg on** encourage, urge, push, drive, goad, prod, prompt.

egghead noun intellectual, academic, scholar, brain, genius, bookworm; *inf.* Einstein.

egoism noun self-interest, self-centeredness, selfishness, egocentricity, egomania, narcissism, vanity, conceit, pride, self-importance.

egotistic adjective egocentric, narcissistic, conceited, vain, proud, arrogant, boastful.

eject verb **1** *eject sewage* emit, discharge, excrete, release, spew out, disgorge. **2** *ejected from the vehicle* propel, thrust out, throw out. **3** *eject him from the stadium* throw out, remove, evict, expel, oust, banish, deport; *inf.* kick out, bounce.

elaborate adjective complicated, detailed, complex, involved, intricate, painstaking; ornate, fancy, showy, ostentatious, extravagant.

elaborate verb expand on, amplify, flesh out; develop, work out, refine, polish, embellish, enhance; ornament, embroider.

elastic adjective stretchy, springy, flexible, pliant, supple, rubbery, resilient.

elated adjective overjoyed, euphoric. *See* ECSTATIC.

elation noun ecstasy, bliss, euphoria, rapture, joy, jubilation, exhilaration, delight.

elderly adjective aged, old, gray-haired, ancient; *inf.* over the hill.

elderly plural noun **the elderly** senior citizens, seniors.

elect verb vote for, choose, pick, select, designate, determine.

electric adjective **1** *electric power* galvanic, voltaic. **2** *an electric moment* tense, charged, exciting, thrilling.

elegance noun style, grace, tastefulness, polish, refinement, finesse, propriety, haute couture.

elegant adjective stylish, graceful, tasteful, fashionable, beautiful, lovely, exquisite, polished, cultivated, refined, dignified, luxurious, sumptuous, opulent.

element noun **1** *an element of truth* basis, ingredient, factor, feature, component, part, segment, member. **2** *in his natural element* environment, habitat, medium, milieu, field, domain.

elementary adjective easy, simple, straightforward, facile, simplistic; basic, fundamental, rudimentary, primary, preparatory, introductory.

elevate verb **1** *elevate the load* raise, lift, hoist. **2** *elevate to management* promote, upgrade, advance; *inf.* kick upstairs. **3** *elevate her spirits* cheer, gladden, brighten, perk up, lighten.

elf noun fairy, pixie, sprite, dwarf, gnome, goblin, imp, leprechaun, troll.

elfin adjective pixielike, little, diminutive, wee, Lilliputian; mischievous, impish, puckish.

elicit verb obtain, draw out, extract, exact, wrest, evoke, derive.

elite noun pick, cream, elect; aristocracy, nobility, gentry, upper crust.

elongate verb lengthen, extend, prolong, protract.

eloquent adjective expressive, well-spoken, articulate, fluent, pithy, persuasive.

elude verb *the fox eluded the hunter* avoid, dodge, evade, escape, lose, duck; *inf.* ditch.

elusive adjective **1** *an elusive person* evasive, slippery, shifty, cagey. **2** *an elusive perfume* indefinable, subtle, intangible, impalpable, fleeting. **3** *an elusive answer* ambiguous, baffling, puzzling, equivocal.

emaciated adjective wasted, gaunt, skeletal, cadaverous, shriveled, shrunken, withered, pinched, wizened.

emanate verb arise, originate, stem, derive, emerge; discharge, emit, exhale, radiate.

emancipate verb free, set free, liberate, release, let loose, deliver; unchain, unfetter, untie.

embargo noun ban, prohibition, interdiction, proscription; restriction, restraint, check, barrier, impediment, obstruction.

embark verb **embark on** *embark on an adventure* begin, start, commence, undertake, initiate.

embarrass verb disconcert, discomfit, fluster, agitate, distress, shame, humiliate.

embassy noun **1** *the British embassy* consulate, legation, ministry. **2** *sent our embassy to China* envoy, representative, legate; delegation.

embellish verb *embellish the ceiling/truth* decorate, adorn, ornament, enhance, embroider, enrich, deck, festoon; elaborate, exaggerate, fabricate.

embezzle verb steal, rob, thieve, pilfer, appropriate, misappropriate, purloin, filch; *inf.* rip off. age

emblem noun crest, badge, symbol, token, mark, sign; insignia.

embody verb incorporate, comprise, include, contain, constitute, encompass, assimilate, integrate, concentrate; personify, represent, symbolize, exemplify.

embrace verb **1** *embrace his wife* hold, hug, cuddle, clasp, squeeze, clutch. **2** *embrace the new philosophy* welcome, accept, take up, adopt; *fml.* espouse.

embrace noun hug, cuddle, squeeze, clasp, hold, clutch.

embroider verb **1** *embroider a tablecloth* sew, decorate. **2** *embroider the truth* embellish, elaborate, exaggerate, invent, fabricate.

emend verb edit, correct, revise, alter, rewrite, improve, polish, refine.

emerge verb come out, appear, surface, materialize, arise, proceed, issue, emanate; become known.

emergency noun crisis, danger, accident, difficulty, plight, predicament.

emigration noun migration, departure, relocation, expatriation, exodus, defection.

eminence noun importance, greatness, prestige, reputation, fame, distinction, renown, preeminence, celebrity, rank.

eminent adjective important, great, distinguished, celebrated, famous, renowned, noted, prominent, esteemed, outstanding, high-ranking, revered, august.

emission noun *the emission of fumes* discharge, issue, excretion, secretion, ejection, emanation, radiation, exhalation, effusion.

emit verb *emit fumes/light* discharge, issue, ooze, leak, excrete, secrete, eject, emanate, radiate, exude.

emotion noun feeling, sentiment, passion, sensation; warmth, ardor, fervor, vehemence.

emotional adjective **1** *emotional person* feeling, passionate, hot-blooded, demonstrative, sentimental, ardent, fervent, sensitive. **2** *an emotional farewell* moving, touching, poignant, heart-rending, soul-stirring, impassioned.

emphasis noun stress, accent, accentuation, weight; importance, attention, priority, significance, intensity, import.

emphasize verb stress, accentuate, underline, call attention to, highlight, point up, spotlight, play up, underscore.

emphatic adjective marked, pronounced, decided, positive, definite, unmistakable, strong, striking, resounding, certain, determined, forceful, earnest, vigorous, unequivocal.

empire noun kingdom, realm, domain, territory, jurisdiction, province, commonwealth; sovereignty, dominion.

employ verb **1** *employ three people* hire, engage, take on, enroll, commission, enlist, retain. **2** *employ cunning* use, apply, exercise, utilize.

employee noun worker, wage earner, hand, hired hand, assistant, laborer, hireling.

employer noun boss, manager, owner, proprietor, contractor, director; firm, organization.

employment noun **1** *the employment of new staff* hiring, engagement, enrollment. **2** *employment as a teacher* job, work, business, line, occupation, profession, trade, vocation, craft, métier, pursuit.

empower verb authorize, license, certify, accredit, qualify, sanction; allow, enable, equip.

emptiness noun **1** *an emptiness in her life* vacuum, void, hollowness. **2** *the emptiness of the house* vacantness, desolation, bareness, barrenness, blankness, clearness. **3** *the emptiness of the threats* meaninglessness, futility, ineffectiveness, uselessness, worthlessness, fruitlessness. **4** *the emptiness of her existence* aimlessness, meaninglessness, worthlessness, barrenness, senselessness, banality, triviality.

empty adjective **1** *empty house* vacant, hollow, void, unoccupied, uninhabited, desolate, bare, blank, clear. **2** *empty threats* meaningless, futile, ineffective, ineffectual, worthless, idle. **3** *empty stare* blank, expressionless, vacant, vacuous, absent.

empty verb **1** *empty the room* vacate, clear, evacuate, unload. **2** *empty the liquid* drain, exhaust, use up, deplete.

enable verb authorize, entitle, qualify, license, sanction, accredit, validate, empower; allow, permit, equip, prepare.

enact verb *a bill enacted by Congress* legislate, rule, pass, approve, ratify, sanction; order, decree, pronounce.

enchant verb bewitch, fascinate, charm, captivate, entrance, enthrall, mesmerize, enrapture.

enchanting adjective bewitching, charming, delightful, captivating, irresistible, fascinating, engaging, entrancing, alluring.

enclose verb **1** *enclosing the garden* surround, circle, ring, confine, circumscribe. **2** *enclose a check* include, insert.

encounter verb meet, run into, run across, confront, accost; *inf.* bump into.

encounter noun meeting; fight, battle, clash, conflict, contest, collision, confrontation, engagement, skirmish, scuffle; *inf.* run-in, brush.

encourage verb **1** *encouraging the runners to press on* cheer, motivate, inspire, stir, incite, animate, hearten, invigorate; urge, prompt, exhort, spur, goad. **2** *exercise encourages good health* help, assist, aid, support, boost, promote, further, foster, advance.

encouragement noun stimulation, motivation, inspiration, incitement; persuasion, exhortation; help, assistance, support, promotion, advocacy, backing.

encumbrance noun **1** *the encumbrance of heavy luggage* hindrance, obstruction, impediment, inconvenience, handicap, constraint. **2** *debts are an encumbrance* burden, weight, load, responsibility, obligation, strain.

end noun **1** *the end of the table* edge, border, boundary, extremity, limit, margin. **2** *the end of the affair* finish, close, conclusion, termination, completion, resolution, finale, epilogue. **3** *the commercial end of the business* side, section, area, field, part, portion, segment. **4** *the end was that he got the promotion* result, consequence, outcome, upshot.

end verb **1** *the show ended | to end a relationship* finish, close, stop, cease, conclude, terminate, complete, dissolve, discontinue, break off. **2** *end his hopes* destroy, annihilate, extinguish.

endanger verb threaten, expose, risk, jeopardize, imperil, compromise.

endearing adjective charming, attractive, adorable, lovable, sweet, engaging, winning, winsome.

endeavor verb try, attempt, strive, venture, aspire, undertake, struggle, labor, essay.

endeavor noun *his best endeavor* try, attempt, trial, effort, venture, struggle, essay; *inf.* crack, shot.

ending noun end, finish, close, conclusion, cessation, termination, expiration, resolution, completion.

endless adjective **1** *endless patience* unending, unlimited, infinite, limitless, boundless, constant, unfading, everlasting, unceasing, untold. **2** *an endless loop* continuous, uninterrupted, unbroken, never-ending. **3** *endless traveling* nonstop, interminable, monotonous, incessant, unremitting, boring.

endorse verb **1** *endorse a check* countersign, sign, autograph, underwrite, validate. **2** *endorse the course of action* approve, support, back, favor, recommend, advocate, champion, authorize, ratify, sanction, warrant.

endow verb **1** *endow with talent* provide, give, present, gift, confer, bestow, supply, furnish. **2** *endow a foundation* bestow, will, finance, fund.

endowment noun **1** *offer an endowment to the school* gift, present, grant, donation, legacy; largesse, funding, revenue, income. **2** *natural endowments* ability, gift, talent, flair, aptitude, capacity, facility, faculty, characteristic, quality.

endurance noun **1** *endurance of his love* durability, stability, permanence, continuance, continuity. **2** *beyond endurance* toleration, sufferance, fortitude, forbearance, perseverance, patience. **3** *a test of endurance* stamina, staying power, fortitude, tenacity; *inf.* guts.

endure verb **1** *love endures* last, continue, persist, remain, stay, survive. **2** *endure the difficult situation* stand, bear, tolerate, suffer, abide; *inf.* stomach, swallow. **3** *endure pain* experience, undergo, bear, tolerate, suffer, brave, withstand, weather.

enduring adjective lasting, durable, permanent, steady, steadfast, eternal, perennial, unwavering, unfaltering.

enemy noun foe, opponent, rival, adversary, antagonist, opposition.

energetic adjective **1** *energetic exercises* active, lively, vigorous, strenuous, brisk, dynamic, spirited, animated, indefatigable, peppy. **2** *energetic approach* forceful, determined, emphatic, aggressive, high-powered.

energize verb activate, stimulate, arouse, rouse, motivate, stir, goad, prompt; enliven, animate, invigorate, electrify, vitalize.

energy noun vigor, strength, stamina, power, drive; enthusiasm, animation, life, liveliness, pep, vivacity, vitality, spirit, exuberance.

enervate verb weaken, exhaust, tire, fatigue, debilitate, sap, incapacitate.

enforce verb **1** *enforce the law* apply, carry out, administer, implement, impose, discharge. **2** *enforce silence* force, compel, require, necessitate, oblige, exact, coerce.

engage verb **1** *engage a housekeeper* employ, hire, take on, appoint, commission. **2** *engaged in a book* occupy, fill, hold; preoccupy, absorb, engross. **3** *engage to marry* contract, promise, agree, guarantee, undertake, pledge, vouch, vow, covenant. **4** *armies engaging at dawn* do battle, fight, wage war, attack, clash, skirmish. **engage in** participate, join, undertake, tackle.

engaged adjective **1** *the conference room is engaged* busy, occupied, unavailable, in use, reserved, booked; *inf.* tied up. **2** *engaged couples* betrothed, affianced, espoused.

engagement noun **1** *a previous engagement* appointment, date, commitment. **2** *an engagement at sea* fight, battle, clash, conflict, attack, assault, confrontation, encounter, offensive.

engaging adjective attractive, charming, appealing, pleasing, pleasant, agreeable, delightful, winning, captivating, winsome.

engineer verb cause, plan, plot, scheme, contrive, devise, manipulate, orchestrate, originate, manage, control, direct, conduct.

engrave verb carve, etch, inscribe, chisel, print; fix, set, imprint, stamp.

engrossed adjective preoccupied, absorbed, engaged, riveted, captivated, immersed, rapt.

engulf verb consume, overwhelm, flood, submerge, immerse, inundate.

enhance verb increase, heighten, strengthen, improve, augment, boost, intensify, magnify, amplify, complement; raise, lift, escalate, elevate.

enigma noun mystery, puzzle, riddle, conundrum, paradox, problem, quandary, dilemma, labyrinth, maze.

enigmatic adjective mysterious, puzzling, baffling, obscure, perplexing, mystifying, cryptic, unfathomable, Sphinxlike; ambiguous, equivocal, paradoxical.

enjoy verb like, love, delight in, appreciate, relish, savor; have, possess, own.

enjoyable adjective entertaining, amusing, nice, pleasant, lovely, fine, agreeable, pleasurable, delicious, delectable, satisfying, gratifying.

enjoyment noun amusement, entertainment, diversion, recreation, pleasure, delight, happiness, gladness, fun, gaiety, satisfaction, gratification, relish, gusto; benefit, advantage, blessing.

enlarge verb **1** *enlarge the living area* expand, extend, amplify, augment, supplement, magnify; widen, broaden, lengthen, elongate, deepen, thicken. **2** *his spleen is enlarged* distend, dilate, swell, inflate, bloat, bulge.

enlighten verb inform, instruct, teach, educate, illuminate, cultivate.

enlightened adjective informed, aware, educated, knowledgeable, learned, wise, literate, intellectual, illuminated, apprised; civilized, refined, cultured, cultivated, sophisticated, open-minded, broad-minded.

enlist verb **1** *enlist staff* recruit, hire, employ, register, take on, engage, muster. **2** *enlist in the army* join, join up, enroll, sign up for.

enliven verb excite, stimulate, rouse, refresh, exhilarate, invigorate, revitalize, vitalize, light a fire under; *inf.* perk up, spice up, jazz up.

enormity noun outrageousness, wickedness, evilness, vileness, monstrousness, hideousness, dreadfulness.

enormous adjective huge, immense, massive, vast, gigantic, colossal, astronomic, mammoth, mountainous, gargantuan, tremendous, titanic.

enough adjective sufficient, adequate, ample, abundant.

enough noun sufficiency, adequacy, abundance, plenty.

enrage verb anger, infuriate, madden, exasperate, provoke, incense, irk, agitate, inflame, incite.

enraged adjective angry, furious, irate, livid, fuming, incensed, provoked, agitated, inflamed.

enroll verb **1** *enroll three new students* register, sign on/up, enlist, recruit, enter, admit, accept. **2** *he enrolled for military service* sign on, volunteer, register, matriculate.

ensemble noun **1** *the parts formed a pleasing ensemble* whole, collection, set, accumulation, sum, entirety, assemblage, aggregate, composite. **2** *a green ensemble* outfit, costume, suit. **3** *a jazz ensemble* group, band, company, troupe, cast, chorus; trio, quartet, quintet.

ensue verb follow, result, occur, happen, transpire, proceed, succeed, issue, derive, stem.

ensure verb guarantee, secure, effect, warrant, certify, confirm; protect, guard, safeguard.

entail verb involve, require, necessitate, ·demand, impose; cause, produce, occasion.

entangle verb **1** *entangle the cords* tangle, twist, knot, intertwine, snarl. **2** *entangle in a net* catch, trap, snare, entrap.

entanglement noun **1** *the entanglement of his business affairs* complication, confusion, mix-up, mess. **2** *his entanglement with his secretary* affair, liaison, amour, intrigue.

enter verb **1** *a river entering the sea* pass into, move into, flow into, penetrate, pierce, puncture. **2** *enter the teaching profession* join, enroll in, enlist in, take up. **3** *enter the date of birth* record, register, note, catalog, document, list, log, file, index. **4** *enter a protest* put forward, offer, present, proffer, submit, register, tender. **5** *enter into negotiations* begin, start, commence, engage in, undertake.

enterprise noun **1** *a challenging enterprise* venture, undertaking, project, operation, endeavor, effort, task, plan, scheme, campaign. **2** *private enterprise* business, industry, firm, corporation, establishment.

enterprising adjective resourceful, entrepreneurial, imaginative, spirited, enthusiastic, eager, keen, zealous, ambitious, energetic, bold, adventurous, audacious.

entertain verb **1** *entertain the guests* amuse, divert, delight, please, charm, cheer, beguile, interest, engage, occupy; treat, welcome, fête. **2** *entertain the idea* consider, contemplate, weigh, ponder.

entertaining adjective amusing, diverting, delightful, pleasurable, engaging, interesting, funny, humorous.

entertainment noun amusement, fun, enjoyment, diversion, recreation, distraction; pastime, hobby.

enthrall verb captivate, enchant, entrance, fascinate, bewitch, rivet, intrigue.

enthusiasm noun eagerness, keenness, ardor, fervor, warmth, passion, zeal, zest, excitement, exuberance, wholeheartedness.

enthusiastic adjective eager, keen, ardent, fervent, warm, passionate, zealous, excited, exuberant, wholehearted.

entice verb lure, tempt, seduce, inveigle, coax, cajole, bait.

entire adjective **1** *one's entire life* whole, complete, total, full, continuous, unbroken. **2** *not an entire success* absolute, total, outright, unqualified. **3** *surprised to find an entire vase in the rubble* sound, intact, undamaged, unharmed, unbroken.

entitle verb *entitle you to claim the estate* qualify, authorize, sanction, allow, permit, enable, empower, warrant, accredit.

entity noun **1** *a living entity* body, being, person, creature, individual, organism, object, article, thing. **2** *the organization's very entity* being, existence, life, substance, essence.

entourage noun retinue, escort, attendant, company, cortege, train, suite, bodyguard; companions, followers; *inf.* groupies.

entrance noun **1** *the entrance to the building* approach, door, doorway, gate, driveway, foyer, lobby, portal, threshold. **2** *the entrance of the gladiators* entry, appearance, arrival, introduction. **3** *refused entrance to the club* entry, admission, admittance, access, entrée.

entreat verb beg, implore, beseech, petition, solicit, pray, exhort, supplicate.

entreaty noun appeal, plea, petition, solicitation, prayer, supplication, suit.

entrust verb commit, assign, consign, deliver; charge, invest, delegate, commend.

entry noun **1** *the main entry to the building* way in, entrance, access, approach, doorway, gate, gateway, driveway, foyer, lobby, portal, threshold. **2** *the entry of the soldiers* entrance, appearance, arrival, introduction. **3** *refuse entry to the protesters* entrance, admission, admittance, access. **4** *an entry in his diary* item, line item, statement, listing, record, note, jotting, memo, account. **5** *fifty entries in the competition* entrant, competitor, contestant, participant, player, candidate. **6** *you can submit four entries* submission, attempt, try, effort.

enumerate verb list, itemize, specify, spell out, name, cite, detail; count, calculate, total, compute, tally.

envelop verb *the fog enveloped him* cover, wrap, cloak, blanket, surround, engulf, conceal, hide, obscure.

envious adjective jealous, covetous, desirous, green-eyed, grudging, begrudging, resentful.

environment noun surroundings, conditions, circumstances; habitat, territory, domain, milieu, element, location, locale, background, setting, scene, context, ambience.

envoy noun **1** *envoys living in the embassy* legate, consul, attaché, chargé d'affaires. **2** *the president's envoy* emissary, courier, representative, intermediary, delegate, deputy, agent.

envy noun covetousness, jealousy, desire; resentment, resentfulness, discontent, spite.

envy verb covet, begrudge, grudge.

epic adjective **1** *an epic poem* heroic, grand, long. **2** *of epic proportions* huge, long, grand, extraordinary, ambitious.

epicure noun gourmet, gastronome, connoisseur.

epidemic noun **1** *a typhoid epidemic* outbreak, plague, scourge. **2** *an epidemic of burglaries* wave, upsurge, upswing, increase.

epidemic adjective *reaching epidemic proportions* rampant, wide-ranging, extensive, widespread, rife, sweeping.

episode noun **1** *the second episode of the story* installment, part, section, chapter, passage, scene. **2** *an episode in his life* incident, occurrence, experience, adventure, occasion, matter, affair.

epitome noun *the epitome of politeness* personification, embodiment, essence, quintessence, archetype, representation, model, type, example, exemplar, prototype.

equal adjective **1** *of equal height* the same, identical, alike, comparable, commensurate. **2** *a sum equal to the previous sum* identical to, equivalent to, commensurate with. **3** *an equal contest* even, balanced, level. **4** *receive equal treatment* like, uniform, unbiased, impartial, nonpartisan, fair, just, evenhanded, egalitarian. **5** *keep it at an equal temperature* even, constant, uniform, steady, stable, level. **equal to** *equal to the task* capable of, fit for, up to, adequate for, sufficient for.

equal verb **1** *four plus five equals nine* be equal to, be equivalent to, come to, amount to, make, total. **2** *she equals him in strength* match, parallel, correspond to, rival. **3** *equal the previous record* match, reach, parallel, achieve.

equip verb *equipped for the sea crossing* fit, rig out, prepare, supply, stock, array, outfit; suit, endow.

equipment noun gear, tools, tackle, apparatus, outfit, matériel; supplies, paraphernalia, accoutrements.

equitable adjective fair, fair-minded, just, evenhanded, proper, reasonable, honest, impartial, unbiased.

equity noun fairness, fair-mindedness, justice, evenhandedness, rightfulness, rectitude, reasonableness, honesty, integrity, uprightness, impartiality.

equivalent adjective *a job with equivalent status* similar, like, alike, comparable, corresponding, commensurate, equal, the same, matching.

era noun age, epoch, eon, period, time, generation, stage.

erase verb remove, rub out, obliterate, efface, expunge, excise, cross out, strike out, delete, cancel.

erect verb build, construct, put up, assemble, set up, raise, elevate.

erect adjective **1** *stand erect* upright, straight, vertical. **2** *an erect penis* hard, rigid, stiff, firm.

erode verb *wind eroded the rocks* wear, eat away at, corrode, abrade, gnaw, consume, disintegrate, deteriorate.

erotic adjective titillating, erogenous, aphrodisiac, seductive, sensual, salacious, suggestive; *inf.* sexy.

errand noun message, task, job, commission, chore, assignment, charge, mission.

erratic adjective inconsistent, variable, irregular, unstable, unreliable, unpredictable, capricious; eccentric, wandering, meandering, wavering, directionless.

erroneous adjective wrong, incorrect, inaccurate, untrue, false, mistaken, fallacious, spurious, invalid, faulty, flawed, unsound, specious.

error noun **1** *detect an error in the arith-*

metic mistake, inaccuracy, miscalculation, fault, flaw, fallacy. **2** *see the error of his ways* wrongdoing, mischief, misconduct, delinquency, sinfulness, evil.

erudite adjective learned, educated, well-read, scholarly, intellectual, knowledgeable, literate, cultured; *inf.* highbrow.

erupt verb **1** *the volcano erupted* belch, gush, vent, spew, boil over. **2** *violence erupted* break out, flare up, explode, pop up, emerge, become visible.

escalate verb **1** *the war escalated* mushroom, increase, heighten, intensify, accelerate. **2** *prices will escalate* go up, mount, soar, climb, spiral.

escapade noun adventure, stunt, prank, caper, romp, frolic, fling, spree; *inf.* lark, shenanigans.

escape verb **1** *the prisoners escaped* get away, break out, flee, bolt, abscond, fly. **2** *escape punishment* avoid, evade, dodge, elude, sidestep, circumvent; *inf.* duck. **3** *gas escaping* leak, seep, gush, spurt, issue, flow, discharge, drain.

escape noun **1** *the escape from jail* breakout, flight, getaway. **2** *an escape from punishment* avoidance, evasion, circumvention. **3** *an escape of gas* leak, leakage, seepage, flow, discharge.

escort noun **1** *the bridal party and its escort* entourage, retinue, train, cortege, protection, defense, convoy; attendant, guide, chaperon, guard, protector. **2** *her escort for the evening* partner, companion, beau; *inf.* date.

escort verb **1** *escort the ambulance* accompany, guide, conduct, lead, usher, shepherd, guard, protect, safeguard, defend. **2** *escort her to the dance* accompany, take out.

esoteric adjective abstruse, obscure, cryptic, recondite, arcane, mysterious, hidden, secret, private, mystic.

especially adverb **1** *especially talented* exceptionally, extraordinarily, uncommonly, unusually, remarkably, notably, eminently. **2** *especially in the summer* particularly, mainly, chiefly, principally. **3** *bought especially for you* specifically, exclusively, expressly, particularly, uniquely.

essence noun **1** *the essence of truth* substance, nature, crux, heart, soul, life, lifeblood, kernel, reality. **2** *essence of peppermint* extract, concentrate, distillate; scent, perfume. **in essence** basically, fundamentally, in effect, substantially, virtually. **of the essence** essential, necessary, indispensable, vital, crucial.

essential adjective **1** *cost-cutting is essential* necessary, indispensable, vital, crucial, requisite. **2** *the essential theme of the* *play* basic, fundamental, inherent, intrinsic, elemental, characteristic, principal. **3** *the essential gentleman* absolute, complete, perfect, ideal, quintessential.

essential noun *experience is an essential* necessity, prerequisite, requisite, sine qua non; *inf.* must.

establish verb **1** *establish a new colony* set up, form, found, institute, start, begin, create, inaugurate, organize, build, construct, install, plant. **2** *establish his guilt* prove, show, demonstrate, certify, confirm, verify, substantiate, corroborate, validate, authenticate.

esteem noun estimation, regard, respect, admiration, honor, deference, veneration, appreciation.

esteem verb regard, respect, value, admire, honor, revere, venerate, appreciate, cherish, prize, treasure.

estimate verb *estimate the cost* assess, compute, gauge, reckon, evaluate, judge, rate, appraise, guess; consider, believe, conjecture, surmise.

estimate noun *the plumber's estimate* price, valuation, evaluation, assessment, appraisal, estimation.

estimation noun opinion, judgment, consideration, mind; view, esteem, regard, respect, admiration.

etch verb engrave, carve, cut, furrow, imprint, inscribe, ingrain.

eternal adjective **1** *life eternal* everlasting, endless, never-ending, immortal, infinite, enduring, deathless, permanent, immutable. **2** *stop that eternal racket* ceaseless, incessant, constant, interminable, tedious, unremitting, relentless.

eternity noun **1** *believe in eternity* immortality, everlasting life, afterlife, heaven, paradise, nirvana. **2** *on the phone for an eternity* age, ages, forever.

ethical adjective moral, honorable, upright, righteous, good, virtuous, decent, principled, honest, just.

ethics plural noun moral code, morality; morals, principles, virtues.

etiquette noun manners; code of conduct, protocol, form, courtesy, propriety, decorum.

eulogy noun panegyric, praise, tribute, accolade, acclamation, paean, panegyric, encomium.

evacuate verb **1** *people evacuated the flooded town* leave, vacate, abandon, quit, flee, desert, forsake. **2** *firemen evacuated the room* empty, clear. **3** *evacuate waste matter* excrete, expel, eject, discharge, eliminate, void, purge, drain.

evacuation noun **1** *the people's evacuation* *of the town* abandonment, withdrawal, retreat, exodus, departure, flight, desertion. **2** *evacuation of waste products* excretion, expulsion, ejection, discharge, elimination, purging, emptying.

evade verb avoid, dodge, elude, sidestep, circumvent, shun, shirk; hedge, parry; *inf.* duck.

evaluate verb assess, appraise, size, gauge, judge, rate, rank, estimate, measure.

evaporate verb **1** *water evaporates in heat* vaporize. **2** *the hot sun evaporated the puddles* vaporize, dry, dry up, dehydrate, desiccate, sear, parch. **3** *the vision evaporated* vanish, fade, disappear, dissolve, dissipate.

evasion noun avoidance, dodging, eluding, elusion, sidestepping, circumvention; subterfuge, deception, trickery, cunning, hedging; *inf.* ducking.

evasive adjective **1** *evasive tactics* avoiding, dodging, escaping, eluding, sidestepping, shunning, shirking. **2** *evasive replies* equivocal, indirect, roundabout, circuitous, oblique; *inf.* cagey.

even adjective **1** *an even surface* level, flat, plane, smooth, uniform, flush, true. **2** *an even temperature* uniform, constant, steady, stable, consistent, unchanging. **3** *even chances of success* equal, identical, like, similar, comparable, commensurate. **4** *an even disposition* even-tempered, placid, serene, composed, calm, tranquil. **get even** take one's revenge, reciprocate.

even adverb **1** *even colder* yet, still, more so. **2** *even the teacher laughed* unexpectedly, paradoxically, surprisingly. **even so** *even so I shall attend* nevertheless, nonetheless, still, yet, notwithstanding.

evening noun **1** *go out in the evening* close of day, twilight, dusk, nightfall, sunset, sundown; *lit.* eve, eventide.

event noun **1** *the party was a successful event* occasion, affair, business, matter, happening, occurrence, episode, experience, circumstance. **2** *the javelin event* competition, contest, game, tournament, heat, match, round, bout, race. **in any event** at any rate, in any case, anyhow, anyway, regardless.

eventful adjective busy, full, lively, active, important, noteworthy, memorable, notable, remarkable, fateful, significant, historic, consequential, decisive.

eventual adjective final, end, concluding, ultimate, resulting, ensuing, consequent, subsequent.

ever adverb **1** *'twas ever thus* always, forever, eternally. **2** *grew ever larger* always, constantly, continually, endlessly, unendingly, incessantly, unceasingly, perpetually.

everlasting adjective **1** *everlasting life* never-ending, endless, eternal, perpetual, undying, immortal, abiding, enduring, infinite, boundless, timeless. **2** *their everlasting complaints* interminable, incessant. *See* ETERNAL adjective 2.

everyday adjective daily, diurnal; ordinary, common, usual, regular, customary, habitual, familiar, routine, plain, workaday, mundane.

evict verb turn out, put out, throw out, eject, expel, oust, remove, dispossess, dislodge.

evidence noun **1** *produce evidence of guilt* proof, confirmation, verification, substantiation, corroboration, support; grounds. **2** *give evidence in court* testimony, deposition, declaration, allegation, affidavit. **3** *evidence of a struggle* sign, indication, mark, manifestation. **in evidence** *with police in evidence* obvious, noticeable, conspicuous, visible.

evident adjective obvious, clear, apparent, plain, unmistakable, noticeable, conspicuous, perceptible, visible, discernible, manifest.

evil adjective **1** *evil deeds* wicked, bad, immoral, sinful, vile, base, corrupt, depraved, heinous, villainous, nefarious, reprobate, sinister, atrocious, malicious, malevolent, demonic, devilish, diabolic. **2** *evil influence* bad, harmful, hurtful, injurious, destructive, detrimental, deleterious, pernicious, malignant. **3** *evil temper* unpleasant, nasty, disagreeable, horrible, foul, vile.

evil noun **1** *more evil in the world than good* wickedness, badness, sin, sinfulness, immorality, vice, iniquity, baseness, corruption, depravity, villainy, atrocity, malevolence. **2** *the evils of war* harm, pain, hurt, misery, sorrow, suffering, misfortune.

evoke verb *evoke a response* cause, bring about, induce, arouse, excite, awaken, kindle, stimulate, elicit; summon, raise, recall.

evolve verb develop, unfold, unroll, grow, progress, mature, expand.

exact adjective precise, accurate, correct, unerring, faithful, true, just, literal, strict.

exaggerate verb overstate, overemphasize, overestimate, magnify, amplify, aggrandize, embellish, amplify, embroider.

exalt verb **1** *exalt to the highest rank* elevate, promote, raise, advance, ennoble. **2** *exalt the composer* praise, extol, glorify, acclaim, laud, worship, revere.

exalted adjective **1** *his exalted position in the firm* high, high-ranking, lofty, grand, eminent, prestigious, elevated, august. **2** *exalted aims* high-minded, lofty, elevated, noble, sublime, inflated.

examination noun **1** *examination of the facts* study, inspection, scrutiny, investigation, analysis, review, exploration, consideration, appraisal. **2** *a medical examination* checkup, observation. **3** *examination of witnesses* questioning, interrogation, cross-examination, third degree. **4** *college examinations* exam, test, midterm, final.

examine verb **1** *examine the facts* study, inspect, survey, scrutinize, investigate, analyze, review, probe, consider, appraise. **2** *examine a patient* inspect, check over, observe. **3** *examine the witnesses* question, test, quiz, interrogate, cross-examine; *inf.* grill.

example noun **1** *an example of cave painting* sample, specimen, instance, illustration. **2** *follow her example* model, pattern, precedent, paradigm, standard, criterion; ideal, paragon. **3** *punished him as an example to others* warning, caution, lesson, admonition.

exasperate verb *exasperate the teacher* anger, annoy, irritate, provoke, irk, vex, gall, pique; *inf.* bug, needle.

excavate verb **1** *excavate a trench* dig, dig out, gouge, cut out, quarry, mine. **2** *excavate an ancient city* unearth, dig up, uncover, disinter, exhume.

exceed verb pass, top, surpass, better, outdo, outstrip, outshine, transcend, overshadow, eclipse; overstep.

exceedingly adverb extremely, exceptionally, extraordinarily, tremendously, enormously, vastly, greatly, highly, hugely, supremely, inordinately.

excel verb stand out, shine; surpass, outshine, eclipse, overshadow, outdo, outclass, top, pass, transcend.

excellence noun merit, eminence, preeminence, distinction, quality, superiority, supremacy.

excellent adjective first-rate, first-class, great, fine, distinguished, superior, superb, outstanding, marvelous, brilliant, notable, eminent, preeminent, admirable, prime, select.

except preposition excluding, but; besides, barring, bar, other than, omitting, saving, save.

exceptional adjective **1** *an exceptional flavor* unusual, uncommon, atypical, odd, anomalous, singular, peculiar. **2** *exceptional ability* excellent, extraordinary, remarkable, outstanding, special, phenomenal, prodigious.

excerpt noun extract, citation, quotation, quote, passage, selection, part, section, fragment, piece, portion.

excess noun **1** *an excess of energy* surplus,

surfeit, overabundance, plethora, glut.
2 *throw out the excess* remainder, residue;
leftovers. **3** *a life of excess* overindulgence, prodigality, debauchery, dissipation,
dissoluteness.

excess adjective extra, additional, surplus,
superfluous, spare.

excessive adjective too much, superfluous,
immoderate, extravagant, lavish, superabundant, unreasonable, undue, uncalled-
for, extreme, inordinate, unwarranted,
unnecessary, needless, disproportionate,
exorbitant.

exchange verb trade, swap, barter, reciprocate.

exchange noun **1** *the exchange of information* interchange, trade, barter, traffic,
reciprocity. **2** *the floor of the exchange* stock
exchange, stock market, market.

excite verb **1** *excite the children too much*
stimulate, rouse, animate, move, thrill; *inf.*
wind up. **2** *excite feelings of love* arouse,
awaken, incite, stimulate, kindle, elicit.
3 *excite a rebellion* cause, incite, stir up,
instigate, foment, provoke.

exciting adjective *an exciting event* thrilling,
stirring, stimulating, exhilarating, rousing,
electrifying, invigorating, moving, inspiring, titillating, provocative, sensational.

exclamation noun call, cry, shout, yell,
ejaculation, interjection; expletive.

exclude verb **1** *exclude women from mem-
bership* bar, prohibit, forbid, prevent, disallow, refuse, ban, blackball, veto, proscribe,
interdict. **2** *exclude the possibility* eliminate, rule out, preclude, reject, except,
repudiate, omit, ignore.

exclusion noun **1** *the exclusion of women*
prevention, refusal, proscription. **2** *the
exclusion of robbery as a motive* elimination,
precluding, rejection, omission.

exclusive adjective **1** *an exclusive club* select, selective, restrictive, private, cliquish, snobbish, fashionable, chic, elegant,
luxurious; *inf.* posh, classy. **2** *my exclusive
attention* complete, undivided, full, absolute, entire, whole, total. **3** *the exclusive
means of travel* sole, only, unique, single.
4 *exclusive of drinks* excluding, omitting,
excepting, barring. **5** *mutually exclusive*
incompatible, antithetical.

excruciating adjective *an excruciating pain*
agonizing, racking, torturous, insufferable, unbearable, severe, intense, extreme,
searing, piercing, acute; *fml.* exquisite.

excursion noun **1** *a shopping excursion*
trip, day trip, expedition, jaunt, outing,
journey, tour. **2** *an excursion from the main
topic* digression, deviation, detour.

excusable adjective forgivable, pardon-

able, defensible, justifiable, understandable, condonable.

excuse verb **1** *excuse the wrongdoer* forgive, pardon, exonerate, absolve, acquit,
indulge. **2** *excuse their behavior* forgive, tolerate, condone, justify. **3** *excuse them from
heavy work* exempt, spare, release, relieve.

excuse noun defense, justification, reason, explanation, apology, vindication,
mitigation, grounds; pretext, pretense,
fabrication; *inf.* cop-out.

execute verb **1** *execute a murderer* put to
death, kill; hang, behead, guillotine, decapitate, electrocute, shoot, crucify; *inf.*
string up, fry. **2** *execute a plan of action*
carry out, accomplish, perform, implement, achieve, complete, fulfill, enact,
enforce, administer, attain, realize.

execution noun **1** *the execution of a murderer* capital punishment; death sentence;
killing, hanging, decapitation, electro-
cution, crucifixion. **2** *the execution of a
plan* implementation, accomplishment,
performance, achievement, completion,
fulfillment, enactment, enforcement, discharge, realization. **3** *execution of a piece of
music | her superb execution of the dance* per-
formance, presentation, staging, rendition,
delivery.

exemplary adjective **1** *exhibiting exemplary behavior* ideal, model, perfect, excellent, admirable, commendable, faultless,
laudable, praiseworthy, meritorious. **2**
exemplary member of the species typical,
representative, illustrative, characteristic,
epitomic.

exemplify verb typify, epitomize, represent,
personify, embody, illustrate.

exempt adjective *exempt from taxation* free
from, excused from, immune to, excepted
from, spared, released from.

exercise noun *physical exercise* activity, exertion, effort, action, work, drill; workout,
warm-up, aerobics, calisthenics.

exercise verb **1** *exercise in order to lose weight*
work out, train, drill. **2** *exercise patience*
employ, use, utilize, apply, implement,
practice, exert.

exert verb **1** *exert pressure* exercise, employ, use, utilize, apply, wield, expend.
2 *exert (yourself) and succeed* strive, endeavor, struggle, labor, toil, strain, work,
push, drive.

exertion noun **1** *physical exertion* effort,
exercise, work, struggle, strain, stress,
toil, labor; pains. **2** *the exertion of pressure*
exercise, employment, use, utilization,
expenditure, application.

exhaust verb **1** *the climb exhausted them*
tire, tire out, wear out, fatigue, weary,
enervate, tax, overtax, debilitate. **2** *ex-*

haust the supply of fuel use up, consume, finish, deplete, expend, spend; empty, drain, void.

exhausted adjective **1** *cold and exhausted* tired out, worn out, fatigued, weary, sapped, enervated, weak, faint, debilitated, spent; *inf.* all in, done in, dead tired, dog-tired, pooped. **2** *exhausted supplies* used up, consumed, finished, depleted.

exhausting adjective tiring, fatiguing, wearying, grueling, punishing, strenuous, arduous, backbreaking, taxing, laborious, enervating.

exhaustive adjective comprehensive, intensive, in-depth, total, encyclopedic, thorough, complete, full, extensive, sweeping.

exhibit verb **1** *exhibit products* display, show, demonstrate, present, model, expose, air, unveil, array, flaunt, parade. **2** *exhibit signs of sadness* show, express, indicate, reveal, display, demonstrate, betray.

exhibit noun *a furniture exhibit* display, show, demonstration, presentation, exhibition.

exhibition noun **1** *a book exhibition* display, show, fair, demonstration, presentation, exhibit, exposition. **2** *an exhibition of bad temper* display, show, expression, indication, revelation, demonstration, manifestation.

exile verb *be exiled from one's country* banish, expatriate, deport, expel, eject, bar, ban.

exile noun **1** *sent into exile* banishment, expatriation, deportation, expulsion. **2** *exiles from their homeland* expatriate, refugee, outlaw, outcast, pariah.

exist verb **1** *doubting that ghosts exist* be, live, subsist, breathe. **2** *cannot exist in a cold climate* survive, subsist, remain, continue, last, endure, prevail. **3** *enough money to exist on* survive, live, stay alive, subsist.

exonerate verb absolve, acquit, clear, discharge, vindicate, exculpate, excuse, pardon.

exorbitant adjective excessive, extreme, unreasonable, immoderate, inordinate, outrageous, preposterous.

exotic adjective foreign, nonnative, tropical, novel, alien; striking, outrageous, colorful, extraordinary, extravagant, sensational, unusual, remarkable, outlandish, bizarre, peculiar, curious, unfamiliar.

expand verb **1** *metals expand when heated* enlarge, increase, swell, inflate, distend, stretch. **2** *expand the business* increase, magnify, amplify, extend, multiply. **3** *expand one's account of the accident* elaborate, amplify, embellish, flesh out, develop.

expanse noun *an expanse of water* area, stretch, region, tract, breadth, extent, sweep, plain, field.

expect verb **1** *don't expect that he will come* think, believe, assume, suppose, imagine, presume, conjecture. **2** *expect a large crowd* anticipate, await, envisage, predict, forecast. **3** *teachers expect your complete attention* require, demand, exact, want.

expectant adjective anticipating, anticipatory, expecting, awaiting, eager, hopeful, ready, watchful, anxious, on tenterhooks.

expedient adjective *expedient to tell a white lie* convenient, advantageous, useful, beneficial, profitable, practical, pragmatic, politic, judicious, opportune.

expedite verb accelerate, speed, hurry, hasten, precipitate, quicken, advance, facilitate, further, promote; dispatch.

expedition noun **1** *an expedition into the jungle* undertaking, enterprise, mission, quest, safari. **2** *a shopping expedition* trip, excursion, outing, journey, jaunt. **3** *members of the expedition* group, team, party, company, crew, band, troop. **4** *carry out orders with expedition* speed, haste, promptness, swiftness, alacrity, quickness, dispatch.

expel verb banish, exile, evict, oust, cast out, deport, proscribe, outlaw; bar, ban, throw out, dismiss.

expend verb **1** *expend time and money on luxuries* spend, disburse, lavish, squander. **2** *expend all one's ammunition* use up, consume, exhaust, deplete, drain, sap, empty.

expendable adjective dispensable, replaceable, nonessential, unimportant.

expense noun **1** *the expense of college* cost, price, charge, fee. **2** *the expense of time and money* outlay, disbursement. **3** *victory at the expense of lives* cost, sacrifice.

expensive adjective costly, high priced, exorbitant, overpriced, lavish, extravagant; *inf.* steep.

experience noun **1** *a frightening experience* event, incident, occurrence, happening, affair, episode, circumstance, ordeal. **2** *practical experience* skill, knowledge, practice, training, understanding, wisdom, maturity; *inf.* know-how.

experience verb *experience hardship* undergo, encounter, meet, feel, know, face, sustain, suffer.

experienced adjective practiced, accomplished, skillful, proficient, seasoned, trained, expert, veteran.

experiment noun **1** *medical experiments with rats* test, investigation, trial, examination, observation, inquiry, pilot study. **2** *results obtained by experiment* research, experimentation, observation, analysis, testing.

experiment verb test, investigate, examine, explore, observe.

expert noun authority, master, specialist, professional, pundit, maestro, virtuoso, wizard, connoisseur.

expert adjective skillful, experienced, practiced, knowledgeable, professional, proficient, adept, brilliant, accomplished, adroit; inf. crack, top-notch.

expertise noun skill, skillfulness, mastery, proficiency, knowledge, command, facility, ability, capability, competence; inf. know-how.

expire verb your license has expired run out, finish, end, terminate, conclude, discontinue, stop, cease, lapse.

explain verb 1 explain the procedure describe, define, spell out, interpret, clarify, decipher, decode, elucidate, expound, explicate, delineate, demonstrate, teach, illustrate. 2 explain their actions justify, defend, vindicate, mitigate.

explanation noun 1 the explanation of the procedure description, definition, interpretation, clarification, elucidation, explication, demonstration, illustration. 2 an explanation of their motives account, justification, reason, excuse, defense, vindication, mitigation, apologia.

explicit adjective 1 explicit instructions detailed, clear, crystal-clear, direct, plain, obvious, precise, exact, straightforward, definite, specific, unequivocal, unambiguous. 2 explicit sexual description outspoken, unrestrained, unreserved, uninhibited, open, candid, frank, forthright.

explode verb 1 the boiler exploded blow up, detonate, burst, erupt. 2 explode in anger blow up, rage, rant and rave; inf. fly off the handle, hit the roof, flip one's lid. 3 world population exploding mushroom, escalate, burgeon, rocket, accelerate.

exploit noun feat, deed, adventure, stunt, achievement, accomplishment, attainment.

exploit verb 1 exploit natural resources utilize, use, profit from, capitalize on; inf. cash in on. 2 exploit the workers take advantage of, abuse, impose upon, misuse.

exploration noun investigation, study, survey, research, inspection, probe, examination, scrutiny, observation, search, inquiry, analysis.

explore verb 1 explore the Antarctic travel, traverse, tour, survey, inspect, scout. 2 explore possibilities investigate, consider, examine, research, survey, scrutinize, study, review.

explosion noun 1 a loud explosion bang, blast, boom, rumble, crash, crack, report, thunder, detonation, discharge, eruption. 2 an explosion of anger outburst, flare-up, fit, outbreak, eruption. 3 an explosion of population mushrooming, escalation, burgeoning, rocketing, acceleration.

explosive adjective 1 explosive substance inflammable, volatile, eruptive, unstable. 2 explosive temperament fiery, angry, touchy, stormy, violent, volatile. 3 an explosive situation tense, charged, critical, inflammable, volcanic, dangerous, perilous, hazardous.

expose verb 1 expose the skin to sunlight uncover, bare, strip, reveal. 2 expose to danger endanger, risk, hazard. 3 expose one's ignorance reveal, show, display, exhibit, disclose, manifest, unveil. 4 expose a criminal uncover, reveal, divulge, unearth, unmask, detect.

exposition noun 1 the exposition of modern educational theories explanation, interpretation, description, elucidation, explication, illustration; commentary, study, treatise, discourse; fml. exegesis. 2 an art exposition exhibition, fair, display, show, presentation.

exposure noun 1 the exposure of the skin to sunlight uncovering, baring, denudation. 2 exposure of one's ignorance revelation, display, exhibition, disclosure, manifestation. 3 exposure of a criminal disclosure, revelation, divulgence, detection, betrayal. 4 resent the exposure given to the affair publicity, advertising, broadcasting, air time.

expound verb 1 expound one's views on education explain, detail, spell out, set forth, describe, discuss. 2 expound (on) the Scriptures interpret, explain, annotate, illustrate, explicate.

express verb 1 express one's feelings state, voice, enunciate, communicate, utter, pronounce, articulate, verbalize, assert, say. 2 express appreciation show, indicate, demonstrate, convey, manifest.

express adjective 1 express service rapid, swift, fast, quick, speedy, prompt, high-speed, expeditious, direct, nonstop. 2 express instructions explicit, clear, plain, distinct, precise, specific, unequivocal.

expression noun 1 public expression of grievances statement, voicing, utterance, articulation, verbalization, assertion; indication, demonstration, conveyance, illustration, manifestation. 2 a particularly apt expression word, phrase, term, wording, language, phrasing, speech, diction, idiom, style, delivery, intonation, execution; fml. locution. 4 a sad expression on her face look, appearance, air, countenance; fml. mien. 5 playing the piano with expression feeling, emotion, passion, intensity, poignancy, depth, ardor.

expressive adjective **1** *an expressive gesture* emotional, eloquent, demonstrative, vivid. **2** *an expressive piece of music* emotional, eloquent, passionate, intense, poignant, moving, evocative, ardent. **3** *expressive of their contempt* indicative, demonstrative, revealing.

expressly adverb **1** *expressly forbidden* absolutely, explicitly, clearly, plainly, distinctly, specifically, unequivocally. **2** *laws expressly made to stop vandalism* purposefully, particularly, specially, especially, specifically.

expulsion noun *expulsion from school* dismissal, removal, eviction, ejection, banishment, discharge.

exquisite adjective **1** *exquisite earrings* beautiful, lovely, delicate, fragile, elegant, fine. **2** *exquisite taste* discriminating, discerning, selective, refined, cultivated, cultured, impeccable, polished.

extemporaneous, extemporary adjective *an extemporaneous vote of thanks* extempore, impromptu, spontaneous, ad lib, improvised, unrehearsed, unplanned, unprepared; *fml.* improvisatory.

extend verb **1** *extend the ladder* expand, lengthen, stretch, elongate. **2** *extend the scope of the law* widen, increase, expand, broaden, enlarge, augment, amplify. **3** *extend the period of credit* prolong, lengthen, protract. **4** *extend a welcome* offer, give, grant, proffer, present, confer, impart. **5** *the road extends for many miles* continue, stretch out, last, unfold, range.

extension noun **1** *the extension of the ladder* expansion, increase, enlargement; elongation. **2** *the extension of a period of credit* prolongation, lengthening, protraction. **3** *an extension to the house* annex, wing, addition.

extensive adjective **1** *extensive grounds around the house* large, sizable, substantial, spacious, considerable, capacious, commodious. **2** *extensive knowledge* comprehensive, thorough, complete, broad, wide, wide-ranging.

extent noun **1** *the full extent of the park* length, area, expanse, stretch, range. **2** *the extent of her knowledge* coverage, breadth, range, scope, degree.

exterior noun *the exterior of the building* outside, façade, covering, shell.

exterior adjective *the exterior layer* outer, outside, outermost, outward, external, surface.

exterminate verb kill, destroy, eradicate, annihilate, eliminate, extirpate.

external adjective **1** *an external wall* outer, outside, outward, exterior, surface, extrinsic. **2** *external affairs* foreign, international, alien.

extinct adjective **1** *an extinct species* dead, defunct, vanished, wiped-out, gone, lost. **2** *an extinct volcano* inactive, extinguished, quenched, doused.

extinguish verb **1** *extinguish the fire* put out, quench, smother, douse, snuff out. **2** *extinguish passion* destroy, kill, end, remove, eliminate, eradicate, erase, expunge.

extol verb praise, applaud, acclaim, laud, eulogize, exalt, commend, congratulate, celebrate, compliment.

extort verb *extort money* extract, force, exact, coerce, wring, wrest, squeeze.

extra adjective **1** *extra money required* more, additional, further, supplementary, supplemental, added, auxiliary. **2** *have extra food* spare, surplus, leftover, excess, superfluous, redundant, reserve, unused.

extract verb **1** *extract a tooth* draw out, pull out, remove, take out, uproot, withdraw, extirpate. **2** *extract money* extort, force, exact, elicit, coerce, wrest, wring, squeeze. **3** *extract juice* squeeze, press, express, distill. **4** *extract a section from a chapter* select, reproduce, copy, quote, cite, cull.

extract noun **1** *vanilla extract* concentrate, essence, distillate, juice. **2** *extracts from newspapers* excerpt, passage, citation, selection, quotation, clipping.

extraneous adjective **1** *extraneous forces* external, outside, exterior, extrinsic, alien, foreign. **2** *extraneous material* irrelevant, immaterial, inapplicable, inappropriate, unrelated, unconnected, peripheral.

extraordinary adjective **1** *extraordinary talent* exceptional, unusual, uncommon, rare, unique, singular, signal, unprecedented, outstanding, striking, remarkable, phenomenal, marvelous, wonderful; *inf.* fabulous. **2** *how extraordinary that we met* amazing, surprising, strange, astounding, curious.

extravagant adjective **1** *extravagant way of life* spendthrift, profligate, prodigal, wasteful, lavish, reckless, imprudent, excessive. **2** *extravagant prices* exorbitant, outrageous, excessive, extortionate, unreasonable, inordinate; expensive, costly, overpriced; *inf.* steep.

extravaganza noun spectacle, pageant, spectacular/impressive show/display.

extreme adjective **1** *extreme cold* utmost, maximum, supreme, greatest, acute, intense, severe, ultimate. **2** *extreme punitive measures* harsh, severe, drastic, radical. **3** *an extreme radical* immoderate, intemperate, fanatical, excessive, overzealous, unreasonable.

exuberant adjective *exuberant with joy* elated, exhilarated, high-spirited, buoyant, cheerful, effervescent, excited, unreserved, ebullient, enthusiastic, irrepressible.

exude verb **1** *sweat exuding through the pores* ooze, seep, filter, leak, trickle, drip, issue; excrete, emit, emanate. **2** *exuding confidence* ooze, emit, emanate, display.

exult verb rejoice, revel; triumph, gloat; be overjoyed, be in ecstasy, be on cloud nine, be in seventh heaven.

eyesore noun blemish, blot, scar, blight, defacement, monstrosity, carbuncle, ugliness; *inf.* sight.

eyewitness noun witness, observer, onlooker, bystander, spectator, watcher, viewer, beholder, passerby.

fable noun **1** *a fable about a fox | Norse fables* tale, fairy tale, moral tale, parable; story, legend, myth, saga, epic, lay. **2** *children telling fables* lie, untruth, falsehood, white lie, fib, fabrication, invention, story, fairy tale, cock-and-bull story, fantasy; *inf.* tall story, yarn.

fabric noun **1** *a silky fabric* cloth, material, textile, stuff, web. **2** *the fabric of the building | the fabric of society* framework, frame, structure, makeup, constitution, essence.

fabricate verb **1** *fabricate the furniture from components* assemble, construct, build, erect, put together, make, form, frame, fashion, shape, manufacture, produce. **2** *fabricate a reason for lateness* make up, invent, think up, concoct, hatch, trump up, devise, formulate. **3** *fabricate a document* forge, falsify, fake, counterfeit.

fabulous adjective **1** *fabulous wealth* incredible, unbelievable, inconceivable, unimaginable, astounding, amazing, astonishing. **2** *a fabulous time at the party* marvelous, wonderful, great, superb, spectacular; *inf.* fab, fantastic, super. **3** *fabulous creatures* mythical, legendary, imaginary, fantastical, fictitious, fictional, made-up, invented, unreal.

façade noun **1** *the façade of the building* front, frontage, face, exterior, outside. **2** *a façade of friendliness* show, appearance, guise, semblance, mask, veneer, masquerade, camouflage, pretense, illusion.

face noun **1** *a beautiful face* countenance, visage, physiognomy; features; *inf.* mug, kisser. **2** *with a furious face* expression, look, air, demeanor, aspect. **3** *make a face* scowl, grimace, frown, pout, moue. **4** *the face of the building* front, frontage. *See* FAÇADE 1. **5** *put a brave/bold face on it* appearance, façade, display, show, exterior, guise. **6** *lose face* prestige, standing, status, dignity, honor, respect, image. **7** *have the face to turn up* audacity, effrontery, impudence, impertinence, cheek, boldness, presumption, temerity; *inf.* nerve, gall.

face verb **1** *face rejection/reality* encounter, meet, come across, be confronted by, come up against, experience; face up to, come to terms with, accept, confront, meet head-on, cope with, deal with, come to grips with. **2** *face criticism/danger* dare, brave, defy, oppose, resist, withstand.

facet noun **1** *one facet of the problem* aspect, angle, side, slant, feature, characteristic, factor, element, point, part, phase. **2** *facet of a gem* side, plane, surface, face.

facetious adjective jocular, playful, frivolous, lighthearted, funny, amusing, humorous, comical, comic, joking, jesting, witty, droll, whimsical, tongue-in-cheek, waggish, jocose.

facilitate verb smooth, assist, help, aid, expedite, speed up, accelerate.

facility noun **1** *perform the task with facility* ease, effortlessness. **2** *facility of expression* ease, smoothness, fluency, eloquence, articulateness, slickness, glibness. **3** *a facility for wood carving* skill, aptitude, ability, gift, talent, knack, proficiency, bent. **4** *a research facility* establishment, structure, building, buildings, complex, system, plant.

facsimile noun copy, replica, reproduction, duplicate, carbon, carbon copy, photocopy, transcript, reprint, clone, image; fax; Xerox (*trademark*), Photostat (*trademark*).

fact noun **1** *fact, not rumor* actuality, reality, certainty, factuality, certitude; truth, naked truth, gospel. **2** *do not omit a single fact* detail, particular, point, item, piece of information/data, factor, element, circumstance. *See* FACTS. **in fact** actually, in point of fact, indeed.

faction noun **1** *a more radical faction* sector, section, group, side, party, band, set, ring, division, contingent, lobby, camp, bloc, clique, coalition, caucus, cabal, junta, splinter group, pressure group, minority (group). **2** *a club full of faction* infighting, dissension, discord, strife, contention, conflict, friction, argument, division, divisiveness, disharmony, disunity, variance, dissidence, rebellion, insurrection, sedition, mutiny, schism.

factious adjective dissenting, contentious, discordant, conflicting, divisive, clashing, warring, at variance, at loggerheads, at odds, dissident, rebellious, insurrectionary, seditious, mutinous.

factor noun element, part, component, ingredient, constituent, point, detail, item, facet, aspect, feature, characteristic, consideration, influence, circumstance, thing, determinant.

facts plural noun *the police just want the facts* information, whole story; details, data; *inf.* info, low-down, poop, word, score, dope.

factual adjective fact-based, real, true to life, true, truthful, accurate, authentic, genuine, exact, precise, strict, honest, faithful, literal, unbiased, objective, unvarnished, unadorned, unadulterated, unexaggerated.

faculties plural noun powers, capabilities, senses, wits; reason, intelligence.

faculty noun **1** *the faculty of speech* power, capability, capacity, attribute, property. **2** *a faculty for learning languages* aptitude, ability, facility, flair, gift, talent, bent, knack, disposition, proficiency, readiness, skill, dexterity, adroitness.

fad noun craze, mania, rage, enthusiasm, fancy, passing fancy, whim, vogue, fashion, trend.

fade verb **1** *the curtains/color faded* become washed out, grow dull/dim, lose luster. **2** *time had faded the colors* pale, bleach, whiten, wash out, dull, discolor, decolorize, dim. **3** *flowers fading* wither, wilt, die, droop, shrivel, decay. **4** *light/hope fading* grow less, dim, die away, dwindle, grow faint, fail, wane, disappear, vanish, die, decline, diminish, dissolve, peter out, melt away, evanesce.

fail verb **1** *their attempt failed* fall through, fall flat, miscarry, founder, misfire, fizzle out, miss the mark, run aground, go astray; *inf.* flop, come a cropper, bite the dust. **2** *fail the exam/failed twice* be found wanting/deficient/defective, not make the grade, not pass muster, be rejected; *inf.* flunk. **3** *words fail me* let down, desert, forsake, abandon, disappoint. **4** *the crops failed* be insufficient, be inadequate, be deficient, fall short. **5** *the light/hope failing* grow less, dim. *See* FADE 4. **6** *the engine failed* break down; *inf.* conk out. **7** *the old

man is failing grow weak/weaker, become feeble, lose strength, flag, sink. **8** *her health failed* decline, fade, diminish, dwindle, wane, ebb, deteriorate, sink, degenerate. **9** *his business failed* collapse, crash, go under, go to the wall, go bankrupt, close down; *inf.* fold.

failing noun fault, shortcoming, weakness, weak spot, imperfection, defect, flaw, blemish, frailty, foible, drawback.

failure noun **1** *the failure of their attempt* abortion, miscarriage, defeat, frustration, collapse, foundering, misfiring, coming to nothing, fizzling out. **2** *their plan was a failure* vain attempt, fiasco, debacle, botch, blunder; *inf.* flop, washout. **3** *he sees himself as a failure* incompetent, loser, nonachiever, ne'er-do-well, disappointment; *inf.* flop, dud, washout. **4** *failure in the line of duty* omission, neglect; negligence, remissness, nonobservance, dereliction, delinquency. **5** *the failure of the crops* insufficiency, inadequacy, deficiency, lack, dearth, scarcity, shortfall. **6** *the failure of his health* failing, decline, fading, dwindling, waning, sinking, deterioration, collapse, breakdown, loss, decay, crumbling, degeneration. **7** *the failure of his business* collapse, bankruptcy, ruin, ruination; *inf.* folding, flop.

faint adjective **1** *a faint mark/noise* indistinct, unclear, dim, obscure, vague, low, soft, muted, weak, feeble. **2** *a faint chance* slight, small, remote, minimal. **3** *feeling faint* giddy, dizzy, light-headed, weak-headed, weak; *inf.* woozy.

faint verb lose consciousness, black out, pass out, collapse; *inf.* keel over, conk out; *lit.* swoon.

faint-hearted adjective timid, timorous, fearful, spiritless, weak, cowardly, unmanly, lily-livered; *inf.* chickenhearted, yellow.

faintly adverb **1** *not faintly amusing* slightly, remotely, vaguely, somewhat, a little, in the least. **2** *call faintly* indistinctly, softly, weakly, feebly, in a whisper, in subdued tones.

fair adjective **1** *a fair decision* just, impartial, unbiased, unprejudiced, objective, disinterested, detached, equitable, aboveboard, lawful, legal, legitimate, proper, square; *inf.* on the level. **2** *a fair person* fair-minded, just, impartial, unbiased, unprejudiced, open-minded, honest, upright, honorable, trustworthy. **3** *fair winds* favorable, advantageous, helpful, beneficial. **4** *fair hair* blond/blonde, yellow, flaxen, strawberry blond, tow-headed. **5** *fair skin* pale, white, creamy, chalky. **6** *fair maidens* beautiful, pretty, lovely, attractive, good-looking, comely; *lit.* beauteous. **7** *a fair number of people* | *a fair* *chance of winning* ample, adequate, sufficient; decent, pretty good, moderate, so-so, average, fair-to-middling.

fair noun exhibition, display, show, exhibit, exposition; *inf.* expo.

fairly adverb **1** *treated fairly* justly, equitably, impartially, evenhandedly. **2** *fairly good* quite, reasonably, passably, tolerably, moderately, rather.

fair-minded adjective just, impartial. See FAIR adjective 2.

fairness noun **1** *treat everyone with fairness* justness, impartiality, objectivity, evenhandedness, disinterest, equitability. **2** *the fairness of the judge* fair-mindedness, justness, impartiality, open-mindedness, honesty, integrity, probity, rectitude, trustworthiness. **3** *the fairness of the maidens* beauty, prettiness, loveliness, attractiveness, comeliness.

fairy noun pixie, elf, sprite, imp, brownie, leprechaun, dwarf, gnome, goblin, hobgoblin.

faith noun **1** *have faith in the doctor* trust, belief, confidence, conviction. **2** *of what faith are they?* religion, church, persuasion, belief, creed, sect, denomination. **3** *keep/break faith* loyalty, allegiance, faithfulness, fidelity, fealty.

faithful adjective **1** *faithful followers* loyal, constant, devoted, dependable, reliable, true, true-blue, trusty, trustworthy, staunch, unswerving, unwavering, steadfast, obedient, dutiful, dedicated, committed. **2** *a faithful copy* accurate, true, exact, precise, close, strict.

faithless adjective **1** *faithless followers* unfaithful, disloyal, false, false-hearted, untrue, untrustworthy, traitorous, treacherous, perfidious, inconstant, fickle, unreliable. **2** *the missionary appealed to the faithless crowd* unbelieving, disbelieving, doubting, skeptical, agnostic, atheistic.

fake adjective **1** *a fake license* counterfeit, forged, sham, imitation, fraudulent, false, bogus, spurious, pseudo; *inf.* phony. **2** *fake furs/pearls* artificial, synthetic, mock, simulated, ersatz. **3** *a fake accent* affected, put-on, assumed, feigned.

fake noun **1** *the document is a fake* counterfeit, forgery, copy, sham, imitation, fraud, reproduction, hoax; *inf.* phony. **2** *the doctor is a fake* charlatan, impostor, mountebank, quack; *inf.* phony.

fall verb **1** *leaves/rain falling* descend, drop, drop down, sink, gravitate, cascade, plop, plummet. **2** *the child fell* fall down, fall over, trip, stumble, slip, slide, tumble, topple over, keel over, go head over heels, collapse, take a spill. **3** *demand/prices fell* fall off, drop off, go down, decline, decrease, grow less, diminish, dwindle,

depreciate, plummet, slump. **4** *empires falling* die, fade, fail, decline, deteriorate, flag, wane, ebb, degenerate, go downhill; *inf.* go to the dogs. **5** *towns falling to the enemy* surrender, yield, submit, give in, give up, give way, capitulate, succumb, resign oneself; be overthrown by, be taken by, be defeated by, be conquered by, lose one's position to, pass into the hands of. **6** *it so fell that she died* occur, happen, take place, come about, come to pass, befall, chance, arise, result. **7** *God punishing angels for falling* sin, do wrong, transgress, err, go astray, yield to temptation. **fall apart** fall to pieces, disintegrate, break up, crumble, dissolve. **fall back** retreat, withdraw, draw back, retire. **fall back on** resort to, call upon, have recourse to, rely on, depend on. **fall behind 1** *fall behind in the race* lose one's place, lag, trail, not keep up. **2** *fall behind with the rent* get into arrears/debt, not keep up with. **fall down** *fall down on the task* fail, not make the grade, not come up to expectations, fall short, disappoint. **fall for 1** *fall for his friend's sister* fall in love with, become infatuated with, be attracted/smitten by. **2** *fall for an old trick* be taken in by, be fooled/deceived/duped by; *inf.* swallow. **fall in** cave in, collapse, sink inward, come down about one's ears, crash in, crumble. **fall in with 1** *fall in with bad company* meet, encounter, get involved with, take up with. **2** *fall in with their plans* agree to/with, go along with, support, back, cooperate with. **fall out** quarrel, argue, squabble, fight, bicker, differ, disagree, clash, wrangle. **fall short (of)** fail to meet/reach, fail to live up to, miss. **fall through** come to nothing, fail, fail to happen, miscarry, abort, go awry; *inf.* fizzle out.

fall noun **1** *the child had a fall* trip, tumble, spill, stumble, topple, nosedive. **2** *a fall in prices* drop, dropping off, decline, decrease, cut, lessening, lowering, dip, diminishing, dwindling, reduction, depreciation, plummeting, slump. **3** *the fall of the Roman empire* death, demise, downfall, ruin, collapse, failure, decline, deterioration, wane, ebb, degeneration, destruction, overthrow. **4** *the fall of the city to the enemy* surrender, yielding, submission, capitulation. **5** *the fall of the land* slope, declivity, descent, downgrade.

fallacy noun misconception, false notion, misapprehension, misjudgment, miscalculation, error, untruth, inconsistency, illusion, delusion, sophism; sophistry.

fallible adjective liable/prone/open to error, erring, errant, imperfect, flawed.

false adjective **1** *a false interpretation/account* incorrect, wrong, erroneous, faulty, invalid, unfounded; untruthful, fictitious, concocted, fabricated, invented, inaccurate, inexact, imprecise, flawed, unreal, counterfeit, forged, fraudulent, spurious, misleading. **2** *a false friend* false-hearted, unfaithful, faithless, treacherous, disloyal, traitorous, perfidious, two-faced, double-dealing, untrustworthy, untrue, deceitful, deceiving, deceptive, dishonorable, dishonest, duplicitous, hypocritical, unreliable, unsound, untruthful, lying, mendacious. **3** *false furs/pearls* artificial, imitation. *See* FAKE adjective 1, 2.

falsehood noun lie, fib, untruth, false statement, falsification, perjury, fabrication, invention; prevarication, equivocation, mendacity.

falsify verb **1** *falsify a document* alter, counterfeit, forge, fake, doctor, tamper with, distort, adulterate, pervert. **2** *falsify their statement* disprove, refute, rebut, contradict, oppose.

falter verb **1** *falter before proceeding* hesitate, waver, oscillate, fluctuate, delay, vacillate, blow hot and cold, shilly-shally, hem and haw, sit on the fence. **2** *falter over her words* stammer, stutter, stumble.

fame noun renown, celebrity, eminence, notability, note, distinction, mark, prominence, esteem, preeminence, glory, honor, illustriousness, stardom, reputation, repute; notoriety, infamy.

familiar adjective **1** *familiar face/task/excuse* well-known, known, recognized, customary, accustomed, common, everyday, ordinary, commonplace, frequent, habitual, usual, repeated, routine, stock, conventional, household. **2** *a familiar atmosphere* informal, casual, relaxed, comfortable, easy, unceremonious, open, natural, simple. **3** *familiar acquaintances* close, intimate, confidential, bosom. **4** *object to him being familiar with the staff* overfamiliar, presumptuous, disrespectful, forward, bold. **familiar with** acquainted with, conversant with, versed in, knowledgeable about, instructed in, no stranger to.

familiarity noun **1** *the familiarity of the atmosphere* informality, casualness, ease, comfortableness, friendliness, lack of ceremony, naturalness, simplicity. **2** *the familiarity of their relationship* closeness, intimacy, nearness, friendliness. **3** *object to his familiarity* overfamiliarity, presumption, presumptuousness, disrespect, forwardness, intrusiveness; liberties. **familiarity with** knowledge of, mastery of, understanding of, experience of, skill with.

family noun **1** *two families living together* household, clan, tribe. **2** *she wants a family* children, offspring, progeny, descendants, issue, scions; brood; *inf.* kids. **3** *the man had no family* relatives, relations, people, kin, kinfolk, kinsmen, one's own flesh and blood. **4** *a noble family* ancestry, extraction, parentage, birth, pedigree, descent, lineage, line, bloodline, blood, race, strain, stock, breed; dynasty, house. **5** *a family of plants* class, genus, species, kind, type, group.

famine noun scarcity, lack, dearth, want, deficiency, shortage, insufficiency, paucity; starvation, hunger.

famished adjective starving, starving to death, starved, ravenous, hungry, undernourished.

famous adjective well-known, renowned, celebrated, famed, prominent, noted, notable, great, eminent, preeminent, distinguished, esteemed, illustrious, acclaimed, popular, legendary.

fan verb **1** *fan the atmosphere* cool, ventilate, air, aerate, blow, freshen, refresh. **2** *fan the flames* stir up, work up, whip up, incite, instigate, provoke. **fan out** spread, spread out, open out/up, unfurl, unfold, outspread, stretch out.

fan noun admirer, lover, enthusiast, devotee, addict, aficionado, zealot, follower, disciple, adherent, supporter, backer, champion, votary; *inf.* buff, fiend, freak, nut, groupie.

fanatic noun zealot, extremist, radical, activist, militant, sectarian, bigot, partisan.

fanatical adjective **1** *a fanatical sect* extremist, extreme, zealous, radical, activist, militant, sectarian, rabid. **2** *a fanatical moviegoer* enthusiastic, eager, fervent, passionate, obsessive, immoderate; *inf.* wild, gung-ho.

fanciful adjective **1** *fanciful notions* imaginary, fancied, fantastic, romantic, mythical, fabulous, legendary, unreal, illusory, visionary, made-up, make-believe, fairytale. **2** *a fanciful child* imaginative, inventive, whimsical, capricious, visionary, chimerical. **3** *fanciful decoration* imaginative, creative, curious, extravagant, fantastic, bizarre.

fancy noun **1** *a child subject to fancy* caprice, whimsy, vagary, eccentricity, peculiarity; whim, quirk, notion, kink. **2** *have a fancy for ice cream* desire, urge, wish, want, yearning, longing, hankering; fondness, liking, partiality, preference; *inf.* yen, itch. **3** *the poet's fancy* imagination, creativity, conception; images, visualizations. **4** *I have a fancy it will rain* idea, guess, thought, notion.

fancy adjective **1** *fancy decorations* ornate, elaborate, ornamented, ornamental, decorated, decorative, adorned, embellished, intricate, lavish, ostentatious, showy, luxurious, sumptuous, baroque, rococo; *inf.* jazzy, ritzy, snazzy, posh, classy. **2** *fancy notions* imaginary, far-fetched, flighty. *See* FANCIFUL 1, 2.

fanfare noun 1 *the queen greeted by a fanfare* flourish, trumpet call, blast of trumpets, fanfaronade. 2 *the store opened with much fanfare* show, showiness, display, ostentation, commotion, fuss, publicity, ballyhoo; *inf.* to-do, hype.

fantastic adjective 1 *fantastic notions* fanciful, imaginary, romantic, unreal, illusory, make-believe, irrational, extravagant, wild, mad, absurd, incredible, strange, eccentric. 2 *fantastic shapes* bizarre, grotesque, freakish, strange, weird, queer, peculiar, outlandish, unreal, extravagant, elaborate, ornate, intricate, rococo, baroque, phantasmagoric. 3 *a fantastic amount of work* tremendous, enormous, huge, impressive, overwhelming. 4 *the movie was fantastic* marvelous, wonderful, sensational, superb, top-notch; *inf.* cool, awesome.

fantasy noun 1 *novels full of fantasy* fancy, imagination, creativity, invention, originality, vision, myth. 2 *indulge in fantasy* fancy, speculation, daydreaming, reverie; flight of fancy, daydream, pipedream. 3 *see fantasies* apparition, phantom, specter, ghost, hallucination, vision, illusion, mirage.

farce noun 1 *starring in a bedroom farce* slapstick, slapstick comedy, burlesque, burlesque show/routine, satire, parody, travesty, buffoonery, absurdity, ridiculousness. 2 *the interviews were just a farce* mockery, absurdity, sham, pretense, joke.

farcical adjective 1 *a farcical situation* ridiculous, ludicrous, absurd, laughable, risible, preposterous, facetious, silly, foolish, nonsensical, asinine. 2 *a farcical play* comic, slapstick, humorous, amusing.

farewell interjection good-bye, so long, adieu, ciao, adios, *auf Wiedersehen, au revoir; inf.* see you, see you later, toodle-oo.

farewell noun good-bye, adieu, leave-taking, parting, send-off, departure.

far-fetched adjective improbable, unlikely, remote, implausible, incredible, unbelievable, dubious, doubtful, unconvincing, strained, labored, fanciful, unrealistic; *inf.* hard to swallow/take.

farm verb *farm the land* cultivate, till, work, plow, plant. **farm out** contract out, subcontract, delegate; rent, rent out, lease, let.

farsighted adjective *farsighted in his choice* prescient, prudent, discerning, judicious, shrewd, provident, wise, sagacious.

fascinate verb captivate, enchant, beguile, bewitch, enthrall, infatuate, enrapture, entrance, hold spellbound, transfix, rivet, mesmerize, hypnotize, allure, lure, tempt, entice, draw, tantalize, charm, attract, intrigue, delight, absorb, engross.

fascinating adjective captivating, enchanting, beguiling, bewitching, enthralling, ravishing, entrancing, compelling, spellbinding, riveting, gripping, alluring, charming, intriguing, absorbing.

fascination noun enchantment, allure, lure, attraction, appeal, charm, magnetism, pull, draw, spell, sorcery, magic, glamour.

fashion noun 1 *the fashion in clothes* style, vogue, trend, latest thing, mode, craze, rage, fad, convention, custom, practice. 2 *she works in fashion* clothes, clothes industry/design, couture; *inf.* rag trade. 3 *working in an untidy fashion* manner, way, style, method, mode, system, approach. 4 *a boat of some fashion* kind, type, sort, make, design, description. **after a fashion** somehow or other, in a rough way, to a certain extent, in a manner of speaking.

fashion verb make, construct, build, manufacture, create, devise, shape, form, mold, forge.

fashionable adjective 1 *fashionable clothes* in fashion, stylish, up-to-date, up-to-the-minute, modern, voguish, in vogue, modish, popular, all the rage, trendsetting, latest, smart, chic, elegant, natty; *inf.* trendy, with it. 2 *fashionable areas* high-class; *inf.* classy, swank.

fast adjective 1 *at a fast pace* quick, rapid, swift, speedy, brisk, fleet-footed, hasty, hurried, accelerated, express, flying. 2 *fast friends* loyal, devoted, faithful, firm, steadfast, staunch, constant, lasting, unchanging, unwavering, enduring. 3 *held fast by a rope* fastened, closed, shut, secured, secure, firmly fixed. 4 *fast women* promiscuous, licentious, dissolute, loose, wanton. 5 *lead fast lives* wild, dissipated, dissolute, debauched, promiscuous, intemperate, immoderate, rakish, unrestrained, reckless, profligate, self-indulgent, extravagant.

fast adverb 1 *run fast* quickly, rapidly, swiftly, speedily, briskly, hastily, hurriedly, post-haste, expeditiously, with dispatch, like the wind, like a shot/flash, hell-bent, hell-bent for leather, like a bat out of hell; *inf.* lickety-split. 2 *stuck fast* firmly, tightly, securely, immovably, fixedly. 3 *live fast* wildly, dissipatedly, intemperately, rakishly, recklessly.

fasten verb 1 *fasten a brooch to the dress* attach, fix, affix, clip, pin, tack. 2 *fasten the door* bolt, lock, secure, make secure/fast, chain, seal. 3 *fasten his gaze on her* direct, aim, point, focus, fix, rivet, concentrate, zero in. 4 *the lions fastening on their prey* take hold of, seize, catch/grab hold of, grab, snatch.

fastidious adjective hard to please, critical, overcritical, hypercritical, fussy, finicky, overparticular; *inf.* choosy, picky, persnickety.

fat adjective **1** *fat people* plump, stout, overweight, obese, heavy, large, solid, corpulent, chubby, tubby, portly, rotund, pudgy, flabby, gross, potbellied, paunchy; *inf.* beefy, roly-poly, elephantine. **2** *fat substances* fatty, greasy, oily, oleaginous, adipose, unctuous, sebaceous. **3** *fat land* fertile, productive, fruitful, rich, lush, flourishing, thriving. **4** *a fat part in a play* substantial, large, sizable, major, important, significant, considerable.

fatal adjective **1** *a fatal blow/illness* mortal, deadly, lethal, death-dealing, killing, terminal, final, incurable. **2** *fatal to our plans* ruinous, destructive, disastrous, catastrophic, calamitous, cataclysmic. **3** *the fatal moment* fateful, critical, crucial, decisive, determining, pivotal, momentous, important.

fatality noun **1** *three fatalities in the accident* dead person, death, casualty, mortality, loss; dead. **2** *the fatality of the blow* deadliness, lethalness.

fate noun **1** *fate meant them to meet* destiny, providence, God's will, kismet, predestination, predetermination, chance, one's lot in life; the stars. **2** *courts deciding our fate* future; outcome, upshot, end. **3** *met his fate in battle* death, end, destruction, ruin, doom.

fated adjective predestined, preordained, foreordained, destined, inevitable, inescapable, sure, ineluctable, doomed.

fateful adjective **1** *a fateful meeting* critical, crucial, decisive, determining, pivotal, momentous, important, fated. **2** *a fateful course of action* disastrous, ruinous, destructive, fatal, lethal, deadly.

father noun **1** begetter, paterfamilias, patriarch; *inf.* dad, daddy, pop, pops, poppa, pa, old man. **2** *investigate the history of his fathers* forefather, ancestor, forebear, progenitor, primogenitor, predecessor, forerunner, precursor. **3** *the father of modern history* founder, originator, initiator, prime mover, architect, inventor, creator, maker, author. **4** *the city fathers* leader, elder, patriarch, senator.

fatherly adjective paternal, kindly, kind, affectionate, tender, caring, protective, supportive, patriarchal.

fathom verb **1** *fathom the depth of the water* sound, plumb, measure, estimate, gauge, probe. **2** *fathom their motives* understand, comprehend, grasp, perceive, penetrate, divine, search out, get to the bottom of, ferret out.

fatigue verb tire, tire out, overtire, make weary, weary, exhaust, wear out, drain, prostrate, enervate; *inf.* take it out of, do in, poop out.

fatigue noun tiredness, overtiredness, weariness, exhaustion, prostration, lassitude, debility, enervation, lethargy, listlessness.

fatuous adjective silly, foolish, stupid, inane, pointless, senseless, nonsensical, childish, puerile, idiotic, brainless, mindless, vacuous, asinine, moronic, witless.

fault noun **1** *a fault in the material* defect, flaw, imperfection, blemish, snag. **2** *a fault in her character* defect, flaw, failing, shortcoming, weakness, weak point, infirmity, lack, deficiency. **3** *a fault in the calculation* error, mistake, inaccuracy, blunder, oversight; *inf.* slipup, booboo. **4** *blame one child for another's faults* misdeed, wrongdoing, offense, misdemeanor, misconduct, sin, vice, lapse, indiscretion, peccadillo, transgression, trespass. **5** *whose fault was it?* culpability, blameworthiness, responsibility, accountability, answerability. **at fault** blameworthy, blamable, in the wrong, culpable, responsible, accountable, answerable. **to a fault** excessively, unduly, in the extreme, needlessly, overly.

faultfinding adjective critical, overcritical, hypercritical, censorious, carping, captious, caviling, quibbling, niggling, hairsplitting; *inf.* nitpicking.

faultless adjective **1** *a faultless piece of work* perfect, flawless, unblemished, impeccable, accurate, correct, exemplary, model. **2** *the wife of the prisoner was faultless* innocent, guiltless, blameless, above reproach, irreproachable, sinless, pure, unsullied.

faulty adjective **1** *a faulty lock* broken, malfunctioning, out of order, damaged, defective, unsound; *inf.* on the blink, kaput. **2** *faulty reasoning* defective, flawed, unsound, wrong, inaccurate, incorrect, erroneous, imprecise, fallacious, impaired, weak, invalid.

faux pas noun blunder, gaffe, mistake, slipup, indiscretion, impropriety, lapse of etiquette, peccadillo; *inf.* booboo.

favor noun **1** *do me a favor* good turn, service, good deed, kindness, courtesy, benefit. **2** *look on him with favor* approval, approbation, esteem, goodwill, kindness, benevolence, friendliness. **3** *owe his job to favor rather than merit* favoritism, bias, partiality, prejudice, partisanship.

favor verb **1** *he favors returning* advocate, approve of, recommend, support, back, endorse, sanction. **2** *the young man favored blondes* prefer, go in for, go for, choose, opt for, select, fancy, like, incline toward. **3** *the wind favored the other team* be advantageous to, benefit, help, assist, aid, advance, abet. **4** *favor us with a smile* oblige, serve, accommodate, satisfy, please.

favorable adjective **1** *a favorable report*

good, approving, commendatory, praising, well-disposed. **2** *the circumstances are favorable* advantageous, beneficial, hopeful, promising, auspicious, propitious, opportune, timely, encouraging, conducive, convenient. **3** *a favorable impression* pleasing, agreeable, successful, positive.

favorite adjective best-loved, most-liked, pet, favored, dearest, preferred, ideal.

favorite noun preference, first choice, choice, pick, pet, beloved, darling, idol, jewel, jewel in the crown; blue-eyed boy, apple of one's eye, teacher's pet.

favoritism noun bias, partiality, prejudice, unfair preference, partisanship, nepotism, unfairness, inequity.

fawn verb *fawn on* kowtow to, bow and scrape to, grovel before, curry favor with, ingratiate oneself with, lick the boots of; *inf.* butter up.

fear noun **1** *filled with fear at the danger* fright, fearfulness, terror, alarm, panic, trepidation, apprehensiveness, dread, fear and trembling, timidity, trembling, quaking, quivering, consternation, dismay; shivers, butterflies, tremors. **2** *all her fears were removed* phobia, aversion, dread, bugbear, nightmare, horror, terror. **3** *express fear that he would die* anxiety, worry, unease, uneasiness, apprehension, nervousness, agitation, concern, disquiet, angst. **4** *fear of the Lord* awe, wonder, amazement, reverence, veneration.

fear verb **1** *she fears spiders* be afraid of, dread, have a horror/dread of, have a phobia about. **2** *they fear God* stand in awe of, revere, reverence, venerate. **3** *I fear you may be right* suspect, have a suspicion, expect, anticipate, have a foreboding. **fear for** worry about, feel anxious/concerned about, have anxieties/qualms about.

fearful adjective **1** *fearful of making a noise* afraid, frightened, scared, terrified, alarmed, apprehensive, uneasy, nervous, tense, panicky, timid, timorous, fainthearted, intimidated, hesitant, disquieted, trembling, quaking, quivering, shrinking, cowering, cowardly, pusillanimous; *inf.* jittery, jumpy. **2** *a fearful accident* terrible, dreadful, appalling, frightful, ghastly, horrific, horrible, horrendous, shocking, awful, atrocious, hideous, monstrous, dire, grim, unspeakable, gruesome, distressing, harrowing, alarming.

fearless adjective unafraid, brave, courageous, valiant, intrepid, valorous, gallant, plucky, lionhearted, stouthearted, heroic, bold, daring, confident, audacious, indomitable, undaunted, unflinching, unshrinking; *inf.* game, gutsy, spunky.

feasible adjective practicable, possible, likely, workable, doable, achievable, attainable, accomplishable, realizable, reasonable, viable, realistic.

feast noun **1** banquet, repast; orgy; revels, festivities; *inf.* blowout, spread, bash. **2** *the feast of St. Stephen* celebration, festival, feast day, saint's day, holy day, holiday, fête, festivity. **3** *a feast for the eyes* pleasure, gratification, delight, treat, joy.

feast verb wine and dine, regale, entertain, treat. **feast on** *feast on a holiday dinner* wine and dine, gorge oneself on, eat one's fill of, partake of, indulge in, overindulge in, gormandize, stuff one's face with, stuff oneself with.

feat noun deed, act, action, exploit, accomplishment, achievement, attainment, move, stunt.

feature noun **1** *one feature of life in the country* aspect, characteristic, facet, side, point, attribute, quality, property, trait, mark, hallmark, trademark, peculiarity, idiosyncrasy. **2** *the tractor pull is a popular feature of the fair* special attraction, attraction, highlight, focal point, focus, draw.

feature verb present, give prominence to, promote, star, spotlight, highlight, emphasize, play up, accentuate.

federal adjective national, civil, nationwide, governmental.

federation noun confederation, confederacy, federacy, league, alliance, coalition, union, syndicate, association, amalgamation, combination, combine, entente, society, fraternity.

fee noun charge, price, cost, payment, remuneration, emolument.

feeble adjective **1** *grow feeble with age* weak, weakly, weakened, frail, infirm, delicate, slight, sickly, puny, failing, ailing, helpless, powerless, debilitated, decrepit, doddering, tottering, enervated, enfeebled, effete. **2** *a feeble attempt at humor* ineffective, ineffectual, unsuccessful, inadequate, unconvincing, futile, poor, weak, tame, paltry, slight. **3** *a feeble light/voice* dim, indistinct, faint, unclear, vague, inaudible.

feebleminded adjective stupid, idiotic, foolish, halfwitted, slow on the uptake; *inf.* boneheaded, dumb, soft in the head, out to lunch.

feed verb **1** *feed the family* nurture, nourish, sustain, cater for, provide for, wine and dine. **2** *feed his self-esteem* gratify, bolster up, strengthen, augment, add to, encourage, minister to, add fuel to. **3** *feed logs to the fire* supply, provide, give, furnish.

feed noun **1** *cattle feed* food, fodder, provender, forage, pasturage, silage. **2** *a good feed* feast, meal, dinner, repast, banquet; *inf.* spread.

feel verb **1** *feel her face* touch, stroke, caress, fondle, finger, thumb; handle, manipulate; paw, maul. **2** *feel the ship's motion* notice, observe, perceive, have a sensation of. **3** *feel pain* experience, know, have, undergo, go through, bear. **4** *feel one's way* grope, fumble, poke, explore. **5** *he feels that he should go* think, believe, consider it right, be of the opinion, hold, judge, deem. **6** *I feel that he's hiding something* sense, get the impression, have a hunch, just know. **7** *the air feels damp* seem, appear, strike one as. **feel for** sympathize with, commiserate with, empathize with. **feel like** wish, desire, fancy; *inf.* have a yen for.

feel noun **1** *the material has a nice feel* texture, surface, finish. **2** *I don't like the feel of the place* atmosphere, ambience, aura, mood, air, impression; *inf.* vibrations, vibes. **3** *a feel for that kind of work* knack, aptitude, flair, talent, gift, art, faculty.

feeling noun **1** *tell what it is by feeling* feel, touch. **2** *a feeling of pain* awareness, consciousness, sensation, sense, perception. **3** *I had a feeling that you would be there* suspicion, notion, inkling, hunch, presentiment, premonition, foreboding. **4** *look at him with feeling* emotion, affection, fondness, warmth, love, sentiment, passion, ardor, fervor. **5** *show feeling for others* sympathy, pity, compassion, understanding, concern, sensitivity, tender-heartedness, empathy. **6** *my feeling is that he will go* instinct, opinion, intuition, impression, point of view, thought, way of thinking, theory, hunch. **7** *a feeling of neglect about the place* atmosphere, ambience. *See* FEEL noun 2.

feeling adjective *a feeling person* sensitive, warm, tender, caring, softhearted, sympathetic, compassionate, responsive, demonstrative.

feign verb fake, simulate, sham, affect, pretend, make believe, act, play-act.

felicitous adjective **1** *a felicitous expression* apt, well-chosen, well-expressed, well-put, fitting, suitable, appropriate, apposite, pertinent, germane, to the point. **2** *a felicitous event* happy, joyful, harmonious, fortunate, lucky, successful, prosperous.

fell verb cut down, hew, level, raze, raze to the ground, demolish, knock down/over, strike down, flatten, ground, floor, prostrate, overthrow, kill.

fellowship noun **1** *a need for fellowship* companionship, companionability, sociability, comradeship, fraternization, camaraderie, friendship, amiability, amity, affability, geniality, kindliness, cordiality, intimacy, social intercourse; *inf.* chumminess. **2** *the church fellowship* association, society, club, league, union, guild, affiliation, order, fraternity, brotherhood.

feminine adjective **1** *a very feminine young woman* delicate, gentle, tender, graceful, womanly, ladylike, girlish, refined, modest. **2** *a man with a feminine manner* effeminate, womanish, effete, unmanly, unmasculine, weak.

fence noun enclosure, barrier, railing, rail, wall, hedge; barricade, rampart, stockade, palisade. **on the fence** uncommitted, uncertain, undecided, vacillating, irresolute, neutral, impartial.

fence verb **1** *fence the garden* enclose, surround, circumscribe, encircle, encompass. **2** *fence when asked questions* hedge, be evasive, beat around/about the bush, dodge the issue, prevaricate, equivocate, fudge the issue, shilly-shally, vacillate. **fence in** shut in, confine, pen, separate off, secure, imprison.

fend verb **fend off** ward off, keep off, turn aside, stave off, divert, deflect, avert, defend oneself against, guard against. **fend for oneself** provide/shift for oneself, take care of oneself, get by.

ferocious adjective **1** *a ferocious animal/criminal* fierce, savage, wild, feral, untamed, predatory, rapacious; ruthless, brutal, brutish, cruel, pitiless, merciless, vicious, violent, inexorable, barbarous, barbaric, inhuman, bloodthirsty, murderous. **2** *ferocious heat* fierce, intense, extreme, acute.

ferret verb **ferret out** unearth, discover, disclose, elicit, bring to light, search out, get at, run to earth, track down, dig up, root out, hunt out, drive out, fish out, nose out, sniff out, smell out.

fertile adjective **1** *fertile soil* fruitful, productive, fecund, rich. **2** *reach the age of being fertile* potent, virile, child-producing, fecund, reproductive, propagative. **3** *fertile imaginations* inventive, creative, original, ingenious, resourceful, visionary, constructive, productive.

fervent adjective passionate, ardent, impassioned, intense, vehement, heartfelt, fervid, emotional, emotive, warm, devout, sincere, eager, earnest.

fervid adjective ardent, intense. *See* FERVENT.

fervor noun fervency, passion, ardor, intensity, vehemency, fervidness, emotion, warmth, devoutness, sincerity, eagerness, earnestness, zeal, enthusiasm.

fester verb **1** *a wound festering* suppurate, matter, come to a head, gather, maturate, run, discharge. **2** *animal corpses festering* rot, decay, go bad, go off, decompose, disintegrate. **3** *resentment festering in their minds* rankle, chafe, gnaw.

festival noun **1** *a church festival* saint's day,

holy day. *See* FEAST noun 2. **2** *the town's annual festival* fair, gala, fête, carnival; celebrations, festivities.

festive adjective joyous, joyful, happy, jolly, merry, gay, jovial, lighthearted, cheerful, cheery, jubilant, convivial, good-time, gleeful, mirthful, celebratory, gala.

festivity noun **1** *the festivity of the occasion* joyfulness, jollity, merriment, pleasure, gaiety, cheerfulness, jubilance, convivialness, cheeriness, gleefulness, glee, mirthfulness, mirth, revelry. **2** *enjoy the festivities* celebration, festival, entertainment, party, revelry, carousal, sport; fun and games.

festoon verb garland, wreathe, hang, drape, decorate, adorn, ornament, array, deck, bedeck, swathe, beribbon.

fetch verb **1** *fetch the doctor* go and get, get, go for, bring, carry, deliver, convey, transport, escort, conduct, lead, usher in. **2** *the vase fetched $40* sell for, go for, bring in, realize, yield, earn, cost.

fetching adjective attractive, charming, enchanting, sweet, winsome, taking, captivating, fascinating, alluring.

fête noun gala, fair, garden party, festival, celebration.

fetish noun **1** *a leather fetish* fixation, compulsion, obsession, mania, idée fixe; *inf.* thing. **2** *carry a fetish* talisman, charm, amulet.

fetter verb **1** *fetter the prisoners* chain, chain up, shackle, bind, tie, tie up, hobble. **2** *fettered by petty restrictions* restrict, hinder, impede, obstruct, constrain, confine, restrain.

fetters plural noun chains, shackles, irons, manacles, trammels; restraint, tether, check.

feud noun vendetta, rivalry, hostility, enmity, conflict, strife, discord, bad blood, animosity, antagonism, unfriendliness, grudge, estrangement, schism; quarrel, conflict, argument, bickering, falling-out.

fever noun **1** *the child's fever subsided* feverishness; *inf.* temperature, temp. **2** *a fever of excitement* ferment, frenzy, furor; turmoil, agitation, excitement, restlessness, unrest, passion, intensity.

feverish adjective **1** *the child is feverish* fevered, febrile, burning, hot, flushed. **2** *feverish excitement* frenzied, frenetic, agitated, worked up, overwrought, frantic.

fiasco noun failure, disaster, catastrophe, mess, ruination, debacle; *inf.* flop, washout.

fib noun lie, white lie, untruth, falsehood, fabrication, piece of fiction, fiction, fairy story/tale.

fiber noun **1** *the fibers of the carpet* thread, strand, tendril, filament, fibril; material,

substance, cloth, stuff. **2** *a person of a different fiber* character, nature, makeup, spirit, disposition, temperament.

fickle adjective capricious, changeable, variable, unpredictable, volatile, mercurial, inconstant, unstable, vacillating, unsteady, unfaithful, faithless, irresolute, flighty, giddy, erratic, fitful, irregular, mutable.

fiction noun storytelling, romance, fable, fantasy, legend; fabrication, invention, concoction, lie, fib, untruth, falsehood, fairy tale/story, tall story, prevarication; *inf.* cock-and-bull story, whopper, fish story.

fictional adjective fictitious, made up, invented, imaginary, unreal, nonexistent.

fictitious adjective **1** *a fictitious character* made up, imaginary. *See* FICTIONAL. **2** *a fictitious address/account* false, untrue, bogus, sham, counterfeit, fake, fabricated, assumed, invented, made up, concocted, spurious, imagined, imaginary, apocryphal.

fiddle verb **1** *fiddling with a pencil* fidget, play, fuss, toy, mess about, fool around; waste time, act aimlessly. **2** *fiddle with the engine* tinker, tamper, interfere; *inf.* monkey around.

fidelity noun **1** *his fidelity to his country* faithfulness, loyalty, devotedness, devotion, allegiance, commitment, constancy, true-heartedness, trustworthiness, dependability, reliability, staunchness, obedience. **2** *the fidelity of the copy* accuracy, exactness, exactitude, precision, preciseness, strictness, closeness, faithfulness, correspondence, conformity, authenticity.

fidget verb wriggle, squirm, twitch, jiggle; *inf.* have ants in one's pants.

fidgety adjective restless, restive, on edge, jumpy, uneasy, nervous, twitchy; *inf.* jittery, like a cat on a hot tin roof.

field noun **1** *cows in the field* pasture, meadow; grassland; *lit.* lea, greensward. **2** *the field of electronics* area, sphere, regime, discipline, province, department, line, specialty, métier. **3** *field of vision* range, scope, purview; limits, confines. **4** *the field for the race is high quality* applicants, candidates, entrants, competitors; competition.

fiend noun **1** *fiends of hell* devil, demon, evil spirit. **2** *the slave driver was a fiend* brute, savage, beast, barbarian, monster, ogre, sadist. **3** *a drug fiend* addict, abuser, user.

fiendish adjective **1** *a fiendish stepfather* wicked, cruel, brutal, brutish, savage, barbaric, ferocious, ruthless, heartless, pitiless, merciless, black-hearted, unfeeling, malevolent, malicious, devilish, diabolical, hellish, demonic, satanic. **2** *a fiendish* *problem* difficult, complex, complicated, intricate.

fierce adjective **1** *a fierce animal/enemy* ferocious, savage, wild, vicious, feral, untamed, bloodthirsty, dangerous, cruel, brutal, murderous, slaughterous, menacing, threatening, terrible, grim. **2** *a fierce love* intense, ardent, passionate, impassioned, fervent, fervid, uncontrolled, violent, strong, tempestuous, raging, furious. **3** *suffer from fierce headaches* severe, intense, grave, awful, dreadful. **4** *fierce competition* keen, intense, strong, relentless.

fight verb **1** *the armies fought* battle, do battle, war, wage war, take up arms, combat, engage, clash, skirmish, struggle, contend, grapple, wrestle, scuffle, tussle, collide, spar, joust, tilt. **2** *the two men fought* come to blows, exchange blows, attack/assault each other, hit/punch each other, box, brawl; *inf.* scrap. **3** *the two families have been fighting for years* feud, quarrel, argue, bicker, squabble, wrangle, dispute, be at odds, disagree, battle, altercate; *inf.* fall out. **4** *fight the council's decision* contest, take a stand against, oppose, dispute, object to, withstand, resist, defy, strive/struggle against, take issue with. **fight back 1** *children told to fight back* defend oneself, retaliate, counterattack, give tit for tat. **2** *fight back tears* suppress, repress, check, curb, restrain, contain, bottle up. **fight off** ward off, beat off, stave off, repel, repulse, hold at bay.

fight noun **1** *the army lost the last fight* battle, engagement, action, clash, conflict, combat, contest, encounter, skirmish, scuffle, tussle. **2** *a fight outside the bar* brawl, affray, fracas, melee, sparring match, free-for-all, disturbance; *inf.* set-to, scrap. **3** *the two families had a fight* quarrel, disagreement, difference of opinion, dispute, argument, altercation, feud. **4** *lose all the fight in him* spirit, will to win, gameness, pluck, aggression, belligerence, militancy, resistance.

figurative adjective nonliteral, metaphorical, allegorical, representative, emblematic, symbolic.

figure noun **1** *add up a column of figures* number, whole number, numeral, digit, integer, cipher. **2** *put a figure on the work involved* cost, price, amount, value, total, sum, aggregate. **3** *figures unrecognizable in the mist* shape, form, outline, silhouette. **4** *a well-developed figure* body, physique, build, frame, torso; proportions; *inf.* vital statistics. **5** *see figure 20* diagram, illustration, picture, drawing, sketch, chart, plan, map. **6** *the lily is a figure of purity* symbol, emblem, sign, representative. **7** *the figures on the wood* pattern, design, motif, device, depiction. **8** *a noted histori-*

cal figure dignitary, notable, personage, somebody, worthy, celebrity, leader, force, personality, presence, character; *inf.* big shot, bigwig.

figure verb **1** *figure a total* calculate, work out, compute, tally, reckon. **2** *she figures in his autobiography* appear, be featured/mentioned, play a part/role. **3** *we figure that they'll go* think, consider, conclude. **figure out 1** *figure out the cost* work out, calculate, compute, reckon, assess. **2** *figure out why they came* understand, comprehend, fathom, decipher, resolve; *inf.* make heads or tails of.

file[1] noun **1** *put documents/data in a file* folder, box, portfolio, document case, filing cabinet. **2** *get out your file* dossier, folder, information; documents, records, data, particulars, case notes. **3** *a file of people* line, column, row, string, chain, queue.

file[2] verb **1** *file the information* categorize, classify, organize, put in place, put in order, pigeon-hole, record, enter, store. **2** *file for divorce* apply, put in, register, sign up. **3** *people filing in* march, parade, troop.

file[3] verb *file one's nails* smooth, shape, buff, rub, rub down, polish, burnish, furbish, refine, scrape, abrade, rasp, sandpaper, pumice.

fill verb **1** *people filled the room* occupy all of, crowd, overcrowd, congest, cram, pervade. **2** *fill the shelves* stock, pack, load, supply, furnish, provide, replenish, restock, refill. **3** *fill the children* feed fully, satisfy, stuff, cram, satiate, sate, surfeit, glut. **4** *perfume/hostility filled the air* pervade, permeate, suffuse, imbue, charge, saturate. **5** *fill the hole* stop, stop up, block up, plug (up), seal, close, clog. **6** *he filled the post of manager* occupy, hold, take up. **fill in 1** *fill in for the manager* substitute, stand in, take over. **2** *fill me in on the events* inform, advise, tell, notify, acquaint, apprise, update; *inf.* put wise, bring up to speed.

film noun **1** *a film of dust* layer, coat, coating, covering, cover, dusting, sheet, blanket, skin, tissue, membrane. **2** *see the mountain through a film* haze, mist, cloud, blur, veil; murkiness. **3** *see a recent film* movie, motion picture, picture; *inf.* video, flick.

film verb **1** *film the wedding* photograph, shoot, videotape. **2** *her eyes filmed (over)* blur, cloud over, mist over, dull, blear.

filmy adjective diaphanous, transparent, see-through, translucent, sheer, gauzelike, gauzy, gossamer, cobwebby, delicate, fine, light, thin, airy, fragile, flimsy, unsubstantial.

filter noun strainer, purifier, cleaner, gauze, netting, cheesecloth.

filter verb 1 *filter the liquid* strain, sieve, sift, filtrate; clarify, purify, clear, refine. 2 *light filtering through* trickle, ooze, seep, leak, dribble, percolate, drain, escape, leach.

filth noun 1 *the floors covered in filth* dirt, muck, grime, mud, mire, sludge, slime, squalor, excrement, dung, manure, sewage, rubbish, refuse, garbage, trash; filthiness, uncleanness, foulness, nastiness; *inf.* crud. 2 *objecting to filth in magazines* pornography, obscenity, indecency, smut; *inf.* porn, hard porn, raunchiness.

filthy adjective 1 *filthy water* dirty, mucky, muddy, murky, slimy, squalid, unclean, foul, nasty, feculent, polluted, contaminated, rotten, decaying, smelly, fetid, putrid. 2 *filthy clothes* unwashed, dirty, dirt-encrusted, grubby, muddy, mucky, black, blackened. 3 *a filthy liar* low-down, despicable, contemptible, base, mean, vile, nasty, sordid. 4 *filthy magazines* pornographic, obscene, indecent, smutty, coarse, bawdy, vulgar, lewd, licentious, dirty, impure; *inf.* blue, raunchy.

final adjective 1 *the final act* last, closing, concluding, finishing, end, ending, terminating, terminal, ultimate, eventual, endmost. 2 *their decision is final* absolute, conclusive, irrevocable, unalterable, irrefutable, incontrovertible, indisputable, unappealable, decisive, definitive, definite, settled.

finale noun end, finish, close, conclusion, climax, culmination, denouement, last act, final scene, final curtain, epilogue; *inf.* wind-up.

finality noun conclusiveness, decisiveness, definiteness, definitiveness, completeness, absoluteness, irrevocableness.

finalize verb complete, conclude, settle, tie up, wrap up, put the finishing touches to; *inf.* sew up, clinch.

finally adverb at last, at long last, ultimately, eventually, at the last minute, in the long run, when all was said and done.

finance noun 1 *she works in finance* money management, commerce, business, investment, banking, accounting. 2 *finances are low* funds, assets, resources, money, capital, cash, wealth, wherewithal, revenue, stock.

finance verb pay for, fund, back, subsidize, underwrite, capitalize.

financial adjective money, monetary, pecuniary, fiscal, economic, budgetary.

find verb 1 *find a gold watch* come across, chance upon, light upon, happen upon, stumble on. 2 *find a cure/answer/hotel* discover, come up with, hit upon, turn up,

bring to light, uncover, unearth, ferret out, locate. 3 *find the missing glove* recover, retrieve, regain, repossess, recoup. 4 *find happiness* get, obtain, acquire, procure, gain, earn, achieve, attain, win. 5 *find it pays to be honest* discover, become aware, realize, learn, conclude, detect, observe, notice, note, perceive. 6 *find the cheese too strong* consider, regard as, think, judge, deem, gauge, rate. 7 *the arrow found its mark* reach, attain, arrive at, gain, achieve. **find out** 1 *we found out they were lying* realize, learn. *See* FIND verb 5. 2 *find out the truth* discover, detect, bring to light, reveal, expose, unearth, disclose, unmask, ferret out, lay bare.

find noun asset, acquisition, lucky discovery, catch, bargain, good buy, godsend, boon, windfall.

finding noun decision, verdict, conclusion, pronouncement, judgment, decree, order, recommendation.

fine adjective 1 *that's fine with me* all right, satisfactory, acceptable, agreeable, convenient, suitable, good; *inf.* OK. 2 *a fine painting/wine* excellent, first-class, first-rate, great, exceptional, outstanding, admirable, quality, superior, splendid, magnificent, beautiful, exquisite, choice, select, prime, supreme, rare; *inf.* A-1, splendiferous, top-notch. 3 *fine china/bones* fragile, delicate, frail, dainty, slight, sheer, light, thin, flimsy. 4 *a fine sand/powder* fine-grained, powdery, powdered, ground, crushed, pulverized. 5 *a fine distinction* subtle, fine-drawn, tenuous, hairsplitting, precise, minute, elusive, abstruse. 6 *a fine taste in art* discriminating, discerning, tasteful, fastidious, critical, sensitive, refined, intelligent. 7 *a fine mind* keen, acute, sharp, quick, clever.

finesse noun tact, discretion, diplomacy, delicacy, refinement, grace, elegance, sophistication, subtlety, polish, *savoir faire*, skill, expertise, craft; tactfulness, adroitness, adeptness, skillfulness, cleverness, artfulness.

finicky adjective fussy, overparticular, fastidious, persnickety, hard to please, overcritical, difficult; *inf.* picky, choosy.

finish verb 1 *finish the task* complete, accomplish, execute, discharge, carry out, do, get done, fulfill, achieve, attain, end, conclude, close, finalize; *inf.* wind up, wrap up, sew up, polish off, knock off. 2 *finish working* stop, cease, discontinue, give up, have done with, suspend. 3 *finish up/off the supply* use, use up, consume, exhaust, empty, deplete, drain, expend, dispatch, dispose of. 4 *the job finished her* \ *finish off the enemy* overcome, defeat, overpower, conquer, overwhelm, get the better of, best, worst, rout, bring down, annihilate, kill, exterminate; *inf.* wipe out, do in. **5** *finish the surface of the table* varnish, lacquer, stain, coat, veneer, wax, gild, glaze.

finish noun **1** *at the finish of the task/race* completion, accomplishment, execution, fulfillment, achievement, consummation, end, conclusion, close, closing, cessation, finale, denouement; last stages; *inf.* winding up. **2** *the finish of the enemy* defeat, overpowering, destruction, rout, end, annihilation, ruination; *inf.* ruin, curtains. **3** *a table with a beautiful finish* surface, texture, grain, veneer, coating, lacquer, glaze, luster, gloss, polish, shine, patina.

finished adjective **1** *finished tasks* completed, accomplished, executed, over and done with, over, in the past; *inf.* wrapped up, sewn up. **2** *the finished carton of milk* empty, drained, used up, exhausted, spent. **3** *a finished performance* accomplished, expert, proficient, masterly, polished, impeccable, consummate, flawless, skillful, elegant, graceful. **4** *the business was finished* over with, doomed, lost, ruined, bankrupt, wrecked; *inf.* washed up.

finite adjective bounded, limited, restricted, delimited, demarcated, terminable.

fire noun **1** *killed in a fire* blaze, conflagration, inferno, holocaust; flames. **2** *enemy fire* gunfire, sniping, flak, bombardment, shelling; volley, barrage, fusillade, salvo. **3** *people of fire* energy, spirit, life, liveliness, animation, vigor, verve, vivacity, sparkle, scintillation, dash, vim, gusto, élan, enthusiasm, fervor, force, potency, vehemence, ardor, passion, intensity, zeal; *inf.* pep. **4** *writings with fire* passion, ardor, intensity, inspiration, imagination, creativity, inventiveness, flair. **on fire 1** *houses on fire* burning, ablaze, blazing, aflame, in flames, flaming, alight, fiery. **2** *on fire with passion* passionate, ardent, fervent, intense, excited, eager, enthusiastic.

fire verb **1** *fire the haystacks* set fire to, set on fire, set ablaze, put a match to, light, ignite, kindle. **2** *fire the guns* shoot, let off, discharge, trigger, set off. **3** *fire a missile* launch, hurl, discharge, eject. **4** *fire the explosives* explode, detonate, touch off. **5** *fired with enthusiasm* arouse, rouse, stir up, excite, enliven, inflame, animate, inspire, motivate, stimulate, incite, galvanize, electrify, impassion. **6** *fire the assistant* dismiss, discharge, give someone his/her marching orders, get rid of, show someone the door, oust, depose, cashier; *inf.* sack, ax.

fireworks plural noun *there were fireworks when she heard the news* tantrums, hysterics, paroxysms, pyrotechnics; outburst, fit, frenzy, uproar.

firm adjective **1** *a firm surface* hard, hardened, stiff, rigid, inflexible, inelastic, unyielding, resistant, solid. **2** *the poles were firm in the ground* fixed, fast, secure, secured, stable, set, established, tight, immovable, anchored, rooted, embedded, riveted, braced, cemented, nailed, tied. **3** *firm plans* fixed, settled, decided, definite, established, unalterable, unchangeable. **4** *a firm handshake* strong, vigorous, sturdy. **5** *a firm friendship* constant, unchanging, enduring, abiding, durable, deep-rooted, long-standing, long-lasting, steady, stable, staunch. **6** *firm about not going* resolute, determined, decided, resolved, unfaltering, unwavering, unflinching, unswerving, unyielding, unbending, inflexible, obdurate, obstinate, stubborn, intransigent, unmalleable.

firm noun company, business, concern, house, establishment, organization, corporation, conglomerate, partnership, cooperative; *inf.* outfit.

firmament noun sky, heaven, the blue, vault of heaven; heavens, skies.

firmness noun **1** *the firmness of the surface* hardness, stiffness, rigidity, inflexibility, inelasticity, resistance, solidity. **2** *the firmness of the handshake* strength, vigor, sturdiness. **3** *the firmness of the friendship* constancy, endurance, durability, steadiness, stability, staunchness. **4** *the firmness of the refusal/teacher* resolution, determination, resolve, obduracy, inflexibility, stubbornness, strictness, intransigence.

first adjective **1** *the first stages of life* earliest, initial, opening, introductory, original, premier, primitive, primeval, primordial, pristine. **2** *first principles* basic, fundamental, key, rudimentary, cardinal. **3** *the first people in the land* leading, foremost, principal, highest, ruling, chief, head, main, major, greatest, preeminent, supreme.

first-rate adjective first-class, second to none, top, premier, superlative, prime, excellent, superb, outstanding, exceptional, tip-top, admirable; *inf.* top-notch, ace, A-1, crack.

fishy adjective *something fishy about it* questionable, dubious, doubtful, suspect, suspicious, odd, queer, peculiar, strange, not quite right; *inf.* funny, shady, not kosher.

fissure noun crack, crevice, cleft, groove, slit, gash, fracture, fault, rift, split, rent.

fit adjective **1** *feeling fit* well, healthy, in good shape, strong, robust, hale and hearty, sturdy, hardy, stalwart, vigorous. **2** *fit to drive* able, capable, competent, adequate, good enough, satisfactory, ready, prepared, qualified, trained, equipped. **3** *a fit occasion* | *fit behavior* fitting, proper, due, seemly, decorous, decent, right, correct, apt, appropriate, suitable, convenient, apposite, relevant, pertinent.

fit verb 1 *facts fitting our theory* agree with, concur with, correspond with, match, dovetail with, tally with, suit, go with. 2 *fit the parts together* join, connect, put together. 3 *fit the carpet* position, lay, fix, insert, arrange, adjust, shape. 4 *the training will fit him for many jobs* make suitable, qualify, prepare, make ready, prime, condition, train. 5 *fit the kitchen with units* fit out, equip, provide, supply, furnish.

fit noun 1 *an epileptic fit* convulsion, spasm, paroxysm, seizure, attack. 2 *a fit of coughing* attack, bout, spell, burst, outburst, outbreak. 3 *she'll have a fit* tantrum, outburst of anger/rage. **by fits and starts** on and off, spasmodically, intermittently, sporadically, erratically, fitfully.

fitful adjective broken, disturbed, irregular, uneven, intermittent, sporadic, spasmodic.

fitness noun 1 *improve your fitness* physical fitness, condition, shape, strength, robustness, sturdiness, vigor. 2 *his fitness to drive* ability, capability, competency, preparedness, qualification, eligibility, worthiness. 3 *the fitness of the occasion* properness, propriety, seemliness, correctness, aptness, suitability, convenience, relevance, pertinence.

fitting adjective proper, due. See FIT adjective 3.

fix verb 1 *fix the shelf to the wall* fasten, secure, make fast, attach, connect, join, couple; stick, glue, cement, pin, nail, screw, bolt, clamp, bind, tie, pinion. 2 *fix the post in the ground* plant, implant, install, anchor, embed. 3 *fix a date/price* decide on, settle, set, agree on, arrange, determine, establish, name. 4 *fix the car* repair, mend, patch up, put right, put to rights, restore, remedy, rectify, adjust. 5 *fix her gaze on them* direct, focus, level at, rivet. 6 *fix something to eat* prepare, make, make ready, put together, cook. 7 *I'll fix him for that* get even with, wreak vengeance on, take retribution on, punish; *inf.* get back at, pay someone back. 8 *fix the outcome of the race* rig, manipulate, maneuver, arrange fraudulently; *inf.* fiddle with. **fix up** *fix you up with a bed* provide, supply, furnish, accommodate.

fix noun *in a bit of a fix* predicament, plight, quandary, dilemma, difficulty, muddle, mess, corner, ticklish/tricky situation, tight spot; *inf.* pickle, jam, hole, spot, scrape, bind.

fixation noun obsession, preoccupation, complex, compulsion, mania, *idée fixe*, phobia; *inf.* hang-up, thing.

fizz verb bubble, effervesce, sparkle, froth, foam; hiss, sputter, fizzle, sibilate.

fizzle verb **fizzle out** peter out, come to nothing, fall through, come to grief, end in failure, fail, miscarry, abort, collapse; *inf.* flop, fold.

flabbergast verb astound, amaze, dumbfound, strike dumb, render speechless, stun, stagger, confound, daze, overcome, overwhelm, nonplus, disconcert; *inf.* bowl over.

flabby adjective flaccid, unfirm, out of tone, drooping, pendulous, limp; *inf.* out of shape.

flaccid adjective unfirm, limp. See FLABBY.

flag noun standard, ensign, banner, pennant, burgee, streamer, bunting; colors.

flagrant adjective glaring, obvious, blatant, egregious, outrageous, scandalous, shocking, disgraceful, shameless; notorious, heinous, atrocious, monstrous, wicked, iniquitous, villainous.

flair noun 1 *a flair for languages* ability, aptitude, capability, facility, skill, talent, gift, knack, bent, feel, genius. 2 *all the women had flair* style, panache, elegance, dash, élan, taste.

flake verb chip, peel, peel off, scale off, blister, exfoliate.

flamboyant adjective 1 *flamboyant gestures* extravagant, theatrical, showy, ostentatious, dashing, swashbuckling. 2 *flamboyant clothes/colors* colorful, bright, exciting, dazzling, glamorous, splendid, resplendent, showy, gaudy, flashy.

flame noun 1 *flames burst from the ashes* fire, blaze, conflagration. 2 *burn with a flame* brilliant light, brightness, glow, gleam. 3 *the flame of love* passion, warmth, ardor, fervor, fire, excitement, enthusiasm. 4 *an old flame* boyfriend, girlfriend, sweetheart, lover, partner, beloved, beau.

flame verb 1 *the wood flamed* burn, blaze, burst into flame, catch fire. 2 *the light flamed* glow, shine, flash, beam, glare, sparkle.

flaming adjective 1 *a flaming bonfire* blazing, ablaze, burning, on fire, afire, in flames, aflame, ignited, fiery, red-hot, raging, glowing. 2 *flaming colors* bright, brilliant, vivid, flamboyant, red, reddish-orange, scarlet. 3 *a flaming idiot* utter, absolute.

flap verb flutter, sway, wave, agitate, vibrate, wag, waggle, shake, swing, oscillate, flail.

flare verb 1 *the fire flared* blaze up, flame, burn unsteadily. 2 *lights flared on the shore* flash, gleam, glow, sparkle, glitter, flicker. 3 *his nostrils flared* broaden, widen, splay. **flare up** 1 *trouble/disease flared up* broke out, burst out, recur. 2 *the two women flared up* lose one's temper, lose control, explode, boil over; *inf.* blow one's top, fly off the handle, lose one's cool.

flash verb **1** *lights flashed* light up, shine out, flare, blaze, glare, beam, gleam, glint, sparkle, flicker, shimmer, twinkle, glimmer, glisten, scintillate, coruscate. **2** *the runners flashed past* dart, dash, tear, shoot, zoom, streak, fly, rush, bolt, race, bound, speed; *inf.* scoot. **3** *flash her new ring* show off, flaunt, flourish, display, exhibit.

flash noun **1** *a flash of light* blaze, burst, glare, flare, shaft, ray, streak, gleam, glint, sparkle, flicker, shimmer, twinkle, glimmer. **2** *he came in a flash* instant, moment, second, split second, minute, trice, twinkling, twinkling of an eye, two shakes of a lamb's tail; *inf.* jiffy, bat of an eye. **3** *a flash of enthusiasm/wit* outburst, burst, outbreak.

flashy adjective ostentatious, showy, tasteless, pretentious, cheap, tawdry, garish, loud, flamboyant, gaudy; *inf.* tacky, snazzy, jazzy, glitzy, ritzy.

flat adjective **1** *a flat surface* level, horizontal, leveled, even, smooth, unbroken, plane. **2** *lying flat on the ground* stretched out, spread-eagle, prone, supine, prostrate, recumbent. **3** *a flat tire* deflated, collapsed, blown out, burst, punctured, ruptured. **4** *a flat denial* outright, direct, out-and-out, explicit, absolute, definite, positive, utter, categorical, unqualified, unconditional, unquestionable, unequivocal. **5** *a flat voice \ flat jokes* monotonous, boring, dull, tedious, uninteresting, lifeless, lackluster, dead, vapid, bland, insipid, prosaic. **6** *the market is flat* slow, inactive, sluggish, slack.

flat adverb **flat out 1** *asked flat out for a raise* directly, bluntly, openly; *inf.* without batting an eye. **2** *the boat passed us flat out* at full speed, at full tilt, full steam ahead; *inf.* hell-bent for leather.

flatten verb **1** *flatten the surface* make flat, level, level out/off, make even, even out, smooth, smooth out/off, plane; compress, press down, crush, squash, compact. **2** *flatten the old buildings* demolish, tear down, raze, raze to the ground. **3** *flatten his opponent* knock down, knock to the ground, floor, knock off one's feet, fell, prostrate; crush, quash, squash, deflate, snub, humiliate; *inf.* put down.

flatter verb **1** *salesmen flattering the customers* compliment, praise, sing the praises of, praise to excess, praise to the skies, eulogize, puff up, blandish, fawn upon, cajole, humor; *inf.* sweet-talk, soft-soap, butter up, lay it on thick to/for, play up to. **2** *that dress flatters her coloring* suit, become, set off, show to advantage, enhance; *inf.* do something for.

flattery noun praise, adulation, false praise, eulogy, puffery, fawning, cajolery; compliments, blandishments; *inf.* sweet talk, soft soap, buttering-up.

flaunt verb show off, parade, exhibit, draw attention to, make a show of, wave, brandish.

flavor noun **1** *dislike the flavor of the herb* taste, savor, tang, relish. **2** *add some flavor to the sauce* flavoring, seasoning, tastiness, piquancy, spiciness, zest; *inf.* zing. **3** *capture the flavor of the place* spirit, essence, soul, nature, character, quality, feel, ambience, tone, style, stamp.

flavor verb season, spice, lace, imbue, infuse.

flaw noun fault, defect, imperfection, blemish, failing, foible, shortcoming, weakness, weak spot; crack, fracture, fissure, tear.

flawless adjective faultless, perfect, impeccable, blemish-free, unimpaired, unmarred, undamaged.

fleck noun spot, mark, speck, speckle, freckle.

flee verb **1** *she fled from the blaze* run, run away, run off, bolt, take flight, make off, fly, abscond, retreat, beat a retreat, beat a hasty retreat, make a quick exit, run for it, make a run for it, take off, take to one's heels, decamp, escape, make one's escape/getaway, do a disappearing act, vanish; *inf.* cut and run, make oneself scarce, beat it, skedaddle, split, scram. **2** *they fled the country* run away from, escape from; *inf.* skip.

fleece verb **1** *fleece the sheep* shear, clip. **2** *a con man fleeced the elderly woman* swindle, defraud, cheat, rob, strip, bilk, overcharge; *inf.* con, take for a ride, rip off, sting, bleed, take to the cleaners, soak.

fleet noun flotilla, naval force, navy, convoy, squadron, armada, argosy.

fleet adjective swift, fast, rapid, quick, speedy, expeditious, nimble, fleet of foot, nimble-footed, swift-footed, like the wind.

fleeting adjective brief, short-lived, momentary, transient, transitory, ephemeral, evanescent, fugacious, vanishing, flying, passing.

flesh noun **1** *flesh and bones* muscle, tissue, brawn. **2** *carry too much flesh* fat; fatness, obesity, corpulence. **3** *not much flesh in the essay* substance, pith, matter, body. **4** *the pleasure of the flesh* body, physical nature, physicality, corporeality, carnality, animality, sensuality, sensualism. **5** *all flesh would perish in such conditions* mankind, man, humankind, people, humanity, *Homo sapiens*; animate life, the living; human beings, living creatures. **flesh and blood** family, kin, kinfolk, relatives, relations. **in the flesh** in person, before one's eyes.

flexible adjective **1** *flexible materials* bendable, pliant, pliable, elastic, springy, plastic, moldable. **2** *my arrangements are flexible* adaptable, adjustable, open, open to change, changeable, variable. **3** *the young man is too flexible* tractable, malleable, compliant, manageable, docile, submissive.

flicker verb **1** *lights flickering* twinkle, sparkle, blink, flash, shimmer, glitter, glimmer, glint, flare. **2** *with eyelids flickering* flutter, quiver, vibrate, bat.

flight noun *the flight of the beaten army* retreat, departure, exit, exodus, decamping, escape, getaway, disappearance, vanishing. **put to flight** chase, chase off, drive off, scare off, rout, scatter, disperse, stampede. **take flight** run away, make off. See FLEE 1.

flighty adjective frivolous, giddy, scatterbrained, harebrained, fickle, changeable, inconstant, unsteady, whimsical, capricious, skittish.

flimsy adjective **1** *a flimsy box* insubstantial, slight, makeshift, jerry-built, gimcrack, rickety, ramshackle, shaky, fragile, frail. **2** *made of a flimsy material* thin, light, lightweight, delicate, sheer, filmy, diaphanous, gossamer, gauzy. **3** *a flimsy excuse* feeble, weak, poor, inadequate, unconvincing, implausible, unsatisfactory, paltry, trifling, trivial, shallow.

flinch verb draw back, pull back, recoil, withdraw, shrink back, shy away, cringe, cower, crouch, quail, wince, blench. **flinch from** *flinch from his duty* dodge, avoid, duck, balk at.

fling verb throw, toss, hurl, cast, pitch, sling, heave, fire, shy, launch, propel, catapult, send flying; *inf.* lob, chuck.

fling noun **1** *with one fling of the javelin* throw, toss, hurl, cast, pitch, shot, heave; *inf.* lob, chuck. **2** *a last fling before marriage* binge, spree, good time, bit of fun, night on the town. **3** *have a fling at winning the match* try, attempt, go, shot, stab, venture; *inf.* crack, whirl.

flip verb **1** *flip a coin* flick, toss, throw, pitch, cast, spin, twist. **2** *flip a switch* flick, click, tap. **flip through** skim (through), flick through, glance over/through, browse through, thumb through, skip over.

flippant adjective frivolous, glib, thoughtless, offhand, disrespectful, impertinent, impudent, irreverent, saucy; *inf.* flip.

flirt verb **flirt with** *she's always flirting with the boys* toy with, trifle with, make eyes at, ogle, lead on; philander with, dally with. **2** *flirt with the idea of going* play with, entertain, consider, give thought to, dabble in.

flirt noun coquette, tease, vamp, heartbreaker, trifler, philanderer.

flirtatious adjective coquettish, provocative, teasing, amorous, philandering, dallying.

float verb **1** *craft floating along* bob, glide, sail, drift. **2** *not working, just floating about* drift, wander, meander; *inf.* bum (around).

flock noun **1** *a flock of sheep* fold, drove, herd. **2** *a flock of birds/geese* flight, bevy, skein, gaggle. **3** *a flock of people* crowd, gathering, assembly, company, collection, congregation, group, throng, mass, host, multitude, troop, herd, convoy.

flood noun **1** *houses damaged in the flood* deluge, inundation, torrent, spate, overflow, flash flood. **2** *a flood of mail* profusion, overabundance, superabundance, plethora, superfluity, glut; *inf.* tons, heaps.

flood verb **1** *rivers flooding/flood the town* overflow, break the banks, brim over, swell, surge, inundate, deluge, immerse, submerge, swamp, drown, engulf. **2** *flood the market with fruit* overfill, oversupply, saturate, glut, overwhelm.

flop verb **1** *flop into a chair* collapse, slump, drop, fall, tumble. **2** *the dog's ears flopped* dangle, droop, sag. **3** *the play flopped* fail, fall flat, founder, close, go over like a lead balloon; *inf.* bomb.

flop noun *the play was a flop* failure, fiasco, loser, disaster, debacle; *inf.* no-go, washout, dud, lemon, bomb, bust.

florid adjective **1** *a florid complexion* ruddy, red-faced, red, reddish, flushed, blushing, rubicund. **2** *florid decorations* ornate, flamboyant, overelaborate, embellished, busy, baroque. See FLOWERY 2.

flounder verb thrash, struggle, stumble, blunder, fumble, grope, falter, muddle, bungle.

flourish verb **1** *flourish the sword/prize* brandish, wave, twirl, wield, swing, hold aloft, display, exhibit, flaunt, parade, vaunt; *inf.* show off. **2** *the plants are flourishing* thrive, burgeon, bloom, blossom, bear fruit, burst forth. **3** *we are all flourishing* be well, be in good health, get on well, prosper, succeed; *inf.* be in the pink, be fine and dandy, go great guns.

flout verb defy, scorn, disdain, show contempt for, spurn, scoff at, mock, laugh at, deride, ridicule.

flow verb **1** *blood/rivers flowing* course, run, circulate, glide, stream, ripple, swirl, surge, sweep, roll, rush, whirl, drift, slide, trickle, gurgle, babble. **2** *blood flowing from the wound* gush, stream, well, spurt, spout, squirt, spew, jet, spill, leak, seep, ooze, drip. **3** *ideas flowing from her pen* arise, issue, spring, originate, derive, emanate, emerge, pour, proceed. **flow with** overflow with, be abundant in, abound in, teem with, be rich in, be full of.

flow noun 1 *the flow of the water* course, current, drift, stream, spate, tide. 2 *stem the flow of blood* gush, stream, welling, spurting, spouting, outflow. 3 *a flow of complaints* flood, deluge, outpouring, abundance, plethora, excess, effusion, succession, train.

flower noun 1 *pick/plant several flowers* bloom, blossom, floweret, floret; annual, perennial. 2 *in the flower of their youth* prime, peak, zenith, acme, height, heyday, springtime; salad days. 3 *the flower of the nation died in battle* finest, best, pick, choice, elite, cream, crème de la crème

flowery adjective 1 *flowery patterns* floral, flower-covered, flower-patterned. 2 *flowery language* high-flown, ornate, fancy, elaborate, overelaborate, grandiloquent, purple, bombastic.

fluctuate verb 1 *prices fluctuating* seesaw, yo-yo, vary, shift, change, alter, swing, oscillate, undulate, ebb and flow. 2 *she fluctuates between going and not going* waver, vacillate, shilly-shally, hem and haw, teeter, blow hot and cold.

fluent adjective 1 *a fluent speaker* articulate, eloquent, smooth-spoken, silver-tongued, voluble. 2 *fluent prose* smooth, flowing, fluid, graceful, effortless, natural, easy, elegant, mellifluous, euphonious.

fluffy adjective 1 *a fluffy blanket* soft, downy, cottony, puffy, airy, light. 2 *a fluffy movie* frivolous, superficial, meaningless, thin, insubstantial, nonintellectual.

fluid noun liquid, gas, solution.

fluid adjective 1 *a fluid substance moving along the pipe* gaseous, gassy, liquid, liquefied, melted, molten, uncongealed, running, flowing. 2 *a fluid prose style* smooth, graceful. See FLUENT 2. 3 *our plans are fluid* flexible, open to change, adaptable, adjustable, not fixed, not settled, variable, mutable. 4 *the situation is fluid* subject/likely to change, unstable, unsteady, ever-shifting, fluctuating, mobile, mercurial.

flurry noun 1 *a flurry of snow/rain* squall, gust, shower; burst, spurt, outbreak, spell, bout. 2 *the hostess in a flurry of excitement* fluster, fuss, bustle, whirl, stir, ferment, hubbub, commotion, hustle.

fluster verb ruffle, unsettle, upset, bother, put on edge, discompose, agitate, panic, perturb, disconcert, confuse, throw off balance, confound, nonplus; *inf.* rattle, faze, throw into a tizzy.

flutter verb 1 *a bird fluttering its wings* flap, beat, quiver, agitate, vibrate, ruffle. 2 *flags fluttering in the breeze* flap, wave, flop, ripple, quiver, shiver, tremble. 3 *with hearts fluttering* pulsate, palpitate.

fly verb 1 *birds flying overhead* flutter, flit, hover, soar, wing, wing its way, take wing, take to the air, mount. 2 *flags flying* flap, wave, flutter, toss. 3 *the runners flew by* race, dash, shoot, rush, tear, bolt, zoom, scoot, dart, speed, hasten, hurry, scamper, career, go like the wind. 4 *watched their beaten opponents fly* run, run away. See FLEE.

foam noun froth, bubbles, fizz, effervescence, head, spume, lather, suds.

foam verb froth, froth up, cream, bubble, fizz, effervesce, spume, lather.

foe noun enemy, opponent, adversary, rival, antagonist, combatant.

fog noun 1 *fog decreasing visibility* mist, mistiness, smog, murk, murkiness, haze; *inf.* pea soup. 2 *a mental fog* haze, daze, stupor, trance; bewilderment, confusion, perplexity, bafflement, vagueness, stupefaction, disorientation.

fog verb 1 *windshields fogging over/up* mist over, become misty, cloud over, steam up. 2 *alcohol fogging their minds* befuddle, becloud, bedim, bewilder, confuse, muddle, perplex, baffle, blind, darken, obscure, daze, stupefy, obfuscate.

foggy adjective 1 *a foggy day* misty, smoggy, dark, dim, gray, overcast, murky, hazy, gloomy; *inf.* soupy. 2 *a foggy recollection of the event* vague, indistinct, dim, hazy, shadowy, cloudy, clouded, dark, obscure, unclear, befuddled, confused, bewildered, muddled.

foible noun weakness, weak point, failing, shortcoming, flaw, blemish, defect, frailty, infirmity, quirk, idiosyncrasy.

foil verb thwart, frustrate, baffle, defeat, check, checkmate, circumvent, counter, impede, obstruct, hamper, hinder, cripple, nip in the bud.

fold noun overlap, layer, pleat, turn, gather, crease, dog-ear; wrinkle, pucker, furrow, crinkle.

fold verb 1 *fold the paper* double, double over, double up, crease, turn under, turn up, bend, overlap, tuck, gather, pleat, crimp, crumple, dog-ear. 2 *fold her in his arms* enfold, wrap, enclose, envelop, clasp, embrace, hug, squeeze. 3 *the firm folded* fail, collapse, go out of business, close, shut down, go bankrupt, crash; *inf.* go bust, go under, flop.

folklore noun legend, myth, mythology, lore, oral history, tradition, folk tradition; legends, fables, myths, old wives' tales.

follow verb 1 *children following after each other* go behind/after, come behind/after, walk behind, tread on the heels of. 2 *dogs following rabbits* chase, pursue, run after, trail, shadow, hunt, stalk, track, dog, hound, course; *inf.* tail. **3** *follow the rules* obey, observe, comply with, conform to, heed, pay attention to, note, have regard to, mind, be guided by, accept, yield to. **4** *the conclusion follows logically* result, arise, develop, ensue, emanate, issue, proceed, spring, flow. **5** *follow an argument* understand, comprehend, take in, grasp, fathom, get, catch on to, keep up with, see; *inf.* latch on to. **6** *he followed the style of Dickinson* copy, imitate, emulate; pattern oneself on, adopt the style of, style oneself on. **7** *he follows science fiction* be a fan/admirer/devotee of, cultivate an interest in, support, keep abreast of, keep up to date with. **follow through (on)** complete, bring to completion, bring to a finish. **follow up (on)** look into, check out, pursue.

follower *noun* **1** *the gang leader and his followers* companion, escort, attendant, henchman, minion, lackey, toady; servant, page, squire; *inf.* hanger-on, sidekick. **2** *Picasso and his followers* imitator, emulator, copier; *inf.* copycat. **3** *followers of Christ* apostle, disciple, adherent, supporter, believer, worshiper, votary, student, pupil. **4** *followers of the Yankees* supporter, enthusiast, fan, admirer, devotee; *inf.* groupie, camp follower, rooter.

following *noun* backing, clientele, public, audience, circle, coterie, retinue, train; supporters, backers, admirers, fans, adherents, devotees, advocates, patrons.

folly *noun* foolishness, absurdity, absurdness, stupidity, silliness, nonsense, senselessness, illogicality, inanity, madness, craziness, idiocy, imbecility, lunacy, ridiculousness, ludicrousness, fatuousness, fatuity, rashness, recklessness, imprudence, indiscretion, irrationality.

foment *verb* instigate, incite, provoke, agitate, excite, stir up, arouse, encourage, urge, actuate, initiate.

fond *adjective* **1** *a fond look* adoring, devoted, loving, affectionate, caring, warm, tender, amorous, doting, indulgent, overindulgent. **2** *fond hopes of success* deep, cherished, heartfelt. **fond of** partial to, keen on, attached to, enamored of, having a soft spot for, addicted to; *inf.* hooked on.

fondle *verb* caress, stroke, touch, pat, pet, cuddle, hug, nuzzle.

fondness *noun* **1** *look upon his brother with fondness* affection, love, warmth, tenderness, kindness, devotion, care, attachment. **2** *a fondness for chocolate* liking, love, taste, partiality, preference, weakness, soft spot, penchant, predilection, fancy, susceptibility.

food *noun* **1** *give food to the children* nourishment, sustenance, nutriment, subsistence, aliment, fare, diet, menu, table, bread, daily bread, board, provender, cooking, cuisine; foodstuffs, refreshments, edibles, meals, provisions, rations, stores, viands, victuals/vittles, commons, comestibles; solids; *inf.* eats, eatables, nosh, grub, chow. **2** *food for the cattle* fodder, feed, provender, forage.

fool *noun* **1** *don't try to explain—he's a fool* idiot, ass, nitwit, halfwit, numskull, nincompoop, ninny, blockhead, dunce, dunderhead, dolt, ignoramus, dullard, moron, simpleton, jackass, loon; *inf.* dope, clod, chump, bonehead, fathead, birdbrain, twit, twerp, nerd, airhead. **2** *make a fool of him* dupe, butt, laughingstock, pushover, easy mark; *inf.* stooge, sucker, sap, fall guy. **3** *the fools of Shakespeare's day* jester, clown, buffoon, comic, jokester, zany, merry andrew, harlequin.

fool *verb* **1** *they certainly fooled the teacher* deceive, trick, play a trick on, hoax, make a fool of, dupe, take in, mislead, hoodwink, bluff, delude, beguile, bamboozle, cozen, gull; *inf.* con, kid, put one over on. **2** *we thought he was sick but he was only fooling* pretend, make believe, feign, put on an act, act, fake, counterfeit; *inf.* kid. **fool around 1** *the boys are always fooling around* jest, joke, clown, caper, cavort. **2** *fool around with the controls* fiddle, play, toy, trifle, meddle, tamper, monkey. **3** *fool around with someone else's wife* have an affair, philander, flirt.

foolhardy *adjective* reckless, rash, daredevil, devil-may-care, impulsive, hotheaded, impetuous, madcap, heedless, precipitate, incautious, imprudent, irresponsible, injudicious, desperate.

foolish *adjective* **1** *a foolish plan/idea* silly, absurd, senseless, nonsensical, unintelligent, inane, pointless, fatuous, ridiculous, laughable, derisible, risible, imprudent, incautious, irresponsible, injudicious, indiscreet, unwise, unreasonable, ill-advised, ill-considered, impolitic; *inf.* damfool, crackbrained, nutty, for the birds. **2** *a foolish fellow* stupid, silly, idiotic, simple, unintelligent, halfwitted, brainless, doltish, dull, dull-witted, dense, ignorant, moronic, witless, weak-minded, mad, crazy; *inf.* dumb, dopey, daft, balmy, batty, dippy, cuckoo, screwy, wacky.

foolishness *noun* **1** *the foolishness of their actions* stupidity, silliness. *See* FOLLY. **2** *talk foolishness* nonsense, rubbish, bunkum, gobbledegook, humbug, balderdash, claptrap, hogwash, rigmarole; *inf.* rot, bunk, poppycock, piffle, hooey, garbage, crap.

foolproof *adjective* infallible, never-failing, unfailing, certain, sure, guaranteed, safe, dependable, trustworthy.

footing *noun* **1** *lose one's footing* foothold, grip, toehold, support. **2** *his business* *was on a secure footing* basis, foundation, groundwork, establishment. **3** *on a friendly footing* relationship, standing, state, condition, position, basis, foundation; relations, terms.

forage verb search, look around, hunt, rummage around, scour; *inf.* scrounge around.

forbear verb refrain from, abstain from, desist from, keep from, restrain oneself from, hold back from, cease, give up, leave off, break off.

forbearance noun tolerance, toleration, patience, resignation, endurance, longsuffering, self-control, restraint, leniency, clemency, indulgence.

forbid verb prohibit, ban, bar, debar, outlaw, veto, proscribe, disallow, interdict, preclude, exclude, rule out, stop.

forbidden adjective prohibited, out of bounds, banned, debarred, outlawed, vetoed, proscribed, interdicted, taboo, verboten.

forbidding adjective **1** *a forbidding manner* stern, harsh, grim, hard, tough, hostile, unfriendly, disagreeable, nasty, mean, abhorrent, repellent. **2** *a forbidding landscape* frightening, threatening, ominous, menacing, sinister, daunting, foreboding.

force noun **1** *requiring a lot of force* strength, power, potency, vigor, energy, might, muscle, stamina, effort, exertion, impact, pressure, life, vitality, stimulus, dynamism; *inf.* punch. **2** *use force to persuade them* compulsion, coercion, duress, pressure, constraint, enforcement, violence; *inf.* arm twisting. **3** *arguments with force* persuasiveness, cogency, validity, weight, effectiveness, efficacy, efficaciousness, influence, power, strength, vehemence, significance; *inf.* bite, punch. **4** *speaking with great force* vehemence, intensity, vigor, drive, fierceness, feeling, passion, vividness. **in force 1** *rules no longer in force* in operation, operative, valid, current, effective, binding. **2** *the fans were out in force* in full strength, in great numbers, in great quantities, in hordes.

force verb **1** *force them to go* compel, coerce, make, pressure, constrain, impel, drive, oblige; *inf.* put the squeeze/bite on, use strong-arm tactics on. **2** *force the door/safe* force open, break open, burst open, blast, prize open, crack. **3** *the wind forced them back* drive, propel, push, thrust, shove, press. **4** *force a confession* wrest, extract, wring, extort, drag.

forced adjective **1** *a forced march* enforced, compulsory, compelled, obligatory, mandatory, involuntary, unwilling. **2** *a forced laugh* strained, unnatural, artificial, feigned, affected, stilted, labored, wooden, self-conscious.

forceful adjective vigorous, powerful, potent, strong, weighty, dynamic, energetic, assertive, effective, cogent, telling, persuasive, convincing, compelling.

forebear noun forefather, ancestor, forerunner, progenitor, primogenitor, predecessor, father.

forebode verb augur, presage, portend, foreshadow, foreshow, foretoken, betoken, prefigure, signify, mean, indicate, point to, foretell, forecast, predict, prophesy, forewarn.

foreboding noun **1** *a foreboding that the car would crash* presentiment, premonition, intuition, sixth sense, feeling, vague feeling, misgiving, suspicion. **2** *the forebodings of the soothsayer* augury, prophecy, prediction, prognostication, forecast, warning, omen, portent.

forecast verb predict, foretell, foresee, prophesy, prognosticate, augur, divine, guess, conjecture, speculate, estimate, calculate.

forecast noun prediction, prophecy, prognostication, augury, guess, conjecture, speculation, prognosis, projection; *inf.* guesstimate.

forefather noun ancestor, forerunner. *See* FOREBEAR.

forefront noun front, fore, foreground, lead, head, van, vanguard, spearhead.

foregoing adjective preceding, precedent, prior, previous, former, above, aforesaid, aforementioned.

foreign adjective **1** *from foreign parts* overseas, alien, distant, remote. **2** *foreign objects* strange, unfamiliar, unknown, exotic, outlandish, odd, peculiar, curious. **3** *matters foreign to the discussion* irrelevant, not pertinent, unrelated, unconnected, inappropriate, extraneous.

foreigner noun nonnative, alien, immigrant, newcomer, stranger, outsider.

foreman noun overseer, supervisor, manager, superintendent; *inf.* boss.

foremost adjective leading, principal, premier, prime, top, first, primary, paramount, chief, main, supreme, highest, preeminent.

forerunner noun predecessor, precursor, ancestor, antecedent, forefather, herald, harbinger, usher, advance guard.

foresee verb anticipate, envisage, predict. *See* FORECAST verb.

foreshadow verb bode, presage. *See* FOREBODE.

foresight noun forethought, discernment, farsightedness, circumspection, prudence, judiciousness, perspicacity, precaution, readiness, preparedness, anticipation, prescience.

forest noun woods, wood, woodland, plantation; trees.

forestall verb preempt, intercept, anticipate, thwart, frustrate, stave off, ward off, fend off, avert, prevent, hinder, impede.

foretell verb 1 *she foretold his death* predict, foresee. *See* FORECAST verb. 2 *the first match foretold the final result* augur, presage. *See* FOREBODE.

forever adverb 1 *loving each other forever* always, evermore, for all time, till the end of time, till the cows come home, till hell freezes over, till doomsday, eternally, undyingly, perpetually, in perpetuity; *inf.* for keeps, for good. 2 *he's forever playing loud music* incessantly, continually, constantly, perpetually, endlessly, unremittingly, interminably, everlastingly.

forewarn verb prewarn, warn, give fair warning to, put on one's guard, tip off, put on the qui vive, alert, caution, advise, apprise, precaution.

foreword noun introduction, preface, preamble, preliminary/front matter, prologue.

forfeit verb relinquish, hand over, give up, surrender, renounce, be stripped/deprived of.

forge verb 1 *blacksmiths forging horseshoes | forge a treaty* hammer out, beat into shape, shape, form, fashion, mold, found, cast, make, manufacture, frame, construct, create. 2 *forge an excuse* invent, make up, devise, coin, fabricate. 3 *forge handwriting/checks* copy, imitate, fake, falsify, counterfeit.

forget verb 1 *forget her phone number* be unable to think of, let slip; *inf.* draw a blank on. 2 *it's best to forget unhappy times* put out of one's mind, disregard, ignore. 3 *I forgot my gloves* overlook, miss. **forget oneself** misbehave, behave improperly.

forgetful adjective 1 *growing forgetful* absentminded, amnesic, amnesiac, abstracted, vague. 2 *forgetful of one's duties* neglectful, negligent, heedless, careless, unmindful, inattentive, oblivious, lax, remiss, disregardful.

forgive verb pardon, excuse, exonerate, absolve, acquit, let off, let bygones be bygones, bear no malice, harbor no grudge, bury the hatchet; *inf.* let someone off the hook.

forgiveness noun pardon, amnesty, exoneration, absolution, acquittal, remission, absence of malice/grudges, mercy.

forgiving adjective lenient, merciful, compassionate, magnanimous, humane, clement, mild, softhearted, forbearing, tolerant, placable.

forgo, forego verb do/go without, waive, renounce, relinquish, sacrifice, surrender, abstain from, refrain from, eschew.

forgotten adjective unremembered, out of mind, beyond/past recall/recollection, consigned to oblivion, obliterated, blotted out, buried, left behind.

forlorn adjective 1 *looking forlorn* unhappy, sad, miserable, wretched, pathetic, woebegone, lonely, disconsolate, desolate, cheerless, pitiable. 2 *a forlorn farmhouse* abandoned, forsaken, deserted, forgotten, neglected. 3 *a forlorn attempt* hopeless, desperate.

form verb 1 *form shapes* make, fashion, shape, model, mold, forge, found, construct, build, assemble, put together, set up, erect, create, produce, concoct, devise. 2 *form plans* formulate, devise, think up, plan, draw up, frame, forge, hatch, develop, organize; *inf.* dream up. 3 *shapes began to form* take shape, materialize, appear, show up. 4 *form bad habits* acquire, develop, get, pick up, contract, grow into; *inf.* get into. 5 *form the children into lines* arrange, draw up, line up, assemble, organize, order, rank. 6 *these books form the complete series* make, make up, comprise, constitute, compose. 7 *forming young children's minds* develop, train, teach, instruct, educate, school, drill, discipline.

form noun 1 *observe the form of the crystals* shape, configuration, formation, conformation, structure, construction, arrangement, disposition, appearance, exterior. 2 *a well-built form* body, physique, figure, shape, build, frame, anatomy, silhouette, contour. 3 *help came to the farmers in the form of rain* shape, appearance, manifestation, semblance, guise, character. 4 *a form of punishment* type, kind, sort, variety, species, genus, genre, stamp. 5 *his literary work lacks form* structure, framework, format, organization, planning, order, orderliness, symmetry, proportion. 6 *put the mixture into a form* mold, cast, shape, matrix, pattern. 7 *not good form to yawn* manners; behavior, conduct, etiquette, convention, protocol. 8 *the ceremony has followed the same form for years* manner, method, mode, style, system, formula, set formula, procedure, convention, custom, ritual, protocol, etiquette; rules.

formal adjective 1 *formal documents/procedures* official, set, fixed, conventional, standard, regular, customary, prescribed, pro forma. 2 *a formal dinner* ceremonial, ceremonious, ritualistic, elaborate, ritual. 3 *a formal manner* reserved, aloof, remote, correct, proper, conventional, precise, exact, punctilious, stiff, unbending. 4 *a formal garden* symmetrical, regular, orderly, arranged, methodical.

formality noun **1** *dislike the formality of the occasion* conventionality, ceremoniousness, ritual, decorum, etiquette, protocol. **2** *obey the formalities* rule, convention, custom, procedure; form, punctilio.

formation noun **1** *planes flying in formation* configuration, format, structure, organization, order, arrangement, pattern, design, disposition, grouping, layout. **2** *the formation of the new buildings/government* construction, building, erecting, fashioning, shaping, setting up, establishment, institution, creation

former adjective **1** *the former ruler* ex-, previous, prior, preceding, precedent, foregoing, earlier, one-time, erstwhile, sometime. **2** *in former times* earlier, past, bygone, ancient, of yore.

formidable adjective **1** *a formidable appearance* intimidating, redoubtable, daunting, alarming, frightening, terrifying, dreadful, awesome, fearsome, menacing, dangerous. **2** *a formidable task* arduous, onerous, difficult, tough, challenging, overwhelming, staggering; *inf.* mind-boggling, mind-blowing. **3** *a formidable opponent* strong, powerful, mighty, impressive, redoubtable.

formula noun recipe, prescription, rubric, blueprint, method, procedure, convention, ritual, modus operandi; principles, rules, precepts.

formulate verb **1** *formulate one's thoughts in plain English* define, articulate, set down, frame, specify, particularize, itemize, detail, designate, systematize, indicate. **2** *formulate our plans* work out, map out, conceive, create, invent, originate, coin, design. *See* FORM *verb* 2.

forsake verb **1** *forsake his wife and children* desert, abandon, leave, leave in the lurch, quit, throw over, jilt, cast off, discard, repudiate, reject, disown; *inf.* leave flat, give someone the air. **2** *forsake her life of luxury* give up, renounce, relinquish, forgo, turn one's back on, repudiate, have done with, discard, set aside.

fort noun fortress, stronghold, citadel, garrison, castle, tower, keep, turret, fortification, redoubt, battlement.

forte noun strong point, strength, métier, specialty, talent, skill, gift, bent; *inf.* bag, thing.

forth adverb **1** *from that day forth* onward, forward. **2** *go forth from the tent* out, outside, away, off.

forthcoming adjective **1** *forthcoming events* future, coming, approaching, expected, prospective, imminent, impending. **2** *no reply was forthcoming* available, ready, at hand, accessible; *inf.* on tap. **3** *the children are not very forthcoming* communicative, talkative, expansive, voluble, chatty, conversational, loquacious, open, unreserved.

forthright adjective direct, frank, candid, blunt, outspoken, plain-speaking, plain-spoken, straightforward, open, honest.

forthwith adverb right away, immediately, at once, this instant, straightaway.

fortification noun **1** *the fortification of the walls* strengthening, reinforcement, bracing. **2** *soldiers manning the fortifications* battlement, rampart, bastion, bulwark, parapet, blockhouse, stronghold, stockade, outwork.

fortify verb **1** *fortify the town* garrison, embattle, guard, cover, protect, secure. **2** *fortify the walls* strengthen, reinforce, shore up, brace, buttress. **3** *fortify himself with a drink* invigorate, energize, revive, embolden, encourage, cheer, hearten, buoy up.

fortitude noun strength, firmness of purpose, backbone, grit, mettle, courage, nerve, pluck, bravery, fearlessness, valor, intrepidity, stoutheartedness, endurance, tenacity, perseverance, resoluteness.

fortress noun stronghold, citadel. *See* FORT.

fortuitous adjective chance, unexpected, unanticipated, unforeseen, serendipitous, random, accidental, unintentional, unplanned; lucky, fortunate, felicitous; *inf.* fluky.

fortunate adjective **1** *a fortunate person* lucky, in luck, favored, blessed, born under a lucky star, having a charmed life, prosperous, well-off, successful, flourishing; *inf.* sitting pretty. **2** *a fortunate position* advantageous, favorable, helpful, auspicious, propitious, opportune, felicitous, profitable.

fortune noun **1** *a merchant of great fortune* wealth, treasure, affluence, opulence, prosperity, substance, property; riches, assets, means, possessions, estates. **2** *the ring cost a fortune* mint, king's ransom; *inf.* packet, bundle, bomb, pile. **3** *by good fortune he won* chance, accident, coincidence, fortuity, serendipity, luck, providence. **4** *tell one's fortune* destiny, fate, lot, cup, portion, kismet; stars. **5** *fortune smiled on him* Lady Luck, Dame Fortune, fate.

fortune-teller noun seer, soothsayer, prophet, prophetess, augur, diviner, sibyl, oracle, clairvoyant, psychic, prognosticator; astrologer, palm reader, phrenologist; *inf.* stargazer.

forum noun meeting, assembly, symposium, round-table conference, debate, discussion place, discussion medium.

forward adjective **1** *a forward movement* onward, advancing, progressing, progressive. **2** *forward for her age* advanced, well-advanced, early, premature, precocious. **3** *a forward young woman* bold, brash, brazen, audacious, presumptuous, overassertive, overweening, aggressive, impudent; *inf.* pushy, cocky, fresh.

forward adverb **1** *move forward* frontward, onward, on, ahead, forth. **2** *step forward for the prize* out, forth, into view, into the open.

foster verb **1** *foster freedom of thought* encourage, promote, further, stimulate, boost, advance, forward, cultivate, foment, help, aid, assist, support, uphold, back, give backing to, facilitate. **2** *foster a child* bring up, rear, raise, care for, take care of, mother, parent. **3** *foster hopes of being rich* cherish, harbor, entertain, nurse, nourish, nurture, hold, sustain.

foul adjective **1** *that drink looks foul* disgusting, revolting, repulsive, nauseating, sickening, loathsome, abominable, odious, offensive, nasty. **2** *that cheese smells foul* evil-smelling, ill-smelling, stinking, fetid, rank, mephitic. **3** *foul water* contaminated, polluted, adulterated, infected, tainted, defiled, impure, filthy, dirty, unclean. **4** *foul carcasses* rotten, rotting, decayed, decomposed, putrid, putrescent, putrefactive. **5** *foul language* foul-mouthed, blasphemous, profane, obscene, vulgar, gross, coarse, filthy, dirty, indecent, indelicate, suggestive, smutty, blue, off-color, low, lewd, ribald, salacious, scatological. **6** *he's a foul creature* horrible, detestable, abhorrent, loathsome, hateful, despicable, contemptible, abominable, offensive, odious, disgusting, revolting, dishonorable, disgraceful, base, low, mean, sordid, vile, wicked, vicious, heinous, execrable, iniquitous, nefarious, notorious, infamous, scandalous, egregious. **7** *foul play by their competitors* unfair, unjust, dishonorable, dishonest, underhand, underhanded, unsportsmanlike, unsporting, unscrupulous, unprincipled, immoral, crooked, fraudulent, dirty; *inf.* shady. **8** *foul clothes* dirty, filthy, unwashed, soiled, grimy, grubby, stained, dirt-encrusted, muddied. **9** *foul weather* nasty, disagreeable, bad, rough, wild, stormy, rainy, wet, blustery, foggy, murky, gloomy.

foul verb dirty, soil, stain, blacken, defile, pollute, contaminate, taint, sully. **foul up** ruin, spoil, bungle, mismanage, mishandle, botch (up), mess up, make a mess of; *inf.* blow, screw up, louse up.

found verb **1** *found a new company* establish, set up, institute, originate, initiate, create, start, inaugurate, constitute, endow, organize, develop. **2** *his story was founded on rumors* base, ground, construct, build, rest.

foundation noun **1** *the foundation of the building* base, bottom, bedrock, substructure, substratum, understructure, underpinning. **2** *lay the foundations of mathematics* basis, groundwork; principles, fundamentals, rudiments. **3** *the foundation of the company* founding, establishing, setting up, institution, initiation, inauguration, constitution, endowment.

founder noun builder, constructor, maker, establisher, institutor, initiator, beginner, inventor, discoverer, framer, designer, architect, creator, author, originator, organizer, developer, generator, prime mover, father, patriarch.

founder verb **1** *ships foundered* sink, submerge, go down, be lost at sea, capsize, run aground, be swamped; *inf.* go to Davy Jones's locker. **2** *plans foundered* fail, fall through, break down, go awry, misfire, come to nothing, miscarry, abort, flounder, collapse; *inf.* come a cropper. **3** *the horse foundered* stumble, trip, stagger, lurch, fall, topple, sprawl, go lame, collapse.

fracas noun disturbance, quarrel, altercation, fight, brawl, affray, row, rumpus, scuffle, tussle, skirmish, free-for-all, brouhaha, melee, donnybrook, riot, uproar, commotion; trouble, tumult, turmoil, pandemonium.

fractious adjective **1** *fractious children* cross, irritable, peevish, petulant, ill-humored, querulous, testy, snappish, touchy. **2** *the fractious element on the committee* unruly, rebellious, insubordinate, contrary, refractory, unmanageable, intractable.

fracture noun **1** *a bone fracture* breaking, breakage, splitting, cleavage, rupture; break, crack, split. **2** *a fracture in the rock* fissure, cleft, rift, slit, rent, chink, crevice, gap, opening, aperture.

fracture verb break, crack, split, splinter, rupture.

fragile adjective breakable, brittle, frangible, splintery, frail, insubstantial, delicate, dainty.

fragment noun **1** *fragments of glass from the bowl* piece, part, particle, chip, chink, shard, sliver, splinter, smithereen. **2** *a fragment of cloth* scrap, bit, snip, snippet, wisp, tatter. **3** *the fragments of a book* remnant, remainder, fraction; remains, shreds.

fragmentary adjective incomplete, disconnected, disjointed, broken, discontinuous, incoherent, sketchy, unsystematic.

fragrance noun **1** *the fragrance of the roses* scent, perfume, bouquet, aroma, smell, redolence. **2** *a bottle of fragrance* scent, perfume, toilet water; cologne, eau de cologne.

fragrant adjective scented, perfumed, aromatic, sweet-smelling, redolent, balmy, odoriferous.

frail adjective **1** *frail china* fragile, breakable, frangible, delicate. **2** *frail old ladies* infirm, weak, slight, slender, puny, unsound, ill, ailing. **3** *frail creatures* easily led/tempted, susceptible, impressionable, vulnerable, fallible.

frailty noun **1** *the frailty of the china* fragility, brittleness, frangibility, flimsiness, insubstantiality, delicacy, daintiness, fineness. **2** *the frailty of the old* infirmity, weakness, delicacy, slightness, puniness, illness. **3** *the frailty of human nature* weakness, susceptibility, impressionability, vulnerability, fallibility; foible, weak point, flaw, blemish, defect, failing, fault, shortcoming, deficiency, peccadillo.

frame noun **1** *a frame of steel* framework, substructure, structure, shell, casing, support, skeleton, scaffolding, foundation, body, chassis. **2** *the man had a huge frame* body, physique, build, figure, shape, size, skeleton, carcass. **3** *alter the frame of society* order, organization, scheme, system, plan, fabric, form, constitution. **4** *a sad frame of mind* state, condition; mood, humor, temper, spirit, attitude.

frame verb **1** *frame the structure* assemble, build, construct, erect, elevate, fashion, mold, shape, forge. **2** *frame a policy* put together, formulate, draw up, plan, draft, map/plot/sketch out, shape, compose, form, devise, create, establish, conceive, think up, hatch; *inf.* dream up, cook up. **3** *frame a picture | hair framing his face* enclose, encase, surround.

framework noun **1** *the framework of the building* shell, skeleton. *See* FRAME noun 1. **2** *the framework of society* order, organization. *See* FRAME noun 3.

frank adjective **1** *a frank person/reply* candid, direct, forthright, plain, plainspoken, straight, straight from the shoulder, downright, explicit, outspoken, blunt, bluff, open, sincere, honest, guileless, artless. **2** *show frank admiration* open, obvious, transparent, patent, manifest, undisguised, unconcealed, unmistakable, evident.

frantic adjective frenzied, wild, hysterical, frenetic, distraught, overwrought, panicky, beside oneself, at one's wits' end, worked up, distracted, agitated, distressed, out of control.

fraternity noun brotherhood, kinship; club, society, association, guild, set, circle.

fraud noun **1** *found guilty of fraud* fraudulence, cheating, swindling, trickery, deceit, double-dealing, duplicity, treachery, chicanery, skulduggery, imposture, embezzlement, crookedness; *inf.* monkey business. **2** *perpetrate a fraud* ruse, trick, hoax, deception, subterfuge, stratagem, wile, artifice, swindle; *inf.* con, rip-off. **3** *the man is a fraud* impostor, fake, sham,

trickster, pretender, charlatan; *inf.* phony, quack, con man. **4** *the vase is a fraud* fake, sham, counterfeit, forgery; *inf.* phony.

fraudulent adjective dishonest, cheating, swindling, criminal, deceitful, double-dealing, duplicitous, dishonorable, unscrupulous; *inf.* crooked, shady.

freak noun **1** *that animal is a freak* freak of nature, aberration, abnormality, irregularity, oddity, monster, monstrosity, malformation, mutant. **2** *the neighbors think he's a bit of a freak* oddity; *inf.* queer fish, oddball, weirdo, nutcase. **3** *sci-fi freaks* enthusiast, fan, fanatic, addict, aficionado, devotee; *inf.* buff, fiend, nut. **4** *the storm was a freak* anomaly, quirk; *inf.* fluke.

freak adjective abnormal, unusual, atypical, aberrant, exceptional, bizarre, queer, odd; *inf.* fluky.

free adjective **1** *a free booklet* free of charge, for nothing, complimentary, gratis, without charge, at no cost; *inf.* for free, on the house. **2** *he is free today* unoccupied, available, not busy, not tied up, idle, at leisure, with time on one's hands. **3** *is this seat free?* empty, vacant, available, spare, unoccupied, untaken, uninhabited, tenantless. **4** *a free nation* independent, self-governing, self-governed, self-ruling, self-directing, sovereign, autonomous, democratic, emancipated, enfranchised, manumitted. **5** *the animals are free* at liberty, at large, loose, on the loose, unconfined, unbound, untied, unchained, unshackled, unfettered, unrestrained, wild. **6** *free to choose* able, allowed, permitted, unrestricted. **7** *a free flow of water* unobstructed, unimpeded, unhampered, clear, unblocked. **8** *the free end of the rope* not fixed, unattached, unfastened, loose. **9** *free with their money* generous, lavish, liberal, openhanded, unstinting, giving, munificent, bountiful, bounteous, charitable, extravagant, prodigal. **10** *a free manner* free and easy, easygoing, natural, open, frank, relaxed, casual, informal, unceremonious, unforced, spontaneous, uninhibited, artless, ingenuous; *inf.* laid-back. **free of** without, devoid of, sans, exempt from, clear of, unencumbered by.

free verb **1** *free the prisoners/animals* set free, release, let go, set at liberty, liberate, set/let/turn loose, untie, unchain, unfetter, unshackle, unmanacle, uncage, unleash, deliver. **2** *free the accident victims from the car* extricate, disentangle, disengage, disencumber. **3** *freed from paying tax* exempt, make exempt, except, excuse, relieve.

freedom noun **1** *colonies seeking their freedom* independence, self-government, sovereignty, autonomy, democracy, emancipation, manumission, enfranchisement, home rule. **2** *prisoners enjoying their freedom* liberty, release, deliverance, nonconfinement. **3** *freedom from tax* exemption, immunity, impunity. **4** *freedom of speech* right, privilege, prerogative. **5** *freedom to move around* scope, latitude, elbowroom, wide margin, flexibility, facility, free rein, license. **6** *admire her freedom of manner* naturalness, openness, casualness, informality, spontaneity, ingenuousness.

freely adverb **1** *speak freely* frankly, openly, candidly, plainly, bluntly, unreservedly. **2** *prisoners not allowed to speak freely* of one's own volition/accord, voluntarily.

freight noun transportation, conveyance, freightage, carriage, portage, haulage; cargo, load, lading, consignment, merchandise; goods.

frenzy noun **1** *go into a frenzy at the news* wildness, hysteria, distraction, agitation; madness, mania, insanity; fit. **2** *a frenzy of activity* bout, outburst, fit.

frequent adjective recurrent, repeated, persistent, continuing, many, numerous; regular, habitual, customary, common, usual, familiar, everyday.

frequent verb visit, attend, haunt, patronize; *inf.* hang out at.

fresh adjective **1** *is the fruit fresh?* garden-fresh, newly harvested, crisp, unwilted, unfaded. **2** *fresh fruit, not canned* raw, natural, unprocessed, unpreserved, undried, uncured, crude. **3** *fresh ideas* new, innovative, original, novel, unusual, unconventional, unorthodox. **4** *feeling fresh and alive* energetic, vigorous, invigorated, refreshed, rested, restored, revived, like a new person, fresh as a daisy; *inf.* full of vim/beans, raring to go, bright-eyed and bushy-tailed, chipper. **5** *a fresh complexion* healthy-looking, clear, bright, youthful-looking, wholesome, glowing, fair, rosy, pink, reddish, ruddy. **6** *curtains looking fresh* bright, clean, spick-and-span, unfaded. **7** *fresh supplies* more, other, additional, further, extra, supplementary, auxiliary. **8** *fresh air* pure, unpolluted, clean, refreshing. **9** *fresh winds* cool, chilly, brisk, bracing, invigorating. **10** *fresh recruits* untrained, inexperienced, untried, raw, callow, green, immature, artless, ingenuous, naïve; *inf.* wet behind the ears. **11** *a fresh young man* familiar, overfamiliar, presumptuous, forward, bold, audacious, brazen, impudent, impertinent, insolent, disrespectful; *inf.* cocky.

freshen verb **1** *a walk will freshen you* | *the swim freshened her up* refresh, rouse, stimulate, revitalize, restore, revive, liven up. **2** *freshen the room* air, ventilate, deodorize, purify. **freshen up** wash, wash up, tidy/spruce oneself up.

fret verb worry, agonize, anguish, be distressed, be upset, be anxious, pine, brood, mope.

fretful adjective peevish, petulant, out of sorts, irritable, bad-tempered, ill-natured, grumpy, crotchety, touchy, captious, testy, querulous, cranky.

friction noun **1** *ropes worn by friction* rubbing, abrading, abrasion, attrition, chafing, gnawing, grating, rasping, scraping, excoriation. **2** *cause friction in the family* dissension, dissent, disagreement, discord, strife, conflict, clashing, contention, quarreling, bickering, squabbling, wrangling, hostility, animosity, antagonism, bad feeling, ill feeling, bad blood, disharmony.

friend noun companion, crony, comrade, playmate, soul mate, intimate, confidante, confidant, familiar, alter ego, ally, associate; *inf.* pal, chum, buddy.

friendly adjective **1** *a friendly person* affable, amiable, warm, genial, agreeable, companionable, cordial, convivial, sociable, hospitable, comradely, neighborly, outgoing, approachable, accessible, communicative, kindly, amenable, sympathetic; *inf.* chummy, buddy-buddy. **2** *on friendly terms* amicable, congenial, cordial, familiar, peaceable, peaceful, conciliatory. **3** *a friendly wind* helpful, favorable, advantageous.

friendship noun **1** *their friendship lasted years* companionship, intimacy, amity, affinity, rapport, harmony, comradeship, fellowship, attachment, alliance. **2** *she always shows friendship to new people* friendliness, affability, amiability, warmth, geniality, cordiality, neighborliness, good-naturedness, kindliness.

fright noun **1** *start back in fright* fear, fear and trembling, terror, alarm, horror, dread, fearfulness, apprehension, trepidation, consternation, dismay, perturbation, disquiet, panic, nervousness, jitteriness; scare, shock; shivers; *inf.* jitters, the heebie-jeebies. **2** *you look a fright* eyesore; *inf.* mess, sight.

frighten verb scare, alarm, startle, terrify, terrorize, petrify, shock, appall, panic, throw into panic, unnerve, intimidate, cow, daunt, dismay, make one's blood run cold; *inf.* scare the living daylights out of, scare stiff, scare out of one's wits, make one's hair stand on end, make one's hair curl, make someone jump out of his/her skin, spook.

frightful adjective **1** *the corpse was a frightful sight* dreadful, terrible, horrible, horrid, hideous, ghastly, grim, dire, abhorrent, revolting, repulsive, loathsome, odious, fearful, fearsome, terrifying, alarming, shocking, harrowing. **2** *a frightful woman* unpleasant, disagreeable, appalling, insufferable, unbearable, annoying, irritating. **3** *a frightful cold* terrible, dreadful, awful, ghastly, nasty.

frigid adjective **1** *frigid conditions* bitter, freezing, frozen, icy, frosty, chilly, wintry, arctic, glacial, Siberian, polar. **2** *a frigid welcome* cold, austere, distant, aloof, remote, stiff, formal, cool, unfeeling, unfriendly, hostile.

frills plural noun ornamentation, decoration, embellishment, fanciness, ostentation, fuss; trimmings, falderals, affectations, extras, additions, superfluities; *inf.* jazz, flash.

fringe noun *on the fringe of the forest* outer edge, edge, borderline, perimeter, periphery, margin, rim; limits, borders, outskirts, verges.

frisky adjective lively, bouncy, active, frolicsome, coltish, playful, romping, rollicking, spirited.

fritter verb **fritter away** squander, waste, overspend, misspend, spend like water, dissipate, run through, misuse.

frivolous adjective **1** *frivolous young girls* giddy, flighty, dizzy, silly, foolish, facetious, zany, lighthearted, merry, superficial, shallow, inane, empty-headed, featherbrained; *inf.* flip. **2** *frivolous details* trivial, trifling, minor, petty, insignificant, unimportant, paltry, niggling, peripheral.

frolic verb frisk, gambol, cavort, caper, skip, leap, romp, skylark, prance, rollick.

frolic noun **1** *enjoy a frolic in the garden* game, romp, lark, antic, caper, escapade, prank, revel, spree. **2** *the children's frolic* fun, fun and games, gaiety, merriment, mirth, amusement, laughter, jollity; *inf.* high jinks.

front noun **1** *the front of the building* fore, forepart, forefront, anterior; frontage, face, facing, façade. **2** *at the front of the line* beginning, head, top, lead. **3** *put on a brave front* look, appearance, face, exterior, air, manner, expression, show, countenance, demeanor, bearing, mien, aspect. **4** *the pawnshop is a front for drug dealing* cover, cover-up, blind, façade, disguise, pretext, mask.

front verb *the house fronts on the lake* face toward, look out on, overlook.

frontier noun border, boundary, bound, limit, edge, rim.

frown verb **1** *frowning at each other* scowl, glower, glare, look daggers at; *inf.* give a dirty look to. **2** *frown at/on sloppy clothes* disapprove of, dislike, discourage, look askance at, not take kindly to, not think much of, take a dim view of.

frugal adjective **1** *a frugal old man* thrifty, sparing, economical, saving, provident,

unwasteful, abstemious, scrimping, niggardly, penny-pinching, miserly, parsimonious, stingy. **2** *a frugal meal* meager, scanty, paltry, insufficient.

fruitful adjective *fruitful discussions* productive, profitable, beneficial, rewarding, gainful, useful, worthwhile, successful, effective.

fruition noun fulfillment, realization, materialization, actualization, achievement, attainment, success, completion, consummation, perfection, maturity, maturation, ripening.

fruitless adjective futile, vain, in vain, useless, abortive, to no avail, worthless, pointless, to no effect, idle, ineffectual, ineffective, inefficacious, unproductive, unsuccessful, unavailing.

frustrate verb **1** *frustrate their attempts* defeat, thwart, check, block, counter, foil, balk, disappoint, forestall, baffle, stymie, stop, spoil, cripple, nullify, obstruct, impede, hamper, hinder, circumvent. **2** *lack of success frustrated him* discourage, dishearten, dispirit, depress, dissatisfy, anger, annoy, vex, irk, irritate, embitter.

frustration noun **1** *the frustration of their plans* defeat, thwarting, foiling, balking, forestalling, hampering, circumvention. **2** *full of frustration at their failure* dissatisfaction, disappointment, discontentment, anger, annoyance, irritation, vexation, resentment, bitterness.

fudge verb **1** *fudge the issue* evade, dodge, skirt, avoid. **2** *fudge the accounts* falsify, fake; *inf.* cook. **3** *fudge his way through the speech* equivocate, hedge, hem and haw, shuffle.

fuel noun **1** *fuel for the furnace/car* coal, wood, oil, gasoline, gas, kerosene. **2** *his answer was fuel to her anger* incitement, provocation, goading, stimulus, incentive, encouragement, ammunition.

fuel verb **1** *fuel the steam engine* fire, stoke up, charge, power. **2** *fuel her anger* fan, inflame, incite, provoke, goad, stimulate, encourage.

fugitive noun escapee, runaway, deserter, refugee.

fulfill verb **1** *fulfill his task* carry out, accomplish, achieve, execute, perform, discharge, implement, complete, bring to completion, finish, conclude, effect, effectuate, perfect. **2** *fulfill his desire* satisfy, realize, attain, consummate. **3** *fulfill the job requirements* fill, answer, meet, obey, comply with, satisfy, conform to, observe.

full adjective **1** *the cup is full* filled, filled up, filled to the brim, brimful, brimming, filled to capacity. **2** *the theater was full* crowded, packed, crammed, chock-full; *inf.* jam-packed, wall-to-wall. **3** *dinner guests feeling full* replete, satisfied, sated, gorged, glutted, cloyed. **4** *a full list of names* complete, entire, whole, comprehensive, thorough, exhaustive, detailed, all-inclusive, all-encompassing, extensive, unabridged. **5** *a full program of events* abundant, plentiful, copious, ample, sufficient, broad-ranging, satisfying, complete. **6** *a full figure* well-rounded, rounded, plump, buxom, shapely, curvaceous, voluptuous; *inf.* busty. **7** *a full skirt* loose-fitting, baggy, voluminous, capacious. **8** *a full voice* rich, deep, resonant, loud, strong. **full of** filled with, abounding in, replete with; *inf.* loaded with.

full-fledged adjective mature, complete; qualified, official.

full-scale adjective thorough, comprehensive, extensive, exhaustive, all-out, all-encompassing, all-inclusive, thoroughgoing, wide-ranging, sweeping, major, in-depth.

fulsome adjective excessive, extravagant, overdone, immoderate, inordinate, overappreciative, insincere, ingratiating, fawning, sycophantic, adulatory, cloying, nauseating, sickening, saccharine, unctuous; *inf.* smarmy.

fumble verb **1** *fumble for his keys* | *fumble in the dark* grope, feel about/around, fish (around), search blindly, stumble, blunder, flounder. **2** *fumble her speech* bungle, botch, mismanage, mishandle, muff, spoil; *inf.* make a mess/hash of, fluff, screw up, foul up, flub.

fume verb be enraged, seethe, boil, be livid, rage, be furious, be incensed, flare up; *inf.* be up in arms, get hot under the collar, be at boiling point, get all steamed up, blow one's top.

fumes plural noun vapor, gas, smoke, exhalation, exhaust, pollution.

fun noun amusement, entertainment, relaxation, recreation, enjoyment, pleasure, diversion, distraction, play, good time, merrymaking; merriment, gaiety, mirth, laughter, hilarity, glee, gladness, cheerfulness, joy; zest; high spirits. **in fun** jokingly, as a joke, in jest, for a laugh. **make fun of** ridicule, rag, deride, mock, scoff at, sneer at, taunt, jeer at, parody, lampoon.

fun adjective **1** *a fun time* amusing, entertaining, enjoyable, diverting, pleasurable. **2** *a fun person* amusing, witty, entertaining, lively, convivial.

function noun **1** *his function in the firm* role, capacity, responsibility, duty, task, chore, job, post, situation, office, occupation, employment, business, charge, concern, province, part, activity, operation, line, mission. **2** *what is that machine's function?* use, purpose, task. **3** *invited to a function* occasion, affair, gathering, reception, party; *inf.* do.

function verb work, go, run, be in working/running order, operate. **function as** serve as, act as, perform, operate as, officiate as, do (the) duty of, have/do the job of, play the role of, act the part of.

fund noun **1** *the church preservation fund* reserve, pool, collection, kitty, endowment, foundation, grant, investment, capital; savings. **2** *a fund of knowledge* stock, store, accumulation, mass, mine, reservoir, supply, storehouse, treasury, treasure-house, hoard, repository.

fund verb finance, back, pay for, capitalize, subsidize, stake, endow, support, float.

fundamental adjective basic, rudimentary, elemental, underlying, primary, cardinal, prime, first, principal, chief, key, central, structural, inherent, intrinsic, vital, essential, important, indispensable, necessary.

fundamentals plural noun basics, first/basic principles, essentials, rudiments; crux, crux of the matter, sine qua non; *inf.* nuts and bolts, nitty-gritty.

funds plural noun money, ready money, cash, hard cash, capital, the wherewithal; means, assets, resources, savings; *inf.* dough, bread, the ready.

funny adjective **1** *a funny story/person* amusing, comic, comical, humorous, hilarious, entertaining, diverting, laughable, hysterical, riotous, sidesplitting, droll, absurd, rich, ridiculous, ludicrous, risible, witty, waggish, jocular, farcical, silly, slapstick. **2** *what a funny hat* strange, peculiar, odd, queer, weird, bizarre, curious. **3** *there's something funny going on* mysterious, suspicious, dubious; *inf.* shady.

furious adjective **1** *furious parents* enraged, raging, infuriated, fuming, boiling, incensed, inflamed, indignant, mad, raving mad, maddened, wrathful, beside oneself, in high dudgeon; *inf.* livid, hot under the collar, up in arms. **2** *a furious struggle* violent, fierce, intense, vehement, tumultuous, turbulent.

furnish verb fit out, outfit, supply, equip, provide, provision, give, grant, present, offer, bestow on, endow.

furor noun **1** *a furor when they found out* commotion, uproar, disturbance, hullabaloo, turmoil, tempest, tumult, brouhaha, stir, excitement, to-do, outburst, outcry. **2** *in a furor* rage, madness, frenzy, fit.

furrow noun **1** groove, trench, channel, rut, trough, hollow, ditch, seam. **2** *furrows on her brow/skin* crease, line, wrinkle, corrugation, crinkle, crow's foot.

further verb advance, forward, promote, back, contribute to, encourage, foster, champion.

furthermore adverb moreover, what's more, additionally, on top of that, over and above that.

furtive adjective secret, secretive, stealthy, surreptitious, sneaky, sneaking, skulking, slinking, clandestine, hidden, covert, cloaked, under the table.

fury noun **1** *the fury of the parents* rage, ire, wrath, furor. **2** *the fury of the storm* fierceness, ferocity, violence, turbulence, tempestuousness, intensity, vehemence, force, power, potency. **3** *she is a real fury* virago, hellcat, termagant, spitfire, vixen, shrew, hag.

fuse verb **1** *fuse the ingredients* blend, intermix, intermingle, merge, meld, coalesce, compound, join, integrate, weld, solder. **2** *fuse the solid* melt, melt down, smelt, dissolve, liquefy.

fuss noun **1** *the fuss over the preparations* fluster, flurry, bustle, to-do, ado, agitation, excitement, bother, stir, commotion, confusion, tumult, uproar, upset, worry, overanxiety; *inf.* tempest in a teacup, much ado about nothing, flap, tizzy, stew. **2** *a fuss in the bar last night* row, altercation, squabble, quarrel, dispute, upset; trouble, bother, unrest.

fuss verb **1** *tell the organizers to stop fussing* | *fuss over details* bustle, bustle about, dash about, rush about, tear around, buzz around; worry, be agitated/worried, make a big thing out of nothing, make a mountain out of a molehill; *inf.* get worked up over nothing, be in a tizzy, be in a stew. **2** *fuss about the service* kick up a fuss, complain, raise an objection; *inf.* grouse, gripe.

fussy adjective particular, overparticular, finicky, persnickety, fastidious, hard to please, difficult, exacting, demanding, discriminating, selective, dainty; *inf.* choosy, picky, nitpicking.

futile adjective **1** *a futile search* vain, in vain, to no avail, unavailing, useless, ineffectual, ineffective, inefficacious, unsuccessful, fruitless, unproductive, unprofitable. **2** *a futile statement* trivial, unimportant, petty, trifling, valueless, worthless, inconsequential, idle.

fuzzy adjective **1** *fuzzy hair* | *a fuzzy peach* frizzy, downy, down-covered, woolly, linty. **2** *everything's gone all fuzzy* out of focus, blurred, blurry, bleary, misty, indistinct, unclear, distorted. **3** *fuzzy recollection* confused, muddled, befuddled, foggy, misty, shadowy.

Gg

gadget noun appliance, apparatus, instrument, implement, tool, contrivance, device, mechanism, invention; *inf.* contraption, widget, gizmo.

gag noun *his gags amused her* joke, jest, witticism, quip; *inf.* wisecrack, crack.

gag verb **1** *gag his mouth* stop up, block, plug, clog, stifle, smother, muffle. **2** *the press have been gagged* silence, muzzle, curb, check, restrain, suppress, repress. **3** *he gagged when he saw the corpse* choke, retch, gasp, vomit.

gaiety noun **1** *the gaiety of the children* merriment, glee, blitheness, gladness, happiness, high spirits, good spirits, delight, joy, joyousness, exuberance, elation, mirth, joviality, liveliness, vivacity, animation, effervescence, buoyancy, *joie de vivre*. **2** *join in the gaiety of the fair* fun, festivity, merrymaking, revelry, revels, celebration. **3** *the gaiety of the dresses* colorfulness, brightness, brilliance, sparkle, glitter, showiness.

gain verb **1** *gain an advantage* obtain, get, acquire, procure, secure, attain, build up, achieve, arrive at, come to have, win, capture, net, pick up, reap, gather. **2** *gain a wage* earn, bring in, make, get, clear, gross, net, realize. **gain on 1** *the police were gaining on the escaped prisoner* catch up with, close in on, overtake. **2** *the escaped prisoner was gaining on the police* leave behind, draw away from, outdistance, do better than. **gain time** stall, procrastinate, delay, temporize.

gain noun **1** *his gain from the deal was negligible* profit, earnings, income, advantage, benefit, reward, emolument, yield, return, winnings, proceeds, dividend, interest. **2** *a gain in experience/weight* increase, augmentation, addition, rise, increment, accretion, accumulation. **3** *their gain against the enemy* advance, advancement, progress, forward movement, headway, improvement, step forward.

gait noun walk, step, stride, pace, tread, bearing, carriage.

gala noun festival, fête, festivities, carnival, pageant, jamboree, party, celebration.

gala adjective *a gala occasion* festive, celebratory, merry, gay, joyous, joyful, jovial, entertaining, spectacular, showy, ceremonial, ceremonious.

gall noun **1** *have the gall to answer back* impudence, insolence, impertinence, nerve, audacity, brashness, effrontery, temerity; *inf.* brass, chutzpah. **2** *words full of gall* bitterness, resentment, rancor, acrimony, malice, spite, venom, sourness, acerbity, animus, bile, spleen.

gall verb **1** *gall the skin* abrade, chafe, rub, rub raw, scrape, excoriate, bark. **2** *her attitude galls him* vex, irritate, irk, annoy, rub the wrong way, exasperate, rile, bother, rankle; *inf.* aggravate, peeve.

gallant adjective **1** *gallant soldiers* brave, courageous, valiant, valorous, bold, plucky, daring, fearless, intrepid, manly, manful, dashing, heroic, lionhearted, stouthearted, doughty, mettlesome. **2** *gallant to the ladies* chivalrous, gentlemanly, courtly, courteous, mannerly, polite, attentive, gracious. **3** *a gallant ship* dignified, stately, noble, elegant, majestic, imposing, glorious, regal, august.

gallop verb canter, lope, run, race, rush, dash, tear, sprint, bolt, fly, shoot, dart, hurry, hasten, speed, career, scamper, scurry, zoom.

gamble verb **1** *he loves to gamble* bet, wager, place a bet, lay a wager/bet, game, try one's luck; *inf.* play the ponies. **2** *he gambled when he invested in that firm* take a chance, take a risk, speculate, venture, buy a pig in a poke; *inf.* stick one's neck out, go out on a limb.

gamble noun risk, hazard, chance, lottery, speculation, venture, pig in a poke.

gambol verb frolic, frisk, cavort, caper, skip, dance, leap, romp, hop, jump, rollick.

game noun **1** *children's games* pastime, diversion, entertainment, amusement, recreation, play, sport, distraction. **2** *we were only playing a game on him* joke, practical joke, prank, jest, trick, hoax. **3** *there's a game tomorrow* match, contest, tournament, meet, round, bout. **4** *he's in the oil game* business, line, occupation, trade, profession, industry, enterprise, activity, calling. **5** *what's his game?* scheme, trick, plot, ploy, stratagem. **6** *they went shooting game* wild animals, wild fowl, quarry, prey,

big game. **make game of** make fun of, ridicule, deride, mock, make sport of.

game adjective **1** *who's game enough to knock at her door?* plucky, brave, courageous, unafraid, fearless, bold, daring. **2** *I'm game to go if you are willing,* ready, prepared, disposed.

gamut noun entire range, whole spectrum, complete scale, whole series, full sweep, full compass, entire scope.

gang noun **1** *a gang of people gathered* group, band, crowd, company, gathering, pack, horde, mob, herd. **2** *the young man and his gang* clique, circle, social set, coterie, lot, ring, club; fraternity, sorority; *inf.* crew. **3** *gang of workers* crew, squad, team, troop, shift, detachment, posse, troupe.

gangster noun racketeer, bandit, brigand, robber, ruffian, thug, hoodlum, tough, desperado, Mafioso, terrorist; *inf.* crook, mobster, hood.

gap noun **1** *a gap in the wall* opening, cavity, hole, aperture, space, breach, orifice, break, fracture, rift, rent, fissure, cleft, chink, crack, crevice, cranny, divide, interstice. **2** *gaps in the program* pause, intermission, interval, interlude, break, recess. **3** *gaps in his account* omission, blank, hole, void. **4** *the gap between the old and the young* breach, difference, divergence, disparity.

gape verb **1** *gape at the procession* stare, stare in wonder, gaze, ogle; *inf.* gawk, rubberneck. **2** *the chasm gaped before them* open wide, yawn, part, crack, split.

garb noun **1** *admire the fine garb | the garb of a soldier* clothes, clothing, garments, dress, attire, apparel, costume, outfit, wear, habit, uniform, array, habiliment, vestments, livery, trappings; style, fashion, look; *inf.* gear, get-up, togs, duds. **2** *wearing the garb of sanity* appearance, guise, exterior, aspect, semblance, look.

garbage noun **1** *put the garbage out* trash, waste, rubbish, refuse, debris, detritus, litter, junk; swill, scraps, leftovers, remains, slops. **2** *talk a lot of garbage* nonsense, rubbish, twaddle, drivel, foolishness, balderdash; *inf.* hogwash, poppycock, rot.

garble verb mix up, jumble, confuse, distort, twist, warp, slant, mutilate, tamper with, doctor, falsify, pervert, corrupt, adulterate, misstate, misquote.

gargantuan adjective gigantic, giant, enormous, monstrous, huge, colossal, vast, immense, tremendous, massive, hulking, towering, mammoth, prodigious, elephantine, mountainous, monumental, titanic; *inf.* jumbo, humongous, whopping.

garish adjective flashy, loud, showy, gaudy, glaring, flaunting, bold-colored, glittering, tinselly, brassy, tawdry, raffish, tasteless, in bad taste, vulgar, cheap, flashy.

garland noun wreath, festoon, lei, laurel, laurels, coronet, crown, circlet, chaplet, fillet, headband.

garment noun clothes, clothing. *See* GARB 1.

garner verb gather, collect, accumulate, heap, pile up, amass, assemble, stack up, store, lay by, put/stow away, hoard, stockpile.

garnish verb decorate, adorn, trim, ornament, embellish, deck, deck out, bedeck, festoon, enhance, grace, beautify, prettify, set off, add the finishing touch to.

garrison noun **1** *the garrison arrived at the fort* platoon, brigade, squadron; troops, militia, soldiers. **2** *the garrison was under siege* fort, fortress, fortification, stronghold, blockhouse, citadel, camp, encampment, command post, base, station; barracks.

garrulous adjective **1** *a garrulous old man* talkative, chatty, chattering, gossiping, loquacious, voluble, verbose, long-winded, babbling, prattling, prating, blathering, jabbering, gushing, effusive; *inf.* mouthy, gabby. **2** *a garrulous account* long-winded, wordy, verbose, rambling, prolix, diffuse.

gash noun cut, slash, wound, tear, laceration, gouge, incision, slit, split, nick, cleft.

gasp verb pant, puff, blow, catch one's breath, gulp, choke, fight for breath, wheeze, huff and puff.

gather verb **1** *people gathered in the church | gather the children* come together, collect, assemble, congregate, meet, group, cluster together, crowd, mass, flock together, convene, converge; call together, summon, round up, muster, marshal. **2** *gather cans of food* get/put together, accumulate, amass, garner, store, stockpile, heap up, pile up, stack up, hoard; *inf.* stash away. **3** *the event gathered a huge audience* attract, draw, pull, pull in. **4** *we gather that he is dead* infer, deduce, conclude, assume, surmise. **5** *gather to one's bosom* embrace, clasp, enfold, hold, hug, cuddle. **6** *gather the harvest* harvest, collect, pick, pluck, cull, garner, crop, reap, glean. **7** *gather in strength* increase, grow, rise, build, expand, enlarge, swell, extend, wax, intensify. **8** *gather the waist of the dress* ruffle, shirr, pleat, pucker, tuck, fold.

gathering noun **1** *a gathering of people* assembly, assemblage, collection, company, congregation, group, party, band, knot, crowd, flock, throng, mass, mob, horde, meeting, meet, convention, conclave, rally. **2** *his gathering of coins* collection, accumulation, assemblage, aggregation, aggregate, mass, store, stock, stockpile, heap, pile, cluster, conglomeration, concentration.

gauche adjective awkward, socially inept, lacking in social graces, inelegant, unpolished, unsophisticated.

gaudy adjective garish, loud, glaring, flashy, showy, ostentatious, tawdry, raffish, tasteless, vulgar, cheap.

gauge verb **1** *gauge the thickness of the metal* measure, calculate, compute, count, weigh. **2** *you must gauge his aptitude* evaluate, appraise, assess, judge, rate, reckon, determine.

gauge noun **1** *find a gauge of his abilities* measure, basis, standard, guide, guideline, touchstone, yardstick, benchmark, criterion, rule, norm, example. **2** *the gauge of a barrel/railroad* area, size, measure, capacity, magnitude, depth, height, width, thickness, span, bore.

gaunt adjective **1** *illness had left her gaunt* haggard, drawn, cadaverous, skeletal, emaciated, bony, angular, rawboned, hollow-cheeked, starved-looking, scrawny, scraggy, shriveled, wasted, withered. **2** *gaunt landscape* bleak, barren, bare, desolate, dreary, dismal, forlorn, grim, stern, harsh, forbidding.

gawky adjective ungainly, ungraceful, uncoordinated, lanky, clumsy, lumbering, maladroit, oafish, loutish.

gay adjective **1** *feeling gay* lighthearted, cheerful, mirthful, jovial, glad, happy, bright, in good spirits, in high spirits, joyful, elated, exuberant. **2** *have a gay time* merry, festive, amusing, enjoyable, entertaining, convivial, hilarious. **3** *gay colors* bright, vivid, brilliant, multicolored, flamboyant, gaudy. **4** *gay men/women* homosexual, lesbian; *derog. inf.* queer, limp-wristed, butch.

gaze verb stare, gape, stand agog, watch in wonder, ogle, eye, take a good look, contemplate; *inf.* gawk, rubberneck, give the once-over.

gear noun **1** *the steering gear of a boat* gears, mechanism, machinery, works. **2** *the workman's gear* equipment, tools, implements, tackle, appliances, contrivances, utensils, supplies, accoutrements, trappings, accessories, paraphernalia; *inf.* stuff. **3** *wearing modern gear* clothes, dress. *See* GARB 1. **4** *their daughter and all her gear* belongings, things, luggage, baggage, effects, paraphernalia, accoutrements, possessions, trappings; *inf.* stuff.

general adjective **1** *the general practice* usual, customary, common, ordinary, normal, standard, regular, typical, conventional, everyday, habitual, run-of-the-mill. **2** *in general use* common, extensive, widespread, broad, wide, accepted, prevalent, prevailing, universal, popular, public, generic. **3** *a general tax hike/rule* across-the-board, blanket, universal, sweeping, broad, broad-ranging, comprehensive, all-inclusive, encyclopedic, indiscrimi-

nate, catholic. **4** *his general knowledge*
mixed, assorted, miscellaneous, variegated,
diversified, composite, heterogeneous.
5 *a general account* loose, approximate,
unspecific, vague, indefinite, imprecise,
rough.

generally adverb **1** *it generally rains there
in the spring* usually, as a rule, normally,
ordinarily, customarily, habitually, typically, for the most part, on the whole, in
most cases. **2** *not generally known* commonly, widely, extensively, comprehensively, universally. **3** *speaking generally*
loosely, approximately, broadly. **4** *they
are generally liked* mostly, mainly, in the
main, largely, chiefly.

generate verb **1** *generate children* beget,
procreate, engender, sire, father, breed,
spawn, produce, propagate. **2** *generate
an argument* cause, give rise to, create,
produce, initiate, originate, occasion, sow
the seeds of.

generic adjective general, common, collective, inclusive, all-inclusive, all-
encompassing, comprehensive, blanket,
sweeping, universal.

generosity noun **1** *the generosity of our host*
liberalness, liberality, kindness, magnanimity, benevolence, beneficence, bounteousness, bounty, munificence, hospitality,
charitableness, charity, openhandedness,
lavishness. **2** *the generosity of his spirit* nobility, nobleness, magnanimity, loftiness,
high-mindedness, honorableness, honor,
goodness, unselfishness.

generous adjective **1** *generous with money* | *a
generous host* liberal, kind, benevolent, beneficent, bountiful, bounteous, munificent, hospitable, charitable, openhanded,
lavish, ungrudging, unstinting. **2** *a generous spirit* noble, magnanimous, lofty,
high-minded, honorable, good, unselfish,
altruistic, unprejudiced, disinterested. **3** *a
generous supply of caviar* abundant, plentiful,
lavish, ample, copious, overflowing.

genesis noun beginning, commencement,
start, outset, birth, origin, source, root,
creation, engendering, inception, generation, propagation.

genial adjective amiable, affable, good-
humored, good-natured, warm, cordial,
amenable, friendly, congenial, amicable,
sociable, convivial, kind, kindly.

genius noun **1** *the boy is a genius* virtuoso,
prodigy, master, mastermind, maestro,
intellectual, intellect, expert; *inf.* brains,
mental giant, Einstein. **2** *a person of genius*
brilliance, intellect, cleverness, brains. **3**
a genius for cooking gift, talent, flair, bent,
knack, aptitude, faculty, ability, capability.

genteel adjective **1** *living in genteel surroundings* well-born, aristocratic, noble,

blue-blooded, patrician, well-bred, respectable, refined, stylish, elegant, ladylike, gentlemanly. **2** *genteel behavior* polite,
well-mannered, mannerly, courteous, civil,
decorous, gracious, courtly, polished, cultivated. **3** *the king's servants were very
genteel* overpolite, mannered, affected,
ultrarefined.

gentle adjective **1** *a gentle person* kind,
kindly, tender, benign, humane, lenient,
merciful, clement, compassionate, tenderhearted, sweet-tempered, placid, mild,
soft, quiet, tranquil, meek, dovelike. **2**
a gentle wind mild, moderate, light, temperate, soft, smooth, soothing. **3** *a gentle
child* docile, manageable, tractable, meek.
4 *a gentle slope* gradual, slight, easy, imperceptible. **5** *of gentle birth* upper-class,
high-born. *See* GENTEEL 1.

genuine adjective **1** *a genuine diamond* real,
authentic, true, pure, actual, bona fide,
veritable, sound, sterling, legitimate, lawful, legal, valid, original, unadulterated,
unalloyed; *inf.* the real McCoy, honest-to-
goodness, kosher. **2** *a genuine person* sincere, truthful, honest, frank, candid, open,
natural, unaffected, artless, ingenuous;
inf. up-front.

germane adjective relevant, pertinent, material, applicable, related, connected, akin,
apropos, apposite, appropriate, apt, fitting,
suited, to the point/purpose.

gesture noun sign, signal, motion,
motioning, wave, indication, gesticulation.

gesture verb gesticulate, sign, signal, motion, wave, indicate.

get verb **1** *where did you get that hat?* acquire, obtain, come by, procure, secure,
buy, purchase. **2** *go and get that book* go
for, fetch, bring, collect, carry, transport,
convey. **3** *get what you want* gain, acquire,
achieve, attain, reach, win, find; *inf.* bag.
4 *get $400 per week* earn, bring in, make,
clear, gross, net, pocket; *inf.* pull in, take
home. **5** *the police got the thief* capture, seize,
grab, lay hold of, grasp, collar, take captive,
arrest, apprehend, take, trap, entrap; *inf.*
nab, bag. **6** *get flu/measles* catch, contract,
come down with, be afflicted by. **7** *try to
get that station* reach, communicate with,
contact, get in touch with. **8** *I didn't get
what he said* hear, catch, take in, perceive.
9 *don't you get what he means?* understand,
grasp, comprehend, see, fathom, follow,
make head or tail of; *inf.* catch on to, get
the hang of. **10** *we got home early* arrive,
reach, come; *inf.* make it. **11** *we got her to
go* persuade, induce, coax, wheedle into,
talk into, prevail upon. **12** *get to see the new
movie* manage, succeed, arrange, contrive.
13 *get fat/wet/old* become, grow, come to
be, turn, turn into, wax. **14** *that music
gets me* affect, move, touch, stir, arouse,

stimulate, impress, leave an impression on; *inf.* send, turn on. **15** *I'll get him for that* avenge oneself on, take vengeance on, get even with, pay someone back, give tit for tat to, settle the score with; *inf.* get back at. **16** *you've really got me there* baffle, puzzle, stump, mystify, confound, nonplus. **get across** communicate, make understood/clear, impart, convey, transmit. **get ahead** make good, do well, succeed, prosper, flourish, rise in the world; *inf.* go places, get somewhere. **get along 1** *I don't get along with his mother* get on, agree, see eye to eye; *inf.* hit it off. **2** *how are you getting along?* get on, fare, manage, cope; *inf.* get by, make out. **get around 1** *get around his objections* circumvent, bypass, outmaneuver, outwit, outsmart. **2** *get around his father* prevail upon, wheedle, coax, win over, convert, sway. **3** *she certainly gets around* travel, visit, circulate, socialize. **get at** suggest, hint, imply, intend, lead up to, mean. **get away** escape, flee, break free, break out, decamp, depart. **get back 1** *get back at dawn* return, come home, come back. **2** *get back her gloves* recover, retrieve, regain, repossess, recoup. **3** *get back at his torturer* avenge oneself on, get even with. *See* 15. **get by** cope, manage, subsist, survive, exist, fare, get along, contrive to get along, make both ends meet, keep the wolf from the door; *inf.* keep one's head above water, make out. **get off** *get off the bus* alight from, climb off, dismount from, leave; descend from, disembark, exit. **get on 1** *get on the bus* board, climb on; mount, ascend, embark. **2** *how are you getting on?* get along, fare, manage, cope; *inf.* get by, make out. **3** *husband and wife do not get on* be on friendly terms, be in harmony. *See* GET ALONG 1. **get out 1** *let's get out now* leave, depart, go away, be off, withdraw; *inf.* vamoose, clear out. **2** *the news has got out* be made public, become known, be revealed, be publicized, be disclosed, leak, be leaked, spread, circulate. **get out of** avoid, dodge, evade, escape, shirk. **get over 1** *get over the flu* recover from, recuperate from, get better after, pull through, survive. **2** *get over one's fear of dogs* overcome, master, get the better of, shake off, defeat. **get to** irritate, get on someone's nerves, annoy, vex, rile, rub someone the wrong way, upset, bother, nettle; *inf.* bug, get someone's goat. **get together 1** *get together the evidence* collect, gather, assemble, accumulate, compile, amass. **2** *we must get together soon* meet, meet up, socialize, congregate.

getaway noun escape, flight, breakout, break, decampment.

get-together noun meeting, party, social gathering, gathering; *inf.* do, bash.

get-up noun outfit, clothes, clothing, dress, garb, apparel, garments.

get-up-and-go noun go, energy, vigor, vitality, vim, enthusiasm, eagerness, drive, push, initiative, ambition; *inf.* bounce.

ghastly adjective **1** *a ghastly murder/accident* terrible, horrible, frightful, dreadful, awful, horrid, horrendous, hideous, shocking, grim, grisly, gruesome, gory, terrifying, frightening. **2** *a ghastly mistake* serious, grave, critical, unforgivable. **3** *what a ghastly man* odious, loathsome, nasty, foul, contemptible, appalling. **4** *her ghastly appearance* deathlike, deathly pale, pale, pallid, wan, ashen, colorless, white, white as a sheet, ghostlike, ghostly, spectral, cadaverous.

ghost noun **1** *haunted by a ghost* specter, apparition, phantom, spirit, phantasm; *inf.* spook. **2** *the ghost of a smile* suggestion, hint, trace, glimmer, semblance, shadow, impression.

ghostly adjective ghostlike, spectral, phantomlike, phantom, phantasmal, unearthly, supernatural, otherworldly, insubstantial, shadowy, eerie, weird, uncanny; *inf.* spooky.

giant noun colossus, Titan, Goliath, behemoth, leviathan; superhuman.

giant adjective gigantic, enormous, colossal, huge, immense, vast, mammoth, monumental, monstrous, gargantuan, titanic, elephantine, prodigious, stupendous; *inf.* jumbo, humongous, industrial-size.

gibberish noun babble, jabbering, nonsense, rubbish, twaddle, drivel, balderdash, mumbo jumbo, blather, double-talk, prattle; *inf.* poppycock, gobbledegook, rot, piffle.

gibe, jibe verb jeer, mock, sneer at, scoff at, taunt, scorn, deride, hold up to ridicule, laugh at, poke fun at, make fun of, tease, twit; *inf.* rib, rag.

giddy adjective **1** *get giddy climbing ladders* dizzy, light-headed, faint, reeling, unsteady; *inf.* woozy. **2** *a giddy girl* flighty, silly, frivolous, skittish, capricious, featherbrained, scatterbrained, fickle, changeable, inconstant, mercurial, volatile, thoughtless, heedless, carefree, insouciant.

gift noun **1** *receive a birthday gift* present, offering, bounty, largesse, donation, contribution, boon, grant, bonus, gratuity, benefaction, bequest, legacy, inheritance, endowment. **2** *a gift for foreign languages* talent, flair, aptitude, facility, knack, ability, faculty, genius, mind for.

gifted adjective talented, brilliant, intelligent, clever, bright, smart, sharp, ingenious, able, accomplished, capable, masterly, skilled, adroit, proficient, expert.

gigantic adjective enormous, colossal. *See* GIANT adjective.

giggle verb titter, snigger, snicker, chuckle, chortle, laugh, cackle; *inf.* tee-hee, ha-ha.

gimmick noun contrivance, stunt, scheme, trick, dodge, ploy, stratagem.

gingerly adverb cautiously, with caution, warily, charily, cannily, carefully, attentively, heedfully, vigilantly, watchfully, judiciously, hesitantly, reluctantly, timidly.

gird verb **1** *gird on his sword* belt, bind, fasten. **2** *trees girded the lake* surround, circle, encircle, ring, enclose, encompass, compass, confine, hem in, pen, enfold, engird, girdle. **3** *gird oneself for battle* prepare, make ready, ready, brace, fortify, steel, buttress.

gist noun essence, quintessence, drift, sense, core, nucleus, nub, kernel, pith, marrow, burden, crux.

give verb **1** *gave him the book* hand, present, donate, bestow, contribute, confer, hand over, turn over, award, grant, accord, leave, will, bequeath, make over, entrust, consign, vouchsafe. **2** *give the impression* show, display, demonstrate, set forth, indicate, manifest, evidence. **3** *give them time* allow, permit, grant, accord, offer. **4** *give a reprimand* administer, deliver, deal. **5** *give advice* provide, supply, furnish, proffer, offer. **6** *give no trouble* cause, be a source of, make, create. **7** *give news of the battle* impart, communicate, announce, transmit, convey, transfer, send, purvey. **8** *land giving a good crop* produce, yield, afford, result in. **9** *the car gave a jolt* perform, execute, make, do. **10** *give a shout/yell* let out, utter, issue, emit. **11** *give his life for his country* give up, sacrifice, relinquish, devote. **12** *gave his seat to the new senator* surrender, concede, yield, give up, cede. **13** *she gave me to believe* lead, make, cause, force. **14** *the chair gave* give way, collapse, break, break down, fall apart, come apart; bend, buckle. **give away 1** *give away secrets* reveal, disclose, divulge, let slip, leak, let out, expose, uncover. **2** *give his friend away* betray, inform on; *inf.* rat on, blow the whistle on. **give in** give up, surrender, admit/concede defeat, concede, yield, capitulate, submit, comply, succumb, quit, retreat; *inf.* throw in the towel. **give off** emit, send out, give out, pour out, throw out, discharge, exude, exhale, release, vent, produce. **give out 1** *give out fumes* emit, send out. *See* GIVE OFF. **2** *give out the prizes* distribute, allocate, allot, mete out, hand out, disperse, apportion, dole out, assign; *inf.* dish out. **3** *give out that he is leaving* announce, declare, make known, communicate, impart, broadcast, publish, disseminate. **4** *supplies were giving out* run out, be used up, be consumed, be exhausted, be depleted, come to an end, fail. **give up 1** *give up smoking* stop, cease, quit, desist from, leave off, swear off, renounce, forswear, abandon, discontinue; *inf.* cut out. **2** *give up in the face of the enemy* surrender, yield. *See* GIVE IN. **3** *she's just given up* despair, lose heart, abandon hope, give up hope.

giver noun donor, contributor, granter, benefactor, backer, fairy godmother; *inf.* angel.

glad adjective **1** *glad you're here* happy, pleased, pleased as Punch, well-pleased, delighted, gratified, thrilled, overjoyed, elated, satisfied, contented, grateful; *inf.* tickled pink. **2** *glad to help* willing, more than willing, eager, ready, prepared, happy, pleased, delighted. **3** *hear the glad news* happy, joyful, delightful, welcome, cheering, cheerful, pleasing, gratifying.

glamorous adjective **1** *a glamorous woman* alluring, dazzling, glittering, well-dressed, smart, elegant, attractive, charming, fascinating, beguiling, bewitching, enchanting, entrancing, irresistible, tantalizing; *inf.* glitzy, ritzy. **2** *a glamorous career* exciting, stimulating, thrilling, high-profile, dazzling, glossy, glittering; *inf.* ritzy, glitzy.

glamour noun **1** *women with glamour* beauty, loveliness, attractiveness, allure, attraction, elegance, charm, fascination; *inf.* glitz, pizzazz. **2** *the glamour of foreign travel* excitement, enchantment, captivation, magic, spell.

glance verb **1** *glance at the stranger* glimpse, peek, peep; *inf.* sneak a look. **2** *glance through the paper* skim, leaf, flip, thumb, scan. **3** *lights glancing on water* flash, gleam, glitter, glisten, glint, glimmer, shimmer, flicker, sparkle, twinkle, reflect. **4** *the arrow glanced off the tree | the car glanced the wall* ricochet, rebound, bounce; graze, skim, touch, brush. **glance at/over** touch upon, mention in passing, mention, skim over.

glance noun **1** *take a glance at* glimpse, peek, peep; *inf.* gander, once-over. **2** *the glance of the sun on the water* flash, gleam, glitter, glint, glimmer, shimmer, flicker, sparkle, twinkle, reflection.

glare verb **1** *glare at the trespassers* glower, scowl, frown, give someone dirty looks, look daggers. **2** *lights glaring* blaze, flare, flame, beam, dazzle.

glare noun **1** *give a glare at his enemy* glower, scowl, frown, dirty look. **2** *the glare of lights* blaze, flare, flame, harsh beam, dazzle.

glaring adjective *a glaring error* conspicuous, obvious, overt, manifest, patent, visible, unconcealed, flagrant, blatant, egregious, outrageous, gross.

glasses plural noun *put on his glasses* eyeglasses, spectacles, bifocals, sunglasses, lorgnette, pince-nez.

glassy adjective **1** *a glassy surface on the table* glasslike, shiny, glossy, smooth, mirrorlike, clear, crystal-clear, transparent, translucent, limpid. **2** *a glassy stare* expressionless, glazed, blank, empty, vacant, vacuous, deadpan, fixed, unmoving, motionless, lifeless.

gleam noun **1** *a gleam of light* beam, flash, glow, shaft, ray, flare, glint. **2** *the gleam of the polished brass* glow, luster, gloss, shine, sheen, brightness, brilliance, flash. **3** *a gleam of hope* glimmer, flicker, ray, trace, suggestion, hint, inkling, grain.

gleam verb shine, radiate, flash, glow, flare, glint, glisten, glitter, beam, shimmer, glimmer, glance, sparkle, twinkle, scintillate.

glee noun exaltation, elation, exuberance, merriment, gaiety, mirth, mirthfulness, delight, joy, joyousness, exhilaration, high spirits, blitheness, cheerfulness.

gleeful adjective elated, exuberant, joyful, overjoyed, joyous, jovial, exhilarated, high-spirited, blithe, cheerful.

glib adjective slick, smooth, smooth-talking, smooth-spoken, fast-talking, plausible, fluent, suave; talkative, voluble, loquacious, unctuous.

glide verb slide, slip, skim, sail, skate, float, drift, flow, coast.

glimmer noun **1** *a glimmer of light* gleam, flash, flicker, glint, shimmer, blink, twinkle, sparkle, glow, ray. **2** *a glimmer of hope* flicker, ray. *See* GLEAM noun 3.

glimmer verb gleam, flash, flicker, shimmer, blink, twinkle, sparkle, glow.

glimpse noun glance, quick look, peek, peep.

glisten verb shine, shimmer, sparkle, twinkle, flicker, blink, wink, glint, glance, gleam, flash, scintillate.

glitter verb sparkle, twinkle, flicker, blink, wink, shimmer, glimmer, glint, gleam, flash, scintillate, coruscate.

glitter noun *the glitter of show business* showiness, flashiness, ostentation, glamour, pageantry, fanfare, splendor; *inf.* razzle-dazzle, glitz, ritziness, pizzazz.

gloat verb relish, take pleasure in, delight in, revel in, rejoice in, glory in, exult in, triumph over, crow about; *inf.* rub it in.

global adjective **1** *global recession* worldwide, world, universal, international, planetary. **2** *a global rule* general, comprehensive, all-inclusive, all-encompassing, all-out, encyclopedic, exhaustive, thorough, total, across-the-board, with no exceptions.

globe noun world, universe, earth, planet; sphere, spheroid, orb, ball.

gloom noun **1** *the gloom of the night* gloominess, dimness, darkness, dark, blackness, murkiness, murk, shadowiness, shadow, shade, obscurity, dusk, twilight. **2** *a state of gloom* low spirits, melancholy, despondency, misery, dejection, glumness, depression, the blues, despair, pessimism, hopelessness.

gloomy adjective **1** *a gloomy day/room* dark, sunless, dull, dim, shadowy, dismal, dreary, black, murky, somber. **2** *a gloomy outlook* distressing, somber, melancholy, depressing, dispiriting, disheartening, disappointing, pessimistic, hopeless. **3** *feeling gloomy* in low spirits, melancholy, woebegone, despondent, disconsolate, miserable, dejected, downcast, downhearted, dispirited, glum, depressed, blue.

glorify verb **1** *glorify God* worship, adore, exalt, extol, pay homage to, pay tribute to, honor, revere, reverence, venerate. **2** *the reports glorified the war* add luster to, aggrandize, ennoble, elevate, raise, lift up, magnify, dignify, advance, boost, promote. **3** *glorify the conqueror* praise, sing/sound the praises of, extol, laud, eulogize, magnify, acclaim, applaud, cheer, hail, celebrate, lionize.

glorious adjective **1** *our glorious history* illustrious, noble, celebrated, famous, famed, renowned, magnificent, majestic. **2** *a glorious day* beautiful, bright, brilliant, sunny, perfect. **3** *have a glorious time* splendid, marvelous, wonderful, delightful, terrific.

glory noun **1** *to the glory of God* worship, adoration, exaltation, extolment, honor, reverence, veneration. **2** *win glory in battle* renown, fame, prestige, honor, distinction, illustriousness, acclaim, credit, accolade, recognition. **3** *the glory of Versailles* splendor, resplendence, magnificence, grandeur, majesty, pomp, pageantry.

gloss noun **1** *the gloss on the furniture* shine, sheen, luster, gleam, brightness, brilliance, sparkle, shimmer, polish, burnish. **2** *a gloss of respectability* façade, front, camouflage, disguise, mask, semblance, show, veneer, surface.

glossy adjective shining, shiny, glassy, gleaming, bright, brilliant, sparkling, shimmering, polished, burnished, glazed.

glow noun **1** *the glow from the light* gleam, glimmer, incandescence, luminosity, phosphorescence. **2** *the glow of the garden flowers* brightness, vividness, brilliance, colorfulness, richness, radiance, splendor. **3** *the glow of her complexion* blush, flush, rosiness, pinkness, redness, crimson, scarlet, reddening, bloom. **4** *induce a warm glow* warmth, happiness, contentment, satisfaction. **5** *the glow of his love* passion, ardor, fervor, vehemence, intensity.

glow verb **1** *the light/fire glowed* shed a glow, gleam, glimmer, shine, smolder. **2** *glow with pleasure* blush, flush, redden, color. **3** *glow with pride* radiate, thrill, tingle.

glower verb scowl, stare angrily, glare, frown, give someone dirty looks, look daggers.

glowing adjective **1** *glowing coals* aglow, smoldering, incandescent, candescent, luminous, phosphorescent. **2** *a glowing complexion* rosy, pink, reddish, red, ruddy, florid. **3** *glowing colors* bright, vivid, brilliant, colorful, rich, radiant. **4** *a glowing report* complimentary, ecstatic, rhapsodic, eulogistic, laudatory, adulatory; *inf.* rave.

glue noun adhesive, fixative, gum, paste, cement, mucilage, epoxy.

glum adjective in low spirits, melancholy. *See* GLOOMY 3.

glut noun surplus, excess, surfeit, superfluity, overabundance, superabundance, oversupply, saturation.

gluttony noun gourmandism, gormandizing, insatiability, voraciousness, voracity, greed, greediness; *inf.* piggishness, hoggishness.

gnaw verb chew, munch, crunch, masticate, bite. **gnaw at** prey on someone's mind, torment, plague, fret, distress, trouble, worry. **gnaw away** erode, corrode, wear away, wear down, eat away, fret, consume, devour.

go verb **1** *I go forward/backward/up* move, proceed, progress, pass, walk, travel, journey, repair. **2** *time to go go* away, leave, depart, withdraw, set off, set out, decamp; *inf.* beat it, scram. **3** *does the machine go?* work, function, operate, run, perform. **4** *go pale/bad* become, grow, get, come to be, wax. **5** *this road goes all the way to the sea* extend, stretch, reach, spread, give access, lead. **6** *where does this book go?* belong, fit in, be located, be situated, be found, lie, stand. **7** *her headache has gone* stop, cease, disappear, vanish, be no more, fade away, melt away. **8** *all my money has gone* be finished, be spent, be used up, be exhausted, be consumed. **9** *the elderly patient has gone* die, pass away, decease, expire, perish; *inf.* give up the ghost, kick the bucket. **10** *these clothes will have to go* be discarded, be thrown away, be disposed of. **11** *some of the staff will have to go* be dismissed, be laid off; *inf.* be fired, be axed, get the ax. **12** *the money will go to charity* be assigned, be allotted, be applied, be devoted, be awarded, be granted/given, be ceded. **13** *how did your interview go?* turn out, work out,

fare, progress, develop, result, end, end up, eventuate. **14** *the carpet and curtains don't go* go together, go with each other, match, harmonize, blend, suit each other, be suited, complement each other, be in accord, accord, be compatible. **15** *this goes to prove his theory* serve, contribute, help, incline, tend. **16** *the bridge went* break, give way, collapse, fall down, cave in, crumble, disintegrate, fall to pieces. **go about** *how do you go about buying a house?* set about, begin, approach, tackle, undertake. **go along with** *I'll go along with your plans* comply with, cooperate with, acquiesce in, follow, agree with, assent to, concur with. **go around** *a rumor going around* circulate, pass around; be passed around, be spread, be broadcast. **go back on** *go back on one's word* renege on, repudiate, retract. **go by 1** *as time goes by* pass, pass by, elapse, move on, proceed, flow, lapse, slip away, tick away, fly. **2** *go by the rules* follow, obey, observe, be guided by, heed. **go down 1** *the ship went down in a storm* sink, be submerged, founder, go under. **2** *prices are going down* decrease, drop, fall, be reduced, decline, plummet. **3** *the champion went down* be beaten, be defeated, suffer defeat, lose, fail, collapse. **4** *his name will go down in history* be commemorated, be remembered, be recalled, be immortalized. **go far** *a young man bound to go far* do well, do well for oneself, be successful, succeed, get on, get on in the world, get ahead, make a name for oneself, advance oneself, set the world on fire. **go for 1** *the dog went for him* attack, assault, assail, launch oneself at, set upon, spring at/upon, rush at. **2** *he doesn't go for quiet women* be attracted to, be fond of, admire, favor, like, prefer, choose, hold with. **go in for** *go in for tennis* engage in, take part in, participate in, practice, pursue, take up, espouse, adopt, embrace. **go into** *the police are going into the evidence thoroughly* investigate, research, inquire into, look into, examine, study, review, check, scrutinize, analyze, delve into, dig into, pursue, probe. **go off 1** *the bomb went off* explode, detonate, blow up, burst, erupt; *inf.* go bang. **2** *we went off at dawn* leave, go away, depart, set out, set off, decamp, move out. **go on 1** *how long did the talk go on?* last, continue, proceed, endure, persist, stay, remain, happen, occur. **2** *she did go on too long* ramble on, talk on and on, chatter, prattle. **go out 1** *he has gone out of the office* leave, exit, depart from. **2** *the lights/passion went out* be extinguished, be turned off, be doused, be quenched, fade, die out. **3** *a boy and girl going out* go with each other, go together, see each other, court; *inf.* go steady, date. **go over** *go over the accounts* read over, look over, inspect, examine, study, scan, run over; *inf.* give the once-over. **go through 1** *go through torture* undergo, suffer, experience, bear, stand, tolerate, endure, weather, brook, brave. **2** *go through money* spend, use up, run through, consume, exhaust. **3** *go through someone's pockets* look through, search, hunt through, check, inspect, examine; *inf.* frisk. **go together 1** *the carpets and curtains do not go together* match, harmonize. *See* GO *verb* 14. **2** *they have been going together for months* see each other, court, keep company. *See* GO OUT 3. **go under 1** *the ship went under* sink, founder. *See* GO DOWN 1. **2** *the firm has gone under* fail, founder, go bankrupt, go into receivership, go to the wall; *inf.* go bust, fold, flop. **go with 1** *the carpets do not go with the curtains* match, complement. *See* GO *verb* 14. **2** *his sister is going with her brother* see; *inf.* go steady with. *See* GO OUT 3.

go *noun* **1** *have a go at hang gliding* try, attempt, effort, bid, essay, endeavor; *inf.* shot, stab, crack, whirl, whack. **2** *people with a lot of go* energy, vigor, dynamism, force, verve, vim, vitality, vivacity, drive, push, enterprise; *inf.* get-up-and-go, pep, oomph.

go-ahead *noun* permission, assent, consent, authorization, sanction, leave, warranty, confirmation; *inf.* green light, OK, thumbs up.

goal *noun* aim, objective, object, end, purpose, target, ambition, design, intention, intent, aspiration, ideal.

go-between *noun* intermediary, mediator, middleman, medium, agent, broker, dealer, factor, liaison, contact, contact person; pander, panderer.

God *noun* God Almighty, the Almighty, the Godhead, the Supreme/Divine Being, the Deity, the Holy One, God the Father, Our Father, the Creator, Our Maker, the Lord, Jehovah, Allah.

god *noun* **1** *tribal gods* deity, divine being, divinity, spirit. **2** *false gods* idol, graven image, icon, golden calf.

godforsaken *adjective* desolate, dismal, dreary, bleak, wretched, miserable, gloomy, deserted, abandoned, forlorn, remote, backward.

godless *adjective* **1** *godless intellectuals* atheistic, agnostic, skeptical, faithless. **2** *preaching to the godless convicts* heathen, pagan, ungodly, impious, irreligious, unrighteous, unprincipled, sinful, wicked, evil, depraved.

godlike *adjective* godly, divine, celestial, heavenly, sacred, holy, saintly, deific, deiform, transcendent, superhuman.

godly *adjective* God-fearing, devout, pious, religious, pietistic, believing, righteous, moral, virtuous, good, holy, saintly.

goings-on *plural noun* misconduct, misbehavior, conduct, behavior, mischief, pranks; *inf.* funny business, monkey business, hanky-panky.

golden *adjective* **1** *golden hair* gold-colored, blond, blonde, yellow, yellowish, fair, flaxen, tow-colored, bright, gleaming, resplendent, brilliant, shining. **2** *a golden future* successful, prosperous, flourishing, thriving, rosy, bright, brilliant, rich. **3** *golden times* happy, joyful, delightful, glorious, precious, treasured. **4** *golden opportunities* fine, superb, excellent, favorable, opportune, promising, rosy, advantageous. **5** *the golden boy of the track team* talented, gifted, special, favorite, favored, cherished, beloved, pet, acclaimed, applauded, praised, lauded.

good *adjective* **1** *a good person* virtuous, moral, ethical, righteous, right-minded, right-thinking, honorable, honest, upright, high-minded, noble, worthy, admirable, estimable, exemplary. **2** *a good child* well-behaved, obedient, well-mannered, manageable, tractable. **3** *that's good* satisfactory, acceptable, adequate, fine, excellent; *inf.* great, OK, hunky-dory. **4** *a good thing to do* right, correct, proper, fitting, suitable, appropriate, decorous, seemly. **5** *a good driver* competent, capable, able, accomplished, efficient, skillful, adept, proficient, dexterous, expert, excellent, first-class, first-rate; *inf.* A-1, tip-top, topnotch. **6** *good brakes/friends* reliable, dependable, trustworthy. **7** *in good condition* fine, healthy, sound, robust, strong, vigorous. **8** *a good party* enjoyable, pleasant, agreeable, pleasing, pleasurable, amusing, cheerful, convivial, congenial. **9** *good of you to come* kind, kindly, kindhearted, good-hearted, friendly, charitable, gracious, benevolent, benign, altruistic. **10** *come at a good time* convenient, fitting, suitable, favorable, advantageous, fortunate, lucky, propitious, auspicious. **11** *broccoli is good for you* wholesome, healthful, nutritional, beneficial, salubrious, salutary. **12** *is this cheese still good?* eatable, edible, untainted, fresh. **13** *the food here is good* delicious, tasty, appetizing; *inf.* scrumptious, yummy. **14** *a good reason for going* valid, genuine, authentic, legitimate, sound, bona fide. **15** *wait a good hour* full, entire, whole, complete, solid. **16** *a good number came* considerable, substantial, goodly, sizable, large, sufficient, ample. **17** *good friends* close, intimate, bosom, fast, dear, valued, treasured. **18** *wear her good clothes* best, finest, newest, nicest, smartest, special, party, Sunday. **19** *good weather* fine, fair, mild, clear, bright, cloudless, sunshiny, sunny, calm, balmy, tranquil, clement, halcyon. **make good 1** *make good the damage* compensate for, make recompense for, make amends for, make restitution for, pay for, reimburse for. **2** *make good a promise* fulfill, carry out, effect, discharge, live up to. **3** *make good a statement* substantiate, back up, confirm, prove, validate, authenticate. **4** *he made good in America* succeed, do well, get ahead, reach the top.

good noun **1** *for your own good* benefit, advantage, behalf, gain, profit, interest, well-being, welfare, usefulness, avail, service. **2** *tell good from bad* virtue, goodness, morality, ethics, righteousness, rightness, rectitude, honor, honesty, uprightness, integrity, probity, worth, merit. **for good** for always, for ever, permanently.

good-bye interjection farewell, au revoir, adieu; *inf.* bye, cheers, see you later, see you, so long, toodle-oo, ciao; *inf.* bye-bye, ta-ta.

good-for-nothing adjective useless, of no use, no-good, lazy, idle, slothful, feckless.

good-for-nothing noun ne'er-do-well, wastrel, black sheep, layabout, idler, loafer, sluggard.

good-humored adjective amiable, affable, easygoing, genial, cheerful, cheery, happy, pleasant, good-tempered.

good-looking adjective attractive, handsome, pretty, lovely, beautiful, personable, comely, fair.

good-natured adjective kind, kindly, kindhearted, warmhearted, generous, benevolent, charitable, friendly, helpful, accommodating, amiable, tolerant.

goodness noun **1** *the goodness of the saint* virtue, virtuousness, morality, righteousness, rectitude, honor, honesty, uprightness, integrity, probity, nobility, worthiness, merit. **2** *she had the goodness to stay* kindness, kindliness, kindheartedness, warmheartedness, generosity, obligingness, benevolence, beneficence, friendliness, goodwill, graciousness, charitableness, unselfishness. **3** *the goodness in the food* nourishment, nutrition, wholesomeness.

goods plural noun belongings, possessions, property, effects, gear, things, paraphernalia, chattels, appurtenances, trappings, accoutrements; *inf.* stuff.

goodwill noun friendliness, kindness, kindliness, benevolence, compassion, amity.

gorge noun chasm, canyon, ravine, abyss, defile, pass, cleft, crevice, rift, fissure.

gorge verb bolt, gobble, wolf (down), devour, stuff down, gormandize; *inf.* shovel in. **gorge on** stuff with, cram with, fill

with, fill up on, glut with, satiate with, surfeit with, overeat.

gorgeous adjective **1** *a gorgeous sight* magnificent, splendid, superb, grand, resplendent, stately, impressive, imposing, sumptuous, luxurious, elegant, opulent, dazzling, brilliant, glittering, breathtaking, stunning. **2** *we had a gorgeous time* wonderful, marvelous, first-rate, delightful, enjoyable, entertaining, excellent.

gory adjective bloody, bloodthirsty, violent, murderous, brutal, savage, horror-filled, horrific; *inf.* blood-and-guts.

gossamer adjective cobwebby, silky, gauzy, chiffony, feathery, light, fine, delicate, frail, flimsy, insubstantial, airy, diaphanous, sheer, transparent, see-through.

gossip noun **1** *have you heard the gossip?* rumors, scandal, hearsay, smear campaign, mudslinging, dirt, low-down. **2** *he's just a gossip* gossipmonger, scandalmonger, busybody, tattletale.

gossip verb spread rumors/stories; talk, blab, tattle.

govern verb **1** *govern the country* rule, reign over, hold sway over, preside over, administer, lead, be in charge of, control, command, direct, manage, oversee, supervise, superintend, steer, pilot. **2** *govern one's passions* control, restrain, keep in check, check, curb, hold back, bridle, rein in. **3** *the weather will govern our decision* determine, decide, sway, rule, influence.

government noun **1** *the country's government* administration, regime, congress, parliament, ministry, council, executive, (the) powers that be. **2** *their government of the country* rule, administration, leadership, command, direction, control, guidance, management, conduct, supervision, superintendence.

gown noun dress, evening gown, ball gown.

grab verb grasp, clutch, grip, clasp, lay hold of, catch hold of, take hold of, fasten upon; seize, snatch, pluck, snap up, appropriate, capture; *inf.* bag, nab.

grab noun **up for grabs** available, accessible, obtainable, to be had, up for sale, for the taking.

grace noun **1** *the grace of the ballerina* gracefulness, suppleness, fluidity of movement, smoothness, ease, agility; *inf.* poetry in motion. **2** *the grace of the women* elegance, refinement, finesse, cultivation, polish, suaveness, good taste, taste, tastefulness, charm, loveliness. **3** *have the grace to apologize* manners, mannerliness, courtesy, courteousness, decency, consideration, tact, tactfulness, breeding, decorum, propriety, etiquette. **4** *fall from grace* favor, goodwill, preferment. **5** *by the grace of our benefactors* goodwill, generosity, kindness, kindliness, benefaction, beneficence, indulgence. **6** *beg for grace from the jury* mercy, leniency, clemency, indulgence, charity, quarter. **7** *ask for a year's grace* delay, postponement, deferment, deferral. **8** *say grace* blessing, benediction, thanks, thanksgiving.

grace verb **1** *paintings gracing the room* adorn, decorate, ornament, embellish, enhance, beautify, prettify, set off, deck, enrich, garnish. **2** *grace the gathering with his presence* dignify, distinguish, honor, favor, glorify, elevate.

graceful adjective **1** *graceful ballerinas* supple, fluid, flowing, smooth, easy, agile, nimble. **2** *graceful women* elegant, refined, cultured, cultivated, polished, suave, charming, lovely.

gracious adjective **1** *a gracious lady* kind, kindly, kindhearted, warmhearted, benevolent, friendly, amiable, affable, cordial, courteous, considerate, polite, chivalrous, well-mannered, beneficent, benign. **2** *a gracious room* elegant, tasteful, comfortable, luxurious. **3** *gracious God* merciful, compassionate, clement.

grade noun **1** *what grade did he reach?* level, stage, echelon, rank, standing, station, position, order, class. **2** *all belonging to the same grade* category, class, classification, type, brand. **3** *a steep grade* gradient, slope, incline, hill, rise, bank, acclivity, declivity. **make the grade** pass, pass muster, measure up, come up to standard, come up to scratch/snuff, qualify, get through.

grade verb classify, class, categorize, sort, group, order, brand, size, rank, evaluate, rate, value, range, graduate.

gradual adjective step-by-step, degree-by-degree, progressive, successive, continuous, systematic, regular, steady, even, moderate, slow, measured, unhurried.

graft noun *get ahead in business by graft* bribery, payola; *inf.* palm-greasing.

grand adjective **1** *grand houses* impressive, magnificent, imposing, splendid, striking, superb, stately, large, monumental, majestic. **2** *a grand feast* luxurious, sumptuous, lavish, opulent, princely. **3** *in the company of grand people* great, noble, aristocratic, distinguished, august, illustrious, eminent, esteemed, prominent, renowned. **4** *make a grand gesture* ostentatious, showy, pretentious, lordly, ambitious, imperious. **5** *the grand total* complete, comprehensive, all-inclusive, inclusive, exhaustive. **6** *the grand hall* principal, main, chief, leading, head, supreme. **7** *have a grand time* wonderful, marvelous, first-rate, outstanding.

grandeur noun **1** *the grandeur of the houses/feast* impressiveness, magnificence, splendor, splendidness, superbness, stateliness, largeness, majesty, luxuriousness,

luxury, sumptuousness, lavishness, opulence. **2** *the grandeur of the ruling classes* greatness, nobility, illustriousness, eminence.

grandiose adjective **1** *grandiose plans* ambitious, overambitious, extravagant, high-flown, high-sounding, pompous, pretentious, flamboyant. **2** *grandiose buildings* impressive, magnificent. See GRAND 1.

grant verb **1** *grant them an interview* agree/consent/assent/accede to give, permit, allow, accord. **2** *grant them an award* bestow on, confer on, give to, impart to, award with, present with, donate to, contribute to, provide with, endow with, furnish with. **3** *I grant you that you may be right* admit to, acknowledge to, concede to, go along with, yield to. **4** *grant property to his heirs* transfer, convey, transmit, pass on, hand over, assign, bequeath.

grant noun award, endowment, donation, contribution, allowance, subsidy, allocation, allotment.

graphic adjective **1** *a graphic description* vivid, striking, expressive, descriptive, lively, forcible, detailed, well-drawn, telling, effective, cogent, clear, lucid, explicit. **2** *a graphic representation* diagrammatic, representational, pictorial, illustrative, drawn, delineative.

grapple verb *grapple (with) the enemy* wrestle, fight, struggle, tussle, clash. **grapple with** tackle, face, cope with, come to grips with.

grasp verb **1** *grasp his hand* grip, clutch, clasp, hold, clench, catch, seize, grab, snatch. **2** *grasp the point* understand, comprehend, perceive, apprehend, get, get the picture, catch on.

grasp noun **1** *take a firm grasp of the rail* grip, hold, clutch, clasp, clench. **2** *beyond the grasp of her enemy* clutches, power, control, command, mastery, dominion, rule. **3** *well within your grasp* capacity, reach, scope, limits, range, compass. **4** *a good grasp of the subject* understanding, comprehension, perception, apprehension, knowledge.

grate verb **1** *grate cheese/onions* shred, pulverize, mince, grind, granulate. **2** *the knife grated against the metal* rasp, scrape, jar, scratch, grind, creak, rub. **grate on** irritate, set someone's teeth on edge, rub someone the wrong way, irk, annoy, vex, gall, nettle, peeve, rile, exasperate, chafe; get on someone's nerves.

grateful adjective **1** *grateful to you* thankful, indebted, obliged, obligated, beholden, appreciative. **2** *a grateful rest* pleasant, agreeable, refreshing, welcome, acceptable.

gratify verb **1** *their appreciation gratified her* please, delight, gladden, satisfy, warm the cockles of the heart. **2** *gratify their desires* fulfill, indulge, humor, comply with, pander to, cater to, give in to.

grating adjective **1** *a grating noise/voice* rasping, scraping, scratching, harsh, raucous, strident, screeching, piercing, shrill, squawking, squawky, hoarse, croaky. **2** *a grating personality* irritating, annoying, vexatious, irksome, galling, exasperating, offensive, disagreeable, unpleasant.

gratitude noun gratefulness, thankfulness, thanks, thanksgiving, appreciation, indebtedness.

gratuitous adjective **1** *gratuitous work* free, gratis, complimentary, voluntary, unasked-for, free of charge, for nothing, on the house. **2** *gratuitous insults* unjustified, unprovoked, groundless, without cause, without reason, uncalled-for, unwarranted, unmerited, needless, unnecessary, superfluous.

gratuity noun tip, perquisite, fringe benefit, bonus, gift, present, donation, reward, recompense, largesse; *inf.* perk.

grave adjective **1** *a grave expression/mood* solemn, earnest, serious, sober, somber, severe, unsmiling, long-faced, pensive, sedate, dignified, staid, dour. **2** *grave matters* serious, momentous, weighty, urgent, pressing, of great consequence, critical, acute, pivotal, life-and-death

graveyard noun cemetery, burial ground, churchyard, memorial park; *inf.* boneyard, potter's field.

gravitate verb **1** *gravitate to the bottom* sink, fall, drop, descend, settle. **2** *gravitate toward the arts* be drawn to, be pulled toward, be attracted to, incline toward.

gravity noun **1** *the gravity of her expression* solemnity, earnestness, seriousness, somberness, severity, pensiveness, sedateness, dignity. **2** *the gravity of the situation* seriousness, significance, weightiness, consequence, criticalness, acuteness.

graze verb **1** *the car grazed the wall* brush, brush against, touch, shave, glance off, skim, kiss. **2** *graze his knee* scrape, abrade, skin, scratch, chafe, bark, bruise.

gray adjective **1** *a gray dress* grayish, silvery, pearly, smoke-colored. **2** *complexion looking gray* ashen, wan, pale, pallid, colorless, bloodless, anemic. **3** *a gray day* cloudy, overcast, dull, dark, sunless, gloomy, dim, dreary, dismal, drab, cheerless. **4** *a gray area* doubtful, unclear, uncertain, indistinct, mixed.

great adjective **1** *a great expanse of forest* large, big, extensive, vast, immense, unlimited, boundless, spacious, huge, enormous, gigantic, colossal, mammoth, monstrous,

prodigious. **2** *describe in great detail* considerable, substantial, pronounced, exceptional, sizable. **3** *the great cities of the world* major, main, leading, chief, principal, capital, paramount, primary. **4** *a great occasion* grand, impressive, magnificent, imposing, splendid, majestic. **5** *the great people of the land* prominent, eminent, preeminent, illustrious, celebrated, famous, renowned, leading, top, high-ranking, noble. **6** *a great thinker/athlete* gifted, talented, outstanding, remarkable, exceptional, first-rate, incomparable, expert, skillful, masterly, adept, adroit, proficient; *inf.* crack, ace, A-1. **7** *a great moviegoer* enthusiastic, eager, keen, zealous. **8** *we had a great time* enjoyable, excellent, marvelous, wonderful. **9** *he's a great friend* thoroughgoing, total, complete, perfect, unqualified, consummate.

greatness noun **1** *the greatness of the forest* largeness, bigness, boundlessness, extensiveness, vastness, immensity, hugeness, enormity, prodigiousness. **2** *the greatness of the occasion* grandeur, impressiveness, magnificence, pomp, splendor, majesty. **3** *the greatness of the leaders* eminence, distinction, luster, illustriousness, renown, nobility. **4** *the greatness of the players* talent, expertise, skill, adeptness, proficiency.

greed noun greediness, avarice, acquisitiveness, rapacity, covetousness, cupidity, miserliness, tight-fistedness, parsimony; avidity, eagerness, hunger, craving, longing.

greedy adjective **1** *a greedy miser* avaricious, acquisitive, grasping, rapacious, grabbing, covetous, hoarding, miserly, niggardly, tight-fisted, close-fisted, parsimonious; *inf.* money-grubbing. **2** *greedy for knowledge* avid, eager, hungry, desirous, craving, longing.

green adjective **1** *green clothes* greenish, aquamarine, aqua, olive, emerald, sage, chartreuse. **2** *green land* verdant, grass-covered, grassy, leafy. **3** *a green apprentice* inexperienced, untrained, raw, immature, unsophisticated, unpolished, naïve, innocent, ingenuous, callow, gullible, wet behind the ears. **4** *look/go green* ashen, sickly, unhealthy, nauseous. **5** *green issues* environmentalist, conservationist, preservationist; environmentally sound/friendly, ecologically sound.

greet verb address, salute, hail, nod to, wave to; receive, meet, welcome.

gregarious adjective sociable, social, company-loving, companionable, convivial, outgoing, friendly, affable.

grief noun sorrow, mourning, mournfulness, bereavement, lamentation, misery, sadness, anguish, pain, distress, agony, heartache, heartbreak, heaviness of heart, trouble, woe, tribulation, trial, remorse, regret. **come to grief** fail, miscarry, meet with failure, meet with disaster; *inf.* come a cropper.

grievance noun **1** *answer the workers' grievances* complaint, charge, protest, ax to grind, bone to pick; *lit.* plaint; *inf.* grouse, gripe, beef. **2** *workers claiming a grievance* wrong, injustice, unfairness, injury, damage, hardship, offense, affront, insult.

grieve verb **1** *the widow is still grieving* mourn, lament, sorrow, weep and wail, cry, sob, suffer, ache, be in anguish, be distressed, eat one's heart out; bewail, bemoan, regret, rue, deplore. **2** *his behavior grieved her* hurt, wound, pain, sadden, break someone's heart, upset, distress.

grievous adjective **1** *a grievous injury* painful, agonizing, hurtful, afflicting, wounding, damaging, injurious. **2** *grievous news* calamitous, disastrous, distressing, dire. **3** *grievous sins/crimes* heinous, flagrant, glaring, outrageous, shocking, appalling, atrocious, dreadful, egregious. **4** *a grievous sound* grief-stricken, anguished, agonized, mournful, sorrowful, tragic, pitiful, heart-rending.

grim adjective **1** *a grim look* stern, forbidding, formidable, fierce, ferocious, threatening, menacing, harsh, somber. **2** *grim determination* resolute, determined, firm, unyielding, obdurate, inflexible, unrelenting, relentless. **3** *a grim sight/accident* dreadful, dire, ghastly, horrendous, appalling, frightful, shocking, harrowing, grisly, gruesome, hideous, macabre.

grimace verb scowl, frown, mouth, sneer, pout.

grimace noun scowl, frown, sneer, face, pout, mouth, moue.

grind verb **1** *grind coffee beans/nuts* crush, pound, pulverize, mill, powder, granulate, grate, crumble, mash, smash. **2** *grind knives* sharpen, file, whet, smooth, polish, sand. **3** *grind one's teeth* gnash, grit, grate, scrape, rasp. **4** *grind away at the task* labor, toil, slog, slave, drudge, plod, sweat; *inf.* plug. **grind down** oppress, torture, torment, molest, harass, harry.

grind noun *his job is a grind* drudgery, chore, slog, travail, toil, hard work, labor, slavery, forced labor, exertion; *inf.* drag, sweat.

grip noun **1** *lose his grip of the railing* hold, grasp, clutch, clasp, clench, hug, embrace; *inf.* clinch. **2** *have a grip of the problem* understanding, apprehension. *See* GRASP noun 4. **3** *in the grip of an addiction* clutches, control. *See* GRASP noun 2. **4** *pack a grip* bag, carryall, overnight bag, valise. **come to grips with** face up to,

meet head on, confront, encounter, deal with, cope with, handle, tackle, grapple with, contend with.

grip verb **1** *grip the railing* grasp, clutch, clasp, clench, hold, latch on to, grab, seize, catch, catch at. **2** *the speech gripped the audience* absorb, engross, rivet, spellbind, hold spellbound, entrance, fascinate, hold.

gripe verb complain, grumble, moan, groan, protest, whine; *inf.* grouse, bellyache, beef, bitch.

gripe noun complaint, grumble, moan, groan, grievance, objection, protest; *inf.* grouse, beef.

gripping adjective riveting, spellbinding, compelling, absorbing, engrossing.

grisly adjective gruesome, ghastly, frightful, horrid, horrifying, horrible, horrendous, grim, hideous, repulsive, revolting, repellent, macabre, spine-chilling, sickening, shocking, appalling, loathsome, abhorrent, odious.

grit noun **1** *boots tracking grit into the carpet* granules, sand, gravel, pebbles, dust, dirt. **2** *he has no grit* pluck, mettle, backbone, spirit, nerve, gameness, courage, bravery, toughness; *inf.* gumption, guts, spunk.

gritty adjective **1** *a gritty substance* sandy, grainy, granular, gravelly, pebbly, powdery, dusty. **2** *a gritty fighter* plucky, mettlesome, spirited, game, courageous, brave, hardy, tough, determined, resolute, dogged; *inf.* gutsy, spunky.

groan verb **1** *groan in pain* moan, cry, call out, sigh, murmur, whimper. **2** *groan about working conditions* complain, object. *See* GRIPE verb. **3** *the gate groaned* creak, grate, squeak, screech.

groggy adjective dazed, in a stupor, dizzy, faint, befuddled, muddled, confused, punch-drunk, shaky, staggering, reeling, unsteady, wobbly; *inf.* woozy.

groom verb **1** *groom one's hair/groom oneself* dress, tidy, brush, comb, smooth, spruce up, smarten up, preen, primp, freshen up. **2** *groom the horses* curry, brush, rub, rub down, clean. **3** *groom the students for college* prepare, prime, make ready, ready, instruct, tutor, drill, train, coach, school.

groove noun **1** *a groove in the ground* furrow, channel, trench, trough, canal, gouge, hollow, indentation, rut, gutter, cutting, cut, score, rabbet. **2** *the same old groove* rut, routine, habit, treadmill; *inf.* daily grind.

grope verb feel, fumble, fish, search, hunt, look, feel.

gross adjective **1** *gross in size* obese, massive, immense, huge, corpulent, overweight, bloated, bulky, cumbersome, unwieldy. **2** *gross jokes* coarse, crude, vulgar, obscene, rude, indecent, indelicate, improper, offensive. **3** *her brother is gross* boorish, loutish, oafish, coarse, crass, vulgar, ignorant, unrefined. **4** *a gross error* flagrant, blatant, glaring, egregious, manifest, obvious, plain, apparent. **5** *gross income* total, whole, entire, aggregate.

grotesque adjective bizarre, weird, outlandish, freakish, odd, peculiar, unnatural, incongruous, misshapen, distorted, twisted, deformed, malformed, misproportioned.

ground noun **1** *fall to the ground* earth, terra firma, floor; *inf.* deck. **2** *The ground is wet* earth, soil, dirt, land, terrain, clay, loam, turf, sod.

groundless adjective baseless, unfounded, unsupported, unsubstantiated, unwarranted, unjustified, uncalled-for, unreasonable, irrational, illogical, empty, idle, chimerical.

grounds plural noun **1** *take a walk around the grounds* surroundings, land, property, estate, lawns, gardens, park, area, domain, holding, territory. **2** *grounds for concern* reason, cause, basis, base, foundation, call, justification, rationale, argument, premise. **3** *coffee grounds* dregs, lees, deposit, sediment, precipitate, settlings, grouts.

groundwork noun foundation, base, basis, cornerstone, footing, underpinning, fundamentals, basics, ABCs, elements, essentials, preliminaries, preparations, spadework.

group noun **1** *divide the books into groups* category, classification, class, set, lot, batch, family, species, genus, bracket. **2** *a group of people/things* band, company, party, body, gathering, congregation, assembly, collection, clump, cluster, crowd, flock, pack, troop, gang, batch; clique, coterie, faction, circle, set; society, association, league, guild, club; *inf.* bunch.

group verb **1** *group students according to ability* classify, class, categorize, sort, grade, rank, bracket. **2** *group the children for a photograph* assemble, collect, gather together, arrange, organize, marshal, line up. **3** *they grouped (together) to form a club* get together, band together, associate, consort.

grovel verb abase oneself, kowtow, bow and scrape, crawl, fawn, curry favor, bootlick, flatter; *inf.* butter someone up, suck up to, throw oneself at someone's feet.

grow verb **1** *the child/pile grew* stretch, heighten, lengthen, enlarge, extend, expand, spread, thicken, widen, fill out, swell, increase, multiply. **2** *the plants are growing* shoot up, spring up, develop, sprout, burgeon, bud, germinate. **3** *her fear grows from her insecurity* arise, originate, stem, spring, issue. **4** *the business*

is growing flourish, thrive, prosper, succeed, progress, make headway, advance, improve, expand. **5** *grow prettier* become, get, turn, wax. **6** *grow corn* cultivate, produce, farm, propagate, raise.

growl verb snarl, howl, yelp, bark.

growth noun **1** *the growth in population* augmentation, increase, proliferation, multiplication, enlargement, expansion, extension, aggrandizement, magnification, amplification. **2** *the growth of the plants* development, maturation, germination, burgeoning, sprouting, blooming. **3** *the growth of the industry* expansion, rise, progress, success, advance, advancement, improvement. **4** *a growth on her body* tumor, lump, excrescence.

grubby adjective dirty, unwashed, grimy, filthy, messy, soiled, smutty, scruffy, shabby, untidy, unkempt, slovenly, squalid; *inf.* grungy, cruddy.

grudge noun resentment, spite, ill-will, pique, umbrage, grievance, hard feelings, rancor.

grueling adjective exhausting, tiring, fatiguing, wearying, taxing, demanding, trying, arduous, laborious, backbreaking, strenuous, punishing, crushing, draining, stiff, grinding, brutal.

gruesome adjective ghastly, frightful. *See* GRISLY.

gruff adjective **1** *a gruff voice* hoarse, harsh, rough, throaty, husky, croaking, rasping, guttural. **2** *a gruff old man* surly, churlish, brusque, curt, blunt, abrupt, grumpy, crotchety, crabby, crusty, bearish, sullen, sour; *inf.* grouchy.

grumble verb **1** *always grumbling about the weather* complain, moan, groan, protest, object, find fault with, carp, whine; *inf.* grouse, gripe, bellyache, beef, bitch, grouch. **2** *stomach was grumbling* rumble, gurgle, murmur, growl, mutter, roar.

grumpy adjective surly, churlish, crotchety, crabby, crusty, bearish, bad-tempered, ill-natured; *inf.* grouchy.

guarantee noun **1** *get a guarantee for the product* warranty, warrant, contract, covenant, bond, guaranty. **2** *give his guarantee that he will return* pledge, promise, assurance, word, word of honor, oath, bond. **3** *the house acts as a guarantee for a loan* collateral, security, surety, earnest, guaranty.

guarantee verb **1** *guarantee a loan* underwrite, sponsor, vouch for, support, back. **2** *I guarantee that I shall return* promise, pledge, give one's word, swear.

guard verb **1** *guard the town* stand guard over, protect, watch over, cover, patrol, police, defend, shield, safeguard, preserve,

save, conserve, secure, screen, shelter.
2 *guard the prisoners* keep under surveillance, keep watch over, mind, supervise.
guard against beware of, keep an eye out for, be on the alert against/for, be on the lookout against/for; *inf.* keep one's eyes peeled for.

guard noun **1** *volunteer as guards* protector, defender, guardian, guarder, bodyguard, custodian, sentinel, sentry, watchman, scout, lookout, watch, picket. **2** *prison guards* jailer, keeper; *inf.* screw. **3** *kept under guard* watch, close watch, watchfulness, vigilance, care, wariness. **4** *a guard for a machine* safeguard, shield, screen, fence, fender, bumper, buffer, cushion, pad. **off one's guard, off guard** unprepared, unready, unalert, unwatchful, napping. **on one's guard** on the alert, vigilant, wary, watchful, on the lookout, on the qui vive, prepared, ready.

guarded adjective careful, cautious, circumspect, wary, chary, reluctant, noncommittal, reticent, restrained, reserved, discreet, prudent; *inf.* cagey.

guardian noun guard, protector, defender, preserver, champion, custodian, warden, keeper, curator, caretaker, steward, trustee.

guess verb **1** *guess the answer* conjecture, surmise, estimate, reckon, fathom, hypothesize, postulate, predict, speculate; *inf.* guesstimate. **2** *I guess that you're right* suppose, believe, think, imagine.

guess noun conjecture, surmise, estimate, guesswork, hypothesis, theory, supposition, feeling, assumption, inference, prediction, speculation; *inf.* guesstimate.

guest noun visitor, caller, company; boarder, lodger, roomer, patron, customer.

guidance noun **1** *under the guidance of the president* direction, leadership, auspices, management, control, handling, charge, rule, teaching, instruction. **2** *career guidance* counseling, counsel, advice, direction, recommendation, suggestion, tip, pointer, instruction.

guide verb **1** *guide them to their seats* lead, conduct, show, usher, shepherd, direct, pilot, steer, escort, accompany, attend. **2** *guide the firm through its problems* control, direct, steer, manage, command, govern, rule, preside over, superintend, supervise, handle, manipulate, maneuver. **3** *guide the young graduates* counsel, advise, give direction to.

guide noun **1** *a tourist guide* leader, conductor, director, courier, pilot, usher, escort, attendant, convoy, chaperon. **2** *act as a career guide* counselor, adviser, mentor, confidant, tutor, teacher, guru, therapist. **3** *the lighthouse was the captain's guide* marker, indicator, pointer, mark, landmark, guiding light, sign, signal, beacon, lodestar,

signpost, key, clue. **4** *use that essay as a guide* model, pattern, example, exemplar, norm, archetype, prototype, paradigm, ideal, precedent. See GUIDELINE. **5** *read a guide to Paris* guidebook, tourist guide, travelogue, directory, handbook, manual, instructions, key, catalog.

guideline noun criterion, measure, standard, gauge, yardstick, benchmark, touchstone, rule, regulation.

guild noun association, society, club, union, league, federation, organization, company, fellowship, order, lodge, brotherhood, fraternity, sisterhood, sorority, alliance.

guile noun cunning, duplicity, craftiness, craft, artfulness, art, artifice, wiliness, wiles, foxiness, slyness, deception, deceit, underhandedness, double-dealing, trickery, trickiness.

guileless adjective ingenuous, artless, open, sincere, genuine, naïve, simple, innocent, unsophisticated, unworldly, trustful, trusting.

guilt noun **1** *prove/admitted his guilt* guiltiness, culpability, blame, blameworthiness, wrongdoing, criminality, misconduct, delinquency, sin, sinfulness, iniquity. **2** *haunted by guilt* remorse, regret, contrition, contriteness, repentance, penitence, compunction, conscience, self-accusation, self-reproach.

guiltless adjective innocent, blameless, unimpeachable, irreproachable, above reproach, clear, pure, sinless, faultless.

guilty adjective **1** *found guilty of the crime* blameworthy, blamable, culpable, at fault, responsible, censurable, criminal, convicted; reproachable, condemnable, erring, errant, wrong, delinquent, offending, sinful, wicked, evil, unlawful, illegal, illicit, reprehensible, felonious, iniquitous. **2** *feel guilty* conscience-stricken, remorseful, ashamed, shamefaced, regretful, contrite, compunctious, repentant, penitent, rueful, sheepish.

guise noun **1** *in the guise of a witch* appearance, likeness, costume, clothes, outfit, dress, habit, style. **2** *under the guise of friendship* pretense, disguise, show, screen, cover, blind.

gulf noun **1** *ships sailing into the gulf* bay, cove, inlet, bight, creek. **2** *a gulf opened up by an earthquake* chasm, abyss, hollow, pit, hole, opening, rift, cleft, fissure, split, crevice, gully, canyon, gorge, ravine. **3** *the gulf between disputing parties* chasm, abyss, split, division, gap.

gullible adjective credulous, trustful, overtrustful, unsuspecting, ingenuous, naïve, green, foolish, wet behind the ears.

gully noun ravine, valley, gulch. *See* GULF 2.

gumption noun initiative, resourcefulness, enterprise, cleverness, astuteness, shrewdness, acumen, common sense, spirit, forcefulness, backbone, pluck, mettle, nerve, courage; *inf.* get-up-and-go, grit, spunk, savvy, horse sense.

gun noun firearm, pistol, revolver, automatic, repeater, six-shooter, handgun; *inf.* gat, piece, rod, heater, Saturday-night special.

gunman noun armed robber, bandit, sniper, gunfighter, assassin, murderer; *inf.* gunslinger, hitman, hired gun, hood, mobster.

guru noun teacher, tutor, sage, swami, maharishi, mentor, leader, master, authority.

gush verb **1** *water gushing from the pipe* stream, rush forth, spout, spurt, surge, jet, well out, pour forth, burst forth, cascade, flood, flow, run, issue, emanate. **2** *she gushed about the beautiful room* effuse, enthuse, wax enthusiastic, wax lyrical, effervesce, bubble over, get carried away, fuss, babble, make too much, overstate the case.

gush noun outpouring, spurt, jet, spout, burst, rush, surge, cascade, flood, torrent, spate, freshet, stream.

gust noun **1** *a gust of wind* blast, flurry, puff, blow, rush, squall, breeze, gale. **2** *a gust of laughter* outburst, burst, outbreak, eruption, explosion, gale, fit, paroxysm, storm, surge.

gusto noun relish, zest, enthusiasm, zeal, fervor, verve, enjoyment, delight, exhilaration, pleasure, appreciation, liking, fondness, appetite.

guts plural noun courage, bravery, valor, backbone, nerve, fortitude, pluck, mettle, gameness, spirit, boldness, audacity, daring, hardiness, toughness, forcefulness, stamina, willpower, tenacity; *inf.* grit, gumption, spunk.

gutter noun drain, sewer, sluice, culvert, conduit, pipe, duct, channel, trough, trench, ditch, furrow.

guzzle verb gulp, gobble, bolt, down, quaff, swill; *inf.* chug, chug-a-lug.

gypsy noun traveler, migrant, rover, roamer, wanderer, rambler; transient, vagrant, vagabond.

gyrate verb rotate, revolve, circle, whirl, pirouette, twirl, swirl, spin, swivel.

Hh

habit noun **1** *it was his habit to take a daily walk* custom, practice, procedure, wont, way, routine, style, pattern, convention, policy, mode, rule. **2** *smoking is a bad habit* addiction, dependence, weakness, fixation, obsession. **habit of** *he had a habit of staring* tendency for, propensity for, predisposition for, proclivity for, penchant for, inclination for.

habitat noun **1** *the animal's natural habitat* environment, setting, element. **2** *the habitat of students* home, abode. *See* HABITATION 2.

habitation noun **1** *fit for habitation* occupancy, occupation, tenancy, living, dwelling, housing, inhabitance, lodging. **2** *settled into a new habitation* home, house, residence, residency, dwelling, dwelling place, abode, domicile, lodging, quarters, living quarters, rooms, apartment, flat, accommodation, housing, roof over one's head; *inf.* pad, digs.

habitual adjective **1** *taking his habitual route* customary, accustomed, regular, usual, normal, set, fixed, established, routine, wonted, common, ordinary, familiar, traditional.

2 *a habitual smoker* persistent, constant, repeated, confirmed, chronic, inveterate.

hackneyed adjective hack, banal, trite, overused, overworked, tired, worn-out, time-worn, stale, stereotyped, clichéd, commonplace, pedestrian, prosaic, run-of-the-mill, stock, conventional; *inf.* played-out, corny, old-hat.

hag noun crone, witch, gorgon, harridan, harpy, shrew, virago; *inf.* battleax, old bat/bag.

haggard adjective drawn, gaunt, pinched, hollow-cheeked, hollow-eyed, peaked, drained, careworn, emaciated, wasted.

haggle verb **1** *haggle over the price* bargain, drive a hard bargain, argue, dicker. **2** *children haggling* squabble, bicker, quarrel, argue, dispute.

hail[1] verb **1** *hail a friend* salute, greet, nod to, wave to, lift one's hat to, acknowledge. **2** *hail a taxi* signal, flag, flag down, call, shout to. **3** *hail the king* acclaim, applaud, cheer, praise, laud, extol.

hail from come from, be a native of, originate in.

hail[2] noun *a hail of bullets* shower, rain, storm, volley, barrage, bombardment, pelting.

hail[3] verb **hail down on** shower, rain down on/upon, pelt, pepper, batter, bombard.

hair noun **1** *brushed her hair* locks, tresses; *inf.* mane, mop. **2** *animal's hair* coat, fur, pelt, hide, wool, fleece, mane. **by a hair, by a hair's breadth** by a narrow margin, by the skin of one's teeth, by a split second, by a whisker. **let one's hair down** relax; *inf.* hang loose, let it all hang out, chill out. **split hairs** quibble, niggle, cavil; *inf.* nitpick.

hair-raising adjective spine-chilling, spine-tingling, bloodcurdling, terrifying, horrifying, frightening; *inf.* scary, creepy.

hairy adjective hair-covered, hirsute, pilose, pileous, woolly, furry, fleecy, fuzzy; bearded, unshaven, bewhiskered, stubbly.

hale adjective well, fit. *See* HEALTH 1.

half-baked adjective *half-baked notions* ill-conceived, unplanned, not thought through, premature, undeveloped, unformed, shortsighted, injudicious, impractical; *inf.* crackpot.

halfhearted adjective lukewarm, unenthusiastic, apathetic, indifferent, uninterested, unconcerned, cool, cursory, perfunctory, superficial.

halfwit noun simpleton, idiot, dolt, blockhead, dunderhead, dullard, dunce, fool, numskull, nitwit; *inf.* moron, dimwit, imbecile, crackpot, nut.

halfwitted adjective simpleminded, feebleminded, simple, stupid, idiotic, doltish, dull-witted, foolish, silly.

hall noun **1** *concerts held in the main hall* auditorium, assembly room, chamber. **2** *guests were greeted in the hall* vestibule, hallway, entry, lobby, foyer, passageway, passage.

hallmark noun *good craftsmanship is his hallmark* mark, trademark, stamp, sign, sure sign, telltale sign, badge, device, symbol.

hallucinate verb fantasize, imagine things, dream, be delirious; *inf.* see things, trip.

hallucination noun illusion, figment of the imagination, imagining, vision, mirage, fantasy, apparition, dream, delirium, phantasmagoria.

halo noun nimbus, aureole, aureola, aura, ring of light, crown of light, corona.

halt[1] verb **1** *halt at the traffic lights* stop, come to a standstill, pull up, draw up, wait. **2** *halt for the day* finish, cease, break off, call it a day, desist, discontinue, rest; *inf.* knock off. **3** *halt progress* arrest, check, block, curb, stem, terminate, end, put an end to, put a stop to, frustrate, obstruct, impede.

halt[2] noun stop, stoppage, cessation, close, end, desistance, discontinuation, discontinuance, standstill, pause, interval, interlude, intermission, break, hiatus, rest, respite, breathing space, time out; *inf.* breather.

halt[3] verb **1** *halt when speaking* falter, hesitate, stammer, stutter, stumble, flounder. **2** *halting between going and staying* hesitate, waver, vacillate, dither.

hammer verb **1** *hammer it on the anvil* beat, shape, form, mold, forge, fashion, make, fabricate. **2** *hammer the punching bag/opposition* beat, batter, pound, pummel, hit, strike; trounce, thrash, worst, drub; *inf.* murder, clobber, wallop. **3** *hammer facts into their heads* drum, drive, drub. **hammer away at** persevere at, persist at; *inf.* stick to/with, plug away at. **hammer out** thrash out, work out, resolve, sort out, settle, negotiate, bring about, produce, carry through, effect.

hamper verb hinder, obstruct, impede, hold back, inhibit, retard, slow down, hold up, restrain, curb, interfere with, cramp, restrict, bridle, handicap, hamstring.

hamstring verb *hamstring the opposition plans* frustrate, thwart, balk, foil, check, curb, hamper, ruin, prevent, stop.

hand noun **1** *large hands* palm, fist; *inf.* paw, mitt, duke. **2** *the hand of a clock* pointer, indicator, needle. **3** *give me a hand* helping hand, help, assistance, aid, support, succor, relief. **4** *hired a number of hands* worker, workman, employee, operative, hired hand, laborer, artisan, crewman. **5** *have a neat hand* writing, handwriting, penmanship, script, calligraphy. **6** *try your hand at baking* ability, skill, art, artistry, craftsmanship. **7** *give the singer a big hand* applause, round of applause, clap, ovation. **at hand 1** *help is at hand* available, accessible. *See* HANDY 1. **2** *your big moment is at hand* close at hand, imminent, approaching, impending. **from hand to mouth** precariously, uncertainly, insecurely, improvidently. **hand in glove** in partnership, in league, in collusion; *inf.* in cahoots. **hand in hand** *work hand in hand* together, closely, side by side, in partnership. **in hand 1** *have the matter in hand* under control, under way. **2** *have money in hand* ready, available, in reserve, put by. **try one's hand** attempt, essay; *inf.* have/take a shot, have a go.

hand verb give, pass, pass over, hand over, deliver, present. **hand down** transfer, transmit, bequeath, will. **hand out** distribute, give out, pass out, deal out, dole out, mete out, dispense, apportion, disburse; *inf.* dish out. **hand over** turn over, deliver, surrender, yield, release; *inf.* fork out/over.

handbag noun purse, bag, shoulder bag, clutch, pocketbook.

handbook noun guide, guidebook, travel guide, manual, instruction manual, instructions.

handful noun **1** *not many, just a handful* few, small number/amount, sprinkling. **2** *the child is a handful* nuisance, pest, bother, irritant; *inf.* pain, pain in the neck.

handicap noun **1** *born with a handicap* disability, disadvantage, abnormality, impairment. **2** *her poverty was a handicap* disadvantage, impediment, hindrance, obstruction, obstacle, encumbrance, barrier, stumbling block, drawback, shortcoming.

handicap verb put at a disadvantage, impede, hinder, impair, hamper, obstruct, check, block, encumber, curb, trammel, bridle, hold back, constrain, restrict, limit.

handle noun shaft, grip, handgrip, hilt, haft, knob, stock.

handle verb **1** *handle the goods* touch, feel, finger, hold, grasp, grip, pick up, caress, stroke, fondle, poke, maul; *inf.* paw. **2** *handle difficult problems/people* cope with, deal with, treat, manage, be in charge of, control, administer, direct, guide, conduct, supervise, take care of. **3** *dealers handling grain* deal in, traffic in, trade in, market, sell, stock, carry.

handout noun **1** *not accepting handouts* alms, charity; gift, sample, free sample; *inf.* freebie. **2** *read the handout* press release, circular, flyer, leaflet, brochure, pamphlet, bulletin.

hands plural noun *in the hands of the enemy* possession, keeping, charge, care, power, authority, command, management, control, custody, guardianship, supervision, jurisdiction. **hands down** *win hands down* easily, with no trouble, effortlessly; *inf.* no sweat.

handsome adjective **1** *a handsome man/woman* good-looking, attractive, elegant, fine, well-formed, well-proportioned, stately, dignified; *inf.* gorgeous, easy on the eyes, foxy. **2** *a handsome gift* generous, magnanimous, liberal, lavish, bounteous, considerable, sizable, large.

handy adjective **1** *is the book handy?* at hand, available, within reach, accessible, near, nearby, close, at one's fingertips, convenient; *inf.* on tap. **2** *a handy instrument* useful, helpful, practicable, practical, serviceable, functional, easy-to-use, convenient. **3** *a handy person* dexterous, deft, nimble-fingered, adroit, adept, proficient, skillful, good with one's hands.

hang verb **1** *mobiles hanging from the ceiling* hang down, be suspended, dangle, swing, sway, be pendent. **2** *hang the picture* suspend, put up, put on a hook. **3** *hang the convicted killer* send to the gallows, put the noose on, send to the gibbet, gibbet, execute; lynch; *inf.* string up. **4** *hang wallpaper* stick on, attach, fix, fasten on, append, paste, glue, cement. **5** *walls hung with tapestries* decorate, adorn, ornament, deck, drape, cover, furnish. **6** *hawks hanging in the air* hover, float, be poised, flutter, flit, drift, remain static. **hang around/about 1** *hang around, he won't be long* linger, loiter, tarry, dally, waste time; *inf.* hang on. **2** *hang around bars* frequent, be a regular at, haunt; *inf.* hang out in. **3** *hang around with thugs* associate, keep company; *inf.* hang out. **hang back** hold back, stay back, stay in the background, be reluctant, hesitate, demur, recoil, shrink back. **hang fire** delay, procrastinate, stall. **hang on 1** *everything hangs on the budget* depend, turn on, hinge on, rest on, be contingent upon, be determined by, be conditioned by. **2** *hang on till things improve* persevere, persist, go on, carry on, continue, remain, endure. **hang on to** cling to, grip, clutch, grasp, cleave to. **hang over** *the threat of layoffs is hanging over them* loom over, menace, threaten.

hang noun **get the hang of** get the knack of, catch on, grasp, comprehend, understand.

hanger-on noun parasite, minion, lackey, vassal, flunky, camp follower, sycophant, fawner, sponger, leech; *inf.* groupie, freeloader.

hang-up noun preoccupation, fixation, obsession, bee in one's bonnet, *idée fixe*; psychological block, block, inhibition, difficulty, problem; *inf.* thing.

hanker verb **hanker after/for** long for, yearn for, crave, desire, hunger for, thirst for, set one's heart on, pine for, lust after; *inf.* be dying for, have a yen for.

hankering noun longing, yearning, craving, desire, hunger, thirst, want, lust; *inf.* yen.

haphazard adjective random, unsystematic, unorganized, unmethodical, orderless, aimless, indiscriminate, slapdash, thrown together, careless, casual, hit-or-miss.

hapless adjective unlucky, luckless, unfortunate, ill-starred, forlorn, wretched, woebegone; *inf.* down on one's luck.

happen verb take place, occur, come about, come to pass, present itself, arise, materialize, appear, come into being, chance, arrive, transpire, crop up, develop; *inf.* come off.

happening noun occurrence, event, incident, occasion, affair, circumstance, action.

happily adverb **1** *I shall happily go with pleasure*, gladly, delightedly, willingly, freely, contentedly, enthusiastically, with all one's heart and soul. **2** *children playing happily* cheerfully, merrily, gaily, lightheartedly, joyfully, blithely. **3** *happily, it turned out all right* luckily, fortunately, as luck would have it, providentially.

happiness noun cheerfulness, cheeriness, merriness, gaiety, good spirits, high spirits, lightheartedness, joy, joyfulness, joviality, glee, blitheness, gladness, delight, exuberance, elation, ecstasy, bliss, blissfulness, euphoria.

happy adjective **1** *a happy mood* cheerful, cheery, merry, gay, lighthearted, joyful, joyous, jovial, gleeful, buoyant, blithe, blithesome, carefree, untroubled, exuberant, elated, ecstatic, blissful, euphoric, in seventh heaven, floating/walking on air; *inf.* on cloud nine, on top of the world. **2** *happy to see you* glad, pleased, delighted, contented, satisfied, gratified, thrilled. **3** *a happy chance* lucky, fortunate, favorable, advantageous, beneficial, helpful, opportune, timely, convenient, propitious, auspicious. **4** *a happy choice* apt, appropriate, fitting, fit, proper, seemly.

happy-go-lucky adjective carefree, lighthearted, devil-may-care, blithe, free and easy, easygoing, nonchalant, casual, untroubled, unworried, unconcerned, insouciant.

harangue noun lecture, tirade, diatribe, sermon, exhortation, declamation; *inf.* spiel.

harass verb **1** *children harassing their mother* bother, pester, annoy, exasperate, worry, fret, disturb, agitate, provoke, badger, hound, torment, plague, persecute, harry, tease, bait, nag, molest, bedevil; *inf.* hassle, give someone a hard time, drive someone up the wall. **2** *troops harassing the enemy* harry, raid, beleaguer, press hard.

harbinger noun herald, forerunner, precursor, sign, portent, omen, augury.

harbor noun port, anchorage, dock, marina; refuge, shelter. *See* HAVEN 1, 2.

harbor verb **1** *harbor criminals* shelter, house, lodge, put up, take in, billet, provide refuge for, shield, protect, conceal, hide, secrete. **2** *harbor resentment* nurture, maintain, hold on to, cherish, cling to, retain, entertain, brood over.

hard adjective **1** *hard ground* firm, solid, solidified, compact, compacted, compressed, dense, rigid, stiff, unyielding, resistant, unmalleable, inflexible, unpliable, tough, strong, stony, rocklike. **2** *hard physical work* arduous, strenuous, heavy, tiring, fatiguing, exhausting, backbreaking, laborious, rigorous, exacting, tough, uphill, toilsome, Herculean. **3** *a hard problem* difficult, complicated, complex, involved, intricate, puzzling, perplexing, knotty, thorny. **4** *a hard master* harsh, severe, stern, cold, grim, ruthless, oppressive, tyrannical, implacable, obdurate. **5** *hard living conditions* unpleasant, disagreeable, uncomfortable, intolerable, unendurable, unbearable, insupportable, distressing, painful. **6** *a hard blow/knock* forceful, violent, heavy, strong, powerful, sharp, fierce. **7** *a hard worker* industrious, diligent. *See* HARDWORKING. **8** *hard words/feelings* angry, acrimonious, bitter, antagonistic, hostile, resentful, rancorous. **9** *the hard facts* actual, definite, undeniable, indisputable, verifiable, plain, cold, bare, unvarnished, unembellished.

hard adverb **1** *push hard* strenuously, energetically, powerfully, heavily, with all one's might, with might and main, vigorously, forcefully, forcibly, fiercely, intensely. **2** *work hard* industriously, diligently, assiduously, conscientiously, enthusiastically, sedulously. **3** *our victory was hard won* with effort, laboriously, after a struggle, painfully. **4** *her death hit him hard* intensely, violently, forcefully, distressingly, painfully, agonizingly. **5** *it was raining hard* heavily, steadily; *inf.* cats and dogs, buckets. **6** *look hard at* keenly, sharply, carefully, closely, painstakingly. **hard** by right by, beside, near, nearby, close to, within a stone's throw of. **hard up** poor, short of money/cash, in financial difficulties, impoverished, destitute, bankrupt, in the red.

hard-and-fast adjective binding, set, strict, stringent, inflexible, rigorous, immutable, unalterable, uncompromising.

hard-boiled adjective cynical, unsentimental, tough.

hard-core adjective **1** *hard-core socialists* diehard, dyed-in-the-wool, staunch, steadfast, dedicated. **2** *hard-core pornography* explicit, blatant.

harden verb **1** *the cement hardened* solidify, set, stiffen, bake, anneal, cake, freeze, congeal, clot, coagulate. **2** *harden one's heart* toughen, deaden, numb, benumb. **3** *harden to cold* accustom, habituate, acclimatize, inure.

hardened adjective chronic, inured, seasoned, inveterate, incorrigible.

hardheaded adjective shrewd, astute, sharp, practical, pragmatic, realistic.

hard-hearted adjective heartless, unfeeling, unsympathetic, uncompassionate, cold, cold-hearted, uncaring, unconcerned, cruel, callous, merciless, pitiless, stony-hearted, stony.

hard-hitting adjective vigorous, tough, uncompromising, unsparing, blunt, frank, critical.

hard-line adjective extreme, uncompromising, inflexible, unyielding, intransigent.

hardly adverb scarcely, barely, only just, just.

hard-pressed adjective overloaded, overburdened, overworked, overtaxed, under pressure, harassed, harried, hounded; *inf.* pushed, up against it.

hardship noun adversity, privation, want, need, destitution, poverty, austerity, desolation, misfortune, distress, suffering, affliction, pain, misery, wretchedness, tribulation.

hardworking adjective diligent, industrious, conscientious, assiduous, sedulous, energetic, keen, enthusiastic, zealous, busy, with one's shoulder to the wheel.

hardy adjective **1** *hardy children* robust, sturdy. *See* HEALTHY 1. **2** *hardy men defying death* brave, courageous, valiant, bold, valorous, intrepid, stouthearted, daring, plucky, mettlesome.

harebrained adjective foolish, foolhardy, rash, reckless, madcap, wild, ridiculous, brainless, giddy, dizzy, whimsical, capricious, flighty. *See* HALF-BAKED.

hark verb harken, listen, pay attention, pay heed, give ear. **hark back** to go back to, turn back to, revert to, regress to, remember, recall, recollect.

harlot noun whore, prostitute, call girl, streetwalker, loose woman, fallen woman, lady of the evening, madam, procuress; *inf.* tramp, hooker.

harm noun **1** *inflict harm* hurt, injury, pain, suffering, trauma, adversity, disservice, abuse, damage, mischief, detriment, destruction, loss, ruin. **2** *full of harm* badness, evil, wrongdoing, wrong, wickedness, vice, iniquity, sin, sinfulness, immorality, nefariousness.

harm verb hurt, injure, wound, abuse, maltreat, ill-treat, ill-use, molest, do violence to, damage, do mischief to, deface, defile, impair, spoil, mar, blemish, destroy.

harmful adjective hurtful, injurious, detrimental, deleterious, disadvantageous, destructive, pernicious, noxious, baneful, toxic.

harmless adjective innocuous, safe, nontoxic, nonirritant, mild, inoffensive, unoffending.

harmonious adjective **1** *a harmonious musical piece* melodious, tuneful, musical, harmonizing, sweet-sounding, mellifluous, dulcet, euphonious, symphonious. **2** *a harmonious relationship* peaceful, peaceable, friendly, amicable, cordial, amiable, agreeable, congenial, in tune, attuned. **3** *a harmonious collection of buildings* compatible, congruous, coordinated, concordant, well-matched, matching.

harmonize verb **1** *the colors/stories harmonize* go together, fit together, be compatible, match, agree, correspond, coincide, be congruent. **2** *harmonize relations* settle differences, reconcile, patch up, negotiate peace between, heal the breach.

harmony noun **1** *working in harmony* agreement, accord, cooperation, unanimity, unity, amity, goodwill, affinity, rapport, fellowship, peace, peacefulness. **2** *the harmony of the colors* compatibility, congruity, consonance, concord, coordination, blending, balance, symmetry, suitability.

harness verb **1** *harness the horses* saddle, yoke, bridle, hitch up, couple. **2** *harness the sun's rays* control, utilize, apply, exploit, channel, mobilize, capitalize on.

harp noun **harp on** dwell on, persist in talking about, nag about, belabor the point about; *inf.* go on and on about.

harridan noun shrew, harpy, virago, termagant, vixen, scold, nag, fishwife, hellcat, spitfire, fury. *See* HAG.

harrowing adjective distressing, agonizing, excruciating, traumatic, painful, racking, chilling, horrifying.

harry verb **1** *invaders harrying the villagers* plunder, rob, raid, sack, pillage, devastate, ravage, despoil, lay waste to. **2** *children harrying their mother* annoy, bother. *See* HARASS 1.

harsh adjective **1** *a harsh noise* grating, jarring, grinding, rasping, strident, raucous, discordant, dissonant, unharmonious. **2** *harsh colors* gaudy, garish, glaring, bold, loud, flashy, showy, crass, crude, vulgar. **3** *harsh conditions/countryside* grim, severe, desolate, stark, austere, barren, bleak, inhospitable, comfortless, spartan. **4** *a harsh reply* abrupt, brusque, blunt, curt, gruff, short, surly, concise, impolite, discourteous, uncivil, ungracious. **5** *a harsh ruler* cruel, brutal, savage, barbarous, hard-hearted, despotic, tyrannical, ruthless, uncompassionate, unfeeling, merciless. **6** *a harsh measure* stern, severe, grim, stringent, austere, uncompromising, inflexible, punitive, draconian.

harvest noun **1** *a good harvest of apples* crop, yield, vintage. **2** *the squirrels have a harvest of nuts* store, supply, stock, stockpile, hoard, cache, accumulation. **3** *the harvest of hard work* product, fruits, return, effect, result, consequence.

harvest verb **1** *harvest the crop* gather in, gather, reap, glean, pick, pluck, collect. **2** *harvest benefits from his experience* acquire, gain, obtain, get, derive, procure, secure, net.

hassle noun **1** *tired of all the hassle* inconvenience, trouble, bother, annoyance, nuisance, harassment, badgering, difficulty, problem, struggle. **2** *a hassle at the bar last night* fight, quarrel, squabble, argument, disagreement, dispute, altercation, tussle.

hassle verb annoy, badger. See HARASS 1.

haste noun **1** *fulfill the order with haste* speed, swiftness, rapidity, quickness, alacrity, promptness, dispatch, expeditiousness, celerity, fleetness, briskness. **2** *haste causes carelessness* hastiness, hurriedness, hurry, rushing, hustling, impetuosity, recklessness, rashness, impulsiveness.

hasten verb **1** *you must hasten to get there on time* make haste, hurry, hurry up, dash, rush, race, sprint, fly, tear along, bolt, scurry, scamper, scuttle; *inf.* get a move on, step on it, hotfoot it, hightail it. **2** *hasten the growth* speed up, accelerate, quicken, advance, precipitate, boost, increase, step up.

hasty adjective **1** *with hasty steps* swift, rapid, quick, fast, speedy, hurried, prompt, expeditious, fleet, brisk. **2** *a hasty visit/glance* brief, short-lived, fleeting, transitory, cursory, perfunctory. **3** *a hasty decision* rushed, impetuous, reckless, rash, foolhardy, precipitate, impulsive, headlong, heedless, ill-conceived. **4** *a hasty nature* hotheaded, quick-tempered, irascible, fiery, excitable, volatile, choleric.

hat noun cap, bonnet, beret, tam-o'-shanter, hard hat, bowler, top hat, deerstalker, Homburg, Stetson, boater, panama, toque, cloche, pillbox, helmet, turban, fez, skullcap, yarmulke.

hatch verb **1** *hatch eggs* incubate, brood, sit on, cover. **2** *hatch a scheme* devise, concoct, contrive, plan, scheme, design, conceive, dream up, think up; *inf.* cook up.

hate verb **1** *hate his job* loathe, detest, abhor, abominate, despise, be unable to abide/bear/stand, be repelled by, recoil from. **2** *I hate to upset her* be reluctant, be loath, be unwilling, feel disinclined, be sorry, dislike, not have the heart.

hateful adjective loathsome, detestable, abhorrent, abominable, despicable, odious, revolting, repugnant, repellent, disgusting, obnoxious, offensive, insufferable, foul, vile, heinous.

hatred noun hate, loathing, detestation, abhorrence, abomination, aversion, hostility, ill will, enmity, animosity, antagonism, antipathy, revulsion, repugnance, odium, rancor.

haughty adjective proud, arrogant, conceited, self-important, egotistical, vain, supercilious, condescending, lofty, patronizing, snobbish, imperious; *inf.* on one's high horse, snooty, high and mighty, stuck-up, hoity-toity, uppity.

haul verb drag, draw, pull, tug, heave, trail, lug, tow; transport, convey, move, cart, carry, convoy, ship.

haunt verb **1** *haunt bars* frequent, be a regular at; *inf.* hang out in, hang around/about. **2** *thoughts of guilt haunted him* obsess, prey on, torment, plague, beset, burden, weigh on, recur to, come back to.

haunt noun stamping ground, favorite spot, resort, rendezvous; *inf.* hangout.

haunting adjective persistent, recurring, recurrent, indelible, unforgettable.

have verb **1** *we have two cars* own, possess, keep, use, hold, retain. **2** *we had news of him* get, receive, obtain, acquire, procure, secure, gain. **3** *the apartment has five rooms* contain, include, comprise, embrace, embody, incorporate. **4** *she had a lot of trouble* experience, undergo, go through, encounter, meet, find, suffer from, endure, tolerate, put up with. **5** *have doubts* feel, entertain, harbor, foster, nurse, cherish. **6** *have the impudence to answer back* show, display, exhibit, demonstrate, manifest, express. **7** *they had her do all their work* make, force to, coerce to, induce to, prevail upon to, talk into, persuade to. **8** *I'll have the technician repair the telephone* ask to, request that, bid to, tell to, order to, command to, direct to. **9** *she won't have such behavior* permit, allow, put up with, tolerate, stand, brook, endure, abide. **10** *she had a daughter* bear, deliver, be delivered of, bring into the world, beget. **11** *they certainly had you* fool, trick, take in, dupe, outwit, deceive, cheat, swindle. **12** *he boasted that he had had all the women there* have sex with, make love to/with, copulate with; *inf.* bed, lay. **have had it** be finished, be out, be defeated, have lost. **have on 1** *I have something on today* have planned, have arranged, be committed to, have on the agenda. **2** *the police have something on him* have information about, have evidence against, know something bad/incriminating about. **have to** must, have got to, be bound to, be obliged to, be under an obligation to, be forced to, be compelled to.

haven noun **1** *ships entering a haven* harbor, port, anchorage, moorage, dock, cove, bay. **2** *refugees seeking a safe haven* refuge, shelter, sanctuary, asylum, retreat, sanctum, sanctum sanctorum, covert.

havoc noun **1** *forest fires wreaking havoc* devastation, destruction, damage, ruination, ruin, rack and ruin, waste, wreckage, desolation. **2** *the havoc in the room after the party* chaos, disorder, confusion, disruption, disorganization, mayhem; *inf.* shambles.

hazard noun danger, peril, risk, jeopardy, threat, menace.

hazard verb **1** *hazard a guess* venture, put forward, proffer, offer, submit, advance, volunteer. **2** *hazard his life* risk, endanger, imperil, jeopardize.

hazardous adjective **1** *a hazardous journey* dangerous, danger-filled, risky, perilous, fraught with danger/risk/peril, precarious; *inf.* dicey, hairy. **2** *a hazardous venture* chancy, uncertain, unpredictable, speculative.

haze noun **1** *haze covered the town* mist, mistiness, fog, cloud, cloudiness, smog, vapor. **2** *her mind is in a haze* vagueness, confusion, befuddlement, bewilderment, obscurity, dimness.

hazy adjective **1** *a hazy day* misty, foggy, cloudy, smoggy. **2** *hazy memories* vague, indefinite, blurred, fuzzy, faint, unclear, obscure, dim, indistinct, ill-defined.

head noun **1** *hurt his head* skull, cranium; *inf.* pate, nut, noodle, noggin, bean. **2** *use your head* mind, intellect, intelligence, brain, brains, mentality, wit, wits, wisdom, sense, reasoning, rationality, understanding; *inf.* gray matter. **3** *a head for business* aptitude, ability, capacity, flair, talent, faculty. **4** *the head of the organization* leader, chief, commander, director, chairman, chair, chairperson, manager, superintendent, controller, administrator, supervisor. **5** *(at) the head of the firm* top, command, control, controls, charge, leadership, directorship. **6** *at the head of the line* front, fore, forefront, van, vanguard. **7** *matters coming to a head* climax, culmination, crisis, critical point, turning point, crossroads. **8** *at the head of the stream* origin, source, fountainhead, fount, wellhead, wellspring, headwater. **9** *the material is listed under various heads* category, classification. *See* HEADING 1. **go to one's head 1** *the wine has gone to my head* make someone intoxicated/dizzy, make someone's head spin; *inf.* make someone woozy. **2** *their praise went to her head* make someone conceited/arrogant/boastful, puff someone up. **head first 1** *fall head first down the stairs* on one's head, head foremost. *See* HEADLONG 1. **2** *rush into things head first* rashly, recklessly. *See* HEADLONG 2. **head over heels** utterly, completely, thoroughly, fully, wholeheartedly, intensely. **keep one's head** keep calm, keep cool, remain unruffled, maintain one's equilibrium. **lose one's head** panic, lose control of oneself, lose control of the situation, get flustered/confused, get angry, get excited, get hysterical; *inf.* lose one's cool, blow one's top, freak out, fly off the handle.

head adjective chief, leading, main, principal, premier, foremost, topmost, supreme, cardinal.

head verb **1** *head the expedition/firm* lead, be the leader of, be at the head of, be in charge of, be in command of, command, control, run, manage, direct, administer, supervise. **2** *a tower headed by a spire* crown, top, surmount, cap, tip. **3** *head for town* make for, aim for, set out for, start out for, go/turn toward, steer toward. **head off** intercept, deflect, turn aside, block off, cut off, ward off, fend off, forestall, avert.

headache noun *her nephew is nothing but a headache to her* nuisance, bother, pest, trouble, vexation, bane, bugbear, worry, inconvenience; *inf.* pain, pain in the neck.

heading noun **1** *materials listed under various headings* head, category, class, classification, subject, topic, division, section. **2** *put headings on the illustrations* title, caption, headline, name, rubric.

headlong adverb **1** *fall headlong into the bushes* head first, on one's head, head foremost, head on diving, plunging. **2** *rush headlong into a decision* hastily, in haste, hurriedly, impetuously, impulsively, without thinking, rashly, prematurely, precipitately, carelessly, heedlessly.

headstrong adjective stubborn, obstinate, obdurate, mulish, intransigent, intractable, pigheaded, refractory, recalcitrant, ungovernable, wayward, contrary, willful, perverse.

headway noun **make headway** make progress, progress, advance, gain ground.

heady adjective **1** *a heady drink* intoxicating, inebriating, potent, strong. **2** *heady with success* exhilarated, excited, overjoyed, thrilled, overwhelmed, euphoric, ecstatic; *inf.* in seventh heaven, on cloud nine. **3** *the heady days of youth* stimulating, rousing, arousing, invigorating, thrilling, electrifying. **4** *a heady action* impetuous, rash, reckless, wild, foolhardy.

heal verb **1** *heal the wound* cure, make well, make better, remedy, treat, mend, restore, regenerate. **2** *heal the breach* reconcile, patch up, settle, set right, put right.

health noun **1** *full of health* healthiness, fitness, well-being, good condition, good shape, soundness, robustness, strength, vigor, salubrity. **2** *his health is poor* constitution, condition, form, tone.

healthy adjective **1** *a healthy young man* in good health, fit, physically fit, able-bodied, in good condition/trim/shape, in fine fettle, in fine/top form, robust, strong, vigorous, hardy, flourishing, hale and hearty, hale, hearty, bursting with health; *inf.* in the pink, fit as a fiddle. **2** *a healthy climate* health-giving, salubrious, invigorating, bracing, stimulating, refreshing, tonic. **3** *a healthy diet* healthful, nutritious, nourishing, wholesome, beneficial.

heap noun pile, stack, mass, mound, mountain, stockpile, accumulation, collection, hoard, store, stock, supply. **heaps, a heap** a lot, lots, a great deal, an abundance, plenty, considerable, a mint; *inf.* oodles, loads, tons.

heap verb **heap on** bestow on, confer on, shower on, load on. **heap up** pile up, stack, stack up, amass, stockpile, accumulate, collect, assemble, hoard, store, stock up, set aside, lay by.

hear verb **1** *I didn't hear what he said* catch, take in, overhear; *inf.* get. **2** *we heard that he was ill* be informed, be told, be made aware, find out, discover, learn, gather, pick up, be given to understand, hear tell, get wind.

hearing noun *present at the hearing* inquiry, trial, inquest, investigation, inquisition, review, examination.

hearsay noun rumor, gossip, idle talk, mere talk, talk of the town, word of mouth; *inf.* buzz, grapevine.

heart noun **1** *love her with all his heart* passion, love, affection, emotions, feelings. **2** *he has no heart* tenderness, compassion, sympathy, empathy, humanity, fellow feeling, benevolence, kindness, kindliness, brotherly love. **3** *I don't have the heart to tell him the truth* courage, bravery, valor, intrepidity, fearlessness, mettle, backbone, nerve, fortitude, purpose, resolution, determination; *inf.* guts, spunk, gumption. **4** *the heart of the matter/universe* center, core, nucleus, middle, kernel, hub, quintessence, essence, crux, marrow, pith, substance, sum and substance. **at heart** basically, fundamentally, in essence, essentially, in reality, really, in fact. **by heart** by rote, word for word, pat, by memory. **do one's heart good** please, gladden, cheer, delight, gratify, satisfy. **eat one's heart out** sorrow, grieve, mourn, agonize, pine, mope, fret, brood, repine. **from the bottom of one's heart** profoundly, deeply, sincerely, devoutly, heartily, fervently, passionately. **have a heart** be kind, be merciful, be lenient, be compassionate, be sympathetic, be considerate. **have one's heart set on** long for, yearn for, desire, be desirous of, crave. **heart and soul** enthusiastically, eagerly, zealously, wholeheartedly, gladly, with open arms, thoroughly, completely. **take heart** cheer up, brighten up, perk up, revive; *inf.* buck up. **with one's heart in one's mouth** fearfully, apprehensively, with fear and trembling, with trepidation, with bated breath.

heartache noun sorrow, grief, sadness, anguish, pain, hurt, agony, suffering, misery, woe, dolor.

heartbreaking adjective sad, pitiful, poignant, tragic, painful, agonizing, distressing, heart-rending, grievous, harrowing, tear-jerking, excruciating.

heartbroken adjective brokenhearted, heartsick, miserable, sorrowful, sad, anguished, grieving, dejected, dispirited, downcast, crestfallen, crushed, despondent, in low spirits.

hearten verb cheer, cheer up, raise the spirits of, invigorate, revitalize, energize, animate, revivify, exhilarate, uplift, elate, comfort, encourage, buoy up, pep up; *inf.* buck up, give a shot in the arm to.

heartfelt adjective deep, profound, sincere, genuine, earnest, ardent, fervent, warm, cordial, enthusiastic, eager.

heartless adjective unfeeling, unsympathetic, uncompassionate, unkind, uncaring, cold, cold-hearted, hard-hearted, cruel, harsh, hard, merciless, pitiless, ruthless.

heart-rending adjective sad, distressing. *See* HEARTBREAKING.

heartsick adjective sick at heart, heavyhearted, dejected, depressed, despondent, disappointed, heartsore.

heartwarming adjective **1** *a heartwarming story* touching, moving, affecting, cheering, gladdening, encouraging, uplifting. **2** *a heartwarming job* gratifying, satisfying, rewarding.

hearty adjective **1** *a hearty welcome* enthusiastic, eager, warmhearted, warm, cordial, jovial, friendly, affable, unreserved, uninhibited, ebullient, exuberant, effusive. **2** *a hearty dislike* wholehearted, complete, total, absolute, thorough. **3** *a hearty young/old man* strong, robust. *See* HEALTHY. **4** *a hearty meal* substantial, solid, abundant, ample, sizable, filling, nutritious, nourishing.

heat noun **1** *the heat of summer* hotness, warmth, sultriness, torridness, swelter, heatwave, hot spell; *inf.* dog days. **2** *caught up in the heat of his speech* warmth, passion, vehemence, intensity, ardor, fervor, zeal, eagerness, enthusiasm, animation, earnestness, excitement, agitation.

heat verb **heat up 1** *heat up the milk* warm, warm up, reheat, cook. **2** *the day heated up* grow hot, grow warm, get hotter/warmer. **3** *the argument heated up* grow passionate/vehement/fierce/angry.

heated adjective passionate, vehement, fierce, angry, furious, stormy, tempestuous, intense, impassioned, violent, excited, inflamed.

heathen noun *missionaries converting heathens* unbeliever, infidel, pagan, idolater, atheist, heretic.

heathen adjective **1** *converting a heathen tribe* infidel, pagan, godless, irreligious, idolatrous. **2** *invaded by heathen tribes* barbarian, barbarous, savage, uncivilized, brutish.

heave verb **1** *heaving heavy weights* lift, haul, pull, tug, raise, hoist, upheave. **2** *heave the hammer in the games* throw, cast, toss, fling, hurl, let fly, pitch, send; *inf.* sling, chuck. **3** *heave a sigh* give, utter, let out, pant, gasp, sigh, sob. **4** *people heaving as the ship sailed* vomit, be sick, spew, retch, gag; *inf.* throw up.

heaven noun **1** *departed souls abiding in heaven* Kingdom of God, paradise, next life, life to come, next world, the hereafter, Zion, nirvana, Valhalla, Elysium, Elysian Fields, empyrean, happy hunting ground. **2** *she was in heaven at the news* ecstasy, bliss, sheer bliss, rapture, supreme happiness, seventh heaven, paradise, Eden, Utopia, dreamland. **3** *the heavens opened* sky, skies, firmament, ether, empyrean, aerosphere, vault of heaven; *inf.* (wild) blue yonder.

heavenly adjective **1** *heavenly concerns* cosmic, extraterrestrial, unearthly, not of this world, otherworldly. **2** *heavenly beings* celestial, divine, angelic, seraphic, cherubic, blessed, beatific, beatified, immortal, superhuman, paradisiacal. **3** *a heavenly party/dress* delightful, pleasurable, enjoyable, marvelous, exquisite, perfect, superb, enchanting, sublime; *inf.* glorious, divine.

heavy adjective **1** *a heavy log/load* weighty, bulky, hefty, substantial, massive, enormous, mighty, colossal, ponderous, unwieldy, cumbersome. **2** *a heavy responsibility* onerous, burdensome, oppressive, unbearable. **3** *a heavy blow* hard, forceful, strong, severe, grievous, harsh, intense, sharp. **4** *a heavy man* stout, overweight, fat, obese, corpulent, portly, tubby, paunchy, lumbering. **5** *heavy traffic/losses* great, large, considerable, abundant, copious, profuse, superabundant. **6** *heavy fighting* severe, intense, serious, grave. **7** *heavy reading* difficult, deep, profound, dull, tedious, boring, uninteresting, dry, wearisome, dry as dust. **8** *feeling heavy after dinner* sluggish, inactive, indolent, listless, torpid. **9** *heavy of heart* sad, sorrowful, dejected, disheartened, despondent, downhearted, depressed. **10** *heavy seas/waves* rough, wild, stormy, tempestuous, turbulent, squally, boisterous, violent. **11** *heavy day/skies* cloudy, overcast, gray, dark, dull, gloomy, dreary, leaden. **12** *heavy pastries* filling, indigestible, dense; sickening.

heavy-handed adjective **1** *heavy-handed and always breaking things* clumsy, awkward, maladroit, bungling, blundering, unhandy, ham-handed, ham-fisted, inept, like a bull in a china shop. **2** *too heavy-handed to deal with the bereaved* insensitive, tactless, thoughtless. **3** *a heavy-handed father* harsh, hard, stern, severe, oppressive, domineering, overbearing, autocratic.

heckle verb shout down, interrupt, disrupt, jeer, taunt, badger, bait, harass.

hectic adjective frantic, frenetic, frenzied, bustling, flustering, flurried, fast and furious, turbulent, tumultuous, confused, exciting, excited, wild.

hedge verb **1** *she hedged when questioned* equivocate, prevaricate, dodge/duck the question/issue, sidestep the issue, hem and haw, beat around the bush, pussyfoot around, temporize, quibble. **2** *hedge yourself against inflation* safeguard, guard, protect, cover, shield, insure. **hedge in 1** *the trees hedge in the garden* surround, enclose, encircle, border, edge, skirt. **2** *hedged in by petty restrictions* hem in, confine, restrict, hinder, obstruct.

heed noun heedfulness, attention, attentiveness, notice, note, regard, mindfulness, consideration, thought, care, caution.

heed verb pay heed to, be heedful of, pay attention to, attend to, take notice of, take note of, notice, note, bear in mind, be mindful of, mind, mark, consider.

heedful adjective attentive, careful, mindful, cautious, prudent, circumspect, wary, chary, observant, watchful, vigilant.

heedless adjective unheeding, inattentive, careless, incautious, unmindful, unthinking, thoughtless, unwary, oblivious, unobservant, negligent, neglectful, rash, reckless.

heel noun **1** *the heel of the loaf* crust, end, remnant, remainder, tail-end, stump, butt, rump. **2** *he's an utter heel* scoundrel, cad, blackguard; *inf.* rat, swine, bounder. **down at (the) heel(s)** shabby, out at the elbows, seedy, rundown, slovenly, slipshod. **take to one's heels** run away, run off, take flight, flee, escape; *inf.* skedaddle, hightail it, hotfoot it, split, vamoose.

hefty adjective **1** *hefty young man* heavy, bulky, hulking, stout, massive, muscular, brawny, strapping, sturdy, rugged, beefy. **2** *a hefty blow* hard, forceful, powerful, vigorous, mighty. **3** *a hefty load* heavy, weighty, big, large, tremendous, immense, bulky, awkward, unwieldy. **4** *a hefty sum* substantial, sizable, expensive, huge, colossal, overpriced.

height noun **1** *measure the height* highness, altitude, loftiness, elevation, tallness, stature. **2** *the height overlooking the valley* top, mountaintop, hilltop, summit, crest, crown, pinnacle, peak, vertex. **3** *at the height of his powers* culmination, crowning point, high point, peak, zenith, apogee, climax, consummation, perfection, apex. **4** *the height of fashion* utmost, uttermost, ultimate, acme, ne plus ultra, limit, extremity, maximum, ceiling.

heighten verb **1** *heighten the ceiling* raise, lift, elevate. **2** *heighten the tension* intensify, raise, increase, augment, build up, boost, strengthen, amplify, magnify, aggravate, enhance, improve.

heinous adjective atrocious, abominable, abhorrent, odious, detestable, loathsome, hateful, execrable, wicked, contemptible, reprehensible, despicable.

heir, heiress noun beneficiary, legatee, inheritor, successor, next in line, scion.

hell noun **1** *wicked spirits in hell* infernal regions, inferno, hellfire, eternal fire, fire and brimstone, nether world, lower world, abode of the damned, perdition, abyss, bottomless pit, Hades. **2** *it was hell in the battle* torment, torture, misery, suffering, affliction, anguish, agony, ordeal, wretchedness, nightmare, woe. **3** *get hell from the teacher* upbraiding, scolding, castigation, vituperation, reprimand, censure, criticism, disapprobation; *inf.* what for. **hell for leather** pell-mell, post-haste, at the double, headlong, full tilt; *inf.* like a bat out of hell. **raise hell 1** *partygoers raising hell* party, carouse, revel. **2** *his father raised hell* be furious, be enraged, protest, complain, object, remonstrate, raise the roof, raise Cain.

helm noun **at the helm** in charge, in command, in control, in authority, at the wheel, in the driver's seat, in the saddle.

help verb **1** *help the neighbors* assist, aid, lend a helping hand to, lend a hand to, be of service to, succor, befriend. **2** *help the charity* contribute to, support, back, promote, boost. **3** *help the pain/situation* soothe, relieve, ameliorate, alleviate, mitigate, assuage, remedy, cure, heal, improve, ease. **help oneself to** *he helped himself to my books* appropriate, commandeer, steal, make free with; *inf.* pinch, walk off with.

help noun **1** *give the woman some help* assistance, aid, helping hand, service, use, guidance, benefit, advantage, avail, support, backing, succor. **2** *no help for the condition* relief, remedy, cure, restorative, corrective, balm, salve. **3** *ask the help for assistance* helper, assistant, employee, worker, hired help, maid, servant.

helper noun assistant, aide, auxiliary, right-hand man/woman, girl/man Friday, helpmate, partner, ally, collaborator.

helpful adjective useful, of use, of service, beneficial, advantageous, valuable, profitable, instrumental, constructive, practical, productive.

helpless adjective **1** *a helpless invalid* weak, feeble, impotent, incapable, infirm, debilitated, powerless, dependent. **2** *left helpless in the wilderness* defenseless, unprotected, vulnerable, exposed.

helter-skelter adverb hastily, hurriedly, pell-mell, headlong.

henceforth adverb from now on, from this day forward, hereafter, in the future, hence, in time to come.

henchman noun follower, right-hand man/woman, subordinate, underling, lackey, flunky, toady, hired killer/assassin; *inf.* hit man, hatchet man.

henpecked adjective *henpecked husbands* bullied, dominated, browbeaten, led by the nose, cringing, cowering, meek, timid, docile; *inf.* under the thumb.

herald verb **1** *companies heralding their new products* announce, make public, make known, proclaim, broadcast, publicize, advertise, promote, promulgate, trumpet, beat the drum about. **2** *prototypes heralding major new inventions* usher in, pave the way for, show in, precede, be the forerunner/precursor of, portend, indicate, augur, presage, promise.

herd noun **1** *a herd of cattle* drove, collection, assemblage, flock, pack, cluster. **2** *a herd of people* crowd, horde, multitude, mob, mass, host, throng, swarm, press. **3** *ignore the tastes of the herd* masses, mob, populace, rabble, riff-raff, hoi polloi, peasants; *inf.* great unwashed.

herd verb **1** *herd the sheep into the pens* drive, round up, shepherd, guide, lead, force, urge, goad. **2** *people herding (together) in the hall* assemble, gather, collect, congregate, flock, rally, muster, huddle. **3** *shepherds herding the sheep* look after, take care of, watch, stand guard over, guard, tend.

hereafter adverb after this, from now on. *See* HENCEFORTH.

hereafter noun **the hereafter** life after death, the afterlife, the afterworld, the next world, the beyond, eternity, immortality. *See* HEAVEN 1.

hereditary adjective genetic, congenital, innate, inborn, inherent, inbred, family, transmissible, transferable, inherited, handed down.

heredity noun genetics, genetic makeup, genes, congenital characteristics/traits.

heresy noun apostasy, dissent, dissension, dissidence, unbelief, skepticism, agnosticism, atheism, nonconformity, unorthodoxy, separatism, sectarianism, freethinking, heterodoxy, revisionism, idolatry, paganism.

heretic noun apostate, dissenter, dissident, unbeliever, skeptic, agnostic, atheist, nonconformist, separatist, sectarian, freethinker, renegade, revisionist, idolater, pagan, heathen.

heritage noun history, tradition, background; ancestry, lineage, descent, extraction, family, dynasty, bloodline, heredity, birth.

hermit noun recluse, solitary, anchorite/anchoress, eremite, ascetic.

hero noun champion, conquering hero, victor, conqueror; man of the hour, celebrity, lion, cavalier; paragon, shining example, exemplar, idol, ideal.

heroic adjective **1** *heroic deeds* brave, courageous, valiant, valorous, intrepid, fearless, gallant, stouthearted, lionhearted, bold, daring, undaunted, dauntless, doughty, manly, virile, chivalrous. **2** *heroic ambitious* epic, epical, high-flown, high-sounding, extravagant, grandiose, pretentious, elevated.

heroism noun bravery, courage, valor, fearlessness, gallantry, stoutheartedness, boldness, daring, dauntlessness, doughtiness, manliness, virility, mettle, spirit, fortitude, chivalry.

hesitant adjective uncertain, unsure, doubtful, dubious, skeptical, irresolute, indecisive, vacillating, wavering, oscillating, shilly-shallying, hanging back, stalling, delaying, disinclined, reluctant, unwilling, halfhearted, diffident, timid, shy.

hesitate verb **1** *he always hesitates before deciding* pause, delay, hang back, wait, be uncertain, be unsure, be doubtful, be indecisive, vacillate, oscillate, waver, shilly-shally, dally, stall, temporize; *inf.* dilly-dally. **2** *she hesitates to interfere* be reluctant, be unwilling, be disinclined, shrink (from), hang back (from), think twice (about), balk (at), have misgivings/qualms (about), be diffident (about). **3** *he hesitates a lot when speaking* stammer, stumble, stutter, falter, hem and haw, fumble for words.

hew verb carve, sculpt, sculpture, shape, fashion, form, model, whittle, chip, chisel, rough-hew. **hew down** chop, chop down, hack, hack down, ax, cut/saw down, fell. **hew off** lop, cut off, chop off, sever, trim, prune.

heyday noun prime, prime of life, bloom, full flowering, flowering, peak, peak of perfection, pinnacle, culmination, crowning point, salad days.

hiatus noun gap, break, lacuna, blank, discontinuity, interruption; interval, intermission, pause, lull, rest, break, suspension, abeyance.

hidden adjective concealed, unrevealed, secret, unseen, out of sight, covered, masked, shrouded, obscure, cryptic, mysterious, covert, under wraps, clandestine.

hide verb **1** *prisoners hiding from the police* go into hiding, conceal oneself, take cover, lie low, keep out of sight, secrete oneself, go underground, cover one's tracks; *inf.* hole up. **2** *hide the jewels* secrete, conceal, store away, stow away, stash, lock up. **3** *clouds hiding the sun* obscure, cloud, darken, block, eclipse, obstruct. **4** *hide one's motives* conceal, withhold, suppress, hush up, mask, veil, shroud, camouflage, disguise; *inf.* keep mum, keep under one's hat.

hide noun skin, pelt, coat, fur, fleece.

hideaway noun hiding place, den, lair, retreat, shelter, refuge, hermitage, hide-out.

hideous adjective **1** *a hideous sight* ugly, unsightly, grotesque, monstrous, repulsive, repellent, revolting, gruesome, disgusting, grim, ghastly, macabre. **2** *a hideous crime* horrible, horrific, horrendous, horrifying, frightful, shocking, dreadful, outrageous, monstrous, appalling, heinous, abominable, foul, vile, odious, loathsome, contemptible, execrable.

hide-out noun hiding place, shelter. *See* HIDEAWAY.

high adjective **1** *a high building* tall, lofty, elevated, soaring, towering, steep. **2** *a high official* high-ranking, leading, top, ruling, powerful, important, principal, chief, main, prominent, eminent, influential, distinguished, notable, exalted, illustrious. **3** *high ideals* noble, virtuous. *See* HIGH-MINDED. **4** *a high wind* intense, extreme, strong, forceful, vigorous, powerful, potent, sharp, violent. **5** *high prices* dear, top, excessive, stiff, inflated, exorbitant, extortionate, high-priced, expensive, costly; *inf.* pricey, steep. **6** *a high lifestyle* high-living, extravagant, luxurious, lavish, rich, grand, prodigal. **7** *a high opinion* favorable, approving, admiring, flattering. **8** *feeling high before the holidays* excited, in high spirits, high-spirited, ebullient, bouncy, elated, ecstatic, euphoric, exhilarated, joyful, merry, happy, cheerful, jolly. **9** *high on drugs* drugged, intoxicated, inebriated, delirious, hallucinating; *inf.* stoned, turned on, tripping, hyped up, freaked out, spaced out. **10** *high voice/notes* high-pitched, acute, high-frequency, soprano, treble, piping, shrill, sharp-toned, piercing, penetrating. **high and dry** stranded, marooned, abandoned, helpless, destitute, bereft. **high and mighty** haughty, arrogant, self-important, proud, conceited, egotistic, overweening, overbearing, snobbish, condescending, disdainful, supercilious, imperious; *inf.* stuck-up, uppity, highfalutin.

high adverb high up, far up, way up, aloft. **high and low** everywhere, all over, far and near, far and wide, in every nook and cranny, exhaustively.

highbrow adjective intellectual, scholarly, bookish, cultured, cultivated, educated, sophisticated; *inf.* brainy.

high-class adjective superior, luxurious, deluxe, select, choice, elite, top-flight, first-rate, elegant, posh, upper-class, up-scale, upmarket; *inf.* tip-top, A-1, super, super-duper, classy.

high-flown adjective extravagant, pretentious, overblown, overdone, overdrawn, exaggerated, elaborate.

high-handed adjective arbitrary, autocratic, dictatorial, domineering, peremptory, imperious, overbearing; *inf.* bossy.

highlight noun main feature, feature, high point, high spot, best part, climax, peak, memorable part, focal point, focus, center of interest, cynosure.

highlight verb call attention to, focus attention on, feature, emphasize, accentuate, accent, stress, underline, spotlight.

highly adverb **1** *highly entertaining* greatly, extremely, decidedly, certainly, exceptionally, tremendously, vastly, immensely, eminently, supremely, extraordinarily. **2** *speak highly of* approvingly, favorably, well, warmly, appreciatively, admiringly.

high-minded adjective noble-minded, moral, virtuous, ethical, upright, righteous, principled, honorable, good, fair, pure, lofty, elevated, high.

high-powered adjective dynamic, aggressive, assertive, energetic, driving, ambitious, effective, enterprising, vigorous, forceful.

high-pressure adjective aggressive, insistent, persistent, intensive, forceful, high-powered, importunate, bludgeoning, coercive; *inf.* pushy.

high-priced adjective expensive, costly. *See* HIGH 5.

high-spirited adjective spirited, lively, full of life, animated, active, energetic, vigorous, boisterous, bouncy, frolicsome, effervescent, buoyant, ebullient, exhilarated, vivacious, full of fun.

high-strung adjective nervous, on edge, edgy, excitable, tense, taut, stressed, temperamental, neurotic, overwrought, restless, wound up.

hijack verb commandeer, seize, expropriate, take over, skyjack.

hike verb walk, march, tramp, trek, trudge, plod, ramble, wander, backpack; *inf.* hoof it. **hike up 1** *he hiked up his pants/load* hitch up, pull up, jack up, lift, raise. **2** *they've hiked up the prices* raise, increase, add to; *inf.* jack up.

hike noun walk, march, tramp, trek, ramble, trudge.

hilarious adjective uproarious, sidesplitting, humorous, entertaining, comical, amusing, merry, jolly, mirthful, animated, vivacious, sparkling, exuberant, boisterous.

hilarity noun mirth, laughter, merriment, levity, glee, high spirits, amusement, comedy.

hill noun **1** *the hills behind the town* elevation, heights, hillock, hilltop, knoll, hummock, mound, tor, mount, ridge. **2** *cars going slowly up the hill* slope, rise, incline, gradient, acclivity. **3** *a hill of garbage* mountain, heap, pile, mound, stack, drift.

hilt noun handle, haft, handgrip, grip, shaft, hold. **to the hilt** completely, fully, wholly, entirely, totally, all the way.

hind adjective rear, back, hinder, posterior, caudal.

hinder verb hamper, impede, hold back, interfere with, delay, hold up, slow down, retard, obstruct, inhibit, handicap, hamstring, block, interrupt, check, trammel, forestall, curb, balk, thwart, frustrate, foil.

hindrance noun impediment, obstacle, interference, obstruction, handicap, block, restraint, check, bar, barrier, drawback, snag, stumbling block, encumbrance, curb, trammel, deterrent.

hinge verb **hinge on** depend on, turn on, be contingent on, hang on, pivot on, revolve around, rest on, center on.

hint noun **1** *give a hint that he was leaving* inkling, clue, suggestion, innuendo, tip-off, insinuation, implication, indication, mention, allusion, intimation, whisper. **2** *write gardening hints* tip, pointer, advice, help. **3** *just a hint of garlic* suspicion, suggestion, trace, touch, dash, soupçon, speck, sprinkling, tinge.

hint verb suggest, insinuate, imply, indicate, intimate, signal.

hire verb appoint, sign on, take on, engage, employ, secure the services of, enlist.

hiss verb sibilate, buzz, whistle, wheeze; boo, jeer, deride, catcall, hoot, taunt, ridicule.

historian noun chronicler, annalist, archivist, recorder, historiographer, antiquarian.

historic adjective notable, celebrated, renowned, momentous, significant, important, consequential, red-letter, memorable, remarkable, outstanding, extraordinary.

historical adjective **1** *a historical account* factual, recorded, documented, chronicled, archival, authentic, actual, attested, verified, confirmed. **2** *historical times* past, former, bygone, ancient.

history noun **1** *the history of the times* annals, chronicles, records, public records, account, study, story, tale, saga, narrative, recital, reports, memoirs, biography, autobiography. **2** *that is history now* the past, the old days, days of yore, antiquity, yesteryear.

hit verb **1** *hit him in anger* strike, slap, smack, buffet, punch, box, cuff, beat, thump, batter, pound, pummel, thrash, hammer, bang, knock, swat; *inf.* whack, wallop, bash, belt, clout, clip, clobber, sock, swipe. **2** *the car hit the truck* run into, bang into, smash into, crash into, knock into, bump into, collide with, meet head-on. **3** *her death really hit him* affect, have an effect on, leave a mark on, move, touch, overwhelm, devastate, damage, hurt. **4** *hit the right tone in his speech* achieve, accomplish, reach, attain, arrive at, gain, secure, touch, strike. **hit it off** get on well, be/get on good terms, take to each other; *inf.* be on the same wavelength. **hit on/upon** stumble on, chance on, light on, come upon, blunder on, discover, arrive at.

hit noun blow, slap, smack, punch, thump; *inf.* whack, wallop, clout, swipe.

hitch verb **1** *hitch the trailer to the car* fasten, connect, attach, join, couple, unite, tie, tether, bind, harness, yoke. **2** *hitching up their skirts* pull up, hike up, jerk up; *inf.* yank up.

hitch noun *what's the hitch?* holdup, delay, catch, difficulty, problem. *See* HINDRANCE.

hit-or-miss adjective haphazard, random, aimless, undirected, disorganized, indiscriminate, careless, casual, offhand, cursory.

hoard noun store, stockpile, supply, reserve, cache, accumulation, heap, pile, mass, aggregation, treasure trove; *inf.* stash.

hoard verb store, store up, stock up, stockpile, pile up, stack up, stow away, accumulate, amass, heap up, collect, gather, squirrel away; *inf.* stash away.

hoarse adjective croaking, croaky, throaty, harsh, rough, gruff, husky, gravelly, grating, rasping, guttural, raucous.

hoary adjective **1** *hoary hair/head* gray, gray-haired, white, white-haired, silvery, silvery-haired, grizzled, grizzly. **2** *hoary gentleman* old, elderly, aged, venerable, time-honored.

hoax noun practical joke, joke, jest, prank, trick, ruse, deception, fraud, imposture, cheat, spoof, swindle; *inf.* con, fast one, scam.

hoax verb trick, fool, deceive, bluff, hoodwink, cozen, delude, dupe, take in, spoof, cheat, swindle; *inf.* con, take someone for a ride, put one over on someone.

hobble verb limp, falter, shuffle, totter, stagger, reel.

hobby noun pastime, diversion, recreation, relaxation, divertissement, sideline.

hobnob verb fraternize, associate, socialize, mingle, mix, keep company, go around, consort; *inf.* hang around, hang out.

hodgepodge noun jumble, mishmash, miscellany, medley, mélange, mess, clutter, odds and ends, potpourri, olio, olla podrida.

hogwash noun nonsense, rubbish, gibberish, gobbledygook, drivel, balderdash, humbug, bunkum; *inf.* piffle, bunk, bosh, tosh, bilge, tripe, rot, tommyrot, crap, hooey.

hoist verb lift, raise, upraise, heave, jack up, hike up, elevate.

hoist noun crane, winch, pulley, jack, elevator, lift.

hold verb **1** *hold his hand* hold on to, clasp, clutch, grasp, grip, seize, clench, cling to. **2** *hold his sweetheart* embrace, hug, enfold, cradle, fondle. **3** *hold the relevant documents* have, possess, own, retain, keep. **4** *will it hold his weight?* bear, carry, take, support, hold up, keep up, sustain, prop up, buttress, brace. **5** *police are holding the suspect* detain, confine, hold in custody, impound, lock up, imprison, put behind bars, incarcerate. **6** *you cannot hold him from going* hold back, restrain, impede, check, bar, curb, stop, retard, delay, prevent. **7** *hold the interest of the audience* keep, maintain, occupy, engage, involve, absorb, engross, immerse, monopolize, arrest, catch, spellbind, fascinate, rivet. **8** *he holds a well-paid post* hold down, be in, occupy, fill, maintain, continue in, enjoy, boast. **9** *the hall holds 400 people* contain, accommodate, take, comprise. **10** *we hold that he is guilty* maintain, think, believe, consider, regard, deem, judge, assume, presume, reckon. **11** *will the good weather hold?* go on, carry on, remain, continue, stay, persist, last, endure, keep up. **12** *the old rule still holds* hold good, stand, apply, be in force, remain valid, exist. **13** *hold a meeting* call, convene, assemble, conduct, run, preside over, officiate at. **hold back 1** *hold back a laugh* keep back, suppress, repress, stifle, smother. **2** *hold back progress* prevent, impede, obstruct, hinder, check, curb, inhibit, restrain, control. **3** *hold back from hitting him* keep, desist, forbear, stop oneself, restrain oneself. **4** *hold back information* withhold, suppress. **hold down 1** *hold down prices* keep low, keep down. **2** *hold down a job* be in, occupy. *See* HOLD verb 8. **hold forth 1** *hold forth about politics* declaim, discourse, lecture, harangue, preach, orate, speechify, sermonize; *inf.* spout, spiel. **2** *hold forth the hand of friendship* hold out, extend, present, proffer, offer. **hold off 1** *hold off the attack* keep off, keep at bay, fend off, stave off, ward off, repel, repulse. **2** *hold off making a decision* delay, postpone, put off, defer, keep from, refrain from, avoid. **hold on** *if the survivors can hold on* survive, last, carry on, keep going,

continue; *inf.* hang on. **hold on to** *hold on to the house* keep, retain possession of, retain ownership of. **hold out** *as long as supplies hold out* last, continue, remain.
hold over put off, postpone, defer, delay, adjourn, suspend, waive. **hold up 1** *hold up traffic* delay, hinder, impede, obstruct, retard, slow, slow down, set back, stop, bring to a halt. **2** *hold up his weight* bear, carry. *See* HOLD *verb* 4. **3** *she held up her father as an example* display, exhibit, show, present, flaunt, brandish. **4** *hold up a bank* rob, waylay, mug; *inf.* stick up. **5** *will his story hold up?* bear examination, be verifiable, hold water. **hold with** approve of, agree with, be in favor of, support, subscribe to, countenance, take kindly to.

hold noun **1** *keep a firm hold of the child's hand* grasp, grip, clutch, clasp. **2** *the government tightened its hold on the country* grip, power, control, dominion, authority, ascendancy, influence, mastery, dominance, sway. **3** *put it on hold* pause, delay, postponement, deferment.

holdup noun **1** *a holdup on the highway* delay, wait, stoppage, obstruction, bottleneck, traffic jam, hitch, snag. **2** *a bank holdup* robbery, theft, burglary, mugging; *inf.* stick-up.

hole noun **1** *a hole in the material* opening, aperture, orifice, gap, space, breach, break, fissure, crack, rift, puncture, perforation, cut, incision, split, gash, rent, slit, vent, notch. **2** *a hole in the ground* excavation, pit, crater, shaft, mine, dugout, cave, cavern, pothole, cavity, chamber, hollow, scoop, pocket, depression, dent, dint, dip. **3** *an animal's hole* burrow, lair, den, covert, nest. **4** *they took us to a real hole for dinner* slum, hovel; *inf.* dump, dive, joint. **5** *the captives were thrown into the hole* dungeon, prison, cell. **6** *spot the hole in their argument* flaw, fault, defect, loophole, inconsistency, discrepancy, error, fallacy. **7** *they are in a financial hole* predicament, mess, plight, difficulty, trouble, corner, spot, tight spot; *inf.* fix, jam, scrape, pickle, hot water. **pick holes in** find fault with, criticize, pull to pieces, run down, cavil at, carp at, disparage, denigrate.

hole verb **hole up** hide, hide out, lie low, go underground, hibernate.

holier-than-thou adjective sanctimonious, self-righteous, pietistic, religiose, priggish, smug; *inf.* goody-goody.

holiness noun sanctity, saintliness, godliness, blessedness, spirituality, religiousness, piety, righteousness, goodness, virtue, virtuousness, purity.

hollow adjective **1** *a hollow vessel* empty, unfilled, vacant, void, hollowed out.

2 *hollow cheeks/marks* sunken, dented, indented, depressed, concave, caved-in, incurvate, cavernous. **3** *a hollow sound* muffled, muted, dull, flat, toneless, dead, sepulchral. **4** *a hollow victory/triumph* valueless, worthless, useless, of no avail, fruitless, profitless, pointless, meaningless, pyrrhic. **5** *hollow compliments* insincere, hypocritical, spurious, unsound, flimsy.

hollow noun **1** *hollows in the ground* depression, indentation, concavity, dent, dint, dip, dimple, hole, crater, cavern, pit, cavity, well, trough, basin, cup, bowl, niche, nook, cranny, recess. **2** *picnic in the hollow* valley, dell, dale, glen, gorge, ravine.

hollow verb **hollow out** scoop out, gouge out, dig out, excavate, furrow, groove.

holocaust noun fire, inferno, conflagration, destruction, devastation, annihilation, massacre, mass murder, extermination, genocide, ethnic cleansing.

holy adjective **1** *a holy person* God-fearing, godly, pious, pietistic, devout, spiritual, religious, righteous, good, virtuous, moral, saintly, saintlike, sinless. **2** *a holy place* blessed, blest, sanctified, consecrated, hallowed, sacred, dedicated, venerated, divine, religious.

home noun **1** *where is his home?* house, abode, domicile, residence, dwelling, dwelling place, habitation. **2** *live a long way from one's home* home town, birthplace. *See* HOMELAND. **3** *agents advertising homes* house, apartment, condominium, bungalow, cottage; *inf.* condo, digs, pad. **4** *couldn't bear to put her mother in a home* institution, shelter, refuge, hostel, hospice, retirement home, nursing home, rest home, convalescent home/hospital, children's home; *inf.* old folk's home. **5** *the home of the buffalo* abode, habitat, natural habitat, environment, stamping ground, haunt, domain. **at home in** familiar with, used to, comfortable in, at ease in, relaxed in, in one's element in, on familiar territory in, on home ground in. **at home with** familiar with, proficient in, conversant with, skilled in, competent at, well-versed in; *inf.* up on. **bring home** emphasize, stress, impress upon someone, underline, highlight. **nothing to write home about** nothing important, nothing worth mentioning, nothing out of the ordinary.

home verb **home in on** aim at, focus on, pinpoint, zero in on, zoom in on.

homeland noun native land, fatherland, motherland, mother country.

homeless adjective down-and-out, destitute, derelict, dispossessed, on the streets, without a roof over one's head, vagrant.

homely adjective **1** *a homely girl* plain, plain-featured, plain-looking, unattractive, ugly; *inf.* not much to look at, short on looks. **2** *homely atmosphere* homelike, homey, comfortable, cozy, snug, welcoming, informal, relaxed, downhome; *inf.* comfy. **3** *a homely but friendly place* plain, simple, modest, unsophisticated, natural, everyday, ordinary, unpretentious.

homespun adjective plain, simple, homely, artless, unpolished, unrefined, coarse, rustic. *See* HOMELY 3.

homicidal adjective murderous, death-dealing, mortal, deadly, lethal, violent, maniacal.

homicide noun **1** *found guilty of homicide* murder, manslaughter, killing, slaying, slaughter, assassination, patricide, matricide, fratricide, infanticide. **2** *a convicted homicide* murderer, killer, slayer, assassin, patricide, matricide, fratricide, infanticide; *inf.* hit man.

homily noun sermon, preaching, lecture, discourse, lesson, talk, speech, address, oration.

homogeneous adjective identical, alike, the same, uniform, unvaried, unvarying, similar, kindred, comparable, analogous.

homogenize verb make uniform, combine, coalesce, fuse, merge, blend, emulsify.

honest adjective **1** *honest people* upright, honorable, moral, ethical, principled, righteous, right-minded, virtuous, good, worthy, decent, law-abiding, high-minded, upstanding, just, fair, incorruptible, trustworthy, scrupulous, reputable. **2** *an honest reply* truthful, sincere, candid, frank, direct, forthright, straightforward, open, plain-speaking, matter-of-fact, outspoken, blunt, unfeigned, unequivocal. **3** *an honest mistake* real, true, genuine, authentic, actual, aboveboard, bona fide, proper; *inf.* on the level, honest-to-goodness.

honesty noun **1** *honesty is its own reward* uprightness, honorableness, honor, integrity, morals, morality, ethics, principle, high principles, righteousness, rectitude, virtue, goodness, probity, worthiness, justness, fairness, incorruptibility, truthfulness, truth, veracity, trustworthiness, reliability, conscientiousness, reputability. **2** *the honesty of his reply* truthfulness, truth, sincerity, candor, frankness, forthrightness, openness, genuineness, bluntness.

honor noun **1** *a man of honor* uprightness, integrity. *See* HONESTY 1. **2** *the honor of winning the battle* fame, renown, glory, prestige, illustriousness, esteem, distinction, notability, credit. **3** *his honor is at stake* reputation, good name, name. **4** *protecting a lady's honor* chastity, virginity, virtue, purity, innocence, modesty. **5** *treat the hero with honor* homage, praise, reverence, veneration, adulation, exaltation.

6 *it was an honor to serve him* privilege, pleasure, joy.

honor verb **1** *all his pupils honor him* esteem, respect, admire, defer to, reverence, revere, venerate, worship, idolize, value, prize. **2** *the crowd honored the victor* acclaim, applaud, pay homage to, pay tribute to, lionize, praise, cheer, compliment, laud, eulogize. **3** *honor the agreement* fulfill, discharge, carry out, observe, keep, be true to, be faithful to, live up to. **4** *honor the check* cash, clear, accept, take, pass.

honorable adjective **1** *honorable men* upright, moral. *See* HONEST 1. **2** *an honorable victory* renowned, prestigious, distinguished, esteemed, notable, noted, great, eminent, noble, illustrious, creditable. **3** *an honorable member of the community* worthy, respected, respectable, reputable, decent, venerable.

honors plural noun rewards, awards, prizes, decorations, commendations, recognition, titles, distinctions, laurels.

honorary adjective nominal, in name only, titular, unofficial, ex officio, complimentary, unpaid.

hoodlum noun **1** *hoodlums vandalizing telephone booths* ruffian, hooligan, thug, rowdy, delinquent, vandal, mugger; *inf.* tough, rough, hood. **2** *hoodlums killing policemen* gangster, mobster, gunman, murderer, assassin, terrorist; *inf.* hit man, hatchet man; hood.

hoodwink verb deceive, delude, dupe, outwit, fool, trick, get the better of, cheat, take in, hoax, cozen, mislead, defraud, swindle, gull, pull the wool over someone's eyes; *inf.* con, bamboozle, pull a fast one on, put one over on, take for a ride, make a sucker of.

hook noun **1** *the hook of the dress is broken* fastener, catch, clasp, clip, link, hook and eye. **2** *a hook in the river* crook, angle, loop, curve, bend, bow, arc, dogleg, horseshoe bend, oxbow, hairpin turn. **by hook or by crook** by fair means or foul, no matter how, somehow or other. **hook, line, and sinker** completely, entirely, thoroughly, wholly, totally. **off the hook** acquitted, cleared, exonerated, let off, vindicated.

hook verb **1** *hook the necklace* fasten, secure, fix, clasp. **2** *finally hooked a marriage partner* snare, ensnare, trap, entrap.

hooked adjective hook-shaped, hooklike, aquiline, curved, bent, bowed, angular. **hooked on** addicted to, devoted to, given to.

hooligan noun ruffian, thug. *See* HOODLUM 1.

hoop noun ring, band, circle, circlet, loop, wheel, girdle.

hoot noun **1** *the owl's hoot* call, screech, whoop, cry. **2** *the hoots of the audience* boo, hiss, jeer, catcall; *inf.* raspberry, Bronx cheer.

hoot verb **1** *the owls hooted* call, screech, whoop, cry. **2** *hooted off the stage* boo, hiss, jeer, deride, mock, taunt, ridicule.

hop verb jump, leap, bound, spring, vault, bounce, skip, caper, dance, frisk.

hop noun jump, leap, bound, spring, vault, bounce, skip.

hope noun hopefulness, expectation, expectancy, anticipation, desire, longing, wish, wishing, craving, yearning, aspiration, ambition, dream, confidence, conviction, faith, trust, optimism.

hope verb expect, anticipate, look forward to, await, contemplate, foresee, desire, long, wish, crave, yearn, dream, believe, rely on, count on, trust in.

hopeful adjective **1** *hopeful candidates* expectant, optimistic, confident, assured, buoyant, sanguine. **2** *hopeful news/signs* promising, encouraging, heartening, gladdening, optimistic, reassuring, auspicious, favorable, propitious.

hopeless adjective **1** *feeling hopeless* despairing, in despair, desperate, pessimistic, defeatist, dejected, downhearted, despondent, demoralized, disconsolate, suicidal. **2** *a hopeless case* lost, beyond remedy, irremediable, beyond recovery, past cure, incurable, beyond repair, irreparable, irreversible, serious, grave. **3** *a hopeless task* impossible, impracticable, futile, useless, vain, pointless, worthless, no-win, unattainable, unachievable. **4** *she's hopeless at math* poor, incompetent, inadequate, inferior; *inf.* no good.

horde noun crowd, mob, throng, mass, multitude, host, army, pack, gang, troop, drove, crew, band, flock, swarm, gathering, assemblage.

horizon noun *broaden the child's horizon* scope, range of experience/knowledge, perspective, perception, prospect, outlook, compass, sphere, purview.

horizontal adjective flat, flat as a pancake, plumb, level, supine, prone.

horrendous adjective **1** *a horrendous sight* dreadful, awful. *See* HORRIBLE 1. **2** *a horrendous child* nasty, disagreeable. *See* HORRIBLE 2.

horrible adjective **1** *a horrible sight/accident* dreadful, awful, horrid, terrible, horrifying, terrifying, frightful, fearful, horrendous, shocking, appalling, hideous, grim, ghastly, harrowing, gruesome, disgusting, revolting, repulsive, loathsome, abhorrent, detestable, hateful, abominable. **2** *horrible child/weather/food/picture/mess* nasty,

disagreeable, unpleasant, mean, unkind, obnoxious, odious, horrid, awful, dreadful, terrible, beastly, ghastly, frightful, horrendous, shocking, appalling, hideous, revolting, abominable.

horrid adjective **1** *a horrid sight* dreadful, awful. *See* HORRIBLE 1. **2** *a horrid child* nasty, disagreeable. *See* HORRIBLE 2.

horrify verb **1** *the apparition horrified the children* terrify, terrorize, intimidate, frighten, frighten out of one's wits, alarm, scare, scare to death, startle, panic, throw into a panic, make someone's blood run cold; *inf.* make someone's hair stand on end, scare stiff, scare the living daylights out of. **2** *his attitude horrifies me* shock, appall, outrage, scandalize, disgust, revolt, repel, nauseate, sicken, offend.

horror noun **1** *full of horror at the sight* terror, fear, fear and trembling, fearfulness, fright, alarm, dread, awe, panic, trepidation. **2** *view his attitude with horror* abhorrence, abomination, loathing, hate, detestation, repulsion, revulsion, disgust, distaste, aversion, antipathy.

horse noun mount, steed, pony, racehorse, draft horse, packhorse, bay, sorrel, pinto, piebald; foal, colt, stallion, mare; *inf.* nag, dobbin, filly.

horseplay noun clowning, fooling, fooling around, antics, capers, high jinks, rough-and-tumble, roughhouse.

horse sense noun common sense, sense one is born with, mother wit, practicality; *inf.* gumption, savvy.

hosiery noun hose, socks, stockings, tights, knee socks, ankle socks, leggings.

hospitable adjective welcoming, sociable, convivial, generous, liberal, bountiful, openhanded, congenial, friendly, neighborly, warm, warmhearted, cordial, kindly, amicable.

hospital noun medical center, clinic, infirmary, sanatorium.

hospitality noun welcome, sociability, conviviality, generosity, liberality, friendliness, neighborliness, warmth, warmheartedness, cordiality, kindness, kindheartedness, amicability.

host¹ noun **1** *the host of the lodge* proprietor, proprietress, landlord, landlady, manager, innkeeper, hotelkeeper, hotelier. **2** *the host of the show* presenter, master of ceremonies, MC, emcee.

host² noun multitude, crowd, throng, horde, mob, army, legion, herd, pack, flock, swarm, troop, band, mass, assemblage, assembly, array, myriad.

hostile adjective **1** *hostile to the idea* antagonistic, opposed, averse, opposite, ill-disposed, against, inimical; *inf.* anti. **2**

hostile weather conditions adverse, unfavorable, unpropitious, disadvantageous, inauspicious. **3** *a hostile crowd* belligerent, bellicose, aggressive, warlike, warring, militant, antagonistic, unfriendly, unsympathetic, spiteful, wrathful, angry.

hostilities plural noun war, warfare, fighting, conflict, militancy, strife, action, battles.

hostility noun antagonism, opposition, aversion, animosity, ill will, enmity, belligerence, bellicosity, militancy, malevolence, malice, spite, wrath, anger.

hot adjective **1** *hot food/weather* boiling, boiling hot, piping, piping hot, scalding, red-hot, sizzling, steaming, scorching, roasting, searing, blazing hot, sweltering, parching, blistering, baking, torrid, sultry. **2** *the curry is very hot* peppery, spicy, pungent, piquant, fiery, sharp, biting. **3** *the child is hot* feverish, fevered, febrile, flushed. **4** *hot on/about the idea of free speech* ardent, eager, enthusiastic, keen, fervent, fervid, zealous, vehement, passionate, animated, excited. **5** *hot with anger* inflamed, furious, infuriated, seething, raging, fuming. **6** *hot young lovers* passionate, impassioned. See HOT-BLOODED. **7** *a hot temper/argument* heated, violent, furious, fierce, ferocious, stormy, tempestuous, savage. **8** *hot from the presses/warehouses* new, fresh, recent, late, brand-new, just out, just released, just issued. **9** *these cameras are not this year* popular, in vogue, in demand, sought-after. **10** *hot on their heels* close, following closely, near. **11** *hot goods* stolen, illegally obtained, smuggled, wanted. **hot air** empty talk, nonsense, bombast, verbiage, wind, blather, claptrap; *inf.* gas, bunkum, guff.

hot-blooded adjective **1** *hot-blooded young lovers* hot, passionate, impassioned, ardent, sensual, sex-hungry, lustful, libidinous; *inf.* horny. **2** *hot-blooded people quarreling* excitable, temperamental, fiery, spirited, impulsive, rash, wild, quixotic.

hotel noun inn, hostelry, motel, boardinghouse, guesthouse.

hotheaded adjective hot-tempered, short-tempered, quick-tempered, fiery, hasty, excitable, volatile, rash, impetuous, impulsive, reckless, foolhardy, wild, unruly.

hound verb **1** *police hounding the criminal* chase, give chase to, pursue, follow, hunt, hunt down, stalk, track, trail, shadow; *inf.* tail. **2** *hound him to do as they wished* nag, bully, browbeat, pester, harass, harry, keep after, urge, badger, goad, prod, pressure.

house noun **1** *his house is over there* abode, residence, domicile, home, habitation; condominium, cottage; *inf.* condo. **2** *descended from a royal house* family, clan, family tree, line, lineage, dynasty, ancestry, ancestors, kindred, blood, race, strain, tribe. **3** *a publishing house* firm, business, company, concern, corporation, enterprise, organization; *inf.* outfit. **4** *a large house for the event* audience, gathering, assembly, congregation, listeners, spectators.

house verb **1** *the building houses 20 people* accommodate, lodge, put up, take in, have room for, have space/capacity for, sleep, shelter, harbor. **2** *the box houses the machinery* cover, sheathe, protect, shelter, guard, contain, keep.

household noun family, family circle, house, home, ménage.

household adjective domestic, family, ordinary, everyday, common, usual, run-of-the-mill.

housing noun **1** *a shortage of housing* accommodations, houses, dwellings, homes, shelter, habitations. **2** *housing for machinery* case, casing, cover, covering, sheath, container, enclosure, jacket, capsule, holder.

hovel noun shack, shanty, hut; *inf.* dump, hole.

hover verb **1** *kites hovering in the air* hang, flutter, float, drift, be wafted. **2** *hover between going and staying* waver, vacillate, fluctuate, oscillate, alternate, seesaw. **hover by/around/near** linger around/by/near, hang around/about, wait near, stay near.

however adverb nevertheless, be that as it may, nonetheless, notwithstanding, anyway, anyhow, regardless, despite that, still, yet, just the same.

howl verb bay, yowl, yelp, wail, yell, bawl, scream, shriek, bellow, caterwaul, cry, weep, ululate; *inf.* holler.

howl noun bay, yowl, yelp, wail, yell, bawl, bellow, roar.

hub noun **1** *the hub of a wheel* pivot, axis, nave. **2** *the hub of the firm* center, core, heart, nerve center, focus, focal point.

huddle verb crowd, press, throng, flock, pack, cram, herd, squeeze, bunch up, cluster, gather, congregate.

hue noun **1** *a blue hue* color, tone, shade, tint, tinge, dye. **2** *political opinions of every hue* complexion, cast, aspect, light.

hug verb **1** *hug his wife* embrace, cuddle, take in one's arms, hold close, enfold in one's arms, clasp/press to one's bosom, squeeze. **2** *hug the shore* keep close to, stay near to, follow closely. **3** *hug his memories* cling to, hold onto, cherish, harbor, nurse.

hug noun embrace, cuddle, squeeze, hold, clasp, bear hug; *inf.* clinch.

huge adjective enormous, immense, great, massive, colossal, vast, prodigious, gigantic, giant, gargantuan, mammoth, monumental, monstrous, elephantine, extensive, bulky, mountainous, titanic, Herculean; *inf.* jumbo.

hullabaloo noun uproar, commotion, roar, racket, din, clamor, disturbance, hubbub, outcry, furor, brouhaha, hue and cry, pandemonium, tumult, turmoil, fuss, to-do, bedlam, babel; *inf.* ruckus.

hum verb 1 *bees/machines humming* drone, murmur, vibrate, throb, thrum, buzz, whirr, purr. 2 *things are humming* be busy, be active, bustle, move quickly, vibrate, pulsate, buzz.

hum noun drone, murmur, vibration, throb, thrum, buzz, whirr, purr.

human adjective 1 *human frailty* mortal, physical, bodily, fleshly, carnal, corporal. 2 *a very human person* kind, kindly. See HUMANE. 3 *they're only human* mortal, flesh and blood, fallible, weak, frail, vulnerable, erring.

humane adjective kind, kindly, kindhearted, good, good-natured, compassionate, considerate, understanding, sympathetic, forgiving, merciful, lenient, forbearing, gentle, tender, mild, clement, benign, benevolent, charitable, generous, magnanimous, approachable, accessible.

humanitarian adjective 1 *humanitarian enemy soldiers* kind, compassionate. See HUMANE. 2 *humanitarian issues* philanthropic, altruistic, welfare, charitable.

humanitarian noun philanthropist, altruist, benefactor, good Samaritan, social reformer, do-gooder.

humble adjective 1 *brilliant but humble* modest, unassuming, self-effacing, unassertive, unpretentious, unostentatious, meek. 2 *born of humble people* plain, common, ordinary, simple, poor, low-ranking, low, lowly, inferior, plebeian, proletarian, unrefined, unimportant, insignificant, inconsequential, undistinguished. 3 *a humble apology* servile, submissive, obsequious, subservient, deferential, slavish, sycophantic.

humble verb 1 *humble them by his criticism* mortify, shame. See HUMILIATE. 2 *feel humbled in the king's presence* belittle, demean, deflate, depreciate, disparage.

humdrum adjective *humdrum life* routine, unvaried, unvarying, mundane, monotonous, repetitious, dull, uninteresting, banal, boring, tedious, tiresome, wearisome.

humid adjective muggy, sticky, steamy, clammy, close, sultry, damp, moist, dank, wet, soggy, misty.

humiliate verb mortify, humble, shame, bring low, put to shame, make ashamed, disgrace, embarrass, discomfit, chasten, subdue, abash, abase, debase, degrade, crush, make someone eat humble pie, take down a peg or two; *inf.* put down; make someone eat crow.

humiliation noun mortification, humbling, shame, disgrace, loss of face, dishonor, indignity, embarrassment, discomfiture, abasement, debasement, degradation, submission, humble pie; *inf.* put-down.

humility noun humbleness, modesty, modestness, meekness, self-effacement, unpretentiousness, unobtrusiveness, diffidence; servility, submissiveness, obsequiousness, subservience, deference, sycophancy.

humor noun 1 *see the humor of the situation* funny side, funniness, comic side, comical aspect, comedy, laughableness, facetiousness, farcicalness, farce, jocularity, hilarity, ludicrousness, absurdness, absurdity, drollness. 2 *entertain them with his humor* comedy, jokes, joking, jests, jesting, gags, wit, wittiness, witticisms, waggishness, pleasantries, buffoonery; *inf.* wisecracks. 3 *what humor is she in today?* mood, temper, temperament, frame of mind, disposition, spirits.

humor verb 1 *humor the child* indulge, pamper, spoil, coddle, mollycoddle. 2 *humor their idiosyncrasies* adapt to, make provision for, give in to, yield to, pander to, go along with, accommodate, acquiesce in, tolerate, permit, allow, suffer.

humorous adjective 1 *a humorous story* funny, comic, comical, witty, jocular, amusing, laughable, hilarious, sidesplitting, rib-tickling, facetious, farcical, ridiculous, ludicrous, absurd, droll, waggish, whimsical.

hump noun protuberance, protrusion, projection, bulge, swelling, lump, bump, knob, hunch, mass, nodule, node, intumescence, tumefaction. **over the hump** out of the woods, in the clear, getting better, making progress.

hunch noun 1 *a hunch on his back* protrusion, bulge. See HUMP. 2 *have a hunch that she will win* feeling, presentiment, premonition, intuition, sixth sense, suspicion, inkling.

hunch verb hump, arch, curve, crook, curl up. **hunch up** crouch over, stoop over, bend over, huddle over.

hunger noun 1 *suffering from hunger* hungriness, ravenousness, starvation, famine, voracity; greed, greediness. 2 *a hunger for knowledge* craving, longing, yearning, desire, want, need, thirst, appetite, pining, itch, lust, hankering; *inf.* yen.

hunger verb **hunger for/after** crave, have a craving for, long for, yearn for, have a yearning for, desire, want, need, thirst for, have an appetite for, pine for, lust after, itch for, hanker after; *inf.* have a yen for.

hungry adjective ravenous, famished, famishing, starving, starved, half-starved; greedy, voracious; *inf.* peckish.

hunt verb **1** *hunt deer/criminals* chase, pursue. *See* HOUND 1. **2** *hunt for her keys* search, look, look high and low, forage, fish, rummage.

hunt noun **1** *the hunt for game* chase, pursuit, course, coursing, stalking, tracking, trailing, shadowing; *inf.* tailing. **2** *the hunt for eggs* search, quest, rummage; foraging, ransacking.

hurdle noun bar, barrier, barricade, obstacle, hindrance, impediment, obstruction, stumbling block, snag, complication, difficulty, handicap.

hurl verb throw, fling, pitch, cast, toss, heave, fire, launch, let fly, propel, project, dart, catapult; *inf.* sling, chuck.

hurried adjective **1** *with hurried steps* quick, fast, swift, rapid, speedy, hasty, breakneck. **2** *a hurried glance* rushed, cursory, superficial, perfunctory, offhand, passing, fleeting, transitory.

hurry verb hurry up, make haste, hasten, speed, speed up, lose no time, press on, push on, run, dash, rush, go hell for leather; *inf.* get a move on, step on it, get cracking, shake a leg, fly, race, scurry, scamper, go like a bat out of hell, hightail it, hotfoot it.

hurry noun haste, urgency, rush, flurry, bustle, hubbub, turmoil, agitation, confusion, commotion.

hurt verb **1** *my foot hurts* ache, smart, nip, sting, throb, tingle, burn. **2** *he has hurt his leg* injure, wound, bruise, cut, scratch, lacerate, maim, mutilate, damage, disable, incapacitate, debilitate, impair. **3** *his cruel words hurt her* upset, sadden, grieve, wound, distress, pain, cut to the quick, sting, offend, give offense. **4** *hurt his reputation* harm, damage, spoil, mar, blight, blemish, impair.

hurt noun **1** *the hurt in his hand* pain, soreness, ache, smarting, stinging, throbbing, suffering, pangs, discomfort. **2** *a hurt on his leg* sore, wound, injury, bruise, cut, scratch, laceration. **3** *the hurt he caused her* upset, sadness, sorrow, suffering, grief, distress, pain, misery, anguish, affliction. **4** *the hurt caused to his reputation* harm, damage, injury, detriment, blight, loss, disadvantage, mischief.

hurt adjective **1** *a hurt leg* wounded, injured, bruised, cut, lacerated, sore, painful, aching, smarting, throbbing. **2** *a hurt expression* upset, aggrieved, distressed, anguished, offended, piqued.

hurtful adjective **1** *hurtful remarks* upsetting, wounding, distressing, unkind, nasty, mean, malicious, spiteful, cutting, cruel, mischievous, offensive. **2** *actions hurtful to his career* harmful, damaging, injurious, detrimental, disadvantageous, deleterious.

hush verb **1** *hush the children* silence, shush; *inf.* shut up. **2** *they suddenly hushed* fall silent, become silent; *inf.* pipe down, shut up. **3** *hush their fears* still, quieten, calm, soothe, allay, assuage, pacify, mollify, compose. **hush up** suppress, conceal, cover up, keep secret, keep dark, smother, stifle, squash.

hush noun quiet, quietness, silence, stillness, still, soundlessness, peacefulness, peace, calm, tranquillity.

hush-hush adjective top secret, secret, confidential, classified, restricted.

husky adjective **1** *a husky voice* throaty, gruff, deep, gravelly, hoarse, coarse, croaking, croaky, rough, thick, guttural, harsh, rasping. **2** *a husky young man* brawny, well-built, strapping, muscular, rugged, burly, sturdy, thickset; *inf.* beefy.

hussy noun minx, seductress, trollop, slut, loose woman; *inf.* vamp, tramp, bimbo, floozy.

hustle verb **1** *hustle them out of the way* push, shove, thrust, crowd, jostle, elbow, nudge, shoulder. **2** *hustle them into making a decision* coerce, pressure, prompt, urge, goad, prod, spur, propel, egg on. **3** *hustle to get there on time* hurry, hasten, dash, rush, fly; *inf.* get a move on, step on it.

hut noun shed, lean-to, shack, cabin, shanty, hovel.

hybrid noun crossbreed, cross, mixed-breed, half-blood, mixture, conglomerate, composite, compound, amalgam; *derog.* half-breed.

hygienic adjective sanitary, clean, germ-free, disinfected, sterilized, aseptic, sterile, unpolluted, uncontaminated, healthy, pure.

hymn noun psalm, anthem, carol, religious song, paean, chant, plainsong, spiritual.

hype noun publicity, promotion, advertising, ballyhoo; *inf.* plugging.

hypnotic adjective mesmerizing, sleep-inducing, sleep-producing, soporific, somniferous, somnific, numbing, sedative, stupefactive.

hypnotize verb **1** *hypnotize the patient* put under, put out, send into a trance, mesmerize, put to sleep. **2** *they were hypnotized by her beauty* fascinate, bewitch, entrance, beguile, spellbind, magnetize.

hypocrisy noun sanctimoniousness, sanctimony, pietism, insincerity, deceptiveness, deceit, deceitfulness, deception, dishonesty, duplicity, imposture, two-facedness, double-dealing, pretense; *inf.* phoniness.

hypocrite noun pharisee, deceiver, impostor, pretender; *inf.* phony.

hypocritical adjective sanctimonious, pietistic, unctuous, insincere, false, deceitful, deceptive, dishonest, duplicitous, two-faced, double-dealing; *inf.* phony.

hypothesis noun theorem, thesis, proposition, theory, postulate, axiom, premise; supposition, assumption, presumption, conjecture, speculation.

hypothetical adjective supposed, assumed, presumed, theoretical, conjectured, imagined, speculative, academic.

hysteria noun hysterics, frenzy, outburst/fit of agitation/panic, madness, delirium.

hysterical adjective **1** *hysterical at the news of his death* frenzied, frantic, out of control, berserk, beside oneself, distracted, distraught, overwrought, agitated, mad, crazed, out of one's mind/wits. **2** *hysterical play/game* hilarious, uproarious, sidesplitting, amusing, comical, farcical, funny.

Ii

icon noun image, idol, likeness, representation, figure, statue.

icy adjective **1** *icy winds/weather* freezing, frigid, chill, chilly, chilling, frosty, biting, bitter, raw, arctic, glacial, Siberian, polar, gelid. **2** *icy roads* frozen over, ice-bound, frosty, rimy, glassy, like a sheet of glass, slippery. **3** *an icy welcome* cold, frigid, frosty, stiff, aloof, distant, unfriendly.

idea noun **1** *the idea of death scares her* concept, conception, conceptualization, image, abstraction, perception. **2** *tell him your ideas on the subject* thought, theory, view, viewpoint, opinion, feeling, outlook, belief. **3** *I had an idea that he would win* feeling, notion, suspicion, fancy, inkling. **4** *could you give me some idea of the cost?* estimation, approximation, guess, surmise; *inf.* guesstimate. **5** *our idea is to open a new store* plan, design, scheme, aim, intention, objective, object, purpose, end, goal, target. **6** *she's not my idea of a good mother* notion, vision, archetype, ideal example, exemplar, pattern.

ideal noun epitome, peak of perfection, paragon, nonpareil; archetype, model, exemplar, paradigm.

ideal adjective **1** *ideal beauty* perfect, consummate, supreme, absolute, complete, flawless, exemplary, classic, archetypal, model, quintessential. **2** *confusing ideal and concrete matters* abstract, conceptual, theoretical, hypothetical. **3** *she dreams of an ideal world* unattainable, Utopian, unreal, impracticable, ivory-towered, visionary, fanciful.

idealistic adjective Utopian, perfectionist, visionary, romantic, quixotic, unrealistic.

ideally adverb in a perfect world, all things being equal, theoretically, hypothetically, in theory.

ideals plural noun principles, standards, morals, morality, ethics.

identical adjective same, very same, one and the same, selfsame; alike, very much the same, indistinguishable.

identification noun **1** *identification of the criminal* recognition, singling out, spotting, pinpointing, naming; *inf.* fingering. **2** *the identification of the best method* establishment, finding out, ascertainment, diagnosis, selection, choice. **3** *show his identification* ID card, ID, badge; papers, credentials. **4** *her identification with her patient* empathy, rapport, bond, sympathy.

identify verb **1** *identify the criminal* recognize, single out, pick out, spot, point out, pinpoint, discern, distinguish, name; *inf.* put the finger on, finger. **2** *identify the problem* establish, find out, ascertain, diagnose, select, choose. **3** *I identify her with my youth* associate, connect. **identify with** empathize with, sympathize with, relate to, respond to.

identity noun **1** *the identity of the criminal* name, specification. **2** *he lost his identity on emigrating* personality, self, selfhood, ego, individuality, distinctiveness, singularity, uniqueness, differentness. **3** *a case of mistaken identity* identification, recognition, naming. **4** *the identity of their interests* identicalness, sameness, indistinguishability, interchangeability.

ideology noun doctrine, creed, credo, teaching, dogma, theory, thesis; tenets, beliefs.

idiocy noun stupidity, stupidness, foolishness, senselessness, inanity, absurdity, fatuity, fatuousness, asininity, lunacy, craziness, insanity; *inf.* dumbness.

idiosyncrasy noun peculiarity, singularity, oddity, eccentricity, mannerism, quirk, habit, characteristic, specialty, quality, feature.

idiot noun blockhead, nitwit, dunderhead, dolt, dunce, halfwit, fool, ass, boob, nincompoop, ninny, ignoramus, cretin, moron; *inf.* numskull, dimwit.

idiotic adjective stupid, foolish, senseless, inane, absurd, fatuous, asinine, unintelligent, halfwitted, harebrained, lunatic, crazy, insane, moronic; *inf.* dumb.

idle adjective **1** *an idle fellow* lazy, indolent, slothful, shiftless, loafing, dronish. **2** *idle machines/workers* not in operation, inoperative, inactive, unused, mothballed; unemployed, out of work, jobless, out of a job, laid off; *inf.* on the dole. **3** *idle hours* unoccupied, empty, vacant, unfilled. **4** *idle rumors* groundless, baseless, lacking foundation. **5** *idle remarks/pleasures* unimportant, trivial, trifling, shallow, foolish, insignificant, superficial, inane, meaningless. **6** *idle threats* useless, vain, worthless, futile, ineffective, ineffectual, inefficacious, unproductive, fruitless.

idle verb **1** *idle away the hours* while, laze, loaf, lounge, loiter, dawdle, dally, fritter, waste. **2** *stop idling and work* laze, loaf, mark time, shirk, slack, vegetate; *inf.* rest on one's oars.

idol noun **1** *pagans worshiping idols* icon, god, false god, effigy, image, graven image, fetish. **2** *the singer is a teenage idol* hero, heroine, favorite, darling, beloved, pet, superstar; *inf.* pinup.

idolatry noun **1** *religion based on idolatry* idolization, idol-worship, fetishism, iconworship, paganism, heathenism. **2** *the fans' idolatry of Elvis* idolizing, worshiping, hero-worship, adulation, adoration, blind adoration, admiration, doting, lionizing, reverence, glorification.

idolize verb **1** *idolize false gods* worship, bow down before, glorify, exalt, revere, adore, deify. **2** *idolize the singer* adulate, love, look up to, admire, dote upon, lionize, venerate.

iffy adjective doubtful, uncertain, unsure, undecided, unsettled, indeterminate, unresolved; *inf.* up in the air.

ignite verb **1** *ignite the fire* light, set fire to, set on fire, fire, kindle, inflame, touch off, put a match to. **2** *the fire ignited* catch/take fire, catch, burst into flames, burn up, burn, flame up.

ignominious adjective shameful, dishonorable, disgraceful, discreditable, disreputable, ignoble, inglorious, scandalous, abject, sorry, base, contemptible, despicable, wicked, vile.

ignominy noun shame, dishonor, disgrace, humiliation, discredit, disrepute, infamy, opprobrium, contemptibleness, wickedness, baseness, vileness, dishonesty, treachery.

ignorance noun **1** *ignorance of the law* unawareness, unfamiliarity, inexperience, greenness, innocence. **2** *appalled at the ignorance of the pupils* illiteracy, unintelligence, stupidity, thickness, denseness, unenlightenment, benightedness.

ignorant adjective **1** *ignorant of legal procedure* unaware of, unfamiliar with, unconversant with, unacquainted with, unconscious of, uninformed about, unenlightened about, inexperienced in, blind to, uninitiated in, unschooled in, naïve about, innocent about; *inf.* in the dark about. **2** *ignorant pupils* unscholarly, uneducated, untaught, unschooled, untutored, untrained, illiterate, unlettered, unlearned, unread, uninformed, unknowledgeable, unintelligent, stupid, unenlightened, benighted; *inf.* thick, dense, dumb.

ignore verb disregard, pay no attention/heed to, take no notice of, brush aside, pass over, shrug off, push aside, shut one's eyes to, be oblivious to, turn a blind eye to, turn a deaf ear to, spurn, cold-shoulder, look right through.

ill adjective **1** *feeling rather ill* unwell, ailing, poorly, sick, sickly, on the sick list, infirm, off-color, afflicted, indisposed, out of sorts, diseased, bedridden, weak, feeble; *inf.* under the weather, laid up, queasy. **2** *the ill feeling in the firm* hostile, antagonistic, acrimonious, belligerent, bellicose, unfriendly, unkind, spiteful, rancorous, resentful, malicious, malevolent, bitter. **3** *his ill temper* fractious, irritable, irascible, cross, cantankerous, crabbed, surly, snappish, gruff, sullen. **4** *an ill wind* adverse, unfavorable, unadvantageous, unlucky, unfortunate, unpropitious, inauspicious, unpromising, ominous, infelicitous. **5** *the ill effects of the medicine* harmful, detrimental, deleterious, hurtful, damaging, pernicious, destructive, ruinous. **6** *a person of ill repute* bad, infamous, wicked, nefarious, vile, evil, foul, sinful, iniquitous, sinister, corrupt, depraved, degenerate. **7** *ill management* unsatisfactory, unacceptable, inadequate, deficient, faulty, poor, unskillful, inexpert. **ill at ease** adjective uncomfortable, uneasy, awkward, self-conscious, out of place, unquiet, disturbed, discomfited, anxious, on edge, nervous.

ill-advised adjective unwise, ill-considered, imprudent, incautious, injudicious, impolitic, misguided, foolish, foolhardy, shortsighted.

ill-bred adjective ill-mannered, bad-mannered, unmannerly, rude, impolite, discourteous, uncivil, ungentlemanly, unladylike, boorish, churlish, loutish, vulgar, coarse, crass, uncouth.

illegal adjective unlawful, illegitimate, illicit, lawless, criminal, actionable, felonious, unauthorized, unsanctioned, unofficial, outlawed, banned, forbidden, barred, prohibited, proscribed, contraband, black-market, under the counter, bootleg.

illegible adjective unreadable, indecipherable, unintelligible, scrawled, scribbled, squiggly, crabbed, faint.

illegitimate adjective 1 *illegitimate use of property* unlawful, illicit. See ILLEGAL. 2 *an illegitimate child* natural, love, born out of wedlock, fatherless, bastard.

ill-fated adjective unlucky, luckless, unfortunate, hapless, unhappy, doomed, blighted, star-crossed, ill-starred, ill-omened.

ill feeling noun ill will, bad blood, hostility, enmity, hatred, no love lost, antipathy, aversion, dislike, antagonism, acrimony, animus, unfriendliness, spite, rancor, grudge, resentment, bitterness, malice, hard feelings.

ill-founded adjective baseless, groundless, without foundation, unjustified, unsupported, unsubstantiated, unproven, unverified, unauthenticated, unreliable.

illicit adjective unlawful, illegitimate. See ILLEGAL.

illiterate adjective unlettered, uneducated, untaught, unschooled, untutored, uninstructed, unlearned, ignorant.

ill-mannered adjective unmannerly, rude. See ILL-BRED.

ill-natured adjective ill-tempered, bad-tempered, ill-humored, moody, irritable, irascible, surly, peevish, petulant, cross, crabbed, testy, grouchy, disagreeable, spiteful, malicious.

illness noun ailment, sickness, disorder, complaint, malady, disease, affliction, attack, disability, indisposition, infection, contagion; ill health, poor health.

illogical adjective unsound, unreasonable, irrational, faulty, spurious, fallacious, fallible, unproved, untenable, specious, unscientific, sophistic, casuistic, inconsistent, invalid.

ill-tempered adjective choleric, cantankerous, grumpy, splenetic. See ILL-NATURED.

ill-timed adjective inopportune, inconvenient, awkward, inappropriate, untimely, mistimed, badly timed, unwelcome, unfavorable, unfortunate.

ill-treat verb abuse, harm, injure, damage, mishandle, ill-use, maltreat, misuse; *inf.* knock about.

illuminate verb 1 *lights illuminating the hall* light, light up, throw/cast light upon, brighten, shine on, irradiate, illumine. 2 *illuminate the problem* clarify, make clear, clear up, shed/cast light on, elucidate, explain, explicate, expound. 3 *illuminate a manuscript* adorn, decorate, ornament, embellish, enhance, illustrate.

illusion noun 1 *the illusion of depth* false/deceptive appearance, deception, faulty perception, misperception. 2 *under the illusion that he was her first love* delusion, misapprehension, misconception, false/mistaken impression, fallacy, error, misjudgment, fancy. 3 *see an illusion* hallucination, figment of the imagination, phantom, specter, mirage, phantasm, fantasy, will-o'-the-wisp, ignis fatuus.

illusive, illusory adjective deceptive, delusory, false, fallacious, mistaken, erroneous, misleading, untrue, specious, unreal, imagined, imaginary, fancied, nonexistent, fanciful, notional, chimerical, dreamlike.

illustrate verb 1 *illustrate the story* adorn, decorate, ornament, embellish. 2 *illustrate his point* exemplify, demonstrate, point up, clarify, bring home, emphasize.

illustration noun 1 *the illustration in the child's book* picture, drawing, sketch, plate, figure; artwork, adornment, decoration, ornamentation, embellishment. 2 *interesting illustrations explaining his theory* example, typical case, case in point, instance, specimen, sample, exemplar.

illustrative adjective exemplifying, explanatory, elucidative, explicative, interpretive.

illustrious adjective renowned, famous, famed, well-known, celebrated, acclaimed, noted, notable, distinguished, esteemed, honored, prominent, preeminent.

ill will noun bad blood, hostility. See ILL FEELING.

image noun 1 *images of the saints* likeness, representation, resemblance, effigy, figure, figurine, doll, statue, statuette, sculpture, bust, idol, icon, fetish, graven image, painting, picture, portrait. 2 *the image formed by the camera* reproduction, representation, reflection; picture, facsimile, photograph, snapshot, photo. 3 *an image of what the new country would be like* vision, concept, conception, idea, perception, impression, fancy, thought. 4 *he is the image of his father* double, living image, replica, clone, copy, reproduction, counterpart, similitude, doppelgänger; *inf.* spitting image, ringer, dead ringer. 5 *he* *is the image of goodness* emblem, symbol, archetype, embodiment, incarnation.

imaginable adjective thinkable, conceivable, supposable, believable, credible, comprehensible, possible, within the bounds of possibility, probable, likely, plausible, feasible.

imaginary adjective fanciful, fancied, unreal, nonexistent, illusory, visionary, dreamy, dreamlike, shadowy, unsubstantial, chimerical, fictitious, fictional, legendary, mythical, mythological, made-up, invented, hallucinatory, phantasmal, phantasmic, spectral, ghostly, ideal.

imagination noun **1** *the project requires imagination* creativity, vision, inventiveness, originality, innovation, resourcefulness, ingenuity, enterprise, cleverness. **2** *it's only your imagination* illusion, fancy, figment of the imagination, vision, dream, chimera, shadow, phantom.

imaginative adjective creative, fanciful, inventive, original, innovative, resourceful, ingenious, enterprising, clever, whimsical.

imagine verb **1** *he imagines a bright future for himself* picture, see in the mind's eye, visualize, envisage, envision, conjure up, dream about, dream up, fantasize about, conceptualize, think up, conceive, think of, plan, project, scheme. **2** *I imagine he will be late* assume, presume, suppose, think, believe, gather, fancy, judge, deem, infer, deduce, conjecture, surmise, guess, reckon, suspect.

imbecile noun fool, idiot, dolt, halfwit, nitwit, dunce, simpleton; *inf.* dimwit, dope.

imbecilic adjective stupid, foolish, idiotic, halfwitted, witless, dull; silly, senseless, absurd, crazy, mad, fatuous, inane, asinine; *inf.* dim-witted, dopey.

imitate verb **1** *imitate the language of Shakespeare* copy, emulate, follow, follow suit, take a page from someone's book, tread in the steps of, walk in the footsteps of, echo. **2** *comics imitating celebrities* mimic, ape, impersonate, do an impression of, parody, mock, caricature, burlesque, travesty; *inf.* send up, take off, spoof, do, make like. **3** *the stage set imitated a city street* look like, simulate, echo, mirror. **4** *imitate the portrait* copy, reproduce, replicate, duplicate, counterfeit, forge, fake.

imitation noun **1** *a house built in imitation of Frank Lloyd Wright* emulation, mimicry, resemblance. **2** *the comic's imitations of celebrities* impersonation, impression, parody, caricature, burlesque, travesty; *inf.* sendup, takeoff, spoof. **3** *a bad imitation of the portrait* copy, reproduction, counterfeit, forgery, fake.

imitation adjective artificial, synthetic, simulated, man-made, ersatz, mock, sham, fake, reproduction, repro; *inf.* pseudo, phony.

imitator noun copier, copyist, emulator, follower, mimic, echo, impersonator, epigone, plagiarist, counterfeiter, forger, ape, parrot.

immaculate adjective **1** *immaculate rooms* clean, spotless, unsoiled, unstained, spick-and-span, neat, neat as a pin, spruce, trim. **2** *of immaculate character* flawless, faultless, stainless, unblemished, spotless, pure, incorrupt, guiltless, sinless, unsullied, undefiled, untarnished, uncontaminated, unpolluted.

immaterial adjective **1** *it's immaterial what he thinks* unimportant, inconsequential, of little account, irrelevant, insignificant, trivial, petty, slight, inappreciable. **2** *as immaterial as ghosts* incorporeal, bodiless, unembodied, disembodied, intangible, impalpable, ethereal, unsubstantial, airy, ghostly, unearthly, supernatural.

immature adjective **1** *immature fruit/plans* unripe, undeveloped, unformed, imperfect, unfinished, incomplete, half-grown, crude, raw, green, unmellowed, unfledged, untimely. **2** *an immature young man* adolescent, childish, babyish, infantile, juvenile, puerile, jejune, callow, inexperienced, green, unsophisticated; *inf.* wet behind the ears.

immaturity noun **1** *the immaturity of the fruit/plans* unripeness, imperfection, crudeness, rawness, greenness. **2** *the immaturity of the men* childishness, babyishness, juvenility, puerility, inexperience.

immeasurable adjective measureless, limitless, boundless, unbounded, illimitable, infinite, incalculable, unfathomable, fathomless, undeterminable, indeterminate, inestimable, extensive, vast.

immediate adjective **1** *an immediate reaction* instant, instantaneous, on the spot, prompt, swift, speedy. **2** *his immediate neighbor* near, nearest, close, closest, adjacent, adjoining, abutting, contiguous. **3** *our immediate plans* present, current, existing. **4** *get immediate experience* direct, firsthand, hands on, in the field, on the job.

immediately adverb right away, right now, straight away, at once, instantly, this instant, directly, promptly, forthwith, posthaste, *tout de suite*; *inf.* before you can say Jack Robinson, in the twinkling of an eye, lickety-split, pronto.

immense adjective huge, vast, massive, enormous, gigantic, colossal, giant, great, extensive, infinite, immeasurable, illimitable, monumental, tremendous, prodigious, elephantine, monstrous, titanic; *inf.* mega.

immerse verb **1** *immerse the cloth in the dye* submerge, plunge, dip, dunk, duck, sink, douse, souse, soak, drench, imbue, saturate. **2** *immerse oneself in one's work* absorb, engross, occupy, engage, preoccupy, involve, engulf, lose.

immigrant noun nonnative, settler, newcomer, new arrival, naturalized citizen, expatriate.

imminent adjective impending, at hand, fast-approaching, close, near, upon us, in the offing, on the horizon, in the air, brewing, threatening, menacing, looming.

immobile adjective immobilized, unmoving, motionless, immovable, still, static, at rest, stationary, at a standstill, stock-still, dormant, rooted, fixed to the spot, riveted.

immobilize verb bring to a standstill, halt, stop, put out of action, inactivate, paralyze, freeze, transfix, disable, cripple.

immoderate adjective excessive, extreme, intemperate, lavish, undue, inordinate, extravagant, unreasonable, unjustified, unwarranted, uncalled-for, outrageous, egregious.

immoral adjective bad, wrong, unprincipled, dishonest, unethical, wicked, evil, sinful, impure, iniquitous, corrupt, depraved, vile, base, degenerate, debauched, abandoned, dissolute, villainous, nefarious, perverted, indecent.

immortal adjective **1** *immortal beings/love* undying, deathless, eternal, everlasting, never-ending, endless, imperishable, perdurable, timeless, indestructible, unfading, undecaying, perennial, evergreen, perpetual, lasting, enduring, constant, abiding, sempiternal. **2** *immortal poets* famous, celebrated, remembered, commemorated, honored, lauded, glorified.

immortalize verb commemorate, memorialize, eternalize, eternize, perpetuate, exalt, laud, glorify.

immovable adjective **1** *immovable pillars* fast, firm, fixed, secure, stable, rooted, riveted, moored, anchored, stuck, jammed, unbudgeable. **2** *the spectators stood immovable* motionless, unmoving, stationary, still, stock-still. **3** *the court was immovable in its ruling* adamant, firm, steadfast, unwavering, resolute, tenacious, obdurate, inflexible, uncompromising, unshakeable.

immune adjective not subject to, not liable to, protected from, safe from, unsusceptible to, secure against, exempt from, clear of, free from, absolved from, released from, excused from, relieved of, spared from, excepted from, unaffected by, resistant to, protected from/against.

immunity noun indemnity, privilege, prerogative, liberty, license, permission. **immunity from 1** *immunity from the disease* nonsusceptibility to, resistance to, protection from. **2** *immunity from tax* exemption from, exception from, freedom from, release from, dispensation from, absolution from, exoneration from, excusal from.

imp noun **1** *devils and imps* demon, hobgoblin, goblin, elf, sprite, puck, gnome, dwarf. **2** *the child's a little imp* scamp, rogue, rascal, mischief-maker, troublemaker, prankster.

impact noun **1** *the impact of the two cars* collision, contact, crash, striking, clash, bumping, banging. **2** *the impact of his talk* influence, effect, impression; results, consequences, repercussions. **3** *he took the full impact of the blow* force, full force, shock, brunt, impetus, pressure.

impair verb weaken, lessen, decrease, reduce, blunt, diminish, enfeeble, debilitate, enervate, damage, mar, spoil, injure, harm, hinder, disable, cripple, impede, undermine, vitiate.

impale verb transfix, pierce, stab, prick, stick, spear, spike, run through, disembowel.

impart verb **1** *impart the news* pass on, convey, communicate, transmit, relate, tell, make known, report, disclose, reveal, divulge, proclaim, broadcast. **2** *age imparts wisdom* bestow, confer, give, grant, lend, accord, afford, assign, offer.

impartial adjective unbiased, unprejudiced, disinterested, detached, objective, neutral, equitable, evenhanded, fair, fairminded, just, open-minded, nonpartisan, with no ax to grind, without fear or favor.

impasse noun deadlock, dead end, stalemate, checkmate, standstill, full/dead stop, stand-off.

impassioned adjective passionate, ardent, fervent, fervid, vehement, intense, violent, fiery, burning, inflamed, emotional, emotive, zealous, eager, enthusiastic, aroused.

impatience noun **1** *wait with impatience* restlessness, restiveness, excitability, anxiety, agitation, nervousness, edginess, fretfulness, jitteriness, fluster, disquiet, disquietude. **2** *answer with impatience* abruptness, brusqueness, shortness, curtness, irascibility, irritability, testiness, snappiness, querulousness, peevishness.

impatient adjective **1** *an impatient crowd* restless, restive, excitable, agitated, nervous, edgy. **2** *an impatient answer* abrupt, brusque, terse, short, short-tempered, quick-tempered, curt, irritated, angry, testy, snappy, querulous, peevish. **3** *impatient to see her boyfriend* anxious, eager, keen, avid, desirous.

impeccable adjective **1** *impeccable behavior* perfect, faultless, flawless, unblemished, exemplary, correct, exact, precise, ideal. **2** *an impeccable young woman* virtuous, innocent, chaste, pure, sinless, irreproachable, unimpeachable, above suspicion, incorrupt.

impede verb hinder, obstruct, hamper, handicap, block, check, bar, curb, hold back, hold up, delay, interfere with, disrupt, retard, slow, slow down, brake, restrain, thwart, frustrate, balk, stop; *inf.* throw a monkey wrench in the works.

impediment noun **1** *an impediment to our plans* hindrance, obstruction, obstacle, handicap, block, stumbling block, check, encumbrance, bar, barrier, curb, brake, restraint, drawback, difficulty, snag, setback. **2** *a speech impediment* stammer, stutter, speech defect, hesitancy, faltering.

impel verb urge, press, exhort, force, oblige, constrain, necessitate, require, demand, make, pressure, spur, prod, goad, incite, prompt, persuade, inspire.

impending adjective approaching, coming. *See* IMMINENT.

impenetrable adjective **1** *impenetrable containers* impervious, impermeable, solid, dense, thick, hard, closed, sealed, tight, unpierceable. **2** *impenetrable forests* impassable, unpassable, inaccessible, thick, dense, overgrown, jungly. **3** *impenetrable jargon* incomprehensible, unintelligible, baffling, puzzling, abstruse, obscure, hidden, inexplicable, unfathomable, recondite, inscrutable, enigmatic.

imperative adjective **1** *it is imperative that you stay* vital, crucial, critical, necessary, required, mandatory, pressing, urgent. **2** *an imperative tone of voice* imperious, authoritative, peremptory, commanding, lordly, masterful, autocratic, dictatorial, domineering, overbearing.

imperceptible adjective unnoticeable, unobtrusive, unapparent, slight, small, gradual, subtle, faint, fine, inappreciable, inconsequential, undetectable, indistinguishable, indiscernible, invisible, indistinct, obscure, vague, indefinite.

imperfect adjective faulty, flawed, defective, blemished, impaired; incomplete, deficient, partial, inadequate, insufficient, lacking.

imperfection noun **1** *an imperfection in the finish* fault, flaw, defect, deformity, blemish; crack, break, scratch, cut, tear, stain, spot. **2** *an imperfection in his character* failing, flaw, foible, deficiency, weakness, weak point, shortcoming, fallibility, frailty, infirmity, peccadillo.

imperial adjective **1** *his/her imperial majesty* royal, sovereign, regal, monarchal, kingly, queenly, princely. **2** *an imperial bearing* majestic, magnificent, grand, great, lofty, imposing, august, stately. **3** *the imperial ruler of the region* supreme, absolute, dominant, predominant, paramount, chief. **4** *an imperial tone of voice* commanding, lordly, masterful, authoritative, imperious, peremptory, domineering.

imperil verb endanger, put in danger/jeopardy, put at risk, risk, jeopardize, hazard, gamble with, take a chance with.

impersonal adjective **1** *an impersonal assessment of the candidates* detached, objective, dispassionate, neutral. *See* IMPARTIAL. **2** *an impersonal manner* cool, aloof, formal, stiff, rigid, wooden, starchy, stilted, stuffy, matter-of-fact, businesslike, bureaucratic.

impersonate verb masquerade as, pose as, pass oneself off as. *See* IMITATE 2.

impertinence noun insolence, impudence, cheek, rudeness, impoliteness, unmannerliness, lack of civility, discourtesy, boldness, brazenness, audacity, effrontery, gall, presumptuousness, brashness; *inf.* nerve, lip.

impertinent adjective **1** *an impertinent youth/act* insolent, impudent, cheeky, rude, impolite, unmannerly, ill-mannered, uncivil, discourteous, disrespectful, bold, brazen, audacious, presumptuous, forward, pert, brash, shameless; *inf.* fresh, flip. **2** *this document is impertinent to the case* irrelevant, inapplicable, inapposite, unrelated, unconnected, not germane.

impervious adjective *impervious containers* impermeable, sealed. *See* IMPENETRABLE 1. **impervious to** *impervious to arguments* unmoved by, unaffected by, proof against, immune to, invulnerable to, unreceptive to, untouched by, closed to.

impetuous adjective **1** *an impetuous action/person* hasty, precipitate, headlong, impulsive, spontaneous, spur-of-the-moment, unthinking, unplanned, unthought out, ill-conceived, ill-considered, unreasoned, reckless, rash, foolhardy, heedless, eager, enthusiastic, impatient, excitable, ardent, passionate, zealous, wild, uncontrolled. **2** *an impetuous wind* violent, forceful, powerful, vigorous, vehement, raging, rampant, unrestrained, uncontrolled, unbridled.

impetus noun **1** *the car lost impetus on the hill* momentum, propulsion, energy, force, power. **2** *the student needs some impetus to start studying* stimulus, instigation, actuation, motivation, inspiration, encouragement, push, urging, pressing, spur, goad.

impish adjective **1** *impish little boys* mischievous, mischief-making, full of mischief, rascally, roguish, prankish, unruly, trouble-making, devilish, sportive. **2** *an impish* *smile* elfin, pixieish, puckish, mischievous, roguish.

implacable adjective unappeasable, unpacifiable, unmollifiable, inexorable, unrelenting, relentless, ruthless, unsympathetic, remorseless, merciless, pitiless.

implausible adjective unlikely, improbable, incredible, unbelievable, hard to swallow, unimaginable, inconceivable.

implement noun 1 *garden/kitchen implements* tool, utensil, appliance, instrument, device, apparatus, contrivance, gadget; *inf.* gizmo. 2 *an implement of peace* agent, medium, channel, expedient, means.

implement verb fulfill, carry out, execute, perform, discharge, accomplish, achieve, realize, put into effect/action, bring about, effect, enforce.

implicate verb involve, concern, include, associate, connect, embroil, entangle; incriminate, compromise, inculpate, accuse, charge, blame.

implication noun 1 *resent the implication that he was lying* suggestion, inference, insinuation, innuendo, hint, allusion, reference, assumption, presumption. 2 *their implication in the events* involvement, concern, association, connection, entanglement.

implicit adjective 1 *implicit criticism* implied, indirect, inferred, deducible, unspoken, unexpressed, undeclared, unstated, tacit, understood, hinted, suggested. 2 *implicit trust* absolute, complete, utter, unconditional, unquestioning.

implied adjective indirect, unspoken. *See* IMPLICIT 1.

implore verb appeal to, beg, entreat, plead with, beseech, pray, ask, request, solicit, supplicate, importune, press; crave, plead for, appeal for.

imply verb 1 *he implied that all was not well* hint, suggest, intimate, give to understand, signal, indicate, insinuate. 2 *being a civil servant implies discretion* involve, entail, presuppose, presume, assume. 3 *war implies bloodshed* signify, mean, indicate, denote, connote, betoken, point to.

impolite adjective unmannerly, ill-mannered, ungracious, ungallant, disrespectful, inconsiderate, rough, crude, unrefined, indelicate, indecorous. *See* ILL-BRED.

importance noun 1 *the importance of the talks* significance, momentousness, seriousness, graveness, urgency, gravity, weightiness, value. 2 *people of importance* prominence, eminence, preeminence, note, notability, noteworthiness, influence, power, high rank, status, prestige, standing, mark.

important adjective 1 *important talks* of import, consequential, significant, critical, crucial, pivotal, momentous, of great moment, serious, grave, urgent, substantial, weighty, valuable. 2 *the important points to remember* salient, chief, main, principal, major. 3 *the important people in the town* prominent, eminent, preeminent, leading, foremost, outstanding, distinguished, esteemed, notable, influential, powerful, high-ranking, high-level, top-level.

impose verb 1 *impose a tax* apply, exact, levy, charge, put on, lay on, set, establish, fix, decree, ordain, institute, introduce, promulgate; require, demand, dictate; *inf.* saddle with. 2 *impose her views on the group* force, foist, inflict, thrust, obtrude. 3 *impose fake antiques on the public* palm off, foist, pass off. **impose on** *impose on her good nature* take advantage of, abuse, exploit, play on. **impose oneself** *impose herself on the company* intrude, break in; *inf.* gatecrash, crash, butt in, horn in.

imposing adjective impressive, striking, splendid, grand, majestic, august, lofty, stately, dignified.

imposition noun 1 *the imposition of new taxes* application, exacting, levying, decreeing, institution. 2 *unfair impositions on the poor* burden, load, charge, onus, encumbrance.

impossible adjective 1 *an impossible task* beyond the realm/bounds of possibility, out of the question, unthinkable, unimaginable, inconceivable, impracticable, unattainable, unachievable, unobtainable, beyond one, hopeless. 2 *an impossible story* unbelievable, incredible, absurd, ludicrous, ridiculous, preposterous, outlandish, outrageous. 3 *impossible behavior* objectionable, unacceptable, intolerable, unbearable, unendurable.

impostor, imposter noun masquerader, pretender, deceiver, fake, fraud, sham, charlatan, quack, mountebank, bluffer, trickster, deluder, duper, cheat, cheater, swindler, defrauder, exploiter, confidence man/woman, rogue; *inf.* phony, con man, con artist.

impotent adjective powerless, helpless, unable, incapable, incapacitated, incompetent; enfeebled, weak, feeble, frail, worn out, exhausted, spent, enervated, debilitated, prostrate, crippled, paralyzed, infirm; ineffective, ineffectual, inefficient, inadequate, inept, useless, worthless, vain, futile, unavailing, unsuccessful, profitless.

impound verb 1 *impound stray animals* pen up/in, fence in, coop up, hem in, tie up, cage, enclose, confine, imprison, incarcerate, immure. 2 *impound legal documents* appropriate, take possession of, seize, commandeer, expropriate.

impoverished adjective **1** *impoverished homeless people* poverty-stricken, destitute, penurious, beggared, indigent, impecunious, penniless, poor, needy, in distressed/reduced/straitened circumstances, down-and-out, bankrupt, insolvent, ruined; *inf.* broke, flat-broke, stone-broke, strapped. **2** *impoverished soil* exhausted, depleted, diminished, weakened, drained, used up, spent, played out.

impractical adjective **1** *an impractical solution* unworkable, useless, ineffective, ineffectual, inefficacious, unrealistic, impossible, nonviable, inoperable, inoperative, unserviceable. **2** *his ideas are too impractical to implement* theoretical, abstract, academic, speculative. **3** *an impractical young woman* unrealistic, unbusinesslike, starry-eyed, visionary, quixotic.

impregnable adjective **1** *an impregnable castle* impenetrable, unattackable, unassailable, inviolable, secure, strong, stout, invulnerable, invincible, unconquerable, unbeatable, indestructible. **2** *an impregnable argument* irrefutable, indisputable, incontestable, unquestionable, flawless, faultless.

impress verb **1** *impress the crowd with his speech* move, sway, bend, influence, affect, affect deeply, stir, rouse, excite, inspire, galvanize; *inf.* grab. **2** *impress upon them the need for action* emphasize, stress, bring home, establish, instill, inculcate, urge. **3** *impress one's name on a metal strip* stamp, imprint, print, mark, engrave, emboss.

impression noun **1** *make an impression on the crowd* effect, influence, sway, impact, hold, power, control. **2** *the impression made by the ring* mark, indentation, dent, hollow, outline, stamp, stamping, imprint, impress. **3** *I have the impression that he is bored* feeling, sense, awareness, perception, notion, idea, thought, belief, opinion, conviction, fancy, suspicion, inkling, intuition, hunch. **4** *his impression of the politician* impersonation, mimicry. *See* IMITATION noun 2.

impressionable adjective susceptible, suggestible, persuadable, receptive, responsive, sensitive, open, gullible, ingenuous, pliable, malleable.

impressive adjective imposing, magnificent, splendid; moving, affecting, touching, stirring, rousing, exciting, powerful, inspiring.

imprint noun print, mark. *See* IMPRESSION 2.

imprison verb put in prison, send to prison, jail, lock up, shut away, take into custody, put under lock and key, put away, incarcerate, intern, confine, detain, constrain, impound, coop up, immure; *inf.* send up, send up the river.

imprisonment noun custody, incarceration, internment, confinement, detention.

improbable adjective unlikely, highly unlikely, doubtful, dubious, questionable, implausible, far-fetched, unconvincing, unbelievable, incredible, ridiculous.

impromptu adjective ad lib, unrehearsed, unprepared, extempore, extemporized, extemporaneous, spontaneous, improvised, unscripted, unstudied, unpremeditated; *inf.* off the cuff.

impromptu adverb ad lib, extempore, spontaneously, on the spur of the moment; *inf.* off the cuff, off the top of one's head.

improper adjective **1** *improper behavior* unseemly, indecorous, unbecoming, unfitting, unladylike, ungentlemanly, impolite, indiscreet, injudicious. **2** *an improper remark* indecent, risqué, off-color, indelicate, suggestive, blue, smutty, obscene, lewd, pornographic. **3** *draw an improper inference* inaccurate, incorrect, wrong, erroneous, false. **4** *an improper tool for the job* inappropriate, unsuitable, unsuited, unfitting, inapt, inapplicable, incongruous.

impropriety noun incorrectness, indecorum, indecorousness, unseemliness, indiscretion, bad taste, immodesty, indecency.

improve verb **1** *improve conditions* make better, better, ameliorate, amend, mend, reform, rehabilitate, set/put right, correct, rectify, help, advance, upgrade, revamp, modernize, gentrify; *inf.* give a face-lift to. **2** *things are improving* get/grow better, advance, come along, develop, progress, pick up, rally, perk up; *inf.* look up, take a turn for the better, get a new lease on life.

improvement noun **1** *the improvement of conditions* betterment, amelioration, reform, rehabilitation, rectifying, rectification, advance, upgrading, gentrification; *inf.* face-lift. **2** *an improvement in the economy* betterment, advance, development, rally, recovery, upswing, comeback; progress, growth.

improvise verb **1** *if you aren't prepared, you will have to improvise* ad lib, extemporize; *inf.* speak off the cuff, play it by ear, wing it. **2** *improvise a shelter* throw/put together, devise, contrive, concoct, rig, jury-rig.

imprudent adjective indiscreet, ill-considered, thoughtless, unthinking, injudicious, unwise, ill-advised, impolitic, careless, hasty.

impudence noun insolence, pertness, sauciness, presumption, bumptiousness. *See* IMPERTINENCE.

impudent adjective insolent, brazen-faced, saucy, bumptious, impolite, rude, ill-mannered, ill-bred, immodest; *inf.* cocky. *See* IMPERTINENT 1.

impugn verb challenge, call into question, question, dispute, cast aspersions on, attack, assail, berate, criticize, denounce, censure.

impulse noun 1 *the impulse driving the machine* impetus, propulsion, impulsion, momentum, force, thrust, push, surge. 2 *the literary impulse* stimulus, inspiration, stimulation, incitement, incentive, inducement, motivation; urge, drive, instinct, appetite, proclivity. 3 *buy the coat on impulse* sudden desire/fancy, (the) spur of the moment, notion, whim, caprice.

impulsive adjective hasty, impromptu, snap, spontaneous, extemporaneous, sudden, quick, precipitate, impetuous, ill-considered, unplanned, unpremeditated, thoughtless, rash, reckless, instinctive, intuitive, passionate, emotional.

impunity noun immunity, indemnity, excusal, nonliability, license, dispensation.

impure adjective 1 *impure chemicals* adulterated, alloyed, mixed, admixed, combined, blended, debased. 2 *impure water* contaminated, polluted, tainted, infected, foul, dirty, filthy, unclean, feculent, sullied, defiled, unwholesome, poisoned. 3 *impure persons/thoughts* unchaste, immoral, loose, promiscuous, wanton, immodest, dissolute, licentious, lascivious, prurient, lustful, lecherous, lewd, obscene, dirty, indecent, ribald, risqué, smutty, pornographic.

impurity noun 1 *the impurity of the chemical* adulteration, admixture, debasement. 2 *the impurity of the water* contamination, pollution, foulness, filthiness, unwholesomeness. 3 *impurities in the chemicals/water* foreign body, contaminant, pollutant, adulterant; dross, dirt, filth, grime, scum. 4 *regretted the impurity of their past/thoughts* immorality, looseness, promiscuity, wantonness, immodesty, lasciviousness, lust, lechery, lewdness, lustfulness, obscenity, ribaldry, smut, smuttiness, impropriety, crudity, vulgarity.

inability noun incapability, incapacity, incompetence, ineptitude, unfitness, powerlessness, uselessness, inefficacy.

inaccessible adjective unreachable, out of reach, beyond reach, unapproachable, impenetrable, unattainable, out of the way, remote, godforsaken.

inaccuracy noun 1 *the inaccuracy of the results* incorrectness, erroneousness, wrongness, mistakenness, fallaciousness, faultiness, inexactness, inexactitude, imprecision. 2 *the accounts were full of inaccuracies* error, mistake, miscalculation, erratum, corrigendum, slip, slip of the pen, fault, blunder, defect; *inf.* slipup, typo, booboo.

inaccurate adjective incorrect, wrong, erroneous, faulty, inexact, imprecise, fallacious, false, imperfect, flawed, defective,

unsound, unreliable, wide of the mark; *inf.* full of holes.

inactive adjective 1 *all the machines lying inactive* idle, inoperative, nonfunctioning, unused, not in use, unoccupied, unemployed, inert, mothballed. 2 *a former athlete now completely inactive* idle, inert, slow, sluggish, indolent, lazy, lifeless, slothful, lethargic, stagnant, vegetating, sedentary. 3 *an inactive volcano* dormant, quiescent, latent, passive.

inadequacy noun 1 *the inadequacy of the supply* inadequateness, insufficiency, dearth, deficiency, meagerness, scantness, scarcity, paucity, shortage, deficit, lack. 2 *the inadequacy of the staff* incompetence, incapability, unfitness, ineffectiveness, ineffectuality, ineptness. 3 *his inadequacies as a manager* shortcoming, fault, failing, flaw, defect, imperfection, weakness, foible.

inadequate adjective 1 *inadequate supplies* insufficient, meager, scanty, scant, niggardly, scarce, sparse, skimpy, sketchy, incomplete. 2 *an inadequate teacher* incompetent, incapable, unfit, ineffective, ineffectual, unskillful, inexpert, unproficient, inept; *inf.* not up to scratch/snuff.

inadvertent adjective 1 *an inadvertent omission* accidental, unintentional, chance, unpremeditated, unplanned, uncalculated, unconscious, unwitting, involuntary. 2 *an inadvertent driver* inattentive, careless, negligent, heedless, unheeding, unmindful, unobservant.

inadvisable adjective ill-advised, unwise, injudicious, ill-judged, imprudent, impolitic, inexpedient, foolish.

inane adjective silly, foolish, stupid, idiotic, absurd, ridiculous, ludicrous, fatuous, frivolous, senseless, mindless, puerile, asinine, futile, worthless, vacuous, vapid; *inf.* daft.

inanimate adjective 1 *inanimate objects* lifeless, exanimate, dead, inert, insentient, insensate. 2 *inanimate people* spiritless, apathetic, lazy, inactive, phlegmatic, listless, lethargic, sluggish, torpid.

inappropriate adjective unsuitable, unfitting, inapt, unseemly, unbecoming, indecorous, improper, inapposite, incongruous, out of place/keeping, untimely.

inapt adjective 1 *an inapt remark* unsuitable, unsuited, unfitting. *See* INAPPROPRIATE. 2 *an inapt plumber* inept, incompetent, unadept, incapable, unskillful, inexpert, clumsy, awkward, maladroit, undexterous, heavy-handed.

inarticulate adjective 1 *inarticulate cries/sounds* unintelligible, incomprehensible, incoherent, unclear, indistinct, blurred, muffled, mumbled, muttered. 2

inarticulate speakers nonfluent, faltering, hesitating, halting, stumbling, stuttering, stammering. **3** *inarticulate emotion* unspoken, unuttered, unexpressed, unvoiced, wordless, silent, mute, dumb, speechless, voiceless.

inattentive adjective distracted, preoccupied, absentminded, daydreaming, woolgathering, lost in thought, with one's head in the clouds, neglectful, negligent, remiss, careless, heedless; *inf.* miles away.

inaudible adjective out of earshot, faint, muted, soft, low, muffled, stifled, hard to make out, indistinct, imperceptible, whispered, murmured.

inaugural adjective first, initial, introductory, opening, maiden, dedicatory.

inaugurate verb **1** *inaugurate the conference proceedings* initiate, begin, start, commence, launch, start off, set in motion, get going, get under way, raise the curtain on, get off the ground. **2** *inaugurate the new president* install, instate, induct, invest, ordain.

inauspicious adjective unpropitious, unpromising, unlucky, unfortunate, infelicitous, unfavorable, ill-omened, ominous, ill-fated, ill-starred, untoward, untimely.

inborn adjective innate, inherent, inherited, congenital, hereditary, in the family, in the blood/genes, inbred, connate, ingrained.

incalculable adjective **1** *the number is incalculable* immeasurable, measureless, inestimable, uncountable, incomputable, infinite, boundless, limitless, fathomless, bottomless, countless, without number, numberless, multitudinous, enormous, immense, vast. **2** *an incalculable risk* unpredictable, indeterminable, unforeseeable.

incantation noun chant, chanting, invocation, conjuration, spell; abracadabra, open sesame.

incapable adjective incompetent, ineffective, ineffectual, inadequate, unfit, unqualified, inept, useless, feeble; *inf.* not up to scratch/snuff. **incapable of** *problems incapable of solution* not open to, impervious to, resistant to, not susceptible to.

incapacitated adjective disabled, debilitated, unfit, immobilized, crippled, indisposed; *inf.* laid up, out of action.

incapacity noun inability, incapability, incompetence, incompetency, inadequacy, unfitness, ineffectiveness, ineffectuality, inefficiency, powerlessness, impotence.

incarcerate verb jail, throw in prison/jail. *See* IMPRISON.

incarceration noun captivity, bondage. *See* IMPRISONMENT.

incendiary adjective **1** *an incendiary bomb* combustible, flammable, fire-producing.

2 *an incendiary speech* inflammatory, incensing, inciting, instigating, arousing, stirring, provocative, rabble-rousing, seditious, subversive.

incendiary noun **1** *buildings set on fire by incendiaries* arsonist, fire-setter, pyromaniac; *inf.* firebug. **2** *crowds driven to rioting by incendiaries* demagogue, agitator, agent provocateur, rabble-rouser, instigator, inciter, insurgent, firebrand, revolutionary.

incense verb anger, enrage, infuriate, exasperate, irritate, madden, provoke, rile, inflame, agitate, vex, irk, get one's hackles up; *inf.* make one's blood boil, make one see red, ruffle one's feathers, get one's dander up.

incentive noun inducement, incitement, stimulus, stimulant, impetus, encouragement, motivation, inspiration, impulse, goad, spur, lure, bait; *inf.* carrot.

inception noun beginning, commencement, start, starting point, outset, opening, debut, inauguration, initiation, institution, birth, dawn, origin, rise; *inf.* kickoff.

incessant adjective ceaseless, unceasing, nonstop, endless, unending, never-ending, everlasting, eternal, constant, continual, perpetual, continuous, uninterrupted, unbroken, ongoing, unremitting, persistent, recurrent.

incidence noun rate, frequency, prevalence, occurrence, amount, degree, extent.

incident noun **1** *unhappy incidents in her life* event, happening, occurrence, episode, adventure, experience, proceeding, occasion, circumstance, fact, matter. **2** *the police were called to an incident in the bar* disturbance, commotion, scene, fracas, contretemps, skirmish, clash, conflict, confrontation.

incidental adjective **1** *her part in the event was incidental* accidental, by chance, chance, fortuitous, random. **2** *incidental expenses* minor, trivial, trifling, petty, small, meager. **incidental to** *travel incidental to her job* related to, connected with, associated with, accompanying, attendant to, concomitant to, contingent to/on.

incidentally adverb by the way, by the by, in passing, speaking of which, while we're on the subject, apropos.

incision noun cut, opening, slit, gash, slash, notch, nick.

incisive adjective **1** *an incisive mind* keen, acute, sharp, penetrating, astute, shrewd, perspicacious, clever, smart, quick. **2** *an incisive remark* caustic, acid, sharp, biting, cutting, stinging, tart, trenchant, mordant, sarcastic, sardonic.

incite verb instigate, provoke, foment, whip up, stir up, prompt, egg on, encourage, urge, goad, spur on, prod, stimulate, drive on, excite, arouse, agitate, inflame.

inclination noun **1** *an inclination to over-eat* tendency, leaning, propensity, proclivity, proneness, liableness, disposition, predisposition, subjectability, weakness. **2** *an inclination for books* penchant, predilection, partiality, preference, affinity, attraction, fancy, liking, fondness, affection, love. **3** *an inclination of the head* bow, bowing, bend, bending, nod, lowering, stooping. **4** *an inclination in the terrain* incline, slope, slant, gradient, bank, ramp, lift, tilt, acclivity, rise, ascent, declivity, descent.

incline verb **1** *the land inclines toward the shore* curve, bend, slope, slant, bank, cant, bevel, tilt, lean, tip, list, deviate. **2** *I'm inclined to believe you* predispose, dispose, influence, bias, prejudice, sway, persuade, bend. **3** *incline the head* bow, bend, nod, lower, stoop, cast down. **incline to/toward** tend to/toward, lean to/toward, swing to/toward, veer to/toward, have a preference/penchant for, be attracted to.

include verb **1** *the group includes all the representatives* contain, hold, take in, admit, incorporate, embrace, encompass, comprise, embody, comprehend, subsume. **2** *include them on the list* allow for, add, insert, put in, enter, count in, take account of, build in, number, incorporate.

incognito adjective/adverb in disguise, disguised, in masquerade, camouflaged, unrecognized, unidentified, sailing under false colors.

incognizant adjective unaware, unconscious, ignorant, unknowing, unsuspecting, unknowledgeable, unenlightened.

incoherent adjective unconnected, disconnected, disjointed, disordered, confused, mixed-up, muddled, jumbled, scrambled, rambling, wandering, discursive, illogical, unintelligible, inarticulate, mumbled, muttered, stuttered, stammered.

income noun salary, pay, remuneration, revenue; earnings, wages, receipts, takings, profits, gains, proceeds, means.

incoming adjective approaching, entering, arriving; new, succeeding.

incomparable adjective beyond compare, inimitable, unequaled, without equal, matchless, nonpareil, unrivaled, peerless, unparalleled, unsurpassed, superlative, supreme.

incompatible adjective *incompatible views/siblings* inharmonious, uncongenial, incongruous, uncomplementary, conflicting, antagonistic, antipathetic, disagreeing, discordant, like oil and water, clashing, jarring. **incompatible with** differing from, contrary to.

See INCONGRUOUS WITH (INCONGRUOUS).

incompetent adjective **1** *incompetent to do the task* unable, incapable, unqualified, inadequate, deficient. **2** *an incompetent performance* unskillful, inexpert, inept, bungling, maladroit, clumsy.

incomplete adjective unfinished, unaccomplished, partial, undone, deficient, lacking, wanting, defective, imperfect.

incomprehensible adjective unintelligible, inapprehensible, beyond comprehension, unfathomable, impenetrable, profound, deep, incapplicable, puzzling, enigmatic, mysterious, abstruse, recondite.

inconceivable adjective unimaginable, unthinkable, incomprehensible, incredible, unbelievable, implausible, impossible, out of the question, preposterous, ridiculous, ludicrous.

inconclusive adjective indefinite, indecisive, indeterminate, undetermined, still open to question, open to doubt, vague, unestablished, unsettled, ambiguous; *inf.* up in the air.

incongruous adjective out of place/keeping, strange, odd, absurd, unsuitable, inappropriate, incompatible, inharmonious, discordant, clashing, jarring. **incongruous with** *behavior incongruous with his principles* incompatible with, inconsistent with, out of keeping/place with, differing from, contrary to, inappropriate to, unsuited to, at odds with, in opposition to, diametrically opposed to, conflicting with, irreconcilable with.

inconsequential adjective insignificant, negligible, inappreciable, unimportant, of minor importance, of little/no account, trivial, trifling, petty; *inf.* piddling.

inconsiderate adjective thoughtless, unthinking, unthoughtful, uncaring, heedless, unmindful, insensitive, tactless, uncharitable, unkind, ungracious, selfish, self-centered, egotistic.

inconsistent adjective changeable, variable, erratic, irregular, inconstant, unstable, unsteady, unpredictable, capricious, fickle, whimsical, mercurial, volatile. **inconsistent with** incompatible with, out of keeping with. *See* INCONGRUOUS WITH (INCONGRUOUS).

inconsolable adjective grief-stricken, brokenhearted, heartbroken, sick at heart, bowed down, miserable, wretched, woebegone, disconsolate, desolate, despairing.

inconspicuous adjective unnoticeable, unobtrusive, indistinct, ordinary, plain, run-of-the-mill, unremarkable, undistinguished, unostentatious, unimposing, hidden, camouflaged, quiet, retiring, in the background; *inf.* low-key.

inconvenience noun trouble, bother, disruption, disturbance, vexation, worry, annoyance, difficulty, nuisance, burden, hindrance; *inf.* pain, drag, bore.

inconvenience verb disturb, bother, trouble, worry, disrupt, put out, impose upon, burden, distract, annoy.

inconvenient adjective awkward, unsuitable, inappropriate, inopportune, disadvantageous, disturbing, troublesome, bothersome, annoying, ill-timed, untimely, unhandy, difficult.

incorporate verb **1** *incorporate the ingredients to form a whole* merge, coalesce, fuse, blend, mix, amalgamate, combine, unite, integrate, unify, compact. **2** *the document incorporates all our thoughts* embody, include, comprise, embrace, absorb, subsume, assimilate.

incorrect adjective **1** *an incorrect answer/account* wrong, inaccurate, erroneous, wide of the mark, mistaken, faulty, inexact, untrue, fallacious, flawed; *inf.* full of holes. **2** *incorrect behavior* improper, unbecoming, unseemly, indecorous, unsuitable, inappropriate, unladylike, ungentlemanly.

incorrigible adjective *an incorrigible criminal* hardened, incurable, inveterate, unreformable, irredeemable, hopeless, beyond hope/redemption, impenitent, uncontrite, unrepentant.

incorruptible adjective **1** *incorruptible members of society* virtuous, upright, high-principled, honorable, honest, moral, ethical, trustworthy, straight, unbribable. **2** *incorruptible materials* imperishable, indestructible, nonbiodegradable, indissoluble, indissolvable, everlasting.

increase verb **1** *demand has increased* grow, expand, extend, multiply, intensify, heighten, mount, escalate, snowball, mushroom, proliferate, swell, wax. **2** *increase the demand* add to, boost, enhance, build up, augment, enlarge, spread, raise, strengthen, magnify, inflate; *inf.* step up.

increase noun growth, rise, enlargement, expansion, extension, increment, addition, development, intensification, heightening, escalation, snowballing, mushrooming, boost, augmentation, strengthening, magnification, inflation.

incredible adjective **1** *find his story incredible* unbelievable, hard to believe, beyond belief, far-fetched, inconceivable, unimaginable, unthinkable, impossible, implausible, highly unlikely, absurd, preposterous, questionable, dubious, doubtful. **2** *an incredible performance* extraordinary, supreme, great, wonderful, marvelous, tremendous, prodigious, astounding, amazing, astonishing, awe-inspiring, awesome, superhuman, fabulous, fantastic.

incredulous adjective disbelieving, unbelieving, skeptical, cynical, distrusting, distrustful, mistrusting, mistrustful, doubtful, doubting, dubious, unconvinced, suspicious.

incriminate verb charge, accuse, indict, impeach, arraign, blame, implicate, inculpate, involve, inform against, blacken the name of, stigmatize; *inf.* finger, point the finger at, stick/pin the blame on, rat on.

incur verb bring upon oneself, expose oneself to, lay oneself open to, provoke, be liable/subject to, contract, meet with, experience.

incurable adjective **1** *an incurable illness* cureless, unhealable, terminal, fatal, untreatable, inoperable, irremediable. **2** *an incurable romantic* inveterate, dyed-in-the-wool, incorrigible, hopeless, beyond hope.

indebted adjective beholden, obliged, obligated; grateful, thankful, appreciative.

indecency noun **1** *the indecency of the remark* suggestiveness, indelicacy, improperness, impurity, ribaldry, bawdiness, foulness, vulgarity, grossness, crudity, dirtiness, smuttiness, smut, coarseness, obscenity, lewdness. **2** *the indecency of the abrupt departure* impropriety, unseemliness, indecorum, indecorousness, inappropriateness, bad taste, tastelessness, unacceptability, offensiveness.

indecent adjective **1** *an indecent suggestion/joke* suggestive, indelicate, improper, impure, risqué, off-color, ribald, bawdy, foul, vulgar, gross, crude, dirty, smutty, coarse, obscene, blue, lewd, lascivious, licentious, salacious, pornographic, scatological; *inf.* raunchy. **2** *marry with indecent haste after the funeral* improper, unseemly, indecorous, unbecoming, unsuitable, inappropriate, unfitting, unbefitting, in bad taste, tasteless, unacceptable, offensive, outrageous.

indecision noun indecisiveness, irresolution, irresoluteness, vacillation, fluctuation, hesitancy, hesitation, tentativeness, ambivalence, doubt, shilly-shallying, uncertainty.

indecisive adjective **1** *an indecisive person* irresolute, vacillating, wavering, fluctuating, hesitant, tentative, faltering, ambivalent, doubtful, of two minds, shilly-shallying, undecided, indefinite, uncertain, unresolved, undetermined, on the fence; *inf.* blowing hot and cold. **2** *an indecisive ballot* inconclusive, open, indeterminate, unsettled, unclear; *inf.* up in the air.

indeed adverb in fact, in point of fact, in truth, truly, actually, really, in reality, certainly, surely, for sure, to be sure, positively, absolutely, doubtlessly, undoubtedly, without doubt, undeniably, veritably.

indefinite adjective **1** *the time of the meeting is still indefinite* undecided, unfixed, undetermined, unsettled, inconclusive, undefined, unknown, uncertain, unspecific, unexplicit, imprecise, inexact, vague, doubtful. **2** *an indefinite shape in the distance* ill-defined, indistinct, blurred, fuzzy, hazy, dim, vague, obscure. **3** *an indefinite answer* vague, unclear, imprecise, inexact, ambiguous, ambivalent, equivocal, confused, evasive, abstruse. **4** *she's a bit indefinite about her plans* undecided, irresolute. *See* INDECISIVE 1. **5** *an indefinite number/amount* indeterminate, unspecified, unlimited, limitless, infinite, immeasurable, boundless.

indelible adjective inerasable, ineradicable, ineffaceable, unexpungeable, indestructible, permanent, lasting, enduring, inextirpable, ingrained, unfading, imperishable.

indelicate adjective **1** *indelicate manners/behavior* vulgar, coarse, rough, unrefined, uncultivated, tasteless, immodest, boorish, churlish, loutish, offensive. **2** *indelicate jokes* risqué, ribald. *See* INDECENT 1.

indemnify verb **1** *indemnify them for their loss* reimburse, compensate, make restitution/amends to, recompense, repay, pay, pay back, remunerate. **2** *indemnify against travel risks* insure, underwrite, guarantee, protect, secure, make secure, give security to, endorse.

indemnity noun **1** *receive indemnity for losses sustained* reimbursement, compensation, restitution, reparation, redress, requital, atonement, payment, repayment, remuneration, recompense; amends. **2** *take out indemnity against lost luggage* insurance, assurance, protection, security, endorsement; guarantee, safeguard. **3** *receive diplomatic indemnity for his crimes* immunity, exemption, privilege, prerogative, impunity.

indentation noun indent, notch, cut, nick, groove, furrow, gouge, score; recess, niche, concavity, hollow, impression, depression, dimple, cranny.

independence noun **1** *states seeking independence* self-government, self-rule, home rule, self-determination, sovereignty, autonomy, nonalignment, freedom, separation, autarchy. **2** *financial independence* self-sufficiency, self-reliance. **3** *independence of spirit* individualism, boldness, liberation, unconstraint, unrestraint, lack of constraint/restraint.

independent adjective **1** *an independent state* self-governing, self-ruling, self-legislating, self-determining, sovereign, autonomous, autonomic, free, absolute, nonaligned, autarchic. **2** *the two firms are independent of/from each other* separate,

unconnected, unrelated, unattached, distinct, individual. **3** *an independent person* self-sufficient, self-supporting, self-reliant, individualistic, unconventional, bold, liberated, unconstrained, unrestrained; *inf.* standing on one's own feet.

indescribable adjective undescribable, inexpressible, undefinable, beyond words/description, surpassing description, incommunicable, ineffable, unutterable, incredible, extraordinary, remarkable, prodigious.

indestructible adjective durable, enduring, unbreakable, infrangible, imperishable, inextinguishable, undecaying, perennial, deathless, undying, immortal, endless, everlasting.

index noun **1** *an index to the information* guide, key, directory, catalog, table of contents. **2** *appearance can be an index of character* mark, token, sign, symptom, indication, clue, hint. **3** *the index on the compass* pointer, indicator, needle, hand.

indicate verb **1** *his visage indicates his distress* reveal, be a sign/symptom of, be symptomatic of, mark, signal, denote, bespeak, betoken, connote, suggest, imply. **2** *he indicated the right direction* point to/out, designate, specify. **3** *he indicated his displeasure* show, demonstrate, exhibit, display, manifest, evince, express, make known, tell, state, reveal, disclose, register, record.

indication noun **1** *his tiredness is an indication of his overwork* sign, symptom, mark, manifestation, signal, omen, augury, portent, warning, hint. **2** *he frowned as an indication of his displeasure* show, demonstration, exhibition, display, manifestation, revelation, disclosure, register, record.

indicative adjective suggestive, symptomatic, typical, characteristic, symbolic, emblematic.

indicator noun **1** *the indicator on the dial* pointer, needle, marker. **2** *a temperature indicator* gauge, meter, display. **3** *an economic indicator* index, guide, mark, sign, signal, signpost.

indict verb accuse, charge, arraign, impeach, prosecute, bring to trial, put on trial, cite, summons, incriminate, inculpate.

indictment noun accusation, charge, arraignment, impeachment, prosecution, citation, summons, incrimination, inculpation.

indifference noun **1** *the indifference of the spectators* apathy, disregard, lack of interest, aloofness, detachment, coldness, coolness, impassivity. **2** *the indifference of the players* mediocrity, adequacy, ordinariness, lack of distinction. **3** *the indifference of the issues* unimportance, insignificance, inconsequence, triviality, slightness, pettiness, irrelevance. **4** *the indifference of the judges* impartiality, disinterest, nonpartisanship, neutrality, objectivity, detachment, equitability, evenhandedness, fairness, fair-mindedness.

indifferent adjective **1** *totally indifferent spectators* apathetic, unconcerned, uncaring, uninterested, unimpressed, aloof, detached, distant, cold, cool, impassive, dispassionate, unresponsive, passionless, unemotional, emotionless, unmoved, unexcited, unfeeling, unsympathetic, uncompassionate, callous. **2** *an indifferent player* mediocre, middling, moderate, medium, fair, not bad, passable, adequate, average, ordinary, commonplace, undistinguished, uninspired; *inf.* OK, so-so. **3** *an indifferent issue* unimportant, insignificant, inconsequential, minor, trivial, trifling, petty. **4** *an indifferent judge* disinterested, unbiased. *See* IMPARTIAL.

indigenous adjective native, original, local, endemic, aboriginal.

indigent adjective poverty-stricken, penniless. *See* IMPOVERISHED 1.

indigestion noun dyspepsia, hyperacidity, acidity, heartburn, pyrosis.

indignant adjective angry, irate, incensed, furious, infuriated, annoyed, wrathful, enraged, exasperated, heated, riled, in a temper, in high dudgeon, provoked, piqued, disgruntled, in a huff, huffy, miffed, fuming, livid, aggravated, mad; *inf.* seeing red, up in arms.

indignation noun anger, fury, rage, wrath, exasperation, pique, disgruntlement, umbrage, offense, resentment, ire.

indirect adjective **1** *an indirect route* roundabout, circuitous, deviant, divergent, wandering, meandering, winding, curving, tortuous, zigzag. **2** *an indirect way of giving the news* oblique, discursive, digressive, long-drawn-out, rambling, circumlocutory, periphrastic, allusive. **3** *an indirect insult* backhanded, left-handed, devious, insidious, deceitful, underhand, surreptitious; *inf.* sneaky. **4** *an indirect result of the talks* incidental, accidental, unintended, secondary, subordinate, ancillary, collateral, contingent.

indirectly adverb **1** *hear the information indirectly* secondhand, in a roundabout way. **2** *tell them the news indirectly* by implication, obliquely, periphrastically.

indiscreet adjective unwise, imprudent, injudicious, impolitic, ill-advised, ill-considered, incautious, careless, tactless, untactful, insensitive, undiplomatic.

indiscretion noun **1** *guilty of indiscretion* imprudence, injudiciousness, foolishness, folly, carelessness, tactlessness, lack of diplomacy. **2** *embarrassed by her indiscretions* gaffe, faux pas, breach of etiquette, slip, blunder, lapse, mistake, error; *inf.* slipup.

indiscriminate adjective **1** *indiscriminate reading habits* undiscriminating, unselective, uncritical, undifferentiating, aimless, haphazard, random, unsystematic, unmethodical, broad-based, wholesale, general, sweeping; *inf.* hit-or-miss. **2** *an indiscriminate collection of furniture* jumbled, mixed, motley, miscellaneous, diverse, varied, mongrel, confused, chaotic, thrown together; *inf.* higgledy-piggledy.

indispensable adjective essential, of the essence, vital, crucial, imperative, key, necessary, requisite, required, needed, important, of the utmost importance, urgent, pressing, high-priority, fundamental.

indisputable adjective incontestable, incontrovertible, undeniable, irrefutable, unquestionable, indubitable, beyond dispute/question/doubt, beyond the shadow of a doubt, unassailable, certain, sure, positive, definite, absolute, final, conclusive.

indistinct adjective blurred, fuzzy, out of focus, bleary, hazy, misty, shadowy, dim, obscure, indefinite, indistinguishable, barely perceptible, undefined.

indistinguishable adjective **1** *the twins are indistinguishable* identical, alike, very similar; *inf.* as like as two peas in a pod. **2** *his identity was indistinguishable in the dark* indiscernible, imperceptible, hard to make out, indefinite, obscure.

individual adjective **1** *each individual flower/house* single, separate, sole, lone, solitary, distinct, distinctive, particular, specific, peculiar, detached, isolated. **2** *an individual style* characteristic, distinctive, peculiar, typical, personal, personalized, own, private, special, especial, singular, original, unique, exclusive, idiosyncratic.

individual noun **1** *a most unpleasant individual* person, personage, human being, creature, mortal, living soul, body, character, type. **2** *she's very much an individual* individualist, free spirit, nonconformist, original, eccentric, bohemian, maverick, rara avis, rare bird, rarity, loner, lone wolf.

individualist noun free spirit, nonconformist. *See* INDIVIDUAL noun 2.

individualistic adjective freethinking, independent, nonconformist, unorthodox, unconventional, original, eccentric, bohemian, maverick.

individuality noun distinctiveness, distinction, originality, uniqueness, singularity, peculiarity, personality, character.

individually adverb one at a time, one by one, singly, separately, independently, apart; personally.

indoctrinate verb instruct, teach, drill, ground, initiate, inculcate, impress (on), instill (in), imbue, impregnate, brainwash, propagandize, proselytize.

indolent adjective lazy, idle, slothful, do-nothing, sluggish, lethargic, slow, slow-moving, slack, shiftless, languid, lackadaisical, apathetic, listless, impassive, inactive, inert, torpid.

induce verb **1** *induce them to go* persuade, talk into, get, prevail upon, prompt, move, inspire, instigate, influence, exert influence on, press, urge, incite, encourage, impel, actuate, motivate, inveigle, coax, wheedle. **2** *induce a reaction* bring about, bring on, cause, produce, effect, create, give rise to, generate, originate, engender, occasion, set in motion.

inducement noun **1** *offer a salary increase as an inducement* incentive, attraction, encouragement, bait, lure, reward, incitement, stimulus, influence, spur, goad, impetus, motive, provocation; *inf.* carrot, come-on. **2** *gave in to their inducement to go* persuasion, prompting, urging, incitement, encouragement, inveigling.

indulge verb **1** *indulge one's appetites* give way to, yield to, pander to, cater to, satisfy, gratify, fulfill, satiate, appease. **2** *indulge in a bout of self-pity* give oneself up to, give rein to, give free rein to, wallow in, luxuriate in, revel in. **3** *indulge the child* pamper, spoil, coddle, mollycoddle, pander to, humor, go along with, baby, pet. **indulge oneself** treat oneself, give oneself a treat, splurge; *inf.* have a spree.

indulgence noun **1** *the indulgence of one's appetites* satisfaction, gratification, fulfillment, satiation, appeasement. **2** *lead a life of indulgence* self-gratification, dissipation, dissoluteness, intemperance, immoderation, immoderateness, debauchery, excess, lack of restraint, unrestraint, prodigality, extravagance. **3** *traveling is his only indulgence* extravagance, luxury, treat. **4** *I was allowed the indulgence of going on board ship* privilege, courtesy, favor, treat. **5** *treat the prisoners with indulgence* tolerance, forbearance, compassion, humanity, sympathy, forgiveness, leniency, mercy, clemency. **6** *too much indulgence was bad for the children* pampering, spoiling, coddling, mollycoddling, cosseting, humoring.

indulgent adjective tolerant, forbearing, forgiving, lenient, merciful, clement; permissive, compliant, pampering, spoiling, mollycoddling, cosseting, humoring.

industrious adjective hardworking, diligent, assiduous, sedulous, conscientious, steady, laborious, busy, busy as a bee, active, bustling, energetic, on the go, vigorous, determined, indefatigable, tireless.

industry noun **1** *involved in heavy industry* manufacturing, production, fabrication, construction. **2** *the publishing industry* business, trade, commercial enterprise, field, line, craft, métier. **3** *work with industry* industriousness, diligence, assiduity, application, sedulousness, sedulity, conscientiousness, concentration, intentness, steadiness, laboriousness, busyness, tirelessness, persistence.

inebriated adjective intoxicated, drunk, drunken, blind drunk, tipsy; *inf.* tight, under the influence, three sheets to the wind, plastered, stoned, loaded, blotto, pickled, out of it, smashed, sloshed, soused, well-oiled, well-lubricated, stewed to the gills, tanked (up).

inedible adjective unedible, uneatable, not fit to eat, unconsumable, unwholesome, off, rotten, bad, putrid, poisonous.

ineffective adjective **1** *ineffective attempts to stem the revolt* ineffectual, vain, to no avail, unavailing, useless, worthless, unsuccessful, futile, fruitless, unproductive, profitless, abortive, inefficacious, idle, feeble, inept, lame, barren, sterile. **2** *ineffective people* ineffectual, powerless, impotent, incompetent, inept, feeble, weak.

ineffectual adjective **1** *ineffectual efforts* vain, unavailing. See INEFFECTIVE 1. **2** *ineffectual people* powerless, inept. See INEFFECTIVE 2.

inefficient adjective ineffective, disorganized, wasteful, uneconomical, lax, slipshod, sloppy, slack.

ineligible adjective unqualified, unfit, unequipped, unsuitable, unacceptable, undesirable, ruled out, disqualified.

inept adjective **1** *an inept mechanic* unadept, unskillful, unskilled, clumsy, awkward, maladroit, undexterous, heavy-handed, ham-handed, incompetent, inadequate, bungling. **2** *an inept remark* out of place, badly timed, inapt, inappropriate, unsuitable, infelicitous. **3** *always doing inept things* absurd, foolish, silly, stupid, inane, nonsensical, senseless, farcical, ridiculous.

inequality noun **1** *inequality of opportunity* unequalness, disparity, imparity, imbalance, unevenness, disproportion, discrepancy, nonconformity, difference, dissimilarity, contrast. **2** *treat women with inequality* bias, prejudice, discrimination, preferentiality.

inequitable adjective unjust, unfair, partial, prejudiced, biased, partisan, discriminatory, preferential, one-sided, intolerant, bigoted.

inequity noun unfairness, injustice, partisanship, partiality, bias, discrimination.

inert adjective **1** *inert bodies* unmoving, motionless, immobile, still, stock-still, stationary, static, lifeless, inanimate, unconscious, passive, out cold, comatose, dormant, dead. **2** *inert members of the company* inactive, dull, sluggish, lethargic, stagnant, listless, torpid.

inertia noun inertness, inactivity, inaction, immobility, stagnation, stasis, passivity, indolence, sloth, dullness, sluggishness, lethargy, languor, listlessness, torpor.

inescapable adjective unavoidable, unpreventable. *See* INEVITABLE.

inestimable adjective immeasurable, measureless, incalculable; priceless, beyond price, precious, invaluable, worth its weight in gold, worth a king's ransom.

inevitable adjective unavoidable, unpreventable, inexorable, inescapable, fixed, settled, irrevocable, fated, destined, predestined, ordained, decreed, out of one's hands, assured, certain, sure, bound/sure to happen, for sure, necessary, ineluctable.

inexact adjective imprecise, approximate; inaccurate, incorrect.

inexcusable adjective unpardonable, unforgivable, unatonable, inexpiable, unjustifiable, unwarrantable, indefensible.

inexhaustible adjective **1** *an inexhaustible supply* unlimited, limitless, infinite, boundless, endless, never-ending, bottomless, measureless. **2** *inexhaustible workers* indefatigable, tireless, untiring, unwearying, weariless, unfaltering, unfailing, unflagging.

inexorable adjective **1** *the inexorable march of progress* relentless, unavoidable, inescapable. *See* INEVITABLE. **2** *inexorable tyrants* adamant, obdurate, unbending, unyielding, immovable, intransigent, implacable, inflexible.

inexpensive adjective low-cost, low-price, low-priced, reasonable, economical, cheap, budget, reduced, sale-price, half-price, marked-down, discount, discounted, cut-rate, bargain, bargain-basement.

inexperienced adjective untrained, untutored, unpracticed, amateur, unskilled, uninitiated, unversed, naïve, unsophisticated, untried, unseasoned, new, callow, immature, fresh, green, raw; *inf.* wet behind the ears.

inexplicable adjective unexplainable, unaccountable, incomprehensible, beyond comprehension/understanding, unfathomable, baffling, puzzling, inscrutable.

infallible adjective **1** *an infallible remedy* unfailing, foolproof, dependable, reliable, certain; *inf.* sure-fire. **2** *an infallible memory* unerring, faultless, flawless, impeccable, unimpeachable, perfect.

infamous adjective **1** *an infamous robber* notorious, disreputable, ill-famed, of

ill-repute. **2** *guilty of infamous conduct* iniquitous, ignominious, dishonorable, discreditable, villainous, bad, wicked, vile, odious, nefarious, abominable, outrageous, shocking, monstrous, disgraceful, shameful, atrocious, heinous.

infant noun baby, babe, newborn, little child, tot, little one; neonate.

infantile adjective babyish, childish, puerile, immature, juvenile.

infatuated adjective in love, head over heels in love, hopelessly in love; enamored, besotted, captivated, bewitched, beguiled, taken with, under the spell of, obsessed, swept off one's feet; ; *inf.* smitten, sweet on, keen on, mad about, wild about, crazy about, nuts about, stuck on, turned on by.

infatuation noun passing fancy, fancy, passion, obsession, fixation, craze, mania; *inf.* puppy love, crush, thing.

infect verb **1** *infect the air/water* contaminate, pollute, taint, make foul, blight, spoil, mar, impair. **2** *infect others with his wickedness* influence, corrupt, pervert, debauch, debase, degrade, vitiate. **3** *infect others with his enthusiasm* imbue, infuse, excite, inspire, stimulate, animate.

infectious adjective **1** *an infectious disease | infectious laughter* infective, communicable, transmittable, transmissible, catching, spreading, contagious. **2** *infectious material* germ-laden, contaminating, polluting, septic, toxic, noxious, virulent, poisonous.

infer verb **1** *from the evidence they inferred that he was guilty* deduce, reason, conclude, gather, conjecture, surmise, theorize, hypothesize. **2** *his conduct inferred a guilty conscience* indicate, point to, signal, signify, bespeak, evidence. **3** *her speech inferred that he was a coward* imply, insinuate, hint, suggest, intimate.

inference noun **1** *dispute the inference from the evidence* deduction, conclusion, ratiocination, conjecture, surmise. **2** *resent her inference that he was a coward* implication, insinuation, suggestion, intimation.

inferior adjective **1** *in an inferior position* lower, lesser, subordinate, junior, secondary, subsidiary, second-class, second-fiddle, minor, subservient, menial. **2** *inferior goods* substandard, low-quality, low-grade, shoddy, reject. **3** *an inferior teacher* second-rate, indifferent, mediocre, incompetent, poor, bad, awful.

inferior noun *despise his inferiors* subordinate, junior, underling, menial.

infernal adjective hellish, diabolical, devilish, demonic, demoniac, fiendish, satanic, malevolent, malicious, heinous, vile, atrocious, execrable, unspeakable, outrageous.

infertile adjective barren, unfruitful, unfructuous, sterile, infecund, childless.

infest verb overrun, spread through, take over, overspread, pervade, permeate, penetrate, infiltrate, invade, swarm over, crawl over, beset, pester, plague.

infidel noun unbeliever, disbeliever, heathen, heretic, pagan, agnostic, atheist, irreligionist.

infidelity noun 1 *discovering the spouse's infidelity* unfaithfulness, adultery, cuckoldry; affair, liaison, intrigue, amour; *inf.* fooling/playing around, cheating, hankypanky. 2 *the servant's infidelity to his master* breach of trust, faithlessness, unfaithfulness, treachery, perfidy, perfidiousness, disloyalty, falseness, traitorousness, treason.

infiltrate verb pervade, penetrate, filter through, percolate through, seep into/through, soak into; sneak into, invade, intrude on.

infinite adjective 1 *infinite space/numbers* boundless, unbounded, unlimited, limitless, without limit/end, extensive, vast, countless, numberless, innumerable, immeasurable, incalculable, indeterminable, enormous. 2 *infinite patience* inexhaustible, interminable, absolute, total.

infinitesimal adjective minute, tiny, microscopic, minuscule, teeny, wee, Lilliputian.

infirm adjective 1 *infirm people* feeble, enfeebled, weak, frail, debilitated, decrepit, disabled, failing, ailing, doddering, tottering, lame. 2 *infirm judgment* indecisive, irresolute, wavering, vacillating, fluctuating, faltering. 3 *infirm furniture* rickety, unsteady, shaky, wobbly, unsound, flimsy, tumbledown, jerry-built.

inflame verb 1 *inflame the passions of the crowd* incite, excite, arouse, rouse, stir up, work up, whip up, agitate, fire, ignite, kindle, foment, impassion, provoke, stimulate, actuate. 2 *inflame the onlookers with his cruelty* enrage, incense, infuriate, exasperate, anger, madden, provoke, rile. 3 *inflame the feud* aggravate, intensify, make worse, exacerbate, fan, fuel.

inflamed adjective 1 *an inflamed arm* swollen, sore, infected, festered, septic. 2 *inflamed passions* excited, aroused, roused, stirred, kindled, impassioned.

inflammation noun swelling, soreness, sore, infection, festering, suppuration.

inflammatory adjective *an inflammatory speech* stirring, fiery, passionate, impassioned, provocative, fomenting, rabble-rousing, demagogic, rebellious, revolutionary, insurgent, seditious.

inflate verb 1 *inflate the air mattress* blow up, pump up, aerate, puff up, puff out, dilate, distend, swell. 2 *he always inflates his stories* amplify, augment, expand, intensify, exaggerate, add to, boost, magnify, escalate, aggrandize.

inflated adjective 1 *inflated prices* increased, raised, escalated, stepped up. 2 *an inflated sense of his own importance* exaggerated, magnified, aggrandized. 3 *inflated prose* high-flown, extravagant, pretentious, pompous, grandiloquent, bombastic.

inflexible adjective 1 *an inflexible substance* rigid, stiff, unbendable, unyielding, taut, hard, firm, inelastic, unmalleable. 2 *inflexible rules* unalterable, unchangeable, immutable, unvarying, fixed, hard and fast. 3 *inflexible people/attitudes* adamant, immovable, unadaptable, dyed-in-the-wool, unaccommodating, uncompliant, stubborn, obdurate, obstinate, unbending, uncompromising.

inflict verb lay on, impose, levy, exact, wreak.

influence noun 1 *have a good/bad influence on them* effect, impact; control, sway, ascendancy, power, mastery, agency, guidance, domination, rule, supremacy, leadership, direction, pressure. 2 *he has influence on the board* prestige, standing, footing; *inf.* clout, pull.

influence verb 1 *his illness influenced his behavior* affect, have an effect on, impact on, sway, bias, incline, motivate, actuate, determine, guide, control, change, alter, transform. 2 *he tried to influence the jury* affect, sway, bias, bring pressure to bear on; *inf.* pull strings with, pull rank on. 3 *he influenced her not to go* persuade, induce, impel, incite, prompt.

influential adjective powerful, important, leading, authoritative, controlling, dominant, guiding, significant, persuasive.

inform verb 1 *inform him of/about the facts* tell, let know, apprise, advise, notify, announce to, impart to, relate to, communicate to, acquaint, brief, instruct, enlighten; *inf.* fill in, clue in/up, put wise, spill the beans to, tip off, give the low-down to, give the inside story to. 2 *optimism informs her writing* characterize, typify, pervade, permeate, suffuse, infuse, imbue. **inform on** betray, denounce, incriminate, inculpate; *inf.* rat on, squeal on, tell on, blow the whistle on, put the finger on, sell down the river, snitch on.

informal adjective 1 *an informal party | informal dress* casual, unceremonious, unofficial, simple, unpretentious, everyday, relaxed, easy. 2 *informal language* colloquial, vernacular, nonliterary, natural; *inf.* slangy.

informality noun casualness, lack of ceremony, simplicity, naturalness, ease.

information noun data, facts; knowledge, intelligence, news, notice, word, tidings, message, report, communiqué, communication; *inf.* info, low-down, dope, poop, inside story, dirt.

informative adjective instructive, illuminating, enlightening, revealing, telling, newsy.

informed adjective knowledgeable, abreast of the facts, well-posted, primed, well-versed, up-to-date, au courant, *au fait*.

informer noun informant, betrayer, traitor, Judas; *inf.* rat, squealer, stool pigeon, tattletale, whistleblower, canary, snitch.

infraction noun breach, violation, transgression, infringement.

infrequent adjective few and far between, rare, occasional, uncommon, unusual, exceptional.

infuriate verb enrage, incense, inflame, madden, exasperate, anger, provoke, rile, make one's blood boil, make one's hackles rise; *inf.* make one see red.

ingenious adjective clever, shrewd, astute, sharp, resourceful, inventive, creative, original, crafty, wily.

ingenuous adjective open, sincere, honest, frank, candid, artless, guileless, simple, naïve, innocent, genuine, undeceitful, undeceptive, undissembling, aboveboard, trustful, unsuspicious.

ingrained adjective fixed, rooted, deep-rooted, deep-seated, permanent, built-in.

ingratiate verb **ingratiate oneself with** curry favor with, toady to, crawl to, grovel to, fawn over, play up to, be a yes-man to; *inf.* suck up to, lick the boots of.

ingratiating adjective sycophantic, toadying, fawning, unctuous, obsequious, servile, overhumble, crawling, flattering, wheedling, cajoling; *inf.* bootlicking.

ingredient adjective constituent, component, element, part, unit, item, feature.

inhabit verb live in, dwell in, reside in, occupy, lodge in, make one's home in, settle in; settle, people, populate.

inhabitant noun resident, resider, dweller, occupant, occupier, habitant, settler.

inherent adjective intrinsic, innate, built-in, inseparable, essential, basic, fundamental, ingrained.

inherit verb **1** *inherit a fortune/estate* become/fall heir to, be bequeathed, be left, be willed, come into/by. **2** *inherit the title* succeed to, accede to, assume, take over, be elevated to.

inheritance noun legacy, bequest, endowment, birthright, heritage, patrimony.

inhibit verb **1** *inhibit progress* hold back, impede, hinder, hamper, interfere with, obstruct, curb, check, restrict, restrain,

constrain, bridle, rein in, balk, frustrate, arrest, prevent, stop. **2** *inhibit them from going* forbid, prohibit, ban, bar, debar, interdict, proscribe.

inhibited adjective *feel inhibited in the presence of parents* self-conscious, reserved, constrained, repressed, subdued, withdrawn; *inf.* uptight.

inhospitable adjective **1** *an inhospitable host* unwelcoming, unsociable, unfriendly, ungracious, uncongenial, ungenerous, aloof. **2** *an inhospitable landscape* uninviting, barren, bleak, desolate, forbidding, hostile.

inhuman adjective **1** *an inhuman cry* nonhuman, animal, ghostly. **2** *inhuman people* unkind, inconsiderate. *See* INHUMANE.

inhumane adjective unkind, unkindly, inconsiderate, uncompassionate, unfeeling, unsympathetic, unforgiving, cold-blooded, heartless, hard-hearted, pitiless, merciless, ruthless, remorseless, brutal, cruel, harsh, savage, vicious, barbaric, barbarous.

inimitable adjective matchless, unmatched, incomparable, unparalleled, unrivaled, unsurpassed, unsurpassable, unique, supreme, perfect, consummate, ideal, nonpareil, peerless.

iniquitous adjective wicked, sinful, evil, immoral, villainous, criminal, heinous, vile, foul, base, odious, abominable, execrable, atrocious, malicious, outrageous, monstrous, shocking, scandalous, reprehensible.

iniquity noun **1** *his falling into iniquity* wickedness, sin, sinfulness, vice, evil, ungodliness, godlessness, wrong, wrongdoing, badness, villainy, knavery, lawlessness, crime, baseness, heinousness. **2** *appalled at his iniquities* sin, vice, offense, crime, transgression, injury, violation, atrocity, outrage.

initial adjective first, beginning, opening, early, introductory, inaugural, inceptive, incipient.

initiate verb **1** *initiate the proceedings* begin, start off, commence, open, institute, inaugurate, get under way, set in motion, lay the foundations of, lay the first stone of, launch, actuate, instigate, trigger, originate, pioneer, sow the seeds of; start the ball rolling for. **2** *initiate the students in science* teach, instruct, coach, tutor, school, train, drill, prime, familiarize, indoctrinate, inculcate. **3** *initiate the new member into the organization* induct, install, instate, ordain, invest.

initiation noun **1** *the initiation of the proceedings* beginning, commencement, opening, institution, inauguration, launch. **2** *rites of initiation* admission, admittance, introduction; induction, installation, ordination, investment, baptism.

initiative noun **1** *take the initiative* first step, first move, first blow, lead, gambit, opening move/gambit. **2** *promotion for those with initiative* enterprise, inventiveness, resourcefulness, originality, creativity, drive, dynamism, ambition, leadership; *inf.* get-up-and-go, zing, push, pep, zip.

injure verb **1** *injure his foot* hurt, harm, damage, wound, maim, cripple, lame, disable, mutilate, deform, mangle. **2** *guilty of injuring his fellow citizens* do an injury to, wrong, do an injustice to, offend against, abuse, maltreat, defame, vilify, malign.

injured adjective **1** *his injured leg* hurt, wounded, broken, fractured, damaged, sore, maimed, crippled, disabled, lame. **2** *the injured party* wronged, offended, abused, maltreated, ill-treated, defamed, vilified, maligned. **3** *an injured look* reproachful, hurt, wounded, upset, disgruntled, displeased.

injurious adjective harmful, hurtful, damaging, deleterious, detrimental, disadvantageous, unfavorable, destructive, pernicious, ruinous, disastrous, calamitous, malignant.

injury noun **1** *machines bound to cause injury* harm, hurt, wounding, damage, impairment, affliction. **2** *injuries taking long to heal* wound, sore, bruise, cut, gash, laceration, abrasion, lesion, contusion, trauma. **3** *do an injury to his neighbors* injustice, wrong, ill, offense, disservice, grievance, evil.

injustice noun **1** *the injustice of the verdict* unjustness, unfairness, inequitableness, inequity, bias, prejudice, favoritism, partiality, one-sidedness, discrimination, partisanship. **2** *injustices done to others* wrong, injury, offense, evil.

inkling noun **1** *he gave no inkling of his intention* hint, clue, intimation, suggestion, indication, whisper, suspicion, insinuation. **2** *no inkling of how to proceed* idea, (the) vaguest idea, notion, glimmering; *inf.* (the) foggiest.

inlet noun cove, bay, arm of the sea, bight, creek, fjord, sound.

inmate noun prisoner, convict, captive, jailbird.

inn noun hotel, lodge, bed and breakfast, hostelry; public house, tavern, bar, pub.

innate adjective **1** *an innate tendency* inborn, inbred, connate, congenital, hereditary, inherited, in the blood/family. **2** *an innate part of the plan* inherent, intrinsic, essential, basic, fundamental, quintessential, organic, radical. **3** *an innate capacity* instinctive, intuitive, unlearned, untaught.

inner adjective **1** *the inner rooms* interior, inside, central, middle, further in. **2** *the inner circle* confidential, intimate, private,

exclusive, secret. **3** *the inner meaning* unapparent, veiled, obscure, esoteric, hidden, secret, unrevealed, deep. **4** *the inner life* spiritual, emotional, mental, psychological, psychic, subconscious, unconscious, innermost.

innermost, inmost adjective **1** *the innermost section* furthest in, deepest within, central. **2** *innermost beliefs* intimate, private, personal, deep, deepest, profound, secret, hidden.

innkeeper noun host, proprietor, manager, landlady, landlord, hotelier; barkeeper, barkeep.

innocence noun **1** *the innocence of the prisoners* guiltlessness, blamelessness, inculpability, unimpeachability, irreproachability, clean hands. **2** *the innocence of their play* harmlessness, innocuousness, inoffensiveness. **3** *the innocence of youth* virtuousness, virtue, purity, sinlessness, decency, righteousness, chastity, virginity, spotlessness. **4** *the innocence of the new recruits* ingenuousness, naïveté, artlessness, guilelessness, frankness, openness, credulity, gullibility.

innocent adjective **1** *innocent prisoners* not guilty, guiltless, blameless, clear, in the clear, above suspicion, unblameworthy, inculpable, unimpeachable, irreproachable, clean-handed. **2** *innocent fun* harmless, innocuous, safe, noninjurious, unmalicious, unobjectionable, inoffensive, playful. **3** *innocent youth* virtuous, pure, sinless, moral, decent, righteous, upright, chaste, virginal, pristine, spotless, stainless, unblemished, unsullied, incorrupt, uncorrupted. **4** *too innocent for the world* ingenuous, naïve, unsophisticated, artless, guileless, childlike, frank, open, unsuspicious, trustful, trusting, credulous, inexperienced, unworldly, green, gullible; *inf.* wet behind the ears. **innocent of** *innocent of guile* free from, without, lacking, devoid of, unacquainted with, ignorant of, unaware of, unfamiliar with.

innocuous adjective **1** *an innocuous substance* harmless, unhurtful, uninjurious, safe, danger-free, nonpoisonous. **2** *an innocuous person* inoffensive, unobjectionable, bland, commonplace, run-of-the-mill, insipid.

innuendo noun insinuation, implication, suggestion, hint, overtone, imputation, aspersion.

innumerable adjective numerous, countless, untold, incalculable, numberless, beyond number, infinite, myriad; *inf.* umpteen, masses, oodles.

inoperative adjective **1** *inoperative machines* not operative, not in operation, not working, out of order, out of service/commission/action, inactive, idle, broken, broken-down, defective, faulty; *inf.*

down, kaput. **2** *an inoperative system* useless, ineffectual, ineffective, inefficient, worthless, unproductive.

inopportune adjective inconvenient, illtimed, badly timed, mistimed, untimely, unseasonable, inappropriate, unsuitable, inapt, ill-chosen.

inordinate adjective excessive, immoderate, extravagant, unrestrained, unrestricted, unlimited, unwarranted, uncalledfor, undue, unreasonable, disproportionate, exorbitant, extreme, outrageous, preposterous, unconscionable.

inquire verb ask, quiz, interrogate; *inf.* grill. **inquire into** investigate, research, look into, examine, explore, probe.

inquiring adjective questioning, investigative, curious, interested, probing, exploring, searching, scrutinizing, inquisitive.

inquiry noun investigation, examination, exploration, probe, search, scrutiny, study, inspection, interrogation.

inquisition noun interrogation, crossexamination, quizzing, questioning; *inf.* grilling, third degree.

inquisitive adjective inquiring, questioning, probing, scrutinizing, curious; overinterested, intrusive, meddlesome, prying, snooping, snoopy, peering, spying; *inf.* nosy.

insane adjective **1** *driven insane by isolation* mad, of unsound mind, deranged, demented, *non compos mentis*, out of one's mind; *inf.* unhinged, crazed, crazy, non compos. **2** *he's insane to take that job* foolish, out of one's mind, unhinged, not all there, crazy; *inf.* bonkers, cracked, crackers, balmy, batty, bats, cuckoo, loony, loopy, nuts, nutty, screwy, bananas, out of one's head, around/round the bend. **3** *an insane idea* idiotic, stupid, senseless, nonsensical, irrational, impracticable, pointless, absurd, ridiculous, ludicrous, bizarre, fatuous; *inf.* daft.

insanity noun **1** *patients suffering from insanity* madness, mental derangement, dementia, frenzy, delirium. **2** *the insanity of the idea* folly, foolishness, craziness, idiocy, stupidity, senselessness, irrationality, absurdity.

insatiable adjective insatiate, unappeasable, unquenchable, greedy, voracious, ravening, gluttonous, omnivorous.

inscribe verb **1** *inscribe one's name on the book/stone* imprint, write, stamp, impress, mark, brand, engrave, etch, carve, cut. **2** *inscribe the candidates in the book* enter, register, record, write, list, enroll.

inscription noun engraving, writing, etching, lettering, legend, epitaph, epigraph.

inscrutable adjective enigmatic, unreadable, impenetrable, cryptic, sphinxlike, mysterious, inexplicable, unexplainable, unfathomable, arcane.

insecure adjective **1** *insecure children* diffident, timid, uncertain, hesitant, anxious, fearful, apprehensive, worried. **2** *insecure fortresses* vulnerable, defenseless, unprotected, unguarded, exposed. **3** *insecure bookshelves* loose, weak, unsubstantial, jerry-built, rickety, wobbly, shaky, unsteady, unstable, unsound.

insecurity noun **1** *the insecurity of the children* diffidence, timidity, uncertainty, anxiety, apprehension, worry. **2** *the insecurity of the fortresses* vulnerability, defenselessness, lack of protection, peril, perilousness. **3** *the insecurity of the bookshelves* looseness, flimsiness, ricketiness, instability.

insensitive adjective unfeeling, callous, thick-skinned, uncaring, unconcerned, uncompassionate, unsympathetic. **insensitive to** unresponsive to, impervious to, indifferent to, unaffected by, unmoved by, oblivious to, unappreciative of.

insert verb **1** *insert a coin into the slot* put in/into, place in, press in, push in, stick in, thrust in, drive in, work in, slide in, slip in, tuck in; *inf.* pop in. **2** *insert a sentence if the paragraph is too short* put in, introduce, enter, interpolate, inset, interpose, interject, implant, infix.

inside adjective **1** *the inside part* interior, inner, internal, inward, on/in the inside, inmost, innermost, intramural. **2** *inside information* confidential, classified, restricted, privileged, private, internal, privy, secret, exclusive, esoteric.

insidious adjective sneaky, cunning, crafty, designing, intriguing, Machiavellian; artful, guileful, sly, wily, tricky, slick, deceitful, deceptive, underhanded, double-dealing, duplicitous, dishonest, insincere, disingenuous, treacherous.

insight noun intuition, perception, awareness, discernment, understanding, penetration, acumen, perspicacity, discrimination, judgment, shrewdness, sharpness, acuteness, vision.

insignia noun/plural noun **1** *insignia of office* badge, decoration, medallion, ribbon, crest, emblem, symbol, sign, mark, seal, signet. **2** *the insignia of the firm* trademark, label, trait, characteristic.

insignificant adjective unimportant, of little import, trivial, trifling, negligible, inconsequential, inconsiderable, not worth mentioning, nugatory, meager, paltry, scanty, petty, insubstantial, unsubstantial, flimsy, irrelevant, immaterial; *inf.* dinky.

insincere adjective disingenuous, dissembling, pretended, devious, hypocritical, deceitful, deceptive, dishonest, underhand, double-dealing, false, two-faced.

insinuate verb 1 *he insinuated that she was dishonest* imply, hint, whisper, suggest, indicate, convey the impression, intimate. 2 *insinuate doubts into their minds* implant, instill, introduce, inculcate, infuse, inject. **insinuate oneself into** worm oneself into, work one's way into.

insinuation noun 1 *resent the insinuation* implication, suggestion, hint, innuendo, intimation, allusion. 2 *the insinuation of doubts* infiltration, implanting, instilling, instillation, introduction.

insipid adjective 1 *an insipid person/book* colorless, anemic, drab, vapid, dull, uninteresting, boring, unentertaining, unimaginative, flat, bland, prosaic. 2 *insipid food* tasteless, flavorless, savorless, bland, unappetizing, unpalatable.

insist verb 1 *if they refuse you must insist* stand firm, be firm, stand one's ground, be resolute, be emphatic, not take no for an answer, brook no refusal. 2 *insist that they go* demand, require, command, importune, entreat, urge, exhort. 3 *she insists that she is innocent* maintain, assert, declare, hold, contend, aver, avow, vow, swear, emphasize, stress, repeat, reiterate.

insistent adjective 1 *she is insistent that you go* emphatic, determined, resolute, tenacious, importunate, persistent, unyielding, obstinate, dogged, unrelenting. 2 *insistent demands for payment* persistent, dogged, incessant, urgent, pressing, compelling, high-pressure, coercive, demanding. 3 *the insistent caw of the crow* constant, incessant, iterative, repeated.

insolence noun impertinence, impudence, cheek, rudeness, disrespect, incivility, insubordination, contempt, contumely, audacity, nerve, boldness, brazenness, brashness, pertness, forwardness, effrontery, gall; *inf.* lip, chutzpah.

insolent adjective impertinent, impudent, cheeky, rude, disrespectful, insubordinate, contemptuous, audacious, bold, brazen, brash, pert, forward; *inf.* fresh.

insoluble adjective insolvable, unsolvable, baffling, unfathomable, complicated, intricate, involved, impenetrable, inscrutable, enigmatic, obscure, mystifying, inexplicable, incomprehensible, mysterious.

insolvent adjective bankrupt, indebted, in debt, liquidated, ruined, in the hands of the receivers; *inf.* gone bust, gone to the wall, on the rocks, in the red.

inspect verb examine, check, go over, look over, survey, scrutinize, audit, study, pore over, view, scan, observe, investigate, assess, appraise; *inf.* give the once-over.

inspection noun examination, check, checkup, survey, scrutiny, view, scan, observation, investigation, probe, assessment, appraisal; *inf.* once-over, going-over, look-see.

inspector noun examiner, checker, auditor, surveyor, investigator, assessor, appraiser.

inspiration noun 1 *acts as an inspiration to his work* stimulus, stimulation, motivation, encouragement, influence, muse, goad, spur, incitement, arousal, rousing, stirring. 2 *his pictures lack inspiration* creativity, originality, inventiveness, genius, insight, vision.

inspire verb stimulate, motivate, encourage, influence, inspirit, animate, fire the imagination of, rouse, stir, spur, goad, energize, galvanize, quicken, inflame, touch off, spark off, ignite, kindle, give rise to, prompt, instigate.

inspired adjective 1 *an inspired operatic performance* brilliant, outstanding, supreme, superlative, dazzling, exciting, thrilling, enthralling, wonderful, marvelous, memorable; *inf.* out of this world. 2 *an inspired guess* intuitive, instinctive.

instability noun 1 *instability of human relationships* impermanence, unendurability, temporariness, transience, inconstancy, unsteadiness, uncertainty, precariousness, shakiness, frailty, insecurity, unpredictability, unreliability; *inf.* chanciness. 2 *upset by her instability* changeableness, variability, capriciousness, volatility, flightiness, vacillation, wavering, fitfulness, oscillation.

install verb 1 *install microwave ovens* put in place, position, place, emplace, fix, locate, situate, station, lodge. 2 *install her as president* induct, instate, institute, inaugurate, invest, ordain, introduce, initiate. 3 *install themselves in the best seats* ensconce, position, settle.

instance noun case, case in point, example, illustration, exemplification, occasion, occurrence.

instant noun 1 *gone in an instant* moment, minute, second, split second, trice, twinkling, twinkling of an eye, flash; *inf.* jiffy, jif, sec, two shakes of a lamb's tail. 2 *at this instant I am not sure* time, present time, juncture, point.

instant adjective 1 *instant recognition* instantaneous, immediate, on-the-spot, prompt, rapid, sudden, abrupt. 2 *at his instant request* urgent, pressing, earnest, importunate, exigent, imperative.

instantaneous adjective immediate, on the spot. *See* INSTANT adjective 1.

instantaneously adverb right away, straight away, immediately, at once, instantly, forthwith, quick as lightning, in a trice, in less than no time, in the twinkling of an eye, before you can say Jack Robinson; *inf.* in a jiffy.

instigate verb **1** *instigate a rebellion* bring about, start, initiate, actuate, generate, incite, provoke, inspire, foment, kindle, stir up, whip up. **2** *instigate them to rebel* encourage, egg on, urge, prompt, goad, prod, induce, impel, constrain, press, persuade, prevail upon, sway.

instigator noun prime mover, inciter, motivator, agitator, fomenter, troublemaker, agent provocateur, ringleader, leader.

instill verb infuse, implant, teach, drill, imbue, permeate, inculcate.

instinct noun **1** *birds migrate by instinct* innate inclination, intuition, sixth sense, inner prompting. **2** *an instinct for poetry* talent, gift, ability, capacity, faculty, aptitude, knack, bent.

instinctive adjective **1** *instinctive behavior* inborn, inherent, innate, inbred, natural, intuitive, intuitional, involuntary, untaught, unlearned. **2** *an instinctive reaction* automatic, reflex, mechanical, spontaneous, involuntary, impulsive, intuitive, unthinking, unpremeditated.

institute verb **1** *institute legal proceedings* begin, start, commence, set in motion, put into operation, initiate. **2** *institute reforms* found, establish, start, launch, bring about, set up, organize, develop, create, originate, pioneer.

institute noun institution, organization, foundation, society, association, league, guild, consortium, academy, school, college, conservatory, seminary.

institution noun **1** *educational/research institutions* organization, society. *See* INSTITUTE. **2** *in an institution for life* hospital, mental hospital, asylum, prison, reformatory. **3** *local institutions* law, rule, custom, tradition, convention, practice. **4** *the traffic cop was an institution in the neighborhood* familiar sight, fixture, habitué; *inf.* part of the furniture.

institutional adjective **1** *institutional food/furniture* uniform, monotonous, bland, dull, insipid. **2** *an institutional atmosphere in the building* cold, clinical, unwelcoming, uninviting, impersonal, formal, forbidding.

instruct verb **1** *instruct the messenger to take a reply* tell, direct, order, command, bid, charge, enjoin, demand, require. **2** *instruct the students in science* teach, educate, tutor, coach, train, school, drill, ground, prime, prepare, guide, inform, enlighten, edify, discipline. **3** *instruct them that I shall be late* inform, tell, notify, acquaint, make known to, advise, apprise, brief.

instruction noun **1** *get good instruction in the arts* teaching, education, tutoring, tutelage, coaching, training, schooling, drilling, grounding, preparation, guidance, information, enlightenment, edification, discipline; lessons, classes, lectures. **2** *his instruction was to leave at once* direction, directive, briefing, order, command, charge, injunction, ruling, mandate.

instructive adjective instructional, informative, informational, educational, enlightening, useful, helpful, edifying.

instructor noun teacher, schoolteacher, schoolmaster, schoolmistress, educator, lecturer, professor, pedagogue, tutor, coach, trainer, adviser, counselor, guide, mentor.

instrument noun **1** *surgical instruments* implement, tool, appliance, apparatus, mechanism, utensil, gadget, contrivance, device, aid; *inf.* contraption. **2** *the instrument of his downfall* agency, agent, prime mover, catalyst, cause, factor, channel, medium, force, mechanism, instrumentality, vehicle, organ; means. **3** *he was just the ringleader's instrument* pawn, puppet, tool, dupe, minion, flunky; *inf.* stooge.

instrumental adjective helpful, useful, contributory, active, involved, influential.

insubordinate adjective rebellious, mutinous, insurgent, seditious, insurrectional, riotous, disobedient, defiant, refractory, recalcitrant, ungovernable, uncontrollable, unmanageable.

insubstantial adjective **1** *insubstantial buildings/arguments* flimsy, fragile, frail, weak, feeble, jerry-built, slight, tenuous. **2** *insubstantial shapes* unsubstantial, unreal, illusory, hallucinatory, phantom, spectral, ghostlike, incorporeal, visionary, imaginary, imagined, fanciful, chimerical, airy, vaporous.

insufferable adjective intolerable, unbearable, unendurable, insupportable, too much to bear, impossible, too much, more than one can stand, more than flesh and blood can put up with, enough to try the patience of Job, enough to test the patience of a saint.

insufficient adjective inadequate, deficient, in short supply, scarce, meager, scant, scanty, not enough, lacking, wanting, at a premium.

insulate verb *cloistered monks are insulated from the world* segregate, separate, isolate, detach, cut off, keep/set apart, sequester, exclude, protect, shield.

insult verb offend, give/cause offense to, affront, slight, hurt the feelings of, hurt, abuse, injure, wound, mortify, humiliate, disparage, discredit, depreciate, impugn, slur, revile.

insult noun **1** affront, slight, gibe, snub, barb, slur; abuse, disparagement, depreciation, impugnment, revilement, insolence, rudeness, contumely; aspersions; *inf.* dig.

insulting adjective offensive, slighting, abusive, injurious, wounding, mortifying, humiliating, disparaging, snubbing, insolent, rude, contumacious.

insurance noun **1** *take out travel insurance* financial protection, indemnity, indemnification, surety, security, coverage, guarantee, warranty, warrant. **2** *he took an umbrella as (an) insurance against the rain* safeguard, precaution, protection, provision.

insurgent noun rebel, revolutionary, mutineer, rioter, insurrectionist, insurrectionary, seditionist, malcontent.

insurgent adjective rebellious, revolutionary, mutinous, rioting, lawless, insurrectionist, insurrectionary, seditious, factious, subversive, insubordinate, disobedient.

insurmountable adjective insuperable, invincible, unconquerable, impassable, overwhelming, unassailable, hopeless, impossible.

insurrection noun rebellion, revolt, revolution, uprising, rising, riot, mutiny, sedition, coup, coup d'état, putsch; insurgency, insurgence.

intact adjective whole, complete, entire, perfect, all in one piece, sound, unbroken, unsevered, undamaged, unscathed, uninjured, unharmed, inviolate, undefiled.

intangible adjective **1** *intangible things* impalpable, untouchable, incorporeal, phantom, spectral, ghostly. **2** *an intangible air of sadness* indefinable, indescribable, vague, subtle, unclear.

integral adjective **1** *an integral part of the organization* essential, necessary, indispensable, requisite, basic, fundamental, intrinsic; constituent, component, integrant. **2** *an integral design* entire, complete, whole, total, full, intact, unified, integrated, undivided.

integrate verb unite, join, combine, amalgamate, consolidate, blend, incorporate.

integrated adjective **1** *integrated parts* united, joined, amalgamated, consolidated, assimilated. **2** *integrated schools* desegregated, nonsegregated, unsegregated, racially mixed, racially balanced.

integrity noun **1** *doubt the integrity of the council* uprightness, honesty, rectitude, righteousness, virtue, probity, morality, honor; principles, ethics. **2** *challenge the integrity of the nation* unity, wholeness, entirety, completeness, totality, cohesion.

intellect noun **1** *a person of little intellect* reason, understanding. See INTELLIGENCE 1. **2** *leave the decisions to the intellects* intellectual, genius, thinker, mastermind; *inf.* brain, mind, egghead, Einstein.

intellectual adjective **1** *an intellectual family* intelligent, academic, well-educated, well-read, erudite, learned, bookish, highbrow, scholarly, studious. **2** *an intellectual approach* mental, cerebral, rational, logical, clinical, unemotional, nonemotional, academic.

intellectual noun **1** *one of the great intellectuals* genius, thinker. See INTELLECT 2. **2** *sought the company of other intellectuals* academic, academician, man/woman of letters, bluestocking, pundit, highbrow, bookworm, pedant; *inf.* egghead, walking encyclopedia.

intelligence noun **1** *people of great intelligence* intellect, mind, brain, brainpower, mental capacity/aptitude, reason, understanding, comprehension, acumen, wit, cleverness, brightness, brilliance, sharpness, quickness of mind, alertness, discernment, perception, perspicacity, penetration, sense, sagacity; brains; *inf.* gray matter. **2** *the intelligence came too late* news, notification, knowledge. See INFORMATION. **3** *he's in military intelligence* information collection, surveillance, observation, spying.

intelligent adjective **1** *intelligent children* clever, bright, brilliant, sharp, quick, smart, apt, discerning, thinking, perceptive, perspicacious, sensible, sagacious, enlightened, knowledgeable; *inf.* brainy. **2** *is there intelligent life on the planet?* rational, reasoning, higher-order.

intemperate adjective immoderate, self-indulgent, excessive, inordinate, extreme, extravagant, unreasonable, unrestrained, uncurbed, unbridled, ungoverned; drunken, drunk, intoxicated, inebriated, dissolute, dissipated, debauched, loose, wild, wanton.

intend verb **1** *he intends to go* mean, plan, have in mind, propose, aim, resolve, expect, contemplate, think of. **2** *they intended the bullet for the leader* destine, purpose, plan, scheme, devise.

intense adjective acute, fierce, severe, extreme, harsh, strong, powerful, potent, vigorous, great, profound, deep, concentrated, consuming, impassioned, passionate, fervent, fervid, burning.

intensify verb heighten, deepen, strengthen, increase, reinforce, magnify, enhance, fan, whet; aggravate, exacerbate, worsen, inflame; extend, augment, boost, escalate, step up.

intensity noun acuteness, fierceness, severity, strength, power, potency, vigor, concentration, fervor, vehemence.

intensive adjective in-depth, concentrated, exhaustive, all-out, thorough, thorough-going, total, all-absorbing.

intent adjective **1** *an intent expression* concentrated, fixed, steady, steadfast, absorbed, attentive, engrossed, occupied, wrapped up, focused, earnest, committed, intense. **2** *intent on getting their own way* set on, bent on, committed to, firm about, determined to, resolved to.

intent noun purpose, aim. *See* INTENTION. **to/for all intents and purposes** virtually, practically, as good as.

intention noun aim, purpose, intent, goal, objective, end, end in view, target, ambition, wish, plan, design, resolve, resolution, determination; premeditation, preconception.

intentional adjective intended, deliberate, meant, done on purpose, willful, purposeful, purposed, planned, calculated, designed, premeditated, preconceived, predetermined.

intentionally adverb deliberately, on purpose, purposefully, by design, willfully.

inter verb bury, consign to the grave, entomb, lay to rest, inhume, inearth, sepulcher.

intercede verb mediate, negotiate, arbitrate, intervene, interpose, step in, plead for, petition for.

intercept verb stop, cut off, deflect, head off, seize, expropriate, commandeer; check, arrest, block, obstruct, impede.

intercession noun mediation, negotiation, arbitration, intervention, interposition, pleading, petition, entreaty, supplication; good offices.

interchangeable adjective exchangeable, transposable, equivalent, corresponding, correlative, reciprocal, comparable.

interest noun **1** *look with interest at the game* attentiveness, attention, absorption, engrossment, heed, regard, notice, scrutiny, curiosity, attraction, appeal, fascination, charm, allure. **2** *a matter of interest to all of us* concern, importance, import, consequence, moment, significance, note, relevance, seriousness. **3** *his interests include reading and music* pastime, hobby, diversion, amusement, pursuit, relaxation; *inf.* thing. **4** *have an interest in the business* share, stake, portion, claim, investment; stock, equity. **5** *you must declare your interest in the case* involvement, partiality, partisanship, preference, onesidedness, favoritism, bias, prejudice. **6** *his commercial interests are in trouble* concern, business, matter, care; affairs. **7** *earn interest on investments* dividend, profit, return, percentage, gain. **8** *it is in their interests to go* benefit, advantage, good, profit, gain. **in the interests of** for the sake/benefit of, to the advantage of, in the furtherance of.

interest verb **1** *the book interests her* attract/hold/engage the attention of, attract, absorb, engross, fascinate, rivet, grip, captivate, amuse, intrigue, arouse curiosity in. **2** *the outcome of the war interests us all* affect, have an effect/bearing on, concern, involve.

interested adjective **1** *the interested children* attentive, intent, absorbed, engrossed, curious, fascinated, riveted, gripped, captivated, intrigued. **2** *interested parties waiting in the lawyer's office* concerned, involved, implicated. **3** *no interested person can judge the contest* partial, partisan, one-sided, biased, prejudiced.

interesting adjective absorbing, engrossing, fascinating, riveting, gripping, compelling, compulsive, spellbinding, captivating, appealing, engaging, amusing, entertaining, stimulating, thought-provoking, diverting, exciting, intriguing.

interfere verb **interfere in** meddle with, butt into, pry into, tamper with, intrude into, intervene in, get involved in, intercede in; *inf.* poke one's nose in, horn in on. **interfere with** hinder, inhibit, impede, obstruct, get in the way of, check, block, hamper, handicap, cramp, trammel, frustrate, thwart, balk.

interference noun *resent her interference in their affairs* meddling, meddlesomeness, prying, intrusion, intervention.

interim noun meantime, meanwhile, interval, interregnum.

interior adjective **1** *the interior part of the building* inner, inside, internal, inward. **2** *the interior parts of the country* inland, noncoastal, central, midland, up-country, remote. **3** *his interior self* inner, spiritual, mental, psychological, emotional, private, personal, intimate, secret, hidden.

interior noun *the interior of the country* center, midland, heartland, hinterland.

interject verb throw in, insert, introduce, interpolate, interpose, insinuate, add, mingle, intersperse.

interloper noun trespasser, invader, intruder, encroacher, gatecrasher.

interlude noun interval, intermission, break, recess, pause, respite, rest, breathing space.

intermediary noun mediator, go-between, broker, agent, middleman, negotiator, arbitrator.

interment noun burial, burying, entombment, inhumation, sepulture, funeral.

interminable adjective **1** *an interminable road* (seemingly) endless, never-ending, without end, everlasting, ceaseless, incessant. **2** *an interminable talk* tedious, wearisome, boring, long-winded, rambling.

intermingle verb mingle, mix, commingle, intermix, blend, fuse, merge, combine.

intermission noun interval, interlude, interim, entr'acte, break, half-time, recess, rest, pause, respite, lull, stop, stoppage, halt, cessation, suspension; *inf.* letup, breather, time out.

intermittent adjective fitful, spasmodic, irregular, sporadic, occasional, periodic, cyclic, recurrent, recurring, broken, discontinuous, on again and off again, on and off.

internal adjective **1** *internal wall* interior, inside, inner, inward. **2** *the country's/firm's internal affairs* home, domestic, civil, interior, in-house, in-company. **3** *his internal opinion* mental, psychological, emotional, subjective, private, intimate.

international adjective cosmopolitan, global, universal, worldwide, intercontinental.

interpret verb **1** *interpret the text* explain, elucidate, expound, explicate, clarify, illuminate, shed light on, gloss, simplify, spell out. **2** *interpret her silence as consent* understand, understand by, construe, take, take to mean, read. **3** *interpret for the foreign ambassador* translate, transcribe, transliterate, paraphrase, decode, decipher. **4** *dancers interpreting the ballet* portray, depict, present, perform, execute, enact.

interpretation noun **1** *the interpretation of the text* explanation, elucidation, expounding, explication, clarification, exegesis. **2** *his interpretation of her silence as consent* understanding, construal, reading. **3** *the scientist's interpretation of the results* analysis, reading, diagnosis. **4** *her interpretation of the foreign ambassador's speech* translation, transcription, transliteration; paraphrase. **5** *the dancer's interpretation of the ballet* portrayal, depiction, presentation, performance, execution, rendering, rendition.

interrogate verb question, put/pose questions to, inquire of, examine, cross-examine, cross-question, quiz, pump, grill, give the third degree to, probe, catechize.

interrogation noun **1** *give way under interrogation* questioning, quizzing, examination, cross-examination, cross-questioning, pumping, grilling, third degree, probing, inquisition. **2** *complain about the policeman's interrogations* question, query, inquiry, poser.

interrupt verb **1** *interrupt his speech* cut in (on), break in (on), barge in (on), intrude (on), disturb, interfere (with); *inf.* butt in (on), chime in (on), horn in (on), muscle in (on). **2** *interrupt the talks for a time* suspend, discontinue, break, break off, hold up, delay, lay aside, leave off, postpone, stop, halt, cease, end, cancel. **3** *only a few trees interrupted the flatness of the landscape* break, break up, punctuate. **4** *the building interrupts our view* obstruct, impede, block, interfere with, cut off.

interruption noun **1** *resent his interruption* cutting in, interference, disturbance, intrusion, obtrusion; *inf.* butting in. **2** *the interruption of/in the talks* suspension, discontinuance, breaking off, delay, postponement, stopping, halt, cessation; intermission, interval, interlude, break, pause, recess, gap, hiatus.

intersect verb cut across/through, halve, divide, bisect; cross, crisscross, meet, connect.

interval noun **1** *in the interval before the next meeting* interim, interlude, period, meantime, meanwhile, wait, space. **2** *drinks served in the theater during the interval* break, pause. *See* INTERMISSION.

intervene verb *intervene in the dispute* mediate, involve oneself, interpose, interfere, intrude. *See* INTERCEDE.

intervention noun intercession, mediation, arbitration, negotiation, agency, involvement, interference, intrusion.

interview noun **1** *candidates nervous at the interview* conference, discussion, meeting, talk, dialogue, evaluation. **2** *give an interview to the press* audience, question and answer session, exchange, colloquy, interlocution.

interview verb talk to, have a discussion/dialogue with, hold a meeting with, confer with, question, put questions to, sound out, examine, interrogate, cross-examine, evaluate.

interweave verb **1** *interweave strands of various fabrics* weave, intertwine, twine, twist, interlace, braid, plait. **2** *their financial affairs are interwoven* intermingle, mingle, interlink, intermix, mix, blend, fuse, interlock, knit, connect, associate.

intimate adjective **1** *intimate friends* close, near, dear, nearest and dearest, cherished, bosom, familiar, confidential; *inf.* thick, buddy-buddy. **2** *in an intimate atmosphere* informal, warm, cozy, friendly, comfortable, snug; *inf.* comfy. **3** *a diary giving intimate details* personal, private, confidential, secret, privy. **4** *his intimate views* private, innermost, inmost, inner, inward, intrinsic, deep-seated, inherent. **5** *an intimate knowledge of the law* experienced, deep, in-depth, profound, detailed, thorough, exhaustive, personal, firsthand, direct, immediate. **6** *the intimate relations of lovers* sexual, carnal.

intimate verb imply, suggest, let it be known, hint, insinuate, give an inkling that, indicate, signal.

intimation noun implication, suggestion, hint, insinuation, inkling, indication, signal, reference, allusion.

intimidate verb frighten, terrify, scare, alarm, terrorize, cow, daunt, domineer, browbeat, bully, tyrannize, coerce, compel, bulldoze, pressure, threaten; *inf.* push around, lean on, twist someone's arm.

intimidation noun **1** *the intimidation of residents by gangs* frightening, terrorization, bullying, coercion, threatening; *inf.* arm-twisting. **2** *leave his premises out of intimidation* fear, terror, alarm, trepidation.

intolerable adjective unbearable, unendurable, beyond endurance. *See* INSUFFERABLE.

intolerance noun bigotry, illiberalism, narrow-mindedness, parochialism, provincialism, insularity, prejudice, bias, partisanship, one-sidedness.

intolerant adjective bigoted, illiberal, narrow-minded, narrow, parochial, provincial, insular, small-minded, prejudiced, biased, partial, partisan, one-sided.

intonation noun pitch, tone, timbre, cadence, lilt, inflection, accentuation, emphasis, stress.

intoxicated adjective inebriated, inebriate, drunk, drunken, dead drunk, under the influence, tipsy, befuddled, stupefied, staggering; *inf.* drunk as a skunk, three sheets to the wind, tight, pickled, soused, under the table, sloshed, plastered, stewed, well-oiled, loaded, stoned, bombed out of one's mind, lit up, tanked up, smashed.

intoxicating adjective **1** *intoxicating drinks* intoxicant, alcoholic, strong, spirituous, inebriant. **2** *intoxicating news* exhilarating, heady, elating, thrilling, animating, exciting.

intoxication noun **1** *suffering from the effects of intoxication* drunkenness, inebriation, inebriety, insobriety, alcoholism, dipsomania, tipsiness, befuddlement, stupefaction. **2** *intoxication following the good news* exhilaration, elation, ecstasy, euphoria, thrill, invigoration, animation, excitement, rapture, delirium.

intrepid adjective fearless, unafraid, undaunted, dauntless, undismayed, unalarmed, unflinching, bold, daring, adventurous, reckless, brave, courageous, gallant, stalwart; *inf.* gutsy, spunky.

intricate adjective **1** *intricate patterns* tangled, entangled, raveled, twisted, knotty, convoluted, mazelike, labyrinthine, serpentine, sinuous, fancy, elaborate, ornate, Byzantine, rococo. **2** *intricate problems* complex, complicated, difficult, involved, thorny, mystifying, enigmatic.

intrigue verb **1** *your behavior intrigues me* interest, absorb, arouse one's curiosity, attract, draw, pull, rivet, fascinate, charm, captivate. **2** *they are intriguing to overthrow the dictator* plot, conspire, scheme, connive, maneuver, machinate, devise.

intrigue noun **1** *an intrigue to overthrow the dictator* plot, conspiracy, collusion, conniving, cabal, scheme, ruse, stratagem, wile, dodge, artifice, maneuver, machination, trickery, double-dealing. **2** *her husband found out about the intrigue* love affair, affair, liaison, amour; adultery; *inf.* carrying on.

intriguing adjective interesting, absorbing, compelling, attractive, appealing, riveting, fascinating, captivating, diverting, titillating, tantalizing.

intrinsic adjective inborn, inbred, natural, native, elemental, true, genuine, real, authentic. *See* INHERENT.

introduce verb **1** *introduce his friends to each other* present, acquaint, make acquainted. **2** *introduce his talk with a joke* preface, precede, lead into, commence, start off, begin. **3** *introduce a new method* bring in, bring into being, originate, launch, inaugurate, institute, initiate, establish, found, set in motion, organize, develop, start, begin, commence, usher in, pioneer. **4** *introduce his ideas* propose, put forward, suggest, broach, advance, bring up, set forth, submit. **5** *introduce a note of solemnity to the party* insert, inject, interject, interpose, add, bring, infuse, instill.

introduction noun **1** *an introduction to the book* foreword, preface, front matter, preamble, prologue, prelude, lead-in; *inf.* intro, prelims. **2** *the introduction of new methods* origination, launch, inauguration, institution, establishment, development, start, commencement, pioneering. **3** *his introduction to a new way of life* baptism, initiation, inauguration, debut. **4** *the course provides an introduction to the subject* basics, rudiments, fundamentals; groundwork. **5** *the introduction of a serious note to the party* insertion, injection, interjection, infusion.

introductory adjective **1** *the speaker's introductory remarks* prefatory, preliminary, lead-in, opening, initial, starting, commencing. **2** *an introductory course* preparatory, elementary, basic, basal, rudimentary, fundamental.

introspective adjective self-analyzing, self-examining, contemplative, reflective, meditative, musing, pensive, brooding, preoccupied.

introverted adjective inward-looking, self-absorbed; withdrawn, shy, reserved.

intrude verb interrupt, push/thrust oneself in, gatecrash, barge in, encroach, butt in, interfere, obtrude; invade, impinge on, infringe on, trespass on, violate.

intruder noun invader, prowler, trespasser; interloper, infiltrator, gatecrasher.

intrusion noun interruption, encroachment, invasion, infringement, trespass, obtrusion, violation.

intrusive adjective interfering, invasive, obtrusive, trespassing, meddlesome, inquisitive; *inf.* pushy, nosy.

intuition noun instinct, sixth sense, divination, presentiment, clairvoyance, second sight, extrasensory perception, ESP, feeling, feeling in one's bones, hunch, inkling, presentiment.

intuitive adjective instinctive, instinctual, innate, unlearned, spontaneous, automatic.

inundate verb **1** *the river inundating the town* flood, deluge, overflow, overrun, swamp, submerge, engulf, drown, cover, saturate, soak. **2** *inundated with correspondence* overwhelm, overpower, overburden, swamp, bog down, glut.

inure verb harden, toughen, season, temper, habituate, familiarize, accustom, acclimatize.

invade verb **1** *the enemy invaded the city* march into, overrun, occupy, storm, take over, descend upon, make inroads on, attack, assail, assault, raid, plunder. **2** *invade their privacy* intrude on, obtrude on, encroach on, infringe on, trespass on, burst in on, violate. **3** *doubts invaded his mind* assail, permeate, pervade, fill, spread over.

invader noun **1** *enemy invaders* attacker, assailant, assaulter, raider, plunderer. **2** *invaders of their privacy* intruder, encroacher, infringer, trespasser, violator.

invalid adjective **1** *the contract is now invalid* inoperative, null, null and void, void, not binding, nullified, revoked, rescinded, abolished. **2** *an invalid assumption* untenable, illogical, irrational, unscientific, false, faulty, fallacious, spurious, ineffectual, unsound, weak.

invalidate verb **1** *invalidate the contract* void, nullify, annul, cancel, quash, veto, negate, revoke, rescind, abolish, terminate, repeal, repudiate. **2** *invalidate the argument* disprove, refute, rebut, negate, discredit.

invaluable adjective priceless, beyond price, inestimable, precious, costly, worth its weight in gold, worth a king's ransom.

invariable adjective unchanging, changeless, unchangeable, constant, unvarying, unalterable, immutable, fixed, stable, set, steady, unwavering, consistent.

invariably adverb always, each and every time, without fail/exception, regularly, consistently, habitually, unfailingly.

invasion noun **1** *the invasion of the city* overrunning, occupation, incursion, offensive, attack, assailing, assault, raid, foray, onslaught, plundering. **2** *the invasion of privacy* interruption, intrusion, obtrusion, encroachment, infringement, breach, infraction, trespass, violation.

invent verb **1** *invent a new machine* originate, create, innovate, discover, design, devise, contrive, formulate, think up, conceive, come up with, hit upon, compose, frame, coin. **2** *he invented that story* make up, fabricate, concoct, hatch, trump up, forge; *inf.* cook up.

invention noun **1** *the invention of the zipper* | *his most famous invention* origination, creation, innovation, discovery, design, contrivance, construction, coinage; *inf.* brainchild. **2** *an artist of great invention* inventiveness, originality, creativity, creativeness, imagination, artistry, inspiration, ingenuity, resourcefulness, genius, skill. **3** *his account of the event was pure invention* fabrication, concoction, fiction, falsification, forgery, fake, deceit, myth, fantasy, romance, illusion, sham, lie, untruth, falsehood, fib, figment of one's imagination, yarn, story; *inf.* tall story.

inventive adjective original, creative, innovative, imaginative, artistic, inspired, ingenious, resourceful.

inventor noun originator, creator, innovator, discoverer, author, architect, designer, deviser, developer, initiator, coiner, father, prime mover, maker, framer, producer.

inventory noun list, listing, checklist, catalog, record, register, tally, account.

invert verb turn inside out, turn upside down, overturn, upturn, turn turtle.

invest verb **1** *the priest will be invested tomorrow* install, induct, inaugurate, instate, ordain, initiate, swear in, consecrate, crown, enthrone. **2** *the bride was invested in silk* clothe, attire, dress, garb, robe, gown, drape, swathe, adorn, deck.

invest in 1 *invest in the business* put/sink money into, lay out money on/for, provide capital for, fund, subsidize. **2** *invest energy in the venture* spend on, expend on/for, devote to, contribute to, give to. **3** *invest power in his heirs* vest in, confer to, bestow to, grant to, entrust to.

investigate verb research, probe, explore, inquire into, make inquiries about, go/look into, search, scrutinize, study, examine, inspect, consider, sift, analyze; *inf.* check out.

investigation noun research, probe, exploration, inquiry, fact-finding, search, scrutiny, study, survey, review, examination, inspection, analysis, inquest, hearing, inquisition.

investigator noun researcher, prober, explorer, inquirer, fact finder, searcher, scrutinizer, reviewer, examiner, inspector, analyzer, questioner, inquisitor. **private investigator** (private) detective; *inf.* private eye, dick, sleuth, Sherlock, gumshoe.

inveterate adjective **1** *an inveterate conservative/drinker* confirmed, habitual, inured, hardened, chronic, diehard, dyed-in-the-wool, long-standing, addicted, hard-core, incorrigible. **2** *an inveterate habit* ingrained, deep-seated, deep-rooted, deepset, entrenched, long-established, ineradicable, incurable.

invigorate verb revitalize, energize, fortify, strengthen, put new strength/life/heart in, brace, refresh, rejuvenate, enliven, liven up, animate, exhilarate, pep up, perk up, stimulate, motivate, rouse, excite, wake up.

invincible adjective **1** *an invincible opponent* unconquerable, undefeatable, unbeatable, unassailable, invulnerable, indestructible, impregnable, indomitable. **2** *an invincible hurdle* insuperable, insurmountable, overwhelming, overpowering.

inviolate adjective intact, unbroken, whole, entire, untouched, undamaged, unscathed, unmarred, unspoiled, unsullied, unstained, undefiled, unpolluted, pure, virgin.

invisible adjective **1** *invisible to the passersby* undetectable, imperceivable, indiscernible, indistinguishable, unseen, unnoticed, unobserved, hidden, concealed. **2** *invisible hairnets* inconspicuous, unnoticeable, imperceptible.

invitation noun **1** *reject their invitation to lunch* asking, bidding, call; *inf.* invite. **2** *accept their invitation to apply for the post* request, call, appeal, petition, solicitation, supplication, summons. **3** *the rebate was an invitation to buy the car* encouragement, overture, attraction, draw, allurement, lure, bait; *inf.* come-on.

invite verb **1** *they invited him to dinner* ask, bid, summon. **2** *invite applications* ask for, request, call for, solicit, look for, seek, appeal for, petition. **3** *invite disaster* cause, bring on, bring upon oneself, draw, make happen, induce, provoke. **4** *they invite trouble by leaving the doors unlocked* welcome, encourage, foster, attract, draw, allure, entice, tempt, court.

inviting adjective attractive, appealing, tempting, enticing, alluring, winning, beguiling, fascinating, captivating, intriguing, irresistible.

invoke verb **1** *invoke God's help* call for, request, supplicate, entreat, solicit, beseech, beg, implore, importune, petition, appeal to. **2** *invoke the constitutional amendment* apply, implement, put into effect/use, resort to, use, have recourse to.

involuntary adjective **1** *an involuntary reaction* reflexive, reflex, automatic, mechanical, unconditioned, spontaneous, instinctive, instinctual, unconscious, unthinking, unintentional, uncontrolled. **2** *their cooperation was involuntary* unwilling, against one's will/wishes, reluctant, unconsenting, grudging, forced, coerced, compelled, compulsory, obligatory.

involve verb **1** *his new job involves total discretion* entail, imply, require, necessitate, presuppose. **2** *try to involve everyone in the party* include, count in, cover, embrace, take in, number, incorporate, encompass, comprise, contain. **3** *the suspect tried to involve others in the crime* implicate, incriminate, inculpate, associate, connect, concern. **4** *introduce the students to something that involves them* interest, be of interest to, absorb, engage, rivet, grip, occupy, preoccupy, engross.

involved adjective **1** *an involved situation* complicated, difficult. *See* INTRICATE. **2** *involved parties should speak up* associated, concerned, participating.

invulnerable adjective impenetrable, secure, safe. *See* INVINCIBLE. **invulnerable to/against** insensitive to, insusceptible to.

inwardly adverb at heart, deep down/within, in one's heart, inside, privately, secretly.

irascible adjective quick-tempered, shorttempered, snappish, testy, irritable, touchy, edgy, surly, cross, crotchety, cantankerous.

irate adjective incensed, enraged, raging, fuming, infuriated, furious, indignant, ireful, ranting, raving, angry, mad, in a frenzy; *inf.* foaming at the mouth.

ire noun anger, wrath, rage, fury, indignation, annoyance, exasperation, resentment, choler, spleen.

iridescent adjective shimmering, glittering, sparkling, dazzling, kaleidoscopic, multicolored, rainbowlike.

irk verb irritate, annoy, provoke, vex, pique, peeve, nettle, exasperate, ruffle, discountenance, anger, infuriate, incense, try one's patience; *inf.* get one's goat, get one's back up.

irksome adjective irritating, annoying, vexing, vexatious, exasperating, infuriating, tiresome, wearisome, tedious, trying, troublesome.

iron verb **iron out 1** *iron out the problems* straighten out, sort out, clear up, settle, solve, resolve, unravel. **2** *iron out their differences* get rid of, eliminate, eradicate, erase, harmonize, reconcile, smooth over.

ironic adjective **1** *an ironic remark/wit* satirical, mocking, scoffing, ridiculing, derisory, derisive, scornful, sneering, sardonic, wry, double-edged, sarcastic. **2** *ironic that Beethoven became deaf* paradoxical, incongruous.

irony noun **1** *use irony in your story* satire, mockery, ridicule, derision, scorn, wryness, sarcasm. **2** *it was a sad irony that the millionaire died a pauper* paradox, incongruity, incongruousness.

irrational adjective **1** *irrational fears* illogical, unreasonable, groundless, implausible, absurd, foolish, senseless, nonsensical, ludicrous, preposterous. **2** *an irrational person* demented, insane, crazy, unstable.

irreconcilable adjective **1** *irreconcilable points of view* incompatible, at odds, at variance, opposite, contrary, incongruous, opposing, conflicting, clashing, discordant. **2** *irreconcilable enemies* implacable, unappeasable, uncompromising, intransigent, hard-line, inflexible.

irregular adjective **1** *an irregular coastline* asymmetric, unsymmetric, nonuniform, uneven, broken, jagged, ragged, serrated, crooked, curving, craggy. **2** *an irregular churchgoer* inconsistent, erratic, sporadic, variable, inconstant, desultory, haphazard, intermittent, occasional, unsystematic, capricious, unmethodical. **3** *his appointment was most irregular* out of order, contrary, perverse, against the rules, unofficial, unorthodox, unconventional, abnormal. **4** *an irregular result* anomalous, aberrant, deviant, abnormal, unusual, uncommon, freak, extraordinary, exceptional, odd, peculiar, strange. **5** *an irregular army* guerrilla, underground, resistance, mercenary.

irregularity noun **1** *the irregularity of the coastline* lack of symmetry, asymmetry, unsymmetricalness, nonuniformity, unevenness, jaggedness. **2** *the irregularity of the pulse* unevenness, unsteadiness, shakiness, fitfulness, fluctuation. **3** *the irregularity of their attendance* inconsistency, inconstancy, desultoriness, haphazardness, intermittence, patchiness. **4** *the irregularity of his appointment* unorthodoxy, unconventionality. **5** *the irregularity of the result* anomaly, anomalousness, aberrance, aberrancy, deviation, abnormality, unusualness, freakishness. **6** *spot the irregularities in the result* anomaly, aberration, deviation, abnormality.

irrelevant adjective nongermane, immaterial, unrelated, unconnected, inappropriate, extraneous, beside the point, not to the point, out of place, nothing to do with it, neither here nor there.

irreparable adjective beyond repair, past mending, irreversible, irrevocable, irretrievable, irrecoverable, irremediable, incurable.

irreplaceable adjective priceless, invaluable, inestimably precious, unique, worth its weight in gold, rare.

irrepressible adjective unrestrainable, uncontainable, insuppressible, uncontrollable, unstoppable, unquenchable, unreserved, unchecked, unbridled.

irresistible adjective **1** *an irresistible impulse* overwhelming, overpowering, compelling, insuppressible, irrepressible, forceful, potent, imperative, urgent. **2** *an irresistible beauty/dessert* fascinating, alluring, enticing, seductive, captivating, enchanting, ravishing, tempting, tantalizing.

irresponsible adjective **1** *irresponsible people* undependable, unreliable, untrustworthy, careless, reckless, rash, flighty, giddy, scatterbrained, erratic, harebrained, featherbrained, immature; *inf.* harumscarum. **2** *irresponsible actions* thoughtless, ill-considered, unwise, injudicious.

irreverent adjective disrespectful, unrespectful, impertinent, insolent, impudent; impious, irreligious, heretical, sacrilegious, blasphemous.

irreversible adjective unalterable, irreparable, unrectifiable, irrevocable, unrepealable, final, fixed, settled.

irrevocable adjective unalterable, unchangeable. *See* IRREVERSIBLE.

irritable adjective bad-tempered, ill-tempered, ill-humored, irascible, cross, snappish, snappy, edgy, testy, touchy, crabbed, peevish, petulant, cantankerous, grumpy, grouchy.

irritate verb **1** *the barking dogs irritate the neighbors* annoy, vex, provoke, irk, aggravate, nettle, peeve, get on one's nerves, exasperate, infuriate, anger, make one's hackles rise, ruffle, disturb, put out, bother, pester, try one's patience; *inf.* rub the wrong way, get one's goat, get one's back up, drive up the wall, drive one bananas. **2** *the rough cloth irritated her skin* chafe, fret, rub, pain, hurt, inflame, aggravate.

irritating adjective annoying, vexing, provoking, irksome, exasperating, infuriating, maddening, disturbing, bothersome, troublesome, pestering, aggravating.

island noun isle, islet, key, cay, atoll.

isolate verb set apart, segregate, cut off, separate, detach, quarantine, sequester, insulate.

isolated adjective **1** *feeling isolated far from her friends* alone, solitary, lonely, separated, segregated, exiled, forsaken, forlorn. **2** *an isolated place* remote, out of the way, off the beaten track, outlying, secluded, hidden, unfrequented, desolate, godforsaken. **3** *an isolated example* single, solitary, unique, uncommon, exceptional, atypical.

isolation noun **1** *the isolation of the patients was necessary* segregation, separation, detachment, abstraction, quarantine, sequestration, insulation. **2** *the prisoner's feeling of isolation* exile, forlornness, aloneness, solitariness, loneliness. **3** *the isolation of the village* remoteness, seclusion, loneliness, desolation.

issue noun **1** *debate the issue for hours* matter, matter in question, point at issue, question, subject, topic, affair, problem, bone of contention, controversy, argument. **2** *the issue is still in doubt* result, outcome, decision, upshot, end, conclusion, consequence, effect. **3** *the next issue of the magazine* edition, number, printing, print run, impression, copy, installment, version. **4** *the issue of the new stamps/paper/shares* issuance, publication, circulation, distribution, dissemination, sending out, delivery. **5** *Abraham and his issue* offspring, progeny, children; heirs, scions, descendants; *inf.* brood. **6** *the issue of the stream* outflow, effusion, discharge, debouchment, emanation. **at issue** to be

discussed, under discussion, for debate, in dispute, to be decided. **take issue with** disagree with, dispute with, challenge, oppose.

issue verb **1** *issue new stamps | issue a statement* put out, give out, deal out, send out, distribute, circulate, release; disseminate, announce, proclaim, broadcast. **2** *smoke issuing from the chimney* emit, exude, discharge, emanate, gush, pour forth, seep, ooze. **3** *people issued from the building* emerge, come out, come forth, appear; leave. **4** *his knowledge issues from a love of books* derive, arise, stem, proceed, spring, originate, result.

itching adjective **1** *an itching scalp* itchy, tingling, prickling. **2** *itching to go/know* longing, yearning, craving, aching, burning, avid, agog, keen, eager, impatient, raring, dying.

item noun **1** *three items for sale* article, thing, piece of merchandise; goods. **2** *several items to be discussed* point, detail, matter, consideration, particular, feature, circumstance, aspect, component, element, ingredient. **3** *a news item* piece, story, bulletin, article, account, report, feature, dispatch.

itemize verb list, inventory, tabulate, detail, particularize, specify, instance, enumerate, number.

itinerant adjective traveling, peripatetic, journeying, wandering, roaming, roving, rambling, wayfaring, unsettled, nomadic, migratory, vagabond, vagrant, gypsy.

Jj

jab verb *jab him in the ribs* poke, prod, dig, nudge, elbow, stab, tap, punch, box; *inf.* sock.

jab noun *a jab in the ribs* poke, prod, dig, nudge, stab, punch.

jabber verb chatter, gibber, prattle, babble, prate, blather, rattle, ramble.

jacket noun *a jacket and matching pants* sport(s) coat, blazer, windbreaker, parka, anorak.

jagged adjective serrated, toothed, notched, spiked, barbed, uneven, rough, ragged, craggy, broken, cleft.

jail noun *sent to jail* prison, lockup, jailhouse, penitentiary; *inf.* pen, clink, inside, stir, slammer, cooler, jug, can, big house.

jail verb *they jailed him for life* imprison, incarcerate, send up, lock up, put away, confine, detain, intern, impound, immure.

jailer noun prison warden, warden, guard, keeper, captor.

jam verb **1** *jam something in the door* wedge, insert, force, ram, stick, press, cram, sandwich, stuff. **2** *the ushers jammed too many people into the hall* cram, pack, crowd, squeeze, crush. **3** *the broken-down vehicles jammed the roads* obstruct, block, clog, congest. **4** *the machine has jammed* stick, stall, halt, stop.

jam noun **1** *caught in a jam on the highway* obstruction, congestion, bottleneck, stoppage, gridlock, traffic jam, holdup. **2** *in a financial jam* predicament, plight, straits, trouble, quandary; *inf.* fix, tight spot, scrape.

jangle verb 1 *the chains jangled* clank, clink, clang, clash, clatter, rattle. 2 *the noise jangled his nerves* irritate, disturb, jar on, grate on.

jangle noun *the jangle of chains* clank, clink, clang, clash, clatter, rattle, cacophony, din, dissonance.

jar verb *the sound jarred his nerves* grate (on), jangle, irritate, disturb, upset, irk, annoy, nettle, vex.

jargon noun 1 *the jargon of the neighborhood kids* cant, slang, argot, idiom, vernacular, dialect, patois; *inf.* lingo. 2 *technical jargon* computerese, legalese, bureaucratese, journalese, buzzword, gobbledegook, psychobabble.

jaundiced adjective 1 *jaundiced skin* yellow, yellowish, sallow. 2 *a jaundiced view of life* cynical, pessimistic, skeptical, distrustful, suspicious, misanthropic, bitter.

jaunt noun outing, drive, excursion, expedition, stroll.

jaunty adjective 1 *in a jaunty mood* sprightly, bouncy, buoyant, lively, breezy, perky, blithe. 2 *a jaunty outfit* smart, stylish, trim, dapper; *inf.* natty.

jealous adjective 1 *jealous of her beauty* grudging, resentful, envious, green-eyed, covetous, desirous. 2 *a jealous lover* suspicious, distrustful, mistrustful, doubting, insecure, possessive.

jealousy noun 1 *show jealousy at her rival's success* resentment, resentfulness, ill-will, bitterness, spite, envy, covetousness. 2 *the jealousy of her husband* suspicion, suspiciousness, distrust, mistrust, doubt, insecurity, possessiveness.

jeer verb *crowds jeering the politician* mock, ridicule, deride, taunt, gibe, scorn, contemn, flout, cry down, tease, boo, hiss; scoff at, laugh at, sneer at; *inf.* knock.

jeer noun *the jeers of the crowd* mockery, ridicule, derision; banter, scoffing, teasing, sneer, taunt, gibe, boo, hiss, catcall, abuse.

jell verb 1 *let the dessert jell* set, stiffen, solidify, harden, thicken, congeal, coagulate. 2 *ideas beginning to jell* take shape, take form, form, crystallize, come together.

jeopardize verb endanger, imperil, put in jeopardy, put at risk, expose to danger, threaten, menace, take a chance with, gamble with.

jeopardy noun risk, danger, endangerment, peril, hazard, precariousness, insecurity, vulnerability, threat, menace.

jerk verb 1 *jerk him by the arm* pull, yank, tug, wrench, tweak, pluck. 2 *the car jerked*

along jolt, lurch, bump, jump, bounce, jounce. 3 *his arm was jerking* twitch, shake, tremble, convulse.

jerk noun 1 *pull it out with a jerk* pull, yank, tug, wrench, tweak. 2 *the car stopped with a jerk* jolt, lurch, bump, start, jar. 3 *he's a complete jerk* fool, idiot, rogue, scoundrel; *inf.* twit, creep.

jest noun 1 *tell jests* joke, witticism, gag, quip, bon mot; *inf.* crack, wisecrack. 2 *play a jest on someone* prank, hoax, practical joke, trick, jape. 3 *they did it in jest* fun, sport, play.

jest verb 1 *they joked and jested all evening* joke, crack jokes, quip, banter; *inf.* wisecrack. 2 *but they were only jesting* fool, fool around, tease, play a prank, play a practical joke, play a hoax, pull someone's leg; *inf.* kid.

jester noun 1 *her uncle's a jester* joker, comic, comedian, humorist, wag, wit, quipster, prankster. 2 *the jesters in Shakespeare's plays* fool, court fool, clown, buffoon, merry-andrew, harlequin.

jet noun 1 *a jet of water* stream, gush, spurt, spout, spray, rush, fountain, spring. 2 *put a jet on the hose* nozzle, spout, sprinkler, rose, atomizer.

jet verb *water jetted out of the hose* shoot, gush, spurt, spout, well, rush, spray, squirt, spew, stream, surge, flow, issue.

jettison verb 1 *jettison heavy goods from a ship* eject, throw overboard, throw over the side, unload. 2 *jettison unwanted clothes* discard, get rid of, toss out, scrap, dump, throw out, throw away.

jetty noun *tie the boat to the jetty* pier, wharf, quay, breakwater.

jewel noun 1 *a crown set with priceless jewels* gem, gemstone, precious stone, bijou; *inf.* rock. 2 *the jewel of his collection* pearl, flower, pride, pride and joy, cream, crème de la crème, plum, boast.

jeweler noun lapidary, gemologist.

jewelry noun jewels, gems, precious stones, treasure, regalia, trinkets, ornaments; costume jewelry.

jiffy noun moment, second, split second, minute, instant, flash, trice, twinkling of an eye; *inf.* two shakes of a lamb's tail.

jilt verb reject, cast aside, discard, throw over, drop, leave, forsake; *inf.* ditch, dump.

jingle verb 1 *money jingling* clink, chink, jangle, rattle, clank. 2 *the bell jingled* tinkle, ding, ring, chime, tintinnabulate.

jingle noun 1 *the jingle of money* clink, chink, jangle, rattle, clank. 2 *the jingle of the bell* tinkle, tinkling, ding, ding-dong, ting-a-ling, ringing, tintinnabulation, chime. 3 *sing a little jingle* ditty, melody, tune, chorus, refrain, catchy tune.

jingoism noun patriotism, excessive patriotism, blind patriotism, nationalism, chauvinism, flag-waving.

jinx noun malediction, curse, spell, plague, affliction; black magic, voodoo, evil eye, bad luck, evil fortune, hex.

jinx verb curse, cast a spell on, put a voodoo spell on, bewitch, hex.

jittery adjective nervous, nervy, uneasy, anxious, agitated, shaky, fidgety, jumpy.

job noun **1** *this job will take hours* task, undertaking, chore, assignment, venture, enterprise, activity, business, affair. **2** *what is his job?* occupation, profession, trade, employment, vocation, calling, career, field of work, métier, position, post, situation, appointment. **3** *it is his job to open the mail* duty, task, chore, errand, responsibility, concern, function, role, charge, office, commission, capacity, contribution. **4** *we must get this job off to the distributors* product, batch, lot, consignment.

jockey verb *jockey for position* maneuver, manipulate, engineer, elbow, insinuate; *inf.* finagle.

jocular adjective humorous, funny, witty, comic, comical, joking, jesting, playful, roguish, waggish, whimsical, droll, jocose, teasing, sportive, amusing, entertaining, diverting.

jog verb **1** *she jogs for exercise* dogtrot, trot, canter, lope. **2** *the sight jogged her memory* stimulate, activate, stir, arouse, prompt. **3** *his backpack jogged up and down on his back* bounce, bob, joggle, jiggle, jounce, jolt, jerk, shake.

join verb **1** *join the pieces of string/metal together* fasten, attach, tie, bind, couple, connect, unite, link, splice, knit, glue, cement, fuse, weld, solder. **2** *the two clubs have joined together* amalgamate, merge, combine, unify, ally, join forces. **3** *we joined them in their venture* join forces with, team up with, band together with, cooperate with, collaborate with, affiliate with. **4** *join the army/club* enlist, sign up, enroll; become a member of, sign up for. **5** *join the search party* join in, participate in, take part in, partake in, contribute to, lend a hand with.

joint noun **1** *reinforce the pipes at the joint* junction, juncture, intersection, nexus, knot, seam, coupling. **2** *drinking in some joint* club, nightclub, bar, place, establishment. **3** *smoke a joint* marijuana cigarette; *inf.* reefer.

joint adjective *a joint interest* common, shared, joined, mutual, combined, collective, cooperative, allied, united.

joke noun **1** *tell a joke* jest, witticism, quip, gag, yarn, pun; *inf.* wisecrack. **2** *play a joke on him* prank, trick, hoax, practical joke.

3 *he is the joke of the class* laughingstock, butt, target.

joke verb **1** *they joked all evening* jest, banter, quip, tell jokes, crack jokes; *inf.* wisecrack. **2** *they were only joking* fool, fool around, tease, pull someone's leg; *inf.* kid.

joker noun comic, comedian, humorist, funny man/woman, jester, wag, wit, quipster, prankster, practical joker, trickster; *inf.* kidder, wisecracker.

jolly adjective merry, gay, jovial, mirthful, gleeful, cheerful, cheery, lively, bright, lighthearted, jocund, exuberant.

jolt verb **1** *the car jolted along* bump, bounce, jounce, start, jerk, lurch. **2** *the accident jolted him* upset, disturb, perturb, shake, shake up, shock, stun, disconcert, disquiet, startle, surprise.

jolt noun **1** *the car moved with a jolt* bump, bounce, jounce, shake, jerk, lurch, start. **2** *her death came as a jolt* shock, bombshell, blow, setback, surprise, thunderbolt.

jostle verb **1** *people jostling each other* bump, knock against, bump into, bang into, collide with, jolt, push, shove, elbow. **2** *jostle her way through* push, thrust, shove, press, squeeze, elbow.

jot noun *not care a jot* iota, whit, bit, scrap, atom, grain, particle, morsel, mite, speck, trace, trifle, smidgen, *inf.* smidge, tad.

journal noun **1** *keep a journal on his travels* diary, daybook, notebook, log, logbook, chronicle, record, register. **2** *publish medical journals* periodical, magazine, trade magazine, review, professional publication. **3** *the proprietor of several national journals* newspaper, paper, daily newspaper, daily, weekly newspaper, weekly, gazette.

journalist noun reporter, newsman/newswoman, newshound, feature writer, columnist, correspondent, contributor, commentator, reviewer, editor; broadcaster; *inf.* stringer. **journalists** the press.

journey noun trip, expedition, excursion, tour, trek, voyage, cruise, safari, peregrination, globe-trotting, odyssey, pilgrimage, outing, jaunt.

journey verb travel, tour, voyage, sail, cruise, fly, hike, trek, roam, rove, ramble, wander, meander, peregrinate, globe-trot.

jovial adjective jolly, jocular, jocose, jocund, happy, cheerful, cheery, glad, merry, gay, mirthful, blithe, buoyant, convivial.

joy noun **1** *receive the gift with joy* delight, pleasure, gladness, enjoyment, gratification, happiness, rapture, glee, bliss, ecstasy, elation, rejoicing, exultation, jubilation. **2** *their daughter is a joy* treasure, prize, gem, jewel, delight. **3** *it is a joy to see you* pleasure, delight, treat, thrill.

joyful adjective **1** *joyful at the news* overjoyed, elated, thrilled, delighted, pleased, gratified, happy, glad, blithe, gleeful, jubilant, exultant; *inf.* tickled pink. **2** *we heard the joyful news* glad, happy, good, pleasing, cheering, gratifying, heartwarming. **3** *a joyful occasion* joyous, happy, cheerful, merry, gay, festive, celebratory.

joyless adjective **1** *a joyless place* gloomy, dreary, drab, dismal, bleak, depressing, cheerless, grim, desolate, comfortless. **2** *joyless people* unhappy, sad, miserable, wretched, downcast, dejected, depressed, despondent, melancholy, mournful.

jubilant adjective rejoicing, overjoyed, exultant, triumphant, elated, thrilled, euphoric, ecstatic, on cloud nine.

jubilation noun exultation, triumph, elation, joy, euphoria, ecstasy, rapture.

jubilee noun celebration, commemoration, anniversary, holiday, feast day, festival, gala, carnival, fête, festivity, revelry.

judge verb **1** *judge the murder case* try, hear evidence in, sit in judgment on/of, give a verdict in, pass sentence in, decree. **2** *judge the contest* adjudicate, adjudge, umpire, referee, arbitrate, mediate. **3** *judge his conduct for yourself* assess, appraise, evaluate, size up, gauge, examine, review, criticize.

judge noun **1** *the judge pronounced sentence* justice, reviewer, magistrate, his/her honor. **2** *the contest judge* appraiser, assessor, evaluator, critic, expert, adjudicator, umpire, referee, arbiter, arbitrator, mediator.

judgment noun **1** *he has no judgment* discernment, acumen, shrewdness, common sense, sense, perception, perspicacity, discrimination, wisdom, judiciousness, prudence, sagacity, understanding, intelligence, powers of reasoning. **2** *the judge gave his judgment* verdict, decision, adjudication, ruling, finding, opinion, conclusion, decree, sentence. **3** *in my judgment he is dishonest* opinion, view, belief, conviction, estimation, evaluation, assessment, appraisal.

judicial adjective **1** *judicial process* judiciary, juridical, judicatory, legal. **2** *a judicial mind* judgelike, impartial, unbiased, critical, analytical, discriminating, discerning, perceptive.

judicious adjective wise, prudent, politic, sagacious, shrewd, astute, sensible, sound, well-advised, well-considered, considered, thoughtful, expedient, practical, discerning, discriminating, informed, intelligent, enlightened, rational, discreet, careful, cautious, circumspect.

jug noun pitcher, ewer, crock, carafe, decanter, jar, urn, vessel, receptacle, container.

juicy adjective **1** *juicy fruit* succulent, moist, lush, watery, wet, flowing. **2** *a juicy tale* racy, risqué, spicy, sensational, thrilling, fascinating, colorful, exciting, vivid.

jumble verb disarrange, disorganize, disorder, muddle, confuse, shuffle, mix, mix up, mingle, put in disarray, make a shambles of, throw into chaos.

jumble noun clutter, muddle, confusion, litter, mess, hodgepodge, mishmash, miscellany, motley collection, mixture, medley, gallimaufry.

jumbo adjective giant, gigantic, immense, huge, extra large, oversized.

jump verb **1** *jump around* spring, leap, bound, hop, bounce, skip, caper, gambol, frolic, frisk, cavort. **2** *jump over the rope* high-jump, leap over, vault, pole-vault, hurdle, clear, sail over. **3** *she jumped when she heard the noise* start, flinch, jerk, recoil, twitch, quiver, shake, wince. **4** *jump (over) a piece of text* skip, miss, omit, leave out, cut out, pass over, overlook, disregard, ignore. **5** *prices jumped* rise, go up, leap up, increase, mount, escalate, surge, soar. **6** *the cat jumped the mouse* pounce on, set upon, fall on, attack, assault; *inf.* mug. **jump at** *jump at the opportunity* grab, snatch. **jump the gun** anticipate, act prematurely.

jump noun **1** *with one jump* spring, leap, vault, bound, hop, bounce, skip. **2** *the jumps in the race* hurdle, fence, rail, hedge, obstacle, barrier, gate. **3** *a jump in the sequence* gap, break, hiatus, interruption, space, lacuna, breach, interval. **4** *she gave a jump at the sight* start, flinch, jerk, twitch, quiver, shake, wince. **5** *a jump in prices* rise, increase, upturn, upsurge, escalation, hike, boost, elevation.

jumpy adjective nervous, edgy, on edge, jittery, agitated, fidgety, anxious, uneasy, restive, tense, apprehensive.

junction noun **1** *reinforcement at the junction of the pipes* joint, juncture, link, connection, seam; joining, coupling, linking, welding, union. **2** *cars stop at the junction* crossroads, crossing, intersection, interchange.

juncture noun point, point in time, time, stage, period, critical point, crucial moment.

jungle noun **1** *wild animals in the jungle* forest, tropical forest, rain forest, wilderness, wilds, the bush. **2** *a jungle of paperwork* jumble, tangle, disarray, confusion, hodgepodge, heap, mass, mess, mishmash, gallimaufry.

junior adjective **1** *the junior member* younger. **2** *the junior position* subordinate, lesser, lower, minor, secondary, inferior.

junk noun rubbish, refuse, litter, scrap, waste, garbage, trash, debris, remnants, castoffs, rejects, odds and ends.

junk verb discard, get rid of, dispose of, throw out, throw away, scrap; *inf.* dump.

jurisdiction noun **1** *under the governor's jurisdiction* authority, control, administration, command, leadership, power, dominion, sovereignty, rule, mastery, sway, say, influence. **2** *living in adjoining jurisdictions* territory, district, province, domain, principality, realm, area, zone. **3** *the jurisdiction of his authority* extent, range, scope, bounds, compass, sphere, area, field, orbit.

just adjective **1** *a just judge* fair, fair-minded, equitable, evenhanded, impartial, unbiased, objective, neutral, unprejudiced, open-minded. **2** *a just man* upright, honorable, honest, ethical, moral, virtuous, principled, good, decent, truthful. **3** *just criticism* valid, sound, well-founded, well-grounded, justified, reasonable. **4** *just deserts* deserved, well-deserved, merited, rightful, due, proper, fitting, appropriate, apt, suitable, condign. **5** *the just heir* lawful, legitimate, legal, licit, rightful, genuine.

just adverb **1** *I just saw him* recently, lately, not long ago, only now, a moment ago. **2** *the house is just right* exactly, precisely, absolutely, completely, totally, entirely, perfectly. **3** *we just made it* barely, scarcely, hardly, by a hair's breadth. **4** *she's just a child* only, merely, simply, but, nothing but, no more than.

justice noun **1** *expect justice from the courts* fairness, fair-mindedness, justness, equity, evenhandedness, impartiality, objectivity, neutrality, lack of prejudice, open-mindedness. **2** *a man of justice* integrity, honor, honesty, ethics, morals, justness, uprightness, virtue, principle, decency,

propriety. **3** *see the justice of his criticism* validity, justification, soundness, reasonableness. **4** *the justice of his heirdom* lawfulness, legitimacy, legality, licitness. **5** *demand justice* amends, recompense, redress, compensation, reparation, requital, retribution, penalty, punishment. **6** *the justice passed sentence* judge, magistrate, sheriff.

justifiable adjective valid, sound, well-founded, lawful, legitimate, legal, tenable, defensible, supportable, sustainable, warrantable, reasonable, acceptable, plausible.

justification noun **1** *give as the justification of his behavior* grounds, reason, just cause, basis, explanation, rationalization, defense. **2** *outline the justification of our fears* warranty, substantiation, verification, reasonableness, confirmation. **3** *the justification of the accused* acquittal, absolution, exoneration, exculpation, pardon.

justify verb **1** *justify his behavior* give grounds for, give reasons for, show just cause for, explain, rationalize, defend, stand up for, uphold. **2** *he had to justify his claim* substantiate, prove, establish, verify, certify, legitimize. **3** *his conduct justified our worries* warrant, substantiate, bear out, confirm. **4** *the accused was finally justified* acquit, clear, absolve, exculpate, exonerate, pardon, excuse.

jut verb stick out, project, protrude, overhang, beetle.

juvenile adjective **1** *juvenile entrants* young, junior, minor. **2** *a juvenile attitude* childish, puerile, infantile, jejune, immature, unsophisticated, naive; *inf.* wet behind the ears.

Kk

keen adjective **1** *a keen edge to the blade* sharp, sharp-edged, fine-edged, razor-sharp. **2** *a keen sense of smell* sharp, acute, discerning, perceptive, sensitive, discriminating. **3** *a keen mind* sharp, astute, quick-witted, sharp-witted, shrewd, perceptive, penetrating, perspicacious, clever. **4** *be the butt of her keen wit* acerbic, acid, biting, caustic, tart, pointed, razorlike, razor-sharp, cutting, stinging, scathing, sardonic. **5** *keen students* willing, eager, enthusiastic, avid, earnest, zealous, fervent. **6** *keen to learn* eager, longing, yearning, impatient, itching.

keenness noun **1** *the keenness of the blade* sharpness, razor-sharpness. **2** *the keenness of her sense of smell* sharpness, acuteness, perceptiveness, sensitivity. **3** *the keenness of his mind* sharpness, astuteness, quick-wittedness, sharp-wittedness, perspicacity, shrewdness, cleverness, intelligence. **4** *the keenness of her wit* acerbity, acidity, causticity, tartness. **5** *the keenness of the students* willingness, eagerness, enthusiasm, avidity, zeal, fervor, devotion, impatience.

keep verb **1** *keep going* carry on, continue, maintain, persist, persevere. **2** *he keeps*

the ring that she gave him retain, hold on
to, keep hold of; preserve, conserve; *inf.*
hang on to. **3** *he keeps all his old newspapers*
save, accumulate, store, hoard, collect. **4**
the druggist keeps (a supply of) insulin sell,
stock, have in stock, carry. **5** *he is responsible
for keeping the estate* look after, tend, mind,
maintain, manage, superintend. **6** *the boy
keeps the sheep | keep him from harm* tend,
care for, look after, mind, guard, safeguard,
protect, watch over, shield, shelter, preserve, protect. **7** *he could not keep a family on
his salary* provide for, support, maintain,
sustain, subsidize, feed, nurture. **8** *keep
it from her* hide, conceal, withhold, hush,
suppress. **9** *keep one's promise* abide by, fulfill, carry out, effectuate, stand by, honor,
obey, observe. **10** *keep the Sabbath* observe,
hold, celebrate, commemorate, respect,
ritualize, solemnize, ceremonialize. **11**
what kept you? delay, detain, hold back,
hold up, retard, hinder, obstruct, impede,
hamper, prevent. **12** *keep myself from falling*
prevent, stop, restrain, check, halt. **keep
at** *the teacher keeps at us to work* badger, nag,
harass. **keep at it** *we'll finish in time if we keep
at it* persist, persevere, carry on, continue.
keep off 1 *keep off his property* stay away
from, stay off, remain at a distance from,
not approach, not trespass on. **2** *keep off the
subject* avoid, steer clear of, not mention,
evade, dodge, shun, eschew. **3** *keep off cigarettes* refrain from, abstain from, give up,
quit. **4** *the rain kept off* stay away, not start,
not begin. **keep on 1** *keep on going* go on,
carry on, continue, persist, persevere. **2**
the boss decided to keep the man on continue to
employ, retain the services of, not dismiss.
keep to 1 *keep to his word* abide by, stand
by, honor. *See* KEEP *verb* 9. **2** *keep to the
subject* not stray from, not wander from, stay
with; *inf.* stick with. **keep up** *keep up the
payments* maintain, continue with, carry on
with. **2** *try to keep up in the race* keep pace,
keep abreast, not lag behind. **keep up with
1** *keep up with the competitors/developments*
keep pace with, keep abreast of, compete
with, vie with, rival; keep informed about,
retain an interest in. **2** *keep up with old
friends* stay in touch with, keep in contact
with, remain in correspondence with.

keep noun **1** *pay for their keep* maintenance, support, board, room and board,
subsistence, sustenance, food, livelihood,
upkeep. **2** *enemies storming the keep* don-
jon, dungeon, tower, stronghold, citadel,
fortress, fort, castle.

keeper noun **1** *prisoners escaping their
keeper* jailer, warden, guard, custodian,
sentry. **2** *a lighthouse keeper* curator, con-
servator, attendant, caretaker, steward,
superintendent, overseer, administrator.
3 *his brother's keeper* guardian, escort,
bodyguard, chaperon, nursemaid, nurse.

keeping noun **1** *children/property in the
keeping of the grandfather* guardianship,
protection, trusteeship, trust, safekeeping, care, charge, custody. **2** *behavior in
keeping with their beliefs* agreement, harmony, accordance, accord, concurrence,
conformity, consistency.

keepsake noun memento, souvenir, remembrance, reminder, token of remembrance.

keg noun barrel, cask, vat, tun, butt, drum,
hogshead, firkin.

kernel noun **1** *grown from a kernel* grain,
seed, germ, stone, nut. **2** *the kernel of the
problem* nub, nucleus, core, center, heart,
marrow, pith, substance, essence.

key noun **1** *key in the lock* latchkey, pass-
key, master key, skeleton key. **2** *the key to
the problem* answer, solution, explanation,
clue, cue, pointer, interpretation, clarification, exposition, translation. **3** *musical
key* tone, pitch, tonality.

keystone noun **1** *the keystone of the pillar* cornerstone, central stone, quoin. **2**
the keystone of the theory principle, basis,
foundation, linchpin.

kick verb **1** *kick the ball* boot, punt. **2**
the gun kicked recoil, spring back. **3** *always kicking about something* protest, resist,
oppose, rebel, spurn, object, complain,
grumble; *inf.* gripe, grouse, beef, bitch.
4 *kick the habit* give up, stop, abandon,
quit. **kick around 1** *kick around the poor
people* abuse, mistreat, maltreat. **2** *kick
around ideas* discuss, talk over, debate.
kick off *kick off the proceedings* start, begin,
commence, open, get under way, initiate.
kick out eject, expel, force out, turn out,
oust, evict, dismiss, discharge; *inf.* send
packing, sack, fire.

kick noun **1** *gave the ball a kick* boot, punt.
2 *she steals for kicks* thrill, excitement,
stimulation, fun, pleasure, enjoyment,
amusement, gratification; *inf.* buzz. **3** *the
drink has quite a kick* strength, potency,
tang, zip; *inf.* punch, zing. **4** *there's no
kick left in the campaign* vigor, force, forcefulness, energy, vitality, verve, animation,
enthusiasm, zest, zip.

kid noun child, young one, youngster, toddler, tot, adolescent, juvenile, teenager,
youth.

kid verb **1** *he was only kidding* tease, joke,
jest, fool around. **2** *don't kid yourself*
deceive, delude, fool, trick, cozen, gull,
hoodwink, bamboozle.

kill verb **1** *he killed three people* slay, murder,
do away with, slaughter, butcher, massa-
cre, assassinate, liquidate, take someone's
life, wipe out, destroy, erase, eradicate,
exterminate, eliminate, dispatch, put to
death, execute; *inf.* bump off, do in, knock
off, rub out. **2** *kill all his hopes* destroy,

ruin, extinguish, scotch, quell. **3** *kill time* pass, spend, expend, while away. **4** *the walk will kill you* exhaust, overtire, fatigue, wear out, overtax, strain. **5** *kill the congressional bill* defeat, veto, vote down, reject, overrule.

killing noun **1** *guilty of killing* murder, slaying, manslaughter, homicide, slaughter, butchery, massacre, bloodshed, carnage, liquidation, destruction, extermination, execution. **2** *make a killing on the stock market* bonanza, fortune, windfall, gain, profit, coup.

killing adjective **1** *a killing blow* deadly, fatal, lethal, mortal, death-dealing, murderous, homicidal. **2** *a killing task* exhausting, tiring, fatiguing, debilitating, taxing, punishing.

killjoy noun spoilsport; *inf.* wet blanket, party pooper.

kin noun *no kin living in the area* relatives, relations, family, connections, folks, people, kindred, kinfolk, kinsfolk.

kind adjective kindhearted, generous, charitable, benevolent, magnanimous, bighearted, warmhearted, altruistic, philanthropic, humanitarian, humane, tenderhearted, softhearted, gentle, mild, lenient, merciful, clement, pitying, forbearing, patient, tolerant, sympathetic, compassionate, understanding, considerate, helpful, thoughtful, good, nice, decent, pleasant, benign, friendly, genial, congenial, amiable, amicable, cordial, courteous, gracious, good-natured, warm, affectionate, loving, indulgent, obliging, accommodating, neighborly.

kind noun **1** *different kinds of creatures* sort, type, variety, brand, class, category; genus, species, family, strain. **2** *a difference in kind rather than degree* nature, character, manner, aspect, disposition, style, stamp, mold.

kindle verb **1** *kindle a fire* light, set fire to, ignite, start, torch. **2** *kindle interest* stimulate, rouse, arouse, excite, stir, awaken, inspire, inflame, touch off.

kindly adjective kindhearted, warmhearted. *See* KIND adjective.

kindness noun **1** *the kindness of the people* kindheartedness, generosity, charitableness, charity, goodwill, benevolence, magnanimity, hospitality, philanthropy, warmheartedness, altruism, humanitarianism, humaneness, tender-heartedness, gentleness, mildness, leniency, clemency, patience, tolerance, sympathy, compassion, understanding, consideration, helpfulness, thoughtfulness, goodness, niceness, decency, pleasantness, friendliness, geniality, congeniality, amiability, cordiality, graciousness, warmth, affection, loving-ness, love, indulgence, neighborliness. **2** *do the neighbors a kindness* kind act, good deed, good turn, favor, help, service, aid.

kindred adjective **1** *kindred members of the wedding party* related, connected, of the same blood, consanguineous. **2** *kindred spirits* like, similar, corresponding, matching, congenial, allied.

king noun **1** *king of Sweden* monarch, sovereign, ruler, crowned head, majesty, royal personage, emperor, sultan, overlord, prince. **2** *king of jazz* luminary, star, superstar, kingpin.

kingdom noun **1** *the ruler's kingdom* realm, empire, domain, country, land, nation, state, province, territory; monarchy, sovereignty. **2** *the plant kingdom* division, grouping, group, classification, class, category, family, genus, kind.

kink noun **1** *a kink in the rope* twist, bend, coil, corkscrew, knot, tangle, entanglement. **2** *a kink in one's hair* curl, wave, crimp, frizz, crinkle. **3** *a kink in the neck* crick, spasm, twinge. **4** *a few kinks in the plan* flaw, defect, imperfection, hitch, snag, difficulty, complication. **5** *a person full of kinks* quirk, whim, whimsy, caprice, vagary, eccentricity, foible, idiosyncrasy.

kinky adjective **1** *a kinky rope* twisted, bent, coiled, curled. **2** *kinky hair* curly, crimped, frizzy. **3** *kinky ideas* quirky, peculiar, odd, strange, queer, bizarre, eccentric, idiosyncratic, weird, outlandish, unconventional, unorthodox, whimsical, capricious, fanciful. **4** *kinky sexual behavior* deviant, abnormal, degenerate, perverted, warped, lascivious, licentious.

kinship noun **1** *kinship was thought more of than friendship* blood relationship, blood ties, family ties, consanguinity, common ancestry, common lineage, kindred. **2** *kinship between their interests* affinity, similarity, likeness, correspondence, concordance, alliance, association.

kismet noun destiny, fate, fortune, providence, portion, lot, predestination, preordination, predetermination.

kit noun **1** *bicycle repair kit* equipment, apparatus, tools, implements, instruments, utensils, gear, tackle, supplies, paraphernalia, accoutrements, effects, stuff, trappings, appurtenances; *inf.* things. **2** *build furniture from a kit* set of parts, set of components; do-it-yourself kit.

knack noun talent, aptitude, gift, flair, bent, forte, ability, capacity, expertise, skill, genius, facility, propensity, adroitness, readiness, quickness, ingenuity, proficiency, handiness.

knave noun scoundrel, blackguard, villain, rogue, reprobate, miscreant, rascal, cur, louse.

knickknack noun trifle, trinket, bauble, gewgaw, gimcrack, bagatelle, bibelot, piece of bric-à-brac.

knife noun blade, cutting tool, dagger, dirk; machete, sword; stiletto, scalpel; Swiss Army (*trademark*) knife; cleaver, paring knife, table knife, steak knife, penknife, pocket knife, bowie knife, jackknife, switchblade.

knife verb stab, pierce, run through, impale, bayonet, cut, slash, lacerate.

knight noun horseman, equestrian, cavalryman, gallant, protector, knight errant, Sir Lancelot, Sir Galahad; dragon slayer.

knit verb 1 *knit wool into a sweater* loop, weave, interweave, crochet. 2 *knit one's brows* wrinkle, crease, furrow, gather, draw in, contract. 3 *the tragedy knitted the community together* join, link, bind, unite, draw (together), ally. 4 *the wound is knitting* heal, mend, become whole, draw together.

knob noun 1 *the knob on the door/machine* doorknob, handle, switch. 2 *iron knobs on the saddle* stud, boss, protuberance, knop.

knock verb 1 *knock on the door* tap, rap, bang, pound, hammer. 2 *knock his head on the low doorframe* strike, hit, slap, smack, box, punch, cuff, buffet, thump, thwack, batter, pummel; *inf.* clip, wallop. 3 *knock the play* criticize, run down, shoot down, carp at, cavil at, deprecate, belittle, disparage, censure, condemn; *inf.* slam, lambaste, pan. **knock about/around** 1 *fighters knocking each other around* strike, hit, beat, beat up, batter, maul, punch, abuse, manhandle, hurt, injure, bruise, wound, damage. 2 *knock about the countryside* travel, wander, roam, ramble, rove, range, saunter, stroll, gallivant, traipse through/about, gad about. **knock down** 1 *knock down the buildings* demolish, pull down, level, raze. 2 *knock down the trees* fell, cut down, hew. **knock off** 1 *they knock off at 5 o'clock* stop work, finish working, close shop, shut down; *inf.* call it a day. 2 *knock off his rival* kill, slay, murder, assassinate, eliminate, do away with, dispose of; *inf.* do in, bump off, rub out. **knock out** 1 *knock him out with the blow* render unconscious, floor, prostrate; *inf.* KO. 2 *knock out his opponent in the first round* eliminate, defeat, beat, vanquish, overthrow. 3 *the storm knocked out the electrical supply* destroy, damage, make inoperative, put out of order. 4 *knocked out by her performance* overwhelm, dazzle, amaze, astound, impress; *inf.* bowl over. **knock up** make pregnant, impregnate, inseminate.

knock noun 1 *a knock at the door* tap, rap, rat-tat, bang. 2 *a knock on the head* slap, smack, blow, punch, cuff, buffet, thump; *inf.* clip, clout, wallop. 3 *the knocks of the reviewers* criticism, strictures, faultfinding, carping, caviling, deprecation, disparagement, censure, condemnation.

knot noun 1 *a knot in the string/tie* loop, twist, bend, ligature, joint. 2 *a knot in the wood* lump, knob, node, nodule, protuberance, knurl, gnarl. 3 *a knot of people/trees* group, cluster, bunch, clump, band, circle, ring, gathering.

knot verb tie, loop, bind, secure, tether, lash.

knotty adjective 1 *a knotty problem* difficult, complicated, intricate, complex, Byzantine, thorny, perplexing, baffling, mystifying, obscure, unfathomable. 2 *a knotty piece of wood* knotted, gnarled, knurled, lumpy, bumpy, nodular, rough, coarse.

know verb 1 *know what they are saying* notice, perceive, realize, be aware of, sense, recognize. 2 *know the rules* understand, comprehend, apprehend, be familiar with. 3 *know tragedy* experience, undergo, go through, be acquainted with. 4 *get to know one's neighbors* be acquainted with, associate with, be friends with, socialize with, fraternize with. 5 *know one brand from another* distinguish, differentiate, tell, identify, discern.

know-how noun knowledge, *savoir faire*, expertise, skill, skillfulness, proficiency, adeptness, aptitude, ability, capability, competence.

knowing adjective 1 *give a knowing look* astute, shrewd, perceptive, meaningful, significant, eloquent, expressive. 2 *a knowing child* aware, astute, shrewd, perceptive, sophisticated, worldly-wise. 3 *a knowing infringement of rules* conscious, intentional, intended, deliberate, willful, purposeful, calculated, on purpose, by design.

knowledge noun 1 *be taught by people of knowledge* learning, erudition, scholarship, letters, education, enlightenment, wisdom. 2 *his knowledge of the subject* understanding, grasp, comprehension, apprehension, cognition, expertise, proficiency, know-how. 3 *his knowledge of the area* acquaintanceship, familiarity, conversance. 4 *where do you acquire the knowledge?* information, facts, intelligence, data; news, reports, rumors.

knowledgeable adjective *knowledgeable people* well-informed, informed, educated, learned, erudite, scholarly, well-read, cultivated, enlightened.

known adjective recognized, acknowledged, admitted, declared, avowed, confessed, published, revealed.

kudos noun prestige, glory, acclaim, acclamation, praise, tribute, honor.

Ll

label noun **1** *put a label on the luggage* identification tag, ID tag, tag, sticker, marker. **2** *his friends gave him the label "Lefty"* epithet, name, nickname, title, sobriquet, designation, characterization; *inf.* moniker. **3** *goods sold under a famous label* brand, brand name, trade name, trademark, proprietary name, logo.

label verb **1** *label the specimens* tag, ticket, stamp, mark, put stickers on. **2** *label him a liar* describe, designate, identify, classify, categorize, brand, call, name, term, dub.

labor noun **1** *paid well for his labor* work, toil, exertion, effort, industry, industriousness, travail, drudgery. **2** *the labors of Hercules* task, job, chore, undertaking, commission, assignment, charge, venture. **3** *a lack of available labor* employees, workers, workforce, hands. **4** *in labor* childbirth, parturition, delivery, contractions, labor pains.

labor verb **1** *labor for little reward* toil, drudge, sweat, struggle, strive, work, endeavor, exert oneself, travail; *inf.* plug away. **2** *labor the point* belabor, overemphasize, overdo, strain, dwell on. **labor under** *laboring under a delusion* suffer from, be a victim of, be burdened by, be disadvantaged by.

labored adjective **1** *labored breathing* difficult, strained, forced, heavy, awkward. **2** *a labored style of writing* contrived, affected, studied, stiff, strained, stilted, forced, unnatural, artificial, overdone, overworked, heavy, ponderous, ornate, elaborate, convoluted, complex, laborious.

laborer noun worker, workman, hand, manual worker, unskilled worker, blue-collar worker, drudge, menial.

laborious adjective **1** *a laborious task* hard, heavy, difficult, arduous, strenuous, fatiguing, tiring, wearying, wearisome, tedious. **2** *the laborious style of the writer* strained, forced. *See* LABORED 2.

labyrinth noun maze, warren, network, convolution, entanglement; jungle, snarl, puzzle, riddle, enigma.

lace verb **1** *lace the shoes* fasten, secure, close, bind, tie, thread, string. **2** *lace the coffee with brandy* mix, blend, flavor, fortify, strengthen, stiffen; *inf.* spike.

lacerate verb tear, gash, slash, cut, mangle, hurt, wound, injure.

lack noun absence, want, need, deprivation, deficiency, privation, dearth, insufficiency, shortage, scarcity, paucity.

lack verb have need of, need, require, want, be short of, be deficient in, miss.

lackadaisical adjective indifferent, halfhearted, lukewarm, apathetic, listless, languid, lethargic, limp, sluggish, spiritless, unanimated, uninterested, unenthusiastic, idle, lazy.

lackey noun toady, sycophant, flatterer, flunky, minion, stooge, hanger-on, parasite, tool, puppet, instrument, pawn, creature; *inf.* yes-man.

lackluster adjective **1** *lackluster prose* bland, insipid, vapid, dull, flat, dry, prosaic, run-of-the-mill, commonplace, unimaginative, uninspired, boring, tedious, wearisome. **2** *lackluster people* dull, uninteresting, spiritless, unanimated, dull-witted.

laconic adjective **1** *a laconic reply* brief, concise, terse, succinct, short, economical, pithy, to the point, incisive. **2** *a laconic person* of few words, reticent, reserved, taciturn, quiet.

lad noun boy, youth, juvenile, youngster, stripling, young man; *inf.* kid.

lady noun **1** *give that lady your seat* woman, female. **2** *the lady and her servants* noblewoman, gentlewoman, duchess, countess, peeress, viscountess, baroness.

ladylike adjective genteel, refined, well-bred, cultivated, polished, decorous, proper, correct, respectable, well-mannered, courteous, polite, civil, gracious.

lag verb **1** *stop lagging and keep up* loiter, linger, dally, straggle, dawdle, hang back, delay, drag one's feet; *inf.* dilly-dally. **2** *their efforts were lagging* flag, wane, ebb, fall off, diminish, decrease, ease up, let up, slacken, abate, fail, falter.

laggard noun loiterer, lingerer, dawdler, straggler, sluggard, snail, slowpoke, loafer, lounger; *inf.* lazybones.

laid-back adjective relaxed, at ease, easy, leisurely, unhurried, casual, easygoing, informal, nonchalant, unexcitable, imperturbable; *inf.* unflappable.

lair noun **1** *the animal's lair* den, hole, covert, burrow, nest, tunnel, dugout, hollow, cave, haunt. **2** *retreat to his lair* retreat, hideaway, refuge, sanctuary, sanctum, sanctum sanctorum, study, den; *inf.* hide-out.

laissez-faire noun free enterprise, private enterprise, individualism, free trade, nonintervention, noninterference.

lambaste verb scold, reprimand, rebuke, chide, reprove, admonish, berate, upbraid, rail at, rant at; *inf.* lace into.

lame adjective 1 *a lame leg* limping, hobbling, halting, crippled, game, disabled, incapacitated, defective. 2 *a lame excuse* weak, feeble, thin, flimsy, unconvincing, unsatisfactory, inadequate, insufficient, deficient, defective, ineffectual.

lament verb 1 *widows lamenting* mourn, grieve, sorrow, wail, moan, groan, weep, cry, sob, complain, keen, ululate, howl, beat one's breast. 2 *lamenting the lack of sports facilities* bemoan, bewail, deplore, complain about.

lament noun 1 *the laments of the bereaved* wail, wailing, lamentation, moan, moaning, groan, weeping, crying, sob, sobbing, complaint, keening, ululation, howl. 2 *recite a lament* dirge, requiem, elegy, threnody.

lamentable adjective 1 *a lamentable state of affairs* deplorable, regrettable, tragic, terrible, wretched, woeful, sorrowful, distressing, grievous. 2 *a lamentable salary* miserable, pitiful, poor, meager, low, unsatisfactory, inadequate; *inf.* measly.

lampoon noun satire, burlesque, travesty, parody, caricature, pasquinade, takeoff; *inf.* send-up.

lampoon verb satirize, parody, caricature, ridicule, mock, make fun of, burlesque, pasquinade, do a takeoff of; *inf.* send up.

land noun 1 *glad to be back on land* ground, solid ground, earth, terra firma. 2 *the land is fertile there* soil, earth, loam, dirt. 3 *houses with plenty of land around them* grounds, fields, open space, open area, expanse, stretch, tract, property, acres, real estate, realty. 4 *born in a far land* country, nation, fatherland, motherland, state, realm, province, territory, district, region, area, domain.

land verb 1 *the plane landed* touch down, alight, make a landing. 2 *we landed at Boston* berth, dock, reach the shore, go ashore, disembark, debark. 3 *how did we land here?* arrive, get, reach, find oneself, end up, turn up; *inf.* wind up. 4 *land a good job* get, acquire, obtain, procure, secure, gain.

landlady, landlord noun owner, proprietor, lessor, householder; innkeeper, hotelkeeper, hotelier, host.

landmark noun 1 *one of the landmarks of the town* feature, monument, distinctive feature, prominent feature. 2 *a landmark in the town's history* milestone, watershed, turning point, critical point, historic

event. 3 *landmarks indicating the distance* milepost, milestone, guidepost, marker.

lane noun 1 *travel through the lanes* narrow road, narrow way, passageway, passage, alley, path, pathway, footpath, track. 2 *traffic lanes* track, course, road division.

language noun 1 *children acquiring language* speech, speaking, talking, words, vocabulary, utterance, verbal expression, verbalization, vocalization, communication, conversation, discourse. 2 *the French language* tongue, speech, parlance, native tongue; *inf.* lingo. 3 *various forms of language throughout the country* speech, dialect, vernacular, patois, lingua franca, colloquialism, slang, idiom, jargon, patter, cant; *inf.* lingo. 4 *admire the language of the speaker/writer* vocabulary, terminology, wording, phrasing, phraseology, style, diction, expression, rhetoric.

languid adjective 1 *languid people* languishing, listless, lackadaisical, spiritless, vigorless, lethargic, torpid, idle, inactive, indolent, lazy, sluggish, slow-moving, indifferent. 2 *feeling languid after her illness* weak, sickly, faint, feeble, frail, limp, flagging, drooping, fatigued. 3 *a languid response* apathetic, lukewarm, halfhearted, unenthusiastic.

languish verb 1 *she languished after the tragedy* droop, flag, wilt, wither, fade, fail, weaken, decline, waste away. 2 *people languishing in institutions* waste away, decay, wither away, be abandoned, be neglected. **languish for** *languish for her lover* pine for, yearn for, long for, sigh for, hunger for, desire, want, grieve for, mourn for.

languor noun 1 *feeling full of languor* listlessness, lethargy, torpor, idleness, indolence, laziness, sluggishness, sleepiness, drowsiness, somnolence. 2 *disturb the languor of the atmosphere* stillness, tranquillity, calm, calmness, lull, silence.

lank adjective 1 *lank hair* lifeless, lusterless, limp, straggling, straight. 2 *lank youths* tall, thin, lean, lanky, skinny, spindly, gangling, gangly, angular, bony, rawboned, gawky, rangy.

lap noun 1 *three laps of the stadium* circuit, circle, loop, orbit, round, compass, ambit. 2 *the last lap of the journey* section, stage, leg.

lap verb 1 *water lapping against the shore* wash, splash, swish, slap, slosh. 2 *cats lapping milk* drink, lick up, sip.

lapse noun 1 *forgive his occasional lapse* slip, error, mistake, blunder, fault, omission, oversight; *inf.* slipup. 2 *after a lapse of time* interval, gap, pause, intermission, interlude, lull, hiatus, break, passage. 3 *a lapse in standards* decline, downturn, fall, drop, deterioration, worsening, degeneration, backsliding. 4 *the lapse of her* *season ticket* expiry, expiration, invalidity, termination. **5** *lapse of faith* abandonment, forsaking, relinquishment, defection, renunciation, repudiation, rejection, disavowal, denial, abjuration, apostasy.

lapse verb **1** *standards have lapsed* decline, fall, fall off, drop, deteriorate, worsen, degenerate; *inf.* go downhill. **2** *our friendship lapsed when we left school* cease, end, stop, terminate. **3** *the season ticket has lapsed* become void, become invalid, expire, run out, terminate. **4** *lapse into sleep* slide, slip, drift, sink, subside, submerge. **5** *time has lapsed* elapse, pass, go by, glide by, run its course.

larceny noun theft, grand larceny, petty larceny, stealing, robbery, pilfering, purloining, burglary, misappropriation.

large adjective **1** *large buildings* big, great, sizable, substantial, goodly, tall, high, huge, immense, enormous, colossal, massive, mammoth, vast, prodigious, gigantic, giant, monumental, stupendous, gargantuan, considerable; *inf.* jumbo, whopping. **2** *a large man* big, burly, heavy, bulky, thickset, powerfully built, heavyset, chunky, strapping, hulking, hefty, ample, fat, obese, corpulent. **3** *a large supply* abundant, copious, plentiful, ample, liberal, generous. **at large 1** *wild animals at large* at liberty, free, unconfined, unrestrained, roaming, on the loose, on the run, fugitive. **2** *society at large* as a whole, as a body, generally, in general, in the main. **by and large** on the whole, generally, in general, all things considered, for the most part, in the main, as a rule.

largely adverb *he is largely to blame* to a large extent, to a great degree, chiefly, for the most part, mostly, mainly, in the main, principally, in great measure.

large-scale adjective extensive, widereaching, wide-ranging, sweeping, wholesale, global.

largesse noun **1** *known for her largesse* generosity, kindness, liberality, openhandedness, munificence, bounty, bountifulness, beneficence, charity, philanthropy. **2** *distributing largesse* gifts, presents, contributions, donations, handouts, endowments, grants, aid, alms.

lark noun prank, horseplay, trick, fooling, antic, mischief, escapade, fun, cavorting, caper, play, game, romp, frolic, sport, rollicking, gambol.

lascivious adjective **1** *lascivious men* lewd, lecherous, lustful, licentious, promiscuous, libidinous, prurient, salacious, lubricious, concupiscent, debauched, depraved, degenerate, dissolute, dissipated. **2** *lascivious magazines* lewd, blue, obscene, pornographic, smutty, bawdy, risqué, suggestive, dirty, salacious; *inf.* raunchy.

lash noun **1** *a lash to beat the horses* whip, horsewhip, bullwhip, scourge, flagellum, cat-o'-nine-tails. **2** *six lashes with a whip* stroke, stripe, blow, hit, strike, thwack, thump; *inf.* swipe, wallop, whack.

lash verb **1** *the driver lashed the horses* whip, horsewhip, scourge, birch, switch, flog, flail, flagellate, thrash, beat, strike; *inf.* wallop, whack. **2** *waves lashing the ship* buffet, pound, batter, strike. **3** *lions lashing their tails* flick, wag, wave, whip, switch. **4** *lash the boat to the side of the ship* fasten, bind, tie, tether, hitch, attach, join, rope, strap, leash, make fast, secure. **lash out at** *lash out at his critics* speak out against, shout at, lose one's temper at, attack verbally, denounce, harangue, rant at, fulminate against, criticize, condemn, censure; *inf.* lace into.

lass noun girl, young woman, young lady, schoolgirl, maid, maiden, miss; *inf.* lassie.

last adjective **1** *the last runner arrived* hindmost, rearmost, final, aftermost. **2** *his last words* final, closing, concluding, ending, finishing, terminating, ultimate, terminal. **3** *the last thing she would want* least likely, most unlikely, least suitable, least wanted, least favorite. **4** *last Thursday* latest, most recent.

last adverb *come last* at the end, at/in the rear, behind, after.

last verb **1** *how long will the symptoms last?* continue, go on, carry on, remain, persist, keep on. **2** *how long will the climbers last in the snow?* survive, exist, live, subsist, hold on, hold out. **3** *those shoes won't last* last long, wear well, stand up to wear, keep, endure.

last-ditch adjective *a last-ditch attempt* desperate, frantic, frenzied, wild, struggling, final, last-chance, last-minute, last-gasp, all-out.

lasting adjective enduring, long-lived, lifelong, abiding, continuing, long-term, persisting, permanent, deep-rooted, durable, constant, eternal, undying, everlasting, perennial, perpetual, unending, never-ending, immortal, ceaseless, unceasing, interminable, imperishable, indestructible.

lastly adverb finally, in conclusion, to conclude, to sum up.

latch noun catch, fastening, hasp, hook, bar, bolt, lock.

latch verb fasten, secure, make fast, bar, bolt, lock.

late adjective **1** *she's always late* tardy, overdue, delayed, behind schedule, behind, not on time, dilatory, slow. **2** *her late husband* deceased, dead, departed. **3** *some* *late news* recent, fresh, new, last-minute, up-to-date, up-to-the-minute.

late adverb **1** *he arrived late* belatedly, tardily, behind time, at the last minute, dilatorily. **2** *we worked late yesterday* past the usual finishing/stopping/closing time, after hours.

lately adverb of late, recently, in the past few days, in recent times.

latent adjective dormant, quiescent, inactive, passive, hidden, unrevealed, concealed, imperceptible, invisible, covert, undeveloped, unrealized, potential.

later adjective *the later bus* subsequent, next, following, succeeding, successive, sequential.

later adverb **1** *I'll come later* later on, at a future time/date, at some point in the future, in time to come. **2** *he arrived first, and she came later* later on, after, afterward, subsequently, by and by, in a while, after a bit.

lateral adjective sidewise, sideways, sidelong, sideward, edgewise, edgeways, indirect, oblique, slanting, askance.

lather noun **1** *soap producing lather* suds, soapsuds, foam, froth, bubbles. **2** *horses covered in lather* sweat, perspiration.

latitude noun **1** *on the same latitude as Moscow* parallel, meridian, grid line. **2** *give his staff latitude in decision-making* scope, freedom of action, freedom, liberty, free play, carte blanche, leeway, elbowroom, license, indulgence, laxity.

latter adjective **1** *the latter is the better* second, second-mentioned, last-mentioned, second of the two. **2** *the latter part of the year* later, hindmost, closing, end, concluding, final. **3** *the technology of latter times* recent, latest, modern.

laudable adjective praiseworthy, commendable, admirable, meritorious, deserving, creditable, worthy, estimable, exemplary.

laudatory adjective acclamatory, commendatory, praising, extolling, admiring, approving, approbatory, complimentary, adulatory, celebratory, eulogizing, eulogistic, panegyric, panegyrical, encomiastical.

laugh verb chuckle, chortle, guffaw, giggle, titter, snigger, ha-ha, tee-hee, burst out laughing, split one's sides, be rolling in the aisles; *inf.* be in stitches, crack up. **laugh at 1** *laugh at the fortune-tellers* mock, ridicule, deride, scoff at, jeer at, sneer at, make fun of, poke fun at, lampoon, satirize, taunt, tease; *inf.* send up. **2** *laugh at danger* laugh off, belittle, make light of, discount, ignore, dismiss, disregard, shrug off, brush aside, scoff at, pooh-pooh.

laugh noun chuckle, chortle, guffaw, giggle, titter, snigger, roar/hoot of laughter, peal of laughter, belly laugh.

laughable adjective **1** *a laughable business proposition* ludicrous, ridiculous, absurd, risible, preposterous, outrageous. **2** *children finding the entertainment laughable* amusing, funny, humorous, hilarious, comical, comic, entertaining, diverting, droll, mirthful, sidesplitting.

laughter noun laughing, chuckling, chortling, guffawing, giggling, tittering, sniggering.

launch verb **1** *launch the ship* set afloat, float. **2** *launch a missile* fire, discharge, propel, project, send forth, throw, cast, hurl, let fly. **3** *launch a project* initiate, instigate, set in motion, begin, start, commence, embark upon, institute, inaugurate, establish, introduce, usher in.

laurels plural noun honors, awards, trophies, prizes, rewards, tributes, praises, acclaim, acclamation, commendation, credit, glory, honor, distinction, fame, renown, prestige, recognition; *inf.* kudos.

lavish adjective **1** *a lavish supply* copious, abundant, superabundant, plentiful, profuse. **2** *lavish in her catering* extravagant, excessive, immoderate, profligate, unrestrained. **3** *a lavish hostess* generous, liberal, bountiful, openhanded, unstinting, free, munificent, overgenerous, extravagant. **4** *a lavish display of flowers* luxuriant, lush, gorgeous, sumptuous, costly, opulent, pretentious, showy.

law noun **1** *the law of the land* legal code, system of laws, body of laws, constitution, charter, rules and regulations, jurisprudence. **2** *the legislature issuing laws* statute, rule, regulation, enactment, act, decree, edict, ordinance, directive. **3** *moral laws* rule, principle, precept, standard, criterion, formula, tenet, doctrine, canon. **4** *law of nature* generalization, general truth, axiom, maxim, truism. **5** *a career in law* the legal profession, the bar. **6** *the law has arrived* police, authorities, officers of the law; *inf.* fuzz, cops.

lawful adjective **1** *lawful actions* legal, legitimate, licit, just, valid, permissible, allowable, rightful, proper, constitutional, sanctioned, authorized, warranted, approved, recognized. **2** *a lawful person* law-abiding, righteous, honorable, orderly, honest, upright, upstanding, peaceable, dutiful.

lawless adjective **1** *a lawless country* without law and order, anarchic, disorderly, ungoverned, unruly, insurrectionary, insurgent, revolutionary, rebellious, insubordinate, riotous, mutinous, seditious, terrorist. **2** *lawless actions* unlawful, illegal, illicit, criminal, felonious, miscreant.

lawsuit noun legal action, legal proceedings, suit, case, proceedings, litigation, trial.

lawyer noun attorney, legal adviser, counsel, criminal lawyer, civil lawyer, advocate, solicitor, legal practitioner.

lax adjective **1** *lax about discipline in the school* slack, slipshod, negligent, neglectful, remiss, careless, heedless, unmindful, inattentive, casual, easygoing, lenient, permissive, indulgent, overindulgent, complaisant. **2** *a lax description* loose, inexact, inaccurate, imprecise, unrigorous, vague, indefinite, nonspecific, broad, general.

lay verb **1** *lay the groceries on the table* put, place, set, deposit, plant, settle, posit. **2** *lay the carpet* position, set out, arrange, dispose. **3** *lay a case before a judge* put forward, bring forward, advance, submit, present, offer, lodge. **4** *lay the blame* attribute, assign, ascribe, allocate, allot, impute. **5** *lay money on it* wager, bet, gamble, stake, give odds, hazard, risk, chance. **6** *lay plans* devise, arrange, contrive, make, prepare, work out, hatch, concoct, design, plan, plot. **7** *lay the burden on him* impose, inflict, encumber, saddle, tax, charge, burden, apply. **8** *lay eggs* deposit, produce, bear, oviposit. **lay bare** *lay bare one's secret thoughts* reveal, make known, disclose, divulge, show, expose, exhibit, uncover, unveil, unmask. **lay down 1** *lay down their weapons* surrender, relinquish, give up, yield, cede, turn over. **2** *lay down the law* set down, stipulate, formulate, prescribe, order, command, ordain, postulate, demand, proclaim, assert, maintain. **lay (one's) hands on 1** *if I ever lay (my) hands on the thief* get (a) hold of, catch, seize, grab, snatch, grasp. **2** *I just can't lay (my) hands on that book* find, locate, unearth, bring to light, discover, acquire, turn up. **3** *priests laying hands on members of the congregation* bless, consecrate, confirm, ordain. **lay in** *lay in a supply of logs* stockpile, store, accumulate, amass, hoard, collect. **lay into 1** *lay into their attackers* set upon, assail, attack, strike out at. **2** *lay into the child for being late* scold, rebuke, chide, berate, upbraid, reproach, reprove, castigate, criticize, censure, condemn, rant at, rave at, harangue; *inf.* lace into, lambaste. **lay it on** *he's laying it on to charm his mother-in-law* exaggerate, overdo it, flatter, soft-soap; *inf.* pile it on, lay it on thick, sweet-talk. **lay off 1** *lay off half of the workforce* let go, dismiss, discharge; *inf.* sack, fire. **2** *lay off alcohol* quit, stop, cease, desist from, refrain from, give up. **lay out 1** *lay out the plans* spread out, set out, arrange, display, exhibit. **2** *lay out a garden* set out, arrange, plan, design. **3** *lay out refreshments* provide, supply, furnish, give. **4** *lay out a lot of money* spend,

expend, pay, disburse, contribute, give, invest; *inf.* shell out, fork out.

lay adjective **1** *a lay preacher* laic, laical, secular, nonclerical, nonordained. **2** *a lay member of the club* nonprofessional, amateur, nonspecialist, dilettante.

layoff noun *many layoffs at the factory* dismissal, discharge; *inf.* sacking, firing.

layout noun **1** *the layout of the house* arrangement, geography, plan. **2** *the magazine's layout* arrangement, design, format, formation.

lazy adjective idle, indolent, slothful, sluggish, lethargic, languorous, listless, torpid, slow-moving, remiss, negligent, lax.

lead verb **1** *lead him to the right spot* guide, conduct, show the way, usher, escort, steer, pilot. **2** *the evidence led her to believe he was guilty* cause, induce, prompt, move, incline, dispose, predispose, persuade, sway, influence, prevail on. **3** *lead the procession* head, be at the head of, be at the front of. **4** *lead the discussion* command, direct, govern, rule, manage, be in charge of, regulate, preside over, head, supervise, superintend, oversee; *inf.* head up. **5** *leading the field* be in the lead, be in front (of), be ahead (of), be first, come first, precede, outdistance, outrun, outstrip, leave behind, outdo, excel, exceed, surpass, outrival, outshine, eclipse, transcend. **6** *lead a happy life* live, pass, spend, experience, undergo. **lead off** begin, start, start off, commence, open; *inf.* kick off. **lead on** *they are just leading her on* deceive, mislead, delude, hoodwink, dupe, trick, beguile, tempt, entice, lure, tantalize, inveigle, seduce; *inf.* string along. **lead the way 1** *he led the way to the spot* guide one, conduct one, show (one) the way. **2** *the scientist led the way in space development* break ground, blaze a trail, lay the foundation, lay the first stone, initiate things, take the first step. **lead to** *his action led to disaster* cause, result in, bring on, call forth, provoke, contribute to.

lead noun **1** *the runner in the lead* first place, advance position, van, vanguard. **2** *take the lead in the market* first position, head place, forefront, primacy, preeminence, supremacy, advantage, edge, precedence. **3** *a lead of half a lap* margin, gap, interval. **4** *she's the lead in the new play* star, principal character, leading role, star/starring role, title role, principal part, leading man, leading lady, hero, heroine. **5** *a dog's lead* leash, tether, rein, cord, rope, chain. **6** *we have no leads in the investigation* clue, pointer, hint, tip, suggestion, indication, tip-off.

leader noun **1** *the leader of the country/committee* ruler, head, chief, commander, director, governor, principal, captain, skipper, manager, superintendent, supervisor, overseer, foreman, kingpin; *inf.* boss, head honcho. **2** *a leader of fashion* pacesetter, trendsetter, front runner. **3** *a leader in the field of genetics* innovator, pioneer, trailblazer, pathfinder, groundbreaker, originator, front runner.

leadership noun rule, command, directorship, direction, governorship, administration, captaincy, management, supervision, control, guidance, authority, superintendency, initiative, influence.

leading adjective **1** *play the leading role* chief, main, principal, foremost, supreme, paramount, dominant, superior, ruling, directing, guiding, controlling; *inf.* number-one. **2** *one of the leading writers* foremost, greatest, best, outstanding, pre-eminent, supreme, principal, top-rank, top-ranking, first-rate. **3** *the leading runner* front, first, in first place.

leaf noun **1** *a leaf from the tree* frond, flag, needle, pine needle, pad, lily pad; *Tech* cotyledon. **2** *a leaf missing from the book* page, sheet, folio, flyleaf. **turn over a new leaf** reform, mend/change one's ways, make a fresh start, start with a clean slate.

leaflet noun pamphlet, flyer, booklet, brochure, handbill, circular.

league noun **1** *a league of nations* alliance, confederation, confederacy, federation, union, association, coalition, combine, consortium, affiliation, guild, corporation, conglomerate, cooperative, partnership, fellowship, syndicate. **2** *a football league* group, band, association. **3** *he is not in the same league as his brother* level, class, category. **in league** in alliance, allied, cooperating, collaborating, linked, hand in glove, in collusion; *inf.* in cahoots.

leak noun **1** *a leak in the bucket* hole, opening, crack, crevice, chink, fissure, puncture, cut, gash, slit, rent, break, rift. **2** *a water/gas leak* drip, leakage, escape, seepage, oozing, discharge. **3** *a leak of secret information* disclosure, divulgence, revelation.

leak verb **1** *water/gas leaking* escape, drip, seep out/through, ooze out, exude, discharge, issue, gush out. **2** *leak information* disclose, divulge, reveal, tell, impart, pass on, relate, give away, let slip; *inf.* spill the beans about.

lean verb **1** *his wife leaning on his arm* rest, be supported, be propped up, recline, repose. **2** *the pole is leaning* incline, bend, slant, tilt, be at an angle, slope, bank, list, heel, careen. **lean on** *they lean on each other* depend on, be dependent on, rely on, count on, have faith in, trust. **lean toward** *she leans toward anarchy* incline toward, tend toward, have a tendency toward, have a propensity for, have

a proclivity for, gravitate toward, have an affinity with.

lean adjective **1** *lean people* thin, slender, slim, spare, lank, skinny, scrawny, bony, rawboned, rangy, gangling. **2** *lean meat* nonfat, low-fat. **3** *a lean harvest* meager, scanty, sparse, poor, inadequate, insufficient. **4** *lean years for art* unproductive, unfruitful, arid, barren, bare, nonfertile.

leap verb **1** *children leaping around* jump, bound, bounce, hop, skip, romp, caper, spring, frolic, frisk, cavort, gambol, dance. **2** *leap to one's feet* jump, jump up, spring. **3** *leap the obstacle* jump, jump over, high-jump, vault over, vault, spring over, bound over, hurdle, clear, sail over. **4** *leap to help* jump, hurry, hasten, rush. **5** *prices have leapt* soar, rocket, skyrocket, shoot up, escalate, mount. **leap at** *leap at the chance* accept eagerly, grasp, grab, take advantage of. **leap to** *leap to conclusions* arrive at hastily, reach hurriedly, form hastily.

leap noun **1** *clear the obstacle at the first leap* jump, vault, spring, bound, hop, skip. **2** *a leap in the number of unemployed* escalation, soaring, surge, upsurge, upswing, rapid increase, sudden rise. **by leaps and bounds** *progress by leaps and bounds* rapidly, swiftly, quickly, speedily, at an amazing rate.

learn verb **1** *learn French* acquire a knowledge of, become competent in, grasp, master, absorb, assimilate, pick up. **2** *learn the poem* memorize, commit to memory. **3** *we learned that he had gone* discover, find out, detect, become aware, gather, hear, be informed, understand, ascertain, discern, perceive.

learned adjective erudite, scholarly, well-educated, knowledgeable, well-read, well-versed, well-informed, lettered, cultured, intellectual, academic, literary, bookish, studious, pedantic, sage, wise; *inf.* highbrow.

learning noun **1** *a woman of learning* erudition, scholarship, knowledge, education, letters, culture, intellect, pedantry, sageness, wisdom. **2** *an opportunity for learning* study, studying, education, schooling, instruction.

lease verb **1** *lease a house/car from an agency* rent, hire, charter. **2** *lease their house to visitors* rent, rent out, let, hire, hire out, sublet, sublease.

leash noun **1** *a dog's leash* lead, rein, tether, rope, cord, chain. **2** *keep a tight leash on his anger* rein, curb, control, check, restraint, hold.

leash verb **1** *leash the dog* tether, tie up, fasten, secure. **2** *leash one's anger* curb, control, keep under control, check, restrain, hold back, suppress.

leather noun skin, hide, kid, doeskin, pigskin, suede.

leave verb **1** *leave hurriedly* depart, go away, go, withdraw, retire, take off, exit, take one's leave, make off, pull out, quit, decamp, disappear; *inf.* push off, shove off, split. **2** *leave for Bermuda* set off, set sail. **3** *leave his wife* abandon, desert, forsake, discard, turn one's back on, leave in the lurch. **4** *has left his job* give up, quit, abandon. **5** *leave his gloves at the hotel* forget, mislay, leave behind. **6** *leave the job to them* assign, allot, consign, hand over, give over, refer, commit, entrust. **7** *he left the estate to his nephew* bequeath, will, endow, hand down, transfer, convey; *fml.* devise. **8** *the quarrel left feelings of resentment* cause, produce, generate, result in. **leave in the lurch** let down, leave stranded, leave high and dry, abandon, desert, forsake. **leave out** *leave out a sentence* omit, fail to include, overlook. **leave out of** *please leave him out of it* exclude from, omit from, except from, eliminate from, count out of, disregard from.

leave noun **1** *get leave to be absent* permission, consent, authorization, sanction, warrant, dispensation, concession, indulgence. **2** *going on (a) leave for three weeks* vacation, break, time off, furlough, sabbatical, leave of absence. **3** *they took their leave* departure, parting, withdrawal, exit, farewell, good-bye, adieu.

lecherous adjective lustful, promiscuous, carnal, sensual, licentious, lascivious, lewd, salacious, libertine, libidinous, lubricious, concupiscent, debauched, dissolute, wanton, intemperate, dissipated, degenerate, depraved; *inf.* horny, raunchy.

lechery noun lust, carnality, sensuality, licentiousness, lasciviousness, lewdness, salaciousness, salacity, libertinism, libidinousness, lubricity, concupiscence, debauchery, dissoluteness, wantonness, intemperance, dissipation, degeneracy, depravity; *inf.* horniness, raunchiness.

lecture noun **1** *attend a lecture on the environment* talk, speech, address, discourse, disquisition, lesson, sermon, homily, harangue. **2** *given a lecture for being late* scolding, chiding, reprimand, rebuke, reproof, reproach, remonstration, upbraiding, berating, tirade, diatribe; *inf.* dressing-down, talking-to.

lecture verb **1** *lectured on local politics* give a lecture, give a talk, talk, make a speech, speak, give an address, discourse, expound, hold forth, give a sermon, sermonize, harangue; *inf.* spout, jaw. **2** *lecture the children for being late* scold, chide, reprimand, rebuke, reprove, reproach, remonstrate with, upbraid, berate, castigate; *inf.* lambaste, tell off.

ledge noun shelf, sill, mantel, mantelpiece, projection, protrusion, overhang, ridge, step.

leech noun hanger-on, parasite, barnacle, sycophant, toady, bloodsucker, extortioner, sponger; *inf.* scrounger, freeloader.

leer verb *leer at* ogle, eye, wink at, watch, stare at, sneer at, smirk at; *inf.* give someone the once-over.

leer noun lascivious look, lecherous glance, wink, stare, sneer, smirk, grin; *inf.* the once-over.

leery adjective wary, chary, cautious, careful, guarded, on one's guard, suspicious, distrustful.

leeway noun room to maneuver, room to operate, latitude, elbowroom, slack, space, margin, play.

left adjective **1** *the left side* left-hand, sinistral, sinister, sinistrous; port. **2** *a left politician* left-wing, leftist, socialist, radical, progressive, liberal, communist.

leftover adjective remaining, excess, surplus, extra, uneaten, unused, unwanted.

leftovers plural noun remainder, excess, surplus, leavings, uneaten food, unused supplies, scraps, odds and ends.

leg noun **1** *her injured leg* lower limb, limb, member, appendage, shank; *inf.* drumstick. **2** *the legs of the tripod* support, upright, prop, brace, underpinning. **3** *the final leg of the journey* part, portion, segment, section, bit, stretch, stage, lap.

legacy noun **1** *a legacy of several million dollars* bequest, inheritance, heritage, bequeathal, endowment, gift, patrimony, heirloom; *fml.* devise. **2** *a legacy of Navajo culture | the legacy of unemployment* inheritance, heritage, tradition, hand-me-down, residue.

legal adjective **1** *legal behavior* lawful, legitimate, licit, valid, permissible, permitted, allowable, allowed, aboveboard, admissible, acceptable, authorized, sanctioned, warranted, licensed; *inf.* legit. **2** *legal processes* judicial, juristictive, forensic.

legate noun envoy, emissary, agent, ambassador, representative, commissioner, nuncio, messenger.

legation noun **1** *part of the American legation in Britain* mission, diplomatic mission, embassy, consulate, ministry, delegation, deputation, representation, envoys. **2** *the address of the American legation* embassy, consulate, diplomatic establishment, ministry.

legend noun **1** *a book of Scandinavian legends* myth, saga, epic, folk tale, folk story, tale, story, narrative, fable, romance. **2** *Greta Garbo became a legend* celebrity, star, superstar, luminary. **3** *the legends under the photographs* caption, inscription, dedication, motto, device. **4** *the legends accompanying the tables* key, code, cipher, explanation, table of symbols.

legendary adjective **1** *legendary figures in Icelandic saga* mythical, heroic, traditional, fabled, fictitious, fictional, storybook, romantic, fanciful. **2** *a legendary actor* celebrated, acclaimed, illustrious, famous, famed, renowned, immortal.

legerdemain noun **1** *magicians practicing legerdemain* sleight of hand, juggling, conjuring, prestidigitation, trickery, hocuspocus, thaumaturgy. **2** *a politician noted for his legerdemain* trickery, cunning, artfulness, craftiness, craft, wiles, deceit, deception, double-dealing, sophistry.

legible adjective readable, decipherable, clear, distinct, plain, neat.

legion noun **1** *legions of soldiers* army, brigade, regiment, battalion, company, troop, division, unit, force. **2** *legions of people arrived for the festival* horde, host, throng, multitude, crowd, drove, mass, mob, gang, swarm, flock, herd.

legislation noun **1** *his office is in charge of legislation* lawmaking, law enactment, law formulation, codification. **2** *dislike the new legislation* law, body of laws, constitution, rule(s), regulation(s), act(s), bill(s), statute(s), enactment(s), charter(s), ordinance(s), measure(s), canon, code.

legislator noun lawmaker, lawgiver, congressman, congresswoman, senator, parliamentarian, politician.

legitimate adjective **1** *legitimate actions* legal, lawful, licit; *inf.* legit. **2** *the legitimate heir* lawful, rightful, genuine, authentic, real, true, proper, correct, authorized, sanctioned, warranted, acknowledged, recognized, approved. **3** *a legitimate reason for being late* valid, sound, admissible, acceptable, well-founded, justifiable, reasonable, plausible, credible, believable, reliable, logical, rational; *inf.* legit, kosher.

leisure noun free time, spare time, idle hours, inactivity, time off, relaxation, recreation, freedom, holiday, vacation, respite; *inf.* time to kill. **at one's leisure** at one's convenience, when it suits one, without haste, unhurriedly, when one gets around to it.

leisurely adjective unhurried, relaxed, easy, easygoing, gentle, comfortable, restful, slow, lazy, lingering; *inf.* laid-back.

lend verb **1** *lend him a book* loan, advance. **2** *the flowers lend beauty to the room* impart, add, give, bestow, confer, provide, supply, furnish. **3** *lend his professional skill to the venture* contribute, donate, grant.

lend a hand help, help out, assist, give assistance, aid, make a contribution; *inf.* pitch in. **lend itself to** *the house does not lend itself to being divided* be suitable for, be suited to, be appropriate for, be adaptable to.

length noun **1** *what length is the yarn?* distance, extent, linear measure, span, reach. **2** *a length of time* period, stretch, duration, term, span. **3** *a length of cloth* piece, portion, section, measure, segment, swatch. **4** *a speech noted for its length* lengthiness, extensiveness, protractedness, prolixity, wordiness, verbosity, verboseness, long-windedness, tediousness, tedium. **at length 1** *speak at length* for a long time, on and on, interminably, endlessly. **2** *deal at length with the problem* fully, to the fullest extent, in detail, in depth, thoroughly, exhaustively, completely. **3** *at length he agreed to accept* finally, at last, eventually, in the end, ultimately, in time.

lengthen verb **1** *lengthen a skirt* make longer, elongate, let down. **2** *the days are lengthening* grow longer, get longer, draw out, stretch. **3** *lengthen the time* extend, prolong, increase, expand, protract, stretch out, draw out.

lengthy adjective **1** *a lengthy affair* long, long-lasting, prolonged, extended, protracted, long-drawn-out. **2** *a lengthy speech* long, protracted, long-drawn-out, diffuse, discursive, verbose, wordy, prolix, long-winded, tedious.

lenient adjective **1** *a lenient judge* merciful, clement, sparing, moderate, compassionate, humane, forbearing, tolerant, liberal, magnanimous, indulgent. **2** *a lenient jail sentence* mild, merciful, moderate.

less adjective *of less importance* smaller, slighter, not so much.

lessen verb **1** *the pain lessened* abate, decrease, diminish, subside, moderate, slacken, die down, let up, ease off, ebb, wane. **2** *the massage lessened the pain* relieve, soothe, allay, assuage, alleviate, palliate, ease, dull, deaden, blunt, take the edge off. **3** *his behavior lessened him in their eyes* diminish, lower, reduce, minimize, degrade, discredit, devalue, belittle.

lesser adjective less important, minor, slighter, secondary, inferior, subordinate.

lesson noun **1** *have a music lesson* class, period of instruction/teaching/coaching/tutoring/schooling. **2** *children doing lessons* exercise, schoolwork, homework, assignment. **3** *reading the lesson in church* Bible passage, Bible reading, scripture, text. **4** *punished as a lesson to others* example, warning, deterrent, message, moral, precept. **5** *hardship taught him valuable lessons* knowledge, wisdom, enlightenment, experience.

let verb **1** *let them play there* allow to, permit to, give permission to, give leave to, authorize to, sanction to, grant to, warrant to, license to; *inf.* give the green light to. **2** *let the people through* allow to go, permit to, give access to, permit to pass. **3** *let it be known* cause, make, enable. **let down 1** *he let them down* fail, disappoint, disillusion, forsake, leave stranded, betray. **2** *let down the skirt* lengthen, make longer. **let in** allow to enter, admit, open the door to, give access to, receive, welcome, greet. **let in on** *let them in on the deal* include in, count in on, admit. **let off 1** *let off the firework* explode, detonate. **2** *letting off fumes* give off, discharge, emit, release, exude, leak. **3** *let the guilty man off* acquit, release, discharge, reprieve, absolve, exonerate, pardon, forgive, exempt, spare. **let on 1** *don't let on that you know him* reveal, make known, tell, disclose, divulge, give away, leak. **2** *he let on that he was deaf* pretend, feign, affect, make believe, simulate, fake. **let out 1** *let the caged animals out* release, liberate, allow to leave, open the door for, let go, free, set free. **2** *she let out a scream* emit, utter, give vent to, produce. **let up 1** *the storm finally let up* lessen, abate, decrease, diminish, subside, moderate, slacken, die down, ease off, ebb, wane. **2** *please let up on the child* treat less severely, be more lenient with, be kinder to; *inf.* go easy on.

letdown noun disappointment, disillusionment, fiasco, anticlimax; *inf.* washout.

lethal adjective fatal, deadly, mortal, death-dealing, murderous, poisonous, toxic, dangerous, virulent, noxious, destructive, disastrous, calamitous, ruinous.

lethargic adjective sluggish, inactive, slow, slothful, torpid, phlegmatic, listless, languid, apathetic, passive.

lethargy noun sluggishness, inertia, inactivity, sloth, idleness, torpor, torpidity, lifelessness, dullness, listlessness, languor, languidness, apathy, passivity, lassitude.

letter noun **1** *written in bold letters* character, alphabetical character, sign, symbol. **2** *send a letter* written message, communication, note, line, missive, epistle, dispatch, billet-doux, fan mail, reply, acknowledgment. **to the letter** *follow our instructions to the letter* strictly, precisely, exactly, accurately, literally, word for word, verbatim.

letup noun lessening, abatement, decrease, diminishing, diminution, moderation, slackening, dying down, easing off, ebbing, waning.

level adjective **1** *a level surface* flat, smooth, even, uniform, plane, flush, horizontal. **2** *keep the temperature level* even, uniform, regular, consistent, constant, stable, steady, unchanging, unvarying, unfluctuating. **3** *hang the pictures level with each other* at the same height, aligned, in line, balanced. **4** *have a level temper* even, equable, steady, stable, calm, serene, tranquil, composed, unruffled.

level noun **1** *at eye level* height, altitude, elevation. **2** *what level is he in the firm?* position, rank, standing, status, station, degree, grade, stage, standard. **3** *levels of rock* layer, stratum, bed. **4** *what level do you live on?* floor, story. **on the level** honest, aboveboard, straight, fair, genuine, true, sincere, open, straightforward; *inf.* upfront.

level verb **1** *level the surface* even off, even out, make flat, flatten, smooth, smooth out, plane. **2** *level the buildings* raze, demolish, flatten, bulldoze, pull down, knock down, tear down, lay waste, destroy. **3** *level his opponent* knock down, knock to the ground, lay out, flatten, floor, fell, knock out; *inf.* KO. **4** *level his gun at the target* aim, point, direct, train, sight, focus, beam, zero in on, draw a bead on. **level with** be honest with, be aboveboard with, tell the truth to, be frank with, be open with, hide nothing from, be straightforward with; *inf.* be upfront with.

levelheaded adjective sensible, prudent, circumspect, reasonable, rational, sane, composed, calm, cool, collected, cool-headed, balanced, self-possessed, unruffled, even-tempered, imperturbable; *inf.* unflappable, together.

leverage noun **1** *not enough leverage to move the load* purchase, force, strength. **2** *not have the leverage to win over the committee* power, influence, authority, weight, ascendancy, rank; *inf.* pull, clout.

levity noun lightheartedness, humor, facetiousness, fun, jocularity, hilarity, frivolity, flippancy, triviality, silliness, giddiness.

levy noun **1** *the levy of taxes* collection, gathering, raising, imposition, exaction, assessment. **2** *unable to pay the levy* tax, taxation, tariff, toll, excise, customs, duty, dues, imposition, impost, assessment.

levy verb **1** *levy taxes* collect, gather, raise, impose, exact, demand, charge, tax. **2** *levy troops* conscript, call up, draft, enlist, muster, mobilize, rally, press.

lewd adjective **1** *lewd behavior* lecherous, lustful, licentious, lascivious, promiscuous, carnal, sensual, prurient, salacious, lubricious, libidinous, concupiscent, debauched, dissipated, dissolute, profligate, unchaste, wanton. **2** *lewd literature* obscene, pornographic, blue, bawdy, salacious, suggestive, ribald, indecent, vulgar, crude, smutty, dirty, coarse; *inf.* raunchy.

liability noun **1** *admit liability for the lost*

goods responsibility, accountability, blame, culpability. **2** *meet his financial liabilities* obligation, debt, indebtedness, debit, arrears, dues. **3** *the extra suitcase proved to be a liability* hindrance, encumbrance, burden, impediment, handicap, nuisance, inconvenience, drawback, drag, disadvantage, millstone around one's neck. **4** *he has a liability to cheat* aptness, likelihood, inclination, tendency, disposition, predisposition.

liable adjective *not liable for customers' lost property* responsible, accountable, answerable, chargeable, at fault. **liable to 1** *liable to injury* exposed to, open to, subject to, susceptible to, vulnerable to, in danger of, at risk of. **2** *liable to burst into tears* apt to, likely to, inclined to, tending to, disposed to, predisposed to, prone to.

liaison noun **1** *no liaison between the offices* communication, contact, connection, interchange, link, linkage. **2** *he acts as liaison between the departments* intermediary, contact person, go-between. **3** *his wife found out about his liaison* affair, adulterous affair, love affair, relationship, romance, intrigue, amour, flirtation; *inf.* hanky-panky.

liar noun fibber, perjurer, falsifier, false witness, fabricator, equivocator, prevaricator, deceiver.

libel noun defamation of character, defamation, slander, false report, denigration, vilification, disparagement, derogation, aspersions, calumny, traducement, obloquy, abuse, slur, smear, smear campaign.

liberal adjective **1** *a liberal supply of food* abundant, copious, ample, plentiful, lavish, profuse, munificent, bountiful, rich, handsome, generous. **2** *hosts liberal with their hospitality* generous, magnanimous, openhanded, unsparing, unstinting, lavish, beneficent, bighearted, kindhearted, kind, philanthropic, charitable, altruistic, unselfish. **3** *too liberal to abide such discrimination* tolerant, unprejudiced, unbiased, unbigoted, impartial, nonpartisan, broad-minded, enlightened, catholic. **4** *a liberal interpretation of the law* broad, loose, flexible, nonrestrictive, free, general, nonliteral, inexact, imprecise. **5** *liberal in his politics* advanced, forward-looking, progressive, reformist, radical, latitudinarian. **6** *a liberal education* wide-ranging, broad-based, general, humanistic.

liberate verb emancipate, set free, free, release, let go, discharge, set loose, unshackle, unfetter, unchain, deliver, rescue, manumit.

libertine adjective licentious, lustful, lecherous, lascivious, dissolute, dissipated, debauched, immoral, wanton, decadent, depraved, profligate, rakish, sensual, promiscuous, unchaste, impure, sinful, intemperate, corrupt.

libertine noun lecher, seducer, profligate, rake, roué, wanton, sensualist, reprobate, womanizer, adulterer, Don Juan, Lothario, Casanova; *inf.* lech.

liberty noun **1** *countries that have liberty* freedom, independence, autonomy, sovereignty, self-government, self-rule. **2** *prisoners gaining their liberty* freedom, liberation, release, discharge, deliverance, emancipation, manumission. **3** *have the liberty to choose* freedom, free will, volition, latitude, option, choice. **4** *given the liberty to leave the grounds* right, prerogative, privilege, permission, sanction, authorization, license, dispensation, exemption. **at liberty 1** *the thief/animal is still at liberty* free, loose, on the loose, at large, unconfined. **2** *you are at liberty to do as you wish* free, permitted, allowed, entitled. **take liberties** *taking liberties with the staff* be overfamiliar, be familiar, be disrespectful, breach etiquette, be impertinent, be insolent, be impudent, be presumptuous, be forward, be audacious.

license noun **1** *license to sell their wares* permission, leave, consent, authority, authorization, sanction, approval, warranty, certification, accreditation, entitlement, privilege, prerogative, right, dispensation, exemption. **2** *they have the license to do as they please* freedom, liberty, latitude, choice, option, independence, self-determination. **3** *a driver's license* permit, certificate, credential, document, documentation, pass.

license verb authorize, permit, allow, entitle, sanction, empower, warrant, certify, accredit, charter, franchise.

licentious adjective dissolute, lustful, lecherous, lascivious, dissipated, debauched, immoral, wanton, decadent, depraved, profligate, sensual, promiscuous, unchaste, impure, intemperate.

lick verb **1** *lick the ice cream* tongue, taste, lap. **2** *flames licking the walls* touch, play over, flick over, dart over, ripple over. **3** *lick the opponents* defeat, beat, conquer, trounce, thrash, rout, vanquish, overcome, overwhelm, overpower, drub; *inf.* wipe the floor with. **4** *lick the problem* get the better of, overcome, solve.

lid noun cover, top, cap, cork, stopper, plug.

lie¹ noun untruth, falsehood, fib, fabrication, invention, piece of fiction, falsification, falsity, prevarication; *inf.* tall tale, whopper.

lie² verb *the witness was lying* perjure oneself, fib, invent/make up a story, prevaricate, depart from the truth.

lie³ verb **1** *he was lying, not sitting* recline,

sprawl, rest, repose, relax, lounge, loll, be recumbent, be prostrate, be supine, be prone, be stretched out. **2** *the town lies on the other side of the hill* be situated, be located, be placed, be positioned, be found. **3** *two poets lie there* be buried, be interred. **4** *lie dormant* remain, continue, stay. **5** *their strength lies in their faith* consist, exist, reside, be inherent. **lie low** *they lay low during the police search* hide, go into hiding, hide out, conceal oneself, keep out of sight, keep a low profile, take cover, go underground; *inf.* hole up.

life noun **1** *as long as there is life in my body* existence, being, animation, viability. **2** *is there life on Mars?* living things, living beings, living creatures, human/animal/plant life, fauna, flora. **3** *many lives were lost in the war* person, human being, individual, mortal, soul. **4** *worked hard all her life* lifetime, days, course of life, life span, time on earth, existence, career. **5** *the life of a battery* duration, active life, period of usefulness. **6** *that's life* the human condition, the way of the world, the way it is, the way things go. **7** *an affluent life* way of living, manner of living, lifestyle, situation, position. **8** *he wrote a life of the poet* biography, autobiography, life story, memoirs, history, career, diary, journal, confessions. **9** *put some life in the party* animation, vivacity, liveliness, vitality, verve, high spirits, sparkle, exuberance, buoyancy, effervescence, enthusiasm, energy, vigor, dynamism; *inf.* pizazz, pep, zing. **10** *he was the life of the firm* life force, vital spirit, spirit, moving force, lifeblood, very essence, essence, heart, core, soul. **give one's life 1** *he gave his life for his friend* die, sacrifice oneself. **2** *give one's life to teaching* dedicate oneself, devote oneself, give oneself, pledge oneself, surrender oneself.

lifeblood noun life force, animating spirit, moving force, driving force, vital spark, inspiration, animus, essence, heart, core, élan vital.

lifeless adjective **1** *lifeless bodies* dead, deceased, cold, defunct; motionless, limp. **2** *lifeless statues lined the corridor* inanimate, inorganic, abiotic. **3** *lifeless stretches of country* barren, sterile, bare, desolate, stark, arid, unproductive, uncultivated, empty, uninhabited, unoccupied. **4** *a lifeless performance* spiritless, lacking vitality, unspirited, lackluster, apathetic, uninspired, colorless, dull, flat, stiff, wooden, tedious, uninspiring.

lift verb **1** *lift the furniture* pick up, uplift, hoist, upheave, raise, raise up, heft. **2** *your visit lifted his spirits* raise, buoy up, boost, elevate. **3** *the mist lifted* rise,

disperse, dissipate, disappear, vanish, be dispelled. **4** *lift the ban* raise, remove, withdraw, revoke, rescind, cancel, annul, void, countermand, relax, end, stop, terminate. **5** *lift one's voice* raise, make louder, amplify. **6** *lift a passage from the book* plagiarize, pirate, copy, abstract. **7** *someone lifted my purse* steal, thieve, rob, pilfer, purloin, filch, pocket, take, appropriate; *inf.* pinch, swipe.

lift noun **1** *give the child a lift up* hoist, heave, push, thrust, shove, help, a helping hand. **2** *the visitors gave the patient a lift* boost, pick-me-up, stimulus; *inf.* shot in the arm. **3** *the new player gave their game a lift* boost, improvement, enhancement, upgrading. **4** *give the children a lift to school* ride, car ride, transportation.

light[1] noun **1** *see by the light of the fire* illumination, luminescence, luminosity, gleaming, brightness, brilliance, glowing, blaze, glare, incandescence, effulgence, refulgence, radiance, luster. **2** *bring the light over here* lamp, flashlight, lantern, beacon, candle, taper, torch. **3** *we like to travel in the light, not the dark* daylight, daylight hours, daytime, day, hours of sunlight. **4** *see things in a different light* aspect, angle, slant, approach, viewpoint, point of view. **5** *light finally dawned on me* enlightenment, illumination, understanding, comprehension, awareness, knowledge, elucidation, explanation. **bring to light** *the search brought to light new evidence* reveal, disclose, expose, uncover, show up, unearth, bring to notice. **come to light** *new evidence came to light* appear, come out, turn up, be discovered, be uncovered, be unearthed, transpire. **in the light of** *in the light of his previous convictions* considering, taking into consideration, taking into account, bearing in mind, keeping in mind, mindful of, taking note of, in view of. **shed/throw (any) light on** *can you shed (any) light on this matter?* elucidate, clarify, clear up, explain, offer an/any explanation for.

light[2] adjective **1** *a light room* full of light, bright, well-lit, well-lighted, well-illuminated, sunny. **2** *wearing light clothes* light-colored, light-toned, pale-colored, pastel, pastel-colored; faded, bleached. **3** *she had light hair* light-colored, fair, blond.

light[3] verb **1** *light the kindling* ignite, kindle, set burning, set fire to, set a match to. **2** *fireworks lit up the sky* illuminate, brighten, lighten, irradiate; *lit.* illumine. **3** *a smile lit up her face* irradiate, brighten, animate, make cheerful, enliven.

light⁴ adjective **1** *the suitcases are light* easy to carry, portable; slight, underweight, small, tiny. **2** *wearing light clothes* lightweight, thin, flimsy, insubstantial, delicate, floaty, gossamer. **3** *a light tap on the shoulder* gentle, slight, soft, weak, faint, indistinct. **4** *light tasks* moderate, easy, simple, undemanding, untaxing, unexacting, effortless, facile; *inf.* cushy. **5** *light entertainment* nonserious, readily understood, lighthearted, entertaining, diverting, recreative, pleasing, amusing, humorous, funny, frivolous, superficial, trivial, trifling. **6** *a light jail sentence* nonsevere, mild, moderate, slight. **7** *this is no light matter* unimportant, insignificant, trivial, trifling, petty, inconsequential. **8** *a light meal* small, modest, scanty, skimpy, frugal, easily digested. **9** *with (a) light heart* carefree, cheerful, cheery, happy, lighthearted, gay, merry, blithe, sunny, untroubled. **10** *was light of foot* nimble, deft, agile, supple, lithe, spry, sprightly, graceful. **11** *feeling light in the head* giddy, dizzy, light-headed, vertiginous, faint, unsteady; *inf.* woozy. **12** *light soil* porous, crumbly, friable.

lighten¹ verb **1** *the sky lightened* become lighter, grow brighter, brighten. **2** *the larger windows lightened the room* brighten, light up, illuminate, shed light on, cast light on, irradiate. **3** *the sun had lightened the colors* whiten, bleach, pale.

lighten² verb **1** *lighten the horse's load* lessen, reduce, ease. **2** *lighten his burden of pain* lessen, ease, alleviate, mitigate, allay, relieve, assuage, ameliorate. **3** *the good news lightened his mood* brighten, cheer up, gladden, hearten, buoy up, perk up, lift, uplift.

light-headed adjective giddy, dizzy, vertiginous, faint, unsteady; *inf.* woozy.

lighthearted adjective carefree, cheerful, cheery, happy, glad, gay, merry, playful, jolly, joyful, gleeful, frolicsome, effervescent, in good spirits, blithe, sunny, untroubled; *inf.* upbeat.

lightly adverb **1** *snow falling lightly* slightly, thinly, softly, gently. **2** *salt the food lightly* sparingly, sparsely, slightly. **3** *get off lightly* easily, without severe punishment, leniently. **4** *jump lightly over the fence* easily, nimbly, agilely, lithely, spryly, gracefully. **5** *dismiss the subject lightly* airily, carelessly, heedlessly, uncaringly, indifferently, thoughtlessly, flippantly, frivolously; *inf.* breezily.

likable, likeable adjective pleasant, nice, friendly, agreeable, amiable, genial, charming, engaging, appealing, winsome.

like adjective *houses of like design* similar, comparable, corresponding, resembling, analogous, parallel, equivalent, of a kind, identical, matching, akin.

like verb **1** *they like each other* be fond of, have a liking/fondness for, be attracted to. **2** *he likes swimming* enjoy, find/take pleasure in, delight in, relish, revel in; *inf.* get a kick from. **3** *would like a piece of cake* wish, want, desire, prefer. **4** *how would you like it if it happened to you?* feel about, regard, think about, appreciate.

likeable adjective. *See* LIKABLE.

likelihood noun probability, chance, good chance, prospect, reasonable prospect, possibility, distinct possibility, strong possibility.

likely adjective **1** *it is likely that he will go* probable, distinctly possible, to be expected, odds-on. **2** *it is likely to rain* apt, inclined, tending, disposed, liable, prone. **3** *he gave a likely enough reason* reasonable, plausible, feasible, acceptable, believable, credible, tenable, conceivable. **4** *a likely place for a picnic* suitable, appropriate, fit, fitting, acceptable, proper, right, qualified, relevant, reasonable.

likeness noun **1** *there is a distinct likeness in the faces of the two friends* resemblance, similarity, sameness, similitude, correspondence, alikeness. **2** *appear in the likeness of Santa Claus* guise, semblance, appearance, outward form, form, shape, character. **3** *he will draw a likeness of your child* picture, drawing, sketch, painting, portrait, photograph, study, representation, image, sculpture.

likewise adverb **1** *she left early and he did likewise* in like manner, in the same way, similarly, in similar fashion, the same. **2** *we enjoyed the food and likewise the company* in addition, also, too, besides, moreover, furthermore, into the bargain, as well.

liking noun fondness, love, affection, desire, preference, partiality, penchant, bias, weakness, soft spot, appreciation, taste, predilection, fancy, inclination, bent, leaning, affinity.

limb noun **1** *injure a limb* arm, leg, wing, member, extremity, appendage. **2** *cut down limbs from the tree* branch, bough. **3** *the society is a limb of an international organization* branch, section, member, offshoot.

limelight noun focus of attention, public eye, publicity, fame, renown, celebrity, stardom, notability, eminence, prominence, spotlight.

limit noun **1** *the 200-mile fishing limit* boundary, boundary line, partition line, demarcation line, endpoint, cutoff point, termination. **2** *push his patience to the limit* extremity, utmost, ultimate, breaking point, endpoint. **3** *cross the limits of his land* boundary, border, bound, fron-

tier, edge, perimeter, confines, periphery.
4 *a speed/spending limit* maximum, ceiling, limitation, restriction, curb, check, restraint.

limit verb **1** *limit their expenditure* place a limit on, restrict, curb, check, keep within bounds, restrain, confine, control, ration. **2** *the bulky jacket limited her movement* restrict, restrain, constrain, hinder, impede, hamper, trammel.

limited adjective **1** *committees having only limited powers* restricted, curbed, checked, controlled, restrained, constrained. **2** *provide limited accommodation* scanty, sparse, cramped, basic, minimal, inadequate. **3** *of limited experience* little, narrow, scanty, basic, minimal, inadequate, insufficient. **4** *he's a hard worker but he's a bit limited* slow, slow-witted, dull-witted, dense, unimaginative, stolid.

limitless adjective **1** *a limitless expanse of forest* infinite, endless, never-ending, interminable, immense, vast, extensive, measureless. **2** *limitless optimism/enthusiasm* boundless, unbounded, illimitable, infinite, endless, never-ending, unceasing, interminable, inexhaustible, constant, perpetual.

limp verb **1** *he still limps after the injury* hobble, shuffle, walk with a limp. **2** *the damaged ship limped into harbor* move slowly, crawl, drag.

limp noun *walk with a pronounced limp* lameness, hobble, jerk, uneven gait, shuffle.

limp adjective **1** *limp leaves* lacking firmness, floppy, drooping, droopy, soft, flaccid, flabby, loose, slack. **2** *feeling limp after the long illness* without energy, tired, fatigued, weary, exhausted, worn-out, lethargic, enervated, feeble, frail, debilitated.

line noun **1** *draw lines* bar, score, stroke, slash, underline, underscore. **2** *lines of white through the black material* band, stripe, strip, belt, seam. **3** *lines on her face* furrow, wrinkle, crease, crow's-foot, groove. **4** *admire the lines of the sculpture* outline, contour, configuration, shape, figure, delineation, silhouette, profile. **5** *the ball went over the line/the state line* boundary, boundary line, limit, border, borderline, frontier, demarcation line, edge, margin, perimeter, periphery. **6** *our line of flight* course, route, track, channel, path, way, road, lane, trajectory. **7** *his line of thought* direction, course, drift, tack, tendency, trend. **8** *what line is he in?* line of work, business, field, area, trade, occupation, employment, profession, work, job, calling, career, pursuit, specialty; *inf.* game. **9** *stocking a new line of cosmetics* brand, kind, sort, type, variety. **10** *a line of figures/people* row, column, series, sequence, succession, queue,

procession, file, string, chain, array. **11** *behind enemy lines* formation, position, disposition, front, front line, firing line. **12** *he comes from a noble line* lineage, descent, ancestry, parentage, family, extraction, heritage, stock, strain, race, breed. **13** *hang the wash on the line/fishing line* rope, string, cord, cable, wire, thread, twine, strand, filament. **14** *drop her mother a line* note, letter, card, postcard, message, word, communication. **15** *give his usual line about having no money* spiel, story, patter, piece of fiction. **draw the line at** *draw the line at lending him money* stop short of, bar, proscribe, set a limit at; *inf.* put one's foot down about. **in line 1** *stand in line to be served* in a row, in a column, in single file, in a queue. **2** *are the two pipes in line?* in alignment, aligned, straight, plumb, true. **3** *their views are very much in line* in agreement, in accord, in harmony, in step, in conformity, in rapport. **4** *keep the junior staff in line* under control, in order, in check, obedient. **in line for** *in line for the promotion* a candidate for, in the running for, on the short list for, being considered for, next in succession for. **lay it on the line** *lay it on the line to him about his drinking* speak frankly, state openly, be direct, pull no punches; *inf.* give it to someone straight. **lay/put on the line** *put his job on the line* risk, put at risk, put in danger, endanger, imperil. **toe the line** *those who do not toe the line are asked to leave* conform, obey the rules, abide by the rules, submit, yield.

line verb **1** *grief had lined her face* mark with lines, furrow, wrinkle, crease. **2** *trees lined the driveway* border, edge, fringe, bound, skirt, hem, rim. **line up 1** *line up the toy soldiers* arrange in a line, arrange in lines, put in rows/columns, group, marshal. **2** *the children lined up* form a line, form lines, get into rows/columns, file, form a queue, group together, fall in. **3** *line up entertainment for the party* get together, organize, prepare, assemble, obtain, procure, secure, produce, come up with.

lineage noun line, descent, ancestry, family, extraction. *See* LINE noun 12.

lineup noun **1** *the lineup for tonight's show/game* list, roster, team, selection, array. **2** *the lineup for inspection* line, row, queue.

linger verb **1** *linger after the others went* stay, remain, hang around, delay, dawdle, loiter, dally, tarry; *inf.* dilly-dally. **2** *the infection lingered* persist, continue, be protracted, endure. **3** *dying man is lingering (on)* stay alive, cling to life, survive, last, continue, hang on.

link noun **1** *a link in the metal chain* ring, loop, connection, coupling, joint, knot. **2** *one of the links in the organization* component, constituent, element, part, piece, member. **3** *a link between smoking and cancer* connection, relationship, association, tie. **4** *strong family links* bond, tie, attachment, connection, relationship, association, affiliation.

link verb **1** *the joint linking the two pieces* join, connect, fasten together, attach, bind, unite, couple. **2** *the press linking their names* join, connect, associate, relate, bracket.

lionhearted adjective brave, courageous, valiant, gallant, intrepid, valorous, fearless, bold, daring, dauntless, stouthearted, stalwart, heroic.

lionize verb glorify, exalt, magnify, acclaim, praise, extol, laud, eulogize, fête, pay tribute to, put on a pedestal, hero-worship, worship, idolize, adulate, aggrandize.

lip noun **1** *the lip of a cup/crater* edge, rim, brim, border, verge, brink. **2** *no one wants to listen to your lip* impertinence, impudence, insolence, rudeness, audacity, effrontery, cheek; *inf.* back talk, sass.

liquid adjective **1** *liquid substances* fluid, flowing, running, runny, watery, aqueous, liquefied, melted, molten, dissolved, hydrous. **2** *liquid eyes* clear, transparent, limpid, unclouded, bright, shining, glowing, gleaming. **3** *liquid assets* convertible, negotiable.

liquidate verb **1** *liquidate debts* pay, pay in full, pay off, settle, clear, discharge, square, make good, honor. **2** *liquidate a business/partnership* close down, dissolve, break up, disband, terminate, annul. **3** *liquidate assets* convert to cash, convert, cash in, sell off, realize. **4** *liquidate an enemy* kill, murder, put to death, do away with, assassinate, eliminate, dispatch, finish off, destroy, annihilate, obliterate; *inf.* bump off, rub out, wipe out.

liquor noun alcohol, alcoholic drink, spirits, drink, intoxicant, inebriant; *inf.* booze, hard stuff, grog, the sauce, hooch, rotgut.

list[1] noun *a list of purchases/films* catalog, inventory, record, register, roll, file, index, directory, listing, enumeration, table, tabulation, schedule, syllabus, calendar, program.

list[2] verb *list the purchases* make a list of, write down, record, register, enter, itemize, enumerate, catalog, file, tabulate, schedule, chronicle, classify.

list[3] verb *vessels listing* lean, tilt, tip, heel, careen, cant, incline, slant, slope.

listen verb *listen to the speaker* pay attention, be attentive, give ear, lend an ear; hang on someone's words, keep one's ears open, prick up one's ears; *inf.* be all ears. **2** *if you had listened in the classroom, you would have passed* take heed, heed, take notice, mind, obey. **listen in on** *listen in on someone's conversation* eavesdrop on, overhear, tap (into), wiretap; *inf.* bug.

listless adjective languid, lethargic, enervated, lackadaisical, spiritless, lifeless, inactive, inert, indolent, apathetic, passive, dull, sluggish, slothful, limp, languorous, torpid, supine, indifferent, uninterested, impassive.

litany noun **1** *church litany* prayer, invocation, petition, supplication, devotion; *lit.* orison. **2** *a litany of complaints* recital, recitation, catalog, list, listing, enumeration.

literacy noun reading ability, reading proficiency, learning, education, culture, knowledge, scholarship, erudition, learnedness, enlightenment, articulateness.

literal adjective **1** *a literal translation* word-for-word, verbatim, line-for-line, exact, precise, faithful, close, strict, accurate. **2** *a literal account* true, accurate, genuine, authentic, veritable, plain, unexaggerated, unvarnished, unembellished, undistorted. **3** *rather a literal person* literal-minded, down-to-earth, prosaic, factual, matter-of-fact, unimaginative, colorless, commonplace, tedious, uninspiring.

literally adverb **1** *translated literally* word for word, verbatim, line for line, exactly, precisely, faithfully, closely, strictly, accurately. **2** *literally thousands of people* actually, really, truly, honestly, certainly, surely, positively, absolutely.

literary adjective **1** *literary works* written, published, printed, in print. **2** *a literary man* well-read, widely read, educated, well-educated, scholarly, learned, intellectual, cultured, erudite, bookish, studious, lettered; *inf.* highbrow. **3** *a literary word* formal, poetic.

literate adjective **1** *scarcely literate* able to read and write, educated, schooled. **2** *the most literate people of his family* educated, well-educated, well-read, scholarly, learned, intellectual, erudite, cultured, cultivated, knowledgeable, well-informed. **3** *literate prose* well-written, stylish, polished, articulate, lucid, eloquent.

literature noun **1** *study English literature* writings, printed works, published works, belles lettres. **2** *receive literature about the course* printed matter, brochure, leaflet, pamphlet, flyer, circular, information, data, facts; *inf.* info.

lithe adjective agile, flexible, supple, limber, loose-limbed, pliant, pliable, lissome.

litigation noun lawsuit, legal case, case, legal dispute, legal action, legal proceedings, suit.

litter noun **1** *litter lying on the grass* trash, rubbish, debris, refuse, junk, detritus, flotsam. **2** *a litter of books everywhere* disorder, untidiness, clutter, jumble, confusion, mess, disarray, disorganization; *inf.* shambles. **3** *a litter of pups* brood, young, offspring, progeny, family, issue. **4** *invalids carried on litters* stretcher, cot.

little adjective **1** *a little person/dog/insect/car* small, short, slight, petite, tiny, wee, miniature, diminutive, minute, minuscule, dwarf, midget, pygmy, bantam; *inf.* teeny, teeny-weeny, pint-sized. **2** *he began painting when he was little* small, young, junior. **3** *after a little period* short, brief, fleeting, short-lived, momentary, transitory. **4** *exaggerate little difficulties* unimportant, insignificant, minor, trivial, trifling, petty, paltry, inconsequential, negligible, nugatory. **5** *gain little advantage* scant, meager, skimpy, sparse, insufficient, exiguous; *inf.* piddling. **6** *nasty little minds* mean, narrow, narrow-minded, small-minded, base, cheap, shallow, petty, illiberal, provincial, parochial, insular.

little adverb **1** *little known as an artist* hardly, barely, scarcely, not much, only slightly, only just. **2** *snow is little seen around here* hardly, scarcely, rarely, seldom, infrequently. **little by little** gradually, slowly, bit by bit, by degrees, step by step, progressively.

little noun *add just a little* small amount, bit, touch, trace, hint, soupçon, trifle, dash, taste, pinch, dab, spot, sprinkling, speck, modicum, grain, fragment, snippet, smidgen; *inf.* smidge.

live verb **1** *when dinosaurs lived* be alive, breathe, draw breath, exist, walk the earth. **2** *patients not expected to live* remain/stay alive, survive, last, endure, persist, abide, continue, stay around. **3** *live quietly* pass/spend one's life, have a life/lifestyle, conduct oneself, lead one's life, behave, comport oneself. **4** *he lives by begging* survive, make a living, earn one's living, subsist, support oneself, maintain oneself, make ends meet. **5** *live in the city* dwell, reside, have one's home, have one's residence, lodge, be settled; *inf.* hang one's hat. **6** *he really lived when he was young* enjoy life, enjoy oneself, have fun, make the most of life, flourish, prosper, thrive. **live it up** live extravagantly, live in clover; *inf.* go on a spree, paint the town red, have a ball. **live on** *live on vegetables* subsist on, feed on, thrive on, eat nothing but.

live adjective **1** *live bodies* alive, living, breathing, animate, vital; *inf.* in the land of the living. **2** *a real live tiger* genuine,

authentic, actual, in the flesh, true-to-life. **3** *a live show* nonrecorded, in real time, unedited, with an audience. **4** *live coals* glowing, aglow, burning, alight, flaming, blazing, hot, smoldering. **5** *live electric wires* charged, connected, active, switched on. **6** *live bombs* unexploded, explodable, explosive. **7** *a live issue* current, topical, active, prevalent, important, of interest, lively, vital, pressing, burning, pertinent, controversial, debatable, unsettled. **live wire** person of energy, self-starter, self-motivator; *inf.* ball of fire, human dynamo, go-getter, hustler.

livelihood noun **1** *earn a livelihood* living, subsistence, means of support, income, keep, maintenance, sustenance, upkeep. **2** *a poorly paid livelihood* job, work, employment, occupation, trade, profession, career.

lively adjective **1** *lively young people* active, animated, energetic, vigorous, spirited, high-spirited, vivacious, enthusiastic, cheerful, buoyant, sparkling, bouncy, perky, sprightly, spry, frisky; *inf.* chipper, peppy. **2** *maintain a lively pace* brisk, quick, rapid, swift, vigorous. **3** *a lively discussion* animated, spirited, stimulating, heated, enthusiastic. **4** *a lively scene at the beach* busy, crowded, bustling, hectic, swarming, teeming, buzzing. **5** *lively writing* vivid, colorful, striking, graphic, stimulating, exciting, effective, imaginative.

liven verb **liven up 1** *liven the party up* enliven, animate, vitalize, vivify, put some life into, brighten up, cheer up, perk up; *inf.* pep up. **2** *livened up when they arrived* cheer up, brighten up, perk up.

livid adjective **1** *livid with his son* furious, infuriated, fuming, seething, beside oneself, incensed, enraged, angry, wrathful, ireful; *inf.* boiling. **2** *a livid patch on his forehead* discolored, bruised, black-and-blue, purplish, bluish.

living adjective **1** *living creatures* animate, vital, alive, live, breathing, existing, existent. **2** *living languages* current, in use, extant, existing, contemporary, operating, active, ongoing, continuing, surviving, persisting.

living noun **1** *earn a living* livelihood, subsistence, means of support, income, keep, maintenance, sustenance, upkeep. **2** *lose his living* job, work, employment, occupation, trade, profession, career. **3** *high living* lifestyle, way of life, conduct, behavior.

load noun **1** *the truck's load* cargo, freight, charge, burden, lading, consignment, shipment. **2** *the heavy load of negotiating a truce | illness added to his load* burden, onus, weight, responsibility, duty, charge, obligation, strain, trouble, worry, encumbrance, oppression, trial, tribulation, cross, millstone, albatross, incubus.

load verb 1 *load the truck* fill, fill up, lade, pack, pile, heap, stack, stuff. 2 *load the staff with responsibility* burden, weigh down, weight, saddle, charge, tax, encumber, oppress, trouble. 3 *load a gun* prime, charge, fill. 4 *load the dice* weight, bias, rig.

loaded adjective 1 *a loaded truck* full, filled, laden, freighted, packed. 2 *a loaded gun* primed, charged, filled. 3 *loaded dice* weighted, biased, rigged 4 *loaded questions* manipulative, cunning, insidious, artful, crafty, tricky. 5 *those people are probably loaded* rich, wealthy, well off, well-to-do, affluent, moneyed; *inf.* well-heeled, flush. 6 *got loaded at the party* drunk, intoxicated, inebriated; *inf.* plastered, smashed.

loaf verb *loafing at home* laze, lounge, idle, lie around, hang about, waste time.

loan noun advance, credit, mortgage.

loan verb lend, advance, give credit, give on loan, let out.

loathe verb hate, detest, abhor, despise, abominate, have an aversion to, shrink from, recoil from, execrate.

loathsome adjective hateful, detestable, abhorrent, odious, repugnant, disgusting, repulsive, revolting, abominable, vile, nasty, obnoxious, horrible, offensive, disagreeable, despicable, contemptible, reprehensible, execrable; *inf.* horrid.

lobby noun 1 *wait for them in the lobby* porch, hall, hallway, entrance hall, entrance, vestibule, foyer, passageway, ante-room, antechamber. 2 *the animal rights lobby* pressure group, interest group, supporters.

lobby verb *lobby the legislators* pressure, solicit, seek to influence, urge, press. **lobby for** *lobby for animal rights* campaign for, press/push for, promote.

local adjective 1 *local politics* community, district, neighborhood, regional, city, town, municipal, provincial, village, parish. 2 *our local store* nearby, near, at hand, close by, neighborhood. 3 *a local anesthetic* confined, restricted, contained, limited, circumscribed, delimited, specific.

locale noun place, site, spot, position, location, venue, area, neighborhood, locality, setting, scene.

locality noun 1 *the locality of the crime* vicinity, surrounding area, area, neighborhood, district, region, environs, locale; *fml.* locus. 2 *identify the locality of the car* location, position, place, whereabouts, bearings; *fml.* locus.

localize verb confine, restrict, contain, limit, circumscribe, delimit.

locate verb 1 *locate the source of infection* find, discover, identify, pinpoint, detect, uncover, track down, unearth, pin down, define. 2 *factories located near the sea* situate, site, position, place, put, build, establish, station, set, fix, settle.

location noun 1 *identify the location of the ship* position, place, situation, whereabouts, bearings, site, point; *fml.* locus. 2 *a pleasant location for a house* position, place, situation, site, spot, scene, setting, venue, locale.

lock verb 1 *lock the door* bolt, fasten, bar, secure, padlock. 2 *pieces of the puzzle locking together* interlock, engage, mesh, join, link, unite. 3 *wheels locked* jam, become rigid. 4 *locked in each other's arms* | *locked in combat* clasp, clench, entangle, entwine, embrace. **lock out** *lock out late arrivals* exclude, bar, ban, refuse entrance to, deny admittance to, ostracize. **lock up** *lock up prisoners* confine, imprison, jail, incarcerate, cage, coop up.

lock[1] noun *force the lock* bolt, catch, fastener, clasp, bar, hasp, padlock.

lock[2] noun *a lock of hair* strand, tuft, tress, curl, ringlet, lovelock.

lodge noun 1 *a ski lodge* house, cottage, cabin, chalet. 2 *the Masonic lodge* branch, chapter, section, association, society, club, group, fraternity, sorority. 3 *an animal's lodge* lair, den, hole, retreat, shelter.

lodge verb 1 *he's lodging at the Smiths'* stay, reside, dwell, room, sojourn, stop. 2 *the Smiths can lodge all of the children* house, accommodate, put up, billet, shelter, harbor, entertain. 3 *lodge a complaint* register, submit, put forward, place, file, lay, put on record, record. 4 *the bullet lodged in his brain* become fixed, become embedded, stick, come to rest.

lodger noun boarder, paying guest, guest, tenant, roomer.

lodging noun 1 *gave them lodging for the night* accommodation, shelter, board, housing, a roof over one's head. 2 *move to new lodgings* accommodation, rooms, place, residence, dwelling, abode, habitation; *inf.* digs.

lofty adjective 1 *lofty peaks* towering, soaring, tall, high, elevated, sky-high, skyscraping. 2 *lofty contempt* arrogant, haughty, proud, self-important, conceited, overweening, disdainful, supercilious, condescending, patronizing, lordly, snobbish, scornful, contemptuous; *inf.* high-and-mighty, stuck-up, snooty, uppity. 3 *lofty ideals* noble, exalted, grand, sublime. 4 *lofty members of the community* eminent, leading, notable, distinguished, famous, renowned, illustrious, esteemed, celebrated.

logic noun **1** *studying logic* science of reasoning, science of deduction, science of thought, dialectics, argumentation, ratiocination. **2** *her logic was flawed* line of reasoning, chain of reasoning, reasoning, argument, argumentation. **3** *no logic in her actions* reason, judgment, wisdom, sense, common sense, rationale, coherence; *inf.* horse sense.

logical adjective **1** *a logical argument* reasoned, rational, sound, cogent, coherent, clear, consistent, relevant. **2** *the logical thing to do* rational, reasonable, sensible, intelligent, wise, judicious. **3** *the logical outcome* likeliest, plausible, obvious. **4** *not a logical person* reasoning, thinking, straight-thinking, rational.

logo noun trademark, emblem, device, symbol, design, seal, stamp, logotype.

loiter verb hang around, linger, wait, skulk, loaf, lounge, idle, dally, waste time; *lit.* tarry.

loll verb **1** *lolling on the sofa* slump, flop, sprawl, relax, recline. **2** *loll around the house* lounge, loaf, idle, loiter, hang around, vegetate, languish. **3** *with his tongue lolling* hang down, hang, hang out, dangle, droop, sag, flap, flop.

lone adjective by oneself, alone, single, solitary, sole, unaccompanied, without companions, companionless, lonely.

lonely adjective **1** *feeling lonely* friendless, companionless, lonesome, forlorn, forsaken, isolated, outcast, despondent. **2** *lead a lonely existence* lone, by oneself, single, solitary, sole, companionless. **3** *a lonely landscape* desolate, barren, isolated, out-of-the-way, remote, secluded, off the beaten track, deserted, uninhabited, unfrequented, unpopulated, godforsaken, lone.

lonesome adjective friendless, forlorn, isolated. *See* LONELY 1.

long adjective **1** *four feet long* in length, lengthways, lengthwise. **2** *a long way* lengthy, extended, extensive, stretched out, spread out. **3** *ten long years* lengthy, prolonged, protracted, extended, long-drawn-out, interminable, tedious.

long verb **long for** wish for, desire, want, yearn for, crave, hunger for, thirst for, itch for, covet, lust after, hope for, dream of, pine for, hanker for/after; *inf.* have a yen for.

longing noun wish, desire, yearning, craving, hunger, thirst, itch, lust, hope, dream, aspiration, pining, fancy, urge, hankering; *inf.* yen.

long-standing adjective established, fixed, long-established, well-established, time-honored, abiding, enduring.

long-suffering adjective patient, forbearing, tolerant, uncomplaining, stoical, resigned, charitable, forgiving.

long-winded adjective verbose, wordy, garrulous, prolix, discursive, diffuse, rambling, lengthy, prolonged, protracted, long-drawn-out, tedious.

look verb **1** *look over there!* see, glance, fix one's gaze, focus, observe, view, regard, eye, take in, watch, scan, scrutinize, survey, consider, peep, peek, glimpse, gaze, stare, gape, ogle; *inf.* take a gander, rubberneck, eyeball. **2** *she looks ill* seem, seem to be, appear, appear to be, look to be, strike someone as being. **3** *the room looks east* face, front, front on. **look after** take care of, care for, attend to, tend, mind, keep an eye on, watch, supervise, protect, guard. **look at** observe, view, eye, watch, examine, study, inspect, scan, scrutinize, survey, check, consider, run one's eyes over. **look down on** scorn, disdain, regard with contempt, hold in disdain, sneer at, spurn, disparage, pooh-pooh, despise; *inf.* turn up one's nose at. **look for 1** *look for the lost glove* search for, hunt for, seek. **2** *look for some improvement* anticipate, expect, await, count on, hope for, look forward to. **look forward to** anticipate, await with pleasure, count the days until. **look into** investigate, explore, research, probe, inquire about, make inquiries about, examine, study, scrutinize, check, follow up on, check up on, check out. **look like** resemble, bear a resemblance to, put someone in mind of, take after; *inf.* be the spitting image of, be a dead ringer for, favor. **look on** *with a crowd looking on* watch, observe, spectate, be a spectator, view, witness. **look on/upon** *look on it as a favor* | *look upon him as a brother* regard, consider, think of, deem, judge, see, take, reckon. **look out** *you'll drop it if you don't look out* watch out, beware, be on guard, be alert, be wary, be vigilant, be careful, pay attention, take heed, keep an eye out, be on the qui vive. **look over** inspect, examine, check, monitor, scan, run through, give something/someone the once-over, check out, peruse; *inf.* eyeball. **look to 1** *look to the future* consider, give thought to, think about, turn one's thoughts to. **2** *look to the family for support* turn to, have recourse to, fall back on, avail oneself of. **look up 1** *look up the information* search for, seek out, research, find, locate. **2** *look them up in San Diego* visit, pay a visit to, call on; *inf.* drop in on. **look up to** *look up to his brother* admire, think highly of, hold in high regard, respect, hold in esteem, esteem, revere, idolize, worship, hero-worship, put on a pedestal, lionize.

look noun **1** *one look at the evidence* sight, glance, observation, view, examination, study, inspection, scan, survey, peep, peek, glimpse, gaze; *inf.* eyeful, gander, looksee, once-over. **2** *an angry look* expression, face, countenance, features, mien. **3** *houses having a Colonial look* appearance, air, aspect, bearing, cast, demeanor, features, semblance, guise, façade, impression, effect. **4** *miniskirts are the look this year* fashion, style, vogue, trend, fad, craze, rage.

lookout noun **1** *on the lookout for danger* watch, guard, vigil, alertness, qui vive. **2** *lookouts located along the coast* observation post, lookout station, lookout tower, watchtower, tower. **3** *the lookout kept watch until dawn* guard, sentry, sentinel, watchman.

loom verb **1** *a shape loomed out of the darkness* appear, emerge, become visible, take shape, materialize. **2** *cliffs loomed above them* tower, soar, rise, rise up, overhang, hang over. **3** *exams are looming* be imminent, impend, be close, threaten, menace.

loop noun coil, hoop, noose, circle, ring, oval, spiral, curl, twirl, whorl, twist, convolution, bend, curve, kink, arc.

loop verb **1** *loop the string* coil, form hoops with, bend into spirals. **2** *loop the sections together* fasten, tie, join, connect. **loop around** *the road loops around the lake* encircle, surround, encompass.

loophole noun escape clause, escape route, ambiguity, omission.

loose adjective **1** *cows loose in the street* at large, at liberty, free, on the loose, unconfined, untied, unchained, untethered, unsecured, unfastened, unrestricted, unbound, freed, liberated, released. **2** *the handle is loose* wobbly, insecure, rickety, unsteady, movable. **3** *loose hair* untied, unpinned, unbound, hanging free, flowing. **4** *loose clothes* loose-fitting, slack, baggy, sagging, sloppy. **5** *a loose translation* inexact, imprecise, vague, indefinite, broad, general. **6** *loose morals* immoral, disreputable, dissolute, corrupt, fast, promiscuous, debauched, dissipated, degenerate, wanton, unchaste, licentious, lascivious, libertine, reprobate. **7** *hang loose* relaxed, informal, uninhibited, unreserved, frank, open, unceremonious, unconstrained. **at loose ends** unsettled, restless, undecided, unemployed, unoccupied, idle, twiddling one's thumbs. **break loose** escape, make one's escape, run away, flee, take to one's heels. **let loose 1** *let the cows loose* set free, unloose, turn loose, loose, untie, unchain, untether, unfasten, detach, unleash, let go, release, free, liberate. **2** *let loose a cry of pain* give, emit, burst out with, shout, yell, bellow. **on the loose** *cows on the loose* at liberty, free, at large, unconfined.

loose verb **1** *loose the dogs* set free, turn

loose. See LET LOOSE (LOOSE *adj.*). **2** *loose her grip* loosen, relax, slacken, weaken, lessen, reduce, diminish, moderate, soften. **3** *loose a missile* discharge, shoot, fire off, eject, catapult.

loosen verb **1** *loosen a nut/belt* slacken, slack, unstick, let out, undo, unfasten, unhook. **2** *the nut loosened* become loose, work loose, work free. **3** *loosen her grip* relax, slacken, lessen. See LOOSE verb 2. **loosen up** relax, calm down, take it easy, ease up; *inf.* hang loose, lighten up, chill, chill out.

loot noun booty, spoils, spoil, plunder, haul, pillage, prize; *inf.* the goods, boodle.

loot verb plunder, pillage, rob, burgle, steal from, ransack, sack, maraud, ravage, despoil, spoliate.

lopsided adjective asymmetrical, unsymmetrical, uneven, unbalanced, off-balance, unequal, askew, squint, tilting, crooked, out of line, awry.

loquacious adjective talkative, garrulous, voluble, long-winded, wordy, verbose, effusive, chattering; *inf.* having the gift of the gab, bigmouthed, gabby.

lord noun **1** *lord of all he surveys* master, lord and master, ruler, leader, chief, monarch, sovereign, king, emperor, prince, governor, commander, captain, overlord, suzerain, baron, potentate, liege. **2** *the lords and ladies* noble, nobleman, peer, aristocrat, landowner, lord of the manor; duke, earl, viscount. **3** *believe in the Lord* God, Jesus, Jesus Christ, Christ, Christ the Lord, the Redeemer, the Savior.

lordly adjective **1** *a lordly disregard for others* imperious, arrogant, haughty, highhanded, overbearing, overweening, overconfident, dictatorial, authoritarian, peremptory, autocratic, tyrannical, supercilious, disdainful, condescending, patronizing; *inf.* high-and-mighty, bossy, stuck-up, snooty, uppity, hoity-toity. **2** *lordly splendor* noble, aristocratic, lofty, exalted, majestic, grand, regal, princely, kingly, imperial, stately, dignified, magnificent, grandiose.

lore noun **1** *researching Cherokee lore* traditions, folklore, beliefs, superstitions, legends. **2** *bird lore* knowledge, learning, wisdom, know-how, skill.

lose verb **1** *has lost his keys* mislay, misplace, drop, forget. **2** *losing a lot of blood* be deprived of, suffer the loss of. **3** *trying to lose the police* outdistance, outstrip, outrun; escape from, evade, elude, dodge, shake off, throw off, duck. **4** *lose the way* stray from, wander from. **5** *lose the opportunity* fail to grasp/take, let pass, miss, forfeit, neglect; *inf.* pass up, lose out on. **6** *lost the battle* suffer defeat, be defeated, be worsted, be beaten, be conquered, be vanquished, be trounced, fail, meet one's Waterloo. **7** *lose time* waste, squander, dissipate, spend, expend, consume, deplete, exhaust, use up.

loss noun **1** *report the loss of the keys* misplacement, mislaying, dropping, forgetting. **2** *loss of prestige* deprivation, privation, forfeiture, bereavement, disappearance, waste, losing, dissipation. **3** *families/firms suffering loss* deprivation, privation, detriment, disadvantage, damage, injury, impairment, harm, hurt, ruin, destruction. **4** *regret the civilian losses* casualty, fatality, dead, death toll. **5** *the company has made significant losses* deficit, debit, debt, deficiency, depletion. **at a loss** *we are at a loss to understand his motives* baffled, nonplussed, mystified, stumped, puzzled, perplexed, bewildered, ignorant, confused; *inf.* clueless.

lost adjective **1** *lost books* missing, gone astray, mislaid, misplaced, vanished, disappeared, forgotten. **2** *lost travelers* stray, astray, off-course, off-track, disorientated, adrift, going around in circles, at sea. **3** *lost opportunities* missed, passed, forfeited, neglected, wasted, squandered, dissipated, frittered; *inf.* down the drain. **4** *lost tribes* extinct, dead, bygone, past, vanished, forgotten. **5** *lost ships* destroyed, ruined, wiped out, wrecked, finished, perished, demolished, obliterated, effaced, exterminated, eradicated, annihilated, extirpated. **6** *lost souls* damned, fallen, irredeemable, hopeless. **lost in** *she was lost in a book* engrossed in, absorbed in, preoccupied by, spellbound by, distracted by, entranced by.

lot noun **1** *draw lots* slip of paper, number, straw, counter. **2** *decided by lot* chance, luck, lottery, drawing lots, accident, serendipity, fortuity. **3** *his lot in life* fate, destiny, fortune, situation, circumstances, portion, plight. **4** *the brothers' lots* share, portion, quota, ration, allowance, percentage, piece; *inf.* cut. **5** *sold as a lot* set, batch, collection, group, bundle, consignment, parcel. **6** *parking lots* plot, patch of ground, tract of land, building lot. **a lot** *smile a lot* much, a good/great deal, often, frequently, many times. **a lot of** *a lot of people* many, a good/great deal of, a great quantity of, numerous, an abundance of, plenty of, masses of, scores of; *inf.* loads of, heaps of, piles of, oodles of, scads of, wads of, oceans of, gobs of. **throw in one's lot** *threw in his lot with thieves* join forces, form an alliance, ally, link up, combine.

lotion noun cream, salve, ointment, moisturizer, balm, emollient, lubricant, unguent, liniment, embrocation, pomade.

lottery noun draw, raffle, sweepstake, game of chance, gamble, lotto, bingo; risk, hazard, venture.

loud adjective **1** *loud noises* blaring,

booming, noisy, deafening, resounding, reverberant, stentorian, roaring, thunderous, tumultuous, clamorous, ear-splitting, ear-piercing, piercing, strident, harsh, raucous. **2** *loud young women* brash, brazen, bold, loudmouthed, vociferous, raucous, aggressive, coarse, crude, rough, crass, vulgar, brassy; *inf.* pushy. **3** *loud demands* vociferous, clamorous, insistent, vehement, emphatic, urgent, importunate, demanding. **4** *loud colors* garish, gaudy, flashy, bold, flamboyant, lurid, glaring, showy, obtrusive.

loudmouth noun **1** *loudmouths showing off* braggart, brag, boaster, blusterer, swaggerer, braggadocio; *inf.* bigmouth. **2** *loudmouths discussing neighbors' affairs* blabbermouth, gossip, gossipmonger, scandalmonger, busybody.

lounge verb laze, lie, lie around, recline, relax, take it easy, sprawl, loaf, idle, loll, repose.

lousy adjective **1** *lousy workmanship* poor, incompetent, inadequate, unsatisfactory, inferior, careless, second-rate, terrible, miserable; *inf.* rotten, no-good. **2** *a lousy trick to play* dirty, low, mean, base, despicable, contemptible, low-down, hateful, detestable, loathsome, vile; *inf.* rotten. **lousy with** *places lousy with tourists* full of, covered in, crowded with, overrun by, swarming with, teeming with, crawling with.

lout noun boor, oaf, dolt, churl, bumpkin, yahoo; brute, rowdy, barbarian; *inf.* slob, clodhopper, clod, lummox.

lovable adjective adorable, dear, sweet, cute, charming, delightful, captivating, enchanting, engaging, pleasing, appealing, winsome, winning, endearing, affectionate, warmhearted, cuddly.

love verb **1** *he loves her* prize, cherish, care for, be fond of, be attracted to, be attached to, hold dear, adore, dote on, worship, idolize, treasure, be devoted to, desire, want, be infatuated with, lust after, long for, yearn for, adulate; *inf.* fancy, have a crush on. **2** *she loves chocolate* like, have a liking for, have a weakness for, be partial to, relish, savor, appreciate, take pleasure in, delight in; *inf.* get a kick out of.

love noun **1** *the couple's love for/of each other* affection, fondness, care, concern, attachment, regard, warmth, intimacy, devotion, adoration, passion, ardor, desire, lust, yearning, infatuation, adulation. **2** *her love of/for chocolate* liking, weakness, partiality, enjoyment, appreciation, relish, passion. **3** *love for/toward one's neighbor* care, caring, regard, solicitude, sympathy, warmth, friendliness, friendship, rapport, brotherhood, kindness, charity. **4** *be brave, my love* beloved, loved one, true love, dear, dearest, darling, sweetheart, angel, lover, inamorato/inamorata. **5** *their love was short-lived* romance, relationship, love affair, affair, liaison. **love affair** affair, romance, relationship, liaison, amour, intrigue, *affaire de coeur.* **in love with** attracted to, infatuated with, enamored of, smitten by, besotted with, devoted to, having a passion for, lusting after; *inf.* having the hots for.

lovely adjective **1** *a lovely face* beautiful, pretty, attractive, good-looking, comely, handsome, sweet, fair, charming, adorable, enchanting, engaging, winsome. **2** *a lovely surprise* delightful, pleasant, nice, agreeable, marvelous, wonderful.

lover noun **1** *send flowers to his/her lover* boyfriend, girlfriend, mistress, ladylove, paramour, beau, loved one, beloved, sweetheart, inamorato/inamorata. **2** *a lover of antiques* admirer, devotee, fan, enthusiast, aficionado; *inf.* buff, freak.

loving adjective affectionate, fond, devoted, caring, adoring, doting, solicitous, demonstrative, tender, warm, warmhearted, friendly, kind, sympathetic, charitable, cordial, amiable, amorous, ardent, passionate.

low adjective **1** *a low table* short, small, little, squat, stubby, stunted, truncated, dwarfish. **2** *low land* low-lying, ground-level, sea-level, flat, sunken, depressed, nether. **3** *of low birth* lowly, humble, low-ranking, plebeian, peasant, poor, common, ordinary, simple, plain, unpretentious, inferior, subordinate. **4** *supplies are low* sparse, meager, scarce, scanty, scant, few, little, deficient, inadequate, paltry, measly, depleted, diminished. **5** *a low hum* soft, quiet, muted, subdued, muffled, hushed, whispered, murmured, gentle, dulcet, indistinct, inaudible. **6** *feeling low* low-spirited, down, depressed, dejected, despondent, disheartened, downhearted, downcast, gloomy, glum, unhappy, sad, miserable, blue, morose, moody, heavy-hearted, forlorn; *inf.* down in the mouth, down in the dumps. **7** *of low intelligence* low-grade, inferior, substandard, below par, second-rate, deficient, defective, wanting, lacking, inadequate, mediocre. **8** *low expectations* modest, unambitious, unpretentious, unaspiring, simple, plain, ordinary, commonplace, run-of-the-mill. **9** *have a low opinion of them* unfavorable, poor, bad, adverse, hostile, negative. **10** *a low thing to do* mean, nasty, foul, bad, wicked, evil, vile, despicable, contemptible, base, dishonorable, unprincipled, dastardly, ignoble, sordid. **11** *low comedy* vulgar, crude, coarse, obscene, indecent, gross, ribald, smutty, bawdy, pornographic, blue, rude, rough, unrefined, offensive. **12** *low prices* cheap, inexpensive, moderate, reasonable, modest, bargain-basement.

lower adjective **1** *of lower status* lesser, subordinate, junior, inferior, minor, secondary. **2** *lower bunk* under, underneath, nether. **3** *lower prices* cheaper, reduced, decreased, cut; slashed.

lower verb **1** *lower the flag/weight* let down, take down, drop, let fall, let sink. **2** *lower the volume* modulate, soften, quieten, hush, tone down, muffle, turn down, mute. **3** *will only lower him in her eyes* degrade, debase, demean, downgrade, discredit, devalue, dishonor, disgrace, belittle. **4** *lower the temperature/prices* reduce, bring down, decrease, lessen, cut, slash. **5** *the winds lowered* abate, die down, subside, let up, moderate, slacken, dwindle, lessen, ebb, wane, taper off.

low-key adjective restrained, muted, subtle, quiet, understated, relaxed, easygoing, modulated, softened; *inf.* laid-back.

lowly adjective **1** *of lowly birth* humble, poor, common. *See* LOW adjective **3**. **2** *feeling lowly before God* humble, meek, submissive, modest, unassuming. **3** *lowly ambitions* low, simple, ordinary, commonplace, run-of-the-mill, modest, unambitious, unpretentious, unaspiring.

loyal adjective faithful, true, true-hearted, trusted, trustworthy, steadfast, staunch, dependable, reliable, devoted, dutiful, patriotic, constant, unwavering, unswerving.

loyalty noun faithfulness, fidelity, fealty, allegiance, trueness, trustworthiness, steadfastness, staunchness, dependability, reliability, devotion, patriotism, constancy.

lubricant noun lubricator, oil, grease, emollient, lard, fat, moisturizer, lotion, unguent.

lucid adjective **1** *a lucid description* clear, clear-cut, comprehensible, intelligible, understandable, plain, simple, direct, straightforward, transparent, cogent. **2** *he is scarcely lucid* sane, rational, in one's right mind, of sound mind, *compos mentis*, sensible, clearheaded; *inf.* all there, with all one's marbles.

luck noun **1** *as luck would have it* serendipity, fate, fortune, destiny, chance, fortuity, accident, hazard. **2** *wishing you luck* good luck, good fortune, success, prosperity, advantage, advantageousness, felicity. **in luck** lucky, fortunate, favored, advantaged, successful. **out of luck** unlucky, unfortunate, luckless, cursed with ill/bad luck, unsuccessful, disadvantaged.

lucky adjective **1** *lucky people* fortunate, favored, born under a lucky star, charmed; successful, prosperous, advantaged. **2** *a lucky guess* fortunate, fortuitous, providential, advantageous, timely, opportune, expedient, auspicious, propitious.

lucrative adjective profitable, profit-making, moneymaking, high-income, well-paid, high-paying, gainful, remunerative, productive, fat, fruitful, rewarding, worthwhile.

ludicrous adjective absurd, ridiculous, laughable, risible, derisible, comical, farcical, silly, funny, amusing, hilarious, crazy, outlandish, preposterous.

luggage noun bags, baggage, suitcases, trunks, things, gear, belongings, effects, impedimenta, paraphernalia, accoutrements.

lugubrious adjective mournful, doleful, melancholy, dismal, gloomy, somber, funereal, sorrowful, morose, miserable, joyless, woebegone, woeful, dirgelike, elegiac.

lukewarm adjective 1 *lukewarm water* tepid, warm, warmish, at room temperature. 2 *lukewarm response* indifferent, cool, halfhearted, apathetic, unenthusiastic, impassive, dispassionate, sluggish, phlegmatic.

lull verb 1 *lull the child to sleep* rock (gently), soothe, quiet, hush, silence, calm. 2 *the storm lulled* abate, die down, subside, let up, moderate, slacken, lessen, dwindle, decrease, diminish, ebb, fade away, wane, taper off.

lull noun 1 *a lull in the proceedings* pause, respite, interval, break, hiatus; *inf.* letup. 2 *the lull before the storm* calm, stillness, quiet, tranquillity, silence, hush.

lumber noun timber, wood, boards, planks, planking, beams.

lumber verb *heard him lumbering around upstairs* clump, stump, plod, trudge, stamp, shuffle, stumble.

luminary noun leading light, star, superstar, notable, dignitary, VIP, celebrity, big name, household name; *inf.* bigwig, big shot.

luminous adjective lighted, lit, illuminated, shining, bright, brilliant, radiant, dazzling, glowing, effulgent, luminescent, phosphorescent, vivid, resplendent.

lump noun 1 *a lump of putty/coal* chunk, wedge, hunk, piece, mass, cake, nugget, ball, dab, pat, clod, gob, wad, clump, mound. 2 *a lump on his head* bump, swelling, bruise, bulge, protuberance, protrusion, growth, carbuncle, hump, tumor, tumescence, node.

lump verb *lump all the expenses together* combine, group, unite, pool, blend, merge, mass, fuse, conglomerate, consolidate.

lumpy adjective 1 *a lumpy mattress* bumpy, knobby, bulging, uneven. 2 *lumpy custard* curdled, clotted, granular, grainy.

lunacy noun 1 *suffering from lunacy* insanity, madness, mental illness/derangement, dementia, dementedness, loss of reason, mania, frenzy, psychosis; *inf.* craziness. 2 *the sheer lunacy of the decision* madness, insanity, foolishness, folly, foolhardiness,

stupidity, idiocy, irrationality, illogicality, senselessness, absurdity, ludicrousness; *inf.* craziness, daftness.

lunatic noun maniac, madman, madwoman, imbecile, idiot, psychopath; *inf.* loony, nut, nutcase, basket case, psycho.

lunatic adjective mad, insane, foolish, foolhardy, idiotic, crackbrained, irrational, illogical, senseless, nonsensical, absurd, silly, asinine, ludicrous, preposterous; *inf.* crazy, daft.

lunge noun 1 *make a lunge toward the open door* spring, jump, leap, bound, dash, charge, pounce, dive. 2 *take a lunge at his attacker* stab, jab, poke, thrust, swing, pass, cut, feint; *inf.* swipe.

lunge verb *lunge toward the door* spring, jump, leap, bound, dash, charge, pounce, dive. **lunge at** *lunge at his attacker* charge, rush, jump, attack, pounce on, lash out at, take a swing at; *inf.* take a swipe at.

lurch verb 1 *drunks lurching home* stagger, sway, reel, weave, stumble, totter. 2 *ships lurching in the storm* list, roll, pitch, toss, sway, veer, swerve.

lure verb entice, attract, induce, inveigle, decoy, draw, lead, allure, tempt, seduce, beguile, ensnare, cajole.

lure noun enticement, attraction, inducement, decoy, draw, temptation, bait, magnet, drawing card, carrot; *inf.* come-on.

lurid adjective 1 *lurid colors/sunsets* overbright, brilliant, glaring, flaming, dazzling, glowing, intense, vivid, showy, gaudy, fiery, blood-red, burning. 2 *lurid descriptions of their affair* sensational, melodramatic, exaggerated, extravagant, graphic, explicit, unrestrained, shocking, startling; *inf.* full-frontal. 3 *lurid details of the murder* gruesome, gory, grisly, macabre, repugnant, revolting, disgusting, ghastly.

lurk verb skulk, lie in wait, hide, crouch, sneak, slink, prowl, steal, tiptoe.

luscious adjective delicious, juicy, sweet, succulent, mouthwatering, tasty, appetizing, delectable, palatable, toothsome; *inf.* scrumptious, yummy.

lush adjective 1 *lush vegetation* luxuriant, abundant, profuse, exuberant, dense, thick, riotous, overgrown, prolific, rank, teeming, junglelike, flourishing, verdant, green. 2 *lush fruits* juicy, succulent, fleshy, pulpy, ripe, soft, tender, fresh. 3 *lush penthouse* luxurious, sumptuous, grand, palatial, opulent, lavish, elaborate, extravagant; *inf.* plush, ritzy.

lust noun 1 *physical lust* sexual desire, sexual appetite, libido, sex drive, sexuality; lechery, lasciviousness, lewdness, carnality, licentiousness, salaciousness, salacity, prurience, concupiscence, wantonness; *inf.* horniness. 2 *a lust for power* greed, greediness, desire, craving, covetousness, avidness, avidity, cupidity, longing, yearning, hunger, thirst, appetite, passion.

lust verb desire, crave, covet, want, need, long for, yearn for, hunger for, thirst for, ache for; *inf.* have the hots for.

luster noun 1 *admire the luster of the table* sheen, gloss, shine, burnish, glow, gleam, sparkle, shimmer. 2 *bring luster to the school* honor, glory, credit, merit, prestige, renown, fame, distinction, notability. 3 *the luster of the stars* brilliance, brightness, radiance, luminousness.

lustrous adjective shiny, shining, glossy, gleaming, glowing, bright, burnished, polished, dazzling, sparkling, glistening, twinkling, shimmering, luminous.

lusty adjective 1 *lusty young men* healthy, strong, vigorous, robust, hale and hearty, hearty, energetic, lively, rugged, sturdy, tough, stalwart, brawny, hefty, husky, burly, powerful, virile, red-blooded. 2 *a lusty cry* loud, vigorous, hearty, powerful, forceful.

luxuriant adjective 1 *luxuriant vegetation* lush, abundant, prolific, verdant. See LUSH adjective 1. 2 *luxuriant prose* florid, flowery, ornate, elaborate, fancy, adorned, decorated, embellished, embroidered, extravagant, flamboyant, ostentatious, showy, high-flown, baroque, rococo.

luxurious adjective 1 *luxurious surroundings* opulent, affluent, sumptuous, expensive, rich, costly, deluxe, lush, grand, splendid, magnificent, lavish, well-appointed, comfortable, extravagant, ornate, fancy; *inf.* plush, posh, ritzy, swanky. 2 *luxurious habits* self-indulgent, sensual, epicurean, hedonistic, sybaritic.

luxury noun 1 *live in luxury* opulence, affluence, sumptuousness, richness, grandeur, splendor, magnificence, lavishness, luxuriousness, lap of luxury, bed of roses. 2 *the luxury of independence* boon, benefit, advantage, delight, bliss, comfort. 3 *one of life's luxuries* extra, nonessential, frill, extravagance, indulgence, treat, refinement.

lying noun untruthfulness, fabrication, fibbing, perjury, falseness, falsity, dishonesty, mendacity, storytelling, dissimulation, dissembling, prevarication, deceit, guile, crookedness, double-dealing.

lyric adjective 1 *lyric poetry* songlike, musical, melodic, melodious, expressive, personal, subjective, emotional, passionate, lyrical. 2 *lyric voices* light, silvery, clear, lilting, flowing, dulcet, sweet, mellifluous, mellow, lyrical.

lyrics plural noun words, libretto, book, text.

Mm

macabre adjective gruesome, grisly, grim, gory, morbid, ghastly, hideous, horrific, horrible, horrifying, dreadful, appalling, loathsome, repugnant, repulsive.

mace noun staff, club, cudgel, bludgeon.

machinations plural noun schemes, plot, intrigues, conspiracies, complots, designs, plans, devices, ploys, ruses, trick, wiles, stratagems, tactics, maneuvers, contrivances, expedients.

machine noun 1 *the washing machine broke down* appliance, apparatus, instrument, tool, device, contraption, gadget, mechanism, engine, motor. 2 *the party machine* organization, system, structure, agency, machinery, council, cabal, clique; *inf.* setup.

machinery noun 1 *factory machinery* equipment, apparatus, mechanism, gear, tackle, instruments, gadgetry. 2 *the machinery of government* workings, organization, system, structure, agency, channel, vehicle;

inf. setup, nuts and bolts, brass tacks, nitty-gritty.

machismo noun masculinity, manliness, virility, toughness, chauvinism, male chauvinism, sexism.

mad adjective 1 *mad with grief* stark (raving) mad, insane, deranged, demented, of unsound mind, crazed, lunatic, *non compos mentis*, unbalanced, unhinged, unstable, distracted, manic, frenzied, raving, distraught, frantic, hysterical, delirious, psychotic, not quite right, mad as a hatter, mad as a March hare, foaming at the mouth; *inf.* crazy, out of one's mind, nuts, nutty, off one's rocker, round/around the bend, balmy, batty, bonkers, crackers, cuckoo, loopy, loony, bananas, loco, dippy, screwy, with a screw loose, out of one's tree, off one's trolley, off the wall, not all there, not right. 2 *the vandalism made them mad* angry, furious, infuriated, irate, raging, enraged, fuming, in a towering rage, incensed, wrathful, indignant, exasperated, irritated, berserk, out of control, beside oneself, livid. **3** *a mad scheme/idea* insane, foolish, stupid, lunatic, idiotic, crackbrained, irrational, illogical, senseless, absurd, impractical, silly, inane, imprudent, preposterous. **4** *mad, passionate love* wild, unrestrained, uncontrolled, abandoned, excited, frenzied, frantic, frenetic, ebullient, energetic, boisterous. **like mad 1** *run like mad* furiously, energetically; *inf.* like crazy, like a house on fire. **2** *love her like mad* madly, enthusiastically, wildly, passionately, intensely, ardently, fervently, to distraction, devotedly. **mad about** *mad about jazz* keen on, fanatical about, devoted to, infatuated with, in love with; *inf.* crazy about, nuts about, hooked on, wild about.

madcap adjective daredevil, impulsive, wild, reckless, rash, hotheaded, daring, adventurous, heedless, imprudent, ill-advised, foolhardy, impractical, harebrained.

madden verb *her behavior maddened them* anger, infuriate, send into a rage, enrage, incense, exasperate, irritate, inflame, annoy, provoke, upset, agitate, vex, irk, pique, gall, make one's blood boil, make one see red.

maddening adjective infuriating, exasperating, irritating, annoying, provoking, upsetting, vexing, irksome, unsettling, disturbing.

made-up adjective **1** *a made-up story* invented, fabricated, trumped-up, concocted, devised, manufactured, fictional, false, untrue, unreal, sham, specious, spurious, imaginary, mythical. **2** *made-up faces* painted, done up, powdered, rouged.

madhouse noun **1** *confined to a madhouse* mental hospital, psychiatric hospital, asylum; *inf.* nuthouse, funny farm, loony bin. **2** *the place is a madhouse!* bedlam, babel, chaos, pandemonium, uproar, turmoil, disarray, disorder, three-ring circus.

madly adverb **1** *behaving madly* insanely, distractedly, frenziedly, maniacally, frantically, hysterically, deliriously, wildly. **2** *rush around madly* furiously, hastily, energetically. **3** *love her madly* enthusiastically, wildly, intensely.

madman noun maniac, lunatic, psychopath; *inf.* loony, nut, nutcase, psycho.

madness noun **1** *madness caused by grief* insanity, insaneness, dementia, mental illness/derangement, dementedness, lunacy, mania, frenzy, psychosis, craziness. **2** *with madness in her voice* anger, fury, rage, wrath, ire, indignation, exasperation, irritation. **3** *the madness of the decision* insanity, folly, foolishness, stupidity, lunacy, idiocy, senselessness, absurdity, silliness, inanity.

maelstrom noun **1** *ships destroyed in a maelstrom* whirlpool, vortex, eddy, swirl, Charybdis. **2** *the maelstrom of war* turbulence, tumult, uproar, commotion, chaos, confusion, upheaval, pandemonium, bedlam.

magazine noun periodical, journal, publication, supplement, color supplement; *inf.* glossy.

magic noun **1** *believers in magic* sorcery, witchcraft, wizardry, enchantment, necromancy, occultism, the occult, black magic, voodoo, thaumaturgy. **2** *skills of magic* sleight of hand, legerdemain, conjuring, illusion, prestidigitation; *inf.* hocus-pocus. **3** *the magic of the stage* allure, enchantment, fascination, charm.

magic adjective magical, enchanting, entrancing, spellbinding, fascinating, captivating, charming, glamorous, magnetic, irresistible, hypnotic.

magician noun **1** *frightened by the magician* sorcerer, sorceress, witch, wizard, warlock, enchanter, enchantress, necromancer. **2** *the magician at the party* illusionist, conjuror, legerdemainist, prestidigitator. **3** *a magician at the piano* genius, master, virtuoso, expert, marvel, wizard, maestro; *inf.* ace, whiz.

magnanimity noun generosity, charitableness, benevolence, bigheartedness, munificence, bountifulness, largesse, unselfishness, selflessness, self-sacrifice, mercy, leniency.

magnanimous adjective generous, benevolent, beneficent, bighearted, greathearted, munificent, bountiful, noble, unselfish, ungrudging, forgiving, merciful, lenient, indulgent.

magnate noun tycoon, captain of industry, baron, industrialist, entrepreneur, financier, VIP, notable, nabob, grandee; *inf.* big shot, bigwig, big wheel, fat cat, mogul.

magnet noun **1** *a magnet attracting iron filings* lodestone, magnetite. **2** *the ad worked as a magnet* lure, attraction, fascination, enticement, draw, temptation, come-on.

magnetic adjective alluring, attractive, captivating, entrancing, enchanting, enthralling, engaging, seductive, inviting, bewitching, charismatic, hypnotic, mesmeric.

magnetism noun allure, attraction, appeal, draw, drawing power, pull, charm, charisma.

magnification noun increase, augmentation, enlargement, extension, expansion, intensification, heightening, enhancement, aggrandizement.

magnificence noun splendor, grandeur, glory, sumptuousness, opulence, luxuriousness, luxury, lavishness, richness, brilliance, radiance, elegance.

magnificent adjective **1** *magnificent processions/apartments* splendid, resplendent, grand, grandiose, impressive, majestic, august, noble, stately, sumptuous, opulent, luxurious; *inf.* splendiferous, ritzy, posh. **2** *a magnificent performance* masterly, virtuoso, impressive, marvelous, wonderful; *inf.* terrific, brilliant, out of this world.

magnify verb **1** *bacteria visible when magnified* increase, augment, enlarge, extend, expand, amplify, intensify, boost, enhance, aggrandize. **2** *magnify their troubles* exaggerate, overstate, overemphasize, overplay, color, embroider, embellish, enhance, inflate; *inf.* blow up, blow up out of all proportion.

magnitude noun **1** *the magnitude of the explosion/epidemic* size, extent, measure, proportions, dimensions, volume, weight, quantity, mass, bulk, amplitude; greatness, largeness, bigness, immensity, vastness, hugeness, enormity, enormousness, expanse. **2** *the magnitude of his rank* importance, significance, weight, moment, consequence, mark, notability, note, greatness, distinction, eminence, fame, renown. **of the first magnitude** of the utmost importance, of the greatest significance.

maid noun maidservant, housemaid, chambermaid, servant, domestic, girl, au pair.

maiden adjective **1** *maiden aunt* unmarried, spinster, unwed, unwedded, single, celibate. **2** *maiden voyage* first, initial, inaugural, introductory, initiatory. **3** *maiden territory* virgin, intact, undefiled, untrodden, untapped, unused, fresh, new.

mail noun letters, packages, parcels, correspondence, communications, airmail, registered mail; electronic mail, E-mail.

maim verb cripple, disable, put out of action, lame, incapacitate, impair, mar, mutilate, disfigure, mangle, wound, injure, hurt.

main adjective **1** *the main office* head, chief, principal, leading, foremost, central, prime, premier, primary, supreme, predominant, preeminent, paramount, cardinal, pivotal. **2** *by main force* sheer, pure, utter, downright, mere, plain, brute, stark, absolute, out-and-out, direct.

mainly adverb for the most part, mostly, in the main, on the whole, largely, by and large, predominantly, chiefly, overall, in general, generally.

mainstay noun chief support, prop, linchpin, pillar, bulwark, buttress, backbone, anchor.

maintain verb **1** *maintain friendly relations* continue, keep up, carry on, preserve, conserve, prolong, perpetuate, sustain.

2 *maintain the roads* keep in repair, keep up, keep intact, care for, take good care of, look after. **3** *maintain a family* support, provide for, keep, finance, feed, nurture, nourish, sustain. **4** *maintain his innocence* declare, assert, state, affirm, aver, avow, profess, claim, allege, contend, asseverate. **5** *maintain a position* uphold, defend, fight for, stand by, support, back, advocate.

maintenance noun **1** *the maintenance of friendly relations* continuation, continuance, preservation, perpetuation. **2** *the maintenance of the property* upkeep, repairs, preservation, conservation, care.

majestic adjective regal, royal, kingly, queenly, princely, noble, lordly, august, exalted, lofty, stately, dignified, magnificent, grand, splendid, resplendent, glorious, impressive, imposing.

majesty noun **1** *the majesty of the procession* nobility, augustness, loftiness, stateliness, dignity, magnificence, grandeur, grandness, splendor, resplendence, glory. **2** *the majesty invested in him* sovereignty, authority, power, dominion, supremacy.

major adjective **1** *the major part is complete* larger, bigger, greater, main. **2** *one of our major poets* greatest, best, most important, leading, foremost, chief, main, outstanding, first-rate, notable, eminent, preeminent, supreme. **3** *a major issue* important, significant, crucial, vital, great, weighty, serious.

make verb **1** *make furniture* build, construct, assemble, put together, put up, erect, manufacture, produce, fabricate, create, form, fashion, model, mold, shape, forge. **2** *make them pay* force (to), compel (to), coerce (into), press (into), drive (into), pressure (into), oblige (to), require (to), prevail upon (to), impel (to); *inf.* railroad (into), put the heat on, put the screws on, strong-arm. **3** *make a noise/scene* cause, create, give rise to, produce, bring about, generate, engender, occasion, effect. **4** *make a bow* perform, execute, do, accomplish, carry out, practice, engage in. **5** *make him chairman* appoint, designate, name, nominate, select, elect, vote in, install, invest, ordain, assign. **6** *make a will/movie* compose, put together, frame, formulate, prepare, write, direct. **7** *make money* gain, acquire, obtain, get, realize, secure, win, earn, net, gross, clear, bring in, take home, pocket. **8** *make tea/dinner* prepare, get ready, put together, concoct, cook; *inf.* whip up, fix. **9** *make laws* draw up, frame, form, formulate, enact, lay down, establish, institute, found, originate. **10** *that makes $100* come to, add up to, total, amount to. **11** *what do you make the total to be?* estimate, calculate, compute, gauge, reckon. **12** *make a decision* come to, settle on, determine on, conclude, establish, seal. **13** *make a speech* give, deliver, utter, give voice to, enunciate, recite, pronounce. **14** *the sofa makes a good bed* act as, serve as, constitute, play the part of, represent, embody. **15** *made the team* achieve, attain, get into, gain access to, gain a place in. **16** *make the bus/party* catch, arrive at, reach, get to. **make as if/though** act as if/though, pretend, feign, give the impression, make a show of, affect, feint; *inf.* put it on. **make believe** pretend, fantasize, indulge in fantasy, daydream, build castles in the air, build castles in Spain, dream, imagine, romance, playact, act, enact. **make do** get by, get along, scrape by, manage, cope, survive, muddle through. **make for 1** *make for a safe place* go toward, head for, aim for, make one's way toward, proceed toward. **2** *this will make for a good relationship* contribute to, be conducive to, promote, facilitate, further, advance, forward, favor. **make off** run away/off, take to one's heels, beat a hasty retreat, flee, bolt, fly, make a getaway, make a quick exit, abscond, decamp; *inf.* clear off, beat it, make tracks, split, cut and run, skedaddle, vamoose, hightail it. **make off with** steal, purloin, appropriate, kidnap, abduct; *inf.* swipe, nab, waltz off with, filch. **make out 1** *make out a figure in the distance* discern, see, distinguish, espy, behold, perceive, descry, notice, observe, recognize, pick out, detect, discover. **2** *unable to make out what she says* understand, comprehend, follow, grasp, fathom, work out, figure out, interpret. **3** *unable to make out the handwriting* decipher, work out, figure out, understand, interpret. **4** *they made out that he was violent* allege, claim, suggest, imply, pretend. **5** *how did you make out?* get on, get along, fare, do, get by, proceed, go, progress, manage, survive. **make over** renovate, remodel, redo, restore, redecorate, brighten up, improve, upgrade; *inf.* do up. **make up 1** *their statements make up the argument* comprise, form, compose, constitute. **2** *make up the balance* supply, furnish, provide. **3** *make up for previous rudeness* make amends, atone, compensate, make recompense, make reparation, make redress. **4** *kiss and make up* be friends again, bury the hatchet, declare a truce, make peace, forgive and forget, shake hands, become reconciled, settle differences, mend fences. **5** *make up a prescription* prepare, mix, concoct, put together. **6** *make up an excuse* invent, fabricate, concoct, hatch, coin, trump up, dream up, think up, devise, manufacture, formulate, frame, construct; *inf.* cook up. **7** *make up a short story* compose, write, create, originate, devise. **8** *make up her face* apply cosmetics to, powder, rouge; *inf.* put on, do, paint, do up, apply warpaint to.

make noun **1** *different makes of car* brand, label, trademark, sort, type, variety, style, mark, marque. **2** *a clumsy make of machine* build, form, frame, structure, construction, shape. **3** *a different make from his brother* character, nature. *See* MAKEUP 3.

make-believe noun pretense, fantasy, daydreaming, dreaming, imagination, romancing, fabrication, playacting, charade, masquerade.

make-believe adjective pretended, feigned, made-up, fantasy, dream, imaginary, unreal, fictitious, mock, sham; *inf.* pretend.

maker noun manufacturer, builder, constructor, producer, creator, fabricator, author, architect, framer.

makeshift adjective stopgap, make-do, provisional, temporary, rough-and-ready, substitute, improvised, standby, jerry-built, thrown-together.

makeup noun **1** *putting on their makeup* cosmetics, greasepaint, foundation; *inf.* warpaint, face paint. **2** *the makeup of the machines* structure, composition, constitution, configuration, construction, assembly, arrangement, organization. **3** *the makeup of a criminal* character, nature, temperament, temper, personality, disposition, humor, make, stamp, mold.

makings plural noun qualities, characteristics, ingredients, materials, essentials, beginnings, basics.

maladjusted adjective disturbed, unstable, neurotic; *inf.* mixed-up, screwed-up.

malady noun disease, disorder, illness, sickness, ailment, affliction, complaint, infection, indisposition, infirmity.

malaise noun lassitude, listlessness, languor, enervation, weakness, feebleness, infirmity, illness, sickness, unease, discomfort, anxiety, angst, disquiet, melancholy, depression, weariness, ennui.

malcontent noun grumbler, complainer, moaner, faultfinder, carper, agitator, troublemaker, mischief-maker, rebel; *inf.* grouser, griper, nitpicker, bellyacher.

male adjective masculine, manlike, manly, virile.

male noun **1** *clothing for males* man, gentleman, boy, lad; *inf.* fellow, guy. **2** *the male has brighter plumage* tomcat, bull, ram, stallion, buck, stag, boar, billy goat, cock, gander, drake.

malevolent adjective malign, malignant, malicious, maleficent, evil-intentioned, evil-minded, ill-natured, hostile, unfriendly, spiteful, baleful, vindictive, revengeful, rancorous, vicious, pernicious, cruel.

malfunction verb go wrong, break down, break, fail; *inf.* conk out, go kaput.

malfunction noun fault, defect, flaw, impairment, glitch; breakdown, failure, collapse.

malice noun malevolence, maliciousness, malignity, evil intentions, ill will, ill feeling, animosity, animus, hostility, enmity, bad blood, hatred, hate, spite, spitefulness, vindictiveness, rancor, bitterness, grudge, venom, spleen.

malicious adjective malevolent, malign, malignant, evil, evil-intentioned, ill-natured, hostile, spiteful, baleful, vindictive, rancorous, bitter, venomous, pernicious, harmful, hurtful, destructive, defamatory; *inf.* bitchy, catty.

malign verb slander, libel, defame, smear, calumniate, vilify, speak ill of, spread lies about, cast aspersions on, misrepresent, traduce, denigrate, disparage, slur, derogate; *inf.* bad-mouth, run down, drag through the mud.

malignant adjective **1** *malignant intentions* malevolent, evil. See MALICIOUS. **2** *a malignant growth/disease* cancerous, dangerous, virulent, uncontrollable, deadly, fatal, life-threatening, lethal.

malleable adjective **1** *malleable substances* workable, shapable, moldable, plastic, pliant, ductile, tractile. **2** *malleable people* pliable, compliant, accommodating, adaptable, amenable, biddable, tractable, manageable, governable.

malnutrition noun undernourishment, starvation, famine, anorexia.

malpractice noun unprofessional conduct, dereliction, negligence, carelessness, unethical behavior, misconduct, wrongdoing.

maltreat verb ill-treat, ill-use. See MISTREAT.

maltreatment noun ill treatment, ill use, mistreatment, abuse, rough handling, manhandling, bullying, injury, harm.

mammoth adjective huge, enormous. See MASSIVE.

man noun **1** *a fine man* male, gentleman; *inf.* fellow, guy. **2** *no man is perfect* human being, human, mortal, person, individual, one. **3** *the evolution of man* mankind, the human race, the human species, *Homo sapiens*, humankind, human beings, humans, people. **4** *employ a man to do the garden* workman, worker, laborer, helper, hand. **5** *the ambassador and his man* valet, manservant, gentleman's gentleman; page, footman; flunky. **6** *his sister and her man* husband, spouse, boyfriend, partner, lover, escort, beau, significant other. **to a man** with no exceptions, without exception, bar none, unanimously, as one.

manacles plural noun handcuffs, chains, irons, hand shackles/fetters; *inf.* cuffs, bracelets.

manage verb **1** *manage the team/organization* run, head, direct, control, preside over, lead, govern, rule, command, superintend, supervise, oversee, administer, organize, conduct, handle, guide, be at the helm of; *inf.* head up. **2** *manage to survive* succeed (in), contrive, engineer, bring about/off, achieve, accomplish, effect; cope, get along, carry on, survive, make do; *inf.* make out, get by. **3** *can you manage the dog?* deal with, handle, control, master, influence. **4** *manage a weapon* wield, use, operate, work, ply, handle, manipulate.

manageable adjective doable, practicable, possible, feasible; controllable, governable, tamable, tractable, docile, accommodating, amenable.

management noun **1** *the dispute with management* managers, employers, owners, proprietors, directors, executives; *inf.* bosses, top brass. **2** *the management of the firm* administration, running, charge, care, direction, command, supervision.

manager noun employer, director, executive, department head, administrator, superintendent, supervisor; *inf.* boss.

mandate noun direction, instruction, order, command, directive, ruling, decree, edict, dictate.

mandatory adjective obligatory, compulsory, binding, required, requisite, essential, imperative, necessary.

maneuver noun **1** *maneuver of troops* movement, deployment, operation, exercise. **2** *with one deft maneuver* move, stroke; trick, stratagem, tactic, machination, artifice, dodge, ploy, ruse, scheme.

maneuver verb **1** *maneuver the car* move, work, negotiate, steer, guide, direct, manipulate. **2** *maneuvers things to suit himself* manage, manipulate, contrive, engineer, devise, plan, plot; *inf.* wangle. **3** *maneuver for the leadership* scheme, intrigue, plot.

mangle verb **1** *the mower mangled the hose* mutilate, hack, cut up, lacerate, maul, tear at, rend, butcher, disfigure, deform. **2** *mangle the piece of music* spoil, ruin, bungle, make a mess of; *inf.* murder.

mangy adjective **1** *mangy animals* scabby, scabious, scaly. **2** *mangy carpets* shabby, scruffy, shoddy, squalid, seedy. **3** *a mangy individual* contemptible, despicable, nasty, mean, base, low.

manhandle verb shove, maul, mistreat, ill-treat, abuse, injure, damage, beat, batter; *inf.* paw, knock about, beat up, rough up.

manhood noun 1 *reach manhood* adulthood, maturity, sexual maturity, puberty. 2 *insult his manhood* maleness, masculinity, virility, machismo. 3 *soldiers demonstrating their manhood* bravery, courage. See MANLINESS 1.

mania noun *a mania for collecting china* passion, enthusiasm, desire, urge, craving, craze, obsession, compulsion, fixation, fetish, fascination, preoccupation; *inf.* thing.

maniac noun madman, madwoman, psychopath, lunatic; *inf.* loony, nutcase, nut, psycho.

manifest verb 1 *manifest strange symptoms* display, show, exhibit, demonstrate, present, evince, express, reveal, indicate, make plain, declare. 2 *manifest his guilt* prove, evidence, substantiate, corroborate, verify.

manifest adjective obvious, clear, plain, apparent, patent, conspicuous, unmistakable, distinct, blatant, glaring.

manifestation noun 1 *a manifestation of solidarity* display, show, exhibition, demonstration, presentation, exposition, illustration, exemplification, indication, declaration. 2 *manifestations of their presence* evidence, proof, testimony, substantiation, sign, indication.

manifesto noun proclamation, pronouncement, declaration, announcement.

manipulate verb 1 *manipulate the tool/weapon* handle, wield, ply, work, operate, use, employ, utilize, exercise. 2 *manipulate his colleagues* influence, control, use to one's advantage, exploit, maneuver, engineer, steer, direct, guide, pull the strings. 3 *manipulate the figures* juggle, massage, falsify, doctor, tamper with, fiddle with, tinker with; *inf.* cook.

manipulator noun exploiter, maneuverer, conniver, intriguer.

manliness noun 1 *show their manliness in battle* manhood, bravery, courage, valor, boldness, fearlessness, stoutheartedness. 2 *cologne said to evoke manliness* masculinity, virility, strength, robustness, muscularity, powerfulness, ruggedness, toughness.

manly adjective 1 *manly characteristics* manful, brave, courageous, gallant, valiant, valorous, bold, fearless, stout, stouthearted, dauntless; *inf.* macho, Ramboesque. 2 *a manly figure* masculine, virile, robust, muscular, powerful, well-built, strapping, sturdy, rugged, tough.

man-made adjective manufactured, synthetic, artificial, imitation, ersatz, plastic.

manner noun 1 *work in an efficient manner* way, means, method, system, approach, technique, procedure, process, methodology, routine, practice, fashion, mode. 2 *an unfriendly manner* look, air, appearance, demeanor, aspect, mien, bearing, cast, deportment. 3 *what manner of person is he?* kind, sort, type, variety, form, nature, breed, class, category.

mannered adjective affected, unnatural, artificial, stilted, theatrical, posed, stagy.

mannerism noun habit, characteristic gesture, trait, idiosyncrasy, quirk, peculiarity.

manners plural noun behavior, conduct; correct behavior, etiquette, good form, protocol, politeness, decorum, propriety, social graces, formalities, politesse.

mansion noun manor house, manor, hall, stately home; palace, castle.

manslaughter noun killing, slaying, murder, homicide.

manual noun handbook, instructions, guidebook, guide; *inf.* how-to book, bible.

manufacture verb 1 *manufacture cars* produce, mass-produce, turn out, process. See MAKE verb 1. 2 *manufacture an excuse* invent, fabricate. See MAKE UP 6 (MAKE verb).

manufacture noun making, production, mass production, construction, assembly, creation, fabrication, processing.

manure noun dung, excrement, muck, guano, droppings, fertilizer.

many adjective numerous, innumerable, countless, scores of, myriad, multitudinous, multiple, copious, abundant, various, sundry, diverse, several, frequent; *inf.* umpteen, lots of, scads of, heaps of, piles of, bags of, tons of, oodles of, an army of, zillions of.

many noun scores, a host, a horde, a crowd, a multitude, a mass, an accumulation, an abundance, a profusion, plenty. **the many** *the wishes of the many* the majority, the people, the masses, the multitude, the rank and file, the crowd, the hoi polloi.

map noun chart, plan, plot, guide, street guide, town plan, road map, atlas, gazetteer.

map verb chart, plot, delineate, depict, portray. **map out** lay out, detail, draw up, sketch out, plan, plot out.

mar verb spoil, detract from, impair, damage, ruin, wreck, disfigure, blemish, scar, deface, harm, hurt, injure, deform, tarnish, taint, sully, stain, blot.

maraud verb raid, plunder, loot, pillage, foray, ransack, forage, ravage, harry, sack, despoil.

marauder noun raider, plunderer, pillager, looter, ravager, robber, pirate, freebooter, buccaneer, corsair, rover, bandit, brigand, rustler, highwayman.

march verb **1** *armies marching* pace, tread, stride, footslog, tramp, hike, trudge, stalk, strut, parade, file. **2** *time marches on* advance, progress, forge ahead, go on, continue on, roll on, develop, evolve.

march noun **1** *scouts on a march* walk, tramp, trek, hike, parade. **2** *a march against the tobacco industry* demonstration, parade, procession, rally. **3** *the march of time* advance, progress, progression, passage, headway, continuance, development, evolution.

margin noun **1** *the margin of the lake* edge, side, verge, border, perimeter, boundary, limits, periphery, brink, brim. **2** *the margin between the countries* border, boundary, frontier, demarcation line. **3** *margin for error* leeway, latitude, scope, room, space, allowance, extra, surplus. **4** *win by a narrow margin* difference, amount.

marginal adjective *marginal ability* slight, small, tiny, minute, low, minor, insignificant, minimal, negligible.

marijuana noun cannabis, hashish, hemp, ganja, sinsemilla; *inf.* dope, hash, grass, pot, mary jane, tea, weed.

marine adjective **1** *marine life* sea, aquatic, saltwater, oceanic, neritic, thalassic. **2** *marine careers* maritime, nautical, naval, seafaring, seagoing.

mariner noun sailor, seaman, seafarer; *inf.* sea dog, (old) salt, bluejacket, tar, gob.

marital adjective matrimonial, marriage, wedding, conjugal, connubial, nuptial, spousal, married, wedded.

mark noun **1** *marks on the table* stain, blemish, blot, smear, trace, spot, speck, dot, blotch, smudge, splotch, bruise, scratch, scar, dent, pit, pock, chip, notch, nick, line, score, cut, incision, gash. **2** *the marks on a horse/cow* marking, blaze, spot, speckle, stripe, brand, earmark. **3** *marks showing the way* marker, guide, pointer, landmark, direction post, signpost, milestone. **4** *mark of respect* sign, symbol, indication, symptom, feature, token, badge, emblem, evidence, proof, clue, hint. **5** *the corporation's mark* seal, stamp, signet, symbol, emblem, device, badge, motto, monogram, hallmark, trademark, logo, watermark, label, tag, flag. **6** *war left its mark on him* impression, imprint, traces, vestiges, remains, effect, impact, influence. **7** *the mark of an honest man* characteristic, feature, trait, attribute, quality, stamp, peculiarity. **8** *the insult missed its mark* target, goal, aim, bull's-eye, objective, object, end, purpose, intent, intention. **9** *work falling below the mark* standard, norm, par, level, criterion, gauge, yardstick, rule, measure, scale. **10** *a person of mark* dis-

tinction, importance, consequence, eminence, preeminence, prominence, note, notability, fame, repute, greatness, prestige, celebrity, glory, standing, rank. **make one's mark** be successful, succeed, prosper, make good, achieve recognition; *inf.* make it. **wide of the mark** irrelevant, inapplicable, inapposite, inappropriate, not to the point, beside the point; inaccurate, incorrect, wrong, erroneous, inexact, off-target.

mark verb **1** *mark the table* stain, smear, smudge, scratch, scar, dent, chip, notch, score, cut, gash. **2** *mark your property* name, initial, put one's seal on, label, tag, stamp, flag, hallmark, watermark, brand, earmark. **3** *mark the places on a map* name, indicate, write down, tag, label, flag. **4** *mark the students' essays* correct, assess, evaluate, appraise, grade. **5** *the children marked his displeasure* see, notice, observe, take note of, discern, spot, recognize. **6** *you should mark his words* heed, take notice of, pay attention to, attend to, note, mind, bear in mind. **7** *a day marked by misfortune* characterize, distinguish, identify, denote, brand, signalize. **8** *mark his birthday* celebrate, commemorate, honor, observe, recognize, acknowledge, solemnize. **mark down** reduce, decrease, lower, cut, slash, put on sale. **mark up** raise, increase, up, hike up, escalate; *inf.* jack up.

marked adjective pronounced, decided, striking, clear, glaring, blatant, unmistakable, prominent, conspicuous, noticeable, distinct, salient, obvious, apparent, evident, manifest, patent.

markedly adverb decidedly, strikingly, remarkably, unmistakably, conspicuously, noticeably, pointedly, distinctly, recognizably, obviously, clearly, plainly.

market noun **1** *shopping at the market* marketplace, mart, shopping center, bazaar. **2** *no market for the product* demand, call, want, desire, need. **3** *the market is sluggish* trade, business, commerce, buying and selling. **in the market for** wishing to buy, in need of, wanting, lacking. **on the market** for sale, purchasable, available, obtainable.

maroon verb abandon, forsake, leave behind, leave, desert, strand, leave stranded.

marriage noun **1** *join in marriage* matrimony, wedlock, conjugal bond. **2** *invited to their marriage* marriage ceremony, wedding, nuptials. **3** *the marriage of their skills* alliance, union, merger, combination, coupling; *inf.* hookup.

married adjective **1** *married couple* wedded, wed, united in wedlock; *inf.* hitched. **2** *married bliss* marital, matrimonial, connubial, conjugal, nuptial, spousal.

marrow noun core, kernel, nucleus, pith,

heart, center, soul, spirit, essence, quintessence, gist, substance.

marry verb **1** *the couple married last year* wed, become man and wife, become espoused; *inf.* tie the knot, walk down the aisle, take the plunge, get hitched, get yoked. **2** *marry their skills* join, join together, unite, ally, merge, unify, combine, link, connect, fuse, weld, couple.

marsh noun marshland, bog, peatbog, swamp, swampland, morass, mire, quagmire, quag, slough, fen, bayou.

marshal verb **1** *tried to marshal his thoughts* gather together, assemble, collect, muster, draw up, line up, align, set/put in order, arrange, deploy, dispose, rank. **2** *marshal the guests to their seats* usher, guide, escort, conduct, lead, shepherd, take.

marshy adjective boggy, swampy, muddy, miry.

martial adjective military, soldierly; militant, warlike, combative, belligerent, bellicose, aggressive, pugnacious.

martial arts plural noun judo, jujitsu, aikido, karate, kung fu, t'ai chi (chu'an), tae kwon do.

martyrdom noun persecution, ordeal, torture, torment, suffering, agony, anguish.

marvel verb be amazed by, be awed by, wonder at, stare at, gape at, goggle at.

marvel noun wonder, wonderful thing, amazing thing, prodigy, sensation, spectacle, phenomenon, miracle; *inf.* something else, something to shout about.

marvelous adjective **1** *his solo climb was marvelous* amazing, astounding, astonishing, awesome, breathtaking, sensational, remarkable, spectacular, stupendous, phenomenal, wondrous, prodigious, miraculous, extraordinary. **2** *a marvelous singer* excellent, splendid, wonderful, magnificent, superb, glorious, super, great, boffo, smashing, fantastic, terrific, fabulous, awesome; *inf.* mean, bad, wicked.

masculine adjective **1** *a masculine physique* virile, robust. *See* MANLY 2. **2** *joined the army to prove he was masculine* brave, courageous. *see* MANLY 1.

masculinity noun **1** *the masculinity of his physique* virility, robustness. *See* MANLINESS 2. **2** *show their masculinity in battle* manhood, bravery. *See* MANLINESS 1.

mash verb crush, pulp, purée, smash, squash, pound, beat.

mash noun pulp, mush, paste, purée, slush, pap.

mask noun *under the mask of being a tourist* disguise, guise, concealment, cover, cover-up, cloak, camouflage, veil, screen, front,

false front, façade, blind, semblance, false colors, pretense.

mask verb disguise, hide, conceal, cover up, obscure, cloak, camouflage, veil, screen.

mass noun **1** *a mass of wood/fibers* concretion, lump, block, chunk, hunk, piece; concentration, conglomeration, aggregation, assemblage, collection. **2** *actors, in the mass, enjoy their work* total, totality, whole, entirety, aggregate. **3** *measure the body's mass* size, magnitude, bulk, dimension, capacity, greatness, bigness. **a mass of** many, a profusion of, numerous, countless. **the mass of** the majority of, the greater part of, the preponderance of, the lion's share of.

mass adjective wholesale, universal, widespread, general, large-scale, extensive, pandemic, popular.

mass verb amass, accumulate, assemble, gather, collect, draw together, join together; marshal, muster, rally, round up, mobilize.

massacre noun mass slaughter, wholesale slaughter, slaughter, mass murder, mass homicide, mass slaying, mass execution, mass destruction, carnage, butchery, blood bath, annihilation, extermination, liquidation, decimation, pogrom, genocide, ethnic cleansing, holocaust.

massacre verb slaughter, butcher, slay, murder, kill, annihilate, exterminate, liquidate, decimate, eliminate, kill off, wipe out, mow down, cut down.

massage noun rub, rubdown, kneading, pummeling, palpation, manipulation; reflexology, acupressure, shiatsu.

masses plural noun common people, populace, proletariat, multitude, commonality, crowd, mob, rabble, hoi polloi; *inf.* great unwashed.

massive adjective huge, immense, enormous, vast, mighty, extensive, gigantic, colossal, mammoth, monumental, elephantine, mountainous, gargantuan, king-size, monstrous, prodigious, titanic, hulking, bulky, weighty, hefty, solid, substantial, big, large, great; *inf.* whopping, humongous.

mast noun **1** *a ship's mast* spar, boom, yard. **2** *the mast atop the building* flagpole, flagstaff, pole, post, support, upright.

master noun **1** *master of the household/hunt* lord and master, lord, overlord, ruler, overseer, superintendent, director, manager, controller, governor, commander, captain, chief, head, headman, principal, owner, employer; *inf.* boss, top dog, big cheese, honcho. **2** *a master of innuendo* expert, adept, professional, authority, pundit, genius, master hand, maestro, virtuoso, prodigy, past master, grand master, wizard; *inf.* ace, pro, maven. **3** *sitting at the feet of the master* guru, teacher, spiritual leader, guide, swami.

master adjective **1** *master craftsmen* expert, adept, proficient, skilled, practiced, experienced; *inf.* crack. **2** *master plan* controlling, ruling, directing, commanding, dominating. **3** *master bedroom* chief, main, principal, leading, prime, predominant, foremost.

master verb **1** *master one's emotions* conquer, vanquish, defeat, overcome, overpower, triumph over, subdue, subjugate, govern, quell, quash, suppress, control, curb, check, bridle, tame. **2** *master the technique* learn, become proficient in, acquire skill in, grasp; *inf.* get the hang of.

masterful adjective **1** *masterful men marrying meek women* dominating, authoritative, powerful, controlling, domineering, tyrannical, despotic, dictatorial, overbearing, overweening, imperious, peremptory, high-handed, arrogant, haughty. **2** *masterful handling of the situation* expert, consummate. *See* MASTERLY.

masterly adjective masterful, expert, consummate, adept, skillful, proficient, adroit, deft, dexterous, accomplished, polished, excellent, superlative, first-rate, talented, gifted; *inf.* crack, ace.

mastermind verb direct, manage, plan, organize, arrange, engineer, conceive, devise, forge, originate, initiate, think up, come up with; *inf.* be the brains behind.

mastermind noun genius, intellect, author, architect, engineer, director, planner, organizer, deviser, originator, manager, prime mover; *inf.* brain, brains.

masterpiece noun magnum opus, masterwork, chef-d'oeuvre, work of art, creation.

mastery noun **1** *mastery over his emotions* control, domination, command, ascendancy, supremacy, superiority, triumph, victory, power, authority, jurisdiction, dominion, sovereignty. **2** *mastery of the language* command, grasp, knowledge, familiarity with, understanding, comprehension, expertise, skill, prowess, proficiency, ability, capability; *inf.* know-how.

masturbation noun autoeroticism, onanism, self-gratification; *inf.* playing with oneself.

mat noun **1** *wipe one's feet on the mat* doormat, welcome mat, rug, carpet. **2** *a mat of hair* mass, tangle, knot, mesh.

match noun **1** *a tennis match* contest, competition, game, tournament, bout, event, test, trial, meet. **2** *she's no match for the champion* equal, peer, rival, competitor. **3** *this glove is a match for that one* mate, fellow, companion, counterpart,

pair, complement. **4** *the new one is an exact match for the previous one* look-alike, double, twin, duplicate, copy, replica; *inf.* spitting image, ringer, dead ringer. **5** *a good match* pairing, alliance, affiliation, combination.

match verb **1** *curtains that match the walls* complement, blend with, harmonize with, go with, coordinate with, correspond to, accord with. **2** *her strength matches his* rival, vie with, compete with, compare with, parallel, keep pace with. **3** *match the socks* pair up, mate, couple, unite, join, combine.

matching adjective corresponding, equivalent, complementing, parallel, analogous, complementary, harmonizing, coordinating, the same, paired, twin, coupled, identical, like.

matchless adjective unmatched, incomparable, beyond compare, unequaled, without equal, unrivaled, unparalleled, unsurpassed, inimitable, peerless, unique, consummate, perfect.

mate noun **1** *she is looking for a mate* husband, wife, spouse, partner, companion, helpmate, lover; *inf.* significant other, other half, better half. **2** *the mate to this sock* twin, match, companion. **3** *they were mates throughout the war* associate, colleague, companion, compeer.

mate verb breed, copulate, couple, pair, join.

material noun **1** *clothes of strong material* fabric, cloth, stuff, textile. **2** *enough material for a book* data, information, facts, facts and figures, evidence, details, notes; *inf.* info.

material adjective **1** *the material world* corporeal, physical, bodily, fleshly, tangible, substantial, concrete, nonspiritual, worldly, earthly, temporal. **2** *a material difference* important, significant, meaningful. **3** *material evidence* relevant, applicable, pertinent, germane.

materialize verb **1** *our plans did not materialize* happen, occur, come about, come to pass, take place; *inf.* shape up. **2** *the guests did not materialize* appear, turn up, come to light, emerge.

mathematical adjective **1** *mathematical problems* arithmetical, numerical, statistical. **2** *mathematical care* precise, exact, rigorous, strict, meticulous, scrupulous, careful.

matrimonial adjective conjugal, connubial, nuptial. *See* MARITAL.

matrimony noun *holy matrimony*, marriage, wedlock, union.

matted adjective tangled, entangled, knotted, tousled, disheveled.

matter noun **1** *organic matter* material, substance, stuff, medium. **2** *concentrate on the matter, not the style* content, subject matter, text, argument, substance, sense, thesis. **3** *no laughing matter* affair, business, proceeding, situation, circumstance, event, happening, occurrence, incident, episode, occasion, experience. **4** *discuss important matters* subject, topic, issue, question, point, case, concern, theme. **5** *issues of little matter* importance, consequence, significance, note, import, moment, weight. **6** *what is the matter?* trouble, upset, distress, worry, problem, difficulty, complication.

matter-of-fact adjective prosaic, down-to-earth, straightforward, plain, unemotional, unsentimental, deadpan, flat, dry.

mature adjective adult, grown-up, grown, fully grown, full-grown, of age; ripe, ripened, mellow, ready, seasoned.

mature verb grow up, develop fully, reach adulthood, be full-grown, come of age; ripen, mellow, maturate.

maturity noun adulthood, manhood/womanhood, puberty, full growth, majority, coming of age; ripeness, mellowness, completion, readiness.

maudlin adjective mawkish, sentimental, oversentimental, tearful, lachrymose; *inf.* weepy, mushy, slushy, schmaltzy.

maul verb handle roughly, manhandle, paw, molest, beat, batter, claw, lacerate, mutilate, thrash, ill-treat; *inf.* belt, wallop, clobber, rough up, kick about.

maverick noun nonconformist, rebel, dissenter, dissident, individualist, bohemian, eccentric.

maxim noun aphorism, proverb, adage, saw, saying, axiom, precept, epigram, gnome.

maximum noun utmost, uttermost, extremity, upper limit, height, ceiling, top, summit, peak, apogee, acme, zenith.

maximum adjective highest, greatest, biggest, largest, topmost, most, utmost, supreme.

maybe adverb perhaps, it could be that, possibly; *lit.* peradventure.

mayhem noun havoc, disorder, confusion, chaos, bedlam, destruction, violence, trouble, disturbance, commotion, tumult, pandemonium.

maze noun labyrinth, network, mesh, web, jungle, tangle, confusion, snarl, imbroglio.

meadow noun field, grassland, pasture, paddock, lea.

meager adjective **1** *meager supplies* paltry, sparse, scant, scanty, spare, inadequate, insufficient, insubstantial, exiguous, short, little, small, slight, slender, poor, puny, skimpy, scrimpy; *inf.* measly, as scarce as hens' teeth. **2** *meager bodies* thin, lean, emaciated, skinny, spare, scrawny, scraggy, bony, gaunt, starved, underfed.

meal noun repast, banquet, feast, picnic, barbecue, buffet.

mean[1] verb **1** *what do the words mean?* indicate, signify, betoken, express, convey, denote, designate, spell out, show, stand for, represent, symbolize, portend, connote, imply, purport, suggest, allude to, intimate, hint at, insinuate, drive at. **2** *not mean to break it* intend, have in mind, plan, set out, aim, aspire, desire, want, wish. **3** *not meant for the army* intend, design, destine, predestine, fate. **4** *this will mean war* involve, entail, lead to, result in, give rise to, cause, engender, produce.

mean[2] adjective **1** *a mean thing to do* nasty, disagreeable, unpleasant, hurtful, unkind, offensive, obnoxious, cross, ill-natured, bad-tempered, irritable, surly, cantankerous, crotchety, crabbed, crabby, grumpy; *inf.* grouchy. **2** *as mean as Scrooge* niggardly, close-fisted, penny-pinching. *See* MISERLY. **3** *a mean creature* base, ignoble, disreputable, despicable, contemptible, hateful. **4** *of mean understanding* inferior, poor, limited, restricted, meager, scant. **5** *a mean hovel* shabby, wretched, dismal, squalid, sordid, seedy, mangy, broken-down, rundown. **6** *of mean birth* low, lowly, lowborn, humble, modest, common, ordinary, undistinguished.

mean[3] noun midpoint, middle, median, norm, middle course, middle ground, happy medium.

mean[4] adjective middle, median, medial, normal, standard, medium.

meander verb wander, roam, ramble, rove, stroll, amble, drift; wind, zigzag, snake, curve, turn, bend; *inf.* mosey.

meaning noun **1** *the meaning of what he said* sense, message, import, drift, gist, essence, substance, purport, implication, significance, thrust. **2** *what is the meaning of the word?* definition, explanation, connotation, denotation, interpretation, elucidation, explication. **3** *it was not our meaning to delay him* intention, purpose, plan, aim, goal, end, object, objective, aspiration, desire, want, wish. **4** *his life has no meaning* significance, point, value, worth, consequence, account. **5** *a glance full of meaning* significance, implication, allusion, intimation, insinuation, eloquence, expression.

meaningful adjective **1** *a meaningful remark* significant, important, relevant, material, valid, worthwhile. **2** *a meaningful glance* pointed, suggestive, eloquent, expressive, pregnant.

meaningless adjective senseless, unintelligible, incomprehensible, pointless, purposeless, motiveless, irrational, inane; empty, futile, worthless, trivial, insignificant, inconsequential.

meanness noun **1** *an act of such meanness* nastiness, disagreeableness, unpleasantness, unfriendliness, crossness, bad temper, irritability, surliness, cantankerousness. **2** *the meanness of the creature* baseness, vileness, sordidness, foulness, nastiness, contemptibility. **3** *the meanness of his intellect* inferiority, poorness, limitations, meagerness. **4** *the meanness of the hovel* shabbiness, wretchedness, squalor, sordidness, seediness. **5** *the meanness of her birth* lowliness, humbleness, commonness.

means plural noun **1** *a means of getting there* way, method, expedient, process, mode, manner, agency, medium, instrument, channel, avenue, course. **2** *a man of means* | *have sufficient means* money, capital, wealth, riches, affluence, substance, fortune, property; resources, funds, wherewithal; *inf.* dough, bread. **by all means** of course, certainly, definitely, surely. **by no means** in no way, not at all, not in the least.

meanwhile adverb meantime, in the meantime, for the time being, for now, for the moment, in the interim; at the same time, simultaneously, concurrently.

measurable adjective **1** *a measurable quantity* assessable, gaugeable, estimable, appraisable, computable, quantifiable, fathomable. **2** *a measurable improvement* significant, appreciable, noticeable, visible, perceptible, obvious, striking, material.

measure noun **1** *find the measure of the material* size, dimension. *See* MEASUREMENT 2. **2** *receive a measure of her father's estate* share, portion, division, allotment, part, piece, quota, lot, ration, percentage. **3** *have a measure of wit* quantity, amount, certain amount, degree. **4** *sales are the measure of the company's success* yardstick, test, standard, touchstone, criterion, benchmark. **5** *take drastic measures* action, act, course, course of action, deed, proceeding, procedure, step, means, expedient, maneuver. **6** *announce measures to control crime* statute, act, bill, law, resolution. **7** *do what you like within measure* moderation, limit, limitation, bounds, control, restraint. **beyond measure** immeasurably, incalculably, infinitely, limitlessly, immensely, extremely. **for good measure** as a bonus, to boot.

measure verb **1** *measure the material* calculate, compute, estimate, quantify, weigh, size, evaluate, rate, assess, appraise, gauge, measure out, determine, judge, survey. **2** *measure one's words* choose carefully, select with care, consider, plan, calculate.

3 *measure his strength against his brother's* pit, set, match, test, put into competition. **measure out** mete out, deal out, dole out, share, divide out, parcel out, allocate, allot, apportion, assign, distribute, administer, dispense, issue. **measure up 1** *he didn't measure up* come up to standard, fulfill expectations, fit/fill the bill, pass muster, be adequate, be suitable; *inf.* make the grade, cut the mustard, be up to snuff. **2** *measure up to the requirements* meet, come up to, match.

measured adjective **1** *measured amounts* measured out, calculated, computed, quantified. **2** *measured steps* regular, steady, even, rhythmical, slow, dignified, stately, sedate. **3** *measured words* carefully chosen, well-thought-out, studied, calculated, planned, premeditated, considered, deliberate, reasoned.

measurement noun **1** *the measurement of the quantity* calculation, computation, estimation, quantification, evaluation, assessment. **2** *the measurements of the carpet are wrong* size, dimension, proportions, magnitude, amplitude, mass, bulk, volume, capacity, extent, expanse, amount, quantity, area, length, height, depth, weight, width, range.

meat noun **1** *meat and drink* flesh, animal flesh, food, nourishment, sustenance, provisions, rations, fare, viands, victuals, comestibles, provender, feed; *inf.* grub, eats, chow, nosh. **2** *the meat of the matter* substance, pith, marrow, heart, kernel, core, nucleus, nub, essence, essentials, gist, fundamentals, basics; *inf.* nitty-gritty, nuts and bolts.

mechanical adjective **1** *a mechanical device* automated, automatic, machine-driven, motor-driven, power-driven. **2** *mechanical gestures* automatic, machinelike, unthinking, unconscious, unfeeling, unemotional, cold, routine, habitual, perfunctory, lackluster, lifeless, unanimated, dead.

mechanism noun **1** *a mechanism for folding paper* apparatus, appliance. *See* MACHINE 1. **2** *the mechanism of the car* motor, workings, works, gears, components; *inf.* innards, guts. **3** *the mechanism for complaints* process, procedure, system, operation, method, technique, means, medium, agency, channel.

meddle verb interfere, butt in, intrude, intervene, interlope, pry, nose; *inf.* stick one's nose in, horn in, snoop.

meddlesome adjective meddling, interfering, intrusive, prying; *inf.* snooping, nosy.

mediate verb **1** *mediate between the warring factions* arbitrate, negotiate, conciliate, intervene, intercede, interpose, moderate, umpire, referee, bring to terms, step in. **2** *mediate a difference of opinion* settle, reconcile, resolve, mend, clear up, patch up. **3** *mediate a peace settlement* bring about, effect, effectuate, make happen, negotiate.

mediation noun arbitration, negotiation, intervention, intercession, good offices.

mediator noun arbitrator, arbiter, negotiator, go-between, middleman, intermediary, peacemaker, moderator, umpire, referee, judge, conciliator, reconciler.

medicinal adjective medical, therapeutic, curative, healing, remedial, restorative, health-giving, analeptic.

medicine noun medication, medicament, drug, remedy, cure, physic. **take one's medicine** accept one's punishment, take the consequences of one's actions.

mediocre adjective indifferent, average, middle-of-the-road, middling, ordinary, commonplace, pedestrian, run-of-the-mill, tolerable, passable, adequate, uninspired, undistinguished, unexceptional, inferior, second-rate, second-class, low-grade, poor, shabby, minor; *inf.* so-so, fair-to-middling, nothing to write home about, no great shakes.

mediocrity noun ordinariness, commonplaceness, inferiority, poorness, shabbiness.

meditate verb *meditating revenge* intend, plan, project, design, devise, scheme, plot. **meditate on/upon** contemplate, think about/over, muse on/about, ponder on/over, concentrate on, reflect on, ruminate about/on/over, brood over.

meditation noun contemplation, thought, musing, reflection, deliberation, rumination, brooding, reverie, brown study, concentration.

medium noun **1** *the medium between extremes* center point, average, standard. *See* MEAN². **2** *the medium of television* means, agency, channel, avenue, vehicle, organ, instrument, instrumentality. **3** *organisms in their natural medium* habitat, element, environment, surroundings, milieu, setting, conditions, atmosphere. **4** *visit a medium to contact the dead* spiritualist, spiritist, necromancer.

medium adjective middle, mean, medial, median, average, midway, midpoint, intermediate.

medley noun assortment, miscellany, mixture, mixed bag, mix, mélange, variety, potpourri, conglomeration, patchwork, gallimaufry, olio, salmagundi.

meek adjective **1** *meek people/animals* patient, long-suffering, forbearing, resigned, gentle, peaceful, docile, modest, humble, unassuming. **2** *feeling meek among aggressive people* submissive, yielding, unresisting, compliant, acquiescent, deferential, weak, timid, frightened, spineless, spiritless.

meet verb **1** *meet an old friend on the train* encounter, run into, run across, come across, come upon, chance upon, happen upon, light upon; *inf.* bump into. **2** *where land and sea meet* come together, abut, adjoin, join, link up, unite, connect, touch, converge, intersect. **3** *the committee met on Saturday* gather, assemble, come together, congregate, convene. **4** *meet the demands of the job* satisfy, fulfill, measure up to, come up to, comply with. **5** *meet one's responsibilities* carry out, perform, execute, discharge, take care of. **6** *meet death bravely* face, encounter, undergo, experience, go through, bear, suffer, endure. **7** *meet the enemy at dawn* confront, engage, engage in battle with, clash with, fight with.

meeting noun **1** *the meeting of the friends* encounter, contact, assignation, rendezvous, tryst. **2** *address the meeting* gathering, assembly, conference, congregation, convention, convocation, conclave; *inf.* get-together. **3** *the meeting of land and sea* abutment, junction, conjunction, union, convergence, confluence, concourse, intersection.

melancholic, melancholy adjective despondent, dejected, depressed, down, downhearted, downcast, disconsolate, glum, gloomy, miserable, dismal, dispirited, low, in the doldrums, blue, mournful, lugubrious, woeful, woebegone, doleful, sorrowful, unhappy, heavy-hearted, low-spirited, somber, pensive; *inf.* down in the dumps, down in the mouth.

melancholy noun despondency, dejection, depression, gloom, gloominess, low spirits, doldrums, blues, woe, sadness, sorrow, unhappiness, pensiveness, melancholia.

mellow adjective **1** *mellow fruit* ripe, mature, well-matured, soft, juicy, tender, luscious, sweet, full-flavored, flavorsome. **2** *a mellow voice* dulcet, sweet, sweet-sounding, tuneful, euphonious, melodious, mellifluous, smooth, full, rich, well-rounded. **3** *a mellow person/mood* gentle, easygoing, pleasant, amiable, good-natured, affable, genial, relaxed.

melodious adjective melodic, musical, tuneful, harmonious, lyrical, dulcet, sweet, sweet-sounding, sweet-toned, silvery, euphonious.

melodramatic adjective theatrical, stagy, overdramatic, histrionic, oversensational, extravagant, overdone, overemotional; *inf.* camp, hammy.

melody noun tune, air, strain, music, refrain, theme, song; melodiousness, tunefulness, musicality, harmony, lyricism, sweetness, euphony.

melt verb **1** *solids melting* liquefy, dissolve, deliquesce, thaw, defrost, soften. **2** *the crowd melted away* disperse, vanish, vanish into thin air, fade away, disappear, dissolve, evaporate, evanesce. **3** *her story melted the jury* soften, touch, disarm, mollify, assuage, move.

member noun **1** *a member of the club* adherent, associate, fellow, participant. **2** *many victims had injured members* organ, limb, appendage, extremity, arm, leg. **3** *a member of the mathematical set* element, constituent, component, part, portion.

memento noun souvenir, keepsake, reminder, remembrance, token, memorial, trophy, relic, vestige.

memorable adjective unforgettable, signal, momentous, significant, historic, notable, noteworthy, remarkable, outstanding, extraordinary, striking, impressive, distinctive.

memorandum noun reminder, note, message, minute, aide-mémoire; *inf.* memo.

memorial noun remembrance, reminder, memento, souvenir.

memory noun **1** *her memory is excellent* remembrance, recollection, powers of recall, recall, reminiscence, powers of retention, retention. **2** *in memory of him* remembrance, commemoration, honor, tribute.

menace noun **1** *an atmosphere full of menace* threat, ominousness, intimidation, warning; danger, peril, risk, hazard. **3** *the child next door is a menace* nuisance, pest, troublemaker, mischief-maker.

menace verb **1** *older boys menacing the young ones* threaten, intimidate, frighten, scare, alarm, terrify, bully, browbeat, cow, terrorize. **2** *bad weather menacing* loom, impend, lower, be in the air, be in the offing.

menacing adjective **1** *a menacing look/silence* threatening, ominous, intimidating, frightening, terrifying, alarming, forbidding, minatory, minacious. **2** *a menacing storm* looming, lowering, impending.

mend verb **1** *mend the furniture* repair, fix, put back together, patch up, restore, rehabilitate, renew, renovate, make whole, make well, cure, heal. **2** *mend socks* sew, stitch, darn, patch. **3** *the patient will soon mend* get better, recover, recuperate, improve. **4** *try to mend matters* put right, set straight, rectify, amend, improve, ameliorate, reform.

menial adjective lowly, humble, low-grade, low-status, unskilled, routine, humdrum, boring, dull.

menstruation noun period, menses, menstrual cycle, monthly flow; *inf.* the curse.

mental adjective **1** *mental work* intellectual, cerebral, brain, thinking. **2** *he's completely mental* mad, insane, deranged, disturbed, unbalanced, mentally ill, unstable.

mentality noun **1** *of a slightly twisted mentality* frame of mind, way of thinking, way one's mind works, mind, psychology, mental attitude, outlook, character, disposition, makeup. **2** *of low-grade mentality* intellect, intellectual capabilities, intelligence, IQ (= intelligence quotient), brainpower, brains, understanding, wit; *inf.* gray matter.

mention verb allude to, refer to, touch on, speak briefly of, hint at, say, state, name, cite, quote, call attention to, speak about/of, utter, communicate, disclose, divulge, reveal. **don't mention it** no thanks necessary, (it was) a pleasure, any time; don't apologize, don't worry; *inf.* no problem, no sweat, no big deal, forget (about) it. **not to mention** to say nothing of, in addition to.

mention noun reference, allusion, observation, remark, statement, announcement, indication, acknowledgment, citation, recognition.

mentor noun guide, adviser, counselor, therapist, guru, spiritual leader, confidant, teacher, tutor, coach, instructor.

mercenary adjective **1** *mercenary people interested only in money* money-oriented, grasping, greedy, acquisitive, avaricious, covetous; *inf.* money-grubbing. **2** *mercenary soldiers* hired, paid, bought, professional, venal.

merchandise noun goods, wares, stock, commodities, produce, vendibles.

merchandise verb **1** *merchandise a wide range of goods* market, sell, retail, buy and sell, distribute, deal in, trade in, traffic in, do business in, vend. **2** *merchandise the new cars* promote, advertise, publicize, push; *inf.* hype, plug.

merchant noun trader, dealer, trafficker, wholesaler, broker, seller, salesman, saleswoman, salesperson, vendor, retailer, store owner, storekeeper, shopkeeper, distributor.

merciful adjective lenient, clement, compassionate, pitying, forgiving, forbearing, sparing, humane, mild, softhearted, tender-hearted, kind, sympathetic, liberal, tolerant.

merciless adjective unmerciful, ruthless, relentless, inexorable, harsh, pitiless, uncompassionate, unforgiving, unsparing, unpitying, implacable, barbarous, inhumane, inhuman, hard-hearted, heartless, callous, cruel, unsympathetic, unfeeling.

mercy noun **1** *the mercy of the judge* leniency, clemency, compassion, pity, charity, forgiveness, forbearance, quarter, soft-heartedness, tender-heartedness, sympathy. **2** *thankful for small mercies* boon, favor, piece of luck, blessing, godsend. **at the mercy of** in the power of, under/in the control of, threatened by, open to, defenseless against, vulnerable to.

mere adjective nothing more than, no better than, no more important than, just a, only a, pure and simple.

merge verb **1** *the two companies merged* join together, join forces, amalgamate, unite, combine, incorporate, coalesce, team up. **2** *the colors merged* blend, fuse, mingle, mix, intermix, homogenize. **merge into** run into, melt into, become assimilated into/in, become lost in, be swallowed up by.

merger noun amalgamation, combination, union, fusion, coalition, alliance, incorporation.

merit noun **1** *the merit of his work* excellence, goodness, quality, high quality, worth, worthiness, value. **2** *the merits of the scheme* good point, strong point, advantage, asset, plus.

merit verb deserve, earn, be worthy of, be entitled to, have a right to, warrant.

meritorious adjective praiseworthy, laudable, commendable, admirable, estimable, creditable, excellent, exemplary, good, worthy, deserving.

merriment noun gaiety, high spirits, jollity, rejoicing, jocundity, conviviality, festivity, merrymaking, revelry, mirth, mirthfulness, glee, gleefulness, laughter, hilarity, amusement, fun.

merry adjective cheerful, cheery, gay, high-spirited, blithe, blithesome, lighthearted, buoyant, carefree, joyful, joyous, jolly, jocund, convivial, festive, mirthful, gleeful. **make merry** have fun, have a good time, enjoy oneself, have a party, party, celebrate, carouse, revel, rejoice; *inf.* have a ball.

mesh noun **1** *wire mesh* network, netting, net, tracery, web, lattice, latticework, lacework, trellis, reticulation, plexus. **2** *the mesh of political intrigue* net, tangle, entanglement, web, snare, trap.

mesh verb connect, interlock, fit together; go together, coordinate, match, harmonize, dovetail.

mesmerize verb hypnotize, put into a trance, hold spellbound, spellbind, entrance, enthrall, bewitch, captivate, enchant, fascinate, grip, magnetize.

mess noun **1** *clean up the mess in the kitchen* disorder, untidiness, disarray, dirtiness, filthiness, clutter, litter; muddle, chaos, confusion, disorganization, turmoil. **2**

have to get out of this mess plight, predicament, tight spot, tight corner, difficulty, trouble, quandary, dilemma, muddle, mix-up, confusion, imbroglio; *inf.* jam, fix, pickle, stew. **3** *he made a mess of the project* muddle, botch, bungle; *inf.* hash, foul-up, screw-up. **4** *cat's mess* dirt, excrement, feces, excreta.

mess verb **mess with the controls** fiddle, play, tinker, toy. **mess around, mess about** amuse oneself, pass the time, fiddle around/about, play around/about. **mess up 1** *mess up the kitchen* dirty, litter, pollute, clutter up, disarrange, dishevel. **2** *mess up the project* botch, bungle, muff, make a mess of, mar, spoil, ruin; *inf.* make a hash of, foul up, screw up.

message noun **1** *leave a message* communication, news, word, tidings, note, memorandum, letter, missive, bulletin, communiqué, dispatch; *inf.* memo. **2** *the message of the sermon* meaning, import, idea, point, purport, intimation, theme, moral.

messenger noun courier, runner, envoy, emissary, agent, go-between, herald, harbinger; *inf.* gofer.

messy adjective untidy, disordered, dirty, filthy, grubby, slovenly, cluttered, littered, chaotic, confused, disorganized, in disarray, disarranged, disheveled, unkempt; *inf.* sloppy.

metamorphosis noun transformation, transfiguration, change, alteration, conversion, changeover, mutation, transmutation, sea change; *inf.* transmogrification.

metaphor noun figure of speech, image, trope, allegory, analogy, symbol, emblem.

mete verb **mete out** deal out, dole out. *See* MEASURE OUT (MEASURE verb).

meteoric adjective rapid, swift, lightning, rapid, swift, fast, quick, speedy, overnight, sudden, dazzling, brilliant, spectacular, flashing, momentary, fleeting, transient, ephemeral, brief, short-lived.

method noun **1** *old-fashioned methods* procedure, technique, system, practice, modus operandi, process, approach, way, course of action, scheme, plan, rule, style, manner, mode. **2** *method in his madness* order, orderliness, organization, arrangement, structure, form, system, plan, design, purpose, pattern, regularity.

methodical adjective orderly, well-ordered, organized, systematic, structured, logical, well-regulated, planned, efficient, businesslike.

meticulous adjective ultracareful, scrupulous, punctilious, painstaking, demanding, exacting, conscientious, thorough, perfectionist, fastidious, particular, exact, precise, detailed, rigorous.

mettle noun **1** *it showed us his true mettle* caliber, character, disposition, nature, temperament, temper, personality, makeup, stamp, kind, sort, variety, mold, kidney. **2** *soldiers of mettle* courage, courageousness, bravery, gallantry, valor, intrepidity, fearlessness, boldness, daring, grit, pluck, nerve, backbone, fortitude, indomitability; *inf.* guts, spunk.

middle adjective **1** *the middle point between two extremes* mid, mean, medium, medial, median, midway, halfway, central, equidistant. **2** *the middle ranks* intermediate, intermedial.

middle noun **1** *the middle of the line* midpoint, halfway point, mean, median, center, dead center. **2** *in the middle of the crowd* heart, center. *See* MIDST. **3** *a thickening middle* midriff, waist, waistline.

middleman noun intermediary, go-between, broker, distributor.

midget noun dwarf, manikin, pygmy, Tom Thumb; homunculus; *inf.* little person.

midnight noun twelve midnight, dead of night, the witching hour.

midst noun middle, center, heart, bosom, core, kernel, nucleus, nub, interior, depths, thick.

mien noun look, appearance, aspect, aura, expression, countenance, demeanor, air, manner, bearing, carriage, deportment.

miffed adjective annoyed, displeased, offended, aggrieved, piqued, nettled, vexed, irked, upset, hurt, put out, resentful, in a huff.

might noun force, power, strength, mightiness, powerfulness, forcefulness, potency, toughness, robustness, sturdiness, muscularity, vigor, energy, stamina, stoutness.

mighty adjective **1** *a mighty blow* forceful, powerful, strong, lusty, potent, tough, robust, sturdy, muscular, strapping, vigorous, energetic, stout. **2** *a mighty mountain* huge, massive, vast, enormous, colossal, giant, gigantic, prodigious, monumental, mountainous, towering, titanic.

migrant adjective traveling, roving. *See* MIGRATORY.

migrant noun vagrant, nomad, itinerant, traveler, gypsy, transient, rover, wanderer, drifter.

migrate verb emigrate, move, resettle, relocate; travel, voyage, journey, trek, hike, rove, roam, wander, drift.

migratory adjective migrant, migrating, traveling, roving, wandering, nomadic, itinerant, vagrant, transient, unsettled.

mild adjective **1** *a mild disposition* tender, gentle, soft, softhearted, tenderhearted, sensitive, sympathetic, warm, warmhearted; placid, meek, docile, calm, tranquil, serene, peaceful; amiable, genial, easygoing, mellow. **2** *mild winds* gentle, moderate, warm, balmy. **3** *mild food* bland, spiceless, insipid, tasteless.

mildness noun tenderness, gentleness, softness, sensitivity, meekness, docility, calmness, tranquillity, serenity, amiability, mellowness.

militant adjective **1** *militant believers* aggressive, assertive, vigorous, active, combative, pugnacious; *inf.* pushy. **2** *militant armies* fighting, warring, contending, clashing, embattled.

militant noun **1** *militants in the party* activist, partisan. **2** *militants on the battlefield* fighter, soldier, warrior, combatant, belligerent.

military noun armed forces, services, militia, soldiery, army, navy, air force, marines.

milk verb **1** *milk sap from a tree* draw, draw off, express, siphon, tap, drain, extract. **2** *milk the poor people* exploit, take advantage of, bleed, suck dry.

mill noun factory, plant, foundry, works, workshop, shop.

mill verb grind, pulverize, pound, crush, powder, crunch, granulate, comminute, triturate. **mill around/about** wander around/about, amble, meander, crowd.

millstone noun burden, weight, onus, misfortune, affliction, cross, albatross.

mimic verb **1** *mimic his friend* impersonate, imitate, copy, ape, caricature, parody; *inf.* take off. **2** *the child's actions mimicked his mother's* resemble, echo, mirror, simulate.

mimic noun impersonator, impressionist, imitator, parodist, copyist, parrot, ape.

mince verb **1** *finely minced beef* chop/cut into tiny pieces, grind, crumble, hash. **2** *I won't mince (my) words* restrain, hold back, moderate, temper, soften, mitigate, refine, weaken.

mind noun **1** *all in the mind* brain, head, psyche, ego, subconscious. **2** *have an active mind* brainpower, intellect, mentality, intelligence, powers of reasoning, brain, brains, wits, understanding, comprehension, sense; *inf.* gray matter. **3** *my mind was wandering* thoughts, thinking, concentration, attention, application, absorption. **4** *bring thoughts of him to mind* memory, recollection, remembrance. **5** *be of the same mind* opinion, way of thinking, outlook, view, viewpoint, point of view, belief, judgment, attitude. **6** *have a mind to go* inclination, desire, wish, urge, will, notion, fancy, intention, intent, aim, purpose, design. **7** *of unsound mind* mental balance, sanity, senses, wits, reason, reasoning, judgment. **8** *one of the great minds* genius, intellect, intellectual, thinker; *inf.* brain, egghead. **be of two minds** be undecided, be uncertain, be hesitant, waver, vacillate, dither, shilly-shally. **bear/keep in mind** remember, be mindful of, take into consideration, consider. **put in mind** remind, call up, conjure up, suggest. **to one's mind** in one's opinion, to one's way of thinking, from one's standpoint.

mind verb **1** *didn't mind their tardiness* object to, care about, be bothered by, be upset by, resent, dislike, disapprove of, look askance at. **2** *mind what the teacher says* take heed of, heed, pay attention to, attend to, concentrate on, listen to, note, take notice of, mark, observe, respect, obey, follow, comply with, adhere to. **3** *mind your own business* attend to, pay attention to, concentrate on. **4** *mind the step* be careful of, be cautious of, watch out for, look out for, keep one's eyes open for. **5** *mind the store/baby* look after, take care of, attend to, tend, have charge of, keep an eye on, watch.

mindful adjective heedful of, watchful of, careful of, wary of, chary of, cognizant of, aware of, conscious of, alert to.

mindless adjective **1** *a mindless idiot* stupid, foolish, brainless, senseless, witless, empty-headed, dull, slow-witted, obtuse, weak-minded, featherbrained; *inf.* birdbrained, dumb, dopey, moronic. **2** *mindless violence* unthinking, thoughtless, careless, gratuitous. **3** *mindless tasks* mechanical, automatic, routine.

mine noun **1** *work in a mine* colliery, pit, excavation, well, quarry, lode, vein, deposit. **2** *the book is a mine of information* source, reservoir, repository, store, storehouse, wealth, mint; *inf.* gold mine.

mine verb excavate, quarry for, dig for, dig up, extract, unearth.

mingle verb **1** *mingle the two colors* mix, blend, combine, compound, homogenize, merge, unite, join, intermingle, intermix, coalesce, blend, commingle. **2** *guests mingling at the party* circulate, socialize, hobnob, fraternize.

miniature adjective small-scale, scaled-down, mini, midget, baby, toy, pocket, dwarf, Lilliputian, small, tiny, wee, minute, minuscule, microscopic; *inf.* pint-sized.

minimize verb **1** *minimize the costs* keep at/to a minimum, reduce, decrease, curtail, cut back on, prune, slash. **2** *minimize the size* reduce, decrease, diminish, abbreviate, attenuate, shrink, miniaturize. **3** *minimize his achievement* belittle, make light of, decry, discount, play

down, deprecate, depreciate, underestimate, underrate.

minimum adjective minimal, lowest, smallest, littlest, least, least possible, slightest.

minion noun **1** *the general and his minions* lackey, flunky, henchman, toady, sycophant, flatterer, fawner, underling, hireling, servant, dependent, hanger-on, parasite, leech; *inf.* yes-man, bootlicker. **2** *the queen's minion* favorite, pet, darling, jewel, apple of one's eye.

minister noun **1** *ministers saying prayers* clergyman, cleric, ecclesiastic, churchman, preacher, priest, parson, pastor, rector, chaplain, padre, curate, vicar. **2** *the British minister in Egypt* ambassador, diplomat, consul, plenipotentiary, envoy, emissary, legate, delegate, representative, chargé d'affaires.

minister verb **minister to** administer to, attend to, tend, look after, take care of, see to, cater to, serve, accommodate, be solicitous of, pander to.

ministry noun **1** *go in for the ministry* the church, the priesthood, holy orders, the pulpit. **2** *the ministry for foreign affairs* department, office, bureau.

minor adjective **1** *a minor poet* little-known, unknown, lesser, insignificant, unimportant, inconsequential, inferior, subordinate. **2** *suffer minor discomfort* slight, small, trivial, negligible, trifling.

minstrel noun musician, singer, bard, troubadour, jongleur, goliard.

mint noun *earn a mint* fortune, small fortune, millions, king's ransom; *inf.* pile, stack, heap, packet, bundle.

mint adjective *in mint condition* brand-new, unblemished, undamaged, unmarred, untarnished, fresh; *inf.* spanking new.

mint verb **1** *mint coins* stamp, stamp out, punch, die, cast, strike, coin, monetize, make, manufacture, produce. **2** *mint new words* coin, invent, make up, fabricate, think up, dream up, hatch up, devise, fashion, forge.

minute noun **1** *I'll only be a minute* moment, short time, second; *inf.* jiffy, jiff. **2** *the minute he appeared* moment, instant. **in a minute** shortly, very soon, in the twinkling of an eye; *inf.* in a jiffy/jiff, in two shakes of a lamb's tail. **up-to-the-minute** up-to-date, ultramodern, modern, fashionable, in vogue, chic, in, all the rage.

minute adjective **1** *a minute creature* tiny, minuscule, microscopic, miniature, diminutive, Lilliputian, little, small; *inf.* knee-high to a grasshopper. **2** *a minute difference* infinitesimal, negligible, trifling, trivial, paltry, petty, insignificant, inconsequential, unimportant, slight, minimal. **3** *in minute detail* detailed, exhaustive, meticulous, punctilious, painstaking, close, strict, exact, precise, accurate.

minutes plural noun record, log, proceedings, transactions, notes, transcript, journal, summary.

miracle noun wonder, marvel, prodigy, phenomenon.

miraculous adjective **1** *Jesus performing miraculous feats* inexplicable, unaccountable, preternatural, superhuman, supernatural, fantastic, magical, thaumaturgic, phenomenal, prodigious, wondrous, remarkable. **2** *a miraculous recovery* amazing, astounding, remarkable, extraordinary, incredible, unbelievable; *inf.* fantastic.

mirage noun optical illusion, illusion, hallucination, phantasmagoria, phantasm.

mire noun marsh, marshland, bog, peatbog, swamp, swampland, morass, quagmire, quag, slough, fen, bayou; mud, slime, muck, dirt, filth.

mire verb **1** *cars mired in the swamp* sink, sink down, bog down, stick in the mud. **2** *mired in financial problems* entangle, catch up, involve, bog down.

mirror noun looking glass, glass, reflector, reflecting surface.

mirror verb reflect, imitate, emulate, simulate, copy, follow, mimic, echo, ape, parrot, impersonate.

mirth noun gaiety, cheerfulness, levity, buoyancy, blitheness, lightheartedness, joviality, enjoyment, amusement, pleasure. *See* MERRIMENT.

mirthful adjective gay, high-spirited, laughter-filled, jocular, lighthearted, jovial, fun-filled, amusing, pleasurable, frolicsome, sportive, playful. *See* MERRY.

misbehave verb behave badly, be naughty, be disobedient, be bad-mannered, show bad/poor manners, be rude, fool around; *inf.* carry on, act up.

misbehavior noun misconduct, bad behavior, disorderly conduct, badness, naughtiness, disobedience, mischief, mischievousness, delinquency, misdeed, rudeness, fooling around; *inf.* carrying on, acting up, shenanigans.

miscarriage noun failure, foundering, ruination, nonfulfillment, misfiring, breakdown, thwarting, frustration.

miscarry verb *our plan miscarried* go wrong, go awry, go amiss, be unsuccessful, fail, misfire, abort, be abortive, founder, come to nothing, come to grief, meet with disaster, fall through, be ruined, fall flat; *inf.* bite the dust, go up in smoke.

miscellaneous adjective varied, assorted, mixed, diverse, sundry, variegated, diversified, motley, multifarious, jumbled, confused, indiscriminate, heterogeneous.

miscellany noun assortment, mixture, collection. *See* MEDLEY.

mischance noun accident, misfortune, bad luck, ill fortune, ill luck, poor luck, misadventure, mishap, setback, failure, contretemps.

mischief noun **1** *involved in mischief* mischievousness, naughtiness, badness, bad behavior, misbehavior, misconduct, pranks, wrongdoing, delinquency; *inf.* monkey tricks, monkey business, shenanigans, goings-on. **2** *with mischief in her eyes* impishness, roguishness, rascality, devilment. **3** *did mischief to their property* harm, hurt, injury, impairment, damage, detriment.

mischievous adjective **1** *mischievous child* naughty, misbehaving, disobedient, troublesome, vexatious; playful, frolicsome, rascally, roguish. **2** *a mischievous smile* playful, teasing, impish, roguish, waggish, arch. **3** *mischievous gossip* malicious, spiteful, malignant, vicious, wicked, evil, hurtful, harmful, injurious, damaging, detrimental, deleterious, destructive, pernicious.

misconception noun misapprehension, misunderstanding, mistake, error, misinterpretation, the wrong idea, a false impression, delusion.

misconduct noun **1** *scolded for their misconduct* bad behavior, naughtiness. *See* MISBEHAVIOR. **2** *doctors guilty of misconduct* unprofessional behavior, unethical behavior, malpractice, impropriety, immorality.

miscreant noun villain, wrongdoer, criminal, evildoer, sinner, scoundrel, wretch, reprobate, blackguard, rogue, rascal.

misdeed noun wrongdoing, evil deed, crime, misdemeanor, offense, error, peccadillo, transgression, sin.

miser noun skinflint, penny-pincher, niggard, Scrooge; *inf.* money-grubber, cheapskate, tightwad.

miserable adjective **1** *feeling miserable* unhappy, sorrowful, dejected, depressed, downcast, downhearted, down, despondent, disconsolate, desolate, wretched, glum, gloomy, dismal, blue, melancholy, low-spirited, mournful, woeful, woebegone, sad, doleful, forlorn, crestfallen; *inf.* down in the mouth, down in the dumps. **2** *a miserable hovel* wretched, mean, poor, shabby, squalid, filthy, foul, sordid, seedy, dilapidated. **3** *miserable wretches* poverty-stricken, needy, penniless, impoverished, beggarly, destitute, indigent, down-at-the-heels, out at the elbows. **4** *miserable scoundrels* contemptible, despicable, base, mean, low, vile, sordid. **5** *miserable salaries* meager, paltry, scanty, low, poor, niggardly, pathetic. **6** *miserable weather* unpleasant, disagreeable, displeasing, uncomfortable, wet, rainy, stormy.

miserly adjective mean, niggardly, parsimonious, tight-fisted, close-fisted, penny-pinching, penurious, greedy, avaricious, ungenerous, illiberal; *inf.* stingy, tight, money-grubbing, cheap.

misery noun **1** *suffer/undergo misery* distress, wretchedness, hardship, suffering, affliction, anguish, torment, torture, agony, pain, discomfort, deprivation, grief, sorrow, despair, depression, woe, sadness, unhappiness. **2** *endure untold miseries* trouble, misfortune, adversity, affliction, ordeal, burden, load, blow, trial, tribulation, woe, catastrophe, calamity, disaster.

misfire verb go wrong, go awry, fail. *See* MISCARRY.

misfit noun fish out of water, square peg in a round hole, nonconformist, eccentric, maverick; *inf.* oddball, weirdo.

misfortune noun **1** *by misfortune we got lost* bad luck, ill fortune, accident, misadventure, mischance. **2** *endure many misfortunes* trouble, setback, reverse, adversity, reverse of fortune, misadventure, mishap, stroke of bad luck, blow, failure, accident, disaster, tragedy, affliction, sorrow, misery, woe, trial, tribulation, catastrophe, calamity.

misgiving noun qualm, doubt, reservation, second thoughts, suspicion, distrust, anxiety, apprehension, unease, uncertainty, hesitation.

misguided adjective **1** *their action was misguided* mistaken, deluded, erroneous, fallacious, wrong, ill-advised, unwise, injudicious, imprudent, foolish. **2** *misguided people believed him* misled, misdirected, misinformed, deluded.

mishandle verb **1** *mishandle the project* mismanage, misdirect, misgovern, misconduct, maladminister, bungle, botch, muff, make a mess of; *inf.* make a hash of, foul up, screw up. **2** *mishandle the prisoners* maltreat, manhandle. *See* MISTREAT.

mishap noun **1** *without further mishap* accident, misadventure, mischance. **2** *after a series of mishaps* accident, trouble, setback, reverse, adversity, misfortune, stroke of bad luck.

mishmash noun hodgepodge, jumble, tangle, confusion, potpourri, pastiche, gallimaufry, olio, salmagundi, mixed bag.

mislay verb lose, misplace, lose track of, miss, be unable to lay one's hands on.

mislead verb misinform, misguide, misdirect, delude, take in, deceive, fool, hoodwink, lead astray, throw off the scent, send on a wild-goose chase, pull the wool over someone's eyes; *inf.* lead up the garden path, take for a ride.

misleading adjective confusing, deceptive, deceiving, delusive, evasive, equivocal, ambiguous, fallacious, spurious, illusory, casuistic, sophistical.

mismanage verb misdirect, misgovern. *See* MISHANDLE 1.

misogynist noun woman-hater, antifeminist, male chauvinist, chauvinist; *inf.* male chauvinist pig, MCP.

misprint noun printing error, typographical error, typing error, mistake, erratum; *inf.* typo.

misrepresent verb misstate, misreport, misquote, misinterpret, falsify, distort, garble.

miss verb **1** *miss a shot* let go, bungle, botch, muff, fail to achieve. **2** *miss the meeting* fail to attend, be too late for, absent oneself from, play truant from, take French leave from; *inf.* skip. **3** *miss an opportunity* let slip, let go, pass up, overlook, disregard. **4** *I'm sorry, I missed what you said* fail to hear/catch, fail to take in, mishear, misunderstand. **5** *they miss their father* regret the absence/loss of, feel the loss of, feel nostalgic for, long to see, long for, pine for, yearn for, ache for. **6** *try to miss the traffic* avoid, evade, escape, dodge, sidestep, steer clear of, give a wide berth to.

miss noun failure, omission, slip, blunder, error, mistake, fiasco; *inf.* flop.

misshapen adjective deformed, malformed, ill-proportioned, misproportioned, twisted, distorted, contorted, warped, curved, crooked, wry, bent, hunchbacked.

mission noun **1** *accomplish his mission* assignment, commission, task, job, errand, work, chore, business, undertaking, operation, duty, charge, trust, goal, aim, purpose. **2** *her mission in life is to heal the sick* vocation, calling, pursuit, quest, undertaking. **3** *scientists asked to join the mission* delegation, deputation, committee, commission, task force, legation.

missionary noun evangelist, apostle, proselytizer, preacher, minister, priest.

missive noun communication, message, letter, note, memorandum, bulletin, communiqué, report, dispatch; *inf.* memo.

misspent adjective dissipated, wasted, squandered, thrown away, prodigal.

mist noun haze, fog, smog, cloud, vapor, condensation, steam, film.

mistake noun error, fault, inaccuracy, slip, blunder, miscalculation, misunderstanding, oversight, gaffe, faux pas, solecism, misapprehension, misreading; *inf.* slipup, booboo.

mistake verb get wrong, misunderstand, misapprehend, misinterpret, misconstrue, misread.

mistaken adjective wrong, erroneous, inaccurate, incorrect, false, fallacious, unsound, unfounded, misguided, misinformed, wide of the mark.

mistreat verb maltreat, treat badly, illtreat, ill-use, misuse, abuse, handle/treat roughly, mishandle, harm, hurt, molest, manhandle, maul, bully; *inf.* beat up, rough up.

mistress noun lover, girlfriend, partner, ladylove, paramour, kept woman, concubine, inamorata.

mistrust verb 1 *mistrust his motives* distrust, have doubts about, be suspicious of, suspect, have reservations about, have misgivings about, be wary of. 2 *mistrust his ability* have no confidence in, question, doubt, lack faith in.

mistrustful adjective distrustful, doubtful, dubious, suspicious, chary, wary, uncertain, cautious, hesitant, skeptical; *inf.* leery.

misty adjective hazy, foggy, cloudy; blurred, fuzzy, dim, indistinct, vague, obscure, nebulous.

misunderstand verb misapprehend, misinterpret, misconstrue, misread, get the wrong idea, receive a false impression.

misunderstanding noun 1 *his misunderstanding of the statement* misapprehension, mistake, error, mix-up, misinterpretation, misconstruction, misreading, misjudgment, miscalculation, misconception, misbelief, wrong idea, delusion, false impression. 2 *the friends had a misunderstanding* disagreement, difference, difference of opinion, clash of views, dispute, quarrel, argument, tiff, squabble, spat; *inf.* falling-out.

misuse verb 1 *misuse their talents* misapply, misemploy, abuse, squander, waste, dissipate. 2 *misuse the furniture* abuse, vandalize. See MISTREAT.

misuse noun 1 *the misuse of their money* misapplication, misemployment, abuse, squandering, waste, dissipation. 2 *this misuse of the verb* misusage, malapropism, barbarism, catachresis. 3 *misuse of the car* maltreatment, mistreatment, ill use, abuse, rough handling, mishandling, manhandling.

mitigate verb alleviate, reduce, diminish, lessen, weaken, attenuate, allay, assuage, palliate, appease, soothe, relieve, ease, soften, temper, mollify, lighten, still, quieten, quiet, tone down, moderate, modify, extenuate, calm, lull, pacify, placate, tranquilize.

mitigating adjective extenuating, exonerative, justificatory, justifying, vindicatory, vindicating, exculpatory, palliative, qualifying, modifying, tempering.

mix verb 1 *mix cement* admix, blend, put together, combine, mingle, compound, homogenize, alloy, merge, unite, join, amalgamate, fuse, coalesce, interweave. 2 *he never mixes at parties* socialize, mingle, associate, fraternize, hobnob. **mix up** 1 *mix up the dates* confuse, get confused, muddle, muddle up, get muddled up, get jumbled up, scramble, mistake. 2 *don't mix me up* confuse, throw into confusion, fluster, upset. 3 *he is mixed up in the crime* involve, implicate, entangle, embroil, draw into, incriminate.

mix noun merger, union, amalgamation, fusion, coalition. See MIXTURE 1.

mixed adjective 1 *a mixed collection* assorted, varied, miscellaneous, diverse, diversified, motley, heterogeneous. 2 *of mixed breed* hybrid, crossbred, interbred, mongrel. 3 *have mixed reactions* ambivalent, equivocal, unsure, uncertain.

mixed-up adjective *a mixed-up kid* maladjusted, ill-adjusted, disturbed, confused; *inf.* screwed-up.

mixture noun 1 *pour out the mixture* compound, blend, mix, brew, combination, concoction, alloy. 2 *a mixture of objects* assortment, variety. See MEDLEY.

mix-up noun confusion, muddle, jumble, misunderstanding, mistake.

moan noun groan, lament, lamentation, wail, whimper, whine, sigh, sough, murmur.

moan verb 1 *he moans in his sleep* groan, wail, whimper, whine, sigh, sough, murmur. 2 *always moaning about the weather* complain, whine, carp; *inf.* grouse, gripe, grouch, beef.

mob noun 1 *the mob of spectators* crowd, horde, multitude, legion, army, throng, host, pack, press, gang, drove, herd, flock, gathering, assemblage. 2 *the cries of the angry mob* masses, populace, commonality, proletariat, rabble, hoi polloi, canaille; *inf.* great unwashed. 3 *those gatecrashers left, but another mob arrived* lot, group, set, troop, company; *inf.* gang.

mob verb 1 *fans mobbed the team* crowd around, swarm around, surround, besiege, jostle. 2 *mob the theater* crowd into, cram full, fill to overflowing, fill, pack.

mobile adjective 1 *mobile library* movable, transportable, portable, traveling, peripatetic, locomotive. 2 *a mobile face* expressive,

animated, ever-changing, changeable.
3 *socially mobile* moving, on the move,
flexible, adaptable, adjustable.

mobilize verb muster, rally, marshal, assemble, organize, make ready, prepare,
ready.

mock verb **1** *rebels mocking government
officials* ridicule, jeer at, sneer at, deride,
treat with contempt, scorn, make fun of,
poke fun at, laugh at, tease, taunt, insult, flout; *inf.* rag, kid, rib. **2** *mocked
their teacher's mannerisms* imitate, mimic,
parody, ape, caricature, satirize, lampoon,
burlesque. **3** *the wind mocked their progress* defy, challenge, thwart, frustrate, foil,
disappoint.

mock adjective *mock leather* imitation, artificial, simulated, synthetic, ersatz, so-called, fake, sham, false, spurious, bogus,
counterfeit, forged, pseudo, pretended;
inf. pretend.

mockery noun **1** *a note of mockery in his
voice* ridicule, jeering, sneer, derision, contempt, scorn, disdain, teasing, taunting,
gibe, insult, contumely; *inf.* ribbing. **2** *the
trial was a mockery* laughingstock, farce,
parody, travesty, caricature, lampoon,
burlesque; *inf.* takeoff, send-up, spoof.

mocking adjective *a mocking smile* sneering,
derisive, derisory, contemptuous, scornful,
disdainful, sardonic, insulting, satirical.

model noun **1** *a model of a train* replica,
representation, mock-up, copy, dummy,
imitation, facsimile, image, mannequin.
2 *the model of the commissioned building*
prototype, protoplast, archetype, type,
mold, original, pattern, design, paradigm,
sample, example, exemplar. **3** *the model
of car I want* style, design, mode, form,
mark, version, type, variety, kind, sort. **4**
a model of tact ideal, paragon, perfect example, perfect specimen, exemplar, (the)
epitome of something, (the) beau ideal,
nonpareil, (the) crème de la crème. **5**
he used his wife as a model sitter, poser,
subject.

model adjective **1** *the model building* prototypical, prototypal, archetypal, illustrative.
2 *a model teacher* ideal, perfect.

moderate adjective **1** *moderate views/demands/behavior* nonextreme, middle-of-the-road, reasonable, within reason, within
due limits, restrained, controlled, temperate, sober, steady. **2** *moderate success*
average, middling, ordinary, fair, fairish,
modest, tolerable, passable, adequate, indifferent, mediocre, run-of-the-mill; *inf.*
so-so, fair-to-middling.

moderate verb **1** *moderate the force/pain*
abate, lessen. *See* MITIGATE. **2** *moderate the
debate* arbitrate, mediate, referee, judge,
chair, take the chair of, preside over.

moderately adverb **1** *moderately expensive*
quite, rather, somewhat, fairly, reasonably, to a certain degree, to some extent,
within reason, within limits. **2** *the work is
moderately good | did moderately well in the
test* fairly, tolerably, passably.

moderation noun **1** *moderation in all things*
moderateness, restraint, self-restraint, control, self-control, temperateness, temperance, nonindulgence. **2** *the moderation of
the force/pain* lessening, decrease, mitigation, appeasement, assuagement, soothing, calming. **in moderation** moderately,
within reason, within due limits.

modern adjective **1** *in modern times* contemporary, present-day, present, current,
existing, existent. **2** *her clothes/ideas are
very modern* up-to-date, up-to-the-minute,
fashionable, in fashion, in, in style, in
vogue, voguish, modish, the latest, new,
newfangled, fresh, modernistic, ultramodern, advanced, progressive; *inf.* trendy,
with-it.

modernize verb update, bring/get up to
date, renovate, remodel, remake, redo,
refresh, revamp, rejuvenate, move with
the times; *inf.* do over, get with it.

modest adjective **1** *modest about his achievements* self-effacing, self-deprecating, humble, unpretentious, unassuming. **2** *too
modest to speak* shy, bashful, self-conscious,
diffident, reserved, retiring, reticent, timid,
fearful, meek. **3** *modest behavior/clothes*
decorous, decent, seemly, demure, proper,
discreet, delicate, chaste, virtuous. **4**
modest improvement moderate, fair, tolerable, passable, adequate, unexceptional,
small, limited. **5** *a modest gift* unpretentious, simple, plain, humble, inexpensive,
low-cost.

modesty noun **1** *admire his modesty* lack
of vanity, humility, self-effacement, lack
of pretension, unpretentiousness. **2** *her
modesty prevented her speaking* shyness,
bashfulness, self-consciousness, reserve,
reticence, timidity, meekness. **3** *modesty
of her behavior/clothes* decorum, decorousness, seemliness, demureness, propriety,
chasteness. **4** *the modesty of their demands*
moderation, fairness, adequacy, acceptability, smallness. **5** *the modesty of the house*
unpretentiousness, simplicity, plainness,
inexpensiveness.

modicum noun bit, particle, iota, jot,
atom, whit, grain, speck, scrap, crumb,
fragment, shred, mite, dash, drop, dab,
pinch, ounce, inch, touch, tinge, trifle;
inf. teeny bit.

modification noun **1** *the modification of the
punishment* lessening, reduction, decrease,
abatement, mitigation, restriction. **2** *the
modification of the design* altering, alteration, adjustment, adaptation, refashioning,

change, variation, revision, refinement, transformation.

modify verb **1** *modify her views* soften, moderate, temper, blunt, dull, tone down, qualify. **2** *modify the design* alter, change, adjust, adapt, vary, revise, recast, reform, reshape, refashion, rework, remold, redo, revamp, reorganize, refine, transform.

mogul noun notable, VIP, magnate, tycoon, baron, captain, lord; *inf.* bigwig, big shot, big cheese.

moist adjective wet, wettish, damp, dampish, clammy, humid, dank, rainy, dewy, soggy.

moisten verb wet, dampen, damp, water, soak, bedew, humidify, irrigate.

moisture noun water, liquid, wetness, wet, dampness, damp, humidity, dankness, wateriness, rain, dew, drizzle, perspiration, sweat.

mold[1] noun **1** *set the mixture in a mold* cast, die, form, matrix. **2** *the mold of history* shape, form, figure, cast, outline, line, configuration, formation, format, structure, frame, construction, build, cut, style, model, pattern, type, kind, brand, make. **3** *people of heroic mold* character, nature, caliber, kind, sort, ilk, stamp, type, kidney.

mold[2] verb **1** *mold the model from clay* shape, form, fashion, model, construct, frame, make, create, design, carve, sculpt, chisel, forge. **2** *mold children's minds* influence, affect, direct, shape, form.

mold[3] noun moldiness, fungus, mildew, blight, smut, must, mustiness, dry rot, rot.

moldy adjective mildewed, blighted, musty, fusty, decaying, rotting, rotten, bad, spoiled.

molest verb **1** *crowds molesting the celebrity* pester, annoy, nag, plague, torment, harass, badger, harry, bother, vex, disturb; *inf.* bug, hassle. **2** *accused of molesting children* abuse, sexually abuse/assault, rape, ravish, assault, attack, injure, hurt, harm, mistreat, maltreat, ill-treat, manhandle.

mollify verb calm, calm down, pacify, placate, appease, soothe, still, quiet, tranquilize.

mollycoddle verb pamper, coddle, cosset, spoil, overindulge, indulge, baby.

moment noun short time, instant. *See* MINUTE noun 1, 2.

momentary adjective brief, short, short-lived, fleeting, passing, transient, transitory, ephemeral, evanescent, fugitive, temporary, impermanent.

momentous adjective important, significant, consequential, fateful, historic; *inf.* earthshaking, earth-shattering.

momentum noun impetus, impulse, propulsion, thrust, push, driving power/force, drive, power, energy, force.

monarch noun sovereign, ruler, crowned head, potentate, king, queen, emperor, empress.

monarchy noun **1** *abolish the monarchy* absolutism, absolute power, autocracy, monocracy, kingship, royalism, sovereignty, despotism. **2** *the country is a monarchy* kingdom, sovereign state, realm, principality, empire.

monastery noun friary, abbey, convent, nunnery, priory.

monastic adjective monastical, cloistered, cenobitic, conventual, canonical, ascetic, celibate, contemplative, meditative, sequestered, secluded, reclusive, recluse, eremitic, anchoritic.

monetary adjective money, cash, financial, capital, pecuniary, fiscal, budgetary.

money noun **1** *not enough money to buy the business* cash, hard cash, ready money, finance, capital, funds, banknotes, currency, coin, coinage, silver, copper, legal tender, specie; *inf.* wherewithal, dough, bread, loot, moolah, filthy lucre, green stuff. **2** *he is a man of money* affluence, wealth, riches, prosperity. **in the money** moneyed, well-to-do, well-off, affluent, rich, wealthy, prosperous, in clover; *inf.* rolling in it, loaded, stinking rich, well-heeled, flush, made of money, on easy street.

moneymaking adjective profitable, lucrative, gainful, paying, remunerative, successful, thriving, going.

mongrel noun crossbreed, cross, half-breed, mixed breed, hybrid, cur.

monitor noun **1** *monitors watching shoppers/workers* detector, scanner, recorder, security system, security camera, observer, watchdog, overseer, supervisor. **2** *computer monitor* screen, cathode-ray tube, CRT.

monitor verb observe, scan, record, survey, follow, keep an eye on, keep track of, check, oversee, supervise.

monk noun brother, monastic, religious, friar, abbot, prior.

monkey noun **1** *monkeys in the jungle* primate, simian. **2** *the child is a little monkey* rascal, scamp, imp, rogue, mischief-maker, devil. **make a monkey of** make a fool of, make a laughingstock of, ridicule, deride, make fun of.

monkey verb **monkey around/about** fool around/about, play around/about; *inf.* mess around/about. **monkey with** fiddle with, play with, tinker with, tamper with, interfere with, meddle with, fool with, trifle with, mess with.

monkey business noun **1** *children up to monkey business* mischief, naughtiness, pranks, clowning; *inf.* shenanigans. **2** *monkey business in the accounts department* dishonesty, trickery, misconduct, misdemeanor, chicanery, skulduggery; *inf.* funny business, hanky-panky.

monologue noun soliloquy, speech, address, lecture, oration, sermon.

monopolize verb corner, control, take over, dominate.

monotonous adjective **1** *a monotonous job* unvarying, unchanging, repetitious, routine, humdrum, run-of-the-mill, commonplace, mechanical, uninteresting, unexciting, prosaic, wearisome, dull, boring, tedious, tiresome. **2** *a monotonous voice* flat, unvarying, toneless, uninflected, droning, soporific.

monotony noun **1** *the monotony of the job* lack of variety, repetition, repetitiveness, sameness, uniformity, routine, routineness, dullness, boredom, tedium, tiresomeness. **2** *the monotony of her voice* flatness, tonelessness, drone.

monster noun **1** *frightened by the monster in the myth* fabulous/mythical creature, ogre, giant, dragon, troll, bogeyman, werewolf, sea monster, behemoth. **2** *Hitler was a monster* fiend, beast, brute, barbarian, savage, villain, ogre, devil, demon. **3** *the sideshow monster was a hoax* monstrosity, miscreation, malformation, freak, freak of nature, mutant, lusus naturae. **4** *a monster of a man* giant, mammoth, colossus, titan, behemoth, leviathan.

monster adjective *a monster truck* huge, enormous, massive, vast, immense, colossal, gigantic, monstrous, stupendous, prodigious, tremendous, giant, mammoth, gargantuan, titanic; *inf.* jumbo, whopping, humongous.

monstrous adjective **1** *Dr. Frankenstein's monstrous creatures* miscreated, malformed, unnatural, abnormal, grotesque, gruesome, repellent, freakish, mutant. **2** *monstrous trucks* huge, enormous. *See* MONSTER adjective. **3** *it was a monstrous thing to do* outrageous, shocking, scandalous, atrocious, heinous, evil, abominable, hideous, loathsome, contemptible, despicable, vicious, cruel, savage, barbaric, inhuman, fiendish, diabolical.

monument noun **1** *a monument to the dead soldiers* memorial, statue, shrine, reliquary, sepulcher, mausoleum, cairn, pillar, column, obelisk, dolmen, megalith. **2** *establish a scholarship as a monument to his talent* memorial, commemoration, remembrance, reminder, testament, witness, token.

monumental adjective **1** *a monumental effort* great, huge, enormous, immense, vast,

exceptional, extraordinary, tremendous, stupendous, prodigious, staggering. **2** *a monumental error* colossal, egregious, catastrophic, staggering, unforgivable, indefensible; *inf.* whopping. **3** *a monumental work of art* massive, impressive, striking, remarkable, magnificent, awe-inspiring, marvelous, majestic, classic, memorable, unforgettable, enduring, permanent, immortal.

mood noun humor, temper, disposition, frame of mind, state of mind, spirit, tenor, vein; bad mood, bad temper, low spirits, depression.

moody adjective **1** *teenagers are often moody* temperamental, changeable, unpredictable, volatile, mercurial, unstable, unsteady, erratic, fitful, impulsive, capricious. **2** *don't say anything—he's moody today* bad-tempered, ill-tempered, ill-humored, irritable, crabby, cross, testy, touchy, petulant, in a pique, sullen, sulky, moping, gloomy, glum, depressed, huffy.

moor verb secure, fix firmly, fasten, make fast, tie up, lash, anchor, berth.

moot adjective *a moot point* debatable, open to debate, open to discussion, questionable, open to question, open, doubtful, disputable, arguable, contestable, controversial, unresolved, undecided.

mop verb clean, wipe, wash, swab, sponge.

mop up **1** *mop up all the profits* absorb, use up, exhaust, consume, swallow up. **2** *mop up the last bits of work* finish off, make an end of, clear up, eliminate, dispatch.

mope verb pine, fret, grieve, brood, sulk, idle, languish, moon.

moral adjective **1** *a moral person/act* ethical, good, virtuous, righteous, upright, upstanding, high-minded, principled, honorable, honest, just, decent, chaste, pure, blameless, right, proper, fit, decent, decorous. **3** *moral support* psychological, emotional, mental.

moral noun lesson, teaching, message, homily, meaning, significance, point.

morale noun self-confidence, confidence, heart, spirit, hope, hopefulness, optimism, determination, zeal.

morality noun **1** *a man/woman of morality* ethics, goodness, virtue, righteousness, rectitude, uprightness, integrity, principles, honor, honesty, justness, decency, chasteness, chastity, purity, blamelessness. **2** *discuss morality* moral code, ethics. *See* MORALS.

morals plural noun ethics, moral code, principles of right and wrong, principles, moral behavior/conduct, standards/principles of behavior, standards, morality, sense of morality, scruples, mores.

morbid adjective **1** *morbid thoughts/details* gruesome, grisly, macabre, hideous, dreadful, horrible, unwholesome; death-orientated, death-obsessed, death-fixated. **2** *don't be so morbid* gloomy, glum, dejected, melancholy, lugubrious, funereal, pessimistic.

more adjective additional, supplementary, further, added, extra, increased, spare, fresh, new.

more adverb *concentrate more* to a greater extent, further, longer, some more.

moreover adverb besides, furthermore, further, what is more, in addition, also, as well, to boot.

morgue noun mortuary, funeral parlor, funeral home, charnel house.

moribund adjective **1** *moribund patients* dying, on one's deathbed, near death, near the end, breathing one's last, fading fast, failing rapidly, having one foot in the grave, *in extremis*. **2** *moribund customs* dying, declining, on the decline, waning, on the way out, obsolescent, on its last legs.

morning noun forenoon, a.m., dawn, daybreak, sunrise; *lit.* morn.

moron noun fool, dolt, dunce, dullard, blockhead, dunderhead, ignoramus, numskull, nincompoop, idiot, imbecile, nitwit, halfwit; *inf.* dope, dimwit, dummy, schmuck.

morose adjective sullen, gloomy, glum, somber, sober, saturnine, lugubrious, funereal, mournful, depressed, dour, melancholy, melancholic, doleful, blue, down, low, moody, sour, scowling, sulky, crabby, cross.

morsel noun bite, nibble, bit, crumb, grain, particle, fragment, scrap, soupçon, taste.

mortal adjective **1** *mortal beings* temporal, transient, ephemeral, passing, impermanent, perishable, human, earthly, worldly, corporeal, fleshly. **2** *a mortal blow* death-dealing, deadly, fatal, lethal, killing, murderous, terminal, destructive. **3** *mortal enemies* deadly, to the death, sworn, out-and-out, irreconcilable, bitter, implacable, unrelenting, remorseless. **4** *mortal pain/fear* terrible, awful, intense, extreme, severe, grave, dire. **5** *of no mortal use* conceivable, imaginable, perceivable, possible.

mortal noun human being, human, earthling, person, man/woman, being, body, individual.

mortality noun **1** *humans subject to mortality* temporality, transience, ephemerality, impermanence, perishability. **2** *appalled at the wartime mortality* bloodshed, death, loss of life, fatalities, killing, slaying, carnage, slaughter.

mortify verb **1** *mortified by failure* humiliate, humble, bring low, disgrace, shame, dishonor, abash, fill with shame, put to shame, chasten, degrade, abase, deflate, embarrass. **2** *mortify one's passions* subdue, control, restrain, suppress, discipline, chasten.

mortuary noun morgue, funeral parlor, funeral home, charnel house.

most noun the majority, the greatest number, nearly all, almost all, the bulk, the mass.

mostly adverb **1** *they were mostly young* for the most part, on the whole, largely, mainly, chiefly, predominantly. **2** *mostly we eat at home* usually, generally, as a rule, ordinarily.

mother noun materfamilias, matriarch, earth mother; *inf.* mom, mommy, ma, mama, mater, old lady.

mother adjective inborn, innate, connate, native, natural.

mother verb look after, care for, tend, raise, rear, foster, cherish, fuss over, indulge, spoil.

motherly adjective maternal, protective, comforting, caring, loving, affectionate, warm, tender, gentle.

motion noun **1** *the motion made her sick* motility, mobility, locomotion, movement, moving. **2** *a motion with her hand* movement, gesture, gesticulation, signal, sign, wave, nod. **set/put in motion** get going, get under way, get in operation, get working/functioning, start, begin, commence.

motion verb gesture, gesticulate, signal, sign, wave, nod.

motionless adjective unmoving, still, stock-still, at a standstill, stationary, immobile, immovable, static, at rest, halted, stopped, paralyzed, transfixed, frozen, inert, lifeless.

motivate verb move, cause, lead, persuade, prompt, actuate, drive, impel, spur, induce, provoke, incite, inspire, give incentive to, stimulate, arouse, stir, goad.

motivation noun incentive, stimulus, inspiration, inducement, incitement, motive; ambition, drive, inspiration.

motive noun reason, rationale, justification, thinking, grounds, cause, basis, occasion; motivation, incentive, inducement, incitement.

motley adjective **1** *motley collection of old clothes* assorted, varied. *See* MISCELLANEOUS. **2** *a motley coat* many-colored, multicolored, parti-colored, many-hued, variegated, kaleidoscopic, prismatic.

mottled adjective blotched, blotchy, splotchy, speckled, spotted, streaked, marbled, flecked, freckled, dappled, stippled, variegated, piebald, pied, brindled.

motto noun **1** *"waste not, want not" should be your motto* maxim, aphorism, adage, saying, saw, axiom, truism, precept, epigram, proverb, byword, gnome. **2** *the club's motto* slogan, catchword, cry.

mound noun **1** *a mound of leaves* heap, pile, stack; *inf.* mountain. **2** *flat country broken by mounds* hillock, hill, knoll, rise, hummock, embankment, bank, dune.

mound verb pile, heap (up), stack (up), accumulate, amass, stockpile.

mount verb **1** *mount the stairs* ascend, go up, climb up, clamber up, make one's way up, scale. **2** *costs mounting up* accumulate, accrue, pile up, grow, multiply. **3** *prices/fear mounting* increase, grow, escalate, intensify. **4** *mount a campaign/exhibition* stage, put on, install, prepare, organize, arrange, set in motion.

mount noun *a plain mount for the gem/picture* setting, fixture, frame, support, stand, base, backing, foil.

mountain noun **1** *snowcapped mountains* peak, height, elevation, eminence, pinnacle, alp; *lit.* mount. **2** *mountains of clothes* heap, pile, mound, stack, abundance; *inf.* ton.

mourn verb grieve, sorrow, keen, lament, wail.

mournful adjective sad, sorrowful, doleful, gloomy, somber, melancholy, lugubrious, funereal, elegiac.

mourning noun grief, grieving, sorrowing, lamentation, keening, wailing, weeping, moaning.

mousy adjective **1** *a mousy person* timid, fearful, timorous, self-effacing, unobtrusive, unassertive, withdrawn, shy. **2** *mousy hair/colors* brownish-gray, grayish, gray, dun-colored, colorless, neutral, drab, dull, lackluster.

mouth noun **1** *open their mouths* lips, jaws, maw, muzzle; *inf.* trap, chops, kisser. **2** *mouth of the cave/trumpet* opening, entrance, entry, inlet, door, doorway, gateway, portal, hatch. **3** *the mouth of the river* estuary, outlet, embouchure. **4** *he's all mouth and no action* empty talk, idle talk, babble, claptrap, boasting, bragging, braggadocio; *inf.* hot air, gas. **5** *don't take any mouth from her* impudence, cheek, insolence, impertinence, rudeness, incivility, effrontery, audacity; *inf.* lip, back talk. **down in the mouth** down, downhearted, dejected, downcast, low in spirits, depressed, dispirited, crestfallen.

move verb **1** *men moving slowly* proceed, progress, advance, pass. **2** *move objects* carry, transport, transfer, transpose, change over, shift, switch. **3** *the government must move soon* take action, act, do something, get moving. **4** *our neighbors are moving* relocate, move away, leave, go away. **5** *she was moved by the performance* affect, touch, impress, upset, disturb, disquiet, agitate. **6** *the sight moved her to tears* provoke, incite, actuate, rouse, excite, urge, incline, stimulate, motivate, influence, persuade, lead, prompt, cause, impel, induce. **7** *as the spirit moves him* propel, drive, push, shift, motivate. **8** *nothing can move him on that* change, budge, change someone's mind; *inf.* do an about-face, do a U-turn. **9** *the goods are not moving* sell, be sold, move from the shelf.

move noun **1** *birds frightened by the slightest move* motion, action. *See* MOVEMENT 2. **2** *arrange our move* removal, relocation, transfer. **3** *plan our next move* action, act, deed, measure, step, tack, maneuver, tactic, stratagem, ploy, ruse, trick. **4** *it's your move* turn; opportunity, chance; *inf.* shot. **get a move on** hurry up, get moving; *inf.* get cracking, make it snappy, step on it, shake a leg. **make a move** take action, act, do something. **on the move 1** *she's always on the move* moving, in motion, going, traveling, journeying. **2** *things are on the move* progressing, advancing, moving/going forward.

movement noun **1** *the movement of the furniture* moving, carrying, transportation, transferal, shifting. **2** *make a sudden movement* move, motion, action, activity, gesture, gesticulation. **3** *the movement of time* progress, progression, advance, passing, passage. **4** *the clock's movement* mechanism, machinery, works, workings, action, wheels; *inf.* innards, guts. **5** *a peace movement* group, party, organization, faction, wing, coalition, front; campaign, crusade, drive. **6** *a movement toward better government* trend, tendency, drift, swing, current. **7** *no movement in the stock market* rise/fall, change, variation, fluctuation. **8** *some movement has been made in the situation* progress, advance, improvement, step forward, breakthrough.

moving adjective **1** *a moving story* affecting, touching, emotive, emotional, poignant, pathetic, stirring, arousing, upsetting, disturbing. **2** *moving parts* movable, mobile, motile, unfixed. **3** *the moving force behind the scheme* driving, dynamic, impelling, motivating, stimulating, inspirational.

much adjective a great deal of, plenty of, ample, copious, abundant; *inf.* a lot of, lots of.

much adverb **1** *I much regret it* greatly, exceedingly, considerably. **2** *he's not here much* often, frequently; *inf.* a lot.

muck noun **1** *clear the muck from the barn* dung, manure, ordure, excrement, guano, droppings, feces. **2** *clean the muck from the* car dirt, grime, filth, mud, slime, sludge, scum, mire; *inf.* gunk, grunge.

mud noun sludge, clay, silt, mire, dirt, soil.

muddle verb **1** *muddle the dates/situation* confuse, mix up, jumble, jumble up, scramble, disarrange, disorganize, throw into disorder, get into a tangle, make a mess of, mess up. **2** *numbers muddle her* confuse, disorient, bewilder, befuddle, daze, perplex, puzzle, baffle.

muddle noun **1** *files in a muddle* chaos, disorder, disarray, confusion, disorganization, jumble, mix up, mess, clutter, tangle. **2** *her mind is in a muddle* state of confusion, disorientation, bewilderment, perplexity, puzzlement, bafflement.

muddy adjective **1** *a muddy substance* mucky, miry, oozy, slushy, slimy. **2** *muddy ground* marshy, boggy, swampy. **3** *muddy shoes* mud-caked, dirty, filthy, grubby, grimy. **4** *muddy stream/liquid* cloudy, murky, smoky, dingy, dull, turbid, opaque. **5** *muddy thinking* confused, jumbled, incoherent, unclear, muddied, woolly.

muffle verb deaden, dull, dampen, stifle, smother, suppress, soften, hush, mute, silence.

muggy adjective close, stuffy, sultry, oppressive, airless, humid, clammy, sticky.

mull verb **mull over** think over, think about, consider, ponder, reflect on, contemplate, meditate on, deliberate about/on, muse on, ruminate over/on, examine, study, review.

multiply verb increase, grow, accumulate, augment, proliferate, spread, breed, reproduce.

multitude noun **1** *multitude of people* crowd, assembly. *See* MOB noun 1. **2** *treat the multitude with disdain* masses, populace. *See* MOB noun 2.

mundane adjective **1** *mundane issues/prose* common, ordinary, everyday, workaday, usual, prosaic, pedestrian, routine, customary, regular, normal, typical, commonplace, banal, hackneyed, trite. **2** *mundane, not spiritual, matters* worldly, earthly, terrestrial, secular, temporal, fleshly, carnal, sensual.

municipal adjective civic, civil, city, metropolitan, urban, town, borough, community, public.

munificence noun liberality, generosity, charity, charitableness, magnanimity, magnanimousness, largesse, bounty, bountifulness, bounteousness.

munificent adjective bountiful, bounteous, liberal, generous, free, openhanded, charitable, hospitable, bighearted, beneficent, benevolent, ungrudging, magnanimous, philanthropic.

murder noun **1** *guilty of murder* killing, slaying, manslaughter, homicide, slaughter, assassination, butchery, carnage, massacre. **2** *the drive was murder* an ordeal, a trial, a misery, agony; *inf.* hell, hell on earth.

murder verb **1** *murder his brother* kill, slay, put to death, take the life of, shed the blood of, slaughter, assassinate, butcher, massacre; *inf.* bump off, do in, eliminate, hit, rub out, blow away. **2** *murder the song* mangle, mutilate, ruin, make a mess of, spoil, mar, destroy. **3** *they murdered our team* trounce, beat soundly, beat decisively, thrash, defeat utterly, give a drubbing to; *inf.* slaughter, hammer, make mincemeat of.

murderer noun killer, slayer, homicide, slaughterer, cutthroat, assassin, butcher, patricide, matricide, fratricide.

murky adjective **1** *murky streets/shadows* dark, dim, gloomy. **2** *murky weather* foggy, misty, cloudy, lowering, overcast, dull, gray, dismal, dreary, cheerless. **3** *murky pools* dirty, muddy, dingy, dull, cloudy, turbid, opaque. **4** *a murky past* dark, questionable, doubtful, obscure, enigmatic, nebulous, mysterious, hidden, secret.

murmur noun **1** *the murmur of the stream* babble, burble, whisper, rustle, buzzing, drone, sigh; *inf.* whoosh. **2** *tell him in a murmur* whisper, undertone, mutter, mumble. **3** *murmurs against his presidency* mutter, grumble, moan, complaint, carping, whisper; *inf.* grouse, gripe, beef.

murmur verb **1** *streams murmuring* babble, burble, whisper, rustle, buzz, drone, sigh; *inf.* whoosh. **2** *murmured her desire to leave* whisper, mutter, mumble. **murmur against** grumble, moan, complain, carp; *inf.* grouse, gripe, beef, bitch.

muscle noun **1** *strain a muscle* sinew, tendon, ligament, thew. **2** *a man with muscle* muscularity, brawn; *inf.* beef. **3** *the new chairperson has no muscle* power, potency, force, forcefulness, might, strength, weight, influence; *inf.* clout, pull.

muscular adjective **1** *muscular men* brawny, strapping, powerfully built, solidly built, hefty, stalwart, sturdy, rugged, burly; *inf.* beefy, husky. **2** *a muscular attempt* vigorous, potent, powerful, strong, energetic, active, dynamic, aggressive, determined, resolute.

muse verb **1** *stand and muse* think, meditate, be lost in contemplation/thought, be in a brown study, reflect, deliberate, daydream, be in a reverie. **2** *muse over the situation* think over, think about. *See* MULL.

mushroom verb spring up, shoot up, sprout, burgeon, burst forth, grow/develop rapidly, boom, thrive, flourish, prosper.

music noun melody, tune, air, rhythm, harmonization, orchestration.

musical adjective tuneful, melodic, melodious, harmonious, lyrical, sweet-sounding, mellifluous, dulcet, euphonious.

muss verb disarrange, misarrange, put out of place, make untidy, make a mess of, mess up, rumple, dishevel, tousle.

muster verb **1** *muster the soldiers* assemble, bring together, call/gather together, call up, summon, rally, mobilize, round up, marshal, collect, convoke. **2** *we must muster at dawn* meet, congregate, convene. **3** *muster one's courage* call up, gather together, summon, rally, screw up.

muster noun **pass muster** measure up, come up to scratch/snuff, be acceptable, qualify; *inf.* make the grade, fill/fit the bill.

musty adjective **1** *musty books/food/rooms* moldy, mildewed, mildewy, fusty, decaying, stale, stuffy, airless, damp, dank. **2** *musty ideas* antiquated, obsolete, ancient, antediluvian, out-of-date, outdated, old-fashioned, out-of-fashion, out-of-style, behind the times, passé, hoary, moth-eaten, worn-out, threadbare, hackneyed, trite, clichéd.

mutation noun change, variation, alteration, modification, transformation, metamorphosis, evolution, transmutation, transfiguration.

mute adjective **1** *mute with surprise* silent, speechless, wordless, unspeaking, taciturn, uncommunicative. **2** *animals born mute* dumb, voiceless, speechless, aphasic, aphonic. **3** *a mute appeal* unexpressed, unspoken.

mutilate verb **1** *mutilated in the accident* maim, lame, cripple, disable, disfigure, damage, injure, impair; dismember, tear limb from limb, amputate limbs from. **2** *mutilate a text* mar, spoil, ruin, damage, butcher, mangle, distort, cut, hack, censor, bowdlerize, expurgate.

mutinous adjective rebellious, insurgent, insurrectionary, revolutionary, anarchistic, subversive, seditious, traitorous, insubordinate, disobedient, riotous.

mutiny noun rebellion, revolt, insurrection, insurgence, insurgency, uprising, rising, riot, revolution, resistance, disobedience, defiance, insubordination, protest, strike.

mutiny verb rebel, revolt, riot, rise up.

mutter verb **1** *going along muttering* talk under one's breath, speak in an undertone, speak sotto voce, mumble, murmur. **2** *mutter against the government* grumble, moan, complain, carp; *inf.* grouse, gripe, beef, bitch.

muzzle verb gag, bridle, silence, censor, suppress, stifle, inhibit, restrain, check, fetter.

myriad noun scores, multitude, host, horde, army, legion, mass, throng, swarm, sea; *inf.* millions, thousands, oodles, zillions.

myriad adjective innumerable, countless, incalculable, immeasurable, numerous, multitudinous, multifarious, manifold, multiple.

mysterious adjective **1** *the ways of nature are mysterious* enigmatic, inscrutable, impenetrable, incomprehensible, inexplicable, unexplainable, unfathomable, unaccountable, insoluble, obscure, arcane, abstruse, cryptic, preternatural, supernatural, uncanny, mystical, peculiar, strange, weird, curious, bizarre, mystifying, baffling, puzzling. **2** *he was mysterious about his whereabouts* secretive, reticent, noncommittal, discreet, evasive, furtive, surreptitious.

mystery noun **1** *his death remains a mystery* enigma, puzzle, secret, problem, riddle, conundrum, question, question mark. **2** *his whereabouts are clothed in mystery* secrecy, concealment, obscurity, vagueness, nebulousness, inscrutability, inexplicability.

mystic, mystical adjective **1** *a mystic experience* spiritual, paranormal, transcendental, otherworldly, supernatural, preternatural, nonrational, occult, metaphysical. **2** *mystic rites* symbolic, representational, allegorical, metaphorical, emblematic. **3** *mystical events* obscure, cryptic. *See* MYSTERIOUS 1.

mystify verb confuse, bewilder, confound, perplex, baffle, puzzle, elude, escape; *inf.* stump, beat.

myth noun **1** *read ancient myths* legend, saga, tale, story, fable, folk tale, allegory, parable, fairy tale/story, bestiary. **2** *her having a rich father was just a myth* invention, fabrication, untruth, lie; *inf.* story, fairy tale/story, tall tale.

mythical adjective **1** *a mythical creature* legendary, mythological, fabled, chimerical, imaginary, imagined, fabulous, fantastical, fairy-tale, storybook, fictitious, allegorical. **2** *a mythical rich uncle* imaginary, pretended, make-believe, unreal, fictitious, invented, fabricated, made-up, untrue; *inf.* pretend.

Nn

nag verb scold, carp, pick on, harp on at, be on someone's back, henpeck, bully, upbraid, berate, criticize, find fault with, complain to, grumble to, badger, pester, plague, torment, harry, goad, vex, harass, irritate; *inf.* go on (and on) at, hassle, drive up the wall.

nag noun shrew, harpy, termagant, fault-finder, carper, caviler, complainer, grumbler.

nail noun **1** *drive a nail into the wood* pin, brad, tack, rivet, spike. **2** *the animal's nails* fingernail, toenail, claw, talon, nipper, pincer.

naïve adjective **1** *they are still young and naïve* innocent, artless, childlike, simple, ingenuous, guileless, trusting, unsophisticated, unworldly, jejune, natural, unaffected, unpretentious, frank, open, candid. **2** *exploited the naïve employees* gullible, overtrusting, overtrustful, credulous, unsuspicious, unsuspecting, deceivable, dupable, callow, raw, green, immature, inexperienced; *inf.* wet behind the ears.

naïveté noun **1** *the young girl's naïveté* innocence, artlessness, simplicity, ingenuousness, guilelessness, lack of guile, unsophistication, lack of sophistication, unworldliness, naturalness, candor. **2** *took advantage of their naïveté* gullibility, credulousness, credulity, overtrustfulness, lack of suspicion, callowness, greenness, immaturity.

naked adjective **1** *naked sunbathers* stark naked, nude, in the nude, bare, stripped, exposed, unclothed, undressed, uncovered, undraped, disrobed, au naturel; *inf.* without a stitch on, in one's birthday suit, in the raw, in the altogether, in the buff, naked as the day one was born, buck naked. **2** *naked landscapes/rooms* bare, barren, stark, uncovered, denuded, stripped, treeless, grassless, unfurnished. **3** *the naked truth* undisguised, unqualified, unadorned, stark, bald, unvarnished, unveiled, unmitigated, unexaggerated, plain, simple, open, patent, evident, apparent, obvious, manifest, overt, unmistakable, blatant, glaring, flagrant. **4** *feeling naked in a foreign country* defenseless, unprotected, vulnerable, exposed, helpless, weak, powerless.

namby-pamby adjective oversentimental, sentimental, mawkish, maudlin, insipid, colorless, anemic, feeble, weak, vapid, spineless, effeminate, effete, prim, prissy, mincing, simpering; *inf.* wishy-washy, wimpish.

name noun **1** *the name of the person/tree* appellation, designation, cognomen, denomination, sobriquet, title, style, label, tag, epithet, first/second name, Christian/given name, surname, family name, maiden name, nickname, pet name, stage name, pseudonym, alias, nom de guerre, nom de plume; *inf.* moniker, handle. **2** *he's a name in the theater* big name, celebrity, luminary, star, dignitary, VIP, lion; *inf.* celeb, megastar, big shot, bigwig. **3** *make his name in motion pictures* reputation, fame, renown, repute, note, distinction, eminence, prominence, prestige.

name verb **1** *name the child/plant* baptize, christen, call, entitle, label, style, term, title, dub, denominate. **2** *name the most suitable day* identify, specify, mention, cite, give. **3** *name his successor* appoint, choose, select, pick, nominate, designate.

nameless adjective **1** *nameless graves* unnamed, untitled, unlabeled, untagged, innominate. **2** *nameless benefactors* anonymous, unidentified, undesignated, unspecified. **3** *nameless fears* unspeakable, unutterable, inexpressible, unmentionable, indescribable.

nap noun catnap, doze, light sleep, rest; *inf.* snooze, forty winks, (some) shut-eye.

narcissistic adjective self-admiring, self-loving, in love with oneself, conceited, vain, egotistic.

narcotic noun drug, opiate, sleeping pill, anesthetic, painkiller, analgesic, anodyne, tranquilizer, sedative, soporific.

narrate verb tell, relate, recount, recite, unfold, give an account of, give a report of, set forth, chronicle, describe, detail, portray, sketch out, rehearse, repeat.

narration noun account, story, storytelling, tale, telling, relation, recital, reciting, report, chronicling, chronicle, description, portrayal, sketch, rehearsal, repetition.

narrative noun account, statement, report, chronicle, history, story, tale.

narrow adjective **1** *narrow roads/waists* narrow-gauged, slender, thin, slim, slight, spare, attenuated, tapering. **2** *narrow spaces* confined, confining, constricted, tight, cramped, close, incommodious, pinched, straitened, squeezed, meager, scant, scanty, spare, scrimped, exiguous. **3** *a narrow range* limited, restricted, select, exclusive. **4** *a* *narrow interpretation* literal, exact, precise, close, faithful. **5** *narrow in her thinking* intolerant, illiberal. *See* NARROW-MINDED.

narrow-minded adjective intolerant, illiberal, unliberal, overconservative, conservative, hidebound, reactionary, close-minded, unreasonable, prejudiced, bigoted, biased, discriminatory, jaundiced, parochial, provincial, insular, small-minded, petty-minded, petty, mean-spirited, prudish, straitlaced.

nasty adjective **1** *a nasty sight/smell* unpleasant, disagreeable, distasteful, horrible, vile, foul, hateful, loathsome, revolting, disgusting, odious, obnoxious, repellent, repugnant, ugly, offensive, objectionable, noisome, squalid, dirty, filthy, impure, polluted, tainted, unpalatable, unsavory, unappetizing, evil-smelling, foul-smelling, smelly, stinking, rank, fetid, malodorous, mephitic; *inf.* yucky. **2** *a nasty situation* dangerous, serious, critical, crucial, severe, alarming, threatening. **3** *a nasty person* ill-tempered, ill-natured, ill-humored, bad-tempered, cross, surly, unpleasant, disagreeable, vicious, spiteful, malicious, mean; *inf.* grouchy. **4** *nasty jokes/videos* obscene, pornographic, indecent, foul, vile, blue, off-color, smutty, bawdy, vulgar, ribald, risqué, lewd, lascivious, licentious.

nation noun country, land, state, kingdom, empire, realm, republic, confederation, commonwealth, people, race, tribe, society, community, population.

nationalistic adjective patriotic, chauvinistic, jingoistic, xenophobic.

native adjective **1** *native instinct* inborn, inherent, innate, connate, built-in, intrinsic, instinctive, intuitive, natural, natural-born, congenital, hereditary, inherited, in the blood, in the family, inbred, ingrained. **2** *native plants/peoples* indigenous, original, homegrown, homemade, domestic, local, aboriginal, autochthonous.

native noun inhabitant, dweller, resident, citizen, national, aborigine, autochthon.

natural adjective **1** *in the natural course of events* usual, normal, regular, common, ordinary, everyday, typical, routine, run-of-the-mill. **2** *her natural instincts* inborn, inherent. *See* NATURE adjective 1. **3** *natural charm* artless, ingenuous, open, frank, genuine, real, authentic, simple, unsophisticated, unaffected, unpretentious, spontaneous, relaxed, unstudied. **4** *natural produce* organic, pure, unrefined, unpolished, unbleached, unmixed, whole, plain, real, chemical-free, additive-free.

naturalistic adjective realistic, real-life, true-to-life, lifelike, factual, graphic, representational; *inf.* warts and all.

naturally adverb **1** *behave naturally* artlessly, ingenuously, candidly, unaffectedly, unpretentiously, spontaneously. **2** *naturally, he is going* of course, certainly, as might be expected.

nature noun **1** *it is in the nature of the species* character, characteristic, essence, constitution, makeup, complexion, stamp, personality, identity. **2** *commune with nature* Mother Nature, natural forces, creation, the environment, the earth, mother earth, the world, the universe, the cosmos; landscape, scenery. **3** *things of this nature* kind, sort, ilk, type, variety, description, category, class, classification, species, style. **4** *he has a pleasant nature* temperament, temper, personality, disposition, humor, mood, outlook.

naughty adjective **1** *a naughty child* mischievous, misbehaving, disobedient, defiant, unruly, roguish, wayward, delinquent, undisciplined, unmanageable, ungovernable, fractious, refractory, perverse, errant. **2** *naughty magazines* indecent, improper, vulgar, bawdy, ribald, lewd, licentious.

nausea noun **1** *travelers overcome by nausea* sickness, vomiting, retching, gagging, biliousness, queasiness, faintness, seasickness, carsickness, airsickness, motion sickness, morning sickness; *inf.* throwing-up. **2** *horror movies causing feelings of nausea* disgust, revulsion, repugnance, distaste, aversion, loathing, abhorrence, detestation, odium.

nauseate verb make sick, sicken, make one's gorge rise, turn one's stomach, revolt, disgust, repel, repulse, offend; *inf.* make someone want to throw up, gross out.

nauseous adjective **1** *nauseous food/sights* nauseating, sickening, disgusting, revolting, repulsive, repellent, repugnant, offensive, loathsome, abhorrent, odious. **2** *feeling nauseous* nauseated, sick, sickly, queasy, green, unwell, indisposed, seasick, carsick, airsick; *inf.* green around the gills.

nautical adjective maritime, naval, marine, seagoing, seafaring, yachting, boating, sailing.

navigate verb **1** *navigate the craft* steer, pilot, maneuver, guide, direct, handle, drive, skipper. **2** *navigate the Atlantic* sail, sail across, cross, traverse, cruise, journey, voyage.

navigation noun **1** *the navigation of the craft* steering, pilotage, maneuvering, guidance, directing, handling, driving. **2** *study navigation* sailing, seamanship, pilotage, helmsmanship, chart-reading, map-reading.

navy noun naval force(s), fleet, flotilla, armada.

near adjective **1** *the store is near* close, close by, nearby, alongside, at close range/quarters, accessible, within reach, close/near at hand, at hand, handy, not far off/away, a stone's throw away, neighboring, adjacent, adjoining, bordering, contiguous, proximate; *inf.* within spitting distance. **2** *the time is near | the near future* close/near at hand, approaching, coming, imminent, forthcoming, in the offing, impending, looming, proximate, immediate. **3** *near relatives* closely related, related, connected, akin, allied, close, intimate, familiar, dear. **4** *a near escape* close, narrow, by a hair's breadth; *inf.* by a whisker/hair. **near miss** narrow escape; *inf.* close shave, close call.

near adverb close, nearby, within earshot, within sight, not far off/away.

near preposition close to, close by, in the neighborhood of, next to, adjacent to, alongside, bordering on, contiguous to.

near verb draw near to, get close to, approach, come close to, come toward, move toward, lean toward.

nearly adverb almost, all but, as good as, virtually, well-nigh, just about, practically, roughly, approximately, not quite.

neat adjective **1** *a neat house* tidy, orderly, well-ordered, straight, in good order, neat and tidy, neat as a pin, in Bristol fashion, shipshape and Bristol fashion, in apple-pie order, spick-and-span. **2** *a neat person* tidy, spruce, trim, smart, dapper, natty; fastidious, organized, well-organized, methodical, systematic. **3** *wearing neat clothes* simple, plain, unadorned, unornamented, unpretentious, unassuming. **4** *a neat solution* elegant, well-put, well-expressed, well-turned, clever, apt. **5** *neat footwork* adroit, skillful, expert, practiced, dexterous, deft, accurate, precise, nimble, agile. **6** *a really neat party* great, terrific, wonderful, excellent, exceptional, first-class, first-rate.

nebulous adjective shapeless, unformed, amorphous, shadowy, dim, indistinct, indefinite, vague, unclear, obscure, misty, cloudy, hazy, fuzzy, uncertain, indeterminate, imprecise, muddled, confused, ambiguous.

necessarily adverb **1** *plans that are necessarily vague* by force of circumstance, like it or not, perforce. **2** *he will not necessarily have to go* certainly, definitely, undoubtedly, inevitably, unavoidably, inescapably, automatically, incontrovertibly, inexorably.

necessary adjective **1** *a necessary reduction in expenditure* needed, needful, essential, required, requisite, vital, indispensable, imperative, mandatory, obligatory, compulsory, de rigueur. **2** *a necessary evil* certain, sure, inevitable, unavoidable, inescapable, inexorable, ineluctable, fated, preordained.

necessitate verb require, demand, call for, entail, involve, exact, oblige, compel, impel, force, leave no choice but to.

necessities plural noun needs, essentials, requisites, requirements, indispensables, fundamentals, necessaries, exigencies.

necessity noun **1** *silence is a necessity* essential, requisite, requirement, prerequisite, necessary, fundamental, sine qua non, desideratum. **2** *she left out of necessity* need, needfulness, force/pressure of circumstance, exigency, obligation. **3** *necessity made them steal* neediness, want, poverty, deprivation, privation, penury, destitution, indigence. **4** *a logical necessity that night follows day* certainty, inevitability, inescapability, inexorability, ineluctability.

need verb require, necessitate, demand, call for, have occasion for; want, lack.

need noun **1** *their needs are few* requirement, want, wish, demand, prerequisite, requisite, essential, desideratum. **2** *he has need of a coat* want, lack, shortage, requirement. **3** *no need to be frightened* necessity, call, obligation. **4** *people in need* neediness, want, poverty, deprivation, privation, penury, destitution, indigence. **5** *in one's hour of need* crisis, emergency, urgency, distress, trouble, extremity, exigency.

needle verb **1** *needle them into action* goad, spur, prod, prick, sting, press, nag, persuade. **2** *deliberately needling the teacher* provoke, bait, harass, annoy, irritate, vex, irk, nettle, taunt, pester; *inf.* aggravate, rile, get to.

needless adjective unnecessary, uncalled-for, gratuitous, undesired, unwanted, pointless, useless, dispensable, expendable, inessential.

needy adjective necessitous, poor, poverty-stricken, deprived, disadvantaged, penurious, impecunious, impoverished, penniless, destitute, indigent, on the breadline, in straitened circumstances.

ne'er-do-well noun good-for-nothing, wastrel, black sheep, loafer, idler, layabout, shirker, sluggard, drone; *inf.* gold brick, lazybones, goof-off.

nefarious adjective wicked, evil, sinful, iniquitous, villainous, criminal, heinous, atrocious, vile, foul, base, abominable, odious, horrible, horrendous, dreadful, terrible, detestable, loathsome, execrable, depraved, shameful, scandalous, monstrous, outrageous, flagitious.

negate verb **1** *facts negating your theory* nullify, render null and void, annul, void, invalidate, cancel, revoke, rescind, abrogate, repeal, retract, countermand, disestablish, reject, disprove, explode, overrule. **2** *try to negate the existence* *of God* deny, dispute, call in/into question, gainsay, contradict, disprove, refute, discredit, disclaim, repudiate, renounce, oppose.

negation noun **1** *the negation of the theory* nullification, voiding, cancellation, revocation, abrogation, repeal, retraction; denial, contradiction, disapproval, repudiation. **2** *anarchy is the negation of government* opposite, reverse, antithesis, contrary, converse. **3** *a life full of negation* nothingness, nothing, nullity, blankness, void, nonexistence, vacuity, nonentity.

negative adjective **1** *negative replies* dissenting, contradictory, contradicting, contrary, opposing, opposite, opposed, rejecting, refusing, denying, gainsaying. **2** *a negative person/reaction* pessimistic, defeatist, gloomy, gloom-laden, cynical, jaundiced, critical, faultfinding, complaining, unhelpful, unconstructive, uncooperative.

neglect verb **1** *neglect their children* fail to look after, fail to provide for, abandon, forsake, leave alone. **2** *neglect his work* let slide, skimp on, shirk, be remiss about, be lax about, pay little/no attention to, leave undone, procrastinate about. **3** *neglect to lock the door* omit, fail, forget. **4** *neglect his warning* disregard, ignore, pay no attention/heed to, overlook, disdain, scorn, slight, spurn, rebuff.

neglect noun **1** *parents/workers guilty of neglect* neglectfulness, dereliction. *See* NEGLIGENCE. **2** *his neglect of her warning* disregard, ignoring, heedlessness, indifference to, disdain, scorn, slight, spurning, rebuff.

neglected adjective uncared for, untended, mistreated, abandoned, forsaken, disregarded, ignored, spurned.

negligence noun neglect, remissness, laxity, laxness, dereliction, dereliction of duty, carelessness, inattention, inattentiveness, heedlessness, thoughtlessness, unmindfulness, forgetfulness, inadvertence, oversight, omission, failure, disregard, default, shortcoming, indifference, slackness, sloppiness.

negligent adjective neglectful, remiss, lax, careless, inattentive, heedless, thoughtless, unmindful, uncaring, forgetful, disregardful, indifferent, offhand, cursory, slack, sloppy, slapdash, slipshod, procrastinating, dilatory.

negligible adjective trivial, trifling, insignificant, paltry, petty, tiny, minute, minor, inconsequential, inappreciable, imperceptible.

negotiable adjective **1** *pay is negotiable* open to discussion, discussable, debatable, subject to bargaining. **2** *negotiable roads* passable, navigable, crossable, traversable, penetrable, unblocked, unobstructed.

negotiate verb **1** *negotiate a deal/settlement* work out, thrash out, arrange, agree on, settle, conclude, pull off, bring off, contract, complete, transact, execute, fulfill, orchestrate, engineer. **2** *union and management negotiate* bargain, drive a bargain, hold talks, confer, debate, discuss, discuss terms, discuss a settlement, parley, haggle, wheel and deal, dicker. **3** *negotiate the hurdles* clear, get over, get through, pass over, make it over, cross, get past, get around, surmount.

negotiator noun arbiter, arbitrator, mediator, go-between, moderator; haggler, wheeler-dealer.

neighborhood noun district, area, region, locality, part, quarter, precinct, community; vicinity, environs, proximity, purlieus; *inf.* stamping ground, neck of the woods, hood. **in the neighborhood of** around, about, approximately, roughly, nearly, almost, close to, just about.

neighboring adjective adjacent, adjoining, bordering, abutting, contiguous, next, nearby.

neighborly adjective friendly, cordial, kind, helpful, obliging, generous, hospitable, companionable, sociable, amiable, affable, genial.

nemesis noun downfall, undoing, ruin, destruction, Waterloo; retribution, vengeance.

neophyte noun novice, beginner, newcomer, initiate, tyro, greenhorn, learner, trainee, apprentice, probationer; *inf.* rookie.

nerve noun **1** *rock climbing requires nerve* courage, courageousness, bravery, fearlessness, daring, coolness, coolheadedness, boldness, pluck, gameness, mettle, spirit, backbone, fortitude, endurance, tenacity, steadfastness; *inf.* grit, guts, spunk. **2** *she had the nerve to ask for more* temerity, impudence, impertinence, effrontery, cheek, insolence, audacity, boldness, presumption, gall, brazenness; *inf.* brass, chutzpah.

nerve-racking adjective stressful, anxious, tense, harrowing, frightening, distressing, difficult, trying, harassing; *inf.* nail-biting.

nerves plural noun strain, anxiety; *inf.* the jitters, the willies. *See* NERVOUSNESS.

nervous adjective **1** *a nervous person* easily frightened, timid, timorous, fearful, apprehensive, anxious, edgy, highly strung, tense, strained, excitable, jumpy, hysterical. **2** *feeling nervous about the interview* on edge, tense, anxious, worried, fretful, uneasy, on tenterhooks, fidgety, apprehensive, fearful, scared, with one's heart in one's mouth, quaking, trembling, shaking, shaking in one's shoes, shaky; *inf.*

with butterflies in one's stomach, jittery, in a state, uptight, wired.

nervousness noun fearfulness, anxiety, tenseness, edginess, tension, nervous tension, stress, agitation, worry, uneasiness.

nervy adjective pushy, presumptuous, impudent, insolent, impertinent, brash, forward, audacious, bold; *inf.* brassy, fresh.

nest noun lair, den, lodge, burrow; retreat, hideaway, shelter, refuge, haunt; *inf.* hide-out.

nestle verb snuggle, curl up, huddle together, cuddle up, nuzzle.

net noun **1** *net curtains* netting, tulle, fishnet, meshwork, mesh, latticework, lattice, openwork, webbing, tracery, reticulum. **2** *fall into the enemy's net* trap, booby trap, snare, mesh, pitfall, stratagem.

net verb take home, clear, earn, make, bring in, get, pocket, receive, gain, obtain, realize; *inf.* pull in.

nether adjective **1** *the nether part of the store* lower, low, low-level, bottom, under, basement, underground. **2** *the nether regions* infernal, hellish, Hadean, Plutonian, Stygian.

nettle verb irritate, provoke, ruffle, try someone's patience, annoy, incense, exasperate, irk, vex, pique, bother, pester, harass, torment, plague, rile, peeve; *inf.* aggravate, rub the wrong way, get under someone's skin, get in someone's hair, get someone's goat, get to.

network noun **1** *a pattern consisting of a network of lines* meshwork, latticework, openwork, mesh, lattice, webbing, tracery, filigree, fretwork. **2** *a network of professional women* nexus, system, complex, organization, structure, arrangement, formulation. **3** *a network of roads | electronic network* interconnection, grid, circuitry, plexus.

neurotic adjective **1** *treating neurotic patients* mentally disturbed, unstable, maladjusted, obsessive, phobic. **2** *his wife is completely neurotic* overanxious, obsessive, phobic, fixated, compulsive, oversensitive, hysterical, irrational.

neuter verb castrate, geld, emasculate; spay; *inf.* fix.

neutral adjective **1** *referees must be neutral* impartial, unbiased, unprejudiced, open-minded, nonpartisan, without favoritism, evenhanded, disinterested, nonaligned, dispassionate, objective, detached, uninvolved, uncommitted. **2** *neutral countries during the war* noncombatant, noncombative, nonfighting, nonparticipating, nonaligned, unallied, uninvolved, noninterventionist. **3** *a neutral personality* indefinite, indeterminate, unremarkable, ordinary, common-place, average, run-of-the-mill, everyday, bland, uninteresting, colorless, insipid, dull. **4** *a neutral color* beige, ecru, gray, taupe, stone-colored, stone, pale, colorless, uncolored, achromatic.

neutralize verb counteract, cancel, nullify, negate, annul, undo, invalidate, frustrate, be an antidote to, offset, counterbalance, compensate for, make up for, negate.

never adverb not ever, at no time, certainly not, under no circumstances; *lit.* ne'er; *inf.* no way, not on your life, not in a million years.

never-ending adjective endless, unending, perpetual, everlasting, interminable, ceaseless, unceasing, incessant, nonstop, continuous, continual, uninterrupted, unbroken, unremitting, relentless, persistent, infinite, limitless, boundless, lasting, enduring, abiding.

nevertheless adverb nonetheless, even so, however, still, yet, just the same, all the same, regardless.

new adjective **1** *new techniques* modern, recent, advanced, state-of-the-art, present-day, contemporary, current, latest, up-to-date, up-to-the-minute, new-fashioned, modish, brand new, ultramodern, avant-garde, futuristic, newfangled; *inf.* wayout, far-out. **2** *in need of new ideas* novel, original, fresh, unhackneyed, imaginative, creative, experimental. **3** *a new book* unused, unworn, pristine, fresh, mint, in mint condition, virgin. **4** *a new job* unfamiliar, unknown, strange, different, unaccustomed, untried. **5** *a new room on the house* additional, added, extra, supplementary, further, another. **6** *feel like a new person* refreshed, renewed, improved, restored, reinvigorated, regenerated, reborn, remodeled.

newcomer noun **1** *newcomers to the town* new arrival, immigrant, settler, stranger, outsider, foreigner, alien, intruder, interloper; *inf.* johnny-come-lately. **2** *a newcomer to the game* beginner, trainee. *See* NOVICE.

newly adverb just, just recently, lately, of late.

news noun information, facts, data, report, story, news item, news flash, account, statement, announcement, press release, communication, communiqué, message, bulletin, dispatch, disclosure, revelation, word, talk, the latest, gossip, rumor, scandal, exposé; *inf.* info, low-down, scuttlebutt, poop, dope.

newspaper noun paper, gazette, journal, tabloid, daily, weekly, scandal sheet; *inf.* rag.

next adjective **1** *the next day* following, succeeding, successive, subsequent, later, ensuing. **2** *the next house* neighboring, adjacent, adjoining, bordering, contiguous, closest, nearest.

nibble verb bite, gnaw, peck at, pick at, pick over, eat, munch; *inf.* snack on.

nice adjective **1** *have a nice time* good, pleasant, enjoyable, pleasurable, agreeable, delightful, amusing, satisfying, gratifying, marvelous. **2** *a nice friend* likable, charming, amiable, friendly, kindly, genial, gracious, sympathetic, understanding, compassionate. **3** *nice manners* polite, courteous, civil, refined, cultivated, polished, genteel, elegant, seemly, decorous, proper, fitting, suitable, appropriate, respectable. **4** *a nice distinction* fine, ultrafine, subtle, minute, precise, exact, accurate, strict, close, careful, meticulous, rigorous. **5** *she is too nice to eat with her fingers* fastidious, delicate, refined, dainty, particular, discriminating, overparticular, fussy, finicky; *inf.* persnickety. **6** *landscapers did a nice job* good, acceptable, commendable, admirable.

nicely adverb **1** *children behaving nicely* well, politely, courteously, decorously, properly, fittingly, suitably, respectably, virtuously. **2** *did nicely on the exam* well, commendably, admirably.

nicety noun finer point, subtlety, nuance, detail; precision, accuracy, exactness, meticulousness, rigor.

niche noun **1** *a niche in the wall* alcove, recess, nook, cranny, cubbyhole. **2** *his niche in life* calling, vocation, place, position, job; *inf.* slot.

nickname noun pet name, family name, familiar name, diminutive; *inf.* moniker, handle.

niggardly adjective **1** *a niggardly person* mean, miserly, stingy, tight-fisted, parsimonious, penny-pinching, avaricious. **2** *a niggardly supply of food* meager, paltry, skimpy, scanty, measly, inadequate, insubstantial, miserable; *inf.* piddling.

night noun nighttime, darkness, dark, hours of darkness. **night and day** all the time, around the clock, ceaselessly, incessantly, continuously.

nightfall noun sunset, sundown, dusk, evening, twilight; *lit.* eventide, gloaming.

nightmare noun **1** *he had nightmares after the accident* bad dream, incubus, phantasmagoria. **2** *the interview was a nightmare* ordeal, horror, torment, torture.

nihilism noun **1** *former believers are turning to nihilism* rejection, repudiation, renunciation, denial, abnegation; disbelief, skepticism; negativism, cynicism, pessimism. **2** *political nihilism* anarchy, lawlessness,

disorder, chaos. **3** *in a state of nihilism* nihility, nothingness, nonexistence, void.

nil noun zero, nothing, naught, none; *inf.* zilch, goose egg.

nimble adjective **1** *nimble movements* agile, lithe, sprightly, spry, lively, quick, graceful, skillful, deft. **2** *nimble of wit* quick-thinking, clever, bright, quick, quick-witted, alert.

nip verb **1** *nip his arm* pinch, tweak, squeeze, grip, bite, nibble. **2** *nip (off) the withered shoots* snip, cut, lop, dock. **3** *frost nipping her cheeks* sting, bite, hurt. **nip in the bud** stop, quash, quell, check, thwart, frustrate.

nirvana noun enlightenment, paradise, heaven; bliss, joy, peace, serenity, tranquillity.

nitpicking adjective captious, hairsplitting, quibbling, faultfinding, hypercritical, caviling.

nitty-gritty noun crux, gist, substance, essence, quintessence; core, heart, center, kernel, nucleus; essentials, basics, facts; *inf.* brass tacks, nuts and bolts.

nitwit noun fool, ninny, idiot, nincompoop, dolt, dunce, ignoramus; *inf.* dope, dimwit.

nobility noun **1** *born to the nobility* lords, peers, plutocracy, aristocracy, high society, elite, upper class; *inf.* upper crust. **2** *the nobility of his deed* magnanimity, generosity, selflessness, honor, integrity, bravery, righteousness, decency.

noble adjective **1** *the noble people of the land* aristocratic, patrician, blue-blooded, highborn, titled, landed, born with a silver spoon in one's mouth. **2** *noble deeds* noble-minded, magnanimous, generous, self-sacrificing, honorable, virtuous, brave, righteous, honest, upright, true, loyal, principled, moral, decent, good. **3** *noble thoughts* lofty, grand, exalted, elevated. **4** *of noble appearance* impressive, magnificent, striking, awesome, stately, grand, dignified.

nod verb **1** *nod one's head* incline, bob, bow, dip, duck. **2** *nod a greeting* signal, gesture, motion, sign, indicate. **3** *the audience began to nod* doze off, drop off, fall asleep, nap, slumber.

node noun protuberance, swelling, lump, growth, excrescence, knob, knot, nodule, bump.

noise noun din, hubbub, clamor, racket, row, uproar, tumult, commotion, rumpus, pandemonium.

noisome adjective disgusting, repugnant, revolting, repulsive, offensive, nauseating, detestable, loathsome.

noisy adjective **1** *noisy neighbors* rowdy, clamorous, boisterous, obstreperous. **2**

noisy music loud, blaring, blasting, deafening, earsplitting.

nomad noun itinerant, traveler, migrant, wanderer, roamer, rover; transient, vagabond, vagrant, tramp.

nominal adjective **1** *the nominal head* in name only, titular, formal; theoretical, self-styled; purported, supposed. **2** *a nominal sum* token, symbolic; minimal, trivial, insignificant.

nominate verb **1** *nominate the candidates* name, propose, put forward, submit, present, recommend; *inf.* put up. **2** *nominate his successor* name, designate, appoint, assign, select, choose.

nonbeliever noun atheist, agnostic, skeptic, doubter, doubting Thomas, unbeliever, disbeliever, cynic, infidel, pagan, heathen.

nonchalance noun coolness, unconcern, indifference, detachment, detachedness, apathy, insouciance; *inf.* cool.

nonchalant adjective unexcitable, calm, cool, unconcerned, indifferent, unemotional, blasé, dispassionate, detached, apathetic, casual, offhand, carefree, insouciant.

noncommittal adjective cautious, guarded, circumspect, wary, careful, discreet, politic, playing one's cards close to one's chest, giving nothing away, sitting on the fence, temporizing, evasive, equivocal, vague, reserved.

nonconformist noun radical, dissenter, protester, maverick, individualist, misfit, eccentric, iconoclast, outsider.

nondescript adjective indefinite, indeterminate, unclassifiable, indescribable, indistinguishable, vague, unremarkable, featureless, undistinguished, ordinary, commonplace, unexceptional, unmemorable, uninteresting, dull, colorless, insipid, bland.

nonentity noun nobody, person of no account, person of no importance, nonperson; *inf.* nothing, lightweight.

nonessential adjective inessential, unessential, unnecessary, needless, unrequired, superfluous, redundant, dispensable, expendable, peripheral, unimportant, insignificant, inconsequential, extraneous.

nonexistent adjective unreal, hypothetical, suppositional, fictional, fictitious, imagined, imaginary, fancied, fanciful, mythical, legendary, fantasy, illusory, hallucinatory, insubstantial.

nonplus verb take aback, stun, dumbfound, confound, astound, astonish, amaze, surprise, disconcert, discomfit, dismay, make one halt in one's tracks, puzzle, perplex, baffle, mystify, stump, confuse, bewilder,

embarrass, fluster; *inf.* faze, flummox, floor.

nonsense noun **1** *talk nonsense* rubbish, balderdash, drivel, gibberish, twaddle; *inf.* tripe, gobbledegook, mumbo jumbo, poppycock, claptrap, bilge, bull. **2** *tired of their nonsense* foolishness, folly, silliness, senselessness, stupidity, ridiculousness, ludicrousness, inanity, fatuity, joking, jesting, clowning, buffoonery, drollery.

nonsensical adjective **1** *nonsensical remarks* meaningless, incomprehensible, unintelligible, senseless, incongruous. **2** *a nonsensical scheme* foolish, absurd, silly, inane, senseless, stupid, ridiculous, ludicrous, preposterous, harebrained, irrational, idiotic, insane; *inf.* crazy, crackpot, nutty, wacky.

nonstop adjective incessant, unceasing, ceaseless, constant, continuous, continual, steady, unremitting, relentless, persistent, endless, never-ending, unending, interminable; *inf.* eternal.

nonstop adverb *talk/rain nonstop* incessantly, unceasingly, constantly, continuously, continually, steadily, unremittingly, relentlessly, persistently, endlessly. *See* NONSTOP adjective.

nook noun **1** *a room full of nooks and crannies* corner, cranny, recess, alcove, niche, opening, cavity, crevice, gap, cubbyhole, inglenook. **2** *find a quiet nook to be alone* hideaway, retreat, refuge, shelter, den, hide-out.

noon noun midday, twelve noon, high noon, noontime, noontide, noonday.

norm noun **1** *measured against the norm* standard, criterion, measure, gauge, yardstick, benchmark, touchstone, scale, rule, pattern, model, type. **2** *six hours a day is the norm* average, mean, normal rate, the usual, the rule.

normal adjective **1** *the normal method* usual, standard, ordinary, conventional, typical, regular, routine, run-of-the-mill, everyday, accustomed, habitual, prevailing, accepted. **2** *of normal size* average, medium, middling, standard, mean. **3** *the patient is not normal* well-adjusted, well-balanced, rational, *compos mentis*, sane.

normally adverb **1** *behave normally* as usual, ordinarily, naturally, conventionally, routinely, typically. **2** *normally, we eat late* usually, ordinarily, as a rule.

north adjective *north winds* northern, northerly, northwardly, Arctic, arctic, polar, boreal.

nose noun **1** *a large nose* proboscis, bill, beak, snout, muzzle, trunk; *inf.* snoot, schnoz. **2** *a nose for a good story* instinct, sixth sense, intuition, insight, perception.

by a nose by a hair's breadth, by a narrow margin, narrowly, by the skin of one's teeth; *inf.* by a whisker/hair. **on the nose** exactly, precisely.

nose verb **1** *dogs were nosing his arm* nudge, push, nuzzle. **2** *nose around the room* pry, search, peer, prowl, have a good look; *inf.* snoop. **3** *nose the car forward* ease, inch, move, run. **nose into** pry into, interfere in, meddle in, inquire into; *inf.* poke one's nose into. **nose out** smell out, sniff out, follow the scent of, scent out, search for, detect, run to ground.

nostalgia noun longing/yearning/pining for the past, regret, recollection, wistfulness, homesickness.

nostalgic adjective wistful, sentimental, maudlin, homesick.

nostrum noun **1** *prescribing nostrums for patients* patent medicine, medicine, medication, drug, potion, pill, quack remedy, elixir. **2** *claiming to have a nostrum for the country's problems* remedy, cure, cure-all, panacea, solution, answer, magic bullet, magic formula, recipe.

nosy adjective prying, inquisitive, quizzing, probing, eavesdropping, curious, interfering, meddlesome, intrusive; *inf.* snooping, snoopy.

notable adjective **1** *a notable achievement* noteworthy, remarkable, outstanding, important, significant, momentous, memorable, unforgettable, pronounced, marked, striking, impressive, extraordinary, rare. **2** *notable people in the town* noted, of note, distinguished, eminent, preeminent, well-known, prominent, illustrious, great, famous, famed, renowned, celebrated, acclaimed.

notable noun dignitary, celebrity, luminary, star, superstar, lion, VIP; *inf.* celeb, megastar, big shot, somebody.

notably adverb *notably successful* remarkably, outstandingly, significantly, markedly, strikingly, impressively, uncommonly, unusually, particularly, especially, extraordinarily, conspicuously, signally.

notation noun system of symbols, symbols, signs, code, cipher, hieroglyphics, shorthand, musical notation.

notch noun **1** *make a notch in the wood* indentation, dent, nick, groove, gouge, cut, mark, incision, score, scratch, gash, slit, cleft. **2** *several notches above the competition* degree, grade, gradation, level, step, stage, rung.

note noun **1** *always kept a note of her purchases* record, account, notation. **2** *write him a note* message, memorandum; letter, epistle, missive; *inf.* memo. **3** *read the notes in the book* footnote, annotation,

commentary, gloss, marginalia, explanation, explication, exposition, exegesis. **4** *worthy of note* notice, attention, attentiveness, heed, observation, consideration, thought, regard, care, mindfulness. **5** *people of note* distinction, eminence, preeminence, illustriousness, greatness, prestige, fame, renown, reputation, acclaim, consequence. **6** *a note of amusement in her voice* tone, intonation, inflection, sound, indication, hint, element.

note verb **1** *note the date in your diary* write down, put down, jot down, mark down, enter, mark, record, register. **2** *note his comments in your report* mention, make mention of, refer to, allude to, touch on, indicate, point out, make known, state. **3** *he noted their concern* observe, take in. *See* NOTICE verb.

noted adjective of note, eminent. *See* NOTABLE adjective 2.

notes plural noun jottings, record, report, observations, impressions, sketch, outline.

noteworthy adjective remarkable, outstanding. *See* NOTABLE adjective 1.

nothing noun **1** *nothing to declare* naught, nil; *inf.* zilch, zip. **2** *the wound is nothing* trifling matter, piece of trivia, bagatelle; *inf.* no big deal. **3** *they treat her like a nothing* nobody, person of no account, nonentity. **4** *pass into nothing* nothingness, nonexistence, nonbeing. **for nothing 1** *work for nothing* free, for free, gratis, without charge, without payment, gratuitously. **2** *do all that studying for nothing* in vain, to no avail, to no purpose, futilely, needlessly. **nothing but** only, solely.

notice noun **1** *escape my notice* attention, cognizance, watchfulness. *See* NOTE noun 4. **2** *the notice on the board* bulletin, poster, handbill, bill, circular, leaflet, pamphlet, advertisement. **3** *receive notice of their arrival* notification, appraisal, announcement, information, intelligence, news, communication, advice, instruction, order, warning. **4** *workers have received/given (their) notice* resignation; dismissal; *inf.* marching orders, walking papers, pink slip, the sack, the boot.

notice verb see, note, take note of, observe, perceive, discern, detect, behold, descry, spot, distinguish, make out, heed, pay attention to, mark, regard.

noticeable adjective observable, visible, discernible, perceptible, detectable, distinguishable, distinct, evident, obvious, apparent, manifest, patent, plain, clear, conspicuous, unmistakable, pronounced, striking, blatant.

notify verb inform, tell, advise, acquaint, apprise, warn, alert, caution.

notion noun **1** *have strange notions about religion* idea, belief, opinion, thought, impression, view, concept, theory. **2** *a notion to go to the sea* impulse, inclination, fancy, whim, wish, desire, caprice.

notoriety noun infamy, ill/evil repute, bad reputation/name, disrepute, dishonor, scandal, opprobrium, obloquy.

notorious adjective **1** *a notorious murderer* infamous, of ill repute, disreputable, dishonorable. **2** *a notorious nightclub* well-known, prominent, legendary, scandalous, opprobrious, obloquial.

nourish verb **1** *nourish the children* feed, nurture, provide for, care for, take care of, tend, attend to, bring up, rear. **2** *nourish growth* encourage, promote, foster, stimulate, boost, further, advance, forward, contribute to, be conducive to, assist, help, aid. **3** *nourish hopes of success* cherish, entertain, harbor, foster, hold.

nourishing adjective wholesome, healthful. *See* NUTRITIOUS.

nourishment noun food, nutriment, nutrition, sustenance, subsistence, aliment, provisions, provender, meat, fare, viands, victuals, daily bread; *inf.* grub, chow, eats.

novel adjective new, fresh, different, original, unusual, uncommon, unfamiliar, rare, unique, singular, imaginative, unhackneyed, unconventional, creative, innovative, groundbreaking, trailblazing, modern, ultramodern, advanced, futuristic.

novelty noun **1** *the novelty of the idea* newness, freshness, difference, originality, unusualness, uniqueness, rareness, imaginativeness, creativity. **2** *a vendor selling novelties* memento, souvenir, knickknack, trinket, bauble, trifle, gimmick, curiosity, gimcrack.

novice noun beginner, newcomer, apprentice, trainee, learner, probationer, student, pupil, (new) recruit, raw recruit, tyro, initiate, neophyte, greenhorn; *inf.* rookie.

now adverb **1** *we do not have any now* at present, at this time, currently. **2** *you must go now* right away, immediately, at once, straight away, instantly, promptly, without delay. **now and again/then** occasionally, on occasion, sometimes.

noxious adjective nocuous, noisome, harmful, hurtful, injurious, damaging, destructive, ruinous, pernicious, detrimental, deleterious, unwholesome, unhealthy, poisonous, toxic.

nuance noun shade, shading, gradation, subtlety, nicety, refinement, degree.

nucleus noun core, kernel, center, heart, nub, basis, pith, meat, marrow, focus, pivot.

nude adjective in the nude, bare. *See* NAKED 1.

nudge noun poke, jab, prod, dig, jog, elbow, bump, touch, push, shove.

nugget noun chunk, lump, piece, mass, clump, wad, hunk.

nuisance noun pest, bother, plague, irritant, annoyance, vexation, trouble, burden, weight, problem, difficulty, worry, bore, inconvenience, disadvantage, handicap, thorn in the side/flesh; *inf.* drag.

null adjective **1** *render the ruling null* null and void, void, invalid, annulled, nullified, canceled, abolished, revoked, rescinded, repealed. **2** *the null effects of the trade embargo* ineffectual, useless, vain, worthless, futile, powerless, unproductive, nonexistent, negative.

nullify verb render null and void, declare null and void, annul, void, invalidate, cancel, abolish, set aside, revoke, rescind, repeal, reverse, abrogate, discontinue, retract, withdraw, countermand, veto, negate, terminate, dissolve, do away with.

numb adjective benumbed, dead, deadened, insensible, insensate, torpid, dull, anesthetized, drugged, dazed, stunned, stupefied, in shock, paralyzed, immobilized.

number noun **1** *add up the numbers* figure, digit, numeral, cipher, character, symbol, unit, integer. **2** *the number of accidents* total, aggregate, score, tally, count, sum, summation. **3** *a large number of people* quantity, amount, group, collection, company, crowd.

number verb **1** *number the items* enumerate, count, add up, total, calculate, compute, reckon. **2** *number them among my friends* count, include, reckon. **3** *his days are numbered* limit, restrict, fix.

numeral noun figure, digit. *See* NUMBER noun 1.

numerous adjective many, very many, innumerable, numberless, countless, myriad, multitudinous, several, quite a few, various, diverse.

nuptial adjective matrimonial, marriage, marital, wedding, conjugal, connubial, bridal, spousal, hymeneal.

nuptials plural noun wedding, marriage.

nurse verb **1** *nurse the patient* take care of, care for, look after, tend, attend to, minister to, treat, doctor. **2** *a mother nursing her baby* suckle, breast-feed, feed, wet-nurse. **3** *nurse her career* nurture, encourage, promote, boost, further, advance, contribute to, assist, help. **4** *nurse* *a grudge* harbor, have, hold, entertain, foster, cherish, nourish.

nurture verb **1** *nurture the children* feed, nourish, provide for, care for, take care of, tend, attend to, bring up, rear. **2** *nurture the students* educate, school, train, tutor, coach. **3** *nurture growth* encourage, promote, foster, stimulate, develop, cultivate, boost, further.

nut noun **1** *a movie nut* fan, enthusiast, aficionado, devotee, follower; *inf.* buff, freak. **2** *acting like a nut* madman, lunatic; *inf.* nutcase, loony, weirdo, oddball, crackpot, screwball.

nutrition noun nutriment, food. *See* NOURISHMENT.

nutritious adjective nourishing, nutritive, wholesome, health-giving, healthy, healthful, beneficial.

nuts adjective mad, insane, deranged, demented, irrational, *non compos mentis*, lunatic, psychopathic; *inf.* nutty, crazy, bananas, loony, loopy, batty, balmy, out of one's mind, with a screw loose, out to lunch.

nuzzle verb **1** *dogs nuzzling their masters* nose, nudge, prod, push. **2** *nuzzle up to her mother* snuggle, cuddle, nestle, curl up.

nymph noun sylph, sprite, water sprite, undine, naiad, dryad, oread.

Oo

oaf noun **1** *that oaf tripped me up* lout, blunderer, bungler, boor, bumpkin, yokel, gorilla, bull in a china shop: *inf.* clodhopper, lummox, galoot. **2** *the foolishness of an oaf* fool, dolt, blockhead, numskull, dunderhead, dunce, dullard, nincompoop, ninny, simpleton; *inf.* goon, schmuck.

oasis noun *an oasis among all the noise* refuge, haven, retreat, sanctuary, sanctum, hiding place, hideaway, hide-out.

oath noun **1** *an oath to tell the truth* vow, promise, pledge, avowal, affirmation, attestation, bond, word of honor, word. **2** *spouting oaths* curse, swearword, expletive, blasphemy, profanity, imprecation, malediction, obscenity, four-letter word.

obedience noun dutifulness, duteousness, duty, sense of duty, deference, respect, compliance, acquiescence, tractability, amenability, malleability, yielding, submission, docility, meekness.

obedient adjective dutiful, duteous, law-abiding, conforming, deferential, respectful, compliant, acquiescent, tractable, amenable, malleable, governable, well-trained, yielding, submissive, docile, meek, subservient, obsequious, servile.

obeisance noun **1** *his obeisance to the emperor* bow, curtsy, kneel, genuflection, stoop, salaam, kowtow. **2** *pay obeisance to the emperor* homage, worship, adoration, reverence, respect, veneration, honor, submission.

obese adjective overweight, fat, plump, stout, ample, chubby, tubby, portly, rotund, corpulent, pudgy, paunchy, fleshy, big, heavy, on the heavy side, large, bulky, chunky, outsize, massive.

obesity noun fatness, corpulence, plumpness, stoutness, rotundness, rotundity, portliness, chubbiness, pudginess, bulk, weight problem, embonpoint.

obey verb **1** *obey the rules/orders* abide by, comply with, adhere to, observe, conform to, respect, acquiesce in, consent to, agree to, follow, perform, carry out, execute, fulfill. **2** *obey your mother* be dutiful to, heed, be governed by.

object noun **1** *wooden objects* thing, something, anything, body, entity, article, item, device. **2** *the object of our discussion* subject, subject matter, substance, issue, concern. **3** *the object of their affection* focus, target, recipient, butt, victim. **4** *our object is to win* aim, goal. *See* OBJECTIVE noun.

object verb raise objections, protest, lodge a protest, demur, beg to differ, remonstrate, expostulate, take exception; oppose, be in opposition to, complain about.

objection noun **1** *their objection to the plan* protest, protestation, demurral, opposition, remonstration, remonstrance, expostulation. **2** *lodge/name their objections* argument, counterargument, doubt, complaint, grievance, scruple, qualm.

objectionable adjective offensive, obnoxious, unpleasant, disagreeable, unacceptable, nasty, disgusting, repulsive, revolting, loathsome, nauseating, hateful, detestable, insufferable, intolerable, odious, vile, horrid, noxious.

objective adjective unbiased, unprejudiced, impartial, neutral, uninvolved, nonpartisan, disinterested, detached, dispassionate, unswayed, evenhanded, equitable, fair, just, open-minded.

objective noun object, aim, goal, target, end, ambition, aspiration, intent, intention, purpose, idea, point, desire, hope, design, plan, scheme, plot.

objectively adverb with objectivity, without bias, impartially, with detachment, with an open mind, without fear or favor.

objectivity noun impartiality, disinterest, detachment, dispassion, dispassionateness, equitability, evenhandedness, openmindedness.

obligation noun **1** *the obligations specified by the contract* requirement, prerequisite, demand, necessity, command, order, constraint. **2** *fulfill/discharge one's obligations* duty, function, chore, task, job, assignment, commission, business, burden, charge, onus, trust, liability, responsibility, accountability, indebtedness, debt. **3** *a sense of obligation* duty, compulsion, necessity, enforcement, duress, pressure. **4** *the obligation is still binding* contract, agreement, deed, covenant, compact, bond, treaty, deal, pact, understanding, transaction.

obligatory adjective **1** *the agreement is obligatory* binding, valid, legal, in force, effective. **2** *attendance is obligatory* compulsory, enforced, prescriptive, mandatory, required, requisite, imperative, de rigueur, unavoidable, unescapable.

oblige verb **1** *friendship obliges me to go* require, necessitate, obligate, compel, call for, force, constrain, press, pressure, impel. **2** *will you oblige me by going?* do someone a favor/kindness/service, serve, accommodate, put oneself out for, indulge, gratify the wishes of, help, assist.

obliging adjective helpful, accommodating, willing, complaisant, indulgent, considerate, cooperative, neighborly.

oblique adjective **1** *an oblique line* slanting, slanted, sloping, sloped, inclined, angled, tilted, listing, diagonal, catercornered; *inf.* kitty-corner. **2** *an oblique compliment* indirect, implied, roundabout, circuitous, circumlocutory, ambagious, evasive, backhanded.

obliterate verb **1** *obliterate all memories of her* erase, eradicate, efface, blot out, rub out, wipe out, expunge, sponge out, delete, cross out, strike out, blue-pencil, remove, cancel. **2** *the village was obliterated* destroy, exterminate, annihilate, wipe out, eliminate, decimate, liquidate, demolish.

oblivion noun obliviousness, heedlessness, unmindfulness, unawareness, unconsciousness, insensibility, inattentiveness, disregard, forgetfulness, absentmindedness, unconcern, abstraction, preoccupation, absorption.

oblivious adjective absentminded, abstracted, distrait, preoccupied, absorbed, faraway. **oblivious of/to** heedless of, unmindful of, unaware of, unconscious of, insensible of, ignorant of, blind to, unobservant of, deaf to, inattentive to, disregardful of, neglectful of, forgetful of, careless of, unconcerned with.

obnoxious adjective repulsive, repellent, abhorrent, repugnant, despicable, contemptible. *See* OBJECTIONABLE.

obscene adjective **1** *obscene jokes* indecent, pornographic, blue, off-color, risqué, lewd, salacious, smutty, lecherous, lascivious, licentious, prurient, lubricious, ribald, scatological, scabrous, bawdy, suggestive, vulgar, dirty, filthy, foul, coarse, gross, vile, nasty, offensive, immoral, impure, immodest, shameless, unchaste, improper, unwholesome, erotic, carnal, sexy; *inf.* raunchy. **2** *the murder was an obscene act* atrocious, heinous, vile, foul, repugnant, revolting, odious.

obscenity noun **1** *the obscenity of the publication* indecency, lewdness, salaciousness, smuttiness, lechery, lasciviousness, licentiousness, prurience, lubricity, ribaldry, scatology, scabrousness, bawdiness, suggestiveness, vulgarity, dirt, dirtiness, filth, filthiness, foulness, coarseness, grossness, vileness, nastiness, immorality, impurity, immodesty, shamelessness, unchasteness, impropriety, unwholesomeness, eroticism, carnality, sexiness. **2** *the obscenity of the crime* atrocity, heinousness, vileness, foulness, repugnance. **3** *a stream of obscenities* curse, swearword, dirty word; *inf.* cuss, cussword. *See* OATH 2.

obscure adjective **1** *obscure references* unclear, indeterminate, opaque, abstruse, recondite, unexplained, concealed, hidden, arcane, enigmatic, deep, cryptic, mysterious, puzzling, perplexing, confusing, intricate, involved, unfathomable, incomprehensible, impenetrable, indefinite, uncertain, doubtful, dubious, ambiguous, equivocal. **2** *obscure shapes looming out of the mist* indistinct, vague, shadowy, hazy, blurred, fuzzy, cloudy. **3** *obscure parts of the forest* dark, dim, black, unlit, murky, somber, gloomy, shady, shadowy. **4** *obscure villages* unknown, unheard-of, out-of-the-way, off the beaten track, remote, hidden, secluded, godforsaken. **5** *obscure poets* little-known, unknown, unheard-of, undistinguished, insignificant, inconspicuous, minor, unimportant.

obscure verb **1** *obscure the main issue* confuse, blur, muddle, complicate, obfuscate, garble, cloud, muddy. **2** *clouds* *obscure the sun* hide, conceal, cover, veil, screen, mask, cloak, shroud, block, block out, eclipse, adumbrate.

obsequious adjective servile, slavish, abject, fawning, groveling, cringing, toadying, truckling, sycophantic, ingratiating, unctuous, oily; *inf.* bootlicking.

observance noun **1** *observance of laws* obedience to, adherence to, abiding by, compliance with, heeding. **2** *observance of duty* performance, execution, discharge, fulfillment. **3** *religious observances* rite, ritual, ceremony, ceremonial, celebration, festival, practice, tradition, custom.

observant adjective **1** *an observant boy spotted the thief* alert, sharp-eyed, eagleeyed, attentive, vigilant, wide-awake, on the qui vive, on the lookout; *inf.* not missing a thing/trick, on the ball. **2** *observant members of the church* dutiful, obedient, conforming, law-abiding, orthodox, practicing.

observation noun **1** *recall our observation of the man* seeing, noticing, watching, viewing, eyeing, witnessing. **2** *keep the thief/patient under observation* scrutiny, scrutinization, watch, monitoring, surveillance, inspection, attention, consideration, study, review, examination. **3** *record your observations on the show* finding, result, remark, comment, note, opinion, thought, reflection. **4** *make a sarcastic observation* remark, comment, statement, utterance, pronouncement, declaration. **observation of** observance of, keeping of. *See* OBSERVANCE 1.

observe verb **1** *we observe him go into the bank* see, catch sight of, notice, note, perceive, discern, detect, espy, behold, watch, view, spot, witness; *inf.* get a load of. **2** *police observe the house | doctors observe the patient* keep under observation, keep watch on, keep under surveillance, keep in sight, keep in view, spy upon, monitor; inspect, study, review, examine, check; *inf.* keep an eye on, keep tabs on. **3** *"A good try," he observed* remark, comment, state, utter, announce, declare, pronounce. **4** *observe the rules* obey, adhere to. *See* OBEY 1. **5** *observe Christmas* celebrate, keep, recognize, commemorate, mark, remember, solemnize.

observer noun watcher, looker-on, onlooker, witness, eyewitness, spectator, bystander; *inf.* rubberneck.

obsess verb preoccupy, haunt, monopolize, have a hold on, possess, consume, engross, have a grip on, grip, dominate, prey on, plague, torment, hound, bedevil.

obsession noun preoccupation, fixation, *idée fixe*, ruling/consuming passion, mania, enthusiasm, infatuation, compulsion, phobia, complex, fetish, craze.

obsessive adjective excessive, overdone, consuming, compulsive, besetting, gripping, haunting.

obsolete adjective outmoded, *démodé*, passé, antiquated, out-of-date, outdated, out, superannuated, out of fashion, out of style, behind the times, old, dated; discontinued, extinct, bygone; *inf.* old hat.

obstacle noun bar, barrier, obstruction, impediment, hindrance, hurdle, barricade, blockade, stumbling block, block, blockage, curb, check, stop, stoppage, deterrent, balk, snag, difficulty, catch, drawback, hitch, interference, fly in the ointment.

obstinate adjective stubborn, mulish, pigheaded, headstrong, willful, perverse, refractory, recalcitrant, contumacious, unmanageable, inflexible, unbending, immovable, intransigent, intractable, uncompromising, persistent, persevering, pertinacious, tenacious, dogged, singleminded, relentless, unrelenting.

obstreperous adjective unruly, disorderly, rowdy, boisterous, rough, riotous, out of hand, wild, rampaging, undisciplined, unrestrained, unbridled, unmanageable, raucous, rambunctious.

obstruct verb **1** *logs obstruct the road/river* block, barricade, bar, cut off, shut off, choke, clog (up), dam up. **2** *obstructing our efforts* hinder, impede, hamper, block, interfere with, interrupt, hold up, frustrate, thwart, balk, inhibit, curb, brake, bridle, hamstring, encumber, restrain, slow, retard, delay, arrest, check, stop, halt, restrict, limit.

obstruction noun impediment, hindrance, blockage. *See* OBSTACLE.

obtain verb **1** *obtain a ticket* get, get hold of, acquire, come by, procure, secure, gain, earn, take possession of, get one's hands on, seize, grab, pick up. **2** *new rules obtain* be in force, exist, stand, prevail, hold, be the case, reign, rule.

obtrusive adjective **1** *obtrusive colors/music* conspicuous, blatant, flagrant. **2** *obtrusive behavior* forward, bold, audacious, intrusive, interfering, meddling, officious, importunate; *inf.* pushy.

obtuse adjective dull-witted, uncomprehending, imperceptive; *inf.* dense, thick, slow on the uptake.

obvious adjective clear, clear-cut, crystalclear, plain, evident, apparent, manifest, distinct, palpable, patent, conspicuous, overt, pronounced, transparent, unmistakable, indisputable, undeniable, as plain as the nose on one's face, staring someone in the face; *inf.* sticking out like a sore thumb, sticking out a mile.

obviously adjective **1** *obviously pregnant* clearly, plainly, visibly, noticeably, unmistakably, undeniably. **2** *obviously, we must go* of course, certainly, undoubtedly.

occasion noun **1** *we met on one or two occasions* time, juncture, point, situation, instance, case, circumstance. **2** *a sad occasion* event, incident, occurrence, happening, episode, affair, experience. **3** *we met at a college occasion* function, party, affair, celebration; *inf.* get-together, do. **4** *if the occasion arises* opportunity, golden opportunity, chance, opening, contingency. **5** *have occasion to believe* reason, cause, grounds, justification, call, excuse, inducement.

occasional adjective infrequent, intermittent, irregular, sporadic, odd, rare, casual.

occasionally adverb now and then, now and again, from time to time, every so often, on occasion, sporadically, infrequently, on and off.

occult adjective supernatural, magic, magical, mystical, mystic, preternatural, transcendental, unrevealed, secret, hidden, concealed, invisible, obscure, recondite, arcane, abstruse, esoteric, inexplicable, unfathomable, mysterious, cryptic, enigmatic.

occult noun **the occult** the supernatural, magic, black magic, witchcraft, sorcery, wizardry, the black arts, devil worship.

occupancy noun occupation, tenancy, tenure, residence, residency, inhabitance, habitation, living, possession, holding.

occupant noun occupier, tenant, renter, leaseholder, lessee, inhabitant, resident, dweller, householder, addressee, incumbent, inmate.

occupation noun **1** *what is his occupation?* job, work, profession, business, employment, employ, career, calling, métier, vocation, trade, craft, line, field. **2** *occupation of the house* tenancy, tenure. *See* OCCUPANCY. **3** *the occupation of their land* invasion, seizure, takeover, conquest, capture.

occupied adjective **1** *everyone is occupied* busy, engaged, working, at work, employed; *inf.* tied up, hard at it. **2** *the rooms are occupied* full, engaged, taken, in use, unavailable.

occupy verb **1** *occupy the apartment* live in, inhabit, reside in, dwell in, stay in. **2** *occupy her time* fill, fill up, take up, use up, utilize. **3** *occupy a top post* hold, fill, have; *inf.* hold down. **4** *occupy oneself* engage, employ, absorb, engross, entertain, divert, amuse, beguile. **5** *the army occupied their country* take possession of, seize, take over, capture, garrison.

occur verb **1** *the accident occurred last year* happen, take place, come about, come to pass, materialize, transpire, arise, crop up, turn up, befall. **2** *the disease occurs in the tropics* be found, exist, appear, present itself, show itself, manifest itself. **3** *an idea occurs to me* come to mind, spring to mind, strike one, hit one, dawn on.

occurrence noun **1** *an everyday occurrence* happening, event, incident, circumstance, affair, episode, proceeding. **2** *the occurrence of the disease* existence, appearance, manifestation.

odd adjective **1** *an odd person/happening* strange, eccentric, queer, peculiar, idiosyncratic, unconventional, outlandish, droll, weird, bizarre, offbeat, freakish, whimsical, unusual, uncommon, irregular, funny, curious, abnormal, atypical, different, out-of-the-ordinary, exceptional, rare, extraordinary, remarkable, singular, deviant, aberrant; *inf.* wacky, freaky, kinky, off-the-wall. **2** *odd jobs/moments* occasional, periodic, irregular, random, chance, fortuitous, various, sundry. **3** *an odd sock* unmatched, unpaired, leftover, spare, remaining, surplus, superfluous. **odd man out** exception, outsider, nonconformist, misfit, maverick.

oddity noun **1** *the house is an oddity* curiosity, rarity, anomaly, aberration, irregularity, phenomenon. **2** *he is an oddity* eccentric, crank, original, misfit, fish out of water, rara avis; *inf.* character, oddball, weirdo, odd/queer fish.

odds plural noun **1** *the odds are in his favor* advantage, lead, edge, superiority, supremacy, ascendancy. **2** *the odds are that he will win* likelihood, probability, chances, balance. **at odds with** in conflict with, in disagreement with, not in keeping with, in opposition to, at variance with. **odds and ends** bits and pieces, oddments, fragments, remnants, scraps, cuttings, snippets, miscellanea, leftovers, leavings.

odious adjective abhorrent, loathsome, detestable, hateful, despicable, contemptible; repugnant, disgusting, repulsive, repellent, unpleasant, disagreeable, objectionable, offensive, abominable.

odor noun **1** *the odor of cologne* aroma, smell, scent, perfume, fragrance, bouquet, redolence, essence, stench, stink. **2** *an odor of ill will* atmosphere, air, ambience, aura, spirit, quality, flavor, emanation.

off adjective **1** *the game/deal is off* canceled, postponed, shelved. **2** *called on the off chance that you were home* unlikely, doubtful, remote, improbable, implausible. **3** *the food/milk is off* bad, rotten, decomposed, moldy, high, sour, rancid, turned.

off adverb off and on sporadically, periodically. See OCCASIONALLY.

offbeat adjective unconventional, unorthodox, idiosyncratic, unusual, strange, outlandish, outré, Bohemian, hippie; inf. way-out, far-out, off-the-wall.

off-color adjective risqué, racy. See OBSCENE 1.

offend verb **1** his behavior offended them wound, affront, upset, displease, annoy, anger, incense, exasperate, vex, pique, put out, gall, irritate, provoke, rile, ruffle, disgruntle, rankle with, outrage, insult, slight, humiliate. **2** offend her sense of taste displease, be disagreeable to, be distasteful to, repel, disgust, revolt, nauseate; inf. turn someone off. **3** apologize for having offended do wrong, sin, go astray, fall from grace, err, transgress.

offender noun wrongdoer, culprit, criminal, lawbreaker, miscreant, delinquent, sinner, transgressor, malefactor.

offense noun **1** commit an offense crime, breach/violation/infraction of the law, wrongdoing, wrong, misdemeanor, misdeed, peccadillo, sin, transgression, shortcoming, fault, lapse. **2** an offense against society affront, injury, hurt, outrage, atrocity, insult, injustice, indignity, slight, snub. **3** her behavior causes offense annoyance, anger, indignation, exasperation, wrath, ire, displeasure, disapproval, dislike, animosity, resentment, pique, vexation. **4** the enemy's offense attack, assault. See OFFENSIVE noun. **take offense at** take umbrage at, get annoyed at, get angry at, resent, get/go into a huff about; inf. be miffed at/by.

offensive adjective **1** an offensive remark/person hurtful, wounding, abusive, displeasing, annoying, exasperating, vexing, galling, irritating, provocative, insulting, humiliating, rude, discourteous, uncivil, impolite, unmannerly, impertinent, insolent, disrespectful. **2** an offensive smell/sight disagreeable, unpleasant, foul, repellent, sickening, unsavory, noisome; inf. yucky. See OBJECTIONABLE.

offensive noun attack, assault, onslaught, drive, invasion, push, thrust, charge, sortie, sally, incursion.

offer verb **1** offer a suggestion put forward, propose, advance, submit, propound, suggest, recommend, make a motion of. **2** the job offers good career prospects afford, provide, supply, give, furnish, make available, present, give an opportunity for.

offer noun proposal, proposition, suggestion, submission, approach, overture.

offering noun **1** collect offerings from the members contribution, donation, subscription, gift, present, alms, charity, handout.

2 offerings to the gods sacrifice, oblation, immolation.

offhand adjective casual, unceremonious, cavalier, blasé, curt, abrupt, terse, brusque.

offhand adverb **1** always acts very offhand casually, unceremoniously, cavalierly, perfunctorily, curtly, abruptly, discourteously, rudely. **2** I cannot say offhand extempore, impromptu, ad lib, extemporaneously, spontaneously; inf. off the cuff, off the top of one's head, just like that.

office noun **1** his office is near his home base, workplace, workroom, room. **2** he has the office of treasurer post, position, appointment, role, place, situation, station. **3** to hold high office work, employment, business, duty, function, responsibility, obligation, charge, tenure.

officer noun **1** the officer in charge of the investigation policeman/policewoman, officer of the law, detective, constable; inf. copper, cop, the law, gumshoe; inf. derog. pig, fuzz. **2** the officers of the club officeholder, office-bearer, official, committee member, board member, administrator, executive, functionary, bureaucrat.

official adjective **1** official permission | his appointment is now official authorized, accredited, approved, validated, authenticated, certified, endorsed, sanctioned, licensed, recognized, accepted, legitimate, legal, lawful, bona fide, proper, ex cathedra; inf. kosher. **2** an official function formal, ceremonial, solemn, conventional, ritualistic, pompous; inf. stuffed-shirt.

official noun **1** party officials officeholder, administrator. See OFFICER 2. **2** officials of the court officer, representative, agent, deputy.

officiate verb be in charge of, be responsible for, chair, preside over, manage, oversee, superintend, conduct, run, operate.

officious adjective interfering, intrusive, meddlesome, meddling, importunate, forward, obtrusive, domineering.

offset verb counterbalance, counterpoise, counteract, countervail, balance, balance out, cancel out, neutralize, compensate for, make up for.

offshoot noun **1** plant offshoots sprout, branch, bough, limb, twig, sucker, tendril, runner, scion, spur. **2** an offshoot of the Hapsburg family descendant, scion, relation, relative, kin. **3** his attitude is an offshoot of his war experiences result, outcome, aftermath, consequence, upshot, product, by-product, spin-off.

offspring noun child, children, family, progeny, young, issue, descendant(s), heir(s), successor(s), spawn; inf. kid(s), young 'un(s).

often adverb frequently, repeatedly, time and time again, time after time, day in (and) day out; *lit.* oft, oft-times.

ogle verb stare at, gaze at, eye amorously, leer at, make eyes at, make sheep's eyes at; *inf.* give someone the once-over, undress with one's eyes.

ogre/ogress noun **1** *a mythical ogre* monster, giant/giantess, troll, bogeyman, bugbear, demon, devil. **2** *ruled by an ogre* fiend, beast, tyrant, despot, brute, sadist.

oily adjective **1** *oily food* greasy, fatty, buttery, swimming in oil/fat, oleaginous. **2** *oily charm* smooth, smooth-talking, unctuous, honey-tongued, flattering, fulsome, glib, suave, urbane.

ointment noun emollient, salve, balm, liniment, embrocation, unguent, gel.

OK noun *give the OK* agreement, consent, assent, permission, authorization, endorsement, sanction, approval, seal of approval, approbation, thumbs up, go-ahead; *inf.* green light, say-so.

OK adjective *an OK job* all right, acceptable, tolerable, passable, satisfactory, adequate, middling; *inf.* not bad, so-so, fair-to-middling.

OK verb *OK the project* consent to, say yes to, agree to, approve, pass, authorize, sanction, give something the/a nod, rubber-stamp.

old adjective **1** *old people* older, mature, elderly, aged, advanced in years, up in years, getting on, gray-haired, grizzled, hoary, past one's prime, ancient, decrepit, senescent, senile, venerable, senior; *inf.* past it, over the hill, long in the tooth. **2** *old clothes/buildings* worn-out, shabby, torn, tattered, ragged, dilapidated, brokendown, rundown, tumbledown, ramshackle, decaying, crumbling, disintegrating. **3** *old ideas* out-of-date, outdated, old-fashioned, outmoded, passé, archaic, obsolete, extinct, antiquated, antediluvian, superannuated; *inf.* old hat. **4** *in the old days* of old, olden, bygone, past, early, earlier, earliest, primeval, primordial, prehistoric. **5** *old customs* age-old, long-standing, long-lived, long-established, time-honored, enduring, lasting. **6** *old for her years* | *he's an old hand* mature, wise, sensible, experienced, knowledgeable, well-versed, practiced, skilled, skillful, adept. **7** *an old girlfriend* ex-, former, previous, one-time, sometime, erstwhile; *lit.* quondam. **old age** elderliness, age, agedness, declining years, advanced years, winter/autumn of one's life, senescence, senility, dotage.

old-fashioned adjective old, former, out of fashion, outmoded, démodé, unfashionable, out of style, out-of-date, outdated, dated, behind the times, past, bygone,

passé, archaic, obsolescent, obsolete, ancient, antiquated, superannuated, antediluvian, old-fogyish, old-fangled; *inf.* old hat, not with it.

old-timer noun senior citizen, senior; veteran; *inf. derog.* old fogy, old geezer, old codger.

omen noun portent, sign, token, foretoken, harbinger, premonition, forewarning, warning, foreshadowing, prediction, forecast, prophecy, augury, straw in the wind, writing on the wall, auspice, presage, presentiment, feeling, foreboding, misgiving; *inf.* funny feeling.

ominous adjective threatening, menacing, minatory, sinister, unpromising, unpropitious, inauspicious, unfavorable, unlucky, ill-fated.

omission noun **1** *the omission of his name* leaving out, exclusion, exception, noninclusion, deletion, erasure, elimination, expunction. **2** *a sin of omission* neglect, neglectfulness, negligence, dereliction, forgetfulness, oversight, disregard, nonfulfillment, default, failure. **3** *note several omissions from the list* exclusion, oversight, gap, lacuna.

omit verb **1** *omit his name from the list* leave out, exclude, except, pass over, drop, delete, erase, eliminate, expunge, rub out, cross out. **2** *omit closing the door* forget, neglect, fail; leave undone, overlook, skip.

omnipotent adjective all-powerful, almighty, supreme, preeminent, invincible.

omniscient adjective all-knowing, all-wise, all-seeing, all-perceiving.

once adverb **1** *they were friends once* at one time, previously, formerly, in the past, long ago. **2** *I saw him only once* on one occasion, one time, one single time. **at once 1** *you must leave at once* immediately, right away, straight away, instantly, forthwith; *inf.* before you can say Jack Robinson. **2** *they both arrived at once* at the same time, together, simultaneously. **once and for all** decisively, conclusively, finally, positively, for good, forever, permanently. **once in a while** occasionally, on the odd occasion, from time to time; *inf.* once in a blue moon.

oncoming adjective approaching, advancing, nearing, onrushing, forthcoming, imminent.

one adjective **1** *one person* a single, a solitary, a sole, a lone. **2** *they are now one* united, allied, joined, unified, bound, wedded, married.

onerous adjective burdensome, heavy, crushing, backbreaking, oppressive, weighty, arduous, demanding, exacting, wearing.

one-sided adjective **1** *one-sided opinions* biased, prejudiced, partisan, partial, biased, prejudiced, partisan, partial, discriminatory, colored, inequitable, unfair, unjust, narrow-minded, bigoted. **2** *a one-sided game* uneven, unequal, unbalanced, lopsided.

ongoing adjective in progress, current, extant, progressing, advancing, successful, developing, evolving, growing, continuous, continual.

onlooker noun looker-on, witness. *See* OBSERVER.

only adverb **1** *only enough for two* just, at most, not more than, barely, scarcely. **2** *he is only saying that* just, merely, simply, purely.

only adjective single, one and only, solitary, sole, lone; individual, unique, exclusive.

onset noun start, beginning, commencement, inception, outbreak; *inf.* kickoff.

onslaught noun assault, attack, charge, onrush, onset, storming, sortie, sally, raid, foray, push, thrust, drive, blitz.

onus noun burden, weight, load, responsibility, liability, obligation, duty, charge, encumbrance, cross to bear, millstone around one's neck, albatross.

ooze verb **1** *pus oozing from the wound* flow, discharge, exude, seep, trickle, drip, dribble, filter, filtrate, percolate, excrete, escape, leak, drain, bleed, sweat. **2** *she was positively oozing charm* exude, pour forth, send out, let loose, display, exhibit, manifest.

opaque adjective **1** *opaque glass* nontransparent, nontranslucent, cloudy, filmy, blurred, hazy. **2** *opaque prose* unclear, unfathomable, unintelligible, incomprehensible.

open adjective **1** *open doors* ajar, wide open, agape, gaping, yawning; unlocked, unbolted, unlatched, unbarred, unfastened, unsecured. **2** *open boxes/drains* uncovered, coverless, unlidded, topless, unsealed. **3** *open spaces* unenclosed, unfenced, exposed, unsheltered, extensive, broad, spacious, sweeping, airy, uncrowded, uncluttered, undeveloped. **4** *open roads* unobstructed, unblocked, clear, passable, navigable. **5** *maps open on the table* spread out, unfolded, unfurled, unrolled, straightened out, extended, stretched out. **6** *quite open about her dislike* frank, candid, honest, forthright, direct, blunt, plainspoken, downright. **7** *an open meeting/competition* public, general, nonexclusive, accessible, nonrestrictive, unrestricted, nondiscriminatory. **8** *the job is still open* vacant, available, unfilled, unoccupied, free. **9** *open hostility* obvious, clear, noticeable, visible, apparent, evident, manifest, overt, conspicuous, patent, unconcealed, unhidden, undis-

guised, blatant, flagrant. **10** *three courses open to us* available, on hand, obtainable, accessible. **11** *the subject is still open* undecided, unresolved, unsettled, arguable, debatable, moot. **12** *keep an open mind* unbiased, unprejudiced. *See* OPEN-MINDED 1. **open to** *open to abuse* allowing of, permitting, vulnerable to, exposed to, susceptible to, liable to, at the mercy of, an easy target for.

open verb **1** *open the door* throw open, unlock, unbolt, unlatch, unbar, unfasten. **2** *open the package* unwrap, undo, untie, unseal. **3** *open the bottle* uncork, broach, crack. **4** *the crack opened* open up, come apart, split, separate, rupture. **5** *we open the campaign tomorrow* start, begin, commence, start the ball rolling; *inf.* kick off. **6** *open his heart* lay bare, bare, uncover, expose, exhibit, disclose, divulge, pour out.

openhanded adjective open, generous, liberal, lavish, free, bountiful, bounteous, munificent; benevolent, charitable, magnanimous.

opening noun **1** *an opening in the wall* gap, aperture, space, hole, orifice, vent, slot, break, breach, crack, split, fissure, cleft, crevice, chink, interstice, rent, rupture. **2** *an opening in the firm* vacancy, position, job, opportunity, chance. **3** *the opening of the season* beginning, start, commencement, outset, inception, launch, birth, dawn; *inf.* kickoff.

open-minded adjective **1** *open-minded judges* unbiased, unprejudiced, prejudice-free, nonpartisan, impartial, nondiscriminatory, objective, disinterested, dispassionate, detached, tolerant, liberal, broad-minded, undogmatic. **2** *writers should be open-minded* receptive, open to suggestions, open to new ideas, amenable.

operate verb work, function, go, run, perform, act, be in action; make go, use, utilize, employ, handle, manipulate, maneuver, ply, manage, be in charge of.

operation noun **1** *operation of the machine* working, functioning, running, performance; using, handling, manipulation. **2** *the operation of radon testing went smoothly* activity, exercise, affair, business, undertaking, enterprise, task, job. **3** *military operations* maneuver, exercise, campaign, assault. **in operation** operational, operative, in force, effective, in use, functioning, working, valid.

operator noun **1** *the operator of a car dealership* manager, businessman, businesswoman, business person, administrator, director, supervisor, superintendent. **2** *a smooth operator* maneuverer, manipulator, machinator, mover, wheeler-dealer.

opiate noun drug, narcotic, sedative, tranquilizer, depressant, bromide, soporific, morphine, opium, laudanum; *inf.* downer.

opinion noun point of view, view, viewpoint, belief, thought, thinking, way of thinking, standpoint, theory, judgment, estimation, feeling, sentiment, impression, notion, assumption, conception, conviction, persuasion, creed, dogma.

opinionated adjective dogmatic, doctrinaire, cocksure, adamant, obstinate, stubborn, pigheaded, inflexible, uncompromising, bigoted.

opponent noun opposer, the opposition, rival, adversary, competitor, enemy, foe, antagonist, contender, dissenter, disputant.

opportune adjective advantageous, favorable, auspicious, propitious, timely, well-timed, fortunate, providential, felicitous, convenient, expedient, suitable, apt, fitting, relevant, applicable, pertinent.

opportunity noun chance, good time, golden opportunity; *inf.* break.

oppose verb **1** *oppose the proposals* disapprove of, be hostile to, contradict, counter, argue against, counterattack, confront, resist, withstand, defy, fight, combat. **2** *oppose memory and imagination* contrast, juxtapose, offset, balance, counterbalance, set against, pit against.

opposite adjective **1** *houses opposite each other* facing, face-to-face with; *inf.* eyeball to eyeball with. **2** *opposite opinions* diametrically opposite, opposing, differing, contrary, reverse, contradictory, conflicting, clashing, discordant, dissident, at variance, antipathetic, poles apart. **3** *on opposite sides* opposing, rival, competitive, enemy, warring, fighting, contending, combatant.

opposition noun **1** *express their opposition* dislike, disapproval, hostility, resistance, defiance. **2** *back the opposition* opponent, opposing side, other side, rival, adversary, competition, antagonist, enemy, foe.

oppress verb **1** *the tyrant oppressed the citizens* tyrannize, crush, suppress, repress, abuse, maltreat, persecute, rule with a rod of iron, trample on, trample underfoot, ride roughshod over. **2** *oppressed by grief* weigh down, lie heavy on, weigh heavy on, burden, crush, depress, dispirit, dishearten, take the heart out of, discourage, sadden, make despondent, deject, desolate.

oppressed adjective tyrannized, subjugated, enslaved, crushed, subdued, repressed, persecuted, browbeaten, downtrodden, disadvantaged, underprivileged.

oppression noun tyranny, suppression, abuse, persecution, despotism, abuse, maltreatment, cruelty, brutality, injustice, ruthlessness, harshness.

oppressive adjective **1** *an oppressive regime* tyrannical, despotic, draconian, iron-fisted, high-handed, repressive, domineering, harsh, crushing, cruel, brutal, ruthless, relentless, merciless, pitiless, inexorable, unjust, undemocratic. **2** *oppressive weather* muggy, close, airless, stuffy, stifling, suffocating, sultry, torrid.

optimistic adjective hopeful, full of hope, Pollyannaish, Panglossian, positive, sanguine, confident, bullish, cheerful, buoyant; *inf.* upbeat.

optimum adjective **1** *the optimum time to choose* most favorable, best, most advantageous, most appropriate, ideal, perfect. **2** *plants in optimum condition* peak, top, best, perfect, ideal, flawless, superlative, optimal; *inf.* tip-top, A-1.

option noun choice, alternative, possibility, preference.

optional adjective noncompulsory, voluntary, discretionary, elective.

opulent adjective **1** *opulent families* affluent, wealthy, rich, well-off, well-to-do, moneyed, prosperous; *inf.* well-heeled, rolling in it. **2** *opulent houses* luxurious, sumptuous, lavishly appointed; *inf.* plush, plushy, ritzy. **3** *opulent vegetation* abundant, superabundant, copious, plentiful, profuse, prolific, luxuriant.

oracle noun **1** *the oracles of classical times* prophet/prophetess, seer, soothsayer, sibyl, augur, sage. **2** *an oracle on architecture* authority, expert, specialist, connoisseur, pundit, guru.

oral adjective spoken, verbal, vocal, uttered, said.

oration noun speech, lecture, address, homily, sermon, discourse, declamation, harangue, tirade; *inf.* spiel.

orator noun speaker, public speaker, speech-maker, lecturer, declaimer, haranguer, rhetorician, Cicero.

orbit noun **1** *the planet's orbit* revolution, circle, circuit, cycle, rotation, circumgyration, path, course, track, trajectory. **2** *his orbit of responsibility* sphere, sphere of influence, range, reach, scope, ambit, sweep, domain.

orbit verb revolve around, circle around, encircle, circumnavigate.

orchestrate verb **1** *orchestrate the music* arrange, score. **2** *orchestrate the event* organize, arrange, put together, set up, manage, stage-manage, mastermind, coordinate, integrate.

ordain verb **1** *ordain a priest* appoint, confer holy orders on, frock, induct, install, invest, anoint, consecrate. **2** *his lack of success seems to have been ordained* fate, predestine, predetermine, preordain. **3** *Congress ordained that taxes be increased* decree, legislate, enact, rule, order, command, enjoin, dictate, prescribe, pronounce.

ordeal noun trial, test, tribulation, suffering, affliction, distress, agony, anguish, torture, torment, calamity, trouble, nightmare.

order noun **1** *restore order to the room* orderliness, neatness, tidiness, trimness, harmony, apple-pie order. **2** *no sense of order in the filing system* method, organization, system, plan, uniformity, regularity, symmetry, pattern. **3** *everything is in working order* condition, state, shape, situation. **4** *in alphabetical/numerical order* arrangement, grouping, system, systemization, organization, form, structure, disposition, classification, categorization, codification, series, sequence, progression, succession, layout, setup. **5** *give orders to fire* command, direction, directive, instruction, behest, decree, edict, injunction, law, rule, regulation, mandate, ordinance, stipulation, dictate, say-so. **6** *lack of order in the land* law, lawfulness, law and order, discipline, control, peace, calm. **7** *place an order for tickets* request, call, requirement, requisition, demand, booking, reservation, commission, notification, application. **8** *the lower orders of society* rank, class, caste, grade, level, degree, position, station. **9** *the social order* grouping, grading, ranking, system, class system, caste system, hierarchy, pecking order. **10** *work of a high order* kind, sort, type, variety, genre, nature. **11** *they all belong to some order* lodge, society, secret society, guild, club, association, league, union, fellowship, fraternity, confraternity, sorority, brotherhood, sisterhood, sodality. **in order 1** *the room is in order* tidy, neat. *See* ORDERLY 1. **2** *is it in order for her to attend?* acceptable, all right, fitting, suitable, appropriate, right, correct. **out of order** *the machine is out of order* broken, broken-down, nonfunctional, inoperative, in disrepair, out of commission; *inf.* down, kaput, on the blink, on the fritz.

order verb **1** *order them to fire* give the order to, command, instruct, direct, bid. **2** *the judge ordered that the courtroom be cleared* decree, ordain, rule, legislate, enjoin, prescribe, pronounce. **3** *order dinner* place an order for, request, call for, requisition, book, reserve, contract for, apply for, send away for. **4** *it was time to order his life* put in order, set in order, organize, systematize, arrange, dispose, classify, catalog, codify, tabulate, sort out, tidy up, regulate.

orderly adjective **1** *an orderly room* in order, neat, tidy, trim, shipshape, shipshape and Bristol fashion, in Bristol fashion, in apple-pie order. **2** *an orderly person* organized, well-organized,

methodical, systematic, systematized, efficient, businesslike. **3** *an orderly class of students* well-behaved, law-abiding, disciplined, quiet, peaceful, controlled, restrained.

ordinarily adverb as a rule, generally, as a general rule, in general, usually, normally.

ordinary adjective **1** *our ordinary procedure* usual, normal, standard, typical, stock, common, customary, habitual, accustomed, wonted, everyday, quotidian, regular, routine, established, settled, fixed, prevailing. **2** *we lead very ordinary lives* run-of-the-mill, conventional, standard, typical, average, commonplace, workaday, humdrum, unremarkable, unexceptional, unmemorable, pedestrian, prosaic, unpretentious, modest, plain, simple, humble. **3** *a very ordinary piece of writing* average, run-of-the-mill, pedestrian, prosaic, uninteresting, dull, uninspired, unimaginative, hackneyed, stale, undistinguished, unexceptional, unremarkable, mediocre, indifferent, second-rate.

organic adjective **1** *organic ingredients* natural, nonchemical, pesticide-free, chemical-free, additive-free. **2** *organic matter* living, live, animate, biotic, biological. **3** *the music in the play is organic, not incidental* fundamental, basic, structural, integral, inherent, innate, intrinsic, vital, essential, indispensable. **4** *society is an organic whole* structured, organized, systematic, systematized, ordered, methodical, methodized.

organism noun **1** *microscopic organisms* being, creature, animal, plant. **2** *the company is a complex organism* structure, system, organization, setup.

organization noun **1** *the organization of the firm/files/party* establishment, development, assembly, arrangement, regulation, coordination, systematization, methodization, categorization, administration, running, management. **2** *the human body is a complex organization* whole, unity. *See* ORGANISM 2. **3** *president of the organization* company, firm, concern, operation, corporation, institution, group, consortium, conglomerate, combine, syndicate, federation, confederation, association, body.

organize verb establish, set up, form, lay the foundations of, found, institute, create, originate, begin, start, develop, build, frame, construct, assemble, structure, shape, mold, put together, arrange, dispose, regulate, marshal, put in order, put straight, coordinate, systematize, methodize, standardize, collocate, group, sort, sort out, classify, categorize, catalog, codify, tabulate.

orgy noun bout, overindulgence, excess, surfeit; carousal, debauch, revel, revels, revelry, bacchanalia, saturnalia; *inf.*

spree, splurge, binge, jag, bender, toot; love-in.

orient, orientate verb **1** *orient himself to his new life* adapt, adjust, accommodate, familiarize, acclimatize. **2** *orient the beach chair toward the sun* direct, guide, lead, position something in the direction of, turn. **3** *orient the course for/toward beginners* aim, direct, slant, angle, intend, design.
orient oneself get/find one's bearings, get the lay of the land, feel one's way.

orientation noun **1** *orientation to his new way of life* adaptation, adjustment, accommodation, familiarization, acclimatization. **2** *establish one's orientation* bearings, location, position, direction.

orifice noun opening, hole, vent, aperture, gap, space, breach, break, rent, slot, slit.

origin noun **1** *the origin of the word* source, derivation, root, roots, provenance, etymology, genesis, etiology. **2** *the origins of life* source, basis, base, wellspring, spring, wellhead, fountainhead, fountain, genesis. **3** *the origin of the age of electronics* birth, dawn, dawning, beginning, start, commencement, emergence, inception, launch, creation, early stages, inauguration, foundation. **4** *explore the family's origin(s)* descent, ancestry, pedigree, lineage, heritage, parentage, extraction, beginnings.

original adjective **1** *the original inhabitants* aboriginal, indigenous, early, earliest, first, initial, primary, primordial, primal, primeval, primitive, autochthonal, autochthonous. **2** *his work is original* innovative, inventive, new, novel, fresh, creative, imaginative, resourceful, individual, ingenious, unusual, unconventional, unorthodox, unprecedented, groundbreaking. **3** *this painting is original* not copied, genuine, authentic, archetypal, prototypical, master.

original noun **1** *this is the original, not a copy* original work/painting, archetype, prototype, master. **2** *among architects, he is an original* standout, paragon, nonpareil, exemplar, one of a kind, nonesuch; individualist, eccentric, nonconformist.

originality noun inventiveness, newness, novelty, break with tradition, freshness, innovation, creativity, imaginativeness, resourcefulness, individuality, unusualness, unconventionality, unprecedentedness.

originally adverb at first, at the start, at the outset, initially.

originate verb **1** *the spring originates in/from the mountains* arise, rise, flow, emanate, issue. **2** *the quarrel originated in/from a misunderstanding* stem, spring, result, derive, start, begin, commence. **3** *he originated the idea* give birth to, be the father/mother of, set in motion, set up, invent, dream

up, conceive, discover, initiate, create, formulate, inaugurate, pioneer, introduce, establish, found, evolve, develop, generate.

originator noun father/mother, inventor, discoverer, initiator, architect, author, prime mover, founder, pioneer, establisher, developer.

ornament noun **1** *a house full of ornaments* knickknack, trinket, bauble, gewgaw, accessory, decoration, frill, whatnot, doodad. **2** *the dress needs little ornament* decoration, adornment, embellishment, trimming, garnish, garnishing. **3** *the diva is the ornament of the opera company* jewel, gem, treasure, pride, flower, leading light, crème de la crème.

ornamental adjective decorative, decorated, ornate, ornamented, embellished, embroidered, fancy, fanciful.

ornate adjective **1** *ornate furnishings* elaborate, overelaborate, decorated, embellished, adorned, ornamented, fancy, fussy, busy, ostentatious, showy, baroque, rococo; *inf.* flashy. **2** *ornate prose* flowery, florid, flamboyant, pretentious, high-flown, high-sounding, grandiose, pompous, bombastic; *inf.* highfalutin.

orthodox adjective *orthodox behavior* conventional, accepted, approved, correct, proper, conformist, established, traditional, prevailing, customary, usual, regular, standard, *comme il faut*, de rigueur.

oscillate verb swing, sway, fluctuate, seesaw, waver, vacillate, vary, hesitate, yo-yo.

oscillation noun swing, swinging, fluctuation, wavering, vacillation, yo-yoing.

ostensible adjective outward, apparent, seeming, professed, alleged, claimed, purported, pretended, feigned, specious, supposed.

ostentatious adjective showy, conspicuous, obtrusive, loud, extravagant, flamboyant, gaudy, flashy, pretentious, affected, overdone, overelaborate, vulgar, kitsch.

ostracize verb exclude, shut out, bar, shun, spurn, avoid, boycott, repudiate, cast out, reject, blackball, blacklist, banish, exile, expel, excommunicate, debar, leave out in the cold, give someone the cold shoulder, send to Coventry.

other adjective **1** *use other means* different, unlike, variant, dissimilar, disparate, distinct, separate, alternative. **2** *need a few other examples* more, additional, further, extra, supplementary.

oust verb drive out, force out, thrust out, expel, eject, put out, evict, throw out, dispossess, dismiss, dislodge, displace, depose, unseat, topple, disinherit; *inf.* fire, sack.

out adverb **1** *the manager is out just now* not here, away, elsewhere, absent. **2** *the* *children have gone out* outside, outdoors, out of doors. **3** *tire them out* completely, thoroughly, entirely, wholly. **4** *the fire is out* extinguished, quenched, doused, dead. **5** *the boxer is completely out* out cold, unconscious, knocked out, senseless; *inf.* KO'd. **6** *your secret is out* revealed, disclosed, divulged, in the open, out in the open, known, exposed, common knowledge, public knowledge. **7** *the flowers are out* open, in bloom, in full bloom, blooming. **8** *long hair is out this year* unfashionable, out of fashion, dated, out-of-date, not in, behind the times, *démodé*, *passé*; *inf.* old hat.

out-and-out adjective absolute, complete, utter, downright, thorough, thoroughgoing, total, perfect, unmitigated, unqualified, consummate, inveterate, dyed-in-the-wool, true-blue.

outbreak noun eruption, flare-up, upsurge, outburst, sudden appearance, start, rash.

outburst noun burst, explosion, eruption, outbreak, flare-up, access, attack, fit, spasm, paroxysm.

outcast noun pariah, *persona non grata*, leper, untouchable, castaway, exile, displaced person, refugee, evictee, evacuee; *inf.* DP.

outclass verb surpass, outshine, eclipse, overshadow, outdistance, outstrip, outdo, outplay, outrank, outrival, trounce, beat, defeat; *inf.* be a cut above, be head and shoulders above, run rings around.

outcome noun consequence, result, end result, sequel, upshot, issue, product, conclusion, aftereffect, aftermath, wake; *inf.* payoff.

outcry noun clamor, protest, complaints, objections, fuss, outburst, commotion, uproar, tumult, hue and cry, hullabaloo, ballyhoo, racket.

outdated adjective out-of-date, out of style, out of fashion, old-fashioned, unfashionable, outmoded, dated, *démodé*, *passé*, behind the times, antiquated, archaic; *inf.* old hat, not with it.

outdo verb surpass, top, exceed, excel, get the better of, transcend, overcome, outsmart, outmaneuver. *See* OUTCLASS.

outer adjective **1** *pierce the outer layer* outside, outermost, outward, exterior, external, surface, superficial. **2** *the outer areas of the estate* outlying, distant, remote, faraway, peripheral, fringe.

outfit noun **1** *wearing a smart outfit* clothes, dress, ensemble, suit, costume, garb, accoutrements, trappings; *inf.* get-up, gear, togs. **2** *pack the fishing outfit* kit, equipment, tools, tackle, apparatus, paraphernalia. **3** *a publishing outfit | soldiers rejoining their outfit* organization, setup, company, firm, business, (military) unit, group, team, coterie, clique.

outfit verb equip, fit out, rig out, supply, furnish with, provide with, stock with, provision, accoutre, attire.

outgoing adjective **1** *outgoing people* extroverted, unreserved, demonstrative, affectionate, warm, friendly, genial, cordial, affable, hail-fellow-well-met, sociable, communicative, open, expansive, talkative, gregarious, approachable, easygoing, easy. **2** *the outgoing president* retiring, departing, leaving, withdrawing.

outing noun trip, excursion, jaunt, expedition, pleasure trip, tour, airing; *inf.* spin.

outlandish adjective strange, odd, peculiar, queer, curious, singular, eccentric, quaint, bizarre, preposterous, fantastic, outré, weird; *inf.* wacky, far-out, off-the-wall.

outlaw noun fugitive, outcast, exile, pariah, bandit, desperado, brigand, criminal, robber.

outlaw verb ban, bar, prohibit, forbid, embargo, disallow, proscribe, interdict.

outlay noun expenditure, expenses, spending, cost, price, charge, payment, disbursement.

outlet noun **1** *water outlets* exit, vent, outfall, valve, safety valve, duct, blowhole, channel, trench, culvert, conduit. **2** *an outlet for her creativity* release, release mechanism, safety valve. **3** *an outlet for their produce* market, marketplace, store, shop.

outline noun **1** *an outline of our plans* draft, rough draft, sketch, skeleton, framework, layout, diagram, plan, design, schema. **2** *give an outline of what happened* thumbnail sketch, quick rundown, summary, synopsis, précis, main points, bones, bare bones. **3** *draw an outline of the building* contour, silhouette, profile, lineaments, delineation, configuration, perimeter, circumference.

outline verb **1** *outline the shape* sketch, delineate, trace, silhouette. **2** *outline your ideas* give a thumbnail sketch of, give a rough idea of, give a quick rundown on, summarize, précis.

outlook noun **1** *a gloomy outlook on life* view, point of view, viewpoint, perspective, attitude, frame of mind, standpoint, slant, angle, interpretation, opinion. **2** *the house has a pleasant outlook* view, vista, prospect, panorama, aspect.

outlying adjective outer, outermost, out-of-the-way, remote, distant, faraway, far-flung, peripheral, isolated, inaccessible, off the beaten path/track, backwoods.

outmoded adjective old-fashioned, unfashionable, out of fashion, out of style, outdated, out-of-date, dated, passé, *démodé*, behind the times, antiquated, archaic, obsolete; *inf.* old hat.

out of the way adjective remote, lonely, obscure, unfrequented. *See* OUTLYING.

output noun production, product, productivity, yield, harvest, achievement, accomplishment.

outrage noun **1** *outrages committed by the soldiers* atrocity, crime, horror, enormity, brutality, barbarism. **2** *the building is an outrage* offense, affront, insult, injury, abuse, indignity, scandal, desecration, violation. **3** *arouse outrage in the citizens* anger, fury, rage, indignation, wrath, annoyance, shock, resentment, horror, amazement.

outrage verb anger, infuriate, enrage, incense, make someone's blood boil, madden, annoy, shock, horrify, amaze, scandalize, offend, insult, affront, vex, distress.

outrageous adjective **1** *outrageous behavior* intolerable, insufferable, insupportable, unendurable, unbearable, impossible, exasperating, offensive, provocative, maddening, distressing. **2** *outrageous acts* atrocious, heinous, abominable, wicked, vile, foul, monstrous, horrible, horrid, dreadful, terrible, horrendous, hideous, ghastly, unspeakable, gruesome. **3** *outrageous prices* immoderate, excessive, exorbitant, unreasonable, preposterous, scandalous, shocking; *inf.* steep.

outright adjective **1** *an outright fool* absolute, complete. *See* OUT-AND-OUT. **2** *the outright winner* definite, unequivocal, unqualified, incontestable, undeniable, unmistakable.

outright adverb **1** *reject the proposal outright* completely, entirely, wholly, totally, categorically, absolutely. **2** *killed outright* instantly, instantaneously, immediately, at once, straight away, then and there, on the spot. **3** *tell her outright* openly, candidly, frankly, honestly, forthrightly, directly, plainly, explicitly, unreservedly.

outset noun start, starting point, beginning, commencement, dawn, birth, inception, opening, launch, inauguration; *inf.* kickoff.

outside adjective **1** *outside layers* outer, outermost, outward, exterior, external. **2** *outside furniture/plumbing* outdoor, out-of-doors. **3** *an outside chance* unlikely, improbable, slight, slender, slim, small, faint, negligible, marginal, remote, distant, vague.

outside noun **1** *brown on the outside* outer side, exterior, surface, outer surface, case, skin, shell, sheath. **2** *the outside of the building* exterior, front, face, façade.

outsider noun alien, stranger, foreigner, outlander, immigrant, emigrant, émigré, newcomer, parvenu, arriviste, interloper, intruder, gatecrasher, outcast, misfit, odd man out.

outsmart verb get the better of, outwit, outfox, outmaneuver, outperform, outplay, steal a march on, trick, dupe, make a fool of; *inf.* put one over on, pull a fast one on.

outspoken adjective candid, frank, forthright, direct, straightforward, straight-from-the-shoulder, plain, plainspoken, explicit, blunt, brusque, unequivocal, unceremonious.

outstanding adjective **1** *an outstanding painter* preeminent, eminent, well-known, notable, noteworthy, distinguished, important, famous, famed, renowned, celebrated, great, excellent, remarkable, exceptional, superlative. **2** *the painting is outstanding* striking, impressive, eye-catching, arresting, memorable, remarkable. **3** *outstanding debts* unpaid, unsettled, owing, due, remaining, pending, ongoing.

outward adjective *no outward sign of grief* external, superficial, visible, observable, noticeable, perceptible, discernible, apparent, evident, obvious.

outwardly adverb **1** *outwardly visible* externally, on the outside. **2** *outwardly he seems all right* on the surface, superficially, on the face of it, to all appearances, to the eye, as far as one can see, to all intents and purposes, apparently, evidently.

outweigh verb be greater than, exceed, be superior to, take precedence over, have the edge on/over, preponderate.

outwit verb get the better of, outmaneuver. *See* OUTSMART.

oval adjective egg-shaped, ovoid, ovate, oviform, elliptical, ellipsoidal.

ovation noun applause, handclap, handclapping, clapping, cheering, cheers, acclaim, acclamation, praise, plaudits, laurels, tribute, accolade, laudation, extolment; *inf.* bouquets.

over adverb **1** *fly over* overhead, above, on high, aloft. **2** *the relationship is over* ended, finished, concluded, terminated, no more, extinct, gone, dead, a thing of the past, ancient history. **over and over** again and again, repeatedly, time and time again, ad nauseam.

overall adjective comprehensive, universal, all-embracing, inclusive, all-inclusive, general, sweeping, complete, blanket, umbrella, global.

overbearing adjective domineering, autocratic, tyrannical, despotic, oppressive, high-handed, lordly, officious, dogmatic, dictatorial, pompous, peremptory, arrogant, haughty, cocksure, disdainful, contemptuous; *inf.* bossy.

overblown adjective extravagant, florid, pompous, overelaborate, pretentious, high-flown, turgid, bombastic, grandiloquent, magniloquent, euphuistic, fustian.

overcast adjective cloudy, clouded, clouded over, sunless, darkened, dark, murky, gray, leaden, lowering, threatening, heavy.

overcome verb conquer, defeat, vanquish, beat, prevail over, get the better of, triumph over, best, worst, trounce, rout, gain mastery over, master, overpower, overwhelm, overthrow, subdue, subjugate, quell, quash, crush; *inf.* lick, clobber, whip, wipe (up) the floor with, blow out of the water.

overconfident adjective cocksure, cocky, swaggering, blustering, brash, overbearing, egotistic, riding/heading for a fall.

overdo verb **1** *overdo the sympathy* exaggerate, do to death, go overboard over, carry too far, carry to extremes, belabor, stretch/strain a point over, overstate, overemphasize, hyperbolize, not know when to stop; *inf.* pile on, lay on thick, lay on with a trowel, make a production of, make a big deal out of. **2** *overdo the meat* overcook, overbake, burn, burn to a crisp. **overdo it** overwork, do too much, overtax oneself, overburden oneself, drive oneself too hard, push oneself too far/hard, wear oneself out, burn the candle at both ends, have too many irons in the fire, have too many balls in the air, burn oneself out, bite off more than one can chew; *inf.* knock oneself out, work/run oneself into the ground.

overdue adjective **1** *our visit is overdue* late, behind schedule, behindhand, delayed, belated, tardy, unpunctual. **2** *overdue bills* unpaid, owed, owing, outstanding, unsettled, in arrears.

overeat verb gorge oneself, stuff oneself, overindulge, surfeit, guzzle, gormandize; *inf.* binge, stuff one's face, eat like a horse, pack it away, make a pig of oneself, pig out.

overflow verb **1** *the water was overflowing* flow over, run over, spill over, brim over, well over, pour forth, stream forth, discharge, surge, debouch. **2** *water overflowed the land* flood, deluge, inundate, submerge, cover, swamp, engulf, drown, soak, drench, saturate. **overflowing with** full of, crowded with, thronged with, swarming with, teeming with, abounding in.

overhaul verb check out/over, investigate, inspect, examine, service, repair, mend, recondition, renovate, revamp, fix up, patch up.

overhead noun expenses, expenditure, outlay, disbursement, running cost(s), operating cost(s).

overjoyed adjective elated, jubilant, thrilled, delighted, euphoric, ecstatic, rapturous, enraptured, transported, delirious with happiness, on top of the world; *inf.* tickled pink, on cloud nine, in seventh heaven.

overlook verb **1** *he overlooked a mistake on the first page* fail to notice/observe/spot, miss, leave; *inf.* slip up on. **2** *overlook tasks* omit, neglect, forget. **3** *decide to overlook his crime* disregard, take no notice of, ignore, let something pass, turn a blind eye to, wink at, blink at, excuse, pardon, forgive, condone; *inf.* let something ride. **4** *the house overlooks the sea* look over, look onto, front onto, have a view of, afford/command a view of.

overly adverb unduly, excessively, inordinately, immoderately.

overpower verb **1** *overpower the enemy* get the upper hand over, conquer. *See* OVERCOME. **2** *his charm overpowered her* overwhelm, move, stir, affect, touch, impress, take aback; *inf.* bowl over, knock/hit for a loop, get to.

overrate verb overestimate, overvalue, overprize, exaggerate the worth of.

override verb **1** *his career overrides all else* take priority/precedence over, supersede, outweigh. **2** *override her objections* trample on, ride roughshod over, set aside, ignore, disregard, discount, pay no heed to, take no account of.

overriding adjective most important, predominant, principal, primary, paramount, chief, main, major, foremost, central, focal, pivotal; *inf.* number one.

overrule verb rule against, disallow, override, veto, set aside, overturn, cancel, reverse, rescind, repeal, revoke, repudiate, annul, nullify, declare null and void, invalidate, void, abrogate.

overrun verb **1** *the enemy was overrunning their country* invade, march into, penetrate, occupy, besiege, storm, attack, assail. **2** *rats overrunning the warehouses* swarm over, surge over, inundate, overwhelm, permeate, infest. **3** *weeds overrunning the garden* spread over, spread like wildfire over, grow over, cover, choke, clog; *inf.* run riot over.

overseer noun supervisor, superintendent, foreman, manager, master, boss; *inf.* super, honcho.

overshadow verb **1** *that runner overshadows the others* outshine, eclipse, put in the shade, surpass, be superior to, outclass, outstrip, outdo, top, transcend, tower above, dwarf, upstage; *inf.* be head and shoulders above, be a cut above. **2** *his death overshadowed the gathering* cast gloom over, blight, take the pleasure out of, mar, spoil, ruin. **3** *clouds overshadowing the sun* darken, bedim, dim, conceal, obscure, eclipse, screen, shroud, veil.

oversight noun **1** *done in oversight* carelessness, inattention, neglect, inadvertence, laxity, dereliction, omission. **2** *an oversight in the article* mistake, error, blunder, gaffe, fault, omission, slip, lapse; *inf.* slipup, goof, booboo. **3** *have oversight of the workforce* supervision, surveillance, superintendence, charge, care, administration, management, direction, control, handling.

overt adjective obvious, noticeable, observable, visible, undisguised, unconcealed, apparent, plain, manifest, patent, open, public, blatant, conspicuous.

overtake verb **1** *cars overtaking each other* pass, get/go past, go by, overhaul, outdistance, outstrip. **2** *misfortune overtook them* befall, hit, strike, fall upon, surprise, catch unawares, catch unprepared, catch off guard.

overthrow verb **1** *overthrow the government* cause the downfall of, remove from office, overturn, depose, oust, unseat, dethrone, disestablish. **2** *overthrow the army of occupation* conquer, vanquish, defeat, beat, rout, trounce, best, worst, subjugate, crush, quash, quell, overcome, overwhelm, overturn, overpower. **3** *squalls overthrowing boats* throw over, turn over, overturn, tip over, topple over, upset, capsize, knock over, upturn, upend, invert.

overthrow noun **1** *the overthrow of the government* downfall, deposition, ousting. **2** *the overthrow of the army* defeat, vanquishing, rout, subjugation, crushing, overwhelming, overturning.

overtone noun implication, innuendo, hint, suggestion, insinuation, association, connotation, undercurrent, nuance, flavor, coloring, vein.

overture noun *peace overtures* advances, move, opening move, conciliatory move, approach, proposal, proposition, offer, suggestion, motion.

overturn verb **1** *the boat overturned* capsize, keel over, tip over, topple over. **2** *high winds overturning trash cans* upturn, turn over. *See* OVERTHROW verb 3. **3** *overturn the previous decision* reverse, rescind. *See* OVERRULE. **4** *overturn the government* depose, oust. *See* OVERTHROW verb

1. **5** *overturn the army of occupation* conquer, vanquish, defeat. *See* OVERTHROW verb 2.

overweight adjective obese, fat, plump, stout, ample, chubby, tubby, corpulent, rotund, portly, pudgy, paunchy, heavy, on the heavy side, big, hefty, large, bulky, chunky, outsize, massive, gross; *inf.* well-padded, well-upholstered, roly-poly.

overwhelm verb **1** *the generous present overwhelmed her* move, daze, dumbfound, shake, take aback, leave speechless, stagger; *inf.* bowl over, knock for a loop, blow one's mind, flabbergast. **2** *overwhelmed with work* inundate, flood, deluge, engulf, submerge, swamp, bury, overload, overburden, snow under. **3** *overwhelm the army of occupation* overpower, conquer, vanquish. *See* OVERCOME.

overwhelming adjective **1** *an overwhelming desire to laugh* uncontrollable, irrepressible, irresistible, overpowering. **2** *an overwhelming amount of mail* profuse, enormous, immense, inordinate, massive, huge, stupendous, prodigious, staggering, shattering; *inf.* mind-boggling, mind-blowing. **3** *the overwhelming majority* vast, massive, great, large.

overwrought adjective **1** *overwrought mothers* tense, agitated, nervous, on edge, edgy, keyed up, highly strung, overexcited, beside oneself, distracted, jumpy, frantic, frenzied, hysterical; *inf.* in a state, in a tizzy, uptight, wound up. **2** *overwrought designs* overornate, overelaborate, overembellished, overblown, overcharged, florid, busy, fussy, strained, contrived, overworked, baroque, rococo.

owe verb be in debt to, be indebted to, be in arrears to, be obligated to, be beholden to.

own adjective personal, individual, particular, private.

own verb **1** *they own three cars* possess, have, keep, retain, maintain, hold, enjoy. **2** *I own that he is right* admit, allow, concede, grant, accept, acknowledge, recognize, agree. **own up** confess, admit; *inf.* come clean.

owner noun possessor, holder, keeper; proprietor/proprietress/proprietrix, landlord, landlady; master/mistress.

Pp

pace noun 1 *take one pace toward her* step, stride. 2 *walk with an ambling pace* gait, walk, tread. 3 *unable to keep up with the pace of the race* speed, swiftness, quickness, rapidity, velocity, tempo; *inf.* clip. 4 *the fast/slow pace of life there* tempo, momentum, measure.

pacific adjective 1 *a pacific nation* peace-loving, peaceable, pacifist, nonviolent, non-aggressive, nonbelligerent, noncombative, dovish. 2 *pacific waters* calm, still, motionless, smooth, tranquil, peaceful, placid, unruffled, undisturbed.

pacify verb calm, calm down, placate, conciliate, propitiate, appease, mollify, soothe, tranquilize, quieten.

pack noun 1 *carry a pack on his back* bag, backpack, rucksack, knapsack, haversack, duffel bag, kitbag, bundle, parcel, bale, truss; *inf.* bindle. 2 *buy a pack of cigarettes* packet, container, package, carton. 3 *a pack of animals* herd, drove, flock, troop. 4 *a pack of thieves* gang, crowd, mob, group, band, company, troop, set, clique; *inf.* crew, bunch. 5 *a pack of lies* collection, parcel, assortment, mass, assemblage, bunch; *inf.* load, heap.

pack verb 1 *pack a suitcase* fill, load, bundle, stuff, cram. 2 *pack clothes in a suitcase* put, place, store, stow. 3 *pack the glass in straw* package, wrap, wrap up, box, bale, cover, protect. 4 *people packing the stadium* fill, crowd, throng, mob, cram, jam, press into, squeeze into. 5 *snow packed by the wind against the wall* compact, compress, press, tamp, ram. **pack in** 1 *a show that has been packing them in for years* draw in, pull in, attract, fill the theater (etc.) with. 2 *pack in one's job* resign, leave, give up, abandon; *inf.* chuck. **pack up** 1 *pack up one's equipment* put away, tidy up, clear up, store. 2 *decided to pack up for the day* finish, leave off, halt, stop, cease; *inf.* call it a day, pack it in.

package noun 1 *a Christmas package* parcel, packet, container, box, carton. 2 *agree to some items but not the (whole) package* lot, combination; agreement, contract, arrangement, deal.

package verb *package the gift* pack, pack up, wrap, wrap up, gift-wrap, box.

packet noun pack, carton, box, container, package, parcel.

pact noun agreement, treaty, deal, contract, settlement, bargain, compact, covenant, bond, concordat, entente, protocol.

pad noun 1 *a pad to prevent friction* padding, wadding, wad, stuffing, buffer. 2 *a pad to rest one's head on* cushion, pillow, bolster. 3 *write one's notes in a pad* notepad, writing pad, notebook; *inf.* memo pad.

pad verb *pad the package with tissue paper* pack, stuff, line, cushion, protect.

paddle noun *use the paddles to row ashore* oar, scull, sweep.

paddle verb *paddle one's way to the shore* row, pull, oar, scull, pole, punt.

pagan noun nonbeliever; heathen, infidel, idolater; pantheist, atheist, polytheist.

pagan adjective paganistic, heathen, heathenish, infidel, idolatrous, pantheistic, atheistic, polytheistic.

page noun 1 *a report 20 pages long* sheet, side, leaf, folio. 2 *his bravery will be recorded in the pages of history* report, account, anecdote, book, volume, writing. 3 *a glorious page in American history* chapter, event, episode, incident, time, period, stage, phase, epoch, era, point.

pageant noun display, spectacle, extravaganza, show, parade, scene, representation, tableau.

pageantry noun display, spectacle, magnificence, pomp, splendor, grandeur, glamour, flourish, glitter, theatricality, show, showiness; *inf.* pizazz.

pain noun 1 *a pain in her leg* soreness, hurt, ache, aching, throb, throbbing, smarting, twinge, pang, spasm, cramp, discomfort, irritation, tenderness. 2 *invalids enduring pain* suffering, agony, affliction, torture, torment. 3 *the pain of losing a loved one* hurt, sorrow, grief, heartache, sadness, distress, misery, wretchedness, anguish, woe. 4 *that job/person is a pain* nuisance, pest, bother, vexation, worry, source of aggravation; *inf.* pain in the neck, drag.

pain verb 1 *the memory of the event still pains her* hurt, grieve, sadden, distress, afflict, torment, torture. 2 *it pained her to tell him to go* worry, distress, trouble, hurt, vex, embarrass.

painful adjective 1 *a painful arm* sore, hurting, aching, throbbing, smarting, cramped, tender, inflamed, irritating, agonizing, excruciating. 2 *endure a painful experience* disagreeable, unpleasant, nasty, distressing, disquieting, disturbing, miserable, agonizing, harrowing. 3 *a painful climb* arduous, laborious, strenuous, rigorous, demanding, exacting, trying, hard, tough, difficult. **4** *it was painful to watch him work so slowly* irksome, tedious, annoying, vexatious.

painkiller noun *take painkillers for headaches* analgesic, anodyne, palliative, lenitive; aspirin, acetaminophen, ibuprofen, codeine, morphine.

painstaking adjective careful, thorough, assiduous, conscientious, meticulous, punctilious, sedulous, scrupulous.

paint noun **1** *buy paint for the walls* coloring, colorant, tint, dye, stain, pigment, gloss (paint), semigloss (paint), enamel, latex (paint), wash, whitewash. **2** *the paint required for his picture* colorant, tint, pigment, watercolor, oil, oil paint. **3** *apply paint to her face* makeup, cosmetic, greasepaint, maquillage; *inf.* warpaint.

paint verb **1** *paint the walls* decorate, color, tint, dye, stain, whitewash. **2** *paint slogans on the walls* daub, smear, plaster, spray-paint. **3** *painted the scene from her window* portray, depict, delineate, draw, sketch, represent. **paint the town red** celebrate; *inf.* go out on the town, whoop it up, carouse, party, step out.

painting noun picture, illustration, portrayal, depiction, delineation, representation, likeness, drawing, sketch, portrait, landscape, seascape, still life, oil painting, watercolor; *inf.* oil.

pair noun **1** *the pair walked down the road* twosome, two, couple, duo. **2** *a pair of pheasants* brace, couple. **3** *a pair of gloves* matched set, matching set. **4** *a coach and pair* team, yoke, span, two horses. **5** *the happy pair after their wedding* married couple, couple, husband and wife, partners, lovers.

pair verb **pair off** *pair off the children for games* arrange/group in pairs, pair up, put together. **pair up** *we paired up to search for clues* join up, link up, team up, unite, form a partnership.

pal noun friend, mate, companion, crony, comrade; *inf.* chum, buddy.

palace noun royal residence, castle; château, mansion, villa.

palatial adjective luxurious, deluxe, imposing, splendid, grand, magnificent, stately, majestic, opulent, sumptuous, plush; *inf.* posh.

pale adjective **1** *a pale complexion* white, white-faced, colorless, anemic, wan, drained, pallid, pasty, ashen, waxen. **2** *pale colors* light, light-colored, pastel, muted, low-key, restrained, faded, bleached, washed-out. **3** *the pale light of dawn* dim, faint, weak, feeble, thin.

pale verb **1** *she paled at the gruesome sight* blanch, grow pale, lose color. **2** *other*

problems paled beside their financial difficulties fade, dim, diminish, lessen, lose significance.

pall verb lose its (etc.) interest, lose attraction, cloy, become tedious, become boring, grow tiresome.

pall noun **1** *a pall of darkness* shroud, mantle, cloak. **2** *the news cast a pall over the gathering* cloud, shadow, gloom, depression, melancholy, somberness, gravity.

pallid adjective **1** *pallid faces* pale, white, white-faced, colorless, anemic, wan, drained, pasty, peaked, ashen, waxen, sickly, ghostly, ghastly, lurid, like death. **2** *a pallid performance* colorless, uninteresting, dull, boring, tedious, unimaginative, lifeless, uninspired, spiritless, bland, vapid.

pallor noun paleness, whiteness, wanness, pallidness, pastiness, ashenness, sickliness, ghastliness, luridness.

palpable adjective **1** *a palpable swelling* tangible, feelable, touchable, solid, concrete. **2** *a palpable error* obvious, apparent, clear, plain, evident, manifest, visible, conspicuous, patent, blatant, glaring, definite, unmistakable.

palpitate verb **1** *with her heart palpitating* pulsate, pulse, throb, flutter, quiver, vibrate, pound, thud, thump, pump. **2** *palpitating with fear* tremble, quiver, quake, quaver, shake.

paltry adjective **1** *a paltry sum of money* small, meager, trifling, minor, insignificant, trivial, derisory; *inf.* piddling. **2** *a paltry excuse/trick* mean, low, base, worthless, despicable, contemptible, miserable, wretched, sorry.

pamper verb spoil, cosset, indulge, over-indulge, humor, coddle, mollycoddle, baby.

pamphlet noun leaflet, booklet, brochure, circular, flyer.

pan noun **1** *pans simmering on the stove* saucepan, pot, frying pan, skillet, kettle, pressure cooker, casserole, wok. **2** *put a pan under the leak* container, vessel, receptacle.

panacea noun cure-all, elixir, nostrum, universal cure, universal remedy.

pancake noun hotcake, flapjack, griddle cake; crêpe, blintz; tortilla.

pandemonium noun uproar, tumult, turmoil, commotion, clamor, din, hullabaloo, hubbub, hue and cry, chaos, confusion, disorder, bedlam.

pang noun **1** *hunger pang* pain, twinge, spasm, ache. **2** *feel a pang of remorse* twinge, qualm, sensation.

panic noun alarm, fright, fear, terror, horror, trepidation, nervousness, agitation, hysteria, perturbation, dismay, disquiet.

panic verb **1** *panic at the sight of smoke* be alarmed, take fright, be scared, be terrified, be agitated, be hysterical, lose one's nerve, overreact, go to pieces; *inf.* lose one's cool, get the jitters, get/go into a tizzy. **2** *the crowd was panicked into a stampede* alarm, frighten, scare, terrify, petrify, startle, agitate, unnerve.

panorama noun **1** *the panorama from the top of the tower* view, vista, spectacle, aerial view, bird's-eye view. **2** *a panorama of political events* survey, overview, perspective, appraisal.

pant verb **1** *panting after climbing the hill* puff, huff and puff, blow, gasp, wheeze. **2** *panting for water/knowledge* long, yearn, pine, ache, hunger, thirst, burn; *inf.* have a yen.

pants plural noun trousers, slacks, jeans, blue jeans; Levis (*trademark*); *inf.* cords.

paper noun **1** *go for the morning paper* newspaper, journal, gazette, tabloid, scandal sheet, daily, weekly; *inf.* rag. **2** *lost the mortgage papers* legal paper, document, certificate, record, deed, instrument, assignment. **3** *write a paper on child development* essay, article, work, dissertation, treatise, thesis, monograph, study, report, analysis. **4** *put striped paper on the walls/shelves* wallpaper, wall covering, shelf paper. **on paper 1** *put your objections on paper* in writing, written down, in black and white. **2** *the plan was good only on paper* in theory, theoretically, hypothetically, in the abstract.

papers plural noun **1** *sign the adoption papers* document, certificate. *See* PAPER noun 2. **2** *escape using forged papers* identification papers, identification documents, identity card, ID. **3** *go through her papers after her death* personal papers, personal documents, letters, records, files.

par noun average, mean, standard, normal, norm. **below par** below average, substandard, inferior, lacking, wanting, second-rate, poor; *inf.* not up to scratch, not up to snuff. **on a par with** equal to, a match for, on a level with, on an equal footing with, of the same standard as, as good as. **par for the course** usual, normal, standard, typical, predictable, what one would expect. **up to par** satisfactory, acceptable, good enough, adequate, passable; *inf.* up to scratch, up to snuff.

parable noun allegory, morality tale/story, fable, lesson.

parade noun *parade of soldiers|Memorial Day parade* march, procession, progression, cavalcade, spectacle, pageant, array.

parade verb **1** *soldiers parading during the celebrations* march, go in columns, file by. **2** *parade their wealth/knowledge* display,

exhibit, show, demonstrate, air, make a show of, flaunt; *inf.* show off. **3** *parade up and down in her new hat* strut, swagger.

paradise noun **1** *believe in paradise after death* heaven, heavenly kingdom, kingdom of heaven, Elysium, the Elysian fields. **2** *Adam and Eve in paradise* the Garden of Eden, Eden. **3** *the resort island is a paradise* Eden, fairyland, Utopia, Shangri-la. **4** *it was paradise to be in love* heaven, bliss, ecstasy, seventh heaven.

paradox noun contradiction, self-contradiction, inconsistency, incongruity, anomaly, enigma, puzzle, absurdity, oxymoron.

paragon noun *a paragon of good behavior* ideal, model, pattern, exemplar, nonpareil, paradigm, standard, criterion, archetype, prototype, quintessence, epitome, apotheosis, acme.

parallel adjective **1** *parallel lines* side by side, equidistant, collateral. **2** *the judge considering a parallel case* similar, like, resembling, analogous, comparable, equivalent, corresponding, matching, duplicate. **3** *parallel processes* concurrent, coexistent, coexisting.

parallel noun **1** *find a parallel for the case* analog, counterpart, equivalent, correspondent, match, duplicate, equal. **2** *draw a parallel between the two cases* similarity, likeness, resemblance, analogy, correspondence, comparison, equivalence, symmetry.

parallel verb **1** *the case parallels the murder of her neighbor* resemble, be similar to, be like, bear a resemblance to, be analogous to, correspond to, compare with, be comparable/equivalent to. **2** *his account of the incident parallels the policeman's* match, correspond to, agree with, be in harmony with, conform to. **3** *his rowing feat has never been paralleled* match, equal, rival, emulate.

paralyze verb **1** *the spider's poison paralyzed the fly | he was paralyzed in the accident* immobilize, render/make powerless, numb, deaden, incapacitate, debilitate, disable, cripple. **2** *paralyze the transport system* immobilize, bring to a halt, bring to a standstill, freeze, put out of order/commission. **3** *paralyzed with fear* immobilize, render motionless, freeze, unnerve, terrify, shock, stun.

parameter noun *within the parameters of the budget* limit, limitation, limiting factor, restriction, constant, specification, guidelines, framework.

paramount adjective *financial considerations are paramount* most important, of greatest importance, of greatest significance, uppermost, supreme, predominant, foremost, first and foremost, preeminent, outstanding.

paramour noun lover, illicit lover; mistress, girlfriend, kept woman, inamorata; boyfriend, inamorato; *inf.* boy toy.

paranoid adjective suspicious, mistrustful, distrustful, fearful, insecure.

parapet noun 1 *the parapet of a balcony* wall, railing, handrail, fence, barrier. 2 *soldiers sheltering behind the parapet* fortification, barricade, rampart, bulwark, bank, embankment.

paraphernalia plural noun 1 *the artist's paraphernalia* equipment, gear, stuff, apparatus, implements, tools, materials, accoutrements, trappings, appurtenances. 2 *loaded down with all her paraphernalia* baggage, luggage, personal belongings, belongings, possessions, things, impedimenta; *inf.* stuff.

paraphrase verb reword, put in other words, rephrase, restate, rehash, interpret, gloss.

parasite noun hanger-on; sponge, sponger, cadger, leech, bloodsucker, drone; *inf.* scrounge, scrounger, freeloader.

parcel noun 1 *tie the parcel with string* package, packet, pack, bundle. 2 *a parcel of land* plot, tract, piece, lot, patch. 3 *a parcel of lies* pack, collection, assortment, mass, assemblage, bunch; *inf.* heap, load.

parcel verb **parcel out** *parcel out the food to the needy* distribute, dispense, allocate, allot, portion out, apportion, mete out, divide out, share out, hand out, deal out, dole out, carve up; *inf.* divvy up.

parched adjective 1 *parched ground/grass* dry, baked, burned, scorched, seared, desiccated, dehydrated, withered, shriveled, dried up, dried out. 2 *parched from walking in the heat* thirsty, dehydrated; *inf.* dry.

pardon noun 1 *seek their pardon* forgiveness, forbearance, indulgence, clemency, lenience, leniency, mercy. 2 *the accused received a pardon* reprieve, release, acquittal, absolution, amnesty, exoneration, exculpation.

pardon verb 1 *pardon me | could never pardon such an offense* forgive, excuse, condone, let off. 2 *the accused man was pardoned* reprieve, release, acquit, absolve, exonerate, exculpate.

parent noun 1 *resembles his parent* mother; father; procreator, progenitor, ancestor. 2 *the parent of all his misfortune* source, root, origin, originator, wellspring, fountain, cause, author, architect.

parentage noun *of humble parentage* family, birth, origins, extraction, ancestry, lineage, descent, heritage, pedigree.

pariah noun *a social pariah* outcast, leper, *persona non grata*, untouchable, undesirable.

parish noun 1 *local administrators of the parish* county, community, district; canton. 2 *the parish choosing a new minister* congregation, parishioners, churchgoers, flock, fold.

park noun 1 *children playing in the park* public park, green, recreation ground, playground, play area. 2 *park surrounding the estate* parkland, grassland, lawns, grounds. 3 *few fans left in the park* stadium, arena, ballpark, ball field, field, playing field.

parliament noun legislative assembly, legislature, lawmaking body, congress, senate, chamber, house, convocation, diet.

parliamentary adjective 1 *parliamentary assemblies* legislative, legislatorial, lawmaking, lawgiving, governmental, congressional, senatorial, democratic, representative. 2 *parliamentary behavior/language* orderly, proper, seemly, by the rules, according to the rule book.

parlor noun 1 *a beauty parlor* salon, shop, establishment, store. 2 *have tea in the parlor* sitting room, living room, drawing room, lounge.

parochial adjective *a parochial attitude to life* provincial, small-town, insular, narrow, narrow-minded, petty, small-minded, limited, restricted.

parody noun 1 *a parody of a Gothic novel* burlesque, lampoon, satire, caricature, mimicry, takeoff; *inf.* spoof, send-up. 2 *trial was a parody of justice* travesty, poor imitation, misrepresentation, perversion, corruption.

parody verb *parody an operatic aria* lampoon, satirize, caricature, burlesque, mimic; *inf.* send up.

parrot verb repeat, echo, copy, imitate, mimic, ape.

parry verb 1 *parry a blow* avert, deflect, block, rebuff, repel, repulse, ward off, fend off, stave off, turn aside, hold at bay. 2 *parry awkward questions* avoid, dodge, evade, elude, sidestep, circumvent; *inf.* duck.

part noun 1 *the early part of her life | part of an orange* portion, division, section, segment, bit, piece, fragment, scrap, slice, fraction, chunk, wedge. 2 *spare parts* component, bit, constituent, element, module. 3 *parts of the body* organ, member, limb. 4 *an unknown part of the country* area, region, sector, quarter, territory, neighborhood. 5 *a book/play in several parts* volume, book, episode. 6 *his part in the project* function, role, job, task, responsibility, capacity, participation, duty, charge. **7** *play the part of Hamlet* role, character. **8** *learn his part* lines, words, script, lyrics. **in part** *success due in part to good luck* partly, partially, to a certain extent/degree, to some extent/degree, somewhat, in some measure. **on the part of** *an error on the part of the instructor* made by, done by, carried out by, caused by, by. **take part in** *take part in the protest* participate in, join (in), engage in, play a part in, contribute to, associate oneself with, be involved in/with, share in, have a hand in. **take someone's part, take the part of** *take his mother's part in the quarrel | take the part of weaker candidates* take the side of, side with, support, lend/give support to, back, back up, abet.

part verb **1** *the crowd parted to let the police through* divide, separate, split, break up, disjoin. **2** *the police parting the crowd* divide, separate, split up, break up, sever, cleave. **3** *couples deciding to part* separate, split up, break up, part company, go their (etc.) separate ways, divorce, get divorced. **4** *exchange kisses before parting* take one's departure, take one's leave, leave, go, go away, say good-bye/farewell/adieu. **part with** *part with her last few dollars* give up, relinquish, forgo, surrender, let go of, renounce, sacrifice, yield, cede.

partake verb **partake of** **1** *partake of Christmas cheer* consume, eat, take, receive, drink, share in. **2** *their manner partook of insolence* suggest, have the qualities/attributes of, hint at, evidence, demonstrate, exhibit, show.

partial adjective **1** *a partial solution/eclipse* limited, incomplete, imperfect, fragmentary. **2** *a partial witness* biased, prejudiced, partisan, colored, one-sided, discriminatory, preferential, unjust, unfair, inequitable. **be partial to** *be partial to dark chocolate* have a liking for, like, love, be fond of, be keen on, have a weakness/taste for, have a soft spot for, have a predilection/proclivity/penchant for.

partiality noun **1** *condemn the partiality of the judge* bias, prejudice, partisanship, discrimination, preference, favoritism, unjustness, unfairness, inequity. **2** *their partiality for chocolate* liking, love, fondness, keenness, taste, weakness, soft spot, inclination, predilection, proclivity, penchant.

partially adverb partly, in part, somewhat, not wholly, not fully, half, to a certain extent/degree, to some extent/degree, fractionally, slightly.

participant noun participator, member, contributor, associate, sharer, partaker.

participate verb **participate in** take part in, join in, engage in, play a part in,

contribute to, associate oneself with, be involved in, share in, have a hand in.

participation noun part, contribution, association, involvement, partaking.

particle noun **1** *particles of dust* speck, spot, mote, atom, molecule. **2** *not a particle of common sense* iota, jot, whit, grain, bit, scrap, shred, morsel, mite, atom, hint, touch, trace, suggestion.

particular adjective **1** *in this particular case* specific, individual, single, distinct, precise. **2** *a matter of particular importance* special, especial, singular, peculiar, exceptional, unusual, uncommon, notable, noteworthy, remarkable, outstanding. **3** *particular about hygiene/food* fastidious, discriminating, selective, fussy, painstaking, meticulous, punctilious, exacting, demanding, critical, finicky; *inf.* persnickety, choosy, picky. **4** *require a particular account of the incident* detailed, exact, precise, faithful, close, thorough, blow-by-blow, itemized, painstaking, meticulous, punctilious, minute.

particularly adverb **1** *a book that is particularly good* especially, specially, singularly, peculiarly, distinctly, markedly, exceptionally, unusually, uncommonly, notably, remarkably, outstandingly, surprisingly. **2** *ask for him particularly* in particular, specifically, explicitly, expressly, specially, especially.

partisan noun **1** *a partisan of the breakaway party* supporter, adherent, devotee, backer, champion, upholder, follower, disciple, fan, votary. **2** *partisans fighting against the ruling power* guerrilla, resistance fighter, underground fighter.

partisan adjective *a partisan attitude to the legal dispute* biased, prejudiced, colored, one-sided, discriminatory, preferential, partial, unjust, unfair, inequitable.

partition noun **1** *the partition of Germany* division, subdivision, separation, splitting-up, breakup, severance. **2** *erect a partition to divide the room* divider, dividing wall, screen, barrier, wall, fence.

partition verb **1** *the Allies partitioned Germany* divide up, separate, split up, break up, sever. **2** *partition the room to make two sleeping areas* divide, divide up, subdivide, separate.

partly adverb in part, partially, somewhat, not wholly, not fully, half, to a certain extent/degree, to some extent/degree, in some measure, fractionally, slightly.

partner noun **1** *his partner in business* associate, colleague, coworker, teammate, collaborator, ally, comrade, consociate. **2** *his partner in crime* accomplice, confederate, accessory, collaborator, fellow conspirator; *inf.* sidekick. **3** *bring your partner* *to the party* wife/husband, spouse, mate, companion, girlfriend/boyfriend; date.

partnership noun **1** *work in partnership with his brother* association, cooperation, collaboration, alliance, union, fellowship, companionship. **2** *a partnership in crime* collusion, connivance, conspiracy. **3** *the partnership was bought out* company, firm, corporation, cooperative, conglomerate, syndicate.

party noun **1** *invite guests to a party* social gathering, social function, reception, celebration, festivity, soirée, orgy, bacchanal; *inf.* get-together, bash, shindig. **2** *a hunting/search party* group, band, company, squad, team, crew, contingent, detachment, unit. **3** *belong to a left-wing party* alliance, affiliation, association, caucus. **4** *both parties declared that they were right* side, faction, camp, set. **5** *a certain party who shall be nameless* person, individual, somebody, someone; *inf.* character.

pass[1] verb **1** *traffic passing along the road* go, move, proceed, progress, run, travel, roll, flow, course. **2** *cars passing us* overtake, outstrip, outdistance. **3** *pass the frontier* cross, traverse, go across, get through. **4** *pass the butter* hand over, give, transfer. **5** *the title passes to his eldest son* be transferred, be turned over, be signed over, go, devolve. **6** *time passed slowly* go by, proceed, progress, advance, roll by, slip by, glide by, flow by, elapse. **7** *how to pass the time* spend, occupy, fill, take up, use, employ, while away. **8** *pass all understanding* exceed, surpass, transcend. **9** *let the matter pass* go, go unheeded, go unnoticed, go unremarked, go undisputed, go uncensored. **10** *students passing their exams* get a passing grade in, get through, succeed in, meet the requirements of, pass muster in. **11** *the examiners passed everyone* let through, declare acceptable/adequate/satisfactory, accept, approve. **12** *pass the motion* accept, approve, adopt, authorize, ratify, sanction, validate, legalize. **13** *pass judgment* pronounce, utter, express, deliver, declare. **14** *after all that has passed* happen, occur, take place, befall, supervene. **15** *the storm passed* blow over, run its course, ebb, die out, fade away, evaporate, disappear, finish, end, terminate. **16** *pass urine* discharge, excrete, eliminate, evacuate, expel, emit. **pass for** *he could pass for 30* be taken for, be regarded as, be mistaken for. **pass off 1** *the demonstration passed off without incident* take place, happen, occur, be completed. **2** *pass him off as her husband* present as genuine, give a false identity, have accepted as genuine. **pass out 1** *passing out in the heat* faint, collapse, lose consciousness, black out, keel over, swoon. **2** *pass out the exam papers* hand out, distribute, give out, deal

out, dole out, allot, allocate. **pass over 1** *pass over the interruption and proceed* ignore, disregard, overlook, forget, pay no attention to, gloss over, take no notice of, turn a blind eye to. **2** *he was passed over for promotion* overlook, ignore, disregard, forget, neglect, omit. **pass up** *pass up an opportunity* fail to take advantage of, waive, reject, refuse, decline, neglect, let slip, ignore, brush aside, forgo.

pass[2] noun **1** *a pass to leave the military base* warrant, permit, authorization, license, passport, visa, safe-conduct. **2** *a pass to the theater* permit, free admission, complimentary ticket; *inf.* freebie. **3** *object to his passes* sexual advance, advance, overture; *inf.* proposition. **make a pass at** *make a pass at his friend's wife* make sexual advances/overtures to; *inf.* make a play for, proposition.

pass[3] noun *a mountain pass* gap, gorge, defile, col, canyon.

passable adjective **1** *a passable knowledge of the subject* adequate, tolerable, fair, acceptable, satisfactory, mediocre, middling, ordinary, average, run-of-the-mill, unexceptional, indifferent; *inf.* so-so, OK. **2** *roads scarcely passable in the snow* crossable, traversable, navigable, unblocked, unobstructed, open, clear.

passage noun **1** *the passage of time* passing, progress, advance, flow, course. **2** *passage through foreign lands* journey, voyage, transit, trek, crossing, trip, tour. **3** *denied passage to the country* access, entry, admission, safe-conduct, warrant, passport, visa. **4** *his passage from boyhood to manhood* change, changeover, transformation, transition, conversion, shift, switch. **5** *underground passages* road, route, path, way, track, trail, lane, channel, course, conduit. **6** *bicycles left in the passage* passageway, corridor, hall, hallway, vestibule. **7** *read aloud passages from the novel* extract, excerpt, quotation, citation, section, verse. **8** *the passage of the bill by Congress* acceptance, approval, adoption, authorization, ratification, sanction, validation, enactment, legalization.

passé adjective out-of-date, outdated, dated, outmoded, old-fashioned, obsolete, obsolescent, out of fashion, out of style, archaic, antiquated, antediluvian; *inf.* old hat, fuddy-duddy.

passenger noun rider, commuter, farepayer, traveler, fare.

passion noun **1** *do everything with great passion* intensity, fervor, fervidness, ardor, zeal, vehemence, fire, emotion, feeling, zest, enthusiasm, eagerness, excitement, animation. **2** *fly into a passion* rage, blind rage, fit of anger, temper, tantrum, fury, frenzy, paroxysm. **3** *his passion for her* love, desire, lust, concupiscence, ardor, infatuation. **4** *a passion for motorcycles* enthusiasm, fascination, keen interest, obsession, fixation, craze, mania.

passionate adjective **1** *a passionate entreaty/person* impassioned, intense, fervent, fervid, ardent, zealous, vehement, fiery, emotional, heartfelt, zestful, enthusiastic, eager, excited, animated. **2** *a passionate lover* ardent, aroused, desirous, hot, sexy, amorous, sensual, erotic, lustful; *inf.* turned-on.

passive adjective **1** *play a passive role in the business* inactive, nonactive, inert, nonparticipating, uninvolved. **2** *a passive attitude to their invaders* unresisting, nonresistant, unassertive, yielding, submissive, compliant, pliant, acquiescent, quiescent, resigned, obedient, tractable, malleable. **3** *look on with a passive expression | a passive person* impassive, emotionless, unmoved, unresponsive, undemonstrative, dispassionate, detached, distant, remote, aloof, indifferent.

password noun watchword, keyword, signal, word, open sesame, shibboleth.

past adjective **1** *in times past* gone by, gone, bygone, elapsed, over, ended, former, long ago. **2** *the past few months* recent, preceding, last, latter, foregone. **3** *past achievements/chairmen* former, previous, prior, foregoing, late, erstwhile, one-time, sometime, ex-.

past noun **in the past** in days gone by, in bygone days, in former times, formerly, previously, before.

pastel adjective *pastel colors* pale, soft, delicate, muted, subdued, faint, low-key.

pastime noun hobby, leisure activity, game, recreation, diversion, amusement, entertainment, distraction, relaxation.

pastor noun minister, vicar, parson, priest, rector, reverend, clergyman, clergywoman, churchman, churchwoman, ecclesiastic, cleric, divine.

pastoral adjective **1** *a pastoral scene* rural, country, rustic, simple, idyllic, innocent, Arcadian, bucolic, georgic. **2** *his pastoral duties* ministerial, vicarial, parsonical, priestly, rectorial, ecclesiastical, clerical.

pastry noun pie, strudel, tart, puff pastry, doughnut, cruller, Danish pastry; *inf.* Danish.

pat verb **1** *pat the child on the head | pat the dog* stroke, caress, pet. **2** *pat the mixture* tap, slap, dab. **pat someone on the back** *pat himself on the back for bringing off the deal* congratulate, praise, commend, compliment, applaud.

pat noun **1** *a pat on the cheek* stroke, touch, caress. **2** *flatten the mixture with a pat* tap,

slap, dab. **3** *a pat of butter* dab, lump, cake, portion.

patch noun **1** *put a patch over the hole* piece of cloth, scrap, piece of material. **2** *a patch over the eye* cover, covering, pad, shield. **3** *patch of ground* plot, area, piece, lot, tract, parcel.

patch verb **1** *patch the pants* cover, mend, repair, sew, sew up, stitch, stitch up. **2** *patch the roof* repair, reinforce, fix. **patch up** *patch up the quarrel* settle, resolve, set right.

patchwork noun *a patchwork of different styles* pastiche, hodgepodge, mishmash, jumble, medley, mélange, miscellany, potpourri, mosaic, blend, mixture.

patent noun license, copyright, registered trademark.

patent adjective **1** *her patent dislike of him* obvious, clear, plain, evident, apparent, manifest, transparent, conspicuous, blatant, unmistakable, unconcealed. **2** *patent medicine* patented, proprietary, licensed, branded, brand-name.

paternal adjective **1** *take a paternal interest in the boy* fatherly, fatherlike, patriarchal, protective, concerned, solicitous, kindly, benevolent. **2** *his paternal grandfather* patrilineal, patrimonial, on the father's side.

path noun **1** *a path through the forest* footpath, track, trail, walk, walkway. **2** *the moon's path around the earth* course, route, circuit, track, orbit, trajectory. **3** *unable to predict the path he will take* course of action, procedure, direction, approach, method, system, strategy. **4** *the path to success* way, road, avenue, route.

pathetic adjective **1** *children in rags were a pathetic sight* pitiful, pitiable, piteous, moving, touching, poignant, affecting, distressing, heartbreaking, heart-rending, sad, wretched, mournful, woeful. **2** *a pathetic attempt/performance* pitiful, lamentable, deplorable, miserable, wretched, feeble, woeful, sorry, poor, contemptible, inadequate, unsatisfactory, worthless.

pathological adjective **1** *a pathological condition* morbid, diseased. **2** *a pathological liar* irrational, compulsive, obsessive.

pathos noun poignancy, pity, piteousness, sadness, plaintiveness, sentiment, compassion.

patience noun **1** *wait in line with patience* calmness, composure, even-temperedness, equanimity, serenity, tranquillity, restraint, imperturbability, tolerance, indulgence, forbearance, resignation, stoicism, fortitude; *inf.* unflappability, cool. **2** *a task requiring patience* perseverance, persistence, endurance, tenacity, assiduity, diligence, staying power, indefatigability, doggedness.

patient adjective uncomplaining, serene, calm, composed, even-tempered, tranquil, restrained, imperturbable, inexcitable, tolerant, accommodating, long-suffering, forbearing, indulgent, resigned, stoical; *inf.* unflappable, cool.

patio noun terrace, veranda, deck, piazza.

patriotic adjective nationalistic, loyal, chauvinistic, flag-waving, jingoistic.

patrol verb *soldiers patrolling the border area* monitor, watch, make the rounds of, guard, range, police, keep watch on, keep guard on.

patrol noun **1** *make regular patrols of the border area* round, sentry duty, policing, watch, guard, vigil, monitoring. **2** *report the matter to the patrol* sentinel, sentry, garrison, guard, watchman, watch, policeman/policewoman.

patron noun **1** *a patron of the arts* sponsor, backer, benefactor/benefactress, promoter, friend, helper, supporter, upholder, champion, protector; *inf.* angel. **2** *parking for patrons only* customer, client, frequenter, shopper, buyer, purchaser; *inf.* regular.

patronage noun **1** *customers taking their patronage elsewhere* trade, custom, business, commerce, shopping, buying, purchasing. **2** *their patronage of the arts* sponsorship, backing, funding, financing, promotion, help, aid, assistance, support, encouragement, championship. **3** *under the patronage of the crime boss* power of appointment, aegis, protection.

patronize verb **1** *patronize her subordinates* condescend to, look down on, talk down to, treat with condescension/disdain, treat contemptuously, be snobbish to. **2** *patronize the new salon* frequent, shop at, buy from, be a customer of, be a client of, do business with. **3** *patronize the arts* sponsor, back, fund, finance, promote, help, aid, assist, support, encourage, champion, protect.

patronizing adjective *a patronizing attitude to younger people* condescending, supercilious, superior, haughty, lofty, lordly, disdainful, scornful, contemptuous, snobbish; *inf.* uppity, snooty.

patter verb **1** *mice pattering across the attic floor* scurry, scuttle, trip. **2** *rain pattering on the window* pitter-patter, tap, drum, beat, pound, pelt.

patter noun **1** *the patter of mice on the floor above* scurrying, scuttling, tripping. **2** *the patter of rain on the window* pitter-patter, tap, tapping, drumming, beat, beating, pounding, rat-a-tat.

pattern noun **1** *the pattern on the wallpaper* design, decoration, motif, marking, ornamentation, device, figure. **2** *study the rats' behavior pattern* system, order, arrangement, method, sequence. **3** *a knitting pattern* design, guide, blueprint, model, plan, template, stencil, instructions.

pattern verb *pattern himself on his father* model, mold, style, form, shape.

paucity noun *a paucity of evidence* scarcity, sparseness, dearth, shortage, insufficiency, deficiency, lack, want, meagerness, paltriness.

paunch noun **1** *developing quite a paunch* potbelly, protruding stomach/abdomen, pot; *inf.* beer belly. **2** *a belt around his paunch* stomach, belly, abdomen; *inf.* gut.

pauper noun beggar, mendicant, down-and-out, penniless person, homeless person.

pause noun break, interruption, lull, respite, stay, discontinuation, gap, interlude, intermission, interval, rest, delay, hesitation; *inf.* letup, breather.

pause verb discontinue, break, stop, halt, cease, take a break, desist, rest, hold back, delay, hesitate, waver; *inf.* let up, take a breather.

pave verb *pave the front path* concrete, asphalt, flag, tile, tar, macadamize. **pave the way** *pave the way for radical change* prepare, clear the way, lay the foundations/groundwork.

pawn verb *pawn her necklace to pay the rent* pledge, give as security, mortgage; *inf.* hock, put in hock.

pawn noun *pawns in the leader's struggle for power* tool, cat's-paw, instrument, puppet, dupe; *inf.* stooge.

pay verb **1** *pay him for work done* remunerate, reimburse, recompense, reward, indemnify, requite. **2** *pay hundreds of dollars for his services* spend, expend, lay out, part with, disburse, hand over, remit, render; *inf.* shell out, cough up. **3** *pay his debts/bill* settle, discharge, meet, clear, square, honor, liquidate, foot, defray. **4** *the business does not pay* make money, be profitable, be remunerative, make a return. **5** *investments paying large sums of money* yield, return, produce, bring in; *inf.* rake in. **6** *pay compliments* give, bestow, extend, offer, proffer, render. **7** *make him pay for his mistakes* atone, suffer, pay a penalty, make atonement. **pay back 1** *pay back the loan* repay, return, reimburse. **2** *pay her back for her cruel behavior* repay, punish, avenge oneself on, get revenge on. **pay off 1** *pay off his debts* pay in full, settle, discharge, meet, clear, square, honor, liquidate. **2** *his hard work paid off* meet with success, be successful, be effective, work, get results, be profitable.

pay noun *get one's pay at the end of the month* salary, wages, earnings, fee, remuneration, recompense, reimbursement, reward, stipend, emoluments.

payable adjective *a bill that is payable now* due, owed, owing, outstanding.

payment noun 1 *receive payment for his services* wages, fee. See PAY noun. 2 *in payment of the account* settlement, discharge, clearance, squaring, liquidation. 3 *make twelve monthly payments* installment, premium, amount, remittance.

peace noun 1 *the peace of the countryside* tranquillity, restfulness, calm, quiet, quietness, stillness. 2 *a mind seeking peace* peacefulness, tranquillity, serenity, calmness, composure, placidity, rest, repose, contentment. 3 *hope for peace between the countries* harmony, accord, concord, amity, goodwill, friendship, cordiality, nonaggression, nonviolence, cease-fire. 4 *the Peace of Versailles* treaty, truce, agreement, armistice, cessation of hostilities.

peaceable adjective 1 *a peaceable person* placid, gentle, mild, nonaggressive, nonviolent, noncombative, easygoing, goodnatured, even-tempered, amiable, pacific, pacifistic, dovish, irenic. 2 *a peaceable set of negotiations* harmonious, amicable, friendly, cordial.

peaceful adjective 1 *in a peaceful setting* tranquil, restful, quiet, calm, still, undisturbed. 2 *a peaceful mind* tranquil, serene, calm, composed, placid, at rest, untroubled, unworried. 3 *peaceful conditions between the two countries* harmonious, amicable, friendly, cordial, nonviolent.

peacemaker noun *call in a third party as a peacemaker* conciliator, mediator, arbitrator, pacifier, appeaser, peacemonger.

peak noun 1 *snow on the mountain peaks* top, summit, crest, pinnacle. 2 *at the peak of his career as a singer* height, high point, climax, culmination, zenith, acme, meridian, apogee, apex, prime.

peak verb *prices peak just before Christmas* climax, culminate, crest, reach the high point.

peaked adjective pale, wan, drained, drawn, pallid, pasty, white, anemic.

peal noun *hear the peal of the bells/thunder* ring, ringing, chime, clang, resounding, reverberation, tintinnabulation, roar, boom, rumble, crash, clap.

peal verb *bells/thunder pealing* ring, chime, clang, resound, reverberate, roar, boom, rumble, crash.

peasant noun farm worker/laborer, sharecropper, peon, rustic; serf; bumpkin, provincial.

peck verb bite, strike, hit, tap, rap, jab.
peck at nibble, pick at, eat sparingly of.

peculiar adjective 1 *a peculiar smell | peculiar clothes* strange, odd, queer, funny, curious, unusual, abnormal, eccentric, unconventional, bizarre, weird, quaint, outlandish, offbeat. 2 *have a peculiar walk* characteristic, distinctive, individual, distinguishing, special, unique, idiosyncratic. **peculiar to** *peculiar to that period of history* belonging to, characteristic of, typical of, representative of, indicative of, exclusive to.

peculiarity noun 1 *the peculiarity of the smell | the peculiarity of her clothes* strangeness, oddness, queerness, curiousness, abnormality, eccentricity, unconventionality, bizarreness, weirdness, outlandishness. 2 *a peculiarity of the breed* characteristic, feature, quality, property, trait, attribute, mark, stamp, hallmark.

pedagogue noun 1 *learning from a pedagogue* teacher, tutor, lecturer, instructor, educator. 2 *a pedagogue without inspiration* dogmatist, pedant.

pedant noun perfectionist, formalist, dogmatist, literalist, precisionist, quibbler, hairsplitter, casuist, sophist, pettifogger; *inf.* nitpicker.

pedantic adjective precise, exact, scrupulous, punctilious, meticulous, formalist, precisionist, dogmatic, literalistic, quibbling, hairsplitting, casuistic, sophistic, pettifogging; *inf.* nitpicking.

peddle verb *peddle goods around town* hawk, sell, tout, market, vend; *inf.* push.

pedestal noun *a bust of Shakespeare on a pedestal* base, support, stand, foundation, pillar, column, plinth. **put on a pedestal** *put his father on a pedestal* idealize, exalt, glorify, adulate, worship, deify.

pedestrian noun walker, stroller, hiker.

pedestrian adjective 1 *pedestrian traffic* on foot, walking. 2 *pedestrian prose* plodding, unimaginative, uninspired, unexciting, dull, flat, prosaic, stodgy, mundane, humdrum, banal, run-of-the-mill, commonplace, ordinary, mediocre.

pedigree noun 1 *proud of his aristocratic pedigree* ancestry, descent, lineage, line, extraction, heritage, parentage, birth, family, strain, stock, blood, stirps. 2 *draw up the dog's pedigree* genealogy, family tree, ancestral record, line of descent.

peek verb peep, glance, take a stealthy look; *inf.* sneak a look.

peek noun peep, glance, glimpse, secret look, sneaky look.

peel verb *peel the fruit | peel the wallpaper from the walls* pare, skin, decorticate, strip, remove, take off.

peel noun *the peel of the fruit* rind, skin, covering, zest, shell, husk, epicarp.

peep[1] verb **1** *peep through the keyhole* peek, glance, take a secret look; *inf.* sneak a look. **2** *crocuses peeping through the snow* appear, emerge, show, come into view, spring up, pop up.

peep[2] noun *take a peep at the secret document* peek, glance. *See* PEEK noun.

peep[3] verb *fledglings peeping in the nest* cheep, chirp, chirrup, tweet, twitter, pipe, squeak.

peep[4] noun **1** *the peep of a baby bird* cheep, chirp, chirrup, tweet, twitter, piping, squeak. **2** *not a peep out of the children* sound, noise, cry, utterance, word.

peer verb *peer at the faded handwriting* squint, look closely, stare, gaze, narrow one's eyes.

peer noun **1** *remained close to his peers from college* compeer, associate, colleague, fellow, equal, match, like, coequal, confrère. **2** *the peers of the realm* noble, nobleman, aristocrat, lord, patrician.

peerless adjective *a peerless performance* incomparable, matchless, unrivaled, unsurpassed, unequaled, unparalleled, superlative, nonpareil.

peeve verb *his behavior really peeved her* irritate, annoy, anger, vex, provoke, upset, exasperate, irk, pique, nettle; *inf.* aggravate, miff.

peevish adjective irritable, fractious, cross, crabby, cranky, petulant, sulky, moody, grumpy, ill-tempered, ill-natured, ill-humored, surly, churlish, touchy, testy, snappish, crusty, splenetic.

peg noun pin, nail, dowel, spike, skewer, brad, screw, bolt, post. **take down a peg or two** humble, humiliate, mortify, abase.

pejorative adjective *pejorative remarks* derogatory, disparaging, deprecatory, slighting.

pell-mell adverb *children rushing pell-mell from the school* helter-skelter, headlong, impetuously, recklessly, hurriedly, hastily.

pelt verb *pelt the fortress with gunfire* bombard, shower, attack, assail, batter, pepper.

pelt noun *a beaver's pelt* skin, hide, fleece, coat, fur.

pen noun *put animals in a pen* enclosure, fold, coop, pound, compound, corral, paddock.

penal adjective **1** *a penal institution* disciplinary, punitive, corrective, retributive. **2** *a penal offense* punishable, indictable, chargeable, impeachable.

penalize verb **1** *penalized for arriving late* punish, discipline, castigate, correct. **2** *people penalized for being poor* handicap, disadvantage.

penalty noun **1** *have to pay a penalty for his crime* punishment, retribution, castigation, penance, fine, forfeit, sentence,

mulct. **2** *one of the penalties of living in the city* handicap, disadvantage, drawback, snag, obstacle.

penance noun atonement, reparation, amends, mortification, expiation; punishment, penalty.

penchant noun *a penchant for bright colors* fondness, preference, taste, partiality, soft spot, inclination, bent, proclivity, predilection, love, passion, desire, fancy, whim, weakness, liking.

pending adjective **1** *the lawsuit then pending* undecided, unsettled, unresolved, uncertain, awaiting action, undetermined, up in the air. **2** *a decision is pending* imminent, impending, on the way, coming, approaching, forthcoming, near, nearing, close at hand.

penetrate verb **1** *penetrate the skin* pierce, bore, perforate, stab, prick, gore, spike. **2** *penetrate the dense forest* enter, infiltrate. **3** *terror penetrated her whole being* permeate, pervade, fill, imbue, suffuse, saturate. **4** *our explanation did not penetrate* register, be grasped, get through, have an impact. **5** *unable to penetrate the mystery* understand, comprehend, apprehend, fathom, get to the bottom of, make out, solve, resolve, work out, figure out, unravel, decipher; *inf.* crack.

penetrating adjective **1** *a penetrating wind* sharp, keen, biting, stinging, harsh. **2** *a penetrating voice* shrill, loud, strong, piercing, ear-piercing, intrusive. **3** *a penetrating mind* keen, sharp, sharp-witted, discerning, perceptive, percipient, intelligent, incisive, astute, shrewd, acute, discriminating. **4** *ask penetrating questions* searching, sharp, incisive, analytic, in-depth.

penetration noun **1** *the penetration of the skin* piercing, perforation, pricking, stabbing. **2** *the penetration of the forest* entry, infiltration. **3** *penetration of the mystery is difficult* comprehension, apprehension, fathoming, resolution, solution, understanding; *inf.* cracking. **4** *impressed by the penetration of their minds* keenness, sharpness, sharp-wittedness, discernment, perception, perceptiveness, insight, intelligence, incisiveness, astuteness, shrewdness, acuteness, acuity, discrimination.

penitence noun *show penitence for his sins* repentance, contrition, compunction, regret, remorse, ruefulness, self-reproach, shame, sorrow.

penitent adjective *feel penitent about his sin* | *penitent children apologizing* repentant, contrite, regretful, remorseful, sorry, apologetic, conscience-stricken, rueful, ashamed, abject.

pennant noun banner, banderole, streamer, flag, ensign, colors, bunting.

penniless adjective impecunious, penurious, impoverished, indigent, poor, poverty-stricken, destitute, bankrupt, hard up; *inf.* broke, flat broke, strapped.

penny-pinching adjective mean, miserly, parsimonious, niggardly, tight-fisted, close-fisted, penurious, scrimping, skimping, close, money-grubbing, Scroogelike; *inf.* stingy, tight.

pensive adjective *in a pensive mood* thoughtful, reflective, contemplative, meditative, pondering, cogitative, ruminative, absorbed, preoccupied, serious, wistful, melancholy.

pent-up adjective *pent-up feelings* bottled-up, repressed, suppressed, restrained, constrained, curbed, bridled.

penury noun *unemployment reduced them to penury* indigence, destitution, privation, pennilessness, impecuniousness, impoverishment, need, want, pauperism, bankruptcy, insolvency.

people noun **1** *plural noun too many people in the hall/country* persons, individuals, human beings, humans, mortals, living souls. **2** *a warlike people* race, tribe, clan, nation, country, population, populace. **3** *plural noun issue to be decided by the people* citizens, general public, public, populace, electorate, masses, rank and file, commonalty, multitude, hoi polloi, rabble.

pep noun *a performance full of pep* spirit, liveliness, animation, life, sparkle, effervescence, verve, ebullience, vivacity, fire, dash, zest, exuberance, élan, vigor, vim, brio; *inf.* zip.

perceive verb **1** *perceive someone walking down the hill* spot, observe, glimpse, notice, make out, discern, behold, espy, detect, witness, see, catch sight of. **2** *perceive the difference between right and wrong* discern, appreciate, recognize, be cognizant of, be aware of, know, grasp, understand, comprehend, apprehend.

perceptible adjective *no perceptible improvement* perceivable, discernible, noticeable, detectable, distinguishable, appreciable, visible, observable, distinct, clear, plain, evident, apparent, obvious, manifest, conspicuous, patent, palpable, tangible.

perception noun **1** *his perception of the problem* discernment, appreciation, recognition, cognizance, awareness, consciousness, knowledge, grasp, understanding, comprehension, apprehension, notion, conception, idea, sense. **2** *show great perception in his performance | his analysis shows great perception* perspicacity, discernment, perceptiveness, understanding, discrimination, insight, intuition, feeling, sensitivity.

perceptive adjective **1** *a perceptive child noticed the fire* observant, alert, sharp-eyed, sharp-sighted, keen-sighted, vigilant. **2** *one of the more perceptive theater critics | a perceptive analysis* discerning, perspicacious, percipient, shrewd, discriminating, intuitive, responsive, sensitive, penetrating, astute.

perch noun pole, rod, branch, roost.

perch verb sit, rest, roost, settle, alight, land.

percolate verb **1** *liquid percolating through the strainer* filter, filtrate, drain, drip, ooze, seep, leach. **2** *percolate the coffee* strain, filter, filtrate, sieve, sift. **3** *coffee percolating in the pot* brew, bubble; *inf.* perk.

perdition noun damnation, hellfire, hell, spiritual destruction.

peremptory adjective **1** *receive a peremptory request from the boss | behave in a peremptory manner* imperious, high-handed, imperative, overbearing, dogmatic, autocratic, dictatorial, domineering, arbitrary, tyrannical, despotic, arrogant, overweening, supercilious, lordly. **2** *a peremptory judgment* incontrovertible, irreversible, binding, absolute, final, conclusive, decisive, definitive, categorical, irrefutable.

perennial adjective *a subject of perennial interest* perpetual, everlasting, eternal, never-ending, undying, ceaseless, abiding, enduring, lasting, persisting, permanent, constant, unfailing, unchanging, continuing, persistent, recurrent.

perfect adjective **1** *a perfect set of china* complete, full, whole, entire. **2** *a perfect fool* absolute, complete, out-and-out, thorough, thoroughgoing, downright, utter, sheer, consummate, unmitigated, unqualified. **3** *a perfect performance/mother* flawless, faultless, unmarred, ideal, impeccable, consummate, immaculate, exemplary, superb, superlative, supreme, excellent, wonderful, model. **4** *a perfect evening* superb, exquisite, superlative, excellent, wonderful, marvelous; *inf.* terrific, fantastic, fabulous. **5** *a perfect copy* exact, precise, accurate, faithful, correct, right, close, true, strict; *inf.* right-on. **6** *the perfect present* ideal, just right, right, appropriate, fitting, fit, suitable, apt.

perfect verb *perfect the technique* polish, refine, elaborate, complete, make perfect, render faultless/flawless, improve, better, consummate, put the finishing touches to.

perfection noun **1** *working on the perfection of their technique* improvement, betterment, polishing, refinement, completion, consummation. **2** *try to achieve perfection in his work* flawlessness, faultlessness, consummation, impeccability, immaculateness, exemplariness, superbness.

perfectionist noun precisionist, precisian, purist, formalist, stickler for perfection.

perfectly adverb **1** *perfectly happy/miserable* absolutely, utterly, completely, altogether, entirely, wholly, totally, thoroughly, fully. **2** *the cake turned out perfectly* to perfection, flawlessly, faultlessly, without blemish, ideally, impeccably, immaculately, superbly, exquisitely, superlatively, wonderfully.

perfidious adjective treacherous, traitorous, treasonous, false, untrue, disloyal, unfaithful, deceitful, double-dealing, duplicitous, dishonest, two-faced.

perforate verb **1** *perforate the skin* pierce, puncture, prick, stab, gore, bore, penetrate, spike. **2** *perforate paper* make holes in, punch holes in, punch, honeycomb.

perform verb **1** *perform acts of charity/perform feats of skill* carry out, execute, discharge, conduct, effect, bring about, bring off, accomplish, achieve, fulfill, complete. **2** *perform in Hamlet/perform a new symphony* act, play, appear, execute. **3** *a car performing well* function, work, operate, run, go.

performance noun **1** *faithful in the performance of his duty* execution, discharge, conducting, effecting, accomplishment, achievement, carrying out, fulfillment. **2** *watch a musical performance* concert, show, production, entertainment, act, presentation; *inf.* gig. **3** *his performance of Hamlet* representation, acting, playing, staging.

performer noun **1** *applaud the performers* actor/actress, player, entertainer, artist, artiste, thespian, trouper, musician, singer, dancer. **2** *performers of charitable acts/a performer of strange feats* executor, worker, doer, operator, architect, author.

perfume noun **1** *the perfume of roses* scent, fragrance, aroma, smell, bouquet, redolence. **2** *buy some French perfume* scent, fragrance, balm, essence, eau de toilette, toilet water, eau de cologne, cologne.

perfunctory adjective *take a perfunctory look at the contract* cursory, superficial, desultory, mechanical, automatic, routine, sketchy, brief, hasty, hurried, rapid, fleeting, quick, fast, offhand, casual, indifferent, careless, inattentive, negligent.

perhaps adverb *perhaps we will meet him on the way* maybe, possibly, it may be that, conceivably, feasibly; *lit.* peradventure.

peril noun danger, jeopardy, risk, hazard, menace, threat.

perilous adjective dangerous, menacing, risky, precarious, hazardous, chancy, threatening, unsafe, fraught with danger.

perimeter noun boundary, border, frontier, limits, confines, edge, margin, fringe, periphery, circumference.

period noun **1** *over a period of several years* time, space, spell, interval, term, stretch, span. **2** *absent for a period* time, while, spell. **3** *the period of the French Revolution* time, days, age, era, epoch. **4** *irregular periods* menstruation, menstrual flow, monthly flow, menses.

periodic adjective recurrent, recurring, repeated, cyclical, cyclic, regular, intermittent, occasional, infrequent, sporadic.

periodical noun *subscribe to periodicals* journal, publication, magazine, newspaper, newsletter, review, organ, almanac, yearbook, annual, quarterly, monthly, weekly, daily; *inf.* paper, rag.

peripatetic adjective itinerant, traveling, wandering, roving, roaming, nomadic, migrant, migratory.

periphery noun *on the periphery of the town/group* outskirts, boundary, border, outer limits, edge, margin, fringe, perimeter.

perish verb **1** *soldiers perishing in battle* die, be killed, lose one's life, breathe one's last; *inf.* bite the dust, kick the bucket. **2** *the old theories having perished* die away, disappear, vanish, disintegrate, be destroyed. **3** *food perishing in the heat* rot, decay, decompose, go bad, go sour.

perk verb **perk up 1** *perking up when his friends arrived* cheer up, brighten up, be gladdened, rally, revive, take heart; *inf.* buck up, pep up. **2** *the vacation perked them up* cheer up, brighten up, give someone a boost/lift.

permanent adjective **1** *the couple's separation is permanent/a permanent disability* everlasting, perpetual, eternal, enduring, perennial, abiding, constant, persistent, unending, never-ending, immutable, unchangeable, inalterable, invariable. **2** *a permanent job* lasting, long-lasting, stable, fixed, established, sound, firm.

permeate verb *cooking smells permeating the whole house/water permeating the soil* spread through, pervade, fill, saturate, be diffused through, imbue, penetrate, infiltrate, percolate through, pass through, soak through, seep through, leak through, leach through.

permissible adjective permitted, allowable, admissible, acceptable, tolerated, authorized, sanctioned, legal, lawful, legitimate, licit, within bounds; *inf.* legit.

permission noun authorization, sanction, leave, license, dispensation, empowerment, allowance, consent, assent, acquiescence, go-ahead, thumbs up, agreement, approval; *inf.* green light.

permissive adjective *a permissive parent/upbringing* indulgent, lenient, unrestricted, overindulgent, liberal, tolerant, broad-minded, open-minded, easygoing, forbearing, latitudinarian, lax, unprescriptive.

permit verb *parents not permitting the children to go | not permit talking in class* allow, let, authorize, give leave, sanction, grant, license, empower, enable, consent to, assent to, acquiesce in, give the goahead to, agree to, approve of, tolerate, countenance, suffer, brook; *inf.* give the green light to.

permit noun *a permit to sell food | a permit to enter the country* license, authorization, warrant, sanction, pass, passport, visa.

pernicious adjective *a pernicious influence on society* destructive, ruinous, injurious, damaging, harmful, hurtful, detrimental, deleterious, deadly, lethal, fatal, wicked, evil, bad, malign, malevolent, malignant, noxious, poisonous, venomous.

perpendicular adjective upright, vertical, at right angles, at 90 degrees.

perpetrate verb *perpetrate a crime* commit, carry out, perform, execute, effect, effectuate, bring about, be guilty of; *inf.* pull off.

perpetual adjective **1** *a state of perpetual bliss | the perpetual snow of the Arctic* everlasting, eternal, never-ending, unending, endless, undying, perennial, permanent, perdurable, lasting, abiding, persisting, enduring, constant, unfailing, unchanging, unvarying, invariable. **2** *work with perpetual noise* incessant, ceaseless, nonstop, continuous, uninterrupted, unbroken, unremitting. **3** *tired of their perpetual complaints* interminable, persistent, frequent, continual, recurrent, repeated.

perpetuate verb *perpetuate the myth that he was a hero* preserve, conserve, sustain, maintain, continue, immortalize, eternalize.

perplex verb *her behavior perplexed him* puzzle, baffle, mystify, stump, bewilder, confound, confuse, nonplus, disconcert, dismay, dumbfound; *inf.* bamboozle.

perplexing adjective **1** *her perplexing behavior* puzzling, baffling, mystifying, mysterious, bewildering, confusing, disconcerting, unaccountable, strange, weird. **2** *a perplexing problem* complicated, involved, intricate, complex, difficult, thorny, knotty, taxing, trying, vexing.

perquisite noun *a perquisite of the job* fringe benefit, benefit, advantage, bonus, dividend, extra, plus; *inf.* perk, freebie.

persecute verb **1** *persecute people for their beliefs* oppress, tyrannize, abuse, mistreat, maltreat, ill-treat, molest, afflict, torment, torture, victimize, martyr. **2** *celebrities persecuted by the press* harass, pester, hound, badger, vex, bother, worry, annoy; *inf.* hassle.

perseverance noun persistence, tenacity, pertinacity, determination, resolve, purposefulness, obstinacy, insistence, intransigence, patience, application, diligence, assiduity.

persevere verb persist, keep going, continue, carry on, struggle, work, be tenacious, be resolute, be purposeful, not give up, be diligent; *inf.* plug away, stick to one's guns, be determined.

persist verb **1** *persist in his efforts to win* continue, carry on. *See* PERSEVERE. **2** *the cold weather persisted* continue, last, remain, linger, hold, carry on, keep on, keep up.

persistence noun *with persistence he got a job* tenacity, determination. *See* PERSEVERANCE.

persistent adjective **1** *persistent people refusing to give up* tenacious, pertinacious, determined, resolute, purposeful, obstinate, stubborn, insistent, intransigent, obdurate, intractable, patient, diligent. **2** *persistent rain* constant, continual, continuous, interminable, incessant, endless, unremitting, unrelenting, relentless. **3** *a persistent cough* chronic, frequent, repetitive, repetitious.

persnickety adjective fussy, punctilious, finicky, fastidious, overparticular, particular; *inf.* nitpicking, choosy, picky.

person noun individual, human being, human, creature, living soul, soul, mortal; *inf.* character.

personable adjective pleasant, agreeable, amiable, affable, likable, charming, nice, presentable.

personage noun *events attended by political personages* public figure, dignitary, notable, celebrity, personality, VIP, luminary; *inf.* big shot.

personal adjective **1** *his reasons for leaving are personal* private, confidential, intimate, secret. **2** *a personal style of prose* individual, idiosyncratic, characteristic, unique, peculiar. **3** *receive the personal attention of the manager* individual, special.

personality noun **1** *an unassuming personality* nature, disposition, character, temperament, makeup, psyche. **2** *man with little personality* character, charisma, magnetism, charm.

personification noun *he is the personification of politeness* embodiment, incarnation, epitome, quintessence, essence, representation, image, portrayal, likeness, semblance.

personify verb *personify all that was good about the country* embody, epitomize, typify, exemplify, symbolize, represent, be the incarnation of.

personnel noun staff, employees, workers, workforce, labor force, manpower, human resources.

perspective noun **1** *young people have a different perspective of such matters* outlook, viewpoint, point of view, standpoint, vantage point, stand, stance, angle, slant, attitude, frame of mind. **2** *get a perspective of the whole valley* view, vista, bird's-eye view, prospect, scene, panorama, aspect, sweep.

persuade verb *persuade her to go | cannot be persuaded* induce, convince, influence, sway, prompt, prevail upon, win over, talk into, coerce, inveigle, cajole, wheedle; *inf.* sweet-talk.

persuasion noun **1** *their successful persuasion of the children to go* prevailing, winning over, inducement, convincing, coercion, inveiglement, cajolery, wheedling; *inf.* sweet-talking. **2** *use their powers of persuasion* persuasiveness, inducement, influence. **3** *Christians of different persuasions* denomination, belief, creed, credo, faith, school of thought, philosophy, sect, affiliation, camp, faction.

persuasive adjective *persuasive arguments* effective, effectual, convincing, cogent, plausible, compelling, forceful, eloquent, weighty, influential, telling.

pert adjective *a pert young girl* impudent, impertinent, saucy, forward, presumptuous, audacious, bold, brash, brazen, bumptious.

pertinent adjective *make a few pertinent comments* relevant, appropriate, suitable, fitting, fit, apt, apposite, applicable, material, germane, apropos, ad rem.

perturb verb disturb, make anxious, worry, alarm, trouble, upset, disquiet, discompose, disconcert, vex, bother, agitate, unsettle, fluster, ruffle, confuse.

peruse verb *peruse the document* study, scrutinize, pore over, inspect, examine; scan.

pervade verb *cooking smells pervaded the entire house | terror pervaded his whole being* spread through, permeate, fill, pass through, suffuse, be diffused through, imbue, infuse, penetrate, infiltrate, percolate.

pervasive adjective prevalent, suffusive, extensive, ubiquitous, omnipresent, permeating, rife, widespread, universal.

perverse adjective **1** *too perverse to get along with others* contrary, wayward, troublesome, unruly, difficult, unreasonable, disobedient, unmanageable, uncontrollable, rebellious, willful, headstrong, capricious, stubborn, obstinate, obdurate, pertinacious, mulish, pigheaded, bullheaded, querulous, fractious, intractable, refractory, intransigent, contumacious. **2** *take a perverse delight in annoying her* contradictory, unreasonable, irrational, illogical, senseless, abnormal, deviant.

pervert verb **1** *pervert the course of justice* turn aside, divert, deflect, avert, subvert. **2** *pervert the English language* misapply, misuse, distort, garble, warp, twist, misinterpret, misconstrue. **3** *pervert young minds* lead astray, corrupt, warp, deprave, debauch, debase, degrade, vitiate.

perverted adjective corrupt, corrupted, depraved, debauched, debased, vitiated, deviant, abnormal, aberrant, warped, distorted, twisted, sick, unhealthy, immoral, evil, wicked, vile; *inf.* kinky.

pessimism noun *his pessimism made everyone gloomy* hopelessness, gloom, gloominess, cynicism, defeatism, fatalism, distrust, doubt, suspicion, resignation, despair.

pessimist noun *pessimists forecasting disaster* prophet of doom, cynic, defeatist, fatalist, alarmist, doubter, doubting Thomas.

pest noun nuisance, bother, vexation, irritant, trouble, worry, inconvenience, trial, tribulation, the bane of one's life; *inf.* pain, pain in the neck, aggravation.

pester verb *photographers pestering the movie star* badger, hound, irritate, annoy, bother, irk, nag, fret, worry, harass, torment, plague, bedevil, harry; *inf.* bug, hassle.

pestilence noun **1** *villagers dying from a pestilence* plague, epidemic, pandemic, disease, contagion, bubonic plague, Black Death, sickness. **2** *the pestilence of war* bane, blight, affliction, scourge, curse, torment.

pet noun *teacher's pet* favorite, darling, idol, apple of one's eye; *inf.* fair-haired boy/girl.

pet adjective **1** *a pet lamb* domesticated, domestic, tame, tamed, housebroken. **2** *a pet theory* favorite, favored, cherished, prized, preferred, particular, special.

pet verb **1** *pet the cat* stroke, caress, fondle, pat. **2** *a couple petting romantically* kiss, cuddle, embrace, caress; *inf.* neck, smooch.

peter verb *peter out* fade, melt away, evaporate, wane, ebb, diminish, taper off, die out, fail, fall through.

petition noun **1** *sign a petition to save the building* appeal, protest document, list of protesters, round robin. **2** *make a petition to God | made petitions for leniency to the judge* entreaty, supplication, plea, prayer, appeal, request, application, suit.

petition verb *petition God | petitioned the court for mercy* entreat, beg, beseech, plead with, make a plea to, pray, appeal to, request, ask, apply to, call upon, press, adjure.

petrify verb **1** *the thought of speaking in public petrified her* terrify, horrify, frighten, panic, alarm, scare, paralyze, stun, stupefy, transfix. **2** *age had petrified the tree* turn to stone, fossilize, calcify, ossify.

petty adjective **1** *waste time discussing petty details* trivial, trifling, minor, small, slight, unimportant, inconsequential, inconsiderable, negligible, paltry; *inf.* piddling. **2** *do it out of petty spite* narrow-minded, narrow, small-minded, mean, grudging.

petulant adjective querulous, complaining, peevish, fretful, impatient, cross, irritable, moody, crabby, snappish, crotchety, touchy, bad-tempered, ill-tempered, ill-humored, irascible, sulky, sullen.

phantom noun ghost, apparition, specter, spirit, revenant, wraith, shadow, phantasm; vision, chimera; *inf.* spook.

phase noun *an exciting phase in history* stage, part, step, chapter, point, period, time, juncture, spell.

phenomenal adjective *enjoying phenomenal success* extraordinary, remarkable, exceptional, singular, uncommon, unheard-of, unique, unparalleled, unprecedented, amazing, astonishing, astounding, marvelous, prodigious, sensational, miraculous; *inf.* fantastic, fabulous, mind-boggling.

phenomenon noun **1** *a social phenomenon peculiar to our times* circumstance, fact, experience, occurrence, happening, event, incident, episode. **2** *the gymnast is a phenomenon* marvel, prodigy, rarity, wonder, sensation, miracle, nonpareil.

philanderer noun Casanova, Don Juan, womanizer, woman-chaser, ladies' man, flirt, lothario, dallier, trifler; *inf.* lady-killer, wolf, stud.

philanthropic adjective humane, humanitarian, public-spirited, socially concerned, solicitous, unselfish, selfless, altruistic, kindhearted, benevolent, beneficent, charitable, almsgiving, generous, kind, munificent, bountiful, bounteous, liberal, openhanded, giving, helping.

philanthropist noun altruist, humanitarian, benefactor, patron, sponsor, almsgiver, donor, contributor, backer, helper.

philanthropy noun humanitarianism, humanity, humaneness, public-spiritedness, social concern, unselfishness, selflessness, altruism, kindheartedness, brotherly love, benevolence, beneficence, charity, generosity, almsgiving, kindness, munificence, bounty, liberality, openhandedness, patronage, sponsorship, backing, help.

philistine noun lowbrow, ignoramus, boor, barbarian, vulgarian, yahoo, lout, clod, oaf.

philosopher noun scholar, metaphysicist, metaphysician, sage, wise man, guru, pundit, seeker after truth, philosophizer, thinker, theorist, theorizer.

philosophical adjective **1** *read philosophical works* philosophic, metaphysical. **2** *in a philosophical mood* thoughtful, reflective, pensive, meditative, contemplative. **3** *remain philosophical in the face of failure* calm, composed, cool, collected, self-possessed, serene, tranquil, stoical, impassive, phlegmatic, unperturbed, dispassionate, unruffled, patient, resigned, rational, logical, realistic, practical.

philosophy noun **1** *the philosophy of Aristotle | studying philosophy* thought, thinking, reasoning, logic, wisdom, metaphysics. **2** *his philosophy of life* beliefs, convictions, ideology, doctrine, tenets, values, principles, attitude, view, viewpoint, outlook.

phlegmatic adjective **1** *a phlegmatic disposition* calm, cool, composed, serene, tranquil, placid, impassive, imperturbable, dispassionate, philosophical. **2** *no enthusiasm in the phlegmatic students* apathetic, indifferent, uninterested, impassive, sluggish, lethargic, listless, languorous, dull, indolent, inert, inactive, stolid, placid, bovine.

phobia noun aversion, abnormal/obsessive fear, dread, horror, terror, hatred, loathing, detestation, distaste, antipathy, revulsion, repulsion; *inf.* thing, hang-up.

phony adjective **1** *phony documents* bogus, counterfeit, imitation, spurious, mock, ersatz, fake, forged, simulated, make-believe, false, fraudulent. **2** *a phony French accent* bogus, sham, imitation, fake, feigned, assumed, affected, contrived, false, mock, pseudo.

phony noun **1** *the doctor is a phony* impostor, pretender, sham, fraud, fake, faker, charlatan, mountebank; *inf.* quack. **2** *the diamond is a phony* counterfeit, fake, forgery, imitation, sham.

photograph noun photo, snap, snapshot, picture, likeness, shot, print.

phrase noun **1** *in phrases and sentences* word group, group of words. **2** *a few well-chosen phrases* expression, idiomatic expression, idiom, remark, saying, utterance, witticism, tag. **3** *an elegant turn of phrase* phraseology, style of speech/writing, style, usage, choice of words, idiom, language, diction, parlance.

phrase verb *phrase the instruction differently* put, word, express, formulate, couch, frame, put into words.

physical adjective **1** *physical and mental well-being* bodily, corporeal, corporal, somatic. **2** *novitiates rising above their physical concerns* nonspiritual, material, earthly, corporeal, carnal, fleshly, mortal. **3** *everything physical in the universe* material, substantial, solid, concrete, tangible, palpable, visible.

physician noun doctor, doctor of medicine, medical practitioner, general practitioner, GP, specialist, consultant; *inf.* doc, medic; *derog.* quack.

pick verb **1** *pick a new sofa from the showroom* | *pick him for the team* choose, select, pick out, single out, handpick, decide upon, settle upon, fix upon, prefer, favor, elect. **2** *picking apples* harvest, gather, collect, take in, pluck, pull, cull. **3** *pick a safe* break into, force open, pry/prize open, crack. **pick at** *picking at their food* nibble at, peck at, toy with, play with, eat like a bird. **pick off** *soldiers picked off by a sniper* shoot, shoot down, gun down, hit, take out. **pick on** *picking on a child* punish repeatedly, criticize, badger. **pick out 1** *picked out from a huge list of applicants* choose, select, single out, handpick. See PICK verb 1. **2** *pick out his face in the crowd* make out, distinguish, tell apart, discriminate, recognize, notice. **pick up 1** *pick up the suitcase* lift, take up, raise, hoist. **2** *business starting to pick up* improve, get better, recover, rally, make a comeback, perk up, make headway, make progress. **3** *manage to pick up a first edition* find, discover, locate, come across, stumble across, happen upon, unearth, obtain, get, acquire, purchase, buy. **4** *pick up tomorrow where we left off today* carry on, go on, continue, take up, begin, begin again. **5** *pick them up on the way* collect, call for, fetch. **6** *pick up a date at the party* strike up an acquaintance with, take up with, fall in with. **7** *pick up the basic skills* | *pick up the local language* learn, get to know, master; *inf.* get the hang of.

pick noun **1** *early shoppers have the pick of the bargains* choice, selection, option, preference. **2** *the pick of the litter/crop* best, choicest, prime, cream, flower, prize, elite, créme de la créme.

picket noun **1** *line of pickets outside the factory* picketer, demonstrator, protester, objector, rebel, dissident. **2** *drive pickets into the ground* stake, post, paling, pale, peg, upright, pike, stanchion, palisade.

picket verb **1** *picket the factory* demonstrate at, protest at, blockade. **2** *picket an area for the animals* enclose, fence off, box in, stake off, secure, rail off, palisade.

pickle noun *in a financial pickle* plight, predicament, mess, trouble, problem, straits, crisis, tight corner; *inf.* jam, fix, scrape, tight spot.

picture noun **1** *paint a picture of the house* painting, drawing, sketch, watercolor, print, canvas, delineation, portrait, portrayal, illustration, likeness, representation, similitude, semblance. **2** *take pictures at the wedding* photograph, photo, snapshot, shot, snap, slide, print, still. **3** *his report*

painted a bleak picture scene, view, image, impression, representation, vision, concept. **4** *write a graphic picture of his despair* description, portrayal, account, report, narrative, narration, story, tale, recital. **5** *the picture of health/happiness* personification, embodiment, epitome, essence, model, exemplar, archetype. **6** *he is the picture of his father* image, living image, double, exact likeness, duplicate, replica, carbon copy, twin; *inf.* spitting image, ringer, dead ringer.

picture verb **1** *I can picture them still* imagine, call to mind, visualize, see, evoke, conjure up an image of. **2** *in the drawing they were pictured against a snowy background* paint, draw, sketch, depict, delineate, portray, illustrate, reproduce, represent.

picturesque adjective **1** *a picturesque village/setting* beautiful, pretty, lovely, attractive, scenic, charming, quaint, pleasing, delightful. **2** *a picturesque description of the events* | *use picturesque language* vivid, graphic, colorful, striking.

piddling adjective **1** *ignore the piddling details* trivial, trifling, minor, small, unimportant, insignificant, petty, paltry, worthless, useless; *inf.* piffling. **2** *a piddling sum of money* meager, trifling, paltry, derisory, negligible, small; *inf.* measly, piffling, Mickey Mouse.

piece noun **1** *a desk delivered in several pieces* part, bit, section, segment, unit. **2** *a vase broken to pieces* | *a dress torn to pieces* bit, fragment, smithereens, shard, shred. **3** *buy a large piece of cheese/wood* bit, section, slice, chunk, lump, hunk, wedge. **4** *a piece of cloth* length, bit, remnant, scrap, snippet. **5** *a piece of his fortune* | *get a piece of the action* share, slice, portion, allotment, allocation, quota, percentage, fraction, quantity. **6** *a fine piece of Colonial furniture* example, specimen, sample, instance, illustration, occurrence. **7** *write a piece on modern theater* | *disagree with his latest piece* article, item, story, report, essay, review, paper, column. **8** *one of the finest pieces by the composer* musical work, work, composition, creation, opus. **9** *one of the artist's finest pieces* work of art, work, painting, canvas, composition, creation, opus. **all in one piece** *find the vase/car/child all in one piece* unbroken, undamaged, unhurt, uninjured, safe, safe and sound. **fall/go to pieces** *people going to pieces in an emergency* panic, lose control, lose one's head, fall apart, break down; *inf.* crack up.

piecemeal adverb *put the story together piecemeal* piece by piece, bit by bit, gradually, in stages, in steps, little by little, by degrees, in fits and starts.

pier noun *stand on the pier to watch the boats* wharf, dock, jetty, quay, promenade.

pierce verb **1** *the spear had pierced his shoulder* penetrate, puncture, perforate, prick, stab, spike, enter, pass through, transfix. **2** *pierce the leather to make a belt* perforate, bore, drill. **3** *a heart pierced by the suffering of others* wound, hurt, pain, cut to the quick, affect, move, sting.

piercing adjective **1** *a piercing glance* penetrating, sharp, keen, searching, alert, shrewd, perceptive, probing. **2** *a piercing shriek* penetrating, shrill, ear-piercing, earsplitting, high-pitched, loud. **3** *a piercing pain* sharp, stabbing, shooting, intense, severe, fierce, excruciating, agonizing, exquisite. **4** *frostbitten in the piercing cold* biting, numbing, bitter, raw, keen, freezing, frigid, arctic.

piety noun **1** *a family noted for its piety* piousness, religiousness, religion, holiness, godliness, devoutness, devotion, veneration, reverence, faith, spirituality, sanctity, religious zeal. **2** *children who were taught filial piety* obedience, duty, respect, respectfulness, deference, veneration.

pig noun **1** *farmers keeping pigs* hog, boar, sow, porker, grunter, swine, piglet; *inf.* piggy, oinker. **2** *pigs who left hardly any food for the others* glutton, guzzler; *inf.* hog. **3** *they live like pigs* slob, messy/filthy/dirty person. **4** *her boss is a real pig* boor, brute, swine, animal, monster; *inf.* bastard, beast, louse.

pigheaded adjective obstinate, stubborn, mulish, bullheaded, obdurate, tenacious, dogged, single-minded, inflexible, uncompromising, adamant, intractable, intransigent, unmalleable, headstrong, self-willed, willful, perverse, contrary, stiff-necked.

pile[1] noun **1** *a pile of clothes* heap, bundle, stack, mound, mass, accumulation, collection, assemblage, store, stockpile, hoard, load, mountain. **2** *a pile of work to do* great deal, quantity, abundance, mountain; *inf.* lot, lots, heap, stacks, oodles, tons. **3** *make a pile on the black market* fortune, money, wealth; *inf.* mint, tidy sum.

pile[2] verb **1** *pile his plate with food* heap, fill, load, stock. **2** *commuters piling on to the train* crowd, charge, tumble, stream, flock, flood, pack, squeeze, crush, jam. **pile up 1** *pile up the cans/apples* heap, stack. **2** *pile up logs for the winter* accumulate, amass, collect, gather, stockpile, hoard, store up, assemble, lay by/in. **3** *snow piled up by the roadsides* heap up, amass, accumulate, form piles, form heaps.

pile[3] noun *the piles supporting the bridge* pillar, column, support, post, foundation, piling, pier, buttress, upright.

pilfer verb *pilfer money from the petty cash* steal, thieve, rob, take, filch, purloin, embezzle, misappropriate; *inf.* walk off with, swipe, lift.

pilgrim noun *pilgrims going to Bethlehem/Mecca* worshiper, devotee, traveler, hajji; Puritan.

pilgrimage noun *make a pilgrimage to Bethlehem/Mecca* religious expedition, holy expedition, trek, excursion, hajj.

pill noun **1** *take a pill for a headache* tablet, capsule, pellet, lozenge, bolus. **2** *she can be a real pill* nuisance, pest, bore, trial; *inf.* pain, pain in the neck, drag.

pillage verb *rival tribes invading and pillaging* plunder, rob, raid, loot, maraud, sack, ransack, ravage, lay waste, despoil, spoil, spoliate, depredate, rape.

pillar noun **1** *pillars supporting the temple* column, post, pole, support, upright, pile, piling, pilaster, stanchion. **2** *a pillar of the community* mainstay, backbone, tower of strength, support, upholder, rock.

pillow noun cushion, bolster, headrest.

pilot noun **1** *the pilot at the aircraft's controls* aviator, aviatrix, aeronaut, captain, commander; *inf.* flier. **2** *the pilot directing the ship into the harbor* navigator, guide, steersman, helmsman.

pilot verb **1** *pilot the aircraft* fly, drive, operate, control, handle, maneuver. **2** *pilot the ship into the harbor* navigate, guide, steer.

pimple noun spot, pustule, boil, swelling, papule; *inf.* blackhead, whitehead, zit.

pin verb **1** *pin the pieces of cloth together* fasten, join, attach, secure. **2** *pin the notice to the board* attach, fasten, affix, fix, stick, tack, nail. **3** *pinned under the fallen tree* pinion, hold, press, restrain, constrain, hold fast, immobilize. **pin down 1** *pinned down by the weight of the car* pinion, hold down, restrain, constrain, hold fast, immobilize. **2** *to get his decision, you must pin him down* force, compel, make, pressure, put pressure on, nail down. **3** *something I dislike about him but I cannot pin it down* define, specify, identify, put one's finger on, put into words, express in words, designate, name. **pin on** *pin the blame on him* lay on, place on, attribute to, impute to, ascribe to.

pin noun **1** *fasten the hem with a pin* straight pin, dressmaker's/dressmaking pin, safety pin. **2** *a broken pin in the machine* peg, bolt, rivet, screw, dowel, post.

pinch verb **1** *pinch her little brother's arm* nip, tweak, squeeze, compress. **2** *shoes pinching her feet* hurt, crush, squeeze, cramp, confine. **3** *have to pinch and scrape to live* scrimp, skimp, stint, economize, be sparing, be frugal, be economical; *inf.* be stingy, be tight. **4** *pinch money from her mother's purse* steal, thieve, rob, take, pilfer, filch, purloin, embezzle, misappropriate; *inf.* swipe, lift.

pinch noun **1** *give her arm a pinch* nip, tweak, squeeze. **2** *a pinch of salt* bit, touch, trace, soupçon; *inf.* smidgen, smidge, tad.

pine verb **1** *pine away* *pine away with grief* decline, weaken, waste away, wilt, fade, languish, droop. **pine for** *pine for her old way of life* long for, yearn for, ache for, sigh for, hunger for, thirst for, hanker for/after, crave.

pink adjective **1** *pink dresses* rose, rose-colored, salmon, salmon-pink, shell-pink. **2** *pink cheeks* rosy, flushed, blushing.

pinnacle noun *the pinnacle of her success* peak, height, culmination, high point, acme, zenith, climax, crowning point, meridian, summit, apex, vertex, apogee.

pinpoint verb *pinpoint the cause of the trouble* identify, discover, distinguish, locate, spot, home in on, put one's finger on.

pioneer noun **1** *the pioneers of the Wild West* settler, colonist, colonizer, frontiersman/frontierswoman, explorer. **2** *a pioneer in/of cancer research* developer, innovator, groundbreaker, trailblazer, front runner, founder, architect.

pious adjective **1** *pious church members* religious, holy, godly, spiritual, devout, devoted, dedicated, reverent, God-fearing, righteous, faithful, dutiful. **2** *patronized by pious do-gooders* sanctimonious, hypocritical, self-righteous, unctuous, pietistic, religiose; *inf.* holier-than-thou, goody-goody.

pipe noun **1** *lay pipes under the street* tube, cylinder; conduit, main, duct, channel, conveyor, pipeline, drainpipe. **2** *smoke a pipe* brier, meerschaum, clay pipe, tobacco pipe, corncob pipe; peace pipe, calumet; hookah. **3** *playing a pipe* whistle, penny whistle, flute, recorder, fife. **pipes** plural noun *playing the pipes* bagpipes, panpipes.

piquant adjective **1** *a piquant sauce/flavor* spicy, highly seasoned, flavorsome, peppery, tangy, pungent, sharp, tart, zesty, biting, stinging. **2** *a piquant piece of gossip* stimulating, intriguing, interesting, fascinating, alluring, racy, salty, provocative. **3** *a piquant wit* lively, sparkling, animated, spirited, sharp, clever, quick.

pique verb **1** *her lack of interest piqued him* irritate, annoy, anger, displease, affront, put out, offend, irk, peeve, vex, nettle, gall, wound; *inf.* aggravate, miff, rile. **2** *pique her curiosity* arouse, rouse, awaken, excite, stimulate, kindle, stir, whet.

pirate noun *pirates boarded the ship* buccaneer, rover, sea robber, corsair, freebooter.

pirate verb *pirate his music/poetry* copy, poach, infringe the copyright of, plagiarize, illegally reproduce; *inf.* crib, lift.

pit[1] noun **1** *fall down a pit* abyss, chasm, crater, hole, cavity, excavation, quarry, mine. **2** *pits in the pottery/skin* depression, hollow, dent, dint, pockmark, indentation, dimple, pock, mark.

pit[2] noun *cherry pits* stone, pip, seed, kernel.

pitch verb **1** *pitch a baseball* *pitch the bales on to the truck* throw, cast, fling, hurl, toss, heave, launch; *inf.* chuck, lob. **2** *pitch a tent* erect, raise, put up, set up. **3** *trip and pitch forward into the lake* tumble, topple, fall headlong, fall, plunge, dive. **4** *ships pitching in the storm* lurch, roll, reel, sway, rock, flounder, keel, list. **pitch in 1** *everyone pitched in to finish the work* help, assist, lend a hand, join in, participate, play a part, cooperate, collaborate. **2** *everyone pitched in to buy a present* contribute, make a contribution; *inf.* chip in.

pitch noun **1** *with one pitch* throw, cast, fling, hurl, toss, heave; *inf.* chuck, lob. **2** *excitement reached such a pitch* level, point, degree, height, extent, intensity. **3** *the pitch of the roof* angle, slope, slant, tilt, cant, inclination. **4** *get the right musical pitch* tone, sound, tonality, modulation. **5** *the pitch of the ship* lurch, roll, reeling, swaying, rocking, keeling, list. **6** *taken in by the salesman's pitch* spiel, sales talk, patter; *inf.* line.

pitcher noun *a pitcher of water* jug, ewer, jar, crock.

piteous adjective *hear a piteous cry/tale* pitiable, pathetic, distressing. *See* PITIFUL 1.

pitfall noun *the pitfalls of running a small business* trap, snare, catch, stumbling block, hazard, peril, danger, difficulty.

pithy adjective *a pithy remark* *a pithy piece of prose* terse, succinct, concise, condensed, compact, summary, epigrammatic, to the point, pointed, expressive, incisive.

pitiful adjective **1** *in a pitiful condition* *a pitiful sight* pitiable, piteous, pathetic, wretched, distressing, affecting, moving, sad, woeful, deplorable, heart-rending, heartbreaking, poignant, emotional. **2** *a pitiful excuse/coward* contemptible, despicable, poor, sorry, miserable, inadequate, worthless, base, shabby; *inf.* pathetic.

pitiless adjective *a pitiless tyrant* merciless, ruthless, relentless, cruel, severe, harsh, heartless, callous, brutal, inhuman, inhumane, cold-hearted, hard-hearted, unfeeling, uncaring, unsympathetic.

pittance noun *earn a pittance* trifling amount, modicum, tiny amount; *inf.* peanuts, chicken feed.

pity noun **1** *show pity for her situation* commiseration, condolence, sympathy, compassion, fellow feeling, understanding, forbearance, mercy, clemency, kindness, charity. **2** *it is a pity that he left* shame, crying shame, misfortune, sin; *inf.* crime.

pity verb *pity the homeless* take pity on, feel sorry for, weep for, grieve for, commiserate with, be sympathetic toward, sympathize with, have compassion for, show mercy to, be merciful toward.

pivot noun **1** *the machine turning on a pivot* axis, fulcrum, axle, swivel, spindle, central shaft. **2** *his job was the pivot of his life* central point, center, focal point, focus, hub, heart, *raison d'être*.

pivot verb *the machine pivots on a central shaft* turn, revolve, rotate, spin, swivel, twirl.

placate verb *placate the angry customer* calm, calm down, pacify, soothe, appease, conciliate, propitiate, mollify, win over.

place noun **1** *the place where the accident happened* location, spot, scene, setting, position, site, situation, venue, area, region, whereabouts, locus. **2** *a sore place on her arm* spot, area, bit, part. **3** *visit a different place each year* town, city, village, hamlet, district, locality, neighborhood, quarter, country, state, area, region. **4** *have a place in town* residence, home, house, apartment, accommodation, abode, dwelling, domicile, property; *inf.* pad. **5** *occupy a lowly place in the company | win first place* position, status, grade, rank, station, standing, footing, role, niche. **6** *find a place in a law firm* position, post, job, appointment, situation, office. **7** *children asked to go back to their places* seat, position, space. **8** *put the book back in its place* position, correct position, space. **9** *not your place to criticize* function, job, role, task, duty, responsibility, charge, concern, affair, prerogative. **in place** *everything must be in place before the meeting* in position, in order, set up, arranged. **in place of** *her sister went in place of her* instead of, in lieu of, in someone's place, in someone's stead, as a substitute for. **out of place 1** *with not a hair out of place* out of position, out of order, in disorder, disarranged, in disarray, disorganized, in a mess. **2** *her remarks were quite out of place* inappropriate, unsuitable, inapposite, unseemly, improper, unfit. **3** *feel out of place at the party* out of one's element, uncomfortable, ill-at-ease, like a fish out of water. **put in (someone's) place** *he was trying to flirt with her but she put him in his place* humble, humiliate, mortify, take down a peg or two; *inf.* cut down to size. **take place** *where did the murder take place?* happen, occur, come about, transpire, crop up, befall, come to pass. **take the place of** *trying to take the place of her mother* replace, substitute for, be a substitute for, act for, stand in lieu of, cover for.

place verb **1** *place the books on the shelves* put, position, set, lay, deposit, rest, stand,

install, settle, station, situate. **2** *place the recruits according to their test scores* order, rank, grade, group, arrange, sort, class, classify, categorize, bracket. **3** *place her trust in him* put, lay, invest, consign. **4** *I know his face, but I cannot place him* identify, recognize, know, remember, put one's finger on, locate. **5** *try to place graduates* find employment for, find a job for, accommodate, find accommodation for, appoint, assign.

placid adjective **1** *the placid waters of the lake* still, calm, peaceful, pacific, tranquil, motionless, smooth, unruffled, undisturbed. **2** *of a placid temperament* calm, cool, coolheaded, collected, composed, self-possessed, serene, tranquil, equable, even-tempered, easygoing, unperturbed, imperturbable, unexcitable, unruffled.

plagiarize verb copy, pirate, poach, borrow, reproduce, appropriate; *inf.* crib, lift.

plague noun **1** *villagers dying from a plague* bubonic plague, Black Death, contagion, disease, pestilence, sickness, epidemic, pandemic. **2** *a plague of locusts* multitude, host, swarm, influx, infestation. **3** *famine and other plagues* affliction, evil, scourge, curse, blight, bane, calamity, disaster, trial, tribulation, torment, visitation.

plague verb **1** *plagued with/by poor health* afflict, torture, torment, bedevil, trouble. **2** *plagued by her little brother* annoy, irritate, bother, disturb, worry, pester, vex, harass, torment, tease; *inf.* hassle, bug.

plain adjective **1** *it was plain that he was guilty* clear, crystal-clear, obvious, evident, apparent, manifest, transparent, patent, unmistakable. **2** *plain indications of his guilt* clear, clear-cut, obvious, visible, discernible, perceptible, distinct, transparent, patent, noticeable, pronounced, marked, striking, unmistakable, conspicuous. **3** *a plain statement of the facts* clear, clear-cut, simple, straightforward, uncomplicated, comprehensible, intelligible, understandable, lucid, unambiguous. **4** *a plain lifestyle | plain furnishings* simple, austere, stark, severe, basic, ordinary, unsophisticated, spartan, restrained, muted, bare, unadorned, undecorated, unembellished, unornamented. **5** *a rather plain child* unattractive, ill-favored, ugly, unprepossessing, unlovely, homely. **6** *a plain man* simple, straightforward, ordinary, average, typical, unpretentious, unassuming, unaffected, artless, guileless, sincere, honest, plain-speaking, plainspoken, frank, candid, blunt, outspoken, forthright, direct.

plain noun lowland, grassland, prairie, meadowland, pasture, savannah, flatland; steppe, tundra; tableland, plateau, mesa.

plainspoken adjective plain-speaking, frank, candid, blunt, outspoken, forthright, direct, downright, unequivocal, unambiguous.

plaintive adjective *plaintive cries* mournful, doleful, melancholy, sad, sorrowful, unhappy, disconsolate, wretched, woeful, grief-stricken, heartbroken, brokenhearted, pathetic, pitiful, piteous.

plan noun **1** *a plan to make money* scheme, system, procedure, method, program, schedule, project, way, means, strategy, tactics, formula. **2** *our plan is to relocate* idea, proposal, intention, intent, aim, hope, aspiration, ambition. **3** *the architect's plan for the new building* drawing, scale drawing, blueprint, layout, sketch, diagram, chart, map, illustration, representation, delineation.

plan verb **1** *plan a picnic for tomorrow* arrange, organize, line up, schedule, program. **2** *plan the reconstruction of the company* devise, design, plot, formulate, frame, outline, sketch out, draft, prepare, develop, shape, build, concoct, contrive. **3** *we are planning to relocate* intend, aim, propose, mean, contemplate, envisage, foresee.

plane noun **1** *on a different intellectual plane* level, stratum, stage, degree, position, rank, footing. **2** *planes taking off* airplane, aircraft, airliner, jet, jumbo jet.

plant noun **1** *buy plants for the garden* herb, shrub, flower, vegetable, weed. **2** *work at the textile plant* factory, works, foundry, mill, workshop, shop, yard.

plant verb **1** *plant tomatoes* put in the ground, implant, sow, scatter, transplant, bed (out). **2** *plant his feet firmly on the ground* place, position, set, situate. **3** *plant an idea in his head* put, place, fix, establish, lodge, embed, insert. **4** *plant a microphone in his bedroom* hide, conceal, secrete.

plastic adjective **1** *as plastic as clay* moldable, shapable, ductile, fictile, pliant, pliable, supple, flexible, malleable. **2** *a plastic charm* false, artificial, synthetic, spurious, sham, bogus, assumed, superficial, specious, meretricious, pseudo; *inf.* phony.

plate noun **1** *serve food on plates* dish, platter, dinner plate. **2** *a plate of spaghetti* plateful, helping, portion, serving. **3** *a book with colored plates* illustration, picture, photograph, print, lithograph. **4** *steel plates used in shipbuilding* sheet, panel, slab.

plateau noun *stand on the plateau to view the valley below* elevated plain, highland, upland, mesa, tableland.

platform noun **1** *deliver a speech from the platform* dais, rostrum, podium, stage, stand. **2** *nothing new in the candidate's platform* plan, program, policy, objectives, principles, tenets, manifesto, party line.

platitude noun *a speech rife with platitudes* cliché, truism, bromide, hackneyed/stock expression, trite/banal phrase, banality, stereotyped phrase, inanity.

platoon noun *the officer in charge of the platoon* squadron, squad, company, patrol, group.

platter noun serving plate, salver, plate, dish, tray.

plaudits plural noun *the plaudits of his colleagues* praise, acclaim, acclamation, applause, ovation, congratulations, compliments, cheers, approval, approbation, commendation, accolade, pat on the back.

plausible adjective *a plausible argument/excuse* tenable, cogent, reasonable, believable, credible, convincing, persuasive, likely, probable, conceivable, imaginable.

play verb **1** *time to play* amuse oneself, entertain oneself, enjoy oneself, have fun. **2** *playing in the park* play games, frolic, frisk, gambol, romp, cavort, sport. **3** *play a musical instrument* perform on. **4** *play Ophelia in Hamlet* act the part of, perform, portray, represent, execute. **5** *play a trick on* perform, carry out, execute, do, accomplish, discharge, fulfill. **6** *play football* take part in, participate in, engage in, be involved in. **7** *play the neighboring team* compete against, contend against, oppose, take on, challenge, vie with, rival. **8** *told not to play with the controls* fiddle, toy, fidget, fool around; *inf.* mess around. **9** *playing with her affections* trifle, toy, dally, amuse oneself. **10** *sunlight playing on the water* move lightly, dance, flit, dart. **play around** philander, womanize, have an affair, fool around, cheat; *inf.* mess around. **play ball** *want to do business, but they refused to play ball* cooperate, collaborate, play along, go along, be willing. **play down** *play down his part in the crime* make light of, gloss over, minimize, diminish, underrate, underestimate, undervalue, think little of; *inf.* soft-pedal. **play it by ear** *we have no plans—we are going to play it by ear* improvise, extemporize, ad lib, take it as it comes. **play up** *car dealers playing up the new safety features* emphasize, accentuate, bring/draw/call attention to, point up, underline, underscore, highlight, spotlight, stress.

play noun **1** *children at play | prefer play to work* amusement, entertainment, recreation, diversion, leisure, enjoyment, fun, merrymaking, revelry. **2** *appear in a play by a local dramatist* drama, stage play, stage show, radio play, comedy, tragedy, farce. **3** *need more play on the fishing line* movement, freedom of movement, slack;

inf. give. **4** *made sarcastic remarks in play* fun, jest, joking, sport, teasing.

playboy noun pleasure seeker, man about town, socialite, rake, roué, womanizer, philanderer, ladies' man, lady-killer, lothario, Casanova, Don Juan, debauchee.

player noun **1** *one of the players in the game* competitor, contestant, participant, team member, athlete, sportsman/sportswoman. **2** *one of the players in the theater company* actor/actress, performer, entertainer, artist, artiste, trouper, thespian. **3** *several of the players in the orchestra* performer, musician, instrumentalist, artist, artiste, virtuoso.

playful adjective **1** *playful kitten | in a playful mood* fun-loving, full of fun, high-spirited, frisky, skittish, coltish, frolicsome, sportive, mischievous, impish, puckish. **2** *a playful remark* in fun, in jest, joking, jesting, humorous, facetious, waggish, tongue-in-cheek, arch, roguish.

playwright noun dramatist, dramaturge, scriptwriter.

plea noun **1** *make a plea to the governor to save his life* appeal, entreaty, imploration, supplication, petition, prayer, request, solicitation, suit, invocation. **2** *evidence in support of his plea against the accused* allegation, case, suit, action, claim.

plead verb *plead insanity as the reason for his crime* put forward, state, assert, argue, claim, allege. **plead with** *plead with the judge to show mercy* appeal to, beg, entreat, beseech, implore, petition, make supplication to, supplicate, importune, pray to, solicit, request, present one's case to.

pleasant adjective **1** *a pleasant experience* agreeable, enjoyable, entertaining, amusing, delightful, pleasing, pleasurable, satisfying, gratifying, nice, good, fine, welcome, acceptable; *inf.* lovely. **2** *a pleasant person/manner* agreeable, friendly, amiable, affable, genial, likable, nice, good-humored, charming, engaging, winning, delightful; *inf.* lovely.

pleasantry noun *exchange pleasantries with his neighbor* good-natured remark, polite remark, joke, jest, quip, witticism, bon mot.

please verb **1** *a gift that will please his mother* be agreeable to, gladden, delight, cheer up, charm, divert, entertain, amuse, tickle, satisfy, gratify, fulfill, content, suit; *inf.* tickle pink. **2** *do as one pleases* want, wish, see fit, will, like, desire, be inclined, prefer, opt.

pleased adjective *give a pleased smile* happy, glad, cheerful, delighted, thrilled, elated, contented, satisfied, gratified, fulfilled.

pleasing adjective **1** *a pleasing experience* agreeable, enjoyable. *See* PLEASANT adjective 1. **2** *he had a pleasing personality* agreeable, friendly, amiable. *See* PLEASANT adjective 2.

pleasure noun **1** *events that bring pleasure | the pursuit of pleasure* happiness, gladness, delight, joy, enjoyment, entertainment, amusement, diversion, satisfaction, gratification, fulfillment, contentment, recreation. **2** *what is your pleasure?* wish, desire, will, inclination, preference, choice, option, purpose.

plebeian adjective **1** *of plebeian origins* lower-class, low, lowborn, working-class, proletarian, common, peasant, mean, ignoble; *inf.* blue-collar. **2** *have plebeian tastes* uncultivated, uncultured, unrefined, coarse, common, base.

plebeian noun commoner, proletarian, peasant.

pledge noun **1** *give his pledge to look after the children* promise, word, word of honor, vow, assurance, oath, covenant, warrant. **2** *give his watch as a pledge* security, surety, guarantee, collateral, bond, earnest, deposit, pawn. **3** *give her a ring as a pledge of his love* token, symbol, sign, mark, testimony, proof, evidence.

pledge verb **1** *he pledged that he would support the children* promise, give one's word, vow, undertake, take an oath, swear, vouch, engage, contract. **2** *pledge one's house/ring as security* mortgage, put up as collateral, guarantee, pawn.

plentiful adjective abundant, copious, ample, profuse, lavish, liberal, generous, bumper, infinite.

plenty noun *the years of plenty* plenteousness, affluence, prosperity, wealth, opulence, luxury, abundance, copiousness, fruitfulness, profusion. **plenty of** *have plenty of money* enough, sufficient, a good deal of; *inf.* lots of, piles of, tons of.

plethora noun *a plethora of good advice* overabundance, superabundance, excess, superfluity, surplus, surfeit, glut.

pliable adjective **1** *a pliable substance* flexible, bendable, pliant, elastic, supple, stretchable, ductile, plastic. **2** *expect the army recruits to be pliable* malleable, yielding, compliant, docile, biddable, tractable, manageable, governable, controllable, amenable, adaptable, flexible, impressionable, persuadable.

plight noun *the plight of the homeless | the plight they are in* predicament, trouble, difficulty, dire straits, extremity, tight corner; *inf.* hole, pickle, spot, jam.

plod verb *plod along the road* trudge, clump, stomp, lumber, tramp.

plot noun **1** *a plot against the dictator* conspiracy, intrigue, secret plan, stratagem. **2** *the plot of the novel* action, theme, subject, story line, story, scenario, thread. **3** *a burial plot* patch, allotment, lot, parcel.

plot verb **1** *plot the new construction site* map out, make a plan/blueprint of, draw, draw a diagram of, draw the layout of, sketch out, outline. **2** *plot the battle sites on the map* mark, chart, map. **3** *rebels plotting against the dictator* scheme, conspire, intrigue. **4** *plot the dictator's downfall* plan, hatch, scheme, concoct, devise, frame, think up, dream up, conceive; *inf.* cook up.

plow verb **1** *plow the field* till, work, cultivate, break up, turn up. **2** *the car plowed into a snowbank* plunge, lunge, career, crash, smash, bulldoze, hurtle. **3** *plow through the mud* plod, trudge, wade, flounder.

ploy noun *a ploy to distract the teacher* dodge, ruse, scheme, trick, stratagem, maneuver.

pluck verb **1** *pluck the burning paper from the fire* pull, remove, extract. **2** *pluck blackberries for jam* gather, collect, pick, harvest, take in, pull, cull. **3** *pluck the string of the guitar* finger, strum, pick, plunk. **pluck at** *plucking at her mother's skirt* tug at, pull at, clutch at, snatch at, catch at, tweak; *inf.* yank (at).

pluck noun *took a lot of pluck to go into the jungle alone* courage, bravery, valor, heroism, intrepidity, fearlessness, mettle, nerve, backbone, determination, boldness, daring, spirit, audacity; *inf.* gumption, grit, guts, spunk.

plug noun **1** *put a plug in the bathtub/jug* stopper, bung, cork, stopple, seal. **2** *a plug of tobacco* cake, chew, twist, quid, wad. **3** *the talk-show host gave his book a free plug* advertisement, commercial, promotion, push, mention; *inf.* ad, hype.

plug verb **1** *plug the hole in the tank* stop up, bung, cork, dam up, block, stopper, stopple, seal off, pack, snuff. **2** *plug his new book on television* publicize, promote, advertise, play up, push, build up; *inf.* hype. **plug away** *keep plugging away* labor, slog away, persevere, grind away.

plumb verb *plumb the mysteries of computer technology* probe, search out, delve into, explore, scrutinize, investigate, inspect, examine, sound out, go into, fathom, unravel.

plummet verb **1** *the kite plummeted to the ground* plunge, hurtle, nosedive, dive, drop. **2** *prices plummeted* plunge, tumble, take a nosedive, drop rapidly.

plump adjective chubby, round, of ample proportions, rotund, buxom, stout, obese, corpulent, fleshy, portly, tubby, dumpy, pudgy, roly-poly.

plunder verb **1** *enemy forces plundering the villages* rob, pillage, loot, raid, ransack,

rifle, strip, fleece, ravage, lay waste, despoil, spoil, spoliate, depredate, harry, maraud, sack, rape. **2** *plunder food* steal, thieve, rob, purloin, filch, make off with.

plunder noun **1** *the plunder of the village* robbery, robbing, pillaging, looting, raiding, ransacking, despoiling, laying waste, harrying, marauding, rapine. **2** *take their plunder back to camp* stolen goods, loot, booty, spoils, prize, pillage.

plunge verb **1** *plunge the dagger into his back* thrust, stick, jab, push, drive. **2** *the pelican plunged into the sea* dive, nosedive, jump, plummet, drop, fall, swoop down. **3** *plunge the house into darkness* throw, cast, pitch. **4** *plunge his burned hand into cold water* immerse, sink, dip, douse. **5** *plunge into matrimony* charge, lurch, rush, dash, hurtle, career. **6** *real-estate prices plunged* plummet, tumble, nosedive, take a nosedive.

plunge noun **1** *his plunge into the sea* dive, nosedive, jump, fall, drop, swoop, descent. **2** *the car's sudden plunge forward* charge, lurch, rush, dash. **3** *an unexpected plunge in prices* fall, drop, tumble, nosedive.

plus noun *use of the company car is a definite plus* bonus, extra, added advantage, fringe benefit, perquisite; *inf.* perk.

plush adjective *plush furnishings* luxurious, deluxe, sumptuous, lavish, gorgeous, opulent, rich, costly; *inf.* ritzy, classy.

ply verb **1** *plying the oars* wield, use, operate, work, utilize, employ, manipulate, handle. **2** *ply his trade as a plumber* practice, work at, engage in, pursue, follow. **3** *ply them with questions* bombard, assail, besiege, beset, harass, importune; *inf.* hassle. **4** *ply them with food and drink* supply, provide, lavish, shower, load, heap.

pocket noun **1** *pockets on the side of the suitcase* pouch, compartment, receptacle. **2** *isolated pockets of resistance to the government* small area, small region, district, zone.

pocket verb *pocketing money from the cash register* appropriate, misappropriate, steal, thieve, purloin, filch; *inf.* lift, swipe.

pod noun *pea pod* shell, husk, hull, case, shuck; pericarp.

poem noun verse, ode, sonnet, ballad, song, lyric, lay, elegy, rhyme, limerick, haiku, jingle.

poetic adjective **1** *write poetic works* metrical, rhythmical, lyrical, elegiac. **2** *poetic language* imaginative, creative, figurative, symbolic, flowery. **3** *a poetic rendering of the symphony* aesthetic, artistic, tasteful, graceful, elegant, sensitive.

poetry noun *write poetry rather than prose* poems, verse, verses, versification, metrical composition, rhythmical composition, rhymes, rhyming.

poignant adjective moving, affecting, touching, emotional, sentimental, heartfelt, sad, sorrowful, tearful, evocative.

point noun **1** *the point of the spear/tool* tapered end, tip, top, extremity, prong, spike, tine. **2** *ships sailing around the point* promontory, headland, head, foreland, cape, bluff. **3** *Gettysburg is a point of great interest* place, position, location, situation, site, spot, area, locality. **4** *abrupt to the point of rudeness* extent, degree, stage. **5** *reach an important point in her life* stage, position, circumstance, condition. **6** *have to go home at some point* time, juncture, stage, period, moment, instant. **7** *at the point where he could not face her* critical point, crux, moment of truth. **8** *explain the situation point by point* detail, item, particular. **9** *get to the point* focal point, salient point, keynote, heart of the matter, essence, nub, core, pith, marrow, meat, crux. **10** *miss the point of the story* meaning, significance, import, essence, gist, substance, drift, thrust, burden, theme, tenor, vein. **11** *raise various points during the discussion* subject, issue, topic, question, matter, item. **12** *the various points of the argument* part, element, constituent, component, ingredient. **13** *what is the point of it?* aim, purpose, object, objective, goal, intention, reason for, use, utility. **14** *kindness is one of his strong points* characteristic, trait, attribute, quality, feature, property. **beside the point** *their religious beliefs are beside the point* irrelevant, immaterial, incidental. **point of view 1** *listen to everyone's point of view* view, viewpoint, opinion, belief, attitude, sentiment, stand, standpoint, stance, position. **2** *look at the situation from a different point of view* angle, slant, perspective, standpoint, viewpoint, outlook. **to the point** *his remarks were very much to the point* pertinent, relevant, germane, applicable, apropos, apposite, appropriate, apt, fitting, suitable.

point verb *point the gun* direct, aim, level, train. **point out** *point out the disadvantages of the proposal* indicate, show, specify, designate, identify, mention, call/draw attention to. **point to** *all the evidence points to her* indicate, show, signify, suggest, be evidence of, evidence.

point-blank adverb **1** *shot him point-blank* at close range, close up. **2** *ask him point-blank for his reasons* bluntly, directly, plainly, straight, straightforwardly, frankly, candidly, forthrightly, openly, explicitly, unequivocally, unambiguously.

pointed adjective **1** *the pointed end of the stick* sharp, sharp-edged, cuspidate, acicular. **2** *a pointed remark* cutting, trenchant, biting, incisive, penetrating, forceful, telling, significant. **3** *treat her with pointed indifference* obvious, evident, conspicuous, striking, emphasized, unmistakable.

pointless adjective **1** *it is pointless to go on* futile, useless, in vain, unavailing, unproductive, senseless, absurd, foolish, nonsensical, stupid, silly. **2** *a few pointless remarks* meaningless, insignificant, vague, empty, worthless, irrelevant, senseless, fatuous, foolish, nonsensical, stupid, silly, absurd, inane.

poise noun **1** *admire her poise in difficulties* composure, equanimity, self-possession, aplomb, self-assurance, self-control, calmness, serenity, dignity, imperturbability, suaveness, urbanity, elegance; *inf.* cool. **2** *admire the poise of the ballet dancers* balance, equilibrium, control, grace, gracefulness.

poise verb **1** *poise oneself to jump* steady, brace, prepare. **2** *the hawk poised in midair* hang, hang suspended, float, hover.

poised adjective **1** *a very poised young woman* composed, serene, self-possessed, self-assured, self-controlled, calm, collected, dignified, imperturbable, unperturbed, unruffled, suave, urbane, elegant; *inf.* unflappable. **2** *poised to take over the president's job* ready, prepared, all set, standing by, waiting, waiting in the wings.

poison noun **1** *the snake's deadly poison* venom, toxin. **2** *a poison in our society* blight, bane, contagion, cancer, canker, malignancy, corruption, pollution.

poison verb **1** *poisoned the victim* administer poison to, give poison to, kill by poison. **2** *poison the environment/soil* contaminate, pollute, blight, spoil, infect, defile, adulterate. **3** *poison their minds* corrupt, warp, pervert, deprave, defile, debauch.

poisonous adjective **1** *poisonous snakes/chemicals* venomous, toxic, mephitic, noxious, deadly, fatal, lethal. **2** *a poisonous influence on society* cancerous, malignant, corrupting, polluting, harmful, injurious, noxious, pernicious, malicious, malevolent, vicious.

poke verb **1** *poke him in the ribs* jab, prod, dig, elbow, nudge, butt. **2** *poke a key through the hole* jab, push, thrust, shove, stick. **poke around** *poke around his possessions* rummage around, ransack, nose around, pry into. **poke fun at** *poking fun at his clumsiness* laugh at, mock, jeer at, ridicule, deride, tease, chaff, taunt; *inf.* rib, rag.

poke noun jab, prod, dig, nudge, elbow, butt, push, thrust, shove.

police noun *wanted by the police* police force, the law, policemen, policewomen, police officers, constabulary; *inf.* the cops, the boys in blue; *derog.* the fuzz, the pigs.

police verb **1** *police the school buildings* patrol, make the rounds of, guard, keep watch on, protect. **2** *police the soccer match* control, keep under control, regulate, enforce, administer, oversee, monitor.

policy noun *the government's educational policy* plan, scheme, program, schedule, code, system, approach, procedure, ·guideline, theory.

polish verb *polish the table* wax, buff, rub, burnish, shine. **polish off** *polish off his meal quickly* finish, eat up, consume, devour, wolf down, down, bolt.

polite adjective **1** *too polite to interrupt* well-mannered, mannerly, courteous, civil, respectful, deferential, well-behaved, well-bred, genteel, polished, tactful, diplomatic. **2** *things not done in polite society* well-bred, civilized, cultured, refined, polished, genteel, urbane, sophisticated, elegant, courtly.

politic adjective wise, prudent, sensible, advisable, judicious, sagacious, expedient, shrewd, astute, discreet, tactful, diplomatic.

political adjective **1** *hold a political position* governmental, ministerial, public, civic, administrative, bureaucratic. **2** *dismissed for political reasons* factional, partisan, power, status.

politician noun statesman, stateswoman, legislator, lawmaker, public servant; senator, congressman, congresswoman, representative; officeholder, bureaucrat.

politics noun **1** *a career in politics* government, affairs of state, party politics. **2** *study politics* political science, civics, statecraft, statesmanship. **3** plural noun *what are his politics?* political alliance, political belief. **4** plural noun *resigned because of the politics within the company* power struggle, manipulation, maneuvering, jockeying for position, Machiavellianism, opportunism, realpolitik.

poll noun **1** *organize a poll to decide on the best candidate* vote, ballot, canvass, headcount, show of hands, straw vote/poll. **2** *a poll heavily in favor of the present administration* returns, count, tally. **3** *conduct a poll to investigate people's eating habits* opinion poll, Gallup poll, survey, market research, sampling.

poll verb *poll one hundred people in a survey* canvass, question, interview, survey, sample, ballot.

pollute verb **1** *pollute the water with chemicals | pollute the environment* contaminate, adulterate, infect, taint, poison, befoul, foul, make dirty, make filthy. **2** *pollute the minds of the young* corrupt, poison, warp, pervert, deprave, defile, debauch.

pollution noun **1** *chemicals involved in the pollution of our water* contamination, adulteration, infecting, tainting, befouling,

fouling, foulness, dirtying, dirtiness, impurity, filthiness. **2** *the pollution of young minds* corruption, corrupting, poisoning, warping, depraving.

pomp noun **1** *the pomp of the coronation* ceremony, ceremoniousness, ritual, display, pageantry, show, spectacle, splendor, grandeur, magnificence, majesty, glory, brilliance, flourish, style. **2** *more interested in pomp than substance* ostentation, exhibitionism, grandiosity, glitter, show, showiness, pomposity, vainglory, fanfaronade.

pompous adjective **1** *a pompous official* self-important, presumptuous, imperious, overbearing, grandiose, affected, pretentious, arrogant, vain, haughty, proud, conceited, egotistic, supercilious, condescending, patronizing. **2** *pompous language* high-sounding, high-flown, bombastic, turgid, grandiloquent, magniloquent, euphuistic, pedantic, stilted, fustian.

pond noun pool, puddle, lake, tarn, millpond, duck pond, fishpond, lagoon.

ponder verb **1** *take time to ponder his previous behavior* consider, reflect on, mull over, contemplate, dwell on, weigh, review. **2** *sit in the dark and ponder* think, consider, reflect, meditate, contemplate, deliberate, brood, ruminate, cogitate, cerebrate.

ponderous adjective **1** *ponderous movements* heavy, slow, awkward, clumsy, lumbering, heavy-footed. **2** *a piece of ponderous prose* awkward, clumsy, labored, forced, stilted, turgid, stodgy, lifeless, plodding, dull, boring, tedious, monotonous, dry, dreary, pedantic, verbose.

pool[1] noun **1** *resting by a mountain pool* pond, water/watering hole, tidal pool, lake, tarn. **2** *a pool of blood* puddle.

pool[2] noun **1** *typing pool* consortium, syndicate, collective, combine, group, team. **2** *a pool of cars for the sales reps* common supply, supply, reserve.

pool[3] verb *pool their resources* put together, combine, amalgamate, merge, share.

poor adjective **1** *poor people with few belongings* poverty-stricken, penniless, hard up, needy, deprived, in need, indigent, impoverished, impecunious, destitute, penurious; *inf.* broke, flat broke. **2** *live in poor surroundings* humble, lowly, mean, modest, plain. **3** *a poor diet/performance | goods of poor quality* inadequate, deficient, insufficient, unsatisfactory, inferior, imperfect, bad, low-grade, defective, faulty, second-rate; *inf.* junky, crummy. **4** *a poor crop of apples* sparse, scanty, meager, scarce, skimpy, reduced, paltry, miserable, exiguous. **5** *a diet poor in nutrients* deficient, lacking, wanting, insufficient. **6** *poor soil* unproductive, barren, unyielding, unfruitful, bare, arid, sterile. **7** *you poor thing* wretched, pitiable, pitiful, unfortunate, unlucky, luckless, unhappy, hapless, ill-fated, ill-starred. **8** *a poor specimen of a man* miserable, sad, sorry, spiritless, mean, low, base, disgraceful, despicable, contemptible, abject, pathetic.

pop verb *guns were popping* explode, go off, bang, crack, burst, detonate. **pop in** *pop in to see his mother* visit, stop by; *inf.* drop in/by. **pop up** *crocuses popping up all over the yard* appear, appear suddenly/abruptly, crop up.

popular adjective **1** *a popular choice | teachers popular with the students* well-liked, liked, favored, favorite, well-received, approved, admired, accepted. **2** *these items are so popular that we have run out* well-liked, in favor, sought-after, in demand, desired, wanted, fashionable, in fashion, in vogue, in. **3** *popular movie stars* well-known, famous, celebrated, renowned. **4** *popular music/science* accessible, simple, understandable, middle-of-the-road, middlebrow, lowbrow, readily understood; *inf.* pop. **5** *issues of popular concern* public, general, civic. **6** *popular beliefs* current, prevalent, prevailing, accepted, recognized, widespread, universal, general, common, customary, usual, standard, stock, conventional.

popularity noun **1** *teachers gaining in popularity* favor, approval, approbation, admiration, acceptance. **2** *restocking the items due to their popularity* demand, fashionableness, vogue, trendiness. **3** *ideas gaining popularity* currency, prevalence, recognition. **4** *the popularity of the entertainer* fame, renown, acclaim, esteem, repute.

population noun **1** *the population of the town* inhabitants, residents, community, people, citizenry, populace, society. **2** *the elderly population* people, folk, society. **3** *populations decreasing in rural areas* population count, numbers of inhabitants, census, headcount.

populous adjective *populous urban areas* densely populated, heavily populated, crowded.

porch noun veranda, portico, stoa, piazza.

pore verb **pore over** *poring over the map* study, read, peruse, scrutinize, examine, review, inspect.

pornography noun **1** *obsessed with pornography* obscenity, salaciousness, lewdness, prurience, erotica, indecency, smut, filth; *inf.* porn. **2** *selling pornography* obscene literature, erotica; *inf.* porn, hard porn, soft porn, porno.

port noun seaport, harbor, haven, anchorage.

portable adjective transportable, movable, conveyable, lightweight, compact, handy, manageable.

portend verb be a warning of, herald, bode, augur, presage, forebode, foreshadow, foretell, be an omen of.

portent noun *dark skies can be a portent of a storm* sign, indication, presage, warning, omen, harbinger, foreshadowing, augury.

portentous adjective **1** *portentous events warning of trouble* ominous, warning, threatening, menacing, foreboding, ill-omened. **2** *a portentous monument* marvelous, remarkable, prodigious, phenomenal, spectacular, wondrous, amazing, astounding.

portion noun **1** *serve generous portions* helping, serving, piece, quantity. **2** *give a portion of his estate to each child* share, division, quota, part, bit, piece, allocation, allotment; *inf.* cut.

portion verb *portion the estate among his children* share, divide, split, partition, carve up, parcel out; *inf.* divvy up. **portion out** *portion out pieces of cake* distribute, dispense, hand out, deal out, dole out, allocate, apportion, allot, parcel out, mete out; *inf.* divvy up.

portly adjective stout, plump, fat, corpulent, obese, tubby, of ample build, stocky.

portrait noun **1** *portraits of his ancestors hung on the walls* painting, picture, drawing, sketch, portrayal, representation, likeness, image, study, canvas. **2** *have the photographer take a portrait of his daughter* photograph, photo, picture, studio portrait, study, shot, snapshot, still. **3** *the writer's portrait of his childhood* description, portrayal, depiction, account, story, chronicle, profile.

portray verb **1** *the artist portrayed the girl in a simple blue dress* paint, draw, sketch, depict, represent, delineate. **2** *portray a scene of abject poverty* describe, depict, characterize. **3** *portray Hamlet's mother in the production* play, act the part of, act, perform, represent, execute.

pose verb **1** *ask him to pose for a portrait* sit, model. **2** *carefully pose the subjects for his still life* arrange, position, lay out, set out, dispose, place, put, locate, situate. **3** *her posing impressed no one* strike an attitude, posture, act, playact, put on airs, show off. **4** *pose a question* put forward, put, submit, advance, propound, posit. **5** *icy roads pose problems for drivers* present, set, create, cause, give rise to. **pose as** *the con artist posed as a stockbroker* pretend to be, impersonate, masquerade as.

pose noun *assume a pose for the photo session* posture, stance, position, attitude, bearing, carriage.

posh · potent

posh adjective luxurious, deluxe, sumptuous, opulent, lavish, rich, grand, elegant, ornate, fancy, plush; *inf.* classy, ritzy, swanky.

position noun **1** *a house in an isolated position* situation, location, site, place, spot, area, locality, locale, scene, setting. **2** *identify the ship's position* location, bearings, whereabouts. **3** *standing in an uncomfortable position* posture, stance, attitude, pose, bearing. **4** *in an unfortunate financial position* situation, state, condition, circumstance, predicament, plight. **5** *declared their position on tax reform* point of view, viewpoint, opinion, outlook, attitude, stand, standpoint, stance. **6** *apply for the position of manager* post, job, situation, appointment, role, office, place, capacity, duty. **7** *what is his position in the class* place, level, grade, grading, rank, status, standing. **8** *people of position in society* rank, status, stature, standing, prestige, influence, reputation, importance, consequence.

position verb *position the soldiers in rows* place, locate, situate, put, arrange, set, settle, dispose, array.

positive adjective **1** *given positive instructions* clear, clear-cut, definite, precise, categorical, direct, explicit, express, firm. **2** *no positive proof of his guilt* real, actual, absolute, concrete, conclusive, unequivocal, incontrovertible, indisputable, undeniable, incontestable, unmistakable. **3** *they are positive that they have the solution* certain, sure, assured, confident, convinced. **4** *the results of the blood test are positive* affirmative. **5** *positive criticism* constructive, productive, helpful, practical, useful, beneficial. **6** *positive thinking* confident, optimistic, assured, assertive, firm. **7** *positive progress* good, favorable, effective, promising, encouraging, heartening.

positively adverb **1** *she assured us positively that he had gone* with certainty, definitely, emphatically, firmly, categorically, absolutely, confidently, dogmatically. **2** *they were positively furious* absolutely, really, indeed, extremely.

possess verb **1** *they possess two cars* own, be the owner of, have, hold, enjoy. **2** *possess a good mind* have, be endowed with, be gifted with. **3** *as if demons had possessed them* influence, control, dominate, bewitch, enchant, obsess.

possessed adjective **1** *like someone possessed* bewitched, enchanted, under a spell, obsessed, haunted, bedeviled, crazed, mad, demented, berserk, frenzied. **2** *a possessed young woman* self-possessed, poised, self-controlled, self-assured, self-confident, confident, calm, cool, even-tempered, composed, imperturbable; *inf.* unflappable.

possession noun **1** *her possession of the jewels* ownership, proprietorship. **2** *their possession of the house* occupancy, occupation, holding, tenure, tenancy. **3** *a possession of which she was very fond* personal item, asset, personal article.

possibility noun **1** *discuss the possibility of the plan working* feasibility, practicability, attainability, likelihood, potentiality, conceivability, probability. **2** *buying a smaller house is one possibility* likelihood, prospect, chance, hope. **3** *a possibility of more violence* likelihood, prospect, potential, promise, chance, risk, hazard.

possible adjective **1** *it is not humanly possible to get there on time* feasible, practicable, doable, attainable, achievable, realizable, within reach. **2** *one of several possible outcomes* likely, potential, conceivable, imaginable, probable, credible, tenable.

possibly adverb **1** *he may possibly arrive tomorrow* perhaps, maybe, likely; *lit.* peradventure. **2** *he will arrive if he possibly can* conceivably, by any means, by any chance, at all.

post[1] noun *put up the posts for the fence* stake, upright, pole, shaft, prop, support, column, stanchion, standard, stock, picket, pillar, pale, palisade, baluster, newel.

post[2] verb **1** *post notices on the walls* put up, attach, affix, hang, display, stick, stick up, pin, pin up, tack, tack up. **2** *details of the exams will be posted* announce, advertise, publish, publicize, circulate, broadcast, make known.

post[3] noun *promoted to a more prestigious post* appointment, assignment, office, position, job, situation; work, employment.

post[4] verb *post guards at the front entrance* station, put, place, position, set, situate, locate.

poster noun **1** *posters advertising the carnival* placard, bill, notice, flyer, advertisement, announcement, bulletin; *inf.* ad. **2** *bedroom walls covered with posters* picture, print, reproduction.

postpone verb defer, put off, delay, hold over, adjourn, shelve, table, pigeonhole; *inf.* put on ice, put on the back burner.

postulate verb *postulate that the population will decrease* assume, presuppose, suppose, presume, posit, hypothesize, theorize.

posture noun **1** *in a reclining posture* position, pose, attitude. **2** *have an elegant posture* carriage, bearing, stance. **3** *adopted a critical posture toward the new policy* attitude, position, point of view, viewpoint, opinion, outlook, stand, standpoint, stance, angle, slant.

potent adjective **1** *potent drugs* powerful, strong, effective, efficacious. **2** *he was a* *potent force in the land* powerful, forceful, strong, vigorous, mighty, influential, authoritative, commanding, dominant, energetic, dynamic; *lit.* puissant.

potential adjective **1** *a potential star* budding, embryonic, developing, promising, prospective, likely, possible, probable. **2** *his potential musical ability* latent, dormant, inherent, embryonic, developing, promising. **3** *a potential disaster* likely, possible, probable.

potential noun **1** *recognize the potential of the young singer* promise, capability, capacity, ability, aptitude, talent. **2** *the potential of the broken-down house* possibilities, promise.

potion noun drink, beverage, brew, concoction, mixture, draft, elixir, philter.

potpourri noun medley, miscellany, mélange, pastiche, collage, blend, mixture, hodgepodge, mishmash, jumble, gallimaufry, farrago, olio, olla podrida.

pouch noun bag, purse, wallet, container.

pounce verb **pounce on** *the fox pounced on the mouse* swoop on, spring on, lunge at, leap at, jump at/on, bound at, make a grab for, take by surprise, attack.

pounce noun *the fox grabbed the mouse with one pounce* swoop, spring, lunge, leap, jump, bound, grab, attack.

pound verb **1** *pound the garlic to a paste* crush, beat, pulverize, smash, mash, grind, comminute, triturate. **2** *pound his opponent with his fists* beat, batter, pummel, strike, hammer, pelt, thump. **3** *with heart pounding* pulsate, pulse, throb, thump, pump, palpitate.

pour verb **1** *she poured cream over the fruit* decant, splash, spill. **2** *water poured from the burst pipe* gush, rush, stream, flow, course, spout, jet, spurt. **3** *it was pouring* rain heavily, come down in torrents/sheets, rain cats and dogs. **4** *people poured from the burning building* stream, swarm, crowd, throng, flood.

pout verb sulk, scowl, glower, lower, look sullen, look petulant.

poverty noun **1** *the poverty of the homeless people* pennilessness, neediness, need, want, hardship, deprivation, indigence, impoverishment, impecuniousness, destitution, penury, privation, beggary, pauperism, straitened circumstances. **2** *the poverty of their surroundings* humbleness, lowliness, meanness, modesty, plainness. **3** *the poverty of their imagination* deficiency, dearth, shortage, scarcity, paucity, insufficiency, lack, want, meagerness. **4** *the poverty of the soil* poorness, barrenness, unfruitfulness, bareness, aridity, sterility.

power noun **1** *the power to corrupt* ability, capability, capacity, potential. **2** *lose*

the power of speech ability, capability, faculty, competence. **3** *the power behind the blow* strength, force, forcefulness, might, weight, vigor, energy, potency. **4** *have him in her power* control, authority, mastery, domination, dominance, rule, command, ascendancy, supremacy, dominion, sway, sovereignty, influence. **5** *have the power to veto the rule* authority, authorization, warrant, license, right, prerogative. **6** *power used for heating* energy, electricity, nuclear power, solar power. **7** *the power of her argument* potency, strength, force, forcefulness, eloquence, effectiveness, cogency, conviction, persuasiveness.

powerful adjective **1** *of powerful build* | *two powerful boxers* strong, sturdy, strapping, stout, stalwart, robust, vigorous, tough, mighty. **2** *powerful members of the committee* influential, controlling, dominant, authoritative, commanding, forceful, strong, vigorous, potent, puissant. **3** *a powerful argument against leaving* forceful, strong, effective, cogent, compelling, convincing, persuasive, eloquent, impressive, telling, influential.

powerless adjective **1** *formerly influential members of the committee now powerless* impotent, weak, feeble, debilitated. **2** *powerless to give them any assistance* helpless, unfit, impotent, ineffectual, inadequate.

practicable adjective feasible, possible, viable, workable, doable, achievable, attainable, accomplishable.

practical adjective **1** *practical experience* hands-on, active, seasoned, applied, empirical, pragmatic, workaday. **2** *practical clothing for walking* functional, useful, utilitarian, sensible. **3** *she is very practical* businesslike, sensible, down-to-earth, pragmatic, realistic. **4** *find a practical solution* expedient, pragmatic, matter-of-fact, sensible, realistic, utilitarian.

practically adverb **1** *practically every day* almost, nearly, virtually, all but, in effect. **2** *behave practically* sensibly, with common sense, realistically, reasonably, pragmatically.

practice noun **1** *put the plan into practice* action, operation, application, effect, exercise, use. **2** *go to tennis practice* training, preparation, study, exercise, drill, workout, rehearsal. **3** *it is standard practice* procedure, method, system, usage, tradition, convention. **4** *it was his practice to visit his mother on Sundays* habit, custom, routine, wont. **5** *he engaged in the practice of law* profession, career, business, work, pursuit. **6** *buy a medical practice* firm, business.

practice verb **1** *to practice self-control* carry out, perform, execute, follow, pursue, observe. **2** *practicing a musical piece* work at, run through, go over, rehearse, polish, refine. **3** *practice law* work at, pursue a career in, engage in, specialize in.

practiced adjective *a practiced liar* experienced, seasoned, skilled, skillful, accomplished, expert, proficient, able, adept, adroit.

pragmatic adjective *she is very pragmatic | a pragmatic approach to the problem* practical, matter-of-fact, down-to-earth, sensible, businesslike, realistic, utilitarian.

praise verb **1** *praise the musician's performance* applaud, acclaim, cheer, compliment, congratulate someone on, pay tribute to, extol, laud. **2** *praise God* worship, glorify, honor, exalt, adore, laud, pay tribute to, give thanks to.

praise noun **1** *receive praise for his efforts* approval, approbation, applause, acclaim, acclamation, cheers, compliments, congratulations, commendation, tributes, accolades, plaudits, eulogy, panegyric, encomium, extolment, laudation, ovation, bouquets. **2** *praise to God* worship, glory, honor, devotion, exaltation, adoration, tribute, thanks.

praiseworthy adjective commendable, laudable, admirable, honorable, estimable, creditable, deserving, meritorious, worthy, excellent, exemplary, sterling, fine.

prank noun trick, practical joke, joke, hoax, caper, stunt; *inf.* lark.

prattle verb chatter, jabber, babble, twitter, blather, run on, rattle on.

pray verb **1** *pray the leaders to seek peace* appeal to, call upon, beseech, entreat, implore, beg, petition, solicit, plead with, importune, supplicate, sue, invoke, adjure. **pray for** *pray for mercy* appeal for, call for, beg for, petition for, solicit, plead for, crave, clamor for. **pray to** *pray to God* offer prayers to.

prayer noun **1** *say a prayer to God* devotion, communion, litany, invocation, intercession. **2** *prayers for mercy* appeal, plea, entreaty, petition, solicitation, supplication, suit, invocation, adjuration.

preach verb **1** *ministers preaching on Sunday* give a sermon, sermonize, evangelize. **2** *preach the word of God* proclaim, teach, spread. **3** *preach economy* advocate, recommend, advise, urge, exhort. **preach at** *tired of being preached at by her father* lecture, moralize, admonish, harangue, sermonize.

preacher noun **1** *a Baptist preacher* minister, reverend, parson, clergyman, clergywoman, ecclesiastic, cleric, missionary, revivalist, evangelist, televangelist. **2** *preachers of economy* advocate, adviser, urger, exhorter.

precarious adjective **1** *a precarious way of earning a living* uncertain, unsure, unpredictable, undependable, unreliable,

risky, hazardous, chancy, doubtful, dubious, unsettled, insecure, unstable; *inf.* dicey. **2** *sitting in a precarious position at the edge of the cliff* risky, hazardous, insecure, unstable, shaky, perilous, dangerous, touch-and-go; *inf.* dicey, hairy.

precaution noun **1** *take a few precautions to avoid accidents* preventative measure, safeguard, provision. **2** *a situation that demands precaution* foresight, forethought, anticipation, prudence, circumspection, caution, care, attentiveness, chariness, wariness.

precede verb **1** *his father preceded him as chairman* go before, be the predecessor of. **2** *she preceded him into the room* lead, usher in, go/come before, go/come ahead of, **3** *the events that preceded the murder/victory* antedate, antecede, lead up to, herald, pave the way for. **4** *precede her lecture with a few informal remarks* preface, prefix, introduce, begin, open, launch.

precedence noun *educational considerations should take precedence over financial considerations* priority, superiority, pre-eminence, supremacy, primacy, transcendence, ascendancy.

precedent noun *is there a precedent for such a punishment?* prior case, pattern, model, example, exemplar, paradigm, criterion, yardstick, standard, previous instance.

preceding adjective *as stated in the preceding paragraph* above, foregoing, previous, earlier, prior, antecedent, anterior.

precept noun **1** *follow the precepts of one's religion* rule, guideline, principle, code, law, tenet, canon, ordinance, statute, command, order, decree, mandate, dictate, dictum, directive, direction, instruction. **2** *precepts that her grandmother used to quote* maxim, axiom, saying, law, adage, aphorism.

precious adjective **1** *precious metals* valuable, costly, expensive, priceless, rare, choice. **2** *precious memories* valued, cherished, prized, treasured, favorite, dear, beloved, adored. **3** *her manners are too precious for words* affected, artificial, chichi, overrefined, effete.

precipice noun escarpment, scarp, cliff, crag, bluff.

precipitate verb *precipitate the crisis* hasten, accelerate, expedite, speed up, propel, trigger.

precipitate adjective **1** *his precipitate dash from the room* hurried, rapid, swift, speedy, headlong, abrupt, sudden, unexpected, breakneck, violent, precipitous. **2** *his precipitate action* hasty, hurried, rash, heedless, reckless, impetuous, impulsive, precipitous, harebrained.

precipitous adjective **1** *a precipitous cliff* steep, sheer, perpendicular, abrupt, high. **2** *his precipitous exit* hurried, abrupt. *See* PRECIPITATE adjective 1. **3** *his precipitous action* hasty, impetuous. *See* PRECIPITATE adjective 2.

precise adjective **1** *a precise record of events* exact, literal, actual, close, faithful, strict, minute, accurate, correct. **2** *at that precise moment she saw him* exact, very, actual, particular, specific, distinct. **3** *precise attention to detail* careful, exact, meticulous, scrupulous, conscientious, punctilious, particular, methodical, fastidious, strict, rigorous.

precisely adverb **1** *at 6 o'clock precisely* exactly, sharp, on the dot, on the button. **2** *write out instructions precisely* exactly, literally, strictly, minutely.

precision noun **1** *the precision of his prose* carefulness, exactness, meticulousness, scrupulousness, conscientiousness, punctiliousness, rigor. **2** *the precision of the mechanism* accuracy, exactness, reliability, regularity.

preclude verb **1** *the rules of the club preclude drinking* prevent, prohibit, debar, interdict, block, bar, hinder, impede. **2** *the findings preclude any doubt as to his guilt* rule out, eliminate.

precocious adjective advanced, gifted, talented, brilliant, bright, quick, intelligent, smart.

preconception noun assumption, presupposition, presumption, prejudgment.

precursor noun **1** *the attacks proved to be the precursors of a full-scale war* forerunner, prelude, harbinger, herald, curtain-raiser. **2** *a precursor of the modern computer* predecessor, forerunner, antecedent, ancestor, forebear, progenitor.

predatory adjective **1** *predatory birds* predacious, carnivorous, rapacious, raptorial. **2** *her predatory relatives have left her penniless* exploitative, exploiting, imposing, greedy, acquisitive, rapacious, vulturine.

predestine verb *he seemed predestined to lead a life of poverty* preordain, foreordain, predetermine, fate, destine.

predetermined adjective *everyone acted on a predetermined signal* prearranged, preplanned, agreed, settled, fixed, set.

predicament noun dilemma, quandary, plight, tight corner, mess, emergency, crisis; *inf.* jam, sticky situation, fix, pickle, scrape, tight spot.

predict verb forecast, foretell, prophesy, foresee, divine, prognosticate, forewarn, forebode, portend, presage, augur.

prediction noun prophecy, forecast, divination, prognostication, forewarning, augury.

predilection noun *a predilection for spicy food* fondness, preference, love, partiality, taste, weakness, soft spot, fancy, inclination, leaning, liking, bias, propensity, bent, proclivity, proneness, penchant, predisposition.

predispose verb **1** *his poverty-stricken childhood predisposed him to save* move, incline, dispose, persuade, influence, sway, induce, prompt. **2** *the child is predisposed to asthma* make susceptible, make prone, make vulnerable.

predominant adjective **1** *the predominant member of the alliance* dominant, controlling, ascendant, ruling, leading, principal, chief, main, supreme, superior. **2** *idleness is his predominant characteristic* chief, main, principal, preponderant, most prevailing.

predominate verb **1** *the largest country predominates in the policymaking* be dominant, rule, hold ascendancy, hold sway, have the upper hand, carry most weight. **2** *blue predominates in the decor* be prevalent, preponderate, be most prominent.

preeminent adjective outstanding, leading, foremost, chief, excellent, distinguished, prominent, eminent, important, famous, renowned, supreme, superior, unrivaled, unsurpassed, transcendent.

preempt verb **1** *preempt the sale of the building by buying it themselves* forestall, prevent, invalidate. **2** *a news bulletin preempting the regular broadcast* supplant, displace, supersede, replace, substitute for.

preen verb **1** *birds preening their feathers* clean, smooth, arrange, plume. **2** *preening himself in front of the mirror* groom, spruce up, beautify, prettify, primp; doll up.

preface noun introduction, foreword, front matter, preamble, prologue, prelude, proem, exordium, prolegomenon; *inf.* intro.

preface verb *preface her speech with a short introduction* precede, prefix, introduce, begin, open, launch.

prefer verb **1** *of the desserts, I prefer pie* favor, incline toward, choose, select, pick, opt for; *inf.* fancy. **2** *prefer to go by bus* would rather, would sooner, favor, choose, opt, elect, wish, want.

preference noun **1** *her preference is for a two-story house* choice, first choice, inclination, liking, fancy, desire, wish, partiality, predilection, leaning, bias, bent. **2** *of the desserts, what is your preference?* choice, selection, option, pick. **3** *applicants with experience will be given preference* priority, advantage, preferential treatment, favor, precedence.

pregnant adjective **1** *discover that she was pregnant* expectant, with child, enceinte; *inf.* expecting, in the family way. **2** *a* *pregnant pause following her announcement* meaningful, significant, eloquent, expressive, suggestive, loaded, charged, pointed, telling.

prejudice noun **1** *have a prejudice against young people* bias, partiality, jaundiced eye, preconceived idea, preconception, prejudgment, predetermination. **2** *racial prejudice* bigotry, bias, discrimination, intolerance, partisanship, partiality, chauvinism, narrow-mindedness, unfairness, unjustness, racism. **3** *without prejudice to any future judgment* detriment, disadvantage, damage, injury, harm, hurt, loss.

prejudice verb **1** *newspaper articles had prejudiced the attitude of the jury* bias, color, poison, jaundice, influence, sway, predispose. **2** *his conviction may prejudice his chances* be detrimental to, damage, injure, harm, hurt, mar, spoil, impair, undermine.

prejudiced adjective *have a prejudiced attitude about foreigners* biased, discriminatory, partisan, partial, one-sided, jaundiced, chauvinistic, bigoted, intolerant, narrowminded, unfair, unjust, racist, sexist.

preliminary adjective **1** *a few preliminary remarks* introductory, prefatory, precursory, opening, initial, beginning, preparatory, initiatory. **2** *preliminary heats* prior, precursory, qualifying, eliminating. **3** *preliminary experiments* introductory, early, exploratory, pilot, test, trial.

preliminary noun **1** *dispense with the preliminaries and get on with the meeting* preparation, groundwork, introduction, preamble, prelude, opening. **2** *advance to the final round after passing the preliminaries* first round, heat, trial, preliminary exam/examination.

prelude noun **1** *the skirmishes were a prelude to full-scale war* precursor, forerunner, curtain-raiser, harbinger, herald, preliminary, introduction, start, beginning. **2** *the prelude to the narrative poem* introduction, preface, prologue, preamble, proem, exordium, prolegomenon; *inf.* intro. **3** *the prelude to the fugue* overture, introductory movement, voluntary.

premature adjective **1** *his premature death* early, untimely, too soon. **2** *it was premature of him to announce his plans* hasty, precipitate, impulsive, impetuous, rash. **3** *announce premature plans* incomplete, undeveloped, immature, embryonic.

premier noun *an international meeting of premiers* head of government, head of state, chief executive, president, prime minister, chancellor.

premise noun *financial advice based on the premise that the recession was over* hypothesis, thesis, assumption, presupposition, presumption, argument, postulation.

premium noun **1** *monthly premiums for life insurance* payment, installment. **2** *earned a premium of $60 on their investment* bonus, dividend. **3** *pay a premium for early delivery* surcharge, additional payment, additional fee. **at a premium 1** *cannot buy a house when real estate is at a premium* high-priced, expensive, costly, upmarket. **2** *parking spaces are at a premium in the city* rare, hard to come by, in short supply, scarce, in great demand, like gold, not to be had. **put a premium on 1** *the teacher puts a premium on creative work* set great store by, hold in high regard, appreciate. **2** *the risk of disease puts a premium on hygiene* make invaluable, make essential, make important.

premonition noun **1** *had a premonition that something terrible was going to happen* foreboding, presage, presentiment, intuition, feeling, hunch, suspicion, misgiving, apprehension. **2** *given a premonition that all was not well in the firm* forewarning, warning, sign, indication, omen, portent.

preoccupied adjective *she seemed rather preoccupied* absorbed, engrossed, pensive, absentminded, distracted, abstracted, distrait, oblivious, rapt.

preoccupy verb *his financial worries were preoccupying him* absorb, engross, distract, obsess.

preparation noun **1** *the preparation of their plans* arrangement, development, assembly, drawing up, production, construction, composition. **2** *finalize their preparations for battle* arrangement, provision, preparatory measure, groundwork, spadework. **3** *the preparation of the students for the exam* coaching, training, grooming, priming.

prepare verb **1** *prepare their plans* make ready, arrange, develop, assemble, draw up, produce, construct, compose, concoct, fashion, work up. **2** *prepare for the president's visit* make preparations, get ready, lay the groundwork, do the spadework. **3** *prepare for the soccer game* train, get into shape, practice, exercise, warm up. **4** *prepare for the exam* study, do homework. **5** *prepare the students for the exam/contest* coach, train, groom, prime. **6** *prepare herself for a shock* brace, steel. **7** *prepare a meal* cook, make, put together, assemble; *inf.* fix, throw together.

preponderance noun *a preponderance of men over women on the staff | a preponderance of red in the room's decor* predominance, dominance, prevalence, majority, bulk.

preposterous adjective *what a preposterous idea!* absurd, ridiculous, foolish, ludicrous, farcical, asinine, senseless, unreasonable, irrational, outrageous, shocking, astonishing, unbelievable, incredible, unthinkable; *inf.* crazy, insane.

prerequisite noun *experience is a prerequisite for the job* requirement, requisite, necessity, essential, precondition, condition, sine qua non; *inf.* must.

prerogative noun *he thinks it is his prerogative to make all the decisions* right, birthright, privilege, due, entitlement, liberty, authority, license.

prescribe verb **1** *the doctor prescribed antibiotics* write a prescription for, order, advise, direct. **2** *prescribe a vacation to cure her depression* advise, recommend, commend, suggest. **3** *the law prescribes strict penalties for drunk driving* lay down, require, direct, stipulate, specify, impose, decree, order, command, ordain, enjoin.

presence noun **1** *the presence of too much acid in the soil* existence, being. **2** *demand his presence at the meeting* attendance, company, companionship. **3** *in the presence of a great man* company, propinquity, proximity, vicinity, closeness, nearness. **4** *a woman of presence* magnetism, aura, charisma, personality, attraction, poise, self-assurance, self-possession, self-confidence, bearing, carriage, dignity. **presence of mind** composure, aplomb, levelheadedness, sang-froid, self-assurance, self-possession, calmness, calm, coolness, alertness, quickness, quick-wittedness.

present[1] adjective **1** *poison was present in the drink* existent, extant. **2** *in the present climate* present-day, existing, current, contemporary. **3** *a doctor had to be present* in attendance, nearby, available, at hand, ready.

present[2] noun *forget the past and think about the present* today, now, here and now, the time being. **at present** *at present he is unavailable* just now, right now, at the moment, currently, presently.

present[3] verb **1** *present a gift to the retiring chairman* award, grant, accord, give, confer, bestow. **2** *present his proposals to the committee* submit, set forth, put forward, proffer, offer, tender, advance. **3** *present his apologies* give, offer, send, tender. **4** *may I present my daughter?* introduce, make known. **5** *present their new product* exhibit, display, put on display, demonstrate, introduce, show, launch. **6** *present a new musical* produce, perform, stage, put on, mount. **7** *present a radio/television program* introduce, host; *inf.* emcee.

present[4] noun *a birthday present* gift, donation, offering, contribution, gratuity, handout, giveaway, presentation, largesse, award, premium, bounty, boon, benefaction.

presentable adjective *make yourself presentable for the interview* well-groomed, smartly dressed, tidy, spruce.

presentation noun **1** *the presentation of his retirement gift* conferral, bestowal, award, granting, according. **2** *the presentation of their proposals to the committee* submission, proffering, tendering, offering. **3** *the presentation of his fiancée to his family* introduction, making known, acquainting. **4** *the presentation of their new product* launch, launching, show, exhibition, display, demonstration. **5** *attend the drama club's presentation of Hamlet* production, performance, staging, mounting, showing, rendition. **6** *improve the presentation of his material* arrangement, organization, ordering, disposition, layout, scheme, system, structure.

presently adverb *he will be here presently* soon, shortly, momentarily, directly, in a moment.

preservation noun **1** *the preservation of the rain forest* conservation, protection. **2** *the preservation of the town from danger* protection, defense, guarding, safeguarding, safekeeping, safety, security, salvation, sheltering, shielding. **3** *the preservation of old traditions* conservation, maintenance, continuation, upholding, perpetuation.

preserve verb **1** *find a substance to preserve the wood* protect, safeguard, care for. **2** *preserve the town from danger* keep, protect, defend, guard, safeguard, secure, shelter, shield. **3** *preserve his work for posterity* save, keep, safeguard, maintain, perpetuate. **4** *preserve the old traditions* keep up, keep alive, maintain, uphold, prolong, perpetuate. **5** *preserve food* cure, smoke, dry, pickle, salt, marinate, kipper, freeze, freeze-dry, can; *inf.* put up, lay by.

preserve noun **1** *an animal preserve* sanctuary, reserve, reservation, game reserve. **2** *he regards the family finances as his preserve* area, domain, field, sphere, realm.

preside verb *the committee members elected him to preside* chair, officiate. **preside over** *preside over the company* be in charge of, head, manage, administer, control, direct, run, conduct, supervise, govern, rule, head up.

president noun **1** *president of the United States* chief of state, head of state, chief executive, commander in chief. **2** *president of the society* head, chief, director, leader, captain.

press verb **1** *press the button* depress, push down, bear down on. **2** *press grapes* crush, squeeze, compress, mash, reduce. **3** *press a pair of pants* iron, smooth out, put creases in, calender, mangle. **4** *press her hand/arm affectionately* squeeze, pat, caress. **5** *they are pressing him to make a decision* urge, entreat, exhort, implore, pressurize, force, compel, coerce, constrain. **6** *press a claim* plead, urge, push forward, advance. **7**

press around the stage to see the performers crowd, surge, cluster, mill, flock, gather, swarm, throng. **press for** *they are pressing for a quick decision* call for, demand, insist on, clamor for. **press on** *we must press on to reach the summit* push on, make haste, hasten, hurry, proceed, continue.

press noun **1** *advertise in the press* newspapers, papers, news media, journalism, the media, journalists, reporters. **2** *get good/bad press* press coverage, press reporting, newspaper articles, write-ups. **3** *he has set up a small press* printing firm, publishing firm, publishing house.

pressing adjective *pressing engagement* urgent, vital, crucial, critical, demanding, important, high-priority, exigent, pivotal.

pressure noun **1** *have to exert pressure on the door to open it | the pressure of the crowd against the barriers* force, weight, heaviness, compression, compressing, squeezing, crushing. **2** *police exerting pressure to get a confession* force, compulsion, coercion, constraint, duress. **3** *the pressure of the job* strain, stress, tension, burden, load, weight, trouble; *inf.* hassle. **4** *find it difficult to work under pressure* adversity, difficulty, urgency, strain, stress, tension.

prestige noun *suffered a loss of prestige when he lost his job* status, standing, stature, importance, reputation, fame, renown, esteem, influence, authority, supremacy, eminence, superiority, predominance.

prestigious adjective **1** *a prestigious school* respected, esteemed, eminent, distinguished, of high standing, well-known, celebrated, illustrious, renowned, famous. **2** *a prestigious job* prominent, impressive, high-ranking, influential, glamorous.

presumably adverb *presumably he will get the job* in all probability, probably, in all likelihood, on the face of it, as likely as not.

presume verb **1** *I presume that your new partner is honest* assume, take for granted, take it, suppose, presuppose, believe, imagine, judge, guess, surmise, conjecture, hypothesize, infer, deduce. **2** *do not presume to offer advice to a more experienced person* have the temerity, have the audacity, be so bold as, have the effrontery, go so far as, dare, venture. **presume on/upon** *presume on/upon his good nature* take advantage of, exploit, take liberties with.

presumption noun **1** *his request for an invitation was pure presumption* arrogance, egotism, boldness, audacity, forwardness, insolence, impudence, bumptiousness, temerity, effrontery. **2** *our presumption is that he has run away* assumption, supposition, presupposition, belief, thought, judgment, guess, surmise, conjecture, hypothesis, premise, inference, deduction.

presumptuous adjective *it was presumptuous to offer advice to someone of her experience* overconfident, cocksure, arrogant, egotistical, conceited, overbold, bold, audacious, forward, insolent, impudent, bumptious, self-assertive, overbearing, overweening; *inf.* pushy.

pretend verb **1** *she is not ill—she is only pretending* act, playact, dissemble, sham, feign, fake, fake it, dissimulate, posture. **2** *she is pretending that she knows nothing about it* make believe, affect, profess, fabricate. **3** *pretend illness* feign, fake, simulate, sham. **4** *pretend to the title* lay claim, make a claim, aspire. **5** *pretend to be her friend* claim, profess, purport.

pretense noun **1** *she is not ill—it is just pretense* acting, dissembling, shamming, faking, dissimulation, make-believe, invention, imagination, posturing. **2** *not taken in by their pretense of grief* false show, semblance, appearance, guise, façade, masquerade, mask, veneer, cover, charade. **3** *on the pretense that he was dying* sham, ruse, wile. *See* PRETEXT. **4** *I have no pretense to being expert* claim, aspiration, purporting, profession. **5** *lead humble lives without pretense* pretentiousness, display, ostentation, affectation, showiness, flaunting, posturing.

pretentious adjective **1** *a pretentious style of writing* affected, ostentatious, showy, overambitious, pompous, artificial, mannered, high-flown, flowery, grandiose, elaborate, extravagant, flamboyant, grandiloquent, magniloquent, bombastic, orotund; *inf.* highfalutin. **2** *a pretentious lifestyle* affected, ostentatious, showy, flaunting, flamboyant.

pretext noun *the thief got into the house on the pretext of checking the phone lines* pretense, false excuse, excuse, cover, guise, sham, ruse, wile, trickery, red herring, lie, falsehood, misrepresentation.

pretty adjective **1** *a pretty child* attractive, lovely, good-looking, nice-looking, comely, prepossessing, appealing, charming, delightful, nice, engaging, pleasing, winning, winsome, cute. **2** *a pretty pattern* attractive, lovely, appealing, pleasant, pleasing, charming, delightful, nice. **3** *cost a pretty penny | make a pretty profit* considerable, large, sizable, substantial, appreciable, fair, tolerable, goodly; *inf.* tidy.

prevail verb **1** *in the end, common sense prevailed* win, win out, triumph, be victorious, carry the day, prove superior, conquer, overcome, gain mastery, gain ascendancy, take the crown, rule. **2** *the economic conditions prevailing at the time* exist, obtain, occur, abound, hold sway, predominate, preponderate, be prevalent, be current, be widespread. **prevail on/upon** *prevail* *upon him to speak at the conference* persuade, induce, convince, sway, prompt, influence, urge, exhort, pressure, cajole, coax; *inf.* sweet-talk.

prevailing adjective **1** *the prevailing attitude toward criminals | the prevailing fashion in hats* prevalent, current, usual, common, general, widespread, established, accepted, popular, fashionable, in style, in vogue. **2** *the prevailing political party* prevalent, dominant, predominant, preponderant, ruling, governing, ascendant, principal, chief, main, supreme. **3** *the prevailing wind in the area* most frequent, most common, commonest.

prevalent adjective **1** *the prevalent opinion in the country is against the war* current, common, widespread. *See* PREVAILING 1. **2** *malaria is prevalent there* common, usual, endemic, widespread, universal, extensive, frequent, ubiquitous, rampant, rife. **3** *the prevalent political party* dominant, preponderant, governing. *See* PREVAILING 2.

prevent verb *prevent the spread of the fire | prevent his daughter from leaving school* stop, halt, arrest, avert, nip in the bud, fend off, turn aside, stave off, ward off, block, check, hinder, impede, hamper, obstruct, balk, foil, thwart, frustrate, forestall, inhibit, restrain, prohibit, bar, deter.

prevention noun *the prevention of crime* stopping, halting, halt, arresting, staving off, warding off, checking, hindrance, hampering, obstruction, balking, foiling, frustration, restraint, prohibition, barring, deterrence.

previous adjective **1** *the previous mayor* former, ex-, preceding, foregoing, past, sometime, onetime, quondam, erstwhile, antecedent, precursory. **2** *in the previous paragraph* preceding, foregoing, earlier, prior, above, precursory, antecedent, anterior. **3** *on a previous occasion* prior, earlier, former, preceding. **previous to** *previous to this everything was fine* before, prior to, until, up to, up until, earlier than, preceding.

previously adverb *previously they lived in Kansas* formerly, earlier on, before, until now/then, hitherto, heretofore, once, at one time.

prey noun **1** *lions looking for prey* quarry, game, kill. **2** *prey for any dishonest salesman* victim, target, dupe; *inf.* sitting duck.

prey verb **prey on 1** *lions preying on deer* eat, devour, hunt, catch, seize. **2** *con men preying on the unsuspecting* victimize, exploit, take advantage of, fleece, attack, bleed; *inf.* con.

price noun **1** *what is the price of the table in the window?* cost, charge, fee, payment, rate, amount, figure, value, valuation, outlay, expense, expenditure, bill. **2** *lack of privacy is the price of fame* consequence, result, cost, penalty, sacrifice, forfeiture, punishment. **3** *outlaws with a price on their heads* reward, bounty, premium, recompense, compensation.

price verb *price the items at $10 each* value, rate, cost, evaluate, assess, estimate, appraise, assay.

priceless adjective *priceless jewels/memories* invaluable, precious, rare, incomparable, expensive, costly, rich, dear, irreplaceable, treasured, prized, cherished, worth its weight in gold, worth a king's ransom.

prick noun **1** *give his finger a prick with a sharp needle* jag, jab, stab, nick. **2** *see the prick on the surface* puncture, perforation, hole, pinhole, nick. **3** *feel a prick on the surface of the skin* prickle, sting, smarting, tingle, tingling, pain. **4** *the pricks of his conscience* pang, twinge, gnawing. **5** *rosebushes with pricks* spike, thorn, barb, spine, prong, tine.

pride noun **1** *his pride was hurt by her criticisms* self-esteem, self-respect, ego, *amour propre*, self-worth, self-image, feelings, sensibilities. **2** *puffed with pride at his achievement* conceit, vanity, arrogance, haughtiness, self-importance, self-conceit, egotism, presumption, hauteur, superciliousness, disdain; *inf.* bigheadedness. **3** *take pride in his work* satisfaction, gratification, pleasure, joy, delight. **4** *the gold medalist is the pride of the swim team* prize, jewel, jewel in the crown, flower, gem, treasure, glory.

pride verb **pride oneself on** *she prided herself on her punctuality* take satisfaction in, congratulate oneself on, revel in, glory in, exult in.

priest noun clergyman, minister, vicar, ecclesiastic, cleric, churchman, churchwoman, man/woman of the cloth, man/woman of God, father, padre.

prig noun prude, puritan, killjoy; *inf.* goodygoody, Goody Two-shoes.

priggish adjective prudish, puritanical, prim, prissy, straitlaced, stuffy, starchy, self-righteous, sanctimonious, narrow-minded, censorious; *inf.* holier-than-thou, goody-goody.

prim adjective proper, demure, formal, precise, stuffy, starchy, straitlaced, prudish, prissy, priggish, puritanical.

prima donna noun diva, leading lady, star.

primarily adverb *his role is primarily an administrative one* basically, essentially, in essence, fundamentally, first and foremost, chiefly, mainly, principally, mostly, for the most part, on the whole, predominantly, predominately.

primary adjective **1** *the children's welfare is our primary consideration* prime, chief, main, principal, leading, predominant, paramount. **2** *finding food to eat is a primary need* basic, fundamental, elemental, rudimentary, essential, prime. **3** *the primary stages of the disease* earliest, original, initial, beginning, first, opening, introductory.

prime adjective **1** *his prime motive was self-interest* chief, main, principal, leading, predominant, major, paramount. **2** *the prime cause of the trouble* basic, fundamental, elemental, rudimentary, essential, primary. **3** *of prime quality* top-quality, highest, top, best, first-class, high-grade, grade A, superior, choice, select; *inf.* A-1. **4** *a prime example of what is wrong with modern society* classic, ideal, excellent, typical, standard.

prime noun *in the prime of his life* | *flowers in their prime* peak, pinnacle, height, zenith, acme, culmination, apex, heyday, full flowering, perfection, blossoming.

prime verb **1** *prime the machines for use* prepare, make ready, get ready, equip. **2** *prime the investigating officer* brief, inform, supply with facts; *inf.* fill in. **3** *the attorney was accused of priming the witness* coach, prepare.

primeval adjective *primeval rocks/species* ancient, earliest, prehistoric, primitive, primordial, primal, autochthonal, pristine.

primitive adjective **1** *in primitive times* | *the primitive church* ancient, earliest, primeval, primordial, primal, autochthonal. **2** *primitive farming tools* crude, simple, rudimentary, undeveloped, unrefined, rough, unsophisticated, rude. **3** *primitive tribes* uncivilized, barbarian, barbaric, savage, wild. **4** *primitive art* simple, natural, unsophisticated, naïve, undeveloped, childlike. **5** *primitive artists* unsophisticated, naïve, untaught, untrained, untutored.

primp verb *primp themselves for the photo* groom, tidy, smarten, spruce, preen, plume; *inf.* doll up.

principal adjective **1** *the principal members of the organization* chief, leading, preeminent, foremost, most influential, dominant, controlling, ruling, in charge. **2** *the principal issues on the agenda* chief, main, major, most important, leading, key, primary, prime, paramount.

principal noun **1** *the principals in the firm* chief, head, director, leader, manager, boss, ruler, controller; *inf.* honcho. **2** *the principals in the play* leading player, leading man/lady, lead, star. **3** *lend him the principal to start up the business* capital, capital funds, working capital, financial resources.

principally adverb *he is interested principally in higher education* chiefly, above all, first and foremost, mainly, primarily, mostly, particularly, especially.

principle noun **1** *the basic principles of geometry* truth, philosophy, idea, theory, basis, fundamental, essence, assumption. **2** *believe in the principle of equal opportunity* rule, law, canon, tenet, code, maxim, axiom, dictum, postulate. **3** *a woman of principle* morals, ethics, integrity, uprightness, righteousness, probity, rectitude, honor, conscience, scruples. **in principle 1** *there is no reason in principle why such a machine could not be built* in theory, theoretically. **2** *they agree in principle to the plan* in essence, in general.

print verb **1** *print books/newspapers* set in print, publish, issue, send to press, run off, put to bed. **2** *print a design on the cloth* imprint, stamp, mark.

print noun **1** *see the story in print* type, letters, lettering, typeface, newsprint. **2** *buy a print of one of Monet's works* copy, reproduction, replica. **3** *buy a set of prints showing presidential homes* picture, design, engraving, lithograph, etching, silkscreen, woodcut. **4** *get enlarged prints* photograph, photo, snapshot. **5** *chairs covered in a print* patterned material/cloth, chintz. **in print 1** *likes to see his name in print* in black and white, on paper. **2** *are her novels still in print?* published, printed, available, on the market. **out of print** *looking for a biography that is out of print* no longer published/printed, unavailable, unobtainable.

prior adjective *a prior claim* earlier, previous, anterior. **prior to** *prior to the conference, they had never met* before, until, up to, preceding.

priority noun **1** *the children's safety is their priority* prime concern, most important thing. **2** *give priority to homeless people* precedence, preference, urgency, superiority.

prison noun jail, penitentiary, lockup, penal institution, dungeon; *inf.* clink, cooler, slammer, pen.

pristine adjective **1** *a pristine copy of the book* unmarked, unblemished, unspoiled, spotless, immaculate, clean, in mint condition. **2** *pristine snow* spotless, clean, fresh, virgin.

private adjective **1** *for her private use* personal, individual, own, particular, especial, special, exclusive. **2** *hold private talks* confidential, secret, unofficial, off-the-record, in camera, closet, privileged; *inf.* hush-hush. **3** *her private thoughts* personal, intimate, secret. **4** *a private place where the lovers meet* secluded, sequestered, quiet, secret, remote, out-of-the-way, withdrawn, retired. **5** *trespassing on private property* privately owned, off-limits. **6** *a private person* reserved, retiring, self-contained, uncommunicative, noncommunicative, diffident, secretive. **7** *the president on a private visit* unofficial, personal. **8** *private industry* privatized, independent.

privation noun *suffering a life of privation* deprivation, want, need, neediness, disadvantage, poverty, penury, hardship, distress, indigence, destitution.

privilege noun **1** *parking there is the privilege of the executives* right, prerogative, entitlement, due, sanction, advantage, benefit, birthright. **2** *enjoy diplomatic privilege* immunity, exemption, dispensation, concession, liberty, freedom. **3** *has always led a life of privilege* advantage, favor, favorable circumstances. **4** *he felt that it had been a privilege to meet her* honor, special benefit.

privileged adjective **1** *coming from a privileged background* advantaged, favored, elite, protected, sheltered. **2** *foreign diplomats are privileged* immune, exempt, excepted. **3** *punished for revealing privileged information* confidential, private, off-the-record, secret, top-secret; *inf.* hush-hush.

prize noun **1** *win a prize in the lottery* jackpot, stakes, purse, winnings. **2** *six prizes awarded in the flower show* trophy, medal, award, accolade, reward, premium, honor, laurels.

prize adjective *wind destroyed his prize roses* prizewinning, award-winning, champion, best, top, choice, select, first-class, first-rate, excellent; *inf.* top-notch, A-1.

prize verb *she prizes her freedom* value, treasure, cherish, hold dear, appreciate, esteem, hold in high regard.

probability noun **1** *what is the probability of the government losing the election?* likelihood, prospect, expectation, chance, chances, odds, possibility. **2** *snow at Christmas is a distinct probability* likelihood, prospect, possibility, reasonable bet.

probable adjective *the probable result is a win for the home team | it is probable that we will arrive late* likely, odds-on, expected, to be expected, anticipated, predictable, foreseeable, credible, possible.

probably adverb *they will probably win* in all probability, likely, in all likelihood, as likely as not, it is to be expected that, perhaps, maybe, possibly.

probe noun *order a probe into the company's accounting procedures* investigation, scrutiny, inquiry, inquest, exploration, examination, study, research, analysis.

probe verb **1** *probe the tooth with his tongue* feel, prod, poke, explore, check. **2** *probe the financial state of the company* investigate, scrutinize, inquire into, examine, study, research, analyze.

problem noun **1** *face a seemingly impossible problem* difficulty, complication, trouble, mess, predicament, plight, dilemma, quandary; *inf.* pickle. **2** *the car's mechanical problems* difficulty, trouble, complication. **3** *he and his wife have had a few problems* difficulty, dispute, bone of contention. **4** *baffled by the word problems* question, puzzle, poser, enigma, riddle, conundrum; *inf.* teaser, brainteaser. **5** *the child is a real problem* source of trouble, bother, nuisance, pest, vexation; *inf.* hassle, aggravation.

problem adjective *a problem child* difficult, troublesome, delinquent, unmanageable, unruly, uncontrollable, intractable, recalcitrant, nuisance.

problematic adjective **1** *a problematic situation* difficult, troublesome, complicated, puzzling, knotty, thorny, ticklish, tricky. **2** *the likely result is still problematic* doubtful, uncertain, unsettled, questionable, open to question, debatable, arguable.

procedure noun **1** *the usual office procedure* course of action, policy, system, method, methodology, modus operandi, technique, means, practice, operation, strategy, way, routine, wont, custom. **2** *essential procedures for setting up the new system* action, step, process, measure, move, operation, transaction.

proceed verb **1** *proceed along Main Street* make one's way, go, advance, carry on, continue, move on, progress. **2** *how shall we proceed?* act, take action, take steps, take measures, go ahead, move, make a start, progress, get under way. **3** *noise proceeding from the floor below | the tragedy that proceeded from a family feud* arise, originate, spring, stem, come, derive, result, follow, ensue, emanate, issue, flow.

proceedings plural noun **1** *the evening's proceedings begin at 7 p.m.* activities, events, action, process, business, affairs, doings, happenings. **2** *the proceedings against him are likely to last several weeks* legal action, case, lawsuit, litigation, trial. **3** *the proceedings of the meeting were made available* minutes, report, account, record, transactions.

proceeds plural noun *donate the proceeds to charity* takings, profits, returns, receipts, gain, income, earnings.

process noun **1** *damaged during the manufacturing process* operation, action, activity, steps, stages. **2** *develop a new process for cleaning stone buildings* method, system, technique, means, practice, way, procedure. **3** *the aging process* development, evolution, changes, stages, steps. **4** *legal processes can be very slow* proceedings, legal action, case, lawsuit, trial. **in the process** *we are in the process of cataloging our* *books* in the midst, in the course, at the stage.

procession noun **1** *a candlelit procession as part of the celebration* parade, march, column, file, train, cortege. **2** *a procession of decorated vehicles* cavalcade, motorcade. **3** *a seemingly endless procession of houseguests* stream, string, succession, series, sequence, run.

proclaim verb **1** *proclaim the news of a royal birth* announce, declare, make known, notify, circulate, advertise, publish, broadcast, promulgate, pronounce, blazon, trumpet, shout something from the rooftops. **2** *proclaim him king* pronounce, announce, declare.

proclamation noun **1** *hear the proclamation of a royal birth* announcement, declaration, notification, circulation, advertisement, publishing, broadcasting, promulgation, pronouncement, blazoning. **2** *the king's proclamation was posted in each town* announcement, declaration, pronouncement, decree, edict, order, command, rule, manifesto.

procrastinate verb delay, stall, temporize, play for time, dally, dilly-dally, drag one's feet/heels.

procure verb **1** *procure a copy of the book from the library* obtain, acquire, get, pick up, find, come by, get hold of, secure, get possession of, gain. **2** *somehow procure the dismissal of his colleague* bring about, cause, contrive, manage, manipulate, rig; *inf.* fix.

prod verb **1** *prod him in the ribs* poke, jab, dig, nudge, elbow, butt, push, shove, thrust. **2** *prod the child into doing some work* urge, encourage, rouse, move, motivate, stimulate, incite, spur, impel, actuate, goad.

prod noun **1** *get a prod in the ribs from someone in the crowd* poke, jab, dig, nudge, elbow, butt, push, shove, thrust. **2** *use a prod to get the cows to go back to the farm* goad, stick, spike. **3** *giving the child a prod to get him to do some work* encouragement, prompt, motivation, stimulus, incitement, spur, goad.

prodigal adjective *a government accused of being prodigal* extravagant, spendthrift, squandering, improvident, imprudent, immoderate, profligate, excessive, wasteful, reckless, wanton.

prodigious adjective **1** *a prodigious achievement* amazing, astonishing, astounding, staggering, stupendous, marvelous, wonderful, phenomenal, miraculous, impressive, striking, startling, extraordinary, remarkable, exceptional, unusual; *inf.* fantastic, fabulous, flabbergasting. **2** *children frightened by the prodigious creatures on the screen* enormous, huge, colossal, gigantic, giant, mammoth, immense, massive, vast, monumental, tremendous, inordinate, monstrous. **3** *charge a prodigious amount of money* huge, large, colossal, immense, massive, considerable, substantial, sizable; *inf.* vast, tremendous.

prodigy noun **1** *the young musician is a prodigy* genius, gifted child, mastermind; *inf.* Einstein. **2** *the pyramids are among the prodigies of the world* wonder, marvel, phenomenon, sensation, miracle.

produce verb **1** *a factory producing high-quality work* make, manufacture, create, construct, build, fabricate, assemble, turn out. **2** *produce great works of art* compose, create, originate, prepare, develop, frame, fashion, turn out. **3** *produce new evidence* bring forward, set forth, present, offer, proffer, advance, show, exhibit, demonstrate, disclose, reveal. **4** *cows producing milk* yield, bear, give, bring forth, supply, provide, furnish. **5** *sows producing litters of piglets* give birth to, bring forth, bear, breed, procreate. **6** *his speech produced an angry reaction* cause, give rise to, evoke, bring about, set off, occasion, generate, engender, induce, initiate, start, spark. **7** *produce plays for television* mount, stage, put on, present, direct.

produce noun *organically grown produce* crops, fruit and vegetables, fruit, vegetables, greens.

product noun **1** *a factory specializing in electronic products* commodity, artifact, manufactured item/article. **2** *good health is the product of good nutrition | he is the product of a Victorian upbringing* result, outcome, effect, consequence, upshot, fruit, spin-off, legacy. **products** *marketing new products* goods, wares, merchandise.

production noun **1** *speed up the production of cars* manufacture, manufacturing, creation, construction, building, fabrication, making, assembly. **2** *his production of great works of literature/art* composition, creation, origination, preparation, development, framing, fashioning. **3** *the production of new evidence* presentation, offering, proffering, advancement, exhibition, demonstration, disclosure. **4** *an increase in production* output, yield. **5** *see a production of her latest play* performance, staging, mounting. **6** *several productions staged by the company* play, film, concert, show, performance, presentation, piece. **7** *this is the writer's/artist's latest production* work, publication, composition, piece, creation, opus.

productive adjective **1** *productive soil* fertile, fruitful, fecund, rich, high-yielding. **2** *a productive worker* prolific, energetic, vigorous, efficient. **3** *not a very productive* *day's work* profitable, gainful, valuable, fruitful, useful, constructive, effective, worthwhile, beneficial, rewarding.

profane adjective **1** *their profane behavior in setting fire to the altar* blasphemous, sacrilegious, impious, irreligious, ungodly, godless, irreverent, disrespectful. **2** *shocked by their profane language* blasphemous, obscene, foul, vulgar, crude, filthy, coarse.

profanity noun **1** *the profanity of brawling in church* profaneness, blasphemy, sacrilege, impiety, irreverence, disrespectfulness, disrespect. **2** *issue a stream of profanities* oath, swearword, swearing, obscenity, four-letter word, curse, execration, imprecation.

profess verb **1** *profess satisfaction with his work | profess one's faith* declare, announce, proclaim, assert, state, utter, affirm, avow, aver, confess, confirm, . **2** *he professed total ignorance of the situation* claim, lay claim to, allege, pretend, feign, fake.

profession noun **1** *a teacher by profession* career, calling, vocation, occupation, line of work, employment, position, situation, post, job, office, appointment, métier, walk of life, business. **2** *they were relieved by his professions of satisfaction | his profession of his faith* declaration, announcement, proclamation, assertion, statement, affirmation, avowal, testimony, averment, confession. **3** *not taken in by his profession of ignorance* claim, allegation, pretense, feigning, shamming, faking, dissembling.

professional adjective **1** *he has a professional job* white-collar. **2** *a very professional worker* skilled, skillful, proficient, expert, adept, competent, efficient, experienced. **3** *a very professional piece of work* skillful, expert, masterly, excellent, fine, polished. **4** *conduct that was hardly professional* ethical, fitting.

professional noun **1** *a new office for the young professional* professional worker, white-collar worker. **2** *this tennis player is a professional now* nonamateur, paid player; *inf.* pro. **3** *the singer/tailor is a real professional* expert, master, past master, adept, authority; *inf.* pro.

proficient adjective *a proficient swimmer | proficient at swimming | proficient in French* accomplished, skillful, skilled, adept, apt, expert, adroit, deft, able, capable, competent, experienced, effective, talented, gifted.

profile noun **1** *look better in profile* sideview, outline. **2** *The profile of the church against the sky* silhouette, outline, contour, lines, shape, form, figure. **3** *write a profile of the author* short biography, sketch, thumbnail sketch, portrait, vignette.

profit noun *the profit made from the sale of the house* takings, proceeds, gain, yield, return, receipts, income, earnings, winnings.

profit verb *it will not profit you to be openly critical of the company* benefit, be of benefit to, be advantageous to, serve, do (someone) good, help, be helpful to, assist, aid, stand (someone) in good stead. **profit from** *profit from his advice* benefit from, gain from, put to good use, learn from; *inf.* cash in on.

profitable adjective **1** *a profitable venture* moneymaking, commercial, gainful, remunerative, paying, lucrative. **2** *a profitable company* sound, solvent, in the black. **3** *find it a profitable experience* beneficial, advantageous, rewarding, helpful, productive, useful, worthwhile, valuable.

profligate adjective **1** *profligate people ending up in debt* extravagant, spendthrift, improvident, prodigal, immoderate, squandering, reckless, wasteful. **2** *a profligate cad* dissolute, dissipated, debauched, corrupt, degenerate, depraved, reprobate, unprincipled, immoral, promiscuous, loose, wanton, licentious, lascivious, lecherous.

profound adjective **1** *a profound thinker* discerning, penetrating, thoughtful, philosophical, deep, weighty, serious, learned, erudite, wise, sagacious. **2** *unable to understand such profound doctrine* learned, erudite, serious, deep, difficult, complex, abstract, abstruse, esoteric, impenetrable. **3** *a profound love for his country* intense, deep, keen, great, extreme, sincere, heartfelt. **4** *a profound silence* deep, pronounced, total, absolute, complete, utter. **5** *profound changes taking place* far-reaching, radical, extensive, exhaustive, thoroughgoing.

profuse adjective **1** *give profuse thanks* lavish, liberal, unstinting, generous, fulsome, extravagant, inordinate, immoderate, excessive. **2** *profuse blossom on the trees* abundant, copious, ample, plentiful, bountiful, luxuriant.

profusion noun *a profusion of roses on the bushes* abundance, superabundance, copiousness, quantities, scores, masses, multitude, plethora, wealth, plenitude, cornucopia; *inf.* heaps, stacks, piles, loads, mountains, tons, scads, oodles.

progeny noun **1** *the parents and all their progeny* children, offspring, young ones, family, issue. **2** *the progeny of John Adams* descendants, successors, lineage, scions, seed, posterity.

program noun **1** *refer to the conference program* agenda, calendar, schedule, syllabus, order of the day. **2** *buy a program at the theater* playbill, list of performers. **3** *the orchestra played a varied program* repertoire, repertory, performance. **4** *watch* *several television programs* production, presentation, show, performance, broadcast. **5** *get the program for next semester's courses* syllabus, prospectus, schedule, list, curriculum, literature. **6** *organize a program of financial investment* schedule, scheme, plan, project.

progress noun. **1** *climbers making progress toward the summit* headway, going, passage, advancement. **2** *the company has made very little progress in the past few years* advancement, improvement, betterment, upgrading, development, growth. **in progress** *work in progress* under way, ongoing, occurring, taking place, proceeding, being done, being performed.

progress verb **1** *the climbers progressed up the mountain* advance, continue, proceed, make one's way, make headway, push forward, forge ahead. **2** *the talks are progressing* make progress, move forward, advance, make headway, make strides, develop, improve.

progression noun **1** *the progression from mail clerk to managing director* passage, advancement, development. **2** *a progression of applicants/jobs* succession, sequence, series, string, stream, parade, chain, train.

progressive adjective **1** *progressive movement* forward, onward, advancing. **2** *a progressive disease* increasing, growing, intensifying, accelerating, escalating. **3** *a progressive office system* modern, advanced, forward-looking, enlightened, enterprising, up-and-coming, innovative; avantgarde. **4** *progressive ideas on education* radical, reforming, innovative, revolutionary, revisionist.

prohibit verb **1** *a regulation to prohibit smoking* forbid, ban, bar, disallow, proscribe, veto, interdict, outlaw. **2** *low salaries prohibit them from buying a house* prevent, stop, rule out, preclude, hinder, impede, hamper, obstruct, restrict, constrain.

prohibition noun **1** *the prohibition of smoking in hospitals* forbidding, banning, barring, disallowing, proscription, vetoing, interdiction, outlawing. **2** *a prohibition on the sale of cigarettes to children* ban, bar, interdict, veto, embargo, injunction, proscription.

prohibitive adjective *the prohibitive cost of housing* prohibitory, forbidding, disallowing, proscriptive, restrictive, suppressive.

project noun scheme, plan, program, enterprise, undertaking, venture, activity, operation, campaign.

project verb **1** *a projected new mall* plan, propose, devise, design, outline. **2** *project missiles into space* launch, discharge, propel, hurl, throw, cast, fling, shoot. **3** *the*

balcony projects over the garden jut, jut out, protrude, extend, stick out, bulge out, beetle, obtrude. **4** *project sales figures for next year* extrapolate, calculate, estimate, gauge, reckon, forecast, predict.

projection noun **1** *a projection of rock* overhang, ledge, shelf, ridge, protuberance, protrusion, jut, bulge. **2** *their sales projection for next year* forecast, prediction, extrapolation, calculation, computation, estimate, estimation, gauge, reckoning.

proletariat noun workers, working class, wage earners, laboring classes, common people, commonalty, lower classes, lower orders, rank and file, masses, mob, rabble, hoi polloi.

proliferate verb multiply, mushroom, increase, extend, expand, burgeon, accelerate, escalate, snowball.

proliferation noun increase, growth, multiplication, spread, expansion, extension, burgeoning, acceleration, escalation, buildup, snowballing, mushrooming.

prolific adjective **1** *prolific vegetation* fertile, fruitful, fecund, luxuriant, abundant, profuse, copious, rank. **2** *a prolific writer* productive.

prologue noun *the prologue to the novel* introduction, foreword, preface, preamble, prelude, preliminary, exordium, proem, prolegomenon.

prolong verb *problems with the car prolonged the journey* lengthen, elongate, extend, stretch out, draw out, drag out, protract.

prominence noun **1** *a prominence on the flat countryside* protuberance, projection, protrusion, jutting, swelling, bulge. **2** *the prominence of the tower on the skyline* conspicuousness, obviousness, obtrusiveness. **3** *newspapers giving prominence to the scandal* importance, weight, conspicuousness, precedence, top billing. **4** *men of prominence in the community* importance, eminence, preeminence, distinction, note, prestige, stature, illustriousness, celebrity, fame, renown, acclaim.

prominent adjective **1** *a prominent feature of the landscape* conspicuous, noticeable, obvious, unmistakable, obtrusive, outstanding, eye-catching, striking. **2** *a prominent member of the local community* leading, outstanding, chief, main, top, important, eminent, preeminent, distinguished, notable, noted, illustrious, celebrated, well-known, famous, renowned, acclaimed.

promiscuous adjective sexually indiscriminating, dissolute, dissipated, fast, licentious, loose, profligate, abandoned, immoral, debauched, wanton, unchaste.

promise verb **1** *promise that he will be present* give one's word, give one's assurance, swear, vow, take an oath, pledge, contract. **2** *skies that promise good weather* augur, indicate, denote, signify, show signs of, hint at, suggest, betoken, presage.

promise noun **1** *a promise that he would be there* word, word of honor, assurance, guarantee, commitment, vow, oath, pledge, bond, contract, covenant. **2** *a promise of spring in the air* indication, hint, suggestion, sign. **3** *a young musician of promise* talent, potential, flair, ability, aptitude, capability, capacity.

promising adjective **1** *it is promising that you have a second interview* encouraging, hopeful, favorable, auspicious, propitious, optimistic, bright. **2** *a promising young writer* with potential, talented, gifted, able, apt; *inf.* up-and-coming.

promontory noun headland, point, cape, head, foreland, bluff, cliff, precipice, overhang, height, projection, prominence.

promote verb **1** *she has been promoted to sales manager* upgrade, elevate, advance, move up, give a higher position to, place in a higher rank, prefer, aggrandize. **2** *he promoted the cause of peace by his actions* advance, further, assist, aid, help, contribute to, foster, boost. **3** *the local council promotes equal rights for all* advocate, recommend, urge, support, back, endorse, champion, sponsor, espouse. **4** *companies promoting their new products* advertise, publicize, push; *inf.* plug, hype.

promotion noun **1** *get a promotion to a managerial post* upgrading, elevation, advancement, preferment, aggrandizement. **2** *his promotion of peace* advancement, furtherance, furthering, assistance, aid, help, contribution to, fostering, boosting. **3** *the council's promotion of equal rights for all* advocacy, recommendation, urging, support, backing, endorsement, championship, sponsoring, espousal. **4** *the company's promotion of their new products* advertising, advertising campaign, publicity, publicizing, push, pushing; *inf.* plug, plugging, hype.

prompt adjective *receive a prompt reply* swift, rapid, speedy, quick, fast, expeditious, early, punctual, timely; immediate, instant, instantaneous.

prompt verb **1** *what prompted them to leave?* cause, make, encourage, move, induce, urge, incite, impel, spur, motivate, stimulate, inspire, provoke. **2** *his actions prompted an angry response* cause, give rise to, induce, occasion, elicit, evoke, provoke. **3** *he forgot his lines, so she prompted him* remind, jog someone's memory, cue.

promulgate verb publicize, announce, spread, communicate, disseminate, circulate, broadcast, publish, proclaim, declare, herald, blazon, trumpet.

prone adjective **1** *lying prone for his rubdown | weary hikers lying prone at their campsite* face down, procumbent, lying down, flat, horizontal, full-length, supine, prostrate, stretched out, recumbent. **2** *prone to lose his temper* inclined, given, likely, liable, apt, disposed, predisposed. **3** *prone to headaches* subject, susceptible, disposed, predisposed.

prong noun point, tip, spike, tine.

pronounce verb **1** *have difficulty in pronouncing the letter 's'* enunciate, articulate, say, utter, sound, voice, vocalize. **2** *pronounce judgment* announce, declare, proclaim, assert, affirm, rule, decree.

pronounced adjective **1** *have a pronounced lisp* marked, noticeable, obvious, evident, conspicuous, striking, distinct, unmistakable. **2** *have pronounced views on the subject* decided, definite, clear, strong, positive, distinct.

proof noun **1** *produce proof of your identity* evidence, certification, verification, authentication, validation, confirmation, attestation. **2** *produce proof of his guilt* evidence, demonstration, substantiation, corroboration, confirmation, attestation, testimony. **3** *send the novelist proofs of her book* galley proof, galley, page proof, trial print.

prop noun **1** *a prop holding up the side of the shed* support, upright, brace, buttress, stay, bolster, stanchion, truss, column, post, rod, pole, shaft. **2** *a prop of the local arts league* pillar, mainstay, anchor, rock, backbone, supporter, upholder, sustainer.

prop verb *prop his bike against the wall* lean, rest, set, lay, stand, balance, steady. **prop up** *prop up the wall of the garage* shore up, bolster, buttress, support, brace, underpin, reinforce, strengthen.

propagate verb **1** *propagate plants* grow, breed. **2** *animals propagating* reproduce, multiply, proliferate, breed, procreate. **3** *propagate new political ideas* spread, communicate, circulate, disseminate, transmit, distribute, broadcast, publish, publicize, promulgate.

propel verb move, set in motion, push forward, drive, thrust forward, force, impel.

propensity noun *a propensity to lie | a propensity for getting into trouble* tendency, inclination, leaning, bent, bias, disposition, predisposition, proneness, proclivity, penchant, susceptibility, weakness.

proper adjective **1** *the proper equipment for the sport* right, suitable, fitting, appropriate, apt. **2** *the proper way to do things* right, correct, precise, accepted, acceptable, established, orthodox, conventional, formal, *comme il faut.* **3** *put the books in* *their proper place* right, correct, own, individual, particular, respective, special, specific. **4** *have a very proper upbringing* seemly, decorous, respectable, decent, refined, genteel, gentlemanly/ladylike, formal, conventional, orthodox, strict.

property noun **1** *the books were her personal property* possessions, belongings, things, goods, effects, chattels, assets, resources. **2** *put his money in property* real estate, buildings, land, estates. **3** *the antiseptic properties of alcohol* quality, attribute, characteristic, feature, power, peculiarity, idiosyncrasy, quirk.

prophecy noun **1** *her prophecy came true* prediction, forecast, prognostication, divination, augury. **2** *the gift of prophecy* prediction, foretelling the future, fortune-telling, second sight, prognostication, divination, augury, soothsaying.

prophesy verb *the seer prophesied his death* predict, foretell, forecast, foresee, presage, prognosticate, divine, augur.

prophet noun seer, soothsayer, fortuneteller, diviner, clairvoyant, prognosticator, prophesier, oracle, augur, sibyl, Cassandra. **prophet of doom** pessimist, Cassandra.

propitious adjective *not a propitious time to try to sell one's house* auspicious, favorable, promising, optimistic, bright, advantageous, fortunate, lucky, rosy, beneficial, opportune, suitable, timely.

proponent noun *a proponent of socialism* advocate, supporter, upholder, adherent, backer, promoter, endorser, champion, defender, sponsor, espouser, friend, well-wisher.

proportion noun **1** *the proportion of women to men on the staff* ratio, distribution, relative amount/number, relationship. **2** *give a large proportion of his income to the poor* portion, part, segment, share, quota, division, percentage, fraction, measure; *inf.* cut. **3** *the pleasing proportions of the room* balance, symmetry, harmony, correspondence, congruity, agreement.

proportional adjective *more work to do, with a proportional increase in salary* proportionate, corresponding, commensurate, equivalent, comparable.

proposal noun **1** *the proposal of new terms of employment* putting forward, advancement, offer, proffering, presentation, submitting. **2** *draw up a financial proposal* scheme, plan, project, program, motion, bid, proposition, presentation, suggestion, recommendation, tender, terms.

propose verb **1** *propose changes in legislation* put forward, advance, offer, proffer, present, submit, tender, propound, suggest, recommend, advocate. **2** *they are proposing to leave now* intend, mean, plan,

aim. **3** *propose his cousin as president of the society* put forward, put up, nominate, name, suggest, recommend. **4** *propose to his girlfriend* offer marriage, ask for someone's hand in marriage, pay suit; *inf.* pop the question.

proposition noun **1** *an attractive business proposition* proposal, scheme, plan, project, program, motion, bid. **2** *getting into the building unnoticed is not an easy proposition* task, job, undertaking, venture, problem. **3** *make a proposition to the man at the bar* sexual advance, indecent proposal; *inf.* come-on.

proprietor noun owner, possessor, titleholder, deed-holder, landowner, landlord/landlady; host, innkeeper, hotelier, manager, restaurateur.

propriety noun **1** *behave with propriety* seemliness, decorum, respectability, decency, correctness, appropriateness, good manners, courtesy, politeness, civility, refinement, gentility, breeding, conventionality, orthodoxy, formality, etiquette, protocol. **2** *question the propriety of your decision* rightness, correctness, fitness, suitability, appropriateness, aptness.

prosaic adjective unimaginative, uninspired, matter-of-fact, dull, dry, humdrum, mundane, pedestrian, lifeless, spiritless, stale, bland, vapid, banal, hackneyed, trite, insipid, monotonous, flat, ordinary, everyday, common, routine, commonplace, workaday, tedious, boring.

proscribe verb **1** *proscribe the sale of alcohol on Sundays* prohibit, forbid, ban, bar, disallow, embargo, interdict, outlaw. **2** *he was proscribed for his part in the conspiracy* outlaw, exile, expel, expatriate, deport, boycott, blackball, ostracize.

prosecute verb *he was prosecuted for drunk driving* bring a charge against, charge, try, put on trial, sue, interdict, arraign.

prospect noun **1** *there is little prospect of success* likelihood, hope, expectation, anticipation, chance, chances, odds, probability, possibility. **2** *the prospect of being unemployed frightens him* thought, idea, contemplation, outlook. **3** *admire the prospect from the hill* view, vista, outlook, perspective, panorama, scene, spectacle.

prospect verb *prospect an area for diamonds* explore, search, inspect, survey, examine, check out. **prospect for** *prospect for gold* search for, seek.

prospective adjective **1** *her prospective father-in-law* future, soon-to-be, intended, expected. **2** *attract prospective customers* would-be, potential, possible, likely, hoped-for, awaited, anticipated.

prosper verb thrive, flourish, succeed, get ahead, progress, advance, make good, become rich, be in clover; *inf.* be on easy street, live the life of Riley.

prosperity noun success, good fortune, ease, plenty, affluence, wealth, riches, the good life, luxury, life of luxury.

prosperous adjective thriving, flourishing, successful, well-off, well-to-do, affluent, wealthy, rich, moneyed, opulent, in clover; *inf.* well-heeled, in the money, on easy street.

prostitute noun call girl, whore, woman of the streets, lady of the evening, streetwalker, woman of ill repute, fallen woman, courtesan, *fille de joie; inf.* hooker, working girl, hustler.

prostrate adjective **1** *found prostrate on the floor* prone, lying down, flat, stretched out, horizontal, full-length, procumbent. **2** *prostrate before the emperor* bowed low, humbled. **3** *prostrate with grief* overcome by/with, overwhelmed by, overpowered by, brought to one's knees by, paralyzed by, laid low by/with, impotent with.

protagonist noun **1** *the protagonist in the new play* hero/heroine, central character, principal, leading man/lady, title role, lead. **2** *a protagonist of feminism* leader, standard-bearer, mainstay, spokesman, spokeswoman, spokesperson, advocate, supporter, upholder, adherent, backer, proponent, promoter, champion.

protect verb **1** *protect the child from injury* keep safe, save, safeguard, shield, preserve, defend, shelter, secure. **2** *soldiers protecting the castle* guard, defend, secure, watch over, look after, take care of. **3** *protect the surface of the table with a plastic sheet* preserve, shield, cover, cover up, conceal, mask.

protection noun **1** *provide protection against violence* safekeeping, safety, preservation, defense, security. **2** *under the protection of the police* safekeeping, care, charge, keeping, defense, protectorship. **3** *wear warm clothes as a protection against the cold* safeguard, shield, barrier, buffer, screen, cover.

protest verb **1** *protesting his treatment of the staff* object to, oppose, make/take a stand against, put up a fight against, take exception to, complain about, express disapproval of, demur at, remonstrate about, demonstrate against; *inf.* gripe about, grouse about, beef about, bitch about. **2** *protest his innocence* declare, announce, profess, proclaim, assert, affirm, argue, attest, testify to, maintain, insist on, aver, avow.

protest noun **1** *register a protest against/about his treatment of the children* objection, opposition, exception, complaint, disapproval, disagreement, dissent, demurral, remonstration, fuss, outcry, demonstration. **2** *listen to his protests that he was*

innocent protestation, declaration, profession, assertion, affirmation, attestation, assurance, avowal, proclamation.

protester noun *a crowd of protesters gathered outside the embassy* objector, opposer, opponent, complainer, demonstrator, dissenter, dissident, rebel, striker, agitator.

protocol noun *observe the protocol associated with royal visits* etiquette, rules of conduct, code of behavior, conventions, formalities, customs, propriety, decorum, manners, courtesies, civilities, good form, politesse.

protract verb *loves to talk at meetings and protract the discussions* prolong, extend, stretch out, draw out, lengthen, drag out, continue.

protrude verb *a piece of rock protruding from the cliff face* jut, jut out, stick out, stand out, project, extend, beetle, obtrude, bulge.

protuberance noun *a protuberance on the trunk of the tree* swelling, bulge, lump, bump, protrusion, projection, knob, growth, outgrowth, tumor, excrescence.

proud adjective **1** *proud parents* pleased, glad, happy, satisfied, gratified, content, appreciative. **2** *they were poor but proud* self-respecting, dignified, independent. **3** *he has become too proud to associate with his old friends* arrogant, conceited, vain, self-important, egotistical, boastful, haughty, disdainful, scornful, supercilious, snobbish, imperious, overbearing, lordly, presumptuous, overweening, high-handed; *inf.* high-and-mighty, stuck-up, uppity, snooty, highfalutin. **4** *it was a proud day when they won the cup* gratifying, satisfying, happy, memorable, notable, redletter, glorious, marvelous. **5** *the ship was a proud sight sailing into the harbor* magnificent, splendid, grand, noble, stately, imposing, majestic, august.

prove verb **1** *prove that he was the murderer* determine, demonstrate, show beyond (a/the shadow of a) doubt, substantiate, corroborate, verify, validate, authenticate, confirm. **2** *the rumor proved to be correct* be found, be shown, turn out.

proverb noun saying, adage, maxim, saw, axiom, aphorism, gnome, dictum, apothegm.

proverbial adjective **1** *her proverbial meanness kept visitors away* legendary, notorious, infamous, famous, famed, renowned, well-known, acknowledged, accepted, traditional, time-honored. **2** *he has become the proverbial good Samaritan* axiomatic, epigrammatic, aphoristic, apothegmatic, well-known.

provide verb **1** *provide the guests with food and shelter* supply, furnish, equip, accommodate, provision, outfit, give, offer. **2**

the novel provides insight into the war give, bring, afford, present, offer, accord, yield, impart, lend. **3** the contract provides that the tenants are responsible for repairs stipulate, lay down, require, state, specify.

provide against provide against an enemy attack make provision for, take precautions against, guard against. **provide for 1** provide for his family support, maintain, keep, sustain, take care of, care for, look after. **2** the organizers of the wedding tried to provide for every eventuality allow for, prepare for, anticipate, plan for.

provident adjective it was provident of them to take out accident insurance | provident people providing for their old age farsighted, prudent, judicious, shrewd, circumspect, wise, sagacious, cautious, careful, canny.

province noun **1** the administrative center of the province state, territory, region, area, district. **2** that part of the business is not my province area of responsibility, field, business, line, charge, concern, duty. **3** in the province of English literature discipline, field, specialty, area.

provincial adjective **1** provincial government regional, local, municipal, state, county, district; topical. **2** unfair in her assumption that all suburbanites are provincial uncultured, uncultivated, unrefined, unpolished, unsophisticated, parochial, limited, small-minded, insular, naïve, uninformed, narrow-minded, bigoted, prejudiced, intolerant.

provision noun **1** the provision of conference facilities providing, supply, furnishing, equipping, outfitting, accommodation, affording. **2** make provision for their old age preparation, plan, prearrangement, arrangement, precaution. **3** the housing policy makes no provision for single people arrangement, allowance, concession. **4** under the provisions of his will, his children inherit his estate term, requirement, specification, stipulation, proviso, condition.

provisional adjective provisory, temporary, interim, stopgap, transitional, conditional, tentative, contingent; inf. pro tem.

provisions plural noun stock up with provisions supplies, stores, groceries, food, foodstuffs, staples, rations, provender, eatables, edibles, victuals, comestibles, viands.

proviso noun they agreed to the change with the proviso that an investigation be held condition, stipulation, provision, clause, rider, qualification, restriction, reservation, limitation, strings.

provocation noun **1** react to the slightest provocation annoyance, irritation, vexation, harassment, affront, insult, exasperation, infuriation, irking; inf. riling, aggravation. **2** hit him under provocation incitement, stimulation, stimulus, motivation,

prompting, inducement, goading. **3** what was the provocation of their anger? evocation, instigation, cause, occasioning, inducement, inspiration, kindling, production, generation, precipitation, promotion.

provocative adjective **1** the fight was started by a provocative remark annoying, irritating, exasperating, infuriating, maddening, vexing, galling, affronting, insulting, inflammatory, goading; inf. aggravating. **2** wear a provocative, low-cut dress alluring, seductive, sexy, tempting, suggestive, erotic, titillating.

provoke verb **1** do not provoke the hornet annoy, anger, incense, enrage, irritate, exasperate, infuriate, madden, pique, nettle, vex, harass, irk, gall, affront, insult; inf. rile, needle, aggravate. **2** provoke her into shouting at them incite, rouse, stir, move, stimulate, motivate, excite, inflame, prompt, induce, spur, goad, prod, egg on. **3** his speech provoked laughter evoke, cause, give rise to, occasion, call forth, elicit, induce, inspire, excite, kindle, produce, generate, engender, instigate, lead to, precipitate, promote, prompt.

prowess noun **1** admire his prowess as a yachtsman skill, skillfulness, expertise, facility, ability, capability, talent, genius, adroitness, adeptness, aptitude, dexterity, deftness, competence, proficiency, know-how, savoir faire. **2** the prowess of the soldiers in battle courage, bravery, gallantry, valor, heroism, intrepidity, fearlessness, mettle, pluck, gameness, nerve, boldness, daring, fortitude, steadfastness, stoutness, sturdiness; inf. grit, guts, spunk.

prowl verb prowling around the building slink, skulk, steal, roam, range, sneak, stalk; inf. snoop.

proximity noun closeness, nearness, propinquity, adjacency, contiguity.

prudence noun **1** question the prudence of his action wisdom, judgment, judiciousness, sagacity, shrewdness, sense, circumspection, farsightedness, foresight, forethought. **2** behave with prudence rather than rashness caution, care, discretion, wariness, vigilance, heedfulness. **3** her prudence allowed her to buy a house providence, thrift, thriftiness, economy, canniness, sparingness, frugality, management, budgeting.

prudent adjective **1** a prudent decision wise, judicious, sagacious, sage, shrewd, sensible, circumspect, farsighted, politic. **2** advised to be prudent cautious, careful, discreet, wary, vigilant, heedful. **3** prudent with her income provident, thrifty, economical, canny, sparing, frugal.

prudish adjective puritan, puritanical, priggish, prim, straitlaced, prissy, stuffy, starchy, Victorian; inf. goody-goody.

prune verb 1 *prune the roses* trim, thin, thin out, cut back, shape. 2 *prune branches from the bushes* cut, lop, chop, clip, snip, remove. 3 *prune expenses* cut back, pare down, cut, trim, reduce, shorten, curtail.

pry verb *she resents it when he pries* interfere, meddle, intrude, be inquisitive, be a busybody; *inf.* snoop. **pry into** 1 *pry into her private affairs* be inquisitive about, nose into, inquire into, interfere in, meddle in; *inf.* be nosy about. 2 *pry into her possessions* peer into, peek into, scrutinize, ferret around in, poke around in, nose around in, spy on; *inf.* poke one's nose into, snoop into.

pseudo adjective *a pseudo interest in the arts* feigned, pretended, simulated, imitation, false, artificial, ersatz, spurious, fake, bogus, sham, mock, fraudulent, counterfeit, forged; *inf.* phony.

pseudonym noun nom de plume, pen name, stage name, professional name, assumed name, alias, allonym, sobriquet, nickname, nom de guerre.

psychic adjective 1 *people thought to be psychic* clairvoyant, telepathic, telekinetic, spiritualistic. 2 *psychic powers* supernatural, preternatural, extrasensory, otherworldly, paranormal, occult. 3 *psychic disorder* spiritual, mental, psychological, psychogenic.

psychological adjective 1 *psychological studies* mental, cerebral, psychic, psychical. 2 *her inability to work is psychological* in the mind, psychosomatic, emotional, irrational, imaginary, subconscious, unconscious.

public adjective 1 *public health services* state, national, civic, civil, social. 2 *increase public awareness* popular, general, common, universal, widespread. 3 *public parks* accessible to all, open to the public, of free access. 4 *make his views public* known, acknowledged, overt, in circulation, published, publicized, plain, obvious. 5 *scandals about public figures* prominent, well-known, eminent, influential, prestigious, famous, celebrated, illustrious.

public noun 1 *the public has a right to know* people, everyone, population, country, nation, community, citizens, populace, masses, commonalty, electorate, voters. 2 *actors/authors worrying about what their public think* audience, spectators, readers, followers, following, fans, admirers, patrons, clientele. **in public** *refuse to appear in public* publicly, openly.

publication noun 1 *the publication of the book/newspaper* publishing, production, issuance. 2 *a widely read publication* book, newspaper, magazine, periodical, journal, daily, weekly, monthly, quarterly, booklet, brochure, leaflet, pamphlet, handbill. 3 *the publication of the committee's*

findings publishing, announcement, notification, reporting, declaration, communication, imparting, proclamation, disclosure, divulgence, broadcasting, publicizing, distribution, spreading, dissemination, promulgation, issuance.

publicity noun 1 *his marriage prompted much publicity* notoriety, public interest, public notice. 2 *seeking publicity for her new book* promotion, advertising; *inf.* hype, buildup.

publicize verb 1 *publicize a description of the wanted man* announce, publish, broadcast, distribute, disseminate, promulgate. 2 *publicize her new book* promote, advertise; *inf.* hype, plug.

publish verb 1 *they publish reference books* produce, issue, print. 2 *publish the committee's findings* make public, announce, report, declare, communicate, impart, proclaim, disclose, divulge, broadcast, publicize, distribute, spread, disseminate, promulgate.

pucker verb 1 *a dress puckered at the waist* gather, shirr, pleat, ruck, ruffle, wrinkle, crease. 2 *the unhappy child's face puckered* screw up, wrinkle, crease, furrow, knit, crinkle, corrugate.

pudgy adjective stout, round, rotund, plump, roly-poly, dumpy, squat, stubby, stumpy, chubby, tubby.

puerile adjective childish, immature, infantile, juvenile, adolescent, foolish, silly, inane, asinine.

puff noun *a puff of wind* gust, blast, whiff, breath, flurry, draft.

puff verb *puffing while climbing the hill* pant, blow, gasp, gulp.

puffy adjective *puffy cheeks/eyes* swollen, distended, inflated, dilated, bloated, bulging, edematous.

pugnacious adjective *in a pugnacious mood* belligerent, bellicose, combative, fighting, battling, aggressive, antagonistic, quarrelsome, argumentative, disputatious, hostile, threatening, irascible, ill-tempered, bad-tempered.

pull verb 1 *the child was pulling a toy behind him* haul, drag, draw, trail, tow, tug. 2 *pull the rope to straighten it* haul, tug, jerk; *inf.* yank. 3 *pull teeth* extract, remove, draw out, take out, root out. 4 *pull a muscle* strain, sprain, wrench, stretch, tear, dislocate, damage. **pull back** *the army pulled back after the defeat* withdraw, retreat, draw back, fall back. **pull down** *pull down old buildings* knock down, demolish, raze, level, destroy, bulldoze, dismantle. **pull in** 1 *the car pulled in to the driveway* drive in, draw in. 2 *plays pulling in large audiences* draw, bring in, attract, lure, entice. 3 *he pulls in $50,000 a year* earn, take home, bring in, make, clear, net, gross, pocket.

pull off 1 *pull the top off the can* remove, detach, tear off. **2** *pull off the export deal* bring off, carry out, accomplish, execute, succeed in. **pull oneself together** regain one's composure, get a grip on oneself; *inf.* snap out of it. **pull out 1** *pull out a gun* take out, withdraw. **2** *pull out of the contest* withdraw, leave, quit, abandon, give up, renege on. **pull someone's leg** *he was only pulling her leg* tease, make fun of, poke fun at, joke with, rag, chaff, twit; *inf.* rib. **pull through** *she was very ill but pulled through* recover, rally, survive, recuperate. **pull up 1** *pull up the weeds* root out, uproot, dig up, grub up, extract. **2** *the car pulled up to the curb* draw up, park alongside, drive up.

pull noun **1** *give a pull at the bell rope* tug, haul, yank, jerk. **2** *the pull of the current* tug, force, power, exertion, effort. **3** *the pull of the sea to sailors* attraction, lure, enticement, draw, magnetism, influence. **4** *he has pull with the boss* influence, weight, leverage, muscle; *inf.* clout.

pulp noun **1** *the pulp of the fruit* flesh, marrow. **2** *reduce the vegetables to a pulp* paste, purée, mush, mash, pap, triturate. **3** *make a fortune out of writing pulp* pulp fiction, rubbish, trash, trivia, drivel, pap.

pulsate verb *loud music pulsating throughout the building* beat, throb, vibrate, pulse, palpitate, pound, thud, thump, drum.

pulse noun *the compelling pulse of the music* beat, rhythm, throb, throbbing, vibration, pulsation, pounding, thudding, thud, thumping, thump, drumming.

pulse verb beat, throb. *See* PULSATE.

pulverize verb **1** *pulverize the solid foods* grind, crush, pound, crumble, powder, crunch, squash, pulp, purée, liquidize, mash, comminute, triturate. **2** *pulverize his opponent in the boxing ring* defeat utterly, overwhelm, trounce, rout, flatten, crush, smash, vanquish, destroy, annihilate; *inf.* hammer.

pump verb **1** *pump the bicycle tires* pump up, blow up, inflate. **2** *pump blood through the body* drive, force, push, send. **3** *pump him for information* question, quiz, interrogate, cross-examine; *inf.* grill.

punch verb strike, hit, knock, thump, thwack, box, jab, cuff, slug, smash, bash, slam, batter, pound, pummel; *inf.* sock, wallop, whack.

punch noun **1** *give his opponent a punch in the jaw* blow, hit, knock, box, jab, cuff, slug, smash, slam; *inf.* sock, wallop, whack, clout, plug. **2** *the speech lacked punch* strength, vigor, force, verve, drive, impact, bite, effectiveness; *inf.* oomph, pizazz.

punctilious adjective careful, scrupulous, meticulous, conscientious, exact, precise, particular, strict, finicky, fussy; *inf.* persnickety.

punctual adjective prompt, on time, on the dot, timely, well-timed, early.

puncture noun *a puncture in the tire* perforation, hole, rupture, cut, nick, slit, leak, prick.

puncture verb *the piece of glass punctured the tire* perforate, pierce, bore, deflate, prick, spike, penetrate, rupture, cut, nick, slit.

pungent adjective **1** *a pungent smell* sharp, acrid, biting, stinging. **2** *a pungent taste* sharp, acid, sour, biting, bitter, tart, tangy, spicy, aromatic, piquant. **3** *pungent wit* caustic, acid, biting, cutting, sharp, incisive, piercing, penetrating, pointed.

punish verb discipline, penalize, castigate, chastise; beat, cane, whip, flog, lash, scourge; mistreat, abuse, manhandle.

punishment noun discipline, penalty, retribution, castigation, redress, chastisement; beating, caning, whipping, flogging, lashing, scourging; mistreatment, abuse, manhandling.

punitive adjective **1** *take punitive measures against the culprits* punishing, penalizing, disciplinary, corrective, castigating, castigatory, chastising. **2** *punitive rates of taxation* harsh, severe, stiff, taxing, cruel, savage.

puny adjective **1** *the bodybuilder claimed that he was once puny* weak, frail, feeble, undersized, underdeveloped, stunted, small, slight, little, dwarfish. **2** *a puny contribution* paltry, petty, trifling, trivial, insignificant, inconsequential, minor, meager; *inf.* piddling.

pupil noun **1** *pupils wearing school uniforms* student, schoolboy, schoolgirl, schoolchild, scholar. **2** *a pupil of Picasso* student, disciple.

puppet noun **1** *puppets amusing children* marionette, hand puppet, finger puppet. **2** *a puppet of management* tool, instrument, cat's-paw, pawn, dupe, mouthpiece; *inf.* stooge.

purchase verb *purchase a new car* buy, acquire, pick up, obtain, invest in, put money into.

purchase noun **1** *proud of her new purchase* acquisition, buy, investment. **2** *difficult to get any purchase on the slippery cliff face* grip, hold, foothold, footing, toehold, support, grasp, leverage, advantage.

pure adjective **1** *pure gold* unalloyed, unmixed, unadulterated, uncontaminated, flawless, perfect, genuine, real, true. **2** *pure water* clean, clear, fresh, unpolluted, untainted, unadulterated, uncontaminated, wholesome, natural. **3** *pure novitiates* virgin, virginal, chaste, virtuous, undefiled, unsullied. **4** *lead a pure life* uncorrupted, moral, righteous, honorable, virtuous, honest, upright, decent, good, worthy, noble, blameless, guiltless, pious, sinless. **5** *of pure character* stainless, spotless, unsullied, unblemished, impeccable, immaculate, blameless, sinless. **6** *pure madness* sheer, utter, absolute, downright, out-and-out, complete, total, perfect, unmitigated, unqualified. **7** *pure mathematics* theoretical, abstract, conceptual.

purely adverb *find out purely by accident* entirely, completely, totally, wholly, solely, only, simply, just, merely.

purge verb **1** *purge their souls of sin* cleanse, clear, purify. **2** *purge the party of dissidents* rid, clear, empty. **3** *purge the dissidents from the party* remove, expel, eject, dismiss, oust, depose, eradicate, root out, weed out.

purge noun **1** *the purge of their souls* cleansing, purification. **2** *the purge of the dissidents from the party* removal, expulsion, ejection, dismissal, ousting, deposal, deposition, eradication, rooting out, weeding out.

purify verb **1** *purify the water* clean, cleanse, decontaminate, depollute, filter, filtrate. **2** *purify the air* clean, cleanse, freshen, deodorize, decontaminate, depollute, refine. **3** *purify their souls* purge, cleanse, clear, absolve.

puritanical adjective ascetic, austere, straitlaced, rigid, stiff, prudish, prim, priggish, prissy.

purity noun **1** *test the purity of the gold* flawlessness, perfection, genuineness. **2** *the purity of the water* cleanness, clearness, freshness, wholesomeness. **3** *the purity of the novitiates* virginity, chasteness, chastity, virtue. **4** *the purity of her character* stainlessness, spotlessness, impeccability, immaculateness, blamelessness, sinlessness.

purport verb **1** *this report purports to be an official statement* claim, allege, profess, assert, pretend, feign. **2** *the document purports that changes are to be made* mean, signify, indicate, denote, suggest, imply, state, convey, express, show, betoken.

purport noun **1** *the purport of his message* gist, substance, drift, implication, meaning, import, tenor, thrust. **2** *his purport is to embarrass them* aim, intention, intent, object, objective, goal, plan, scheme, design, purpose.

purpose noun **1** *the purpose of his visit* reason, point, basis, motivation, cause, justification. **2** *his only purpose in life* aim, intention, object, objective, goal, end, target, ambition, aspiration, desire, wish,

hope. **3** *to little purpose* benefit, advantage, use, usefulness, value, gain, profit, avail, result, outcome, effect. **on purpose** *cheated us on purpose* purposely, intentionally, deliberately, by design, willfully, wittingly, knowingly, consciously.

purposeful adjective determined, resolute, resolved, firm, steadfast, single-minded, persistent, persevering, tenacious, dogged, unfaltering, unwavering.

purposely adverb on purpose, intentionally, deliberately, by design, willfully, wittingly, knowingly, consciously.

purse noun **1** *carry money in her purse* wallet, pouch; bag, handbag, pocketbook. **2** *a purse of $50,000* prize, award, reward.

pursue verb **1** *the detective pursued the thief* chase, follow, hunt, stalk, track, trail, shadow; *inf.* tail. **2** *decide not to pursue the line of inquiry* follow, proceed with, carry on with, continue with, continue, persist in. **3** *pursue a career in science* follow, engage in, work at, practice, prosecute, conduct, ply, apply oneself to. **4** *pursue his goal of happiness* strive toward, work toward, seek, search for, aim at, aspire to. **5** *she pursued every eligible young man* chase after, chase; play up to.

pursuit noun **1** *take part in the pursuit of the thief* chase, hunt, stalking, tracking; *inf.* tailing. **2** *give up the pursuit of that line of inquiry* continuance, persistence, following, proceeding. **3** *his pursuit of a life of crime* engagement, occupation, work, practicing, prosecution, conducting, plying. **4** *his pursuit of happiness* striving toward, search, aim, goal, objective, aspiration.

push verb **1** *push his friend into the swimming pool* shove, thrust, propel, drive, ram, butt. **2** *push one's way through the crowd* shove, thrust, force, press, squeeze, jostle, elbow, shoulder. **3** *push the button* press, depress. **4** *push him into applying for the job* encourage, prompt, press, urge, egg on, spur, prod, goad, incite, impel, dragoon, force, coerce, constrain, browbeat, strong-arm. **5** *pushing their latest products* promote, advertise, publicize, boost; *inf.* plug, hype. **push around** *older boys pushing him around* bully, trample on, tread on, browbeat, tyrannize, intimidate, domineer. **push off** *they told him to push off* go away, leave, depart, get out; *inf.* shove off, make oneself scarce, beat it, get lost, hit the road.

push noun **1** *gave his friend a push into the pool* shove, thrust, butt. **2** *the general launched a big push* attack, assault, advance, onslaught, onset, charge, sortie, sally.

pushy adjective assertive, self-assertive, aggressive, forceful, forward, bold, brash, bumptious, presumptuous, cocksure, loud, obnoxious.

put verb **1** *put the books on the shelf* place, lay, set, deposit, position, rest, stand, locate, situate, settle, install, posit. **2** *put it in layman's terms* translate, transcribe, render, construe, interpret, word, express, phrase, frame, formulate, couch, say, utter, voice, speak, state, pronounce. **3** *put them to work* set, apply, employ, use, utilize, assign, allocate, devote. **4** *put to death* commit, consign, subject, condemn, sentence, convict, doom. **5** *put its worth at $500* assess, evaluate, value, estimate, calculate, reckon, guess, measure, establish, fix, place, set. **6** *put money on a horse* place, bet, wager, gamble, stake, risk, chance, hazard. **7** *put his fist through the window* thrust, drive, plunge, stick, push, force, lunge, knock, bang, smash, bash. **put across** *successfully put across the message* convey, communicate, explain, express, make understood, clarify. **put aside 1** *put aside money for a rainy day* lay by, save, reserve, keep in reserve, store, stockpile, hoard, deposit, salt away, squirrel away. **2** *put aside the newspaper* set aside, cast aside, discard, abandon, drop. **3** *put aside their differences* set aside, forget, disregard, ignore, bury. **put away 1** *put away food for a rainy day* lay by, set aside, save, keep in reserve, store, stockpile. **2** *put away the books* replace, tidy up, clear away. **3** *put away all thoughts of him* lay aside, discard, cast aside, forget, disregard, rid oneself of, jettison. **4** *put the criminal away* confine, lock up, shut away, commit, imprison, hospitalize, institutionalize, certify. **5** *put away quantities of food* consume, eat, swallow, gulp down, devour, down, gobble up, bolt, wolf down. **put down 1** *put down a rebellion* crush, suppress, quash, quell, stamp out, stop, repress, smash, extinguish. **2** *put their names down* write down, make a note of, jot down, take down, enter, list, record, register, log. **3** *put it down to experience* attribute, ascribe, impute, chalk up to, blame on. **4** *put down the sick animal* euthanize, put to sleep, put out of its misery, destroy. **5** *always putting down his wife* snub, disparage, deprecate, belittle, denigrate, deflate, slight, humiliate, mortify. **put forward** *his name was put forward for the candidacy* submit, present, suggest, advance, tender, propose, move, introduce, offer, proffer, recommend, suggest, nominate, name. **put off 1** *put off the meeting* postpone, defer, delay, adjourn, hold over, reschedule, shelve; *inf.* put on ice, put on the back burner. **2** *put off by his surly behavior* discourage, dissuade, dishearten, distress, dismay, discomfit, daunt, repel, offend, disgust, revolt. **put on 1** *put on her new suit* get dressed in, change into, slip into, don. **2** *put on a play* stage, mount, present, produce. **3** *she is just putting on the grief* feign, fake, sham, simulate, affect. **4** *put the blame on the father* place on, attribute to, ascribe to, impute to, fix on, attach to, assign to, allocate to, lay on, pin on. **put one over on** *he really put one over on us* trick, deceive, hoodwink, mislead, delude, fool, take in, dupe, lead on, outwit, bamboozle; *inf.* pull a fast one on, con, make a sucker of. **put out 1** *she is easily put out* annoy, anger, irritate, exasperate, infuriate, provoke, irk, vex, gall, disturb, perturb, disconcert, agitate, harass. **2** *don't put yourself out* inconvenience, trouble, bother, impose upon, discommode, incommode. **3** *put out the fire* extinguish, quench, douse, snuff out, stamp out. **4** *put out a report on the drought* issue, circulate, release, disclose, publish, broadcast, publicize. **put to** *put it to the committee* set before, lay before, present to, submit to, tender to, offer to, proffer to, set forth to, advance to, posit to. **put up 1** *put up new houses* build, construct, erect, raise. **2** *put up his friends for the night* accommodate, house, give accommodations to, give a bed to, entertain. **3** *put his friend up for chairman* put forward, nominate, propose, recommend. **4** *put up the money for the campaign* provide, supply, furnish, give, donate, pay, advance, pledge. **5** *put up posters* post, display, exhibit. **put up to** *put his friend up to the burglary* egg on to do/commit/(etc.), persuade to do/commit/(etc.), goad to do/commit/(etc.). **put up with** endure, tolerate, bear, stand, abide, suffer, take, stomach, brook, accept, swallow. **put upon** *she is so obliging that she gets put upon* take advantage of, impose upon, exploit, overburden, saddle.

puzzle verb *he was puzzled by her behavior* perplex, baffle, stump, mystify, confuse, bewilder, nonplus, dumbfound, daze, confound; *inf.* flummox.

puzzling adjective perplexing, knotty, baffling, enigmatic, abstruse, nonplussing, mystifying, bewildering, unfathomable, inexplicable, incomprehensible.

pygmy noun **1** *insultingly called him a pygmy* midget, dwarf; *inf.* shrimp, munchkin, Tom Thumb. **2** *a pygmy among intellectual giants* nonentity, nobody, lightweight.

Qq

quack noun *quacks selling fake medicines* charlatan, mountebank, impostor, fraud, fake, pretender, humbug; *inf.* con man, phony.

quagmire noun **1** *avoiding the muck of the quagmire* quag, bog, peat bog, marsh, swamp, morass, mire, slough, fen. **2** *in a quagmire with no place to live* quandary, dilemma, predicament, plight, tight corner, muddle, imbroglio, impasse; *inf.* jam, scrape, pickle, fix.

quail verb flinch, shrink, recoil, shy away, cower, cringe, shudder, shiver, tremble, shake, quake, blanch.

quaint adjective old-world, droll, curious, whimsical, attractive, charming, sweet.

quake verb shake, tremble, quiver, shiver, shudder, rock, vibrate.

qualification noun **1** *qualification to be a teacher* certification, training, competence, competency, accomplishment, eligibility, acceptability, suitability, preparedness, fitness, proficiency, skillfulness, adeptness, capability, aptitude; skill, ability, attribute, endowment. **2** *say what you mean without qualification* modification, limitation, restriction, reservation, stipulation, adaptation, adjustment; condition, proviso, provision, caveat.

qualified adjective **1** *a qualified doctor* certified, trained, fit, equipped, prepared, competent, accomplished, proficient, skilled, skillful, adept, practiced, experienced, expert, capable, able. **2** *a qualified approval* modified, limited, conditional, restricted, contingent, confined, circumscribed, reserved, guarded, equivocal, stipulated, adapted, adjusted.

qualify verb **1** *his training qualifies him to teach* certify, license, empower, authorize, allow, permit, sanction, warrant, fit, equip, prepare, train, educate, coach, teach, instruct. **2** *qualify her statement* modify, limit, make conditional, restrict. **3** *qualify her criticism* modify, temper, soften, modulate, mitigate, reduce, lessen, diminish.

quality noun **1** *the material is of poor quality* standard, grade, level, make, sort, type, kind, variety. **2** *his quality has been recognized* excellence, superiority, merit, worth, value, caliber, talent, eminence, preeminence, distinction. **3** *they have many good qualities* feature, trait, attribute, characteristic, aspect, property, peculiarity.

qualms plural noun **1** *have some qualms about going* doubt(s), misgivings, hesitation, hesitancy, reluctance, disinclination, anxiety, apprehension, disquiet, uneasiness, concern(s). **2** *have no qualms about having hurt them* pangs of conscience, scruples, compunction, remorse.

quandary noun dilemma, predicament, plight, tight spot, muddle, impasse; *inf.* jam, pickle, fix.

quantity noun **1** *what quantity of books/paper do you need?* number, amount, total, aggregate, sum, quota, weight. **2** *estimate the quantity* size, capacity, mass, volume, bulk, extent, length, area. **a quantity of** *found a quantity of books/paper* a number of, several, numerous, many, considerable amounts of.

quarrel noun **1** *the couple had a quarrel* argument, fight, disagreement, dispute, squabble, altercation, wrangle, tiff, row, misunderstanding; *inf.* falling-out, spat, scrap. **2** *I have no quarrel with him* bone of contention, complaint, grievance, resentment.

quarrel verb *the couple quarreled* argue, fight, dispute, squabble, bicker, spar, wrangle. **quarrel with** *I cannot quarrel with his logic* fault, criticize, object to, take exception to.

quarrelsome adjective argumentative, belligerent, disputatious, contentious, pugnacious, combative, bellicose, litigious, hot-tempered, irascible, choleric, irritable.

quarter noun **1** *live in the Latin quarter of the city* district, area, region, part, side, neighborhood, locality, zone, territory, province. **2** *accept help from any quarter* direction, place, point, spot, location.

quarters plural noun rooms, chambers, barracks; lodging(s), accommodations, billet, residence, abode, dwelling, domicile, habitation, cantonment; *inf.* digs, pad.

quash verb **1** *quash the jail sentence* annul, nullify, invalidate, void, cancel, overrule, override, overthrow, reverse, revoke, rescind, repeal. **2** *quash the rebellion* crush, put down, squash, quell, subdue, suppress, repress, quench, extinguish, stamp out, end, terminate, defeat, destroy.

quaver verb *his voice quavered* quiver, vibrate, tremble, shake, waver.

queasy adjective sick, nauseated, nauseous, ill, indisposed, dizzy.

queen noun **1** *the queen reigned for 50 years* monarch, sovereign, empress, ruler. **2** *she* *was the queen of Broadway* star, shining star, prima donna, idol, paragon, doyenne.

queer adjective **1** *queer behavior* odd, strange, unusual, extraordinary, funny, curious, peculiar, weird, outlandish, singular, eccentric, unconventional, unorthodox, atypical, abnormal, irregular, anomalous, deviant, outré, offbeat; *inf.* off-the-wall. **2** *something queer going on* strange, peculiar, suspicious, suspect, irregular, questionable, dubious, doubtful; *inf.* fishy, shady.

quell verb **1** *quell the rebellion* quash, defeat, conquer, vanquish, overpower, overcome, overwhelm, rout, crush, suppress, subdue, extinguish, stamp out, put down. **2** *quell their fears* allay, lull, put at rest, quiet, silence, calm, soothe, appease, assuage, abate, deaden, dull, pacify, tranquilize, mitigate, palliate.

quench verb **1** *quench one's thirst* satisfy, slake, sate, satiate. **2** *quench their desire* suppress, extinguish, stamp out, smother, stifle.

query noun *his behavior raises a query as to his sanity* question, doubt, uncertainty, inquiry, reservation, suspicion; skepticism.

query verb **1** *"where are we?" he queried* ask, inquire, question. **2** *he queried their fitness for the job* call into question, question, doubt, challenge, express reservations about.

quest noun **1** *in quest of a better life* search, pursuit, chase, hunt. **2** *their quest was the Holy Grail* goal, aim, objective, purpose. **3** *knights setting out on a quest* adventure, expedition, journey, voyage, exploration, crusade.

question noun **1** *answer her questions* query, inquiry, interrogation. **2** *there is no question that he is ill* doubt, dispute, argument, debate, controversy, reservation. **3** *there is the question of safety* issue, problem, matter, point, subject, topic, theme. **beyond question** without (a) doubt, undoubtedly, indisputably, incontestably, incontrovertibly. **in question** *the matter in question* under consideration, at issue. **out of the question** impossible, inconceivable, unthinkable, unimaginable, absurd, ridiculous, preposterous.

question verb **1** *question the witnesses* interrogate, cross-examine, cross-question, quiz, catechize, interview, sound out, examine, give the third degree to; *inf.* grill, pump. **2** *question his motives* call into question, query, challenge, express reservations about.

questionable adjective *his motive/ability is questionable* doubtful, dubious, uncertain, debatable, in dispute, arguable, controversial, controvertible.

quibble verb **1** *quibble about/over a minor detail* cavil, carp, pettifog, split hairs; *inf.*

nitpick. **2** *he quibbles so that it is difficult to get a straight answer* be evasive, equivocate, hedge, fudge; *inf.* beat about the bush.

quick adjective **1** *a quick reader* fast, rapid, speedy, swift, fleet, express. **2** *a quick response* prompt, immediate, expeditious. **3** *a quick look at the map* brief, brisk, fleeting, momentary, hasty, hurried, cursory, perfunctory. **4** *the child is very quick* sharp-witted, alert, intelligent. See QUICK-WITTED.

quicken verb **1** *his pulse quickened* speed up, accelerate. **2** *they quickened their steps* speed up, accelerate, expedite, hasten, hurry, precipitate. **3** *the documentary quickened his interest in wildlife* stimulate, arouse, rouse, whet, inspire, kindle, fan, refresh, strengthen, revitalize, resuscitate, pique, sharpen.

quickly adverb **1** *run quickly* fast, rapidly, speedily, swiftly, on the double, post-haste; *inf.* hell-bent for leather, like a bat out of hell. **2** *respond quickly* promptly, without delay, immediately, expeditiously. **3** *read the letter quickly* rapidly, briskly, hastily, hurriedly, cursorily, perfunctorily.

quick-tempered adjective irascible, irritable, hot-tempered, fiery, hasty, impatient, touchy, testy, snappish, quarrelsome, petulant, choleric, splenetic, volatile; *inf.* on a short fuse.

quick-witted adjective quick, sharp-witted, nimble-witted, alert, intelligent, bright, lively, smart, perceptive, discerning, shrewd; *inf.* quick on the uptake.

quiet adjective **1** *the house was quiet* silent, hushed, noiseless, soundless, peaceful. **2** *a quiet voice* soft, low, inaudible. **3** *a quiet person* calm, serene, composed, placid, untroubled, peaceful, tranquil, gentle, mild, temperate, restrained, phlegmatic, reserved, uncommunicative, taciturn. **4** *quiet colors/clothes* unobtrusive, unostentatious, restrained, muted, understated, subdued, subtle, conservative, sober, modest, demure. **5** *live in a quiet village* peaceful, sleepy, undisturbed, unfrequented, private, secluded, sequestered, isolated; *inf.* off the beaten track. **6** *have a quiet word with him* private, confidential, secret, discreet, unofficial, off the record. **7** *we kept his presence quiet* secret, unrevealed, undisclosed, uncommunicated; *inf.* hush-hush.

quiet noun *in the quiet of the evening* stillness, silence, hush, noiselessness, peace, peacefulness, calmness, tranquillity, serenity.

quiet verb **1** *quiet the noisy children* silence, hush, shush. **2** *the children soon quieted* grow silent, settle down; *inf.* shut up. **3** *quiet the frightened horse/quiet their fears* calm, soothe, tranquilize, allay, appease, lull, pacify, mollify, palliate, suppress, quell, stifle, dull, deaden.

quietly adverb **1** *speak quietly* softly, in a whisper, in an undertone, inaudibly. **2** *creep out quietly* silently, noiselessly, soundlessly. **3** *tell him quietly that he must leave* privately, confidentially, secretly, discreetly. **4** *she is quietly confident* calmly, patiently, placidly, serenely, undemonstratively, unemotionally. **5** *dress quietly* unobtrusively, unostentatiously, with restraint, conservatively, soberly, modestly, demurely.

quip noun witticism, wisecrack, joke, jest, bon mot, epigram, aphorism; *inf.* crack.

quirk noun *it is one of his quirks to polish his car every day* idiosyncrasy, peculiarity, oddity, eccentricity, foible, whim, vagary, caprice, kink, mannerism, habit, characteristic, trait.

quit verb **1** *quit smoking* give up, stop, cease, discontinue, drop, leave off, abandon, abstain from, desist from. **2** *quit his job* leave, vacate, walk out on. **3** *he has decided to quit* leave, depart, take off; *inf.* call it quits, pack it in.

quite adverb **1** *he has quite recovered* completely, fully, entirely, totally, wholly, absolutely, in all respects. **2** *he is quite talented* extremely, exceedingly, considerably, hugely, enormously, very. **3** *it is quite delicious* truly, really, definitely, absolutely, certainly, unequivocally.

quiver verb *quiver with fear* tremble, shiver, vibrate, quaver, quake, shudder, palpitate.

quiz noun test, examination, questioning, interrogation, catechism, inquiry.

quiz verb *quiz them about their movements* question, ask, interrogate, cross-examine, cross-question, catechize; *inf.* pump, grill.

quizzical adjective *a quizzical look* questioning, puzzled, perplexed, baffled, mystified, mocking, teasing.

quota noun share, allowance, allocation, portion, ration, part, slice, measure, proportion, percentage; *inf.* cut.

quotation noun **1** *full of quotations from Shakespeare* citation, reference, allusion, excerpt, extract, selection, passage, line; *inf.* quote. **2** *give them a quotation for the work* estimate, cost, charge, figure; *inf.* quote.

quote verb **1** *quote verses from the sonnet* repeat, iterate, recite. **2** *he could not quote an example of what he meant* cite, name, refer to. **3** *quote the job at $800* estimate, price.

Rr

rabble noun **1** *a rabble gathered to protest the verdict* mob, horde, swarm, crowd, throng. **2** *inciting the rabble to revolt* populace, commonality, rank and file, peasantry, hoi polloi, riff-raff; masses.

rabid adjective **1** *rabid dogs* rabies-infected, mad, foaming at the mouth, hydrophobic. **2** *rabid socialists/conservatives* fanatical, extreme, overzealous, overenthusiastic, fervent, unreasonable, frenzied, irrational, raging, raving, intolerant, bigoted.

race[1] noun **1** *the competitors in the race* competition, chase, pursuit, relay. **2** *the race for the presidency* contest, competition, rivalry, contention.

race[2] verb **1** *horses racing at Churchill Downs* run, contend, compete. **2** *race to the finish line* run, sprint, dash, dart, bolt, speed, fly, tear, zoom, accelerate, career.

race[3] noun **1** *humankind divided into races* people, ethnic group. **2** *discrimination on grounds of race* ancestry, racial type, blood, bloodline, stock, line, lineage, breed, strain, stirps, extraction, parentage.

racism noun racial discrimination, racial prejudice, bigotry, apartheid, segregation, racial bias.

racist adjective discriminatory, prejudiced, bigoted, intolerant, illiberal.

rack noun frame, framework, stand, form, trestle, structure, holder, shelf.

racket noun **1** *a racket coming from next door* noise, din, row, commotion, disturbance, uproar, hubbub, hullabaloo; clamor, pandemonium, tumult. **2** *he is involved in a drugs racket* illegal enterprise, fraud, scheme, swindle.

racy adjective risqué, suggestive, off-color, ribald, bawdy, vulgar, coarse, crude, rude, smutty, dirty, blue, indecent, indelicate, immodest, naughty; *inf.* spicy.

radiance noun **1** *the radiance of the sun* light, shining, brightness, brilliance, luminosity, effulgence, incandescence, glow, gleam, glitter, sparkle, shimmer. **2** *the radiance of the bride* joyfulness, joy, elation, rapture, blitheness, happiness, delight, pleasure, gaiety, warmth. **3** *the radiance of her beauty* resplendence, splendor, dazzlingness.

radiant adjective **1** *the radiant sun/light* shining, bright, brilliant, luminous, luminescent, effulgent, refulgent, incandescent, beaming, glowing, gleaming, glittering, sparkling, shimmering. **2** *the bride was radiant* joyful, elated, ecstatic, delighted, glowing; *inf.* in seventh heaven, on cloud nine. **3** *her radiant beauty* splendid, resplendent, magnificent, dazzling, glowing.

radiate verb **1** *radiating heat* emit, emanate, scatter, disperse, diffuse, spread. **2** *radiate joy* transmit, emanate; *inf.* be the picture of.

radical adjective **1** *radical change needed* thorough, complete, comprehensive, exhaustive, sweeping, far-reaching, profound, drastic, violent. **2** *radical views* extremist, extreme, immoderate, revolutionary, militant, fanatic, leftist, left-wing.

rag noun (piece of) cloth, scrap, remnant, fragment; dishrag, dishcloth, dustcloth, dust rag.

rage noun **1** *be filled with rage* fury, anger, wrath, ire, frenzy, madness. **2** *fly into a rage* frenzy, tantrum, rampage. **all the rage** *miniskirts are all the rage* ultrafashionable, ultrapopular; *inf.* trendy.

rage verb **1** *the dissatisfied customer is raging* seethe, lose one's temper, boil over, rant, rave, storm, fume, fulminate; *inf.* foam at the mouth, blow one's top, blow a gasket, hit the ceiling, flip one's lid. **2** *rage against the new rules* fulminate, storm, inveigh, rail. **3** *the storm is raging* be violent, be turbulent, be tempestuous.

ragged adjective **1** *ragged clothes* tattered, torn, rent, worn to shreds, threadbare, frayed. **2** *ragged children* in rags, shabby, unkempt, destitute, indigent. **3** *a ragged coastline* jagged, notched, serrated, sawtoothed, craggy, rugged, uneven, irregular. **4** *a ragged band of soldiers* straggling, straggly, disorganized, fragmented.

raid noun *make a raid on the enemy* | *a police raid* surprise attack, assault, onslaught, invasion, incursion, foray, charge, thrust, sortie, sally; *inf.* bust.

raid verb **1** *raid the enemy lines* attack, assault, invade, charge, assail, storm, rush, set upon. **2** *raid the enemy supplies* | *raid the refrigerator* plunder, pillage, loot, rifle, forage, ransack.

rail verb **rail against** *rail against the new rules* criticize, censure, condemn, inveigh against, rage against, protest; *inf.* lambaste.

railing noun balustrade, fencing, barrier.

rain noun **1** *farmers needing rain* rainfall, precipitation, drizzle, shower, rainstorm,

cloudburst, torrent, downpour, deluge, thunderstorm. **2** *a rain of arrows* shower, hail, deluge, volley.

rain verb *it is raining* pour, precipitate, shower, drizzle; *inf.* rain cats and dogs, come down in buckets.

raise verb **1** *raise one's eyes* | *raise the ship* lift, lift up, elevate, uplift, hoist, heave up. **2** *raise his prices* increase, escalate, inflate; *inf.* hike, jack up. **3** *raise the volume/temperature* increase, heighten, augment, amplify, intensify. **4** *raise a statue* construct, build, erect, put up. **5** *raise money/troops* collect, assemble, muster, levy, accumulate, amass, scrape together. **6** *raise objections* put forward, introduce, advance, bring up, broach, suggest, present. **7** *raise hopes* cause, engender, create, kindle, arouse, awaken, excite, provoke, activate, evoke, incite. **8** *raise three children* bring up, rear, nurture, educate. **9** *raise chickens* breed, rear. **10** *raise crops* grow, farm, cultivate, propagate, till, produce. **11** *raise him to captain* promote, advance, upgrade, elevate, exalt. **12** *raise a ghost* call up, call forth, summon, conjure up.

raise noun *a raise in salary* gain, (pay/wage) increase, growth, addition, appreciation; *inf.* boost.

rake noun roué, debauchee, playboy, libertine, profligate.

rakish[1] adjective *the playboy's rakish behavior* dissolute, debauched, dissipated, profligate, wanton, degenerate, depraved.

rakish[2] adjective *wears his hat at a rakish angle* dashing, jaunty, sporty, breezy, debonair, smart, dapper, spruce; *inf.* natty.

rally verb **1** *rally to support the school* come together, assemble, convene, unite. **2** *rally the forces* call together, assemble, summon, round up, muster, marshal, mobilize. **3** *they were defeated, but they rallied* regroup, reassemble, re-form, reunite. **4** *she was ill, but she rallied* recover, recuperate, revive, improve, perk up, pull through, turn the corner.

rally noun **1** *a political rally* mass meeting, gathering, assembly, convention, conference. **2** *a rally on the stock exchange* resurgence, recovery, recuperation, improvement, revival, comeback.

ram verb **1** *ram the tobacco into the pipe* force, cram, stuff, compress, thrust, tamp. **2** *ram fence posts into the ground* drive, hammer, pound, beat, hit. **3** *his car rammed ours* strike, hit, bump, slam.

ramble verb **1** *ramble through the countryside* wander, stroll, saunter, amble, roam, range, rove, roam, trudge, jaunt. **2** *the speaker rambled on* digress, wander, go off on tangents, maunder, gibber, blather, babble, chatter, rattle on.

ramble noun wander, stroll, saunter, amble, roam, traipse, jaunt, trip, excursion, tour.

rambling adjective *rambling speeches* digressive, wandering, roundabout, circuitous, diffuse, periphrastic, disconnected, disjointed, maundering, long-winded, verbose, wordy, prolix.

ramification noun *the action had many ramifications* consequence, implication, aftermath, outcome, result, upshot.

rampage noun uproar, furor, mayhem, turmoil. **on the rampage** running amok, going berserk, out of control.

rampant adjective *rampant crime* uncontrolled, rife, unrestrained, unchecked, unbridled, widespread, pandemic, epidemic.

rampart noun *the ramparts of the fortress* embankment, earthwork, parapet, fortification, fort, stronghold, bulwark, bastion, barbican.

ramshackle adjective tumbledown, broken-down, rundown, dilapidated, derelict, decrepit, neglected, crumbling, rickety, shaky, unsteady, tottering, flimsy, jerry-built.

rancor noun resentment, malice, spite, ill will, hatred, malevolence, malignancy, animosity, antipathy, enmity, hostility, acrimony, venom, vindictiveness.

random adjective haphazard, chance, accidental, fortuitous, serendipitous, adventitious, arbitrary, hit-or-miss, indiscriminate, sporadic, stray, spot, casual, unsystematic, disorganized, unplanned, unpremeditated. **at random 1** *chose numbers at random* randomly, haphazardly, arbitrarily. **2** *trees planted at random* unsystematically, erratically, indiscriminately, sporadically.

range noun **1** *range of vision* | *the range of his influence* scope, compass, radius, span, scale, gamut, reach, sweep, extent, area, field, orbit, province, domain, latitude; limits, bounds, confines. **2** *a range of mountains* row, line, file, rank, string, chain, series, sequence, succession, tier. **3** *a wide range of flavors* assortment, variety. **4** *animals on the range* pasture, pasturage, grassland, grazing land.

range verb **1** *range from very hot to freezing* extend, stretch, reach, cover, go, run, pass, fluctuate, vary. **2** *sheep ranging over the hills* roam, rove, ramble, traverse, wander, meander, amble, stroll, stray, drift.

rank noun **1** *salary according to rank* grade, level, stratum, class, status, position, station, echelon, standing. **2** *persons of rank* nobility, aristocracy, high birth, eminence, distinction, influence, power, prestige, weight, importance. **3** *break rank* array, alignment, order, arrangement, organization. **rank and file 1** *the officers separated from the rank and file* ordinary soldiers, soldiers, men, troops. **2** *government ignoring the wishes of the rank and file* ordinary people, public, general public; populace, commonality, rabble.

rank adjective **1** *rank vegetation* lush, luxuriant, abundant, dense, profuse, flourishing, exuberant, vigorous, overgrown. **2** *a rank smell* strong, pungent, acrid, malodorous, foul-smelling, evil-smelling, stinking, rancid, putrid, fetid, offensive, revolting, sickening, noxious, mephitic. **3** *condemn his rank language* indecent, immodest, indecorous, coarse, gross, vulgar, shocking, outrageous, lurid, crass, scurrilous, nasty, foul, filthy, vile, obscene, smutty, profane. **4** *rank disobedience* utter, complete, total, absolute, out and out, downright, thorough, sheer, unqualified, unmitigated, arrant, flagrant, blatant, glaring, egregious.

rankle verb *their insults still rankle* fester, annoy, irk, vex, peeve, irritate, rile, chafe, gall; *inf.* get one's goat.

ransack verb **1** *raiders ransacking the area* plunder, pillage, raid, rob, loot, despoil, rifle, strip, fleece, sack, ravage, harry, maraud, devastate, depredate. **2** *ransack the house looking for the will* search, scour, comb, explore, turn inside out.

ransom noun **1** *pay the kidnappers a ransom* payoff, payment, price. **2** *obtain the kidnapped child's ransom* release, freedom, deliverance, liberation, rescue, redemption, restoration.

ransom verb *succeed in ransoming the kidnapped child* release, free, deliver, liberate, rescue, redeem, restore to freedom.

rant verb bluster, harangue, vociferate, declaim, hold forth, roar, bellow, bawl, rave; *inf.* spout.

rap noun **1** *a rap on the knuckles* tap, hit, blow, whack, bang, cuff, clip, clout. **2** *hear a rap at the door* knock, knocking, tap, bang, rat-a-tat. **3** *take the rap for the accident* blame, responsibility, accountability, punishment, penalty, castigation.

rap verb **1** *rap him on the knuckles* tap, hit, strike, whack, bang, cuff, clip, clout, batter; *inf.* bash. **2** *rap at the door* knock, tap, bang.

rapacious adjective **1** *rapacious moneylender* acquisitive, greedy, avaricious, covetous, insatiable, predatory, usurious. **2** *rapacious invaders* plundering, pillaging, robbing, marauding, looting, piratical.

rapid adjective quick, fast, swift, speedy, fleet, hurried, hasty, expeditious, express, brisk, lively, prompt, precipitate.

rapidly adverb quickly, fast, swiftly, speedily, hurriedly, in a hurry, hastily, in haste, expeditiously, briskly, promptly, precipitately, at full tilt; *inf.* before one can say Jack Robinson.

rapport noun affinity, bond, empathy, harmony, sympathy, understanding, link.

rapt adjective **1** *rapt attention* absorbed, engrossed, preoccupied, intent, concentrating, pensive, meditative. **2** *a rapt smile* enraptured, enchanted, entranced, charmed, thrilled, transported, blissful, ecstatic.

rapture noun joy, ecstasy, elation, exaltation, exhilaration, bliss, euphoria, rhapsody, enchantment, delight, delectation; *inf.* cloud nine, seventh heaven.

rare adjective **1** *a rare specimen* unusual, uncommon, extraordinary, exceptional, atypical, singular, remarkable, phenomenal, strange, recherché, unique. **2** *one of his rare appearances* infrequent, scarce, sparse, sporadic, scattered. **3** *exhibit a rare skill* outstanding, superior, first-rate, special, choice, excellent, incomparable, unparalleled, peerless, matchless; *inf.* A-1, top-notch.

rarely adverb seldom, infrequently, hardly, scarcely; *inf.* once in a blue moon.

rascal noun **1** *the child is a little rascal* imp, scamp, scalawag, mischief-maker, devil. **2** *that man is a real rascal* scoundrel, villain, rogue, blackguard, ne'er-do-well, wastrel, reprobate, cad.

rash adjective reckless, impetuous, hasty, impulsive, madcap, audacious, brash, daredevil, foolhardy, harum-scarum, devil-may-care, headstrong, hotheaded, incautious, careless, heedless, thoughtless, imprudent, ill-advised, ill-considered, foolish, hare-brained.

rash noun **1** *a rash on his face* outbreak, eruption, breaking out; erythema, hives, heat rash, nettle rash, diaper rash. **2** *a rash of burglaries* outbreak, spate, torrent, flood, wave, plague, epidemic, succession, series, run.

rasping adjective *a rasping noise/voice* grating, scratchy, jarring, discordant, creaky, harsh, rough, gravelly, croaking, croaky, gruff.

rate noun **1** *rate of interest* percentage, ratio, proportion, scale, degree, standard. **2** *the rate per day* payment, fee, remuneration, price, cost, charge, rent, tariff; *inf.* damage. **3** *walk at a rate of 4 miles per hour* pace, speed, tempo, velocity, measure. **at any rate** in any case, anyhow, anyway, nevertheless, in any event.

rate verb **1** *how would you rate his performance?* adjudge, judge, assess, appraise, evaluate, value, measure, grade, rank, classify, categorize. **2** *I rate him a complete fool* regard as, consider, count, deem, reckon, esteem. **3** *he rates re-*

spect be worthy of, deserve, merit, be entitled to.

rather adverb **1** *I would rather not go* sooner, preferably, more willingly, more readily. **2** *not a notebook, but rather a leaflet* on the contrary, instead, actually, in reality, strictly speaking, to be precise. **3** *he is rather outspoken* quite, fairly, a bit, a little, slightly, somewhat, relatively, to some degree/extent; *inf.* kind of, pretty.

ratify verb confirm, endorse, sign, countersign, corroborate, sanction, warrant, approve, authorize, authenticate, certify, validate, accept, consent to, uphold, bear out.

ratio noun proportion, correlation, correspondence, percentage, fraction, quotient.

ration noun allowance, quota, allotment, portion, share, measure, part, lot, amount, helping, proportion, percentage, budget.

ration verb *ration the amount per person* limit, restrict, control, conserve, budget. **ration out** *ration out the week's supplies* distribute, issue, allocate, allot, divide out, apportion, give out, hand out, dole out, measure out, mete out, parcel out.

rational adjective **1** *based on purely rational considerations* cognitive, mental, cerebral, logical, analytical, conceptual. **2** *a rational course of action* sensible, reasonable, logical, sound, intelligent, wise, judicious, sagacious, prudent, circumspect, politic, astute, shrewd, perceptive, well-advised. **3** *the patient does not always seem rational* lucid, coherent, sane, in sound mind, in one's right mind, compos mentis, well-balanced, normal; *inf.* all there.

rationale noun theory, hypothesis, thesis, logic, philosophy, reason, *raison d'être*; grounds.

rationalize verb *rationalize his behavior* explain away, account for, make excuses for, make plausible, justify.

rattle verb **1** *the windows/chain rattled* bang, clatter, clang, clank, jangle, clink. **2** *the car rattled along* bounce, bump, jiggle, jounce, shake, jolt, vibrate, jar. **3** *he rattled on about his job* chatter, babble, gabble, prattle, jabber, gibber, blather, prate; *inf.* yak. **4** *she was rattled by the experience* disconcert, disturb, fluster, upset, shake, perturb, discompose, discomfit, frighten, scare; *inf.* faze.

raucous adjective strident, shrill, screeching, piercing, ear-piercing, harsh, sharp, grating, rasping, discordant, dissonant, jarring.

ravage verb devastate, lay waste, ruin, wreak havoc on, destroy, level, raze, demolish, wreck, shatter, pillage, plunder, despoil, harry, maraud, ransack, sack, loot.

rave verb **1** *the invalid is raving* talk wildly,

babble, ramble. **2** *her parents raved at her* rant, rage, storm, fulminate, explode, lose one's temper, lose control, go into a frenzy, run amok; *inf.* fly off the handle, flip one's lid. **rave about/over** *rave about her performance* | *rave over his car* go into raptures over, rhapsodize over, gush over, acclaim; *inf.* go wild about, be mad about.

rave adjective *rave reviews* rapturous, ecstatic, enthusiastic, laudatory, excellent, favorable.

ravenous adjective starving, starved, famished; greedy, gluttonous, voracious, insatiable, insatiate, ravening, wolfish.

ravine noun chasm, gorge, canyon, abyss, gulf, gully, gulch, defile, pass, gap.

raving adjective **1** *raving patients* delirious, out of one's mind, irrational, frenzied, deranged, hysterical, frantic, berserk, demented, insane, mad, crazed, wild; *inf.* crazy. **2** *a raving beauty* extraordinary, singular, striking, outstanding, stunning.

ravishing adjective stunning, gorgeous, dazzling, radiant, enchanting, bewitching, charming.

raw adjective **1** *raw food* uncooked, fresh. **2** *raw sugar/silk* unrefined, crude, coarse, unprocessed, unprepared, untreated, unfinished. **3** *raw recruits* inexperienced, untrained, unskilled, untutored, unschooled, unpracticed, untried, untested, unseasoned, undisciplined, new, callow, immature, green, ignorant, naive, unsophisticated; *inf.* wet behind the ears. **4** *raw flesh/wounds* excoriated, skinned, grazed, abraded, scratched, chafed, open, exposed, unhealed, sore, tender. **5** *raw weather* damp, wet, cold, chilly, chilling, freezing, bitter, biting, nippy, piercing, penetrating.

ray noun **1** *rays of light* beam, shaft, streak, stream, gleam, glint, flash, glimmer, flicker, twinkle. **2** *a ray of hope* flicker, glimmer, spark, trace.

raze verb flatten, demolish, tear down, level, pull down, knock down, fell, bulldoze, ruin, wreck.

reach verb **1** *he reached out* | *reach out a hand* stretch, outstretch, extend, hold out. **2** *reach one's destination* get to, arrive at, come to, get foot on. **3** *reach perfection* attain, achieve, gain, accomplish. **4** *we could not reach him that day* contact, get in touch with, get through to. **reach for** *reach for the book* grasp, seize, grab at, clutch at.

reach noun **1** *the rope was beyond her reach* | *within reach of safety* grasp, stretch, spread, extension, extent, span, distance. **2** *within the reach of his influence* scope, range, compass, latitude, ambit, orbit,

sphere, area, field, territory, authority, jurisdiction.

react verb **1** *react to the drug* respond, behave in response to. **2** *how did she react on hearing the news?* behave, act, conduct oneself, proceed, operate, function, cope.

reaction noun **1** *receive a reaction to their proposal* response, answer, reply, feedback. **2** *his harsh regime was a reaction to total disorder* counteraction, counterbalance, counterpoise, recoil, reversal.

reactionary adjective ultraconservative, conservative, diehard, rightist, right-wing.

read verb **1** *read the book* peruse, study, scan, pore over, scrutinize, run one's eye over, look at, refer to, browse through; *inf.* wade through, dip into. **2** *read his silence as consent* interpret, construe, take to mean, decipher, understand, comprehend. **3** *the thermometer is reading zero* register, record, display, show, indicate. **read into** *read too much into their statement* infer from, interpolate from.

readable adjective **1** *readable exam papers* legible, decipherable, clear, intelligible, understandable, comprehensible. **2** *readable works of fiction* enjoyable, entertaining, interesting, gripping, enthralling, stimulating.

readily adverb **1** *he will readily help you* willingly, without hesitation, gladly, happily, cheerfully, with pleasure, eagerly. **2** *the sofa readily converts into a bed* easily, with ease, without difficulty, effortlessly.

ready adjective **1** *dinner is ready* prepared, completed, finished, organized. **2** *ready for battle* | *ready to go* prepared, equipped, organized, all set, fit. **3** *ready to help* willing, inclined, disposed, given, eager, keen, happy, glad; *inf.* game. **4** *a ready source of income* available, accessible, handy, convenient, on hand, present, near, near at hand, on call, at one's fingertips; *inf.* on tap. **5** *a ready answer* prompt, quick, rapid, swift, speedy, punctual, timely. **ready to** *ready to collapse* about to, on the verge/brink of, in danger of, liable to.

real adjective **1** *the real world* actual, existent, factual, unimaginary. **2** *real leather* authentic, genuine, bona fide, veritable. **3** *real emotion* sincere, heartfelt, earnest, fervent, unfeigned, unaffected, honest, truthful.

realistic adjective **1** *be realistic as to your prospects* practical, pragmatic, rational, down-to-earth, matter-of-fact, sensible, commonsensical, levelheaded, hardheaded, businesslike, sober; *inf.* with both feet on the ground, no-nonsense. **2** *a realistic model of a dinosaur* lifelike, true-to-life, true, faithful, close, representational, graphic, naturalistic, authentic.

realize verb 1 *realize that they are rich* grasp, know, comprehend, apprehend, be aware, appreciate, recognize, perceive, discern, conceive; *inf.* get it. 2 *realize one's dreams* fulfill, achieve, accomplish, bring to fruition, consummate, effect, effectuate, actualize, reify. 3 *realize a profit* make, clear, acquire, gain, bring in, obtain, earn.

really adverb 1 *the guard dog is really a gentle pet* in reality, actually, in fact. 2 *this is really useful* certainly, surely, truly, undoubtedly, indubitably, assuredly, unquestionably, indeed, absolutely, categorically. 3 *a really charming person* very, extremely, thoroughly, truly, decidedly. 4 *his career is really over* to all intents and purposes, virtually, for all practical purposes, just about, almost.

realm noun 1 *the realm of Denmark* kingdom, country, land, state, province, empire, domain, monarchy, principality. 2 *the realm of the imagination | the realm of science* world, field, sphere, area, department, region, province, orbit, zone.

reap verb harvest, gather in, take in, realize, obtain, acquire, secure, procure.

rear noun 1 *at the rear of the garage* back, back part, hind part. 2 *at the rear of the line* end, tail, tail end.

rear verb 1 *rear three children* raise, bring up, care for, nurture, parent, educate, train, instruct. 2 *rear one's head* raise, lift up, hoist, elevate.

reason noun 1 *the reason for his behavior* grounds, cause, basis, motive, motivation, impetus, actuation, instigation. 2 *give a reason for your absence* explanation, exposition, justification, argument, case, defense, vindication, apologia, rationalization, excuse, apology. 3 *follow reason not emotion* reasoning, intellect, intelligence, mind, judgment, logic, rationality, ratiocination; brains. 4 *he has lost his reason* sanity, mind, soundness of mind; senses. 5 *keep a sense of reason in your expenditure* common sense, sense, practicality, practicability, moderation, propriety. **within reason** *have anything you like within reason* in moderation.

reason verb 1 *unable to reason when upset* think, think straight, use one's head, analyze, cerebrate, intellectualize, ratiocinate. 2 *he reasoned that two could live as cheaply as one* deduce, infer, conclude, work out, reckon, think, surmise. **reason with** *try reasoning with him* use logic on, argue with, debate with, dispute with, try to persuade, plead with.

reasonable adjective 1 *he is a reasonable man* fair, just, equitable, impartial, aboveboard. 2 *it seemed a reasonable idea* logical, practical, rational, sensible, intelligent, wise, sound, judicious, advisable, well-thought-out, tenable, plausible. 3 *reasonable prices* moderate, inexpensive, modest.

reasoning noun 1 *let reasoning, not emotion, dictate your actions* thought, logic, rationalization, deduction, analysis, cerebration, ratiocination. 2 *his reasoning is faulty* argument, rationale, case, hypothesis, interpretation.

reassure verb encourage, hearten, put one's mind at rest, put at ease, restore confidence to, buoy up, cheer up.

rebate noun refund, repayment, deduction, discount, allowance, reduction.

rebel noun revolutionary, insurrectionist, insurgent, revolter, mutineer, seditionist, agitator, resistance fighter, anarchist; dissenter, nonconformist.

rebel verb *the troops are rebelling* mutiny, riot, revolt, rise up, take to the streets. **rebel against** *rebel against authority* defy, disobey. **rebel at** *his stomach rebelled at the thought of food* recoil from, shrink from, flinch from.

rebellion noun revolt, revolution, insurrection, insurgence, insurgency, uprising, mutiny, riot, civil disobedience, resistance; defiance, disobedience, dissent, nonconformity.

rebellious adjective 1 *rebellious children* unruly, ungovernable, unmanageable, disorderly, intractable, recalcitrant, incorrigible, contumacious. 2 *the rebellious protestors were imprisoned* revolutionary, insurrectionary, insurgent, mutinous, rioting. 3 *the rebellious students were expelled* defiant, disobedient, resistant, dissentient, nonconformist.

rebuff verb reject, refuse, decline, turn down, spurn, repudiate, repel, discourage, fend off, stave off, snub, slight; *inf.* brush off.

rebuke verb reprimand, scold, chide, admonish, reproach, reprove, lecture, reprehend, censure, berate, upbraid, castigate, take to task; *inf.* tell off, call on the carpet, lambaste, chew out, bawl out.

rebuke noun reprimand, scolding, admonition, reproach, reproof, reproval, remonstration, lecture, censure, upbraiding, castigation; *inf.* tongue-lashing, dressing-down, bawling out.

recalcitrant adjective intractable, refractory, unmanageable, ungovernable, disobedient, insubordinate, defiant, contrary, wayward, willful, headstrong, perverse, contumacious, obstinate, obdurate.

recall verb 1 *unable to recall his name* call to mind, remember, recollect, summon, evoke.

recall noun *have total recall* memory, recollection, remembrance.

recant verb disavow, disclaim, disown, deny, renounce, relinquish, abjure, forswear, repudiate, renege on, recall, revoke, retract, countermand.

recapitulate verb restate, repeat, reiterate, summarize, sum up; *inf.* recap.

recede verb **1** *the water receded* ebb, abate, subside, retreat, withdraw, fall back. **2** *the coastline receded as we sailed away* grow less visible, become distant, fade into the distance. **3** *danger receded in time* lessen, fade, diminish, decrease, dwindle, shrink, wane, fall off, taper off, peter out. **4** *his chin recedes* slant, slope backward, fall away.

receipt noun **1** *the receipt of the goods* | *receipt of his apology* receiving, recipience, arrival, reception, acceptance, obtaining, acquisition. **2** *get a receipt for the goods* sales slip, proof of purchase, stub, voucher. **3** *make a list of receipts for the auditor* payment received, income, proceeds, profits, gains, earnings.

receive verb **1** *he did receive the goods* accept, take possession of. **2** *receive good news* get, obtain, acquire, come by, gain, gather, collect, hear. **3** *receive bad treatment* undergo, experience, meet with, encounter, sustain, be subjected to, bear, suffer. **4** *receive guests* welcome, greet, entertain.

recent adjective **1** *recent developments* new, fresh, novel, latest, late, modern, contemporary, latter-day, current, up-to-date, up-to-the-minute. **2** *his recent illness* occurring recently, not long past.

reception noun **1** *the reception of the goods* receiving, acceptance. See RECEIPT 1. **2** *the reception of the guests* welcoming, greeting, entertaining. **3** *the show got a warm reception* response, acknowledgment, reaction, treatment, welcome. **4** *a wedding reception* party, function, entertainment, soirée; *inf.* do, bash.

receptive adjective open, flexible, willing, perceptive, sensitive, keen.

recess noun **1** *books arranged in a recess* alcove, niche, nook, corner, cavity, bay, oriel. **2** *in the recesses of my memory* interior, heart, retreat, refuge, sanctum; depths; *inf.* innards. **3** *Congress will resume discussions after the recess* break, respite, rest, interval, intermission, time off, vacation, holiday, closure, cessation of business; *inf.* breather, time out.

recession noun **1** *the recession cost many stockbrokers their jobs* economic downturn, depression, slump; hard times. **2** *the recession of floodwaters* receding, retreat, withdrawal, ebbing, subsiding, abatement.

recipe noun **1** *follow the recipe for pancakes* directions, instructions; guide. **2** *his suggestions are a recipe for disaster* method, technique, system, procedure, modus operandi, process, means, way, formula, prescription.

reciprocal adjective **1** *a reciprocal favor* return, in return, requited, retaliated. **2** *reciprocal affection* mutual, shared, common, exchanged, give-and-take, complementary, corresponding, correlative.

reciprocate verb return, requite, repay, give back; respond in kind.

recital noun **1** *the recital of the poem* rendition, declamation, reading, delivery. **2** *the recital of the events* enumeration, detailing, itemizing, specification; account, report, chronicle, recounting, relation, record, story, tale. **3** *a piano recital* performance, concert, show.

recite verb **1** *recite a poem* declaim, speak, render, say, repeat, deliver. **2** *recite a list of disasters* enumerate, detail, list, itemize, reel off, rattle off, specify, particularize, describe, recount, relate, narrate, recapitulate.

reckless adjective rash, careless, thoughtless, incautious, heedless, inattentive, daredevil, devil-may-care, madcap, harum-scarum, wild, precipitate, headlong, hasty, irresponsible, harebrained, foolhardy, ill-advised, imprudent, unwise, indiscreet, mindless, negligent, temerarious.

reckon verb **1** *he reckoned that she was lying* think, believe, suppose, assume, surmise, conjecture, imagine, fancy, guess. **2** *she was reckoned a good painter* regard as, consider, judge, hold to be, look upon as, account, deem, rate, evaluate, gauge, count, estimate, appraise. **3** *reckon the cost* count, calculate, add up, compute, total, tally. **reckon with** *he will have her father to reckon with* cope with, deal with, contend with, handle, face.

reckoning noun **1** *according to my reckoning, the total is wrong* calculation, addition, computation, total, tally, counting, summation, score. **2** *according to their reckoning, she is the best* opinion, judgment, evaluation, estimation, appraisal. **3** *the reckoning of the account* settlement, payment, discharging, defrayal, squaring, clearance. **4** *the day of reckoning* settlement, retribution, judgment, fate, doom.

recline verb lie, lie down, lean, be recumbent, rest, repose, loll, lounge, sprawl, stretch out.

recluse noun hermit, anchorite, ascetic, eremite, monk, nun, solitary, lone wolf, loner.

recognition noun **1** *recognition of the thief* identification, spotting, knowing, recollection. **2** *his recognition of his mis-*

take realization, awareness, consciousness, perception, appreciation, understanding, acknowledgment, acceptance. **3** *their recognition of his claim* acknowledgment, acceptance, admittance, granting, endorsement, sanctioning, approval, validation, ratification. **4** *receive recognition as an artist* acknowledgment, appreciation, reward, honor, homage, applause.

recognize verb **1** *recognize an old friend* know, identify, place, spot, recall, recollect, remember. **2** *recognize his own mistake* realize, see, perceive, discern, appreciate, understand, apprehend, acknowledge, accept, admit, concede, allow, grant, confess, own. **3** *recognize his claim* acknowledge, accept, admit, allow, grant, endorse, sanction, approve, validate, ratify, uphold. **4** *recognize his achievement* reward, honor, salute, applaud.

recoil verb **1** *recoil from him in terror* shrink, shy away, flinch, start, wince, cower, quail. **2** *the spring/gun recoiled* rebound, resile, kick back.

recollect verb *I cannot recollect his name* remember, recall, call to mind, think of, summon up, place; *inf.* put one's finger on.

recommend verb **1** *recommend this as a cure* advocate, commend, endorse, approve, vouch for, suggest, offer, put forward, propose, advance. **2** *recommend that you go home* advise, counsel, guide, urge, exhort, enjoin.

recommendation noun **1** *accept your recommendation as to the wine* endorsement, suggestion, tip, hint, proposal, commendation, praise; *inf.* plug. **2** *accept the judge's recommendation as to how to act* advice, counsel, guidance, exhortation, enjoinder. **3** *fast service is the restaurant's only recommendation* advantage, benefit, blessing, good point, boon.

reconcile verb **1** *mother and daughter have been reconciled* reunite, bring together, bring to terms, pacify, appease, placate, · propitiate, mollify. **2** *reconcile themselves to her death* resign, come to accept, accept, accommodate, submit, yield. **3** *reconcile their differences* settle, resolve, square, put to rights, mend, remedy, patch up, rectify. **4** *reconcile his philosophy and his actions* harmonize, make compatible, adjust, attune, make coincide, make congruent.

reconnaissance noun survey, exploration, probe, scan, inspection, investigation, scrutiny, observation, scouting.

reconsider verb review, reexamine, reevaluate, reassess, think better of; think twice, have second thoughts, change one's mind.

record noun **1** *the records are missing* official document, register, log, logbook, file, chronicle, diary, journal; documentation; documents, minutes, notes, annals, archives. **2** *play a record* album, phonograph record, disc; compact disc; single, recording, release; *inf.* LP, CD. **3** *what do you know of his record?* employment history, past performance, curriculum vitae, history, background, reputation; *inf.* track record. **4** *does he have a record?* criminal record; *inf.* rap sheet. **5** *this is a record of his achievement* remembrance, souvenir, testimony, testimonial, witness; documentation, evidence. **6** *climate records* information, collected information; data, reports, accounts. **off the record** confidential, in confidence, unofficial, private, secret, sub rosa. **on record 1** *the wettest winter on record* registered, documented, officially noted. **2** *he is on record as promising improvements* officially noted, documented, publicly known.

record verb **1** *record the details* document, register, chronicle, set down, write down, take down, enter, put on file, docket, list, log, catalog, transcribe. **2** *record a very low temperature* register, read, indicate, show, display. **3** *record a music video* make, produce, cut, tape, videotape.

recoup verb *recoup the lost property* regain, recover, win back, retrieve, repossess, redeem.

recover verb **1** *recover their stolen possessions* regain, recoup, retrieve, reclaim, repossess, redeem, recapture. **2** *the invalid will recover in time* recuperate, convalesce, get well, heal, get back on one's feet, improve, mend, rally, revive, pull through, bounce back.

recreation noun **1** *for recreation he rows* relaxation, refreshment, leisure, amusement, entertainment, distraction, diversion, pleasure, enjoyment, fun, play, sport. **2** *his favorite recreation is reading* leisure activity, pastime, hobby, diversion.

recruit verb **1** *recruit new members* enlist, enroll, sign up, draft, conscript, levy, engage, obtain, acquire, procure, take on, round up, muster. **2** *recruit an army* form, raise, muster, assemble.

recruit noun **1** *army recruits* enlistee, draftee, conscript. **2** *new recruits to the industry* newcomer, initiate, beginner, learner, trainee, apprentice, novice, tyro, neophyte; *inf.* rookie, greenhorn.

rectify verb remedy, repair, right, correct, amend, emend, fix, make good, redress, reform, improve, better, ameliorate, adjust, square.

recuperate verb **1** *he is recuperating after an illness* recover, convalesce, improve, mend, rally, revive, pull through, bounce back. **2** *recuperate costs* recover, recoup, regain, retrieve, reclaim.

recur verb happen again, return, reappear, repeat itself, happen repeatedly.

recurrent adjective recurring, repeated, repetitive, reiterative, periodic, cyclical, regular, habitual, continual, frequent, intermittent, chronic.

recycle verb reuse, reprocess, salvage, save.

red adjective **1** *red dresses/flowers* crimson, scarlet, vermilion, cherry, ruby, cardinal, carmine, ruby-colored, maroon, wine, wine-colored, claret, russet, coral, cochineal, rose. **2** *she had a red face* flushed, blushing, florid, ruddy, rubicund, roseate. **3** *with red eyes* bloodshot, inflamed. **4** *red hair* flaming-red, flame-colored, auburn, copper, Titian, chestnut, carroty, ginger.

redeem verb **1** *redeem pawned goods* reclaim, regain, recover, retrieve, repossess, recoup, buy back, repurchase. **2** *redeem the vouchers* exchange, cash in, convert, turn in. **3** *he redeemed himself by helping his neighbor* vindicate, absolve, remove guilt from. **4** *redeem his obligations* fulfill, discharge, make good, carry out, execute, keep, adhere to, abide by, obey, meet, satisfy.

redress verb **1** *redress a wrong* rectify, remedy, make amends for, compensate for, make reparation/restitution for, recompense for, atone for. **2** *redress the balance of power* put right, even up, regulate, adjust, correct.

redress noun amends; compensation, reparation, restitution, recompense, atonement.

reduce verb **1** *reduce the size of the garden | reduce the volume* decrease, diminish, lessen, lower, cut, curtail, contract, shorten, abbreviate, moderate, dilute, mitigate, alleviate, abate. **2** *they were reduced to tears* bring to, bring to the point of, force to, drive to. **3** *they were reduced to a lower grade/rank* demote, downgrade, lower, humble. **4** *reduced yesterday's stock* lower, make cheaper, cut, mark down, slash, discount, put on sale. **5** *she is trying to reduce* slim down, lose weight, diet, shed some pounds, slenderize.

redundant adjective **1** *his presence was redundant* not required, unnecessary, inessential, unwanted, de trop, surplus, supernumerary, in excess, extra. **2** *redundant writings* padded, wordy, verbose, tautological, periphrastic, diffuse, pleonastic.

reel verb **1** *drunks reeling down the street* stagger, lurch, sway, stumble, totter, wobble, falter, waver, pitch, roll. **2** *reeling from the blow* feel giddy/dizzy, feel confused, be shaken, be in shock, be upset. **3** *her mind was reeling* whirl, spin, revolve, swirl, twirl, swim.

refer verb **refer to 1** *refer to his notes* consult, turn to, look at, look up in, have recourse to. **2** *refer the question/person to a higher court* pass (on) to, hand on to, send on to, transfer to, remit to, direct to. **3** *he referred to her death in his speech* mention, make reference to, allude to, touch on, speak of, cite, advert to, hint at. **4** *these figures refer to last year* apply to, be relevant to, concern, relate to, pertain to, have a bearing on.

referee noun umpire, judge, adjudicator, arbitrator, arbiter, mediator; *inf.* ref.

referee verb **1** *referee the game* umpire, judge, adjudicate. **2** *referee in the dispute* arbitrate, mediate, intercede.

reference noun **1** *a reference to her death in his speech* mention, allusion, citation, hint. **2** *with reference to yesterday's meeting* regard, respect, relation, bearing, application, relevance, pertinence, connection, correlation. **3** *give a list of your references for the book* source, citation, authority. **4** *the teacher gave her a reference* recommendation, character reference, testimonial, good word; credentials.

refine verb **1** *refine sugar* purify, rarefy, clarify, clear, cleanse, strain, sift, filter, distill, process. **2** *sent to a school that would refine them* civilize, make cultivated, polish, improve, make elegant. **3** *refine the art of conversation* improve, perfect, consummate, elaborate, hone, fine-tune, complete.

refined adjective **1** *refined sugar* purified, pure, rarefied, clarified, clear, filtered, distilled, processed. **2** *a refined lady/gentleman* cultivated, cultured, polished, civilized, civil, gracious, stylish, elegant, sophisticated, urbane, courtly, well-mannered, well-bred, gentlemanly, ladylike, genteel. **3** *refined tastes/manners* discriminating, discerning, tasteful, sophisticated, fastidious.

refinement noun **1** *the refinement of sugar* purification, processing, distillation, filtration. **2** *a person of refinement* cultivation, culture, taste, discrimination, polish, civility, grace, graciousness, style, elegance, finesse, sophistication, urbanity, courtliness, good breeding, politeness, gentility, politesse; good manners. **3** *the term paper needs refinement* revision, improvement, enhancement, correction, amendment. **4** *refinements of logic/language* subtlety, nicety, nuance, fine point.

reflect verb **1** *the surface reflects heat/light* throw back, send back, give back, scatter, diffuse. **2** *their faces reflected in the pool* mirror, image. **3** *reflect sound* bounce back, echo. **4** *his complexion reflects his state of health* indicate, express, bespeak, communicate, show, display, demonstrate, exhibit, reveal, manifest. **reflect on** 1 *it will reflect on the school if he does badly* discredit, damage the reputation of, detract from. 2 *reflect on her problems* consider, mull over, contemplate, deliberate over, ponder, meditate about, muse about, ruminate about, cogitate about, cerebrate, dwell on, brood about.

reflection noun 1 *the reflection of sound/images* throwing back, echoing, mirroring; diffusion, radiation. 2 *look at her reflection* image, mirror image. 3 *the ring is a reflection of the way he feels about her* indication, expression, display, demonstration, manifestation. 4 *his behavior is a reflection on the school* imputation, slur, aspersion, source of discredit, derogation. 5 *on reflection, he decided to go* thought, second thought, consideration, contemplation, deliberation, meditation, rumination, cogitation, cerebration. 6 *write down your reflections on the subject* thought, opinion, view, idea, impression, comment; findings.

reform verb 1 *reform the system* improve, better, ameliorate, amend, mend, rectify, correct, rehabilitate, change, revise, revolutionize, reorganize, reconstruct, rebuild, refashion, remodel, remake, revamp, renovate. 2 *he has reformed since you knew him* mend one's ways, turn over a new leaf, improve; *inf.* go straight.

reform noun *the reform of the system* improvement, betterment, amelioration, amendment, rectification, correction, rehabilitation, change, revision, reorganization, reconstruction, rebuilding, refashioning, remodeling, renovation.

refrain verb *refrain from drinking* desist, abstain, forbear, forgo, avoid, eschew, cease, stop, give up, leave off, quit, renounce.

refresh verb 1 *refreshed by a long walk* invigorate, revitalize, revive, brace, fortify, enliven, stimulate, energize, exhilarate, reanimate, resuscitate, rejuvenate, regenerate, inspirit; *inf.* perk up. 2 *refresh one's memory* stimulate, prompt, prod, jog, activate, rouse, arouse.

refreshments plural noun food and drink, sustenance; snacks, finger foods, drinks; *inf.* grub, nosh, chow.

refuge noun 1 *seek refuge from the elements* shelter, safety, security, protection, asylum, sanctuary. 2 *regard their house as a refuge* shelter, haven, retreat, sanctuary, harbor.

refugee noun displaced person, émigré, exile, fugitive, escapee.

refund verb *refund her deposit* return, repay, pay back, reimburse, make good, restore, replace.

refund noun *give the disappointed audi-*

ence a refund repayment, reimbursement, rebate.

refurbish verb renovate, revamp, overhaul, redecorate, spruce up, recondition, refit, reequip, remodel, repair, mend; *inf.* do up, fix up.

refusal noun 1 *four acceptances and one refusal to the invitation* rejection, spurning, decline, nonacceptance, dissent, no, demurral, negation, thumbs down, rebuff; regrets; *inf.* brush-off. 2 *you can have first refusal* option, choice, consideration, opportunity.

refuse verb 1 *refuse an invitation* turn down, decline, reject, spurn, rebuff, repudiate; *inf.* pass up. 2 *refuse to go* decline, be unwilling; balk at, demur at, avoid, resist, protest at. 3 *refuse permission to go* withhold, not grant.

refuse noun rubbish, garbage, trash, waste, debris, litter, dross; dregs, leavings, flotsam; *inf.* junk.

regain verb recover, recoup, retrieve, reclaim, repossess, redeem, retake, recapture, get back, win back.

regal adjective royal, majestic, noble, proud, stately, magnificent, sumptuous; kingly, queenly, princely.

regard verb 1 *he seldom regards her advice* heed, pay attention to, listen to, mind, take into consideration/account. 2 *regard the prospect with horror* look upon, view, consider, contemplate, reflect on. 3 *his work is well regarded* judge, adjudge, rate, value, estimate, gauge, appraise, assess, deem, consider, look upon.

regard noun 1 *pay no regard to his warning* heed, attention, notice, consideration, thought, mind. 2 *looked upon with regard* respect, esteem, admiration, approval, approbation, appreciation, favor, deference, affection, love. 3 *in this regard I disagree with you* respect, aspect, point, particular, detail, item, feature.

regardless adjective **regardless of** despite, notwithstanding, heedless of, indifferent to.

regardless adverb *he decided to go, regardless* anyway, anyhow, in any case, nevertheless, nonetheless.

regime noun government, rule, reign, command, administration, establishment, direction, management, leadership.

region noun 1 *the western region of the country* area, province, territory, division, section, sector, zone, tract, part, quarter. 2 *the lumbar region of the body* part, place, section, locality, site. 3 *work in the region of metaphysics* field, sphere, orbit, ambit, realm, domain, world.

register noun 1 *be in the medical register* official list, roll, roster, index, directory, catalog. 2 *historians consulting county reg-*

isters record, chronicle, journal, log; annals, archives, files. **3** *the register of her voice* range, compass, scope, scale, gamut, reach, spectrum.

register verb **1** *register a birth* record, put on record, enter, chronicle, enroll, inscribe, write down, note, list, catalog. **2** *the speedometer registered 50 miles per hour* read, record, indicate, show, display. **3** *her face registered surprise* show, express, display, exhibit, evince, betray, reveal, manifest, demonstrate, reflect. **4** *his danger did not register* make an impression, get through, sink in, penetrate.

regress verb retrogress, revert, relapse, lapse, backslide, degenerate, recidivate.

regret verb **1** *she regrets her action* repent, rue, feel contrite about, feel remorse about. **2** *she regrets their going* feel sorry about, lament, bemoan, mourn, grieve over, deplore.

regret noun **1** *she looks upon her actions with regret* remorse, contrition, repentance, compunction, ruefulness, self-reproach, penitence. **2** *she regarded their going with regret* sorrow, disappointment, lamentation, grief, mourning, pining.

regrettable adjective deplorable, reprehensible, blameworthy, unfortunate, unwelcome, distressing, ill-advised.

regular adjective **1** *his regular route to work* usual, normal, customary, habitual, routine, typical, everyday, daily, unvarying, common, average, commonplace. **2** *regular breathing* rhythmic, periodic, steady, even, uniform, constant, unchanging. **3** *trees placed at regular intervals* even, uniform, consistent, orderly, systematic, fixed. **4** *he is a regular charmer* real, thorough, absolute, utter, complete.

regulate verb **1** *regulate one's expenditure* control, direct, guide, govern, rule, manage, order, administer, handle, arrange, organize, conduct, run, supervise, oversee, superintend, monitor. **2** *regulate the mechanism* adjust, balance, set, synchronize, modulate.

regulation noun **1** *the regulation of expenditure* control, direction, guidance, government, rule, management, administration, organization, handling, supervision, monitoring. **2** *the regulation of the mechanisms* adjustment, balancing, synchronization, modulation. **3** *new government regulations* rule, ruling, order, directive, act, law, decree, statute, edict, ordinance, pronouncement, dictum, command, procedure, requirement, prescription, precept.

rehabilitate verb **1** *rehabilitate the injured athlete* restore to health, reintegrate, readapt, retrain. **2** *rehabilitate slum*

areas/houses restore, redevelop, recondition, renovate, renew, refurbish, redecorate, mend, repair, fix up, rebuild, reconstruct. **3** *rehabilitate the criminal* reform, reclaim, reeducate, redeem, transform.

rehearse verb **1** *rehearse the play* practice, prepare, try out, run through, go over. **2** *rehearse the actors* drill, train, prepare.

reign verb **1** *she reigned for thirty years* be king/queen, be monarch/sovereign, occupy the throne, wear the crown, wield the scepter. **2** *the present committee has reigned for years* govern, rule, be in command/charge/control, administer, hold sway; *inf.* be at the helm. **3** *chaos reigned* prevail, predominate, obtain, hold sway, be supreme, be rife, be rampant.

reign noun **1** *during the reign of the king* monarchy, sovereignty. **2** *under the reign of the present government* government, rule, command, control, administration, charge, influence, sway, ascendancy, dominion, power, supremacy.

rein noun *act as a rein on their expenditure* check, curb, restraint, constraint, restriction, limitation, control, bridle, brake.

rein verb *try to rein in his impatience|rein your expenditure* check, curb, restrain, constrain, restrict, control, bridle.

reinforce verb **1** *reinforce the bridge|reinforce his argument* strengthen, fortify, bolster, shore up, buttress, prop up, brace, support, back up, uphold, stress, underline, emphasize. **2** *reinforce the troops* augment, increase, add to, supplement.

reiterate verb repeat, restate, belabor, dwell on, harp on, stress.

reject verb **1** *reject an offer* refuse, turn down, decline, spurn, rebuff, repudiate, veto, deny; *inf.* pass up. **2** *reject the bill|reject his wife* cast aside, discard, jettison, renounce, abandon, forsake, scrap, exclude, eliminate.

rejection noun **1** *the rejection of their offer* refusal, turning down, declining, spurning; *inf.* brush-off. **2** *the rejection of the bill|his rejection of his family* casting out, discarding, jettisoning, renunciation. **3** *receive a rejection* refusal, no, demurral, negation, thumbs down; *inf.* brush-off.

rejoice verb **1** *people rejoicing on hearing the good news* celebrate, revel, be joyful, be delighted, be elated, be overjoyed, be jubilant, be euphoric, jump for joy, exult, glory, triumph, make merry. **2** *rejoice in her new baby* take delight/pleasure in, find joy in.

rejoicing noun jubilation, happiness, celebration, revelry, merrymaking, gladness, delight, elation, euphoria, exultation, glory, triumph.

rejoinder noun answer, response, reply, riposte, retort; *inf.* comeback.

relapse verb **1** *business improved but then relapsed* regress, retrogress, revert, backslide, degenerate, retrograde, recidivate. **2** *the patient relapsed* worsen, take a turn for the worse, sicken, deteriorate, sink.

relapse noun **1** *the business had a relapse after its improvement* regression, retrogression, reversion, recidivism. **2** *the patient suffered a relapse* turn for the worse, setback, deterioration.

relate verb **1** *relate the story of the accident* recount, tell, narrate, describe, report, impart, communicate, recite, present, detail, delineate, chronicle, set forth. **2** *it is sometimes difficult to relate cause and effect* connect, associate, link, correlate, ally, couple, join. **relate to** *this information does not relate to the matter in hand* concern, apply to, be relevant to, refer to, pertain to, bear on.

relation noun **1** *the relation of the story* recounting, telling, narration, description, reporting, reciting. **2** *the relation between cause and effect* connection, association, link, tie-in, correlation, alliance, bond, interdependence. **3** *have no relation to the problem in hand* applicability, application, relevance, reference, pertinence, bearing. **4** *he is my one Scandinavian relation* relative, kinsman, kinswoman.

relationship noun **1** *the relationship between cause and effect* connection, association, link, correlation, alliance, bond, parallel, correspondence, conjunction. **2** *enter into a new relationship* friendship, love affair, partnership, liaison.

relative adjective **1** *consider the relative merits of the candidates* comparative, respective, correlative, parallel, corresponding. **2** *the salary scale is relative to production* proportionate, in proportion/ratio, proportional. **3** *facts relative to the issue* applicable, relevant, pertaining, pertinent, germane, material, apposite, appropriate, apropos, appurtenant.

relative noun *a relative of his wife* relation, member of the family, kinsman, kinswoman, connection; kin.

relax verb **1** *relax one's grip* loosen, slacken, weaken, untighten, lessen, let up, reduce, diminish. **2** *relax the rules* moderate, make less strict, soften, ease. **3** *relax one's efforts* lessen, reduce, diminish, decrease, ease off, slacken off, let up on, abate. **4** *this will relax you* loosen up, calm, calm down, tranquilize, soothe, pacify; *inf.* unwind. **5** *he relaxes by playing the piano* loosen up, enjoy oneself, amuse oneself, entertain oneself, ease up, rest; *inf.* unwind, take it easy, let one's hair down. **6** *relax by the*

pool rest, lounge, repose, take one's ease, idle, put one's feet up.

relaxation noun **1** *the relaxation of his grip* loosening, slackening, weakening, letting-up. **2** *relaxation of rules* moderation, softening, easing. **3** *relaxation of one's efforts* lessening, reduction, easing off, abatement. **4** *the relaxation of the patients* calming, tranquilization, soothing, pacification. **5** *for relaxation he plays the piano* leisure, recreation, enjoyment, amusement, entertainment, fun, pleasure, rest.

release verb **1** *release the prisoners* set free, free, let go, turn loose, liberate, deliver, emancipate, manumit. **2** *release those who had been tied up* set free, free, untie, unloose, unbind, unchain, unfetter, unshackle, extricate. **3** *release her from her promise* let off, excuse, absolve, acquit, exonerate, exempt. **4** *release the news* make public, issue, break, announce, reveal, divulge, unveil, present, disclose, publish, broadcast, circulate, disseminate, distribute, spread.

release noun **1** *the release of the prisoners* liberation, deliverance, emancipation, manumission, freedom. **2** *the release of the bound victims* freeing, untying, unbinding, unchaining, extrication. **3** *the release from her promise* absolution, acquittal, dispensation, exemption, excusing. **4** *the release of the news* issuing, breaking, announcement, divulging, publication, broadcasting, circulation. **5** *write a press release* announcement, bulletin, publication, proclamation. **6** *the artist's latest release* recording; record, disc, compact disc; single, album; book; movie, motion picture, film; *inf.* CD; flick.

relent verb **1** *the judge relented and reduced the sentence* soften, become lenient, show mercy/pity, melt, capitulate, yield, give in, forbear, change one's mind; *inf.* do a U-turn. **2** *the wind relented* let up, ease, slacken, relax, abate, drop, fall off, die down, weaken.

relentless adjective *a relentless tyrant* ruthless, merciless, pitiless, remorseless, unforgiving, implacable, inexorable, cruel, grim, harsh, hard, cold-hearted, fierce, strict, obdurate, unyielding.

relevant adjective applicable, pertinent, apposite, material, appurtenant, germane, admissible, appropriate, apt, fitting.

reliable adjective **1** *a reliable friend* dependable, trustworthy, true, faithful, steady, steadfast, constant, unfailing, certain, sure, responsible. **2** *reliable evidence* dependable, trustworthy, well-founded, well-grounded, authentic, genuine, credible, sound.

reliance noun **1** *place no reliance on what she says* confidence, trust, faith, belief, conviction. **2** *his total reliance on his colleagues* dependence, leaning.

relic noun **1** *relics on view in the museum* artifact, antique, heirloom. **2** *a tradition that is a relic of another age* vestige, trace, survivor, remnant. **3** *regard the ring as a relic of a former relationship* souvenir, memento, keepsake, remembrance, reminder.

relief noun **1** *the relief of the pain* alleviation, mitigation, allaying, soothing, dulling, lessening, reduction, assuagement, palliation, ease, abatement. **2** *bring relief to the starving people* aid, help, assistance, succor. **3** *relief from the monotony* respite, remission, interruption, break, variation, diversion; *inf.* letup. **4** *the soldier's relief* replacement, substitute, stand-in, fill-in, alternate, understudy; *inf.* sub. **5** *details bringing the story out in sharp relief* distinctness, vividness, intensity, sharpness, focus, clarity, precision. **6** *relief from his burden* freedom, release, liberation, deliverance, exemption, extrication, discharge.

relieve verb **1** *relieve his pain* alleviate, mitigate, assuage, allay, soothe, soften, palliate, appease, ease, dull, abate, reduce, lessen, diminish. **2** *relieve the victims* aid, help, assist, rescue, save, succor. **3** *relieve the monotony* interrupt, break up, vary, lighten. **4** *relieve the soldier on guard* take over from, take the place of, stand in for, substitute for. **5** *relieve them of their burdens* free, release, liberate, deliver, exempt, extricate, discharge, unburden, disencumber.

religion noun faith, belief, creed, persuasion, doctrine, theology, church, denomination.

religious adjective **1** *religious festivals/discussions* church, holy, divine, theological, doctrinal, spiritual, sectarian. **2** *religious people* churchgoing, God-fearing, godly, pious, devout.

relinquish verb **1** *relinquish her right to the title* renounce, resign, abdicate, surrender, give up, sign away. **2** *relinquish his position* leave, quit, vacate, abandon, forsake. **3** *relinquish the habit* give up, discontinue, stop, cease, drop, abstain from, forbear from, forgo, desist from. **4** *relinquish her grip* release, let go, loosen, unloose.

relish noun *tells a story with relish* gusto, enjoyment, delight, pleasure, satisfaction, gratification, appreciation, liking, zest.

relish verb *the children relish the beach* enjoy, delight in, fancy, like, love, adore, appreciate, revel in, luxuriate in.

reluctant adjective **1** *a reluctant hero* unwilling, hesitant, unenthusiastic, grudging. **2** *reluctant to go* unwilling, disinclined, loath, averse.

rely verb *you can rely on me* depend, count, bank, trust, lean, bet.

remain verb **1** *only a handful remained* be left, stay behind, survive, last, abide, endure, prevail. **2** *remain at home* stay, wait, linger, tarry; *inf.* stay put. **3** *remain calm* stay, continue, persist in being.

remainder noun remnant, residue, residuum, balance, surplus, excess, superfluity; remains, remnants, relics, vestiges, leavings, dregs.

remark verb mention, say, state, declare, pronounce, assert, observe. **remark on/upon** *she remarked on his appearance* comment on, mention.

remark noun **1** *ignore his nasty remarks* comment, statement, utterance, pronouncement, observation, reference, opinion. **2** *a performance worthy of remark* comment, attention, mention, notice, observation, heed, acknowledgment, recognition.

remarkable adjective extraordinary, unusual, uncommon, conspicuous, singular, signal, rare, exceptional, outstanding, striking, impressive, considerable, notable, noteworthy, memorable, preeminent, significant, important, momentous, phenomenal, wonderful, distinctive, peculiar, special, curious, unique.

remedy noun **1** *given a remedy for asthma* cure, treatment, medicine, medication, medicament, therapy, antidote, restorative, nostrum, panacea. **2** *find a remedy for the situation* corrective, solution, redress, panacea.

remedy verb **1** *unable to remedy her condition* cure, heal, treat, counteract, control. **2** *remedy the situation* rectify, solve, put right, redress, fix, sort out.

remember verb **1** *I cannot remember his name* recall, call to mind, recollect, think of. **2** *remember that it is raining* keep/bear in mind, not forget. **3** *remembering the past* recall, recollect, reminisce; reminisce about, look back on, hark back to, summon up.

remembrance noun **1** *their remembrance of times past* recollection, reminiscing, memory. **2** *give her a remembrance of their meeting* keepsake, souvenir, memento, token, commemoration, memorial.

remind verb cause one to remember, jog/refresh one's memory, prompt, awake one's memories of.

remiss adjective negligent, neglectful, lax, slack, slipshod, careless, forgetful, inattentive, heedless, thoughtless, unthinking, unmindful, culpable, delinquent; *inf.* sloppy.

remit verb **1** *remit a penalty* cancel, revoke, repeal, rescind, stop, halt. **2** *remit payment* send, dispatch, forward, transmit, post, mail. **3** *remit the case to another court* refer, pass on, hand on, send on, transfer, direct. **4** *remit the offense* pardon, forgive, excuse, overlook, pass over.

remittance noun payment, fee, transmittal.

remnant noun **1** *the remnant of the army* remainder, residue, balance; remains, vestiges. **2** *a remnant of material* piece, fragment, scrap.

remorse noun regret, sorrow, contriteness, compunction, penitence, repentance, guilty conscience, guilt, shame, self-reproach, ruefulness; pangs of conscience.

remote adjective **1** *the remote past* distant, far, far-off, faraway, far-removed. **2** *in remote mountain villages* out-of-the-way, outlying, inaccessible, off the beaten track, isolated, secluded, lonely. **3** *a remote possibility* outside, unlikely, improbable, implausible, negligible, insignificant, doubtful, dubious, inconsiderable, slight, slender, slim, small, poor. **4** *she is rather remote among strangers* aloof, distant, detached, withdrawn, reserved, uncommunicative, unapproachable, standoffish, cool, haughty, uninvolved, indifferent.

remove verb **1** *remove the dishes from the table* take away, shift, convey, transfer, transport. **2** *remove him from office* get rid of, dismiss, evict, eject, expel, cast out, oust, throw out, dislodge, relegate, unseat, depose, displace; *inf.* sack, fire. **3** *remove their coats* take off, doff, pull off. **4** *remove their privileges* withdraw, do away with, abolish. **5** *remove the errors* delete, eliminate, erase, rub out, cross out, strike out, blue-pencil, efface, obliterate. **6** *remove the weeds/opposition* take out, pull out, uproot, eradicate, extirpate, destroy, exterminate, annihilate. **7** *remove a branch* cut off, amputate, lop off, chop off, excise.

remuneration noun payment, pay, salary, fee, emolument, stipend, honorarium, income, profit, reward, recompense, reimbursement; wages, earnings.

renaissance noun rebirth, reemergence, reappearance, resurgence, renewal, reawakening, revival, resurrection, rejuvenation, regeneration.

render verb **1** *render them helpless* make, cause to become, leave. **2** *pay for services rendered* give, contribute, provide, supply, furnish; do, perform. **3** *render insult for insult* exchange, trade, swap, return. **4** *render a verdict* present, send in, submit, tender; deliver, hand down. **5** *the artist rendered her in a wistful mood* paint, portray, depict, represent. **6** *the piano solo was well rendered* play, execute, perform, interpret. **7** *render the passage into Russian* translate, transcribe, construe, put, express. **8** *they rendered their land to the emperor* hand over, deliver, turn over, give up, yield, cede, surrender, relinquish. **9**

render the lands (back) to the original owners give back, return, restore.

rendezvous noun **1** *have a rendezvous with her lover* appointment, date, engagement, tryst, meeting, assignation. **2** *their rendezvous is the café* meeting place, venue, tryst.

renegade noun defector, deserter, turncoat, betrayer, traitor, dissenter, apostate, revolutionary, rebel, mutineer.

renege verb default, go back on one's word, break one's promise, back out, pull out; *inf.* cop out, welsh.

renounce verb **1** *renounce his claim* give up, relinquish, resign, abdicate, abnegate, surrender, waive, forgo. **2** *renounce his son* repudiate, disown, cast off, discard, reject, disinherit, spurn, shun. **3** *renounce strong drink* give up, abstain from, desist from, swear off, eschew. **4** *renounce one's religion* abandon, forsake, renege on, turn one's back on, abjure.

renovate verb modernize, recondition, refurbish, rehabilitate, overhaul, restore, revamp, remodel, repair, redecorate, refit; *inf.* do up, fix up.

renown noun fame, repute, acclaim, celebrity, distinction, illustriousness, eminence, preeminence, prominence, note, consequence, prestige.

renowned adjective famous, famed, well-known, acclaimed, celebrated, distinguished, illustrious, eminent, preeminent, prominent, noted, notable, prestigious.

rent noun *what is the rent for the boat?* rental, payment, fee.

rent verb *rent a boat from the owner* lease, hire, charter. **rent out** *they rent out houses/boats* let, lease, hire out.

renunciation noun **1** *the renunciation of his claim* resignation, abdication, abnegation, surrender, waiving. **2** *the renunciation of his son* repudiation, disowning, discarding, rejection, disinheriting, shunning, spurning. **3** *the renunciation of strong drink* giving up, abstention. **4** *the renunciation of their friendship* abandonment, forsaking, reneging, abjuration.

repair verb **1** *repair the machine* fix, service, adjust, regulate, overhaul. **2** *repair the torn clothes* mend, darn, sew, patch. **3** *repair the rift in their friendship* mend, fix, patch up, heal. **4** *repair the omission* rectify, correct, redress, put right, make good, compensate for.

repair noun **1** *the repair of the car* fixing, restoration, servicing, overhaul. **2** *you will not notice the repair* mend, darn, patch. **3** *the car is in good repair* condition, state, form, fettle, kilter; *inf.* shape.

reparation noun redress, atonement, restitution, satisfaction, compensation, recompense, indemnity; amends, damages.

repartee noun witty conversation, badinage, banter, raillery, wordplay.

repay verb **1** *repay him for the money owed* refund, reimburse, recompense, remunerate, settle up with, indemnify. **2** *repay him for the crime against her family* retaliate against, get even with, settle the score with. **3** *repay the wrong* avenge, revenge.

repeal verb *repeal the bill* revoke, rescind, abrogate, annul, nullify, void, invalidate, cancel, countermand, retract, withdraw, recall, abjure, overrule, override, reverse.

repeal noun *the repeal of the bill* revocation, rescission, abrogation, annulment, nullification, voiding, invalidation, cancellation, countermanding, retraction, withdrawal, recall, abjuration, overruling, overriding, reversal.

repeat verb **1** *repeat the statement* say again, restate, retell, iterate, recapitulate; *inf.* recap. **2** *she repeated his words* restate, echo, parrot, quote, duplicate, copy, reproduce. **3** *repeat the task* do again, redo, duplicate.

repeat noun **1** *a repeat of his statement* repetition, restatement, retelling, iteration, recapitulation; *inf.* recap. **2** *a repeat of his actions* repetition, echoing, duplication, copy, reproduction. **3** *watch a repeat of the sitcom's first episode* rerun, replay, rebroadcast.

repeated adjective recurrent, frequent, continual, incessant, constant, endless.

repel verb **1** *repel attackers* repulse, drive back, beat back, hold off, ward off, fend off, stave off, parry, keep at bay, foil, check, frustrate, put to flight. **2** *repel his advances* repulse, reject, decline, rebuff. **3** *the sight of blood repels her* revolt, disgust, sicken, nauseate, turn one's stomach, offend, shock.

repellent adjective repulsive, revolting, disgusting, sickening, nauseating, distasteful, repugnant, abhorrent, offensive, obnoxious, loathsome, hateful, vile, nasty, shocking, despicable, reprehensible, contemptible, odious, abominable, horrible, horrid, foul, heinous, obscene.

repent verb regret, rue; be penitent, be sorry, be contrite, feel remorse/remorseful, reproach oneself, be ashamed; *inf.* see the light.

repentance noun penitence, sorrow, regret, contrition, contriteness, remorse, conscience, self-reproach, ruefulness, shame, guilt.

repercussion noun **1** *the repercussions of his action* effect, result, consequence, backlash. **2** *he heard/felt the repercussion* echo,

reverberation, reflection, recoil, rebound.

repetition noun **1** *a repetition of the statement* restatement, retelling, iteration, recapitulation; *inf.* recap. **2** *her repetition of his words* restatement, echoing, parroting, quoting, copying. **3** *a repetition of his actions* duplication, repeat, redoing. **4** *a lot of repetition in the essay* redundancy, tautology.

repetitive adjective *repetitive work* recurrent, unchanging, unvaried, monotonous, tedious, boring, mechanical, automatic.

replace verb **1** *replace the book on the shelf* put back, return, restore. **2** *he will replace the retired teacher* take the place of, succeed, supersede, follow after, supplant, substitute for, stand in for, act for, fill in for, cover for, understudy; *inf.* sub for.

replacement noun *find a replacement for the retired teacher* successor, substitute, stand-in, fill-in, understudy, proxy, surrogate, *inf.* sub.

replenish verb **1** *replenish one's plate* refill, top off, fill up, recharge, reload. **2** *replenish stocks of food* stock up, fill up, make up, replace, renew.

replica noun copy, carbon copy, duplicate, facsimile, model, reproduction, imitation.

reply verb answer, respond, rejoin, retort, return, riposte, come back, counter.

reply noun answer, response, acknowledgment, rejoinder, retort, return, riposte, comeback.

report noun **1** *a report of the accident* account, statement, record, exposition, delineation. **2** *newspaper/television reports* article, piece, account, story, write-up, communication, communiqué, dispatch, bulletin. **3** *a company's financial report* statement, record, register, chronicle. **4** *the report of a gun/explosion* bang, boom, crack, crash, rumble, reverberation, noise, echo.

report verb **1** *report the latest findings* announce, pass on, communicate, relay, relate, tell, recount, document, delineate, detail, divulge, disclose, circulate. **2** *report the child for cheating* tell on, inform on, expose, accuse, charge; *inf.* squeal on, rat on. **3** *they will report at noon* present oneself, appear, arrive, check in; *inf.* show up.

reporter noun journalist, newsman, newswoman, pressman, correspondent, writer, broadcaster, announcer, presenter, news commentator; *inf.* newshound, hack.

repose noun **1** *seek repose after work* rest, relaxation, leisure, ease, inactivity, respite, sleep, slumber. **2** *a place of repose in the mountains* quiet, quietude, calm, calmness, tranquillity, peace, peacefulness, stillness, silence, hush.

reprehensible adjective blameworthy, reproachable, censurable, condemnable, reprovable, culpable, errant, wrong, bad, shameful, disgraceful, discreditable, dishonorable, ignoble, objectionable, odious, opprobrious, unpardonable, indefensible, unjustifiable, inexcusable.

represent verb 1 *X represents the larger number* stand for, correspond to, equal, be equivalent to, symbolize. 2 *the Statue of Liberty represents the spirit of democracy* stand for, symbolize, personify, epitomize. 3 *he represents their idea of a Frenchman* embody, incorporate, typify, exemplify. 4 *Cupid is usually represented as a winged boy* depict, portray, delineate, illustrate, picture, denote, paint, draw, sketch, exhibit, show, display. 5 *he represented the children at the hearing* act for, appear for, speak for.

representative adjective 1 *a representative specimen* typical, archetypal, exemplary, characteristic, indicative, illustrative. 2 *the bald eagle is representative of the United States* emblematic, symbolic, evocative. 3 *a representative government* elected, elective, democratic, representational, delegated.

representative noun 1 *a typical representative of its class* example, exemplar, specimen, type, archetype, illustration, epitome, embodiment. 2 *he is the society's representative* spokesman, spokeswoman, spokesperson, agent, deputy, proxy. 3 *he is a sales representative* salesman, agent; *inf.* rep. 4 *our country's representative at the conference* delegate, commissioner, ambassador, envoy. 5 *the state's representative in Congress* congressman, congresswoman, member of Congress, senator.

repress verb 1 *tyrants repressing the people* subjugate, oppress, tyrannize, crush, master, dominate, domineer, bully, intimidate. 2 *repress a rebellion* put down, quell, quash, squash, subdue, suppress, extinguish, stamp out. 3 *repress a laugh* bite back, restrain, suppress, check, inhibit, bottle up, silence, muffle, stifle, smother.

repressive adjective *a repressive regime* tyrannical, despotic, dictatorial, authoritarian, oppressive, coercive, suppressive, harsh, severe, strict, cruel.

reprieve noun *the condemned man has had a reprieve* postponement of punishment, remission/cancellation of punishment, stay of execution, pardon.

reprimand noun *receive a reprimand from the teacher* rebuke, scolding, chiding, reproach, reproof, lecture, admonition, berating, upbraiding, castigation, tonguelashing; *inf.* talking-to, dressing-down, bawling-out.

reproach noun 1 *words of reproach* criticism, faultfinding, censure, admonition, condemnation, abuse, reprimand, scolding, reproof, reproval, upbraiding. 2 *her behavior brought reproach to the family* discredit, disgrace, shame, dishonor, disrepute, ignominy, opprobrium, odium, obloquy, stigma.

reproduce verb 1 *the copier can reproduce color photographs* copy, duplicate, replicate, photocopy, print, transcribe, clone; Xerox (*trademark*). 2 *reproduce the effect* recreate, repeat, redo, remake, imitate, emulate, echo, mirror, parallel, match, mimic, ape. 3 *the animals seem unable to reproduce* breed, procreate, bear young, produce offspring, multiply, propagate, proliferate, spawn.

reproduction noun 1 *the reproduction of color photographs* copying, duplicating, photocopying, printing; Xerox (*trademark*). 2 *a reproduction of the painting* copy, duplicate, replica, facsimile, imitation, print. 3 *a reproduction of the photograph* copy, duplicate, facsimile, fax, photocopy, mimeograph, print; Xerox (*trademark*). 4 *animal reproduction* breeding, procreation, multiplying, propagation, proliferation.

reproof noun 1 *without a word of reproof* reproval, disapproval, disapprobation, reproach, admonition, castigation, criticism, censure, blame, condemnation. 2 *ignore their reproofs* rebuke, scolding, chiding, reproach, lecture, admonition, berating, upbraiding, castigation, criticism, faultfinding, censure.

reprove verb rebuke, scold, chide, reproach, lecture, admonish, berate, upbraid, castigate, take to task, criticize, censure, blame, condemn; *inf.* tell off, bawl out.

repudiate verb 1 *repudiate one's son/faith* disown, cast off, cut off, abandon, forsake, desert, discard, reject, renounce, disavow, abjure. 2 *repudiate a charge/claim* deny, contradict, gainsay, disclaim, disavow. 3 *repudiate a treaty* reject, rescind, revoke, cancel, disregard, flout, spurn, dishonor, disobey.

repugnant adjective abhorrent, revolting, repulsive, repellent, disgusting, sickening, nauseating, disagreeable, distasteful, offensive, objectionable, obnoxious, loathsome, hateful, despicable, reprehensible, contemptible, abominable, horrible, horrid, foul, nasty, vile, ugly, odious, heinous.

repulsive adjective abhorrent, revolting, disgusting. *See* REPUGNANT.

reputable adjective respectable, respected, well-thought-of, esteemed, estimable, worthy, creditable, reliable, dependable, trustworthy, honest, honorable, aboveboard, legitimate, upright.

reputation noun 1 *have a dishonest reputa-*

tion name, estimation, character, repute, standing, position, status. **2** *she has lost her reputation* good name, good character, standing, respect, respectability, repute, status, stature, esteem.

repute noun **1** *a house of ill repute* character, estimation. *See* REPUTATION 1. **2** *they are companies of repute* good reputation, good name, high standing, stature, esteem, fame, renown, celebrity, distinction.

repute verb *he is reputed to be a good player* think, believe, consider, hold, suppose, reckon, judge, assume, presume.

request noun **1** *come at his request* asking, entreaty, solicitation, petitioning, application, imploration, pleading, behest, supplication, demand, summons, requisition. **2** *make several requests* entreaty, appeal, petition, plea, behest, demand, call, suit.

request verb *request a favor* ask for, solicit, seek, apply for, put in for, entreat, beseech, petition, implore, requisition.

require verb **1** *we require peace and quiet* need, lack, want, wish, desire, crave, miss. **2** *absolute obedience is required* demand, order, command, call for, insist on, ask for, request. **3** *they required him to go* order, instruct, command, oblige, enjoin, bid, compel. **4** *the job requires patience* call for, demand, necessitate, involve, take.

required adjective *required reading* compulsory, obligatory, mandatory, prescribed, recommended, set, essential, necessary, vital.

requirement noun **1** *list your travel requirements* need, want, lack, must, necessity, essential, demand. **2** *what are the requirements for the job?* prerequisite, requisite, precondition, specification, qualification, sine qua non, stipulation.

requisite adjective *the requisite amount* required, prerequisite, needed, necessary, essential, indispensable, vital, obligatory, mandatory.

requisition noun *put in a requisition for supplies* application, order, claim, request, call, demand, summons.

rescind verb repeal, revoke, reverse, abrogate, retract, countermand, overturn, annul, nullify, void, invalidate, cancel.

rescue verb save, deliver from danger, come to the aid of, free, release, liberate, emancipate, extricate, redeem, salvage, relieve.

rescue noun saving, deliverance, release, liberation, emancipation, extrication, redemption, salvage, relief.

research noun *carry out medical research* investigation, experimentation, fact-finding, testing, exploration, analysis, examination,

scrutiny; experiment, assessment, study, review, inquiry, probe, inspection; tests.

research verb *research the new drug* investigate, inquire into, look into, probe, explore, analyze, study, examine, scrutinize, review, inspect, experiment with, do tests on, assess.

resemblance noun likeness, similarity, similitude, sameness, uniformity, correspondence, parallelism, parity, analogy, affinity, closeness, nearness, agreement, congruity, concurrence, conformity.

resemble verb look like, bear a resemblance to, be similar to, remind one of, take after, echo, mirror, duplicate, parallel; *inf.* favor.

resent verb take offense/umbrage at, take exception to, take amiss, begrudge, dislike.

resentment noun offense, indignation, irritation, displeasure, annoyance, anger, ire, pique, grudgingness, bitterness, animosity, hostility; hard feelings.

reservation noun **1** *make a reservation* advance booking, booking, engagement, accommodation. **2** *have reservations concerning the plan* qualification, proviso, provision, condition, stipulation, limitation, qualm, scruple; hesitancy, doubt. **3** *an American Indian reservation* reserve, preserve, enclave, sanctuary, tract, area, territory.

reserve verb **1** *reserve some food for later* put/set aside, put away, keep, withhold, conserve, save, retain, store, hoard, stockpile; *inf.* hang on to. **2** *reserve a room* book, engage, arrange for, charter, hire. **3** *reserve judgment* put off, postpone, defer, delay, withhold. **4** *reserve the right to refuse* keep, retain, secure; *inf.* hang on to.

reserve noun **1** *we have reserves of steel* store, stock, supply, reservoir, pool, cache, fund, stockpile, accumulation, backlog, hoard. **2** *her reserve puts people off* restraint, aloofness, detachment, distance, remoteness, formality, coolness, reticence, unapproachability, unresponsiveness, shyness, diffidence, secretiveness, silence.

reserved adjective **1** *the table/room is reserved* booked, engaged, taken, spoken for, chartered, hired. **2** *she is reserved, but he is outgoing* aloof, detached, remote, formal, unemotional, undemonstrative, cool, reticent, unapproachable, uncommunicative, unsociable, unfriendly, unresponsive, unforthcoming, shy, retiring, diffident, secretive, taciturn, silent.

reside verb **1** *he resides in Utah* live, dwell, stay, sojourn, inhabit, occupy, be settled. **2** *the strength residing in his personality* be inherent, be intrinsic, rest, dwell, abide, exist.

residence noun **1** *his residence is in London*

house, home, place, dwelling, domicile, habitation; quarters. **2** *take up residence tomorrow* occupation, occupancy, habitation, inhabitation, tenancy.

resident noun *all residents pay taxes* inhabitant, occupant, householder, dweller, sojourner, tenant, local, denizen.

residue noun remainder, remnant, rest, surplus, extra, excess, balance; remains, leftovers, dregs, lees, residuum.

resign verb **1** *he resigned yesterday* give notice, leave, quit. **2** *resign his position* relinquish, give up, renounce, abdicate, surrender, cede. **3** *resign oneself to losing* reconcile, submit, yield, accede, bow.

resigned adjective **1** *resigned to the fact that he would fail* reconciled, acquiescent. **2** *take a resigned attitude* compliant, unresisting, passive, submissive, subdued, docile, patient, tolerant, stoical.

resilient adjective **1** *a resilient material* elastic, springy, rubbery, flexible, pliant, supple, pliable, plastic. **2** *she was usually resilient after disappointments* quick to recover, irrepressible, tough, strong, hardy.

resist verb **1** *resist the march of progress* check, stem, curb, obstruct, hinder, impede, block, thwart, frustrate, inhibit, restrain. **2** *resist fatty foods* abstain from, forgo, avoid. **3** *resist the invading army* stand up to, withstand, repel, defy, oppose, confront.

resistance noun *the invaders met with resistance* opposition, obstruction, hindrance, impediment, defiance, confrontation, struggle, contention.

resolute adjective determined, resolved, decided, firm, fixed, set, intent, steadfast, earnest, staunch, bold, courageous, serious, purposeful, deliberate, inflexible, unyielding, unwavering, unfaltering, unhesitating, unswerving, unflinching, obstinate, obdurate, strong-willed, dogged, persevering, persistent, tenacious, relentless, unshakable, dedicated.

resolution noun **1** *admire the resolution of the competitors* resolve, determination, firmness, intentness, steadfastness, staunchness, boldness, courage, seriousness, purpose, purposefulness, obstinacy, obduracy, willpower, doggedness, perseverance, persistence, tenacity, dedication. **2** *it is our resolution to proceed* resolve, decision, aim, intent, intention, purpose, object, plan, design, aspiration. **3** *the committee/court passed a resolution* motion, declaration, decree, verdict, judgment. **4** *the resolution of the problem will take time* solving, solution, sorting out, working out, unraveling, disentanglement.

resolve verb **1** *he resolved to leave* decide,

make up one's mind, determine, undertake. **2** *resolve the problem* solve, sort out, work out, clear up, unravel, disentangle. **3** *resolve their doubts* dispel, remove, banish, clear up.

resolve noun **1** *their resolve is to win* aim, intent, purpose. *See* RESOLUTION 2. **2** *set out with resolve* determination, purposefulness. *See* RESOLUTION 1.

resort verb **resort to** *resort to force* fall back on, turn to, have recourse to, look to, use, utilize, exercise.

resort noun **1** *a health resort* vacation spot, retreat; spa. **2** *your only resort is to ask the police* recourse, expedient, measure, alternative, choice, chance, possibility, hope.

resound verb **1** *caves resounding with the noise of waves* reverberate, resonate, echo, ring. **2** *her fame resounded throughout Europe* spread, circulate, be proclaimed, be celebrated.

resource noun **1** *use any resource to find help* expedient, resort, course, way, device; means. **2** *draw on one's coal resources* reserve, reservoir, store, stock, supply, pool, fund, stockpile, accumulation, hoard. **3** *person of resource* resourcefulness, initiative, ingenuity, inventiveness, talent, ability, capability. **4** *rely on their country's resources* assets, reserves, materials; wealth.

resourceful adjective ingenious, inventive, creative, imaginative, bright, sharp, talented, gifted, able, capable.

respect noun **1** *their respect for their teacher* esteem, regard, admiration, appreciation, veneration, reverence, deference, honor, homage. **2** *treat the old lady with respect* deference, consideration, thoughtfulness, attentiveness, politeness, courtesy, civility. **3** *without any respect for/to rhythm* heed, regard, consideration, attention, notice. **4** *correct in all respects* aspect, facet, feature, way, sense, characteristic, particular, point, detail, matter. **5** *with respect to the matter in hand* reference, relevance, regard, relation, connection, bearing.

respect verb **1** *they respect their teacher* esteem, think highly of, admire, appreciate, venerate, revere, value, honor. **2** *respect her wishes | respect the treaty* heed, observe, comply with, follow, abide by, adhere to, obey.

respectable adjective **1** *a respectable person/background* reputable, upright, honorable, trustworthy, aboveboard, worthy, decent, good, virtuous, admirable, wellbred, proper, decorous. **2** *a respectable effort/salary* reasonable, fair, passable, tolerable, adequate, decent, worthy, considerable, substantial, satisfactory; *inf.* not bad.

respite noun rest, break, breathing spell, interval, intermission, recess, lull, pause, hiatus, halt; relief, relaxation; reprieve, stay, suspension, postponement, adjournment, deferment, delay, moratorium; *inf.* breather, letup.

respond verb *"no," she responded* answer, reply, rejoin, retort, riposte, come back, counter.

response noun **1** *they gave no response to the question* answer, reply, acknowledgment, rejoinder, retort, riposte, comeback. **2** *receive a good response to their questionnaire* reaction, feedback.

responsibility noun **1** *it is his responsibility to get us there* charge, duty, onus, task, role, liability, accountability, answerability. **2** *people of responsibility* maturity, reason, common sense, soundness, stability, reliability, dependability, trustworthiness, conscientiousness. **3** *a post of responsibility* authority, control, power.

responsible adjective **1** *he is responsible for the confusion* accountable, answerable, to blame, at fault, guilty, culpable. **2** *he is responsible to the president* answerable, accountable. **3** *the children are very responsible* mature, adult, levelheaded, rational, reasonable, sensible, sound, stable, reliable, dependable, trustworthy, conscientious. **4** *a responsible position* authoritative, executive, powerful, high, important.

responsive adjective *a responsive audience* receptive, sensitive, perceptive, sympathetic, impressionable, open, alive, awake, aware, sharp.

rest[1] noun **1** *seek rest after work* repose, relaxation, leisure, ease, inactivity, respite, time off. **2** *have a rest after work* sleep, nap, doze, slumber, siesta; *inf.* breather, snooze, forty winks. **3** *a place of rest in the mountains* repose, quiet, quietude, calm, calmness, tranquillity, peace, peacefulness, stillness, silence, hush.

rest[2] verb **1** *resting after work* relax, lie down, sleep, take a nap, nap, doze, slumber; *inf.* take it easy, snooze. **2** *the result rests on the decision of the jury* depend, rely, hang, hinge.

rest[3] noun *some will go; the rest will stay* remainder, residue, residuum, balance, remnant, surplus, excess, remains, leftovers.

rest[4] verb *you may rest assured* remain, stay, continue, be left.

restful adjective **1** *a restful effect* calming, relaxing, soothing, tranquilizing. **2** *a restful place* quiet, calm, tranquil, relaxed, peaceful, placid, still, languid, undisturbed, unhurried, sleepy.

restitution noun reparation, redress, atonement, recompense, compensation, indemnification, indemnity, requital, retribution, remuneration, reimbursement, repayment; amends.

restless adjective **1** *pass a restless night* sleepless, wakeful, fitful. **2** *the crowd grew restless* uneasy, on edge, agitated. **3** *restless children* restive, fidgety.

restore verb **1** *restore the building* renovate, repair, fix, recondition, rehabilitate, refurbish, rebuild, reconstruct, remodel, revamp, redecorate, touch up; *inf.* fix up. **2** *a rest will help to restore him* build up, resuscitate, revitalize, refresh, revive, revivify. **3** *restore the vase to the shelf* put back, return, replace, reinstate. **4** *restore democracy* reestablish, reinstitute, reinstate, reimpose.

restrain verb **1** *restrain the unruly crowd* control, hold in check, curb, subdue. **2** *restrain one's anger* control, check, suppress, repress, contain, smother, stifle, rein in. **3** *restrain the boy from jumping* prevent, hold back, hinder, impede, inhibit. **4** *restrain the thieves* tie up, bind, chain up, fetter, pinion, confine, detain.

restraint noun **1** *he acts as a restraint on their impulsiveness* constraint, check, curb, barrier, block, hindrance, impediment, deterrent, inhibition. **2** *behave with restraint* self-restraint, self-control, self-discipline, moderation, temperateness, prudence, judiciousness. **3** *her restraint puts people off* self-possession, reserve, formality, aloofness, detachment, reticence. **4** *put the thieves in/under restraint* confinement, detention, imprisonment, incarceration, bonds, chains.

restrict verb **1** *restrict movement* hinder, impede, hamper, retard, handicap, cramp. **2** *restrict your food consumption* limit, regulate, control, moderate.

restriction noun **1** *impose currency restrictions* constraint, limitation, control, check, curb, regulation, condition, provision, proviso, stipulation, qualification. **2** *the restriction of the space* confinement, constraint. **3** *restriction of movement* hindrance, impediment, handicap.

result noun *pleased with the result of the talks* outcome, consequence, upshot, effect, reaction, repercussion, conclusion, termination, aftermath, product, by-product; fruits.

result verb **1** *a fight resulted from the discussion* follow, ensue, issue, develop, stem, arise, evolve, emerge, emanate, occur, happen, come about, eventuate. **2** *it resulted in a draw* end, culminate, finish, terminate.

resume verb **1** *resume after lunch* carry on, continue, proceed, go on, recommence, restart. **2** *resume negotiations* reopen, reinstitute, take up, carry on, continue, recommence.

résumé noun **1** *present a résumé of the events* summary, précis, synopsis, abstract, outline, sketch, abridgment, digest. **2** *send your résumé with your application* work history, curriculum vitae; *inf.* CV.

resuscitate verb **1** *resuscitate him after his collapse* administer CPR to, bring around, revive. **2** *resuscitate old practices* revive, resurrect, breathe new life into, restore, reintroduce.

retain verb **1** *retain his job* keep, hold on/fast to; *inf.* hang on to. **2** *retain the old system* keep, maintain, continue, preserve. **3** *retain the facts* memorize, remember, recall, recollect. **4** *retain a gardener* hire, employ, engage, commission, pay.

retaliate verb return like for like, make reprisal(s), take/exact revenge, avenge oneself, counter, reciprocate, even the score.

retard verb slow down, hold up, delay, hinder, hamper, obstruct, impede, check, arrest, thwart, frustrate.

reticent adjective reserved, restrained, taciturn, diffident, uncommunicative, secretive, tight-lipped, closemouthed, quiet, silent; *inf.* mum.

retire verb **1** *he retires at 65* give up work, stop working. **2** *the jury retired* withdraw, go out, depart, exit, leave, absent oneself. **3** *they retire at midnight* go to bed, go to one's room; *inf.* turn in, call it a day.

retiring adjective *a retiring young woman* shy, diffident, bashful, self-effacing, shrinking, unassuming, unassertive, reserved, reticent, timid, timorous, modest, demure.

retract verb *retract one's statement* take back, withdraw, revoke, repeal, rescind, annul, cancel, abrogate, disavow, abjure, renounce, recant, disclaim.

retreat verb *the army retreated* withdraw, pull back, fall back, give ground, decamp, depart, leave, flee, take flight, turn tail.

retreat noun **1** *the retreat of the army* withdrawal, departure, flight, evacuation. **2** *he has a retreat in the mountains* refuge, haven, shelter, den, sanctuary, sanctum sanctorum, hideaway, resort.

retribution noun punishment, justice, reckoning, reprisal, requital, retaliation, revenge, vengeance, redress, reparation, recompense, restitution; just deserts.

retrieve verb **1** *retrieve one's property* get back, recover, regain, recoup, redeem, reclaim, repossess, recapture, salvage, rescue. **2** *dogs retrieving sticks* fetch, bring back.

retrospect noun **in retrospect** on reflection, on reconsideration, with hindsight.

return verb **1** *they returned at dawn | the symptoms returned* go back, come back, reappear, reoccur, come again. **2** *return soda bottles | return his love letters* give back, send back, take back, remit. **3** *return the books to the shelves* put back, replace, restore, reinstate, reinstall. **4** *return her greetings* reciprocate, repay, requite. **5** *the firm returned a profit* yield, bring in, earn, make, net. **6** *return a guilty verdict* bring in, deliver, announce, submit.

return noun **1** *look forward to their return* homecoming, reappearance, reoccurrence. **2** *the return of the books to the shelf* replacement, restoration, reinstatement, reinstallment. **3** *the return on the investment* profit, yield, gain, income, revenue, interest, benefit. **4** *fill in a tax return* statement, report, account, summary, form. **5** *done in return for your help* reciprocation, repayment, response, exchange.

reveal verb **1** *the coat blew back to reveal a red dress* show, display, exhibit, expose. **2** *examination revealed a deep cut* bring to light, uncover, expose, lay bare, unearth, unveil, unmask. **3** *reveal the details of the affair* disclose, divulge, tell, let slip, give away, leak, betray, broadcast, publicize, publish.

revel verb *partygoers reveling all night* celebrate, make merry, party, carouse; *inf.* whoop it up, rave, paint the town red. **revel in** *revel in her victory* delight in, take pleasure in, bask in, rejoice in, relish, savor, luxuriate in, wallow in.

revelation noun *the revelation of the details* disclosure, divulgence, leak, betrayal, publication, communication.

revelry noun celebration, festivities; merrymaking, mirth, carousal.

revenge noun **1** *seek revenge* vengeance, retaliation, retribution, reprisal, requital, redress, satisfaction. **2** *a heart full of revenge* vengefulness, vindictiveness, spite, spitefulness, malice, ill will, animosity, hostility.

revenge verb *revenge an injustice | revenge oneself* avenge, retaliate, exact retribution for, requite.

revenue noun income, return, yield, interest, gain; profits, receipts, proceeds.

reverberate verb resound, echo, ring, vibrate.

revere verb admire, respect, esteem, defer to, honor, venerate, worship, adore, hold in awe, exalt, put on a pedestal, idolize.

reverence noun *regard the leader with reverence* admiration, respect, deference, honor, veneration, worship, homage, adoration, devotion, awe, exaltation.

reverent adjective respectful, deferential, admiring, adoring, loving, devoted, awed, submissive.

reverse verb **1** *reverse the collar* turn inside out, transpose. **2** *reverse the barrel* turn upside down, upend, invert. **3** *reverse roles* change, exchange, trade, swap. **4** *reverse the decision* alter, change, countermand, overturn, revoke, repeal, rescind, annul, nullify, void, invalidate.

reverse adjective *in reverse order* backward, inverted, transposed, opposite, inverse.

reverse noun **1** *the reverse is the case* opposite, contrary, converse, antithesis. **2** *write on the reverse* other side, back, flip side, verso. **3** *the firm has suffered reverses* reversal, upset, setback, failure, misfortune, mishap, misadventure, blow, disappointment; adversity, hardship, affliction, vicissitude, defeat.

review noun **1** *a review of the whole situation* survey, study, analysis, examination, scrutiny, assessment, appraisal. **2** *the salary structure is under review* reconsideration, reexamination, reassessment, reevaluation, reappraisal, revision. **3** *the general conducting a military review* inspection, parade, display, procession. **4** *his review of the play* criticism, critique, assessment, evaluation, judgment, rating.

review verb **1** *review the situation* survey, study, analyze, examine, scrutinize, assess, appraise. **2** *it is more than time to review salaries* reconsider, reexamine, reevaluate, reassess, reappraise, revise. **3** *review the troops* inspect, view, scrutinize. **4** *review the play* criticize, critique, evaluate, assess, appraise, judge.

revile verb criticize, rail, abuse, berate, vilify, vituperate.

revise verb **1** *revise the text* emend, amend, correct, alter, change, edit, rewrite, redraft, rework, update, revamp. **2** *revise our opinions* reconsider, review, reassess, alter, change.

revive verb **1** *revive the man who collapsed* bring around, resuscitate, administer CPR to, save. **2** *a cup of tea revived her* refresh, restore, enliven, revitalize. **3** *revive old traditions* breathe new life into, bring back, restore, resuscitate, resurrect, revitalize, reintroduce, reestablish.

revoke verb repeal, rescind, abrogate, countermand, annul, nullify, void, invalidate, cancel, retract, withdraw, recall, abjure, overrule, override, reverse.

revolt verb **1** *the citizens revolted against the army* rise up, take to the streets, take up arms, rebel, mutiny. **2** *the filthy sight revolted me* repel, disgust, sicken, nauseate, be repugnant to, put one off, offend, shock; *inf.* turn one off.

revolting adjective repulsive, repellent, disgusting, sickening, nauseating, distasteful, repugnant, abhorrent, offensive, obnoxious, loathsome, hateful, foul, vile, nasty, shocking, abominable, despicable, reprehensible, contemptible, odious, heinous, obscene.

revolution noun **1** *the French Revolution* rebellion, revolt, insurrection, uprising, insurgence, mutiny, riot, coup, coup d'état. **2** *a revolution in the fashion industry* drastic change, metamorphosis, upheaval, upset, transformation, innovation, reformation, cataclysm. **3** *a revolution of the wheel* rotation, whirl, spin.

revolutionary adjective **1** *revolutionary troops* rebellious, insurgent, insurrectionist, mutinous, seditious, factious, insubordinate, subversive, extremist. **2** *revolutionary changes in education* drastic, progressive, radical, innovative, avant-garde, experimental.

revolve verb **1** *the wheel revolved slowly* turn, rotate, spin, whirl. **2** *revolve around the sun* circle, orbit, gyrate, whirl.

revulsion noun repulsion, disgust, nausea, distaste, aversion, repugnance, abhorrence, loathing, hatred, detestation, contempt.

reward noun **1** *a reward for finding the wallet* recompense, payment, remuneration, bonus, bounty, present, gift, tip, gratuity, prize; *inf.* cut. **2** *the criminal got his (just) reward* retribution, requital, retaliation; just deserts, deserts; *inf.* comeuppance.

reward verb *reward them for their efforts* recompense, pay, remunerate, tip.

rhetoric noun **1** *the use of rhetoric to win over the crowd* oratory, eloquence, elocution. **2** *the literary work was spoiled by rhetoric* bombast, grandiloquence, hyperbole, pomposity, verbosity, wordiness, prolixity, turgidity, purple prose, fustian.

rhyme noun *a nursery rhyme* verse, ditty, poem, song, ode.

rhythm noun beat, cadence, meter, tempo, pulse, throb, lilt, flow.

ribald adjective bawdy, risqué, blue, smutty, vulgar, coarse, earthy, off-color, rude, naughty, racy, suggestive, indecent, indelicate, lewd, salacious, licentious, concupiscent.

rich adjective **1** *rich and powerful people* wealthy, affluent, well off, well-to-do, prosperous, moneyed, propertied; *inf.* wellheeled, loaded, flush, on easy street. **2** *rich furnishings* opulent, expensive, costly, precious, valuable, priceless, luxurious, lush, sumptuous, splendid, superb, resplendent, elegant, fine, exquisite, magnificent, grand, gorgeous. **3** *rich in talent* abounding, overflowing, replete, rife. **4**

rich supplies of minerals copious, abundant, ample, plentiful, plenteous, bountiful. **5** *a rich soil* fertile, productive, fecund, fruitful, lush. **6** *rich food* creamy, fatty, heavy, spicy. **7** *rich colors* strong, deep, intense, vivid, brilliant, warm, vibrant. **8** *rich voices* full, sonorous, resonant, deep, mellow, mellifluous, melodious.

rid verb *rid the park of litter* clear, cleanse, purge, purify, free, relieve, deliver. **get rid of** dispose of, do away with, throw away, remove, dispense with, eliminate, dump, unload, jettison, expel, eject, weed out.

riddle noun puzzle, poser, conundrum, brainteaser, problem, enigma, mystery.

ride verb **1** *ride a horse* sit on, mount, manage, control. **2** *ride in a car* travel, go, move, progress.

ridicule noun derision, mockery, laughter, scorn, jeering, gibing, teasing, taunting, banter, badinage, raillery, satire, sarcasm; *inf.* kidding, ribbing, ragging.

ridicule verb deride, mock, laugh at, scoff at, scorn, jeer at, gibe at, tease, taunt; *inf.* kid, rag.

ridiculous adjective **1** *telling ridiculous jokes* absurd, comical, funny, laughable, hilarious, humorous, droll, farcical, facetious, ludicrous. **2** *what a ridiculous thing to do* foolish, inane, nonsensical.

rife adjective **1** *disease is rife* rampant, prevalent, predominant, widespread, common, extensive, ubiquitous. **2** *the territory is rife with disease/vermin* abounding, overflowing, alive, swarming, teeming.

riff-raff noun rabble, mob, commonality, hoi polloi, scum.

rifle verb *looters rifling stores during the blackout* plunder, pillage, loot, ransack. **rifle through** *rifle through her belongings* ransack, rummage through, search.

rift noun **1** *a rift in the rock* fault, split, break, breach, fissure, cleft, crevice, gap, crack, cranny, slit, chink, cavity, opening, hole, aperture. **2** *a rift between family members* breach, division, estrangement, schism, split, alienation, quarrel, disagreement, conflict, feud; *inf.* falling-out.

right adjective **1** *his actions were not right* just, fair, equitable, righteous, proper, moral, ethical, honorable, honest, principled, lawful, legal. **2** *the right answer* correct, accurate, unerring, exact, precise, valid. **3** *he is the right owner* rightful, true, genuine, authentic, lawful, legal, legitimate. **4** *the right person for the job* suitable, appropriate, fitting, fit, proper, ideal. **5** *he came at the right moment* opportune, favorable, convenient, suitable, appropriate, propitious. **6** *in his right mind* sane, sound, rational, lucid. **7** *the engine does not sound right* fine, healthy, well, fit, normal, sound; *inf.* up to scratch. **8** *the right wing of politics* conservative, reactionary.

right adverb **1** *go right on* straight, directly. **2** *he will be right down* immediately, instantly, promptly, quickly, straightaway, without delay. **3** *come right off its hinges* all the way, completely, entirely, totally, wholly, altogether, utterly, quite. **4** *right in the middle* exactly, precisely, just, squarely; *inf.* smack-dab. **5** *if I remember right* accurately, correctly, exactly, precisely. **6** *treat them right* justly, fairly, properly, honorably, honestly, morally, ethically. **7** *it will come out right* well, for the best, favorably, advantageously. **right away** at once, immediately, straight away, this instant, promptly, directly, forthwith.

right noun **1** *know the difference between right and wrong* lawfulness, legality, goodness, righteousness, virtue, virtuousness, integrity, rectitude, propriety, morality, truth, honesty, honor, justice, fairness, equity. **2** *his position gives him the right to dismiss people* prerogative, privilege, authority, power, license, permission, warrant, sanction, entitlement.

right verb **1** *right the pole* stand/set upright. **2** *right the situation* put to rights, sort out, straighten out, rectify, fix, tidy up, repair. **3** *right a wrong* set/put right, rectify, redress, vindicate.

righteous adjective **1** *righteous people* good, virtuous, upright, moral, ethical, law-abiding, honest, honorable, blameless, guiltless, pure, noble, God-fearing. **2** *righteous indignation* rightful, justifiable, well-founded, defensible, admissible, allowable, reasonable.

rigid adjective **1** *a rigid substance* stiff, hard, taut, inflexible, unbending, unyielding, unmalleable. **2** *a rigid schedule* fixed, set, firm, inflexible, unalterable, unchangeable, unvarying, invariable, hard and fast. **3** *a man of rigid principles* strict, severe, stern, stringent, rigorous, uncompromising.

rigorous adjective **1** *rigorous discipline* strict, severe, stern, stringent, austere, spartan, tough, hard, harsh, rigid, inflexible, intransigent, uncompromising, demanding, exacting. **2** *rigorous attention to detail* meticulous, punctilious, painstaking, thorough, laborious, scrupulous, conscientious.

rim noun **1** *the rim of a cup* brim, lip. **2** *the rim of a lake* edge, border, brink, circumference.

ring[1] noun **1** *wore a ring on her finger* band, circlet. **2** *a ring around the moon* circle, circlet, loop, halo. **3** *a boxing ring* arena, enclosure. **4** *a spy ring* gang, syndicate, cartel, mob, organization, confederacy, league, cabal, junta.

ring[2] verb *a fence ringed the area* circle, encircle, circumscribe, encompass, enclose, surround, hem in, fence in, seal off.

ring[3] noun *the ring of the bells* ringing, toll, tolling, peal, pealing, knell, chime, clang, tinkle.

ring[4] verb **1** *ring the bells* toll, sound. **2** *the halls rang with music* resound, reverberate, resonate, echo. **ring in** *bells ringing in the new year* herald, signal, announce, usher in.

riot noun *there was a riot when he was arrested* rebellion, revolt, uprising, insurrection, insurgence, commotion, disturbance, uproar, tumult, melee, row, scuffle, fracas, fray, brawl, free-for-all.

riot verb *crowds rioting in the streets* rebel, revolt, take to the streets, rampage, run wild/amok, fight, brawl.

ripe adjective **1** *ripe fruit/cheese* mature, full-grown, ready, mellow, seasoned, tempered. **2** *the time is ripe* suitable, convenient, opportune, favorable, advantageous, auspicious.

ripen verb **1** *fruit ripening on the trees* mature, come to maturity, mellow. **2** *our plans are ripening* develop, come to fruition.

rise verb **1** *mountains rising above the town* tower, soar, loom. **2** *prices rose* increase, soar, rocket, escalate. **3** *standards have risen* improve, advance. **4** *her voice rose* grow, increase, swell, intensify. **5** *the children rose on the arrival of the guest* stand up, get up, jump up. **6** *he rose at dawn* arise, get up, wake up. **7** *rise from the ranks* climb, ascend, advance, be promoted. **8** *citizens rising against the troops* rebel, revolt, mutiny, take up arms. **9** *the river rises in the mountains | the argument rose from a misunderstanding* originate, begin, start, commence, issue, spring, flow, emanate. **10** *the ground rises here* slope/slant upward, ascend, climb.

rise noun **1** *the rise in prices* increase, escalation, upsurge, upswing. **2** *a rise in standards* improvement, advance, upturn. **3** *his rise to power* climb, ascent, advancement, promotion, aggrandizement. **4** *a rise in the ground* incline, elevation, upward slope, acclivity, hillock, hill.

risk noun *an element of risk in the game* chance, hazard, uncertainty, speculation, venture.

risk verb **1** *risk his life* endanger, imperil, jeopardize. **2** *risk $5 on the bet* gamble, hazard, chance, venture.

risky adjective dangerous, hazardous, perilous, unsafe, precarious, tricky, uncertain; *inf.* chancy, dicey.

risqué adjective off-color, indelicate, improper, suggestive, naughty, bawdy, spicy, racy, salacious, licentious, lewd, ribald.

rite noun ritual, ceremony, observance, service, sacrament, celebration, performance, act, practice, tradition, convention, formality, procedure, usage.

rival noun **1** *they are rivals for her love* opponent, adversary, antagonist, contestant, competitor, challenger, vier, contender. **2** *in tennis she has no rival* equal, match, equivalent, fellow, peer.

rival verb compete with, vie with, match, equal, emulate, measure up to, compare with.

rival adjective *rival teams* opposed, opposing, competing, contending, in conflict.

road noun street, avenue, roadway, boulevard, thoroughfare; highway, turnpike, expressway, parkway, freeway.

roam verb wander, rove, ramble, meander, drift, range, tramp, traverse, trek, peregrinate.

roar verb **1** *the sergeant roared at the recruits* bellow, yell, bawl, shout, howl, thunder, scream, cry, bay. **2** *roar at the comedian's jokes* howl with laughter, guffaw; *inf.* split one's sides, roll in the aisles.

rob verb **1** *rob a bank* hold up, stick up, burgle, burglarize, break into. **2** *rob a tourist* mug; *inf.* rip off. **3** *rob them of their savings* defraud, swindle, cheat, mulct; *inf.* bilk.

robber noun burglar, thief, mugger, pilferer, housebreaker, looter, raider, bandit, brigand, pirate, highwayman.

robbery noun **1** *commit robbery* burglary, theft, thievery, stealing, housebreaking, larceny, embezzlement, misappropriation, swindling, fraud. **2** *a robbery at the bank* mugging, holdup, break-in, raid.

robe noun **1** *judges' robes* vestment, habit, costume, gown. **2** *wearing a robe over pajamas* bathrobe, dressing gown, housecoat, kimono, peignoir.

robust adjective *robust young athletes* healthy, strong, vigorous, hearty, energetic, muscular, powerful, rugged, sturdy, stalwart, strapping, brawny, burly.

rock noun **1** *rocks dislodged from the cliff* boulder, stone. **2** *that department is the rock on which the company is built* foundation, cornerstone, support, prop, mainstay.

rock verb **1** *the cradle/boat was rocking* move to and fro, swing, sway, roll, lurch, pitch, reel, wobble, undulate, oscillate. **2** *the world was rocked by his death* stun, shock, stagger, astound, astonish, amaze, dumbfound, surprise, shake, take aback, bewilder.

rod noun **1** *rods of iron* bar, stick, pole, baton, staff. **2** *spare the rod and spoil the child* cane, stick, birch, switch, wand.

rogue noun scoundrel, rascal, reprobate, wretch, cad, blackguard, ne'er-do-well, wastrel, good-for-nothing, scamp, imp, rascal, devil, mischief-maker.

role noun **1** *play the role of King Lear* part, character, representation, portrayal. **2** *in his role as mayor* capacity, function, position, place, situation, job, post, task.

roll verb **1** *the wheels rolled* turn, revolve, spin, whirl, wheel. **2** *roll up a newspaper* furl, coil, fold. **3** *roll the pastry* flatten, level, smooth, press down, crush. **4** *ships rolling on the ocean* toss, rock, pitch, lurch, sway, reel. **5** *waves rolling* billow, toss, tumble.

roll noun **1** *a roll of tape* spool, reel, bobbin, cylinder. **2** *buy rolls for lunch* bun; hard roll, croissant. **3** *on the electoral roll* register, list, file, index, roster, directory, catalog. **4** *a roll of drums* boom, reverberation, thunder, rumble. **5** *the roll of the sea* undulation, billowing, swell, tossing, pitching, rocking.

romance noun **1** *she wrote about a world of adventure and romance* fantasy, glamour, mystery, legend. **2** *their romance is over* love affair, affair, liaison, attachment, intrigue, courtship, amour. **3** *write romances* love story, romantic fiction, melodrama; *inf.* tearjerker.

romantic adjective **1** *present a romantic picture of his life* unrealistic, fanciful, idealistic, Utopian, starry-eyed, optimistic. **2** *romantic words* loving, amorous, passionate, fond, tender, sentimental; *inf.* mushy. **3** *a romantic figure in black* fascinating, mysterious, glamorous, exotic, exciting.

room noun **1** *take up a lot of room* space, area, territory, expanse, volume, elbowroom. **2** *room for improvement* scope, capacity, margin, leeway, latitude, occasion. **3** *she has a room in that building* bedroom, apartment, office.

room verb *we roomed together in college* board, stay, dwell, reside, lodge.

roomy adjective spacious, commodious, capacious, voluminous, ample, extensive.

root noun **1** *the plant's roots* radicle, radix, rhizome, tuber. **2** *the root of the problem* source, origin, fountainhead, basis, foundation, seat, nucleus, kernel, nub, cause, reason, rationale, occasion, motivation.

root verb **1** *the idea rooted* take root, become established, set. **2** *her fear was deeply rooted* fix, establish, embed, implant, entrench.

rope noun *tie the logs with a rope* / *hang the clothes on a rope* cord, cable, line, strand, hawser.

roster noun list, rota, roll, register, schedule, agenda, calendar, directory, index, table.

rosy adjective **1** *rosy cheeks* pink, red, ruddy, rubicund, blushing, glowing. **2** *a rosy future* optimistic, promising, auspicious, hopeful, encouraging, bright, favorable, sunny.

rot verb **1** *the material is rotting* decompose, decay, crumble, disintegrate, corrode. **2** *the food is rotting* spoil, molder, putrefy.

rot noun **1** *material suffering from rot* decomposition, decay, disintegration, corrosion, putrefaction, mold, blight. **2** *combating the rot of urban society* degeneracy, deterioration, decline, dissoluteness. **3** *talk rot* rubbish, nonsense, bunkum, claptrap, drivel, moonshine; *inf.* bunk, tommyrot, gobbledegook, hogwash, poppycock, bull.

rotate verb **1** *the wheels are rotating* turn, revolve, spin, whirl, swivel, reel, wheel, gyrate. **2** *the directorship rotates* alternate, take turns.

rotten adjective **1** *rotten food* bad, moldy, moldering, spoiled, tainted, rancid, rank, decaying, decomposed, putrid, putrescent, fetid; *inf.* off. **2** *rotten material/teeth* decomposing, decaying, crumbling, disintegrating, corroding. **3** *he is a rotten creep* corrupt, dishonorable, dishonest, untrustworthy, immoral, unprincipled, unscrupulous, villainous. **4** *that was a rotten thing to do* nasty, foul, mean, bad, dirty, filthy, contemptible, despicable, base, scurrilous. **5** *we had a rotten time* miserable, unpleasant, disagreeable. **6** *it is a rotten idea* ill-considered, ill thought out, ill-advised, injudicious. **7** *what a rotten selection of goods* poor, inadequate, inferior, substandard, unsatisfactory, unacceptable; *inf.* lousy, crummy. **8** *feeling rotten with the flu* ill, sick, unwell, unhealthy, below par; *inf.* under the weather, poorly, lousy, yucky.

rotund adjective plump, chubby, buxom, roly-poly, tubby, well-rounded, portly, stout, corpulent, pudgy, fat, obese, heavy, fleshy.

rough adjective **1** *rough surfaces* uneven, irregular, bumpy, broken, rugged, craggy, lumpy, nodulous. **2** *dogs with a rough coat* shaggy, hairy, bushy, fuzzy, bristly, hirsute. **3** *get involved in some rough play* boisterous, rowdy, disorderly, wild, violent, savage. **4** *rough seas* turbulent, tumultuous, choppy. **5** *rough weather* inclement, stormy, squally, tempestuous. **6** *he is a rough character* coarse, crude, uncouth, vulgar, unrefined, loutish, boorish, churlish, brutish, ill-bred, ill-mannered, impolite, discourteous. **7** *receive rough treatment* harsh, severe, hard, tough, difficult, unpleasant, disagreeable, nasty, cruel. **8** *he was rough on his son* harsh, hard, stern, unrelenting, merciless, unfeeling, unfair, unjust. **9** *rough wood* crude, raw, unpolished, undressed, uncut, rough-hewn, unrefined, unprocessed. **10** *rough voices* husky, gruff, hoarse, harsh. **11** *a rough sketch* hasty, sketchy, cursory, crude, incomplete, rudimentary, basic, unpolished, unrefined. **12** *a rough estimate* approximate, inexact, imprecise, vague, hazy.

round adjective **1** *a round shape* circular, ring-shaped, annular, cycloid, discoid, spherical, spheroid, ball-shaped, globular, orblike, orbicular, balloonlike. **2** *spent, in round figures, $600* approximate, rough; *inf.* ballpark.

round noun **1** *cut it in rounds* circle, circlet, ring, hoop, band, disk, cylinder, sphere, ball, globe, orb. **2** *a round of parties* succession, sequence, series, cycle. **3** *two rounds left in the gun* bullet, cartridge, shell. **4** *the first round of the competition* stage, level, division, lap, heat, game.

round verb *round Cape Horn* go around, travel around, sail around, circumnavigate. **round up** gather together, drive together, assemble, collect, group, muster, marshal, rally.

roundabout adjective *a roundabout route* indirect, circuitous, meandering, winding, tortuous.

rouse verb **1** *rouse the sleeping children* wake, wake up, call, awaken, get up. **2** *rouse the crowds to protest* stir up, excite, incite, egg on, inflame, agitate, whip up, galvanize, stimulate. **3** *rouse feelings of guilt* stir up, kindle, evoke, call up, conjure up.

rout noun **1** *troops put to rout* retreat, flight, headlong flight. **2** *suffer a rout at the hands of the enemy* defeat, drubbing, trouncing, conquest, subjugation, beating, thrashing; *inf.* licking.

rout verb **1** *they routed the enemy troops* put to flight, dispel, scatter. **2** *they easily routed their opponents* defeat, drub, trounce, worst, conquer, subjugate, overthrow, crush, beat, thrash; *inf.* lick.

route noun course, way, itinerary, road, path.

routine noun **1** *he hates to upset his routine* pattern, procedure, practice, custom, habit, wont, program, schedule, formula, method, system, order, way. **2** *have heard the comic's routine before* act, performance, piece, line; *inf.* spiel.

routine adjective **1** *carry out routine procedures* usual, normal, everyday, common, ordinary, typical, customary, habitual, conventional, standard. **2** *he finds the work too routine* boring, tedious, tiresome, monotonous, predictable, unexciting, uninspiring.

row[1] noun **1** *a row of people* line, column, queue, procession. **2** *a row of vegetables* column, sequence, series. **3** *a row of seats* tier, rank, bank.

row[2] noun argument, dispute, disagreement, controversy, quarrel, squabble, tiff, fight, altercation, scuffle, fracas, melee; *inf.* set-to, scrap.

rowdy adjective unruly, disorderly, noisy, boisterous, loud, obstreperous, rough, unrestrained, lawless.

rowdy noun ruffian, thug, hooligan, troublemaker, brawler; *inf.* tough.

royal adjective **1** *a royal wave* kingly, queenly, princely, regal, monarchical, sovereign. **2** *royal surroundings* majestic, magnificent, impressive, glorious, splendid, imposing, grand, superb. **3** *he is a royal pain in the neck* extreme, unmitigated, absolute, relentless, outright, sheer.

rub verb **1** *rub her sore neck* massage, knead. **2** *rub the silver lamp* polish, buff up, burnish. **rub in** *rub in the ointment* apply, smear, spread, work in.

rubbish noun **1** *throw out the rubbish* garbage, trash, waste, refuse, litter, junk, debris, detritus, dross, rubble. **2** *talking rubbish* nonsense, drivel, gibberish, balderdash, bunkum, twaddle; *inf.* rot, tommyrot, bunk, gobbledegook, hogwash.

ruddy adjective *a ruddy complexion* red, pink, rosy, rosy-cheeked, rubicund, flushed, blushing, glowing.

rude adjective **1** *offended by rude people* ill-mannered, impolite, discourteous, impertinent, insolent, impudent, uncivil, disrespectful, churlish, curt, brusque, blunt. **2** *rude tools* primitive, crude, rudimentary, rough, rough-hewn, simple. **3** *rude peasants* simple, artless, uncivilized, uneducated, ignorant, illiterate, uncultured, unrefined, rough. **4** *rude jokes* vulgar, coarse, indelicate, smutty, dirty, naughty, risqué, blue, ribald, bawdy, licentious. **5** *a rude awakening* sudden, abrupt, startling, harsh, unpleasant, disagreeable, nasty.

rudimentary adjective **1** *rudimentary arithmetic* elementary, basic, fundamental, introductory. **2** *rudimentary tools* primitive, crude, rough, simple.

rue verb *live to rue her actions* regret, be sorry about, feel remorseful about.

ruffian noun thug, villain, scoundrel, hoodlum, hooligan, rogue, rascal, miscreant; *inf.* tough, rowdy.

ruffle verb **1** *ruffle feathers* disorder, rumple, dishevel, tousle, tangle, mess up; *inf.* muss. **2** *she gets ruffled in a crisis* vex, exasperate, fluster, agitate, harass, upset, disturb, discompose, unsettle, disconcert, worry, trouble, confuse; *inf.* rattle, shake up.

rugged adjective **1** *rugged terrain* rough, uneven, irregular, bumpy, rocky, jagged, craggy. **2** *rugged features* wrinkled, furrowed, lined, weather-beaten. **3** *a rugged beauty* unrefined, unpolished, coarse, crude. **4** *you have to be rugged to survive there* tough, hardy, robust, sturdy, strong, vigorous, stalwart. **5** *a rugged way of life* tough, harsh, austere, spartan, exacting, taxing, demanding, difficult, hard, arduous, rigorous, strenuous.

ruin noun **1** *cities in a state of ruin* ruination, destruction, devastation, havoc, demolition, dilapidation, desolation, decay. **2** *the ruin of the army | the ruin of his hopes* ruination, downfall, overthrow, defeat, undoing, conquest, elimination, termination, end. **3** *businesses facing ruin* ruination, failure, bankruptcy, insolvency, disaster. **4** *castle ruins* remains, relics, remnants, vestiges.

ruin verb **1** *it ruined our plans* damage, spoil, wreak havoc on, mar, wreck, botch, shatter. **2** *the recession ruined him* bankrupt, make insolvent, impoverish, pauperize. **3** *invading armies ruining cities* destroy, devastate, lay waste, raze, demolish.

ruinous adjective disastrous, devastating, calamitous, catastrophic, cataclysmic, injurious, damaging, crippling, destructive.

rule noun **1** *obey the rules of the realm* law, bylaw, regulation, statute, ordinance, tenet, canon, order, decree, commandment, directive. **2** *it is a good rule to wait for others to speak* principle, precept, standard, axiom, truth, truism, maxim, motto. **3** *as a general rule, children are not allowed* practice, procedure, routine, custom, habit, convention. **4** *the rule of the present government* reign, dominion, sovereignty, regime, government, administration, jurisdiction, authority, control, direction, leadership, command, ascendancy, supremacy, power, sway, influence.

rule verb **1** *the last administration ruled for only a few months* be in power, reign, control, be in authority, administer, command, be in charge, govern; *inf.* be at the helm. **2** *the judge ruled that he be released* order, decree, direct, pronounce, decide, determine, resolve, settle, establish. **3** *let common sense rule* prevail, obtain, hold sway, predominate. **rule out** *rule out the possibility of arson* preclude, exclude, eliminate, reject, dismiss.

ruler noun sovereign, monarch, king, queen, emperor, empress, head of state, governor, president, overlord, chief, chieftain, lord, commander, leader.

ruling noun judgment, adjudication, finding, verdict, resolution, decree, pronouncement.

ruminate verb *sit and ruminate* think, contemplate, deliberate, ponder, brood, meditate, muse, cogitate. **ruminate on** *ruminating on her problems* give thought to, consider, mull over.

rumor noun **1** *rumor has it that he has gone* gossip, hearsay, talk; *inf.* the grapevine. **2** *hear a rumor that he has gone* report, story, whisper, canard; *inf.* buzz.

rumor verb *they are rumored to be wealthy* say, report, think, gossip, hint, suggest.

rumple verb **1** *rumple clothes* crumple, crease, wrinkle, crush, crinkle. **2** *rumple hair* disarrange, tousle, dishevel, ruffle, mess up.

rumpus noun disturbance, row, uproar, commotion, brouhaha, fracas, brawl, melee.

run verb **1** *she ran to catch the bus* race, rush, hasten, hurry, dash, sprint, bolt, dart, gallop, speed, scurry, scamper, scramble; *inf.* hotfoot it. **2** *the thief ran from the police* abscond, flee, take flight, make off, bolt, make a run for it, clear out, escape; *inf.* beat it, skedaddle, split, cut and run, hightail it. **3** *trains run on tracks* move, go, travel. **4** *leave the engine running* go, operate, function. **5** *the lease runs for 20 years* continue, operate, be valid, be current. **6** *the play runs until Christmas* be staged, be presented, be performed, be put on. **7** *the road runs along the coast* go, continue, proceed, extend, stretch. **8** *the horse will run* compete, take part, enter, race. **9** *run for president* stand, stand as candidate, campaign, put oneself forward. **10** *water running* flow, issue, stream, pour, gush, cascade, spurt, course, jet, trickle, leak. **11** *the dye from the shirt ran all over the pants* spread, be diffused, bleed. **12** *joggers running the course* travel, traverse. **13** *run an errand* go on, do, carry out, perform, fulfill, execute. **14** *the newspaper ran a story about the accident* publish, print, feature, carry. **15** *run a business* operate, conduct, carry on, direct, manage, administer, control, head, lead, look after, organize, coordinate, supervise, superintend, oversee. **16** *run them out of town* chase, drive, propel, hunt. **17** *ideas running through my mind* go, pass, dart, flow, slide. **18** *run your eye over the page* pass, slide, flick. **19** *stockings running* unravel, tear, be snagged. **20** *her eyes are running because of the cold* stream, water, tear. **run across** *run across an old friend* run into, come across, chance upon, stumble upon; *inf.* bump into. **run away** *the thieves have run away* abscond, flee. *See* RUN verb

2. **run away with** 1 *run away with his daughter* run off with, elope with, abduct, make off with. 2 *run away with the race* win easily; *inf.* win hands down, win by a mile. **run into** 1 *another car ran into ours* bump into, knock into, collide with, crash into, hit, strike, ram. 2 *I ran into an old friend* run across, chance upon, stumble upon; *inf.* bump into. 3 *the cost runs into thousands of dollars* reach, extend to, be as high/much as. **run low** *supplies are running low* dwindle, diminish, become depleted, become exhausted. **run off** 1 *the dog ran off* run away, flee, bolt, clear out, escape; *inf.* beat it, hightail it. 2 *run off several copies* copy, duplicate; *Xerox (trademark).* **run off with** 1 *run off with her daughter* run away with, elope, abduct, make off with. 2 *run off with the company funds* abscond with, snatch, steal, purloin; *inf.* pinch, swipe, lift. **run out** *supplies have run out* | *run out of food* be finished, give out, dry up, fail, be exhausted; exhaust. **run out on** *he has run out on his family* desert, abandon, forsake, jilt; *inf.* leave high and dry, leave in the lurch. **run over** 1 *nearly ran over a rabbit with his car* run down, knock down, knock over, hit. 2 *the bathwater is running over* overflow, spill over. 3 *run over the figures for tomorrow* run through, look over, go over, go through. **run through** 1 *run through the figures for tomorrow* run over, go over, look over, look through. 2 *run through money* squander, fritter away, dissipate, waste; *inf.* blow. 3 *sadness runs through the book* pervade, permeate, suffuse. **run to** 1 *the cost runs to thousands* run into, reach, extend to, be as high/much as. 2 *the family runs to fat* tend to, be disposed/inclined to.

run noun 1 *break into a run* jog, sprint, dash, gallop, canter. 2 *the run from Providence to Boston* trip, route. 3 *a run of luck* period, spell, stretch, streak, chain, string, cycle, sequence, series, succession. 4 *a run on silver* demand, rush, clamor. 5 *different from the general run of applicants* kind, variety, type, sort, class. 6 *the chickens' run* enclosure, pen, coop. 7 *a run in her tights* rip, tear, snag.

rundown noun *give them the rundown on/of the situation* analysis, briefing, brief, review, summary, résumé, sketch, outline; *inf.* low-down.

run-down adjective 1 *run-down property* dilapidated, tumbledown, ramshackle, decaying, in ruins, seedy, shabby. 2 *feel run-down after an illness* debilitated, below par, drained, exhausted, fatigued, tired, enervated, worn-out; *inf.* under the weather.

run-of-the-mill adjective ordinary, average, common, middling, mediocre, commonplace, everyday, undistinguished, unexceptional, passable, tolerable, acceptable, fair, not bad; *inf.* so-so.

rupture noun 1 *a rupture in the defenses* break, fracture, crack, split, rent, tear, rift, fissure; breaking, cracking, splitting, bursting. 2 *ruptures exist within the party* rift, estrangement, schism, breach, division, alienation, variance, disagreement, quarrel, feud; *inf.* falling-out.

rupture verb 1 *rupture the defenses* | *rupture an organ* break, fracture, crack, split, breach, burst, rend, tear, puncture. 2 *rupture East-West relations* sever, cut off, break off, disrupt, breach.

rural adjective country, pastoral, rustic, agricultural, agrarian.

ruse noun trick, stratagem, subterfuge, artifice, device, wile, dodge, ploy, machination, maneuver, tactic, deception, hoax, blind.

rush verb 1 *rush to the door* hurry, hasten, run, race, dash, sprint, speed, scurry, scamper; *inf.* step on it, get a move on, hotfoot it. 2 *rush the enemy* attack, assault, charge, storm. 3 *rush the job through* hurry, hasten, expedite, speed up, accelerate, advance, hustle, press, push.

rush noun 1 *make a rush on the enemy* onslaught, attack, surge, charge. 2 *a rush of water* surge, flow, gush, stream, flood. 3 *no rush for the goods* hurry, haste, speed, swiftness, rapidity, dispatch. 4 *a rush for toys* demand, clamor, run (on). 5 *the Christmas rush* activity, bustle, hubbub, flurry.

rustic adjective 1 *rustic scenes* country, rural, pastoral, agricultural, agrarian, Arcadian, bucolic. 2 *rustic pleasures* unsophisticated, plain, simple, homely, homespun. 3 *rustic peasants* artless, plain, simple, naïve, ingenuous, unsophisticated, uncultured, unrefined, unpolished, homespun; coarse, rough, indelicate.

rustic noun countryman, countrywoman, peasant, country bumpkin, yokel; *inf.* hillbilly, hayseed.

rut noun 1 *farm roads full of ruts* furrow, groove, track, crack, hollow, hole, pothole, trough, gutter, ditch. 2 *in a rut in his job* humdrum existence, routine, boring pattern; *inf.* daily grind, treadmill, dead end.

ruthless adjective merciless, pitiless, unrelenting, remorseless, unsparing, inexorable, implacable, heartless, unfeeling, hard, harsh, severe, stern, grim, cruel, vicious, brutal, barbarous, callous, savage, fierce, ferocious.

Ss

sabotage noun **1** *the fire at the factory was an act of sabotage* deliberate destruction/damage, vandalism, subversion, treachery. **2** *the sabotage of our plans* disruption, spoiling, ruination, wrecking; *inf.* fouling up.

saccharine adjective oversweet, cloying; mawkish, maudlin, sentimental; *inf.* sappy, mushy.

sack noun bag, pack, pouch; knapsack, backpack. **the sack** *delinquent workers getting the sack* a dismissal, a discharge, a termination; *inf.* one's walking papers, a pink slip, the boot, the ax.

sack verb *enemy soldiers sacking the city* plunder, ransack, raid, loot, rifle, pillage, maraud, harry, lay waste, wreak havoc on, destroy, ruin, devastate, ravage, vandalize, despoil, rape.

sacred adjective **1** *a sacred place* holy, blessed, blest, hallowed, consecrated, sanctified. **2** *sacred music* religious, spiritual, devotional, church, churchly, ecclesiastical. **3** *in Hinduism the cow is sacred* sacrosanct, inviolable, inviolate, unimpeachable, protected.

sacrifice noun **1** *the job was not worth the sacrifice of her principles* giving up, renunciation, abandonment, surrender, relinquishment, forfeiture. **2** *make many sacrifices to educate their children* renunciation, relinquishment, loss, self-sacrifice. **3** *give the goat as a sacrifice to their god* offering, gifts, oblation, burnt offering.

sacrifice verb **1** *sacrifice her principles for the job* give up, forgo, renounce, abandon, surrender, relinquish, yield, cede, forfeit. **2** *sacrifice the goat to the god* offer up, offer, immolate.

sacrilege noun *sacrilege to vandalize the cross* desecration, profanity, profanation, blasphemy, godlessness, disrespect.

sad adjective **1** *feeling sad about his departure* unhappy, miserable, sorrowful, gloomy, melancholy, blue, mournful, woebegone, wretched, dejected, downcast, despondent, in low spirits, low, downhearted, depressed, doleful, glum, cheerless, dispirited, disconsolate, heartbroken, sick at heart, grief-stricken; *inf.* down, down in the dumps, down in the mouth, in the pits. **2** *the sad events of the past* unhappy, unfortunate, sorrowful, miserable, sorry, depressing, upsetting, distressing, dispiriting, heartbreaking, heart-rending, grievous, tragic, disastrous, calamitous. **3** *the country is in a sad state* sorry, wretched, deplorable, lamentable, regrettable, unfortunate, pitiful, pitiable, pathetic, shameful, disgraceful.

sadden verb deject, depress, dispirit, dampen one's spirits, upset, distress, grieve, break one's heart, make one's heart bleed.

safe adjective **1** *the children are safe in bed* secure, protected, sheltered, guarded, safe and sound, out of harm's way. **2** *the flood victims are safe* unharmed, alive and well, unhurt, uninjured, unscathed, undamaged, out of danger. **3** *the building is quite safe* secure, sound, impregnable, unassailable. **4** *he is a safe person to leave the children with* reliable, dependable, responsible, trustworthy, upright, honest, honorable. **5** *he is a safe driver | on the safe side* reliable, cautious, circumspect, prudent, unadventurous, conservative, timid, unenterprising. **6** *these crayons are safe for children* harmless, innocuous, nontoxic, nonpoisonous.

safe noun *put jewelry in the safe* safe-deposit box, cashbox, depository, locker, vault, crypt.

safeguard noun *they need to have some safeguard against fraud* protection, defense, precaution, security, surety.

safeguard verb *you must safeguard your investment* protect, look after, defend, guard, preserve, secure.

sag verb **1** *the ceiling sags* sink, subside, curve down, slump. **2** *the hem of the skirt sags* hang unevenly, droop. **3** *his spirit sagged* fall, flag, fail, wilt, falter. **4** *industrial production has sagged* fall, decline, decrease, diminish, sink, plummet, tumble.

saga noun epic, chronicle, legend, history, myth, adventure.

sage adjective **1** *give sage advice* wise, judicious, prudent, sensible, shrewd, politic. **2** *a sage old man* wise, sagacious, learned, intelligent, acute, shrewd, discerning, perspicacious; *lit.* sapient.

sage noun wise man/woman, philosopher, thinker, savant, pundit, authority, expert, guru.

sail verb **1** *learn to sail* boat, cruise, yacht, ride the waves. **2** *we sail tonight* set sail, embark, put to sea, raise sail, shove off. **3** *he is sailing the ship* steer, captain, pilot, navigate.

sailor noun seaman, seafarer, mariner, marine, (old) salt, sea dog, yachtsman, yachtswoman; *inf.* tar, gob.

saintly adjective sainted, holy, godly, pious, God-fearing, religious, devout, blessed, virtuous, righteous, good, moral, ethical, sinless, blameless, pure, angelic.

sake noun **1** *stop smoking for the baby's sake* good, well-being, welfare, behalf, benefit, advantage, interest, gain, profit, consideration, regard, concern, account, respect. **2** *for the sake of peace we agreed* cause, reason, purpose, aim, end, objective, object, goal, motive.

salary noun pay, earnings, remuneration, fee, emolument, stipend, honorarium.

sale noun *not concerned in the actual sale of the cars* selling, vending, deal, transaction. **on sale** reduced, marked down, discounted.

salient adjective *discuss the salient points* important, main, prominent, conspicuous, striking, noticeable, obvious.

sallow adjective *a sallow complexion* yellowish, jaundiced-looking, pallid, wan, pale, waxen, anemic, colorless, pasty, pasty-faced.

sally noun **1** *enemy troops making a sally into our territory* charge, sortie, foray, thrust, offensive, drive, attack, raid, assault, onset, rush, onrush. **2** *coming out with a series of quick sallies* witticism, bon mot, quip, joke, jest, barb; *inf.* wisecrack, crack.

salon noun shop, boutique, parlor.

salt noun *conversation in need of a little salt* spice, flavor, piquancy, pungency, zest, bite, liveliness, vigor; *inf.* zing, zip. **with a grain of salt** with reservations, skeptically, cynically, doubtfully, suspiciously.

salubrious adjective *living in a salubrious climate* healthy, healthful, beneficial, wholesome, salutary, refreshing, invigorating, bracing.

salute noun *raise his hat as a friendly salute* greeting, salutation, address, welcome.

salute verb **1** *salute one's neighbor in passing* greet, address, hail, acknowledge. **2** *salute the director's achievement* pay tribute to, honor, recognize, acknowledge; *inf.* take one's hat off to.

salvage verb *succeed in salvaging the ship | salvage valuable articles from the fire* rescue, save, recover, retrieve, reclaim.

salvation noun **1** *the salvation of sinners* redemption, deliverance, saving, rescue. **2** *regard his work as his salvation* lifeline, preservation, conservation.

same adjective **1** *the same person I saw yesterday* identical, selfsame, one and the same. **2** *family members having the same mannerisms* identical, alike, duplicate, twin, indistinguishable, interchangeable,

corresponding, equivalent. **3** *the same old food/story* unchanging, unvarying, invariable, unfailing, constant, consistent, uniform.

sample noun **1** *a sample of his handwriting* specimen, example, instance, illustration, model, pattern. **2** *polled a sample of the population* cross section, sampling, test.

sample verb *sample the wine* try, try out, test, examine, inspect, taste.

sanctify verb **1** *sanctify the building* consecrate, bless, hallow, set apart, dedicate. **2** *sanctify sinners* free from sin, absolve, purify, cleanse. **3** *a practice sanctified by tradition* sanction, ratify, confirm, warrant, legitimize.

sanctimonious adjective self-righteous, holier-than-thou, overpious, pietistic, unctuous, smug, hypocritical, pharisaic; *inf.* goody-goody.

sanction noun **1** *receive the sanction of the church/authorities* authorization, warrant, accreditation, license, endorsement, permission, consent, approval, seal of approval, stamp of approval, go-ahead, approbation, acceptance, thumbs-up; *inf.* the green light, OK. **2** *laws receiving sanction* ratification, validation, confirmation. **3** *sanctions imposed against certain crimes* penalty, punishment, penalization, penance, sentence. **4** *impose trade sanctions on the belligerent country* embargo, ban, boycott.

sanction verb *unwilling to sanction the sale* authorize, warrant, accredit, license, endorse, permit, allow, consent to, approve, accept, back, support; *inf.* OK.

sanctuary noun **1** *priests standing in the sanctuary* holy place, church, temple, shrine, altar, sanctum. **2** *find a sanctuary from his pursuers* refuge, haven, shelter, retreat, hide-out. **3** *seek sanctuary in the church* safety, safekeeping, protection, shelter, immunity. **4** *a bird sanctuary* preserve, reserve, reservation.

sane adjective **1** *patients not absolutely sane* of sound mind, in one's right mind, *compos mentis*, rational, lucid; *inf.* all there. **2** *a sane course of action* sensible, reasonable, sound, balanced, levelheaded, judicious, responsible, prudent, wise, politic, advisable.

sanguine adjective *a sanguine disposition* optimistic, confident, assured, hopeful, buoyant, cheerful, spirited.

sanitary adjective *sanitary conditions in the hospital* hygienic, clean, germ-free, antiseptic, aseptic, sterile.

sanity noun **1** *question the patient's sanity* saneness, soundness of mind, mental health, reason, rationality, lucidness. **2** *acknowledge the sanity of the decision* sense, common sense, reasonableness, rationality, soundness, judiciousness, prudence, wisdom, advisability.

sap verb *completely sapped by the heat* drain, enervate, exhaust, weaken, enfeeble, debilitate.

sarcasm noun derision, scorn, sneering, scoffing, irony, satire, causticness, acerbity, acrimony, mordancy, bitterness, spitefulness.

sarcastic adjective derisive, derisory, scornful, mocking, sneering, ironic, sardonic, satirical, caustic, trenchant, acerbic, mordant, bitter, spiteful.

sardonic adjective dry, wry, derisory, scornful, mocking, cynical, sneering, jeering, scoffing, contemptuous, sarcastic, caustic, trenchant, acerbic, mordant, bitter, spiteful.

Satan noun the Devil, the Evil One, Old Nick, Prince of Darkness, Lucifer, Beelzebub, Moloch, Belial.

satanic adjective diabolical, fiendish, devilish, demonic, hellish, infernal, accursed, wicked, evil, sinful, iniquitous, malevolent.

satiate verb *satiated with food/pleasure* sate, overfill, surfeit, stuff, glut, gorge, cloy.

satire noun **1** *write a satire* burlesque, parody, travesty, caricature, lampoon, skit, pasquinade; *inf.* takeoff, spoof, send-up. **2** *treat them with satire* mockery, ridicule, irony, sarcasm.

satirical adjective mocking, ridiculing, taunting, ironic, sarcastic, sardonic, caustic, biting, trenchant, mordant, acerbic, pungent, critical, cynical.

satisfaction noun **1** *derive satisfaction* fulfillment, gratification, pleasure, enjoyment, happiness, pride, comfort, contentment. **2** *the satisfaction of her demands* fulfillment, gratification, appeasement. **3** *demand satisfaction for the trouble caused* damages, compensation, recompense, amends, reparation, redress, indemnity, restitution, requital, atonement, reimbursement, remuneration, payment.

satisfactory adjective adequate, acceptable, sufficient, competent, up to standard, up to scratch, passable.

satisfy verb **1** *satisfy their appetites/thirst* satiate, sate, slake, quench. **2** *satisfy their desires* fulfill, gratify, appease, indulge. **3** *satisfy the qualification requirements* fulfill, meet, comply with, answer. **4** *satisfy a debt* pay, settle, discharge, square up. **5** *satisfy the police that he is innocent* convince, persuade, assure, reassure.

saturate verb **1** *the rain saturated our clothing* wet through, drench, soak, souse, douse. **2** *saturate the market* overfill, surfeit, glut, satiate.

saucy adjective impudent, impertinent, insolent, rude, disrespectful, audacious, presumptuous, bold, brazen, cheeky, pert, brash; *inf.* fresh.

saunter verb stroll, amble, wander, meander, traipse, walk, ramble, roam, promenade; *inf.* mosey.

savage adjective **1** *a savage blow* vicious, ferocious, fierce, brutal, cruel, bloody, murderous, inhuman, harsh, terrible, merciless, ruthless, pitiless, sadistic, barbarous. **2** *a savage animal* fierce, ferocious, wild, untamed, feral. **3** *explorers encountering savage tribes* primitive, uncivilized, uncultivated.

savage noun **1** *sailors attacked by island savages* barbarian, native, primitive, heathen. **2** *her attacker was a savage* brute, beast, monster, barbarian, ogre.

save verb **1** *save the children from danger* rescue, free, liberate, deliver, snatch, salvage, redeem. **2** *save them from their sinful desires* protect, safeguard, guard, keep, shield, screen, preserve. **3** *save a lot of trouble* prevent, obviate, forestall, spare, rule out. **4** *save some money* set aside, put by, keep, reserve, conserve, salt away, stockpile, store, hoard. **5** *time to save, not spend* economize, scrimp, budget, cut costs, cut expenditure.

savings plural noun capital, assets, resources, cache, reserves, funds, nest egg.

savior noun rescuer, liberator, deliverer, emancipator, champion, knight in shining armor.

Savior noun *worshiping the Savior* Christ, Jesus, Jesus Christ, the Redeemer, the Messiah, Our Lord.

savoir faire noun finesse, poise, aplomb, social graces, style, diplomacy, discretion, smoothness, urbanity, suaveness; *inf.* savvy.

savor verb *savor the taste of the soup | savor the joys of freedom* taste, enjoy, appreciate, delight in, take pleasure in, relish, revel in, luxuriate in.

savory adjective *savory smells from the kitchen | savory entrées* appetizing, mouthwatering, fragrant, flavorful, palatable, tasty, delicious, delectable, luscious, toothsome; *inf.* scrumptious.

say verb **1** *refuse to say his name* speak, utter, mention, voice, pronounce, give voice to, vocalize. **2** *"it is too expensive," he said* state, remark, announce, affirm, assert, maintain, declare, aver, allege, profess, avow; *lit.* opine. **3** *finding it difficult to say how one feels* express, put into words, tell, phrase, articulate, communicate, convey, reveal, divulge, disclose. **4** *say a short poem* recite, repeat, deliver, declaim, orate, read, perform. **5** *what do the instructions say?* indicate, specify, designate, tell, explain, suggest. **6** *people said to be spying* suggest, allege, claim, report, rumor.

saying noun *old sayings about the weather* proverb, maxim, aphorism, axiom, adage, saw, epigram, dictum, gnome, apothegm, platitude, cliché.

scale[1] noun *weigh it on the scale* scales, weighing machine, balance.

scale[2] noun **1** *on the Richter scale | social scale* graduated system, calibrated system, measuring system, progression, succession, sequence, series, ranking, register, ladder, hierarchy; *inf.* pecking order. **2** *a scale of a hundred miles to the inch* ratio, proportion. **3** *entertain on the grand scale* extent, scope, range, degree, reach.

scale[3] verb *scale the high wall* climb, ascend, mount, clamber up, escalade. **scale down** *scale down the extent of the alterations* reduce, cut down, cut back on, decrease, lessen, lower, trim.

scamp noun rascal, rogue, imp, devil, monkey, scalawag, mischief-maker, prankster, miscreant.

scamper verb scurry, scuttle, dart, run, rush, dash, race, sprint, hurry, hasten, scramble; *inf.* scoot.

scan verb **1** *scan the horizon/evidence* study, examine, scrutinize, survey, inspect, take stock of, search, scour, sweep. **2** *scan the pages of the document* skim, look over, glance over, run one's eye over, read through, leaf through, flip through.

scandal noun **1** *corruption scandals destroying political careers* impropriety, misconduct, transgression. **2** *caused a scandal in the village* outrage, disgrace, embarrassment. **3** *bring scandal on the family* disgrace, shame, dishonor, disrepute, discredit, odium, opprobrium, censure, obloquy. **4** *spread scandal about the politician* calumny, defamation, aspersion, gossip, rumors, dirt, muckraking, smear campaign.

scandalous adjective **1** *public figures guilty of scandalous behavior* disgraceful, shameful, dishonorable, shocking, disreputable, improper, unseemly, discreditable, opprobrious. **2** *spread scandalous rumors* slanderous, libelous, defamatory, scurrilous, malicious, gossiping.

scant adjective *pay scant attention* little, minimal, limited, insufficient, inadequate.

scanty adjective *scanty supplies of food* meager, sparse, small, paltry, slender, negligible, skimpy, thin, poor, insufficient, inadequate, deficient, limited, restricted, exiguous.

scar noun **1** *a scar left by the wound* mark, blemish, blotch, discoloration, disfigure-

ment, defacement. **2** *cruelty leaves an emotional scar* damage, trauma, injury.

scarce adjective **1** *money being scarce* in short supply, meager, scant, scanty, sparse, paltry, insufficient, deficient, inadequate, lacking, exiguous. **2** *red squirrels being scarce* rare, infrequent, sparse, uncommon, unusual.

scarcely adverb **1** *I scarcely know them* hardly, barely, only just. **2** *I can scarcely expect them to believe that* hardly, certainly not, surely not, not at all, on no account, by no means.

scarcity noun **1** *scarcity of money in the recession* dearth, shortage, paucity, meagerness, sparseness, insufficiency, deficiency, inadequacy, lack, exiguity. **2** *the scarcity of red squirrels* rarity, infrequency, uncommonness.

scare verb frighten, alarm, startle, make fearful, make nervous, terrify, terrorize, petrify, horrify, appall, shock, intimidate, daunt, cow, panic, make one's blood run cold, make one's hair stand on end; *inf.* scare the living daylights out of.

scare noun *recovering from a scare* fright, alarm, start, fearfulness, nervousness, terror, horror, shock, panic.

scarf noun muffler, kerchief, cravat, bandanna, headscarf.

scary adjective *a scary experience* frightening, alarming, startling, nerve-racking, terrifying, petrifying, hair-raising, horrifying, appalling, daunting.

scathing adjective *scathing criticism* virulent, savage, fierce, ferocious, brutal, stinging, biting, mordant, trenchant, caustic, vitriolic, withering, scornful, harsh, severe, stern.

scatter verb **1** *scatter breadcrumbs for birds* disseminate, diffuse, spread, sow, sprinkle, strew, toss. **2** *the crowd scattered* break up, disperse, disband, dissolve.

scatterbrained adjective irresponsible, forgetful, dreamy, featherbrained, harebrained, erratic, giddy.

scene noun **1** *the scene of the accident* place, location, site, position, spot, setting, locale. **2** *against a scene of confusion* background, backdrop, setting, set. **3** *look out on beautiful rural scenes* scenery, view, outlook, landscape, vista, panorama, prospect. **4** *the scene created by the bickering couple* fuss, exhibition, outburst, commotion, to-do, upset, tantrum, furor, brouhaha.

scenic adjective **1** *the scenic route* picturesque, pretty, beautiful, pleasing. **2** *the scenic advantages of the area* landscape, panoramic.

scent noun **1** *the scent of new-mown hay* aroma, perfume, fragrance, smell, bouquet, redolence, odor. **2** *dogs losing the scent of the fox* track, trail, spoor.

schedule noun **1** *projects going according to schedule* timetable, plan, scheme, program. **2** *a busy schedule* list of appointments, diary, calendar, itinerary, agenda.

schedule verb *schedule the meeting for tomorrow* time, arrange, organize, plan, program, book.

scheme noun **1** *a scheme for recycling paper* plan, program, project, system, procedure, strategy, design, device, tactics, contrivance. **2** *an attractive color scheme* arrangement, system, organization, disposition. **3** *produce the scheme for the new shopping center* outline, blueprint, design, delineation, diagram, layout, sketch, chart, map, schema. **4** *police discovering his little scheme* plot, ruse, ploy, stratagem, maneuver, machinations, subterfuge, intrigue, conspiracy; *inf.* game, racket.

scheme verb *rebels scheming to overthrow the government* plot, conspire, intrigue, maneuver, plan, lay plans.

scheming adjective calculating, conniving, wily, crafty, cunning, sly, tricky, artful, foxy, slippery, underhanded, duplicitous, devious, Machiavellian.

scholar noun man/woman of letters, academic, intellectual, pundit, savant; *inf.* bookworm, egghead.

scholarship noun **1** *works showing scholarship* learning, knowledge, education, erudition, letters. **2** *on a scholarship to the college* fellowship, endowment, award, grant.

school noun **1** *attend the local school* educational institution, academy, nursery school, primary school, secondary school, grammar school, high school, seminary. **2** *belonging to the Impressionist school of art* group, set, proponents, adherents, devotees, circle, class, sect, clique, faction, following, disciples, votaries, pupils, students. **3** *teachers belonging to the old school* school of thought, outlook, persuasion, opinion, point of view, belief, faith, creed, doctrine.

school verb **1** *schooled locally* educate, teach, instruct. **2** *school oneself in patience* train, coach, instruct, drill, discipline, direct, guide, prepare, prime, verse.

scientific adjective *requiring a scientific approach* systematic, methodical, orderly, regulated, controlled, exact, precise, mathematical.

scintillating adjective *scintillating conversation* sparkling, dazzling, vivacious, effervescent, lively, animated, ebullient, bright, brilliant, witty, exciting, stimulating, invigorating.

scion noun *a scion of a noble family* descendant, heir, offspring, issue, child.

scoff verb **scoff at** revile, deride, belittle, jeer at, mock, sneer at, gibe at, taunt, laugh at, ridicule, poke fun at, make sport of, rag, pooh-pooh, scorn; *inf.* knock.

scold verb *scolded them for being late* rebuke, reprimand, chide, reprove, reproach, remonstrate with, upbraid, berate, censure, lecture, castigate; *inf.* tell off, bawl out.

scope noun **1** *within the scope of the inquiry* extent, range, sphere, area, field, realm, compass, orbit, reach, span, sweep, confine, limit. **2** *a job with much scope* latitude, capacity, room to maneuver, elbowroom, opportunity, freedom.

scorch verb **1** *scorched by an iron* burn, singe, char, sear. **2** *grass scorched by the sun* burn, parch, wither, brown.

score noun **1** *a score of five to two* result, outcome, total. **2** *a score on the table/wall* notch, mark, scratch, scrape, groove, cut, nick, chip. **3** *a score to settle* dispute, grievance, grudge, injury, a bone of contention.

score verb **1** *score a point/goal* win, gain, achieve; *inf.* chalk up, notch up. **2** *score the woodwork* notch, mark, scratch, scrape, cut, nick, chip, gouge.

scorn noun *treat the poor with scorn* contempt, disdain, haughtiness, derision, mockery, contumely.

scorn verb **1** *scorn their attempts at playing* hold in contempt, disdain, disparage, slight, deride, mock, scoff at, sneer at. **2** *scorn his invitation* rebuff, spurn, shun, refuse, reject, turn down.

scornful adjective contemptuous, disdainful, haughty, supercilious, disparaging, scathing, derisive, mocking.

scoundrel noun villain, rogue, rascal, miscreant, reprobate, cad, good-for-nothing, ne'er-do-well, wastrel.

scour verb **1** *scour the bathtub* scrub, cleanse, abrade, polish, buff, burnish. **2** *scour the countryside* search, comb, ransack, hunt through, rummage through.

scourge noun **1** *poverty was the scourge of her life* bane, curse, affliction, plague, trial, torment, burden, cross to bear. **2** *punished with a scourge* whip, horsewhip, bullwhip, switch, lash, cat-o'-nine-tails, thong, flail, strap, birch.

scourge verb **1** *scourge the offenders* whip, horsewhip, flog, lash, strap, birch, cane, thrash, beat. **2** *scourge them with cruel words* curse, afflict, plague, torment, burden, punish.

scout noun **1** *scouts returning with no information* advance guard, vanguard, lookout, outrider, spy. **2** *a scout in the* *audience* talent scout, talent spotter, recruiter.

scout verb **scout for** *scout for information* search for, seek, hunt for. **scout out** *scout out the territory* reconnoiter, make a reconnaissance of, survey, inspect, investigate, examine, scan, study, observe; *inf.* check out, case.

scowl verb frown, glower, glare, look daggers, grimace.

scowl noun frown, glower, glare, dirty look.

scramble verb **1** *scramble over the fence* clamber, climb, crawl. **2** *scramble to get there on time* hurry, hasten, rush, race, scurry. **3** *scramble for a place in the finals* jockey, struggle, jostle, strive, contend, compete, vie. **4** *the tools were scrambled together* mix up, jumble, tangle, disorganize.

scramble noun **1** *a scramble to get there on time* hurry, rush, race. **2** *a scramble for concert tickets* jockeying, struggle, tussle, jostle, competition.

scrap[1] noun **1** *a scrap of material* fragment, piece, bit, snippet, remnant, tatter. **2** *not a scrap of truth in it* bit, grain, iota, trace, whit, particle, sliver, snatch. **3** *collect scrap* waste, junk, rubbish, scrap metal.

scrap[2] verb *scrap the van/plans* throw away, get rid of, discard, toss out, abandon, jettison; *inf.* ditch, junk, throw on the scrap heap.

scrap[3] noun fight, quarrel, argument, squabble, wrangle, tiff, row, fracas, brawl, scuffle, clash; *inf.* set-to, run-in.

scrape verb **1** *scrape the surface to smooth it* scour, rub, scrub, file, sandpaper. **2** *scraping a knife across metal* grate, rasp, grind, scratch. **3** *fall and scrape one's knee* graze, scratch, abrade, skin, cut, lacerate, bark. **4** *scrape the side of a car* scratch, gouge, damage, deface, spoil, mark.

scrape noun **1** *the scrape of a knife on metal* grating, rasping, grinding, scratching. **2** *wash the scrape on the child's knee* graze, scratch, abrasion, cut, laceration, wound. **3** *a scrape on the woodwork* scratch, mark, defacement. **4** *a financial scrape* trouble, difficulty, straits, mess, muddle, predicament, plight, tight spot; *inf.* fix.

scratch verb **1** *skin scratched by rose bushes* graze, scrape, abrade, skin, cut, lacerate, bark. **2** *scratch an itchy part* rub, scrape, tear at. **3** *scratch a knife over metal* scrape, grate, rasp, grind. **4** *scratch his name from the list* cross out, strike out, delete, erase, remove, eliminate. **5** *runners being scratched from the race* withdraw, take out, pull out, remove, eliminate.

scratch noun **1** *a scratch on the skin* graze, scrape, abrasion, cut, laceration, wound.

2 *a scratch on the paint* scrape, mark, line, defacement. **up to scratch** up to par, satisfactory, acceptable, passable, sufficient, adequate, competent; *inf.* OK, up to snuff.

scrawny adjective scraggy, thin, skinny, gaunt, bony.

scream noun *a scream of pain* shriek, howl, shout, yell, cry, screech, yelp, squeal, wail, squawk.

scream verb *scream in pain* shriek, howl, shout, cry out, call out, yell, screech, yelp, squeal, wail, squawk, bawl; *inf.* holler.

screech noun *a screech of fright* shriek, howl, squeal, squawk.

screech verb *screeching in pain* shriek, howl, shout, yell.

screen noun **1** *change clothes behind a screen* partition, (room) divider, curtain. **2** *a screen on a window* mesh, net, netting. **3** *act as a screen from the wind* shelter, shield, protection, guard, safeguard, buffer. **4** *coal put through a screen* sieve, strainer, colander, filter, winnow.

screen verb **1** *screen them from the wind* shelter, shield, protect, guard, safeguard. **2** *their activities screened by darkness* conceal, hide, cover, cloak, veil, mask, camouflage, disguise. **3** *employees screened by security* evaluate, check, test. **4** *screen people for cancer* check, test, examine, investigate, scan. **5** *screen coal* sieve, sift, strain, filter, winnow.

screw verb *screw the planks down* fasten, clamp, rivet, bolt, batten. **screw in** *screw in the bolt* tighten, turn, twist, work in. **screw up 1** *screw up one's face in the sun* wrinkle up, pucker, contort, distort. **2** *screw up a business deal* make a mess of, bungle, botch, ruin, spoil.

scrimp verb skimp, economize, be frugal, be thrifty, tighten one's belt.

script noun **1** *written in a careful script* handwriting, hand, pen, calligraphy. **2** *read over the script of the play* text, book, libretto, score, lines, words, manuscript.

Scripture noun Holy Writ, the Bible, the Holy Bible, the Gospel, the Good Book, the Word of God.

scrounge verb *scrounge money* cadge, beg, borrow; *inf.* sponge, bum.

scrub verb **1** *scrub the floor/bathtub* rub, scour, clean, cleanse, wash. **2** *scrub the plans* cancel, drop, discontinue, abandon, call off, give up, discard, abort.

scrub noun *land covered in scrub* brushwood, brush, copse, coppice, thicket.

scruffy adjective untidy, unkempt, disheveled, ungroomed, shabby, ragged, tattered, slovenly.

scruples plural noun *have no scruples about stealing* qualms, twinge of conscience, compunction, hesitation, doubt, misgivings, uneasiness, reluctance, restraint.

scrupulous adjective **1** *pay scrupulous attention to detail* meticulous, careful, painstaking, thorough, rigorous, strict, conscientious, punctilious, exact, precise, fastidious. **2** *scrupulous in his business dealings* honest, honorable, upright, moral, ethical.

scrutinize verb examine, study, inspect, survey, scan, investigate, peruse, probe, analyze, dissect.

scrutiny noun examination, study, inspection, perusal, investigation, inquiry, analysis, dissection.

scuffle noun *involved in a barroom scuffle* struggle, fight, tussle, row, quarrel, fracas, brawl, disturbance.

scuffle verb *arrested for scuffling in the street* struggle, fight, tussle, brawl; *inf.* scrap.

sculpture noun *a sculpture of Jefferson* statue, bust, figure, figurine.

sculpture verb *sculpture his head in bronze* sculpt, chisel, model, fashion, shape, cast, carve, hew.

scum noun **1** *scum forming on the surface of the pond* froth, foam; algae, filth, dirt. **2** *regard his neighbors as scum* lowest of the low, dregs of society, riff-raff, rabble.

scurrilous adjective *a scurrilous attack on her character* abusive, vituperative, insulting, offensive, disparaging, defamatory.

scurry verb hurry, hasten, rush, race, dash, run, sprint, scamper, scramble.

sea noun **1** *sail on the sea* ocean, brine; *lit.* deep, main. **2** *rough seas* waves, swell, breakers. **3** *a sea of daffodils* expanse, mass, multitude, host, profusion, abundance, plethora.

seal noun *the presidential seal* emblem, symbol, insignia, badge, crest, token, mark, monogram.

seal verb **1** *seal the parcel/jars* fasten, secure, shut, close, cork, stopper, stop up. **2** *seal off the area* close, shut, cordon, fence. **3** *seal the bargain* secure, clinch, settle, decide, complete, confirm, validate.

seam noun **1** *the seam between the lengths of material* joint, join, junction. **2** *seams of coal* layer, stratum, vein, lode. **3** *seams on her brows* furrow, line, ridge, wrinkle.

sear verb **1** *cloth seared by an iron* burn, singe, scorch, char. **2** *grass seared by the sun* burn, scorch, wither.

search verb **1** *search the house* look through, scour, ransack, comb, rummage through, rifle, sift through, turn inside out. **2** *search one's soul* examine, explore, investigate,

inspect. **3** *search the prisoner* examine, inspect, check; *inf.* frisk. **search for** *search for clues* look for, seek out, hunt for, scout out; track down, uncover.

search noun **1** *conduct a search of the house* hunt, rummage, forage, rifling, ransacking. **2** *a search for truth* exploration, pursuit, quest, probe. **in search of** *in search of happiness* seeking, hunting for, in pursuit of.

season noun *in the warm season* period, time of year, spell, term. **in season** *when strawberries are in season* available, obtainable, common, plentiful.

season verb **1** *season the sauce* flavor, add salt/pepper/herbs/spice(s) to, spice; *inf.* add zing to. **2** *letters seasoned with gossip* enliven, leaven, spice, pep up. **3** *season the wood* mature, mellow, prime, prepare.

seasoned adjective *seasoned travelers* experienced, practiced, well-versed, established, habituated, veteran, hardened, battle-scarred.

seasoning noun *add seasoning to the sauce* flavoring, salt and pepper, herbs, spices.

seat noun **1** *enough seats for the spectators* chair, bench, settee, stool. **2** *the seat of government* headquarters, location, site, base, center, hub. **3** *fall on one's seat* bottom, buttocks, posterior, rump, hindquarters; *inf.* behind, backside, butt, tail, fanny, ass.

seat verb **1** *seat them next to each other* place, position, put, situate. **2** *the hall seats 500* hold, take, accommodate.

secede verb **secede from** *secede from the organization* withdraw from, break away from, sever relations with, quit, resign from, pull out of, drop out of, repudiate, reject, renounce.

secluded adjective *a secluded place | the cabin was secluded* concealed, hidden, private, unfrequented, solitary, lonely, sequestered, out-of-the-way, remote, isolated, sheltered, off the beaten path, tucked away, cut off.

seclusion noun *celebrities now living in seclusion* privacy, solitude, retreat, retirement, sequestration, isolation, concealment, hiding, secrecy.

second adjective **1** *take a second pair of climbing boots* extra, additional, other, alternative, backup, substitute, further. **2** *move from the second team to the first* secondary, lower, subordinate, lesser, lower-grade, inferior. **3** *regarded as a second Einstein* duplicate, replicate. **second to none** *as a player he is second to none* unparalleled, without equal, unmatched, unique, in a class of one's own.

second verb **1** *seconded in his research by a student* assist, help, aid, support. **2**

second the proposal support, back, approve, endorse, promote.

second noun *I will be with you in a second* moment, minute, instant, trice, twinkling of an eye; *inf.* sec, jiffy, two shakes of a lamb's tail.

secondary adjective **1** *ignore the secondary issues* lesser, subordinate, minor, ancillary, subsidiary, nonessential, unimportant. **2** *a secondary line of action* backup, reserve, relief, auxiliary, extra, alternative, subsidiary.

second-rate adjective **1** *regarded as second-rate citizens* second-class, inferior, lesser, unimportant. **2** *second-rate goods* inferior, substandard, poor-quality, low-grade, shoddy; *inf.* tacky.

secrecy noun **1** *the secrecy of the information* confidentiality, privateness. **2** *the secrecy of their love affair* clandestineness, furtiveness, surreptitiousness, stealth, covertness. **3** *the secrecy of their meeting place* seclusion, concealment, privacy, sequestration, remoteness.

secret adjective **1** *keep the matter secret* confidential, private, unrevealed, undisclosed, under wraps, unpublished; *inf.* hush-hush. **2** *a secret drawer in the table* hidden, concealed, camouflaged, disguised. **3** *a secret love affair* clandestine, furtive, conspiratorial, undercover, surreptitious, stealthy, cloak-and-dagger, covert; *inf.* closet. **4** *a secret code/message* mysterious, cryptic, abstruse, recondite, arcane. **5** *a secret place* secluded, concealed, hidden, sheltered, private, solitary, sequestered, out-of-the-way, remote, tucked away. **6** *a secret person* reticent, uncommunicative. *See* SECRETIVE.

secret noun **1** *unable to keep a secret* confidential matter, confidence, private affair. **2** *the secrets of nature* mystery, enigma, puzzle, riddle. **3** *the secret of their success* recipe, formula, key, answer, solution. **in secret 1** *talks held in secret* behind closed doors, in camera. *See* SECRETLY 1. **2** *conduct their love affair in secret* privately, discreetly. *See* SECRETLY 2.

secrete verb **1** *secrete a watery discharge* discharge, emit, excrete, exude, ooze, leak, give off. **2** *secrete the package in a hidden drawer* hide, conceal, cover up, cache; *inf.* stash.

secretive adjective *a secretive nature* secret, reticent, uncommunicative, reserved, taciturn, silent, quiet, tight-lipped, close-mouthed; *inf.* cagey.

secretly adverb **1** *committees meeting secretly* in secret, confidentially, privately, behind closed doors, in camera, sub rosa. **2** *conducting their love affair secretly* in secret, clandestinely, furtively, conspiratorially, surreptitiously, stealthily, on the sly, covertly; *inf.* on the q.t.

sect noun group, denomination, order, faction, camp, splinter group, wing, division.

section noun **1** *divide the fruit into sections* part, segment, piece, portion, bit, slice, fraction, fragment. **2** *the various sections of the book* part, division, component, chapter. **3** *the reference section of the library* part, division, department, branch.

sector noun **1** *the manufacturing sector of the economy* part, division, area, branch, category, field. **2** *forbidden to enter the military sector* zone, quarter, district, area, region.

secular adjective *secular music/matters* lay, nonreligious, nonspiritual, nonchurch, laical, temporal, worldly, earthly.

secure adjective **1** *the children/jewels will be quite secure there* safe, free from danger, out of harm's way, invulnerable, protected, sheltered, shielded. **2** *the windows are secure* fastened, closed, shut, locked, sealed. **3** *feeling secure in his job* safe, unworried, at ease, comfortable, confident, assured. **4** *look forward to a secure future* settled, fixed, established, solid.

secure verb **1** *secure the building from attack* make safe, fortify, strengthen, protect. **2** *secure the doors and windows* fasten, close, shut, lock, bolt, chain, seal. **3** *secure the boat* tie up, moor, anchor. **4** *secure their rights* ensure, guarantee, underwrite, confirm, establish. **5** *finally secure all they needed* acquire, obtain, gain, get, procure, get possession of.

security noun **1** *the security of the children/jewels* safety, invulnerability, protection, safekeeping, shielding. **2** *children losing their feelings of security* safety, certainty, confidence, assurance. **3** *the security of the job* reliability, dependability, solidity. **4** *tight security for the president's visit* safety measures, safeguards, surveillance, defense, protection. **5** *use one's house as security for a loan* collateral, surety, guarantee, pledge.

sedate adjective *remained sedate during the excitement* calm, composed, tranquil, placid, serene, unruffled, imperturbable, unflappable.

sedative noun tranquilizer, depressant, sleeping pill, narcotic, opiate.

sedative adjective *drugs with a sedative effect* calming, tranquilizing, soothing, calmative, relaxing, soporific, narcotic.

sedentary adjective *sedentary workers/people* sitting, seated, deskbound, inactive.

sediment noun lees, dregs, grounds, deposit, residue, precipitate.

sedition noun incitement to riot/rebellion, agitation, rabble-rousing, fomentation, civil disorder, insurrection, insurgence, mutiny, subversion, treason.

seduce verb 1 *seducing the younger employees* lead astray, corrupt, deflower, ravish, violate. 2 *seduced into crime by the promise of wealth* attract, allure, lure, tempt, entice, beguile, ensnare.

seductive adjective 1 *seductive smiles* alluring, tempting, provocative, exciting, arousing, sexy. 2 *seductive salaries* attractive, appealing, inviting, alluring, tempting, enticing, beguiling.

see verb 1 *I can see the house* make out, glimpse, spot, notice, observe, view, perceive, discern, espy, distinguish, identify, recognize. 2 *see that man over there* look at, regard, note, observe, heed, mark, behold; *inf.* get a load of. 3 *saw a movie last night* watch, look at, view. 4 *see what they mean* understand, grasp, get, comprehend, follow, know, realize. 5 *go and see what he wants* find out, discover, learn, ascertain, determine, ask, inquire. 6 *we will have to see* consider, reflect, deliberate. 7 *see that the door is locked* see to it, take care, mind, make sure, make certain. 8 *see trouble ahead* foresee, predict, forecast, anticipate, envisage. 9 *see an old friend in the street* meet, encounter, run into, chance upon. 10 *see the doctor* visit, pay a visit to, consult. 11 *he is seeing someone else now* go out with, take out, court; *inf.* go steady with, date. 12 *see her to her car* escort, accompany, show, lead, take. **see through** 1 *see through his disguise* be undeceived by, not be taken in by, be wise to, fathom, penetrate; *inf.* not fall for, have someone's number. 2 *see the job through* keep at, persevere with, persist with; *inf.* stick (it) out. 3 *see a friend through misfortune* support through, help through, stand by through, stick by through. **see to** *see to the travel arrangements* deal with, arrange, organize, attend to, cope with, look after, take care of.

seed noun 1 *growing plants from seeds* ovule, germ. 2 *issue of his seed* sperm, semen, spermatozoa. 3 *the seed of her discontent* source, origin, root, cause, reason, grounds, basis, motivation. **go/run to seed** *the farm has gone to seed* deteriorate, decline, degenerate, decay; *inf.* go to pot.

seedy adjective *seedy little hotels* shabby, scruffy, shoddy, run-down, dilapidated, squalid, mean, sleazy, sordid, tatty; *inf.* crummy.

seek verb 1 *seek up-to-date information* search for, look for, hunt for, be in pursuit of. 2 *seek help from a counselor* ask for, request, solicit, entreat, beg for. 3 *seek to please* try, attempt, endeavor, strive, aim, aspire.

seem verb *seem a pleasant place* appear, appear to be, look, look like.

seeming adjective *his seeming charm* apparent, ostensible, outward, external, surface, superficial, pretended, feigned, assumed, supposed.

seemly adjective decorous, proper, decent, becoming, fitting, suitable, appropriate, meet, *comme il faut*, in good taste.

seep verb ooze, leak, exude, drip, drain.

seer noun prophet, soothsayer, augur, sibyl.

seethe verb *seething at the lateness of the bus* be furious, be livid, be incensed, rant and rave, storm, fume, foam at the mouth.

segment noun *divide the fruit into segments* section, part, piece, portion, slice, wedge.

segregate verb separate, set apart, isolate, dissociate, cut off, sequester, ostracize.

seize verb 1 *a drowning man seizing a lifeline* | *seize power/control* grab, grab hold of, take hold of, grasp, grip. 2 *police seizing a shipment of drugs* confiscate, impound, commandeer, appropriate, sequester. 3 *criminals seizing a hostage/van* snatch, abduct, kidnap, hijack. 4 *police seizing the criminals* catch, arrest, apprehend, take into custody; *inf.* collar, nab. 5 *seize the meaning of the message* grasp, understand, comprehend, discern, perceive.

seizure noun 1 *the vice squad's seizure of the drugs* confiscation, commandeering, appropriation, sequestration. 2 *the seizure of the hostage/van* snatching, abduction, kidnapping, hijacking. 3 *the seizure of the criminals* arrest, apprehension; *inf.* collaring, nabbing.

seldom adverb rarely, hardly ever, infrequently; *inf.* once in a blue moon.

select verb choose, pick, hand-pick, single out, opt for, decide on.

select adjective 1 *a select range of goods* choice, hand-picked, prime, finest, best, top-quality, supreme, superb, excellent. 2 *a select club* exclusive, elite, privileged, cliquish; *inf.* posh.

selection noun 1 *offer a wide selection of goods* choice, pick, option. 2 *publish a selection of his works* anthology, variety, assortment, miscellany, collection, range.

selective adjective *able to be selective about houses* particular, discriminating, discerning, fussy; *inf.* choosy, picky.

self-assurance noun self-confidence, assertiveness, positiveness.

self-centered adjective egocentric, egotistical, self-absorbed, self-seeking, selfish, narcissistic.

self-confidence noun self-assurance, self-possession, poise, aplomb, composure, sang-froid.

self-conscious adjective awkward, shy, diffident, bashful, timorous, nervous, timid, ill-at-ease, embarrassed, uncomfortable.

self-control noun self-restraint, restraint, self-discipline, willpower.

self-esteem noun self-respect, self-regard, self-confidence, pride.

self-important adjective pompous, vain, conceited, arrogant, egotistical, presumptuous, overbearing, overweening, haughty, swaggering.

selfish adjective self-seeking, self-centered, egocentric, egotistic, self-interested.

selfless adjective unselfish, altruistic, generous, self-sacrificing, magnanimous.

self-respect noun self-esteem, self-regard, pride, self-confidence.

self-righteous adjective sanctimonious, holier-than-thou, pietistic, pharisaic; *inf.* goody-goody.

self-satisfied adjective pleased with oneself, proud of oneself, complacent, smug.

sell verb **1** *sell their house* put up for sale, dispose of, vend, auction off, trade. **2** *selling fruit and vegetables* trade in, deal in, stock, carry, market, peddle, hawk. **3** *selling for $5* retail, go, be found. **4** *sell the idea of self-support* promote, win approval for, get support for. **5** *you have been sold!* betray, cheat, swindle, defraud, fleece, deceive, trick, double-cross, sell down the river; *inf.* con, stab someone in the back. **sell on** *try to sell him on the plan* persuade of, convince of, talk someone into. **sell out 1** *supplies of tickets sold out* be bought up, be depleted, be exhausted. **2** *he used to have principles but he sold out for money* prostitute oneself, sell one's soul.

semblance noun *only a semblance of honesty* appearance, show, air, guise, pretense, façade, front, veneer, mask, pretext.

send verb **1** *send a letter* dispatch, forward, mail, post, remit. **2** *send a message* transmit, convey, communicate, broadcast. **send for** *send for a doctor* call for, summon, request, order.

senior adjective **1** *senior officer* high-ranking, superior. **2** *the senior of the two* older, elder.

sensation noun **1** *awake with a sensation of fear* feeling, sense, awareness, consciousness, perception, impression. **2** *their affair caused a sensation* stir, excitement, agitation, commotion, furor, scandal. **3** *the new show is a sensation* great success; *inf.* hit, smash.

sensational adjective **1** *a sensational news story* spectacular, exciting, startling, dramatic, amazing, shocking, scandalous, lurid. **2** *looking sensational in the evening*

dress marvelous, superb, exceptional; *inf.* fabulous, out of this world.

sense noun **1** *a sense of touch* feeling, sensation, faculty, sensibility. **2** *detect a sense of hostility* atmosphere, impression, aura. **3** *a sense of guilt* feeling, awareness, consciousness, perception. **4** *a sense of humor* appreciation, awareness, understanding, comprehension. **5** *have the sense to keep quiet* practicality, wisdom, sagacity, discernment, perception, intelligence, understanding, logic, brains. **6** *a word with several senses* meaning, definition, signification, implication, nuance, drift, gist, purport, denotation. **7** *no sense in what she said/did* intelligibility, coherence, logic, rationality, purpose, point.

sense verb *sense their hostility* feel, be conscious of, perceive, discern, grasp, pick up, suspect, divine, intuit.

senseless adjective **1** *a senseless act/comment* nonsensical, stupid, foolish, silly, inane, idiotic, mindless, irrational, illogical, meaningless, pointless, absurd, ludicrous, fatuous. **2** *knocked senseless by the blow* unconscious, insensible, out cold, numb, insensate.

sensibility noun sensitivity, delicacy, taste, discrimination, discernment.

sensible adjective **1** *a sensible person/approach* practical, realistic, down-to-earth, wise, prudent; judicious, sagacious, discerning, perceptive, reasonable, rational, logical. **2** *a sensible rise in temperature* perceptible, discernible, appreciable, noticeable, observable, palpable.

sensitive adjective **1** *sensitive skin* delicate, fine, soft, fragile. **2** *sensitive rather than coarse people* responsive, perceptive, discerning, sympathetic, understanding, empathetic. **3** *too sensitive to withstand criticism* thin-skinned, touchy, temperamental. **4** *a sensitive issue* delicate, problematic, ticklish. **sensitive to** *sensitive to unfriendly atmospheres* responsive to, susceptible to, reactive to, sentient of.

sensual adjective **1** *sensual rather than spiritual pleasures* physical, carnal, bodily, fleshly, animal, epicurean. **2** *sensual lips* voluptuous, sexy, erotic.

sentiment noun **1** *no room for sentiment in business* emotion, tenderness, softness. **2** *a revolutionary sentiment obvious in her writings* attitude, opinion, view, point of view. **3** *romantic novels full of sentiment* emotionalism, mawkishness. *See* SENTIMENTALITY.

sentimental adjective **1** *singing sentimental love songs* overemotional, romantic, mawkish, maudlin, soppy; *inf.* mushy, schmaltzy, corny. **2** *a sentimental attachment to the town* emotional, nostalgic, affectionate.

sentimentality noun *criticizing the sentimentality of the novels* emotionalism, overemotionalism, romanticism, mawkishness; *inf.* mush, corniness.

separate adjective **1** *have separate residences* individual, distinct, autonomous, independent. **2** *the problems being quite separate* unconnected, distinct, different, disconnected, unrelated, detached, divorced, divided, discrete.

separate verb **1** *separate the joined pieces of wood* detach, sever, disconnect, uncouple, divide, disjoin, sunder. **2** *old pipes separating at the joints* come apart, break off, divide. **3** *the fence separating the two gardens* divide, come between, stand between, partition. **4** *the roads separated at the foot of the hill* part, part company, diverge, split, divide. **5** *the couple separated last year* break up, split up, become estranged, divorce. **6** *separate the misbehaving child from the rest* set apart, segregate, single out, isolate. **separate from** *a splinter group separating from the society* break away from, secede from, withdraw from, sever relations with.

separation noun **1** *the separation of the pieces* detachment, disconnection, severance, uncoupling, division, disjunction, segregation. **2** *upset by her parents' separation* breakup, split, parting, estrangement, rift, divorce.

sequel noun *an unfortunate sequel of/to the party* follow-up, development, result, consequence, outcome, upshot, conclusion.

sequence noun *sequence of events* chain, course, cycle, series, progression, succession, order, pattern.

serene adjective *calm*, composed, tranquil, peaceful, placid, still, quiet, unperturbed, imperturbable, undisturbed, unruffled, unworried.

serenity noun *calm*, calmness, composure, tranquillity, peace, placidity, stillness, quietness.

series noun *a series of numbers* succession, progression, sequence, chain, string, set, row, arrangement.

serious adjective **1** *serious expressions* solemn, earnest, unsmiling, thoughtful, grave, somber, sober, stern, grim. **2** *serious problems* important, significant, consequential, momentous, urgent, pressing, crucial, vital, life-and-death. **3** *serious injuries* acute, grave, bad, critical, grievous, dangerous, perilous. **4** *serious about reforming* earnest, sincere, honest, resolute, determined.

sermon noun **1** *sermons from the pulpit* homily, preaching, teaching, speech, address, oration. **2** *her father gave her a ser-*

mon *on lateness* lecture, tirade, harangue, diatribe, reprimand; *inf.* talking-to.

servant noun *kitchen servants* domestic, domestic help, maid, housekeeper, butler, steward, valet; menial, drudge; attendant, lackey.

serve verb **1** *willing to serve his fellow men* be of use to, help, assist, aid, lend a hand to, do a good turn to, benefit, support, minister to, succor. **2** *serve on the committee* sit, perform duties, fulfill duties. **3** *will the car serve us for another year?* be good for, be adequate for, suffice; *inf.* fill the bill for, do. **4** *serve three years as an apprentice* spend, carry out, complete, discharge. **5** *serve food* dish up, give out, distribute, set out, present, provide. **6** *serve a customer* attend to, take care of, assist. **serve as** *sofas serving as beds* act as, do duty as, function as.

service noun **1** *retire after fifty years' service* work, employment, labor, duties. **2** *do him a service by telling him* good turn, advantage, benefit. **3** *wedding service* ceremony, ritual, rite, sacrament. **4** *cars due for service* servicing, overhaul, maintenance check, repair. **5** *pay extra for service in a restaurant* serving, waiting at table. **6** *have had good service from it* treatment, behavior, conduct, handling.

service verb *service the washing machine* overhaul, maintain, repair.

serviceable adjective **1** *serviceable rather than fashionable shoes* functional, utilitarian, practical, plain, useful. **2** *machinery no longer serviceable* usable, of use, functional, operative.

servile adjective **1** *made to do servile tasks* menial, lowly, humble, mean, base. **2** *surrounded by servile employees* subservient, obsequious, sycophantic, fawning, toadying, groveling; *inf.* bootlicking.

servitude noun *slavery*, enslavement, subjugation, domination, bondage, serfdom.

session noun **1** *the afternoon sessions of the summit talks* meeting, sitting, assembly, conference, discussion. **2** *studied French during the fall session* semester, term.

set verb **1** *set the books (down) there | a house set in the woods* put, place, lay, deposit, position, situate, station, posit; *inf.* stick, park, plunk. **2** *set a jewel in the ring* fix, embed, insert, lodge, mount, arrange, install. **3** *set pen to paper* put, apply, touch. **4** *set your mind to it* apply, direct, aim, turn, address, focus. **5** *set one's watch* adjust, regulate, synchronize, coordinate, calibrate. **6** *set the table* lay, make ready, prepare, arrange. **7**

set her hair fix, style, arrange, curl. **8**
a dress set with sequins decorate, adorn,
ornament, deck, embellish. **9** *set things
in motion* | *set it on fire* start, actuate, in-
stigate. **10** *the gelatin/concrete will not set*
solidify, stiffen, thicken, gel, jell, harden,
congeal, coagulate. **11** *the sun setting*
go down, sink, disappear. **12** *set them
thinking* start, motivate, cause. **13** *set a
new record* establish, fix, create, institute.
14 *set a date for the meeting* fix, settle
(on), appoint, decide on, name, specify,
stipulate, determine, designate, select,
choose, arrange, schedule, confirm. **15**
set rules impose, establish, define, stipulate, prescribe. **16** *teachers setting classroom tasks* assign, allocate, allot, give
out, distribute, dispense, mete out. **17**
set her services at a high price evaluate,
value, assess, price, rate. **18** *footsteps
set toward home* direct, steer, orientate,
point, incline, train, aim. **set about** *set
about clearing up* begin, start, commence,
tackle, undertake; *inf.* get cracking on.
set apart *behavior setting him apart from
the rest* differentiate, distinguish, single
out, demarcate, characterize. **set aside**
1 *set aside money for later* lay by, put away,
save, reserve, keep in reserve, store, stockpile, hoard, deposit, salt away, squirrel
away; *inf.* stash. **2** *set aside the newspaper*
put aside, discard, abandon, drop. **3**
set aside our differences put aside, forget,
disregard, ignore, bury. **4** *set aside the
judge's ruling* overrule, overturn, reverse,
nullify, annul, dismiss. **set back** *set back
their progress* hinder, impede, obstruct,
hold up, delay, retard, check, thwart. **set
forth 1** *set forth for the city* start out,
depart. *See* SET OUT 1. **2** *set forth their
demands* declare, state, describe, detail,
submit, present, advance. **set in** *winter
has set in* begin, start, commence, arrive, come. **set off 1** *set off for the city*
start out, depart. *See* SET OUT 1. **2** *set
off a bomb* detonate, explode, blow up,
ignite, light. **3** *set off a flurry of selling
on the stock market* cause, start, initiate,
prompt, touch off, stimulate. **4** *a dress
setting off the blue of her eyes* enhance,
bring out, heighten, intensify, emphasize. **set on** attack, assault, strike, beat,
beat up, fall upon, pounce on, fly at.
set out 1 *they set out for the city early*
set off, set forth, start out, depart, leave,
get under way, embark, sally forth; *inf.*
hit the road. **2** *I did not set out to hurt
them* intend, aim, mean, aspire. **set up.
1** *they set up a statue in his memory* put
up, erect, raise, construct, build. **2** *we
set up a business/scholarship* establish, institute, found, create, start, initiate, inaugurate, organize. **3** *we must set up a
meeting* arrange, organize, prepare, plan,
devise, fix.

set noun **1** *a set of articles for sale* collection, group, assemblage, series, batch,
array, assortment, selection. **2** *the golfing
set* circle, crowd, clique, group, gang, coterie, faction, company; *inf.* crew. **3** *the
set of his shoulder* bearing, carriage, cast,
posture, position, inclination. **4** *paint the
set* stage setting, scenery, backdrop, *mise
en scène.*

set adjective **1** *set meals* fixed, prescribed,
scheduled, specified, predetermined, prearranged, established. **2** *her set routine*
customary, regular, normal, usual, habitual, accustomed. **3** *give a set speech*
stock, standard, routine, hackneyed, con-
ventional. **4** *people of set opinions* | *set in
their ways* fixed, firm, rooted, immovable,
deep-seated, ingrained, entrenched, rigid,
inflexible, hidebound. **5** *all set for the journey* ready, prepared, equipped, primed,
fit. **set on** *set on getting his own way* intent
on, determined to be, resolute about.

setback noun *their progress/plans suffered
a setback* reversal, stumbling block, hitch,
hindrance, impediment, obstruction, disappointment, misfortune, blow.

settle verb **1** *settle in Chicago* make one's
home, take up residence, put down roots,
move to. **2** *the Mormons settled (in) Utah*
colonize, occupy, people, inhabit, populate. **3** *the children will not settle after the
excitement* calm down, be quiet, be still,
relax. **4** *the sedative will settle her* calm, calm
down, tranquilize, quiet, soothe, sedate.
5 *a butterfly settling on the leaf* alight, light,
land, repose, rest. **6** *settle a dispute* resolve,
clear up, patch up, reconcile. **7** *settle one's
affairs* put in order, arrange, straighten
out, organize, systematize. **8** *settle one's
debts* pay, discharge, square, clear, liquidate. **9** *the dust settled* sink, subside, fall,
gravitate. **settle for** *settle for a smaller sum*
compromise on, accept, agree to, assent
to. **settle on** *settle on a date* decide on,
agree on, determine, confirm, arrange,
fix, choose, appoint, select.

settlement noun **1** *the settlement of the area*
founding, peopling, colonization. **2** *a remote settlement* community, colony, town,
village, encampment, outpost. **3** *the settlement of the dispute* resolution, patching
up, reconciliation, conclusion. **4** *reach a
financial settlement with management* agreement, contract, pact, compact. **5** *the
settlement of his finances* ordering, arrangement, organization, systematization. **6**
in settlement of debts payment, discharge,
defrayal, liquidation.

settler noun colonist, pioneer, frontiers-
man, immigrant.

sever verb **1** *sever a branch* cut off, chop
off, lop off, hack off. **2** *sever the log in two
pieces* divide, split, cleave, halve. **3** *sever*

relations with them break off, discontinue, suspend, dissolve, terminate.

several adjective **1** *several people came* some, a number of, a few. **2** *go their several ways* separate, different, diverse, divergent, respective, individual, own, various, sundry.

severe adjective **1** *severe criticism* harsh, stringent, rigorous, unsparing, relentless, merciless, ruthless, painful, caustic, biting, scathing. **2** *a severe regime* harsh, hard, stern, stringent, strict, grim, inflexible, uncompromising, merciless, pitiless, ruthless, brutal, cruel, iron-handed, autocratic, tyrannical, despotic. **3** *a severe shortage of food* extreme, serious, grave, acute, critical, dire, dangerous, perilous. **4** *severe headaches* fierce, strong, intense, powerful. **5** *a severe test of their stamina* demanding, taxing, exacting, tough, difficult, arduous, rigorous, punishing. **6** *a severe expression* stern, grim, cold, austere, forbidding, dour, disapproving, tight-lipped, unsmiling, grave, sober, serious. **7** *a severe style of decoration* austere, stark, spartan, ascetic, plain, bare, unadorned, unembellished. **8** *a severe winter* harsh, extreme, inclement, cold, freezing, frigid.

sew verb stitch, seam, embroider, mend, darn.

sex noun **1** *identify the sex of the animal* gender. **2** *attraction based on sex* sexuality, sexual attraction, desire, sex drive, sexual appetite, libido. **3** *sex education* facts of life, reproduction; *inf.* the birds and the bees. **4** *have sex with him* intimacy, coitus, copulation, making love, mating, fornication.

sexuality noun **1** *differences based on sexuality* sex, gender. **2** *identifying one's sexuality* sexual desire, sexiness, eroticism, sensuality; sexual orientation, sexual preferences.

sexy adjective **1** *sexy pictures/clothes* erotic, titillating, suggestive, arousing, exciting, stimulating, provocative, seductive, sensuous. **2** *sexy women/men* sexually attractive, alluring, seductive.

shabby adjective **1** *shabby houses* dilapidated, broken-down, run-down, tumbledown, ramshackle, scruffy, dingy, seedy, squalid; *inf.* tacky. **2** *shabby clothes* worn, worn-out, threadbare, ragged, frayed, tattered, faded, scruffy. **3** *shabby treatment of the old lady* contemptible, despicable, dishonorable, disreputable, mean, base, low, shameful, ignoble, unworthy, shoddy.

shackle verb **1** *shackle the prisoner* chain, fetter, put in irons, manacle, tie up, bind, handcuff. **2** *no longer shackled by convention* deter, restrain, restrict, limit, impede, hinder, hamper, encumber, check, curb, constrain.

shackles plural noun **1** *prisoners in shackles* chains, fetters, bonds, irons, manacles, ropes, handcuffs. **2** *throw off the shackles of convention* restraint, impediment, hindrance, check, curb, constraint.

shade noun **1** *sit in the shade of a tree* shadow, shelter, cover. **2** *a darker shade for the carpets* color, hue, tone, tint, tinge. **3** *act as a shade against the light* screen, shield, curtain, blind, canopy, veil. **4** *a word with several shades of meaning* nuance, degree, gradation. **a shade** *better* slightly, marginally, a bit, a touch.

shade verb **1** *trees shading the garden* cast a shadow over, screen, darken, dim. **2** *shading the light* cover, obscure, mute, hide, conceal, veil.

shadow noun **1** *sit in the shadow of the building* shade, cover. **2** *their shadows on the wall* silhouette, outline, shape. **3** *cast a shadow on their happiness* gloom, cloud, blight. **4** *her younger sister was her shadow* constant companion, intimate, alter ego; *inf.* sidekick. **5** *the policewoman acting as a shadow* watch, follower; *inf.* tail. **6** *not a shadow of a doubt* bit, shade, trace, modicum, hint, suggestion, ghost. **7** *a shadow of his former self* ghost, specter, phantom, remnant.

shadowy adjective **1** *shadowy parts of the garden* shady, shaded, dim, murky, crepuscular, tenebrous. **2** *shadowy shapes on the horizon* indistinct, indeterminate, unclear, nebulous.

shady adjective **1** *shady parts of the garden* shaded, shadowy, sheltered, covered, dim, dark, leafy, bowery, umbrageous, tenebrous. **2** *shady character* disreputable, suspicious, questionable, dishonest, untrustworthy, devious, shifty, slippery, underhanded, unscrupulous; *inf.* fishy.

shaft noun **1** *the shafts of the mine* passage, duct, tunnel, flue. **2** *shafts of light* ray, beam, gleam, streak, pencil. **3** *the shaft of a spade* pole, rod, staff, shank, stem, handle, upright.

shaggy adjective hairy, hirsute, long-haired, unkempt, untidy.

shake verb **1** *the truck shaking on the rough roads* jolt, bounce, roll, sway, wobble, rattle, vibrate. **2** *shaking with fear* shiver, tremble, quiver, quake, shudder. **3** *shake the can of coins* jiggle, joggle, jerk, rattle, agitate. **4** *shaken by the accident/news* agitate, upset, distress, shock, alarm, disturb, perturb, fluster, unsettle, disquiet, disconcert, unnerve, ruffle, jolt; *inf.* rattle. **5** *shake a stick at them* brandish, wave, flourish, swing, wield. **shake off** *shake off their pursuers* escape, elude, give the slip to, throw off. **shake up 1** *shake up the dressing/cocktail* mix, churn up, agitate. **2** *shaken up by the accident* agitate, upset, disturb, unsettle. **3**

shake up the firm reorganize, revolutionize, stir up.

shake noun **1** *the children had the shakes* shivering, trembling, tremor, quiver, quivering, convulsion. **2** *with one shake of the can* jiggle, joggle, jerk, rattle. **3** *get quite a shake from the accident/news* upset, shock, jolt. **4** *with a shake of his fist* brandish, wave, flourish, swing.

shaky adjective **1** *with shaky limbs* trembling, tremulous, quivering, shaking, unsteady, weak. **2** *take a few shaky steps* unsteady, faltering, wobbly, tottering, staggering. **3** *rather shaky reasoning* questionable, dubious, tenuous, flimsy, weak, nebulous, unsound, ungrounded, unfounded.

sham verb *shamming an illness* fake, pretend, feign, counterfeit, simulate, affect, imitate.

sham noun **1** *his charm is only a sham* pretense, feint, counterfeit, imposture, simulation. **2** *the doctor was a sham* impostor, fake, fraud, pretender, dissembler, charlatan; *inf.* phony. **3** *the document is a sham* counterfeit, fake, forgery, copy, imitation, hoax.

sham adjective **1** *sham sympathy* pretended, feigned, contrived, simulated, affected, insincere, false, bogus, spurious; *inf.* phony. **2** *sham gold watches* fake, counterfeit, imitation, artificial, synthetic, ersatz; *inf.* phony, pseudo.

shame noun **1** *I feel shame at being imprisoned* humiliation, mortification, loss of face, remorse, compunction, embarrassment. **2** *bring shame on the family* disgrace, dishonor, scandal, discredit, degradation, ignominy, disrepute, infamy, odium, stigma, opprobrium. **3** *a shame he could not be there* pity, misfortune, bad luck, ill luck, source of regret. **put to shame** *put their efforts to shame* outshine, outclass, overshadow, eclipse, surpass, outdo.

shamefaced adjective *too shamefaced to appear after his crime* ashamed, embarrassed, remorseful, contrite, penitent, regretful, humiliated, mortified.

shameful adjective **1** *shameful behavior* disgraceful, base, mean, low, vile, outrageous, shocking, dishonorable, unbecoming, deplorable, despicable, contemptible, reprehensible, scandalous, atrocious, heinous.

shameless adjective **1** *shameless about his prison sentence* unashamed, unabashed, uncontrite, impenitent. **2** *shameless behavior* brazen, impudent, bold, brash, forward, audacious, immodest, unseemly, improper, unbecoming, wanton, indecent.

shape noun **1** *pieces of plastic in all shapes and sizes* form, figure, configuration, formation, contour, outline, silhouette. **2** *in the shape of the devil* form, guise, appearance, likeness, semblance, image, aspect. **3** *athletes in good shape* condition, state, health, trim, fettle, kilter.

shape verb **1** *shape the clay into a figure* form, fashion, make, design, mold, model, cast, carve, sculpt. **2** *attitudes shaped by childhood experiences* form, mold, create, influence, determine, define. **shape up** **1** *new recruits shaping up* improve, make progress, show promise. **2** *plans shaping up* take shape, develop, crystallize, fall into place, come along, progress.

shapeless adjective **1** *shapeless hunks of clay* amorphous, formless, undeveloped, embryonic. **2** *shapeless clothes* formless, sacklike, ill-proportioned, inelegant.

shapely adjective *shapely legs* well-proportioned, elegant, curvaceous, curvy.

share noun *each receiving a fair share* division, quota, allowance, ration, allocation, allotment, portion, part, lot; *inf.* cut.

share verb *share the workload/profits* divide (up), split, distribute, apportion, parcel out; *inf.* divvy (up). **share in** *sharing in their good fortune* participate in, take part in, partake of, have a stake in.

sharp adjective **1** *a sharp utensil* razor-edged, pointed, keen. **2** *a sharp drop to the sea* steep, sheer, abrupt, precipitous, vertical. **3** *a sharp pain* intense, acute, piercing, stabbing, shooting. **4** *a sharp taste* pungent, biting, bitter, acid, sour, tart. **5** *a sharp smell* acrid, pungent, burning. **6** *a sharp noise* piercing, shrill, high-pitched, earsplitting, harsh, strident. **7** *exchange sharp words* harsh, curt, brusque, bitter, cutting, scathing, caustic, biting, barbed, acrimonious, hurtful. **8** *a sharp student* sharp-witted, intelligent, bright, clever, quick. **9** *sharp intelligence/wits* keen, acute, quick, shrewd, discerning, perceptive, penetrating. **10** *a sharp customer* unscrupulous, cunning, wily, crafty, artful. **11** *a sharp dresser* smart, stylish, fashionable, chic; *inf.* snappy, natty.

sharp adverb *arrive at 9 a.m. sharp* promptly, punctually, on the dot.

sharpen verb edge, whet, hone, strop, grind.

shatter verb **1** *shatter the windshield* smash, break into pieces, splinter, fracture, pulverize, crush, crack. **2** *shatter one's hopes* destroy, demolish, wreck, ruin, dash, blight, torpedo. **3** *shattered by their betrayal* devastate, crush.

sheath noun **1** *a sheath for a sword* scabbard, case, casing, cover. **2** *a contraceptive sheath* condom, contraceptive; *inf.* rubber.

shed noun hut, outhouse, lean-to, shack.

shed verb **1** *trees shedding their leaves* let fall, let drop. **2** *snakes shedding their skins* cast off, slough off. **3** *shed clothes* take off, remove, strip off, doff. **4** *shed blood* pour forth, spill, discharge. **5** *shed light* diffuse, radiate, disperse, scatter.

sheen noun shine, luster, gleam, gloss, patina.

sheepish adjective embarrassed, ashamed, shamefaced, blushing, abashed, bashful.

sheer adjective **1** *sheer folly* utter, complete, total, absolute, downright, out-and-out, unmitigated. **2** *a sheer drop to the sea* steep, abrupt, sharp, precipitous, vertical, perpendicular. **3** *sheer silk* transparent, diaphanous, see-through, translucent, filmy, gossamer.

sheet noun **1** *sheets and blankets* bedsheet, bed linen. **2** *a sheet of lacquered veneer on the table* layer, stratum, overlay, coating, coat, veneer, film. **3** *sheets of plastic* pane, panel, plate, slab. **sheet of paper** leaf, page, folio.

shell noun **1** *the shell of a crab* carapace, case. **2** *the shell of a nut* casing, husk, pod, integument. **3** *shells in the army magazine* bullet, shot, cartridge, case. **4** *the shell of a car/ship under construction* framework, frame, chassis, hull, skeleton.

shell verb **1** *shell peas* husk, shuck. **2** *troops shelling the city* bomb, bombard, blitz, strafe, fire on. **shell out** *shell out money* pay out, spend, disburse; *inf.* fork out.

shelter noun **1** *provide shelter from danger/cold* protection, shield, cover, safety, security, refuge, sanctuary, asylum. **2** *a shelter for battered wives* refuge, sanctuary, retreat, haven.

shelter verb **1** *shelter them from the weather* protect, shield, screen, safeguard. **2** *shelter the criminal from the police* guard, harbor, conceal, hide.

sheltered adjective **1** *a sheltered spot for the picnic* protected, shielded, secluded. **2** *lead a sheltered life* secluded, isolated, protected, cloistered, reclusive.

shelve verb *shelve expansion plans* lay aside, put off, postpone, defer, delay, suspend, table, mothball, put on the back burner.

shepherd verb *shepherd the children to their classes* escort, conduct, usher, guide, marshal, steer.

shield noun *a shield against disease* protection, defense, safeguard, bulwark.

shield verb *shield one's eyes from the dust* protect, screen, guard.

shift verb *shift one's position on the new project* alter, vary, modify, change, reverse.

shift noun **1** *a shift in public opinion* change, alteration, variation, modification, about-face, reversal. **2** *an eight-hour shift* work period, stint.

shiftless adjective lazy, idle, indolent, slothful, unenterprising, good-for-nothing.

shifty adjective evasive, slippery, devious, underhanded, wily, crafty, artful, sly, scheming, contriving.

shilly-shally verb vacillate, waver, hesitate, hem and haw.

shimmer verb glisten, flicker, twinkle, sparkle, gleam, scintillate, dance.

shine verb **1** *lights shining in the distance* gleam, glow, sparkle, twinkle, flicker, glitter, glisten, shimmer, flash, dazzle, beam, radiate, illuminate, luminesce. **2** *with face shining* glow, beam, radiate. **3** *shine the shoes* polish, burnish, buff, wax, gloss. **4** *shine in a crowd* stand out, be conspicuous, excel, dominate, star.

shine noun **1** *the shine of the street lights* brightness, gleam, glow, sparkle, twinkle, flicker, glitter, shimmer, flash, dazzle, glare, beam, radiance, illumination, luminescence, effulgence. **2** *put a shine on the table* polish, burnish, gloss, luster, sheen, patina.

shiny adjective polished, burnished, gleaming, glossy, lustrous.

shirk verb avoid, evade, dodge, sidestep, shun; *inf.* duck.

shiver verb *shiver with cold* tremble, quiver, shake, shudder, quake.

shiver noun *a shiver of fear* quiver, shake, quaver, shudder.

shock[1] noun **1** *the shock of the two cars hitting each other* impact, blow, concussion, jolt. **2** *the news came as a shock* surprise, blow, disturbance, revelation, bolt from the blue, bombshell. **3** *suffering from shock after the accident* trauma, stupor, stupefaction, collapse.

shock[2] verb *shocked by the scenes of famine* appall, horrify, outrage, astound, dumbfound, stagger, amaze, astonish, stun, flabbergast, overwhelm.

shock[3] noun *a shock of red hair* mass, mop, mane, thatch.

shocking adjective *a shocking sight* appalling, horrific, dreadful, awful, frightful, terrible, horrible, scandalous, outrageous, disgraceful, ghastly, hideous, repellent, revolting, repulsive, repugnant, disgusting, distressing, disturbing, staggering, amazing, overwhelming.

shoddy adjective poor-quality, inferior, tawdry, trashy, junky; *inf.* tacky.

shoot verb **1** *shoot a deer* hit, wound, injure, bring down, bag, fell, kill, slay; *inf.* pick off, plug. **2** *shoot a round of bullets/arrows* fire, discharge, launch, let fly. **3** *runners shooting past* race, dash, sprint, bound, charge, dart, fly, hurtle, bolt, streak, flash, speed. **shoot at** *shoot at the fugitives* fire at, open fire on, snipe at, shell. **shoot up** *plants shooting up* bud, burgeon, sprout, germinate, spring up.

shoot noun *shoots of a tree* bud, slip, scion, sucker, sprout, branch, twig, sprig, cutting, graft.

shop noun **1** *a dress shop* store, boutique. **2** *mechanics working in the shop* workshop; plant, factory.

shop verb *shop for a dress/house* go shopping, look to buy, browse.

shore noun seaside, beach, coast, waterfront, strand.

shore verb *shore up the broken wall* prop up, support, underpin, strengthen, brace, buttress.

short adjective **1** *short people* small, little, petite, tiny, squat, dwarfish, diminutive, Lilliputian; *inf.* pint-sized. **2** *short bushes* low, stubby, miniature. **3** *a short report* brief, concise, succinct, compact, terse, pithy, abbreviated, condensed, truncated. **4** *a short affair* brief, temporary, shortlived, short-term, cursory, fleeting, passing, transitory, transient, ephemeral. **5** *the short route* direct, straight. **6** *money is a bit short* deficient, lacking, wanting, scarce, scanty, meager, sparse, tight. **7** *he was short with her* curt, sharp, abrupt, brusque, terse, gruff.

short adverb *stop short* abruptly, suddenly, unexpectedly. **cut short** shorten, curtail, truncate, abbreviate, reduce, interrupt. **fall short** be deficient, be inadequate, disappoint, fail, not fulfill expectations. **in short** briefly, in a word, in a nutshell. **short of 1** *short of eggs* deficient in, lacking, wanting, in need of, low on. **2** *short of breaking a window, how will you get into your locked car?* other than, apart from, aside from, besides, except (for), without, disregarding.

shortage noun dearth, scarcity, lack, deficiency, insufficiency, paucity, deficit, shortfall, want.

shortcoming noun *forgive his shortcomings* defect, fault, flaw, imperfection, failing, drawback, weakness, foible.

shorten verb *shorten the text* abbreviate, condense, abridge, cut, compress, reduce, decrease, diminish, curtail, trim, pare down.

shortly adverb **1** *she will be with you shortly* soon, in a little while, presently, directly. **2** *he replied shortly* curtly, sharply, abruptly, bluntly, brusquely, tersely, gruffly.

shortsighted adjective **1** *wear spectacles because of being shortsighted* myopic, nearsighted. **2** *a shortsighted attitude to business* lacking foresight, ill-considered, imprudent, injudicious, unwise, ill-advised, thoughtless, unthinking, heedless.

short-tempered adjective quick-tempered, hot-tempered, irascible, touchy, testy; *inf.* on a short fuse.

shot noun **1** *hear a shot* gunfire, report (of a gun), crack, bang, blast, explosion. **2** *shot for the guns* bullets, slugs, projectiles, ammunition. **3** *got the ball through the hoop with one shot* throw, toss, lob, fling, hurl. **4** *a better shot than his brother* shooter, marksman, markswoman, rifleman. **5** *have a shot at getting there* attempt, try, effort, endeavor; *inf.* go, stab, crack. **6** *have shots before going to the tropics* injection, vaccination. **a shot in the arm** *a shot in the arm for the tourist industry* boost, fillip, lift, encouragement, stimulus. **a shot in the dark** *her answer was a shot in the dark* wild guess, random guess. **like a shot** *he flew out of here like a shot* without hesitation, immediately, instantly, like a flash.

shoulder verb **1** *shoulder a heavy responsibility* bear, carry, support, take on. **2** *shoulder his way to the front* push, shove, jostle, elbow. **give (someone) the cold shoulder** ostracize, shun, snub, ignore, rebuff. **put one's shoulder to the wheel** apply oneself, exert oneself, get down to work, strive; *inf.* buckle down. **rub shoulders with** associate with, socialize with, fraternize with, hobnob with.

shout verb cry out, call out, yell, roar, howl, bellow, bawl; *inf.* holler.

shout noun *a shout of pain* cry, call, yell, roar, howl, bellow.

shove verb *shove her out of the way* push, thrust, drive, force, jostle.

shove noun *give him a shove* push, thrust, jostle.

shovel noun spade, scoop.

show verb **1** *gray hairs beginning to show* be visible, appear. **2** *show the new merchandise* exhibit, display, present, demonstrate, reveal. **3** *show his grief* express, manifest, reveal, make plain, disclose, betray, divulge. **4** *show (them) the new procedures* demonstrate, point out, explain, clarify, teach, instruct in. **5** *show them to their seats* escort, accompany, usher, conduct, attend, guide, lead, direct, steer. **6** *he never showed* show up, appear, turn up, come, arrive. **show off 1** *models showing off the dresses* display, exhibit, demonstrate, parade, flaunt. **2** *showing off in front of the guests* put on airs, boast, brag, swagger. **show up 1** *sunshine showing up the dust* expose, reveal, make obvious, highlight. **2** *the red showing up well against the white* be visible, stand out, catch the eye. **3** *show him up in front of his rich friends* expose, shame, mortify, humiliate, embarrass. **4** *the guest did not show up* appear, turn up, come.

show noun **1** *a brilliant show of flowers | a boat show* display, array, arrangement, exhibition, demonstration, presentation, exposition, spectacle; *inf.* expo. **2** *put on a musical show* performance, production. **3** *a show of courage* appearance, air, guise, semblance, pretense, pose, affectation. **4** *doing it only for show* display, ostentation, affectation, window-dressing.

shower noun **1** *a shower of rain/snow* drizzle, flurry, sprinkling. **2** *a shower of arrows* volley, barrage, fusillade. **3** *a shower of gifts* abundance, profusion, plethora.

shower verb **1** *arrows showered on them* rain, fall. **2** *shower them with gifts* deluge, inundate, lavish, overwhelm.

show-off noun exhibitionist, braggart, boaster, braggadocio; *inf.* blowhard.

showy adjective *showy clothes/lifestyle* ostentatious, flamboyant, elaborate, fancy, pretentious, glittering.

shred noun **1** *shreds of material* scrap, fragment, sliver, bit, remnant, snippet. **2** *not a shred of evidence* bit, iota, whit, particle, atom, modicum, trace, speck.

shred verb *shred paper/cabbage* cut up, tear up, rip up, grate.

shrew noun virago, termagant, fury, harpy, nag.

shrewd adjective *a shrewd businessman* astute, sharp, clever, quick-witted, discerning, discriminating, canny, cunning, artful, crafty, wily, calculating.

shriek verb *shriek with laughter* scream, screech, squeal, howl.

shriek noun *a shriek of terror* scream, screech, squeal, howl, shout, cry, wail.

shrill adjective high-pitched, sharp, piercing, penetrating.

shrine noun **1** *a shrine in memory of the dead soldiers* memorial, monument, tomb, cenotaph. **2** *worship in the shrine* holy place, temple, church.

shrink verb **1** *markets shrinking* become smaller, contract, diminish, lessen, reduce, dwindle, narrow, decline, fall off, shrivel. **2** *shrinking in fear* draw back, pull back, shy away, recoil, retreat, flinch, cringe, wince.

shrivel verb *leaves shriveled by the sun* dry up, wither, desiccate, dehydrate, wrinkle.

shroud noun *a shroud of mist over the hills* covering, pall, cloak, mantle, blanket, cloud, veil.

shroud verb *hills shrouded in mist* cover, enshroud, swathe, envelop, cloak, blanket, veil, conceal, hide.

shudder verb *shudder in horror* shake, shiver, tremble, quiver, quake, convulse.

shudder noun *a shudder of horror* shake, shiver, tremor, quiver, convulsion, spasm.

shun verb avoid, evade, eschew, steer clear of, cold-shoulder.

shut verb *shut the doors* close, fasten, bar, lock, secure, seal. **shut down 1** *the factory has shut down* close, close down, cease production, come to a halt. **2** *shut down the machinery* switch off, stop, halt. **shut out 1** *shut out intruders* lock out, keep out. **2** *during negotiations, he was shut out* exclude, omit, keep out, bar, ostracize, blackball, banish. **shut up 1** *shut the sheep up in a pen* lock in, confine, imprison, coop up. **2** *please shut up* be quiet, keep silent; *inf.* hold one's tongue, pipe down. **3** *the sound of the siren shut up the crowd* quiet, silence, hush, shush.

shy adjective bashful, diffident, reserved, reticent, self-effacing, withdrawn, timid, timorous, hesitant, self-conscious.

shy verb **shy away from** shrink from, recoil from, flinch from, balk at, quail at.

sick adjective **1** *unable to work when sick* unwell, ill, ailing, indisposed, out of sorts, laid up; *inf.* under the weather. **2** *feel sick on a boat* nauseated, queasy, bilious; *inf.* green around the gills. **3** *be sick on the boat* vomit, retch, be sick to one's stomach; *inf.* throw up, puke. **4** *a sick joke* morbid, macabre, ghoulish, gruesome, sadistic, perverted, cruel. **sick of** *sick of that music* tired of, weary of, bored with, satiated with; *inf.* fed up with.

sicken verb *sickened by the smell of garbage* nauseate, revolt, disgust, repel, shock, appall.

sickly adjective **1** *a sickly child* unhealthy, delicate, frail, weak, feeble, puny. **2** *a sickly complexion* pale, wan, pallid, anemic, languid.

sickness noun **1** *a terminal sickness* illness, disease, ailment, affliction, malady, infirmity; *inf.* bug. **2** *a bout of sickness* vomiting, retching, upset stomach; *inf.* throwing up, puking. **3** *a feeling of sickness on the swaying boat* nausea, queasiness, biliousness.

side noun **1** *by the side of the lake/road* edge, border, verge, boundary, margin, rim, fringe, flank, brink, brim, periphery. **2** *on the east side of the city* part, quarter, section, sector. **3** *the upper side of the paper/wood* surface, face, facet. **4** *both sides of the question* aspect, angle, facet, point of view, standpoint, position, slant. **5** *on the chairman's side in the dispute* camp, faction, caucus, party. **6** *which side do you root for?* team, squad, group. **side by side** *walk/fight side by side* together, alongside each other, shoulder to shoulder, cheek by jowl, arm in arm. **take the side of**

take the side of the likely winner side with, support, favor.

side adjective **1** *on the side position of the battle* lateral, wing, flank. **2** *a side issue* minor, lesser, secondary, subordinate, subsidiary, ancillary, marginal.

sideways adverb **1** *walk sideways* crabwise, to the side. **2** *bring the table in sideways* side first, edgeways, edgewise. **3** *look sideways at her* obliquely, indirectly, sidelong.

siege noun blockade, beleaguerment.

sieve noun *use a sieve to strain the mixture* strainer, sifter, filter, colander, screen.

sift verb **1** *sift flour onto a board* shake, sprinkle, scatter, strew. **2** *sift the lumps from the flour* filter, strain, screen, winnow. **sift through 1** *sift through the evidence* examine, scrutinize, study, pore over, investigate, analyze, screen, review, probe. **2** *sift through the debris* search through, look through, rummage through.

sigh verb **1** *sigh with boredom* groan, exhale. **2** *the wind sighing through the trees* whisper, rustle. **3** *sigh for times past* yearn, pine, long, mourn.

sight noun **1** *have excellent sight* eyesight, vision. **2** *within (the) sight of her father* range of vision, view. **3** *love at first sight* view, glimpse, glance. **4** *in her father's sight, she was perfect* view, judgment, estimation, perception. **5** *memorable sights* spectacle, scene, display, curiosity, rarity, marvel. **catch sight of** glimpse, see, spot, sight, espy, set eyes on. **set one's sights on** aim at/for, aspire to, strive toward.

sign noun **1** *a sign of weakness* indication, symptom, hint, suggestion, mark, manifestation, token. **2** *signs indicating the offices in the building* signpost, notice, placard, marker. **3** *make a sign to follow him* gesture, signal, motion, gesticulation. **4** *mathematical signs* | *decipher the signs* symbol, mark, hieroglyph. **5** *look for a sign from above* omen, portent, warning.

sign verb **1** *sign one's name* write, inscribe. **2** *sign the agreement* autograph, initial, endorse, certify. **sign on/up 1** *soldier signing on for five years* enlist, join up. **2** *sign up for music classes* enroll, register. **3** *sign on new employees* employ, take on, engage, hire, recruit. **sign over** *sign over the estate to his son* transfer, hand over, turn over, assign, consign.

signal noun **1** *the signal to stop* sign, indicator, cue. **2** *a signal that winter is coming* sign, indication, token, hint.

signal verb **1** *signal to her to follow* give a sign, beckon, gesture, motion, gesticulate. **2** *signaled his displeasure* indicate, show, express, communicate.

significance noun **1** *not comprehend the significance of his remark* meaning, sense,

import, purport, point, gist, essence, implications. **2** *the significance of the medical discovery* importance, consequence, momentousness, magnitude, impressiveness, seriousness.

significant adjective **1** *a significant few words* meaningful, eloquent, expressive. **2** *make significant progress* important, momentous, material, impressive, vital.

signify verb **1** *dark clouds signifying rain* indicate, mean, betoken, suggest, portend. **2** *what do the symbols signify?* mean, denote, represent, symbolize. **3** *signify one's agreement* indicate, show, express, communicate.

silence noun **1** *in the silence of the night* still, stillness, quiet, hush, peacefulness, tranquillity, soundlessness. **2** *their behavior reduced him to silence* speechlessness, wordlessness, muteness, taciturnity. **3** *the need for silence about their whereabouts* secrecy, secretiveness, concealment, reticence.

silence verb **1** *silence the noisy children* quiet, hush, calm, pacify, subdue. **2** *silence the noise of the engine* muffle, deaden, extinguish. **3** *silence their complaints* put an end to, put a stop to, cut short.

silent adjective **1** *in their silent surroundings* still, quiet, hushed, peaceful, tranquil, noiseless. **2** *silent in the face of the opposition* speechless, wordless, dumb, mute, taciturn, tight-lipped; *inf.* struck dumb. **3** *silent criticism* unspoken, wordless, unvoiced, tacit, implicit, implied.

silhouette noun *see her silhouette on the wall* outline, contour, profile, form, shape.

silly adjective **1** *a silly person* foolish, stupid, idiotic, brainless, witless, thoughtless, reckless, foolhardy, irresponsible, scatterbrained, featherbrained, flighty, frivolous, giddy, inane, immature, childish, naïve. **2** *silly actions* foolish, stupid, senseless, mindless, idiotic, pointless, meaningless, irrational, thoughtless, foolhardy, irresponsible, harebrained, absurd, ridiculous, ludicrous, preposterous, asinine; *inf.* half-baked.

similar adjective *have similar houses* like, alike, comparable, corresponding, comparable, analogous, parallel, equivalent.

similarity noun *a degree of similarity* resemblance, sameness, similitude, correspondence, equivalence, closeness.

simmer verb **1** *a stew simmering on the stove* boil gently, bubble, stew. **2** *simmering with rage* fume, seethe, smolder.

simple adjective **1** *a simple task* easy, uncomplicated, straightforward, effortless, elementary; *inf.* like falling off a log. **2** *simple instructions* clear, plain, intelligible, comprehensible, lucid, straightforward, uncomplicated. **3** *simple clothes* plain, unelaborate, unadorned, undecorated, unembellished, austere, spartan. **4** *simple chemical substances* pure, basic, uncompounded, unmixed, unblended, unalloyed, single, elementary, fundamental. **5** *the simple truth* plain, straightforward, candid, honest, unvarnished, bald, unembellished. **6** *a simple country girl* unsophisticated, natural, unaffected, innocent, guileless, childlike, naïve, ingenuous. **7** *lead a simple life* ordinary, commonplace, unpretentious, modest, humble, rustic.

simpleton noun idiot, halfwit, dolt, fool, nincompoop; *inf.* nitwit, dope.

simplicity noun **1** *the simplicity of the task* simpleness, easiness, straightforwardness, effortlessness, facility. **2** *the simplicity of the directions* clarity, plainness, intelligibility, lucidity, straightforwardness. **3** *the simplicity of the clothes* clean lines, absence of adornment/decoration, plainness, absence of ornamentation/embellishment, austerity, starkness, restraint, naturalness. **4** *the simplicity of the statement* straightforwardness, frankness, directness, candor. **5** *the simplicity of their lifestyle* unpretentiousness, modesty, humbleness, lowliness.

simplify verb **1** *simplify the instructions* make simpler, make plainer, clarify, decipher, explain, paraphrase, translate, condense. **2** *simplify the procedure* make simpler, make easier, streamline.

simulate verb **1** *simulate grief* feign, pretend, fake, sham, affect. **2** *simulate flight landing conditions* reproduce, mimic, parallel, do a mock-up of.

simultaneous adjective *simultaneous events* concurrent, contemporaneous, concomitant, coinciding, coincident, synchronous, coexistent, parallel.

sin noun **1** *commit a sin in the eyes of the church* wrong, act of evil/wickedness, crime, offense, misdeed, transgression, lapse, fall from grace; *lit.* trespass. **2** *guilty of sin* wrongdoing, evil, evildoing, wickedness, iniquity, immorality, unrighteousness, ungodliness, impiety.

sin verb *sin against the church* commit a sin, do wrong, commit a crime/offense, transgress, go astray, stray from the straight and narrow, fall from grace.

sincere adjective **1** *sincere affection* genuine, real, true, honest, unfeigned, unaffected, honest, heartfelt, earnest. **2** *sincere people* honest, trustworthy, frank, candid, straightforward, genuine, guileless, ingenuous; *inf.* up-front.

sincerely adverb **1** *thank them sincerely* wholeheartedly, earnestly, fervently. **2** *mean it most sincerely* genuinely, truly, without pretense, honestly, in good faith.

sincerity noun **1** *doubt the sincerity of his beliefs* genuineness, truth, honesty, good faith, wholeheartedness, earnestness. **2** *misled by their seeming sincerity* openness, honesty, trustworthiness, frankness, candor, straightforwardness, genuineness, ingenuousness.

sinful adjective evil, wicked, bad, iniquitous, immoral, corrupt, unrighteous, ungodly, irreverent, profane, impious, dissolute, depraved.

sing verb **1** *children singing happily* carol, pipe, croon, chant, yodel. **2** *birds singing* trill, warble, chirp.

singer noun vocalist, soloist, songster, songstress, chorister, crooner, chanteuse, minstrel; balladeer, diva.

single adjective **1** *send a single rose* sole, lone, solitary, unique, isolated, exclusive. **2** *remove every single item* individual, particular, separate, distinct. **3** *preferring to remain single* unmarried, unwed, wifeless/husbandless, spouseless, partnerless, unattached, free.

singular adjective **1** *a singular talent* extraordinary, exceptional, rare, unusual, unique, remarkable, outstanding, notable, noteworthy. **2** *singular occurrences happening in the village* strange, unusual, odd, peculiar, curious, weird.

sinister adjective **1** *a sinister figure* evil-looking, menacing, threatening, frightening. **2** *sinister motives* evil, wicked, villainous, malevolent. **3** *sinister signs* ominous, inauspicious, portentous.

sink verb **1** *sink to one's knees | the sun sinking* fall, drop, descend, plunge, plummet, slump. **2** *ships sinking* go under, submerge, founder, capsize. **3** *feel the ground sinking* collapse, cave in, fall in. **4** *empires/patients sinking rapidly* decline, fade, fail, deteriorate, weaken, flag, degenerate, decay; *inf.* go downhill. **5** *would not sink to that level* stoop, lower oneself. **6** *sink a well/shaft* dig, bore, drill, excavate. **7** *having sunk their savings into the venture* invest, put, venture, risk.

sinner noun wrongdoer, evildoer, offender, miscreant, transgressor, reprobate; *lit.* trespasser.

sip verb *sip the drink* taste, sample, sup.

sip noun *take a sip* mouthful, swallow, drop, thimbleful, taste.

sit verb **1** *please sit* take a seat, settle down, be seated; *inf.* take a load off. **2** *the books sitting on the shelf* rest, perch. **3** *committees sitting until midnight* be convened, meet, assemble, be in session.

site noun **1** *the site of the battle* location, position, place, locality, setting, scene. **2** *the building site* ground, plot, lot.

situate verb *factories situated near the river* place, position, locate, site.

situation noun **1** *their financial situation* circumstances, affairs, state, state of affairs, condition, predicament, plight. **2** *from a lowly situation in life* status, station, standing, rank. **3** *apply for a situation in the new firm* post, position, place, job, employment.

size noun dimensions, measurements, proportions, magnitude, vastness, bulk, extent.

skeleton noun **1** *the skeleton of the building/car* framework, frame, structure, shell, bare bones, chassis. **2** *the human skeleton* bones.

skeptic noun **1** *supporters of his theories arguing with the skeptics* doubter, disbeliever, dissenter, cynic. **2** *ministers of the church challenging skeptics* agnostic, unbeliever, doubter, doubting Thomas, atheist.

skeptical adjective doubtful, distrustful, mistrustful, suspicious, disbelieving, incredulous, unconvinced, cynical.

sketch noun **1** *draw a rough sketch of the house* preliminary drawing, outline, diagram, plan, delineation. **2** *give a sketch of his plans* outline, summary, abstract, précis, skeleton, draft.

sketch verb *sketch the landscape on paper* draw, rough out, outline, pencil, delineate. **sketch out** *sketch out his plans* outline, summarize, précis, draft.

sketchy adjective **1** *plans still a bit sketchy* preliminary, provisional, unpolished, rough, crude. **2** *sketchy knowledge* slight, superficial, cursory, perfunctory, meager, skimpy, imperfect, incomplete.

skill noun *the skill of the performer* skillfulness, ability, accomplishment, adeptness, competence, adroitness, deftness, aptitude, expertise, talent.

skillful adjective *a skillful performer* skilled, able, accomplished, adept, competent, adroit, deft, masterly, expert, first-rate, practiced, talented, gifted.

skim verb *skim through the report* glance at, scan, run one's eye over, leaf through, thumb through.

skimp verb **skimp on** *skimp on food/material* be sparing with, economize on, be frugal with, scrimp on, limit; *inf.* be stingy with.

skimpy adjective **1** *skimpy meals* small, meager, scanty, insubstantial, inadequate, paltry. **2** *skimpy dresses* short, brief, insubstantial.

skin noun **1** *damage the skin* integument, epidermis, cuticle, corium, derma. **2** *fair skin* complexion, coloring. **3** *animal skin* hide, pelt, fleece, fell. **4** *banana skin* peel, rind, hull, husk. **5** *a skin forming on the gravy* film, coating, layer, crust. **by the skin of one's teeth** only just, narrowly, barely, by a hair's breadth; *inf.* by a whisker. **get under one's skin** *noisy neighbors getting under her skin* irritate, annoy, irk, vex, grate on, nettle; *inf.* needle.

skin verb *skin one's knee* scrape, graze, abrade, cut, bark, excoriate.

skinflint noun miser, penny-pincher, Scrooge; *inf.* cheapskate, tightwad.

skinny adjective thin, lean, scrawny, emaciated; *inf.* skin and bone.

skip verb **1** *children skipping along* hop, bounce, dance, caper, prance, trip, cavort, gambol, frisk. **2** *skip from subject to subject* pass quickly, flit, dart, zoom. **3** *skip the more boring parts of the text* omit, pass over, bypass, skim over. **4** *skip lectures* play truant from, miss; *inf.* cut, play hooky from.

skirmish noun battle, fight, clash, conflict, engagement, combat, contest, tussle, scrimmage, fracas, melee, altercation; *inf.* set-to, scrap.

skirmish verb fight, engage, combat, clash, tussle.

skittish adjective highly strung, nervous, restive, jumpy, fidgety, excitable.

sky noun upper atmosphere, heaven, firmament, blue, blue yonder; *lit.* ether.

slab noun **1** *a slab of cheese* hunk, chunk, lump, slice, wedge. **2** *a slab of wood/stone* plank, block, lump.

slack adjective **1** *slack clothes* loose, baggy, hanging, flapping. **2** *slack muscles* relaxed, limp, flaccid, flabby. **3** *a slack rope* not taut, relaxed, flexible; pliant. **4** *business a bit slack* slow, quiet, sluggish. **5** *rather slack about punctuality* lax, negligent, remiss, neglectful, careless, inattentive, slipshod, sloppy, disorderly.

slack noun **1** *take up the slack of the rope* looseness, play; *inf.* give. **2** *no more slack left in personnel* surplus, excess, leeway.

slacker noun idler, shirker, loafer, dawdler, layabout, malingerer, gold brick.

slake verb *slake one's thirst/desire* satisfy, quench, assuage, relieve, gratify.

slander noun defamation, misrepresentation, calumny, libel, aspersion, vilification, muckraking.

slander verb defame, libel, malign, vilify, smear, slur, disparage.

slang noun **1** *use slang rather than formal language* colloquialism, informal language. **2** *cannot understand the technicians' slang* jargon, lingo, cant, argot.

slant verb **1** *the old floor slants* slope, tilt, be askew, lean, dip, list. **2** *accuse the newspaper of slanting the news* give a slant to, give a bias to, angle, distort.

slant noun **1** *the slant of the floor/picture* slope, tilt, dip, inclination. **2** *giving a political slant to the news* bias, leaning, prejudice, angle, distortion. **3** *require a woman's slant on the new product* angle, point of view, opinion, attitude.

slap noun *a slap on the back* smack, blow, whack, thump, cuff, spank; *inf.* wallop. **slap in the face** *giving the job to his assistant was a slap in the face* snub, insult, rebuff, humiliation, blow to one's pride.

slap verb **1** *slap him on the back* smack, strike, hit, whack, spank; *inf.* belt. **2** *slap the money (down) on the table* plunk, plop, slam, fling, throw. **3** *slap paint on* daub, plaster, spread.

slash verb **1** *slash the fencing dummy* cut, gash, lacerate, hack, slit, score, knife. **2** *slash prices* reduce, lower drastically, cut, drop, mark down.

slaughter verb **1** *slaughter animals for food* kill, butcher. **2** *slaughter the enemy soldiers* massacre, murder, butcher, put to the sword, slay, exterminate, annihilate. **3** *slaughter the opposition* defeat utterly, rout, trounce, thrash, vanquish, conquer, crush, overwhelm, give a drubbing to.

slaughter noun massacre, murder, butchery, extermination, annihilation; bloodshed, carnage.

slave noun **1** *the master and his slaves* bondsman, bondswoman, bondservant, serf, vassal. **2** *slaves in the kitchen* drudge, laborer, menial worker, servant; *lit.* scullion.

slave verb *slaving (away) at the stove* toil, drudge, slog, labor, grind.

slavery noun **1** *sold into slavery* enslavement, bondage, servitude, subjugation. **2** *working there is sheer slavery* drudgery, toil, hard labor, grind.

slavish adjective **1** *slavish admiration* servile, subservient, obsequious, sycophantic, deferential, groveling, fawning, abject. **2** *slavish imitation* unoriginal, uninspired, unimaginative.

slay verb *slay his enemy* kill, murder; slaughter, put to death, assassinate.

sleek adjective *sleek hair* smooth, glossy, shiny, lustrous, silky, satiny, burnished.

sleep verb *sleep for a few hours* be asleep, slumber, doze, nap; *inf.* snooze, crash, catch some Z's, have forty winks.

sleep noun *have a short sleep* slumber, doze, nap, rest, siesta; *inf.* snooze, forty winks, (bit of) shut-eye.

sleepy adjective **1** *feeling sleepy* drowsy, tired, somnolent, languid, languorous, lethargic, comatose. **2** *sleepy little villages* inactive, quiet, peaceful, slumberous.

slender adjective **1** *slender figures* slim, thin, slight, lean, svelte, willowy. **2** *a*

slender hope of success small, slight, slim, faint, remote, feeble, flimsy, tenuous, fragile.

slice noun *a slice of cake* piece, portion, segment, sliver, wedge.

slice verb *slice the cake/meat* cut, carve, divide, segment, sever, separate.

slick adjective **1** *a slick presentation* smooth, well-organized, streamlined, efficient, polished. **2** *a slick reply* smooth, glib, fluent, specious. **3** *a slick operator* smooth, skillful, deft, adroit, sharp, shrewd, suave, urbane, sophisticated, polished.

slide verb **1** *slide on the ice* slip, skid, slither, skate. **2** *drawers sliding in easily* slip, glide, slither. **let slide** *let the housework slide* neglect, forget, ignore, gloss over.

slight adjective **1** *a slight change* small, little, tiny, minute, imperceptible, subtle, modest. **2** *of slight importance* little, minor, unimportant, petty, insignificant, inconsequential, negligible, trivial, trifling, scant. **3** *a slight figure* slim, slender, spare, delicate, frail.

slight verb *slight him by not inviting him* snub, insult, rebuff, give the cold shoulder to, disregard, ignore, neglect, scorn.

slight noun *upset by the slight* snub, insult, affront, rebuff, cold shoulder, disregard, neglect, scorn, disdain; *inf.* a slap in the face.

slim adjective **1** *slim girls* slender, thin, slight, lean, svelte, willowy. **2** *slim hopes of success* slight, faint. See SLENDER 2.

slimy adjective **1** *slimy surfaces* sludgy, mucky, oozy, muddy, slippery, viscous. **2** *a slimy character* despicable, contemptible, vile, low, scurvy.

slink verb *slinking around dark corners* steal, sneak, creep, skulk, lurk.

slip[1] verb **1** *slip on the ice* skid, slither, lose one's footing. **2** *slip from her hands* fall, slide, drop. **3** *slip from the room unnoticed* steal, creep, sneak, slink. **4** *slip through the police net* escape, evade, dodge. **5** *the standard of the work slipped* drop, fall off, decline, deteriorate, degenerate. **let slip** *let slip the secret* let out, reveal, disclose, divulge, give away, leak. **slip on** *slip on a sweater* put on, pull on, don. **slip up** blunder, miscalculate, err; *inf.* screw up.

slip[2] noun *accused of making a slip* slipup, mistake, error, blunder, miscalculation, oversight; *inf.* booboo. **give the slip** *the pickpocket gave the policeman the slip* lose, evade, dodge, elude, shake off.

slip[3] noun **1** *written on a slip* of paper scrap, shred; sales slip, receipt. **2** *a slip from the plant* cutting, offshoot, scion, sprout, sprig.

slippery adjective **1** *slippery surfaces* smooth, slick, oily, icy, glassy. **2** *a slippery character* shifty, devious, duplicitous, cunning, foxy, tricky, sneaky, treacherous, unreliable.

slipshod adjective *slipshod methods* careless, slovenly, sloppy, slapdash, unsystematic.

slipup noun mistake, error, blunder. *See* SLIP².

slit verb *slit the material* cut, split open, slash, gash, rip, knife, lance.

slit noun *make a slit in the material* cut, gash, rip, incision, tear, split, rent, fissure, opening.

sliver noun chip, flake, splinter, shred, fragment, scrap.

slobber verb slaver, drool, dribble.

slogan noun motto, catchword, jingle, rallying cry, shibboleth.

slop verb *water slopping over* spill, splash, slosh, splatter.

slope verb drop away, slant, incline, lean, tilt, dip.

slope noun **1** *floors on a slope* slant, inclination, angle, tilt, dip, gradient. **2** *grassy slopes* hill, hillock, bank, rise.

sloppy adjective **1** *a sloppy mixture* wet, soggy, slushy, sludgy. **2** *sloppy work* careless, slapdash, slipshod, disorganized, unmethodical, untidy, messy, slovenly.

slot noun **1** *money in the slot* slit, crack, hole, opening, aperture, groove, notch. **2** *broadcast a show in the noon slot* place, position, niche, space, opening, time, period.

sloth noun laziness, indolence, idleness, sluggishness, lethargy, languor, torpor.

slothful adjective lazy, indolent, idle, sluggish, inactive, lethargic, languid, torpid.

slouch verb slump, hunch, stoop, droop.

slovenly adjective **1** *of slovenly appearance* slatternly, untidy, messy, unkempt, disheveled, tousled, rumpled. **2** *slovenly methods* careless, sloppy, slapdash, slipshod.

slow adjective **1** *at a slow pace* slow-moving, unhurried, leisurely, measured, deliberate, ponderous, creeping, sluggish, snail-like. **2** *he was incorrectly labeled as slow* backward, retarded, slow-witted, dull-witted, stupid, dense; *inf.* dumb. **3** *the service being a bit slow* delayed, dilatory, unpunctual, tardy. **4** *a slow process* long-drawn-out, time-consuming, protracted, prolonged. **5** *a slow part of the world* sleepy, unprogressive, backward, stagnant. **6** *business being slow* slack, quiet, sluggish, dead. **7** *slow to make a decision* reluctant, hesitant, loath, unwilling, disinclined.

slow verb **slow down 1** *slow down at the corner* reduce speed, decelerate, put the brakes on. **2** *weather slowed the runners down* hold back, keep back, delay, detain, restrain. **3** *workaholics told to slow down* take it easy, ease up, relax; *inf.* let up.

sluggish adjective **1** *feeling sluggish with a hangover* listless, lethargic, languid, languorous, torpid, phlegmatic. **2** *business being sluggish* slow, slack, inactive, stagnant.

slumber verb sleep, doze; *inf.* snooze; be in the land of Nod.

slumber noun sleep, doze; *inf.* snooze, shut-eye.

slump noun *a slump in sales* plunge, falling-off, drop, downturn, slide, decline, decrease, depreciation, depression.

slump verb **1** *slump into a chair* collapse, sink, fall. **2** *prices slumped* plummet, plunge, nosedive, fall, drop, slide, decline, decrease.

slur verb *slur his words* mumble, stammer, drawl.

slur noun **1** *slurs made against/on her character* insult, slight, aspersion, imputation, smear, stain, stigma. **2** *avoid all suggestion of a slur* insult, affront, defamation, slander, libel, calumny.

slut noun trollop, hussy, prostitute, harlot, whore, streetwalker; *inf.* floozy, hooker.

sly adjective **1** *a sly character* cunning, crafty, wily, foxy, conniving, scheming, devious, shrewd. **2** *in a sly manner* furtive, underhand, stealthy, surreptitious, covert, clandestine. **3** *a sly smile* roguish, impish, mischievous, playful, arch. **on the sly** *have another job on the sly* secretly, stealthily, surreptitiously, covertly, clandestinely.

smack noun **1** *a smack on the face* slap, blow, whack, cuff, punch, rap, bang; *inf.* wallop, clout, swipe. **2** *the object hit the car with a smack* thud, thump, bang.

smack verb *smack him on the back* slap, hit, strike, whack, thump; *inf.* wallop, belt.

smack adverb *run smack into the police* headlong, right, straight, directly, bang, plumb.

small adjective **1** *a small toy* little, tiny, wee, petite, slight, minute, miniature, minuscule, diminutive, undersized, puny; *inf.* pocket-size, pint-sized. **2** *a small mistake* slight, minor, unimportant, trifling, trivial, insignificant, inconsequential. **3** *from small beginnings* humble, modest, lowly, simple, unpretentious. **4** *a small mind* narrow-minded, mean, petty.

smart adjective **1** *wedding guests looking smart* well-dressed, well turned out, fashionable, stylish, elegant, chic, spruce, trim; *inf.* natty, spiffy. **2** *smart children* clever, bright, intelligent, gifted, sharp, quick-witted, shrewd, ingenious. **3** *at a smart pace* brisk, quick, fast, swift, lively, energetic, spirited, vigorous.

smart verb *eyes smarting with the smoke* sting, burn, bite.

smash verb **1** *smash the dishes* break, shatter, pulverize, splinter. **2** *smash the car* crash, demolish, wreck. **3** *smash their hopes* destroy, ruin, shatter, devastate.

smash noun *hear the smash of dishes* breaking, shattering, crashing.

smashing adjective *a smashing time at the fair* marvelous, magnificent, sensational, stupendous, superb, wonderful, excellent, first-rate; *inf.* terrific, fantastic, super, great, fabulous.

smattering noun *a smattering of French* bit, modicum, rudiments.

smear verb **1** *children smearing paint on the walls* spread, daub, slap, plaster. **2** *smear the windows* smudge, streak, blur. **3** *smear his reputation* sully, tarnish, blacken, taint, stain, slur, defame, defile, vilify, slander, libel, calumniate.

smear noun **1** *a smear of paint on the walls* daub, spot, splotch. **2** *smears on the windows* smudge, streak. **3** *the smears on their reputation* taint, stain, slur, blot.

smell verb **1** *smell something rotten* sniff, get a whiff of. **2** *drains smelling* stink, reek, be malodorous.

smell noun **1** *the smells of the countryside* odor, scent, whiff. **2** *the smell of new-mown hay* scent, aroma, perfume, fragrance, bouquet, redolence. **3** *what a smell from the drains!* stink, stench, reek.

smile verb grin, beam.

smirk verb leer, sneer, simper, grin.

smitten adjective *smitten with the pretty girl* taken with, infatuated with, enamored of, captivated by, enchanted by; *inf.* bowled over by, swept off one's feet by.

smog noun haze, fog, pollution.

smoke verb **1** *fires smoking* smolder, reek. **2** *smoke the salmon* cure, dry, preserve.

smoky adjective **1** *a smoky atmosphere* smoke-filled, hazy, smoggy, murky. **2** *smoky walls* grimy, sooty.

smolder verb **1** *fires smoldering* smoke, reek. **2** *smoldering with resentment* seethe, fume, burn, boil, simmer.

smooth adjective **1** *paint smooth surfaces* even, level, flat, plane, flush, unwrinkled. **2** *smooth hair/tabletops* glossy, shiny, sleek, silky, satiny, polished, burnished. **3** *smooth sea* calm, still, tranquil, glassy. **4** *smooth progress* easy, effortless, trouble-free. **5** *the smooth running of the machine* steady, regular, rhythmic, uninterrupted, fluid. **6** *smooth young men* suave, urbane, courteous, gracious, glib, slick.

smooth verb **1** *smooth the surface* level, even, flatten, plane, steamroll. **2** *smooth the troubled situation* ease, soothe, pacify, calm, alleviate, appease, palliate. **3** *smooth his promotion* ease, facilitate, pave the way for, expedite, assist, help along.

smother verb **1** *nearly smothered by the fumes* suffocate, stifle, asphyxiate. **2** *smother them with kindness* overwhelm, shower, inundate, envelop. **3** *smother a fire* extinguish, dampen, snuff out. **4** *smother a laugh* stifle, muffle, suppress. **5** *smother the steak in onions* cover with, pile with, heap with.

smudge noun *smudges on the walls* mark, spot, smear, streak, stain, blotch, blot.

smug adjective self-satisfied, complacent, pleased with oneself, conceited.

snack noun light meal, refreshments, bite, tidbit; *inf.* bite to eat.

snack verb eat between meals, nibble, munch; *inf.* graze.

snag noun **1** *discover a snag in our plans* catch, drawback, hitch, stumbling block, obstacle, complication. **2** *a snag in her tights* rip, tear, run.

snag verb *snag one's tights* catch, rip, tear.

snap verb **1** *the rod/rope snapped* break, fracture, splinter, separate, crack. **2** *suddenly snap after years of stress* have a nervous breakdown, collapse, lose one's mind, go mad. **3** *snap one's fingers | burning logs popping and snapping* crack, click, crackle. **4** *dogs snapping* bite, nip. **5** *snap into action* hurry, hasten, rush, race. **6** *snapping at the children* speak sharply, bark, lash out; *inf.* fly off the handle. **snap out of it** get over it, recover, perk up; *inf.* pull oneself together, get a grip on oneself. **snap up** *snap up the bargains* snatch at, take advantage of, grab, seize, grasp, pounce upon.

snap noun **1** *a snap of one's fingers | the snap of twigs beneath our feet* crack, click, crackle. **2** *with a snap of its teeth* bite, nip. **3** *a snap of cold weather* spell, period, stretch, interval.

snappy adjective *a snappy dresser* smart, fashionable, stylish, chic, modish, dapper; *inf.* natty, spiffy, trendy. **make it snappy** hurry up, be quick, look lively; *inf.* get a move on, step on it.

snare verb **1** *snare rabbits* trap, catch, net. **2** *snare a rich spouse* ensnare, trap, catch, capture.

snare noun **1** *rabbits caught in a snare* trap, springe, net, noose. **2** *unaware of the snares set by the opposition* trap, pitfall, danger, hazard, peril.

snarl[1] verb **1** *dogs snarling* show one's teeth, growl. **2** *snarling at everyone first thing in the morning* snap, lash out; *inf.* fly off the handle.

snarl[2] verb **1** *ropes getting snarled* tangle, entangle, entwine, twist, knot. **2** *snarl plans for reorganization* complicate, confuse, muddle; *inf.* mess up.

snatch verb **1** *snatch the last sandwich from the plate* seize, grab, pluck. **2** *snatch the tourist's wallet* grab, steal, make off with, appropriate; *inf.* nab, swipe. **3** *snatch the millionaire's child* kidnap, abduct. **4** *snatch victory toward the end of the game* pluck, wrest, seize, secure.

snatch noun **1** *at one snatch* grab, pluck, grip, clutch. **2** *snatches of the broadcast* fragment, snippet, bit, scrap, piece.

sneak verb **1** *sneak out of the lecture* steal, creep, slip, slink. **2** *hear people sneaking around outside* creep, skulk, lurk, prowl. **3** *sneak a quick look* snatch, take, catch.

sneer verb *sneering rather than smiling* smirk, snicker, snigger. **sneer at** *sneer at their unsuccessful attempts* scoff at, scorn, disdain, mock, jeer at, ridicule, deride, insult.

sneer noun **1** *give a sneer* smirk, snicker. **2** *endure the sneers of her enemies* jeer, jibe, taunt, insult, slight.

snicker verb snigger, smirk, titter, giggle.

sniff verb **1** *people with colds sniffing* snuffle, sniffle. **2** *sniff the aroma of fresh-baked bread* smell, get a whiff of.

sniff noun **1** *the sniffs of people with colds* snuffle, sniffle. **2** *take a sniff of the sea air* smell, scent, whiff.

snip verb **1** *snip the piece of cloth* cut, nick, slit, notch, incise. **2** *snip off a lock of hair* cut, clip, dock, trim, crop, prune.

snip noun **1** *cut it with one snip* cut, nick, slit, notch, incision. **2** *snips of cloth* scrap, cutting, bit, piece, fragment, remnant, tatter.

snobbish adjective arrogant, proud, condescending, haughty, disdainful, supercilious, patronizing; *inf.* snooty, stuck-up, hoity-toity.

snub verb *snub him in public* ignore, disregard, shun, rebuff, repulse, spurn, slight, give the cold shoulder to; *inf.* give the brush-off to, put down.

snub noun *embarrassed by the snub* rebuff, slight, insult, affront; *inf.* brush-off, put-down.

snug adjective **1** *a snug little house* cozy, comfortable, warm, sheltered; *inf.* comfy. **2** *a snug fit* close-fitting, tight.

snuggle verb nestle, cuddle, nuzzle.

soak verb **1** *soaked by the rain* drench, saturate. **2** *soak the soiled dress in soapy water* steep, immerse, souse. **3** *ink soaking through the paper* permeate, penetrate, infuse, imbue.

soar verb **1** *birds/planes soaring into the air* fly, take flight, ascend, climb, rise. **2** *prices soaring* rise/increase rapidly, spiral, climb.

sob verb weep, cry, blubber, snivel, howl, bawl.

sober adjective **1** *he was drunk but is now sober* abstemious, teetotal, abstinent, temperate, moderate; *inf.* on the wagon, dry. **2** *sober speakers* serious, solemn, thoughtful, grave, earnest, composed, sedate, staid, dignified. **3** *discuss sober matters* serious, solemn, grave, important, crucial, weighty, ponderous. **4** *a sober account* factual, dispassionate, objective, rational, logical, circumspect. **5** *wearing sober clothes/colors* dark, somber, quiet, restrained, severe, austere.

sociable adjective social, friendly, affable, cordial, neighborly, companionable, gregarious, convivial, genial.

social adjective **1** *social problems* civic, public, societal. **2** *social clubs* entertainment, recreational, amusement. **3** *not a very social person* friendly, affable, gregarious. *See* SOCIABLE.

society noun **1** *enemies of society* civilization, the general public, the people, the community. **2** *urban and rural societies* community, culture, civilization. **3** *marry into society* high society, polite society, the aristocracy, the gentry, the upper classes, the elite; *inf.* the upper crust. **4** *enjoy the society of friends* company, companionship, fellowship, camaraderie. **5** *join a society* association, club, group, circle, fraternity, brotherhood, sisterhood, league, union, alliance, federation.

sodden adjective **1** *sodden clothes* soaking wet, drenched, saturated, sopping, dripping. **2** *sodden ground* saturated, soggy, boggy, swampy, waterlogged.

soft adjective **1** *soft ground* spongy, swampy, boggy, miry. **2** *pieces of a soft substance* pliable, supple, elastic, flexible, malleable. **3** *the soft surface of the curtains* smooth, velvety, cushiony, downy, silky, satiny; *inf.* like a baby's bottom. **4** *soft winds blowing* gentle, light, mild, calm, balmy, delicate. **5** *soft lights* low, faint, dim, subdued, muted, mellow. **6** *soft colors* pale, light, pastel, subdued, muted, understated. **7** *he spoke in soft tones* hushed, whispered, murmured, low, faint, quiet, mellow, melodious, mellifluous. **8** *soft words* sympathetic, kind, gentle, soothing, tender, affectionate, warm, sweet. **9** *teachers too soft with the students* easygoing, tolerant, lenient, indulgent, permissive, liberal, lax. **10** *too soft to be a good leader* tenderhearted, sensitive; spineless, feeble. **11** *soft muscles* flabby, flaccid, limp. **12** *lead a soft life* easy, comfortable; pampered,

409

indulged; *inf.* cushy. **13** *soft in the head* feebleminded, simple, silly; *inf.* daft.

soften verb **1** *soften the blow* ease, cushion, temper, mitigate, assuage. **2** *the winds softened* abate, moderate, lessen, diminish, calm down. **3** *they softened their harsh approach* moderate, temper, tone down.

soggy adjective wet, saturated, sodden, boggy, swampy, waterlogged.

soil noun **1** *plant in light soil* earth, ground, dirt. **2** *on American soil* land, country, terra firma.

soil verb **1** *soil her white gloves* dirty, stain, muddy, spot, smudge. **2** *soil his reputation* sully, stain, taint, blot, smear.

sojourn noun stay, visit, stop, stopover; holiday, vacation.

solace noun *bring solace to the bereaved* comfort, consolation, condolence.

soldier noun fighter, warrior, trooper; *inf.* cannon fodder.

solemn adjective **1** *a solemn occasion* serious, grave, profound; formal. **2** *a solemn procession* dignified, ceremonious, stately, majestic. **3** *a solemn child* serious, somber, unsmiling; pensive, thoughtful. **4** *a solemn promise* earnest, sincere, heartfelt.

solicit verb **1** *solicit information* ask for, request, seek, beg, plead for. **2** *solicit him for financial help* ask, beg, beseech, implore, entreat, petition, importune, supplicate.

solicitous adjective *solicitous about your health* concerned, caring, attentive, anxious.

solid adjective **1** *a solid rather than liquid substance* firm, hard, dense, compressed. **2** *made of solid silver* pure, unalloyed, unadulterated, genuine. **3** *solid houses* sound, substantial, strong, sturdy, durable, well-built, stable. **4** *solid arguments* sound, well-founded, valid, logical, cogent, authoritative, convincing, plausible. **5** *a solid friendship* reliable, dependable, trustworthy, stable, steadfast. **6** *solid citizens* sensible, decent, law-abiding, upright. **7** *a solid company* financially sound, solvent, creditworthy, secure. **8** *a solid line of people* continuous, uninterrupted, unbroken, undivided. **9** *solid political support* unanimous, united, undivided.

solidarity noun *the solidarity of the workers* unity, unanimity, like-mindedness, team spirit, camaraderie, harmony, esprit de corps.

solitary adjective **1** *forced to lead a solitary life* reclusive, cloistered, lonely, companionless, friendless, antisocial, hermitical. **2** *seek a solitary spot for a honeymoon* lonely, remote, out-of-the-way, isolated, secluded, hidden, private, unfrequented, sequestered. **3** *a solitary tree on the horizon* lone, single, sole.

solitude noun loneliness, remoteness, isolation, seclusion, privacy.

solution noun **1** *the solution to the mathematical problem* answer, result, key, resolution. **2** *the solution of the problem will take years* solving, resolving, explanation, clarification, elucidation, unraveling. **3** *a solution of brine* suspension, emulsion, mixture, mix, blend, compound.

solve verb *solve the problem* answer, resolve, work out, figure out, fathom, decipher, clear up, unravel; *inf.* crack.

solvent adjective financially sound, debt-free, creditworthy; *inf.* in the black.

somber adjective **1** *dress in somber clothes* dark, dull, drab. **2** *in a somber mood* | *a somber expression* gloomy, depressed, sad, melancholy, doleful, mournful, joyless, cheerless, lugubrious, funereal.

sometimes adverb *we see her sometimes* occasionally, on occasion, now and then, from time to time, once in a while, every so often, off and on.

song noun **1** *a beautiful song* tune, air, melody; ballad, ditty, chorus, chantey, carol, canticle. **2** *the song of the birds* warble, chirp, trill, whistle, pipe.

sonorous adjective **1** *the sonorous tones of the minister* deep, rich, full, round, resonant, ringing. **2** *a sonorous style of prose* majestic, lofty, grandiloquent, orotund.

soon adverb **1** *be there soon* shortly, in a little while, before long, in a moment, any minute, in the twinkling of an eye; *inf.* before you know it, before you can say Jack Robinson, pronto, in two shakes of a lamb's tale. **2** *How soon can you get here?* quickly, promptly, speedily.

soothe verb **1** *soothe the baby* quiet, calm, pacify, settle down, hush, lull, mollify. **2** *soothe the pain* ease, assuage, alleviate, allay, mitigate, palliate, lessen, reduce.

soothsayer noun seer, augur, prophet, diviner, sibyl.

sophisticated adjective **1** *sophisticated people* worldly, suave, urbane, cultured, refined, elegant, cosmopolitan. **2** *sophisticated production techniques* advanced, highly developed, ultramodern, complex, elaborate, intricate.

soporific adjective *soporific drugs* sleep-inducing, somnolent, sedative, tranquilizing, narcotic, opiate, somniferous.

sorcery noun black magic, magic, witchcraft, wizardry, necromancy, thaumaturgy.

sordid adjective **1** *a sordid creature* vile, foul, base, low, degenerate, despicable, ignoble. **2** *sordid moneylenders* mean, greedy, avaricious, mercenary. **3** *sordid hovels* filthy, dirty, foul, squalid, shabby, seedy, slummy.

sore adjective 1 *a sore leg* painful, aching, hurting, tender, inflamed, raw, irritated, bruised, injured. 2 *feel sore at her distressed*, upset, resentful, vexed, aggrieved, offended, hurt, annoyed, angry, irritated, irked, nettled; *inf.* peeved. 3 *in sore need of some food* dire, urgent, pressing, desperate, critical, acute, extreme.

sore noun *a sore on his leg* wound, scrape, abrasion, cut, laceration, abscess.

sorrow noun 1 *the sorrow of the widow* sadness, unhappiness, grief, misery, distress, heartache, anguish, suffering, wretchedness. 2 *one of the great sorrows of his life* worry, woe, misfortune, affliction, trial, tribulation.

sorrowful adjective *sorrowful expressions* sad, unhappy, tearful, woebegone, dejected, mournful, doleful, melancholy.

sorry adjective 1 *sorry for his actions* regretful, apologetic, repentant, penitent, remorseful, contrite, ashamed. 2 *feel sorry for them* sympathetic, full of pity, compassionate, moved, empathetic. 3 *sorry to hear about his accident* sad, unhappy, distressed, grieved, regretful. 4 *a sorry sight* wretched, miserable, pitiful, piteous, pathetic.

sort noun 1 *a different sort of plant/car* kind, type, variety, class, category, style, set, genre, genus, family, order, breed, make, brand. 2 *a good sort* person, individual, soul; *inf.* fellow, chap, guy. **out of sorts** 1 *having been out of sorts with a bad cold* unwell, sick, ill, indisposed; *inf.* under the weather. 2 *avoid him when he is out of sorts* in a bad mood, ill-tempered, irritable, cross, testy, crotchety, grumpy, snappish. 3 *out of sorts after her broken engagement* in low spirits, dejected, depressed, downcast, glum, melancholy, miserable; *inf.* down.

sort verb *sort the potatoes according to size* classify, class, categorize, grade, group, divide, arrange, order, organize. **sort out** 1 *sort out the weaker plants and dispose of them* separate out, segregate, sift, pick out, select. 2 *sort out the problem/mess* clear up, put right, solve, tidy up, put in order.

so-so adjective mediocre, average, indifferent, unexceptional, undistinguished, uninspiring, tolerable, passable.

soul noun 1 *the soul as opposed to the body* spirit, psyche, inner self, vital force. 2 *the soul of discretion* personification, embodiment, incarnation, essence, epitome. 3 *not a soul in sight* person, human being, individual, creature. 4 *the life and soul of the party* essence, heart, core, driving force. 5 *performed without soul* feeling, emotion, intensity, fervor, ardor, vitality, animation, energy, inspiration.

sound noun 1 *not a sound was heard* noise. 2 *she made not a sound* utterance, cry. 3 *the sound of the flute* noise, music, note, chord. 4 *they do not like the sound of her plans* impression, idea, tone, tenor. 5 *within sound of the church bells* hearing, distance, earshot, range.

sound verb 1 *sound the trumpet* play, blow. 2 *the trumpet sounded* resound, reverberate, resonate. 3 *sound the alarm* operate, set off, ring. 4 *sound the letter "f" or "t"* pronounce, utter, voice, enunciate, articulate, vocalize. 5 *sound a word of warning* utter, express, voice, pronounce, declare, announce.

sound adjective 1 *sound lungs* healthy, in good condition, physically fit, disease-free, undamaged, uninjured, in fine fettle. 2 *sound rafters in the building* solid, substantial, sturdy, well-constructed, intact. 3 *sound arguments* solid, well-founded, well-grounded, valid, reasonable, logical, cogent, authoritative, convincing, plausible. 4 *a sound judge of character* reliable, dependable, trustworthy, good, sensible, judicious, astute. 5 *sound business* solvent, creditworthy, solid, secure. 6 *a sound sleep* deep, undisturbed, untroubled. 7 *a sound thrashing* thorough, complete, out-and-out, severe.

sour adjective 1 *sour substances* tart, bitter, acid, acidulous, sharp, vinegary, pungent. 2 *sour milk* turned, curdled, fermented, rancid, bad. 3 *a sour old man* embittered, nasty, unpleasant, disagreeable, bad-tempered, irritable, crotchety, cross, peevish, grumpy; *inf.* grouchy.

sour verb *people soured by his treatment of them* embitter, disenchant, alienate; *inf.* turn off.

source noun 1 *the source of the river* wellspring, fountainhead, headwater. 2 *the source of the rumor* origin, derivation, cause, wellspring, fountainhead, provenance, originator. 3 *sources listed in the essay* reference, authority.

souvenir noun memento, keepsake, token, reminder, relic, memorabilia.

sovereign noun ruler, monarch, king, queen, emperor, empress, tsar, crowned head, potentate.

sovereign adjective 1 *sovereign power* supreme, absolute, unlimited. 2 *the children are her sovereign concern* chief, paramount, predominant, ruling. 3 *a sovereign state* independent, self-governing, autonomous. 4 *our sovereign lord* ruling, royal, regal, majestic, noble.

sovereignty noun 1 *hold sovereignty over adjoining states* supremacy, dominion, power, ascendancy, jurisdiction, control, sway. 2 *an island sovereignty* kingdom, realm, country.

sow verb 1 *sow seed* scatter, disperse, strew, disseminate, distribute, spread. 2 *sow a field with wheat* plant. 3 *sow doubt in their minds* implant, plant, lodge, instigate, foster.

space noun 1 *houses taking up a lot of space | not enough space for them all* room, expanse, capacity, area, volume, spaciousness, scope, elbowroom, leeway. 2 *a large space between houses* interval, gap, opening. 3 *write your name in the space provided* blank, gap. 4 *no spaces left in the theater* seat, place, berth, accommodation. 5 *green spaces at the edge of the city* expanse, stretch. 6 *within the space of three hours* time, duration, period, span, stretch, interval. 7 *staring into space* the blue, the vacuum, the void. 8 *travel in space* outer space, the universe, the galaxy, the solar system; infinity.

space verb 1 *space the trees around the garden* place at intervals, arrange, order. 2 *space out the plans* interspace, set apart.

spacious adjective *a spacious house | spacious grounds* roomy, commodious, capacious, sizable, large, ample, extensive, broad, wide, expansive.

span noun 1 *the span of the bird's wings* length, extent, reach, stretch, spread, distance. 2 *within a short span of time* duration, period, space, stretch, interval.

span verb 1 *a life spanning almost a century* extend over, stretch across, cover, range over. 2 *bridges spanning the Hudson* bridge, cross, traverse.

spank verb smack, slap, put over one's knee; *inf.* tan someone's hide, belt.

spare adjective 1 *a spare blanket* extra, additional, reserve, supplementary, auxiliary, surplus, supernumerary. 2 *have little spare time* free, leisure, unoccupied. 3 *of spare build* lean, thin, slim, slender, skinny, wiry, lank; *inf.* skin and bones. 4 *a spare helping* meager, frugal, scanty, skimpy, modest. **to spare** *a few plants to spare* left over, superfluous, surplus.

spare verb 1 *can you spare a few dollars?* afford, part with, give, provide, relinquish. 2 *spare the culprit* pardon, show mercy to, be lenient to; *inf.* let off. 3 *spare the tree from destruction* save, protect, guard, defend.

sparing adjective *be sparing with money* economical, frugal, thrifty, careful, prudent, cautious, parsimonious, niggardly; *inf.* stingy, tight-fisted.

sparkle verb 1 *lights/diamonds sparkling* twinkle, flicker, shimmer, flash, glitter, glint, wink, dance, shine, gleam, coruscate. 2 *people sparkling at the party* be vivacious, be animated, be effervescent, be witty. 3 *wine sparkling* bubble, effervesce.

sparkle noun 1 *the sparkle of lights on the river* twinkle, flicker, shimmer, flash, glitter, glint, winking, dancing, gleam, coruscation. 2 *require employees with some sparkle* vivacity, liveliness, animation, vitality, enthusiasm, dash, élan, panache; *inf.* pizzazz, zip, zing.

sparse adjective scanty, meager, slight, scattered.

spartan adjective *a spartan life* austere, harsh, stringent, rigorous, strict, severe, ascetic, abstemious.

spasm noun 1 *stomach spasms* contraction, convulsion, cramp, twitch. 2 *a spasm of coughing/laughter* fit, paroxysm, attack, bout, seizure, outburst.

spasmodic adjective intermittent, fitful, irregular, sporadic, periodic, recurrent.

speak verb 1 *speak the truth* utter, voice, express, say, pronounce, articulate, enunciate, state, tell. 2 *the lecturer spoke for two hours* talk, lecture, hold forth, discourse, orate. 3 *speak volumes with her eyes* convey, impart, suggest, communicate, express. **speak for** 1 *a lawyer speaking for the accused* represent, act on behalf of, intercede for. 2 *speak for the motion* support, uphold, defend, advocate. **speak of** *speak of his faults* talk about, discuss, mention, refer to, allude to, comment on. **speak out/up** 1 *speak up to be heard in the crowd* raise one's voice, make oneself heard. 2 *speak out against the cruelty* speak one's mind, sound off. **speak to** 1 *she spoke to him angrily* address, talk to, converse with, have a word with. 2 *speak to the insubordinates* reprimand, rebuke, scold, lecture, admonish; *inf.* tell off. 3 *speak to the motion* comment on, touch upon, remark on.

speaker noun *an accomplished speaker* speech-maker, lecturer, orator, demagogue.

spearhead noun *the spearhead of the opposition* vanguard, forefront, driving force.

spearhead verb *spearhead the opposition* lead, head, initiate, launch, pioneer.

special adjective 1 *have a special talent* exceptional, remarkable, unusual, rare, extraordinary, singular, outstanding, unique. 2 *words with a special meaning* particular, individual, distinctive. 3 *take special care of it* especial, particular, exceptional. 4 *a special occasion* significant, momentous, memorable, festive, gala, red-letter. 5 *a special tool* specific, particular, custom-built. 6 *his special interest* particular, chief, main, major, primary.

specialist noun *a specialist in electronics* expert, authority, professional, consultant.

specialty noun 1 *many specialties in the field of medicine* area of specialization, field of study. **2** *putting people at ease is her specialty* forte, métier, talent, gift, claim to fame.

species noun *a species of plant* sort, kind, type, variety, class, category, genus, breed, genre.

specific adjective **1** *give very specific instructions* well-defined, clear-cut, unambiguous, unequivocal, exact, precise, explicit, express, detailed. **2** *for a specific purpose* particular, specified, fixed, set, distinct, definite.

specify verb *specify your housing requirements* state, name, stipulate, define, itemize, detail, list, spell out, enumerate.

specimen noun sample, representative, example, illustration, instance, exhibit.

speck noun **1** *specks of soot on the curtains* spot, fleck, stain, mark, smudge. **2** *not a speck of food left* particle, bit, atom, iota, grain, trace.

speckled adjective *speckled eggs/horses* mottled, flecked, spotted, dotted, dappled, brindled.

spectacle noun **1** *the spectacle of snow-capped mountains* sight, vision, scene, picture. **2** *the circus act was quite a spectacle* display, show, exhibition, extravaganza. **3** *making a spectacle of himself* laughingstock, fool, curiosity.

spectacular adjective striking, impressive, magnificent, splendid, breathtaking, glorious, dazzling, sensational, stunning, outstanding, extraordinary, dramatic, astonishing, singular.

spectator noun watcher, viewer, observer, onlooker, witness, bystander.

specter noun apparition, ghost, phantom, spirit, vision; *inf.* spook.

speculate verb **1** *speculate that he left unwillingly* conjecture, theorize, hypothesize, guess, surmise. **2** *speculate on their future* muse, reflect, deliberate, consider. **3** *speculate on the stock market* gamble, take a risk, venture.

speech noun **1** *express opinions in speech* communication, conversation, discussion, dialogue, colloquy. **2** *slurred speech* diction, articulation, enunciation, pronunciation. **3** *give an after-dinner speech* talk, lecture, address, discourse, oration, sermon, harangue. **4** *the speech of the Deep South* language, tongue, idiom, dialect, parlance; *inf.* lingo. **5** *given to obscene speech* utterance, remarks, comments.

speechless adjective **1** *speechless with rage* dumbstruck, dumbfounded. **2** *speechless with modesty* tongue-tied, inarticulate, dumb. **3** *speechless disappointment* silent, unspoken, tacit.

speed noun rapidity, swiftness, quickness, haste, expeditiousness, expedition, alacrity, celerity, velocity.

speed verb **1** *commuters speeding homeward* hurry, hasten, rush, race, dash, sprint, scurry, charge; *inf.* tear. **2** *speed their recovery* expedite, hasten, hurry up, accelerate, advance, facilitate, boost. **speed up 1** *need to speed up to win the race* hurry up, rush, accelerate; *inf.* step on it. **2** *speed up the process* expedite, hasten. *See* SPEED verb 2.

speedy adjective **1** *a speedy form of transport | a speedy reply* rapid, swift, quick, fast, expeditious, fleet; prompt, immediate.

spell[1] noun **1** *recite a spell* incantation, conjuration, charm. **2** *put under a spell* trance, state of enchantment, enthrallment. **3** *fall under his spell* allure, charm, attraction, beguilement.

spell[2] noun **1** *a spell of warm weather* time, period, interval, stretch, span, patch. **2** *a spell of coughing* bout, fit. **3** *do a spell at the wheel* turn, stint, term, shift.

spellbound adjective riveted, entranced, enthralled, enraptured, rapt, bewitched, fascinated, captivated, mesmerized, hypnotized.

spend verb **1** *spend a great deal of money on clothes* pay out, lay out, expend, disburse; *inf.* fork out, shell out. **2** *spend hours on the task* occupy, fill, pass. **3** *spend a lot of effort* employ, apply, devote. **4** *soldiers having spent all their ammunition* use up, consume, exhaust, finish off, deplete.

spendthrift noun squanderer, prodigal, profligate, wastrel; *inf.* big spender.

spendthrift adjective *spendthrift habits* extravagant, prodigal, profligate, wasteful, improvident.

spent adjective **1** *a spent force* used up, consumed, exhausted, finished, depleted, drained; *inf.* played-out, burnt-out. **2** *feeling spent after the long walk* exhausted, worn-out, tired-out, fatigued, weary; *inf.* done in, bushed.

spew verb *lava spewing from the volcano* gush, pour, spurt, issue, discharge, spout.

sphere noun **1** *ornaments in the shape of spheres* globe, ball, orb, globule. **2** *spheres in the sky* planet, star, moon, celestial body. **3** *a limited sphere of influence* area, field, range, scope, extent, compass, jurisdiction. **4** *in the sphere of economics* field, discipline, specialty, domain, realm, province.

spice noun **1** *add spices to food* flavoring, seasoning, herb, condiment. **2** *add a bit of spice to food* flavor, piquancy, pungency, relish, tang, bite, zest, savor; *inf.* punch, kick. **3** *add spice to life* excitement, interest, color, zest, gusto, pep; *inf.* zip, zing.

spicy adjective **1** *spicy sauces* well-seasoned, sharp, tart, hot, peppery, piquant, pungent. **2** *spicy stories about her colleagues* lively, spirited, suggestive, risqué, racy, off-color; *inf.* raunchy.

spill verb **1** *milk spilling from the jug* pour, flow, overflow, brim over, slop. **2** *spill the scandalous details* reveal, disclose, divulge, leak; *inf.* blab.

spin verb **1** *wheels spinning* revolve, rotate, turn, circle, whirl, gyrate. **2** *spin around to face him* wheel, whirl, twirl, turn, twist, swivel, pirouette. **3** *spin a yarn about his successes* tell, relate, narrate, recount, concoct, invent, fabricate. **4** *her head was spinning* whirl, reel, swim. **spin out** *have to spin out his lecture* protract, draw out, drag out, prolong, extend, pad out. ·

spin noun **1** *a spin of the coin* turn, revolution, rotation, whirl, gyration. **2** *a spin in the car* drive, ride, trip, run, jaunt, journey, outing, turn; *inf.* joyride.

spine noun **1** *injure his spine* spinal column, vertebrae, vertebral column, backbone, dorsum. **2** *a weak man lacking spine* mettle, grit, pluck, determination, resolution, fortitude, courage, bravery, valor.

spineless adjective weak, feeble, indecisive, cowardly, timorous, timid, lily-livered; *inf.* chicken, yellow, yellow-bellied, gutless.

spiral adjective *spiral staircases* coiled, corkscrew, winding, twisting, whorled, helical, cochlear.

spiral noun *a spiral of smoke* coil, twist, whorl, corkscrew, curlicue, helix.

spire noun **1** *a church spire* steeple, belfry. **2** *mountain spires* peak, pinnacle, crest.

spirit noun **1** *a healthy body but a troubled spirit* soul, psyche, inner self, ego. **2** *the spirit of nature* vital spark, life force. **3** *haunted by spirits* apparition, ghost, phantom, specter, wraith; *inf.* spook. **4** *take the criticism in the wrong spirit* attitude, way, mood, frame of mind, humor. **5** *the spirit of the age* ethos, essence, quintessence, embodiment, quiddity. **6** *lack the spirit to carry out the task* courage, mettle, pluck, grit, willpower, motivation, backbone, stoutheartedness, vigor, energy, determination, resoluteness; *inf.* guts, spunk. **7** *play the song with spirit* animation, liveliness, vivacity, enthusiasm, fervor, fire, passion, energy, verve, zest, dash, élan; *inf.* pizzazz, zing, zip. **8** *the spirit of the new rule* implication, essence, gist, tenor, drift, meaning, sense, purport. **spirit away** *spirit away the celebrity from the photographers* whisk away, carry off, make off with, snatch, seize.

spirited adjective **1** *put up a spirited defense* courageous, brave, valiant, valorous, heroic, plucky, gritty. **2** *a spirited playing of the song* animated, lively, vivacious, enthusiastic, fiery, passionate, energetic.

spiritual adjective **1** *spiritual needs* incorporeal, ethereal, intangible, otherworldly, unworldly. **2** *spiritual music* religious, sacred, divine, holy, ecclesiastic, devotional.

spit verb **1** *not allowed to spit in public* expectorate, hawk. **2** *spit blood* discharge, issue, eject. **3** *"get out," he spat* hiss, rasp, snort.

spit noun spittle, saliva, sputum.

spite noun *say it out of spite* malice, illwill, malevolence, malignance, hostility, resentment, rancor, envy, hatred, vengefulness, vindictiveness. **in spite of** *happy in spite of being poor* despite, notwithstanding, regardless of.

spite verb *do it to spite her sister* annoy, harass, irritate, vex, provoke, peeve, pique, frustrate.

spiteful adjective malicious, malevolent, venomous, hostile, resentful, snide, rancorous, vengeful, vindictive, splenetic.

splash verb **1** *splash water/paint around* spatter, sprinkle, spray, shower, splatter, slosh, slop. **2** *waves splashing against the rocks* dash, beat, batter, buffet, break, wash, surge. **3** *children splashing about in water* paddle, wade, wallow, dabble. **4** *his name splashed across the newspapers* blazon, exhibit, plaster, broadcast, trumpet.

splash noun **1** *the splash of water against the rocks* dashing, beating, battering. **2** *splashes of mud on the walls* spot, splotch, smudge, smear. **3** *the scandal made a front-page splash* display, exhibition, sensation. **4** *a splash of color* patch, burst, streak. **make a splash** cause a sensation, cause a stir, attract attention.

spleen noun *vent one's spleen on the innocent* bad temper, ill-humor, irritability, irascibility, peevishness, cantankerousness, resentment, spitefulness, bitterness, hostility, rancor, maliciousness, malevolence, bile.

splendid adjective **1** *splendid furnishings* magnificent, imposing, superb, grand, sumptuous, resplendent, opulent, luxurious, gorgeous, elegant. **2** *a splendid reputation* distinguished, impressive, illustrious, brilliant, notable, outstanding, eminent, celebrated, venerable. **3** *splendid colors* glorious, brilliant, gleaming, radiant, dazzling, refulgent. **4** *a splendid meal* excellent, fine, first-rate, marvelous, wonderful; *inf.* fantastic, terrific, fabulous.

splendor noun **1** *the splendor of the furnishings* magnificence, grandeur, sumptuousness, opulence, luxury, luxuriousness, elegance. **2** *the splendor of his reputation* illustriousness, brilliance, eminence, renown. **3** *the splendor of the colors* gloriousness, brilliance, radiance.

splinter noun *splinters of wood* sliver, fragment, shiver, shard, chip, shaving, shred, bit.

splinter verb *the glass splintered* break into fragments, shatter, shiver, fracture.

split verb **1** *split the material in two* break, chop, cut, hew, cleave, rip, tear, slash, snap, rive. **2** *split the party in two* divide, separate, sever, sunder, bisect, partition. **3** *split the profits* share, divide, halve, apportion, distribute, parcel out, allocate; *inf.* divvy. **4** *the road splits over the hill* divide, fork, bifurcate. **5** *her husband split* leave, depart, take off, decamp, exit; *inf.* push off, shove off. **split up** *the couple split up* break up, separate, part, part company, become estranged, divorce.

split noun **1** *a split in the material* break, cut, rent, rip, tear, slash, slit, crack, fissure, breach. **2** *a split in the political party* division, rift, schism, rupture, separation.

spoil verb **1** *spoil the material by washing it* damage, disfigure, injure, harm, ruin, destroy. **2** *spoil our plans* upset, mess up, ruin, destroy, wreck. **3** *spoil her little boy* pamper, overindulge, mollycoddle, cosset, coddle, baby, spoonfeed. **4** *the food will spoil* go bad, turn, rot, become tainted, decompose, decay.

spoils plural noun **1** *the spoils of high rank* benefit, advantage, gain, profit. **2** *divide up the spoils from the burglary* booty, loot, plunder, pickings.

spoken adjective oral, verbal, voiced, expressed, unwritten.

spokesman noun spokeswoman, spokesperson, mouthpiece, voice, negotiator, mediator, representative.

sponsor noun *a sponsor of the new art gallery* patron, backer, promoter, guarantor, supporter; *inf.* angel.

sponsor verb *companies sponsoring the softball teams* back, fund, finance, promote, subsidize, support.

spontaneous adjective **1** *spontaneous offers of help* voluntary, unforced, unconstrained. **2** *a spontaneous vote of thanks* unplanned, unpremeditated, unrehearsed, impromptu, extempore, spur-of-the-moment, extemporaneous. **3** *a spontaneous smile* instinctive, involuntary, automatic, impulsive.

sporadic adjective irregular, intermittent, scattered, occasional.

sport noun **1** *play a variety of sports* physical activity, game, physical exercise, recreation, pastime, athletics. **2** *flying kites for sport* amusement, entertainment, diversion, play, fun, pleasure, enjoyment. **make sport of** make fun of, laugh at, poke fun at, mock, jeer at, ridicule.

sporting adjective *a sporting gesture* sportsmanlike, fair, honorable, generous.

spot noun **1** *black spots on the cloth* mark, dot, speck, fleck, smudge, stain, blotch, splotch, patch. **2** *a spot on her face* pimple, blemish, pustule, boil, pock. **3** *a dark spot on her reputation* stain, blemish, flaw, brand, stigma. **4** *a picnic spot* area, place, site, location, scene, setting, situation. **5** *a regular spot on the program* place, position, niche. **6** *in a spot* difficulty, mess, plight, predicament, quandary, tight corner; *inf.* fix, jam.

spot verb **1** *spot someone following him* catch sight of, notice, observe, espy, discern, detect. **2** *the mud spotted her dress* mark, stain, dirty, soil, spatter.

spotless adjective **1** *spotless houses* clean, ultraclean, spick-and-span, immaculate, shining, gleaming. **2** *of spotless character* pure, flawless, faultless, unsullied, untainted, unimpeachable.

spotted adjective **1** *a spotted dog/horse* dappled, mottled, pied, piebald, speckled. **2** *a spotted dress* polka-dot, flecked.

spout verb **1** *oil spouting from the well* spurt, gush, spew, squirt, erupt, disgorge, pour, spray. **2** *tired of politicians spouting* declaim, orate, rant, harangue, speechify, sermonize.

sprawl verb **1** *people sprawling on the sofa* stretch out, lounge, repose, recline, flop, loll. **2** *suburbs sprawling out into the countryside* spread, stretch, spill, ramble.

spray noun **1** *a spray from the sea* shower, jet, mist, drizzle, foam, froth. **2** *buy a deodorant spray* atomizer, vaporizer, aerosol.

spray verb disperse, disseminate, sprinkle, shower.

spread verb **1** *spread the map out* stretch, extend, unfurl, unroll. **2** *the town is spreading out* stretch out, extend, enlarge, widen, grow, develop, branch out. **3** *the view spread out before them* stretch out, unfold, be unveiled, be revealed. **4** *spread manure on the fields* lay, put, apply, smear; *inf.* plaster. **5** *spread the bread with butter* cover, coat, layer. **6** *the disease is spreading* mushroom, extend, advance, proliferate, escalate. **7** *spread rumors* disseminate, circulate, transmit, broadcast, publicize, propagate, promulgate, bruit.

spread noun **1** *measure the spread of the bird's wings* extent, stretch, span, reach, compass, sweep. **2** *the spread of the disease* advance, expansion, proliferation, escalation, diffusion. **3** *the spread of rumors* dissemination, circulation, transmission, broadcasting, publicizing, propagation. **4** *a birthday spread* feast, banquet, repast.

spree noun outing, fling, revel, orgy, debauch, bacchanal; *inf.* binge.

sprightly adjective spry, lively, energetic, agile, nimble, spirited, brisk, jaunty, perky.

spring verb **1** *springing to his feet* jump, leap, bound, vault, hop. **2** *her family springs from a relative of James Madison* descend, originate, derive, issue. **3** *disapproval springs from ignorance* originate, derive, stem, arise, emanate, proceed, start. **4** *spring his resignation on them* present unexpectedly, introduce suddenly. **spring back** *the branch sprang back* rebound, recoil. **spring up** *new houses springing up everywhere* appear, shoot up, mushroom, burgeon, crop up; *inf.* pop up.

spring noun **1** *reach her in one spring* jump, leap, bound, vault. **2** *a mattress with little spring* springiness, bounce, elasticity, resilience, flexibility, stretch, recoil, tensility. **3** *put a spring in his step* bounce, buoyancy, liveliness, lightheartedness.

sprinkle verb **1** *sprinkle water on the grass* spray, shower, splash, trickle, spatter. **2** *sprinkle salt on the icy steps* scatter, strew. **3** *sprinkle the cake with powdered sugar* dust, powder.

sprinkling noun **1** *a sprinkling of snow on the ground* scattering, dusting. **2** *only a sprinkling of people in the audience* handful, trickle.

sprint verb *sprinting for the bus* run, race, rush, dash; *inf.* scoot, tear.

sprout verb **1** *deer sprouting antlers* send forth, grow, develop. **2** *potatoes sprouting* bud, germinate. **3** *weeds sprouting up everywhere* shoot up, spring up, grow, develop, appear, mushroom, proliferate.

spry adjective sprightly, lively, energetic, active, agile, nimble, quick.

spunk noun courage, bravery, valor, pluck, mettle, daring, spirit, backbone; *inf.* guts.

spur noun **1** *the use of spurs to speed up the animals* goad, prick, prod. **2** *act as a spur to his ambition* stimulus, incentive, encouragement, impetus. **on the spur of the moment** impulsively, on impulse, impetuously, suddenly, unexpectedly, out of the blue.

spur verb **1** *spur the animal to go faster* goad, prick, prod. **2** *his early success spurred him on to try hard* stimulate, induce, encourage, motivate, prompt, urge, impel.

spurious adjective counterfeit, fraudulent, fake, bogus, sham, contrived, fictitious, deceitful, specious; *inf.* phony.

spurn verb reject, repulse, rebuff, repudiate, snub, slight, disdain, scorn.

spurt verb *oil spurting from the well* gush, squirt, shoot, surge, pour, stream, flow, issue, emanate.

spurt noun **1** *a spurt of water* gush, jet, spray. **2** *a sudden spurt of energy/speed* burst, fit, surge. **3** *put on a spurt at the end* burst of speed, sprint, rush.

spy noun *documents stolen by an enemy spy* enemy agent, foreign agent, secret agent, undercover agent, operative, informer; *inf.* mole.

spy verb *spy someone on the horizon* catch sight of, spot, see, notice, observe, discern. **spy on** *spy on the rival firm* keep under surveillance, watch, observe, shadow; *inf.* tail.

squabble noun quarrel, row, dispute, argument, tiff; *inf.* scrap, spat.

squabble verb quarrel, argue, bicker, wrangle; *inf.* scrap.

squalid adjective **1** *squalid hovels* dirty, filthy, grubby, grimy, slumlike, wretched, mean, nasty, seedy, slovenly, neglected, dilapidated, ramshackle. **2** *squalid tales of corruption* sordid, vile, nasty, shameful.

squander verb *squander his savings on bad investments* waste, misspend, dissipate, fritter away, run through; *inf.* blow.

square noun **1** *a band playing in the square* town square, village square, market square, quadrangle. **2** *regard parents as squares* old fogy, traditionalist, conformist; *inf.* stick-in-the-mud, fuddy-duddy.

square adjective **1** *a businessman square in all his dealings* fair, just, equitable, honest, straight, aboveboard; *inf.* on the level. **2** *regard her parents as being square* old-fashioned, behind the times, conservative, conventional, straitlaced, stuffy; *inf.* fuddy-duddy.

square verb **1** *the two accounts do not square with each other* tally, agree, correspond, fit, conform, harmonize. **2** *square the bill* settle, pay, discharge. **3** *square matters before we go* straighten out, set right, put in order.

squash verb **1** *squash the berries with a spoon* crush, squeeze, flatten, compress, smash, mash, pulverize. **2** *the audience was squashed into the hall* crowd, cram, pack, jam, squeeze, wedge. **3** *squash the rebellion* put down, quash, quell, crush, suppress, squelch.

squat verb *squat behind the hedge* crouch, sit on one's heels.

squat adjective *a squat figure* dumpy, stubby, chunky, stocky.

squeak verb **1** *mice squeaking* squeal, peep, whimper. **2** *gates squeaking in the wind* creak, scrape, grate.

squeal verb **1** *children squealing with pain/excitement* shriek, yell, scream, howl, shout, cry, wail. **2** *the burglar squealing on his associates* inform, tell tales on; *inf.* blow the whistle on, rat, snitch.

squeamish adjective queasy, nauseous, sickish, sick.

squeeze verb 1 *squeeze the sweater to re-move moisture* wring, twist, press. 2 *squeeze the juice from the orange* extract, press, force, express. 3 *squeeze the oranges* compress, crush, squash, mash. 4 *squeeze his arm* grip, clutch, pinch, compress. 5 *the audience was squeezed into the hall* crowd, cram, pack, jam, squash, wedge. 6 *squeeze his fiancée* embrace, hug, cuddle, clasp, hold tight. 7 *squeeze money out of them* extort, wring, wrest, pressure, strong-arm, blackmail, milk; *inf.* bleed.

squeeze noun 1 *give his fiancée a squeeze* embrace, hug, cuddle. 2 *give her hand a squeeze* clasp, grip, grasp, clutch. 3 *it was a bit of a squeeze in the hall* crowd, crush, jam, press, congestion. 4 *a squeeze of lemon juice* drop, dash, bit.

squirm verb wriggle, wiggle, writhe, twist, turn, shift.

squirt verb 1 *squirt water from a water pistol* discharge, expel, shoot, spurt. 2 *water squirting from the water pistol* eject, discharge, spurt, spout, stream, spray, gush, surge. 3 *squirting people with water* splash, wet, spray, shower, sprinkle.

squirt noun 1 *a squirt of water* jet, stream, spray, flow. 2 *a nasty little squirt* insignificant person; *inf.* pipsqueak, twerp.

stab verb knife, pierce, puncture, stick, skewer, gash, slash.

stab noun 1 *receive a stab in the leg* puncture, gash, slash, incision. 2 *feel a stab in the chest* pain, shooting pain, pang, twinge, spasm. 3 *take a stab at writing a novel* try, attempt, endeavor, essay, effort, venture; *inf.* go, shot, crack.

stability noun 1 *the stability of the structures | the stability of their relationship* firmness, solidity, steadiness, secureness, strength, stoutness, sturdiness, sureness, durability, constancy, permanence, reliability, dependability. 2 *question her stability* soundness, sense, responsibility, self-control, sanity.

stable adjective 1 *stable structures* firm, solid, steady, secure, fixed, strong, fast, stout, sturdy, immovable. 2 *a stable relationship* secure, strong, sure, steadfast, unwavering, unfaltering, deep-rooted, well-grounded, abiding, durable, enduring, lasting, permanent, reliable, dependable. 3 *a stable person* well-balanced, sound, steady, sensible, responsible, sane.

stack noun 1 *a stack of logs* heap, pile, store, stock, stockpile, mound, mountain. 2 *a stack of money* abundance, amplitude; *inf.* load, heap, ton, scads.

stack verb *stack logs* heap, pile, accumulate, store, stockpile.

stadium noun arena, field, amphitheater, coliseum; ballpark.

staff noun 1 *a shepherd's staff* rod, pole; stick, cane, crook. 2 *the staff of office* rod, mace, scepter. 3 *reduce staff in the office* employees, workers, workforce, personnel.

stage noun 1 *a stage in the development* period, step, juncture, level. 2 *the last stage of a journey* lap, leg, phase. 3 *stand on a stage in the theater* platform, dais, rostrum, podium. 4 *the stage for many international meetings* setting, scene, site, arena, backdrop. **the stage** *a career connected with the stage* the theater, drama, show business.

stage verb 1 *stage a production of Shakespeare* produce, direct, perform, mount, present. 2 *stage a protest rally* arrange, organize, engineer, orchestrate.

stagger verb 1 *stagger drunkenly up the road* reel, sway, teeter, totter, wobble, lurch. 2 *staggered by the price of the toys* amaze, astound, dumbfound, astonish, flabbergast, shock, stupefy, stun. 3 *stagger the lines of bricks* alternate, vary, step.

stagnant adjective 1 *stagnant water* still, motionless, standing, stale, brackish. 2 *stagnant business economy* sluggish, slow-moving, inactive, static.

staid adjective sedate, quiet, serious, sober, proper, decorous, formal, prim, stiff.

stain verb 1 *fabric stained with rust* soil, discolor, smudge, smear. 2 *stain her reputation* blacken, tarnish, sully, blemish, mar, besmirch, taint. 3 *stain the wood* varnish, dye, paint.

stain noun 1 *the stains made by the blood* mark, spot, blotch, blemish, smudge, smear. 2 *stains on her character* blemish, taint, blot, slur, stigma. 3 *use a brown stain on the wood* varnish, dye, paint.

stake[1] noun *stakes for plants to grow up* post, pole, stick, upright, rod, spike.

stake[2] noun 1 *card players laying down $50 stakes* wager, bet, ante. 2 *have a stake in the firm* financial interest, share, investment.

stake[3] verb *stake $10 on the race | stake his life on the outcome* wager, bet, gamble, chance, venture, risk, hazard.

stale adjective 1 *stale bread/cheese* dry, hard, hardened, moldy. 2 *stale air* stuffy, close, musty, fusty. 3 *stale beer* flat, sour, turned, spoiled. 4 *stale jokes* hackneyed, tired, worn-out, threadbare, banal, trite, stock, clichéd.

stalemate noun *reach a stalemate in their talks* deadlock, impasse, standstill, standoff.

stalk noun *the stalk of a plant* stem, branch, shaft.

stalk verb pursue, follow, shadow, hunt; *inf.* tail.

stall noun **1** *the vendor's stall* booth, stand, kiosk. **2** *animals in their stalls* pen, coop, sty, corral.

stall verb **1** *stall until he thinks of the answer* play for time, delay, hem and haw; *inf.* drag one's feet. **2** *stall his creditors* hold off, stave off, keep at bay, evade, avoid.

stalwart adjective **1** *stalwart young men* strong, sturdy, robust, hardy, brawny, strapping, burly, rugged. **2** *stalwart adventurers* brave, courageous, valiant, intrepid, heroic, bold, daring, adventurous.

stamina noun endurance, staying power, fortitude, strength, vigor, energy, robustness, toughness; *inf.* grit.

stammer verb stutter, stumble, mumble, splutter, hesitate, falter.

stamp verb **1** *stamp his name on the book* imprint, inscribe, engrave, emboss. **2** *her last words stamped on his mind* imprint, impress, fix. **3** *he was stamped a criminal* brand, characterize, categorize, style, term, label, dub, tag. **stamp out** *stamp out the rebellion* quash, suppress, put down, quell, crush, squelch, extinguish, eradicate, eliminate.

stamp noun *have the stamp of genius* mark, hallmark, label, quality.

stampede noun charge, rush, flight.

stand verb **1** *ask the children to stand* rise, get to one's feet, get up. **2** *a house once stood there* be situated, be located. **3** *stand the ladder against the wall* set, place, put, position. **4** *the orders stand* remain in force, remain valid, hold. **5** *unable to stand his attitude* put up with, tolerate, bear, take, endure, abide, suffer, brook, countenance, cope with; *inf.* stomach. **stand by 1** *stand by his friend* support, back, uphold, be loyal to, defend, stick up for, champion, side with. **2** *stand by his word* adhere to, stick to, observe. **3** *soldiers asked to stand by* wait, be prepared. **stand for 1** *what do the initials stand for?* represent, mean, signify, denote, imply, symbolize. **2** *he stands for all that is good* advocate, favor, support, uphold, promote. **3** *refuse to stand for her behavior* tolerate, bear. *See* STAND verb 5. **stand in for** *stand in for the leading lady* replace, act as substitute for, cover for, act as understudy for. **stand out 1** *sculptures standing out from the building* project, jut out, protrude, extend, stick out. **2** *she stood out in the crowd* be noticeable, be conspicuous, be striking, be distinctive, be prominent, attract attention, catch the eye. **stand up 1** *that argument will not stand up in court* be valid, have force, be effective, be plausible. **2** *stand her up on a date* fail to meet, let down. **stand up for 1** *stand up for his friend in trouble* support, defend, champion. *See* STAND BY 1.

2 *stand up for what one believes* uphold, promote, argue for. **stand up to** *stand up to the bully* confront, face up to, brave, defy, challenge.

stand noun **1** *come to a stand* standstill, halt, stop. **2** *take a stand against the new policies* defensive position, resistance, opposition. **3** *take a liberal stand* stance, standpoint, position, line, policy, attitude. **4** *selling books in his stand* stall, booth, kiosk. **5** *put books in stands* display case, shelf, rack, frame. **6** *give a speech from the stand* platform, stage, dais, rostrum.

standard noun **1** *a standard by which quality is judged* yardstick, benchmark, gauge, measure, criterion, touchstone, paradigm, ideal, archetype, principle, law, canon. **2** *works of a low standard* level, grade, quality, worth, merit. **3** *raise the battle standard* flag, banner, pennant, streamer, ensign, colors. **4** *trees supported by standards* support, prop, post, upright. **5** *maintain old-fashioned standards* principle, code of behavior, code of honor, morals, ethics, ideals.

standard adjective **1** *standard shoe sizes* usual, ordinary, average, normal, common, regular, stock, conventional. **2** *the standard work on Shakespeare* definitive, classic, recognized, accepted, authoritative.

standardize verb make uniform, regulate, systematize, normalize.

standing noun **1** *his standing in the community* status, rank, position, station, footing, place, circumstances. **2** *people of standing in the community* reputation, repute, eminence, prominence, note. **3** *her husband of many years' standing* duration, continuance, endurance.

standoffish adjective aloof, distant, cool, remote, detached, unapproachable.

standpoint noun *from the standpoint of the customer* point of view, viewpoint, perspective, angle, frame of reference.

staple adjective *staple foods* primary, main, principal, basic, fundamental, essential, indispensable, necessary.

star noun **1** *stars in the sky* heavenly body; planet, asteroid. **2** *born under a lucky star* destiny, fate, fortune, lot. **3** *read his stars* horoscope, forecast, augury. **4** *one of the stars of the film* principal, leading lady, leading man, lead. **5** *some of the stars on the local council* celebrity, dignitary, notable, name; *inf.* VIP, big shot.

stare verb *stare into space* gaze, gape, look; *inf.* gawk.

stark adjective **1** *in stark contrast* sharp, obvious, evident, clear, clear-cut. **2** *a stark landscape* desolate, bare, barren, vacant, empty, forsaken, bleak, grim, harsh. **3** *stark madness* sheer, utter, absolute, downright, out-and-out, outright, total, complete, pure, unmitigated, unqualified, consummate, patent. **4** *the stark facts* bald, bare, simple, blunt, straightforward, unadorned, unembellished, harsh, grim.

stark adverb *stark (raving) mad* completely, totally, entirely, wholly, altogether, utterly, absolutely, quite. **stark naked** nude, bare, undressed, unclad, au naturel; *inf.* in the buff, in the altogether, in the raw, in one's birthday suit.

start verb **1** *when her illness started* commence, get underway, begin, appear, come into existence, arise, originate, crop up. **2** *have to start now to finish the job in time* begin, commence, get going, get things moving, buckle down, start the ball rolling; *inf.* get moving, get down to business, get the show on the road, kick off. **3** *start now to be there by tonight* set out, depart, leave; *inf.* hit the road, push off. **4** *start the machine* set in motion, turn on, activate. **5** *start the campaign* set up, establish, create, institute, initiate, launch, originate, pioneer, organize; *inf.* kick off. **6** *start in pain* jump, jerk, twitch, recoil, flinch, wince, shy. **7** *chipmunks starting out of the bushes* jump, leap, spring, bound, dart.

start noun **1** *present at the start of the event* beginning, commencement, opening, inception, inauguration, dawn, birth; *inf.* kickoff. **2** *at the start of her illness* beginning, onset, emergence. **3** *the start of the trouble* origin, source, root, basis, derivation, wellspring. **4** *at the start of the campaign* establishment, foundation, institution, launch, origination. **5** *get a start in the race* head start, advantage, edge, lead, jump. **6** *finally got her start in show business* opening, opportunity, chance, introduction; *inf.* break. **7** *give a start from the pain* jump, leap, jerk, twitch, wince.

startle verb disturb, agitate, perturb, unsettle, frighten, alarm, surprise, astonish.

starvation noun extreme hunger, famine, fasting, malnourishment.

starving adjective starved, famished, ravenous, malnourished, fasting; *inf.* able to eat a horse.

state noun **1** *in its previous state* condition, shape, situation, circumstances, state of affairs, position. **2** *in a nervous state* condition, mood, humor, frame of mind. **3** *she often gets into a state* state of agitation, panic, fluster, pother; *inf.* flap, tizzy. **4** *look at the state of this room* mess, chaos, disorder, disarray, confusion, clutter. **5** *a meeting of the world's states* country, nation, land, realm, kingdom, republic. **6** *feel the state is too powerful* government, administration, establishment. **7** *occasions of state* pomp, ceremony, display, majesty, grandeur.

state verb *state one's objections* express, voice, utter, declare, set out, assert, announce, pronounce, articulate, present.

stately adjective ceremonial, dignified, solemn, majestic, royal, regal, magnificent, grand, splendid, elegant, imposing, impressive, august, lofty, pompous; measured, deliberate.

statement noun *a statement of one's views* declaration, account, recitation, report, assertion, announcement, pronouncement, articulation, presentation.

static adjective unmoving, unvarying, changeless, constant, steady, stationary, motionless.

station noun **1** *get the bus at the bus station* terminus, terminal, stop, depot. **2** *police station* base, office, headquarters, seat. **3** *security staff at their stations* post, place, position, location. **4** *different stations in life* class, level, rank, grade, standing, status, caste.

stationary adjective **1** *stationary traffic* unmoving, motionless, at a standstill. **2** *stationary price patterns* unchanging, constant, unvarying.

statuesque adjective dignified, stately, majestic, magnificent, imposing, regal.

stature noun **1** *ill-developed in stature* height, tallness, size. **2** *catering to people of stature* status, importance, standing, consequence, eminence, prominence, note, fame, renown.

status noun *of uncertain social status* standing, rank, level, grade, position, importance.

staunch adjective *staunch supporters* loyal, faithful, dependable, reliable, steadfast, unswerving, unwavering, unfaltering.

stay verb **1** *stay there till we call you* remain, wait, continue, delay, tarry. **2** *stay loyal to him* remain, continue to be. **3** *stay judgment until tomorrow* put off, postpone, suspend, defer, delay. **4** *stay the progress of the disease* check, curb, arrest, stop, delay, hold, prevent, hinder, impede, obstruct. **5** *stay at a hotel* lodge, take a room, visit, reside, dwell.

stay noun **1** *a brief stay at a hotel* visit, sojourn, stop, vacation. **2** *a stay of judgment* postponement, suspension, adjournment, deferment, delay. **3** *a stay in his old age* prop, support, brace, bolster, buttress.

steadfast adjective **1** *a steadfast friend* faithful, loyal, true, constant, devoted, dependable, reliable, staunch. **2** *steadfast in his views* steady, firm, determined, resolute, unchanging, unwavering, unfaltering. **3** *a steadfast gaze* steady, fixed, intent, immovable, unwavering, unfaltering.

steady adjective **1** *make the posts steady* firm, fixed, stable, secure. **2** *a steady hand* still, unshaking, motionless, sure. **3** *a steady gaze* steadfast, fixed, immovable, unwavering, unfaltering. **4** *a steady faith* constant, unchanging, invariable, continuous, ceaseless, perpetual, persistent, unremitting, unending, endless. **5** *walk at a steady pace* uniform, even, regular, rhythmic, consistent. **6** *a steady boyfriend* regular, habitual, usual, customary. **7** *a steady young man* balanced, sensible, levelheaded, rational, down-to-earth, calm, equable, reliable, dependable.

steal verb **1** *steal money* take, misappropriate, pilfer, purloin, filch, walk off with, embezzle, pocket, shoplift; *inf.* pinch, swipe, rip off. **2** *steal someone else's work* plagiarize, copy, pirate, appropriate, poach; *inf.* lift. **3** *steal a child* kidnap, snatch, abduct, seize, shanghai. **4** *steal a kiss* snatch, obtain surreptitiously. **5** *steal out of the room* slip, tiptoe, sneak, creep, slink, glide.

stealth noun *get into the house by stealth* secrecy, furtiveness, surreptitiousness, slyness, covertness.

stealthy adjective *stealthy maneuvers* secret, furtive, surreptitious, sly, sneaky, clandestine, covert, underhand, undercover.

steep adjective **1** *steep cliffs* sheer, abrupt, precipitous, perpendicular, vertical. **2** *a steep rise in share prices* sharp, rapid, sudden, precipitate. **3** *prices at that restaurant are a bit steep* high, costly, expensive, excessive, exorbitant.

steep verb **1** *steep the stained clothes in cold water* soak, saturate, immerse, submerge, souse. **2** *steep the meat in wine* marinate, souse. **steep in 1** *a family steeped in misery* imbue with, permeate with, pervade with, infuse with. **2** *they were steeped in the classics* submerge in, immerse in.

steeple noun spire, tower, bell tower, turret.

steer verb **1** *steer the car* guide, navigate, drive, pilot, be at the wheel of. **2** *steer the guests to the garden* guide, lead, direct, conduct, usher. **steer clear of** keep away from, give a wide berth to, avoid, evade, dodge, eschew, shun.

stem noun **1** *the stem of a bush* trunk, stock, peduncle. **2** *flowers on a stem* stalk, shoot, branch, twig.

stem verb **1** *stem the flow of blood* check, stop, halt, hold back, contain, curb, staunch. **2** *troubles stemming from poverty* arise, originate, derive, spring, emanate.

stench noun stink, foul smell, odor, reek.

step noun **1** *reach her in one step* stride, pace. **2** *hear steps on the stairs* footstep, footfall, tread. **3** *police examining steps in the mud* footprint, impression, track. **4** *walk with a cheerful step* walk, gait, bearing, carriage. **5** *live just a step away* pace,

stone's throw, spitting distance. **6** *the steps of a ladder* rung, tread. **7** *take a foolish step* course of action, move, act, deed. **8** *a step toward international peace* advancement, development, progression, stage, move. **9** *another step in his promotion* stage, level, grade, rank, degree. **in step** *in step with the views of the committee* in agreement, in accord, in harmony, in line, in conformity. **watch one's step 1** *watch your step on the broken pavement* step carefully, tread cautiously. **2** *watch your step when doing business with him* be careful, be cautious, be wary, be circumspect, take care, take heed, be on one's guard, look out. **out of step** *out of step with modern thinking* in disagreement, at odds, out of line, at variance. **step by step** *follow the instructions step by step* by stages, by degrees, progressively, gradually, bit by bit.

step verb *step lightly down the street* walk, tread, stride. **step down** *step down to make way for a younger person* resign, retire, abdicate. **step in** *the police had to step in* intervene, intercede, take action. **step up 1** *police stepping up their efforts* increase, boost, augment, intensify, escalate. **2** *step up the pace of production* increase, speed up, accelerate.

stereotype verb typecast, pigeonhole, label, tag, categorize.

stereotyped adjective *stereotyped images of a woman's role* typecast, conventional, hackneyed, clichéd, trite, platitudinous.

sterile adjective **1** *sterile female* infertile, barren. **2** *sterile soil* infertile, unproductive, unfruitful, unyielding, arid, dry, barren, unprolific. **3** *sterile discussions* unproductive, fruitless, useless, futile, vain, ineffectual, worthless. **4** *sterile conditions in the hospital* sterilized, germ-free, antiseptic, disinfected, aseptic, uncontaminated.

sterling adjective **1** *have done sterling service* excellent, first-rate, exceptional, outstanding, splendid, superlative. **2** *sterling friends* genuine, real, true, dependable, trustworthy, faithful, loyal.

stern adjective **1** *a stern regime* strict, harsh, severe, rigorous, stringent, rigid, exacting, demanding, relentless, unsparing, inflexible. **2** *a stern expression* severe, forbidding, unsmiling, sober, austere.

stew verb **1** *stew the meat* simmer, fricassee. **2** *stewing in the doctor's waiting room* be anxious, be nervous, be agitated, worry, fret, agonize.

stew noun **1** *make a beef stew* casserole, ragout, fricassee. **2** *get in a stew about the lost document* state of agitation, fluster, panic, dither, pother; *inf.* flap, tizzy.

stick noun **1** *gather sticks for kindling* branch, twig, switch. **2** *sticks supporting plants* cane, pole, post, stake, upright. **3** *punished with a stick* cane, birch, switch, rod. **4** *beaten with a stick* cudgel, truncheon, blackjack, baton. **the sticks** *bored with living in the sticks* the backwoods, the hinterland, the backwater; *inf.* the middle of nowhere, the boondocks, boonies.

stick verb **1** *stick a fork in the potato* thrust, push, insert, jab, poke. **2** *stick the pictures to a sheet of paper* glue, paste, tape, fasten, attach, fix, pin, tack. **3** *events that stick in the mind* remain, stay, linger, dwell, lodge, persist, continue. **4** *the car stuck in the mud* become bogged down, become embedded, become immobilized. **5** *machines sticking* jam, come to a standstill, stop, halt, cease to work. **6** *stick it in the drawer* put, place, lay, deposit, drop; *inf.* plunk, stuff. **7** *a needle sticking his finger* pierce, penetrate, puncture, prick, stab. **stick by** *stick by his friend in his misfortune* stand by, be loyal to, remain faithful to, support, back, defend. **stick it out** *the work is hard but he can stick it out* see it through, endure it, grin and bear it, soldier on; *inf.* take it, hang in there, tough it out. **stick out 1** *sculptures sticking out from the wall* stand out, jut out, project, extend, protrude, bulge. **2** *she stuck out in the crowd* stand out, be noticeable, be obvious.

sticky adjective **1** *sticky tape* adhesive, gummy, tacky. **2** *sticky substances* gluey, glutinous, viscous; *inf.* gooey. **3** *a sticky summer day* humid, muggy, clammy, sultry, sweltering, oppressive. **4** *a sticky situation* awkward, difficult, tricky, ticklish, delicate, thorny; *inf.* hairy.

stiff adjective **1** *stiff cardboard* rigid, inflexible, firm, hard, brittle. **2** *stiff muscles* tight, tense, taut, aching, arthritic, rheumatic. **3** *a stiff climb* difficult, arduous, tough, laborious, demanding, formidable, challenging, Herculean. **4** *a stiff penalty* severe, harsh, stringent, rigorous, heavy. **5** *put up a stiff resistance* strong, vigorous, determined, resolute, dogged, tenacious. **6** *a stiff occasion* formal, ceremonious, dignified, proper, decorous, pompous. **7** *stiff behavior* formal, prim, punctilious, chilly; *inf.* starchy. **8** *a stiff drink* strong, potent. **9** *a stiff breeze* vigorous, brisk, fresh.

stiffen verb **1** *the mixture needs time to stiffen* thicken, set, gel, jell, solidify, harden, congeal, coagulate. **2** *something to stiffen their resolve* strengthen, harden, fortify, brace, steel, reinforce. **3** *his muscles have stiffened* tighten, tense, become taut.

stifle verb **1** *stifle a yawn* smother, check, keep back, withhold, choke back, muffle, suppress, silence. **2** *stifle a rebellion* suppress, quash, quell, put down, extinguish, stamp out, crush, subdue, repress. **3** *it is stifling in here* suffocating, sweltering, airless, close.

stigma noun shame, disgrace, dishonor, stain, taint.

still adjective **1** *completely still bodies* motionless, unmoving, immobile, inert, lifeless, stock-still, stationary. **2** *the house was completely still* quiet, silent, hushed, soundless, noiseless. **3** *a still evening* calm, mild, tranquil, peaceful, serene, windless.

still noun *in the still of the night* quiet, silence, hush, calm, tranquillity, peacefulness, serenity.

still verb **1** *try to still her fears* quiet, calm, pacify, soothe, allay, assuage, appease, silence, subdue. **2** *the wind stilled* abate, die down, moderate, slacken.

stilted adjective **1** *a stilted way of speaking* stiff, unnatural, wooden, forced, labored, awkward. **2** *stilted prose* pompous, pretentious, high-flown, grandiloquent, pedantic.

stimulant noun **1** *a stimulant to the system* tonic, restorative, energizer, analeptic; *inf.* pep pill, upper, pick-me-up, bracer. **2** *a stimulant to further economic growth* incentive, impetus, fillip. See STIMULUS.

stimulate verb *stimulate economic activity* encourage, prompt, spur, stir up, excite, kindle, incite, fan.

stimulus noun *a stimulus to economic growth* stimulant, incentive, fillip, spur, push, drive, encouragement, incitement, goad, jog, jolt; *inf.* shot in the arm.

sting noun **1** *get a sting from a bee* prick, wound, injury. **2** *take the sting out of the burns* irritation, smarting, tingle, pain. **3** *the sting of unrequited love* pain, hurt, distress, anguish, agony, torment. **4** *crooks planning a sting* swindle, fraud; *inf.* rip-off.

sting verb **1** *stung by a jellyfish* prick, wound, injure, hurt. **2** *eyes stinging in the smoke* smart, tingle, burn. **3** *stung by their son's treatment of them* hurt, wound, distress, grieve, torment. **4** *stung by the dishonest dealer* swindle, defraud, cheat, fleece; *inf.* rip off.

stingy adjective mean, miserly, parsimonious, niggardly, tight-fisted, penny-pinching; *inf.* tight, cheap.

stipulate verb *stipulate a delivery date* specify, set down, demand, require, make a condition of.

stir verb **1** *stir the mixture* mix, blend, beat, whip. **2** *stirred in his sleep* move, quiver, tremble, twitch. **3** *wind stirring the leaves* disturb, agitate, rustle. **4** *refuse to stir from the fireside* move, budge, get up. **5** *stirring early on Christmas Day* get up, rise, be up and about; *inf.* shake a leg, look lively. **6** *stir his imagination* stimulate, excite, rouse, kindle, inspire. **7** *speakers stirring the men to action* rouse, incite, provoke, inflame, goad, spur, egg on, urge, motivate, drive, impel.

stir noun *their arrival caused a stir* excitement, commotion, disturbance, fuss, to-do, bustle.

stock noun **1** *a stock of goods for sale* store, supply, range, selection, assortment, variety. **2** *run out of stock before Christmas* supplies, goods, merchandise, wares, commodities. **3** *lay in a stock of wood for the winter* store, supply, stockpile, reserve, reservoir, accumulation, load, hoard, cache. **4** *employed to look after the farm stock* livestock, cattle, beasts, herd. **5** *have stock in the company* shares, investment, holding, capital. **6** *his stock in the company is rising* standing, status, reputation, position. **7** *born of good stock* descent, lineage, ancestry, extraction, family, parentage, pedigree. **8** *stock for soup* bouillon, broth. **9** *the stock of an implement* handle, haft, grip, shaft, shank. **in stock** *a range of goods in stock* for sale, on sale, available; *inf.* on tap. **take stock of** *take stock of the situation* review, weigh, appraise; *inf.* size up.

stock adjective **1** *stock sizes of clothes* standard, regular, average, readily available. **2** *stock items in a kitchen cupboard* regular, common, customary, staple, basic, fundamental, essential, indispensable. **3** *stock responses to his requests* usual, routine, run-of-the-mill, commonplace, conventional, traditional, clichéd.

stock verb **1** *stores stocking children's clothes* sell, deal in, market, supply. **2** *stock the factory with modern machinery* equip, fit, outfit, furnish, supply, provide. **stock up** **1** *stock up the shelves* fill, fill up, load, replenish. **2** *stock up (on) cans of soup* collect, gather, accumulate, amass, lay in, stockpile, hoard; *inf.* squirrel away.

stockings plural noun hosiery, hose, nylons; panty hose, tights.

stocky adjective heavyset, thickset, squat, chunky, solid, sturdy.

stodgy adjective **1** *a stodgy young man* staid, sedate, stuffy. **2** *stodgy prose* dull, uninteresting, boring, tedious, dry, wearisome, unimaginative, uninspired, monotonous, labored, wooden, turgid.

stoical adjective impassive, unemotional, self-disciplined, forbearing, patient, long-suffering, resigned, philosophical, fatalistic.

stomach noun **1** *a pain in the stomach* abdomen, belly, paunch, potbelly; *inf.* tummy, gut, bread basket. **2** *have no stomach for rich food | have no stomach for the battle* appetite, taste, hunger, desire, inclination, liking, fancy, fondness, relish, gusto.

stomach verb **1** *unable to stomach rich food* eat, digest, swallow. **2** *unable to stomach his arrogance* stand, bear, tolerate, abide, endure, suffer; *inf.* weather.

stony adjective **1** *stony ground* rocky, pebbly, gravelly, gritty, rough. **2** *a stony stare* cold, frosty, icy, rigid, fixed. **3** *a stony heart* unfeeling, uncaring, unsympathetic, insensitive, callous, heartless, unmoved, unresponsive, severe, harsh, hard, cruel, cold-hearted, merciless, pitiless, ruthless, unforgiving.

stoop verb **1** *stoop to pick something up* bend down, lean over, crouch down. **2** *stoop his head to get into the car* bend, bow, lower, duck. **3** *very tall people often stoop* slouch, slump, hunch one's shoulders. **4** *never stoops to talk to her inferiors* condescend, deign, lower oneself. **5** *refuse to stoop to crime* sink, descend, resort.

stop verb **1** *stop the fight* halt, end, put an end to, finish, terminate, discontinue, interrupt. **2** *unable to stop laughing* cease, refrain from, leave off, quit; *inf.* knock off. **3** *work has stopped for the day* come to a halt, end, finish, come to a close, cease, conclude, terminate. **4** *stop their getaway flight* prevent, hinder, obstruct, impede, block, check, curb, frustrate, thwart, foil, restrain. **5** *stop off at Newport on the way to Boston* stay, sojourn, lodge, rest. **stop up** *stop up a leak* plug (up), seal (up), block (up), bung up, stem.

stop noun **1** *come to a stop* halt, end, finish, close, cessation, conclusion, termination, standstill, stoppage. **2** *there are ten stops on the bus route* terminus, terminal, depot, station. **3** *aim for a stop at Miami* stopoff, stopover, stay, sojourn, overnight.

stopgap noun substitute, fill-in, makeshift, improvisation, expedient, last resort.

stoppage noun **1** *the stoppage of some forms of welfare* end, discontinuation, cessation, termination. **2** *another stoppage at the factory* strike, walkout, shutdown. **3** *a stoppage in the pipe* blockage, obstruction, occlusion. **4** *a stoppage in the supply* obstruction, obstacle, impediment, check, snag.

store noun **1** *a store of logs for the winter* supply, stockpile, reserve, accumulation, pile, cache, reservoir. **2** *get supplies from the store* storeroom, storehouse, warehouse, repository. **3** *buying shoes/food/books at the store* shop, department store, supermarket, retail outlet, emporium. **set store by** think highly of, hold in regard, admire, appreciate, value, prize, esteem.

store verb *store food in case of a shortage* stock up on, stockpile, collect, gather, accumulate, amass, put away, deposit; *inf.* salt away, stash.

storm noun **1** *ships damaged in the storm* gale, hurricane, cyclone, tempest, squall, cloudburst, downpour, torrent. **2** *a storm of protest* outcry, outburst, commotion, furor, clamor, tumult, disturbance; *inf.*

to-do. **3** *a storm on the castle* assault, attack, offensive, onslaught, charge, raid, foray, sortie. **4** *a storm of missiles* shower, deluge, volley, salvo.

storm verb **1** *storm the castle* attack, charge, rush. **2** *storm out of the room* charge, rush headlong, stamp; *inf.* stomp. **3** *storming at the incompetent recruits* rage, rant, rave, fume, bellow, thunder; *inf.* raise the roof, raise hell.

stormy adjective blustery, windy, gusty, squally, tempestuous, turbulent.

story noun **1** *have a story published | read the children a story* short story, tale, fairy tale, fable, legend; *inf.* yarn. **2** *their stories of the accident did not agree* account, report, record. **3** *the novel's complicated story* story line, plot. **4** *journalists looking for a story* news item, article, feature; *inf.* scoop. **5** *told a story when she was caught* lie, untruth, falsehood, fib.

stout adjective **1** *stout people advised to lose weight* fat, plump, portly, tubby, obese, corpulent, rotund, heavy, thickset, overweight, burly, fleshy; *inf.* beefy. **2** *a stout stick* strong, heavy, solid, substantial, sturdy. **3** *a stout defender of the city* stouthearted, valiant, gallant, intrepid.

stouthearted adjective *stouthearted defenders of the city* courageous, valiant, valorous, gallant, fearless, plucky, intrepid, brave, bold.

straight adjective **1** *in a straight line* direct, undeviating, unswerving, uncurving. **2** *three straight wins* successive, consecutive, in a row, running, uninterrupted, nonstop. **3** *is the picture straight?* level, symmetrical, even, true, in line, aligned. **4** *get the room straight* in order, orderly, neat, tidy, spruce, shipshape, organized, arranged, sorted out. **5** *a straight answer* direct, honest, sincere, frank, candid, forthright, straightforward, plainspoken, plain, unequivocal, unambiguous, unqualified. **6** *incapable of straight thinking* logical, rational, sound, intelligent, unemotional, dispassionate. **7** *straight spirits* unmixed, undiluted, pure, neat.

straight adverb **1** *go straight there* directly, by a direct route, without deviating; without delay. **2** *tell them straight* directly, honestly, frankly, candidly, plainly, straight from the shoulder, with no holds barred, unequivocally, unambiguously. **3** *not thinking straight* logically, rationally, intelligently, dispassionately. **straight away** *the work must be done straight away* right away, immediately, at once, without delay; *inf.* pronto. **straight out** *tell him straight out that he is fired* directly, honestly, frankly, candidly.

straightforward adjective **1** *a straightforward answer* direct, honest, frank, candid.

See STRAIGHT adjective 5. **2** *a straightforward task* uncomplicated, simple, elementary, undemanding, routine.

strain verb **1** *strain a rope till it snaps* tighten, make taut, stretch, extend, distend. **2** *strain a muscle* pull, wrench, twist, sprain. **3** *strain one's eyes by reading too much* tax, overtax, overwork, fatigue, tire. **4** *strain to win* make every effort, strive, struggle, labor. **5** *strain at the rope* pull, tug, heave, haul, jerk; *inf.* yank. **6** *strain the mixture* sieve, filter, sift, screen, riddle, separate.

strain noun **1** *the rope snapped under the strain* tension, tightness, tautness. **2** *suffer muscle strain* wrench, twist, sprain, pull. **3** *the strain of his job* demands, exertions, burdens, pressure, stress, tension. **4** *suffer from strain* stress, tension, overwork, exhaustion, anxiety.

strainer noun *put the food through a strainer* sieve, colander, filter, sifter, screen, riddle.

strait noun *the boat crossing the strait* sound, narrows, channel, inlet, arm of the sea.

straitlaced adjective puritanical, prudish, prim, proper, priggish, stuffy; *inf.* fuddy-duddy.

straits plural noun *in dire straits* predicament, plight, difficulty, trouble, crisis, mess; *inf.* tight corner, hot water, jam, hole, scrape.

strand¹ noun **1** *the strands of the wool* thread, fiber, filament. **2** *strands of hair* lock, wisp, tress. **3** *the last volume drawing together the strands of the trilogy* element, component, strain, story line, theme.

strand² noun *walk on the strand* shore, seashore, beach, coast, seaside, waterfront.

stranded adjective **1** *she was stranded when her purse was stolen* left helpless, abandoned, forsaken, in dire straits, left in the lurch, left high and dry. **2** *stranded ships* grounded, beached, shipwrecked, wrecked, marooned.

strange adjective **1** *he had a strange expression on his face* peculiar, odd, bizarre, unusual, atypical, abnormal, weird, funny, unfamiliar. **2** *a strange land* unknown, unfamiliar. **3** *a strange phenomenon* inexplicable, anomalous, unexpected, extraordinary.

stranger noun **1** *he was a complete stranger to her* unknown person, alien. **2** *strangers being welcomed into the community* new person, outsider, newcomer, foreigner. **a stranger to** *a stranger to the area* unfamiliar with, unacquainted with, unaccustomed to, new to, unused to, inexperienced in, unversed in.

strangle verb **1** *he strangled his victim with a scarf* throttle, choke, garrotte. **2** *strangle artistic expression* suppress, inhibit, repress, restrain, curb, stifle, gag.

strap noun *straps fastening the trunk* band, belt, thong, cord, tie.

strap verb **1** *strap the trunk with leather thongs* fasten, secure, tie, bind, lash, truss, pinion. **2** *strap the naughty children* flog, lash, whip, scourge, beat; *inf.* belt.

stratagem noun trick, ruse, plot, scheme, maneuver, plan, tactic, artifice, machination, wile, subterfuge, dodge, deception.

strategic adjective **1** *strategic schemes* tactical, diplomatic, calculated, planned, plotted, cunning, wily. **2** *strategic bases in the war* crucial, key, vital, critical.

strategy noun **1** *the government's economic strategy* policy, approach, program, scheme, plan of action, blueprint, game plan. **2** *the general's strategy* art of war, military science, military tactics.

stray verb **1** *cows straying into the neighbor's field* wander, roam, rove, go astray. **2** *strayed in later life* go astray, go wrong, stray from the straight and narrow, err, sin, transgress. **3** *stray from the point* digress, wander, deviate, get sidetracked, go off on a tangent.

stray adjective **1** *a stray dog* lost, homeless, wandering, vagrant, abandoned, unclaimed. **2** *a stray bullet* odd, random, isolated, scattered, occasional, incidental, accidental, chance, freak.

streak noun **1** *a streak of light in the dark sky* line, band, strip, stripe. **2** *a streak of cowardice* strain, vein, element, trace. **3** *a streak of lightning* bolt, flash, beam. **4** *streaks on the windows* smear, smudge, mark. **5** *on a winning streak* spell, period, course, stretch, series.

streak verb **1** *a blue sky streaked with white* striate, fleck, band, stripe. **2** *dirty cloths streaking the glass* smear, smudge, mark. **3** *runners/cars streaking past* race, rush, speed, dash, sprint, hurtle, fly, flash, zoom, zip; *inf.* whiz.

stream noun **1** *mountain streams* river, brook, creek, rivulet, rill, freshet. **2** *a stream of blood* flow, rush, gush, surge, efflux, current, cascade. **3** *people going with the stream* flow, current, tide, drift.

stream verb **1** *water streaming from the pipe* flow, run, pour, course, spill, gush, surge, flood, cascade. **2** *flags streaming in the breeze* float, swing, flap, flutter. **3** *people streaming out of the building* surge, pour, crowd.

street noun road, thoroughfare, boulevard, avenue, drive, lane.

strength noun **1** *men of great physical strength* power, might, force, brawn, muscle, stamina. **2** *regain his strength* health, robustness, vigor. **3** *adversity gave him inner strength* fortitude, courage, firmness,

stamina, backbone. **4** *test the strength of the castle doors* solidity, toughness, resistance, impregnability. **5** *the strength of the feeling against him* intensity, force, forcefulness, vehemence, ardor, fervency. **6** *the strength of their argument* cogency, potency, weight, soundness, validity. **7** *workers who are the strength of the firm* mainstay, support, anchor, foundation stone. **8** *the firm's reliability is its main strength* advantage, asset, strong point, forte. **9** *the strength of the workforce* size, extent, magnitude.

strengthen verb **1** *strengthen children's bones* make stronger, make healthy, nourish, build up. **2** *the wind strengthened* gain strength, intensify, heighten. **3** *strengthen their determination* fortify, harden, stiffen, toughen, steel. **4** *his evidence strengthened their argument* reinforce, support, back up, bolster, substantiate, corroborate.

strenuous adjective **1** *a strenuous task* arduous, laborious, taxing, demanding, exhausting, tiring, fatiguing. **2** *make strenuous efforts to reach the top* energetic, active, vigorous, forceful, strong, spirited, determined, zealous.

stress noun **1** *the stress of his new job* strain, pressure, tension. **2** *in times of stress* worry, anxiety, trouble, difficulty, distress, trauma. **3** *place stress on education* emphasis, priority, importance, weight, significance, value, worth. **4** *place stress on the first syllable* emphasis, accent, accentuation.

stress verb **1** *stress the importance of education* emphasize, accentuate, underscore, highlight, spotlight, dwell on. **2** *stress the first syllable* place emphasis on, place the accent on, accentuate. **3** *discover that the workers have been stressed for years* overtax, pressurize, overwork, overburden, push too far.

stretch verb **1** *the material stretches* be elastic, distend, be tensile, enlarge, expand. **2** *stretch the piece of elastic* extend, elongate, lengthen, expand, draw out. **3** *stretched a hand out* reach out, hold out, proffer, offer. **4** *the forests stretched for miles* extend, spread, unfold, range. **5** *a job that will stretch her* challenge, tax, push to the limit. **6** *stretch the truth* strain, exaggerate, overdraw, push too far. **stretch out** *stretch out on the sofa* lie down, recline, sprawl (out), lounge.

stretch noun **1** *stretches of forest* expanse, area, tract, extent, spread. **2** *a four-hour stretch* period, time, spell, term, stint.

strict adjective **1** *a strict interpretation of the rules* precise, exact, close, faithful, scrupulous, meticulous, conscientious, punctilious. **2** *a strict upbringing* stringent, rigorous, authoritarian, rigid, austere, inflexible, unyielding, uncompromising. **3**

in strict confidence absolute, utter, complete, total, perfect. **4** *strict members of the religious sect* orthodox, fundamentalist.

stride verb *stride along swinging their arms* step, pace, walk.

stride noun *take huge strides* long/large step, pace.

strident adjective shrill, loud, harsh, raucous, rough, grating, discordant, jarring, screeching.

strife noun conflict, friction, discord, dissension, dispute, bickering, controversy, contention.

strike verb **1** *strike the gong* bang, beat, hit, pound. **2** *struck his opponent* hit, slap, smack, beat, batter, thump, punch, cuff, box, knock, rap; *inf.* wallop, belt, clout, whack, clobber, bop, sock. **3** *the ship struck a rock* run into, bang into, bump into, smash into, collide with, dash against. **4** *strike the ball a good distance* hit, drive, propel. **5** *strike a match* light, ignite. **6** *the enemy struck our army at dawn* attack, charge, assault, storm, fall upon. **7** *disaster struck the family* come upon, afflict, smite. **8** *strike a balance* reach, achieve, arrive at, find, attain. **9** *strike a bargain* agree on, settle on, sign, endorse, ratify, sanction. **10** *strike a dramatic pose* assume, adopt, affect, feign. **11** *strike oil/gold* discover, find, happen upon, stumble upon, unearth, uncover, turn up. **12** *an idea struck him* occur to, come to, dawn on. **13** *the house strikes me as unfriendly* seem to, appear to, impress, affect. **14** *workers striking for higher wages* go on strike, protest, walk out. **15** *strike the disputed clause from the record* delete, cross out, erase, rub out, obliterate. **strike up 1** *the band struck up* commence playing, begin/start to play. **2** *they struck up an acquaintance* begin, start, commence, embark on, initiate.

strike noun **1** *stunned his opponent with one strike* hit, slap, smack, thump, punch, cuff, box, knock; *inf.* wallop, whack. **2** *a lucky strike* discovery, find. **3** *an unexpected enemy strike* attack, assault, blitz. **4** *declare a strike* walkout, protest.

striking adjective **1** *a striking resemblance* obvious, conspicuous, prominent, unmistakable, remarkable, extraordinary. **2** *a striking floral display* impressive, splendid, magnificent, superb, marvelous, dazzling; *inf.* smashing. **3** *married to a striking woman* beautiful, glamorous, stunning, gorgeous.

string noun **1** *tie the package with string* twine, cord, yarn, rope, line. **2** *own a string of stores* chain, series, succession. **3** *a string of people waiting to get in* line, row, queue, procession, file, column, succession, sequence. **4** *a string of beads* strand, necklace.

stringent adjective **1** *a stringent ban on smoking* strict, firm, rigid, severe, harsh, tough, exacting, demanding, inflexible, uncompromising. **2** *stringent economic conditions* difficult, tight, hard, tough.

strip verb **1** *they stripped and got into dry clothes* undress, take one's clothes off, disrobe. **2** *strip the wet child* undress, unclothe. **3** *strip the bark from the tree* peel, pare, skin, excoriate. **4** *strip paint from the doors* remove, take off, peel off, flake off. **5** *strip a machine* dismantle, break down, take apart. **6** *the burglars stripped the house* empty out, clean out, plunder, ransack, rob. **strip of** *strip him of his rank* take away from, deprive of, confiscate from.

strip noun *strips of paper* piece, bit, band, belt, ribbon, stripe, swathe, slip.

stripe noun *a white stripe on a black background* strip, band, belt, bar.

strive verb *strive to succeed* try, attempt, endeavor, make an effort, exert oneself, strain, struggle, bend over backward; *inf.* go all out, give it one's best shot. **strive against** *strove all his life against oppression* struggle against, fight, battle, combat, contend with, grapple with.

stroke noun **1** *felt the stroke of his opponent* blow, hit, slap, smack, thump, punch, cuff, knock; *inf.* wallop, clout, whack. **2** *swimming strokes* movement, action, motion. **3** *a stroke of genius/diplomacy* accomplishment, achievement, feat, attainment, coup. **4** *with one stroke of the pen* movement, action, mark, line. **5** *put the finishing strokes to the plan* touch, detail, bit, addition. **6** *hear five strokes of the church bell* striking, peal, ring, knell. **7** *in the hospital since he had a stroke* thrombosis, embolism, seizure, apoplexy.

stroke verb *stroke the cat* caress, fondle, pat, touch, rub, massage, soothe.

stroll verb *stroll (along) in the sunshine* saunter, amble, wander, meander, ramble, promenade, stretch one's legs; *inf.* mosey (along).

stroll noun *go for a stroll* saunter, walk, amble, wander, turn, constitutional, promenade.

strong adjective **1** *strong men lifting heavy weights* powerful, mighty, brawny, muscular, strapping, sturdy, burly. **2** *invalids becoming strong again* healthy, well, robust, vigorous. **3** *strong enough to refuse the blackmailer's demands* courageous, brave, resolute; *inf.* gutsy. **4** *intimidated by strong individuals* determined, forceful, high-powered, tough, formidable. **5** *the vault's strong doors* solid, well-built, heavy, secure, well-fortified, impregnable, impenetrable. **6** *strong material* heavy-duty, sturdy, durable, long-lasting. **7** *arouse strong feelings* forceful, intense, acute, vehement, passionate, fervent. **8** *a strong supporter of the local team* keen, eager, enthusiastic, dedicated, staunch, loyal, steadfast, passionate, fierce, fervent. **9** *a strong argument* powerful, cogent, potent, weighty, compelling, convincing, plausible, effective, sound, valid, well-founded. **10** *a strong resemblance* marked, pronounced, distinct, definite, obvious, unmistakable, remarkable. **11** *strong colors* deep, intense, vivid, graphic. **12** *in strong light* bright, brilliant, intense, dazzling, glaring. **13** *strong measures to reduce crime* firm, energetic, active, forceful, severe, drastic, extreme. **14** *strong coffee* concentrated, undiluted. **15** *strong drink* alcoholic, intoxicating, heady. **16** *strong garlic* sharp, pungent, biting, spicy.

stronghold noun **1** *assault the enemy stronghold* fortress, fort, castle, citadel. **2** *a conservative stronghold at the last election* bastion, center, refuge, hotbed.

structure noun **1** *wooden structures* building, edifice, construction, erection, complex. **2** *the structure of the firm* construction, form, configuration, shape, constitution, composition, makeup, organization, system, arrangement, design.

struggle verb **1** *struggle to obtain power* strive, endeavor, exert oneself, battle, labor, toil, strain. **2** *boys struggling with each other* fight, grapple, wrestle, scuffle, brawl; *inf.* scrap. **3** *rivals struggling for supremacy* fight, compete, contend, vie, lock horns, cross swords.

struggle noun **1** *his struggles to obtain power* battle, endeavor, effort, exertion, labor, pains. **2** *a barroom struggle* fight, wrestling match, scuffle, brawl, tussle; *inf.* scrap, set-to. **3** *opposing armies engaged in a struggle* battle, fight, combat, conflict, contest, hostilities, clash, skirmish. **4** *a struggle on the committee for supremacy* competition, contention, vying, rivalry. **5** *a struggle just to survive* effort, fight, trial, labor; *inf.* grind, hassle.

strut verb swagger, prance, parade, flounce, sashay.

stub noun end, butt, stump, remnant.

stubborn adjective obstinate, headstrong, willful, strong-willed, pigheaded, mulish, dogged, persistent, adamant, inflexible, uncompromising, unbending, unyielding, obdurate, intractable, refractory, recalcitrant, contumacious.

stuck adjective **1** *posters stuck to the wall* glued, fixed, mired, fastened. **2** *stuck in the mud* immobile, fast, fixed, mired, rooted. **3** *the problem has her stuck* baffled, stumped, at a loss, perplexed. **stuck on** *stuck on the new girl* attracted to, infatuated with, fond of, in love with, obsessed by; *inf.* mad about, hung up on.

student noun pupil, schoolboy, schoolgirl; undergraduate; trainee, apprentice.

studied adjective *with studied indifference* deliberate, willful, conscious, calculated, purposeful, forced.

studio noun workshop, workroom, atelier.

studious adjective *a studious pupil* scholarly, academic, intellectual, bookish, serious, earnest.

study noun **1** *a life devoted to study* learning, scholarship, education, academic work, research, reading. **2** *make a study of rural transport* investigation, inquiry, examination, analysis, review, survey. **3** *writing in his study* office, workroom, studio, library. **4** *write a study on/of Shakespeare's late plays* paper, work, essay, review.

study verb **1** *study history* learn, read, work at; *inf.* bone up on, cram. **2** *study the effects of sleeplessness* investigate, inquire into, research, examine, analyze, review, survey, scrutinize. **3** *study the suspect's movements* watch, observe, keep an eye on, keep under surveillance.

stuff noun **1** *made out of durable stuff* material, fabric, matter, substance. **2** *get rid of the stuff in the hall* things, objects, articles, items. **3** *travelers carrying their stuff* luggage, baggage, belongings, possessions, paraphernalia.

stuff verb **1** *stuff a pillow* fill, pack, pad. **2** *too much furniture stuffed into the room* pack, cram, squeeze, crowd, stow, press, force, compress, jam, wedge. **3** *stuff the money into his wallet* thrust, shove, push, ram. **4** *stuff themselves with turkey* fill, gorge, overindulge, satiate.

stuffing noun **1** *stuffing for cushions* filling, filler, packing, padding, wadding. **2** *stuffing for the duck* filling, dressing, forcemeat.

stuffy adjective **1** *a stuffy atmosphere* airless, close, muggy, stifling, suffocating. **2** *a stuffy young man* staid, stiff, formal, pompous, starchy, prim, priggish, straitlaced, conservative, stodgy; *inf.* fuddy-duddy, square. **3** *a stuffy nose* stuffed-up, blocked.

stumble verb **1** *stumble and fall* trip, lose one's balance, slip. **2** *drunks stumbling home* blunder, lumber, lurch, stagger, reel. **3** *stumble a little when giving her speech* stammer, stutter, hesitate, falter; *inf.* fluff one's lines. **stumble upon** *stumble upon an unpublished work of the novelist* chance upon, happen upon, come across, find, discover, encounter.

stump noun end, stub, butt, remnant, remains.

stump verb *the last question stumped him* baffle, outwit, foil, perplex, puzzle, confound, bewilder; *inf.* flummox, stymie.

stun verb **1** *the blow stunned him* daze, stupefy, knock senseless. **2** *stunned by the news of his death* shock, astound, dumbfound, stupefy, overwhelm, devastate, stagger, take one's breath away, confound, bewilder; *inf.* flabbergast.

stunning adjective **1** *a stunning range of electronic equipment* impressive, extraordinary, staggering, incredible, amazing, astonishing, marvelous; *inf.* mind-boggling. **2** *looking stunning in a new evening dress* sensational, ravishing, dazzling, wonderful, magnificent, glorious, exquisite, beautiful; *inf.* gorgeous, fabulous, smashing.

stunt verb *stunt the child's growth* retard, slow, impede, hamper, hinder, check, curb, restrict, arrest.

stupefy verb **1** *a boxer stupefied by the first blow* stun, daze, knock senseless. **2** *stupefied by the news* shock, astound, dumbfound. *See* STUN 2.

stupendous adjective **1** *a stupendous achievement* amazing, astounding, astonishing, extraordinary, wonderful, phenomenal; *inf.* fantastic, mind-boggling. **2** *a stupendous beast* colossal, immense, gigantic, massive, huge, enormous.

stupid adjective **1** *a stupid fellow* dense, brainless, mindless, dull-witted, slow-witted, slow, simpleminded, halfwitted; *inf.* thick, dim, dumb, dopey, moronic, imbecilic. **2** *stupid error/behavior* foolish, silly, idiotic, mindless, senseless, irresponsible, unthinking, ill-advised, ill-considered, unwise, injudicious, shortsighted, inane, absurd, ludicrous, ridiculous, asinine, pointless, meaningless, insane.

stupor noun *in a drunken stupor* daze, insensibility, oblivion, coma, blackout.

sturdy adjective **1** *sturdy young men* well-built, muscular, athletic, strong, strapping, brawny, powerful, solid, substantial, robust, vigorous, tough, hardy, stalwart. **2** *put up a sturdy resistance* strong, vigorous, stalwart, firm, determined, resolute, tenacious, staunch, steadfast, unyielding, unwavering, uncompromising.

stutter verb stammer, stumble, hesitate, falter, splutter.

style noun **1** *an unusual style of house* kind, type, variety, sort, design, pattern. **2** *try to copy the style of her favorite artist* technique, method, approach, manner, way, mode, system. **3** *a young man with style* elegance, polish, suaveness, urbanity, flair, dash, panache, élan; *inf.* pizzazz. **4** *used to living in style* comfort, elegance, affluence, wealth, luxury. **5** *styles popular in the 1920s* fashion, trend, vogue, mode.

6 *criticize both the content and style of the novel* mode of expression, phraseology, wording, language.

style verb **1** *style the clothes to suit a warm climate* design, fashion, tailor. **2** *he styled himself professor* designate, call, term, name, dub, label, tag.

stylish adjective *stylish clothes* fashionable, smart, elegant, chic, modish, à la mode; *inf.* trendy, natty, classy, snazzy.

suave adjective smooth, glib, sophisticated, urbane, worldly, charming, polite, diplomatic, polished.

subconscious adjective subliminal, latent, suppressed, repressed, hidden, underlying, deep, intuitive, instinctive.

subdue verb **1** *subdue the rebel forces* conquer, defeat, vanquish, overpower, subjugate, master, crush, quell, tame. **2** *subdue one's desire to hit him* control, curb, restrain, check, inhibit, repress, suppress, stifle.

subject noun **1** *the subject of the discussion* topic, theme, question, gist, thesis. **2** *subjects studied at university* course of study, course, discipline. **3** *a suitable subject for hypnosis* case, client, patient, participant; *inf.* guinea pig. **4** *his disappearance was the subject of much speculation* occasion, basis, grounds, source. **5** *a British subject* citizen, national. **6** *the king's subjects* liege, subordinate, underling, vassal.

subject adjective **subject to 1** *subject to the terms of the contract* conditional upon, contingent upon, dependent on. **2** *subject to colds in the winter* susceptible to, liable to, prone to, vulnerable to. **3** *subject to the laws of the land* bound by, constrained by, accountable to.

subject verb **subject to** *subjected us to his anger* put through, expose to, lay open to, submit to.

subjective adjective *a highly subjective view of the situation* personal, individual, biased, prejudiced.

sublime adjective **1** *sublime devotion/beauty* noble, exalted, awe-inspiring, majestic, imposing, glorious, supreme, virtuous, high-principled. **2** *a sublime meal* excellent, outstanding, first-rate, first-class, superb, perfect, ideal, wonderful, marvelous; *inf.* fantastic, fabulous. **3** *a sublime lack of concern for the truth* total, complete, utter, arrogant.

submerge verb **1** *watch the submarines submerging* go under water, dive, sink, plummet. **2** *submerge the dress in soapy water* immerse, dip, plunge, dunk. **3** *floodwaters submerged the streets* flood, inundate, deluge, engulf, swamp. **4** *submerged in a backlog of correspondence* inundate, deluge, swamp, bury, engulf.

submission noun **1** *he sought their submission to his demands* yielding, capitulation, agreement, acceptance, consent, accession, compliance. **2** *the submission of our army to the enemy forces* surrender, laying down one's arms. **3** *the submission of a planning proposal* presentation, tendering, entry, proposal, introduction. **4** *accept his submission that his client is innocent* argument, assertion, contention, claim. **5** *after years of submission, they rebelled* passivity, obedience, submissiveness, compliance, acquiescence, tractability, nonresistance, docility, meekness, resignation, humility, deference, subservience, servility, subjection.

submissive adjective yielding, compliant, acquiescent, tractable, nonresisting, passive, obedient, dutiful, docile, meek, resigned, humble, deferential, obsequious.

submit verb **1** *submit a planning proposal* put forward, present, proffer, tender, advance, propose, introduce. **2** *submit a claim* put in, enter, refer. **3** *submit that his client was innocent* argue, assert, contend, state, claim, aver, propound. **4** *submit to his demands* give in, yield, bow, capitulate, agree, accept, consent, accede, acquiesce, conform. **5** *submit to the enemy forces* surrender, yield, lay down one's arms, raise the white flag, bend the knee.

subordinate adjective **1** *his subordinate officers* lower-ranking, junior, lesser, inferior. **2** *subordinate issues* lesser, minor, secondary, subsidiary, ancillary, auxiliary.

subordinate noun *be patronizing to his subordinates* junior, assistant, second, deputy, aide, underling, inferior; *inf.* sidekick.

subscribe verb **subscribe to 1** *subscribe to several learned journals* pay a subscription to, contract to buy. **2** *subscribe to several charities* donate to, give to, pledge money to, contribute to. **3** *subscribe to the theory of evolution* agree with, accede to, consent to, accept, believe in, endorse, back, support.

subsequent adjective *on subsequent visits* following, ensuing, succeeding, later. **subsequent to** *subsequent to his illness* following, after, in the wake of.

subservient adjective servile, submissive, deferential, obsequious, sycophantic, groveling, fawning, ingratiating, toadying, unctuous; *inf.* bootlicking.

subside verb **1** *storms subsiding* abate, let up, moderate, calm, slacken, die down/out, peter out, taper off, recede, lessen, diminish. **2** *water levels subsiding* go down, recede, sink, fall back.

subsidiary adjective *discuss subsidiary issues* subordinate, secondary, ancillary, auxiliary, minor.

subsidy noun *government subsidies for the arts* grant, contribution, backing, support, aid, sponsorship, funding, subvention.

subsist verb **1** *subsist on bread and water | old customs still subsist* live, exist, survive, be in existence, continue, last. **subsist in** *her attractiveness subsists in her personality* lie in, reside in, be attributable to.

subsistence noun **1** *their subsistence on bread and water | the subsistence of old customs* existence, survival, continuance. **2** *contribute to the child's subsistence* keep, support, maintenance, livelihood; sustenance, provisions.

substance noun **1** *a hard substance* matter, material, stuff, mass. **2** *ghostly figures with no substance* solidity, body, corporeality, materiality, concreteness, tangibility. **3** *an argument with little substance* meaningfulness, significance, weight, soundness, validity. **4** *a person of very little substance* character, backbone, mettle. **5** *the substance of the novel* subject matter, theme, topic, content, essence, gist, sense, import. **6** *born poor, he became a man of substance* wealth, affluence, prosperity, capital, means, resources, assets, property.

substantial adjective **1** *confuse the substantial world with the world of the imagination* material, real, actual, concrete. **2** *make a substantial contribution to the project* sizable, considerable, meaningful, significant, important, major, material, marked, valuable, useful, worthwhile. **3** *substantial houses* solid, sturdy, strong, well-built, durable. **4** *a substantial figure of a man* large, big, solid, sturdy, stout, hefty, bulky. **5** *put forward a substantial argument* solid, meaningful, weighty, powerful, sound, valid. **6** *run a substantial business* successful, prosperous, wealthy, affluent, well-to-do. **7** *in substantial agreement* essential, basic, fundamental.

substantiate verb support, uphold, back up, bear out, validate, corroborate, verify, authenticate, confirm.

substitute noun *act as a substitute for the manager* replacement, deputy, relief, proxy, surrogate, fill-in, stand-in.

substitute verb **substitute for 1** *substitute sparkling wine for champagne* replace with, use instead of, exchange for, switch with; *inf.* swap for. **2** *she substituted for him when he was ill* replace, relieve, fill in for, cover for, take over from, hold the fort for.

subterfuge noun **1** *think of a subterfuge to get past the doorman* trick, ruse, wile, ploy, stratagem, artifice, dodge, maneuver, pretext, intrigue, scheme, deception. **2** *use subterfuge to gain entry* trickery, intrigue, deviousness, evasion, deception, duplicity.

subtle adjective **1** *a subtle flavor* elusive, delicate, understated, low-key, muted, toned down. **2** *a subtle distinction* fine, nice, slight, minute, indistinct. **3** *a subtle intelligence* perceptive, discerning, sensitive, discriminating, penetrating, astute, keen, acute, shrewd, sagacious. **4** *subtle devices to trap the unwary* clever, ingenious, intricate, crafty, artful, devious.

subtract verb take away, take, deduct; *inf.* knock off.

subversive adjective *spread subversive rumors about the boss* inflammatory, seditious, revolutionary, treasonous, disruptive.

subvert verb **1** *subvert the government* overthrow, overturn, sabotage, destroy, wreck, disrupt, undermine, weaken. **2** *subverted by gifts from the enemy* corrupt, pervert, warp, deprave, contaminate, vitiate.

succeed verb **1** *plans that succeed* be successful, turn out well, work; *inf.* pan out. **2** *he succeeded him as chairman* come after, follow, replace, supplant. **3** *he succeeded as a lawyer* achieve success, make good, prosper, flourish, thrive, triumph; *inf.* make it, arrive. **succeed in** *succeed in his ambition* accomplish, achieve, bring off, attain, reach, arrive at, complete, fulfill, realize. **succeed to** *succeed to the throne* accede to, inherit, assume, take over, come into.

succeeding adjective *grow weaker in the succeeding days* subsequent, following, ensuing, next.

success noun **1** *gain success in his endeavor* accomplishment, achievement, attainment, fulfillment, victory, triumph. **2** *envy his success* prosperity, affluence, wealth, fame, eminence. **3** *the book/play was a success* best seller, box-office success, winner, sellout, triumph; *inf.* hit, box-office hit, smash hit, sensation. **4** *became a success in Hollywood* celebrity, big name, somebody, VIP, star.

successful adjective **1** *successful in his endeavor* victorious, triumphant. **2** *envying successful people* prosperous, affluent, wealthy, well-to-do, famous, eminent. **3** *a successful business* flourishing, thriving, profitable, moneymaking, lucrative.

succession noun **1** *a succession of events leading to disaster* sequence, series, progression, course, cycle, chain, train. **2** *his succession to the throne* accession, inheritance, assumption, elevation. **3** *the succession is through his eldest son* line of descent, ancestral line, dynasty, lineage. **in succession** *several firms closed in (quick) succession* successively, one after the other.

successor noun **1** *the successor to the throne* heir, heir apparent, next-in-line. **2** *select the chairman's successor* heir, replacement, supplanter.

succinct adjective short, brief, concise, compact, crisp, terse, to the point, pithy.

succor noun *give succor to the wounded* assistance, aid, help, comfort, relief, support.

succor verb *succor the wounded* assist, aid, help, minister to, comfort, bring relief to, support.

succumb verb **1** *succumb to temptation* give in, yield, submit, surrender, capitulate, fall victim. **2** *succumb to his injuries* die, pass away, expire.

sudden adjective **1** *a sudden change in the temperature* immediate, instantaneous, abrupt, unexpected, unforeseen, unanticipated. **2** *his sudden rise to fame* rapid, swift, speedy, quick, meteoric.

suddenly adverb all of a sudden, instantaneously, abruptly, unexpectedly, without warning; *inf.* out of the blue.

sue verb take one to court, bring an action against, bring charges against, charge, bring a suit against, prosecute, summons, indict.

suffer verb **1** *suffered from the illness* be in pain, endure agony, hurt, ache. **2** *the divorce caused him to suffer* be distressed, experience hardship, be miserable, be wretched. **3** *suffer loss* experience, undergo, sustain, encounter, endure. **4** *his work suffered because of tardiness* deteriorate, fall off, decline, be impaired. **5** *cannot suffer his arrogance* put up with, tolerate, bear, stand, abide. **suffer from** *suffer from headaches* be affected by, be afflicted by, be troubled with.

suffering noun **1** *distressed by the patient's suffering* pain, agony, torment. **2** *endured the suffering of poverty* distress, hardship, misery, wretchedness, hurt, pain, anguish.

suffice verb be enough, be sufficient, be adequate, do, serve, meet one's needs; *inf.* fill the bill, hit the spot.

sufficient adjective enough, adequate, plenty of, ample.

suffocate verb *was nearly suffocated by the fumes* smother, stifle, asphyxiate.

suffuse verb spread over, cover, bathe, mantle, permeate, pervade, imbue.

suggest verb **1** *suggest him as a replacement* propose, put forward, move, submit, recommend, advocate. **2** *an aroma suggesting fresh-baked bread* bring to mind, evoke. **3** *an appearance suggesting that he lived rough* indicate, lead (one) to believe, give the impression. **4** *a letter suggesting that he is lying* insinuate, hint, imply, intimate.

suggestion noun **1** *put forward a suggestion that we leave* proposal, proposition, plan, motion, submission, recommendation. **2** *a suggestion of a French accent in* *her speech* hint, trace, touch, suspicion. **3** *object to the suggestion that he was making* insinuation, hint, implication, intimation.

suggestive adjective **1** *make suggestive remarks* provocative, sexual, indelicate, improper, off-color, racy, risqué. **2** *an aroma suggestive of freshly cut grass* redolent, indicative, evocative, reminiscent.

suit noun **1** *a woman wearing a blue suit* set of clothes, outfit, costume, ensemble. **2** *bring a suit against his employers* lawsuit, court case, action, proceedings, prosecution. **3** *take one's suit to the king* petition, appeal, request, plea, entreaty. **4** *pay suit to his friend's sister* courtship, wooing, attentions.

suit verb **1** *a color that suits her* become, look attractive on, go well with. **2** *the suggested date does not suit him* be suitable for, be convenient for, be acceptable to, meet requirements. **3** *rich food does not suit him* agree with, be good for, be healthy for. **4** *suit your speech to the occasion* make appropriate, tailor, fashion, accommodate, adjust, adapt, modify.

suitable adjective **1** *find a suitable date* convenient, acceptable, satisfactory. **2** *shoes suitable for dancing* right, appropriate, fitting, ideal, apt. **3** *not suitable behavior* appropriate, fitting, becoming, seemly, decorous, proper. **suitable for** *a speech suitable for the occasion* suited to, befitting, appropriate to, in keeping with, in character with.

suitcase noun case, grip, valise, overnight bag.

suitor noun **1** *unable to choose among her suitors* admirer, beau, wooer, boyfriend; *lit.* follower. **2** *the king giving audience to several suitors* petitioner, supplicant, plaintiff, appellant.

sulk verb mope, pout, be sullen, be put out, be grumpy.

sullen adjective morose, uncommunicative, resentful, sulky, sour, glum, gloomy, surly, cross, glowering, grumpy.

sultry adjective **1** *a sultry day* stuffy, stifling, close, oppressive, muggy, humid, sticky, hot, sweltering. **2** *a sultry singer* sensual, sexy, voluptuous, seductive, alluring, passionate, erotic.

sum noun **1** *find the sum of the figures* total, grand total, tally, aggregate. **2** *a large sum of money* amount, quantity. **3** *look at the problem in its sum* entirety, totality, whole. **sum up 1** *when the judge sums up* review the evidence, summarize the argument. **2** *sum up the situation* form an opinion of, form an impression of, get the measure of; *inf.* size up. **3** *sum up the facts* summarize, précis, abstract, encapsulate, put in a nutshell.

summarily adverb *summarily dismissed when caught stealing* immediately, straight away, on the spot, directly, forthwith, promptly, speedily, suddenly, abruptly, peremptorily, without discussion, without formality.

summarize verb sum up, give a synopsis of, précis, abstract, abridge, condense, outline, sketch, give a rundown of, review.

summary noun *a summary of the plot* synopsis, précis, résumé, abstract, abridgment, digest, epitome, outline, sketch, rundown, review, summing-up.

summary adjective **1** *summary dismissal* immediate, instantaneous, prompt, speedy, swift, rapid, sudden, abrupt, hasty, peremptory. **2** *a summary account of the long debate* abridged, abbreviated, shortened, condensed, brief, concise, succinct, thumbnail.

summit noun **1** *the summit of the mountain* top, peak, crest, crown, apex, vertex, apogee. **2** *the summit of her stage career* peak, height, pinnacle, climax, zenith, acme.

summon verb **1** *summoned by the principal* send for, call for, bid. **2** *summon a committee meeting* order, call, convene, assemble, convoke, muster. **3** *summon a witness* summons, serve with a summons, cite, serve with a writ, subpoena. **summon up 1** *summon up the courage to act* gather, collect, muster, rally. **2** *summon up half-forgotten memories* call to mind, call up, conjure up, evoke, recall, revive.

summons noun **1** *a summons to give evidence in court* citation, writ, subpoena. **2** *obey the principal's summons to attend* order, directive, command, instruction, dictum.

sumptuous adjective lavish, luxurious, opulent, magnificent, splendid, costly, expensive, extravagant; *inf.* plush, ritzy.

sundry adjective **1** *sundry items* various, varied, miscellaneous, assorted, diverse. **2** *on sundry occasions* several, some, various, different.

sunny adjective **1** *a sunny day* sunlit, bright, clear, fine, cloudless. **2** *a sunny nature* cheerful, lighthearted, bright, gay, merry, joyful, buoyant, bubbly, blithe, hopeful, optimistic.

sunrise noun dawn, daybreak, sunup, first light; *lit.* aurora.

sunset noun sundown, nightfall, close of day, evening, twilight, dusk, gloaming.

superb adjective superlative, excellent, first-rate, first-class, outstanding, remarkable, dazzling, brilliant, marvelous, magnificent, wonderful, splendid, exquisite; *inf.* fantastic, fabulous, A-1.

supercilious adjective arrogant, haughty, conceited, proud, vain, disdainful, scornful, condescending, patronizing, lordly, snobbish; *inf.* hoity-toity, high-and-mighty, uppity, snooty, stuck-up.

superficial adjective **1** *superficial damage* surface, exterior, peripheral, slight. **2** *a superficial examination* cursory, perfunctory, hasty, hurried, slapdash. **3** *a superficial similarity* outward, apparent, ostensible. **4** *rather a superficial person* shallow, trivial, frivolous, silly. **5** *a superficial book* lightweight, insignificant, trivial.

superfluous adjective **1** *sell off the superfluous furniture* spare, surplus, extra, excess, supernumerary. **2** *their presence was superfluous* unnecessary, unneeded, unwarranted, gratuitous.

superhuman adjective **1** *require a superhuman effort* Herculean, phenomenal, prodigious, heroic, extraordinary. **2** *superhuman intervention* divine, godlike, holy. **3** *a cry that seemed superhuman* supernatural, preternatural, otherworldly.

superintendent noun director, administrator, manager, supervisor, overseer, boss, chief.

superior adjective **1** *the superior player* better, greater, more skillful, more advanced. **2** *hold a superior position* higher, higher-ranking, higher-up. **3** *goods of superior leather* high-quality, first-rate, top-quality, high-grade, choice, select, prime, fine. **4** *give her a superior look* haughty, disdainful, condescending, supercilious, patronizing, lordly, snobby; *inf.* high-and-mighty, hoity-toity, uppity, snooty, stuck-up.

superior noun boss, manager, chief, supervisor, foreman.

superlative adjective best, greatest, supreme, consummate, first-rate, first-class, excellent, magnificent, outstanding, unsurpassed, unparalleled, unrivaled, peerless.

supernatural adjective **1** *supernatural beings* otherworldly, unearthly, spectral, ghostly, magical. **2** *supernatural powers* paranormal, supernormal, psychic, miraculous, extraordinary.

supersede verb **1** *workers superseded by machines* replace, displace, supplant, oust. **2** *supersede him as chairman* replace, take over from, succeed.

supervise verb **1** *supervise the factory* superintend, direct, administer, manage, run. **2** *supervise the trainees* oversee, watch, observe, guide.

supervision noun **1** *the supervision of the factory* administration, management, direction, control. **2** *children playing under supervision* observation, guidance.

supervisor noun **1** *the supervisor of the factory* director, administrator, manager, overseer, boss, chief, superintendent. **2**

the supervisors of the children overseer, observer, guide, adviser.

supplant verb replace, displace, supersede, oust, overthrow, unseat.

supple adjective **1** *supple gymnasts* lithe, loose-limbed, limber. **2** *supple leather* pliant, pliable, flexible, bendable.

supplement noun **1** *dietary supplement* addition, additive, extra. **2** *add a supplement to the book/document* appendix, addendum, codicil, rider. **3** *a newspaper supplement* pullout, insert.

supplement verb *supplement his salary with an evening job* add to, augment, increase, complement.

supplicate verb plead, entreat, beseech, beg, implore, petition, appeal, solicit, pray.

supplies noun provisions, stores, rations, food, victuals, provender; equipment, materials, matériel.

supply verb **1** *supply the necessary money* provide, give, furnish, contribute, donate, grant; *inf.* shell out. **2** *supply him with tools* provide, equip, outfit.

supply noun **1** *organize the supply of wood* provision, furnishing. **2** *a supply of logs* stock, store, reserve, reservoir, stockpile, hoard, cache.

support verb **1** *beams supporting the roof* bear, carry, hold up, prop up, bolster up, brace, underpin, buttress. **2** *work to support his family* maintain, provide for, sustain, take care of. **3** *support him in his hour of need* comfort, help, sustain, encourage, fortify. **4** *bring evidence to support his argument* back up, substantiate, corroborate, confirm, verify, validate, authenticate, endorse, ratify. **5** *support several charities* contribute to, donate to, subsidize, fund, finance. **6** *support the candidate* back, champion, side with, vote for, stand behind, stand up for. **7** *support conservation measures* back, advocate, promote, further, champion, espouse, recommend, defend.

support noun **1** *the supports of the bridge* base, foundation, pillar, post, prop, underpinning, substructure, brace, buttress, abutment, bolster, stay. **2** *pay toward his family's support* keep, maintenance, sustenance, subsistence, aliment. **3** *discouraged and in need of support* friendship, encouragement, fortification. **4** *give support to charities* contribution, donation, money, subsidy, funding, funds, capital. **5** *give his support to the candidate* backing, assistance, vote. **6** *in support of conservation measures* backing, advocacy, promotion, championship, espousal, recommendation. **7** *he was a great support to his mother* help, assistance, comfort, tower of strength, prop, backbone, mainstay.

supporter noun **1** *supporters of the charity* backer, contributor, donor, sponsor, patron, friend, well-wisher. **2** *the candidate's supporters* backer, helper, adherent, follower, ally, voter. **3** *supporters of animal welfare* adherent, advocate, promoter, champion, defender, apologist. **4** *football supporter* fan, follower.

suppose verb **1** *I suppose you are right* dare say, assume, presume, expect, imagine, believe, suspect, guess, surmise, reckon, conjecture. **2** *suppose we arrive late* take as a hypothesis, hypothesize, postulate, posit; *inf.* let's say. **3** *creation supposes a creator* presuppose, require, imply.

supposition noun **1** *his suppositions proved correct* assumption, presumption, suspicion, guess, surmise, conjecture, speculation, theory. **2** *on the supposition that he is right* assumption, hypothesis, postulation.

suppress verb **1** *suppress the rebellion* conquer, vanquish, crush, quell, squash, stamp out, extinguish. **2** *suppress his anger* restrain, keep a rein on, hold back, check, curb. **3** *suppress the information* keep secret, conceal, hide, withhold, cover up, smother, stifle.

supremacy noun **1** *a country holding supremacy over its neighbors* ascendancy, predominance, dominion, sway, authority, mastery, control, power, rule, sovereignty, lordship. **2** *challenge her supremacy as top tennis player* preeminence, dominance, superiority, ascendancy, inimitability, matchlessness, peerlessness.

supreme adjective **1** *the supreme commander* highest-ranking, chief, foremost, principal. **2** *a supreme effort* extreme, utmost, maximum, extraordinary, remarkable. **3** *the supreme sacrifice* final, last, ultimate.

sure adjective **1** *we cannot be sure that he is honest* certain, definite, positive, confident, assured. **2** *a sure success* assured, certain, guaranteed, inevitable. **3** *in the sure knowledge* true, certain, absolute, categorical, proven, unquestionable, indisputable, incontestable, irrefutable, incontrovertible, undeniable. **4** *a sure remedy* unfailing, infallible, reliable, dependable, trustworthy, tested, tried and true, foolproof, effective, efficacious; *inf.* sure-fire. **5** *sure friend* true, reliable, dependable, trusted, trustworthy, loyal, faithful, steadfast. **6** *with a sure hand* firm, steady, stable, secure, confident, unhesitating, unfaltering, unwavering. **be sure** *be sure to arrive on time* be certain, be careful, take care, remember.

surely adverb **1** *they will surely fail* certainly, definitely, assuredly, undoubtedly, without doubt, indubitably, unquestionably, irrefutably, incontrovertibly, undeniably, inevitably. **2** *walk slowly but surely* firmly, steadily, confidently, unhesitatingly.

surface noun outside, exterior, top, façade. **on the surface** *on the surface, the business seems profitable* at first glance, to the casual eye, outwardly, to all appearances, apparently, superficially.

surge noun **1** *a surge of water* gush, rush, outpouring, stream, flow, efflux. **2** *a sudden surge in prices* increase, rise, upswing, escalation.

surge verb *the water surged from the broken pipe|crowds surging from the hall* gush, rush, stream, flow.

surly adjective bad-tempered, ill-natured, grumpy, crotchety, grouchy, cantankerous, irascible, gruff, churlish, sullen.

surmise verb guess, conjecture, suspect, deduce, assume, presume, gather, think, believe, imagine.

surmount verb **1** *many obstacles to surmount* get over, overcome, conquer, triumph over, prevail over, beat. **2** *climbers struggling to surmount the mountain* climb, ascend, scale, mount.

surpass verb beat, exceed, excel, transcend, outdo, outshine, outstrip, overshadow, eclipse.

surplus noun *get rid of the surplus* excess, remainder, residue, surfeit.

surplus adjective *surplus food going to waste* excess, superfluous, leftover, unused, remaining, extra, spare.

surprise verb **1** *their sudden appearance surprised him* astonish, amaze, nonplus, take aback, startle, astound, flabbergast. **2** *surprise the burglars opening the safe* take by surprise, catch unawares, catch off guard, catch red-handed.

surprise noun **1** *look up in surprise* astonishment, amazement, incredulity, wonder. **2** *it was a surprise when she left* shock, bolt from the blue, bombshell.

surrender verb **1** *surrender his right to the title* give up, relinquish, renounce, forgo, forsake, cede, abdicate, waive, hand over, let go of. **2** *surrender to the enemy* give oneself up, yield, submit, capitulate, lay down one's arms, raise the white flag. **3** *surrender all hope* give up, abandon, lose.

surrender noun **1** *the surrender of his title* relinquishment, renunciation, forgoing, ceding, cession, abdication, waiving. **2** *their surrender to the enemy* yielding, capitulation, submission.

surreptitious adjective stealthy, clandestine, secret, sneaky, furtive, underhand, covert.

surround verb encircle, enclose, encompass, ring, gird, fence in, hem in.

surroundings plural noun *brought up in squalid surroundings* environment, setting, milieu, element.

surveillance noun *under surveillance* observation, watch, scrutiny, espionage.

survey verb 1 *survey the burned building* observe, view, regard, examine, inspect. 2 *survey the evidence* scan, study, consider, review, examine, scrutinize, take stock of; *inf.* size up. 3 *survey a building* make a survey of, value, appraise, assess, prospect, triangulate.

survey noun 1 *undertake a survey of the evidence* study, consideration, review, overview, examination, inspection, scrutiny. 2 *carry out a survey of the building* valuation, appraisal. 3 *a survey of TV viewing habits* investigation, inquiry, research, study, review, probe, questionnaire.

survive verb 1 *old customs surviving in the village* live on, continue, remain, last, persist, endure, exist. 2 *fathers surviving their sons* outlive, outlast. 3 *people surviving in the freezing conditions* remain alive, live, subsist.

susceptible adjective 1 *con artists preying on susceptible people* impressionable, gullible, vulnerable. 2 *susceptible to colds* subject, liable, prone, inclined, predisposed.

suspect verb 1 *I suspect that you are right* feel, fancy, surmise, guess, conjecture, speculate, have a hunch, suppose, believe, think. 2 *suspect the truth of his statement* doubt, harbor suspicions about, have misgivings about, distrust, mistrust.

suspend verb 1 *suspend a light from the tree* hang, swing, dangle. 2 *suspend the proceedings* adjourn, interrupt, discontinue, break off, put off, postpone, delay, defer, shelve, pigeonhole, table; *inf.* put on ice. 3 *suspend him from his job* debar, shut out, exclude, keep out, remove.

suspense noun uncertainty, doubt, anticipation, expectation, excitement, tension, anxiety, nervousness, apprehension.

suspicion noun *his suspicion is that she will appear* feeling, surmise, guess, conjecture, speculation, hunch, supposition, belief; *inf.* gut feeling. **suspicions** *have suspicions about his motives* doubts, misgivings, qualms, skepticism; *inf.* a funny feeling.

suspicious adjective 1 *give him suspicious looks* doubtful, wary, chary, skeptical, distrustful, mistrustful. 2 *police observing a suspicious character* guilty-looking, dishonest-looking; *inf.* shifty, shady. 3 *suspicious circumstances* questionable, doubtful, odd, strange, irregular, queer, funny; *inf.* fishy.

sustain verb 1 *beams sustaining the weight of the roof* bear, support, carry, prop up, shore up. 2 *sustain one's courage* keep up, continue, carry on, maintain. 3 *sustain him in his hour of need* support, comfort, help, assist, encourage. 4 *enough food to sustain them* keep alive, keep going, maintain, preserve, feed, nourish. 5 *sustain defeat* experience, undergo, suffer, endure. 6 *the court sustained his claim* uphold, validate, ratify, vindicate. 7 *evidence sustaining his allegations* confirm, verify, corroborate, substantiate.

swagger verb *swagger down the street in his new coat* strut, parade, prance; *inf.* show off.

swallow verb 1 *swallow the meat with difficulty* gulp down, eat, consume, devour, ingest. 2 *swallow two drinks in quick succession* gulp down, drink, swill; *inf.* swig, chug. 3 *swallow one's pride* repress, restrain, choke back, control; eat. **swallow up** 1 *the waves swallowed him up* engulf, swamp, overwhelm. 2 *big companies swallowing up small ones* take over, absorb, assimilate, overrun.

swamp noun *get stuck in a swamp* marsh, bog, quagmire, mire, morass, fen, quag.

swamp verb 1 *heavy rains swamping the town* flood, inundate, deluge, wash out, drench, saturate. 2 *swamped with applications* inundate, flood, deluge, overwhelm, engulf, snow under, besiege.

swap verb 1 *children swapping toys* exchange, trade, barter, switch. 2 *swap jokes* exchange, trade, bandy.

swarm noun *a swarm of people* crowd, multitude, horde, host, mob, throng, mass, army, drove.

swarm verb *shoppers swarming to the sales* flock, crowd, throng. **swarming with** *a barn swarming with flies* overrun with, teeming with, bristling with, crawling with, infested with.

swarthy adjective dark, dark-skinned, dark-complexioned, dusky.

sway verb 1 *trees swaying in the breeze* swing, shake, bend, lean, incline. 2 *drunks swaying on their way home* roll, stagger, wobble. 3 *swaying her hips* swing, shake. 4 *swaying between emigrating and staying* waver, hesitate, fluctuate, vacillate, oscillate. 5 *swayed by their arguments* influence, affect, persuade. 6 *swayed by ambition* rule, govern, control, direct, guide.

sway noun *colonies under the sway of the monarchy | under the sway of her parents* jurisdiction, rule, government, sovereignty, dominion, control, command, power, authority, influence, guidance, direction. **hold sway** *the aged emperor still holds sway* hold power, rule, be in control, predominate.

swear verb 1 *swear to take care of the child* solemnly promise, pledge oneself, vow, give one's word, take an oath. 2 *he swore that he was fit to drive* vow, insist, declare, assert, maintain, contend, aver. 3 *swear* *at the other driver* curse, blaspheme, utter profanities, swear like a trooper/sailor; *inf.* cuss. **swear by 1** *swear by Almighty God* call as one's witness, appeal to, invoke. **2** *swear by her remedy for colds* have faith in, have trust in, place reliance on, depend on, believe in.

sweat noun **1** *sweat pouring from his brow* perspiration; *Med.* diaphoresis. **2** *in a sweat until the results came through* fluster, dither, fuss, panic; *inf.* tizzy, stew, lather.

sweat verb **1** *sweating in the heat* perspire, drip with perspiration. **2** *they were sweating until the results came through* fret, dither, fuss, panic, worry, agonize, lose sleep; *inf.* be on pins and needles. **3** *sweat to get the work done* work like a Trojan, labor, toil, slog.

sweep verb **1** *sweep the floor* brush, whisk, clean. **2** *swept away by the waves* carry, pull, drag. **3** *fire sweeping through the building* race, hurtle, streak, whip; *inf.* tear. **sweep aside** *sweep aside their objections* cast aside, discard, disregard, ignore, dismiss.

sweep noun **1** *with one sweep of her hand* gesture, movement, action, stroke, wave. **2** *the sweep of the road* curve, curvature, bend, arc. **3** *within the sweep of his power* span, range, scope, compass, reach. **4** *a sweep of pasture lands* stretch, expanse.

sweeping adjective **1** *sweeping reforms* extensive, wide-ranging, global, broad, comprehensive, far-reaching. **2** *make sweeping statements* blanket, wholesale, unqualified, indiscriminate. **3** *a sweeping victory* decisive, overwhelming, thorough, complete, total, absolute, out-and-out.

sweet adjective **1** *sweet types of food* sugary, honeyed, syrupy, saccharine. **2** *sweet fruit* ripe, mellow, luscious. **3** *the sweet smell of roses* fragrant, aromatic, perfumed, scented, balmy. **4** *the sweet sound of children's voices* musical, tuneful, dulcet, mellifluous, harmonious, euphonious. **5** *the sweet sight of home* pleasing, delightful, welcome. **6** *have a sweet nature* good-natured, amiable, pleasant, agreeable, friendly, kindly, charming, engaging. **7** *sweet faces* attractive, beautiful, lovely, comely. **8** *his sweet wife* dear, darling, beloved, cherished, precious, treasured. **sweet on** *sweet on the boy next door* fond of, taken with, in love with, enamored of, keen on.

sweetheart noun **1** *his teenage sweetheart* girlfriend, boyfriend, lover, suitor, admirer, beau, paramour, inamorato, inamorata; *inf.* steady, flame. **2** *good-bye, sweetheart* dear, dearest, darling, love, beloved; *inf.* honey, sweetie.

swell verb **1** *his ankle swelled up* expand, bulge, distend, inflate, dilate, become bloated, blow up, puff up, balloon. **2** *the numbers have swelled* increase, rise, mount, escalate, snowball, mushroom. **3** *the music swelled* grow louder, intensify, heighten.

swell noun **1** *the swell of the sea* billowing, undulation, surging. **2** *a swell in numbers* increase, rise, escalation, mushrooming.

swelling noun *treat the swelling on his head* bump, lump, bulge, inflammation, protuberance.

swerve verb veer, turn aside, skew, deviate, sheer.

swift adjective **1** *a swift runner* fast, rapid, quick, speedy, fleet. **2** *at a swift pace* fast, rapid, brisk, lively, expeditious. **3** *a swift change of plan* rapid, sudden, abrupt, hasty, hurried. **4** *a swift reply* rapid, prompt, immediate, instantaneous.

swill verb *swill bottles of beer* gulp down, drink, quaff, swallow, down, drain, guzzle; *inf.* swig, knock off.

swill noun *remove the swill from the pigsties* waste, slop, refuse, scourings.

swindle verb *swindle the old lady* defraud, cheat, trick, fleece, dupe, deceive; *inf.* con, rip off, pull a fast one on, bilk.

swindle noun *get the money through a swindle* fraud, trick, deception, scam; *inf.* con, rip-off.

swindler noun fraud, cheat, trickster, rogue, mountebank; *inf.* con man, con artist, shark.

swing verb **1** *lights swinging from the roof* hang, be suspended, dangle. **2** *the pendulum swings* sway, undulate, oscillate. **3** *he swings from optimism to despair* change, fluctuate, oscillate, waver, seesaw, yo-yo. **4** *manage to swing an interview with the chairman* achieve, obtain, acquire, get, maneuver.

swing noun **1** *the swing of the pendulum* swaying, oscillation, undulation. **2** *music with a swing rhythm* beat, pulse. **3** *a swing to the left at the election* move, change, turn-around.

swirl verb *water swirling round and round* whirl, eddy, circulate, spin, churn, swish.

switch noun **1** *a switch from a tree* shoot, twig, branch. **2** *hit the mutineer with a switch* cane, rod, stick, whip. **3** *a sudden switch in direction* change, shift, reversal, about-face, swerve, U-turn. **4** *the switch from one method to another* change, changeover, transfer, conversion. **5** *get a new book in a switch with his friend* exchange, trade; *inf.* swap.

switch verb **1** *switch directions* change, shift, reverse. **2** *switch cars* exchange, interchange, trade, barter; *inf.* swap.

swollen adjective bulging, distended, inflated, dilated, bloated, puffy.

swoop verb *hawks swooping on their prey* pounce, dive, descend. **swoop up** *swoop* *up the baby in her arms* take up, pick up, scoop up, seize, grab.

sword noun blade, rapier, saber, cutlass. **cross swords** fight, do battle, quarrel, engage in conflict, lock horns. **put to the sword** *put the traitor to the sword* put to death, execute, kill, slay, murder.

sycophant noun toady, flatterer, Uriah Heep; *inf.* bootlicker, yes-man.

symbol noun **1** *the dove is the symbol of peace* emblem, token, sign, badge, representation, image. **2** *mathematical symbol* sign, character, mark. **3** *the symbol of the company* stamp, emblem, trademark, logo, monogram.

symbolic adjective **1** *the dove being symbolic of peace* emblematic, representative. **2** *a symbolic dance* representative, illustrative, figurative, allegorical.

symbolize verb stand for, represent, personify, exemplify, betoken, denote, signify.

symmetrical adjective **1** *symmetrical features* balanced, well-proportioned, even, harmonious. **2** *the two sides of the building must be symmetrical* regular, even, uniform, proportional, consistent, in agreement.

symmetry noun **1** *the symmetry of her features* balance, proportions, regularity, harmony. **2** *the symmetry of the two sides of the building* regularity, evenness, uniformity, consistency, congruity, conformity, agreement, correspondence.

sympathetic adjective compassionate, commiserating, pitying, consoling, comforting, supportive, caring, concerned, solicitous, considerate, kindhearted, warmhearted, understanding, charitable, empathetic. **sympathetic to** *not very sympathetic to their*

cause favorably disposed to, approving of, supportive of, encouraging of.

sympathize verb **sympathize with 1** *sympathize with the bereaved* be sympathetic toward, show compassion for, commiserate with, offer condolences to, console, comfort, be supportive of, empathize with. **2** *sympathize with their cause* be sympathetic toward, be in favor of, approve of, commend, back, support, encourage.

sympathy noun **1** *express their sympathy to the bereaved* compassion, commiseration, pity, condolence, consolation, support, concern, consideration, charity, understanding, empathy. **2** *a bond of sympathy between them* empathy, harmony, compatibility, closeness. **3** *show sympathy for their cause* favor, approval, approbation, good will, support, encouragement.

symptom noun **1** *a symptom of the disease* sign, indication, warning, mark, characteristic, feature. **2** *his bad behavior was a symptom of his unhappiness* expression, sign, indication, signal, token, evidence, demonstration, display.

synthetic adjective manufactured, man-made, fake, artificial, mock, ersatz.

system noun **1** *the railroad system* structure, organization, arrangement; *inf.* setup. **2** *a new system for teaching languages* method, methodology, technique, procedure, approach, means, way, modus operandi. **3** *absolutely no system in his accounting methods* method, order, planning, logic.

systematic adjective *a systematic approach to the problem* structured, organized, methodical, orderly, logical, efficient, businesslike.

Tt

table noun **1** *put the plates on the table* counter, bar, buffet, bench, stand. **2** *table of data* list, catalog, tabulation, inventory, digest, itemization, index; chart, diagram, figure, graph, plan.

table verb postpone, defer, suspend, shelve; *inf.* put on ice.

taboo adjective forbidden, prohibited, banned, proscribed, vetoed, ruled out, outlawed.

tabulate verb chart, systematize, systemize, arrange, order, dispose, organize, catalog,

list, classify, class, codify, group, range, grade.

tacit adjective implicit, understood, implied, unstated, undeclared, unspoken, unexpressed, unmentioned, unvoiced, silent, wordless.

taciturn adjective unforthcoming, uncommunicative, reticent, secretive, untalkative, tight-lipped, closemouthed, quiet, silent, mute, dumb; reserved, withdrawn, aloof, cold, detached.

tack noun **1** *attach the notice with a tack* nail, pin, staple, rivet. **2** *take an unusual* *tack* course/line of action, method, approach, process, way, policy, tactic, plan, strategy, attack.

tack verb 1 *tack the picture to the wall* nail, pin, staple, fix, fasten, affix, put up/down. 2 *in politics it is necessary to know when to tack* change course/direction, alter one's approach, change one's mind/attitude, have a change of heart, do an about-face; *inf.* do a U-turn. 3 *tack a postscript on the letter* add, attach, append, tag, annex.

tackle noun *fishing tackle* gear, equipment, apparatus, outfit; tools, implements, accoutrements, paraphernalia, trappings; *inf.* things, stuff.

tackle verb 1 *tackle the task/problem* undertake, attempt, apply/address oneself to, get to grips with, set/go about, get to work at, take on. 2 *tackle the intruder* grapple with, seize, take hold of, confront, accost, waylay.

tacky adjective tasteless, garish. *See* TAWDRY.

tact noun diplomacy, *savoir faire*, sensitivity, delicacy, subtlety, finesse, skill, adroitness, perception, judgment, prudence.

tactful adjective diplomatic, politic, discreet, sensitive, understanding, subtle, skillful, adroit, prudent, judicious.

tactic noun maneuver, device, stratagem, trick, scheme, plan, ploy, method, approach, tack. *See* TACTICS.

tactics plural noun strategy, campaign, policy; plans, battle/game plans.

tactless adjective undiplomatic, impolitic, indiscreet, insensitive, crude, clumsy, awkward, inept, bungling, maladroit, gauche.

tag noun label, ticket, sticker, docket.

tag verb 1 *tag the items* label, put a ticket/sticker on, mark. 2 *tag him Lefty* name, call, nickname, title, entitle, label, dub, term, style, christen. 3 *tag a postscript to the letter* add, attach, append, affix, tack. **tag along with** accompany, follow, trail behind, tread on the heels of, dog.

tailor noun outfitter, dressmaker, couturier, clothier, costumier.

tailor verb *tailor the schedule to your needs* fit, suit, fashion, style, mold, shape, adapt, adjust, modify, convert, alter, accommodate.

taint verb contaminate, pollute, adulterate, infect, blight, befoul, spoil; tarnish, sully, blacken, stain, besmirch, smear, blot, blemish, muddy, damage, injure, harm.

take verb 1 *take the book from her* get/lay hold of, grasp, grip, clutch. 2 *take first prize* get, receive, obtain, gain, acquire, secure, procure, come by, win, earn. 3 *take prisoners* seize, catch, capture, arrest,

carry off, abduct. 4 *who took my pen?* remove, appropriate, make off with, steal, filch, pilfer, purloin, pocket; *inf.* pinch, swipe. 5 *she showed me several dresses but I took the blue one* pick, choose, select, decide on, settle on, opt for. 6 *take some nourishment* consume, eat, devour, swallow; drink, imbibe. 7 *the vaccination did not take* be effective/efficacious, work, operate, succeed. 8 *the journey takes three hours* use, use up, require, call for, need, necessitate. 9 *take the box home with you* carry, fetch, bring, bear, transport, convey, cart; *inf.* tote. 10 *will you take his sister home?* escort, accompany, conduct, guide, lead, usher, convoy. 11 *take the child's temperature* find out, discover, ascertain, determine, establish. 12 *I take it that you agree* understand, interpret as, grasp, gather, comprehend, apprehend, assume, believe, suppose, consider, presume. 13 *take the news badly* receive, deal with, cope with. 14 *take the offer* accept, receive, adopt. 15 *take a course of study* enter upon, undertake, begin, set about. 16 *take French at school* study, learn, be taught, take up, pursue. 17 *take an oath/look* perform, execute, effect, do, make, have. 18 *the bucket takes three gallons* hold, contain, have the capacity for, have space/room for, accommodate. 19 *I cannot take his rudeness* bear, tolerate, stand, put up with, stomach, brook. 20 *the machine takes its name from the inventor* derive, obtain, come by. 21 *the passage is taken from the Bible* extract, quote, cite, excerpt, derive. 22 *take three from five* subtract, deduct, remove. 23 *taken by her beauty* captivate, enchant, charm, delight, please, attract, win over, fascinate. **take after** resemble, look like, be like, favor; *inf.* be a chip off the old block, be the spitting image of. **take back** 1 *take back the accusation* retract, withdraw, renounce, disclaim, unsay, disavow, recant. 2 *the store will not take the goods back* give a refund for, exchange, trade, swap. 3 *his wife has taken him back* accept back, welcome back, forgive. 4 *take back the land won by the enemy* regain, repossess, reclaim, recapture, reconquer. **take down** 1 *take down the details* write down, note down, make a note of, jot down, set down, record, put on record, commit to paper, document. 2 *take down the scaffolding/fence* remove, dismantle, disassemble, take apart, take to pieces, demolish, tear down, level, raze. 3 *take down the flag* pull down, let down, haul down, lower, drop. 4 *that should take him down a bit* humble, deflate, humiliate, mortify, take down a peg or two; *inf.* put down. **take for** regard as, consider as, view as, look upon as. **take in** 1 *take in paying guests* admit, let in, receive, welcome, accommodate, board. 2 *he didn't* *seem to take the news in* grasp, understand, comprehend, absorb, assimilate. **3** *said nothing but took everything in* observe, see, notice, take note of, note, perceive, regard. **4** *they were completely taken in by the con man* deceive, delude, hoodwink, mislead, trick, dupe, fool, cheat, defraud, swindle, gull; *inf.* con, bilk, pull the wool over someone's eyes. **5** *the court's jurisdiction takes in these three districts* include, encompass, embrace, contain, comprise, cover. **6** *try to take in a concert there* go to, go to see, attend, visit. **take off 1** *take the lid off the jar* remove, detach, pull off. **2** *take off one's clothes* remove, discard, strip off, peel off, throw off, divest oneself of, doff. **3** *take money off the bill for poor service* deduct from, subtract from, take away from. **4** *the children took off when they saw the police* run away, take to one's heels, flee, decamp, disappear, leave, go, depart; *inf.* split, beat it, skedaddle, vamoose, hightail it. **5** *the business/scheme has really taken off* succeed, do well, become popular, catch on. **take on 1** *take on extra work* undertake, accept, tackle. **2** *take on extra staff* employ, engage, hire, enroll, enlist; *inf.* take on board. **3** *take him on at chess* compete against, oppose, challenge, face, pit/match oneself against, contend with, vie with, fight. **4** *suddenly his words took on new meaning* acquire, come to have, assume. **take out 1** *take out a tooth* remove, extract, pull out, yank out. **2** *take out the girl next door* go out with, escort; *inf.* date. **take over** take/assume/gain control of, take charge/command of, assume responsibility for. **take to 1** *she's taken to smoking* begin, start, commence, make a habit of, resort to. **2** *he did not take to her friend* like, get on with. **3** *he has really taken to swimming* develop an ability/aptitude for, develop a liking for, like, enjoy, become interested in. **take up 1** *take up surfing* become involved/interested in, engage in, begin, start, commence. **2** *practicing the piano takes up a great deal of time* use, use up, occupy, fill, consume, absorb, cover, extend over. **3** *take up the story where they left off* resume, recommence, restart, begin again, carry on, continue, pick up. **4** *take up with the wrong sort of people* become friendly/friends, go around; *inf.* hang around.

take noun takings; proceeds, returns, receipts, profits, winnings, purse, pickings, earnings; gain, income, revenue.

tale noun **1** *a fairy tale* story, short story, narrative, anecdote, legend, fable, myth, parable, allegory, epic, saga; *inf.* yarn. **2** *hear tales of her wild behavior* talk, rumor, gossip, hearsay; report, allegation. **3** *don't believe her story—it's just a tale* lie,

fib, falsehood, untruth, fabrication; *inf.* tall story, cock-and-bull story, whopper.

talent noun gift, flair, aptitude, facility, knack, bent, ability, faculty, endowment.

talented adjective gifted, accomplished, able, capable, apt, deft, adept, proficient, brilliant.

talk verb **1** *talk incessantly* speak, chat, chatter, gossip, prattle, prate, gibber, jabber, babble, rattle on; *inf.* yak, gab. **2** *talk nonsense* speak, say, utter, voice, express, articulate, pronounce, enunciate, verbalize. **3** *they do not talk any more* communicate, converse, confer, parley, palaver, confabulate; *inf.* have a confab, chew the fat, jaw, rap. **4** *torture made the prisoner talk* tell, reveal all, tell tales, give the game away, open one's mouth, let the cat out of the bag; *inf.* blab, squeal, spill the beans, sing. **5** *if they divorce, people will talk* gossip, spread rumors, pass comment, make remarks, criticize. **6** *the professor is talking tonight* give a talk, speak, lecture, discourse. **talk back** answer defiantly/impertinently, answer back, be sassy; *inf.* give lip. **talk big** brag, boast, crow, exaggerate; *inf.* blow one's own horn, shoot one's mouth off. **talk down to** speak condescendingly to, condescend to, speak haughtily to, patronize. **talk into** persuade to, cajole to, coax into, influence. **talk of** speak about, discuss, mention, make mention of, refer to, make reference to. **talk out of** dissuade from, persuade against, discourage from, deter from, stop.

talk noun **1** *their noisy talk kept me awake* talking, speaking, chatter, chatting, gossiping, prattling, gibbering, jabbering, babbling, gabbling; *inf.* yakking, gabbing. **2** *baby/seamen's talk* words; speech, language, dialect, jargon, cant, slang, idiom, idiolect, patois; *inf.* lingo. **3** *have a talk about their future* conversation, chat, discussion, tête-à-tête; dialogue; *inf.* confab, rap. **4** *give a talk to the society* lecture, speech, address, discourse, oration, sermon, disquisition. **5** *there is talk of a merger* gossip, rumor, hearsay.

talkative adjective loquacious, garrulous, voluble, chatty, gossipy, conversational, long-winded, gushing, effusive, gabby, mouthy; *inf.* bigmouthed.

talker noun **1** *the talker bored the audience* speaker, lecturer, orator. **2** *they are a family of talkers* conversationalist, chatter, chatterbox, gossip.

tall adjective **1** *tall people/buildings* lanky, rangy, gangling, high, lofty, towering, soaring, sky-high, skyscraping. **2** *a tall story* exaggerated, unlikely, incredible, far-fetched, implausible.

tally noun count, record, running total, reckoning, enumeration, register, roll, census, poll; score, result, total, sum.

tally verb *the two accounts do not tally* agree, accord, concur, coincide, conform, correspond, match, fit, harmonize.

tame adjective **1** *tame animals* domesticated, gentle, docile. **2** *the supposedly rowdy children were quite tame* subdued, docile, submissive, compliant, meek, obedient, tractable, manageable. **3** *the horror movie turned out to be quite tame* unexciting, uninteresting, dull, bland, flat, insipid, vapid, run-of-the-mill, mediocre.

tame verb **1** *tame the wild cat* domesticate, break, train, gentle. **2** *tame the unruly element in the class* subdue, discipline, curb, control, master, overcome, suppress.

tamper verb **tamper with 1** *tamper with the exam papers* meddle with, interfere with, monkey around with, mess about with, tinker with, fiddle with. **2** *tamper with the jury* influence, get at, rig, manipulate, bribe, corrupt; *inf.* fix.

tang noun **1** *the tang of orange* flavor, taste, savor; smell, odor, aroma. **2** *add some tang to the occasion* spice, spiciness, piquancy, relish, sharpness, zest; *inf.* ginger, punch, zip.

tangible adjective **1** *tangible changes to the skin* touchable, palpable, tactile. **2** *tangible proof* concrete, real, actual, solid, substantial, hard, definite, clear, distinct, unmistakable.

tangle verb **1** *the net became tangled in the rose bush* entangle, intertwine, twist, snarl, ravel, knot. **2** *do not tangle with the authorities* come into conflict, dispute, argue, quarrel, fight, wrangle, squabble, contend, cross swords, lock horns.

tantalize verb tease, torment, make one's mouth water, lead on, entice, titillate, allure, beguile.

tap[1] noun spigot, faucet, stopcock, valve. **on tap** at/on hand, available, ready, in reserve, standing by.

tap[2] verb **1** *tap cider from a cask* draw off, siphon off, drain, bleed. **2** *tap a cask* broach, open, pierce. **3** *tap sources of information* use, make use of, draw on, exploit, milk, explore, probe. **4** *tap their telephone calls* wiretap, eavesdrop on; *inf.* bug.

tap[3] noun knock, rap, beat, touch, pat.

tap[4] verb knock, rap, strike, beat, drum, touch, pat.

tape noun **1** *the first-place runner breaking the tape* band, strip, string, ribbon. **2** *play a tape* recording, cassette, videotape, videocassette, video, audiotape, audiocassette.

tape verb **1** *tape the pieces together* bind, tie, fasten, stick, seal, secure; Scotch (*trademark*) tape. **2** *tape the concert/conversation* record, tape-record, videotape.

taper verb narrow, thin. **taper off** dwindle, diminish, lessen, decrease, reduce, subside, die off, die away, fade, peter out, wane, ebb, wind down, slacken off, thin out.

target noun objective, goal, object, aim, end, intention, desired result.

tariff noun tax, duty, toll, excise, levy, impost.

tarnish verb **1** *time had tarnished the brass* dull, dim, discolor, rust. **2** *tarnish his reputation* sully, besmirch, blacken, stain, blemish, blot, taint, befoul.

tart adjective **1** *a tart dessert* sour, tangy, piquant, pungent, bitter, acid, acidulous, vinegary. **2** *a tart remark/wit* astringent, caustic, sharp, biting, cutting, stinging, mordant, trenchant, incisive, piercing, scathing, sardonic.

task noun job, duty, chore, charge, odd job, assignment, mission, undertaking, errand, quest. **take to task** rebuke, reprimand, reprove, reproach, upbraid, scold, berate, lecture, castigate, censure, criticize, blame; *inf.* tell off.

taste noun **1** *the taste of fresh raspberries* flavor, savor, relish, tang. **2** *a taste of the pudding/sauce* bit, morsel, bite, mouthful, spoonful, sample, sip, drop, swallow, touch, soupçon. **3** *a taste for the unknown* liking, love, fondness, fancy, desire, preference, penchant, predilection, inclination, partiality. **4** *furnish the house with taste* discrimination, discernment, judgment, cultivation, culture, refinement, polish, finesse, elegance, grace, stylishness. **5** *her remark lacked taste* decorum, propriety, tact, tactfulness, diplomacy, delicacy, nicety, discretion.

taste verb **1** *taste the sauce while cooking it* sample, test, try, nibble, sip. **2** *I cannot taste the garlic* make out, perceive, discern, distinguish, differentiate. **3** *not taste food for days* eat, partake of, consume, devour. **4** *taste success/defeat* experience, undergo, encounter, meet, come up against, know.

tasteful adjective **1** *a tasteful display* in good taste, pleasing, elegant, graceful, discriminating, refined, restrained. **2** *tasteful behavior* decorous, proper, seemly, fitting, refined, cultivated.

tasteless adjective **1** *tasteless food* flavorless, savorless, bland, insipid, unappetizing, vapid. **2** *tasteless decorations* vulgar, crude. See TAWDRY. **3** *tasteless behavior* indecorous, improper, unseemly, rude, unfitting, unrefined, uncultured, uncultivated, vulgar, crude, uncouth, crass.

tasty adjective flavorsome, flavorful, full-flavored, appetizing, palatable, toothsome, delectable, delicious, luscious, mouthwatering, piquant, pungent, spicy; *inf.* scrumptious, yummy.

tatter noun **in tatters 1** *clothes in tatters* ragged, torn, in shreds, in bits. **2** *his career in tatters* in ruins, ruined, destroyed, demolished.

tattle verb gossip, chatter, prattle, prate, babble, rattle on; *inf.* gab.

taunt noun gibe, jeer, sneer, insult, barb, dig, catcall; provocation, derision, mockery; *inf.* put-down.

taunt verb gibe at, jeer at, sneer at, insult, chaff, tease, torment, provoke, ridicule, deride, mock.

taut adjective **1** *taut ropes/muscles* tight, stretched, rigid, tightened, flexed, tensed. **2** *a taut expression* tense, strained, stressed, drawn; *inf.* uptight. **3** *run a taut ship* orderly, shipshape, tight, trim, neat, tidy, spruce.

tawdry adjective showy, gaudy, flashy, garish, loud, tasteless, cheap, cheapjack, shoddy, meretricious; *inf.* tacky, kitsch.

tax noun **1** *a tax on imports* levy, charge, duty, toll, excise, tariff; customs. **2** *they became a tax on her resources* burden, load, weight, encumbrance, strain, pressure, stress, drain.

tax verb *the work taxes his strength* make demands on, weigh down, burden, load, encumber, overload, stretch, strain, try, wear out, exhaust, sap, drain, enervate, fatigue, tire, weary, weaken.

teach verb instruct, educate, school, tutor, coach, show, guide, train, drill, ground, enlighten, edify.

teacher noun schoolteacher, instructor, educator, tutor, coach, trainer, lecturer, professor, pedagogue, guide, mentor, guru.

team noun band, bunch, party, gang, crew, troupe, set, squad, side, lineup.

tear[1] noun rip, split, hole, rent, run, rupture.

tear[2] verb **1** *tear the paper/cloth* rip, pull apart, split, rend, sever, rive, sunder, rupture. **2** *tear the flesh* lacerate, gash, slash, pierce, stab, scratch, cut, mutilate, hack. **3** *tear off the cover* wrench, yank, wrest, extract, peel, snatch, pluck, grab, seize. **4** *torn by guilt* distress, upset, harrow, torture, torment. **5** *children tearing down the street* run, race, sprint, gallop, rush, dash, bolt, career, dart, fly, shoot, hurry, speed, hasten, whiz, zoom, zip; *inf.* hotfoot it.

tear[3] noun teardrop, drop, droplet, globule, bead. **in tears** crying, weeping. *See* TEARFUL.

tearful adjective **1** *in a tearful state* in tears, crying, weeping, weepy, sobbing, blubbering, sniveling, whimpering, wailing; emotional, upset, distressed. **2**

a tearful parting heartbreaking, heartrending, sad, poignant, mournful, melancholy, lamentable, dolorous.

tease verb **1** *tease the cat* torment, provoke, badger, bait, goad, needle, aggravate, pest, bother, worry, vex, irritate, annoy, gibe, rag, twit, mock, ridicule. **2** *he was only teasing her* joke (with), fool (with); *inf.* kid, rib, put on.

technical adjective *technical training* mechanical, practical, scientific, nontheoretical.

technique noun **1** *new business techniques* method, modus operandi, system, procedure, manner, way, course of action, mode, fashion; means. **2** *admire the violinist's technique* execution, performance, skill, proficiency, expertise, mastery, artistry, art, craftsmanship, craft, ability, adroitness, deftness, dexterity, knack.

tedious adjective wearisome, wearying, tiresome, tiring, fatiguing, long-drawn-out, overlong, long-winded, prolix, dull, boring, uninteresting, dry, uninspired, flat, monotonous.

teem verb abound, swarm, crawl, bristle, seethe, brim; be abundant, be plentiful, be copious.

teeter verb **1** *teeter down the street on high heels* totter, wobble, stagger, stumble, reel, sway, roll, lurch. **2** *teeter between accepting and refusing* waver, vacillate, fluctuate, oscillate, dither, hesitate, shilly-shally, seesaw.

tell verb **1** *tell the news to everyone* make known, impart, communicate, announce, proclaim, broadcast, divulge, reveal, disclose, declare, state, mention, utter, voice, say, speak. **2** *tell a story* narrate, relate, recount, report, chronicle, recite, rehearse, describe, portray, sketch, delineate. **3** *tell them tomorrow that you are going* inform, let know, make aware, apprise, notify. **4** *I tell you that he is guilty* assure, promise, guarantee, warrant. **5** *tell them to go home* instruct, bid, order, command, direct, charge, enjoin, require. **6** *he knows, but he promised not to tell* talk, tell tales, blab, give the game away, open one's mouth, let the cat out of the bag, spill the beans. **7** *his friend told on him* report, inform; *inf.* sing, squeal, rat, blow the whistle. **8** *his expression told how he felt* reveal, disclose, show, display, exhibit, indicate. **9** *unable to tell his reaction from his expression* deduce, make out, discern, perceive, recognize, discover, understand, comprehend. **10** *unable to tell one from the other* distinguish, differentiate, discriminate. **11** *breeding tells* have an effect, count, carry weight, have influence/force, register.

telling adjective significant, important, striking, impressive, forceful, effective, effectual, cogent, influential, decisive.

temerity noun effrontery, impudence, audacity, cheek, gall, presumption, presumptuousness, brazenness, rashness, recklessness, foolhardiness.

temper noun 1 *he is of an equable temper* disposition, nature. *See* TEMPERAMENT 1. 2 *the temper of the times* tenor, tone, attitude, vein. 3 *he is in a temper* fury, rage, passion, fit of pique, tantrum. 4 *a display of temper* anger, annoyance, fury, rage, irritation, irascibility, hotheadedness, resentment, surliness, churlishness. 5 *lose one's temper* composure, equanimity, self-control, coolness, calm, tranquillity; *inf.* cool.

temper verb 1 *temper the metal* toughen, anneal, harden, strengthen, fortify. 2 *temper justice with mercy* moderate, soften, tone down, modify, mitigate, alleviate, allay, palliate, mollify, assuage, lessen, weaken.

temperament noun 1 *of a nervous temperament* disposition, nature, humor, mood, makeup, constitution, complexion, temper, spirit, mettle, frame of mind, cast of mind, mind, attitude, outlook, stamp, quality. 2 *actors often are people of temperament* excitability, volatility, capriciousness, moodiness, oversensitivity, touchiness, petulance; moods.

temperamental adjective 1 *temperamental differences between them* constitutional, inherent, innate, deep-rooted, ingrained. 2 *actors are often temperamental* excitable, emotional, volatile, mercurial, oversensitive, touchy, moody, hotheaded, explosive, impatient, petulant.

temperate adjective 1 *lead a temperate life* moderate, self-restrained, restrained, abstemious, self-controlled, continent, austere, self-denying. 2 *temperate winds* mild, gentle, clement, balmy, pleasant, agreeable.

tempest noun 1 *ships buffeted by the tempest* storm, gale, hurricane, squall, cyclone, tornado, typhoon, whirlwind. 2 *their squabble erupted into a tempest* uproar, commotion, furor, disturbance, tumult, turmoil, upheaval.

tempestuous adjective 1 *tempestuous weather* stormy, turbulent, blustery, squally, windy, gusty, breezy. 2 *a tempestuous affair* tumultuous, turbulent, wild, uncontrolled, unrestrained, emotional, intense, fierce, heated, feverish, hysterical, frenetic.

tempo noun beat, rhythm, cadence, pulse; pace, rate, speed, measure.

temporal adjective *temporal affairs* secular, nonspiritual, worldly, material, earthly, carnal.

temporary adjective short-term, impermanent, interim, provisional, pro tem, pro

tempore; passing, short-lived, transient, transitory, ephemeral, evanescent.

tempt verb 1 *she is tempted to run away* entice, incite, induce, egg on, urge, goad, prompt, sway, influence, persuade, cajole, coax. 2 *displays to tempt buyers* allure, lure, entice, attract, whet the appetite of, make one's mouth water, captivate, appeal to, beguile, inveigle, woo, seduce, tantalize. 3 *tempt fate* fly in the face of, risk, bait, provoke.

temptation noun allurement, lure, attraction, draw, bait, pull, enticement, inducement, invitation, decoy, snare; *inf.* come-on.

tempting adjective alluring, enticing, attractive, captivating, appealing, beguiling, fascinating, tantalizing, appetizing, mouthwatering.

tenacious adjective 1 *a tenacious grip* clinging, fast, tight, strong, forceful, powerful, unshakable, iron. 2 *tenacious efforts/individuals* persistent, pertinacious, determined, dogged, resolute, firm, steadfast, purposeful, unswerving, relentless, inexorable, unyielding, inflexible, stubborn, obstinate, intransigent.

tenant noun occupier, occupant, resident, inhabitant, renter, leaseholder, lessee, holder, possessor.

tend verb *tend the sick/cows* look after, take care of, care for, attend to, minister to, see to, cater to, nurse, wait on, watch over, watch, guard, keep an eye on, keep.

tendency noun 1 *a tendency to dishonesty* inclination, disposition, predisposition, proclivity, propensity, proneness, aptness, bent, leaning, penchant, susceptibility, liability. 2 *the upward tendency of the graph* movement, direction, course, drift, bias, trend.

tender adjective 1 *tender meat* succulent, juicy, soft. 2 *tender blossoms/shoots* fragile, frail, delicate, sensitive, slight, feeble. 3 *they are still of tender years* young, youthful, early; immature, callow, inexperienced, green, raw. 4 *a tender heart* compassionate, softhearted, kind, kindly, sympathetic, warm, caring, humane, gentle, solicitous, generous, benevolent, loving, affectionate. 5 *a tender spot on her arm* sore, painful, aching, smarting, throbbing, inflamed, irritated, red, raw, bruised. 6 *a tender subject requiring tact* delicate, sensitive, tricky, ticklish.

tender verb *tender a proposal* offer, proffer, present, extend, give; volunteer, put forward, propose, suggest, advance, submit.

tenderness noun 1 *the tenderness of the blossoms/shoots* fragility, frailness, frailty, delicacy, sensitivity, sensitiveness, slightness, feebleness. 2 *the tenderness of their years* youthfulness, immaturity, callowness, inexperience, greenness. **3** *the tenderness of her heart* compassion, compassionateness, softheartedness, kindness, kindliness, sympathy, warmth, humaneness, gentleness, solicitousness, generosity, benevolence, sentimentality, emotionalism; fondness, love, affection, emotion, amorousness. **4** *the tenderness of the topic* delicacy, delicateness, sensitivity, sensitiveness, difficulty, trickiness, ticklishness. **5** *the tenderness of the wounded area* soreness, pain, painfulness, ache, aching, smarting, throbbing, inflammation, irritation, redness, rawness, bruising.

tenet noun doctrine, creed, credo, principle, belief, conviction, persuasion, view, opinion.

tense adjective **1** *tense ropes* tight, taut, rigid, stretched, strained. **2** *feeling tense about the interview* nervous, keyed up, worked up, overwrought, distraught, anxious, uneasy, worried, apprehensive, agitated, jumpy, edgy, on edge, restless, jittery, fidgety; *inf.* uptight, wound up, strung out. **3** *there were some tense moments in the negotiations* nerve-racking, stressful, worrying, fraught, exciting, cliff-hanging.

tension noun **1** *the tension of the ropes* tightness, tautness, rigidity, stretching, straining. **2** *the tension of waiting* stress, stressfulness, pressure, anxiety, unease, disquiet, worry, apprehensiveness, agitation, jumpiness, edginess, restlessness; nerves. **3** *the tension between the two sides grew* strain, unease, ill feeling, hostility, enmity.

tentative adjective **1** *a tentative plan* experimental, exploratory, trial, provisional, test, pilot. **2** *take a few tentative steps* hesitant, hesitating, faltering, wavering, uncertain, unsure, doubtful, cautious, diffident, timid.

tenuous adjective **1** *a tenuous connection between the two events* fragile, slight, flimsy, weak, insubstantial, shaky, sketchy, doubtful, dubious, nebulous, hazy, vague, unspecific, indefinite. **2** *a tenuous thread* fine, thin, slender.

term noun **1** *fail to understand the technical term* word, expression, phrase, name, title, denomination, appellation, designation. **2** *the chairman's term of office* period, time, spell, interval, stretch, span, duration, space.

terminal adjective fatal, deadly, mortal, lethal, killing; dying, on one's deathbed, near death, in the throes of death.

terminal noun **1** *the terminal of the railroad line* terminus, last stop, depot. **2** *the computer terminal* workstation, visual display unit, monitor; *inf.* VDU.

terminate verb close, end, conclude, finish, stop, wind up, discontinue; cease, cancel, expire, run out, lapse; abort, put an end to.

termination noun **1** *the termination of the meeting* closing, close, ending, end, conclusion, finish, winding-up, wind-up. **2** *the termination of his contract* cessation, discontinuance, expiration, lapse, cancellation.

terms plural noun **1** *tell them in no uncertain terms* words, phrases, expressions, language. **2** *on good terms with their neighbors* relations; standing, footing, relationship. **3** *under the terms of the will* stipulations, specifications, conditions, provisions, provisos, particulars. **4** *offer reduced terms in the winter* prices, rates, charges, costs, fees. **come to terms with 1** *they finally came to terms with the neighbors* come to an agreement/understanding with, reach a compromise with. **2** *come to terms with her loss* become reconciled with, reach an acceptance of, learn to live with.

terrible adjective **1** *he is a terrible tennis player* bad, poor, incompetent, useless, talentless; *inf.* rotten. **2** *hostages enduring terrible experiences* dreadful, terrifying, frightening, frightful, horrifying, horrible, horrific, horrendous, harrowing, hideous, grim, unspeakable, appalling, awful, gruesome. **3** *the terrible heat/pain* extreme, severe, harsh, unbearable, intolerable, insufferable. **4** *what is that terrible smell?* nasty, foul, offensive, odious, obnoxious, vile, revolting, repulsive, abhorrent, loathsome, hateful, unpleasant, disagreeable, dreadful, awful, horrible, horrid.

terrific adjective **1** *a terrific bang/speed* tremendous, great, huge, sizable, considerable, intense, extreme, extraordinary, excessive. **2** *she is a terrific singer* excellent, superb, ace, remarkable, magnificent, wonderful, marvelous, great, super, sensational, fabulous; *inf.* fantastic, A-1, unreal, awesome. **3** *there has been a terrific accident* dreadful, frightful, horrible, horrific, hideous, grim, appalling, awful.

terrify verb terrorize, frighten to death, frighten, scare stiff, scare, petrify, horrify, make one's blood run cold, make one's flesh crawl, make one's hair stand on end, alarm, panic, intimidate, dismay, appall, shock, paralyze with fear, put the fear of God into; *inf.* spook.

territory noun **1** *territories governed by the same ruler* country, state, domain, county, district. **2** *an unexplored territory* region, area, terrain, tract. **3** *leave me out of it—that's your territory* area of concern, province, field, sector, department, bailiwick, beat.

terror noun **1** fright, fear, fear and trembling, dread, alarm, panic, shock, horror.

2 *imagining all manner of terrors* bogeyman, bugbear, monster, demon, fiend, devil. **3** *that child is a little terror* hooligan, ruffian, hoodlum, rogue, rascal, troublemaker, holy terror.

terrorize verb **1** *terrorize the hostages* strike terror in/into, petrify. *See* TERRIFY. **2** *terrorize them into leaving their homes* coerce, browbeat, bully, intimidate, menace, threaten, bulldoze; *inf.* strong-arm.

terse adjective **1** *a terse description of the event* concise, succinct, compact, brief, short, to the point, crisp, pithy. **2** *she sounded terse on the phone* abrupt, curt, brusque, blunt.

test noun **1** *a test to distinguish the competent from the incompetent* examination, check, assessment, evaluation, appraisal, investigation, inspection, analysis, study, probe. **2** *take the bike out for a test* trial, tryout, try, probation, assay. **3** *studying for a test* exam, quiz, questionnaire. **4** *the test of a good cake* criterion, touchstone, yardstick, standard, measure, model.

test verb **1** *test their knowledge of local history* put to the test, examine, check, assess, evaluate, appraise, investigate, scrutinize, study, probe. **2** *their behavior tested his patience* try, tax, strain. **3** *test the water for pollution* analyze, assay, check, investigate, scrutinize, explore, probe.

testament noun *the sculpture was a testament to his skill* attestation, testimony, evidence, proof, witness; demonstration, indication, exemplification, tribute.

testify verb **1** *she testified to his honesty* swear to, attest to, corroborate, substantiate, verify, vouch for, endorse, support, back up, uphold. **2** *testify that she had witnessed the accident* swear, declare, assert, affirm, state, allege, pledge, profess, avow. **testify to** *tears that testified to her guilt* be evidence/proof of, confirm, bear out, show, demonstrate, indicate.

testimony noun **1** *challenge the testimony of the witness* evidence, attestation, sworn statement, deposition, affidavit; statement, declaration, assertion, protestation, affirmation, profession, allegation. **2** *her academic record was a testimony to her ability* proof, evidence, verification, corroboration, support; demonstration, manifestation, indication.

testy adjective touchy, irritable, irascible, petulant, cross, ill-tempered, crotchety, crabby, crabbed, snappish, querulous, peevish, grouchy, grumpy, cantankerous, fractious.

tether noun rope, cord, chain, lead, leash, line.

tether verb tie, tie up, fasten, secure, chain, rope.

text noun **1** *the text of the speech* words, wording, script, transcript. **2** *the speaker took foreign policy as his text* theme, subject matter, topic. **3** *the texts chosen for the funeral service* passage, verse, quotation, extract, line, abstract, paragraph.

texture noun **1** *the texture of her skin* feel, touch, appearance, surface, grain. **2** *fabrics of varying texture* weave, structure, composition, constitution, constituency.

thankful adjective **1** *she was thankful to reach home safely* grateful, appreciative, pleased, relieved. **2** *she was thankful to them for taking her in* indebted, obliged, beholden.

thankless adjective **1** *thankless children* ungrateful, unappreciative, ungracious. **2** *thankless tasks* unappreciated, unrewarded, unrewarding, unacknowledged.

thanks plural noun gratitude, gratefulness, appreciation, acknowledgment, recognition.

thaw verb defrost, unfreeze, melt, soften, liquefy; relax, loosen up.

theater noun drama, dramatic art, dramaturgy, the stage, show business, thespian art; *inf.* showbiz.

theatrical adjective **1** *theatrical careers* dramatic, stage, dramaturgical, show business, thespian. **2** *theatrical gestures* dramatic, melodramatic, histrionic, exaggerated, overdone, ostentatious, showy, affected, mannered, stilted, forced, stagy; *inf.* hammy.

theft noun stealing, robbery, thieving, thievery, burglary, larceny, misappropriation, pilfering, purloining, shoplifting, embezzlement, swindling, fraud; *inf.* swiping, rip-off.

theme noun **1** *the theme of the speech* topic, subject, subject matter, matter, thesis, text, argument, burden, idea, keynote. **2** *play the theme from the TV series* theme song, melody, tune, air, leitmotif. **3** *students writing themes in French* essay, composition, paper, dissertation.

theoretical adjective conceptual, abstract, hypothetical, conjectural, suppositional, speculative.

theorize verb speculate, conjecture, suppose, hypothesize.

theory noun hypothesis, thesis, conjecture, supposition, speculation, guess, notion, postulation, assumption, presumption, opinion, view.

therapy noun treatment, remedy, cure.

thereafter adverb afterward, after that, then, next, subsequently.

therefore adverb and so, so, then, thus,

accordingly, consequently, as a result, for that reason.

thesis noun **1** *his thesis is that the territory is uninhabited* theory, hypothesis, contention, argument, proposal, proposition, premise, postulation. **2** *present a thesis for his doctorate* dissertation, paper, treatise, disquisition, essay, composition, monograph.

thick adjective **1** *two feet thick* across, wide, broad, deep. **2** *thick legs* large, big, bulky, solid, substantial, fat, beefy. **3** *a thick forest* dense, close-packed, concentrated, crowded, condensed, compact, impenetrable, impassable. **4** *thick cream* coagulated, heavy, firm. **5** *thick mists* dense, heavy, opaque, smoggy, soupy, murky, impenetrable. **6** *too thick to understand* stupid, dense, unintelligent, dull-witted, dull, slow-witted, slow, doltish; *inf.* dim, dimwitted, boneheaded. **7** *a voice thick with emotion* husky, hoarse, throaty, guttural, rough, indistinct, muffled. **8** *a thick accent* broad, pronounced, marked, strong, rich, obvious, distinct, decided. **9** *those two are thick these days* intimate, close, devoted, hand and/in glove, inseparable, familiar; *inf.* palsy-walsy, chummy. **lay it on thick** flatter, overpraise, toady; *inf.* butter up. **thick with 1** *the ground thick with ants* teeming with, swarming with, crawling with, alive with. **2** *the room thick with smoke* full of, filled with; *inf.* chock-full of.

thicken verb set, gel, solidify, congeal, clot, coagulate, cake.

thicket noun dense growth, tangle, copse, grove, wood.

thickset adjective burly, brawny, muscular, bulky, sturdy, stocky, beefy.

thick-skinned adjective insensitive, unfeeling, tough, unsusceptible, impervious, invulnerable, hardened, case-hardened, callous, hard-boiled.

thief noun robber, burglar, housebreaker, larcenist, pilferer, stealer, purloiner, filcher, shoplifter, pickpocket, embezzler, bandit, swindler, fraudster, mugger.

thin adjective **1** *thin lines* narrow, fine, attenuated. **2** *thin materials* fine, light, delicate, flimsy, diaphanous, gossamer, unsubstantial, sheer, transparent, seethrough, gauzy, filmy, translucent. **3** *their models have to be thin* slim, slender, lean, slight, svelte, light, spare. **4** *thin and ill-looking* skinny, spindly, lank, lanky, scrawny, scraggy, bony, skeletal, wasted, emaciated, shrunken, anorexic, undernourished, underweight. **5** *thin hair* sparse, scanty, wispy, skimpy. **6** *the audience was rather thin* sparse, scarce, scanty, meager, paltry, scattered. **7** *a thin mixture* dilute, diluted, weak, watery, runny. **8** *a thin voice* weak, small, low, soft, faint,

feeble. **9** *a thin excuse* flimsy, unsubstantial, weak, feeble, lame, poor, shallow, unconvincing.

thin verb **thin down** *thin down the mixture* dilute, water down, weaken. **thin out** lessen, decrease, diminish, dwindle.

thing noun **1** *people matter more than things* object, article, item. **2** *where did you get that thing?* object; *inf.* what-d'you-call-it, whatchamacallit, what's-its-name, whatsit, thingamabob, thingamajig. **3** *what a silly/difficult thing to do* action, act, deed, exploit, feat, undertaking, task, job, chore. **4** *what a silly thing to think* idea, thought, notion, concept, theory, conjecture. **5** *say silly things* statement, remark, comment, declaration, utterance, pronouncement. **6** *a terrible thing to happen* event, happening, occurrence, incident, episode. **7** *patience is a useful thing* quality, characteristic, attribute, property, trait, feature. **8** *the poor thing has no home* soul, creature, wretch. **9** *there is another thing you should know* fact, point, detail, particular, aspect. **10** *the latest thing in swimwear* style, fashion, specimen, example. **have a thing about 1** *have a thing about spiders* phobia of, fear of, aversion to/toward; *inf.* hang-up about. **2** *have a thing about champagne* liking for/of, love for/of, fancy for, predilection for, penchant for, preference for, taste for, obsession with, fixation on/with/about. **the thing 1** *the thing is to avoid annoying him* the aim, the intention, the idea, the objective, the object, the purpose. **2** *the thing is that he has no money* the fact, the fact of the matter, the point, the issue, the problem.

things plural noun **1** *put on dry things* | *take night things* clothing, attire, apparel; clothes, garments, gear; *inf.* togs. **2** *I will watch your things while you get a ticket* belongings, possessions, paraphernalia; *inf.* stuff. **3** *her painting things* equipment, apparatus, gear, tackle; implements, tools. **4** *things are getting worse* matters, affairs, circumstances, conditions, relations; the state of affairs, the situation.

think verb **1** *I think they will come* believe, suppose, expect, imagine, surmise, conjecture, guess, fancy. **2** *he is thought to be clever* consider, deem, hold, reckon, regard as, assume, presume, estimate. **3** *he is sitting thinking* ponder, meditate, deliberate, contemplate, muse, cogitate, ruminate, cerebrate, concentrate, brood, rack one's brains, be lost in thought, be in a brown study. **think better of** have second thoughts about, reconsider, change one's mind about, decide against. **think over** contemplate, consider, deliberate about, muse over, mull over, ponder, reflect on, weigh up, consider the pros and cons of.

think up dream up, come up with, devise, invent, create, concoct.

thinking noun *the latest thinking on tax reform* view, opinion, outlook, judgment, assessment, appraisal, evaluation, position, theory, reasoning; conclusions, thoughts.

thin-skinned adjective sensitive, hypersensitive, supersensitive, easily offended/hurt, touchy.

thirst noun **1** *dying of thirst in the desert* thirstiness, dryness, parchedness, dehydration. **2** *a thirst for knowledge* desire, craving, longing, hankering, yearning, avidity, hunger, lust, appetite; *inf.* yen.

thirst verb **thirst for/after** desire, crave, long for, hanker after, yearn for, hunger after, lust after.

thorn noun prickle, spike, barb, spine, bristle.

thorny adjective **1** *thorny branches* prickly, spiky, barbed, spiny, spined, bristly, sharp, pointed. **2** *a thorny situation/issue* problematic, awkward, ticklish, difficult, tough, troublesome, bothersome, trying, taxing, irksome, vexatious, worrying, harassing, complicated.

thorough adjective **1** *a thorough investigation* in-depth, exhaustive, complete, comprehensive, full, intensive, extensive, widespread, sweeping, all-embracing, all-inclusive, detailed. **2** *he is slow but thorough* meticulous, scrupulous, assiduous, conscientious, painstaking, punctilious, methodical, careful. **3** *he is a thorough villain* thoroughgoing, out-and-out, utter, downright, sheer, absolute, unmitigated, unqualified, complete, total, perfect.

thoroughbred adjective pure, pure-blooded, full-blooded, pedigreed; well-bred, highborn, aristocratic, blue-blooded, elegant, graceful, refined.

thoroughfare noun road, roadway; main road, street; highway, freeway, turnpike, parkway, expressway, throughway; *inf.* pike.

thoroughly adverb **1** *search the place thoroughly* exhaustively, completely, fully, intensively, extensively, meticulously, scrupulously, assiduously, conscientiously, painstakingly, methodically, carefully. **2** *she is thoroughly spoiled* completely, utterly, absolutely, totally, entirely.

thought noun **1** *lost in thought* thinking, reasoning, pondering, meditation, deliberation, cogitation, rumination, musing, mulling, reflection, introspection, contemplation. **2** *a thought came to me about how to do it* idea, notion, theory, opinion. **3** *I had no thought of going* intention, plan, design, purpose, aim. **4** *what are your thoughts on this?* judgment, stance, stand, feeling, sentiment. *See* THINKING. **5** *give the matter thought* consideration, attention, heed, regard, scrutiny, care, carefulness. **6** *give up all thought of winning* expectation, anticipation, hope, prospect, aspiration, dream. **7** *he has no thought for his widowed mother* thoughtfulness, consideration, care, regard, concern, solicitude, kindness, kindliness, compassion, tenderness.

thoughtful adjective **1** *a thoughtful mood* pensive, reflective, introspective, meditative, contemplative, ruminative, cogitative, absorbed. **2** *a thoughtful essay* profound, deep, serious, pithy, meaty, weighty. **3** *every action he takes is thoughtful* considered, circumspect, prudent, careful, cautious, heedful, wary, guarded. **4** *he is a thoughtful son* considerate, attentive, caring, solicitous, helpful, kind, kindly, compassionate.

thoughtless adjective **1** *thoughtless remarks* tactless, undiplomatic, indiscreet, insensitive, inconsiderate, impolite, rude. **2** *his thoughtless actions* unthinking, heedless, careless, absentminded, injudicious, ill-advised, ill-considered, imprudent.

thrash verb **1** *rebels thrashed by the dictator's guards* beat, whip, horsewhip, flog, lash, birch, cane, flagellate, scourge, spank, chastise; *inf.* belt, wallop, lambaste, tan. **2** *the home team thrashed the opposition* trounce, rout, vanquish, drub, crush; *inf.* lick, clobber, hammer, slaughter, wipe (up) the floor with. **3** *thrashing around in pain* thresh, flail, jerk, twitch, squirm, writhe.

threadbare adjective **1** *threadbare upholstery* worn, frayed, tattered, ragged, holey, shabby; *inf.* tatty. **2** *threadbare arguments* hackneyed, tired, stale, worn-out, trite, banal, platitudinous, clichéd, cliché-ridden; *inf.* played out.

threat noun warning, menace, risk, danger, hazard, omen, foreboding, portent.

threaten verb **1** *bullies threatening younger children* make threats to, menace, intimidate, browbeat, bully; *inf.* lean on. **2** *rain is threatening* be imminent, impend, hang over, loom, foreshadow. **3** *a sky threatening rain* warn of, presage, portend, augur. **4** *pollution threatening the environment* be a threat to, endanger, imperil, put at risk, jeopardize.

threshold noun **1** *guests standing at/on the threshold* doorway, doorstep, entrance, entry. **2** *on the threshold of a new era* beginning, commencement, start, outset, inception, opening, dawn, brink, verge, debut; *inf.* kickoff.

thrift noun thriftiness, economy, frugality, scrimping, parsimony, penny-pinching, miserliness.

thrifty adjective economical, economizing,

frugal, sparing, scrimping, parsimonious, penny-pinching, miserly.

thrill noun **1** *seeing his hero gave him a thrill* glow, tingle, joy, delight, pleasure; *inf.* buzz, charge, kick. **2** *a thrill of terror ran through him* throb, tremble, tremor, quiver, flutter, shudder, vibration.

thrill verb excite, stimulate, arouse, stir, electrify, move, give joy/pleasure to; *inf.* give a buzz/charge/kick to. **thrill to** tingle from, feel joy from; *inf.* get a buzz/charge/kick out of.

thrilling adjective **1** *a thrilling experience* exciting, stirring, stimulating, electrifying, hair-raising, rousing, moving, gripping, riveting, joyful, pleasing. **2** *a thrilling sensation through the body* throbbing, trembling, tremulous, quivering, shivering, fluttering, shuddering, vibrating.

thrive verb flourish, prosper, boom, burgeon; succeed, advance, get ahead.

throb verb beat, pulse, pulsate, palpitate, pound, vibrate, go pit-a-pat, thump.

throes plural noun **1** *the throes of childbirth* agony, suffering, excruciation, pain, torture, distress; pangs. **2** *in the throes of changing jobs* turmoil, upheaval, disruption, tumult.

throng noun crowd, horde, mob, mass, host, multitude, swarm, flock, pack, herd, drove.

throng verb **1** *people thronged to see the play* flock, troop, swarm. **2** *fans thronging around the star* crowd, mill, congregate, converge. **3** *fans thronging the stadium* pack, cram, jam, fill.

throttle verb choke, strangle, strangulate, garrotte; gag, muzzle, silence, stifle, suppress, control, inhibit.

through adverb **through and through** thoroughly, completely, utterly, altogether, totally, to the core, entirely, wholly, fully, unreservedly, out and out.

through adjective finished, completed, done, ended, terminated; *inf.* washed up.

throw verb **1** *throw a brick* hurl, toss, cast, sling, pitch, shy, lob, propel, launch, project, send, heave, chuck. **2** *throw an opponent/rider* fell, floor, prostrate; unseat, dislodge. **3** *his question threw me* disconcert, discomfit, disturb, confound, astonish, surprise, dumbfound. **4** *threw the switch* operate, turn/switch on, move. **5** *the potter throwing a vase* shape, form, mold, fashion. **6** *she threw on her clothes* pull/put on quickly, don, slip into. **throw away 1** *throw away his textbooks* throw out, discard, get rid of, dispose of, jettison, scrap, reject, dispense with; *inf.* dump, ditch. **2** *throw away a good opportunity* waste, squander, fritter away, lose; *inf.*

blow. **throw off 1** *throw off their shackles* cast off, shake off, abandon. **2** *throw off one's pursuers* evade, escape from, get away from, elude, give someone the slip, lose.

throw out 1 *throw out the troublemakers* eject, evict, expel, show the door to, put out; *inf.* kick out. **2** *throw out a proposal* reject, give the thumbs down to, turn down, dismiss, disallow. **3** *fires throwing out heat* emit, radiate, give off, diffuse, disseminate.

throw noun hurl, toss, cast, sling, pitch, lob, heave, chuck. **a throw** *jackets at $50 a throw* each, apiece; *inf.* a pop.

thrust verb **1** *thrust open the door | thrust their way through the crowd* push, shove, drive, press, prod, propel, force, shoulder, elbow, jostle. **2** *thrust responsibility on him* force, impose, push, press, urge. **3** *fencers learning to thrust* stab, pierce, stick, jab, lunge at.

thrust noun **1** *with one thrust of his fist* push, shove, ram, drive, press, prod. **2** *surprised by the enemy's sudden thrust* advance, drive, attack, offensive, assault, charge, onslaught, incursion, raid. **3** *upset by her nasty thrust* criticism, censure. **4** *the thrust of the speech* gist, drift, substance, essence, theme, subject, thesis.

thud noun thump, clunk, crash, smack, wham.

thug noun ruffian, tough, rough, hoodlum, bully, hooligan, villain, gangster, robber, bandit, murderer, killer, assassin; *inf.* hood, goon, mobster, hit man.

thumb verb *thumb through the book* leaf, flick, flip, riffle, browse, skim, scan.

thump verb **1** *he thumped her attacker* strike, hit, punch, thwack, wallop, smack, slap, batter, beat, cudgel, knock, thrash; *inf.* whack, belt, clout, lambaste. **2** *my heart/head is thumping* pound, thud, pulse, pulsate, throb, palpitate. **3** *thumping on the table* bang, batter, beat, crash, knock, rap.

thump noun **1** *give the attacker a thump* blow, punch, thwack, wallop, smack, slap; *inf.* whack, belt, clout, lambasting. **2** *give the table a thump* bang, knock, rap. **3** *the shoe landed with a thump* thud, clunk, crash, smack, wham.

thunder verb **1** *his voice thundered in my ear* boom, rumble, roar, blast, resound, reverberate. **2** *thundering at the crowd to be quiet* roar, bellow, bark, yell, shout.

thus adverb **1** *I hold the apparatus thus* like this, in this way, so, like so. **2** *he is the eldest son and thus inherits the estate* so, therefore, accordingly, hence, consequently, as a result, ergo.

thwart verb frustrate, foil, balk, check, block, stop, prevent, defeat, impede, obstruct, hinder, hamper, stymie.

tic · time

tic noun twitch, spasm, jerk.

tick noun ticking, click, beat, tap, tapping, tick-tock.

tick verb click, beat, tap, sound, tick-tock. **tick off** annoy, irritate, rile, aggravate, peeve.

ticket noun pass, token, stub, coupon, card.

tickle verb **1** *tickle one's fancy* interest, excite, stimulate, arouse, captivate, please, gratify, delight. **2** *tickled by the antics of the children* amuse, entertain, divert, cheer, gladden.

ticklish adjective *a ticklish situation* difficult, problematic, awkward, delicate, sensitive, tricky, thorny, knotty, touchy, risky, uncertain, precarious; *inf.* sticky.

tide noun *the tide of events* course, movement, direction, trend, current, drift, run, tendency.

tidings plural noun news, notification, word, communication, information, intelligence, advice; reports; *inf.* info, low-down.

tidy adjective **1** *a tidy room/garden* neat, trim, orderly, in order, in good order, well-ordered, spruce, shipshape, well-kept, clean, spick-and-span. **2** *people who are tidy by nature* organized, well-organized, methodical, systematic, businesslike. **3** *leave a tidy sum* considerable, sizable, substantial, goodly, handsome, generous, ample, largish, large.

tidy verb clean, clean up, put to rights, put in order, straighten, make shipshape, spruce up, groom, smarten, neaten.

tie verb tie up, fasten, attach, fix, bind, secure, tether, moor, lash, join, connect, link, couple, rope, chain. **tie down** restrict, confine, curb, limit, constrain, restrain, hamper, hinder, impede, cramp. **tie in** fit in, tally, concur, conform, dovetail. **tie up 1** *tie up the package* wrap, wrap up, bind, truss. **2** *his capital is tied up* invest, commit. **3** *the meeting will tie him up all morning* occupy, engage, keep busy, engross, take up one's attention. **4** *we should tie up the arrangements* finalize, conclude, wind up, complete, finish off; *inf.* wrap up.

tie noun **1** *trash bags fastened with a tie* ligature, link, fastening, fastener, clip, catch. **2** *business ties* bond, connection, relationship, kinship, affiliation, allegiance. **3** *the game ended in a tie* draw, dead heat, deadlock, stalemate.

tier noun row, level, bank, line; layer, echelon, rank.

tight adjective **1** *keep a tight grip* fast, secure, fixed, clenched, clinched. **2** *tight ropes/muscles* taut, rigid, stiff, tense, stretched, strained. **3** *a tight mass of fibers* compact, compacted, compressed. **4** *space was a*

bit tight with so many people cramped, restricted, limited, constricted. **5** *the box must be tight* impervious, impenetrable, sound, sealed, hermetic; watertight, airtight. **6** *money is a bit tight just now* scarce, scant, sparse, in short supply, limited, insufficient, inadequate. **7** *security was tight at the press conference* strict, rigorous, stringent, tough, rigid, uncompromising, exacting. **8** *in a tight situation* problematic, difficult, precarious, hazardous, dangerous, perilous, tricky, ticklish, worrying, delicate; *inf.* sticky. **9** *a piece of tight prose* concise, succinct, terse, crisp, pithy, epigrammatic. **10** *it was a tight race* close, even, evenly matched, neck and neck. **11** *tight with his money* tight-fisted, mean, miserly, parsimonious, stingy, niggardly.

tighten verb **1** *she tightened the leash* secure, make fast, tauten, stretch, make rigid, stiffen, tense. **3** *tighten security* increase, make stricter, make rigorous/stringent. **3** *his throat tightened* narrow, constrict, contract.

till verb cultivate, farm, plow, dig.

tilt verb lean, list, slope, slant, incline, tip, cant.

timber noun wood, lumber; beam, spar, pole.

time noun **1** *in the time of the dinosaurs* age, era, epoch, period. **2** *he worked there for a time* while, spell, stretch, span, period, term. **3** *the last time I saw him* occasion, point, juncture. **4** *now is the time to act/leave* moment, point, instant, stage. **5** *the places I have been in my time* lifetime, life, life span. **6** *have a hard time* condition, circumstance; situation, experience. **7** *in waltz time* rhythm, measure, tempo, beat, meter. **8** *he never has any time to himself* freedom, leisure, leisure time, spare time; moments, odd moments. **ahead of time** early, in good time, with time to spare. **all the time** *he works all the time* constantly, always, at all times, perpetually, continuously, continually. **at one time 1** *at one time he worked there* once, previously, formerly, hitherto. **2** *several matches going on at one time* simultaneously, concurrently, at once, at the same time, together. **at the same time** *he is wealthy; at the same time, he lives frugally* nevertheless, nonetheless, however, but, still, yet, just the same. **at times** from time to time, every now and then, periodically, on occasion, occasionally. **behind time** late, running late, behind schedule. **behind the times** old-fashioned, out-of-date, dated, outmoded, obsolete, passé, antiquated; *inf.* old hat. **from time to time** now and then, every so often, at times. **in no time** rapidly/quickly/swiftly, speedily, at great speed, expeditiously, with dispatch. **in good time** punctually, on time; early, ahead of time, with time to spare. **in time** *they will forget in time* eventually, ultimately, as time goes on/by, by and by, one day, someday, sooner or later, in the long run. **many a time** often, frequently, many times, on many occasions. **on time** punctually, early enough, in good time, sharp, on the dot. **time after time** again and again, many times over, repeatedly, time and again, time and time again, recurrently.

time verb 1 *time the meeting for the afternoon* schedule, fix, set, arrange, program. 2 *time his progress* clock, measure, calculate, regulate, count.

timeless adjective ageless, enduring, lasting, permanent, abiding, unending, ceaseless, undying, deathless, eternal, everlasting, immortal, changeless, immutable, indestructible.

timely adjective opportune, well-timed, convenient, appropriate, seasonable, felicitous.

timetable noun schedule, program, calendar, list, agenda.

timid adjective 1 *too timid to stand up to the bully* timorous, fearful, apprehensive, afraid, frightened, scared, faint-hearted, lily-livered, cowardly, pusillanimous; *inf.* chicken, yellow. 2 *too timid to speak to strangers* shy, diffident, bashful, reticent, unselfconfident, timorous, shrinking, retiring, coy, demure.

tinge verb color, tint, shade, dye, stain, suffuse, imbue, flavor.

tinge noun 1 *a tinge of silver in the wallpaper* color, tint, shade, tone, tincture, cast, dye, stain, wash. 2 *a tinge of sadness in her attitude* hint, suggestion, trace, touch, bit, dash, soupçon.

tingle verb prickle, prick, tickle, itch, sting, quiver, tremble.

tingle noun 1 *the tingle in her fingers* tingling, prickling, pricking, tickle, itch, quiver, trembling, pins and needles. 2 *feel a tingle of excitement* quiver, tremor, thrill, throb.

tinker verb fiddle, play, toy, tamper, fool (around), mess (about).

tinkle verb ring, chime, peal, ding, jingle.

tint noun 1 *several tints to choose from* shade, color. *See* TINGE noun 1. 2 *a hair tint* dye, rinse, colorant, coloring.

tiny adjective minute, diminutive, miniature, mini, minuscule, infinitesimal, microscopic, dwarfish, midget, pocket-sized, Lilliputian, wee, petite, small, little, insignificant, trifling, negligible, inconsequential; *inf.* teeny, teeny-weeny, itsy-bitsy, pint-sized.

tip[1] noun point, peak, top, summit, apex, crown.

tip[2] verb *the table tends to tip* tilt, lean, list, cant, slant. **tip over** topple (over), overturn, fall over, turn topsy-turvy, capsize, upset, upend.

tip[3] noun 1 *give the waiter a tip* gratuity, pourboire, baksheesh; *inf.* little something. 2 *tips on how to take out stains* hint, suggestion, recommendation, piece of advice; advice.

tip[4] verb **tip off** warn, forewarn, advise, inform, notify, caution, alert.

tipsy adjective drunk, intoxicated, inebriated; *inf.* tiddly, tight, under the influence.

tirade noun diatribe, harangue, lecture, upbraiding, denunciation, obloquy, philippic; invective, vituperation, fulmination.

tire verb 1 *climbing the hill tired him* tire out, fatigue, wear out, weary, exhaust, drain, enervate, debilitate; *inf.* take it out of. 2 *he tires easily* flag, droop; *inf.* poop out. 3 *their constant boasting tires me* bore, weary, irk, irritate, get on one's nerves, annoy, exasperate; *inf.* get to.

tired adjective 1 *feel tired after the climb* fatigued, worn out, weary, wearied, exhausted, drained, enervated, debilitated; *inf.* done in, all in, beat, dog-tired, bushed, pooped (out), dead on one's feet, ready to drop. 2 *tired children ready for bed* sleepy, drowsy, weary; *inf.* asleep on one's feet. 3 *tired jokes* stale, hackneyed, familiar, worn-out, outworn, well-worn, clichéd, stock, platitudinous, trite, banal. 4 *made tired by their chatter* bored, wearied, irked, irritated, annoyed, exasperated.

tireless adjective untiring, unflagging, indefatigable, energetic, industrious, vigorous, determined, resolute, dogged.

tiresome adjective 1 *tiresome work* wearisome, laborious, wearing, tedious, boring, monotonous, dull, uninteresting, unexciting, humdrum, routine. 2 *she is a tiresome child* troublesome, irksome, vexatious, irritating, annoying, exasperating, trying.

titillate verb excite, arouse, stimulate, thrill, fascinate, tantalize, seduce; *inf.* turn on.

titillating adjective exciting, arousing, stimulating, provocative, tantalizing, suggestive, seductive, erotic.

title noun 1 *picture/illustration titles* credit, caption, legend, inscription, heading, name. 2 *what is the title of the ship's officer?* designation, appellation, name, denomination, epithet, sobriquet; *inf.* moniker, handle. 3 *disputing his title to the land* entitlement, right, claim, ownership, proprietorship, possession, holding. **4** *boxers contending for the title* championship, first place, crown; laurels.

title verb entitle, name, call, designate, label, tag, style, term.

titter noun snicker, snigger, giggle, tee-hee, laugh, chuckle, cackle, chortle.

titular adjective *the titular head of state* nominal, so-called, self-called, self-styled, *soi-disant*, token, puppet, putative.

toady noun sycophant, fawner, flatterer, groveler, lackey, flunky, minion; hanger-on, parasite, leech, jackal; *inf.* yes-man, bootlicker.

toady verb **toady to** bow and scrape to, be obsequious to, fawn on, flatter, grovel to, kowtow to, curry favor with; *inf.* butter up, fall all over, suck up to.

toast verb **1** *toast the bread* brown, crisp, grill. **2** *toast the winner* drink (to) the health of, drink to, pledge, salute.

toddle verb totter, teeter, wobble, falter, dodder. **toddle off** go, leave, depart.

together adverb **1** *friends who work together* in conjunction, jointly, conjointly, in cooperation, as one, in unison, side by side, hand in hand, hand and/in glove, shoulder to shoulder, cheek by jowl. **2** *they arrived together* simultaneously, concurrently, at the same time, at once, all at once, synchronously. **3** *they have got it together at last* organized, sorted out, straight, to rights, settled, fixed, arranged.

toil verb labor, slog, struggle, slave, push oneself, drive oneself, strive, drudge, work like a dog/slave/Trojan; *inf.* work one's fingers to the bone, sweat, grind.

toil noun labor, slaving, drudgery, striving, industry, effort, exertion, travail, sweat of one's brow; *inf.* elbow grease, grind.

toilet noun lavatory, bathroom, rest room, washroom, men's room, ladies' room, powder room, convenience, urinal, latrine, privy, outhouse; *inf.* john, can.

token noun **1** *a token of friendship* symbol, sign, emblem, badge, representation, indication, mark, manifestation, expression, demonstration. **2** *keep the menu as a token of the celebration* memento, souvenir, keepsake, remembrance, reminder, memorial.

token adjective *offer token resistance* perfunctory, superficial, nominal, minimal, slight, hollow.

tolerable adjective **1** *the pain/noise level was scarcely tolerable* endurable, bearable, sufferable, supportable, acceptable. **2** *his work was only tolerable* fair, passable, adequate, so-so, mediocre, middling.

tolerance noun **1** *treat the young with*

tolerance toleration, open-mindedness, forbearance, patience, magnanimity, understanding, charity, lenience, indulgence, permissiveness, complaisance, laxness. **2** *his tolerance of pain* endurance, sufferance, acceptance, fortitude, stamina, hardiness, resilience, toughness.

tolerant adjective open-minded, unprejudiced, unbiased, unbigoted, broad-minded, liberal, magnanimous, sympathetic, understanding, charitable, lenient, indulgent, permissive.

tolerate verb **1** *tolerate other people's views* permit, allow, admit, sanction, warrant, countenance, brook, recognize, acknowledge. **2** *unable to tolerate the pain/noise* endure, bear, suffer, take, stand, put up with, abide, accept, stomach, submit to.

toll noun **1** *pay a toll to use the road* charge, fee, payment, levy, tariff. **2** *the death toll* cost, damage, loss.

tomb noun grave, burial place/chamber, sepulcher, vault, crypt, catacomb, mausoleum.

tomfoolery noun horseplay, mischief, fooling, foolery, clowning, skylarking, buffoonery, nonsense; pranks, tricks, capers, antics, larks; *inf.* shenanigans, monkey business.

tone noun **1** *the pleasant tone of the flute* sound, color, pitch, timbre, tonality. **2** *speak in an angry tone* intonation, inflection, modulation, accentuation. **3** *the tone of his letter was optimistic* mood, air, attitude, character, manner, spirit, temper, tenor, vein, drift, gist.

tongue noun *speak in a foreign tongue* language, speech, parlance, dialect, idiom, patois, vernacular; *inf.* lingo.

tonic noun restorative, refresher, stimulant, analeptic, pick-me-up, boost, fillip; *inf.* shot in the arm, picker-upper.

too adverb **1** *the dog came, too* as well, also, in addition, besides, furthermore, moreover, to boot. **2** *she is too busy* excessively, overly, unduly, inordinately, extremely.

tool noun **1** *the tools of his trade* implement, instrument, utensil, device, apparatus, gadget, appliance, machine, contrivance, contraption, aid. **2** *he is the manager's tool* puppet, pawn, minion, lackey, flunky, henchman, toady.

top noun **1** *the top of the hill* summit, peak, pinnacle, crest, crown, tip, apex, vertex, apogee. **2** *he is at the top of his career* height, zenith, acme, culmination, climax, crowning point, prime, meridian. **3** *put the top on the jar* cap, lid, stopper, cork, cover. **4** *she wore a blue top* shirt, T-shirt, blouse, jersey, sweater, sweatshirt.

top adjective **1** *the top drawer/floor* topmost, uppermost, highest. **2** *top scientists* foremost, leading, principal, preeminent, greatest, finest. **3** *the top positions in the firm* leading, chief, principal, main, highest, ruling, commanding. **4** *top goods* top-quality, top-grade, best, finest, prime, choicest, quality; *inf.* A-1, top-notch. **5** *at top speed* maximum, maximal, greatest, utmost.

top verb **1** *ice cream topped with chocolate sauce* cap, cover, finish, garnish. **2** *she tops the list of candidates* head, lead. **3** *he topped his previous record* surpass, exceed, go beyond, transcend, better, best, beat, excel, outstrip, outdo, outshine, eclipse.

topic noun subject, subject matter, theme, issue, matter, point, question, argument, thesis.

top-notch adjective first-rate, top-grade, excellent, ace, choice, superior; *inf.* A-1, crack.

topple verb **1** *the load was unstable and toppled* fall over, tip over, keel over, overturn, capsize. **2** *the rebels toppled the tyrant* overthrow, oust, unseat, bring down.

topsy-turvy adverb/adjective in disorder, in confusion, in a muddle, in chaos, in disarray, in a mess, upside down.

torment noun **1** *the torment of grief* agony, suffering, torture, pain, excruciation, anguish, hell, misery, distress, affliction, wretchedness. **2** *he was a torment to them* scourge, curse, plague, bane, affliction, thorn in the flesh, irritation, irritant, annoyance, worry, nuisance, bother.

torment verb **1** *tormented by conscience* afflict, harrow, plague, torture, distress, worry, trouble. **2** *tormented the new teacher* tease, irritate, vex, annoy, pester, harass, badger, bother.

torn adjective **1** *torn clothes* ragged, tattered, ripped, split, slit, cut, lacerated, rent. **2** *I am torn between the two dresses* divided, wavering, vacillating, irresolute, uncertain, undecided.

torpid adjective sluggish, slow-moving, slow, dull, lethargic, heavy, inactive, stagnant, inert, somnolent, sleepy, languorous, languid, listless, apathetic, passive, slothful, indolent, lazy.

torrent noun **1** *torrents of floodwaters* flood, deluge, inundation, spate, cascade, rush, stream, current; downpour, rainstorm. **2** *a torrent of abuse* stream, volley, outpouring, barrage, battery.

torrid adjective **1** *the torrid conditions in the desert* hot, arid, sweltering, scorching, boiling, parching, sultry, stifling. **2** *torrid love scenes* passionate, impassioned, ardent, fervent, fervid, amorous, erotic; *inf.* steamy.

tortuous adjective **1** *a tortuous mountain path* twisting, winding, curving, curvy, sinuous, coiling, serpentine, snaking, snaky, zigzag, meandering. **2** *a tortuous description of the incident* convoluted, roundabout, circuitous, indirect, involved, complicated, ambiguous. **3** *his tortuous policy* devious, cunning, tricky, deceptive.

torture noun **1** *use torture to extract a confession* persecution, pain, suffering, abuse, ill-treatment, punishment, torment. **2** *the torture of a toothache* agony, anguish. *See* TORMENT noun 1.

torture verb **1** *torture the hostages* persecute, abuse, ill-treat, punish, torment; *inf.* work over. **2** *tortured by his conscience* rack, afflict. *See* TORMENT verb 1.

toss verb **1** *toss the book over here* throw, hurl, cast, sling, pitch, shy, lob, propel, launch, project, heave, chuck. **2** *tossing around unable to sleep* thrash, wriggle, writhe, squirm, roll, tumble. **3** *ships tossing around on the waves* rock, roll, sway, undulate, pitch, lurch, heave.

total noun sum, sum total, aggregate, whole, entirety, totality.

total adjective **1** *the total number of votes* complete, entire, whole, full, comprehensive, combined, aggregate, composite, integral. **2** *a total disaster* complete, thorough, thoroughgoing, all-out, utter, absolute, downright, out and out, unmitigated, unqualified.

total verb **1** *these figures total more than $1,000* add up to, come to, amount to. **2** *total these figures rapidly* add up, sum, count up, count, calculate, reckon.

totalitarian adjective one-party, monocratic, undemocratic, autocratic, authoritarian, absolute, despotic, dictatorial, tyrannical, oppressive, fascist.

totally adverb completely, entirely, wholly, fully, thoroughly, utterly, absolutely, quite.

totter verb **1** *tottering on high heels* teeter, wobble, stagger, stumble, reel, sway, roll, lurch. **2** *tables/buildings tottering in the explosion* shake, sway, rock, lurch, shudder. **3** *the regime is tottering* be unstable, be unsteady, be shaky, be on the point of collapse, falter.

touch verb **1** *the wires are touching* be in contact, meet, converge, be contiguous, adjoin, abut. **2** *he touched her arm* tap, brush, graze, feel, stroke, pat, fondle, caress. **3** *do not touch the glassware* handle, hold, pick up, move, play with, toy with, fiddle with. **4** *she did not touch her meal* eat, consume, drink, take, partake of. **5** *they were touched by the child's plight* affect, move, influence, upset, disturb, sadden; *inf.* get to. **6** *the recession did not touch him* affect, concern, involve. **7** *they would not touch anything illegal* be associated with, have dealings with, deal with, handle, be a party to. **8** *no one can touch him at tennis* come near (to), come up to, compare with, be on a par with, equal, match, be in the same league as, rival, hold a candle to. **9** *they touched rock bottom* reach, attain, arrive at. **touch off 1** *touch off the explosive* ignite, trigger, explode, detonate. **2** *the statement touched off a storm of protest* set off, start, begin, set in motion, initiate, instigate, trigger, launch. **touch on/upon 1** *touch on the subject in his speech* refer to, mention, comment on, remark on, allude to. **2** *his actions touched on treason* come close to, verge on, be tantamount to. **touch up** patch up, fix up, repair, refurbish, renovate, revamp, give a face-lift to, improve, enhance.

touch noun **1** *feel a touch on his arm* pressure, tap, strike, hit, blow, brush, stroke, pat, caress. **2** *sense its presence by touch* feel, feeling, tactility. **3** *material with a velvety touch* feel, texture, grain, finish, surface, coating. **4** *a touch of garlic* bit, trace, dash, taste, spot, drop, pinch, speck, smack, suggestion, hint, soupçon, tinge, tincture, whiff, suspicion. **5** *admire the player's touch* craftsmanship, workmanship, artistry, performance, dexterity, deftness, skill, virtuosity, adroitness. **6** *the room needs a few extra touches* detail, feature, addition, accessory. **7** *I think the teacher is losing his touch* skill, skillfulness, expertise, technique, knack, adeptness, ability, talent, flair. **8** *the house needs a woman's touch* influence, effect, hand, handling, direction, management, technique, method. **9** *in touch with old friends* contact, communication, correspondence.

touch-and-go adjective uncertain, precarious, risky, hazardous, dangerous, critical, suspenseful, cliff-hanging.

touching adjective moving, impressive, affecting, warming, heartwarming, emotive, stirring; upsetting, disturbing, saddening, pitiful, piteous, poignant.

touchy adjective **1** *he is very touchy about his height* sensitive, oversensitive, hypersensitive, easily offended, thin-skinned; testy, irascible, irritable, grouchy, grumpy, peevish, querulous, cross, surly. **2** *a touchy situation* tricky, ticklish, delicate, precarious, chancy, risky.

tough adjective **1** *a tough substance* strong, durable, resistant, resilient, sturdy, firm, solid, hard, rigid, stiff. **2** *tough meat* chewy, leathery, gristly, stringy, fibrous, sinewy. **3** *have to be tough to survive those conditions* hardy, strong, fit, sturdy, rugged, stalwart, vigorous, strapping, robust. **4** *a tough job managing the firm* difficult, hard, arduous, onerous, heavy, uphill, laborious, strenuous, exacting, taxing, stressful. **5** *teachers getting tough with the children* firm,

strict, stern, severe, harsh, hard-hitting, adamant, inflexible. **6** *a tough way of life* hard, harsh, austere, bleak, grim, dire, rough. **7** *led astray by tough kids* rough, rowdy, unruly, disorderly, violent, wild, lawless, lawbreaking, criminal.

toughen verb **1** *toughen the glass* strengthen, fortify, reinforce, harden. **2** *toughen the laws* stiffen, tighten; *inf.* beef up.

tour noun **1** *a world tour* trip, excursion, journey, expedition, jaunt, outing, peregrination. **2** *on a golfing tour* circuit, ambit, round, course, beat. **3** *troops doing a tour in the Persian Gulf* tour of duty, stint, stretch, turn.

tour verb travel, journey, explore, vacation, visit, sightsee.

tournament noun competition, contest, series, meeting, event, match, tourney.

tousled adjective rumpled, disheveled, unkempt, disordered, untidy, messy; *inf.* mussed up.

tow verb pull, draw, drag, haul, tug, trail, lug.

tower noun steeple, spire, belfry, bell tower, turret, column, pillar, obelisk, minaret.

tower verb soar, rise, ascend, mount, rear. **tower above** surpass, excel, outshine, outclass, outdo, leave behind, overshadow, cap, top, transcend, eclipse, be head and shoulders above, put in the shade, run circles around.

towering adjective **1** *towering skyscrapers* high, tall, lofty, elevated, sky-high. **2** *in a towering rage* extreme, mighty, fierce, terrible, intense, violent, vehement. **3** *one of the towering intellects of his age* outstanding, extraordinary, preeminent, surpassing, incomparable, unrivaled, peerless.

town noun community; borough, municipality, township.

toxic adjective poisonous, venomous, virulent, noxious.

toy noun **1** *children's toys* plaything, game. **2** *the rich woman surrounds herself with toys* trinket, bauble, knickknack, gewgaw, trifle.

toy verb **toy with 1** *he is just toying with her* amuse oneself with, play around with, flirt with, dally with, sport with, trifle with. **2** *the child was toying with his food* play around with, fiddle with, fool/mess around with.

trace noun **1** *there was no trace left of the picnic* mark, sign, vestige, indication; evidence; remains, remnants, relics. **2** *traces of poison in the drink* bit, touch, hint, suggestion, suspicion, trifle, drop, dash, tinge, tincture, shadow, jot, iota.

trace verb **1** *unable to trace the letter* find,

discover, detect, unearth, uncover, track down, turn up, dig up, ferret out, hunt down. **2** *trace the bear to the forest* follow, pursue, track, trail, tail, shadow, stalk, dog. **3** *trace out the policies for the year* draw up, sketch, draft, outline, delineate, rough out, map, chart.

track noun **1** *follow the tracks of the burglar/bear/motorbike* marks, impressions, prints, imprints, footprints, footsteps; trail, spoor, scent. **2** *follow in the track of the great explorers* trail, path, pathway, way, course, route, line, orbit, trajectory. **keep track of** keep up with, follow, monitor, record. **lose track of** forget about, be unaware of, misplace, lose/cease contact with.

track verb *track the bear to the forest* follow, pursue. *See* TRACE verb 2. **track down** hunt down/out, run to earth, unearth, uncover, turn up, dig up, ferret out, nose out, bring to light, expose, discover, find out, detect.

tract[1] noun area, region, zone, stretch, expanse, extent, plot.

tract[2] noun pamphlet, booklet, leaflet, brochure, monograph, essay.

trade noun **1** *he is in the export trade* commerce, buying and selling, dealing, traffic, trafficking, business, marketing, merchandising. **2** *what trade is his father in?* line of work, line, occupation, job, career, profession, craft, vocation, calling, métier; work, employment. **3** *I will do a trade of my car with yours* swap, trade-off, exchange, switch, barter.

trade verb **1** *the firm is trading at a loss* do business, deal, run, operate. **2** *they trade in diamonds* buy and sell, traffic, market, merchandise. **3** *he traded his stamps for comics* swap, exchange, switch, barter. **trade on** take advantage of, exploit, capitalize on.

trader noun merchant, dealer, buyer, seller, buyer and seller, marketer, merchandiser, broker.

tradition noun custom, belief, practice, convention, ritual, observance, habit, institution; oral history, lore, folklore.

traditional adjective **1** *traditional holiday fare* customary, accustomed, conventional, established, ritual, habitual, routine, usual, wonted, old, time-honored, familial, ancestral. **2** *keeping alive traditional customs* handed-down, folk, unwritten, oral.

traffic noun *drug traffic* trafficking, trade, trading, dealing, commerce, business, peddling, smuggling, bootlegging.

traffic verb **traffic in** trade in, deal in, do business in, peddle, smuggle.

tragedy noun disaster, calamity, catastrophe, misfortune, misadventure, affliction, adversity.

tragic adjective **1** *a tragic accident* disastrous, calamitous, catastrophic, fatal, terrible, dreadful, appalling, dire, awful. **2** *listen to her tragic tale* pitiful, piteous, melancholy, doleful, mournful, dismal, gloomy. **3** *it is tragic what they have done to the river* dreadful, deplorable, lamentable, regrettable.

trail noun **1** *follow the trail left by the leader* track, scent, spoor; traces, marks, signs, footprints, footmarks; path, pathway, footpath, track, road, route. **2** *the rock star had a trail of young admirers* line, queue, train, file, column, procession, following, entourage. **3** *leave a trail of disaster behind them* chain, series. *See* TRAIN noun 2.

trail verb **1** *the child trailed the toy behind him* tow, pull, drag, draw, haul. **2** *her long skirt trailing on the floor* drag across, sweep, dangle, hang down, droop. **3** *children trailing behind their parents* trudge, plod, dawdle, straggle, loiter, linger, lag. **4** *plants/creatures trailing along the ground* creep, crawl, slide, slink. **5** *they trailed him to his lair* follow, pursue. *See* TRACE verb 2. **6** *his voice trailed away* fade, fade away/out, disappear, vanish, peter out, die away, melt away.

train noun **1** *leaving a train of vapor* trail, stream, track, path, wake, wash. **2** *a train of disasters followed* trail, chain, string, series, sequence, set, progression. **3** *a train of people climbing the mountain* procession, line, file, column, convoy, caravan. **4** *the princess and her train* retinue, entourage, cortege, following.

train verb **1** *train the students in reading* instruct, teach, coach, tutor, school, educate, drill, prepare, ground, guide, indoctrinate, inculcate. **2** *she is training to be a teacher* study, qualify, learn, prepare. **3** *athletes train daily* exercise, do exercises, work out, practice, prepare. **4** *train the binoculars on the bird* aim, point, focus, direct, level, line up.

trait noun characteristic, attribute, feature, quality, property, idiosyncrasy, peculiarity, quirk.

traitor noun betrayer, backstabber, turncoat, double-crosser, double-dealer, renegade, defector, deserter, apostate, Judas, quisling, fifth columnist; *inf.* snake in the grass, two-timer.

tramp verb **1** *hear him tramping upstairs* trudge, plod, stamp, stump, stomp. **2** *spend the day tramping over the hills* trek, hike, march, slog, walk, ramble, roam, range, rove; *inf.* traipse.

tramp noun **1** *tramps sleeping on freight trains* vagrant, vagabond, hobo, derelict, down-and-out, itinerant, drifter. **2** *hear* *the tramp of the soldiers* footstep, footfall, tread, stamp, stomping. **3** *labeled her a tramp* loose woman, slut, wanton, trollop, prostitute, whore.

trample verb **1** *trample on the grass* tramp on, tread on, walk over, stamp on, squash, crush, flatten. **2** *trample on other people* ride roughshod over, treat with contempt, disregard, show no consideration for, encroach on, infringe.

trance noun daze, stupor, dream, reverie, brown study.

tranquil adjective **1** *a tranquil life* peaceful, restful, reposeful, calm, quiet, still, serene, placid, undisturbed. **2** *a tranquil person* calm, placid, composed, even-tempered, unexcitable, unflappable, unruffled, unperturbed.

tranquillity noun **1** *love the tranquillity of the place* peace, peacefulness, restfulness, reposefulness, calm, quiet, quietness, quietude, stillness, serenity, placidity. **2** *her tranquillity is never disturbed* composure, coolness, serenity, equanimity, even-temperedness, unexcitability, unflappability.

transact verb carry out, conduct, do, perform, execute, enact, manage, handle, negotiate, take care of, see to.

transaction noun **1** *the transaction took less than an hour* business, deal, undertaking, affair, bargain, negotiation; proceedings. **2** *the transaction of business in private* conducting, performance, execution, enactment, handling, negotiation.

transcend verb **1** *transcend human belief* go beyond, exceed, overstep, rise above. **2** *her performance transcended that of her opponents* surpass, excel. *See* TOWER ABOVE (TOWER verb).

transcendental adjective mystical, mystic, mysterious, preternatural, supernatural, otherworldly.

transfer verb **1** *transfer the material from the house to the garage* convey, move, shift, remove, take, carry, transport, change, relocate. **2** *transfer his property to his son* turn over, sign over, hand on, hand down, pass on, transmit, convey, devolve, assign, delegate.

transfer noun move, shift, relocation, change.

transfix verb *transfixed with/in terror* root to the spot, paralyze, petrify, stop dead, hypnotize, mesmerize, rivet, spellbind, fascinate, engross, stun, astound.

transform verb change, alter, convert, metamorphose, revolutionize, transfigure, remodel, redo, reconstruct, rebuild, reorganize, rearrange, renew, translate, transmute; *inf.* transmogrify.

transgression noun **1** *transgression of the law* overstepping, infringement, breach, breaking, contravention, violation, defiance, disobedience. **2** *punished for their transgressions* wrong, misdemeanor, misdeed, lawbreaking, crime, offense, lapse, fault, sin; wrongdoing, misbehavior.

transgressor noun wrongdoer, lawbreaker, criminal, miscreant, delinquent, villain, felon, offender, culprit, sinner, trespasser, malefactor.

transient adjective short-lived, impermanent. *See* TRANSITORY.

transition noun passage, change, transformation, conversion, changeover, metamorphosis, shift, switch, jump, leap, progression, gradation, development, evolution.

transitory adjective transient, short-lived, short-term, impermanent, temporary, brief, short, ephemeral, evanescent, momentary, fleeting, flying, passing, fugitive, fugacious, mutable.

translate verb **1** *translate the jargon into plain English* construe, interpret, render, convert, transcribe, transliterate, paraphrase, reword, decipher, decode, explain, elucidate. **2** *translate ideas into action* turn, change, convert, transform, alter, metamorphose, transmute.

transmission noun **1** *the transmission of mail* sending, conveyance, transport, dispatch, remission. **2** *the transmission of information/disease* transference, transferal, passing on, communication, imparting, dissemination, spreading. **3** *a radio transmission* broadcasting, relaying, sending out; broadcast, program.

transmit verb **1** *transmit the package by air* send, convey, transport, dispatch, forward, remit. **2** *transmit information/disease to others* transfer, pass on, hand on, communicate, impart, disseminate, spread, carry, diffuse. **3** *transmit late-night programs* broadcast, air, relay, send out, put on the air.

transparent adjective **1** *transparent plastic/streams* clear, see-through, translucent, lucid, pellucid, crystal-clear, crystalline, limpid, glassy, transpicuous. **2** *made of transparent material* sheer, diaphanous, filmy, gauzy. **3** *his transparent dishonesty* obvious, patent, manifest, undisguised, unmistakable, clear, plain, visible, noticeable, evident. **4** *done with transparent sincerity* frank, open, candid, direct, forthright, plainspoken, straight, ingenuous, artless.

transpire verb **1** *it transpired that he had been married before* become known, come to light, emerge, come out. **2** *tell me what transpired at the meeting* come about, take place, happen, occur, turn up, arise, chance, befall.

transport verb **1** *transport the goods to the warehouse* convey, take, transfer, move, shift, bring, fetch, carry, bear, haul, lug, cart, run, ship. **2** *transport criminals to an island* banish, exile, deport, drive away, expatriate. **3** *she was transported by the music* enrapture, entrance, enchant, enthrall, captivate, delight, ravish, carry away.

transport noun transportation, conveyance, transit, carriage, freight; vehicle, car.

trap noun **1** *rabbits caught in a trap* snare, net, mesh, ambush, pitfall, booby trap. **2** *the question was a trap to get him to confess* stratagem, setup, artifice, ruse, wile, trick, device, deception, subterfuge. **3** *lay a trap for the criminal* ambush, lure, decoy, bait.

trap verb **1** *trap the rabbits* snare, ensnare, enmesh, entrap, catch, corner. **2** *trapped into making a confession* trick, dupe, deceive, lure, inveigle, beguile, set up. **3** *they were trapped in the building* cut off, corner, confine, imprison.

trappings plural noun accoutrements, appurtenances, appointments, trimmings, paraphernalia, fittings, things; equipage, equipment, apparatus, gear, livery, adornment, ornamentation, decoration, finery, frippery; panoply.

trash noun **1** *talk trash* rubbish, garbage, nonsense, drivel, poppycock, balderdash, bunkum, twaddle; *inf.* bunk, tripe, bilge, rot, tommyrot. **2** *empty out the trash* rubbish, waste, refuse, litter, garbage. **3** *he regards his neighbors as trash* riff-raff, scum, rabble, canaille, vermin; dregs, good-for-nothings.

traumatic adjective agonizing, shocking, scarring, disturbing, distressing, damaging, injurious, harmful.

travel verb **1** *she plans to travel after she retires* journey, take a trip, tour, voyage, sightsee. **2** *news travels fast* proceed, progress, advance, be transmitted, carry. **3** *travel the length of the country* cross, traverse, cover, wander, ramble, roam, rove, range, wend, make one's way over. **4** *the car was certainly traveling* speed, go at breakneck speed; *inf.* hellbent for leather, go like a bat out of hell, tear up the miles.

traveler noun tourist, vacationer, excursionist, explorer, passenger, voyager, sightseer, globe-trotter.

traverse verb **1** *traversing the desert* cross, go across, travel over, journey over, make one's way across, pass over, wander, roam, range. **2** *beams traversing the ceiling* go across, lie across, stretch across, extend across, cross, cut across, bridge. **3** *traverse all aspects of the subject* consider, examine, check, study, review, investigate, inspect, scrutinize, look into.

travesty noun misrepresentation, distortion, perversion, corruption, poor imitation, mockery, parody, caricature, sham, burlesque, satire, spoof, lampoon, takeoff; *inf.* send-up.

treacherous adjective **1** *betrayed by a treacherous follower* traitorous, backstabbing, double-crossing, double-dealing, disloyal, faithless, unfaithful, perfidious, duplicitous, deceitful, false-hearted, false, untrue, untrustworthy, unreliable, undependable; *inf.* two-timing. **2** *the weather conditions can be treacherous* precarious, unreliable, undependable, unstable, unsafe, risky, hazardous, dangerous, perilous, deceptive; *inf.* dicey.

treachery noun traitorousness, backstabbing, double-crossing, double-dealing, disloyalty, faithlessness, unfaithfulness, perfidy, perfidiousness, treason, duplicity, deceit, deceitfulness, deception; *inf.* two-timing.

tread verb **1** *tread softly so as not to wake the baby* walk, step, go, pace. **2** *tread the long road home* hike, tramp, stride, step out, trek, march, trudge, plod. **3** *tread grapes* trample, tramp on, step on, stamp on, squash, crush, flatten, press down. **tread on** ride roughshod over, oppress, repress, suppress, subdue, subjugate, quell, crush.

tread noun step, footstep, footfall, walk, tramp.

treason noun high treason; betrayal, traitorousness, treachery, disloyalty, perfidy, sedition, subversion, mutiny, rebellion, lese-majesty.

treasure noun **1** *find buried treasure* riches, valuables; wealth, fortune, hoard; jewels, gems, coins, gold, money, cash. **2** *she is her father's treasure* darling, pride and joy, apple of one's eye, jewel, jewel in the crown, gem, pearl, precious, prize.

treasure verb **1** *she treasures her friendship/children* value, prize, set great store by, think highly of, hold dear, adore, cherish, love, worship, revere, venerate, dote on. **2** *treasure the souvenirs of their travels* save, collect, accumulate, hoard, store up, lay by, stow away, squirrel away, salt away; *inf.* stash away.

treat noun **1** *think of a treat for her birthday* surprise, celebration, entertainment, amusement, diversion. **2** *bringing a treat for the child* gift, present, tidbit, delicacy; *inf.* goodie. **3** *it was a treat to see her again* pleasure, delight, thrill, joy, gratification, satisfaction; fun.

treat verb **1** *treat his car recklessly* deal with, handle, cope with, contend with, manage, use. **2** *treat his remarks as jokes* regard, consider, view, look upon, deal with. **3** *treat the sick patient* medicate, doctor, nurse, care for, attend to, minister to, cure, heal. **4** *her book treats the question of religious doubt* deal with, discuss, go into, discourse upon, be concerned with, touch upon, refer to, consider, study, review, analyze. **treat to 1** *treat (them) to dinner* pay for, buy for, pay/foot the bill for, finance, take out to. **2** *we were treated to a wonderful performance* entertain by, amuse by, divert by, cheer by, gratify by, delight by, regale by. **treat with** *treat the wood with creosote* apply to, put on, use on, ply with.

treatise noun discourse, exposition, dissertation, thesis, disquisition, study, essay, paper, monograph, tract, pamphlet.

treatment noun **1** *his treatment was fair/cruel* action, behavior, conduct, handling, management, use; dealings. **2** *patients/wounds responding to treatment* medication, medicament, therapy, doctoring, nursing, first aid, care, ministration; cure, remedy; drugs, therapeutics.

treaty noun agreement, pact, deal, compact, covenant, bargain, pledge, contract, alliance, concordat, convention, entente.

trek verb trudge, tramp, plod, travel, journey. *See* TRAMP verb 2.

trek noun expedition, trip, journey, hike, march, walk, odyssey.

tremble verb **1** *fingers trembling with excitement* shake, quiver, shiver, quake, twitch, wiggle. **2** *buildings trembling in the earthquake* shudder, teeter, totter, wobble, rock, vibrate, oscillate, rattle. **3** *I tremble at the thought* fear, be frightened, be apprehensive, worry, be anxious.

tremendous adjective **1** *people of tremendous girth* great, huge, enormous, immense, massive, vast, colossal, prodigious, stupendous, gigantic, gargantuan, mammoth, giant, titanic; *inf.* whopping. **2** *she is a tremendous cook* excellent, marvelous, extraordinary, exceptional, wonderful, incredible, fabulous; *inf.* fantastic, terrific, super.

tremor noun tremble, trembling, shake, shaking, shiver, quiver, quaver, vibration, twitch, spasm, paroxysm.

trench noun ditch, excavation, earthwork, furrow, duct, trough, channel, conduit, cut, drain, waterway, moat, fosse.

trenchant adjective **1** *a trenchant wit* incisive, cutting, pointed, sharp, biting, pungent, caustic, piercing, penetrating, razor, razor-edged, mordant, scathing, acrid, acid, tart, acidulous, acerbic, astringent, sarcastic. **2** *trenchant divisions between the political parties* clear, clear-cut, distinct, defined, well-defined, sharp, crisp, unequivocal, unambiguous.

trend noun **1** *an upward trend in prices* tendency, drift, course, direction, bearing, current, inclination, bias, leaning, bent, swing. **2** *they like to follow the trend* fashion, vogue, style, mode, look, craze, fad.

trespasser noun **1** *trespassers will be prosecuted* intruder, interloper, encroacher, infringer, invader, obtruder. **2** *trespassers asking for forgiveness* wrongdoer, evildoer, criminal, offender, transgressor, sinner, malefactor.

trial noun **1** *the murder trial lasted several weeks* court case, case, hearing, inquiry, tribunal, litigation. **2** *give the applicant/car a trial* probation, test, audition, testing, tryout, check, assay; *inf.* dry run. **4** *climb the mountain at the third trial* try, attempt, endeavor, effort, venture, go; *inf.* shot, stab, crack. **5** *she was never a trial to her mother* nuisance, pest, bother, worry, vexation, annoyance, irritant, irritation, bane, curse, burden, cross to bear, thorn in one's flesh; *inf.* pain in the neck. **6** *the trials of life* trouble, worry. *See* TRIBULATION.

tribe noun **1** *the tribes of Israel* family, dynasty, clan, sept. **2** *a tribe of doctors at the conference* group, crowd, company, party, band, number, collection; *inf.* bunch.

tribulation noun trouble, worry, anxiety, vexation, load, burden, cross to bear, blow, affliction, trial, adversity, hardship, ordeal, pain; suffering, distress, misery, wretchedness, unhappiness, sadness, woe, grief.

tribute noun **1** *give tributes to the heroes* gift, present, accolade, commendation, testimonial, paean, eulogy, panegyric, encomium; gratitude, applause, praise, homage, honor, exaltation, laudation, extolment, glorification; congratulations, compliments, bouquets. **2** *the success is a tribute to their hard work* acknowledgment, recognition, testimonial, indication, manifestation; evidence, proof. **3** *foreign governments paying tributes to the emperor* charge, tax, duty, levy, tariff, ransom.

trick noun **1** *he got the job by a trick* stratagem, ploy, artifice, ruse, dodge, wile, device, maneuver, trick of the trade, deceit, deception, subterfuge, swindle, fraud; *inf.* con. **2** *he has the trick of making guests feel welcome* knack, art, gift, talent, technique, ability, skill, expertise, know-how. **3** *play tricks on the old man* hoax, practical joke, leg-pull, prank, jape, antic; *inf.* gag, put-on. **4** *he has an annoying trick of repeating himself* idiosyncrasy, habit, mannerism, quirk, peculiarity, foible, eccentricity, characteristic, trait, practice.

trick verb deceive, delude, mislead, take in, cheat, hoodwink, fool, outwit, dupe, hoax, gull, cozen, defraud, swindle; *inf.* con, pull a fast one on, put one over on.

trickery noun guile, artifice, wiliness, deceit, deception, cheating, subterfuge, craft, craftiness, chicanery, pretense, dishonesty, fraud, swindling, imposture, double-dealing, duplicity; *inf.* conning, monkey/funny business, hanky-panky.

trickle verb drip, dribble, leak, ooze, seep, exude, percolate.

tricky adjective **1** *a tricky situation* difficult, problematic, awkward, delicate, sensitive, ticklish, thorny, knotty, touchy, risky, uncertain, precarious; *inf.* sticky. **2** *a tricky character* cunning, crafty, wily, artful, devious, scheming, foxy, sly, slippery, deceitful, deceptive.

trifle noun **1** *her mind is occupied with trifles* trivia, inessentials; triviality, bagatelle. **2** *buy a few trifles for gifts* bauble, knickknack. *See* TRINKET. **3** *it cost a mere trifle* next to nothing, hardly anything, pittance, piddling sum. **4** *a trifle confused* bit, touch.

trifle verb **trifle with 1** *he is just trifling with the young woman* amuse oneself, dally with. *See* TOY WITH (TOY *verb*). **2** *he is not a man to be trifled with* treat lightly, deal with casually, treat in a cavalier fashion, dismiss.

trifling adjective **1** *discuss trifling matters* petty, trivial, unimportant, insignificant, inconsequential, shallow, superficial, frivolous, silly, idle, foolish, empty. **2** *cost a trifling amount* small, tiny, minuscule, infinitesimal, negligible, paltry, piddling.

trim adjective **1** *looking trim in her uniform* neat, tidy, neat and tidy, smart, spruce, well-groomed, well-dressed, well-turned-out, dapper, natty. **2** *trim gardens* orderly, well-maintained, shipshape, well-looked-after, well-cared-for, spick-and-span. **3** *have a trim figure* slim, slender, lean, svelte, streamlined, willowy, lissome, sleek, in good shape, fit, physically fit.

trim verb **1** *trim one's hair/beard* cut, clip, snip, shear, prune, pare, even up, neaten, tidy up. **2** *trim the fat from the meat* | *trim the branches from the tree* chop, hack, remove, take off. **3** *trim the annual budget* cut down, decrease, reduce, diminish, cut back on, curtail, dock, retrench. **4** *trim the Christmas tree* decorate, adorn, ornament, embellish, festoon. **5** *trim the dress with lace* edge, pipe, border, fringe.

trim noun **1** *admire the trim on the dress* trimming, decoration, adornment, ornamentation, embellishment, edging, piping, border, fringe, frill, edging. **2** *give the boy/hedge a trim* haircut, cut, clip, snip, shearing, pruning, paring. **3** *the old man is still in trim* good health, good

condition, good shape/form, fine fettle, shape.

trinket noun bauble, ornament, knick-knack, trifle, gimcrack, gewgaw, piece of bric-à-brac, bibelot, doodad, whatnot.

trip noun **1** *go on a trip to China* excursion, tour, expedition, voyage, jaunt, outing, run. **2** *the trip on the sidewalk* stumble, misstep, false step, slip, slide, fall, tumble, spill.

trip verb **1** *she tripped on the broken pavement* stumble, lose one's footing/balance, stagger, totter, slip, slide, misstep, fall, tumble. **2** *she tripped across the dance floor* skip, dance, hop, prance, bound, spring, gambol, caper, frisk, cavort, waltz. **trip up 1** *she tripped up when she tried to alter the accounts* make a mistake, blunder, go wrong, err, lapse, bungle, botch, slip up. **2** *the defending lawyer tripped the witness up* trap, outwit, outsmart, confuse, disconcert, unsettle, discountenance; *inf.* throw.

trite adjective hackneyed, banal, commonplace, ordinary, common, platitudinous, clichéd, stock, stereotyped, overused, overdone, stale, worn-out, threadbare, unimaginative, unoriginal, uninspired, dull, pedestrian, run-of-the-mill, routine, humdrum.

triumph noun **1** *his triumph over his opponent* conquest, victory, win, ascendancy, mastery, success. **2** *it was a triumph of American engineering* coup, tour de force, feat, masterstroke, achievement, attainment, accomplishment, supreme example, sensation, hit. **3** *expressions of triumph on their faces* exultation, jubilation, jubilance, elation, rejoicing, joy.

triumph verb **1** *the better team triumphed* win, succeed, be the victor, be victorious, gain a victory, carry the day, take the honors/prize/crown. **2** *the defeated team watching the winners triumph* exult, rejoice, jubilate, celebrate, revel, glory, gloat, swagger, brag, boast. **triumph over** beat, defeat, conquer, vanquish, best, worst, overcome, overpower, get the better of, prevail against.

triumphant adjective **1** *the triumphant team took a bow* winning, victorious, successful, prizewinning. **2** *giving triumphant shouts* exultant, jubilant, elated, rejoicing, joyful, joyous, proud, gloating, boastful.

trivial adjective unimportant, insignificant, inconsequential, flimsy, insubstantial, petty, minor, of no account/matter, negligible, paltry, trifling, foolish, frivolous, worthless, piddling.

troop noun band, group, company, assemblage, gathering, body, crowd, throng, multitude, horde, host, mob, squad, pack, drove, flock, swarm, stream, gang, crew.

troop verb flock, stream, swarm, surge, crowd, throng, mill.

troops plural noun armed forces, army, military, services, soldiers, soldiery, fighting men/women.

trophy noun cup, prize, award, laurels; spoil, booty; souvenir, memento, keepsake, relic.

tropical adjective hot, torrid, sweltering, boiling, sultry, steamy, humid, sticky.

trouble noun **1** *his car is causing him trouble* worry, bother, anxiety, disquiet, unease, irritation, vexation, inconvenience, annoyance, agitation, harassment, difficulty, distress; problems. **2** *there has been a lot of trouble in her life* difficulty, misfortune, adversity, hardship, bad luck, ill luck, burden, distress, pain, suffering, affliction, torment, woe, grief, unhappiness, sadness, heartache. **3** *please do not go to any trouble* bother, inconvenience, disturbance, fuss, effort, exertion, work, labor, attention, care, thoughtfulness; *inf.* hassle. **4** *the trouble with him is he's too nice* problem, difficulty, failing, weakness, shortcoming, fault, imperfection, defect, blemish. **5** *he has stomach trouble* disorder, disease, illness, dysfunction. **6** *the bartender does not want any trouble* disturbance, disorder, unrest, fighting, strife, conflict, tumult, commotion, turbulence, lawbreaking. **in trouble** in difficulty, having problems, in dire straits, in a predicament, in a tight corner, in hot water, in a jam/pickle, in a mess/spot.

trouble verb **1** *he is troubled by neighbors/finances* worry, annoy, irritate, vex, irk, fret, pester, torment, plague, upset, perturb, agitate, discompose, harass, distress; *inf.* hassle. **2** *he is troubled by back pain* afflict, oppress, weigh down, burden, incapacitate. **3** *I am sorry to trouble you, but may I use your phone?* bother, disturb, inconvenience, put out, impose upon, discompose, incommode.

troublesome adjective worrying, worrisome, bothersome, tiresome, disturbing, annoying, irritating, irksome, upsetting, perturbing, harassing, distressing, difficult, problematic, demanding, taxing.

trounce verb **1** *they trounced the other team* rout, drub, thrash, crush, overwhelm; *inf.* make mincemeat (out) of, walk all over, wipe the floor with, hammer, clobber, slaughter, give a pasting to. **2** *trounced for disobeying the emperor* thrash, beat, whip, flog, lash, birch, cane, spank, chastise; *inf.* belt, wallop, lambaste, tan the hide of.

truce noun cease-fire, armistice, suspension/cessation of hostilities, peace, respite, moratorium.

truculent adjective belligerent, pugnacious, bellicose, combative, contentious, hostile, obstreperous, violent, fierce, defiant, sullen, surly, cross, bad-tempered, ill-natured.

trudge verb plod, lumber, shuffle, drag one's feet, clump, slog, trek, tramp, hike.

true adjective **1** *what you say is true | a true account* truthful, accurate, correct, right, valid, factual, exact, precise, faithful, genuine, reliable, veracious, honest. **2** *a true witch doctor* real, genuine, authentic, actual, bona fide, valid, legitimate; *inf.* honest-to-goodness. **3** *a true friend* loyal, faithful, trustworthy, trusty, dependable, staunch, firm, fast, steady, constant, unswerving, unwavering, devoted, sincere, dedicated.

truly adverb **1** *she is truly his daughter* in truth, really, in reality, actually, in fact, genuinely, certainly, surely, definitely, decidedly, positively, absolutely. **2** *tell me truly what you think* truthfully, honestly, frankly, candidly, openly. **3** *truly, I did not know* indeed, veritably. **4** *they are truly grateful* sincerely, very, extremely, exceptionally. **5** *the novel does not truly depict the era* exactly, precisely, faithfully, closely, accurately, correctly, unerringly.

truncate verb shorten, reduce, diminish, decrease, cut short, prune, trim, lop, curtail, abbreviate.

trunk noun chest, case, portmanteau, crate, storage box, box, coffer.

truss verb tie up, wrap up, bind up, bundle up.

truss noun support, brace, prop, strut, buttress.

trust noun **1** *have trust in the surgeon* faith, confidence, belief, conviction, credence, assurance, certainty, reliance, hope, expectation. **2** *a position of trust* responsibility, duty, obligation. **3** *the money is kept in trust* trusteeship, guardianship, care, custody.

trust verb **1** *you can trust him to behave well* have faith/confidence in, rely on, depend on, bank on, count on, be sure of, swear by. **2** *I trust you will come* hope, assume, presume, expect, believe, suppose. **3** *he trusted his son to her* entrust, put in the hands of, turn over, assign, consign, commit, delegate.

trustful adjective trusting, unsuspicious, unquestioning, credulous, ingenuous, naive.

trustworthy adjective reliable, dependable, stable, staunch, loyal, faithful, trusty, responsible, honest, honorable, upright, ethical, righteous, principled.

truth noun **1** *no truth in what she says* truthfulness, accuracy, correctness, rightness, validity, fact, genuineness, veracity, verity, honesty. **2** *truth is stranger than fiction* reality, actuality, factuality. **3** *he is a man of truth* integrity, uprightness, righteousness, honor, honorableness, sincerity, candor. **4** *cite an old truth* truism, axiom, maxim, proverb, adage, aphorism.

truthful adjective **1** *a truthful child* honest, trustworthy, veracious, candid, frank, open, forthright, straight. **2** *a truthful account* true, accurate, correct, right, valid, factual.

try verb **1** *try to do well* attempt, aim, endeavor, make an effort, exert oneself, undertake, strive, seek, struggle, do one's best; *inf.* have a go/shot/crack/stab. **2** *try a new brand* try out, test, put to the test, experiment with, investigate, examine, appraise, evaluate, assess, experience, sample, check out. **3** *the children try her patience* tax, strain, sap, drain, exhaust. **4** *she has been sorely tried by the children* irk, vex, annoy, irritate, harass, afflict, nag, pester, plague, torment. **5** *try the case* hear, adjudge, adjudicate. **try out** test, appraise. *See* TRY 2.

trying adjective **1** *the visitors were very trying* troublesome, bothersome, tiresome, irksome, vexatious, annoying, irritating, exasperating. **2** *have a trying day* taxing, demanding, stressful, difficult, arduous, hard, tough, tiring, fatiguing, exhausting, upsetting.

tuck verb **1** *tuck the shirt into the skirt* gather, push, ease, insert, stuff. **2** *tuck the material* gather, fold, ruck, ruffle, pleat. **tuck in** cover up, wrap up, put to bed, make snug/comfortable.

tuck noun gather, fold, ruck, ruffle, pleat.

tug verb **1** *tug the rope hard* pull, jerk, yank, wrench, wrest. **2** *the dog was tugging him along the road* draw, drag, haul, tow.

tumble verb **1** *the toddler tumbled suddenly* fall over, fall down, fall headlong, topple, fall head over heels, fall end over end, lose one's footing/balance, stumble, stagger, trip up; somersault, flip. **2** *share prices have tumbled* plummet, plunge, slump, dive, drop, slide, fall, decrease, decline. **3** *ships tumbling about on the waves* roll, toss, pitch, heave, thrash. **4** *tumble out of bed* blunder, stumble. **5** *the wind had tumbled her hair* dishevel, ruffle, disarrange, disorder, mess up; *inf.* muss up.

tumbledown adjective dilapidated, ramshackle, crumbling, disintegrating, decrepit, ruined, in ruins, rickety, shaky, tottering, teetering.

tumult noun **1** *we cannot hear you above the tumult* din, uproar, commotion, racket, hubbub, hullabaloo, clamor, shouting, yelling, pandemonium, babel, bedlam. **2** *the meeting ended in tumult* disorder, disarray, disturbance, chaos, upheaval. **3** *police sent to deal with a tumult* riot, protest, insurrection, rebellion, brawl, fight, fracas. **4** *emotions in tumult* turmoil, confusion, ferment.

tumultuous adjective **1** *tumultuous applause* loud, noisy, clamorous, ear-shattering, deafening, ear-piercing, blaring, uproarious, unrestrained. **2** *a tumultuous crowd* rowdy, unruly, boisterous, disorderly, obstreperous, wild, violent, lawless, vociferous. **3** *tumultuous emotions* raging, unrestrained, uncontrolled, frenzied, in turmoil, turbulent.

tune noun **1** *play a folk tune* melody, air, song, theme, strain, motif. **2** *his ideas are not in tune with modern thinking* agreement, accord, accordance, harmony, correspondence, congruence, conformity, sympathy.

tune verb adjust, regulate, pitch, attune.

turbulent adjective **1** *turbulent seas* tempestuous, stormy, raging, foaming, rough, choppy. **2** *turbulent crowds* rowdy, agitated. *See* TUMULTUOUS 2. **3** *turbulent emotions/moods* disturbed, agitated, unsettled, unstable, troubled, distraught, in turmoil.

turgid adjective **1** *turgid ankles* swollen, enlarged, puffy, puffed up, bloated, distended, tumescent. **2** *turgid prose* bombastic, high-flown, high-sounding, grandiloquent, magniloquent, extravagant, pretentious, pompous, flowery, orotund, fustian.

turmoil noun agitation, ferment, confusion, disorder, disarray, upheaval, chaos, pandemonium, bedlam, tumult; disturbance, bustle, flurry, commotion.

turn verb **1** *the wheel is turning* go around/round, rotate, revolve, circle, roll, spin, wheel, whirl, twirl, gyrate, swivel, pivot. **2** *he turned in the driveway* turn around/round, change direction/course, go back, return, reverse direction, make a U-turn. **3** *he turned toward her* veer, wheel around/round, swing around/round. **4** *turn the meat* turn over, reverse, invert, flip over, turn upside down, turn topsy-turvy. **5** *turn the hose on them* aim, direct, point, train, level, focus. **6** *his expression turned from amusement to horror* change, alter, transform, metamorphose, mutate. **7** *he turned nasty* become, come to be, get, go. **8** *the milk/butter turned* go/turn sour, sour, curdle, spoil, become rancid, go bad. **9** *the sight turned my stomach* nauseate, sicken, upset, unsettle. **10** *my head is turning* spin, feel dizzy/giddy. **11** *turn the corner* go/come around, round, negotiate, take. **12** *turn somersaults* perform, execute, do, carry out. **13** *turn a profit* make, bring in, gain, acquire, obtain, get, procure, secure. **14** *turn a pot* shape, mold, fashion, form, cast, construct. **15** *he used to be a loyal follower, but he turned* change sides, go over, defect, desert, renege, turn renegade, break faith, apostatize, tergiversate. **turn away** send away, reject, rebuff, repel, cold-shoulder; *inf.* give the brush-off to. **turn back** *turn back if the weather is bad* go back, retrace one's steps, return, retreat. **turn down 1** *he turned down the proposal* reject, decline, give the thumbs down to, rebuff, repudiate, spurn, veto. **2** *turn down the gas* lessen, lower, reduce, decrease, diminish. **turn in 1** *turn in your homework* hand in, submit, tender, hand over, deliver. **2** *it is time to turn in* retire, call it a day; *inf.* hit the hay/sack. **3** *turn him in to the police* hand over, turn over, deliver, inform on, betray; *inf.* squeal on, blow the whistle on, rat on, finger, put the finger on. **turn off 1** *turn off the heater* switch off, shut off, flick off, unplug. **2** *the driver suddenly turned off the main road* branch off, leave, quit, depart from, deviate from. **3** *she was turned off by his table manners* put off, turn against; disenchant, alienate, repel, disgust, nauseate, sicken. **turn on 1** *turn on the electricity* put on, switch on, flick on, plug in, operate. **2** *the dog turned on his master* attack, launch an attack on, fall on, set upon, become hostile to; *inf.* lay into, tear into. **3** *the result turns on the number voting* depend on, hang on, hinge on, be contingent on. **4** *she is turned on by muscular men* arouse, excite, titillate, stimulate, thrill, attract, please. **turn out 1** *turn her out of her house* put out, throw out, kick out, eject, evict, oust; *inf.* chuck out, bounce. **2** *turn out the delinquent workers* dismiss, discharge, ax; *inf.* fire, sack. **3** *turn out the light* turn off, put off, switch off, shut off, flick off, unplug. **4** *turn out thousands of toys per year* bring out, put out, produce, make, manufacture, fabricate, yield, process. **5** *a big crowd turned out to hear him* go, come, be present, attend, put in an appearance, appear, turn up, arrive, assemble, gather; *inf.* show up, show. **6** *it turned out that she was right* happen, occur, come about, end up, transpire. **7** *she turned out a beautiful girl* develop into, end up, emerge as. **turn over 1** *the boat turned over* overturn, topple, upturn, capsize, keel over, turn turtle. **2** *turn over the pages* flick over, flip over, leaf over. **3** *turn over the pros and cons* consider, think about, ponder, reflect on, mull over, ruminate about. **4** *turn over the estate to his brother* hand over, transfer, consign, assign, commit. **turn to 1** *turn to drink* have recourse to, resort to, take to. **2** *turn to him for help* look to, apply to, approach, appeal to, have recourse to. **turn up 1** *turn up*

the volume increase, raise, amplify, make louder, intensify. **2** *turn up some interesting information* uncover, unearth, discover, bring to light, find, hit upon, dig up, ferret out, root out, expose. **3** *he has mislaid the book, but it will turn up* be found, be located, come to light. **4** *they did not turn up at the party* appear; *inf.* show up. *See* TURN OUT 5 (TURN *verb*). **5** *he hopes a job will turn up* present itself, crop up, pop up, arise, come on the scene.

turn *noun* **1** *give the wheel a few turns* rotation, revolution, circle, spin, whirl, twirl, gyration, swivel. **2** *take a turn to the left* deviation, divergence, veer. **3** *a road full of turns* turning, bend, curve, corner, twist, winding. **4** *dislike the turn of events* trend, tendency, bias, leaning, direction, drift. **5** *a turn for the better/worse* change, alteration, variation, difference, deviation, divergence, shift. **6** *he is of an academic turn of mind* bent, tendency, inclination, bias, propensity, affinity, leaning. **7** *it is your turn to play* time, opportunity, chance, stint, spell, move, try. **8** *take a turn in the park* walk, stroll, airing, constitutional, promenade, drive, ride, outing, jaunt; *inf.* spin. **9** *do him a good/bad turn* act, action, deed, service, gesture, favor. **10** *you gave me quite a turn* shock, start, surprise, fright, scare.

turning point *noun* crossroads, crisis, crux, moment of truth/decision.

turnout *noun* number, gathering, crowd, assembly, assemblage, audience, attendance, gate.

tussle *noun* struggle, wrestle, conflict, fight, battle, skirmish, scuffle, brawl; *inf.* set-to, scrap.

tutor *noun* teacher, instructor, coach, lecturer, educator.

tutor *verb* teach, instruct, coach, educate, school, train, drill, direct, guide.

twig *noun* branch, stick, offshoot, shoot, spray, stem.

twilight *noun* **1** *walk home at twilight* dusk, gloaming. **2** *scarcely able to see her in the twilight* half-light, semidarkness, dimness. **3** *in the twilight of his career* decline, ebb, waning.

twin *noun* **1** *where is the twin of that glove?* mate, match, fellow, counterpart, complement. **2** *she is an absolute twin for the queen* double, look-alike, likeness, image, duplicate, clone; *inf.* spitting image, ringer, dead ringer.

twine *noun* **1** *a ball of twine* cord, string, yarn, thread. **2** *vines in a twine* coil, spiral, whorl, convolution, twist, tangle.

twinge *noun* **1** *a twinge of rheumatism* spasm, pain, pang, ache, throb, tweak, tingle, cramp, stitch. **2** *a twinge of conscience* pang, uneasiness, discomfort, qualm, scruple, misgiving.

twinkle verb glitter, glint, sparkle, flicker, shimmer, glimmer, gleam, dazzle, flash, wink, blink, shine, scintillate, coruscate.

twinkle noun twinkling, glitter, glint, sparkle, flicker, shimmer, glimmer, gleam, dazzle, flash, wink, blink, shining, scintillation, coruscation.

twirl verb **1** *she twirled around/round to the music* spin, whirl, turn, pirouette, wheel, gyrate, revolve, rotate, pivot, twist. **2** *twirl a curl of hair around/round her finger* twist, coil, wind, curl.

twist verb **1** *twist the metal rod | twist it off the wall* bend, warp, misshape, deform, contort, distort; wrench, wrest. **2** *his face twisted in agony* contort, screw up. **3** *he twisted his ankle* wrench, turn, sprain. **4** *the plant had twisted itself around the tree* twine, entwine, coil, wind, weave, wrap. **5** *twist a garland* twine, weave, plait, braid. **6** *twist a curl of hair around/round her finger* twirl, coil, wind, curl. **7** *the path twisted around/round the mountain* wind, curve, bend, twine, zigzag, meander, snake, worm. **8** *the child twisted out of his grasp* wriggle, writhe, squirm, wiggle. **9** *twist their words* distort, pervert, warp, garble, misrepresent, falsify, misquote, misreport, change, alter. **10** *she twisted her head around* swivel, turn, rotate, spin, pivot.

twist noun **1** *with a twist of his arm* wrench, wrest, turn, contortion, pull, jerk, yank. **2** *try to repair the twist in the wire* bend, warp, kink, contortion, distortion. **3** *a painful twist of the ankle* wrench, turn, sprain. **4** *a twist of hair* coil, twirl, curl, braid. **5** *the twists in the mountain path* bend, turn, curve, winding, arc, zigzag, meander. **6** *a slight twist to his character* aberration, peculiarity, quirk, oddity, eccentricity, idiosyncrasy, foible.

twitch verb jerk, jump, quiver, shiver, quaver, blink, flutter.

twitch noun spasm, jerk, jump, quiver, tremor, shiver, quaver, blink, flutter, jump, tic.

twitter verb chirrup, cheep, tweet, trill, warble, whistle, sing.

two-faced adjective hypocritical, insincere, deceitful, deceiving, dissembling, duplicitous, false, untrustworthy, treacherous, perfidious, double-dealing, Janus-faced.

tycoon noun magnate, baron, captain of industry, industrialist, financier, merchant prince, mogul; *inf.* fat cat.

type noun **1** *a rare type of plant* kind, sort, variety, form, class, classification, category, group, order, set, genre, strain, species, genus, ilk. **2** *they regard her as the very type of womanhood* example, exemplar, model, pattern, essence, personification, epitome, quintessence, archetype, prototype. **3** *set in a different kind of type* print, font, face, character.

typical adjective **1** *a typical New England winter* representative, classic, standard, stock, orthodox, conventional, true-to-type, quintessential, archetypal. **2** *what would be your typical day?* normal, average, ordinary, regular, general, customary, habitual, routine. **3** *it is typical of him to be rude* characteristic, in character, in keeping, to be expected, usual.

typify verb **1** *he typifies the self-made man* exemplify, characterize, personify, epitomize, symbolize, embody, sum up, incarnate. **2** *they have tried to typify the various sectors of society* represent, indicate, illustrate, denote.

tyranny noun despotism, absolutism, authoritarianism, arbitrariness, high-handedness, imperiousness, oppressiveness, oppression, coercion, bullying, severity, cruelty, brutality, unjustness, unreasonableness; autocracy, dictatorship.

tyrant noun despot, autocrat, dictator, absolute ruler, authoritarian, oppressor, martinet, slave driver, bully.

Uu

ubiquitous adjective everywhere, omnipresent, ever-present, in all places, all over, all over the place, pervasive, universal.

ugly adjective **1** *ugly people/buildings* ill-favored, hideous, plain, unattractive, unlovely, homely, unprepossessing, unsightly, displeasing; *inf.* not much to look at. **2** *an ugly sight met their eyes* hideous, horrible, horrid, frightful, terrible, disagreeable, unpleasant, foul, nasty, shocking, distasteful, disgusting, revolting, repellent, repugnant, loathsome, hateful, nauseating, sickening. **3** *he is an ugly character* objectionable, offensive, obnoxious, foul, vile, base, dishonorable, dishonest, rotten. **4** *an ugly situation* threatening, menacing, ominous, sinister, dangerous, nasty, unpleasant, disagreeable. **5** *the crowd grew ugly* nasty, angry, bad-tempered, ill-natured, hostile, surly, sullen, mean, sour, spiteful, malevolent, evil.

ulterior adjective hidden, concealed, unrevealed, undisclosed, undivulged, secret, covert.

ultimate adjective **1** *take ultimate responsibility* last, final, eventual, concluding, conclusive, terminal, end, furthest. **2** *ultimate truths* basic, fundamental, primary, elemental, radical. **3** *the ultimate gift* supreme, superlative, paramount, greatest, highest, unsurpassed, unrivaled.

umbrella noun *under the corporate umbrella* agency, aegis, cover, protection, support, patronage, backing.

umpire noun adjudicator, arbitrator, arbiter, judge, moderator, referee; *inf.* ref.

umpire verb adjudicate, arbitrate, judge, moderate, referee; *inf.* ref.

unabridged adjective uncut, unshortened, unreduced, uncondensed, unexpurgated, full-length, complete, entire, whole, intact.

unacceptable adjective unsatisfactory, inadmissible, unsuitable, insupportable, intolerable, objectionable.

unaccompanied adjective alone, on one's own, by oneself, unescorted, solo, lone, solitary, single.

unaccountable adjective **1** *an unaccountable increase in births* inexplicable, unexplainable, insoluble, unsolvable, incomprehensible, unfathomable, puzzling, baffling, mysterious, inscrutable, peculiar, unusual, curious, strange. **2** *she is unaccountable for the error* not responsible, not answerable, not liable, free, clear, exempt, immune.

unaccustomed adjective unusual, unfamiliar, uncommon, unwonted, new, exceptional, out of the ordinary, extraordinary, special, remarkable, singular. **unaccustomed to** unused to, new to, unpracticed at/in, unfamiliar with, inexperienced at/in, unversed in.

unaffected adjective **1** *unaffected children* artless, guileless, ingenuous, naive, unsophisticated, unassuming, unpretentious, down-to-earth, without airs, natural, plain, simple. **2** *unaffected sincerity* unfeigned, unpretended, genuine, real, sincere, honest, true, candid. **unaffected by** unchanged by, unaltered by, uninfluenced by, untouched by, unmoved by, impervious to, unresponsive to, insensible to, invulnerable to.

unanimity noun agreement, accord, con-

cord, unity, consensus, like-mindedness, solidity, concertedness, uniformity, consistency, congruence.

unanimous adjective in complete agreement/accord, of one mind, like-minded, with one voice, united, concordant, concerted, uniform, consistent, congruent.

unapproachable adjective **1** *unapproachable places* inaccessible, remote, out-of-the-way, out of reach, beyond reach, unreachable, off the beaten path/track. **2** *the new teacher is unapproachable* aloof, standoffish, distant, remote, detached, reserved, uncommunicative, unsociable, cool.

unassuming adjective modest, self-effacing, humble, meek, retiring, demure, restrained, reticent, diffident, shy, bashful, unassertive, unobtrusive, unostentatious, unpretentious, unaffected, natural, genuine, simple.

unattached adjective **1** *she is still unattached* unmarried, unwed, uncommitted, free, available, footloose and fancy free, partnerless, single, on one's own, by oneself, unescorted. **2** *a merger was discussed, but the firm is still unattached* independent, unaffiliated, unassociated, autonomous, nonaligned, self-governing, self-ruling.

unauthorized adjective uncertified, unaccredited, unlicensed, unofficial, unsanctioned, unwarranted, unapproved, disallowed, prohibited, forbidden, illegal.

unavoidable adjective inescapable, inevitable, bound to happen, inexorable, ineluctable, certain, fated, predestined, necessary, compulsory, required, obligatory, mandatory.

unaware adjective unknowing, unconscious, ignorant, heedless, unmindful, oblivious, uninformed (about), unenlightened (about), undiscerning, incognizant; *inf.* in the dark.

unawares adverb **1** *come upon him unawares* unexpectedly, by surprise, without warning, suddenly, abruptly, unprepared, off guard; *inf.* with one's pants down. **2** *I must have dropped my keys unawares* unknowingly, unwittingly, unintentionally, unconsciously, inadvertently.

unbalanced adjective **1** *unbalanced since the death of her husband* unstable, of unsound mind, mentally ill, deranged, demented, crazed, distracted, insane, mad, crazy, lunatic; *inf.* not all there, off one's head. **2** *an unbalanced report of the events* one-sided, biased, prejudiced, partisan, partial, inequitable.

unbearable adjective intolerable, insufferable, unsupportable, unendurable, unacceptable, more than flesh and blood can stand; *inf.* too much, enough to try the patience of a saint.

unbeatable adjective invincible, indomitable, unconquerable, unstoppable, unsurpassable.

unbecoming adjective 1 *an unbecoming hat* unflattering, unattractive, unsightly. 2 *unbecoming behavior* unfitting, inappropriate, unsuitable, inapt, improper, indecorous, unseemly.

unbelievable adjective beyond belief, incredible, unconvincing, far-fetched, implausible, improbable, inconceivable, unthinkable, unimaginable, astonishing, astounding, preposterous.

unbending adjective 1 *an unbending material/manner* rigid, stiff, inflexible, unpliable, inelastic, unmalleable, hard-line, uncompromising, tough, harsh, strict, stern, severe, firm, resolute, determined, unrelenting. 2 *an unbending person* formal, stiff, aloof, reserved; *inf.* uptight.

unbiased adjective impartial, unprejudiced, nonpartisan, neutral, objective, disinterested, dispassionate, detached, evenhanded, open-minded, equitable, fair, fair-minded, just.

unbounded adjective boundless, unlimited, limitless, infinite, unrestrained, unconstrained, uncontrolled, unchecked, unbridled, vast, immense, immeasurable.

unbridled adjective unrestrained, unconstrained, uncontrolled, unchecked, uncurbed, ungoverned, rampant, excessive, intemperate.

unbroken adjective 1 *unbroken china/sets* intact, whole, undamaged, unimpaired, complete, entire. 2 *an unbroken series* uninterrupted, continuous, unremitting, ceaseless, unceasing, endless, incessant, constant, nonstop. 3 *unbroken sleep* undisturbed, untroubled, sound.

unburden verb 1 *unburden the horse* unload, disburden, unpack, disencumber. 2 *unburden one's sins/guilt* confess, confide, acknowledge, disclose, reveal, divulge, expose, lay bare, make a clean breast of; *inf.* come clean.

uncalled-for adjective 1 *uncalled-for advice* unsought, unasked, unsolicited, unrequested, unprompted, unwelcome, gratuitous. 2 *uncalled-for rudeness* unnecessary, needless, undeserved, unmerited, unjustified, unreasonable, inappropriate.

uncanny adjective 1 *uncanny happenings in the old house* strange, mysterious, odd, queer, weird, eerie, unnatural, preternatural, supernatural, unearthly, ghostly; *inf.* creepy, spooky. 2 *bear an uncanny resemblance to the president* remarkable, striking, extraordinary, exceptional, astounding, astonishing, incredible.

uncertain adjective 1 *the outcome is uncertain* unknown, undetermined, unsettled, pending, in the balance, up in the air. 2 *feel uncertain about what to do* unsure, doubtful, dubious, undecided, unresolved, indecisive, irresolute, hesitant, wavering, vacillating, equivocating, vague, hazy, unclear, ambivalent, of two minds. 3 *the future is uncertain* unpredictable, unforeseeable, incalculable, speculative, unreliable, untrustworthy, undependable, risky, chancy. 4 *uncertain weather* changeable, variable, irregular, fitful, unpredictable, unreliable.

uncharitable adjective uncompassionate, unsympathetic, ungenerous, unfeeling, unkind, hard-hearted, censorious, unforgiving, merciless.

uncharted adjective unmapped, unsurveyed, unexplored, unresearched, unplumbed, unfamiliar, unknown, strange.

uncivil adjective discourteous, rude, impolite, unmannerly, bad-mannered, ill-bred, ungracious, disrespectful.

uncivilized adjective 1 *uncivilized tribes* barbarian, barbarous, barbaric, primitive, savage, wild. 2 *some of their friends are so uncivilized* uncouth, coarse, rough, boorish, vulgar, philistine, uneducated, uncultured, uncultivated, unsophisticated, unrefined, unpolished.

uncomfortable adjective uneasy, ill-at-ease, nervous, tense, edgy, self-conscious, awkward, embarrassed, discomfited, disturbed, troubled, worried, anxious, apprehensive, distressing, disturbing.

uncommon adjective 1 *an uncommon name* unusual, rare, uncustomary, unfamiliar, strange, odd, curious, out of the ordinary, novel, singular, peculiar, queer, bizarre, weird. 2 *those birds are uncommon here* rare, scarce, infrequent, few and far between, occasional. 3 *an uncommon resemblance* remarkable, extraordinary, exceptional, singular, outstanding, notable, noteworthy, distinctive, striking.

uncommunicative adjective taciturn, reserved, shy, retiring, diffident, reticent, quiet, unforthcoming, unconversational, untalkative, silent, tight-lipped, secretive, unresponsive, close, distant, remote, aloof, withdrawn, standoffish, unsociable, antisocial.

uncompromising adjective unyielding, immovable, dogged, obstinate, obdurate, tenacious, relentless, inexorable, intransigent. *See* UNBENDING 1.

unconcerned adjective unworried, untroubled, unperturbed, unruffled, insouciant, nonchalant, carefree, blithe, relaxed, at ease. **unconcerned with** indifferent about, apathetic about, uninterested in,

461   **unconditional · undermine**

uninvolved with/in, dispassionate about, detached from, aloof from, remote from.

unconditional adjective complete, total, entire, full, outright, absolute, downright, out-and-out, utter, all-out, thoroughgoing, unequivocal, conclusive, definite, positive, indubitable, incontrovertible, categorical, unqualified, unlimited, unreserved, unrestricted.

unconscious adjective **1** *fall unconscious* senseless, insensible, comatose, knocked out, stunned, dazed; *inf.* blacked out, KO'd, out like a light, out cold, out. **2** *unconscious of the noise* unaware, heedless, ignorant, incognizant, oblivious, insensible. **3** *deliver an unconscious insult* unintentional, unintended, accidental, unthinking, unwitting, inadvertent, unpremeditated. **4** *unconscious prejudice* instinctive, automatic, reflex, involuntary, inherent, innate, subliminal, subconscious, latent.

unconventional adjective unorthodox, irregular, unusual, uncommon, uncustomary, rare, out of the ordinary, atypical, singular, individual, individualistic, different, original, idiosyncratic, nonconformist, bohemian, eccentric, odd, strange, bizarre; *inf.* offbeat, way-out.

uncoordinated adjective clumsy, awkward, inept, maladroit, butterfingered, all thumbs, bungling, blundering, bumbling, lumbering, heavy-footed, graceless, ungainly; *inf.* like a bull in a china shop, klutzy.

uncouth adjective rough, coarse, uncivilized, uncultured, uncultivated, unrefined, unpolished, unsophisticated, provincial, crude, gross, loutish, boorish, oafish, churlish, uncivil, rude, impolite, discourteous, unmannerly, bad-mannered, ill-bred, vulgar.

uncover verb expose, lay bare, bare, reveal, discover, detect, unearth, dig up, bring to light, unmask, unveil, make known, divulge, disclose.

unctuous adjective **1** *unctuous behavior* sycophantic, ingratiating, obsequious, fawning, servile, toadying, honey-tongued, gushing, effusive, suave, urbane, glib, smooth. **2** *unctuous substance* oily, oleaginous, greasy, soapy, saponaceous.

undaunted adjective undismayed, unalarmed, unafraid, unflinching, unfaltering, indomitable, resolute, unflagging, intrepid, bold, valiant, brave, courageous.

undecided adjective **1** *the result is as yet undecided* uncertain, unsettled, unresolved, indefinite, unknown, unestablished, unascertained, pending, in the balance, up in the air. **2** *they are undecided as to what to do* unsure, doubtful, dithering. *See* UNCERTAIN 2.

undeniable adjective indisputable, indubitable, unquestionable, beyond doubt/question, inarguable, incontrovertible, incontestable, irrefutable, unassailable, certain, sure, definite, positive, proven, clear, obvious, evident, manifest, patent.

under preposition **1** *under the tree* below, beneath, underneath, at the foot/bottom of. **2** *prices under $5* | *numbers under 20* below, less than, lower than, smaller than. **3** *ranks under major* inferior to, subordinate to, junior to, secondary to, subservient to, reporting to, subject to, controlled by, at the mercy of, under the heel of. **4** *under the water* submerged by, immersed in, sunk in, engulfed by, inundated by, flooded by, drowned by. **5** *it is under his mother's name* listed under, classified under, categorized under, placed under, positioned under, included under, subsumed under. **6** *living under threat* subject to, liable to, bound by.

undercover adjective secret, hidden, concealed, masked, veiled, shrouded, private, confidential, covert, clandestine, underground, surreptitious, furtive, stealthy, sly; *inf.* hush-hush.

undercurrent noun *an undercurrent of discontent* undertone, overtone, hint, suggestion, implication, whisper, murmur, atmosphere, aura, tenor, flavor; vibrations; *inf.* vibes.

undercut verb undersell; weaken, impair, damage. *See* UNDERMINE 1.

underestimate verb miscalculate, misjudge, underrate, undervalue, set little store by, not do justice to, misprize, minimize, hold cheap; *inf.* sell short.

undergo verb go through, experience, sustain, be subjected to, submit to, endure, bear, tolerate, stand, withstand, put up with, weather.

underground adjective **1** *underground shelters* subterranean, subterrestrial, belowground, buried, sunken, hypogeal. **2** *an underground organization* secret, clandestine, surreptitious, covert, undercover, concealed, hidden. **3** *underground literature* unconventional, unorthodox, experimental, avant-garde, alternative, radical, revolutionary, subversive.

underhand, underhanded adjective deceitful, devious, sneaky, furtive, covert, dishonest, dishonorable, unethical, immoral, unscrupulous, fraudulent, dirty, unfair, treacherous, double-dealing, below the belt, two-timing; *inf.* crooked.

underline verb underscore, emphasize, stress, highlight, point up, accentuate, call attention to, give prominence to.

undermine verb **1** *undermine their authority* weaken, impair, damage, injure, sap, threaten, subvert, sabotage; *inf.* throw a monkey wrench in/into the works of, foul up. **2** *undermine the foundations* tunnel under, dig under, burrow under, excavate.

underprivileged adjective disadvantaged, deprived, in need, needy, in want, destitute, in distress, poor, impoverished, impecunious, badly off.

understand verb **1** *understand his meaning* comprehend, apprehend, grasp, see, take in, perceive, discern, make out, glean, recognize, appreciate, get to know, follow, fathom, get to the bottom of, penetrate, interpret; *inf.* get the hang/drift of, catch on, latch on to, figure out. **2** *I understand your feelings/position* appreciate, accept, commiserate with, sympathize with, empathize with. **3** *I understand that he has left* gather, hear, learn, believe, think, conclude.

understanding noun **1** *it depends on your understanding of his meaning* comprehension, apprehension, grasp, perception, discernment, appreciation, interpretation. **2** *his powers of understanding are limited* intelligence, intellect, mind, brainpower; brains; *inf.* gray matter. **3** *it is my understanding that he has gone* belief, perception, view, notion, idea, fancy, conclusion, feeling. **4** *treat the difficult problem with understanding* compassion, sympathy, empathy, insight. **5** *we have an understanding, although not a signed contract* agreement, gentleman's agreement, arrangement, bargain, pact, compact, (verbal) contract.

understanding adjective compassionate, sympathetic, sensitive, considerate, kind, thoughtful, tolerant, patient, forbearing, lenient, merciful, forgiving.

understate verb downplay, play down, make light of, minimize, de-emphasize; *inf.* soft-pedal.

understudy noun substitute, replacement, reserve, stand-in, fill-in, locum, backup, relief.

undertake verb take on, set about, tackle, shoulder, assume, enter upon, begin, start, commence, embark on, venture upon, attempt, try.

undertone noun *undertones of unrest* murmur, whisper, undercurrent, hint, suggestion, intimation, inkling, insinuation.

underwater adjective submarine, subaqueous, undersea, submerged, immersed.

underwear noun underclothes, undergarments; underclothing, lingerie, underthings; *inf.* undies, unmentionables.

underworld noun **1** *the underworld revenged his death* (crime) syndicate, organized crime; criminals, gangsters; Mafia, Cosa Nostra, gangland; *inf.* mob. **2** *Orpheus in the underworld* abode of the dead, nether/infernal regions, hell, Hades.

underwrite verb **1** *underwrite the agreement* agree to, approve, sanction, confirm, ratify, validate; *inf.* OK. **2** *underwrite the new project* fund, finance, back, support, sponsor, subsidize, contribute to, insure.

undesirable adjective unwanted, unwished-for; unpleasant, disagreeable, objectionable, offensive, repugnant, repellent, distasteful, unsavory.

undisciplined adjective unruly, disorderly, disobedient, obstreperous, wild, willful, wayward; disorganized, erratic, lax.

undisguised adjective open, obvious, evident, patent, manifest, transparent, overt, unconcealed, unhidden, unmistakable.

undisputed adjective uncontested, unchallenged, unquestioned, not in question/doubt, accepted, acknowledged, recognized, incontestable, unquestionable, incontrovertible.

undo verb **1** *undo buttons/laces* unfasten, untie, loosen, loose, disentangle, release, free, open. **2** *undo the agreement* cancel, annul, nullify, invalidate, revoke, repeal, rescind, reverse, set aside, wipe out. **3** *undo all his work/hopes* destroy, ruin, wreck, smash, shatter, annihilate, eradicate, obliterate.

undoing noun destruction, ruin, ruination, downfall, defeat, overthrow, collapse.

undoubtedly adverb indubitably, doubtless, doubtlessly, beyond a doubt, unquestionably, beyond question, undeniably, positively, absolutely, certainly, decidedly, definitely.

undress verb strip, disrobe, unclothe.

undue adjective unwarranted, unreasonable, inappropriate, improper, excessive, immoderate, disproportionate, inordinate, fulsome, uncalled-for, unnecessary, nonessential, unrequired.

unduly adverb excessively, overly, disproportionately, immoderately, inordinately, unnecessarily.

undying adjective deathless, immortal, eternal, infinite, perpetual, unending, never-ending, unceasing, ceaseless, incessant, permanent, lasting, abiding, unfading, imperishable, inextinguishable.

unearth verb **1** *dogs unearthing bones* dig up, excavate, exhume, disinter, unbury. **2** *unearth new evidence* uncover, discover, find, come across, hit upon, bring to light, reveal, expose, turn up, root up, dredge up, ferret out.

unearthly adjective **1** *unearthly sounds* otherworldly, not of this world, supernatural, preternatural, ghostly, spectral, phantom, haunted, uncanny, eerie, strange; *inf.* spooky, creepy. **2** *come home at an* *unearthly hour* unreasonable, preposterous, abnormal, extraordinary, absurd, ridiculous; *inf.* ungodly, unholy.

uneasy adjective **1** *feel uneasy about what was happening* ill at ease, troubled, worried, anxious, apprehensive, alarmed, disturbed, agitated, nervous, on edge, edgy, jittery, restive, restless, unsettled, discomposed, discomfited. **2** *an uneasy peace* strained, constrained, tense, awkward, precarious, unstable, insecure. **3** *an uneasy suspicion that all was not well* dismaying, disturbing, perturbing, disquieting, unsettling, upsetting.

unemotional adjective undemonstrative, passionless, cold, frigid, cool, reserved, restrained, self-controlled, unfeeling, unresponsive, unexcitable, unmoved, impassive, apathetic, indifferent, phlegmatic, detached.

unemployed adjective jobless, out of work, out of a job, workless, laid off, idle, on the dole.

unending adjective endless, never-ending, interminable, perpetual, ceaseless, incessant, unceasing, nonstop, uninterrupted, continuous, continual, constant, unremitting, relentless.

unequal adjective **1** *unequal in size/talent* different, differing, dissimilar, unlike, unalike, disparate, varying. **2** *unequal to the task* not up to, inadequate, insufficient. **3** *the sides of the box are unequal* asymmetrical, unbalanced. *See* UNEVEN 3. **4** *unequal contest* unfair, one-sided. *See* UNEVEN 4.

unequaled adjective peerless, unmatched, unrivaled, unparalleled, unsurpassed, incomparable, beyond compare, inimitable, second to none, nonpareil, unique.

unequivocal adjective unambiguous, clear, clear-cut, crystal-clear, unmistakable, plain, well-defined, explicit, unqualified, categorical, outright, downright, direct, straightforward.

unethical adjective immoral, unprincipled, unscrupulous, dishonorable, dishonest, disreputable, dirty, unfair, underhand, underhanded; *inf.* shady.

uneven adjective **1** *uneven surfaces* rough, bumpy, lumpy. **2** *his work is uneven* variable, varying, changeable, irregular, fluctuating, erratic, patchy. **3** *the sides of the box are uneven* unequal, asymmetrical, unsymmetrical, unbalanced, lopsided, irregular, disproportionate, not matching. **4** *an uneven contest* unequal, unfair, unjust, inequitable, one-sided, ill-matched.

unexpected adjective unforeseen, unanticipated, unlooked-for, unpredicted, not bargained for, surprising, out of the blue.

unfair adjective **1** *unfair treatment* unjust, inequitable, partial, partisan, prejudiced, biased, one-sided, unequal, uneven, unbalanced. **2** *the punishment was unfair* undeserved, unmerited, uncalled-for, unreasonable, unjustifiable, disproportionate, excessive, immoderate. **3** *unfair play* foul, unsporting, unsportsmanlike, dirty, below-the-belt, underhanded, unscrupulous, dishonorable; *inf.* crooked.

unfaithful adjective **1** *unfaithful friends* disloyal, false, false-hearted, faithless, perfidious, treacherous, traitorous, untrustworthy, unreliable, undependable. **2** *unfaithful spouses* adulterous, fickle, untrue, inconstant; *inf.* cheating, two-timing.

unfamiliar adjective unknown, new, strange, alien, unaccustomed, uncommon. **unfamiliar with** unacquainted with, unused to, unaccustomed to, unskilled in, uninformed of, uninitiated in.

unfavorable adjective **1** *unfavorable reviews* adverse, critical, hostile, inimical, unfriendly, negative, discouraging, poor, bad. **2** *unfavorable circumstances* disadvantageous, adverse, unfortunate, unhappy, detrimental. **3** *come at an unfavorable moment* inconvenient, inopportune, untimely, untoward.

unfeeling adjective uncaring, unsympathetic, hard-hearted, hard, harsh, heartless, apathetic, cold, callous, cruel, pitiless, inhuman.

unfit adjective *too unfit to compete in the race* out of condition, in poor condition/shape, flabby, unhealthy, debilitated, weak. **unfit for** unsuited for/to, ill-suited for/to, unsuitable for, unqualified for, unequipped for, unprepared for, untrained for, incompetent for, not up to, not equal to, not good enough for; *inf.* not cut out for.

unfold verb **1** *unfold the map* open out, spread out, stretch out, flatten, straighten out, unfurl, unroll, unravel. **2** *unfold a tale of horror* narrate, relate, recount, tell, reveal, make known, disclose, divulge, present. **3** *when our plans unfold* develop, evolve, grow, mature, bear fruit.

unforeseen adjective unpredicted, unanticipated. *See* UNEXPECTED.

unforgettable adjective memorable, impressive, striking, outstanding, extraordinary.

unfortunate adjective **1** *unfortunate circumstance* adverse, disadvantageous, unfavorable, untoward, unpromising, disastrous, calamitous. **2** *the unfortunate girl* unlucky, luckless, ill-starred, hapless, wretched, miserable. **3** *an unfortunate remark* regrettable, deplorable, ill-advised, inappropriate, unsuitable, inapt, tactless.

unfounded adjective groundless, baseless, unsubstantiated, unproven, unsupported, uncorroborated, speculative, conjectural, spurious.

unfriendly adjective **1** *unfriendly neighbors* unamicable, uncongenial, unsociable, inhospitable, unneighborly, unkind, unsympathetic, aloof, cold, cool, distant, disagreeable, unpleasant, hostile, antagonistic, aggressive, quarrelsome. **2** *an unfriendly climate* unfavorable, disadvantageous, unpropitious, inauspicious.

ungainly adjective awkward, clumsy, ungraceful, graceless, inelegant, gawky, gangling, maladroit, inept, bungling, bumbling, lumbering, uncoordinated, hulking, lubberly.

ungodly adjective **1** *ungodly people/acts* godless, irreligious, impious, blasphemous, profane, immoral, sinful, wicked, iniquitous. **2** *come home at an ungodly hour* unreasonable, preposterous. *See* UNEARTHLY 2.

unhappy adjective **1** *feeling unhappy* sad, miserable, wretched, sorrowful, dejected, despondent, disconsolate, brokenhearted, down, downcast, dispirited, crestfallen, depressed, melancholy, blue, gloomy, glum, mournful, woebegone, long-faced, joyless, cheerless. **2** *unhappy circumstances* unfortunate, disadvantageous, unlucky, adverse. **3** *an unhappy choice of phrase* unfortunate, regrettable, inappropriate.

unhealthy adjective **1** *unhealthy children* in poor health, unwell, ill, ailing, sick, sickly, indisposed, unsound, weak, feeble, frail, delicate, debilitated, infirm. **2** *an unhealthy diet* unwholesome, unnourishing, detrimental, injurious, damaging, deleterious, noxious, insalubrious.

unholy adjective **1** *unholy people/acts* godless, irreligious. *See* UNGODLY 1. **2** *an unholy commotion* unreasonable, preposterous, outrageous, appalling, shocking, dreadful; *inf.* ungodly.

unidentified adjective nameless, unnamed, unknown, anonymous, incognito.

unification noun union, junction, merger, fusion, alliance, amalgamation, coalition, combination, consolidation.

uniform adjective **1** *a uniform temperature* constant, consistent, invariable, unvarying, unvaried, unchanging, undeviating, stable, regular, even, equal, equable. **2** *all of uniform length* same, alike, like, selfsame, identical, similar, equal.

uniform noun livery, regalia, habit, suit, dress, costume, garb.

unify verb unite, bring together, merge, fuse, amalgamate, coalesce, combine, blend, mix, bind, link up, consolidate.

unimaginable adjective unthinkable, inconceivable, incredible, unbelievable, unheard-of, unthought-of, implausible, improbable, unlikely, impossible.

unimaginative adjective unoriginal, uninspired, commonplace, pedestrian, mundane, ordinary, prosaic, vapid, insipid, bland.

unimportant adjective insignificant, inconsequential, of no account, nonessential, immaterial, irrelevant, not worth mentioning, minor, slight, trifling, trivial, petty, paltry; dinky.

uninhabited adjective vacant, empty, unoccupied, untenanted, unpopulated, unpeopled, unsettled, abandoned, deserted, forsaken, desolate.

uninhibited adjective unreserved, unrepressed, unconstrained, unselfconscious, spontaneous, relaxed, informal, open; unrestrained, uncontrolled, uncurbed, unchecked, unbridled.

unintelligible adjective incomprehensible, meaningless, unfathomable, incoherent, indistinct, inarticulate, confused, muddled, jumbled.

unintentional adjective unintended, accidental, inadvertent, unpremeditated, uncalculated, unconscious, involuntary, unwitting, unthinking.

uninterested adjective indifferent, unconcerned, uninvolved, apathetic, blasé, unresponsive, impassive, dispassionate, aloof, detached, distant.

uninteresting adjective unexciting, dull, unentertaining, boring, tiresome, wearisome, tedious, dreary, flat, monotonous, humdrum, dry, pedestrian, prosaic, hackneyed, stale.

uninviting adjective unappealing, unattractive, unappetizing, repellent, revolting, repugnant.

union noun **1** *the union of three firms* joining, merging. *See* UNIFICATION. **2** *the union is made up of several organizations* association, alliance, league, coalition, consortium, syndicate, guild, confederation, federation. **3** *the union of the man and the woman* marriage, wedding; coupling, intercourse, coition, coitus, copulation. **4** *we are all in union about the plans* agreement, accord. *See* UNITY 3.

unique adjective **1** *a unique specimen* only, one and only, single, sole, lone, solitary, *sui generis*, exclusive, in a class by itself. **2** *a unique opportunity* unequaled, unparalleled, unmatched, matchless, peerless, incomparable, beyond compare.

unit noun **1** *the family regarded as a unit* entity, whole. **2** *the course is divided into units* component, part, section, element, constituent, subdivision, portion, segment, module, item, member. **3** *a unit of length* measurement, measure, quantity.

unite verb **1** *unite the two parties/firms* join, link, connect, combine, amalgamate, fuse,

465

weld, splice. **2** *unite the two substances* combine, mix, commix, admix, blend, mingle, homogenize. **3** *unite this man and this woman* marry, wed, join in wedlock, tie the knot between. **4** *they united to fight the common enemy* join together, join forces, band together, ally, cooperate, work/act/pull together.

united adjective **1** *a united effort* combined, amalgamated, allied, cooperative, concerted, collective, pooled. **2** *united in their opinion of the plan* in agreement, agreed, in unison, of the same opinion/mind, of like mind, like-minded, at one, in accord, unanimous.

unity noun **1** *detract from the unity of the painting* oneness, singleness, wholeness, entity, integrity. **2** *their strength lies in their unity* union, undividedness. See UNIFICATION. **3** *strive for political unity* agreement, harmony, accord, concord, concurrence, unanimity, consensus, concert, togetherness, solidarity.

universal adjective general, all-embracing, all-inclusive, comprehensive, catholic, across the board, worldwide, global, widespread.

unjust adjective **1** *an unjust verdict* inequitable, prejudiced. See UNFAIR 1. **2** *an unjust accusation* wrongful, wrong, undue, unwarranted. See UNFAIR 2.

unkempt adjective untidy, disheveled, disordered, disarranged, tousled, rumpled, windblown, uncombed, ungroomed, messy, messed up, scruffy, slovenly, sloppy; *inf.* mussed up.

unkind adjective **1** *unkind remarks* unfriendly, unamiable, uncharitable, inhospitable, ungenerous, nasty, mean, cruel, vicious, spiteful, malicious, pitiless, unsympathetic, unfeeling, hard-hearted. **2** *an unkind climate* inclement, harsh, intemperate.

unknown adjective **1** *the results of the test are as yet unknown* unrevealed, undisclosed, undivulged, undetermined, undecided, unestablished, unsettled, unascertained, up in the air. **2** *the donor is unknown* unnamed, nameless. See UNIDENTIFIED. **3** *unknown territory* unfamiliar, unexplored, uncharted, untraveled, undiscovered. **4** *unknown poets* unheard-of, little-known, obscure, undistinguished, unrenowned, unsung.

unlawful adjective illegal, illicit, illegitimate, criminal, felonious, actionable, prohibited, banned, outlawed, proscribed.

unlike adjective unalike, dissimilar, different, distinct, disparate, contrary, diverse, divergent, incompatible, ill-matched, incongruous; *inf.* like day and night.

unlikely adjective improbable, doubtful, dubious, faint, slight, remote.

unlimited adjective **1** *unlimited freedom* unrestricted, unconstrained, uncontrolled, unrestrained, unchecked, unhindered, unhampered, unimpeded, unfettered, untrammeled; absolute, total, unqualified, unconditional. **2** *unlimited supplies of money* limitless, boundless, unbounded, immense, vast, great, extensive, immeasurable, incalculable, untold, infinite, endless.

unlucky adjective **1** *an unlucky young man* luckless, out of luck, down on one's luck, unfortunate, hapless, ill-fated, ill-starred, star-crossed, wretched, miserable. **2** *an unlucky set of circumstances* adverse, disadvantageous, unfavorable, unfortunate, untoward, unpromising, inauspicious, unpropitious.

unmarried adjective single, unwed, unwedded, spouseless, partnerless, divorced, unattached, bachelor, celibate; husbandless, wifeless.

unmistakable adjective clear, plain, obvious, evident, manifest, patent, palpable, distinct, conspicuous, well-defined, pronounced.

unmitigated adjective absolute, unqualified, unconditional, categorical, complete, total, thorough, thoroughgoing, downright, utter, out and out, veritable, perfect, consummate.

unmoved adjective **1** *unmoved from their purpose* firm, steadfast, unshaken, staunch, unwavering, unswerving, undeviating, determined, resolute, decided, resolved. **2** *unmoved by the sad sight* unaffected, untouched, unstirred, unconcerned, uncaring, indifferent, impassive, unfeeling, impervious.

unnatural adjective **1** *his face turned an unnatural color* unusual, uncommon, extraordinary, strange, queer, odd, bizarre, preternatural. **2** *an unnatural laugh | unnatural behavior* affected, artificial, forced, labored, studied, strained, mannered.

unnecessary adjective needless, unneeded, inessential, nonessential, uncalled-for, unrequired, gratuitous, useless, dispensable, expendable, redundant, superfluous.

unnerve verb discourage, dishearten, demoralize, daunt, alarm, frighten, dismay, disconcert, perturb, upset, unsettle, disquiet, fluster, agitate, shake; *inf.* rattle.

unobtrusive adjective low-key, restrained, subdued, quiet, unostentatious, unshowy, inconspicuous, unnoticeable.

unoccupied adjective **1** *unoccupied houses/places* vacant, unpopulated. See UNINHABITED. **2** *he is unoccupied just now* not busy, at leisure, idle, inactive, unemployed.

unofficial adjective informal, casual, unauthorized, unsanctioned, unaccredited, unconfirmed, unsubstantiated.

unorthodox adjective 1 *unorthodox beliefs* heterodox, uncanonical, heretical, nonconformist. 2 *unorthodox methods* unconventional, unusual, uncommon, out of the ordinary, irregular, abnormal, divergent, aberrant, anomalous.

unparalleled adjective matchless, peerless. *See* UNEQUALED.

unperturbed adjective calm, composed, cool, collected, serene, tranquil, self-possessed, placid, unruffled, unflustered, unexcited, undismayed, untroubled, unworried; *inf.* laid-back.

unpleasant adjective disagreeable, disgusting, repugnant, revolting, nauseating, sickening, offensive, obnoxious, foul.

unpopular adjective disliked, unliked, unloved, friendless, unwanted, unwelcome, avoided, ignored, rejected, shunned, out in the cold, out of favor.

unprecedented adjective unparalleled, unheard-of, uncommon, out of the ordinary, unusual, exceptional.

unpredictable adjective 1 *unpredictable results* unforeseeable, undivinable, uncertain, unsure, in the balance, up in the air; *inf.* iffy. 2 *unpredictable behavior* erratic, fickle, capricious, whimsical, mercurial, volatile, unstable, undependable, unreliable.

unpretentious adjective simple, plain, modest, ordinary, humble, unostentatious, unshowy, unimposing, unassuming, unaffected.

unprincipled adjective immoral, amoral, unethical, dishonorable, dishonest, unprofessional, deceitful, devious, unscrupulous, corrupt, crooked.

unproductive adjective fruitless, futile, vain, idle, useless, worthless, valueless, ineffective, ineffectual, inefficacious, unprofitable, unremunerative.

unprofessional adjective 1 *unprofessional conduct* unethical, unprincipled, improper, unseemly, indecorous, lax, negligent. 2 *unprofessional workers* amateur, amateurish, unskilled, inexpert, untrained, unqualified, inexperienced, incompetent.

unqualified adjective 1 *unqualified teachers* uncertificated, unlicensed, untrained. 2 *unqualified to comment* ineligible, unfit, incompetent, incapable, unequipped, unprepared. 3 *unqualified approval* without reservations, utter, perfect, consummate. *See* UNCONDITIONAL.

unquestionable adjective undoubted, indisputable. *See* UNDENIABLE.

unravel verb 1 *unravel knots* untangle, disentangle, straighten out, unknot, undo.

2 *unravel the problem* solve, resolve, work out, clear up, get to the bottom of, fathom; *inf.* figure out.

unreal adjective imaginary, make-believe, fictitious, mythical, fanciful, fantastic, fabulous, hypothetical, nonexistent, illusory, chimerical, phantasmagoric.

unrealistic adjective impractical, impracticable, unworkable, unreasonable, irrational, illogical, improbable, foolish, wild, absurd, quixotic; *inf.* half-baked.

unreasonable adjective 1 *unreasonable demands* excessive, immoderate, undue, inordinate, outrageous, extravagant, preposterous, unconscionable, exorbitant. 2 *unreasonable people* irrational, illogical, opinionated, obstinate, obdurate, willful, headstrong, temperamental, capricious. 3 *unreasonable behavior* unacceptable, inappropriate.

unrelenting adjective 1 *unrelenting demands/rain* relentless, unremitting, continuous, continual, constant, incessant, unceasing, nonstop, endless, unending, perpetual, unabating. 2 *unrelenting judge* implacable, inexorable, inflexible, rigid, hard, strict, harsh, stern.

unreliable adjective undependable, irresponsible, untrustworthy, suspect, questionable, open to question/doubt.

unrepentant adjective impenitent, unrepenting, unremorseful, shameless, unregenerate.

unresolved adjective undecided, to be decided, unsettled, undetermined, pending, unsolved, unanswered, debatable, open to debate/question, doubtful, in doubt, moot, up in the air; *inf.* iffy.

unrest noun dissatisfaction, discontent, discontentment, unease, disquiet, dissension, dissent, discord, strife, protest, rebellion, agitation, turmoil.

unruly adjective unmanageable, uncontrollable, refractory, recalcitrant, intractable, contumacious, disobedient, rebellious, mutinous, insubordinate, defiant.

unsavory adjective 1 *unsavory food/smell* unpalatable, unappetizing, unpleasant, disagreeable, disgusting, loathsome, repugnant, revolting, nauseating, sickening. 2 *unsavory characters* objectionable, offensive, disreputable, degenerate, coarse, gross, vulgar, boorish.

unscrupulous adjective unprincipled, unethical, amoral, immoral, conscienceless, shameless, corrupt, exploitative.

unseemly adjective unbecoming, unfitting, unbefitting, indecorous, improper, inappropriate, undignified, unrefined, indelicate, tasteless.

unselfish adjective altruistic, self-sacrificing, selfless, kind, self-denying, openhanded, generous, liberal, unsparing, ungrudging, unstinting, charitable, philanthropic.

unsettle verb **1** *the move unsettled the children* disturb, discompose. *See* UPSET verb **2**. **2** *unsettle the smooth workings of the firm* throw into confusion/disorder, disrupt, disorganize, disarrange, derange.

unsightly adjective ugly, unattractive, unprepossessing, hideous, horrible, repulsive, revolting, offensive, distasteful.

unskilled adjective untrained, unqualified, inexpert, inexperienced, amateurish.

unsociable adjective unfriendly, unamiable, unaffable, uncongenial, reclusive, reticent, withdrawn, aloof, distant, remote, standoffish.

unsolicited adjective unsought, unasked-for, unrequested, uninvited, unwelcome, gratuitous, volunteered.

unsophisticated adjective **1** *unsophisticated country girls* naive, simple, innocent, childlike, artless, guileless, ingenuous, natural, unaffected, unrefined, unpolished, provincial. **2** *unsophisticated tools* crude, basic, rudimentary, primitive, undeveloped. **3** *unsophisticated approach to the problem* simple, straightforward, uncomplicated, unspecialized.

unsound adjective **1** *in unsound health* unhealthy, unwell, ailing, delicate, weak, frail. **2** *of unsound mind* disordered, diseased, deranged, demented, unbalanced, unhinged. **3** *unsound furniture* defective, disintegrating, broken, broken-down, rotten, rickety, flimsy, shaky, wobbly, tottery, insubstantial, unsafe. **4** *unsound reasoning* flawed, defective, faulty, weak, unreliable, unfounded, untenable, specious, spurious, false, fallacious, erroneous.

unspeakable adjective **1** *unspeakable joy* beyond words, inexpressible, unutterable, indescribable, ineffable, overwhelming, marvelous, wonderful. **2** *an unspeakable crime* appalling, abominable, despicable, contemptible, repellent, loathsome, odious, monstrous, heinous, execrable.

unspoken adjective **1** *unspoken criticism* unexpressed, unstated, tacit, implicit, implied, understood. **2** *unspoken plea for mercy* mute, silent, wordless, unuttered.

unstable adjective **1** *unstable chairs* unsteady, infirm, rickety, shaky, wobbly, tottery, unsafe, unreliable, insecure, precarious. **2** *emotionally unstable* unbalanced, volatile, moody, mercurial, capricious, giddy, erratic, unpredictable. **3** *unstable prices* changeable, variable, unsettled, fluctuating, inconstant, unpredictable.

unsuccessful adjective failed, vain, unavailing, futile, useless, worthless, abortive, ineffective, ineffectual, inefficacious, fruitless, unproductive, unprofitable, unprosperous; frustrated, thwarted, foiled.

unsuitable adjective inappropriate, inapt, inapposite, unfitting, unbefitting, incompatible, incongruous, out of place/keeping.

unsure adjective **1** *he was a bit unsure at first* unselfconfident, insecure, hesitant, diffident. **2** *unsure what to do* undecided, irresolute, of two minds, ambivalent. **3** *unsure about his motive* uncertain, unconvinced, dubious, doubtful, skeptical, distrustful, suspicious.

unsuspecting adjective unwary, off guard, trusting, trustful, gullible, credulous, ingenuous.

unsympathetic adjective uncompassionate, compassionless, unpitying, pitiless, uncaring, unfeeling, insensitive, unconcerned, indifferent, unresponsive.

untenable adjective indefensible, undefendable, insupportable, unsustainable, refutable, unsound, weak, flawed, defective, faulty, implausible, specious.

unthinkable adjective **1** *it is unthinkable that the territory is unexplored* inconceivable, unimaginable, unbelievable, beyond belief. **2** *it is unthinkable that he should represent us* out of the question, absurd, preposterous, outrageous.

unthinking adjective **1** *hurt by an unthinking remark* thoughtless, inconsiderate, tactless, undiplomatic, injudicious, indiscreet, insensitive, blundering, careless, rude. **2** *an unthinking kick of the ball* mechanical, automatic, instinctive, involuntary.

untidy adjective **1** *untidy children* disheveled, rumpled. *See* UNKEMPT. **2** *untidy desks/rooms* disordered, disorderly, disarranged, disorganized, chaotic, confused, muddled, jumbled, topsy-turvy, at sixes and sevens, higgledy-piggledy, every which way.

untimely adjective **1** *an untimely visit* ill-timed, mistimed, inconvenient, inopportune. **2** *his untimely death* premature, early.

untiring adjective tireless, indefatigable, unfailing, unfaltering, unwavering, unflagging, unremitting, constant, resolute, steady.

untold adjective **1** *her untold story* unrecounted, unrelated, unnarrated, unreported, unmentioned, unstated, unspoken, unrevealed, undisclosed, undivulged, unpublished, secret. **2** *untold joy* unspeakable, indescribable, inexpressible, unutterable, ineffable, unimaginable, inconceivable. **3** *untold millions* countless, innumerable, myriad, incalculable, immeasurable, measureless.

untrue adjective **1** *untrue stories* false, fallacious, fictitious, fabricated, erroneous, in error, wrong, incorrect, inaccurate, unsound, distorted, misleading. **2** *untrue friends* disloyal, faithless, unfaithful, false, treacherous, perfidious, deceitful, untrustworthy, double-dealing, insincere, unreliable, inconstant.

untrustworthy adjective treacherous, two-faced, double-dealing, duplicitous, deceitful, dishonest, dishonorable, unreliable, undependable, slippery.

unusual adjective uncommon, out of the ordinary, atypical, abnormal, rare, singular, extraordinary, exceptional, remarkable, outstanding; odd, strange, curious, queer, bizarre, different, unconventional, unorthodox, irregular; *inf.* weird.

unveil verb uncover, reveal, lay open/bare, expose, bring to light, disclose, divulge, make known/public.

unwarranted adjective unauthorized, unsanctioned, unapproved, unjustifiable, unjustified, indefensible, inexcusable, uncalled-for, gratuitous.

unwelcome adjective unwanted, undesired, uninvited; displeasing, distasteful, undesirable.

unwieldy adjective cumbersome, unmanageable, unmaneuverable, awkward, clumsy, massive, hefty, bulky, hulking.

unwilling adjective reluctant, disinclined, averse, loath, opposed.

unwind verb **1** *unwind the balls of yarn* undo, unravel, uncoil, unroll, untwist, disentangle. **2** *unwind by watching television* wind down, relax, calm down, slow down, loosen up.

unwise adjective imprudent, injudicious, inadvisable, ill-considered, ill-judged, ill-advised, impolitic, indiscreet, irresponsible, foolish, unintelligent, mindless.

unwitting adjective **1** *an unwitting offender* unknowing, unconscious, unaware, ignorant. **2** *an unwitting slight* unintentional, unintended, inadvertent, unplanned, accidental, chance.

unwonted adjective unusual, uncommon, uncustomary, atypical, abnormal.

unworldly adjective **1** *unworldly considerations* spiritual, spiritualistic, nonmaterial, religious. **2** *too unworldly to cope on her own* naive, inexperienced, uninitiated, unsophisticated, gullible, ingenuous, trusting, credulous, idealistic. **3** *unworldly beings* otherworldly, unearthly, extraterrestrial, ethereal, ghostly, spectral, phantom, preternatural, supernatural.

unworthy adjective **1** *unworthy conduct for a teacher* unsuitable, inappropriate, unbefitting, unseemly, improper, incompatible, incongruous, degrading. **2** *an unworthy cause* worthless, inferior, second-rate, undeserving, ignoble, disreputable.

3 *an unworthy wretch* disreputable, dishonorable, base, contemptible, reprehensible.

upbraid verb scold, rebuke, reproach, reprove, chide, reprimand, berate, remonstrate with, castigate, criticize, censure.

upgrade verb improve, better, ameliorate, enhance, promote, advance, elevate, raise.

upheaval noun disruption, disturbance, revolution, disorder, confusion, turmoil, cataclysm.

uphill adjective **1** *an uphill path* upward, ascending, climbing, mounting, rising. **2** *an uphill job* arduous, difficult, laborious, strenuous, hard, tough, taxing, grueling.

uphold verb **1** *uphold the committee's decision* confirm, endorse, support, back up, stand by, champion, defend. **2** *uphold the old traditions* maintain, sustain, hold to, keep.

upkeep noun maintenance, running, preservation, conservation, repairs, keep, support, subsistence.

uplift verb raise, upraise, lift, elevate; improve, edify, inspire.

upper adjective higher, loftier; superior, higher-ranking, elevated, greater.

uppermost adjective **1** *the uppermost shelf* highest, furthest up, loftiest, top, topmost. **2** *uppermost in our minds* foremost, greatest, predominant, dominant, principal, chief, main, paramount, major.

upright adjective **1** *upright posts* erect, on end, vertical, perpendicular, standing up, rampant. **2** *upright members of the community* honest, honorable, upstanding, decent, respectable, worthy, reputable, good, virtuous, righteous, law-abiding, ethical, moral.

uprising noun rebellion, revolt, insurrection, insurgence, mutiny, riot, revolution, coup, coup d'état, overthrow, putsch.

uproar noun tumult, turmoil, turbulence, disorder, confusion, commotion, mayhem, pandemonium, bedlam; din, noise, clamor, hubbub, racket; row, rumpus, brouhaha, hullabaloo, furor, fracas, brawl, scuffle, conflict.

uproarious adjective **1** *an uproarious party* noisy, loud, rowdy, disorderly, unruly, boisterous, wild, unrestrained, rollicking. **2** *an uproarious show* hilarious, sidesplitting; *inf.* rib-tickling.

upset verb **1** *upset the bucket/boat* overturn, knock over, push over, upend, tip over, topple, capsize. **2** *the news upset them* perturb, disturb, discompose, unsettle, disconcert, dismay, disquiet, trouble, worry, bother, agitate, fluster, ruffle, shake, frighten, alarm, anger, annoy, distress, hurt, grieve; *inf.* rattle. **3** *upset the* *smooth running of the firm* disturb, disarrange, mess up, mix up, turn topsyturvy. **4** *upset Napoleon's army* defeat, beat, conquer, vanquish, rout, overthrow, overcome, triumph over, get the better of, worst.

upset adjective **1** *the upset bucket* overturned, upturned, upended, toppled, capsized, upside down. **2** *upset by the news* perturbed, disturbed, discomposed, unsettled, disconcerted, dismayed, disquieted, troubled, worried, bothered, anxious, agitated, shaken, annoyed, distressed, hurt. **3** *an upset stomach* queasy, ill, sick. **4** *our upset plans* disordered, confused, in confusion, disarranged, in disarray, jumbled up, messed up, chaotic, in chaos, topsy-turvy, higgledy-piggledy.

upshot noun result, outcome, conclusion, issue, end, end result, denouement, effect, repercussion, reaction; *inf.* payoff.

up-to-date adjective modern, current, present-day, up-to-the-minute, fashionable, in fashion, in vogue, voguish; *inf.* all the rage, trendy, with-it, now.

urban adjective city, cityish, citified, innercity, metropolitan, municipal, civic.

urbane adjective suave, debonair, sophisticated, smooth, worldly, elegant, cultivated, cultured, civilized, polished, refined, gracious, courtly, polite, courteous, well-mannered.

urge verb **1** *urge the horses on* push, drive, propel, impel, force, hasten, hurry. **2** *urge the contestants to greater effort* spur, incite, stir up, stimulate, prod, goad, egg on, encourage, prompt; *inf.* psych up. **3** *urged him to go* entreat, exhort, implore, appeal, beg, beseech, plead. **4** *urge caution* advise, counsel, advocate, recommend, suggest, support, endorse.

urge noun desire, need, compulsion, longing, yearning, wish, fancy, impulse, itch; *inf.* yen.

urgent adjective **1** *it is urgent that we operate | urgent matters* imperative, vital, crucial, critical, essential, exigent, top-priority, high-priority, necessary, important, pressing, serious, grave. **2** *an urgent whisper/demand* importunate, insistent, clamorous, earnest, pleading, begging.

usage noun **1** *damaged by rough usage* treatment, handling, management. *See* USE noun 1. **2** *old usages now forgotten* custom, practice, habit, way, procedure, method, mode, form, tradition, convention.

use verb **1** *use tools* make use of, utilize, employ, work, operate, wield, ply, maneuver, manipulate, avail oneself of, put to use, put into service. **2** *use him roughly* treat, handle, deal with, act/behave toward. **3** *he just uses people for his own ends* exploit,

take advantage of, impose upon, abuse. **4** *we have used up all the food* consume, get through, exhaust, deplete, expend, spend, waste, fritter away. **used to** accustomed to, at home with, habituated to, inured to.

use noun **1** *for external use* usage, application, utilization, employment, operation, manipulation, maneuvering. **2** *fall to pieces from use* using, usage, wear, wear and tear. **3** *his use of other people for his own ends* exploitation, manipulation. **4** *what use is this to you?* usefulness, good, advantage, benefit, service, help, gain, profit, avail. **5** *established by long use* practice, custom, habit, wont. **6** *we have no use for this machine* need, necessity, call, demand, purpose, reason.

used adjective secondhand, cast-off, hand-me-down.

useful adjective **1** *a useful tool* of use, functional, utilitarian, of service, practical, convenient. **2** *a useful experience* beneficial, advantageous, of help, helpful, worthwhile, profitable, rewarding, productive, valuable.

useless adjective **1** *a useless attempt* vain, in vain, to no avail/purpose, unavailing, unsuccessful, futile, purposeless, ineffectual, inefficacious, fruitless, unprofitable. **2** *he is a useless player* worthless, ineffective, ineffectual, incompetent, incapable, inadequate; *inf.* no good.

usher noun escort, guide, attendant.

usher verb escort, show, conduct, direct, guide, lead. **usher in** herald, pave the way for, announce, introduce, bring in, get going, get under way, launch.

usual adjective **1** *his usual route* habitual, customary, accustomed, wonted, normal, regular, routine, everyday, established, set, familiar. **2** *not usual behavior* common, typical, ordinary, average, run-of-the-mill, expected, standard, stock, regular.

usually adverb generally, as a rule, normally, by and large, in the main, mainly, mostly.

utilize verb use, put to use, make use of, employ, avail oneself of, have recourse to, resort to, take advantage of, turn to account.

utmost adjective **1** *have the utmost confidence in them* maximum, supreme, paramount, greatest, highest, most. **2** *the utmost ends of the earth* uttermost, furthest, farthest, remotest, outermost, extreme, ultimate.

utter adjective absolute, sheer. *See* UNMITIGATED.

utter verb voice, say, speak, pronounce, express, enunciate, articulate, verbalize, vocalize.

utterly adverb absolutely, completely, totally, entirely, thoroughly, positively, extremely, perfectly.

Vv

vacancy noun **1** *a vacancy in the firm* opening, position, post, job, opportunity, slot. **2** *the vacancy of his expression* blankness, expressionlessness, emotionlessness, vacuousness.

vacant adjective **1** *a vacant space* empty, void. **2** *a vacant position/seat* unoccupied, unfilled, free, empty, available, unengaged, not in use, unused; *inf.* up for grabs. **3** *a vacant house* uninhabited, untenanted, tenantless, to let, abandoned, deserted. **4** *a vacant expression* blank, expressionless, inexpressive, deadpan, poker-faced, emotionless, uninterested, vacuous, inane.

vacate verb leave, quit, depart from, evacuate, abandon, desert.

vacation noun break, recess, furlough, holiday, rest, respite; leave, time off.

vacillate verb shilly-shally, waver, dither, hesitate, equivocate, hem and haw, keep changing one's mind, beat about the bush; *inf.* blow hot and cold.

vacuum noun emptiness, void, nothingness, vacuity; gap, empty space, lacuna, need, want.

vagabond noun wanderer, itinerant, nomad, wayfarer, traveler, rover, gypsy, hobo, tramp, vagrant, derelict, beachcomber, down-and-out, bird of passage, rolling stone; *inf.* bum.

vagrant noun tramp, hobo, beggar. *See* VAGABOND noun.

vague adjective **1** *a vague shape* indistinct, indeterminate, ill-defined, unclear, nebulous, amorphous, shadowy, hazy, dim, fuzzy, foggy, blurry, bleary, out of focus. **2** *a vague description* imprecise, inexact, unexplicit, nonspecific, loose, generalized, ambiguous, equivocal, hazy, woolly. **3** *she is rather vague about her plans* uncertain, unsure, hesitant, wavering, shilly-shallying, blowing hot and cold. **4** *her plans are rather vague* undecided, indefinite, indeterminate, doubtful, open, speculative, conjectural; *inf.* up in the air. **5** *she is rather vague* absentminded, abstracted, dreamy, vacuous; *inf.* with one's head in the clouds.

vain adjective **1** *vain people* conceited, narcissistic, self-admiring, peacockish, egotistical, proud, haughty, arrogant, boastful, swaggering, imperious, overweening, cocky, affected, vainglorious; *inf.* stuck-up, bigheaded, swellheaded. **2** *vain triumphs* futile, worthless, insignificant, pointless, meaningless, valueless, meritless, empty, hollow,

idle. **3** *vain attempts* unsuccessful, futile. *See* USELESS 1.

valiant adjective brave, courageous, valorous, heroic, stouthearted, lionhearted, gallant, manly, intrepid, fearless, undaunted, undismayed, bold, daring, audacious, staunch, stalwart, indomitable, resolute, determined.

valid adjective **1** *valid reasons/objections* sound, well-founded, well-grounded, substantial, reasonable, logical, justifiable, defensible, authentic, bona fide. **2** *the ruling is still valid* lawful, legal, licit, legitimate, binding, contractual, in force, in effect.

validate verb **1** *validate the contract | validate his appointment* ratify, legalize, legitimize, authorize, sanction, warrant, license, approve, endorse, set one's seal to. **2** *validate a statement* verify, prove, authenticate, substantiate, confirm, corroborate, justify.

valley noun dale, dell, hollow, vale, glen, depression.

valor noun bravery, courage, heroism, stoutheartedness, gallantry, manliness, intrepidity, fearlessness, boldness, daring, staunchness, fortitude.

valuable adjective **1** *a valuable watch* costly, high-priced, expensive, priceless, precious. **2** *a valuable contribution/lesson* useful, helpful, beneficial, advantageous, worthwhile, worthy, important.

value noun **1** *place a value on the ring* price, market price, cost. **2** *the value of a healthy diet* worth, merit, usefulness, advantage, benefit, gain, profit, good.

value verb **1** *value the watch* set a price on, price, evaluate, assess, appraise. **2** *we value his contribution greatly* rate highly, appreciate, esteem, hold in high regard, think highly of, set store by, respect, admire, prize, cherish, treasure.

values plural noun *moral values* principles, ethics, morals, standards.

vanguard noun advance guard, forefront, front, front line, front rank, leading position, van; leaders, spearheads, trailblazers, trendsetters.

vanish verb **1** *she vanished in the mist* disappear, be lost to sight/view, be/become invisible, evaporate, dissipate, fade, fade away, evanesce, melt away. **2** *hopes of success have vanished* pass away, die out, come to an end, end, become extinct/obsolete.

vanity noun **1** *his vanity about his looks/achievements* conceit, conceitedness, self-conceit, self-admiration, self-love, narcissism, egotism, pride, haughtiness, arrogance, boastfulness, braggadocio, vainglory; airs; *inf.* bigheadedness, swellheadedness, showing off. **2** *the vanity of human triumphs* worthlessness, futility, futileness, insignificance, pointlessness, meaninglessness, emptiness, hollowness.

vanquish verb conquer, defeat, triumph over, beat, overcome, best, worst, master, subdue, subjugate, put down, quell, quash, repress, rout, overwhelm, overrun, overthrow, crush, trounce, thrash, drub; *inf.* clobber.

variable adjective varying, changeable, changeful, changing, mutable, chameleonic, protean, shifting, fluctuating, wavering, vacillating, inconstant, unsteady, unstable, fitful, capricious, fickle; *inf.* blowing hot and cold.

variation noun **1** *subject to variation* change, alteration, modification, diversification. **2** *noted for its variation* variability, changeability, fluctuation, vacillation, vicissitude. **3** *show variation from the norm* deviation, divergence, departure, difference.

varied adjective diversified, diverse, assorted, miscellaneous, mixed, motley, heterogeneous.

variety noun **1** *introduce variety into your selection* variation, diversification, diversity, multifariousness, many-sidedness, change, difference. **2** *a variety of flowers were exhibited* assortment, miscellany, range, mixture, medley, motley, collection, multiplicity. **3** *a variety of rose/humor* strain, breed, kind, type, sort, class, category, classification, brand, make.

various adjective **1** *come in various shapes* varying, different, differing, dissimilar, unlike, disparate, assorted, mixed, miscellaneous, variegated, heterogeneous. **2** *for various reasons* varied, sundry, diverse.

varnish noun coating, lacquer, shellac, enamel, glaze, veneer.

vary verb **1** *they tend to vary in size* differ, be different, be dissimilar. **2** *the sky varies constantly* change, alter, metamorphose, suffer a sea change, vacillate, fluctuate. **3** *our opinions vary* be at variance, disagree, conflict, clash, be at odds, be in opposition, diverge. **4** *vary the speed/appearance* change, alter, modify, transform, permutate. **5** *vary from the norm* deviate, diverge, depart.

vast adjective **1** *a vast shape loomed* immense, huge, enormous, massive, bulky, tremendous, colossal, prodigious, gigantic, monumental, elephantine, hulking. **2** *vast forests* extensive, broad, wide, expansive, boundless, limitless, infinite.

vault noun **1** *hide in the vault* cellar, basement, underground chamber, tomb. **2** *valuables stored in the vault* safe, strongbox, strongroom, repository, depository. **3** *take a vault over the fence* jump, leap, spring, bound.

vault verb jump, leap, jump over, leap over, spring over, bound over.

veer verb change course/direction, shift direction, turn, swerve, swing, sidestep, sheer, tack.

vegetation noun plant life, herbage, greenery, verdure; plants, flora.

vehement adjective passionate, ardent, impassioned, fervent, fervid, strong, forceful, forcible, powerful, emphatic, vigorous, intense.

vehicle noun **1** *park the vehicle* transportation, conveyance; car, bus, truck. **2** *a vehicle for their propaganda* channel, medium, means, agency, instrument, mechanism, organ, apparatus.

veil noun *a veil of secrecy* covering, cover, screen, curtain, film, mantle, cloak, mask, blanket, shroud, canopy, cloud.

veil verb **1** *try to veil his contempt* hide, conceal, cover up, camouflage, disguise, mask, screen. **2** *mist veiling the mountains* cover, envelop, mantle, cloak, blanket, shroud, canopy.

vein noun **1** *a vein of ore* lode, seam, stratum. **2** *veins of blue in the white marble* streak, stripe, line, thread, marking. **3** *there was a vein of wickedness in him* streak, strain, trait, dash, hint. **4** *a humorous vein* mood, temper, attitude, inclination, tendency, tenor, tone.

velocity noun speed, swiftness, fastness, quickness, rapidity, celerity.

vendor noun seller, salesperson, dealer, trader, merchant, peddler, hawker.

veneer noun **1** *a veneer of mahogany* facing, covering, coat, finishing coat, finish. **2** *a veneer of politeness* façade, front, false front, show, outward display, appearance, semblance, guise, mask, pretense, camouflage.

venerable adjective venerated, respected, revered, reverenced, worshiped, honored, esteemed, hallowed.

veneration noun respect, reverence, worship, adoration, honor, esteem.

vengeance noun revenge, retribution, requital, retaliation, reprisal, an eye for an eye, tit for tat, measure for measure, blow for blow, quid pro quo. **with a vengeance 1** *the rain came down with a vengeance* forcefully, violently, vehemently, furiously, wildly. **2** *go at the job with a vengeance* to the utmost, to the limit, all out, flat out.

venom noun **1** *suck the venom of the snake bite* poison, toxin, toxicant. **2** *speak with venom about his rival* spite, spitefulness, rancor, vindictiveness, malice, malevolence, malignity, ill will, animosity, bitterness, resentment, acrimony, virulence, hostility, enmity.

venomous adjective **1** *a venomous snake/bite* poisonous, toxic, lethal, deadly, fatal, noxious. **2** *a venomous remark/look* spiteful, rancorous, vindictive, malicious, malevolent, malignant, baleful, bitter, resentful, grudging, virulent, antagonistic, hostile, hate-filled, vicious.

vent noun **1** *an air vent* opening, aperture, hole, gap, orifice, duct, flue. **2** *give vent to his anger* outlet, expression, release.

vent verb *vent his anger* give vent to, express, air, utter, voice, verbalize, let out, release, pour out, emit, discharge, come out with.

ventilate verb **1** *ventilate a room* air, aerate, oxygenate, air-condition, freshen, cool, purify. **2** *ventilate one's views* air, give an airing to, bring into the open, discuss, debate, talk over.

venture noun **1** *explorers engaged in a new venture* adventure, exploit, mission. **2** *a business venture* enterprise, undertaking, project, speculation, fling, plunge, gamble.

venture verb **1** *venture to voice an opinion* dare, be so bold as, presume. **2** *venture an opinion* volunteer, advance, put forward, chance, risk. **3** *venture his life for her* risk, put at risk, endanger, hazard, put in jeopardy, jeopardize, imperil, chance, gamble.

verbal adjective *a verbal account* oral, spoken, said, uttered, articulated.

verbatim adjective word for word, literal, verbal, exact.

verbatim adverb word for word, literally, to the letter, faithfully, exactly, precisely.

verbose adjective wordy, loquacious, garrulous, long-winded, prolix, diffuse, pleonastic, circumlocutory, periphrastic, tautological.

verdict noun decision, judgment, adjudication, finding, conclusion, ruling, opinion.

verge noun **1** *the verges of the lake* edge, border, margin, rim, limit, boundary, end, extremity. **2** *on the verge of a discovery* brink, threshold.

verify verb confirm, substantiate, prove, corroborate, attest to, testify to, validate, authenticate, bear out, justify, give credence to.

versatile adjective **1** *a versatile member of staff* all-around, multifaceted, resourceful, ingenious, clever. **2** *a versatile tool* adaptable, adjustable, multipurpose, all-purpose, handy.

verse noun **1** *a poem in several verses* stanza, strophe, canto, couplet. **2** *a verse about the countryside* poem, lyric, sonnet, ode, limerick, piece of doggerel, ditty, song, lay, ballad.

version noun **1** *tell us your version of the events* account, report, story, rendering, interpretation, construction, understanding, reading, impression, side. **2** *published in several versions* adaptation, interpretation, translation. **3** *there are several versions of the song going around* variant, variation, form, copy, reproduction.

vertical adjective upright, erect, on end, perpendicular.

vertigo noun dizziness, giddiness, lightheadedness; *inf.* wooziness.

verve noun enthusiasm, vigor, force, energy, vitality, vivacity, liveliness, animation, sparkle, spirit, life, élan, dash, brio, fervor, gusto, zing, vim; zip, punch, get-up-and-go, pizzazz.

very adverb extremely, exceedingly, to a great extent, exceptionally, uncommonly, unusually, decidedly, particularly, eminently, remarkably, really, truly; *inf.* awfully, terribly.

very adjective **1** *his very words* actual, exact, precise. **2** *that is the very thing for the task* ideal, perfect, appropriate, suitable, fitting, right, just right. **3** *its very simplicity appeals to us* sheer, utter, simple, pure, plain, mere. **4** *at the very beginning* extreme, absolute.

vessel noun **1** *a seagoing vessel* ship, boat, yacht, craft, argosy. **2** *pour the milk into several vessels* container, receptacle.

vest verb *vest in the power vested in him* bestow on/upon, confer on/upon, endow, entrust to/with, invest in, lodge in/with, place in/on/with, put in the hands of.

vestige noun **1** *see vestiges of a pack of wolves* trace, mark, sign, indication, print, imprint, impression, track. **2** *vestiges of a lost civilization* remains, relics; evidence. **3** *not a vestige of proof* scrap, hint, suggestion, touch, tinge, suspicion, soupçon, inkling, drop, dash, jot, iota.

veteran noun old hand, old-timer, past master, master; *inf.* pro, warhorse.

veteran adjective long-serving, seasoned, old, adept, expert; *inf.* battle-scarred.

veto verb reject, turn down, give the thumbs down to, prohibit, forbid, interdict, proscribe, disallow, outlaw, embargo, ban, bar, preclude, rule out; *inf.* kill, put the kibosh on.

veto noun rejection, prohibition, interdict, proscription; embargo, ban.

vex verb anger, annoy, irritate, incense, irk, enrage, infuriate, exasperate, aggravate, pique, provoke, nettle, disturb, upset, perturb, discompose, put out, try one's patience, try, bother, trouble, worry, agitate, pester, harass, fluster, ruffle, rile, hound, nag, torment, distress, tease, fret, gall, molest, peeve; *inf.* miff, bug, hassle, get one's goat, drive up the wall, get to.

viable adjective *a viable plan* workable, sound, feasible, practicable, applicable, usable.

vibrant adjective **1** *vibrant music* throbbing, pulsating, resonant, reverberating, ringing, echoing. **2** *vibrant with excitement* trembling, quivering, shaking, shivering. **3** *a vibrant personality* lively, energetic, spirited, vigorous, animated, sparkling, vivacious, dynamic, electrifying. **4** *vibrant colors* vivid, bright, strong, striking.

vibrate verb **1** *the pendulum vibrated* oscillate, swing. **2** *the noise vibrated through the house* throb, pulsate, resonate, resound, reverberate, ring, echo. **3** *vibrating with excitement* pulsate, tremble, quiver, shake, quaver, shiver, shudder.

vibration noun **1** *the musical vibration* throb, pulsation, resonance, reverberation. **2** *the vibration of the engine* pulsating, trembling, tremble, quivering, quiver, shake, shaking, quaver, shiver, shivering.

vicarious adjective indirect, secondhand, surrogate, by proxy.

vice noun **1** *vice is rampant* sin, sinfulness, wrong, wrongdoing, wickedness, badness, immorality, iniquity, evil, evildoing, venality corruption, depravity, degeneracy; transgression, offense, misdeed, error, violation. **2** *chocolate/shopping is one of her vices* failing, flaw, defect, imperfection, weakness, foible, shortcoming.

vice versa adverb conversely, inversely, the other way around, contrariwise.

vicinity noun **1** *he lives in the vicinity* neighborhood, locality, area, district; environs, precincts, purlieus; *inf.* neck of the woods. **2** *the town's vicinity to Nashville* nearness, closeness, proximity, propinquity. **in the vicinity of** *in the vicinity of $3000* in the neighborhood of, near to, close to.

vicious adjective **1** *vicious dogs* fierce, ferocious, savage, dangerous, ill-natured, bad-tempered, surly, hostile. **2** *vicious remarks* malicious, malevolent, malignant, spiteful, vindictive, venomous, catty, backbiting, rancorous, caustic, mean, cruel; *inf.* bitchy. **3** *a vicious attack* violent, brutal, inhuman, barbarous, fiendish, sadistic, monstrous, heinous. **4** *a vicious band of people* corrupt, degenerate, depraved, debased, wicked, evil, immoral, unprincipled, disreputable.

victim noun **1** *they were victims of his sales patter* dupe, easy target/prey, fair game; *inf.* sitting duck, sucker, sap, fall guy, pushover. **2** *track down their victim(s)* prey, quarry, game, the hunted, target. **3** *a sacrificial victim for the gods* offering, sacrifice, scapegoat.

victimize verb **1** *bullies victimizing their classmates* persecute, bully, pick on, discriminate against, punish unfairly. **2** *con artists victimizing the naïve couple* exploit, prey on, take advantage of, swindle, dupe, cheat, trick, hoodwink.

victor verb conqueror, vanquisher, winner, champion, prizewinner, conquering hero; *inf.* champ, top dog, number one.

victorious adjective conquering, vanquishing, triumphant, winning, champion, successful, prizewinning, top, first.

vie verb compete, contend, contest.

view noun **1** *come into view* sight, field/range of vision, vision, eyeshot. **2** *the view from the mountain* outlook, prospect, scene, spectacle, vista, panorama; landscape, seascape. **3** *radical views* viewpoint, opinion, belief, judgment, thinking, thought, notion, idea, conviction, sentiment. **4** *a private view of the exhibition* viewing, sight, look, contemplation, observation, inspection, scrutiny, scan. **in view of** considering, taking into consideration, bearing in mind, taking into account. **on view** on display, on exhibition, on show.

view verb **1** *view the birds through binoculars* look at, watch, observe, contemplate, regard, behold, scan, survey, inspect, gaze at, stare at, peer at. **2** *view the house* survey, examine, scrutinize, take stock of. **3** *view the prospect with dismay* look on, consider, contemplate, think about, reflect on, ponder. **4** *view himself as an upright man* see, consider, judge, deem.

viewpoint noun point of view, way of thinking, frame of reference, perspective, angle, slant, standpoint, position, stance, vantage point.

vigilance noun watchfulness, observation, surveillance, attentiveness, attention, alertness, guardedness, carefulness, caution, wariness, circumspection, heedfulness, heed.

vigilant adjective watchful, attentive, alert, on the alert, on the qui vive, awake, wide awake, unsleeping, on one's guard, cautious, wary, circumspect, heedful.

vigor noun **1** *the natural vigor of country children* robustness, healthiness, strength, sturdiness, fitness, toughness. **2** *return to* *work with renewed vigor* energy, vitality, vivacity, vim, verve, animation, dynamism, sparkle, zest, dash, élan, gusto, zing, pep; *inf.* zip, oomph.

vigorous adjective **1** *vigorous children brought up in the country* robust, healthy, in good health, hale and hearty, strong, sturdy, fit, in good condition/shape. **2** *feel more vigorous after exercise* energetic, lively, active, spry, sprightly, vivacious, animated, dynamic. **3** *a vigorous attempt at winning* strenuous, forceful, forcible, spirited, keen, enthusiastic, ardent, fervent, vehement, intense.

vile adjective **1** *a vile taste/smell* foul, nasty, unpleasant, disagreeable, horrid, horrible, offensive, obnoxious, odious, repulsive, repellent, revolting, repugnant, disgusting, distasteful, loathsome. **2** *a vile creature | a vile thing to do* base, low, mean, wretched, dreadful, disgraceful, appalling, shocking, ugly, abominable, monstrous, wicked, evil, iniquitous, sinful, vicious, corrupt, depraved, degenerate, contemptible, despicable, reprehensible.

villain noun rogue, scoundrel, blackguard, wretch, cad, reprobate, evildoer, wrongdoer, ruffian, hoodlum, hooligan, criminal, miscreant; *inf.* baddy, crook, rat, louse.

vindicate verb **1** *he was vindicated when his alibi was proved* acquit, clear, absolve, free from blame, exonerate, exculpate. **2** *time vindicated his suspicions* justify, warrant, substantiate, testify to, verify, confirm, corroborate. **3** *vindicate his claim* defend, support, back, fight for, champion, uphold, maintain, sustain, stand by.

vindictive adjective vengeful, out for revenge, revengeful, avenging, unforgiving, resentful, implacable, unrelenting, spiteful.

vintage noun year, harvest, crop; era, epoch, period, time, generation.

vintage adjective **1** *vintage wines* high-quality, quality, prime, choice, select, superior, best. **2** *vintage comedy* classic, ageless, enduring. **3** *this story is vintage Poe* characteristic, typical, supreme, at his/her/its best.

violate verb **1** *violate a law/treaty* break, breach, infringe, contravene, infract, transgress, disobey, disregard, ignore. **2** *violate a grave* desecrate, profane, defile, blaspheme. **3** *violate their privacy* disturb, disrupt, intrude on, interfere with, encroach on, invade, upset, shatter, destroy. **4** *he was accused of violating his niece* rape, ravish, abuse, molest.

violence noun **1** *the violence of his temper* strength, forcefulness, wildness, passion. **2** *the violence of the blow* forcefulness, powerfulness, might, savagery, ferocity, destructiveness, brutality. **3** *the violence of his*

dislike strength, intensity, vehemence. **4** *use violence to get his way* force, brute force, roughness, ferocity, brutality, savagery; strong-arm tactics.

violent adjective **1** *a violent temper* strong, powerful, forceful, uncontrolled, unrestrained, unbridled, uncontrollable, ungovernable, wild, passionate, raging. **2** *he is a violent person* brutal, vicious, destructive, savage, fierce, wild, intemperate, hotheaded, hot-tempered, bloodthirsty, homicidal, murderous, maniacal. **3** *a violent blow* forceful, powerful, mighty, savage, ferocious, destructive, damaging, brutal. **4** *a violent dislike* strong, great, intense, extreme, vehement, inordinate, excessive, acute.

virgin adjective *virgin territory* pure, immaculate, unblemished, spotless, stainless, unused, untouched, untainted, unspoiled, untarnished, unadulterated.

virile adjective manly, masculine, male, all-male, strong, vigorous, robust, powerfully built, muscular, rugged, strapping, sturdy, red-blooded; *inf.* macho.

virtual adjective near, effective, in effect, tantamount to, for all practical purposes, in all but name; functioning as, operating as.

virtually adverb more or less, nearly, practically, as good as, effectively, essentially, for all practical purposes, to all intents and purposes.

virtue noun **1** *admires the virtue of workers* goodness, righteousness, morality, uprightness, integrity, rectitude, honesty, honorableness, honor, incorruptibility, probity, decency, respectability, worthiness, worth, trustworthiness. **2** *the virtue of youth* virginity, celibacy, purity, pureness, chastity, chasteness, innocence, modesty. **3** *generosity is one of her virtues* good point, merit, asset, credit, attribute, advantage, benefit, strength, plus. **4** *there is no virtue in the use of such drugs* merit, usefulness, efficacy, efficaciousness, power, potency. **by virtue of** by reason of, by dint of, on account of, as a result of, owing to, thanks to.

virtuoso noun master, genius, expert, artist, maestro, wizard.

virtuous adjective **1** *virtuous, hardworking people* good, righteous, moral, ethical, upright, upstanding, honest, honorable, incorruptible, decent, respectable, worthy, trustworthy. **2** *virtuous youth* virginal, celibate, pure, chaste, innocent, modest.

visible adjective **1** *hills scarcely visible in the mist* perceptible, perceivable, discernible, detectable, seeable. **2** *his distress was visible to all* apparent, evident, noticeable, observable, recognizable, manifest, plain, clear, obvious, unconcealed, undisguised, conspicuous.

vision noun **1** *have good vision* eyesight, sight, eyes. **2** *the prophet saw a vision* apparition, specter, phantom, ghost, wraith, phantasm, chimera, revelation. **3** *saw wild horses in one of his visions* dream, hallucination, optical illusion, mirage, illusion, delusion, figment of the imagination, daydream, pipe dream, fantasy. **4** *artists must have vision* perception, perceptiveness, insight, intuition, imagination. **5** *in need of political vision* foresight, farsightedness, prescience, breadth of view, discernment. **6** *she was a vision in white* dream, spectacle, picture, feast for the eyes, beautiful sight.

visionary adjective **1** *visionary schemes* idealistic, impractical, unrealistic, utopian, romantic, quixotic, starry-eyed, unworkable, unfeasible, theoretical, hypothetical. **2** *visionary artists* perceptive, intuitive, insightful, imaginative. **3** *visionary politicians* farsighted, discerning, wise, prescient. **4** *visionary figures* unreal, imaginary, imagined, fanciful, fancied, illusory, phantasmagoric, spectral, ghostly, wraithlike.

visionary noun **1** *ancient visionaries* mystic, seer, prophet. **2** *too much of a visionary to run a business* dreamer, daydreamer, idealist, romantic, romanticist, fantasist, theorist, utopian.

visit verb **1** *visit his aunt* pay a visit to, go/come to see, pay a call on, call on, look in on, stop by (to see); *inf.* pop/drop in on, look up. **2** *a city visited with the plague* attack, assail, afflict, smite, descend on, trouble, harrow, torture.

visit noun call, social call; stay, sojourn, stopover.

visitor noun caller, guest; tourist, traveler, pilgrim.

visualize verb conjure up, envisage, picture in the mind's eye, picture, envision, imagine.

vital adjective **1** *the vital organs* life-giving, life-preserving, life-sustaining, basic, fundamental. **2** *matters of vital importance* essential, necessary, key, important, significant, urgent, critical, crucial, life-and-death. **3** *such a vital person* lively, animated, spirited, vivacious, vibrant, zestful, dynamic, energetic, vigorous, forceful. **4** *a vital error* deadly, lethal, fatal, fateful.

vitality noun life, liveliness, animation, spirit, spiritedness, vivacity, vibrancy, zest, zestfulness, dynamism, energy, vigor, forcefulness.

vitriolic adjective caustic, mordant, bitter, acerbic, astringent, acid, acidulous, acrid, trenchant, virulent, scathing, withering, sarcastic, sardonic.

vituperation noun invective, condemnation, denunciation, castigation, chastisement, rebuke, abuse, vilification, denigration.

vivacious adjective lively, full of life, animated, effervescent, bubbling, ebullient, sparkling, scintillating, lighthearted, spirited, high-spirited, gay, merry, jolly, vibrant, dynamic, vital.

vivid adjective **1** *vivid colors* strong, intense, colorful, rich, glowing, bright, brilliant, clear. **2** *a vivid description* graphic, clear, realistic, lifelike, true to life. **3** *a vivid personality* strong, striking, flamboyant, memorable, dynamic, lively, animated, spirited, vibrant, vital.

vocal adjective **1** *vocal noises* voiced, vocalized, spoken, said, uttered, expressed. **2** *people vocal in their criticism* vociferous, outspoken, forthright, clamorous, strident, loud, noisy.

vocation noun profession, calling, occupation, walk of life, career, life's work, métier, trade, craft, job, work, employment, business, line, specialty.

vociferous adjective loud, noisy, clamorous, vehement, strident, vocal, outspoken.

vogue noun **1** *the vogue for short skirts* fashion, mode, style, trend, taste, fad, craze, rage, latest thing, last word. **2** *a hairstyle in vogue in the 1920s* fashionableness, modishness, popularity, currency, prevalence, favor, acceptance.

voice noun **1** *give voice to her feelings* expression, utterance, verbalization, vocalization, airing. **2** *the voice of the people* opinion, view, comment, feeling, wish, desire, vote. **3** *he is the voice of the company* spokesman, spokeswoman, spokesperson, mouthpiece, organ, agency, medium, vehicle.

voice verb express, give utterance to, utter, articulate, enunciate, mention, talk of, communicate, declare, assert, divulge, air, ventilate, come out with.

void adjective **1** *a void space* empty, vacant, bare, clear, free, unfilled. **2** *the ticket is now void* null and void, invalid, canceled, inoperative, ineffective, not binding, not in force.

void noun emptiness, blankness, vacuum; space, gap, lacuna, hole, hollow, chasm, abyss.

void verb **1** *void the decision* annul, nullify, disallow, invalidate, quash, cancel, repeal, revoke, rescind, reverse, abrogate. **2** *void the bowels* empty, drain, evacuate; excrete, eject, expel, emit, discharge.

volatile adjective **1** *a volatile person* mercurial, changeable, variable, capricious, whimsical, fickle, flighty, giddy, inconstant, erratic, unstable. **2** *a volatile international situation* explosive, eruptive, charged, inflammatory, tense, strained.

volition noun **of one's own volition** of one's own free will, of one's own choice, by one's own preference, voluntarily.

volley noun barrage, cannonade, battery, broadside, salvo, fusillade, shower, stream, deluge.

volume noun **1** *a volume on butterflies* book, publication, tome. **2** *measure the volume* bulk, capacity, quantity, amount, mass. **3** *turn down the volume* loudness, sound, amplification.

voluminous adjective capacious, roomy, commodious, ample, full, big, vast, billowing.

voluntary adjective **1** *attendance is voluntary* of one's own free will, volitional, of one's own accord, optional, discretional, at one's discretion, elective, noncompulsory, nonmandatory. **2** *undertake voluntary work* unpaid, honorary, volunteer.

volunteer verb offer, tender, proffer, present, put forward, advance; offer one's services, present oneself, step forward.

voluptuous adjective **1** *voluptuous pleasures* hedonistic, sybaritic, epicurean, pleasure-loving, self-indulgent, sensual, carnal, licentious, lascivious. **2** *a voluptuous woman* curvy, shapely, full-figured, buxom, seductive; *inf.* curvaceous.

vomit verb **1** *he suddenly vomited* be sick, retch, heave, spew, throw up; *inf.* puke, barf, toss one's cookies, lose one's lunch, upchuck, hurl. **2** *vomit blood* bring up, regurgitate, spew up, spit up. **3** *chimneys vomiting smoke* belch, eject, emit, send forth.

voracious adjective **1** *a voracious eater* gluttonous, greedy, ravenous, ravening,

starving, hungry. **2** *a voracious reader* insatiable, insatiate, unquenchable, prodigious, compulsive, enthusiastic, eager.

vortex noun whirlpool, maelstrom, eddy, swirl, whirlwind.

vote noun **1** *have a vote on who should be mayor* ballot, poll, election, referendum, plebiscite. **2** *get the vote* franchise, suffrage.

vouch verb **vouch for 1** *vouch for his honesty* attest to, bear witness to, give assurance of, answer for, be responsible for, guarantee. **2** *vouch for the painting's authenticity* certify, warrant, confirm, verify, validate, substantiate.

vow noun oath, pledge, promise.

vow verb swear, state under oath, pledge, promise, undertake, give one's word of honor.

voyage noun crossing, cruise, passage; journey, trip, expedition; travels.

vulgar adjective **1** *vulgar language/jokes* indecent, indecorous, indelicate, unseemly, offensive, distasteful, obnoxious, risqué, suggestive, off-color, blue, ribald, bawdy, obscene, lewd, salacious, licentious, concupiscent, smutty, dirty, filthy, pornographic, scatological; *inf.* raunchy. **2** *vulgar table manners* rude, impolite, ill-mannered, unmannerly, ill-bred, common, coarse, boorish, rough, crude. **3** *vulgar decorations* tasteless, gross, crass, unrefined, tawdry, ostentatious, showy, flashy, gaudy. **4** *the vulgar masses* common, ordinary, low, lowborn, ignorant, unsophisticated, unrefined, uneducated, illiterate, uncultured, uncouth.

vulnerable adjective open to attack, attackable, assailable, exposed, liable, subject, unprotected, unguarded, defenseless, easily hurt/wounded/damaged, powerless, helpless, weak, sensitive, thin-skinned.

Ww

wade verb **1** *wade the stream* ford, cross, traverse. **2** *wade through piles of papers* plod, plow, labor, toil/plug/peg away.

wag verb swing, sway, vibrate, quiver, shake, rock, twitch, waggle, wiggle, wobble, wave, nod, bob.

wag noun *he's quite a wag* wit, humorist, jester, joker, jokester, comic, comedian, comedienne, wisecracker, punner.

wage noun pay, remuneration. *See* WAGES 1.

wage verb carry on, conduct, execute, engage in, pursue, undertake.

wager noun bet, gamble, stake, pledge, hazard.

wager verb lay a wager, bet, place/make/lay a bet, lay odds, put money on, speculate.

wages plural noun **1** *collect one's wages* pay, payment, fee, remuneration, salary, emolument, stipend; earnings. **2** *the wages of sin* recompense, requital, retribution; returns, deserts.

waif noun stray, foundling, orphan.

wail verb cry, lament, weep, sob, moan, groan, whine, complain, howl, yowl, ululate.

wait verb **1** *wait here* stay, remain, rest, linger, tarry, abide. **2** *you will just have to wait and see* be patient, hold back, stand by, bide one's time, hang fire, mark time, cool one's heels; *inf.* sit tight, hold one's horses, sweat it out. **3** *wait his arrival* await, wait for, look/watch out for, anticipate, expect, be ready for, be in readiness for.

wait noun *have a wait of two hours for the bus* period of waiting, interval, stay, delay, holdup.

waive verb **1** *waive one's right to appeal* relinquish, renounce, give up, abandon, surrender, yield, cede. **2** *waive the rules* set aside, forgo, disregard, ignore. **3** *waive the decision until tomorrow* postpone, defer, put off, delay, shelve; *inf.* put on the back burner.

wake verb **1** *wake at dawn* awake, awaken, waken, wake up, rouse, stir, come to, get up, arise. **2** *wake him out of depression* rouse, stir up, activate, stimulate, spur, prod, galvanize, provoke. **3** *wake to the fact that he is dishonest* become aware/conscious, become alert, become mindful/heedful. **4** *wake old memories* evoke, call up, conjure up, rouse, stir, revive, resuscitate, revivify, rekindle, reignite.

wakeful adjective **1** *wakeful children* unsleeping, restless, tossing and turning, insomniac. **2** *wakeful security staff* alert, on the alert, vigilant, on the lookout, on one's guard, on the qui vive, watchful, observant, attentive, heedful, wary.

walk verb **1** *we walked rather than take the car* go by foot, travel on foot; *inf.* hoof it. **2** *walk, don't run* stroll, saunter, amble, plod, trudge, hike, tramp, trek, march, stride, step out. **3** *walk her home* accompany, escort, convoy. **walk off/away with 1** *walk off with the firm's money* make/run off with, snatch, steal, filch, pilfer, embezzle. **2** *walk off with the prize* win easily, win hands down. **walk out 1** *he had a fight with the boss and walked out* storm out; *inf.* take off. **2** *the workers walked out at lunchtime* go on strike, call a strike, stop work. **walk out on** desert, abandon, forsake, leave, leave in the lurch, throw over, jilt.

walk noun **1** *go for a walk* stroll, saunter, amble, promenade, ramble, hike, tramp, march, constitutional, airing. **2** *he has a distinctive walk* gait, pace, step, stride. **3** *the walk up to the house* promenade, path, pathway, footpath, track, lane, alley. **4** *the postman's usual walk* route, beat, round, run, circuit. **walk of life** social status, sphere, area, line of work, profession, career, vocation, job, employment, trade, craft, métier.

wall noun **1** *areas of the house separated by walls* partition, divider. **2** *the city walls are still standing* fortification, rampart, barricade, parapet, bulwark, stockade, breastwork.

wallow verb **1** *a hippopotamus wallowing in mud* roll, tumble about, lie around, splash around. **2** *wallow in self-pity* luxuriate, bask, indulge oneself, delight, revel, glory.

wan adjective **1** *looking wan after illness* pale, pallid, ashen, white as a sheet/ghost, anemic, colorless, bloodless, waxen, pasty, peaked, washed out, sickly. **2** *a wan light* dim, faint, weak.

wand noun baton, stick, rod, staff, twig, sprig.

wander verb **1** *wander over the hills* ramble, roam, meander, rove, range, prowl, saunter, stroll, amble, peregrinate, drift; *inf.* traipse. **2** *rivers wandering along* wind, meander, curve, zigzag. **3** *wander from the straight and narrow* stray, depart, diverge, veer, swerve, deviate. **4** *the narcotics make him wander* babble, talk nonsense, rave, be delirious. **wander off** lose one's way, get lost, go off course, go astray, go off on a tangent.

wanderer noun rambler, roamer, rover, drifter, traveler, itinerant, wayfarer, nomad, bird of passage, rolling stone, gypsy; vagabond, vagrant, hobo, tramp, derelict; *inf.* bum.

wane verb decrease, decline, diminish, dwindle, shrink, contract, taper off, subside, sink, ebb, dim, fade away, vanish, die out, draw to a close, evanesce, peter out, wind down, be on the way out, abate, fail.

want verb **1** *the child wants candy* wish, wish for, desire, demand, call for, long for, hope for, yearn for, pine for, fancy, crave, hanker after, hunger for, thirst for, lust after, covet, need; *inf.* have a yen for. **2** *he wants to emigrate* wish, desire, long, yearn. **3** *the garden wants weeding | the poor wanting food* need, be in need of, require; lack, be without, be devoid of, be bereft of, be short of, be deficient in.

want noun **1** *for want of time* lack, absence, dearth, deficiency, inadequacy, insufficiency, shortness, paucity, shortage, scarcity, scarceness, scantiness. **2** *children expressing their wants* wish, desire, demand, longing, yearning, fancy, craving, hankering, hunger, thirst. **3** *give aid to* *people in want* need, neediness, privation, poverty, destitution, penury, indigence.

wanting adjective **1** *find the service wanting* lacking, deficient, inadequate, imperfect, not up to standard/par, not good enough, disappointing, not acceptable, not up to expectations, flawed, faulty, defective, inferior, second-rate. **2** *something wanting in the machine/organization* lacking, missing, absent, not there, short.

wanton adjective **1** *wanton behavior* promiscuous, fast, immoral, loose, immodest, shameless, unchaste, impure, lustful, lecherous, lascivious, libidinous, licentious, libertine, dissolute, dissipated, debauched, degenerate. **2** *wanton destruction* willful, malicious, malevolent, spiteful, cruel, unmotivated, arbitrary, groundless, unjustified, uncalled-for, unprovoked, gratuitous, senseless, pointless. **3** *a wanton wind* capricious, playful, sportive, careless, heedless, devil-may-care. **4** *weeds growing in wanton profusion* wild, unrestrained, uncontrolled, immoderate, lavish, extravagant, abundant, profuse, luxuriant.

war noun **1** *a state of war between the nations* conflict, strife, hostility, enmity, antagonism, animus, ill will, bad blood. **2** *the war lasted five years* warfare, combat, fighting, struggle, battle, fight, confrontation, skirmish; hostilities. **3** *the war against poverty* battle, fight, campaign, crusade.

war verb wage/make war, be at war, do battle, fight, take up arms, cross swords, quarrel, wrangle.

ward verb *ward off* fend off, stave off, parry, avert, deflect, turn aside, drive back, repel, repulse, beat back, put to flight, keep at bay, keep at arm's length, rebuff, foil, frustrate, thwart, checkmate.

warden noun custodian, keeper, guardian, protector, guard, watchman.

wares plural noun goods, products, commodities, lines; merchandise, produce, stuff, stock.

warfare noun conflict, strife. *See* WAR noun 1, 2.

warlike adjective aggressive, belligerent, bellicose, pugnacious, combative, militaristic, militant, martial.

warm adjective **1** *warm water* heated, tepid, lukewarm. **2** *a warm day* sunny, balmy. **3** *a warm person* kindly, kind, friendly, affable, amiable, genial, cordial, sympathetic, affectionate, loving, tender, caring. **4** *a warm welcome* hearty, enthusiastic, eager, sincere, heartfelt, ardent, vehement, passionate, intense, fervent. **5** *the international situation is getting rather warm* heated, tense, strained, dangerous, perilous, hazardous, tricky, difficult, unpleasant, uncomfortable.

warm verb *warm the food in the oven* warm up, make warm, heat, heat up, reheat.

warm up 1 *warm the party up* liven, enliven, put some life into, cheer up, animate; *inf.* get going. **2** *warm up for the race* loosen up, limber up, condition, prepare, exercise, practice, train.

warmth noun **1** *feel the warmth of the fire/sun* warmness, heat, hotness. **2** *the warmth of her personality* kindliness, friendliness, affability, amiability, geniality, cordiality, sympathy, tenderness, charitableness, charity, sincerity, genuineness. **3** *the warmth of the welcome* heartiness, hospitality, enthusiasm, eagerness, sincerity, ardor, vehemence, passion, intensity, fervor.

warn verb **1** *call to warn them of the coming storm* inform, notify, give notice, let know, alert, acquaint, give fair warning, forewarn; *inf.* tip off, put wise. **2** *warn them to be careful* advise, exhort, urge, counsel, caution, forewarn.

warrant noun authorization, consent, sanction, permission, validation, license, imprimatur, seal of approval.

warrant verb **1** *the law warrants the procedure* authorize, sanction, permit, license. **2** *her interference was not warranted* justify, vindicate, excuse, be a defense of, explain away, account for. **3** *unable to warrant the truth of the statement* guarantee, swear to, vouch for, testify to, bear witness to, support, endorse.

warrior noun fighter, fighting man, combatant, soldier, champion.

wary adjective **1** *be wary when you walk alone at night* careful, cautious, circumspect, chary, on one's guard, alert, on the alert/look out, on the qui vive, attentive, heedful, watchful, vigilant, observant. **2** *you should be wary of strangers* suspicious, distrustful, mistrustful, leery.

wash verb **1** *I must wash before breakfast* wash oneself, bathe, shower, take a bath/shower. **2** *wash one's face | wash the floor* clean, cleanse, sponge, scrub. **3** *waves washing against the rocks* splash, dash, break, beat. **4** *his story just won't wash* hold up, hold water, stand up, bear scrutiny. **5** *the current washed the boat away* carry, bear, sweep, convey, transport. **6** *wash away the riverbank* erode, abrade, wear, denude.

wash noun washing, clean, cleaning, cleansing; bath, shower, laundry.

waspish adjective petulant, peevish, querulous, touchy, testy, irritable, cross, snappish, splenetic, ill-tempered, crabby, crabbed.

waste verb **1** *waste resources/money* squander, dissipate, fritter away, misspend, misuse, spend recklessly, throw away, go through, run through; *inf.* blow. **2** *the disease had wasted his legs* weaken, enfeeble, sap the strength of, wither, debilitate, atrophy, emaciate, shrivel, shrink. **3** *the invading army wasted the land* destroy, devastate, wreak havoc on, pillage, plunder, sack, spoliate, loot, maraud.

waste noun **1** *a waste of money/time* squandering, dissipation, frittering away, misspending, misuse. **2** *dispose of the waste* rubbish, refuse, garbage, trash, debris, dross; dregs, leavings. **3** *lost in the waste of Antarctica* desert, wasteland, wilderness, barrenness, emptiness.

waste adjective **1** *waste material* left over, unused, superfluous. **2** *the land was waste* desert, barren, uncultivated, unproductive, arid, bare, desolate.

wasteful adjective prodigal, profligate, thriftless, spendthrift, extravagant, lavish.

watch verb **1** *watch the moon* look at, observe, view, eye, gaze at, stare at, gape at, peer at, contemplate, behold, inspect, scrutinize, survey, scan, examine. **2** *watch the children* mind, take care of, look after, supervise, superintend, tend, guard, protect, keep an eye on. **watch out 1** *watch out and don't get mugged* look out, pay attention, take heed/care, be careful, be on the alert/lookout, be vigilant, be wary; *inf.* keep one's eyes peeled. **2** *watch out for the delivery truck* look (out) for, wait for; *inf.* keep an eye open for. **watch over** look after, tend. *See* WATCH verb 2.

watch noun **1** *the time by my watch* wristwatch, pocket watch, timepiece, chronometer. **2** *on watch at night* guard, vigil, surveillance.

watchful adjective observant, alert, vigilant, attentive, heedful, sharp-eyed, eagle-eyed, wary, circumspect.

watchman noun security guard, guard, custodian, caretaker.

water noun **1** *drink water* H_2O; tap water, drinking water, mineral water, bottled water. **2** *have a picnic by the water* sea, ocean, sound, bay, river, lake, pond, pool, reservoir. **hold water** be tenable, ring true, bear examination, work out.

water verb **1** *water the garden* sprinkle, moisten, dampen, wet, water down, douse, hose, spray, drench, saturate, sodden, flood. **2** *water the drinks* water down, dilute, thin, weaken, adulterate. **water down** *water down the extent of the disaster* play down, downplay, tone down, soft-pedal, understate, underemphasize.

waterfall noun cascade, cataract; falls.

watery adjective **1** *a watery substance* aqueous, liquid, liquefied, fluid, hydrous. **2** *watery terrain* wet, damp, moist, sodden, soggy, saturated, waterlogged, marshy,

boggy, swampy, miry. **3** *a watery soup/batter* thin, runny, weak, dilute, diluted, watered down, adulterated, tasteless, flavorless.

wave verb **1** *wheat waving in the breeze* undulate, ripple, stir, flutter, flap, sway, swing, shake, quiver, oscillate. **2** *wave one's hand/flag* wag, waggle, flutter. **3** *wave a sword in the air* brandish, swing, shake. **4** *wave to them to follow* gesture, gesticulate, signal, sign, beckon, indicate.

wave noun **1** *children playing in the waves* breaker, billow, roller, ripple, whitecap; swell, surf. **2** *a wave of visitors* stream, flow, rush, surge, flood. **3** *a wave of enthusiasm* surge, upsurge, groundswell, welling up, rush, outbreak, rash.

waver verb **1** *his gaze did not waver* falter, wobble, hesitate. **2** *waver between staying and leaving* hesitate, dither, hem and haw, vacillate, shilly-shally. **3** *lights wavering* flicker, quiver, tremble.

wavy adjective undulating, curvy, curling, squiggly, rippled, curving, winding.

wax verb **1** *his power waxed in time of war* increase, develop, enlarge, magnify, extend, widen, broaden, spread, mushroom. **2** *wax lyrical about his achievements* become, grow.

way noun **1** *walk along the paved way* road, roadway, street, thoroughfare, track, path, pathway, lane, avenue, drive. **2** *is this the way to their house?* route, course, direction. **3** *the right way to cook the meat* method, procedure, technique, system, plan, scheme, manner, modus operandi; means. **4** *the American way* conduct, behavior, practice, wont, manner, style, nature, personality, temperament, disposition, character; habit, custom, characteristic, trait, attribute, mannerism, peculiarity, idiosyncrasy. **5** *a long way from here* distance, length, stretch, journey. **6** *things are in a bad way* state, condition, situation, shape. **7** *can I help in any way?* feature, aspect, detail, point, particular, respect, sense. **by the way** incidentally, by the by, in passing. **give way 1** *the bridge gave way* collapse, give, fall to pieces, crumble, cave in. **2** *he refused to help but finally gave way* yield, back down, acquiesce. **on the/one's way** coming, going, proceeding, journeying, traveling.

waylay verb lie in wait for, ambush, hold up, attack; accost, intercept, pounce on, swoop down on.

wayward adjective **1** *wayward children* willful, contrary, uncooperative, refractory, recalcitrant, contumacious, unruly, ungovernable, unmanageable, incorrigible, intractable, difficult, fractious, disobedient, insubordinate. **2** *wayward fancies* capricious, whimsical, fickle, inconstant, changeable, unpredictable, mercurial, volatile, flighty.

weak adjective **1** *too weak to walk* weakly, frail, fragile, delicate, feeble, infirm, shaky, debilitated, incapacitated, ailing, indisposed, decrepit, puny, faint, enervated, tired, fatigued, spent. **2** *too weak to stand up for his rights* timid, spineless, ineffectual, powerless, impotent, namby-pamby, soft, weak-kneed. **3** *weak eyesight* defective, faulty, poor, inadequate, deficient, imperfect, substandard. **4** *weak excuses* unsound, feeble, flimsy, lame, unconvincing, untenable, implausible. **5** *a weak sound/signal* faint, low, muffled, stifled, muted. **6** *weak coffee* diluted, watery, thinned down, thin, adulterated, tasteless, flavorless, insipid; *inf.* wishy-washy.

weaken verb **1** *the illness had weakened her* enfeeble, debilitate, incapacitate, sap one's strength, enervate, tire, exhaust, wear out. **2** *weaken the force of the argument* lessen, reduce, decrease, diminish, moderate, temper, sap. **3** *the force of the storm weakened* abate, dwindle, ease up, let up. **4** *weaken the argument* impair, undermine, invalidate. **5** *they first refused to help but weakened later* relent, give in, yield, give way, accede, come around. **6** *too much milk weakened the coffee* dilute, water down, thin, adulterate.

weakling noun coward, mouse, milksop, namby-pamby, sissy; *inf.* wimp, chicken, yellowbelly, fraidy-cat, scaredy-cat.

weakness noun **1** *the weakness of the invalid* frailty, fragility, delicateness, delicacy, feebleness, infirmity, debility, incapacity, indisposition, decrepitude, puniness, enervation, fatigue. **2** *despise his weakness* cowardliness, timidity, spinelessness, ineffectuality, ineptness, powerlessness, impotence. **3** *the weakness of her eyesight* defectiveness, faultiness, inadequacy, deficiency. **4** *the weakness of the excuses* unsoundness, feebleness, flimsiness, lameness, untenability, implausibility. **5** *the weakness of the sound/light* faintness, mutedness, dimness. **6** *the weakness of the coffee* wateriness, thinness, tastelessness, flavorlessness; *inf.* wishy-washiness. **7** *extravagance is one of her weaknesses* weak point, failing, foible, fault, flaw, defect, shortcoming, imperfection, blemish, Achilles' heel, chink in one's armor. **8** *a weakness for chocolate* soft spot, fondness, liking, partiality, preference, leaning, inclination, proclivity.

wealth noun **1** *amass wealth* money, cash, capital, treasure, fortune, finance, property; riches, assets, possessions, resources, goods, funds, wherewithal; *inf.* dough, bread. **2** *people of wealth* richness, money, affluence, prosperity, substance; means. **3** *a wealth of opportunities* mass, abundance, profusion, plenitude, amplitude, bounty, cornucopia.

wealthy adjective rich, well off, well-to-do, moneyed, affluent, prosperous, of means, of substance; *inf.* well-heeled, rolling in it/money, in the money, made of money, filthy/stinking rich, loaded, flush, on easy street.

wear verb **1** *wear beautiful clothes* be dressed in, dress in, be clothed in, cloth oneself in, have on, put on, don, sport. **2** *she wore an anxious expression* have, assume, present, show, display, exhibit. **3** *wind and rain have worn the rock* erode, corrode, abrade, wash away, rub away, rub down, grind away, wear down/away. **4** *the carpet is starting to wear* become worn, show signs of wear, wear thin, fray, become threadbare. **5** *she is worn by the whole experience* fatigue, exhaust. *See* WEAR OUT 2 (WEAR verb). **6** *this carpet has worn well* last, endure, hold up, survive, bear up, stand up to wear, prove durable. **wear down 1** *the steps have become worn down* wear away, erode. *See* WEAR verb 3. **2** *wear down their resistance* erode, undermine; *inf.* chip away at. **wear off** *the novelty will soon wear off* fade, peter out, dwindle, decrease, diminish, disappear, subside, ebb, wane. **wear on** *as time wore on* pass, go by, move on, roll on. **wear out 1** *children wear out their clothes quickly* wear thin, make threadbare, fray. **2** *the job has quite worn her out* fatigue, tire, weary, exhaust, drain, strain, stress, weaken, enfeeble, prostrate, enervate; *inf.* wear to a frazzle, poop out.

wear noun **1** *clothes/items for everyday wear* use, service, employment. **2** *pack away her winter wear* clothing, attire, apparel, wardrobe; clothes, garments, outfits; *inf.* gear. **3** *showing signs of wear and tear* erosion, corrosion, abrasion, deterioration, degeneration, damage.

weary adjective **1** *weary at the end of a hard day's work* fatigued, tired, exhausted, drained, worn, worn out, spent, wearied; *inf.* dead tired/beat, dead on one's feet, dog-tired, all in, done in, pooped (out), bushed. **2** *a weary journey* wearisome, fatiguing, tiring, exhausting, wearing, trying, taxing, irksome, tiresome, laborious, boring, tedious, dull. **3** *she is weary of the job* bored, fed up, discontented, jaded.

weary verb fatigue, tire, exhaust, drain, wear out; *inf.* wear to a frazzle, poop out.

weather noun **under the weather** below par, unwell, out of sorts, indisposed, ailing, ill, sick.

weather verb **1** *weather the wood* dry, season, expose. **2** *rocks weathered by storms* erode, wear, bleach. **3** *weather the recession* survive, withstand, bear up against, stand, endure, ride out; *inf.* stick out.

weave verb **1** *weave flowers into garlands* interlace, intertwine, interwork, entwine, braid, plait. **2** *weave a story* make up, fabricate, put together, construct, invent, create, contrive. **3** *weave in and out of the crowds* zigzag, wind, crisscross.

web noun lacework, lattice, latticework, mesh, net, netting; network, tissue, tangle, knot.

wed verb **1** *they wed tomorrow* get married, marry; *inf.* get hitched, tie the knot. **2** *the two firms have been virtually wedded for years* unite, join, merge, amalgamate, fuse, link, ally.

wedded adjective married, marital, matrimonial, connubial, conjugal, nuptial.

wedge noun chunk, lump, block.

wedge verb *wedged himself into the crowded backseat* thrust, stuff, pack, ram, force, cram, squeeze, jam.

weep verb cry, shed tears, sob, blubber, snivel, whimper, whine, moan, lament, grieve, mourn, keen, wail; *inf.* boo-hoo.

weigh verb **1** *the child weighs 50 pounds* have a weight of; *inf.* tip the scales at. **2** *weigh one plan against the other* balance, compare, evaluate. **weigh down** load (down), overload, burden, overburden, weigh on, bear down on, press down on, oppress, trouble. **weigh up** *weigh up the situation* consider, contemplate, think over, mull over, ponder, deliberate upon, meditate on, muse on, brood over, reflect on.

weight noun **1** *what is the weight of the flour?* heaviness; poundage, tonnage. **2** *lack of money is a weight on his mind* burden, load, onus, millstone, albatross, strain, millstone around one's neck, cross to bear. **3** *how much weight is attached to his statement?* importance, significance, consequence, value, substance, force, influence; *inf.* clout.

weighty adjective **1** *weighty loads* heavy, massive, burdensome, cumbersome, ponderous, hefty. **2** *weighty responsibility* burdensome, onerous, oppressive, worrisome, stressful. **3** *weighty matters* important, of great import, significant, momentous, of moment, consequential, of consequence, vital, crucial, serious, grave. **4** *weighty arguments* cogent, powerful, potent, forceful, effective, persuasive.

weird adjective **1** *weird things were happening* strange, uncanny, eerie, mysterious, mystifying, unnatural, unearthly, ghostly; *inf.* spooky, creepy. **2** *she wears weird clothes* odd, eccentric, bizarre, outlandish, freakish, grotesque; *inf.* offbeat, far-out, way-out.

welcome noun *receive a welcome from their hostess* greeting, salutation, reception.

welcome verb bid welcome to, greet, receive, embrace, receive with open arms, roll out the red carpet for, meet, usher in.

welcome adjective *welcome guests/news* wanted, appreciated, desirable, pleasant, agreeable, to one's liking.

welfare noun **1** *concern for the welfare of the firm* well-being, health, soundness, security, prosperity, success, good fortune. **2** *poor families on welfare* state aid, public assistance; social security, dole.

well adverb **1** *behave well* satisfactorily, correctly, rightly, properly, fittingly, suitably, nicely. **2** *get on well* agreeably, pleasantly, happily; *inf.* famously, capitally. **3** *he plays the piano well* ably, competently, proficiently, adeptly, skillfully, expertly, admirably, excellently. **4** *treat their guests well* kindly, in a kind/kindly way, genially, affably, generously, hospitably, civilly, politely. **5** *polish it well* thoroughly, completely, efficiently, effectively, conscientiously, industriously, carefully. **6** *we don't know her well* fully, deeply, profoundly, intimately, personally. **7** *listen to it well* closely, attentively, carefully, conscientiously. **8** *speak well of him* highly, admiringly, with praise, glowingly, approvingly, favorably, warmly. **9** *live well* comfortably, in comfort, prosperously. **10** *you may well be right* probably, possibly, likely, undoubtedly, certainly. **11** *he is well over forty* considerably, markedly, substantially. **12** *it bodes well for the future* auspiciously, propitiously. **as well** too, also, in addition, besides, into the bargain, to boot.

well adjective **1** *the patient is quite well now* healthy, in good health, fit, strong, robust, hale and hearty, able-bodied. **2** *all is well now* satisfactory, all right, (just) fine, good, thriving, flourishing; *inf.* OK, fine and dandy. **3** *it would be well to leave early* advisable, fitting, proper, wise, prudent, sensible.

well-being noun good health, happiness, comfort. *See* WELFARE 1.

well-bred adjective well brought up, mannerly, well-mannered, courteous, polite, civil, ladylike, gentlemanly, gallant, chivalrous, cultivated, refined, polished, cultured.

well-known adjective known, familiar; famous, famed, renowned, celebrated, noted, notable, illustrious, eminent.

well off adjective **1** *his parents are poor but he is very well off* rich, well-to-do. *See* WEALTHY. **2** *he doesn't know when he is well off* fortunate, lucky, comfortable, thriving, successful, flourishing.

well-spoken adjective articulate, eloquent, fluent, silver-tongued, smooth-talking.

wet adjective **1** *wet clothes/ground* damp, dampened, moist, moistened; soaked, drenched, saturated, sopping/dripping/wringing wet, sopping, dripping, soggy, waterlogged. **2** *a wet day* rainy, raining, pouring, showery, drizzling, damp, humid, dank, misty. **wet blanket** killjoy; *inf.* party pooper, gloomy Gus.

wet noun **1** *the wet damaged the table/land* wetness, damp, dampness, moisture, condensation, humidity, water, liquid. **2** *get in out of the wet* rain, drizzle, damp.

wet verb dampen, damp, moisten, sprinkle, spray, splash, water, irrigate, douse, wet through, soak, saturate.

wharf noun pier, quay, dock, jetty; mooring(s).

wheedle verb coax, cajole, beguile, charm, flatter, inveigle, win over, talk into, persuade, induce, entice, influence; *inf.* butter up.

wheel noun disk, hoop, circle, ring. **at the wheel** driving, steering; in charge, in command, in control; *inf.* at the helm, in the driver's seat.

wheel verb **1** *birds wheeling around* circle, rotate, revolve, spin. **2** *wheel a stroller* push, shove, trundle.

wheeze verb gasp, whistle, hiss, rasp.

whet verb **1** *whet a blade* sharpen, put an edge on, edge, hone, strop, file, grind, rasp. **2** *whet the curiosity* stimulate, excite, arouse, rouse, kindle, quicken.

whiff noun **1** *a whiff of air* puff, breath, gust, draft. **2** *a whiff of the perfume* smell, scent, odor, aroma, stink, reek. **3** *a whiff of scandal* hint, suggestion, trace, suspicion, soupçon.

while noun time, spell, period, interval.

whim noun **1** *have a sudden whim* notion, fancy, idea, impulse, urge, caprice, vagary. **2** *behavior ruled by whim* whimsy, capriciousness, caprice, volatility, fickleness.

whimper verb whine, cry, sniffle, snivel, moan, wail, groan.

whimsical adjective fanciful, fantastical, playful, waggish, quaint, unusual, curious, droll.

whine verb whimper, cry; complain, grumble, moan, groan, fuss, lament; *inf.* grouse, gripe, bellyache, beef.

whip verb **1** *condemned for whipping his crew* lash, flog, scourge, flagellate, birch, switch, strap, cane, thrash, beat, strike, castigate; *inf.* belt, tan, give a hiding to, beat the living daylights out of. **2** *whip a handkerchief from his pocket* whisk, flash, snatch, pull, yank, jerk, produce, remove. **3** *he whipped around the corner* dart, dash, dive, dodge, shoot, tear, rush, fly, bolt, zoom. **4** *whip the opposition at football* defeat, overcome, overpower, overwhelm, thrash, trounce, crush, rout. **5** *whip them into a frenzy* rouse, stir up, incite, goad, prod, spur, prompt, agitate.

whip noun lash, scourge, flagellum, horsewhip, bullwhip, cat o'nine tails, knout, birch, switch, thong, crop, riding crop, cane.

whirl verb **1** *dancers whirling* circle, spin, rotate, revolve, wheel, twirl, swirl, gyrate, reel, pirouette, pivot. **2** *buses whirling past* speed, rush, race, shoot, tear, charge, whip. **3** *my head is whirling* go round, spin, reel.

whirl noun **1** *give the wheel a whirl* turn, spin, rotation, revolution, wheel, twirl, swirl, gyration, reel, pirouette, pivot. **2** *the social whirl* activity, bustle, flurry, to-do, hurly-burly. **3** *a whirl of parties* round, succession, series, sequence, progression, string, chain, cycle. **4** *with heads in a whirl* spin, dither, daze, muddle, jumble. **5** *give the new game a whirl* try, tryout, test, go; *inf.* shot, stab.

whirlpool noun vortex, maelstrom, eddy.

whirlwind noun cyclone, tornado, twister, dust devil.

whirlwind adjective lightning, swift, rapid, quick, speedy, hasty, headlong, impulsive.

whisk verb **1** *the horse whisked its tail* wave, flick, brandish. **2** *whisk the table clean / whisk away the crumbs* brush, sweep, wipe. **3** *whisk a handkerchief out of his pocket* snatch, pull. *See* WHIP verb 2. **4** *the cat whisked around the corner* dart, dash. *See* WHIP verb 3.

whisper verb **1** *whisper endearments* murmur, mutter, breathe, say under the breath. **2** *trees whispering in the wind* rustle, sigh, sough, swish, swoosh.

whisper noun **1** *speak in a whisper* murmur, mutter, hushed tone, undertone. **2** *the whisper of trees in the wind* rustle, sigh, sough, swish, swoosh. **3** *there is a whisper that he has been promoted* rumor, report, insinuation, suggestion, hint; gossip, word. **4** *a whisper of hostility about the room* whiff, trace, tinge, hint, suggestion, suspicion.

white adjective **1** *a white face* white as a ghost/sheet, chalk-white, pale, wan, pallid, ashen, waxen, pasty, peaky. **2** *white hair* gray, silver, hoary, snow-white.

white-collar adjective office, clerical, professional, executive, salaried.

whittle verb cut, hew, pare, shave, trim; carve, shape, model. **whittle away 1** *inflation whittled away their savings* wear away, eat away, erode, consume, use up, undermine, destroy. **2** *the number of employees has been whittled away* reduce, lessen, decrease, diminish, cut back.

whole adjective **1** *three whole days* entire, complete, full, total, solid, integral, unabridged, unreduced, undivided, uncut. **2** *he came home whole* intact, sound, flawless, in one piece, unimpaired, undamaged, unharmed, unhurt, uninjured, unmutilated.

whole noun entity, unit, ensemble, totality, entirety. **on the whole 1** *on the whole, he is perfect for the job* all in all, all things considered, by and large. **2** *on the whole, he works late* as a rule, as a general rule, generally, in the main, for the most part.

wholehearted adjective enthusiastic, zealous, earnest, committed, unreserved, unqualified, unstinting, complete, sincere, genuine.

wholesome adjective health-giving, healthful, good for one, salubrious, salutary; uplifting, edifying, helpful, beneficial.

wholly adverb **1** *wholly in favor of the scheme* completely, fully, entirely, totally, utterly, thoroughly, altogether, unreservedly, heart and soul; *inf.* one hundred percent. **2** *the burden rests wholly on his shoulders* only, solely, exclusively, purely.

whoop noun cry, call, shout, yell, scream, shriek, hoot, cheer, hurrah; *inf.* holler.

whore noun prostitute, call girl, streetwalker, harlot, lady of the evening/night, *fille de joie*, woman of ill repute, wanton, loose woman, trollop, slut, fallen woman, courtesan; *inf.* tart, hooker, hustler.

wicked adjective **1** *a wicked man* evil, sinful, bad, black-hearted, villainous, base, vile, vicious, dishonorable, unprincipled, unrighteous, criminal, lawless, perverted, immoral, amoral, unethical, corrupt, dissolute, abandoned, dissipated, degenerate, reprobate, debauched, depraved, unholy, impious, irreligious, ungodly, godless, devilish. **2** *his wicked deeds* sinful, iniquitous, wrong, foul, mean, gross, odious, obnoxious, nefarious, heinous, flagitious, infamous, dreadful, dire, grim, horrible, hideous, gruesome, monstrous, atrocious, abominable, abhorrent, loathsome, hateful, detestable, reprehensible, dishonorable, disgraceful, shameful, ignoble, ignominious, unlawful, illicit, illegal, villainous, dastardly, blackguardly, profane, blasphemous, irreverent, damnable, demonic, diabolic. **3** *hurt by her wicked remarks* spiteful, malicious, malignant, nasty, offensive, hurtful, distressing, galling, vexatious. **4** *aim a wicked blow* dangerous, perilous, destructive, harmful, injurious, ferocious, fierce, terrible, mighty. **5** *a wicked sense of humor* mischievous, impish, roguish, arch, rascally, naughty. **6** *the weather has been wicked* nasty, unpleasant, disagreeable, dreadful, terrible, awful.

wide adjective **1** *a wide river/building* broad, extensive, spacious, spread out, ample. **2** *a wide range of subjects* extensive, vast, far-ranging, immense, wide-ranging, expansive, sweeping, encyclopedic, comprehensive, general, all-embracing, catholic, compendious.

wide adverb **1** *open your mouth wide* as far as possible, fully, completely. **2** *he shot wide* wide of the mark/target, off target, off course, astray. **wide awake 1** *still wide awake at dawn* fully awake, open-eyed. **2** *you have to be wide awake to do business with them* alert, vigilant, wary, chary, watchful, observant, attentive, heedful, aware; *inf.* on one's toes, on the ball. **wide open 1** *with eyes wide open* fully open, dilated, gaping. **2** *with arms wide open* outspread, spread open, outstretched. **3** *wide open to attack* exposed, vulnerable, unprotected, unguarded, defenseless, at risk, in danger. **4** *the outcome of the game was wide open* uncertain, unsure, indeterminate, unsettled, unpredictable, in the balance, up in the air, anyone's guess.

widen verb broaden, expand, extend, enlarge, increase, augment, add to, supplement.

widespread adjective universal, common, general, far-reaching, far-flung, prevalent, rife, extensive, sweeping, pervasive, epidemic.

width noun wideness, breadth, broadness, span, diameter, thickness, ampleness, scope, range, span, extensiveness, vastness.

wield verb **1** *wield a sword* brandish, flourish, wave, swing, shake, use, put to use, employ, handle, ply, manipulate. **2** *wield the power in the country* exercise, exert, be possessed of, have, hold, maintain, command, control, manage.

wife noun spouse, mate, consort, woman, helpmate, squaw, bride; *inf.* better/other half, missus; *derog.* old woman/lady, the little woman, the lady of the house.

wild adjective **1** *wild cats/horses* untamed, undomesticated, unbroken, feral, savage, fierce, ferocious. **2** *wild plants* uncultivated, natural, native, indigenous. **3** *wild peoples/tribes* uncivilized, primitive, ignorant, savage, barbaric, barbarous, brutish, ferocious, fierce. **4** *wild countryside* unpopulated, uninhabited, unsettled, unfrequented, empty, barren, waste, desolate, forsaken, godforsaken, isolated. **5** *a wild night* stormy, tempestuous, turbulent, blustery, howling, violent, raging, furious, rough. **6** *a wild life* undisciplined, unrestrained, unconstrained, uncontrolled, out of control, uncurbed, unbridled, unchecked, chaotic, disorderly. **7** *a wild crowd* rowdy, unruly, disorderly, noisy, turbulent, violent, lawless, riotous, unmanageable, ungovernable. **8** *the crowd went wild* beside oneself, berserk, frantic, frenzied, in a frenzy, hysterical, crazed, mad, distracted, distraught; *inf.* crazy. **9** *lost his temper and was wild* angry, infuriated, incensed, exasperated, in a temper, seething, mad. **10** *wild schemes* extravagant, fantastical, impracticable, foolish, ill-advised, ill-considered, imprudent, unwise, madcap, impulsive, reckless, rash, outrageous, preposterous. **11** *wild about rock music* enthusiastic, eager, avid, agog; *inf.* crazy, mad, nuts. **12** *a wild guess* arbitrary, random, hit-or-miss, haphazard, uninformed, unknowledgeable. **13** *wild hair* uncombed, unkempt, disheveled, tousled, windblown, disarranged, untidy.

wilderness noun **1** *the Arctic wilderness* desert, wasteland, waste, jungle, no-man's land; wilds. **2** *a wilderness of cars* confusion, tangle, jumble, muddle, clutter, miscellany, hodgepodge.

wile noun trickery, craftiness, craft, cunning, artfulness, slyness, guile, chicanery, fraud, deception; trick, dodge, ruse, subterfuge, ploy, stratagem, lure, artifice, maneuver, device, contrivance.

will[1] verb *come when you will* wish, want, desire, please, see/think fit, think best, choose, prefer, opt, elect.

will[2] verb **1** *God willed it* decree, order, ordain, command, direct, bid, intend, wish, desire. **2** *will him all her books* bequeath, leave, give, hand/pass down to, pass on to, transfer to.

will[3] noun **1** *freedom of will* volition, choice, option, decision, discretion, prerogative, desire, wish, preference, inclination, fancy, mind. **2** *it is the will of God* decree, ordinance, dictate. **3** *he lacks the will to succeed* willpower, determination, resolution, resolve, firmness of purpose, purposefulness, doggedness, single-mindedness, commitment, moral fiber, pluck, mettle, grit, nerve. **4** *bear him ill will* feeling, disposition, attitude. **at will** *come and go at will* as one wishes/pleases, as one thinks fit, to suit oneself.

willful adjective **1** *willful neglect* deliberate, intentional, intended, conscious, purposeful, premeditated, planned, calculated. **2** *coping with willful children* headstrong, strong-willed, obstinate, stubborn, stubborn as a mule, mulish, pigheaded, bullheaded, obdurate, intransigent, intractable, refractory, recalcitrant, contrary, perverse, wayward.

willing adjective **1** *willing helpers* ready, eager, keen, enthusiastic, avid. **2** *willing to accept responsibility* prepared, ready, disposed, agreeable, amenable, in the mood, compliant; *inf.* game. **3** *willing help* cooperative, accommodating, obliging.

willpower noun strength of will, determination. *See* WILL[3] 3.

wilt verb **1** *plants wilting* droop, wither, shrivel, sag, languish. **2** *their courage wilted* diminish, dwindle, lessen, grow less, flag, fade, melt away, ebb, wane, weaken, fail.

wily adjective crafty, cunning, artful, sharp, astute, shrewd, scheming, intriguing, shifty, foxy, sly, guileful, deceitful, deceptive, underhanded.

win verb **1** *win first prize* achieve, attain, earn, gain, receive, obtain, acquire, procure, get, secure, collect, pick up, come away with, net; *inf.* bag. **2** *may the best side win* be victorious, gain the victory, overcome, achieve mastery, carry the day, finish first, come out ahead, come out on top, succeed, triumph, prevail, win out. **win over** bring around, persuade, induce, influence, sway, prevail upon, convert.

win noun victory, conquest, success, triumph.

wince verb grimace, start, flinch, blench, quail, shrink, recoil, cringe, squirm.

wind noun **1** *a day almost entirely without wind* zephyr, breeze, gust, blast, gale. **2** *need a lot of wind to play the trombone* breath, respiration; *inf.* puff. **3** *a pompous fool full of wind* empty talk, talk, babble, blather, boasting, bluster, braggadocio; *inf.* hot air, baloney, gas. **4** *wind of a scandal* rumor, gossip, hint, suggestion, inkling, intimation; news, information, report, intelligence. **in the wind** about to happen, in the offing, on the way, coming near, close at hand, approaching, impending, looming, in the cards.

wind verb **1** *the road winds up the hill* twist, twist and turn, curve, bend, loop, zigzag, snake, spiral, meander, ramble. **2** *smoke winding up into the sky* curl, spiral, wreathe, snake. **3** *wind the yarn into a ball* twist, twine, coil, wrap, roll. **wind down 1** *the runners need to wind down after a race* unwind, relax, ease up, calm down, cool off. **2** *schoolwork is winding down for the summer* slacken off, taper off, dwindle, diminish, lessen, decline, come to an end/close. **wind up 1** *he gets wound up easily* make tense, strain, make nervous, work up, put on edge, agitate, fluster, disconcert, discompose. **2** *it's time to wind up the meeting* end, conclude, terminate, finish; *inf.* wrap up. **3** *we wound up in a remote village* end up, finish, find oneself.

windy adjective **1** *a windy day* breezy, blowy, blustery, blustering, gusty, gusting, boisterous, squally, stormy, wild, tempestuous, turbulent. **2** *a windy speech* long-winded, loquacious, wordy, verbose, rambling, meandering, prolix, diffuse, turgid, bombastic.

wing noun **1** *the extreme wing of the party* arm, side, branch, section, segment, group, grouping, circle, faction, clique, set, coterie, cabal. **2** *the east wing of the house* extension, annex, addition, ell.

wing verb **1** *birds winging through the air* fly, glide, soar. **2** *winged to the finish line* zoom, speed, race, hurry, hasten. **3** *the bullet winged the bird/soldier* wound, hit, clip.

wink verb **1** *wink an eye* blink, flutter, bat, nictitate. **2** *lights winking across the water* flash, twinkle, sparkle, glitter, gleam. **wink at** *wink at the child's mistakes* turn a blind eye to, close/shut one's eyes to, blink at, ignore, overlook, disregard, let pass, condone, tolerate.

winner noun champion, victor, vanquisher, conqueror, conquering hero, prizewinner.

wintry adjective **1** *a wintry day* cold, chilly, icy, frosty, freezing, frozen, snowy, arctic, glacial, biting, piercing, nippy. **2** *a wintry look* unfriendly, cool, chilly, cold, distant, remote, bleak, cheerless.

wipe verb rub, brush, dust, mop, sponge, swab, clean, dry. **wipe off** rub off, brush off, mop up, sponge off, clean off, remove, get rid of, take off, take away, erase, efface. **wipe out** destroy, demolish, annihilate, exterminate, eradicate, eliminate, extirpate, obliterate, expunge, erase, blot out, extinguish.

wiry adjective **1** *wiry youths* lean, spare, sinewy, tough, strong. **2** *wiry brushes* bristly, prickly, thorny, stiff, rigid.

wisdom noun **1** *the wisdom of the old man* sageness, sagacity, enlightenment, reason, philosophy, discernment, perception, insight. **2** *admire their wisdom in leaving early* sense, common sense, prudence, judiciousness, judgment, shrewdness.

wise adjective **1** *she is a wise woman* sage, sagacious, enlightened, philosophic, deep-thinking, discerning, perceptive, experienced. **2** *a wise decision* sensible, prudent, well-advised, judicious, politic, shrewd, astute, smart, reasonable.

wish verb **1** *wish to travel abroad* want, desire, long, yearn, aspire. **2** *they wish you to go now* demand, bid, ask, require, instruct, direct, order, command. **wish for** fancy, crave, hunger for, thirst for, lust after, covet, sigh for, set one's heart on; *inf.* hanker after, have a yen for.

wish noun desire, longing, hope, yearning, want, fancy, aspiration, inclination, urge, whim, craving, hunger, thirst, lust; *inf.* hankering, yen.

wishy-washy adjective **1** *he is a bit wishy-washy* weak, feeble, puny, ineffectual, effete, spineless, irresolute, weak-kneed. **2** *wishy-washy soup* tasteless, flavorless, insipid, watery, weak, diluted.

wistful adjective yearning, longing, melancholy, sad, mournful, dreaming, dreamy, daydreaming, in a reverie, pensive, reflective, musing.

wit noun **1** *he did not have the wit to understand* intelligence, intellect, cleverness, wisdom, sageness, sagacity, judgment, common sense, understanding, comprehension, reason, sharpness, astuteness, shrewdness, acumen, discernment, perspicacity, perception, percipience, insight, ingenuity; brains. **2** *a person of great wit* wittiness, humor, jocularity, drollery, waggishness, repartee, badinage, banter, raillery. **3** *one of the great wits of his time* humorist, wag, comic, jokester, farceur; *inf.* card.

witch noun **1** *the witch cast a spell* sorceress, enchantress, magician, necromancer. **2** *dressed up as an ugly old witch* hag, ogress, crone, gorgon; virago, termagant, shrew, harridan.

witchcraft noun witchery, sorcery, black art/magic, magic, necromancy, wizardry, occultism, the occult, sortilege, thaumaturgy.

withdraw verb **1** *withdraw the poker from the fire* take back, pull back, take away, extract, remove. **2** *asked to withdraw their remarks* retract, recall, unsay. **3** *Congress withdrew the bill* revoke, annul, nullify, declare void, rescind, repeal, abrogate. **4** *withdraw from the group* draw back, go back, absent oneself, detach oneself. **5** *the troops withdrew* pull back, fall back, retire, retreat, disengage, depart, go, leave.

withdrawn adjective retiring, reserved, uncommunicative, unsociable, taciturn, silent, quiet, introverted, detached, aloof, distant, private, shrinking, timid, timorous, shy, bashful, diffident.

wither verb dry up/out, desiccate, shrivel, go limp, wilt; fade, ebb, wane, die.

withhold verb **1** *unable to withhold their laughter* hold back, keep back, restrain, check, curb, repress, suppress. **2** *withhold permission* refuse, decline.

without preposition **1** *they were three days without food* lacking, short of, wanting, requiring, deprived of, destitute of. **2** *he arrived without her* unaccompanied by, unescorted by, in the absence of. **3** *that is the price without tax* exclusive of, excluding, not including, not counting.

withstand verb hold out against, resist, fight, combat, oppose, endure, stand, tolerate, bear, put up with, take, cope with, weather, brave, defy.

witness noun **1** *a witness to the accident* eyewitness, observer, spectator, onlooker, looker-on, viewer, watcher, beholder, bystander. **2** *his ragged clothes were witness* *of his poverty* evidence, testimony, confirmation, corroboration, proof. **bear witness to** testify to, attest to, be evidence of, confirm, corroborate, be proof of, prove, bear out, vouch for, betoken.

witness verb **1** *they witnessed the accident* see, observe, view, watch, look on at, behold, perceive, be present at, attend. **2** *witness his will/signature* endorse, countersign, sign. **witness to** testify to, attest to. *See* BEAR WITNESS TO (WITNESS noun).

witty adjective clever, ingenious, scintillating, humorous, amusing, jocular, funny, facetious, droll, waggish, comic.

wizard noun **1** *wizards casting spells* sorcerer, warlock, enchanter, witch, necromancer, magician. **2** *he is a wizard at the piano* expert, master, genius, virtuoso, maestro, star, ace, whiz.

wobble verb **1** *the table/runner wobbled* rock, sway, seesaw, teeter, shake, vibrate, totter, stagger, waddle, waggle. **2** *her voice wobbled with emotion* shake, tremble, quiver, quaver. **3** *the politicians were wobbling* waver, vacillate, hesitate, dither, shilly-shally.

woe noun **1** *a tale of woe* misery, wretchedness, grief, anguish, affliction, suffering, pain, agony, torment, sorrow, sadness, unhappiness, distress, heartache, heartbreak, despondency, desolation, dejection, depression, gloom, melancholy. **2** *she told everyone her woes* trouble, misfortune, adversity, trial, tribulation, ordeal, burden, affliction, disaster, calamity, catastrophe; trials and tribulations.

woeful adjective **1** *woeful tales of poverty* sad, saddening, unhappy, sorrowful, miserable, dismal, wretched, doleful, gloomy, tragic, pathetic, grievous, pitiful, plaintive, heart-rending, heartbreaking, distressing, anguished, agonizing, dreadful, terrible. **2** *the army will meet a woeful fate* disastrous, ruinous, calamitous, catastrophic. **3** *a woeful piece of work* poor, bad, inadequate, substandard, lamentable, deplorable, disgraceful, wretched, appalling, terrible, shocking; *inf.* rotten, lousy.

woman noun **1** *women and children first* female, lady, girl, she; *derog. inf.* chick, dame. **2** *he has a new woman* girlfriend, female friend, lady love, sweetheart, partner, lover, wife.

womanizer noun lady-killer, ladies' man, philanderer, seducer, lecher, lech, Casanova, Don Juan, lothario; *inf.* wolf.

wonder noun **1** *children gazing with wonder at the Christmas tree* wonderment, awe, surprise, astonishment, amazement, bewilderment, stupefaction, fascination, admiration. **2** *one of the wonders of the world* marvel, phenomenon, miracle, prodigy, curiosity, rarity.

wonder verb **1** *she wondered what to do next* think, speculate, ponder, muse, ask oneself, puzzle. **2** *they wondered at the beauty of the church* marvel, stand in awe, gape, gawk, look agog; *inf.* be flabbergasted.

wonderful adjective **1** *the church ceiling was wonderful to behold* marvelous, awe-inspiring, awesome, remarkable, extraordinary, phenomenal, prodigious, miraculous, fantastic, amazing, astonishing, astounding, surprising, incredible, unprecedented, unparalleled, unheard-of; *lit.* wondrous. **2** *a wonderful mother* superb, marvelous, magnificent, brilliant, sensational, stupendous, excellent, first-rate, fabulous, outstanding, terrific, ace, tremendous, admirable, very good; *inf.* great, super, fantastic, tip-top, A-1.

woo verb **1** *woo the boss's daughter* court, pay court/suit to, seek the hand of, set one's cap at, make love to. **2** *woo fame* seek, seek to win/gain, pursue, chase after. **3** *wooing consumers into buying their goods* importune, press, urge, entreat, beg, implore, supplicate, solicit, coax, wheedle.

wood noun lumber, timber; firewood, kindling, fuel.

wooden adjective **1** *a wooden performance* stiff, stolid, stodgy, graceless, inelegant, ungainly, gauche, awkward, clumsy, maladroit. **2** *a wooden expression* expressionless, inexpressive, blank, deadpan, empty, vacant, impassive, lifeless, spiritless, unanimated.

woods plural noun forest, woodland, wood, copse, thicket, grove; trees.

word noun **1** *what's another word for "fame"?* term, expression, name. **2** *he said not a word* remark, comment, statement, utterance, expression, declaration. **3** *she gave him her word* word of honor, solemn word, promise, pledge, assurance, guarantee, vow, oath. **4** *have a word with the teacher* chat, chitchat, talk, conversation, discussion, tête-à-tête, consultation, exchange of views; *inf.* confab, powwow. **5** *they have had word of his death* news, notice, communication, information, intelligence; tidings; message, report, account, communiqué, dispatch, bulletin; *inf.* low-down. **6** *word has it that he is a spy* rumor, talk, hearsay, gossip, grapevine. **7** *give the word to begin* command, order, signal, go-ahead, thumbs up; *inf.* green light. **8** *the king's word is law* decree, edict, mandate, bidding, will. **9** *our word now must be success* slogan, watchword, password, catchword. **in a word** in short, in a nutshell, briefly. **word for word** verbatim, literal, exact, precise, accurate.

word verb express, phrase, couch, put, say, utter, state.

words plural noun **1** *the words of the song/opera/play* lyrics, libretto, book, text, script. **2** *she has had words with her sister* argument, disagreement, row, altercation.

wordy adjective long-winded, verbose, loquacious, garrulous, voluble, prolix, protracted, discursive, diffuse, rambling, digressive, maundering, tautological, pleonastic.

work noun **1** *building a house involves a lot of work* effort, exertion, labor, toil, sweat, drudgery, trouble, industry; *lit.* travail; *inf.* grind, elbow grease. **2** *your work is to answer the phone* job, task, chore, undertaking, duty, charge, assignment, commission, mission. **3** *out of work* employment, occupation, business; job, profession, career, trade, vocation, calling, craft, line, field, métier, pursuit. **4** *he regards it as his life's work* achievement, accomplishment, deed, feat, handiwork, fulfillment, performance, production. **5** *a work of art* composition, creation, opus, piece, oeuvre, masterpiece. **6** *admire the work that has gone into the statue* art, craft. *See* WORKMANSHIP.

work verb **1** *he works in industry* be employed, have a job, hold down a job, be engaged, earn one's living, do business, follow/ply one's trade. **2** *work hard to pass the exam* exert oneself, put in effort, labor, toil, sweat, drudge, slave, peg away; *inf.* grind, plug away, knock oneself out. **3** *work the machine* operate, control, drive, manage, direct, use, handle, manipulate, maneuver, ply, wield. **4** *this machine will not work* go, operate, function, perform, run. **5** *your idea/plan will not work* succeed, go well, be effective. **6** *work the land* cultivate, till, dig, farm. **7** *they can work miracles* bring about, achieve, accomplish, perform, carry out, execute, create, cause, contrive, effect, implement. **8** *they worked it so that the criminal got off* arrange, handle, manipulate, maneuver, contrive, bring off, carry off, pull off; *inf.* fix, swing. **9** *work the clay* knead, shape, form, mold, fashion, model. **10** *work the peg into the hole* maneuver, manipulate, negotiate, guide, engineer, direct, edge. **11** *work one's way through the crowd* maneuver, progress, penetrate, move, make, push, elbow. **work on** coax, cajole, wheedle, pester, press, nag, importune, persuade, influence, sway. **work out 1** *work out the puzzle* solve, resolve, figure out. **2** *work out a plan* develop, evolve, formulate, devise, arrange, organize, elaborate, construct, put together, plan, contrive. **3** *the plan did not work out* work, succeed, go well. **4** *things worked out well/badly* go, turn out, come out, develop, evolve, result; *inf.* pan out. **5** *work out to keep fit* exercise, do exercises, train, drill, warm

up. **work up 1** *work up to a climax* advance, progress, proceed, make headway. **2** *unable to work up any enthusiasm* stir up, arouse, rouse, awaken, excite, instigate, prompt, generate, kindle, foment. **3** *the speaker worked up the crowd* agitate, stir up, arouse, excite, animate, inflame.

worker noun **1** *workers and employers* employee, hand, workman, working man/woman/person, blue-collar worker, white-collar worker, laborer, artisan, craftsman, craftswoman, wage-earner, proletarian. **2** *workers of miracles* doer, performer, perpetrator, executor, operator. **3** *he is a real worker* hard worker, toiler, workhorse, busy bee; *inf.* workaholic.

working adjective *working machines* functioning, operating, going, running, in working order.

working noun **1** *understand the working of the machine* functioning, operation, modus operandi. **2** *the working of miracles* doing, performing, performance, perpetration, execution, operation. **3** *the workings of the clock* mechanism, machinery; works.

workmanship noun craftsmanship, craft, artistry, art, handicraft, handwork, expertise, skill, technique, work.

workout noun exercises, gymnastics, aerobics; *inf.* daily dozen.

workshop noun **1** *the car is still in the workshop* factory, plant, mill; garage. **2** *craftsmen in their workshop* workroom, studio, atelier, shop. **3** *hold a workshop in self-assertiveness* seminar, study/discussion group, class.

world noun **1** *travel around the world* earth, globe, sphere, planet. **2** *the world was shocked by the nuclear attack* whole world, mankind, man, humankind, humanity, people everywhere, people, everyone, everybody, public, general public. **3** *God created the world* universe, creation, cosmos. **4** *the earth and other worlds* planet, satellite, moon, star, heavenly body, orb. **5** *the academic world* society, sector, section, group, division. **6** *he works in the world of finance* area, field, department, sphere, province, domain, realm. **7** *the world of the Roosevelts* age, epoch, era, period; times. **8** *it made a world of difference* vast/huge amount; *inf.* great deal, immensity.

worldly adjective **1** *worldly pleasures* earthly, terrestrial, secular, temporal, material, materialistic, human, carnal, fleshly, corporeal, physical. **2** *traveling has made her more worldly* worldly-wise, experienced, knowing, sophisticated, cosmopolitan, urbane.

worn adjective **1** *worn clothes* worn-out, threadbare, tattered, in tatters, ragged, frayed, shabby. **2** *worn furniture* dilapidated, crumbling, broken-down, rundown, tumbledown, decrepit, deteriorated, on its last legs. **3** *rescue workers looking worn* haggard, drawn, strained, careworn; *inf.* all in, done in, dog-tired, dead on one's feet, played out, bushed, pooped. **4** *workers worn by long hours* exhausted, overtired, tired out, fatigued, weary, wearied, spent. **5** *worn ideas/jokes* obsolete, antiquated, old, hackneyed, stale, played out. **worn-out** worn, dilapidated, exhausted.

worry verb **1** *she worries too much* be worried, be anxious, fret, brood. **2** *his absences worry her* make anxious, disturb, trouble, bother, distress, upset, concern, disquiet, discompose, fret, agitate, unsettle.

worry noun anxiety, disturbance, trouble, bother, distress, concern, care, upset, uneasiness, unease, disquiet, fretfulness, agitation, edginess, tenseness, apprehension, fearfulness.

worsen verb **1** *his statement worsened the situation* aggravate, exacerbate, damage, intensify, increase, heighten. **2** *the financial situation worsened* take a turn for the worse, deteriorate, degenerate, retrogress, decline, sink, slip, slide, go downhill.

worship noun **1** *acts of worship* reverence, veneration, homage, respect, honor, adoration, devotion, praise, prayer, glorification, exaltation, laudation, extolment. **2** *the fans' worship of the star* adulation, admiration, adoration, devotion, idolization, hero-worship.

worship verb **1** *worship God* revere, venerate, pay homage to, honor, adore, praise, pray to, glorify, exalt, laud, extol. **2** *he worships his wife* be devoted to, cherish, treasure, admire, adulate, idolize, hero-worship, lionize; *inf.* be wild about.

worth noun **1** *the jewels are of little worth* value, price, cost; valuation, assessment, appraisal. **2** *his advice is of little worth to you* use, usefulness, advantage, benefit, service, gain, profit, avail. **3** *persons of great worth in the community* worthiness, merit, credit, eminence, importance.

worthless adjective **1** *the jewels are worthless* valueless, of little/no value, rubbishy, trashy. **2** *his advice was worthless* useless, of no benefit, to no avail, futile, ineffective, ineffectual, pointless. **3** *their worthless son ended up in prison* good-for-nothing, useless, despicable, contemptible, base, low; *inf.* no-good, no-account.

worthwhile adjective worth it, worth the effort, valuable, of value, useful, of use, beneficial, advantageous, helpful, profitable, constructive, justifiable.

worthy adjective virtuous, good, moral, upright, righteous, honest, decent, honorable, respectable, reputable, trustworthy, reliable, irreproachable, blameless, unimpeachable, admirable, praiseworthy, laudable, commendable, deserving, meritorious.

wound noun **1** *a wound in the leg that is not healing* lesion, cut, graze, scratch, gash, laceration, tear, puncture, slash, injury, sore. **2** *a wound to his pride* blow, insult, slight, offense, affront; hurt, harm, damage. **3** *mental/emotional wounds* pain, pang, ache, distress, grief, trauma, anguish, torment, torture.

wound verb **1** *the shot wounded his arm* cut, graze, scratch, gash, lacerate, tear, puncture, pierce, stab, slash, injure, hurt, damage, harm. **2** *their words wounded his pride* harm, damage, insult, slight, offend, affront. **3** *his actions wounded her feelings* distress, grieve, mortify, pain, shock, traumatize.

wrap verb **1** *wrap the child in blankets* envelop, enfold, fold, encase, enclose, cover, swathe, bundle up, swaddle. **2** *wrap the present* wrap up, package, do up, tie up, gift-wrap. **wrap up** *try to wrap up the meeting early* finish, conclude, terminate, wind up.

wrap noun shawl, stole, cloak, cape, mantle.

wrapper noun wrapping, cover, covering, packaging, paper; jacket, casing, case, sheath; capsule, pod, shell.

wrath noun anger, ire, rage, fury, annoyance, indignation, exasperation, dudgeon, high dudgeon, bad temper, ill humor, irritation, crossness, displeasure, irascibility.

wreath noun **1** *wreaths of flowers* garland, chaplet, circlet, coronet, crown, diadem, festoon, lei. **2** *wreaths of smoke* ring, loop, circle.

wreck noun **1** *the wreck of the car/house/dreams* wreckage, debris, rubble, detritus; ruins, remains, remnants, fragments, pieces, relics. **2** *upset by the wreck of their car/house/dream* wrecking, destruction, devastation, ruination, ruin, demolition, smashing, shattering, disruption, disintegration, undoing.

wreck verb **1** *wreck the car* smash, demolish, ruin, damage; *inf.* write off. **2** *wreck their plans/hopes* destroy, devastate, smash, shatter, disrupt, undo, spoil, mar, play havoc with. **3** *the new crew wrecked the ship* shipwreck, sink, capsize, run aground.

wrench noun **1** *remove the root with one wrench* twist, pull, tug, yank, wrest, jerk, jolt. **2** *the wrist injury is just a wrench* sprain, twist, strain. **3** *the wrench of a broken heart* pain, ache, pang, anguish, distress, trauma.

wrench verb **1** *wrench the root from the ground* twist, pull, tug, yank, wrest, jerk, tear, rip, force. **2** *wrench one's ankle/wrist* sprain, twist, strain.

wrest verb twist, wrench, pull, snatch, take away, remove.

wrestle verb **wrestle with** struggle with, grapple with, fight with, contend with, battle with, combat with, come to grips with, face up to, pit oneself against.

wretch noun **1** *pity the wretches living on the streets* poor creature/soul/thing, unfortunate, poor devil. **2** *the wretch who stole her purse* scoundrel, villain, ruffian, rogue, rascal, blackguard, reprobate, criminal, delinquent, miscreant; *inf.* rat, swine, skunk.

wretched adjective **1** *feeling wretched at leaving home* miserable, unhappy, sad, brokenhearted, sorrowful, sorry, distressed, disconsolate, downcast, down, downhearted, dejected, crestfallen, cheerless, depressed, melancholy, gloomy, mournful, doleful, forlorn, woebegone, abject. **2** *feeling wretched during the sea voyage* ill, unwell, sick, sickly, ailing, below par; *inf.* under the weather, out of sorts. **3** *lead a wretched existence* hard, harsh, grim, difficult, unfortunate, sorry, pitiful, tragic. **4** *wretched people living in poverty* unfortunate, unlucky, hapless, pitiable. **5** *the wretched drug dealer is back in prison* contemptible, despicable, base, low, vile. **6** *the food was wretched* poor, bad, substandard, low-quality, inferior, pathetic, worthless.

wring verb **1** *wring the clothes* twist, squeeze. **2** *wring the information from him* extract, force, coerce, exact, extort, wrest, wrench, screw.

wrinkle noun crease, fold, pucker, gather, furrow, ridge, line, corrugation, crinkle, crumple, rumple; crow's-foot.

write verb **1** *write their names* write down, put in writing, put in black and white, commit to paper, jot down, note, set down, take down, record, register, list, inscribe, scribble, scrawl. **2** *write an essay/letter* compose, draft, create, pen, dash off. **3** *don't forget to write* write a letter, correspond, communicate; *inf.* drop a line/note. **write off** forget about, disregard, dismiss, give up for lost, cancel, annul, nullify, wipe out.

writer noun author, wordsmith, penman, hack; novelist, essayist, biographer, journalist, columnist, scriptwriter; scribe; *inf.* scribbler, pen/pencil pusher.

writhe verb twist about, twist and turn, roll about, squirm, wriggle, fidget, jerk, thrash, flail, toss, struggle.

writing noun **1** *the writing is illegible* handwriting, hand, penmanship, script, print, calligraphy, scribble, scrawl. **2** *have his writing published* work, opus, book, volume, publication, composition.

wrong adjective **1** *the wrong answer* incorrect, inaccurate, erroneous, mistaken, inexact, imprecise, unsound, faulty, false, wide of the mark, off target; *inf.* barking up the wrong tree. **2** *chose the wrong moment to speak* unsuitable, inappropriate, inapt, inapposite, undesirable, unacceptable, unfitting, improper, unseemly, indecorous, unconventional. **3** *it is wrong to steal* unlawful, illegal, illicit, lawless, criminal, delinquent, felonious, dishonest, dishonorable, corrupt, unethical, immoral, bad, wicked, evil, sinful, iniquitous, blameworthy, culpable; *inf.* crooked. **4** *something wrong with his phone/heart* amiss, awry, out of order, not right, faulty, defective. **5** *iron the dress on the wrong side* inside, reverse, opposite, inverse.

wrong adverb **get wrong** misunderstand, misinterpret, misapprehend, misconstrue. **go wrong 1** *you cannot go wrong if you follow the instructions* make a mistake, go astray, err; *inf.* slip up, make a booboo. **2** *things went wrong from the start* go badly, go amiss, go awry. **3** *when did he go wrong?* go astray, err, stray from the straight and narrow, fall from grace; *inf.* go to the dogs.

wrong noun **1** *not know right from wrong* badness, immorality, sin, sinfulness, wickedness, evil, iniquity, unlawfulness, crime, dishonesty, dishonor, injustice, transgression, abuse; *inf.* crookedness. **2** *commit a wrong | do us a wrong* misdeed, offense, injury, crime, infringement, infraction, injustice, grievance, outrage, atrocity. **in the wrong** in error, mistaken, at fault, to blame, blameworthy, culpable, guilty.

wrong verb **1** *he wronged his wife* abuse, mistreat, maltreat, ill-treat, ill-use, harm, hurt, do injury to. **2** *you wrong him by calling him a thief* malign, dishonor, impugn, vilify, defame, slander, libel, denigrate, insult; *inf.* bad-mouth.

wrongdoer noun lawbreaker, criminal, delinquent, culprit, offender, felon, villain, miscreant, evildoer, sinner, transgressor, malefactor.

wry adjective **1** *make a wry face* twisted, distorted, contorted, crooked, lopsided, askew. **2** *a wry wit* ironic, sardonic, mocking, sarcastic, dry, droll, witty, humorous.

Xx

Xerox (*trademark*) verb *Xerox the document* photocopy, copy, duplicate, reproduce; Photostat (*trademark*).

Yy

yank verb *yank the weeds out* pull, tug, jerk, wrench.

yardstick noun measure, standard, gauge, scale, guide, guideline, touchstone, criterion, benchmark, model, pattern.

yarn noun **1** *use a fine yarn* thread, fiber, strand. **2** *tell a good yarn* story, tale, anecdote, fable; *inf.* tall tale/story, cock and bull story.

yearn verb long, pine, crave, desire, want, wish, hanker, have a fancy, hunger, thirst; *inf.* have a yen.

yearning noun longing, craving, desire, want, wish, hankering, fancy, hunger, thirst, lust, ache, burning; *inf.* yen.

yell verb shout, cry out, howl, scream, shriek, screech, squeal, roar, bawl, whoop; *inf.* holler.

yell noun shout, cry, howl, scream, shriek, screech, squeal, roar, bawl, whoop; *inf.* holler.

yen noun hankering, desire. *See* YEARNING.

yet adverb **1** *he has not appeared yet* as yet, so/thus far, up till/to now. **2** *there is yet more to come* still, in addition, besides, into the bargain, to boot. **3** *I was not expecting him yet* now, just/right now, by now, already, so soon.

yield verb **1** *fields yielding a good crop* produce, bear, give, give forth, supply, provide. **2** *investments yielding a good profit* return, bring in, fetch, earn, net, produce, supply, provide, generate, furnish. **3** *yield the crown to the conqueror* give up, relinquish, part with, deliver up, turn over, give over, remit, cede, renounce, resign, abdicate, forgo. **4** *the army yielded*

after a long battle surrender, capitulate, submit, lay down one's arms, give in, give up the struggle, succumb, raise/show the white flag; *inf.* throw in the towel, cave in. **5** *the material yields on pressure* give, bend, stretch, be flexible/pliant.
yield to submit to, bow down to, comply with, accede to, agree to, consent to, go along with.

yoke noun **1** *the yoke of the oxen* harness, collar, coupling. **2** *under the yoke of the tyrant* oppression, tyranny, enslavement, slavery, servitude, bondage, thrall. **3** *the yoke of marriage* tie, link, bond.

yokel noun rustic, countryman, countrywoman, peasant, country bumpkin, provincial, country cousin; *inf.* hayseed, hillbilly.

young adjective **1** *young people* youthful, juvenile, junior, adolescent, in the springtime of life, in one's salad days. **2** *young industries* new, recent, undeveloped, fledgling, in the making.

young noun *bear young* offspring, progeny, family, issue; little ones, babies; litter, brood.

youngster noun young adult/person, youth, juvenile, teenager, adolescent, young hopeful; lad, boy, young man/woman, lass, girl; *inf.* kid, shaver, young 'un.

youth noun **1** *in their youth they were beautiful* young days, early years, teens; early life, adolescence; boyhood, girlhood. **2** *the coach was a good friend to the youths* juvenile, teenager. *See* YOUNGSTER. **3** *the youth of today* young people, young, younger generation; *inf.* kids.

youthful adjective *he is a youthful sixty-five* young, active, vigorous, spry, sprightly.

Zz

zany adjective eccentric, weird, peculiar, daft, odd, ridiculous, absurd, comic, clownish, madcap, funny, amusing; *inf.* wacky, screwy, kooky.

zeal noun **1** *his zeal for life/hockey* ardor, fervor, fervency, passion, fire, devotion, vehemence, intensity, enthusiasm, eagerness, keenness, earnestness, vigor, energy, verve, gusto, zest. **2** *put off by their religious/political zeal* fanaticism, extremism. *See* ZEALOTRY.

zealot noun enthusiast, fanatic, extremist, radical, militant; *inf.* fiend.

zealotry noun zeal, fanaticism, extremism, single-mindedness, radicalism, militancy.

zealous adjective ardent, fervent, fervid, passionate, impassioned, devoted, intense, enthusiastic, eager, keen, earnest, vigorous, energetic, zestful, fanatical.

zenith noun crowning point, height, top, acme, peak, pinnacle, climax, prime, meridian, apex, apogee, vertex.

zero noun **1** *a series of zeros | win absolutely zero* naught, nothing, cipher, nil; *inf.* zilch, nada, goose egg, zippo. **2** *economic growth is at zero* lowest point, nadir, rock bottom.

zest noun **1** *approach the project with zest* relish, gusto, enthusiasm, zing, eagerness, zeal, vigor, liveliness, energy, enjoyment, joy, delectation, appetite; *inf.* oomph. **2** *add zest to the dish/occasion* piquancy, spice, pungency, flavor, relish, tang, savor, interest; *inf.* kick.

zip noun zest, enthusiasm, zing, eagerness, gusto, life, liveliness, spirit, animation, sparkle, pep, élan, brio; *inf.* oomph, pizzazz.

zip verb rush, dash, hurry, speed. *See* ZOOM.

zone noun area, sector, section, belt, district, region, province.

zoom verb rush, dash, pelt, race, tear, shoot, fly, scurry, speed, hurry, hasten, whiz, zip.

Writer's Toolkit

Punctuation Guide

Punctuation is an essential element of good writing because it makes the author's meaning clear to the reader. Although precise punctuation styles may vary somewhat among published sources, there are a number of fundamental principles worthy of consideration. Discussed below are these punctuation marks used in English:

> comma
> semicolon
> colon
> period
> question mark
> exclamation point
> apostrophe
> quotation marks
> parentheses
> dash
> hyphen

Comma

The comma is the most used mark of punctuation in the English language. It signals to the reader a pause, which generally clarifies the author's meaning, and establishes a sensible order to the elements of written language. Among the most typical functions of the comma are the following:

1. It can separate the clauses of a compound sentence when there are two independent clauses joined by a conjunction, especially when the clauses are not very short:

> *It never occurred to me to look in the attic, and I'm sure it didn't occur to Rachel either.*

> *The Nelsons wanted to see the Grand Canyon at sunrise, but they overslept that morning.*

2. It can separate the clauses of a compound sentence when there is a series of independent clauses, the last two of which are joined by a conjunction:

> *The bus ride to the campsite was very uncomfortable, the cabins were not ready for us when we got there, the cook had forgotten to start dinner, and the rain was torrential.*

3. It is used to precede or set off, and therefore indicate, a nonrestrictive dependent clause (a clause that could be omitted without changing the meaning of the main clause):

> *I read her autobiography, which was published last July.*

They showed up at midnight, after most of the guests had gone home.

The coffee, which is freshly brewed, is in the kitchen.

4. It can follow an introductory phrase:

Having enjoyed the movie so much, he agreed to see it again.

Born and raised in Paris, she had never lost her French accent.

In the beginning, they had very little money to invest.

5. It can set off words used in direct address:

Listen, people, you have no choice in the matter.

Yes, Mrs. Greene, I will be happy to feed your cat.

6. The comma can separate two or more coordinate adjectives (adjectives that could otherwise be joined with *and*) that modify one noun:

The cruise turned out to be the most entertaining, fun, and relaxing vacation I've ever had.

The horse was tall, lean, and sleek.

Note that cumulative adjectives (those not able to be joined with *and*) are not separated by a comma:

She wore bright yellow rubber boots.

7. Use a comma to separate three or more items in a series or list:

Charlie, Melissa, Stan, and Mark will be this year's soloists in the spring concert.

We need furniture, toys, clothes, books, tools, housewares, and other useful merchandise for the benefit auction.

Note that the comma between the last two items in a series is sometimes omitted in less precise style:

The most popular foods served in the cafeteria are pizza, hamburgers and nachos.

8. Use a comma to separate and set off the elements in an address or other geographical designation:

My new house is at 1657 Nighthawk Circle, South Kingsbury, Michigan.

We arrived in Pamplona, Spain, on Thursday.

9. Use a comma to set off direct quotations (note the placement or absence of commas with other punctuation):

"Kim forgot her gloves," he said, "but we have a pair she can borrow."

There was a long silence before Jack blurted out, "This must be the world's ugliest painting."

"What are you talking about?" she asked in a puzzled manner.

"Happy New Year!" everyone shouted.

10. A comma is used to set off titles after a person's name:

Katherine Bentley, M.D.

Martin Luther King, Jr., delivered the sermon.

Semicolon

The semicolon has two basic functions:

1. It can separate two main clauses, particularly when these clauses are of equal importance:

> *The crowds gathered outside the museum hours before the doors were opened; this was one exhibit no one wanted to miss.*

> *She always complained when her relatives stayed for the weekend; even so, she usually was a little sad when they left.*

2. It can be used as a comma is used to separate such elements as clauses or items in a series or list, particularly when one or more of the elements already includes a comma:

> *The path took us through the deep, dark woods; across a small meadow; into a cold, wet cave; and up a hillside overlooking the lake.*

> *Listed for sale in the ad were two bicycles; a battery-powered, leaf-mulching lawn mower; and a maple bookcase.*

Colon

The colon has five basic functions:

1. It can introduce something, especially a list of items:

   In the basket were three pieces of mail: a postcard, a catalog, and a wedding invitation.

   Students should have the following items: backpack, loose-leaf notebook, pens and pencils, pencil sharpener, and ruler.

2. It can separate two clauses in a sentence when the second clause is being used to explain or illustrate the first clause:

   We finally understood why she would never go sailing with us: she had a deep fear of the water.

   Most of the dogs in our neighborhood are quite large: two of them are St. Bernards.

3. It can introduce a statement or a quotation:

   His parents say the most important rule is this: Always tell the truth.

   We repeated the final words of his poem: "And such is the plight of fools like me."

4. It can be used to follow the greeting in a formal or business letter:

   Dear Ms. Daniels:

   Dear Sir or Madam:

5. In the U.S., use a comma to separate minutes from hours, and seconds from minutes, in showing time of day and measured length of time:

   Please be at the restaurant before 6:45.

   Her best running time so far has been 00:12:35.

Period

The period has two basic functions:

1. It is used to mark the end of a sentence:

   It was reported that there is a shortage of nurses at the hospital. Several of the patients have expressed concern about this problem.

2. It is often used at the end of an abbreviation:

   On Fri., Sept. 12, Dr. Brophy noted that the patient's weight was 168 lbs. and that his height was 6 ft. 2 in. (Note that another period is not added to the end of the sentence when the last word is an abbreviation.)

Question Mark and Exclamation Point

The only sentences that do not end in a period are those that end in either a question mark or an exclamation point.

Question marks are used to mark the end of a sentence that asks a direct question (generally, a question that expects an answer):

Is there any reason for us to bring more than a few dollars?

Who is your science teacher?

Exclamation points are used to mark the end of a sentence that expresses a strong feeling, typically surprise, joy, or anger:

I want you to leave and never come back!

What a beautiful view this is!

Apostrophe

The apostrophe has two basic functions:

1. It is used to show where a letter or letters are missing in a contraction:

   The directions are cont'd [continued] on the next page.

   We've [we have] decided that if she can't [cannot] go, then we aren't [are not] going either.

2. It can be used to show possession:

   a. The possessive of a singular noun or an irregular plural noun is created by adding an apostrophe and an s:

   the pilot's uniform

   Mrs. Mendoza's house

   a tomato's bright red color

   the oxen's yoke

   b. The possessive of a plural noun is created by adding just an apostrophe:

   the pilots' uniforms [referring to more than one pilot]

   the Mendozas' house [referring to the Mendoza family]

   the tomatoes' bright red color [referring to more than one tomato]

Quotation Marks

Quotation marks have two basic functions:

1. They are used to set off direct quotations (an exact rendering of someone's spoken or written words):

> *"I think the new library is wonderful," she remarked to David.*

> *We were somewhat lost, so we asked, "Are we anywhere near the art gallery?"*

> *In his letter he had written, "The nights here are quiet and starry. It seems like a hundred years since I've been wakened by the noise of city traffic and squabbling neighbors."*

Note that indirect quotes (which often are preceded by that, if, or whether) are not set off by quotation marks:

> *He told me that he went to school in Boston.*

> *We asked if we could still get tickets to the game.*

2. They can be used to set off words or phrases that have specific technical usage, or to set off meanings of words, or to indicate words that are being used in a special way in a sentence:

> *The part of the flower that bears the pollen is the "stamen."*

> *When I said "plain," I meant "flat land," not "ordinary."*

> *Oddly enough, in the theater, the statement "break a leg" is meant as an expression of good luck.*

> *What you call "hoagies," we call "grinders" or "submarine sandwiches."*

> *He will never be a responsible adult until he outgrows his "Peter Pan" behavior.*

Note that sometimes single quotation marks (the 'stamen.'), rather than double quotation marks as above (the "stamen."), may be used to set off words or phrases. What is most important is to be consistent in such usage. Single quotation marks are also used to set off words or phrases within material already in double quotation marks, as:

> *"I want the sign to say 'Ellen's Bed and Breakfast' in large gold letters," she explained.*

Parentheses

Parentheses are used, in pairs, to enclose information that gives extra detail or explanation to the regular text. Parentheses are used in two basic ways:

1. They can separate a word or words in a sentence from the rest of the sentence:

> *On our way to school, we walk past the Turner Farm (the oldest dairy farm in town) and watch the cows being fed.*

> *The stores were filled with holiday shoppers (even more so than last year).* (Note that the period goes outside the parentheses, because the words in the parentheses are only part of the sentence.)

2. They can form a separate complete sentence:

> *Please bring a dessert to the dinner party. (It can be something very simple.) I look forward to seeing you there.* (Note that the period goes inside the parentheses, because the words in the parentheses are a complete and independent sentence.)

Dash

A dash is used most commonly to replace the usage of parentheses within sentences. If the information being set off is in the middle of the sentence, a pair of dashes is used; if it is at the end of the sentence, just one dash is used:

On our way to school, we walk past the Turner Farm—the oldest dairy farm in town—and watch the cows being fed.

The stores were filled with holiday shoppers—even more so than last year.

Hyphen

A hyphen has three basic functions:

1. It can join two or more words to make a compound, especially when so doing makes the meaning more clear to the reader:

We met to discuss long-range planning.

There were six four-month-old piglets at the fair.

That old stove was quite a coal-burner.

2. It can replace the word "to" when a span or range of data is given. This kind of hyphen is sometimes also called a dash:

John Adams was president of the United States 1797-1801.

Today we will look for proper nouns in the L-N section of the dictionary.

The ideal weight for that breed of dog would be 75-85 pounds.

3. It can indicate a word break at the end of a line. The break must always be between syllables:

It is important for any writer to know that there are numerous punctuation principles that are considered standard and proper, but there is also flexibility regarding acceptable punctuation. Having learned the basic "rules" of good punctuation, the writer will be able to adopt a specific and consistent style of punctuation that best suits the material he or she is writing.

Usage Guide

Even the best writers are sometimes troubled by questions of correct usage. A guide to some of the most common questions is provided below, with discussion of the following topics:

> singular or plural
> -s plural or singular
> comparison of adjectives and adverbs
> nouns ending in -ics
> group possessive
> *may* or *might*
> *I* or *me*, *we* or *us*, etc.
> *we* (with phrase following)
> *I who*, *you who*, etc.
> *you and I* or *you and me*
> collective nous
> *none* (pronoun)
> *as*

singular or plural

1. When subject and complement are different in number (i.e., one is singular, the other plural), the verb normally agrees with the subject, e.g.,

> (Plural subject)
> *Their wages were a mere pittance.*
>
> *Liqueur chocolates are our specialty.*

(The Biblical *The wages of sin is death* reflects an obsolete idiom in which *wages* took a singular verb.)

> (Singular subject)
> *What we need is customers.*
>
> *Our specialty is liqueur chocolates.*

2. A plural word or phrase used as a name, title, or quotation counts as singular, e.g.,

> Sons and Lovers has *always been one of Lawrence's most popular novels.*

3. A singular phrase (such as a prepositional phrase following the subject) that happens to end with a plural word should nevertheless be followed by a singular verb, e.g.,

> *Everyone except the French* wants (not *want*) *Britain to join.*
>
> *One in six* has (not *have*) *this problem.*

See also *-ics, s plural or singular.*

-s plural or singular

Some nouns, though they have the plural ending -s, are nevertheless usually treated as singular, taking singular verbs and pronouns referring back to them.

1. *News*

2. Diseases:

measles	rickets
mumps	shingles

Measles and *rickets* can also be treated as ordinary plural nouns.

3. Games:

billiards	craps
dominoes	quoits
checkers	darts

4. Countries:

the Bahamas	the Netherlands
the Philippines	the United States

These are treated as singular when considered as a unit, which they commonly are in a political context, or when the complement is singular, e.g.,

The Philippines is *a predominantly agricultural country.*

The United States has *withdrawn its ambassador.*

The Bahamas and *the Philippines* are also the geographical names of the groups of islands that the two nations comprise, and in this use can be treated as plurals, e.g.,

The Bahamas were *settled by British subjects.*

See also *-ics.*

comparison of adjectives and adverbs

The two ways of forming the comparative and superlative of adjectives and adverbs are:

(*a*) Addition of suffixes -*er* and -*est*. Monosyllabic adjectives and adverbs almost always require these suffixes, e.g., *big* (*bigger*, *biggest*), *soon* (*sooner*, *soonest*), and normally so do many adjectives of two syllables, e.g., *narrow* (*narrower*, *narrowest*), *silly* (*sillier*, *silliest*).

(*b*) Use of adverbs *more* and *most*. These are used with adjectives of three syllables or more (e.g., *difficult*, *memorable*), participles (e.g., *bored*, *boring*), many adjectives of two syllables (e.g., *afraid*, *awful*, *childish*, *harmless*, *static*), and adverbs ending in -*ly* (e.g., *highly*, *slowly*).

Adjectives with two syllables sometimes use suffixes and sometimes use adverbs.

There are many that never take the suffixes, e.g.,

antique	*bizarre*
breathless	*constant*
futile	*steadfast*

There is also a large class that is acceptable with either, e.g.,

clever	*pleasant*
handsome	*tranquil*
solemn	*cruel*
common	*polite*

The choice is largely a matter of preference.

nouns ending in -*ics*

Nouns ending in -*ics* denoting subjects or disciplines are sometimes treated as singular and sometimes as plural. Examples are:

apologetics	*mechanics*
genetics	*politics*
optics	*economics*
classics (as a study)	*metaphysics*
linguistics	*statistics*
phonetics	*electronics*
mathematics	*obsterics*
physics	*tactics*
dynamics	*ethics*

When used strictly as the name of a discipline they are treated as singular:

Psychometrics is *unable to investigate the nature of intelligence.*

So also when the complement is singular:

Mathematics is *his strong point.*

When used more loosely, to denote a manifestation of qualities, often accompanied by a possessive, they are treated as plural:

His politics were *a mixture of fear, greed, and envy.*

I don't understand the mathematics of it, which are *complicated.*

The acoustics in this hall are *dreadful.*

So also when they denote a set of activities or pattern of behavior, as commonly with words like:

acrobatics	*athletics*
dramatics	*gymnastics*
heroics	*hysterics*

E.g., *The mental gymnastics required to believe this* are *beyond me.*

group possessive

The group possessive is the construction by which the ending -'s of the possessive case can be added to the last word of a noun phrase, which is regarded as a single unit, e.g.,

The king of Spain's daughter

John and Mary's baby

Somebody else's umbrella

A quarter of an hour's drive

Expressions like these are natural and acceptable.

may or *might*

There is sometimes confusion about whether to use *may* or *might* with the perfect tense when referring to a past event, e.g., *He may have done* or *He might have done.*

1. If uncertainty about the action or state denoted by the perfect remains, i.e., at the time of speaking or writing the truth of the event is still unknown, then either *may* or *might* is acceptable:

> *As they all wore so many different clothes of identically the same kind . . . there* may *have been several more or several less.*

> *For all we knew our complaint went unanswered, although of course they* might *have tried to call us while we were out of town.*

2. If there is no longer uncertainty about the event, or the matter was never put to the test, and therefore the event did not in fact occur, use *might*:

> *If that had come ten days ago my whole life* might *have been different.*

> *You should not have let him come home alone; he* might *have gotten lost.*

It is a common error to use *may* instead of *might,* as here:

> *If they had not invaded, then eventually we *may* have agreed to give them aid.*

> *I am grateful for his intervention, without which they *may* have remained in the refugee camp indefinitely.*

> *Schoenberg *may* never have gone atonal but for the breakup of his marriage.*

In each of the three sentences above *might* should be substituted for *may.*

I or *me*, *we* or *us*, etc.

There is often confusion about which case of a personal pronoun to use when the pronoun stands alone or follows the verb *to be*.

1. When the personal pronoun stands alone, as when it forms the answer to a question, strictly formal usage requires it to have the case it would have if the verb were supplied:

> *Who called him?*—I (in full, *I called him* or *I did*).

> *Which of you did he approach?*—Me (in full, *he approached me*).

Informal usage permits the objective case in both kinds of sentence, but this is not acceptable in formal style. However, the subjective case often sounds stilted. One can avoid the problem by providing a verb, e.g.,

> *Who likes cooking?*—I do.

> *Who can cook?*—I can.

> *Who is here?*—I am.

2. When a personal pronoun follows *it is, it was, it may be, it could have been*, etc., formal usage requires the subjective case:

> *Nobody could suspect that it* was *she.*

> *We are given no clues as to what it must have felt like to be* he.

Informal usage favors the objective case (not acceptable in formal style):

> *I thought it might have been* him *at the door.*

> *Don't tell me it's them* again!

When *who* or *whom* follows, the subjective case is obligatory in formal usage and quite usual informally:

> *It was* I *who painted that sign.*

The informal use of the objective case often sounds incorrect:

> *It was* her *who would get into trouble.*

In constructions that have the form *I am* + noun or noun phrase + *who*, the verb following *who* agrees with the noun (the antecedent of *who*) in number (singular or plural)

> *I am the sort of person who* likes *peace and quiet.*

> *You are the fourth of my colleagues who's told me that* ('s = has, agreeing with *the fourth*).

we (with phrase following)

Expressions consisting of *we* or *us* followed by a qualifying word or phrase, e.g., *we Americans, us Americans,* are often misused with the wrong case of the first person plural pronoun. In fact the rules are exactly the same as for *we* or *us* standing alone.

If the expression is the subject, *we* should be used:

> (Correct)
> *Not always laughing as heartily as* we *Americans are supposed to do.*

> (Incorrect)
> *We all make mistakes, even* us *judges* (substitute *we judges*).

If the expression is the object or the complement of a preposition, *us* should be used:

> (Correct)
> *To* us *Americans, personal liberty is a vital principle.*

> (Incorrect)
> *The president said some nice things about* we *reporters in the press corps* (substitute *us reporters*).

I who, you who, etc.

The verb following a personal pronoun (*I, you, he,* etc.) + *who* should be the same as what would be used with the pronoun as a subject:

> *I, who* have *no savings to speak of, had to pay for the work.*

> *They made me, who* have *no savings at all, pay for the work* (not *who has*).

When *it is* (*it was,* etc.) precedes *I who,* etc., the same rule applies: the verb agrees with the personal pronoun:

> *It's I who* have *done it.*

> *It could have been we who* were *mistaken.*

you and I or *you and me*

When a personal pronoun is linked by *and* or *or* to a noun or another pronoun, there is often confusion about which case to put the pronoun in. In fact the rule is exactly as it would be for the pronoun standing alone.

1. If the two words linked by *and* or *or* constitute the subject, the pronoun should be in the subjective case, e.g.,

Only she *and her mother cared for the old house.*

That's what we would do, that is, John and I *would.*

Who could go?—Either you or he.

The use of the objective case is quite common in informal speech, but it is non-standard, e.g.,

Perhaps only her *and Mrs. Natwick had stuck to the christened name.*

That's how we look at it, me *and Martha.*

Either Mary had to leave or me.

2. If the two words linked by *and* or *or* constitute the object of the verb, or the complement of a preposition, the objective case should be used:

The afternoon would suit her *and John better.*

It was time for Kenneth and me *to go down to the living room.*

The use of the subjective case is very common informally. It probably arises from an exaggerated fear of the error indicated under 1 above. •It remains, however, non-standard, e.g.,

It was this that set Charles and I *talking of old times.*

Why is it that people like you and I *are so unpopular?*

Between you and I . . .

This last expression is very commonly heard. *Between you and me* should always be substituted.

collective nouns

Collective nouns are singular words that denote many individuals, e.g., *audience, government, orchestra, the clergy, the public.*

It is normal for collective nouns, being singular, to be followed by singular verbs and pronouns (*is, has, consists,* and *it* in the examples below):

> *The government is determined to beat inflation, as* it has *promised.*

> *Their family is huge:* it consists *of five boys and three girls.*

> *The bourgeoisie is despised for not being proletarian.*

The singular verb and pronouns are preferable unless the collective is clearly and unmistakably used to refer to separate individuals rather than to a united body, e.g.,

> *The cabinet has made* its *decision.*

but

> *The cabinet* are *sitting at* their *places around the table with the president.*

The singular should always be used if the collective noun is qualified by a singular word like *this, that, every,* etc.:

> *This family is divided.*

> *Every team has* its *chance to win.*

none (pronoun)

The pronoun *none* can be followed either by singular verb and singular pronouns, or by plural ones. Either is acceptable, although the plural tends to be more common.

Singular: *None of them* was *allowed to forget for a moment.*

Plural: *None of the orchestras ever* play there.

None of the authors expected their *books to become best-sellers.*

as

In the following sentences, formal usage requires the *subjective* case (*I, he, she, we, they*) on the assumption that the pronoun would be the subject if a verb were supplied:

You are just as intelligent as he (in full, *as he is*).

He . . . might not have heard the song so often as I (in full, *as I had*).

Informal usage permits *You are just as intelligent as* him.

Formal English uses the *objective* case (*me, him, her, us, them*) only when the pronoun would be the object if a verb were supplied:

I thought you preferred John to Mary, but I see that you like her just as much as him (which means . . . *just as much as you like him*).

Diacritical Marks

(to distinguish sounds or values of letters)

′   acute (as in the French word *née*)
‵   grave (as in the French word *père*)
~   tilde (as in the Spanish word *piñata*)
^   circumflex (as in the word *rôle*)
‾   macron (as used in pronunciation: *āge, īce*)
˘   breve (as used in pronunciation: *tăp, rĭp*)
¨   dieresis (as in the word *naïve*)
¸   cedilla (as in the word *façade*)

Proofreader's Marks

℘	delete	✎ ℈	quotation marks
✑	delete and close up	⟨ ⟩	parentheses
℘ #	delete and leave space	⟦ ⟧	square brackets
∧	insert	=	hyphen
#	space	1/M	em-dash
⊙	period	1/N	en-dash
∧	comma	¶	new paragraph
⸱∧	semicolon	dictionᣴary	break line or word
∴ or ⊙	colon	✌	set as superscript
✌	apostrophe	⸕	set as subscript

dictionᣴᣴary	transpose
(tr)	transpose (note in margin)
(s)	spell out
(sp)	spell out (note in margin)
dictionary	capitalize
(cap)	set as capitals (note in margin)
₧ictionary	make lower case
(lc)	set in lower case (note in margin)
dictionary	make boldface
(bf)	set in boldface (note in margin)
dictionary	make italic
(ital)	set in italic (note in margin)
dictionary	small caps
(sc)	set in small caps (note in margin)
(lf)	lightface (note in margin)
(rom)	set in roman (note in margin)